Business Organizations for Paralegals

Editorial Advisory Board for Paralegal Education

Business Organizations for Paralegals

◆ ◆ ◆

Second Edition

Deborah E. Bouchoux

Georgetown University
Member, California and District of Columbia bars

Aspen Law & Business
A Division of Aspen Publishers, Inc.
Gaithersburg New York

Permissions
Aspen Law & Business
1185 Avenue of the Americas
New York, NY 10036

Printed in the United States of America.

ISBN 0-7355-1734-7

1 2 3 4 5 6 7 8 9 0

Library of Congress Cataloging-in-Publication Data

Bouchoux, Deborah E., 1950–
Business organizations for paralegals/Deborah E. Bouchoux. — 2nd ed.
p. cm.
Includes index.
ISBN 0-7355-1734-7
1. Corporation law — United States. 2. Business enterprises — Law and legislation — United States. 3. Legal assistants — United States — Handbooks, manuals, etc. I. Title.

KF1414.3 .B68 2000
346.73'065 — dc21 00-046882

About Aspen Law & Business Legal Education Division Paralegal Textbooks

With a dedication to preserving and strengthening the long-standing tradition of publishing excellence in legal education, Aspen Law & Business continues to provide the highest quality teaching and learning resources for today's paralegal education community. Careful development, meticulous editing, and an unmatched responsiveness to the evolving needs of today's discerning educators combine in the creation of our outstanding textbooks and supplementary materials.

ASPEN LAW & BUSINESS
A Division of Aspen Publishers, Inc.
A Wolters Kluwer Company
www.aspenpublishers.com

In memory of my beloved father
Millard C. Eckmann

Summary of Contents

Contents

1

Introduction to Business Organizations and Agency Law

2

Sole Proprietorships

3

General Partnerships

4

Limited Partnerships

5

Registered Limited Liability Partnerships

6

Limited Liability Companies

7

Other Unincorporated Organizations

8

◆ ◆ ◆

Introduction to Corporations

9

Formation of Corporations

10

Corporate Finances

11

Corporate Management

12

Corporate Dividends

13

◆ ◆ ◆

Securities Regulation and the Stock Exchanges

14

◆ ◆ ◆

Changes in the Corporate Structure and Corporate Combinations

15

◆ ◆ ◆

Qualification of Foreign Corporations

16

Termination of Corporate Existence

17

Corporate Variations

18

Employee Compensation and Employment Agreements

19

Special Topics in Business Law

Preface

The concepts of business organizations surround us every day. References are made to the stock market during each evening's news broadcasts. Newspapers and television reports often refer to partnerships and other forms of business entities. The ups and downs of major companies such as Microsoft, Coca Cola Company, and Intel are studied and analyzed in depth. Mergers and dissolutions of companies are reported as events significantly affecting the economy. Employees eagerly await the granting of stock options. Commercials promote online trading. Most newspapers in large cities devote an entire section of each daily issue to business or finance. Nevertheless, many of us have only a vague notion of the import and effect of the news of business organizations that we hear about each day. Some individuals are intimidated by the financial section of the newspaper or weekly news magazines, assuming that only those with degrees in business can appreciate and comprehend the business news.

This text is intended to provide readers with a basic and thorough understanding of the various types of business organizations operating in the United States. Learning about the advantages and disadvantages of different forms of business entities will provide you with the foundation to understand the business concepts that surround us. Equally important, understanding the nature of the various ways in which business is conducted in the United States will enhance your ability to perform competently as a paralegal.

While the study of business organizations is undoubtedly most useful for paralegals intending to participate in the field of corporate law, the concepts discussed in this text cross over to many other practice fields. Litigation paralegals will need to know whether partners in a partnership are personally liable for business debts, under which circumstances shareholders in a corporation may be liable for a corporation's obligations, and whether all members of a limited liability company can be sued. Paralegals engaged in the field of estates and trusts need to understand that the effect of a shareholder's buy-sell agreement requires that shares owned by an individual at the time of death must be transferred to the corporation rather than to the decedent's heirs. Paralegals working with general practitioners will need to know how to form all of the business organizations described in this text, draft resolutions, prepare corporate bylaws, and take minutes of meetings.

Each of the varieties of business organizations will be discussed thoroughly. The nature of the entity, its advantages and disadvantages, the relative ease with which it may be formed, its dissolution, and its tax consequences will be addressed. Each chapter includes an introduction to the material to be covered in that chapter, a complete discussion of the pertinent topic, a section devoted to the possible tasks to be performed by paralegals regarding that business enterprise, a guide to both conventional and Internet resources enabling you to locate additional materials and forms of interest, discussion questions challenging you to apply the concepts discussed in the chapter to fact patterns, and a brief summary of the key features covered in that chapter.

The text begins with an introduction to the various business entities, and then progresses from the simplest, the sole proprietorship, through partnerships to the most complex, the business corporation. The newest forms of business organizations, the registered limited liability partnership and the limited liability company, are also discussed. Chapters include sample forms to illustrate the principles discussed and key terms highlighting concepts discussed. Appendices provide additional forms and model or actual statutes from which business concepts are derived. A glossary is included for easy reference to the many and difficult terms used in the law of business organizations.

There are a number of additions and enhancements to this second edition of the text, including discussions of family limited partnerships, real estate investment trusts, the Securities Litigation Reform Act, intellectual property, and unfair competition. Additionally, there is significant treatment of modern trends in the corporate field, including discussion of cybermeetings (meetings held via the Internet), e-proxies (voting via the Internet), and cybertrading, including day trading and online trading. Additional forms and agreements have been included, including a letter of intent for a stock purchase transaction. Finally, this edition of the text includes a separate section at the end of each chapter on Internet resources, identifying Web sites for secretaries of state, online form banks, and other useful research and practice tools now available through the Internet.

When you begin reading this text, you may be unfamiliar with most, if not all, of the business enterprises and concepts discussed. As you progress in class and through the chapters and discussion questions, you will readily be able to measure your progress. When you complete this text and your class, you will have gained a thorough introduction to business organizations as well as familiarity with the terms and concepts required by paralegals in the business or corporate fields and those which we hear and read about each and every day.

Deborah E. Bouchoux
October 2000

Acknowledgments

I would like to express my deep appreciation to the many individuals who contributed greatly to the development of this text. As always, my first thoughts and gratitude go to Susan M. Sullivan, Director of Graduate Career Programs at the University of San Diego, who gave me my first teaching job and opened a door to an exciting and challenging field. Susan has been a valued friend as well as a competent professional whom I greatly admire.

My current Program Director, Gloria Silvers of the Legal Assistant Program at Georgetown University in Washington, D.C., has been steadfast in her support and encouragement. Her constant enthusiasm and love for her profession galvanizes all of her teachers into doing their best. Gloria's willingness to listen and her innovative and creative ideas have been of invaluable help.

A special thank you to my family: my husband Don, and my children Meaghan, Elizabeth, Patrick, and Robert for their patience and understanding while I completed this text and its second edition.

Many thanks also to the various reviewers who evaluated the manuscript on behalf of the publisher. I have also received continuing evaluation from my students throughout my twenty-year career as a paralegal educator. Their comments and insights regarding methods of teaching, productive assignments, and effective class discussion have been a great help.

The author wishes to expressly acknowledge the following states and commonwealths, which generously granted permission to reprint their state forms in this textbook: California, Colorado, Connecticut, Delaware, Florida, Illinois, Louisiana, Maine, Commonwealth of Massachusetts, Michigan, Montana, Nevada, New York (prepared by the New York State Department of State, reprinted with permission), North Carolina (reprinted courtesy of the North Carolina Department of the Secretary of State, Elaine F. Marshall, Secretary), Ohio, Commonwealth of Pennsylvania, Tennessee, Commonwealth of Virginia — State Corporation Commission, Washington, and Wisconsin.

Additionally, the author would like to acknowledge and thank Foundation Press, 11 Penn Plaza, New York, NY, for its permission to reprint selected Delaware statutes from its text *Corporations and Business Associations, Statutes, Rules, Materials and Forms* (1999 ed.) and the National Conference of Commissioners of Uniform State Legislation, which graciously granted permission to reprint the Uniform Partnership Act (1914), (1994), (1997) and the Uniform Limited Partnership Act (1976) with 1985 amendments. The author wishes to expressly acknowledge and thank the American Bar Association for granting permission to reprint the Revised Model Business Corporation Act. West Group graciously granted permission to reprint from *Uniform Laws Annotated* (Volumes 6 and 6A) the charts provided in Appendices B, C, and E, showing which states have adopted uniform acts and the citations to each state's pertinent statutes.

Finally, a special thank you to the individuals at Aspen Law & Business who generously provided guidance and support throughout the development of the second edition of this text, including Carol McGeehan, Director of Acquisitions; Dan Mangan, Publisher; Melody Davies, Editorial Director; Betsy Kenny, Development Editor; Curt Berkowitz, Project Editor; and Karen Quigley, designer.

Business Organizations for Paralegals

1

Introduction to Business Organizations and Agency Law

CHAPTER OVERVIEW

There are many different ways in which business is conducted in this country. Selecting the most appropriate form of business enterprise for an individual or a group of individuals involves careful consideration of a variety of factors. These factors must be balanced against each other to ensure the most appropriate form of business enterprise is selected for the client. Businesses often act through designated individuals, called agents, to conduct their operations, and many legal relationships in business are governed by the law of agency. Agency relationships can arise by express agreement or by a course of conduct between the parties. The acts of agents will bind the businesses they serve if the agent has either actual or apparent authority to act.

A. Types of Business Enterprises

This book will explore the nine most common ways of doing business in this country. While each type of business structure will be described in detail in the following chapters, a brief overview follows:

1. Sole Proprietorship

In a **sole proprietorship,** one individual owns all of the business assets and is the sole decision-maker. The sole proprietor has unlimited personal liability for

Sole proprietorship
Business owned and operated by one person

all business debts. This form of enterprise is the most commonly selected form of business for new enterprises.

2. *General Partnership*

General partnership
Business co-owned by two or more persons

In a **general partnership,** two or more persons co-own all of the business assets and share decision-making, profits, and losses. General partners suffer unlimited personal liability for all business debts and obligations. The general partnership is easily formed and is managed by mutual agreement.

3. *Limited Partnership*

Limited partnership
Business created under a state statute in which some partners have limited liability

A **limited partnership** is a type of investment vehicle created so persons can invest in a business enterprise and yet not have unlimited personal liability. A limited partnership is managed by one or more general partners, all of whom have unlimited personal liability for business debts and obligations. The limited partners do not manage or control this enterprise and their liability is limited to the amount they invested in the business. Limited partnerships are more complex to form than general partnerships and can only be created by strict compliance with the pertinent state statutes.

Registered limited liability partnership
Business entity providing limited liability for its members

4. *Registered Limited Liability Partnership*

This new form of business enterprise alters a basic principle of partnership law: partners in this enterprise are not liable for the torts or acts of misconduct of their partners. In some states, the partners are not liable either for the torts of their partners or contractual obligations incurred by the entity or other partners. Ideally suited to legal, medical, and accounting practices, partners in one office are not liable for acts of partners in their office or a branch office simply because of the partner relationship. This form of business enterprise, which can be formed only through adherence to state statutes, combines some of the best features of partnerships and corporations.

5. *Limited Liability Company*

Limited liability company
Business providing limited liability and pass-through tax status for its members

Another new form of business organization is the **limited liability company.** This business structure continues the modern trend of combining the best features of a partnership with those of a corporation. Its primary characteristics are that its owners have limited liability (like shareholders in a corporation) and it is taxed as a partnership, meaning that all income earned by the entity is passed through to the owners who pay taxes at whatever rate is applicable to them. A limited liability company can be created only by complying with pertinent state statutes.

6. *Business Corporation*

Business corporation
Legal entity existing under the authority of the state legislature

A **business** (or *for profit*) **corporation** is an entity created by the person or persons who organize it. This legal entity may own property, enter into contracts, and sue and be sued. Because it is a "person," it is subject to taxation. Its owners, called *shareholders,* also pay tax on certain distributions made to them, such as cash dividends. This is often referred to as *double taxation.* Shareholders are protected from liability and their loss is limited to the amount of money they invest in the corporation. Although the shareholders own the corporation, the corporation is managed by its board of directors. The directors typically appoint officers to carry out the directors' policies and goals for the corporation. A corporation is subject to regulatory control by the state in which it is formed as well as any other states in which it does business.

7. *Professional Corporation*

Professional corporation
Corporation formed by professionals

Professionals such as doctors, lawyers, accountants, and engineers may incorporate to obtain certain tax and other benefits available to a business corporation. Nevertheless, these professionals remain personally liable for their own negligence and for the negligence of those working for them, such as nurses or paralegals.

8. *S Corporation*

S corporation
Corporation that passes through all income to its shareholders, who pay tax on income received

Certain small business corporations which adhere to specific requirements of the Internal Revenue Code are provided relief against double taxation, typically common to business corporations. Called an **S corporation** after the original subchapter of the Internal Revenue Code providing such relief, the corporation itself does not pay tax and all income earned is passed through to the shareholders. All shareholders (who must not number more than 75) must agree to the election of S status and only eligible corporations may apply for this status. A typical business corporation is referred to as a "C corporation" to distinguish it from an S corporation.

9. *Close Corporation*

Close corporation
Small corporation whose shareholders are active in managing the business and that operates informally

Close corporations are generally small corporations owned by family members and friends. Unlike shareholders in a large corporation, such as General Motors Corporation, these shareholders are active in operating the business. Only certain types of corporations can qualify to be treated as close corporations. The shareholders are allowed more flexibility in the operation and management of the corporation and usually function without adhering to all of the formalities required of business corporations.

Other enterprises such as joint ventures and nonprofit corporations will also be examined. In many business structures, the more management and control an individual exercises, the greater the liability. For example, the sole proprietor makes all business decisions and therefore his liability extends beyond what he has invested in the enterprise to personal assets such as his car and art collection. On the other hand, shareholders in a corporation exercise very limited management and control. Their participation in the corporation is typically limited to voting for directors and voting on extraordinary corporate action such as mergers or dissolution. Because they are not managing or controlling the enterprise, shareholder liability is limited: the stock they purchased may fall in value to zero, but they are not personally liable for debts and obligations of the corporation. A newer trend in many business structures is to combine the ability to manage with limited liability, thus affording the best of all worlds to investors. The limited liability partnership and limited liability company are enterprises allowing their members to manage the enterprise and yet retain limited liability, thus accounting for their enormous popularity.

Key Types of Business Enterprises

- Sole Proprietorships
- General Partnerships
- Limited Partnerships
- Registered Limited Liability Partnerships
- Limited Liability Companies
- Business Corporations
- Professional Corporations
- S Corporations
- Close Corporations

B. Considerations in Selection of Business Enterprise

While a sole proprietorship may be ideal for one client, it may be inappropriate for another. Determining which form of business enterprise is the most advantageous for a client involves careful consideration of a number of factors. The attorney you work with will counsel the client to consider the following factors:

1. Ease of Formation

The ease with which an enterprise can be formed should be carefully considered. Some enterprises, such as sole proprietorships, are easily formed, while others, such as limited partnerships and corporations, require compliance with state statutes and may be more expensive to organize. Consideration should always be given as to how easy, expeditious, and expensive it is to form the enterprise.

2. *Management*

Some individuals prefer to manage their business themselves. For them, a sole proprietorship or general partnership may afford them the greatest ability to manage and control the enterprise. With this management and control, however, generally comes unlimited personal liability. Other individuals may prefer to invest in a business knowing their maximum potential loss as they enter the enterprise. For these individuals, limited partnerships or corporations may be ideal so long as they understand that their ability to influence and control the business is limited as well.

3. *Liability and Financial Risk*

The financial exposure an individual faces is one of the most critical factors to consider in selecting a form of business enterprise. Some enterprises shield the individual from unlimited personal liability while others expose the individual to greater risk. Clients must be fully informed of the potential liability consequences when selecting a particular form of business.

4. *Continuity of Existence*

Some business organizations, such as corporations, are capable of existing perpetually. Other forms of business enterprises do not have such continuity of existence. For example, a sole proprietorship generally terminates with the death of the sole proprietor and limited liability companies are subject to a term of duration in some states. Consideration should be given to the intended duration of the enterprise.

5. *Transferability*

Clients should consider the ease with which they can "get into" and "get out of" the business enterprise. It may be difficult to transfer out of a general partnership because the partnership may severely restrict the ability of partners to transfer their interests. On the other hand, to get out of a corporation, one need only sell his or her stock to another. If clients foresee a need to liquidate their investment in an enterprise for a cash return, they should evaluate how easy or difficult it may be to transfer into and out of the enterprise.

6. *Profits and Losses*

While a sole proprietor maintains all profits, he or she is also solely liable for all losses. In a partnership, partners have the ability to bind each other and, thus, while a partner may be able to share a loss with a co-partner, the very reason the partner may have a loss is due to the co-partner's activities. Clients must carefully consider the division of profits and losses when evaluating the form of business enterprise to select.

7. *Taxation*

Clients should consider applicable tax considerations. For some, the individual tax rates may be best; for others, the corporate tax rates may yield the best advantages. (See Figure 1-1, Checklist for New Businesses.)

Considerations
in Selecting a Business Enterprise

- Ease of Formation
- Management
- Liability and Financial Risk
- Continuity of Existence
- Transferability
- Profits and Losses
- Taxation

FIGURE 1-1
Checklist for New Businesses

- ❑ Do I want to be my own boss?
- ❑ Do I have sufficient expertise to make all business decisions by myself, or do I need the advice and expertise of others to make the business a success?
- ❑ Do I have sufficient capital to form the business and maintain it, or do I need partners or shareholders to help provide needed capital?
- ❑ Am I prepared to accept the unlimited personal liability that attaches to sole proprietors and general partners?
- ❑ Do I have considerable wealth that will be exposed to creditors if I form a sole proprietorship or become a general partner in a general or limited partnership?
- ❑ Do I want to be actively involved in the business, or do I prefer to be a passive investor with limited liability?
- ❑ What are the tax advantages and disadvantages of each form of business structure?

C. How Business Is Conducted in This Country

Many individuals perceive that business in the United States is conducted by huge corporations which impact nearly every aspect of financial growth and development. Most would be surprised to find that sole proprietorships (businesses conducted by one person) dominate the business landscape.

According to the *Statistical Abstract of the United States* 540 (118th ed. 1998), nearly 75 percent of business in this country is conducted by sole proprietorships. According to returns filed with the Internal Revenue Service in 1995, there were approximately 16.4 million sole proprietorships, 1.6 million partnerships, and 4.5 million business corporations. Nevertheless, business corporations account for a disproportionately high share of revenue. In 1995, business receipts for sole proprietorships were approximately $807 billion, while business receipts for partnerships were approximately $854 billion, and business receipts for business corporations were nearly $13 trillion (see Figure 1-2). Similarly, while corporations account for a disproportionately high amount of business receipts, the number of huge corporations is smaller than expected. For example, more than half of all workers employed by business firms work in establishments employing fewer than 100 workers. (See Figure 1-3 for a chart showing where individual employees worked.)

FIGURE 1-2
Business Receipts (1995)

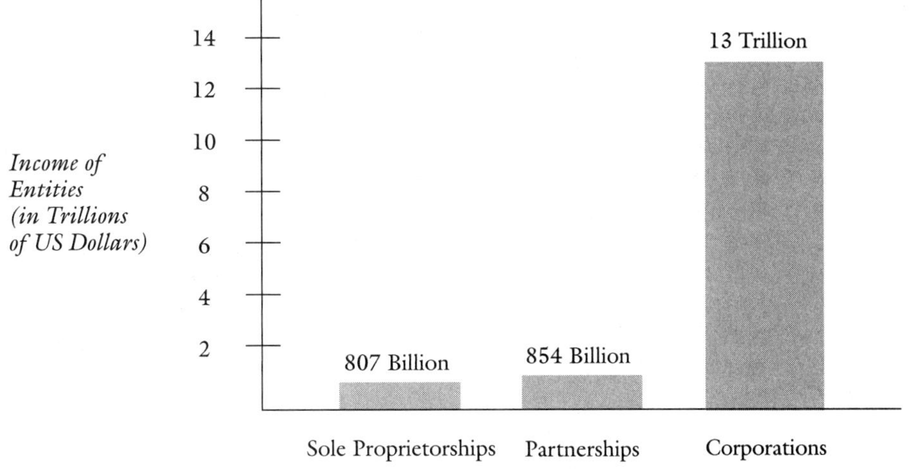

Source: *United States Statistical Abstract* 540 (118th ed. 1998)

FIGURE 1-3
Companies Indexed by Numbers of Employees (1995) (In thousands)

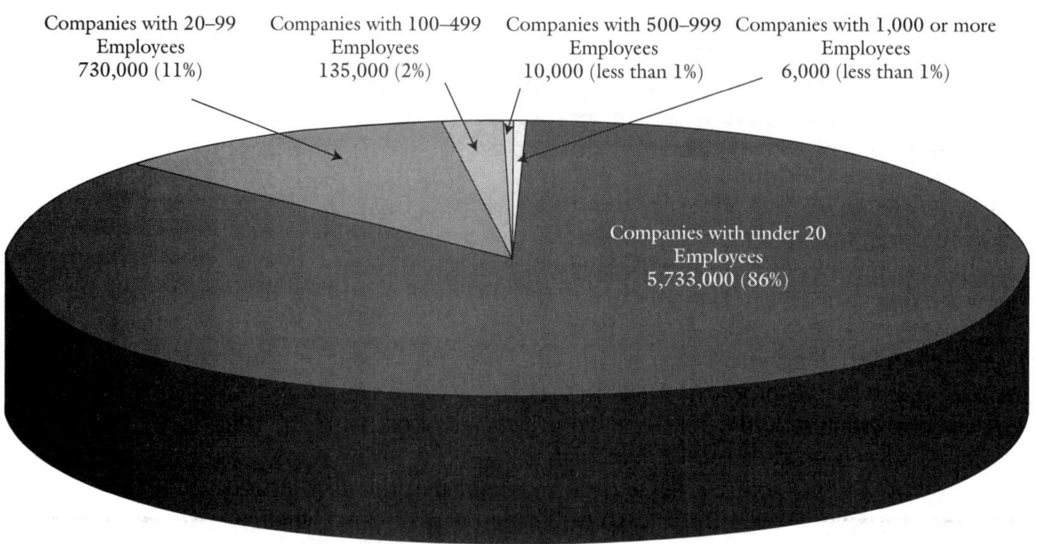

Source: *United States Statistical Abstract* 547 (118th ed. 1998)

D. Agency in Business Organizations

Agent
One who acts for or represents another

Principal
The person for whom an agent acts

Understanding the basic concepts of agency is necessary to understand the way many business enterprises operate. Simply put, an **agent** is one who agrees to act for or represent another, called the **principal.** Because businesses often act through third parties, it is important to determine whether these third parties have the authority to obligate or bind the business.

Agency relationships arise in a variety of settings. When a client asks a law firm to prepare a will, the law firm acts as the agent for the client, who is the principal. When an employee of a store sells goods, he does so as the agent of the store owner, the principal. When a partner in a partnership signs a contract, she may bind the partnership under the principles of agency law.

1. *Formation of Agency Relationship*

There are three primary ways in which an agency relationship can be created.

Agreement. Most agency relationships are created by mutual consent: one party agrees to act for the other, either orally or in writing. For example, if Candy

Ellis decides to sell her house and lists it with a real estate agency, Candy is the principal who has granted permission to the agency to act on her behalf with regard to the sale. In this instance, a written agreement will likely set forth the relationship and duties of the parties. This is an **express agency** agreement. Nevertheless, an agency relationship can be created without a written agreement. An agreement whereby an individual makes an oral agreement with another for child care also creates an express agency relationship.

Express agency
An agency agreement, written or oral

Agency relationships can also be implied. For example, individuals employed by small retail stores or restaurants seldom have formal employment agreements. Yet the acts they perform on behalf of their employers (ordering goods, selling goods, agreeing to give a discount) bind their employers, the principals. These are examples of **implied agency;** there is no formal agreement, yet the parties have agreed to a course of conduct by their actions. In an implied agency relationship, the rights and obligations of the parties have not been expressed (either orally or in writing), yet the parties act as if one of them can bind the other. Their words, conduct, or prior dealings show the existence of their agency relationship.

Implied agency
An agency relationship in which there is no express agreement, but the parties' words, conduct, or prior dealings show the existence of their agency relationship

Ratification. An agency relationship can also be created by **ratification** or acceptance of an agent's act by a principal. If Candy's real estate agent has been instructed to present no offer to Candy for her house under $200,000, and yet presents an offer to Candy for $190,000 which Candy accepts, Candy has ratified this unauthorized act by her agent. Ratification thus occurs when the principal accepts the agent's act even though the agent had no authority to do the act, or the act exceeded the scope of the agent's authority.

Ratification
Acceptance of an act; may be express or implied

Estoppel. Sometimes an agency relationship arises because it would be inequitable to allow the principal to deny the relationship. In such a circumstance, the principal is precluded or "estopped" from denying that an agency relationship existed. For example, suppose that Jean, an interior decorator, visits the home of one of her customers. Accompanying her is Linda, a new employee just learning the business. At the customer's house, Jean repeatedly tells the customer that "We can supply all your needs" and "We are the best decorators in the county." If the customer then calls an order in to Linda, Jean is estopped to deny that Linda is her agent inasmuch as she created the reasonable impression that Linda was authorized to act for Jean with regard to the decorating business. In such cases, agency by estoppel arises from acts that lead third parties to believe an agency relationship exists.

Agency by estoppel
An agency arising from acts that lead others to believe an agency relationship exists

2. *Authority of Agents*

Often a third party seeks to hold a principal liable for acts of the agent. A principal may attempt to avoid liability by distancing herself from the agent's acts by denying that the agent had the authority to do certain acts on the principal's behalf. The third party will attempt to prove that the agent had the authority to act for the principal and could thus bind the principal.

An agent has the ability to bind the principal in two ways: by being granted actual authority to do an act, whether the authority is express or implied, or by apparent authority. Even when an agent exceeds the scope of his or her authority, the principal may nevertheless ratify the agent's acts and thus become obligated for those acts.

Actual Authority. A person may properly appoint another to perform any act he or she could perform. A principal may grant actual authority to an agent to act for him or her. This actual authority can be express or implied. **Express authority** may be given in writing or orally, and refers to those acts specifically directed or authorized by the principal. For example, if parents go out of town leaving their children with a neighbor, they may expressly grant the neighbor **power of attorney,** the authority to approve emergency medical care for the children. A **special power of attorney or agency** limits the agent (the neighbor) to performing acts specifically authorized, in this case approving essential medical services. A **general power of attorney or agency,** by contrast, would authorize the agent to transact any kind of activity on behalf of the principal. Theoretically, the neighbor could take the children for a routine dental check-up as easily as to the emergency room under a general power of attorney or general agency.

Express authority
Actual authority granted by one to another, whether in writing or orally

Power of attorney
The authority to act for another

Special power of attorney or agency
Authority to act for another only as to specifically authorized matters

General power of attorney or agency
Authority to act for another as to any matter

In some instances, express authority *must* be given in writing. The **equal dignity rule** in most state statutes provides that if an agreement or contract to be entered into must be in writing (such as a contract to sell land or one that cannot be performed within one year), then the agent's authority must be granted in writing also.

Equal dignity rule
Rule that if an agreement must be in writing, then agent's authority to act in regard to the agreement must also be in writing

An agent also has the **implied authority** to perform acts customarily performed by such an agent or those acts reasonably necessary to allow the agent to carry out express authority. For example, a hotel may hire a manager and grant express authority to the manager to operate the hotel. The manager also has the implied authority to perform acts reasonably necessary to operate the hotel (obtaining insurance, hiring and firing employees, ordering supplies, and advertising the hotel's services) or acts customarily performed by hotel managers (giving complimentary meals to unhappy patrons, arranging transportation services to the airport, or arranging to fax documents for a guest).

Implied authority
Power to performs acts customarily performed by an agent

Apparent Authority. Actual authority refers to authority granted by the principal to the agent. **Apparent authority** arises when by his conduct, a principal causes a third person reasonably to believe the agent has the authority to act for the principal. Assume that a landlord informs tenants that rent must be delivered by mail to him by the first of every month. One tenant who does not get paid until the last day of each month begins personally delivering the monthly rent check to the on-site manager who accepts the checks and thereafter delivers them to the landlord. One month, the on-site manager allows the check to fall into the hands of another and the landlord insists that the tenant repay the rent. In this case, the tenant could assert that by the principal's previous conduct of allowing the checks to be hand-delivered rather than mailed, the tenant reasonably believed the on-site manager had the authority to receive the payments. The landlord will be precluded or estopped from asserting that the on-site manager, his agent, lacked authority to accept the rent check and is thus bound by his agent's act of accepting the check. Because the tenant has paid the rent to the agent, it need not be paid again.

Apparent authority
Authority that arises through conduct of principal leading others to believe agent has authority to act for principal

3. *Duties of Agents and Principals*

Agents and principals owe **fiduciary duties** to each other: each party owes the utmost duty of good faith, candor, and fair dealing to the other due to the trust each reposes in the other. Other duties also arise from the agency relationship.

Fiduciary duties
Duty to act in utmost good faith and fair dealing

Agent's Duties. Generally, an agent owes four duties to his or her principal:

Performance. An agent must perform the work or duties required by the principal. These duties may be set forth in the agency agreement or may be implied from the nature of the agency relationship. The agent is required to perform these duties with reasonable diligence and due care. The level of performance expected of the agent is usually that of an ordinarily prudent person in similar situations. Some agency relationships, however, may impose higher standards of care on the agent. For example, in the attorney-client relationship, the attorney has held himself or herself out as possessing a certain amount of expertise. Thus, agents such as these will be held to a higher standard of care: that possessed by others in the field. Failure to exercise the duty of care required of the agent will render the agent liable to the principal.

Notification. An agent must provide all information relating to the agency to his or her principal. Assume a real estate agent has been hired by the Hunters to sell their home. The agent has a duty to notify the Hunters, the principals, of all offers on the house. The agent cannot decide for himself, "This offer is so low I won't bother telling the Hunters about it." In agency law, it is assumed the principal knows all that the agent knows. Failure to provide information and notification to a principal will subject an agent to liability for breach of contract.

Loyalty. The agent must act solely for the benefit of the principal and cannot engage in any transaction that could be detrimental to the principal. Thus, the agent cannot make a secret profit for his or her own benefit. Furthermore, the agent cannot represent anyone whose interests conflict with the principal's unless the principal agrees. For example, an attorney cannot represent both the plaintiff and the defendant in a matter unless each party knows of the representation and agrees to it. The agent's loyalty to the principal must be total and undivided.

Accounting. Agents are subject to account to the principal for all money or property received on the principal's behalf. Thus, an attorney could not settle a case and keep an extra $10,000 for herself by telling the principal that the settlement was $10,000 less than it actually was. This act is also a violation of the agent's fiduciary duty and of the duties of notification and loyalty. The agent must maintain separate accounts for the principal's funds and cannot commingle funds. In fact, attorneys who commingle money paid by clients for future legal services (typically called a **retainer**) with money used to pay for office expenses are subject to disciplinary proceedings.

Retainer
Money paid in advance for services to be rendered

Principal's Duties. Principals typically owe three duties to their agents:

Compensation. Principals must pay agents for their services. Sometimes the compensation is fixed in a written agreement. An example is the standard real estate listing agreement which obligates sellers of a dwelling to pay a 6 percent commission based on the purchase price of the property. If no sum certain is stated, the agent is entitled to compensation in a reasonable and customary amount.

Reimbursement and Indemnification. The principal must reimburse the agent for costs and expenses incurred on the principal's behalf. For example, law firms typically charge clients for long-distance phone calls, postage, and photocopying. Similarly, business brokers are generally reimbursed for travel expenses incurred on behalf of their principals.

In addition to the duty to reimburse agents for costs and expenses reasonably incurred in the course of performance by the agent, the principal is generally required to indemnify or compensate the agent for liability incurred by the agent while performing duties for the principal. While the agent will not be indemnified or compensated for acts of reckless or willful misconduct, the agent will be indemnified for acts directed or authorized by the principal. Using our example, assume the real estate agent provides an offer to the Hunters for their house. The Hunters accept the offer and agree to vacate the house by the first of the next month. If the Hunters fail to vacate on time, the buyers may be required to incur costs for staying in hotels and eating in restaurants. The Hunters, as principals, are required to indemnify the real estate agent for this liability if the buyers attempt to hold the agent responsible.

Cooperation. The principal must not hinder the agent in the performance of his or her duties. Assume the Hunters have a change of heart and decide not to sell their house. Because they have listed the house with an agent they are required to cooperate with the agent so the agent can perform his duty to sell the house. If the Hunters refuse to show the house, purposefully ruin the appearance of the house, or destroy appliances so that the house will not be attractive to buyers, the agent may sue for breach of contract. Similarly, the Hunters cannot list the house with two agents. Finally, the duty to cooperate encompasses a duty to provide the agent with what he will need to perform duties. This may include a credit card, an office, or equipment. (See Figure 1-4 for chart of duties owed in agency relationships.)

FIGURE 1-4
Duties Owed in Agency Relationships

Duties Owed by Agent	*Duties Owed by Principal*
Performance (using due care and diligence)	Compensation
Notification (duty to inform principal)	Reimbursement and Indemnification
Loyalty	Cooperation
Accounting of Profits	

4. *Liability for Agent's Torts*

An agent is liable for his or her own **torts** or civil wrongs. Such torts might include assault, battery, false imprisonment, negligence, or professional malpractice. The question often arises whether the principal is liable for torts committed by the agent. The answer to this question depends on several variables. The general rule is that a principal is liable for the torts of her agent committed in the course and scope of the agency. Thus, if an employee of a restaurant accidentally spills scalding coffee on a patron, the restaurant may be liable because this act was performed in the routine course of duties by the employee-agent for her employer-principal. On the other hand, if the employee *throws* scalding coffee on a patron, the employer-principal is not likely to be held liable. Employers can be liable for failure to properly supervise an employee and even for improper selection of an employee, as is the case when an employer hires an obviously unqualified person for a position or hires a person with a known history of criminal activity. Similarly, the employer can be liable for wrongful retention of an employee, which occurs when the employee is allowed to remain employed after the employee threatens others or commits violent acts at the workplace.

Tort
A civil wrong

Courts often examine whether the agent is truly acting in the scope of his assigned duties or whether the employee is on a personal "frolic" or "detour." For example, a trucking company may be liable for accidents caused by its drivers while they are in the process of performing their duties for their employer-principal. On the other hand, if the driver left his designated route to visit a friend and in the course of this act was involved in an accident, the employer-principal would likely not be held liable because the employee-agent was engaged in activity on his own behalf rather than on behalf of the principal.

This liability theory is referred to as ***respondeat superior*** (literally, "let the master answer") and results in liability being imposed on the employer-principal even though he did not actually commit the wrong. This doctrine imposes **vicarious liability** on the employer-principal, meaning that liability is imposed without regard to actual fault.

Respondeat superior
Liability imposed on employers for acts of employees

Vicarious liability
Liability imposed on one for another's acts, without regard to actual fault

While a principal is liable for the torts of his agent committed in the course and scope of the agency, a principal is usually not held liable for torts committed by an independent contractor. In general, one is vicariously liable for the acts of others, such as employees, that he or she can direct and control. Some individuals, however, are **independent contractors** who, rather than being subject to the direction of another, as are employees, exercise independent discretion and control as to their activities. Generally, employer-principals are not liable for the acts of independent contractors, unless they have directed or authorized the wrongful act. (See Chapter Eighteen for further discussion of independent contractors.)

Independent contractor
Individuals performing services for another who are not employees and who exercise independent discretion and control over their own activities

5. *Termination of Agency*

Upon termination of the agency relationship, the agent no longer has the authority to bind the principal. Agency relationships may be terminated when the stated time period expires if the agreement provides a period of duration (such as a six-month listing period for a real estate agent), when the purposes of the agency have been fulfilled, by mutual agreement, by death or bankruptcy of either

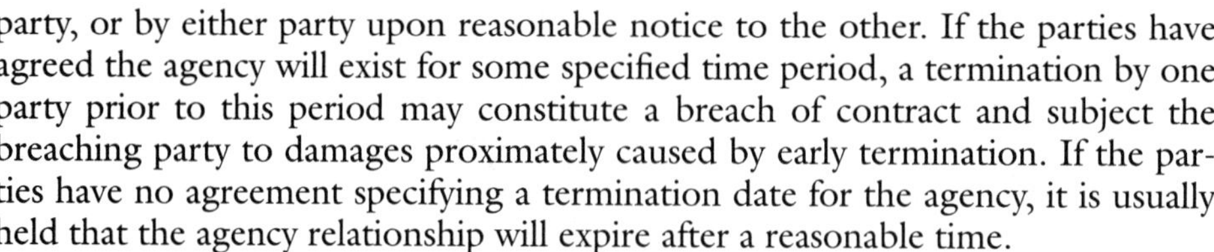

party, or by either party upon reasonable notice to the other. If the parties have agreed the agency will exist for some specified time period, a termination by one party prior to this period may constitute a breach of contract and subject the breaching party to damages proximately caused by early termination. If the parties have no agreement specifying a termination date for the agency, it is usually held that the agency relationship will expire after a reasonable time.

6. *Agency in Business Relationships*

This overview of the relationship, duties, and obligations of agents and principals is fundamental to an understanding of many forms of business enterprise. For example, when sole proprietorships are discussed in the next chapter, you will see that a sole proprietor is vicariously liable for the acts of her employees. When general partnerships are discussed in Chapter Three, you will learn that partners are both agents and principals for each other and that any partner in a partnership has the ability to sign contracts, hire employees, and purchase goods for the partnership and that these acts bind the partnership and the other partners as well. You will learn that directors and officers are agents of a corporation and thus may be reimbursed for expenses incurred on behalf of the corporation, will be indemnified for acts performed on behalf of the corporation, owe fiduciary duties to the corporation, and owe undivided loyalty to the corporation (and thus cannot serve as a director or officer of a competitor corporation).

Agency relationships permeate almost all forms of business enterprise. You will see that even without express agreements, certain individuals in a business have the authority to bind others by their actions. A thorough understanding of some of the basic principles of agency law is thus critical to an understanding of the various forms of business enterprise to be discussed in this book.

Key Features of Agency Relationships

- Formation of agency occurs through express agreement, implied agreement, or estoppel.
- Agents have actual authority or apparent authority to act for their principals.
- Agents and principals owe fiduciary duties to each other.
- Agents are liable for their own torts and principals are liable for an agent's torts and acts committed in the course and scope of the agency.

Resource Guide

While specific resources will be given for each type of business enterprise examined in this book, there are two excellent sources, legal encyclopedias, that provide further information about all of the topics discussed in this chapter. These sources are competitive, meaning that you should select one to read rather than reading both. Each set provides clear and articulate summaries of various topics of law. Each set has a general index. Use those alphabetically arranged indices for direction to the specific volume needed.

1. Am. Jur. 2d (American Jurisprudence, Second Series) (published by Lawyers' Cooperative Publishing).
2. C.J.S. (Corpus Juris Secundum) (published by West Group).

WEB RESOURCES

Forming businesses is easier than ever due to the vast number of forms and "how to" guides available on the Internet. Nearly all states have basic business forms available to download. In some cases, one can submit the forms electronically to the appropriate state agency, authorizing payment by credit card. There are a number of Web sites that provide excellent introductory information on business structures. Try the following:

http://www.sba.gov
The U.S. Small Business Administration site offers excellent information on starting a business, a "Small Business Startup Kit," and a tutorial on preparing a business plan.

http://www.nass.org
This Web site of the National Association of Secretaries of State allows you to link directly to the home page for each state's secretary of state. Many states offer guides to starting businesses with basic information, forms, checklists, and phone numbers. Select "States" and then point the cursor to your state's name and flag, and proceed to locate information on forming businesses in your state.

www.irs.gov
The Web site of the Internal Revenue Service offers a wealth of information about taxes, businesses, and provides hundreds of forms that can be downloaded and printed.

The following Web sites will be discussed in greater depth in following chapters, but a brief listing may be helpful.

www.hoovers.com
This Web site offers addresses, phone numbers, and brief capsules on hundreds of companies doing business in America.

www.sec.gov
Access to the documents filed with the Securities and Exchange Commission by publicly traded companies is available through the SEC's online system, EDGAR.

www.amex.com
This is the Web address for the American Stock Exchange.

www.nasdaq.com
This is the Web address for the National Association of Securities Dealers Automated Quote system.

www.nyse.com
This is the Web address for the New York Stock Exchange.

www.ll.georgetown.edu
When you access this site for Georgetown University Law Center, select "State, Local & Territorial." You will be presented with a map of the United States. Point your cursor to the state in which you are interested, and you will be provided with links to a variety of legal sources relating to that state. Select "Statutes" or "Codes," and you will be linked to that state's statutes. In some states, searching can be done by either keywords or by section number. In other states, searching is accomplished exclusively by keywords.

The following sites provide excellent business and corporate forms, including forms for bylaws, agreements, articles of incorporation, minutes of shareholders' and directors' meetings, and various resolutions for corporate action:

- www.findlaw.com/16/forms/index.html
- http://legal-resource.com/forms
- www.siccode.com/forms.php3
- www.lectlaw.com (select "Rotunda" then "Forms Room")

Discussion Questions

1. Franklin Tech Co. is in the process of obtaining quotes for insurance for its business and instructed its insurance agent to insure the business premises for $1,000,000. The agent believes such insurance is excessive and has independently insured the premises for $750,000. Have any of the agent's duties to the principal been breached? Discuss.

2. Assume the same set of facts as given above. The agent's uncle owns a reputable insurance company, Harrison Property Insurance, and the agent obtains insurance from the uncle's company, although the insurance could have been provided by at least one other company for less than what Harrison Property Insurance is charging for premiums. Has the agent violated any duties to the principal? Discuss.

3. A waiter employed by Pasta Perfect restaurant has decided to impose an automatic 15% tip onto every bill at the restaurant. The employer is unaware of the charge, and restaurant patrons have complained to a local licensing board about the excess charge. According to local license regulations, such a charge is an unfair business practice unless disclosed in advance to patrons. Is the employer liable under the principle of respondeat superior? Would your answer change if the employer had heard rumors among the staff that the tips were being imposed and failed to act?

2

Sole Proprietorships

CHAPTER OVERVIEW

The sole proprietorship, sometimes called an "individual proprietorship," is the most common way of doing business in this country. Nearly three-quarters of all of the businesses formed in the United States are conducted as sole proprietorships. As its very name indicates, the sole proprietorship is carried on by one person. The primary reason that so many businesses are conducted as sole proprietorships is due to the ease of forming and operating the business. Sole proprietors own and manage their businesses and incur sole liability for any business obligations.

A. Characteristics of Sole Proprietorships

Many people dream of owning their own business. For most of these entrepreneurs, the sole proprietorship is an ideal way of pursuing this dream. The **sole proprietorship** is a business owned and conducted by one person, generally called the **sole proprietor.** Almost any kind of business can be conducted as a sole proprietorship: a law office; a restaurant; a child care center; or an auto repair service. The key feature of a sole proprietorship is that it is managed and owned by one person. This person may hire managers and employees to assist him or her in running the business, but the business is characterized by a sole decision-maker. There are no limits on how many people may be employed in this type of enterprise; a sole proprietorship may be a large business with numerous employees and great revenue.

Sole proprietorship
A business owned and operated by one person

Sole proprietor
Owner of a sole proprietorship

It is often difficult to determine the nature of businesses operated by families. It is common in family-run businesses, for example, for one spouse to work in the shop, the other spouse to do some of the accounting and bill-paying, and the children to fill in as employees during summer vacations. To determine the nature of this enterprise, examine how decisions are made. If one person makes the key business decisions, such as whom to hire and fire, what products and services to offer, and whether additional shops will be opened, it is likely a sole proprietorship. If both spouses, however, share such critical decisions, and either has the ability to enter into contracts, then the business is likely a partnership. It does not matter whether the parties believe the business is a sole proprietorship; a court is not bound by what parties believe, but will examine the actual business structure. If one person manages and controls the business, it is a sole proprietorship; if there is shared decision-making, the business is likely a partnership.

B. Governing Law

Sole proprietorships are governed exclusively by state and local laws rather than by federal law (except for federal laws relating to taxes, civil rights, and so forth, to which all sole proprietors are subject). Each state regulates businesses that operate within the state through a variety of laws relating to names under which the businesses may operate, licensing considerations, and state tax obligations. Local jurisdictions, such as counties and states, typically require sole proprietorships that will be operating under an assumed or fictitious name (a business name that does not include the sole proprietor's surname or one that implies other owners are involved) to file a statement identifying the true owner of the business. Other than these laws and regulations, sole proprietorships are subject to minimal statutory burdens.

C. Advantages of Sole Proprietorships

One of the reasons the sole proprietorship is such a popular way of doing business is that this enterprise is easily and inexpensively formed and offers great flexibility to the business owner. Sole proprietorships themselves are not created or governed by state or federal statutes, and thus their formation is readily accomplished. The owner is free to make all decisions regarding the business. The sole proprietor can select the name of the business, establish its location, decide what products and services will be offered by the business, hire and fire employees, and establish the business policies and hours of operation for the business. Vacations can be taken when the sole proprietor desires and the sole proprietor does not have to secure permission from others to make decisions affecting the business. Furthermore, the sole proprietor retains all of the profits generated by the business and does not have to share them with any co-owner. Finally, the owner is not vulnerable to the incompetence or dishonesty of partners and is free to sell the business without having to secure approval from partners.

D. Disadvantages of Sole Proprietorships

1. *Unlimited Personal Liability*

The chief disadvantage of doing business as a sole proprietor is that the sole proprietor is personally liable for the debts, obligations, and liabilities of the business. Assume a sole proprietor is operating a restaurant. If rent is owed to the owner of the building or money is owed to the restaurant's chief wine supplier, these creditors are not limited to seizing only money in the restaurant's business accounts. The sole proprietor's liability extends beyond what has been invested in the business to his or her personal assets. In most states, statutes exist to provide that certain property is exempt from attachment, so that the sole proprietor is not stripped of all assets. For example, household furnishings, appliances, and other personal effects may be exempt if they are personally used by the sole proprietor and are reasonably necessary. Similarly, certain heirlooms, jewelry, and artworks may be exempt to the extent they do not exceed some stated statutory value, often $2,500. In general, however, view the front door of the sole proprietor's house as wide open and the contents therein available for picking by any creditors of the business. Thus, the sole proprietorship is so closely affiliated with the sole proprietor that its debts become his or her debts.

Sole proprietors are liable not only for business obligations but also for the torts or civil wrongs they commit or that are committed by their employees or agents acting in the course and scope of their employment. For example, if one of the restaurant's employees negligently trips a patron or spills scalding coffee on a patron, the sole proprietor will be liable for such acts. On the other hand, if the employee causes a car accident while not on duty, the sole proprietor would not likely have any liability for this act.

Because the risk of a sole proprietor extends to personal assets, the sole proprietorship may not be the best form of business enterprise for a wealthy individual, all of whose assets and wealth are subject to the debts and liabilities of the sole proprietorship.

To protect against the disadvantage of unlimited **personal liability,** the sole proprietor may seek to obtain insurance. General liability insurance, however, is usually costly to secure and may not be available to cover every type of risk. The sole proprietor may also seek to enter into contractual arrangements with creditors whereby, in return for obtaining the proprietor's business, they agree not to look to his or her personal assets to satisfy debts. Additional protection is provided by the fact that the sole proprietor has total control over decision-making and does not have to worry that a partner is obligating the business for unnecessary items.

Personal liability
Liability extending beyond what is invested in a business to an individual's personal assets (also called *unlimited liability*)

Generally, when people realize the extent of the liability of a sole proprietor, they often wonder why anyone would select this form of business enterprise. Some businesses, however, such as a typical retail store, often have slight exposure to unknown liabilities. A skating rink, chemical manufacturing plant, or a child care center, however, are far riskier businesses, and thus the sole proprietorship may not be appropriate for such enterprises that have increased exposure to potential liability.

2. *Lack of Continuity*

Because the sole proprietorship is so closely affiliated with the sole proprietor, the sole proprietorship generally terminates upon the death of the sole proprietor. While some state statutes provide for continuity of certain types of businesses, the general rule is that the sole proprietorship cannot survive the death of the sole proprietor. If the business assets descend to an heir who continues to operate the business, a new sole proprietorship has been created. The restaurant may look the same and offer the same products and services, but a new sole proprietorship has been created.

Sole proprietorships can be sold to another. However, because the business is so closely identified with its owner, a change in ownership may dramatically affect the business itself. To provide some continuity, the new owner may employ the previous owner or retain his or her services as an advisor or consultant during a transition period. The new owner, who has created a new sole proprietorship, should obtain a covenant from the previous owner not to compete against the new business for some reasonable period of time. (See Chapter Eighteen for discussion of covenants not to compete.)

3. *Difficulties in Raising Capital*

Capital
Money used to form and operate a business or other venture

If a partnership needs to raise additional **capital,** or money, to meet an unforeseen need or to expand the business, there may be several partners who can contribute this needed capital. Corporations can raise money by selling shares. The sole proprietor, on the other hand, is limited in his or her ways of obtaining additional money. The sole proprietor can look only to his or her own funds or can attempt to obtain loans. If banks or other parties do not believe the business has a proven track record, they may refuse to make loans, and the sole proprietorship may collapse just as it is on the verge of becoming a success. This difficulty in obtaining and raising capital is a disadvantage of a sole proprietorship. The Small Business Administration offers a variety of loan programs and loan guaranty programs to small businesses that are unable to secure financing on reasonable terms through normal business channels.

4. *Management Difficulties*

The sole proprietor has the flexibility of making all management decisions; however, sometimes this can be a disadvantage. The business may need special assistance or expertise as it grows. A partnership may admit new partners to respond to these needs. A corporation can rely on its board of directors and officers to provide managerial expertise. The sole proprietor, however, is also the sole decision-maker and may lack certain skills to respond to a changing economy, a changing market, or a growing business. Thus, sole proprietors may have to hire experts and advisors.

Sole proprietors tend to work very hard. They often invest their emotion as well as their money into the enterprise. It may be difficult to take a vacation if the sole proprietor cannot find committed employees or managers. The sole proprietor may work in the business all day and then spend evenings doing bookkeeping and marketing. Most sole proprietors find operating the business both exhilarating and exhausting. (See Figure 2-1 for a chart comparing the advantages and disadvantages of sole proprietorships.)

E. Formation of Sole Proprietorships

One of the greatest advantages of a sole proprietorship is the lack of formalities in organizing and forming this enterprise. Most of the requirements involved in forming the sole proprietorship are common to almost any business and are not imposed on this enterprise simply because it is a sole proprietorship.

1. *Licensing Considerations*

If the sole proprietor will be engaged in a business that has licensing requirements, he will need to comply with these. For example, attorneys must acquire a license to practice law, real estate and insurance agents must pass a test to become licensed, and restaurants that serve liquor must obtain liquor licenses from the appropriate alcoholic beverage control authority.

To determine whether the business is one that requires a license, review your state's statutes, your state's administrative code (which generally includes all information relating to any testing for the license or prerequisites that must be met), or contact any association which may govern the profession, such as the department of realtors or your state's bar association.

Sole proprietorships can conduct business in other localities or states so long as their licensing and name requirements are followed.

FIGURE 2-1
Sole Proprietorships

Advantages	*Disadvantages*
Easy to form and maintain	Unlimited personal liability
Inexpensive to form	Limited ways of raising capital
Owner is sole decision-maker	Lack of continuity
Management is informal and flexible	Possible lack of expertise in management

2. *Name Considerations*

Fictitious name
A name that must be registered with state or local officials because it does not disclose the surname of the business owner

DBA
"Doing business as"; another name for a fictitious business name statement

Fictitious business name statement
Record filed with public officials to identify the owner of a business operating under a name other than the owner's surname

Many sole proprietors choose to operate their businesses under a name other than their own. This is often referred to as an ***assumed name, trade name,*** or a **fictitious name.** For example, assume Susan Sullivan intends to operate a restaurant. She may prefer to call the restaurant "The Venetian Garden" rather than "Susan Sullivan's Restaurant." Because The Venetian Garden is a fictitious name, Susan must generally file a document with her local or state authority informing the public that she intends to "do business as" or "trade as" The Venetian Garden. Sometimes this document is referred to as the **dba** statement (for "doing business as"). An example of a **fictitious business name statement** is shown in Figure 2-2. This document protects consumers who can then determine the actual owner of the restaurant if a lawsuit must be filed against the sole proprietor. Most jurisdictions provide a form to be completed. The form is generally quite simple to complete and, while a fee may be charged, it is often less than $25.

While standards vary from state to state, the general rule in determining whether the fictitious business name statement must be filed is as follows: If the business name includes the sole proprietor's last name and does not imply that others are involved (by using terms such as "Associates," "Brothers," and so forth), no statement need be filed. Consumers are always entitled to know who may be sued, and signals such as "Associates" or "and Company" imply other owners may be involved in the business. Thus, such names must be registered. Because the cost of filing the statement is so low, and because the form is so easy to complete, when in doubt, file the fictitious business name statement. Failure to file the statement may result in a fine or refusal to allow the sole proprietor to institute or defend a legal action, although the sole proprietor can usually cure the defect and file the statement in order to litigate. The statement is usually valid for a few years and can be renewed. Some states, such as California, require that the name be published in a newspaper of general circulation in the area in which the business will be located to afford notice to the public of the sole proprietor's intent to conduct business under an assumed or fictitious name.

When selecting a name, the sole proprietor cannot operate under a name likely to cause confusion with another enterprise. The agency with which you file the statement will generally check to see if the name is available in that locality. For a more thorough check, the sole proprietor can have searches conducted of business names throughout the nation. Sole proprietors who intend to conduct business in various localities or jurisdictions should conduct these more thorough searches. Two companies that specialize in such name searches are:

Corsearch Inc.	*Thomson & Thomson*
28 West 23rd St., 7th Floor New York, NY 10010 1-800-SEARCH-1® (212) 627-0330 www.corsearch.com	500 Victory Road North Quincy, MA 02171 (800) 692-8833 (617) 786-8273 www.thomson-thomson.com

These companies will check trade associations, telephone directories, Internet uses, and other sources to determine if a name is already being used. Alternatively, you can access the trademark database of the U.S. Patent and Trademark Office

FIGURE 2-2
California Fictitious Business Name Statement

WARREN SLOCUM, Assessor-County Clerk-Recorder
Attn: Special Services
400 County Center, 6th Floor
Redwood City, California 94063-1647

REMINDER
1. Submit Original and 3 copies.
2. Filing Fee $28.00 for 1st Business Name and Registrant, $5.00 for each additional Business Name, and Partner.
3. Provide Return Envelope, if mailed.

PLEASE PRINT OR TYPE **SEE REVERSE SIDE FOR INSTRUCTIONS**

FICTITIOUS BUSINESS NAME STATEMENT (FILE No.)

THE FOLLOWING PERSON(S) IS (ARE) DOING BUSINESS AS:

* ....
(Type/Print Fictitious Business Name[s] on Line Above)
USE SEPARATE SHEET OF PAPER FOR ADDITIONAL BUSINESS NAMES

** **LOCATED AT:** ....
(Street Address of Business — if No Street Address Assigned — Give Exact Location of Business Plus P.O. Box or Rural Route)

IN: ....
(City and Zip)

IS [ARE] HEREBY REGISTERED BY THE FOLLOWING OWNER[S]:

*** (#1) .... (#2) ....
(Full Name — Type/Print) (Full Name — Type/Print)

(Residence Address or state of incorporation if incorporated) (Residence Address or state of incorporation if incorporated)

(City and Zip) (City and Zip)

(#3) .... (#4) ....
(Full Name — Type/Print) (Full Name — Type/Print)

(Residence Address or state of incorporation if incorporated) (Residence Address or state of incorporation if incorporated)

(City and Zip) (City and Zip)

(If More Than 4 Registrants - Attach Additional Sheet Showing Owner Information)

**** **This business is conducted by:** ☐ **an Individual** ☐ **Individuals — Husband and Wife** ☐ **a General Partnership** ☐ **Co-Partners** ☐ **a Limited Partnership** ☐ **a Corporation** ☐ **a Business Trust** ☐ **a Joint Venture** ☐ **Limited Liability Company** ☐ **an Unincorporated Association — other than a Partnership** ☐ **Other** *(Specify)* ....

***** The registrant commenced to transact business under the fictitious business name or names listed above on ________________.

SIGNATURE OF REGISTRANT: ....

(Print name of person signing and, if a Corporate Officer, also state title)

THIS STATEMENT WAS FILED WITH WARREN SLOCUM, ASSESSOR-COUNTY CLERK-RECORDER, SAN MATEO COUNTY ON DATE INDICATED BY FILE STAMP ABOVE

A FICTITIOUS BUSINESS NAME STATEMENT EXPIRES FIVE YEARS FROM THE DATE IT WAS FILED IN THE OFFICE OF THE COUNTY CLERK.

THE FILING OF THIS STATEMENT DOES NOT OF ITSELF AUTHORIZE THE USE IN THIS STATE OF A FICTITIOUS BUSINESS NAME IN VIOLATION OF THE RIGHTS OF ANOTHER UNDER FEDERAL, STATE, OR COMMON LAW (SEE SECTION 14400 ET SEQ., BUSINESS AND PROFESSIONS CODE).

COUNTY CLERK

Rev. 7-98

(<www.uspto.gov>) to review trademarks applied for or registered with the Patent and Trademark Office.

3. Business and Sales Tax Permits

Many jurisdictions require that the sole proprietor obtain a basic license to do business. For example, New York City requires that an application be completed for any business to be conducted in the city, whether it is a sole proprietorship, a partnership, or a corporation. In addition to including routine items such as names and addresses, the applicant must indicate whether he or she has been convicted of any offenses or violations of the law and whether any other type of license has previously been denied to the applicant.

If the sole proprietor will be selling goods, arrangements must be made to pay sales tax to the appropriate authority. Contact your state's taxing agency to obtain a sales tax permit.

A sole proprietor who hires employees must apply for an employer identification number in order to make arrangements to withhold federal income tax. Application for the number is made by obtaining Form SS-4 from the Internal Revenue Service and filing it with the Service. This form (see Figure 2-3) is easily completed. Forms can be obtained by calling the IRS at (800) 829-1040 or accessing the IRS Web site at <http://www.irs.gov>.

F. Taxation of Sole Proprietorships

Because the sole proprietorship itself is so closely identified with the individual operating it, it is not recognized as a separate taxable entity. Thus, the sole proprietorship itself does not pay any federal income tax. Income derived from the sole proprietorship is simply added to any other income the sole proprietor makes (whether from leasing of a rental unit, game-show winnings, or income earned through receipt of a cash dividend on shares of stock the sole proprietor may own), and the sole proprietor pays tax on this entire amount. The income earned from the business, however, is reported on a separate form called Schedule C (see Figure 2-4) which is attached to the proprietor's individual income tax return (Form 1040). Sole proprietors who meet certain criteria, such as having no employees and claiming less than $2500 for business expenses, may use a new schedule, called Schedule C-EZ, which is simple and easy to complete (see Figure 2-5). The sole proprietor may declare and deduct various business expenses such as advertising, business insurance, and interest paid, and use these to offset income. The sole proprietor pays tax on all net income, even money retained for anticipated business expenditures.

The sole proprietor pays tax at whatever rate or "bracket" is appropriate. (See Figure 2-6 for schedule of tax rates for individuals.) Thus, depending on the individual's income and the income earned from the business, the tax rate may be lower than the corporate tax rate (especially in the first few years of the business when expenses are high and the business may not be an immediate success). If tax circumstances change, the sole proprietor can later incorporate the business to take advantage of corporate tax rates.

FIGURE 2-3
IRS Form SS-4

Form **SS-4**
(Rev. February 1998)
Department of the Treasury
Internal Revenue Service

Application for Employer Identification Number
(For use by employers, corporations, partnerships, trusts, estates, churches, government agencies, certain individuals, and others. See instructions.)
▶ Keep a copy for your records.

EIN
OMB No. 1545-0003

Please type or print clearly.

1 Name of applicant (legal name) (see instructions)

2 Trade name of business (if different from name on line 1)
3 Executor, trustee, "care of" name

4a Mailing address (street address) (room, apt., or suite no.)
5a Business address (if different from address on lines 4a and 4b)

4b City, state, and ZIP code
5b City, state, and ZIP code

6 County and state where principal business is located

7 Name of principal officer, general partner, grantor, owner, or trustor—SSN or ITIN may be required (see instructions) ▶

8a Type of entity (Check only one box.) (see instructions)
Caution: *If applicant is a limited liability company, see the instructions for line 8a.*

☐ Sole proprietor (SSN)
☐ Estate (SSN of decedent)
☐ Partnership
☐ Personal service corp.
☐ Plan administrator (SSN)
☐ REMIC
☐ National Guard
☐ Other corporation (specify) ▶
☐ State/local government
☐ Farmers' cooperative
☐ Trust
☐ Church or church-controlled organization
☐ Federal government/military
☐ Other nonprofit organization (specify) ▶ (enter GEN if applicable)

Sole proprietors are entitled to establish qualified retirement plans for themselves, typically called **Keogh plans** after the Keogh Act, which allows self-employed individuals to make tax deductible contributions for retirement plans for themselves. (See Chapter 18 for additional information on Keogh plans.)

Keogh plan
A retirement plan for sole proprietors

Key Features of Sole Proprietorships

- Business is owned and managed by one person.
- Sole proprietor retains all profits and bears all losses.
- Sole proprietor's personal assets can be reached to satisfy business obligations ("personal liability").
- Business is easily and inexpensively formed.
- All income earned is passed through to sole proprietor, who pays tax at appropriate individual tax bracket.

FIGURE 2-4
IRS Schedule C

SCHEDULE C (Form 1040)
Department of the Treasury Internal Revenue Service (99)

Profit or Loss From Business
(Sole Proprietorship)
▶ Partnerships, joint ventures, etc., must file Form 1065 or Form 1065-B.
▶ Attach to Form 1040 or Form 1041. ▶ See Instructions for Schedule C (Form 1040).

OMB No. 1545-0074
1999
Attachment Sequence No. 09

Name of proprietor | Social security number (SSN)

A Principal business or profession, including product or service (see page C-1) | B Enter code from pages C-8 & 9 ▶

C Business name. If no separate business name, leave blank. | D Employer ID number (EIN), if any

E Business address (including suite or room no.) ▶
City, town or post office, state, and ZIP code

F Accounting method: (1) ☐ Cash (2) ☐ Accrual (3) ☐ Other (specify) ▶
G Did you "materially participate" in the operation of this business during 1999? If "No," see page C-2 for limit on losses . ☐ Yes ☐ No
H If you started or acquired this business during 1999, check here . . . ▶ ☐

Part I Income

1	Gross receipts or sales. **Caution:** *If this income was reported to you on Form W-2 and the "Statutory employee" box on that form was checked, see page C-2 and check here* . . . ▶ ☐	1	
2	Returns and allowances . . .	2	
3	Subtract line 2 from line 1 . . .	3	
4	Cost of goods sold (from line 42 on page 2) . . .	4	
5	**Gross profit.** Subtract line 4 from line 3 . . .	5	
6	Other income, including Federal and state gasoline or fuel tax credit or refund (see page C-3) . . .	6	
7	**Gross income.** Add lines 5 and 6 . . . ▶	7	

G. Role of Paralegal

Because forming a sole proprietorship is relatively simple, only a few tasks may be required of a paralegal.

1. Paralegals should determine whether the business to be engaged in is one requiring a license, such as the sale of liquor, construction work, or the sale of real estate.
2. Pertinent state statutes should be reviewed to determine whether a fictitious business name statement must be filed.
3. Consideration should be given as to whether a name search should be conducted to ensure the name selected by the sole proprietor does not infringe a name already in use.
4. If the sole proprietorship is engaged in a business subject to local or state sales taxes, a sales tax certificate must be filed with the pertinent authority.
5. If the business employs people, arrangements must be made to contribute to Social Security and a federal employer identification number must be obtained by completing and filing IRS Form SS-4.

FIGURE 2-5
IRS Schedule C-EZ

SCHEDULE C-EZ (Form 1040)

Department of the Treasury
Internal Revenue Service (99)

Net Profit From Business
(Sole Proprietorship)

▶ Partnerships, joint ventures, etc., must file Form 1065 or 1065-B.
▶ Attach to Form 1040 or Form 1041. ▶ See instructions on back.

OMB No. 1545-0074
1999
Attachment Sequence No. **09A**

Name of proprietor | **Social security number (SSN)**

Part I **General Information**

You May Use Schedule C-EZ Instead of Schedule C Only If You:

- Had business expenses of $2,500 or less.
- Use the cash method of accounting.
- Did not have an inventory at any time during the year.
- Did not have a net loss from your business.
- Had only one business as a sole proprietor.

And You:

- Had no employees during the year.
- Are not required to file **Form 4562,** Depreciation and Amortization, for this business. See the instructions for Schedule C, line 13, on page C-3 to find out if you must file.
- Do not deduct expenses for business use of your home.
- Do not have prior year unallowed passive activity losses from this business.

A Principal business or profession, including product or service | **B Enter code from pages C-8 & 9** ▶

C Business name. If no separate business name, leave blank. | **D Employer ID number (EIN), if any**

E Business address (including suite or room no.). Address not required if same as on Form 1040, page 1.

City, town or post office, state, and ZIP code

FIGURE 2-6
Federal Taxation (1998)

Taxable Income Taxpayers Filing Jointly	*Taxable Income Taxpayer Filing Singly*	*Tax Rate*
$0 – $42,350	$0 – $25,350	15%
$42,351 – $102,300	$25,351 – $61,400	28%
$102,301 – $155,950	$61,401 – $128,100	31%
$155,951 – $278,450	$128,101 – $278,450	36%
More than $278,450	More than $278,450	39.6%

Resource Guide

Several resources are available to assist paralegals working to form a sole proprietorship. The most common are:

1. The Internal Revenue Service

To obtain various IRS forms (including Schedule C, C-EZ, and form SS-4), contact the toll-free IRS tax forms number: (800) 829-3676. The forms will be sent to you within 7 to 15 working days.

2. U.S. Small Business Administration

The SBA is an independent government agency providing small businesses with practical guidance on business issues. It also assists small businesses in obtaining low-cost loans and government contracts and provides assistance to minority-owned businesses. The national office of the SBA is located at 409 Third Street, S.W., Washington, D.C. 20416. The SBA maintains a toll-free line to answer inquiries at (800) 827-5722 (800-UASK-SBA). A Small Business "Startup Kit" can be obtained from your local SBA office. It contains a wealth of information regarding starting a business. The Startup Kit will be sent to you within two to three weeks.

The SBA has offices in most large cities. Check your telephone directory to obtain the local number or call the toll-free Answer Desk number given above.

Information from the SBA is free and includes a variety of pamphlets and materials on forming and operating small businesses, financing businesses, counseling and training, procurement assistance, women's business ownership, and other topics.

3. Local Government Agencies

Many agencies in your county and city can provide advice and forms needed in forming sole proprietorships. Check the telephone directory listings for Business Licenses, Assessments, Licenses and Permits, or Business and Economic Development. In smaller localities, contact your town clerk and ask for information.

4. State Statutes

You must review the pertinent statutes in your state to determine which state laws govern the formation and operation of sole proprietorships. Nearly every state has statutes relating to requirements for fictitious business names or trade names. Review these statutes carefully to determine whether the name selected for the sole proprietorship requires the filing of a fictitious business name statement.

5. Secretaries of State

Each of the 50 states and the District of Columbia has an office dedicated to business enterprises. In each state's capital, there will be a secretary of state's office maintaining records and information related to businesses in that state. In the District of Columbia, the agency is called the Department of Consumer and Regulatory Affairs (Corporate Division). These offices will provide you with additional information as to any state requirements relating to sole proprietorships as well as forms and checklists. A list of all of these offices, together with their addresses, phone numbers, and Web sites is found in Appendix A.

6. General Business Organizations

Contact your local chamber of commerce for information on small businesses and start-up assistance. The National Association for the Self-Employed

(2121 Precinct Line Road, Hurst, TX 76054, (800) 232-NASE) offers introductory information and guides for small businesses, including information on hiring procedures, raising money, and advertising.

◆ ◆ ◆

WEB RESOURCES

While a few states and jurisdictions have made fictitious business name statements available on the Internet, most have not. Nevertheless, there is a vast array of information available to the small business owner or sole proprietor.

www.nass.org
This Web site of the National Association of Secretaries of State allows you to link directly to the home page for each state's secretary of state. Point the cursor at "States," and you will be presented with a list of all states and flags for all states. Point and click on your state's name or flag. Look for information about business structures in the state or guides on forming businesses in the state.

www.irs.gov
The Web site of the Internal Revenue Service offers guides and pamphlets on tax obligations as well as hundreds of tax forms (and their instructions) to download and print.

www.sba.gov
The Web site of the Small Business Association offers the Small Business Startup Kit, as well as several excellent publications about forming and operating small businesses.

http://sbinformation.about.com/msub7.htm
This site provides direct links to each state's secretary of state, department of revenue, and so forth, as well as directing you to links providing information on starting businesses in the state selected.

Discussion Questions

1. Is the name "Sam Baker & Sons" a fictitious name such that it would have to be registered with an appropriate agency? Discuss.

2. Randall operates a dry cleaning establishment as a sole proprietor. The county has received a judgment against Randall for $90,000, the cost of cleaning up chemicals buried by Randall on his property. Randall has only $60,000 in his business accounts to pay the judgment. From what other sources, if any, may the county recover? Is there anything Randall could have done to protect himself?

3. Kate operates a catering company as a sole proprietor. In the course of catering a dinner party, one of Kate's employees becomes involved in a heated dis-

pute with the customer and pushes her in trying to grab payment for the services from the customer. Kate has been sued for assault and battery. Discuss Kate's liability for this act.

4. A law firm's client, Janet, is extremely wealthy. She plans to operate a child care business as a sole proprietor. Discuss the advantages and disadvantages to Janet of operating her business as a sole proprietor.

3

General Partnerships

CHAPTER OVERVIEW

A partnership is a voluntary agreement between two or more persons to do business together for profit. No particular written document is needed to create a partnership; the agreement may be oral or written. Partnerships range in size from two persons to hundreds of persons. The "persons" in a partnership may be individuals, other partnerships, or even corporations. A partnership is often referred to as a "general partnership" to distinguish it from a "limited partnership." In brief, in general partnerships all partners have rights to manage and control the business and all suffer the disadvantage of unlimited liability. As you will see in Chapter Four, in a limited partnership, some partners (called the "limited" partners) cannot manage or control the business and their liability is limited to the amount they have invested in the enterprise. General partnerships can be created with very little formality, while limited partnerships can be formed only by strict compliance with statutory requirements.

A. Characteristics of General Partnerships

A general partnership is a voluntary association of two or more persons who agree to carry on business together for profit. The agreement may be either written or oral, although a written agreement is strongly recommended because it provides certainty in the event of a dispute among partners. General partnerships are easy and inexpensive to form, and there is little state regulation. The partners share decision-making and equally manage the business. In return for their ability to jointly manage the business enterprise and the flexibility in operating the business,

Unlimited personal liability
Liability for business debt, which extends beyond what is invested in a business to an individual's personal assets

partners suffer the disadvantage of **unlimited personal liability,** meaning that their personal assets can be reached by creditors. Because partners are agents of each other and the partnership, one partner can bind the partnership and co-partners by his or her acts, resulting in ruinous personal liability for an act other partners may not have approved or even known about. Partnerships operate with great flexibility, and the partners are free to agree to manage the business in almost any way they desire, so long as they do not engage in unlawful acts.

B. Governing Law

UPA
Uniform Partnership Act, model for partnership legislation in about one-half of the states

Much of the law governing partnerships is located in the **Uniform Partnership Act (UPA).** This model statute was drafted by the National Conference of Commissioners on Uniform State Laws, a group of more than 300 legal scholars, which recommended that each state adopt the Act to govern partnerships so there would be a certain amount of uniformity among the states in their treatment of partnerships.

The UPA acts as a "safety net" for partnerships. Generally, partners can agree to manage and conduct their partnership any way they see fit, so long as they do not engage in some illegal act. Oftentimes, however, a dispute may arise between the partners regarding some issue on which the partnership agreement is silent. If partners have not agreed among themselves how to deal with an issue, the UPA will govern the issue. It therefore acts as a safety net or default statute to provide terms and conditions relating to the partnerships when the partners have failed to reach an understanding.

RUPA
Revised Uniform Partnership Act, model for partnership legislation in about one-half of the states

In 1992, the National Conference of Commissioners adopted a **Revised Uniform Partnership Act (RUPA).** Additional changes were incorporated in 1994, 1996, and 1997, and approved by the American Bar Association. The RUPA retains most of the basic features of the UPA but does include some significant changes. Various states are in the process of adopting the RUPA so that eventually most states will be governed by the RUPA rather than the UPA. At the time of this writing, 23 states and the District of Columbia have adopted the RUPA. The remainder of the states (except for Louisiana) continue to follow the UPA. See Figure 3-1 for designation of which states follow each act. Thus, because the U.S. jurisdictions are nearly evenly divided as to which act is followed, a thorough understanding of the differences between the UPA and RUPA is necessary. Additionally, while some states adopt the UPA or RUPA verbatim, other states will make changes to the "uniform" acts. Thus, while there is a great deal of similarity between the partnership laws in California and Minnesota, both of which have adopted the RUPA, there may be some differences as well. Louisiana has adopted neither the UPA nor the RUPA. Louisiana partnerships are governed by case law developed in Louisiana and by various statutes relating to partnerships. See Appendix B for selected UPA provisions and Appendix C for selected RUPA provisions. The states that have adopted the UPA and those that have adopted the RUPA, as well as their governing statutes, are also identified in Appendixes B and C, respectively.

General partnership
A voluntary association of two or more persons to carry on a business for profit

Under the RUPA, a **general partnership** is an entity that operates independently of its member-partners, much like a corporation. Thus the partnership owns property in *its* name, *it* can be a plaintiff or defendant, and *it* is the party which enters into contracts or other obligations. Under the UPA, a partnership was an en-

FIGURE 3-1
Table of Jurisdictions Following UPA and RUPA

UPA	*RUPA*
Alaska	Alabama
Arkansas	Arizona
Delaware	California
Georgia	Colorado
Hawaii	Connecticut
Illinois	District of Columbia
Indiana	Florida
Kentucky	Idaho
Maine	Iowa
Massachusetts	Kansas
Michigan	Maryland
Mississippi	Minnesota
Missouri	Montana
Nevada	Nebraska
New Hampshire	New Mexico
New Jersey	North Dakota
New York	Oklahoma
North Carolina	Oregon
Ohio	Texas
Pennsylvania	Vermont
Rhode Island	Virginia
South Carolina	Washington
South Dakota	West Virginia
Tennessee	Wyoming
Utah	
Wisconsin	

tity in some respects but not in others. In general, under the UPA, a partnership is merely an aggregate collection of its members rather than a separate legal entity. Other significant differences between the UPA and RUPA relate to the rules governing breakups of partnerships. Under the UPA, a partnership is dissolved whenever a partner departs, for any reason. The RUPA attempts to provide more stability to partnerships by providing that only certain departures trigger a dissolution. Many dissociations or departures of partners result merely in a buyout of the withdrawing partner's interest. A chart comparing some of the more significant distinctions between the UPA and RUPA is found at Figure 3-10.

C. Partnership Defined

According to the UPA and the RUPA a partnership is "an association of two or more persons to carry on as co-owners a business for profit." An examination of each element of this definition is needed to fully understand the nature of a general partnership.

The element of "association" means that the partners have voluntarily agreed to associate or do business together. The agreement may be written, it may be oral, or it may be implied from conduct.

The "two or more persons" element of a partnership excludes sole proprietorships, which are, of course, managed and controlled by one person. The "persons" in the partnership may be individuals, or they may be other business enterprises, such as a partnership (either general or limited) or a corporation.

"Co-ownership" refers to the fact that the partners jointly own partnership property and have rights to participate in management and control of the enterprise and share profits and losses.

The word "business" refers to every trade, occupation, or profession.

By definition, a partnership must be carrying on a business "for profit." Naturally, not all businesses are profitable. Nevertheless, so long as there is the expectation of earning a profit, an enterprise will be deemed a partnership. Nonprofit organizations such as charitable and fraternal groups may not operate as partnerships.

A partnership can be formed for any purpose so long as it is legal. As seen in Figure 3-2, there are by far more partnerships devoted to finance, insurance, and real estate than any other businesses.

D. Partnership Property

1. *Property or Services Contributed by Partners or Acquired by Partnership*

Partners may contribute almost any type of property or service to the partnership—cash, real estate, office furniture, a car, a trademark—or services such as legal, accounting, or decorating services. Once contributed, and unless a partner specifies otherwise, the property then becomes the property of the partnership itself. The partner who contributed it cannot change her mind and tell the remaining partners, "Remember that car I provided as my $15,000 contribution? Well, I need it back to give to my husband." The car is no longer owned by that partner; it has become the property of the partnership. If something other than cash is contributed, the value of this contribution should be determined. If the partners cannot agree among themselves as to the value of a contribution, such as land or accounting services, they should retain an expert to value the contribution. If cash is contributed and then used to purchase office supplies and furniture, these items now become property of the partnership as well. The UPA provides that unless a contrary intention appears, property acquired with partnership funds is partnership property. UPA Section 8(2).

FIGURE 3-2
Partnerships (In Thousands) (1995)

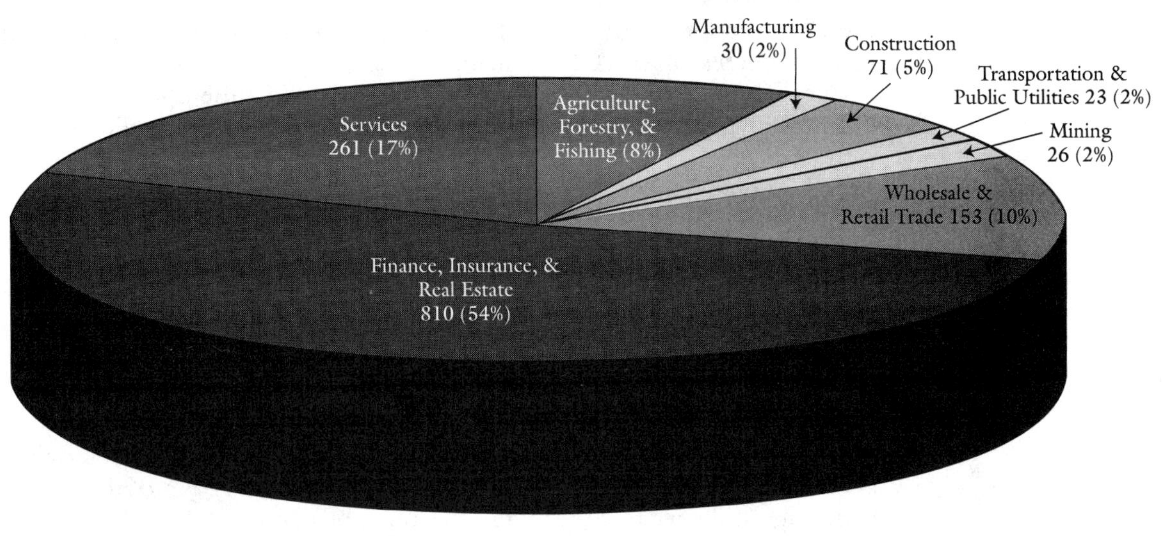

When it is not clear whether property belongs to the partnership or to some individual partner, a court will look to the parties' intentions. This is another example why a written partnership agreement clearly setting forth the rights and duties of all partners is important. If a partner intends to retain some right to property contributed, his or her rights should be clearly set forth in the agreement. The money or value of any property contributed by a partner forms the partner's **capital account.** A partner's capital account is increased if a partner makes additional contributions and decreased as distributions are made to the partners.

Capital account
Money or value of any property contributed by a partner

2. *Property Rights of Partners*

Partners, as individuals, have three property rights: their rights to specific partnership property; their interest in the partnership; and their right to participate in management. UPA Section 24.

Specific Partnership Property. Under the UPA, an individual partner has rights in specific partnership property. Thus, a car purchased for the partnership is co-owned by the partners under a theory entitled **tenancy in partnership.** Ownership rights to specific partnership property (cars, inventory, accounts receivable, promissory notes) are very limited: a partner cannot use the specific

Tenancy in partnership
Property co-owned by partners

property for her own benefit without the consent of the other partners; the property cannot be seized by a creditor of the partner; a partner cannot transfer or assign the specific property to another; and upon the death of a partner, the partner's heirs have no rights to such property. Section 203 of the RUPA clarifies the ambiguity in Sections 8 and 24 of the UPA by eliminating the theory of tenancy in partnership and clearly providing that property acquired by the partnership is owned by the partnership itself, rather than by the individual partners, who therefore cannot assign or transfer that property. This determination avoids the conflict inherent in the UPA which provides that a partner has "rights in specific partnership property" and then virtually cancels all of the rights one expects to flow from "ownership" (the right to use or transfer property and the right to leave it to one's heirs). Property acquired in the name of an individual partner, without an indication of partnership capacity and without use of partnership funds, is presumed to be owned by the individual partner, even if the property is used by the partnership. RUPA Section 204(d).

Interest in partnership
A partner's right to profits

Partnership Profits. A partner has an "interest in the partnership." Simply put, a partner's **interest in the partnership** refers to a partner's share of partnership profit. Typically, a partner's share of profits is based upon his initial contribution to the partnership. Thus, if Michael provides 34 percent of the initial assets or services contributed to the partnership, Michael will usually have the right to 34 percent of the partnership profits, will have to bear 34 percent of the partnership losses, and will have to contribute 34 percent of any additional capital which may be needed. The need to clearly value each partner's original contribution is critical: it typically is "etched in stone" and forms the basis for division of profits and losses.

The right to profit, if any, is a personal property right and a partner may transfer or assign this right to another. For example, if Michael owes spousal support to his ex-wife, he can have the partnership write a check to his ex-wife each month for his share of the partnership profits rather than writing a check directly to Michael. Similarly, Michael's share of earned profits can be reached by his individual creditors (such as a landlord or utility company) and will descend to his heirs upon his death. The mere fact that the ex-wife receives Michael's share of the profits does not make her a partner. A partnership is a voluntary arrangement and the other partners did not agree to do business with Michael's ex-wife, but rather with Michael. In brief, it is of no consequence to the partnership who ultimately receives any partner's share of profits.

Management. Partners also have the right to participate in management of the partnership. This right to manage and control the affairs of the partnership is typically exercised through voting at partnership meetings. A partner cannot assign or transfer this right to another, even if the partner believes another is more competent to act. Once again, a partnership is a voluntary arrangement; allowing some unknown third party to manage or control the partnership destroys this basic element of the partnership.

E. Advantages of General Partnerships

Many of the advantages of doing business as a general partnership are similar to those of doing business as a sole proprietor. A general partnership can be easily formed. While no written agreement is required (in which case, the UPA or RUPA, as the case may be, will "fill in the gaps"), it is always better to have a written agreement. Hiring an attorney to draft a partnership agreement can be somewhat expensive, but it is still easily accomplished. Often no filings need be made with any state agency and, thus, general partnerships are simple and relatively inexpensive to form.

Another advantage is shared management. A partner will have other partners to rely on to provide expertise in needed areas. Decisions can be made jointly after thorough discussion. Of course, this feature of shared decision-making may also be a disadvantage when a quick decision is needed. While sole proprietors can make all decisions themselves, partners must consult with each other on significant issues. Partnerships, however, have the flexibility of appointing certain partners as managers for the business, and they can be delegated the authority to make certain decisions by themselves.

Other partners can also serve as additional sources for capital. If additional money is needed for the partnership, there is more than one person to help. Other partners may have additional capital to make loans to the partnership or perhaps have strong credit backgrounds and can readily obtain a loan from a bank. The partnership can also consider admitting new partners to provide additional funds for the partnership.

While partners must share profits with each other, they also share losses in proportion to their contributions or as agreed upon. Thus, no one partner need bear all of the burden of losses sustained by the partnership.

Finally, as discussed in Section M, partnerships do not pay federal income tax. Net money earned is passed through to the individual partners who declare and pay tax on their respective share of partnership profits.

F. Disadvantages of General Partnerships

1. *Unlimited Personal Liability*

The primary disadvantage of doing business in a general partnership is that each partner has unlimited personal liability for debts and obligations of the partnership. Additionally, because partners have the authority to act for and bind each other, one partner may find herself facing unlimited personal liability for an obligation she did not know was incurred by another partner. Thus, personal assets are vulnerable to seizure by partnership creditors, assuming no statutory exemptions exist protecting certain assets.

Not only do partners have unlimited personal liability, that liability is joint and several for any wrongful acts of partners or breaches of trust. **Joint and several liability** means that a creditor can sue all partners for the wrongful act, can sue the partnership itself for the wrongful act, or may pick and choose among the

Joint and several liability
Theory that each partner and the partnership is liable for all debts and wrongful acts

partners as to which ones may be sued. Thus, a wealthy partner may find he is the sole target in a lawsuit arising because of his partner's misconduct, behavior of which he was not even aware. The theory used by courts to justify this somewhat harsh rule is that outside third parties injured by a partner's misconduct or breach of trust must be protected above all others. If the wealthy partner is "targeted," and he must pay the entire damages sum, he may later seek appropriate contribution from his co-partners. In essence, the message is that the innocent third party will be protected first, and it is up to partners later on to sort out the true allocation of the damages among themselves, according to either their partnership agreement, the UPA, or the RUPA.

A judgment obtained by a creditor against a partnership is not by itself a judgment against any individual partner. Thus, for the broadest scope of protection, creditors should name both the partnership and all of its members as defendants in any lawsuit. Then the judgment may be satisfied from partnership assets first and thereafter from individual partners' assets on the basis of joint and several liability.

As in sole proprietorships, partners can attempt to protect themselves against this unlimited personal liability by obtaining insurance or by attempting to secure agreements from third parties so they will not look to a partner's personal assets to satisfy debts. Using a corporation as a general partner will also minimize or eliminate personal liability because corporations have limited liability. Additional protection is derived from the **marshaling of assets** doctrine, requiring partnership creditors to first exhaust all partnership assets before they can attack the personal assets of any partner.

Marshaling of assets
Partnership theory requiring creditors to first exhaust partnership assets before pursuing partners' individual assets

2. *Lack of Continuity*

Like a sole proprietorship, a partnership under the UPA cannot survive the death or withdrawal of a partner (unless the partners have specified otherwise in their partnership agreement). This lack of continuity is an unattractive feature of a general partnership and provides less stability than does a corporation, which can endure perpetually. If the remaining partners continue doing business together, they have formed a new partnership different from the original partnership inasmuch as its membership is different.

3. *Difficulty in Transferring Partnership Interest*

If a shareholder no longer wishes to own stock in a corporation, the stock can usually be sold freely. A partner, however, may have more difficulty in leaving the partnership or transferring his interest in the partnership to another. As discussed above, the only transferable property right a partner has is his share of profits. Because a partnership is a voluntary arrangement, one partner cannot simply sell his partnership interest to another; the other partners have not agreed to do business with the newcomer. Admission of a new partner requires consent from the other partners; when the new partner enters the business, a new partnership is formed.

Withdrawing from a partnership may also be a breach of the partnership agreement. If all partners have signed an agreement stating that the term of the partnership is five years, and one partner withdraws early, she may be liable to the other partners for resulting damages. For example, if the wealthiest partner withdraws, banks may be unwilling to lend money to the partnership inasmuch as there is no longer a wealthy individual to guarantee repayment. Oftentimes, partnership agreements make it difficult for partners to withdraw early by providing a term for the existence of the partnership; partners may withdraw earlier than the set term but may be unable to withdraw their contributions to the partnership. Partners are thus faced with the unhappy choice of leaving the partnership, leaving their money behind, and then being unable to control the management of their money because they will no longer be a partner with any right to manage the business. Provisions setting forth a specified term for the partnership or prohibiting a return of contributions to partners who withdraw early are useful for discouraging withdrawal.

G. Formation of General Partnerships

The very definition of a general partnership, namely, that it is an association of two or more persons to operate a business for profit, ensures that there are few formalities involved in creating a general partnership. A partnership can be created by a simple oral agreement to form a catering business or even by a course of conduct in which parties act like partners in that they co-manage the business and share decision-making. There are usually no state filings needed to create a general partnership; the essence of the formation of this entity is the **agreement** to do business together, whether this agreement is memorialized in a document or not.

Partnership agreement
An agreement by two or more persons to do business together as a partnership; may be written or oral

Nevertheless, certain formalities may apply when creating a general partnership. Similar to a sole proprietorship, the partnership may choose to operate under a fictitious name. The general rule is that if all of the partners' surnames are included in the business name, then it is not fictitious. For example, suppose a partnership of Dave Adams, Susan Baker, Alan Carr and Geri Dolan is formed. If the partnership operates as "Adams, Baker, Carr & Dolan," no fictitious business name filing need be made. If, however, the business operates as "Adams & Baker" or "Adams & Company," then a fictitious business name statement must be filed. The use of signals such as "and Company" or "and Associates" makes the name fictitious in many states, since the signal implies the existence of other partners.

The **fictitious business name statement** is highly similar to, or in some instances, identical to, that required of a sole proprietor. The fictitious business name statement shown as Figure 2-2 may be used by partnerships as well as sole proprietors. Once again, public policy protects consumers, so they know who is responsible for operating the business and who can be sued for a debt or other obligation. Failure to file the appropriate fictitious business name statement, when required, will result in the same penalties being imposed upon a general partnership as are imposed on a sole proprietorship—generally, fines or inability to sue in that jurisdiction until the defect is cured. In no case may a partnership conduct business under a name likely to cause confusion with another business.

Fictitious business name statement
Statement filed with public official to indicate names of owners of a business

Just as with sole proprietorships, if the business is one that is subject to licensing requirements, the partnership must comply with these requirements. Thus, a real estate sales agency, a liquor store, or a general construction business may all have to comply with various statutes relating to the licensing of these businesses.

In most instances, a partnership can do business in a state other than the one in which it was formed without filing any documents or notices. Thus, a partnership operating in Maryland could expand and offer its services in Virginia and Delaware without any formal requirements. One state, however, New Hampshire, imposes requirements on partnerships that are formed outside New Hampshire and elect to do business therein. New Hampshire requires that the out-of-state partnership (called a **foreign partnership**) qualify to do business within its borders and that the foreign partnership appoint an agent who will be available to receive any summons and complaint (**service of process**) filed against the partnership. This is clearly a minority approach and may perhaps be viewed as a way to raise revenue rather than a scheme of strict state regulation of partnerships.

Foreign partnership
A partnership doing business in a state other than the one in which it was formed

Service of process
Providing litigation notices (summons and complaint)

H. Operation of General Partnerships

1. *Duties and Rights of Partners*

Partners owe each other fiduciary duties. They are required to deal with each other in good faith and to act in good faith for the benefit of the partnership. Partners stand in the same relationship to each other as do principals and agents. Therefore, they cannot engage in any activities that are detrimental to or competitive with the partnership (unless they disclose this conflict and receive consent from the other partners). While partners can vary or eliminate many UPA or RUPA provisions by their agreement, under RUPA Section 103(b), partners cannot eliminate the duties of good faith, loyalty, and fair dealing, or unreasonably reduce the duty of due care each partner owes to the other partners and the partnership.

Each partner is an agent of the partnership for business purposes and the act of any partner in carrying out the usual business of the partnership will bind the partnership, unless the partner had no authority to so act, and the person with whom the partner was dealing knew or had notice that the partner lacked authority. UPA Section 9(1); RUPA Section 301(1). This is referred to as **general agency** and, simply put, means that each partner has the authority to sign contracts, execute documents, and make purchases that will bind the partnership. For example, assume Patricia, Allen, and Doug are in a partnership engaged in selling auto supplies and performing automotive services. If Patricia routinely buys supplies for the business at Cars R Us but one day, using a company credit card, buys a CD player, car phone, and spoiler for her own use, the partnership is likely liable to Cars R Us for these purchases. The owners of Cars R Us had no knowledge that Patricia was not acting on behalf of the partnership. In fact, it appeared as if Patricia was acting for the partnership. The partnership must now pay for this debt. Because Patricia has violated her fiduciary duties to the partnership, her partners can then sue her for this breach and recover the money the partnership had to pay on her account. A court, however, will always protect the most innocent party. In this transaction, the most innocent party, Cars R Us, had no way of knowing that the goods sold were for Patricia's personal use rather than for the partnership business. Because Patricia is an agent for the partnership, her acts have bound the partnership. It is obviously important to know fully and trust

General agency
The authority of a partner to act for and bind the partnership and other partners

one's partners because these partners have the authority, under agency principles, to bind the partnership and its partners, whether those partners receive any specific benefit from the transaction or whether they even know about the transaction.

If a partnership is aware that one of its partners is acting irrationally by purchasing unneeded items for the partnership, the partnership should send written notices to as many of its suppliers and creditors as possible, stating that the partner no longer has the authority to bind the partnership and those creditors who sell items or provide credit to the partnership do so at their own risk and will have to look solely to that partner, rather than the partnership, for payment. In many instances, banks will not loan money to a partner for the partnership business without first reviewing the partnership agreement to ensure that such an act is authorized by the agreement.

Due to the risk inherent in the partnership principle that partners are agents of the partnership and thus their acts bind the partnership (assuming the partner's act is apparently taken for the purpose of carrying out the ordinary business of the partnership), RUPA Section 303 allows partnerships to file an optional **Statement of Authority** with state officials to provide public notice of the specific partners who are authorized to execute instruments transferring real estate. The Statement may also grant or limit partners' authority to enter into other transactions (see Figure 3-3).

Another new document, allowed by RUPA Section 304, is the **Statement of Denial,** typically filed by a partner to deny information given in the Statement of Authority, often filed by a withdrawing partner to provide notice that the partner denies his status as a partner (see Figure 3-4).

Statement of Authority
Document filed with secretary of state providing notice of partners who are authorized to act for partnership

Statement of Denial
Document filed with secretary of state denying information in statement of authority or providing notice of withdrawal from partnership

2. *Management of the Partnership*

Unless the partners decide otherwise, all partners have equal rights in the management of the partnership business. UPA Section 18(e); RUPA Section 401(f). Thus, regardless of initial capital contributions, if the partners have not agreed on a formula for voting, each partner has one vote in management matters. Assume that a partnership is composed of Ellen and James. Ellen contributed $60,000 to the partnership while James contributed $40,000. Ellen is likely to assume that because she has contributed more than James her voting and management rights should be greater. This is not the case. Unless Ellen and James agree on how management is to be conducted, the UPA and RUPA supply this missing term and mandate that Ellen and James have equal rights to manage and conduct the partnership's business.

Unless the partners agree otherwise, decision-making in the partnership is by majority vote. Certain extraordinary matters that dramatically affect the partnership usually require unanimous approval. According to UPA Section 9, unanimous consent of partners is needed for the following extraordinary activities:

- assigning the partnership property in trust for creditors
- disposing of the goodwill of the business
- performing any act which would make it impossible to carry on the ordinary activities of the partnership

FIGURE 3-3
California Statement of Authority

State of California
Secretary of State
Bill Jones

Form GP-1

STATEMENT OF PARTNERSHIP AUTHORITY

IMPORTANT-- Read instructions on back before completing form.

1. NAME OF PARTNERSHIP

2. STREET ADDRESS OF CHIEF EXECUTIVE OFFICE — CITY/STATE/COUNTRY — ZIP CODE

3. STREET ADDRESS OF A CALIFORNIA OFFICE, IF ANY — CITY — ZIP CODE
CALIFORNIA

4. ☐ A. LIST THE FULL NAMES AND MAILING ADDRESSES OF ALL PARTNERS (ATTACH ADDITIONAL PAGES, IF NECESSARY)

NAME:
ADDRESS:
CITY: STATE/COUNTRY: ZIP CODE:

NAME:
ADDRESS:
CITY: STATE/COUNTRY: ZIP CODE:

OR: ☐ B. STATE THE FULL NAME AND MAILING ADDRESS OF AN AGENT APPOINTED AND MAINTAINED BY THE PARTNERSHIP WHO WILL MAINTAIN A LIST OF THE NAMES AND MAILING ADDRESSES OF ALL PARTNERS.

NAME:
ADDRESS:
CITY:
STATE/COUNTRY:
ZIP CODE:

5. NAMES OF ALL PARTNERS AUTHORIZED TO EXECUTE INSTRUMENTS TRANSFERRING REAL PROPERTY HELD IN THE NAME OF THE PARTNERSHIP (ATTACH ADDITIONAL PAGES, IF NECESSARY)

PARTNER NAME: PARTNER NAME:
PARTNER NAME: PARTNER NAME:
PARTNER NAME: PARTNER NAME:

6. OTHER MATTERS, IF ANY: (ATTACH ADDITIONAL PAGES, IF NECESSARY)

7. NUMBER OF PAGES ATTACHED, IF ANY :

8. I DECLARE UNDER PENALTY OF PERJURY UNDER THE LAWS OF THE STATE OF CALIFORNIA THAT THE FOREGOING IS TRUE AND CORRECT.

SIGNATURE OF PARTNER — DATE EXECUTED
TYPE OR PRINT NAME OF PARTNER — COUNTY AND STATE EXECUTED

SIGNATURE OF PARTNER — DATE EXECUTED
TYPE OR PRINT NAME OF PARTNER — COUNTY AND STATE EXECUTED

For Secretary Of State Use
FILE #
DOCUMENT #

9. **RETURN TO:**
NAME:
ADDRESS:
CITY: STATE/COUNTRY: ZIP CODE:

FIGURE 3-4
California Statement of Denial

State of California
Secretary of State
Bill Jones

Form GP-2

STATEMENT OF DENIAL

IMPORTANT-- Read instructions on back before completing form.

1. NAME OF PARTNERSHIP	2. SECRETARY OF STATE FILE NUMBER

3. FACT DENIED, WHICH MAY INCLUDE DENIAL OF AUTHORITY OR STATUS AS A PARTNER:

4. NUMBER OF PAGES ATTACHED, IF ANY:

5. I DECLARE UNDER PENALTY OF PERJURY UNDER THE LAWS OF THE STATE OF CALIFORNIA THAT THE FOREGOING IS TRUE AND CORRECT.

SIGNATURE OF PARTNER — DATE EXECUTED

TYPE OR PRINT NAME OF PARTNER — COUNTY AND STATE EXECUTED

For Secretary Of State Use

DOCUMENT #__________

6. **RETURN TO:**

NAME:

ADDRESS:

CITY: STATE: ZIP CODE:

- confessing a judgment (permitting a judgment to be entered against one without the necessity for instituting legal proceedings) or submitting a partnership claim or liability to arbitration

While the UPA includes the foregoing detailed list of extraordinary activities that require unanimous approval of partners, the RUPA includes no equivalent provision, leaving it to the courts to determine which actions are beyond the authority of individual partners. Because, however, the acts identified by the UPA (such as assigning partnership property or submitting a claim to arbitration) are arguably not in the apparent scope of partnership business anyway, such a list may not be necessary, and its omission from the RUPA is thus understandable.

In a partnership with a large number of partners, it may be impractical for all partners to manage the business equally. Therefore, some partnerships will appoint a managing partner or a committee of partners for the management of some activities. For example, there may be a compensation committee, a hiring committee, and a marketing committee. These committees may study various proposals and then make reports to the entire membership which will then vote on these matters. Alternatively, the committees may have some limited authority to act on their own; for example, the hiring committee may be able to hire anyone whose salary will be less than $40,000. Individuals who will be hired at salaries in excess of $40,000 may then need to be approved by the majority vote of all partners.

3. *Compensation, Profits, and Accounting*

Ordinarily, general partners do not receive a salary for their services to the partnership. It is assumed that they will devote their undivided loyalty to the partnership business and therefore they will be paid from the profits of the business. Both the UPA and RUPA expressly provide that no partner is automatically entitled to remuneration for acting in the partnership business. UPA Section 18(f); RUPA Section 401(h). Partners often provide otherwise in their partnership agreement so they will be able to anticipate their monthly income. Oftentimes, partners will receive a monthly *draw* against the anticipated profits of the partnership, and at the end of the year, the draw is deducted from that partner's percentage of profits. Some partnerships, however, adhere strictly to the rule that partners are paid only from profits. In those partnerships, during a lean time, partners may have to borrow from a bank to pay their personal expenses such as mortgage or rent payments, insurance, and food. When the partnership receives funds, it may then distribute a large profit to its members who then repay the bank for their short-term loans, retaining the remainder until the next division of profits occurs. A partner having special responsibilities, such as a managing partner, may be paid a stated salary as a partnership expense, one not deducted from his share of the profits.

Because partners do not ordinarily receive compensation merely for performing services for the partnership, they typically expect to receive profits arising from the partnership's business operations. According to UPA Section 18(a) and RUPA Section 410(b), unless the partners agree otherwise, each partner is entitled to an equal share of the partnership profits (and is chargeable with a share of losses in the same proportion as profits), regardless of capital contributions to the partnership. To avoid these default provisions of the UPA and RUPA, most partnership agreements provide for the sharing of profits and losses in proportion to the amount contributed to the partnership by each partner. Nevertheless, partners are free to devise any arrangement they desire regarding the sharing of profits and losses.

Partners who incur or pay for expenses related to the partnership from their own money are entitled to be reimbursed by the partnership. UPA Section 18(b); RUPA Section 401(c). Thus, if needed inventory is delivered to the business and the partnership accounts are too low to pay for it, a partner advancing this money from her personal checking account is entitled to be reimbursed by the partnership, whether this action has been agreed upon or not. Otherwise, partners would be discouraged from taking actions to aid the partnership.

To determine whether the distribution of profits is correct, all partners have the right to inspect and copy the partnership's books of account. Partners also have a duty to supply information on matters affecting the partnership to their copartners. UPA Sections 19, 20; RUPA Section 403. In fact, because partners have fiduciary relationships to one another, any knowledge one partner has regarding partnership matters is imputed to all other partners. Finally, under UPA Section 22, a partner can demand a formal accounting if he is wrongfully excluded from the partnership affairs or whenever circumstances render such an accounting reasonable and just.

I. The Partnership Agreement

Although partnerships can be formed by oral agreement or even by a course of conduct, it is better practice to have a formal written partnership agreement that fully sets forth the partners' rights, duties, and liabilities. Failure to have a definitive agreement can cause many unanticipated consequences. For example, in our earlier scenario, Ellen and James formed a partnership, with Ellen contributing 60 percent of the capital and James contributing 40 percent of the capital. Because Ellen has contributed more than James she will likely expect to have more power than James in voting issues and to receive a greater portion of the profits. Without an agreement, however, UPA Section 18 and RUPA Section 401 supply these missing terms and provide that Ellen and James will be equal partners with regard to management, control, and sharing of profits and losses. Thus, if the partnership has net profits of $100,000, Ellen and James will share the profits equally ($50,000 each) without regard to their initial contributions.

Moreover, a partnership agreement will provide guidance in the event of a dispute among partners. If the partnership agreement is oral, it may be difficult to prove what the partners' agreement was with regard to various issues. Finally, investors and bankers prefer the clarity provided by a partnership agreement.

The *partnership agreement,* sometimes called the *articles of partnership,* can provide any terms with regard to operation, management, and control of the partnership so long as the terms are not illegal or contrary to statute or public policy. Thus, the parties are free to distribute profits and losses as they like, allowing one partner a greater share of profits because he provides the partnership with expertise and then indemnifying that partner against partnership debts or obligations.

A partnership agreement should be carefully drafted to accomplish the purposes and goals of its partners. Generally, however, a partnership agreement should include provisions relating to the following issues (see Appendix D for a sample partnership agreement):

1. *Name of Partnership*

The partnership can operate under the names of its partners or under a fictitious business name, so long as the appropriate filing is made. If all of the partners' last names are included in the name of the partnership, it is likely that the name is not fictitious. In any event, the partnership cannot operate under a name that is likely to cause confusion with another.

2. *Names and Addresses of the Partners*

The names and addresses of all partners should be set forth. Addresses are provided so that various notices and information can be communicated to the partners.

3. *Recitals*

Recitals
Introductory clauses in agreements setting forth basis for agreement

A **recital** clause simply states that it is the intent of the parties to the agreement to form a partnership. In the event of any dispute later, a partner will be precluded from alleging that the business arrangement was something other than a partnership.

4. *Purpose*

The purpose of the partnership should be stated. Be sure that the purpose is not so limited that it restricts the partnership from related activities or discourages growth of the business. It may be a good idea to state a somewhat specific purpose and then broaden it as follows: "The purpose of this partnership is to engage in the purchase and sale of real estate and any other acts incidental thereto or necessary therefor or as may be agreed upon by the partners."

5. *Address*

The principal place of business of the partnership should be provided so that partners and others can provide communications and notices to the partnership.

6. *Term*

The term or duration of the partnership should be provided. There are several alternatives that the partners can elect.

a. The partners may specify that the partnership shall have a definite term by stating, for instance, "This partnership shall come into existence on May 24, 1999 and shall terminate on December 31, 2003."
b. Because a partnership is a voluntary arrangement, the partners can agree that it will terminate upon their mutual agreement.
c. The partners can state that the partnership will terminate once its purposes have been accomplished; for example, the construction of a certain housing development.
d. The partnership may be terminable at will upon notice by any partner. If such a provision is elected, the partners should consider whether they may wish to continue doing business upon the withdrawal of one member and whether the withdrawing member is entitled to receive a return of his contribution and any profits before the partnership's stated term expires.

Under the UPA, partners who continue doing business after the withdrawal of a member will have formed a new partnership, and this new partnership is usually viewed as operating under or having adopted the prior written terms of the agreement.

7. *Financial Provisions*

Various provisions relating to financial items should be set forth, including the following:

a. The initial contributions of the partners should be specified. If partners contribute money, the exact amount contributed should be set forth. Often, contributions by partners are identified in a separate exhibit or attachment to the partnership agreement. If legal, accounting, management, decorating or other services are provided, or if property such as real estate is contributed, they should be valued so each partner's initial contribution is clearly set forth.
b. The agreement should indicate under what circumstances additional capital might need to be contributed. For example, if the business sustains a loss or needs additional money to operate, the agreement should state the amount of each partner's expected additional contribution.

Typically, calculation of additional contributions is determined by the initial contributions made by each partner. Thus, if Anna contributed 34 percent of the initial capital, Bob contributed 22 percent of the initial capital, and David contributed 44 percent of the initial capital, additional contributions will be made in the same proportion, so that if $100,000 additional capital is needed, Anna must contribute $34,000; Bob must contribute $22,000; and David must contribute $44,000.

The partners may make alternative arrangements. For example, if one partner is contributing expertise and business acumen to the partnership and is assuming all responsibilities of managing the partnership, he or she may be excused from additional contributions. If a partner cannot make the required additional contribution, another partner may make it and thereby increase his ownership interest in the partnership.

This section of the agreement should also specify whether partners may make loans or advances to the partnership, what interest will be paid on such loans, and how they are to be repaid. Under both UPA Section 18(c) and RUPA Section 401(e), payments or advances made by partners to aid the partnership are viewed as loans to the partnership that automatically carry interest.

The partners may wish to retain some profit in a bank account so that in the event of an emergency (for example, replacement of the roof of the apartment building owned by the partnership) additional contributions are not required.

If the partners wish to withdraw their capital prior to the termination of the partnership, the terms and conditions of such withdrawal should be expressly provided. Many agreements provide that no withdrawal of capital from the partnership is allowed prior to dissolution of the partnership.

8. Profits and Losses

The agreement should clearly specify each partner's share of profits and the losses to be borne by each partner. There are several alternatives:

a. Profits and losses may be shared equally by the partners.
b. Profits are shared and losses may be borne in proportion to the initial contributions to the partnerships. Thus, using our example, Anna would be entitled to 34 percent of any profits, Bob would be entitled to 22 percent of any profits, and David would be entitled to 44 percent of any profits. This is the most common scheme.
c. Certain profits may be guaranteed for a partner and he or she may bear no losses or may bear losses in an amount less than the initial contribution. For example, assume Anna is a real estate expert who spent quite a bit of time selecting the apartment building to be purchased by the partnership and manages the partnership business. If she contributed 22 percent of the initial contribution, she may receive 22 percent of the profits and bear only 10 percent of the losses. Bob and David, the remaining partners, will have to make up the difference and bear losses disproportionate to their profits or initial contributions.
d. The agreement may specify that losses caused by reckless conduct or fraud be borne by the partner committing such acts. Such a provision is common.
e. If salaries are to be paid, they should be set forth in this section.
f. The agreement may provide that partners will be indemnified by the partnership for obligations incurred in the ordinary course of partnership business.

9. *Management and Control*

This section should specify the management policies for the partnership business. Designations of managing partners or committees should be made and each partner's voting power should be set forth. If the partners desire that certain activities, such as selling partnership assets, settling litigation claims, and borrowing, should be subject to a greater than majority vote (for instance, two-thirds voting approval or unanimous approval), the specifications should be set forth.

The partnership may elect to meet at regular intervals to discuss partnership business. The time and place for any such meeting, whether weekly, monthly, or quarterly, should be set forth in the agreement.

There are several alternatives for the management and control of a partnership.

a. One partner can be appointed the managing partner with the right to make all decisions in the ordinary course of the partnership business. This partner's rights and duties as well as any limitations on his authority should be clearly specified so that it is clear what activities the managing partner may undertake. For example, the managing partner may be given the authority to run the day-to-day business operations of the partnership but may be precluded from incurring debt or admitting new partners without the other partners' consent.
b. There may be various committees established for certain functions. For example, there may be a compensation committee, a recruiting committee, and a business development committee, each with certain specified powers and rights.
c. The partners may agree to manage the partnership equally, with each partner having an equal vote.
d. The partnership may be managed by all partners who vote in accord with their initial contributions. In our example, Anna would have 34 percent of the votes to cast on any issue, Bob would have 22 percent, and David would have 44 percent. This is the most common approach in smaller partnerships.
e. Decisions can be made by majority vote or a greater than majority vote. Certain matters, such as the expulsion of a partner, may require unanimous approval.

10. *Admission of New Partners and Withdrawal of Partners*

A partnership is a voluntary association and, therefore, there can be no admission of new partners unless all partners agree, or the partners provide otherwise. The partnership agreement may state that the admission of a new member is subject to unanimous approval or subject to the approval of partners holding a certain percentage of the partnership interest. If new members are to be admitted, provisions should be made for their contributions to the partnership. This usually requires reallocating the interests of the existing partners so the new partner has an interest in the partnership.

All matters pertaining to the withdrawal of a partner should be specified. The partners may provide that a withdrawing partner must offer to sell his or her interest to the partnership or to the remaining partners. Partners who wish to retire or withdraw should provide advance written notice to the partnership. The agreement may specify that a withdrawing partner shall not be repaid his or her contribution until the partnership dissolves or terminates.

If partners may be expelled, the reasons for and methods of expulsion should be clearly provided. For example, a partner may be expelled for willful misconduct detrimental to the partnership, committing a felony, or breaching any duties required by the terms of the partnership agreement.

11. Dissolution

This section of the agreement should not only specify what particular actions may cause a dissolution of the partnership but should also describe the actual process of dissolving the partnership and winding up its affairs.

The partners should identify any acts that may cause a dissolution of the partnership, such as unanimous agreement, completion of the business for which it was formed, or expiration of its term. Similarly, the partners should consider whether the death, retirement, or bankruptcy of a partner will cause a dissolution. Unless the partners agree that the partnership may continue, the death or bankruptcy of a partner will cause a dissolution of the partnership. UPA Section 31(4), (5). Under the UPA, a partner may petition a court to declare a dissolution when a partner is incapable of performing duties under the partnership or when a partner's conduct prejudicially affects the carrying on of the business. UPA Section 32(1)(b), (c).

The partners may wish to designate one partner, or perhaps a committee of partners, who will liquidate or "wind up" the affairs of the partnership. These partners will complete outstanding contracts, collect and dispose of partnership assets, pay creditors, and then distribute the remaining sums to the partners. Third-party creditors must always be fully paid before the partnership can distribute any money to members of the partnership. The UPA sets forth a distribution scheme as follows: outside creditors must be paid first; partners are repaid money owed to them for advances, loans, or anything other than a return of their capital or any profit; partners then receive a return of their capital; and, finally, partners receive profits. UPA Section 40(b). RUPA Section 807 also requires that partnership assets must first be applied to discharge any liabilities to creditors. Thereafter, remaining sums may be distributed to partners. Thus, under both the UPA and RUPA, third party creditors, including claims for taxes and wages, must always be fully satisfied before any money or assets can be distributed to partners.

12. Miscellaneous Provisions

Non-compete clauses
Clauses in agreement restricting signatory from competing with another during and after parties' relationship terminates

There are many other provisions that may be included in a partnership agreement. The partners may wish to provide that any withdrawing partner cannot engage in any activity competitive with the partnership business. Known as **non-compete clauses,** these provisions ensure that a withdrawing partner will not take customer lists and knowledge acquired within the partnership and use it for his benefit to the detriment of former partners. Many states specifically regulate the terms of such non-compete clauses because they impose restrictions on a person's ability to earn a living. California forbids their use entirely unless they are bargained for in connection with the sale of a business. Generally, the clause must be reasonable in length of time, scope, and geographic area. Thus, it would be unreasonable to forbid a withdrawing partner to carry on a similar business anywhere in the United States for ten years. (See Chapter Eighteen for additional information on non-compete clauses.)

The agreement also should include provisions for resolving disputes among partners. The partners may elect to resolve disputes by binding arbitration. They may also provide that the prevailing party in any litigation or dispute is entitled to be paid attorney's fees and costs by the losing party. This provision may serve as a disincentive to those partners who might be tempted to litigate minor issues.

Various provisions may be included regarding partnership books and accounting. The agreement may provide that any partner has a right to an accounting upon reasonable advance notice, that reports of the partnership's affairs shall be distributed quarterly, that the partnership books and records are available to any partner for inspection upon reasonable advance notice, and that the banking of the partnership shall be done at a specific institution. The agreement may specify the manner in which partners are to be reimbursed for incurring expenses, such as travel expenses, on behalf of the partnership. A tax year for the partnership may be selected.

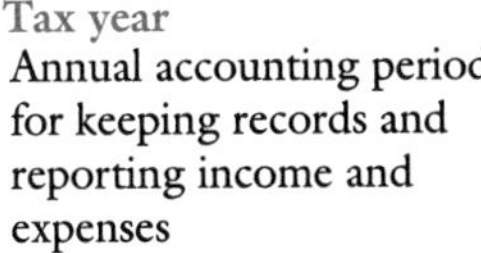
Tax year
Annual accounting period for keeping records and reporting income and expenses

A **tax year** is an annual accounting period for keeping records and reporting income and expenses. A tax year can be a calendar year (from January 1 through December 31) or a fiscal year (any 12-consecutive month period). A tax year is adopted when the partnership files its first income tax return. Generally IRS approval is needed to change a tax year.

Cash method of accounting
Listing expenses and income in business records only when they are paid or received

Accrual method of accounting
Listing expenses and income in business records when they are incurred or billed rather than when they are actually paid or received

The partnership should establish the method by which its accounting will be done. Under the **cash method of accounting,** expenses and income are listed in record and ledger books only when paid or received. Under the **accrual method of accounting,** income is recorded or "booked" as received at the time the customer is billed (which may be several weeks or months before actual receipt), and expenses are recorded or "booked" at the time they are incurred rather than when they are actually paid.

A variety of other "standard" provisions may be included, such as the following: how notice of any partnership meeting or matter is to be given; that the agreement will be construed under the laws of a certain state; that no modifications can be made to the agreement unless in writing and consented to by all partners; that the use of masculine pronouns includes the feminine, and the use of the singular includes the plural; and that if any portion of the agreement is invalid, that provision is severable from the remaining portions of the agreement so that they remain in effect.

13. *Signatures and Date*

The agreement should be signed and dated by all partners. If a partner is a corporation, it should be signed by the appropriate corporate officer. If a partner is another partnership, it should be signed by the managing partner.

J. Transferability of Partnership Interest

As discussed earlier, partners have various property rights in the partnership. While they may assign their profits in the partnership to another, they cannot, without the consent of the other partners, substitute another partner for themselves. Because a partnership is a voluntary association, one cannot be forced to be a partner with another. In fact, RUPA Section 502 expressly states that the only transferable interest of a partner is his or her share of the profits and losses of the partnership.

Under the UPA, if there is no definite term of the partnership agreement, the withdrawal by one partner causes a dissolution. UPA Section 31(b). Because most partnerships will not wish to dissolve due to the withdrawal of one partner, the agreement should provide a procedure for the withdrawal of partners and the admission of new partners. The agreement can provide that a partner may withdraw upon 30 days' notice and the remaining partners may continue to do business without that partner. The agreement should specify whether and how the withdrawing partner will be paid the value of her interest. The agreement can provide that upon the withdrawal of any partner, she must sell to the partnership her interest in the partnership. The agreement can establish a method to value the partner's interest and a method of payment (for example, installment payments) if there is not enough cash to pay off the withdrawing partner. If the withdrawing partner has breached the partnership agreement (for instance, by withdrawing before the term specified for the partnership) she may be liable for damages caused by this breach. Once the partner leaves, she will not be liable for debts incurred thereafter although the partner will continue to be liable for debts incurred while she was a partner.

New partners can be admitted upon the consent of all existing partners (or upon less than unanimous consent, if provided by the partnership agreement). They should sign the existing partnership agreement and thereby become bound to its terms. The incoming partner will not be held personally liable for debts or obligations arising before his admission to the partnership; this liability can be satisfied only out of partnership property. The new partner will have personal liability only for debts or obligations incurred after admission. UPA Section 17; RUPA Section 306(b).

K. Dissolution and Winding Up Under the UPA

Dissolution and **winding up** are not synonymous terms. The UPA specifically provides that dissolution is the change in the relation of the partners caused by any partner's ceasing to be associated in the carrying on of the business. UPA Section 29. Thus, under the UPA, whenever a partner leaves the partnership for any reason, the partnership is dissolved. Upon dissolution, partnership relationships end so the fiduciary relationships among partners are terminated. The partnership will continue its existence until its business affairs have been "wound up" by satisfying all obligations and collecting all assets. If the partnership continues its business rather than winding up, it is technically a new partnership.

Dissolution
Change in the relation of partners caused when a partner leaves the business; generally, a termination of a partnership

Winding up
Wrapping up business affairs, terminating business, satisfying obligations, selling assets, and collecting debts

Dissolution can occur by acts of the partners or by decree of court.

1. *Dissolution by Acts of Partners*

Under the UPA, dissolution is caused by the following events:

a. by completion of the partnership's term of existence or its purpose;
b. by the will of any partner when no definite term or purpose is specified;
c. by mutual agreement of all of the partners;
d. by the expulsion of a partner according to the terms of the partnership agreement;
e. by the express will of any partner, even if this is in violation of the terms of the partnership agreement;
f. by any event which makes it unlawful for the business of the partnership to be continued, for example, a change in a zoning law that would prohibit the partnership, a bar, from serving alcoholic beverages within a certain radius of a school;
g. by the death of any partner;
h. by the bankruptcy of any partner; or
i. by the decree of a court. [UPA Section 31.]

If the partnership agreement contains terms, however, allowing the partnership to continue doing business after the death, withdrawal, expulsion, or bankruptcy of a partner, the partnership can continue and need not wind up. The partnership that continues is new in the eyes of the law because it does not comprise the same individuals who made up the original membership of the partnership. It is now a **partnership at will** and can be dissolved upon the withdrawal of any partner. If the partners continue to act according to the terms and conditions of the partnership agreement, they may be viewed as having adopted or ratified its terms by their conduct.

Partnership at will
Partnership without a definite term or undertaking

To ensure that the partnership will not have to do business with a deceased partner's estate, the partnership agreement can provide that upon the death of a partner, that partner's interest in the partnership must be sold to the partnership. To fund such a provision, the partnership may purchase life insurance policies, sometimes called **key person policies,** for each partner, naming the partnership as beneficiary. Then upon the death of a partner, the partnership will have sufficient funds to pay to the deceased partner's estate to compensate for the value of the decedent's interest in the partnership. (See Chapter Eighteen.)

Key person policies
Insurance policies on the life of key individuals in a business

2. *Dissolution by Decree of Court*

Upon application by a partner, a court may decree a dissolution if any of the following occurs:

a. a partner is shown to be of unsound mind;
b. a partner becomes incapable of performing his or her partnership obligations;
c. a partner has committed an act that prejudicially affects the carrying on of the business;

d. a partner's conduct is such that it is not reasonably practicable to continue doing business with him or her;
e. the partnership business can be carried on only at a loss; or
f. other circumstances render a dissolution equitable. [UPA Section 32.]

3. *Winding Up*

Winding up is the process of terminating all partnership business, satisfying all obligations, selling assets, and collecting debts. After the assets are collected they must be distributed as specified by UPA Section 40, which provides that third-party creditors are to be repaid first, partners are then reimbursed for loans or advances to the partnership, partners are returned their capital, and only then do partners receive profits.

The distribution of profits after winding up is generally in accord with the percentage of initial capital contribution. In our example, Anna would expect to receive 34 percent of all assets remaining after creditors were paid, Bob would expect to receive 22 percent, and David would expect to receive 44 percent. The partners, by agreement, however, may provide otherwise.

If the partnership is unable to satisfy its third-party creditors, the partners must make the appropriate personal contributions to pay these debts.

L. Dissociation and Dissolution Under the RUPA

Dissociation
A withdrawal of a partner from a partnership; does not necessarily cause a dissolution or termination of partnership

The RUPA seeks to avoid the harsh UPA approach that any withdrawal from a partnership automatically triggers a dissolution by creating a new concept of **dissociation,** thus allowing the partnership to continue although a partner may have departed. The RUPA's position that a partnership is an entity in and of itself justifies the partnership continuing, although a partner has withdrawn from the entity.

A dissociation is a withdrawal of a partner from a partnership. Under the RUPA, the dissociation of a partner does not necessarily cause a dissolution or termination of the partnership. According to RUPA Section 601, a dissociation occurs whenever a partnership receives notice of a partner's express will to leave the partnership, when a partnership agreement provides for events that cause dissociation, upon a partner's expulsion, upon court decree (usually initiated by the partnership because a partner's conduct threatens the partnership business), or upon a partner's death or bankruptcy.

Wrongful dissociation
A dissociation caused by a breach of partnership agreement

Under the RUPA, partners have the absolute power to dissociate from a partnership at any time, even if the dissociation breaches a provision in the partnership agreement or even if the partner wishes to depart before the term of a partnership expires. Such events are referred to as **wrongful dissociations.** The significance of wrongful dissociation is that it may give rise to damages caused to the partnership by the dissociation.

The consequences of dissociation vary and depend largely upon whether the partnership is an at-will partnership (one formed for no definite term or undertaking) or whether it is one with a definite term or undertaking. Recall that under the UPA, the withdrawal of a partner for any reason always results in dissolution (usually leading to winding up of the partnership business). To prevent such a technical dissolution, the RUPA provides that only the following departures trigger a dissolution and winding up:

- In a partnership at will, when a partnership receives notice of a partner's will to depart or dissociate; and
- In a partnership for a definite term or undertaking, when a wrongful dissociation occurs, or when a dissociation occurs due to death or bankruptcy. In these events, however, a majority of the partners may, within 90 days, determine whether they wish to continue doing business as a partnership.

In all other instances of dissociation (for example, dissociation due to the bankruptcy of a partner in an at-will partnership), no dissolution is caused, and the effect of the dissociation is only that the departing partner is bought out. RUPA Section 701 provides that the partnership must buy out the ownership interest of the dissociated partner, although a partner who wrongfully dissociates by voluntarily departing from a partnership before its term expires (assuming the partnership has decided to continue) is not entitled to payment of the buyout price until the partnership term expires. The RUPA provides a method and process for calculating the buyout price. The partnership will then pay the buyout price to the dissociated member, and the partnership itself continues and is not dissolved merely because a member departed. Thus, the RUPA ameliorates the harsh effects of the UPA by allowing partnerships to survive the dissociation of their members in some instances.

In the case of any dissociation, the partnership remains bound for two years for the dissociating partner's acts before dissociation. The partnership may, however, file a voluntary **Statement of Dissociation** with its state agency, identifying the partner who dissociated. Third parties will be bound by this notice 90 days after it is filed, thereby reducing the two-year period of potential liability for the dissociating partner's acts to 90 days (see Figure 3-5).

Statement of Dissociation
Document filed with state identify dissociating partner and filed to limit period for which partnership will be liable for dissociating partner's acts

If the partnership does dissolve and its business must be wound up, creditors must be paid prior to partners. Although the UPA requires third-party creditors' claims to be paid prior to claims of partners and requires partners to be repaid their contributions before they receive profits, the RUPA draws no such distinctions and merely requires creditors' claims (including those of partners) to be paid before partners receive any assets.

Under RUPA Section 802(b), even if the partnership is dissolved, at any time before winding up is completed, the partners can agree to continue doing business, much the same way the UPA allows the creation of a technically new partnership after the dissolution of a partnership due to the departure of any partner for any reason. Finally, because both the UPA and RUPA are default statutes, nearly all of the procedures relating to dissociation and dissolution can be varied by the terms of the partners' agreement. Thus, the partnership agreement should be carefully drafted to provide as much continuity as possible and to avoid a forced dissolution and winding up.

FIGURE 3-5
California Statement of Dissociation

State of California
Secretary of State

Form GP-3

Bill Jones

STATEMENT OF DISSOCIATION

IMPORTANT -- Read instructions on back before completing form.

1. NAME OF PARTNERSHIP	2. SECRETARY OF STATE FILE NUMBER

3. NAME OF DISSOCIATED PARTNER ______________________ .

4. STATEMENT THAT THE PARTNER IS DISSOCIATED FROM THE PARTNERSHIP. (ATTACH ADDITIONAL PAGES, IF NECESSARY)

5. NUMBER OF PAGES ATTACHED, IF ANY: ____

6. I DECLARE UNDER PENALTY OF PERJURY UNDER THE LAWS OF THE STATE OF CALIFORNIA THAT THE FOREGOING IS TRUE AND CORRECT.

SIGNATURE OF PARTNER	DATE EXECUTED
TYPE OR PRINT NAME OF PARTNER	COUNTY AND STATE EXECUTED
SIGNATURE OF PARTNER	DATE EXECUTED
TYPE OR PRINT NAME OF PARTNER	COUNTY AND STATE EXECUTED

For Secretary of State Use

DOCUMENT #____________

7. **RETURN TO:**

NAME:

ADDRESS:

CITY: STATE: ZIP CODE:

M. Taxation of Partnerships

Although a partnership is an entity and can sue and be sued in its own name, it is not a taxpaying entity. All profits or losses earned are "**passed through**" to the partners, who report their respective income or losses on a separate form called Schedule K (see Figure 3-6) attached to their individual tax returns. Thus, the taxation of partners is much like the taxation of sole proprietors. The partners simply add their share of the partnership income to any income gained from any other sources and pay tax according to the personal income tax rates or "brackets" established by the Internal Revenue Service (see Figure 2-6).

Pass-through tax status
The tax status of a partnership in which all income is passed through to partners who pay at their individual rates

Partners must declare and pay taxes on any income earned, whether or not that income is distributed. Thus, if the partners decide to reserve an emergency account of $10,000 for anticipated repairs to partnership property, each partner must declare and pay tax on his or her respective share of the money reserved, even though the partner has not received that income.

Similarly, losses experienced by the partnership can be declared on each partner's individual tax return, thus offsetting other income and lowering tax liability. The income or losses declared will be determined by the partnership agreement. In our example, if the partnership had income of $100,000, whether or not that income

FIGURE 3-6
IRS Schedule K

Form 1065 (1999) Page **3**

Schedule K **Partners' Shares of Income, Credits, Deductions, etc.**

	(a) Distributive share items		(b) Total amount
Income (Loss)	1 Ordinary income (loss) from trade or business activities (page 1, line 22)	1	
	2 Net income (loss) from rental real estate activities *(attach Form 8825)*	2	
	3a Gross income from other rental activities ... 3a		
	b Expenses from other rental activities *(attach schedule)* ... 3b		
	c Net income (loss) from other rental activities. Subtract line 3b from line 3a	3c	
	4 Portfolio income (loss):		
	a Interest income	4a	
	b Ordinary dividends	4b	
	c Royalty income	4c	
	d Net short-term capital gain (loss) *(attach Schedule D (Form 1065))*	4d	
	e Net long-term capital gain (loss) *(attach Schedule D (Form 1065)):*		
	(1) 28% rate gain (loss) ▶ ________ (2) Total for year ▶	4e(2)	
	f Other portfolio income (loss) *(attach schedule)*	4f	
	5 Guaranteed payments to partners	5	
	6 Net section 1231 gain (loss) (other than due to casualty or theft) *(attach Form 4797)*	6	
	7 Other income (loss) *(attach schedule)*	7	
Deductions	8 Charitable contributions *(attach schedule)*	8	
	9 Section 179 expense deduction *(attach Form 4562)*	9	
	10 Deductions related to portfolio income (itemize)	10	
	11 Other deductions *(attach schedule)*	11	

is actually distributed to the partners Anna would pay tax on 34 percent of that income, Bob would pay tax on 22 percent of the income, and David would pay tax on the remaining 44 percent of the income earned. If the partners did not agree how income and losses were to be allocated, each partner would declare and pay tax on one-third of the income earned regardless of that partner's initial contribution.

While the partnership does not pay tax, it does file an information return, Form 1065 (see Figure 3-7). This form is used to report the income, deductions, gains, and losses from the operation of the partnership. One general partner must sign the form. Information returns also can now be filed electronically. Generally, the partnership must file the information tax form by the fifteenth day of the fourth month following the date its tax year ended. While the most common tax year for an entity is the calendar year, namely January 1 through December 31, other tax years can be selected; for example, July 1 through June 30. Extensions can be obtained upon request. All partnerships, even those without employees, must apply with the IRS for an employer identification number. (See Form SS-4 at Figure 2-3).

Corporations are treated quite differently from partnerships regarding taxation. Partnerships do not pay tax although the partners pay tax on income earned,

FIGURE 3-7
IRS Form 1065

Form **1065** — **U.S. Partnership Return of Income** — OMB No. 1545-0099 — **1999**

Department of the Treasury
Internal Revenue Service

For calendar year 1999, or tax year beginning ______, 1999, and ending ______, ______.
▶ See separate instructions.

A Principal business activity	Use the IRS label. Otherwise, please print or type.	Name of partnership	D Employer identification number
B Principal product or service		Number, street, and room or suite no. If a P.O. box, see page 12 of the instructions.	E Date business started
C Business code number		City or town, state, and ZIP code	F Total assets (see page 12 of the instructions) $

G Check applicable boxes: (1) ☐ Initial return (2) ☐ Final return (3) ☐ Change in address (4) ☐ Amended return
H Check accounting method: (1) ☐ Cash (2) ☐ Accrual (3) ☐ Other (specify) ▶ ______
I Number of Schedules K-1. Attach one for each person who was a partner at any time during the tax year ▶ ______

Caution: *Include **only** trade or business income and expenses on lines 1a through 22 below. See the instructions for more information.*

Income

1a Gross receipts or sales	1a		
b Less returns and allowances	1b	1c	
2 Cost of goods sold (Schedule A, line 8)		2	
3 Gross profit. Subtract line 2 from line 1c		3	
4 Ordinary income (loss) from other partnerships, estates, and trusts *(attach schedule)*		4	
5 Net farm profit (loss) *(attach Schedule F (Form 1040))*		5	
6 Net gain (loss) from Form 4797, Part II, line 18		6	
7 Other income (loss) *(attach schedule)*		7	
8 **Total income (loss).** Combine lines 3 through 7		8	

whether distributed or not. Corporations themselves are taxpaying entities and pay at different rates than do individuals (see Chapter Ten). Moreover, when profits are distributed to shareholders as dividends, those shareholders then pay tax on the money they receive. Thus, corporations may retain certain income that will not be taxed to the shareholders (inasmuch as they have not received the distribution).

To afford such opportunities to partnerships, a late 1996 change to the tax code (see 26 C.F.R. Sections 301.7701-1, et seq.) allows partnerships to "**check the box**" on a designated IRS Form (Form 8832) and elect to be taxed as a corporation. Because taxation is a complex issue and election to be taxed as a corporation may not be beneficial to all partners, careful consideration should be given as to whether the partnership wishes to "check the box" and elects to be taxed at corporate rates. Generally, one partner signs on behalf of all partners and states, under penalty of perjury, that she is authorized to do so.

Check the box
Method by which businesses elect how they wish to be taxed, namely, whether as partnerships or corporations

According to the regulations, if no election is affirmatively made, the "default" provision is that the partnership will automatically be treated as having the typical pass-through status of a partnership rather than the two-tier tax status of a corporation with its different tax rates. Thus, any partnership desiring to elect corporate tax status must file the election (see Figure 3-8 for IRS Form 8832). The election is made by attaching IRS Form 8832 to the partnership's informational return or to a corporate tax return. Generally, once the election is made, it cannot be changed for five years.

Key Features of General Partnerships

- Partnerships are formed by agreement, either oral or written.
- All partners share rights to manage the partnership.
- Partners share profits and losses according to their agreement; if no agreement, profits and losses are shared equally, regardless of capital contribution.
- Partners have unlimited personal liability for partnership obligations.
- Liability is joint and several, meaning that any partner is completely liable for any debt.
- Partnerships are easily and inexpensively formed.
- Partners owe each other fiduciary duties.
- Partners can transfer their partnership interest (share of profits) but transferee becomes a partner only upon consent of other partners.
- Withdrawal of a partner may not necessarily cause a dissolution and winding up of the partnership; in many instances the dissociating partner is bought out.
- Partnerships file information tax returns but do not pay taxes; all income, whether distributed or not, is passed through to the partners who pay tax at their appropriate individual rates.

FIGURE 3-8
IRS Form 8832

Form **8832**
(December 1996)
Department of the Treasury
Internal Revenue Service

Entity Classification Election

OMB No. 1545-1516

Please Type or Print	Name of entity	**Employer identification number (EIN)**
	Number, street, and room or suite no. If a P.O. box, see instructions.	
	City or town, state, and ZIP code. If a foreign address, enter city, province or state, postal code and country.	

1 Type of election (see instructions):

a ☐ Initial classification by a newly-formed entity (or change in current classification of an existing entity to take effect on January 1, 1997)

b ☐ Change in current classification (to take effect later than January 1, 1997)

2 Form of entity (see instructions):

a ☐ A domestic eligible entity electing to be classified as an association taxable as a corporation.

b ☐ A domestic eligible entity electing to be classified as a partnership.

c ☐ A domestic eligible entity with a single owner electing to be disregarded as a separate entity.

d ☐ A foreign eligible entity electing to be classified as an association taxable as a corporation.

e ☐ A foreign eligible entity electing to be classified as a partnership.

f ☐ A foreign eligible entity with a single owner electing to be disregarded as a separate entity.

3 Election is to be effective beginning (month, day, year) (see instructions) . . . . ▶ __/__/__

...mation | 5 That person's telephone number

N. Role of Paralegal

While the attorney must determine which form of business enterprise is most appropriate for a client, paralegals play an integral role in the formation of a general partnership. The paralegal will likely prepare and file the fictitious business name statement, if needed. He can review the results of searches to determine if a partnership name is available by consulting one of the search firms identified in Chapter Two. The paralegal may also be tasked with obtaining appropriate forms for tax identification numbers and income tax forms. Most importantly, the paralegal will have an active role in drafting the partnership agreement.

Many law firms have various partnership agreements on file. The various forms should be reviewed to determine which provisions are "standard" (such as partnership name, addresses of the partners, and so forth) and must be included.

The paralegal can then discuss these issues with the attorney or client. Preparing a partnership agreement is more than just an exercise in selecting the right form from a database or form file and changing names and addresses; it should be carefully tailored to suit the needs and particular requirements of each partnership client and to comply with the appropriate state statutes.

It may be useful to prepare a form or checklist of questions for the client. These can be asked during a conference or even mailed to the client for completion to assist in drafting the agreement. A sample for such a questionnaire is provided in Figure 3-9.

Resource Guide

There are several sources to consult to obtain information about the formation and operation of partnerships as well as the preparation of partnership agreements.

1. Statutes

As always, the starting point should be your state's statutes. The UPA and RUPA have been adopted by every state except Louisiana, but you will need to review your state's version to determine if any additions or omissions have been made. Obtain a copy of your state's annotated codes or statutes. Use the general index to the set and look for "partnerships," "partners," or "general partnerships." You will be directed to the specific sections governing partnerships in your state. Review the statutes as well as the annotations or summaries of cases that follow the statutes. Review and brief any cases, if necessary, and consult with your attorney.

You may also obtain a copy of the UPA and RUPA from the National Conference of Commissioners on Uniform State Laws by writing to 211 E. Ontario, Suite 1300, Chicago, Illinois 60611, by calling (312) 915-0195, or by accessing its Web site at <nccusl@nccusl.org>.

2. Encyclopedias

For basic information about partnerships, consult a legal encyclopedia. If your state has its own encyclopedia, consult this. Otherwise, review either C.J.S. (Corpus Juris Secundum) or Am. Jur. 2d (American Jurisprudence, Second Series). These encyclopedias are arranged alphabetically by topic. Thus, retrieve the volume for "partnerships" and you will be provided with excellent introductory and general information about partnerships.

3. Form Books

Various form books exist that will assist you in drafting partnership agreements. Some of the better known sets are:

a. Rabkin and Johnson, *Current Legal Forms*
b. Am. Jur. Legal Forms 2d
c. West's Legal Forms, 2d

These form books will provide short-form partnership agreements, long-form partnership agreements, and dozens of alternative provisions for inclusion in partnership agreements, as well as tips for drafting agreements and practice strategies.

FIGURE 3-9
Partnership Checklist and Questionnaire

1. Proposed Name of Partnership: ______________________
   Alternative Names[s] ______________________
2. Names and Addresses of all Partners
   a. ______________ b. ______________
      ______________ ______________
      ______________ ______________
   c. ______________ d. ______________
      ______________ ______________
      ______________ ______________
3. Address of Partnership ______________________
   ____
4. Purpose of Partnership ______________________
   ____
5. Duration of Partnership ______________________
6. Capital Contributions of Partners
   a. ______________ b. ______________
   c. ______________ d. ______________
7. Distribution of Profits and Losses
   a. ______________ b. ______________
   c. ______________ d. ______________
8. Management of Partnership/Voting/Decisions That Require Unanimous Approval
   ____
   ____
   ____
9. Designation of Managing Partner ______________________
10. Rights to Admit New Partners ______________________
    ____
11. Rights of Partners to Withdraw ______________________
    ____
    ____
12. Events That Will Cause Dissolution and Winding Up ______________________
    ____
    ____
13. Manner of Resolving Disputes (namely, litigation or arbitration) ______________
14. Fiscal Year ______________________
15. Banking Information ______________________
16. Other ______________________
    ____
    ____
    ____

FIGURE 3-10
Comparison of UPA and RUPA Provisions

	UPA	*RUPA*
Nature of Partnership	Partnership is an aggregate of individuals	Partnership is an entity for nearly all purposes
Acts Requiring Unanimity	Lists certain acts requiring unanimous consent	No list of acts requiring unanimous consent
Public Filing of Statements of Authority, Denial, Dissociation, Merger, and Conversion	Not provided for	Statements may be filed with state officials
Fiduciary Duties	Generally provides only that partners are accountable as fiduciaries	Provides that partners are subject to the duties of loyalty and due care, which cannot be waived or eliminated; partners must exercise their duties consistent with good faith and fair dealing
Right to Accounting	Partners have a right to formal account of partnership affairs	Partner may bring an action for an accounting
Property Rights	Partner is a co-owner with his partners of specific partnership property (the theory of tenancy in partnership)	Abolishes concept of tenancy in partnership and provides that partnership property is owned by the entity and not by individual partners
Withdrawal by Partner	Withdrawal of a partner for any reason causes a dissolution of the partnership	Provides for dissociation of partner, which causes a dissolution and winding up only in certain situations; otherwise, partnership buys out dissociating partner's interest and continues unaffected by dissociation
Settlement of Accounts upon Dissolution	Outside third party creditors are paid first, followed by partners' claims, followed by return of partners' capital, and then distribution of profits	Creditors claims are paid first (including claims by partners) and then surplus is paid to partners

FIGURE 3-10 *Continued*
Comparison of UPA and RUPA Provisions

	UPA	*RUPA*
Limited Partnerships	Provided for under UPA	Not governed under RUPA
Limited Liability Partnerships	Not provided for under UPA	Provided for under RUPA
Conversion and Mergers of Partnerships	Not provided for	RUPA allows the merger of two or more partnerships and the conversions of general partnerships to limited partnerships (and the reverse)

4. *Government Authorities*

Check with your secretary of state (see Appendix A) or local governing authorities for information about fictitious business names, sales tax licenses, and so forth.

5. *Internal Revenue Service*

To obtain tax information relating to partnerships, Form 1065 (the information tax return filed for partnerships) or Schedule K (the schedule to be prepared by each individual partner), contact the Internal Revenue Service at (800)-TAX-FORM. General tax information is provided in Publication No. 541, sent upon request.

6. *Periodicals*

Review periodical articles for new information relating to partnerships and for information relating to the adoption of the RUPA. The best known index to periodicals is the *Index to Legal Periodicals.* An alternative is *Current Law Index.* Both indices can be accessed by subject. Therefore, look up "partnership," "partners," "general partnerships," or other relevant subject names and you will be referred to articles written about these topics.

7. *SCORE*

The Service Corps of Retired Executives (SCORE) is composed of retired businessmen and businesswomen who volunteer their services and offer free counseling and low-cost training for prospective and existing business owners.

SCORE Chapter #1
c/o Small Business Administration
1110 Vermont Avenue, N.W.
Suite 900
Washington, D.C. 20005
phone: (202) 606-4000

WEB RESOURCES

A number of sites provide general information about partnerships with clear and concise discussions of the partnership entity, comparing and contrasting it to other forms of business entities. Many of the sites listed below provide forms for partnership agreements. As with all forms, exercise caution in using the form, inasmuch as it will likely not be suitable for all partnerships. As with any form, you should modify it to suit your needs. Review the Web site Disclaimer or Legal Terms sections to determine if there are any prohibitions on use or reproduction of the forms. In any event, the forms serve as useful starting places.

http://www.nass.org
This Web site of the National Association of Secretaries of State allows you to link directly to the home page for each state's secretary of state. Many states offer guides to forming partnerships with basic information, forms, checklists, and phone numbers. Select "States" and then point the cursor to your state's name and flag, and proceed to locate information on forming a partnership in your state. Statements of Partnership Authority, Statements of Partnership Denial, and Statements of Merger and Dissolution are offered on most state Web sites.

www.irs.gov
The Web site of the Internal Revenue Service offers a wealth of information about taxes, businesses, and provides Form 1065 and Schedule K, the partnership tax forms that can be downloaded and printed.

www.ask.com
"Ask Jeeves" is an Internet "butler" who will help you find what you need. Simply type in your question, in natural English, and you will be referred to numerous useful sites. For example, type in "Where can I find a form for a partnership agreement?" You will then be directed to sites offering information on partnerships and forms of agreements. "Ask.com" is often the first site many individuals access to find information on nearly any topic. Bookmark this site, and use it often.

www.tannedfeet.com
Billed as "The Entrepreneurs' Help Page," this site provides a wealth of information regarding the formation and operation of businesses, including partnerships. Access <www.tannedfeet.com/html/partnerships.htm> for specific information about partnerships.

www.about.com
"About.com" offers a wide variety of information relating to many topics. After you access the site, point your cursor to "Business/Careers" and then to "Small Business Information" for information on starting businesses, tax strategies, and information about types of entities, including partnerships.

www.ilrg.com
The Internet Legal Research Guide is a great source of information and provides a form for a partnership agreement in its "Legal Forms Archive."

www.law.com
"Law.Com" is a well-known site used by legal professionals. After viewing the home page, go to "Business" and then to "Resources for Business." Scroll down the page for access to business forms, including a form of partnership agreement.

www.lectlaw.com
The 'Lectric Law Library provides a vast array of information on legal topics. Access "The Rotunda" and then "Forms Room" for a form of partnership agreement.

www.lawsmart.com
Access the home page and enter "partnership" as a key term. You will be referred to a form of partnership agreement.

www.LegalWiz.com
This legal resource for entrepreneurs offers articles, general information about businesses, a glossary of business and legal terms, and a form of partnership agreement. Access "Legal Forms" and you will be provided with the partnership agreement form.

http://www.siccode.com/forms.php3
This Web site, entitled "SICCode.com" provides numerous business and legal forms. When you access the site, point your cursor to "free legal forms." You will be provided with hundreds of forms, including a form for a partnership agreement, which you are invited to cut and paste into your word processor.

www.findlaw.com/16forms/index.htm
The forms section of "FindLaw.com," a well-known legal Web site, offers numerous links to forms collections and forms indexes.

Discussion Questions

Fact Scenario. Tom, Mary, and Bob are partners in a construction business that routinely buys supplies from Home Depot. The partnership has no written agreement and no oral agreement as to management or division of profits and losses, although the partners orally agreed to continue the partnership for five years. Tom contributed $40,000 to the partnership, Mary contributed $18,000 to the partnership, and Bob contributed $42,000 to the partnership.

1. Bob has purchased construction supplies from Home Depot for his own personal residence using the partnership checkbook. The bill from Home Depot has now arrived. Who is responsible to pay the bill? Discuss. What partnership principle governs your answer? Discuss each partner's possible liability for the obligation.

2. Given the facts above, assume that the partnership's paint supplier has delivered paint to the partnership. Funds in the partnership account are low, and Mary pays for the paint from her personal checking account. Is Mary entitled to be reimbursed from the partnership? If so, will she receive interest? What section of the RUPA governs your answer?

3. Assume that the partnership made $180,000 this year. Discuss how the profits will be allocated.

4. Discuss the tax implications to the partnership on its revenues of $180,000. Assume the partnership has decided to retain $15,000 in its accounts for moving expenses for next year.

5. On the weekends, Tom does minor home repairs for others in his neighborhood, for which he charges fees. Is this a violation of any partnership duties? Discuss.

6. Mary has decided to withdraw from the partnership in its third year of existence. What effect does this withdrawal have? Discuss using both UPA and RUPA principles. Under the RUPA, is there any action Mary may take to notify others of her status?

4

Limited Partnerships

CHAPTER OVERVIEW

A limited partnership is a unique type of partnership. You will recall from Chapter Three that in a general partnership, all of the partners have the right to manage and control the partnership and they all suffer the risk of unlimited personal liability for business debts, torts, and obligations. In a limited partnership, some of the partners, called *limited partners,* do not have unlimited personal liability. Their liability is limited to what they invested in the enterprise. While the value of this investment may fall to zero, at the outset of the enterprise limited partners can determine what their maximum risk or exposure will be, namely, the amount they invested in the business. These limited partners also have little ability to manage or govern the partnership. Another critical distinction between general partnerships and limited partnerships relates to the organization of the enterprise. A general partnership may be formed with few formalities; a limited partnership, however, can only be created by strict compliance with pertinent statutes.

A. Characteristics of Limited Partnerships

Unlike sole proprietorships and general partnerships, which are formed with either no or minimal governmental involvement, limited partnerships are creatures of statute and can only be formed in compliance with state law, by the filing of a certificate of limited partnership with the appropriate state official. A limited partnership includes one or more general partners and one or more limited partners. The primary advantage of a limited partnership is that it affords limited liability to the limited partners, making a limited partner similar to a shareholder in a corporation, so that the maximum potential loss is the investment in the enterprise. In exchange for this protection, limited partners forego any management of the

Silent partner
An older term for "limited partner"

partnership. Years ago, limited partners were referred to as "**silent partners,**" in recognition of the fact that they played no role in managing the partnership business. Thus, all management and control of a limited partnership is provided by the general partners who face the same risks and have the same responsibilities as do general partners in general partnerships, primarily unlimited personal liability. Limited partnerships allow pass-through tax treatment, meaning that the limited partnership does not pay taxes. All taxable income is passed through to the partners, who pay taxes according to their respective tax brackets.

B. Governing Law

Limited partnership
Business entity created in accord with state statutes that provides limited liability to some of its members, called limited partners

ULPA
Uniform Limited Partnership Act, predecessor to RULPA

RULPA
Revised Uniform Limited Partnership Act; the model for limited partnership legislation in all states (except Louisiana)

Most of the law governing **limited partnerships** is found in either the **Uniform Limited Partnership Act (ULPA),** approved in 1916, or in the **Revised Uniform Limited Partnership Act (RULPA),** approved in the mid-1970s and later amended in 1985. All states except Louisiana follow the RULPA. Most states rapidly adopted the RULPA, as it provided a much more streamlined approach to creating limited partnerships and reduced the paperwork and administrative burdens of the ULPA. Remember that some states modified the RULPA and thus there will be minor changes from state to state. Because a limited partnership can be created only by complying with pertinent state statutes, a thorough review is necessary for a complete understanding of how limited partnerships operate and are governed in your state. The text of the RULPA is found in Appendix E.

Earlier chapters have discussed that the sole proprietorship and general partnership may not be attractive business enterprises to wealthy individuals because the risks to sole proprietors and general partners extend beyond what has been invested in the business to their personal assets. Thus, an investment of only $10,000 could result in potential loss of hundreds of thousands of dollars.

The limited partnership originated in continental Europe so that a wealthy individual could invest in a business enterprise and yet not expose all of his or her other assets and funds to unlimited liability. Limited partnerships were first recognized in the United States in the early 1800s. All states, except Louisiana, recognize the limited partnership by adoption of the RULPA. Louisiana recognizes limited partnerships, but has statutes differing slightly from the ULPA or RULPA. Additionally, there is some linkage with the RUPA governing general partnerships, as RULPA Section 1105 provides that matters not governed by the RULPA are governed by RUPA. Thus, because duties of general partners in limited partnerships are not discussed in the RULPA, those duties are controlled by the RUPA. In sum, limited partnerships are governed by state statutes, all of which (except for Louisiana) are based upon the RULPA, which itself is supplemented by the RUPA.

Due to the existence of two relatively recently recognized entities, limited liability partnerships and limited liability companies, both of which offer their members limited liability as well as the opportunity to manage the enterprise, limited partnerships are not nearly as popular now as they once were. The new forms of business structures (discussed in Chapters Five and Six) are part of a recent trend to create new forms of business that afford limited liability coupled with management rights.

C. Limited Partnership Defined

A *limited partnership* is a partnership formed by two or more persons pursuant to a statute, having as its members one or more general partners and one or more **limited partners.** RULPA Section 101(7). An examination of each element of this definition follows.

Limited partner
A member of a limited partnership who does not participate in managing the business and whose liability is limited to amount invested in the business

The "persons" referred to in the definition can be natural persons, general partnerships, limited partnerships, trusts, estates, associations, or corporations. When the members of a business organization are other businesses, it can be extremely complicated to determine who is actually managing and controlling the enterprise. For example, assume that a limited partnership is formed with one general partner. That general partner may be a general partnership consisting of three corporations engaged in business as partners. The controlling stock of the corporations in turn may be held by another partnership or even another corporation. When presented with one of these puzzles, you may need to prepare an organizational tree or flow chart clearly outlining the relationship of each entity to another and identifying the majority owner or decision-maker for each entity.

Perhaps the most critical part of the definition of a limited partnership is the phrase referring to the formation of the entity "under the laws of [a state]," which confirms that the creation of a limited partnership is strictly controlled and regulated by state law. Failure to comply with the appropriate state statutes will result in a failure to create a limited partnership. When presented with an entity not in compliance with the necessary requirements to form a limited partnership, courts often determine that because the entity cannot be a limited partnership it must be a general partnership (in which case, all partners have unlimited personal liability). In most states, substantial compliance with the pertinent statutes is sufficient to form a limited partnership. Thus, an inadvertent or insignificant error or omission may not result in the entity being forbidden status as a limited partnership.

The general partner in a limited partnership is the same as a general partner in a general partnership. RULPA Section 403(a). This general partner will manage and control the limited partnership and consequently may face unlimited personal liability.

The "limited partner" in a limited partnership differs from a general partner in two critical respects:

1. Limited partners do not suffer the risk of unlimited liability. Their maximum loss is the amount invested in the business.
2. Limited partners cannot manage or control the partnership business.

D. Partners' Rights and Duties

1. *General Partners*

General partner
Member in a limited partnership who manages and controls the business and has unlimited personal liability

Because limited partners cannot participate in the operation and management of the limited partnership, every limited partnership must have at least one **general partner** who will be fully responsible for managing the business. This general partner also has personal liability for the limited partnership's debts and obligations, meaning that his or her personal assets can be taken by creditors.

If a corporation is the general partner, it will manage and control the business through its board of directors. Corporations have limited liability, meaning that the only funds and assets available to creditors are those owned by the corporation itself. Its directors, officers, and shareholders have no personal liability for the corporation's debts and obligations. Thus, if a corporation is the general partner of a limited partnership, no one in the limited partnership has personal liability, and, assuming there has been no fraud, the only assets available to satisfy creditors would be those of the limited partnership itself and those owned by the corporate general partner.

The management rights and responsibilities of general partners in a limited partnership are the same as those of general partners in a general partnership. Thus, general partners have fiduciary duties to the limited partners and to the limited partnership. They are the agents of the partnership who bind the partnership for contractual and other obligations. They cannot compete with the partnership business. Because the limited partners cannot manage the business without losing their limited liability status, the general partner or partners have full responsibility for management of the limited partnership business. If there is more than one general partner, their specific duties and responsibilities will be set forth in the partnership agreement. If the agreement fails to provide specific duties and responsibilities, management and control will be shared equally between general partners.

Under the ULPA, a general partner had no authority to perform certain acts, such as admitting a new general partner or confessing a judgment against the partnership, without the approval of the limited partners. Under the newer RULPA, there are no such restrictions on general partners; however, admission of a new general partner must be pursuant to the terms of a partnership agreement, and, if the agreement does not so provide, can only be done with the consent of all of the partners, including the limited partners. RULPA Section 401.

Under new statutory provisions, a few states, notably Delaware and Texas, allow a limited partnership to file a registration statement with the secretary of state, which results in the general partner(s) having protection from limited liability. This variety of limited partnership, called a *limited liability limited partnership,* is discussed in Chapter Five, Section J.

2. *Limited Partners*

A limited partner is basically a passive investor in this business enterprise. A limited partner invests his money in the limited partnership and knows that this represents the maximum loss he or she will face. Because limited partners cannot manage or control the limited partnership business, they have no personal liability for partnership debts and obligations. In general, limited partners can freely assign or transfer their interest in the partnership. This interest, namely, their share of the profits, is viewed as the limited partners' personal property. The transferee may become a limited partner if the agreement so provides or all other partners consent. Many agreements allow the general partner to unilaterally admit new partners. Because limited partners do not manage or control the business, the general partner is unlikely to care whether it is *A's* money which has been contributed or *B's* money. The partnership agreement may, however, restrict such transfers and assignments.

A limited partner may lose his or her limited liability status by acting as a general partner. While limited partners have the right to be provided copies of the partnership tax returns, the right to be informed of the partnership's business and affairs, and the right to review the corporate books and accounts, they cannot "control" the business. Numerous cases have attempted to interpret what types of activities constitute control of the partnership. Under the RULPA, if a limited partner participates in the control of the business, she is liable only to those persons who transacted business with the limited partnership reasonably believing, based upon the limited partner's conduct, that the limited partner was a general partner. RULPA Section 303(a). No such limitation existed under the ULPA.

In an attempt to clarify what activities are permissible for a limited partner, the RULPA specifically provides that a limited partner may engage in the following activities without subjecting himself to personal liability:

1. being a contractor for or an agent or employee of the limited partnership;
2. consulting with and advising a general partner with respect to the limited partnership business;
3. acting as a guarantor of partnership obligations;
4. bringing a derivative action in the name of the limited partnership;
5. requesting or attending a meeting of partners;
6. proposing, approving, or disapproving one or more of the following matters:
   - the dissolution and winding up of the limited partnership;
   - the sale, transfer, or mortgage of all or substantially all of the assets of the limited partnership;
   - the incurrence of indebtedness by the limited partnership other than in the ordinary course of its business;
   - a change in the nature of the business;
   - the admission or removal of a general or limited partner;
   - a transaction involving an actual or potential conflict of interest between a general partner and the limited partnership or limited partners;
   - an amendment to the partnership agreement or certificate of limited partnership; or
   - matters related to the business of the limited partnership not otherwise enumerated which the partnership agreement states may be subject to the approval or disapproval of limited partners;
7. winding up the limited partnership; or
8. exercising any right or power permitted to limited partners under the RULPA. [RULPA Section 303(b).]

The RULPA also specifies that conduct or activities undertaken by limited partners that are not specifically enumerated in the preceding list does not necessarily constitute an act of control by a limited partner that would render him subject to personal liability. Thus, a limited partner may perform some act not on this list and it will not necessarily be viewed as an act of control which would subject him to personal liability.

Additionally, a limited partner's last name cannot be used in the name of the limited partnership (unless it is also the name of a general partner or the business operated under that name before that partner's admission). Using a limited partner's surname in the partnership name will render that limited partner liable to creditors who do not know she is a limited partner. RULPA Section 303(d).

The general prohibition against a limited partner "managing or controlling" the business or having her last name in the business name seems to be based upon what third parties and creditors are likely to perceive. If a third party sees an individual engaged in the management and control of a business or notes that person's last name in the partnership name, he is likely to believe that person is a general partner whose personal assets are vulnerable.

The same person can serve as both a general partner and a limited partner. Wearing a hat as a general partner, that individual has full rights to manage the business and has personal liability. Wearing a hat as a limited partner, liability is "capped" at the initial contribution to the limited partnership, and the limited partnership interest can be transferred without causing a dissolution of the partnership. RULPA Section 702.

E. Advantages of Limited Partnerships

1. *Attracting Capital*

A limited partnership is an ideal way of attracting capital for an enterprise. Wealthy individuals who might not prefer to be sole proprietors or general partners can invest a certain amount of money in an enterprise knowing in advance their maximum exposure is limited to the amount of their contribution. Because new limited partners can easily be admitted to the business, a limited partnership that finds itself in financial difficulties can raise money by admitting new limited partners who will bring an influx of cash with them and will neither have personal liability nor interfere with the enterprise's management. While prior laws based upon the ULPA allowed limited partners to contribute only cash or property, RULPA Section 501 now allows limited partners to contribute cash, property, services, or even a promissory note or other obligation promising to contribute cash, property, or services in the future.

2. *Limited Liability*

From a wealthy individual's perspective, the limited partnership is an attractive business venture. One of the greatest advantages a limited partnership offers is limited liability to its limited partners. They can invest money in a business and, so long as they do not manage or control the business or allow their surname to be used in the business name, they will not be liable for any amount beyond their original contribution to the limited partnership.

3. *Easy Transferability of Partnership Interest*

Limited partners can easily transfer their interests to another. An assignment will not cause a dissolution of the limited partnership. The assignee, however, does not become a new limited partner but is merely entitled to receive any distribution the original limited partner would receive. The assignee may, however, become a new limited partner if all other partners agree or if such is allowed by limited partnership agreement. General partners have the same rights to assign their partnership interests as limited partners.

Moreover, unless the limited partnership provides a specific term or provides specific events which give rise to a right to withdraw, according to RULPA Sections 603 and 604, a limited partner has the right to withdraw from the limited partnership and demand a return of her contribution upon giving six months' written notice to the general partner[s].

4. *Continuity of Existence*

While sole proprietorships and general partnerships governed by the UPA cannot survive the death or withdrawal of the sole proprietor or a partner, the limited partnership will not necessarily dissolve upon the withdrawal of a general partner provided there is at least one other general partner and the limited partnership agreement permits the business to be carried on by the remaining general partner. Additionally, the RULPA provides that if an event of withdrawal occurs that would ordinarily cause dissolution, such as the resignation or removal of a general partner, the limited partnership need not wind up and dissolve if within 90 days after the withdrawal, all partners agree in writing to continue the limited partnership business and appoint one or more general partners. RULPA Section 801(4). Additionally, because limited partners do not manage or control the business, their withdrawal, death, or removal generally does not end the existence of the limited partnership, but instead may require only that an amendment to various documents be filed with the state. Thus, limited partnerships can survive events that might ordinarily force a dissolution and winding up of general partnerships.

F. Disadvantages of Limited Partnerships

1. *Lack of Control*

Although one of the greatest advantages to being a limited partner is limited liability, it comes at a price. Limited partners cannot manage or control the business or they risk unlimited personal liability. While they have a right to be informed about the operation of the business, they cannot participate in that operation. Thus, for individuals who prefer to manage their own affairs and control decisions relating to their investments, the limited partnership may not be an ideal form of business. Similarly, because the general partner has full responsibility for managing the business, the limited partners must have full confidence in the general partner and should therefore conduct some investigation, often called **due diligence,** to inquire about the background and trustworthiness of the general partner before contributing their money and then taking their traditional passive roles.

Due diligence
Investigation and research conducted before entering into agreements or transactions

2. *Unlimited Liability for General Partner*

Each limited partnership must have at least one general partner. General partners assume all of the responsibility for management of the limited partnership business. Thus, the disadvantage of being a general partner in a limited partnership is the same as being a general partner in a general partnership: unlimited personal liability for the debts and obligations of the business. If a limited partnership has a corporation as its general partner, the corporation will manage the business through its officers and directors, meaning the corporation will not have unlimited liability. Creditors of the limited partnership could reach only the assets in the limited partnership accounts and those in the corporate general partner's accounts. No individuals would have personal liability.

3. *Formalities and Expenses of Organization*

A general partnership can be formed with a handshake. No written agreement is required to form a general partnership. A limited partnership, however, is often said to be a "creature of statute," meaning it cannot be formed without compliance with statutory formalities. Various documents must be filed with the state in which the limited partnership operates. Annual reporting requirements may be imposed. Filing fees must be paid to the appropriate state authority. To do business in another state, the limited partnership is usually required to become formally authorized by the foreign state. This will involve filing documents with that state and paying filing fees.

Because it is necessary to comply with state statutes to create a limited partnership, most limited partnerships will require legal counsel. Thus, legal fees will likely be incurred.

G. Formation of Limited Partnerships

1. *Contents of the Limited Partnership Certificate*

Limited partnership certificate
The document filed with the state that creates a limited partnership

To form a limited partnership, a **limited partnership certificate** must be prepared, signed, and filed with the secretary of state of the state in which the partnership will operate. Under the original ULPA, the certificate needed to provide 14 items, including the nature of the business, an identification of each limited partner's contribution, how additional contributions were to be made, and each limited partner's share of the profits. ULPA Section 2. Under RULPA Section 201, the contents of the certificate are streamlined in recognition of the fact that the partnership agreement, not the certificate of limited partnership, is the authoritative document for a limited partnership, and only the following must be included:

a. the name of the limited partnership;
b. the address of the office and the name and address of the agent for service of process (namely, litigation summonses and complaints);
c. the name and business address of each general partner;
d. the latest date upon which the limited partnership is to dissolve; and
e. any other matters the general partners determine to include.

As stated earlier, each state may have some modifications and may require additional information. For example, Figure 4-1 shows the form required by the state of Delaware, which requires even fewer than the four items required by the RULPA. Filing fees charged by states can vary from $10 to hundreds of dollars.

The following elements are included in the certificate of limited partnership:

Name. The rule that sole proprietorships and general partnerships may not select names that are the same as or deceptively similar to that of another business also applies to limited partnerships. To determine name availability, one can contact the secretary of state and inquire whether the client's proposed name is available. See Appendix A for a listing of the secretary of state offices for each state. For a more thorough search, contact one of the search companies identified in Chapter Two.

According to RULPA Section 102(1), the name of a limited partnership must include without abbreviation the words "limited partnership." Some states have modified this requirement slightly. For example, in Illinois and Washington, a limited partnership name must include either the words "limited partnership" or the abbreviation "L.P." The purpose of these requirements is to afford public notice that the partnership is not a general partnership and that the assets of certain partners may not be available to creditors of the business.

The name of the limited partnership may not include the surname of a limited partner unless a general partner shares that surname or unless the limited partnership operated under that name prior to the admission of the limited partner. RULPA Section 102(2).

Registered Office and Agent. The limited partnership must designate an office in the state to which documents and notices can be sent. This need not be the limited partnership's principal place of business; however, an address must be provided so that notices and documents can be sent to the limited partnership. RULPA Section 105 provides that certain records must be kept at the office, including lists of general partners and limited partners, copies of tax records for the three most recent years, copies of any partnership agreements, and information relating to the contributions made by each partner and their right to receive distributions. Equally important, an **agent for service of process** must be identified. The agent is either an individual residing in the state or a company which is authorized to receive *service of process* for the limited partnership, meaning notices of litigation filed against the limited partnership. In the event any individual wishes to file suit against the limited partnership, the agent has been appointed to receive the summons and complaint. Upon receipt of the appropriate papers by

Agent for service of process
One who agrees to accept litigation notices for another

FIGURE 4-1
Delaware Certificate of Limited Partnership

STATE *of* DELAWARE
CERTIFICATE *of* LIMITED PARTNERSHIP

- **The Undersigned,** desiring to form a limited partnership pursuant to the Delaware Revised Uniform Limited Partnership Act, 6 Delaware Code, Chapter 17, do hereby certify as follows:
- **First:** The name of the limited partnership is ______________________________

  ____
- **Second:** The name and address of the Registered Agent is ____________________

  ____

  ____
- **Third:** The name and mailing address of each general partner is as follows:

  ____

  ____

  ____

  ____

  ____

  ____

  ____
- **In Witness Whereof,** the undersigned has executed this Certificate of Limited Partnership of ____as of

  __________________________.

BY: ______________________________
(General Partner)

NAME: ______________________________
(Type or Print)

the registered agent, the period for answering the complaint begins, and failure of the limited partnership to respond in a timely fashion may result in a default judgment entered against the partnership. In most states one can determine the name and address of a registered agent by calling the secretary of state.

Names and Addresses of General Partners. The names and addresses of the general partner or partners must be identified. Because the limited partners do not participate in the management and control of the business, they should be able to conduct due diligence to investigate the background of the general partner[s]. The identification of the general partner[s] not only provides an official address for correspondence with the limited partnership, but also provides sufficient information that the limited partners, if desired, can conduct some investigation into the general partner[s] to determine whether the general partner has been involved in previous lawsuits, has filed a petition for bankruptcy, or has engaged in other conduct that would influence the decision of a limited partner to invest money in this enterprise.

Dissolution Date. The date for dissolution of the limited partnership is given to provide notice to limited partners so they know when final distributions may be made and when their involvement with the limited partnership ends.

Other Matters. The general partner may include other items in the limited partnership certificate, including events triggering dissolution, names and addresses of limited partners, information regarding additional contributions that may need to be made by limited partners, and how contributions will be returned to limited partners. Because the certificate of limited partnership is a public document, however, most general partners comply narrowly with the requirements of their state and do not include other matters. The inclusion of additional matters may necessitate amendments to the certificate in the future. Thus, most limited partnerships comply strictly with what their state requires and provide no additional information.

2. *Filing the Certificate of Limited Partnership*

In most states, the form of the certificate of limited partnership is provided by the state. Contact your secretary of state's office (see Appendix A) and request a form for a limited partnership certificate. Alternatively, most states now make the forms available for downloading from the home page of the secretary of state. Some states may also require that the certificate be filed in the county in which the limited partnership will principally conduct its business. Carefully review your state statutes to ensure compliance with your state's requirements.

The certificate of limited partnership must be signed by all general partners. A limited partnership is formed at the time of the filing of the certificate with the office of the secretary of state. Filing fees are required in all states and many states require that a duplicate certificate be filed as well.

If there is an error in the certificate, it must be determined whether there has been substantial compliance with the pertinent state statute. If substantial compliance has been achieved, the limited partnership certificate will be valid and limited partners will be protected from unlimited liability. If, however, there is no substantial compliance with the appropriate state statutes, all of the members of the enterprise will be treated as if they were members in a general partnership with resulting individual liability. Sometimes, individuals invest in a business enterprise believing they are limited partners but the general partner, through mistake, inadvertence, or willfulness, fails to file the limited partnership certificate. Individuals who erroneously believe they are limited partners are not subject to liability as general partners to creditors of the business if, upon discovering the mistake, they cause the appropriate certificate to be filed or if they renounce their future profit in the enterprise. RULPA Section 304(a).

If the certificate contains a false statement, one who suffers loss by reliance on the statement may recover damages from anyone who knew the statement was false or from any general partner who knew or should have known the statement was false.

3. *Amendment of the Limited Partnership Certificate*

In the event of significant changes in the limited partnership, a certificate of amendment must be prepared and filed with the secretary of state. RULPA Section 202(b) provides that an amendment to the certificate of limited partnership shall be filed within 30 days after any of the following events:

a. admission of a new general partner;
b. withdrawal of a general partner; or
c. the continuation of the business after the withdrawal of a general partner.

Amendments may be filed for any other purpose the general partners determine. Moreover, in the event a general partner becomes aware that the certificate of limited partnership contains a false statement, or that any other facts set forth in the original certificate of limited partnership have changed, the general partner must promptly amend the certificate. Amending the original certificate will require preparation of the appropriate form designated for use in that state, signature by a general partner and any new general partner, and payment of a filing fee.

Under the original ULPA, the certificate of limited partnership was required to be amended for a variety of events, including any admission or withdrawal of a limited partner. For a limited partnership with a large number of limited partners, this was an expensive and cumbersome requirement. Thus, the RULPA provides a much more narrow list of events that require the filing of an amendment to the certificate of limited partnership. See Figure 4-2 for a sample certificate of amendment.

4. *Foreign Limited Partnerships*

Foreign limited partnership
A limited partnership doing business in a state other than the one in which it was formed

A limited partnership formed under the laws of one state may decide to expand its operations and conduct business in another state. A limited partnership formed in one state doing business in another is referred to as a **foreign limited partnership** by the second state, inasmuch as it was not originally created in the second state.

FIGURE 4-2
California Certificate of Amendment

State of California
Secretary of State
Bill Jones

AMENDMENT TO CERTIFICATE OF LIMITED PARTNERSHIP

A $30.00 filing fee must accompany this form.
IMPORTANT— Read instructions before completing this form.

This Space For Filing Use Only

1. SECRETARY OF STATE FILE NUMBER
2. NAME OF LIMITED PARTNERSHIP

3. COMPLETE ONLY THE BOXES WHERE INFORMATION IS BEING CHANGED. ADDITIONAL PAGES MAY BE ATTACHED, IF NECESSARY.

A. LIMITED PARTNERSHIP NAME (END THE NAME WITH THE WORDS "LIMITED PARTNERSHIP" OR THE ABBREVIATION "L.P.")

B. THE STREET ADDRESS OF THE PRINCIPAL OFFICE
ADDRESS
CITY STATE ZIP CODE

C. THE STREET ADDRESS IN CALIFORNIA WHERE RECORDS ARE KEPT
STREET ADDRESS
CITY STATE CA ZIP CODE

D. THE ADDRESS OF GENERAL PARTNER(S)
NAME
ADDRESS
CITY STATE ZIP CODE

E. NAME CHANGE OF A GENERAL PARTNER FROM: TO:

F. GENERAL PARTNER(S) CESSATION

G. GENERAL PARTNER ADDED
NAME
ADDRESS
CITY STATE ZIP CODE

H. THE PERSON(S) AUTHORIZED TO WIND UP AFFAIRS OF THE LIMITED PARTNERSHIP
NAME
ADDRESS
CITY STATE ZIP CODE

I. THE NAME OF THE AGENT FOR SERVICE OF PROCESS

J. IF AN INDIVIDUAL, CALIFORNIA ADDRESS OF THE AGENT FOR SERVICE OF PROCESS
ADDRESS
CITY STATE CA ZIP CODE

K. NUMBER OF GENERAL PARTNERS' SIGNATURES REQUIRED FOR FILING CERTIFICATES OF AMENDMENT, RESTATEMENT, MERGER, DISSOLUTION, CONTINUATION AND CANCELLATION.

L. OTHER MATTERS (ATTACH ADDITIONAL PAGES, IF NECESSARY).

4. TOTAL NUMBER OF PAGES ATTACHED (IF ANY)

5. I CERTIFY THAT THE STATEMENTS CONTAINED IN THIS DOCUMENT ARE TRUE AND CORRECT TO MY OWN KNOWLEDGE. I DECLARE THAT I AM THE PERSON WHO IS EXECUTING THIS INSTRUMENT, WHICH EXECUTION IS MY ACT AND DEED.

SIGNATURE POSITION OR TITLE PRINT NAME DATE

SIGNATURE POSITION OR TITLE PRINT NAME DATE

SEC/STATE (REV. 10/98)
FORM LP-2 – FILING FEE: $30.00
Approved by Secretary of State

To protect its citizens, a state can require that a foreign limited partnership apply to do business within its borders. Many activities, such as bringing or defending a lawsuit, holding meetings, or engaging in an isolated transaction are not considered "**doing business**" such that an application must be filed in the other state. Check state statutes to determine which activities require the foreign limited partnership to apply. In the application, the foreign limited partnership must appoint an agent for service of process so that any citizens injured by acts of the limited partnership in that state will be able to bring claims against the limited partnership. RULPA Section 902 sets forth the elements that must be met when a foreign limited partnership wishes to conduct business in a state other than the state of creation. In many respects, the application mimics the requirements of a certificate of limited partnership. Further, a limited partnership conducting business in another state will be required to comply with all of that state's laws, for example, any laws relating to the requirement of the words "limited partnership" or the abbreviation "L.P." in the business name.

Doing business
Activities enumerated by a state that require an entity to qualify before entering the state to transact business

Request the appropriate application form from the secretary of state for the state in which the limited partnership wishes to conduct business. Generally, the form must be signed by the general partner and accompanied by a filing fee. Failure to receive permission from a state to transact business may prohibit the limited partnership from maintaining any lawsuit in that state until the defect is cured. A limited partner of a foreign limited partnership is not liable as a general partner, however, merely because the general partner failed to file the appropriate form to become authorized to do business in the state. Figure 4-3 provides a model application for registration of a foreign limited partnership. Amendment of the application will be required in the event of significant changes in the foreign limited partnership, and the application should be canceled or withdrawn when the foreign limited partnership ceases to do business in the foreign state.

5. *Limited Partnership Agreement*

According to RULPA Section 101(9), a **limited partnership agreement** is any valid agreement among the partners, whether written or oral, governing the affairs of the limited partnership and the conduct of the business. Although the definition permits an oral agreement, for the sake of certainty a written agreement should always be prepared. The agreement will cover many matters not included in the certificate of limited partnership. The certificate, as a public record, should comply with the state's requirements; to include additional elements not required may only necessitate filing an amendment and paying a filing fee later. Under the prior act, the ULPA, the agreement could be filed as the certificate in many states so long as it complied with the statutory formalities for the certificate.

Limited partnership agreement
Agreement among partners in a limited partnership, usually written but may be oral

Limited partners will obviously desire a comprehensive agreement because their involvement in the business is so strictly curtailed. In many respects, the limited partnership agreement will be similar to a general partnership agreement because the important elements of the two, such as sharing of profits and losses, events causing dissolution, and the general partner's responsibilities, are common. A form of limited partnership agreement is available from your instructor.

The following elements should be included in a limited partnership agreement:

FIGURE 4-3
North Carolina Foreign Limited Partnership Application

State of North Carolina
Office of the Secretary of State

Office Use Only

Limited Partnership
Application for Certificate of Authority to do Business in North Carolina

A. Return Acknowledgement to:
Name:
Mailing Address:
City/State/Zip:

Read Instructions on reverse before beginning. Attach additional pages as needed.

No. pages attached:

B. Limited partnership name(s):
1. Name under which limited partnership formed:
2. Name under which limited partnership proposes to do business in N.C. (Must contain words "limited partnership"):

C. Jurisdiction in which limited partnership formed:

D. Dates of limited partnership
1. Date formed: 2. Period of duration:

E. Address of limited partnership in jurisdiction where formed:

Street/Number:	City:	State or Country:	Zip:	County:

F. Registration in North Carolina

1. Name of proposed registered agent in NC:
2. Address of proposed registered office in NC:

Street/Number:	City:	NC	Zip:	County:

G. General Partners

	1.	2.
Name		
Street/Number		
City		
State/Zip		
County		

	3.	4.
Name		
Street/Number		
City		
State/Zip		
County		

H. Limited partners (select 1 or 2 as appropriate)

1. ___ attached is a list of the names and addresses of all limited partners (full name/street address/city/state/zip code/county), or
2. ___ location of office where list will be as long as limited partnership transacts business in NC:

Street/Number:	City:	State or Country	Zip

I. This limited partnership appoints the N.C. Secretary of State as its agent to receive service of process, notice, or demand if it fails to maintain a registered agent in NC or if such agent cannot be located.

J. The following signature of one general partner signifies acceptance of all conditions of doing business in N.C. and constitutes an affirmation under the penalties of perjury that the facts herein are true:

Type or print name	Title	Signature	Date

NOTES: Filing fee is $50.00. This document and one exact or conformed copy must be filed with the Secretary of State.

Form LP-04 *(Revised Sept. 1998)*

CORPORATIONS DIVISION 300 N. SALISBURY STREET RALEIGH, NC 27603-5909

Name of Partnership. Consult the appropriate state statutes to ensure compliance in selecting the name of the limited partnership. After ensuring availability, determine whether the state requires the signal "limited partnership" or "L.P." Recall that a limited partner's surname cannot be used in the business name unless it is also the surname of a general partner or the business was carried on under that name prior to that limited partner's admission.

Names and Addresses of Partners. The names and addresses of all partners should be stated. Additionally, the agreement should designate whether a partner is a general or limited partner. Many limited partnerships that have a large number of limited partners identify the limited partners in an exhibit or attachment to the agreement.

Recitals. The recital clause confirms the intent of the partners to create a limited partnership. This clause clarifies that this is a unique partnership in which individuals who manage the enterprise will have unlimited liability, while others are mere passive investors not subject to any risk beyond their original contributions.

Purpose. A clause should be included stating the purpose of the limited partnership, for example, real estate development, the maintenance and management of shopping centers, or the operation of a chain of restaurants. The limited partnership can conduct any lawful activity. This clause should not be so restrictive as to limit the limited partnership from carrying on other activities. Thus, after the specific purpose is given, include a broader provision, such as ". . . and any other activities reasonably related to the purposes of this partnership or that are lawful in this State."

Address. The principal place of business of the partnership should be provided. Certain documents must be kept by limited partnerships and all partners should be provided with the location of these documents, because, under RULPA Section 105(b), the records are subject to inspection by any partner. Furthermore, this address will provide a location for certain notices and communications to be sent to the limited partnership.

Term. The date for termination of the limited partnership should be stated. Alternatively, this section can set forth any events that will cause a dissolution of the limited partnership. If no time limit is set, a limited partner may withdraw from the partnership and demand a return of capital on six months' notice.

Certificate of Limited Partnership. The agreement should mandate that the certificate of limited partnership be recorded in the appropriate state office (or confirm the filing of the certificate). A specific general partner should be designated to be in charge of the original filing of the certificate as well as any needed amendments to it.

Financial Provisions. A variety of provisions relating to finances should be included. First, the initial contributions of all partners should be identified. Originally, limited partners were only allowed to contribute cash or property to a limited partnership and were prohibited from contributing services. This prohibition against contributing services was related to the prohibition against management of the business by limited partners. Under the RULPA, limited partners may contribute money, property, services rendered, a promissory note, or some other obligation to contribute cash or property or to perform services. RULPA Section 501. If property or services are contributed, their value should be set forth so that if a limited partner contributes office furniture and then demands a return of capital, all partners are in agreement as to what this return should be.

The need for additional contributions also should be addressed so that if the partnership needs additional capital, there is a procedure for effecting this. Typically, as in general partnerships, additional contributions will be required in the same percentage as initial contributions, so that if a limited partner contributed 27 percent of the original capital, she will need to contribute 27 percent of additional capital needed. If desired, limitations can be set so that no limited partner is required to contribute more than a certain percentage of her original contribution.

Profits and Losses. This section of the agreement should set forth the share of profits to be distributed to each partner and the losses allocated to each partner. As with general partnerships, agreements usually provide that profits and losses be shared in proportion to the contributions to the limited partnerships. If the agreement fails to provide for allocation of profits and losses, RULPA Section 503 provides that profits and losses will be allocated on the basis of the contributions made by partners that are received and not returned by the partnership. This is quite different from the approach taken by the UPA and the RUPA, which both provide that in the absence of agreement, profits and losses will be shared equally, regardless of contributions. Because general partners have complete responsibility for management and control of the business and face unlimited liability, they are often provided a salary or perhaps an additional percentage of profit. Any losses caused by the reckless or willful conduct of any partner should be borne by that partner alone.

Rights and Duties of General Partner. Because the general partner has the sole responsibility to conduct partnership business, express authority should be granted to him to conduct such business. Arrangements should be made for the general partner to pay the partnership's obligations, such as rent and insurance, and the general partner should be given the authority to conduct ordinary business on behalf of the partnership. If there are to be any limitations on the general partner's authority, they should be clearly expressed. For example, the partners may wish to limit to a stated dollar amount the general partner's authority to borrow money on behalf of the partnership or to sell partnership assets, to limit the general partner's authority to admit another general partner, or to prohibit the general partner from instituting any litigation or settling any claim without notice to all partners. Unless restrictions are provided, a general partner in a limited partnership has all of the powers and rights of a general partner in a general partnership. RULPA Section 403(a). Additionally, if there is more than one general partner, the agreement should provide a formula for their voting.

Rights and Duties of Limited Partners. The agreement should incorporate the provisions of RULPA Section 303(b) setting forth the activities that may be undertaken by limited partners without risk of losing their limited liability status. Furthermore, the provisions of RULPA Section 305 allowing limited partners to inspect and copy partnership records, to obtain information from the general partner regarding the state of affairs and financial conditions of the limited partnership, and to obtain copies of the limited partnership's various tax returns should be incorporated. Further expansion of the rights of limited partners will jeopardize their limited liability status. Provisions may be included to allow removal of a general partner for certain acts of misconduct.

Admission of New General Partners. Under RULPA Section 401, after the filing of a limited partnership's original certificate of limited partnership, additional general partners may be admitted as provided by the written agreement of the partners or, if the partnership agreement does not provide in writing for the admission of an additional general partner, with the written consent of *all* partners. Thus, if the agreement so provides, a general partner can be admitted upon a less-than-unanimous vote by all partners.

Admission of New Limited Partners. As to admission of additional limited partners, RULPA Section 301(b) provides that after the filing of the original certificate of limited partnership, a person may be admitted as a new limited partner upon compliance with the provisions in the limited partnership agreement, or if the partnership agreement is silent, upon the written consent of *all* partners. Thus, the agreement can provide for the admission of new limited partners solely by the consent of the general partner or a simple majority vote of the partners.

Any new partners, whether general or limited, should be required to sign the agreement and agree to be bound by its provisions.

Events of withdrawal
Events relating to a general partner that cause dissolution of a limited partnership

Withdrawal of General Partners. According to RULPA Section 402, unless agreed otherwise by all partners in writing, the following are **events of withdrawal** of a general partner that will cause a dissolution of the partnership:

1. the general partner withdraws by giving notice to the other partners; however, if this withdrawal violates the terms of the partnership agreement, which might specify a definite date of duration, the limited partnership can recover any damages from the general partner caused by this breach of agreement;
2. the general partner transfers all of her interest to a transferee;
3. the general partner is removed from the partnership in accord with the terms of the partnership agreement (such as removal by a certain percentage of the limited partnership interests);
4. unless allowed by a written partnership agreement, the general partner:
   (a) makes an assignment for the benefit of creditors;
   (b) is adjudicated bankrupt; or
   (c) files a petition under the Bankruptcy Act or consents to the appointment of a receiver for his or her property; or
5. the general partner dies.

The agreement may, of course, provide that the partnership can survive any of these events. Nevertheless, if the general partner withdraws in violation of the terms of the limited partnership agreement, she may be held liable for damages caused by this breach of agreement.

An event of withdrawal, however, will not cause a dissolution if there is at least one other general partner and the written partnership agreement permits the business to be conducted by the remaining general partner or, if within 90 days after the withdrawal, *all* partners agree in writing to continue the partnership business and a new general partner is appointed, if needed. RULPA Section 801.

Withdrawal of Limited Partners. According to RULPA Section 603, a limited partner may withdraw from a limited partnership in accordance with the provisions of the limited partnership agreement, such as those relating to the term of the agreement or the occurrence of certain events. If the agreement does not specify such events, a limited partner may withdraw from the partnership upon giving six months' written notice to each general partner. At the time of withdrawal, the limited partner is entitled to receive any distribution to which he or she may be entitled under the terms of the agreement, or, if not otherwise provided, may receive the fair value of his interest in the limited partnership, so long as partnership assets exceed liabilities.

The limited partnership does not dissolve upon the death or withdrawal of a limited partner. Because limited partners are merely passive investors, their membership in the partnership is not critical to the operation of the partnership business, and thus they may freely withdraw from a limited partnership without causing a dissolution.

Transfer of Partnership Interests. According to RULPA Section 702, both general and limited partners may assign their **partnership interest,** meaning their share of the profits of the partnership. Such an assignment does not dissolve the partnership or immediately allow the assignee to become a partner. The assignee is entitled to receive only the distribution to which the assignor would be entitled. The assignee may, however, become a partner if the assignor so agrees and the partnership agreement provides for such, or if all other partners consent. Naturally, any assignee should be required to execute the limited partnership agreement. Generally, one ceases to be a partner upon assignment of all of his or her partnership interest.

Partnership interest
A partner's share of partnership profits

Dissolution. There are two types of dissolution of a limited partnership: nonjudicial and judicial. As the very names indicate, nonjudicial dissolution occurs without the involvement of a court while judicial dissolution involves court action.

As to **nonjudicial dissolution,** a limited partnership is dissolved and its business wound up upon the following:

Nonjudicial dissolution
Dissolution of an entity without involvement by a court

1. the time specified in the certificate of limited partnership;
2. upon the occurrence of any events specified in a written partnership agreement;
3. written consent of all partners; or
4. an event of withdrawal of a general partner (unless, of course, there is another general partner to carry on the business and the agreement permits the business to be carried on *or* if within 90 days after the withdrawal, all partners agree in writing to continue the partnership business).

As to **judicial dissolution,** any partner may apply to a court to dissolve the limited partnership when it is no longer reasonably practicable to carry on the business in conformity with the partnership agreement. RULPA Section 802.

Judicial dissolution
Dissolution of an entity ordered by a court

Liquidation. Unless a general partner has wrongfully dissolved a limited partnership, the general partner will be responsible for winding up the business affairs of the limited partnership. Additionally, upon application by any partner, a court may wind up the partnership's business affairs.

Upon the winding up of a limited partnership, its assets must be distributed as follows:

1. to creditors, including partners who are creditors (having made loans to the partnership or having incurred expenses on behalf of the partnership);
2. to partners and former partners who have withdrawn, to satisfy the return of their contributions; and
3. to partners for the return of their contributions, and then to partners for profits, according to their respective partnership interests (except as provided in the partnership agreement). RULPA Section 804.

Miscellaneous Provisions. Just as seen in general partnership agreements, numerous other provisions may be included in a limited partnership agreement.

1. Non-compete clauses can be provided to prohibit general partners from competing with the partnership business for a reasonable period of time within a reasonable geographic area.
2. The partners should provide a method for resolving disputes. They may elect arbitration or may agree upon a court in which to bring actions. Attorney's fees and costs may be allowed to the prevailing party.
3. "Standard" or "boilerplate" provisions may be included, such as how notice of certain matters is to be given; that the agreement will be interpreted according to the laws of a certain state; that if part of the agreement is invalid, the rest remains valid; that the agreement supersedes and replaces any prior written or oral agreements; that the agreement can be modified only in writing upon the consent of all partners; and that use of masculine and singular terms includes the feminine and plural.

Signatures. All partners should sign and date the limited partnership agreement. Any new partners, whether general or limited, should also be required to sign the agreement. Corporate partners should sign by an authorized officer of the corporation. General partners which are themselves general partnerships should sign by an authorized general partner.

H. Transferability of Interest

The transfer or assignment of a limited partner's interest in a limited partnership is much more easily accomplished than such an assignment by a general partner in a general partnership.

RULPA Section 702 provides that a limited partner's interest in the partnership, namely, his right to profits, is assignable in whole or in part. No permission is required from any partner. Thus, the limited partner can easily transfer his interest in the partnership to another. The assignment, however, does not automatically entitle the assignee to become a member of the partnership. Nevertheless, an assignee of either a general or limited partner may become a limited partner if the assignor gives that right in accordance with the terms of the limited partnership agreement *or* all the other partners consent.

The reason for such ready transferability by limited partners is that they are passive investors who do not participate in the management or control of the business. Therefore, business operations and management are not greatly affected by the transfer in and out of limited partners. In essence, they may be viewed as simply "moneymen" who make financial contributions to the partnership and hope that the general partner's expertise and management skills will enhance the value of their investment. General partners may also assign their interest in the partnership to another, unless the agreement provides otherwise. The assignee receives only the distribution to which the transferring general partner would be entitled. A new general partner may be admitted as provided in the agreement, or if the agreement is silent, upon the written consent of all partners.

Generally, unless the agreement provides otherwise, a partner (whether general or limited) ceases to be a partner upon assignment of all of his or her partnership interest. Such an action by a general partner is an event of withdrawal that triggers dissolution and winding up unless the partnership agreement allows the business to continue or all partners, within 90 days, agree to continue the business.

I. Actions by Limited Partners

If a limited partner has been directly injured by the limited partnership, for example, she is refused the right to inspect the books, the limited partner may institute an action for this injury to her. This type of action is called a **direct action** because the limited partner has been directly injured.

Direct action
Action brought by one to redress a wrong done to him or her

In some instances, however, the limited partnership itself is injured and refuses to enforce its own cause of action. For example, assume that a limited partnership loans $50,000 to one of the friends of a general partner. If the loan is not paid when due, the general partner may be reluctant to initiate an action against his or her friend. The failure to recover the loan, however, deprives the limited partnership of capital. In such a case, a limited partner may institute a **derivative suit** to enforce the obligation due to the limited partnership. The action is referred to as derivative because the limited partner is not suing for himself but rather to enforce rights derived from his ownership interests in the limited partnership. The action can be instituted by a limited partner if the general partner has refused to bring the action or if an effort to cause the general partner to bring the action is not likely to be successful. To ensure that individuals do not join partnerships solely to litigate actions, RULPA Section 1002 provides that the plaintiff partner must have been a partner at the time of the transaction being complained of. If the derivative action is successful, the recovery will belong to the limited partnership although the limited partner who brought the action is entitled to be reimbursed for expenses and attorneys' fees. (See RULPA Sections 1001–1004.) The rules and procedures for derivative actions by limited partners are highly similar to those for derivative actions by stockholders discussed in Chapter Eleven.

Derivative suit
Action brought by one to enforce an obligation owed to another, usually to a business

J. Dissolution and Winding Up of Limited Partnerships

As noted above, a limited partnership is dissolved and its business affairs must be wound up when one of the following events occurs:

1. the time specified for the duration of the limited partnership expires;
2. upon the happening of any events specified in writing in the limited partnership agreement (such as an agreement to dissolve when property is sold, when revenue drops below a certain level, or when a change in tax laws may make it unwise to operate as a limited partnership);
3. written consent of all partners;
4. an act of withdrawal of the general partner unless there is at least one general partner to conduct the business and the written agreement so provides, or, if within 90 days after the withdrawal, all partners agree in writing to continue the business and to appoint an additional general partner, if necessary; or
5. a decree of judicial dissolution is entered upon application of any partner who shows that it is not reasonably practicable to continue the limited partnership business.

Unless a general partner has wrongfully caused a dissolution (for example, by withdrawing before the term set in the agreement), the general partner may wind up or liquidate the limited partnership by collecting its assets and completing its obligations. Otherwise, a court may oversee the winding up upon the application of any partner.

After creditors are paid (including partners' claims for reimbursement for expenses incurred or loans made on behalf of the partnership), former partners will then receive their distributions. Then partners will receive a return of their contributions and, finally, their profits. While the original ULPA preferred limited partners to general partners by requiring distributions to limited partners before distributions to general partners, the RULPA allows for no such distinctions between the two types of partners in the distribution of assets.

K. Cancellation of Limited Partnership Certificate

The creation of a limited partnership is accomplished by the filing of a certificate of limited partnership. When the limited partnership is dissolved and wound up, a certificate of cancellation should be filed with the secretary of state. It will contain basic information about the limited partnership, including the reason for discontinuance of the business. The certificate must be filed by a general partner, signed by a general partner, and must be accompanied by a filing fee. (Figure 4-4 provides a certificate of cancellation of limited partnership.) If the partnership is doing business in any other states, it should cancel or withdraw any applications in those foreign states.

FIGURE 4-4
North Carolina Cancellation of Certificate of Limited Partnership

State of North Carolina
Department of the Secretary of State

Cancellation of Certificate of Domestic or Foreign Limited Partnership

A. Return Acknowledgement to:	Office Use Only
Name:	
Mailing Address:	
City/State/Zip:	

Read Instructions on reverse before beginning. Attach additional pages as needed and complete appropriate section.

☐ B. **DOMESTIC LIMITED PARTNERSHIP CANCELLATION** — No. of pages attached:

1.Name of limited partnership:	
2.Date originally filed with Secretary of State:	3.Number originally assigned by Secretary of State:
4.Reason for cancellation:	
5.Effective date of cancellation (not to exceed 90 days from this filing by Secretary of State):	
6.Any other information partners wish to present:	

7.The following signatures by each general partner constitute an affirmation under the penalties of perjury that the facts herein are true.

Complete for each general partner.	Signature	Date
1. Name		
Title		
2. Name		
Title		
3. Name		
Title		

☐ C. **FOREIGN LIMITED PARTNERSHIP CANCELLATION** — No. of pages attached:

1.Name of limited partnership:	
2.Name used to transact business in N.C., if different:	
3.Date originally filed with N.C. Secretary of State:	4.Number originally assigned by N.C. Secretary of State:
5.Reason for cancellation:	
6.Effective date of cancellation (not to exceed 90 days from this filing by N.C. Secretary of State):	
7.Any other information partners wish to present:	

8.The following signature by one general partner constitutes an affirmation under penalty of perjury that the facts herein are true:

Type or print name	Title	Signature	Date

NOTES:
1. Filing fee is $25.00. This document and one exact or conformed copy must be filed with the Secretary of State.

(Revised May 1998) *Form LP-03*
CORPORATIONS DIVISION 300 N. SALISBURY STREET RALEIGH, NC 27603-5909

L. Taxation of Limited Partnerships

In general, taxation of a limited partnership is highly similar to taxation of a general partnership. Thus, all of the income earned by the partnership is "passed through" to the partners, who declare their share of the profits on their own individual tax returns. Similarly, losses can be used to offset other income of the partners. Although the limited partnership, itself not a separate taxable entity, does not pay tax (unless it has sufficient characteristics of a corporation that it can be treated and taxed as such by the Internal Revenue Service), it will complete and file an information tax return, just as a general partnership does. In fact, the similarities between general and limited partnerships regarding tax treatment are so great, that the very form used by a general partnership to file its information tax return, Form 1065 (see Figure 3-7), is also used by the limited partnership. Similarly, individual general partners and limited partners in a limited partnership report their respective income or losses on Schedule K and attach it to their individual tax returns. Schedule K, shown in Figure 3-6, is used by general partners of general partnerships as well. Although limited partnerships are treated as general partnerships for tax purposes, like general partnerships, a limited partnership can elect to be taxed as a corporation by "checking the box" on the appropriate tax form. (See Chapter Three and Figure 3-8.)

Key Features of Limited Partnerships

- Limited partnerships must have at least one general partner and one limited partner.
- The general partner in a limited partnership functions identically to and has the same risks as a general partner in a general partnership.
- Limited partners do not have personal liability for the limited partnership's obligations (so long as they do not manage the business); their liability is limited to the amount invested in the enterprise.
- Formation of limited partnerships requires filing a Certificate of Limited Partnership with the appropriate state agency.
- Limited partners can freely enter and exit the partnership.
- Limited partnership agreement may be oral or written; if no agreement on profits and losses, they are allocated on basis of contributions made by partners.
- Limited partnerships offer "pass through" taxation, meaning that the entity does not pay tax, but, rather, all income is passed through to the partners who pay at their respective tax rates.

M. Family Limited Partnerships

A relatively new twist on limited partnerships is the **family limited partnership,** which is not truly a different form of limited partnership, but a vehicle to achieve certain estate and tax planning benefits. In a family limited partnership (sometimes called a *family limited liability company*), all partners are family members (or spouses of family members) and income-producing capital assets, such as rental property or securities, are transferred into the family limited partnership. In most cases, parents act as general partners, and children and other family members are limited partners.

Family limited partnership
An investment vehicle entered into by family members to achieve estate and tax planning benefits (sometimes called a *family limited liability company*)

Because the first $675,000 of income is excluded from one's estate tax, the parents each initially make a gift of limited partnership interests in this amount to their children/limited partners (for a total of $1.35 million). Thereafter, because individuals can annually give away or "gift" up to $10,000 each year and the giver neither pays gift tax on the amount nor does the recipient pay tax on the amount received, additional fractional interests in the family limited partnership are transferred or gifted from the parents to the children/limited partners. In essence, money is shifted out of the parents' estates so the estates will not be subject to taxation upon death of the parents; yet the parents, as general partners, maintain control and management of the limited partnership business itself. In most cases, the parents own far less interest in the family limited partnership than do the children. The parents, as general partners, often receive a management fee of some type to provide them with a stream of income. The Internal Revenue Service carefully scrutinizes family limited partnerships to ensure that they comply with federal tax regulations. Note that the amounts provided herein will increase over time, so that by 2006, the estate tax exclusion will be $1 million, and the gift tax exclusion will be indexed to inflation.

A family limited partnership is created just as any other limited partnership. It is essentially a device to minimize or eliminate estate taxes through the transfer of property into the partnership, most of the interest of which is held by the children/limited partners.

N. Role of Paralegal

Because limited partnerships can be formed only by compliance with appropriate state statutes, the organization of limited partnerships offers unique opportunities for paralegals to provide an integral role in the creation of limited partnerships.

The paralegal can check the availability of the desired name, determine what signals (such as "limited partnership" or "L.P." must be included in the name), and ensure that a limited partner's surname is not used improperly in the partnership name.

The paralegal will likely have an active role in drafting and filing the certificate of limited partnership. Review state statutes carefully to determine what information is required. Changes in the limited partnership should also be monitored to determine when an amendment to the certificate must be filed.

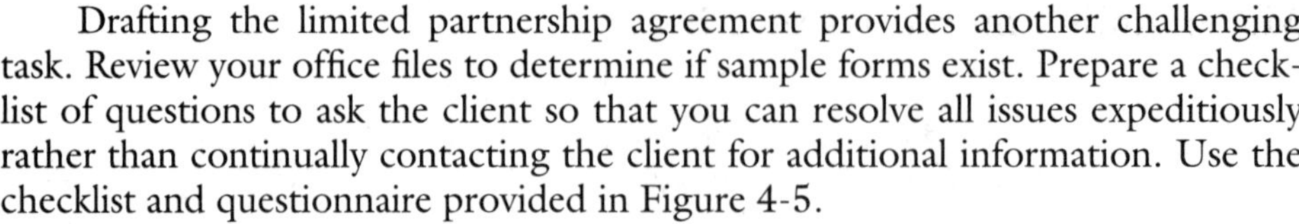

Drafting the limited partnership agreement provides another challenging task. Review your office files to determine if sample forms exist. Prepare a checklist of questions to ask the client so that you can resolve all issues expeditiously rather than continually contacting the client for additional information. Use the checklist and questionnaire provided in Figure 4-5.

Resource Guide

Most of the resources available for information about the formation of general partnerships are the same for the formation and operation of limited partnerships.

1. Statutes

Because a limited partnership cannot be created by a simple private agreement, but only by compliance with pertinent state statutes, you will need to consult carefully the applicable statutes, particularly with regard to the preparation and filing of the limited partnership certificate. Many states provide forms and you should consider contacting your secretary of state (see Appendix A for a listing of the secretary of state offices) for the forms suggested by that state. In most instances, the forms are free and can be easily obtained.

2. Encyclopedias

If you need general background information on limited partnerships, consult one of the two legal encyclopedias: C.J.S. or Am. Jur. 2d. Both of these sets will provide you with thorough and articulate information about the development, formation, operation, and dissolution of limited partnerships.

3. Form Books

Form books will provide guidance in drafting a limited partnership agreement. Some of the better known form books are:

a. Rabkin and Johnson, *Current Legal Forms*
b. Am. Jur. Legal Forms 2d
c. West's Legal Forms, 2d

These form books include a variety of form agreements and suggested provisions for limited partnership agreements. These can then be discussed with the client to determine the provisions most appropriate for that client's needs.

4. Periodicals

Review periodical articles for new information relating to limited partnerships.

5. Associations

Join your local paralegal association or bar association and sign up for a section devoted to business or corporate law. You will then be kept informed of recent developments and will be notified of lectures and seminars relating to proposed changes in the law relating to limited partnerships.

6. WESTLAW

West Group's computer assisted research service, WESTLAW, provides access to limited partnership records from the states and the District of Columbia. A limited partnership's name, address, and the states in which it conducts business are readily determined. To search all available states at once, access the ALLCORP database.

FIGURE 4-5
Limited Partnership Checklist and Questionnaire

1. Proposed Name of Partnership: ______
   Alternative Names[s] ______
2. Names and Addresses of General Partner[s]
   a. ______ b. ______
   ______ ______
   ______ ______
3. Names and Addresses of Limited Partner[s]
   a. ______ b. ______
   ______ ______
   ______ ______
   c. ______ d. ______
   ______ ______
   ______ ______
4. Address of Limited Partnership ______
   ______
5. Purpose of Limited Partnership ______
6. Duration of Limited Partnership ______
7. Contributions of Limited Partnership ______
   Name ______ Profits/Losses ______ Contribution ______
   Name ______ Profits/Losses ______ Contribution ______
8. Contributions and Profits and Losses of Limited Partners
   Name ______ Profits/Losses ______ Contribution ______
   Name ______ Profits/Losses ______ Contribution ______
   Name ______ Profits/Losses ______ Contribution ______
   Name ______ Profits/Losses ______ Contribution ______
9. Conditions Regarding Transferability of Partnership Interests ______
   ______
   ______
   ______
10. Designation of Managing Partner ______
11. Manner of Resolving Disputes ______
    ______
12. Events of Dissolution ______
    ______
    ______
13. Fiscal Year ______
14. Banking Information ______
15. Other Provisions ______
    ______
    ______

◆ ◆ ◆

WEB RESOURCES

A number of sites provide general information about partnerships with clear and concise discussions of limited partnerships, comparing and contrasting them to other forms of business entities. Many of the sites listed below provide forms for partnership agreements. Only a few provide forms specifically for limited partnership agreements, since many professionals use a general partnership agreement as a starting point and then modify it to use for limited partnerships. As with all forms, exercise caution in using the form, as it will likely not be suitable for all partnerships. As with any form, you should modify it to suit your needs. Because most of the partnership agreements provided on the Internet are for general partnerships rather than limited partnerships, you will need to revise many agreements. Review the Web site's Disclaimer or Legal Terms section to determine if there are any prohibitions on use or reproduction of the forms. In any event, the forms serve as useful starting places.

Of most importance is review of a state's statutes regarding limited partnerships. To review state statutes online, access <www.ll.georgetown.edu>, the Web site of Georgetown University Law Center. Select "State, Local & Territorial," and you will then be presented with a map of the United States. Point your cursor to the desired state, and you will then be able to select whether you wish to view that state's constitution, statutes, cases, or other legal information. By selecting "Statutes" or "Code," you will be able to search the state's statutes and find relevant statutory material. In some instances, you can search by statute number; in other instances, you can search by keyword. Some states allow you to browse various titles. Search for "Corporations" and then view the limited partnership statutes usually included either within or near this title.

Other Web sites of interest are as follows:

http://www.nass.org
This Web site of the National Association of Secretaries of State allows you to link directly to the home page for each state's secretary of state. Many states offer guides to forming partnerships with basic information, forms, checklists, and phone numbers. Point the cursor to your state's name and flag and proceed to locate information on forming a limited partnership in your state. Forms for limited partnership certificates, certificates for correction, and certificates for cancellation of limited partnerships are offered on most state Web sites.

www.irs.gov
The Web site of the Internal Revenue Service offers a wealth of information about taxes, businesses, and provides Form 1065 and Schedule K, the partnership tax forms that can be downloaded and printed.

www.ask.com

"Ask Jeeves" is an Internet "butler" who will help you find what you need. Simply type in your question, in natural English, in the box presented, and you will be referred to numerous useful sites. For example, type in "Where can I find information about limited partnerships?" You will then be directed to sites offering information on limited partnerships and forms of agreements. "Ask.com" is often the first site many individuals access to find information on nearly any topic. Bookmark this site, and use it often.

www.tannedfeet.com

Billed as "The Entrepreneurs' Help Page," this site provides a wealth of information regarding the formation and operation of businesses, including partnerships. Access <www.tannedfeet.com/html/partnerships.htm> for specific information about partnerships.

www.about.com

"About.com" offers a wide variety of information relating to many topics. After you access the site, point your cursor to "Business/Careers" and then to "Small Business Information" for information on starting businesses, tax strategies, and information about types of entities, including limited partnerships.

www.ilrg.com

The Internet Legal Research Guide is a great source of information and provides a form for a partnership agreement in its "Legal Forms Archive."

www.law.com

"Law.Com" is a well-known site used by legal professionals. After viewing the home page, go to "Business" and then to "Resources for Business." Scroll down the page for access to business forms, including a form of partnership agreement.

www.lectlaw.com

The 'Lectric Law Library provides a vast array of information on legal topics. Access "the Rotunda" and then "Forms Room" to locate a form of partnership agreement.

www.lawsmart.com

Access the home page and enter "partnership" as a key term. You will be referred to a form of partnership agreement.

www.LegalWiz.com

This legal resource for entrepreneurs offers articles, general information about businesses, a glossary of business and legal terms, and a form of partnership agreement. Access "Legal Forms" and you will be provided with the partnership agreement form.

http://www.siccode.com/forms.php3
This Web site, entitled "SICCode.com" provides numerous business and legal forms. When you access the site, point your cursor to "free legal forms." You will be provided with hundreds of forms, including a form for a partnership agreement, which you are invited to cut and paste into your word processor.

www.findlaw.com/16forms/index.htm
The forms section of "FindLaw.com," a well-known legal Web site offers numerous links to forms collections and forms indexes.

Discussion Questions

Fact Scenario. Anne Reynolds is the general partner in Reynolds L.P., a Connecticut limited partnership engaged in real estate investment. The limited partners are Francine and Tim Talbot, Judith Harris, and Anne's husband, Michael. While the limited partnership has a written agreement, it is silent on matters of sharing of profits and losses and on withdrawals of partners. Each limited partner invested $10,000, and Anne invested $40,000.

1. Does the partnership name have any adverse consequences for Michael?
2. Francine has seen a vacant lot she believes would be a good investment for the partnership business and has signed a contract for its purchase, placing $20,000 down as a deposit with its owner. What are the possible consequences to Francine of such action?
3. Judith routinely stops by the partnership office to inquire about the partnership's activities and has requested that Anne hold quarterly partnership meetings. Are there any possible adverse consequences of such action for Judith?
4. The partnership owes a debt of $150,000 to one of its bankers and has only $50,000 in its bank accounts and as assets. Describe each partner's share of the debt.
5. Anne believes that the purchase and sale of various New York properties would afford the partnership unique opportunities for profit. What should the partnership do in order to commence doing business in New York?

5

Registered Limited Liability Partnerships

CHAPTER OVERVIEW

A registered limited liability partnership is a new form of business organization. Recognized in all states and the District of Columbia, this entity modifies a fundamental principle of partnership law. You will recall that under the RUPA and general partnership law, a partner in a general partnership has unlimited personal liability for the wrongful acts or omissions of his or her partners. In this new form of partnership, the liability of all partners is limited so they are not subject to unlimited personal liability for the wrongful acts and omissions of their partners or, in some states, for the contractual obligations of the partnership. To protect the public from acts of negligence, some states mandate certain liability insurance requirements. This new form of business organization combines some of the best features of partnership law and corporation law and is ideally suited to partnerships composed of professionals, such as doctors, accountants, and lawyers. The registered limited liability partnership thus continues a trend in modern business law of combining limited liability and pass-through taxation to afford its members a flexible business structure with single taxation.

A. Characteristics of Registered Limited Liability Partnerships

In the late 1980s a number of savings and loan institutions failed. The injured investors could not bring effective causes of action against the institutions because those institutions were insolvent. They therefore began commencing actions for damages against the law firms that had provided legal advice and against the accounting firms that had provided accounting services to the institutions.

In brief, professional malpractice claims were made against the law and accounting firms that provided professional services to the failed institutions. Many of those firms were general partnerships. Under general partnership law, partners in one office found themselves subject to unlimited liability for advice given by their partners in another office, perhaps thousands of miles away. In many cases, the savings and loan institutions had been represented by only a few attorneys or accountants in a firm and only those individuals had provided any professional services to the financial institutions; yet hundreds of other partners across the country and around the world found themselves facing unlimited liability for advice they had not given to clients of whom they had never heard.

The *registered limited liability partnership* (RLLP), sometimes called simply a **limited liability partnership** (LLP), was created in response to this situation. An LLP is highly similar to a general partnership; however, one critical feature of general partnership law is changed: unlimited personal liability. American jurisdictions are nearly evenly divided as to the extent to which personal liability can be avoided in an LLP. There are two approaches:

Limited liability partnership
Partnership providing protection against liability for wrongful conduct of other partners; formed by compliance with statutes

Partial shield states
States in which partners in an LLP retain liability for contractual obligations

Full shield states
States in which partners in an LLP are fully protected from personal liability, whether arising in tort or contract

- **Partial Shield States.** In these states, a partner in an LLP will not have personal liability for the wrongful acts or omissions of his or her partners. Partners in partial shield states retain personal liability for other partnership obligations, such as those arising from contract.
- **Full Shield States.** In these states (and under RUPA Section 306(c)), a partner is not personally liable for either the wrongful acts or omissions of his or her partners or for commercial, contractual, or other obligations of the partnership, making the LLP partner much like a shareholder in a corporation with regard to liability.

The initial LLP statutes were all of the partial shield variety, with states later electing or converting to a full shield protection beginning in 1994. In all jurisdictions, however, partners in an LLP retain liability for their own acts of negligence, those of others in the partnership whom they supervise or direct and, in many states, those of which they know (and fail to prevent or stop).

LLPs are governed by state statute. Thus, they cannot be created by a simple oral or written agreement as can a general partnership. An LLP can only be created by compliance with state statutes; in this way, it is similar to a limited partnership. An existing general partnership may convert to an LLP or a business may begin its existence as an LLP. In most states, an existing limited partnership can convert to an LLP. In all states, LLPs are subject to state registration requirements and, in some states, mandatory insurance requirements.

Although the LLP is ideal for professional businesses, such as those practicing law or accounting, and was created with those professions in mind, in most states any other partnership or business may also form as an LLP so long as the business it conducts is lawful. A few jurisdictions, however, including California, Nevada, Oregon, and New York, limit LLPs solely to the practice of specified professions, such as law and accounting, and the LLP form is not available in those states to other businesses.

B. Governing Law

LLPs are partnerships and are thus governed nearly exclusively by partnership laws and principles, except as specifically modified by state legislation. In 1996, the RUPA (governing general partnerships and discussed in Chapter Three) was expressly amended to add a new Uniform Limited Liability Partnership Act. While many states and the District of Columbia have adopted the RUPA, many have modified its provisions as they relate to LLPs. Citation to each state's relevant statutes is provided in Appendix A.

Thus, LLPs are governed by state statutes and by the agreement of their members. In the absence of agreement, the state statutes (based upon the RUPA) control and serve as default statutes, identical to the way the RUPA serves as a default statute to provide terms and conditions relating to general partnerships when the parties fail to reach agreement on certain terms.

In sum, LLPs are recognized in all states and the District of Columbia, they are governed by state statutes (based largely upon the RUPA), the parties are free to modify many of the provisions of those statutes by their agreement, and, in the absence of agreement, the state statutes serve as default laws to fill in the gaps. Particular attention must therefore be paid to the state statutes, especially in cases in which the LLP is formed in one state and will do business in others that may have varying statutory schemes. Like limited partnerships, LLPs can only be formed by compliance with state statutes.

C. Advantages of LLPs

The greatest advantage of an LLP is the one already discussed: In all states, partners in an LLP will not suffer unlimited personal liability for the negligent acts and misconduct of their partners or other representatives of the partnership business. This protection will not exist, however, if any of the following occurs:

1. a partner supervised or directed the partner who committed the act of liability at the time the act was committed;
2. the partner was directly involved in the act giving rise to liability; or
3. the partner had knowledge or notice of the act of liability and failed to prevent or stop it (in many states).

Partners in LLPs always retain personal liability for their own negligence, misconduct, or wrongful acts.

1. Partial Shield States

In partial shield states, the protection against unlimited liability does not apply to all acts of one's partners but only to wrongful acts and omissions, such as negligence. Thus, in those states, a partner in an LLP remains liable for other debts and obligations incurred by a partner, such as money borrowed, contractual commitments, rent, insurance, and other such debts or obligations. Moreover, the partnership itself (as opposed to the individual assets of the LLP members) is fully liable for the negligent acts or omissions of any partner. Therefore, these partnerships, upon collecting assets, will generally distribute them to the partners, so as to avoid a "deep pocket" ready and waiting to be reached by a malpractice claim.

For example, assume a law firm has offices in Cleveland, Chicago, and Houston. The partnership is composed of 100 attorneys employed throughout these offices. Two partners in the Houston office begin working on a case. As a result of legal malpractice, they miss a statute of limitations deadline and their client therefore cannot bring an action. No one else in the Houston office is aware of the case and the partners in the other cities have never worked on the case, seen any files relating to this matter, or even heard of the client. Under general partnership law, the partnership itself and all partners in all the offices would have unlimited personal liability for this claim of malpractice. If the partnership is an LLP, however, only the partnership itself and the two attorneys who actually committed the act of malpractice would face liability. The individual assets of the other partners in Houston, Cleveland, and Chicago cannot be reached to satisfy the claim of malpractice. This feature of an LLP makes the partners in an LLP much like shareholders in a corporation who are protected from liability for the corporation's acts.

2. *Full Shield States*

In the roughly half of American jurisdictions that follow the full shield approach (which is also the approach of RUPA Section 306(c)), a partner in an LLP is not, solely by reason of being a partner, personally liable for any obligation of the LLP, whether arising in tort, contract, or otherwise, unless the partner knows of the act (and fails to stop it or prevent it), supervised it, or committed it. Even in full shield states, partners in LLPs retain liability for their own wrongful acts and omissions and those of others under their control or supervision.

Full shield statutes appear to be gaining in popularity, primarily due to concern in some states that the entire justification for LLP statutes could be eviscerated by clever plaintiffs who can merely construct their pleadings to file malpractice actions as breach of contract actions, rather than as actions sounding in tort, in order to hold all partners in an LLP liable for an act of malpractice. Only full shield statutes avoid such circumvention.

For example, assume that an accounting company operates as an LLP in New York (a full shield state). Dana, an accountant in the firm, will not be liable for acts of malpractice committed by her partners. Moreover, she will not be personally liable for the partnership's obligation to pay its rent, its bank loan, or its car leases. If, however, Dana is employed by the LLP's Indiana office (Indiana being a partial shield state), while Dana would not be liable for acts of malpractice committed by her partners, she would be personally liable (jointly and severally) for the partnership's rent, bank loan, and car lease obligations. In either jurisdiction, Dana would be personally liable for her own acts of malpractice, negligence, and misconduct (and for those of her partners under her supervision and control and,

FIGURE 5-1
Chart Identifying Full Shield and Partial Shield States

Full Shield States	*Partial Shield States*
Alabama	Alaska*
Arizona	Arkansas
California*	Florida*
Colorado	Hawaii*
Connecticut	Illinois
Delaware*	Iowa
District of Columbia	Kansas
Georgia	Kentucky
Idaho	Louisiana
Indiana	Maine
Maryland	Michigan
Massachusetts*	Mississippi
Minnesota	Nebraska
Missouri	Nevada
Montana	New Hampshire
New Mexico	New Jersey
New York	North Carolina
North Dakota	Ohio
Oregon	Oklahoma
South Dakota	Pennsylvania*
Vermont	Rhode Island*
Virginia	South Carolina*
Wisconsin	Tennessee
Wyoming	Texas*
	Utah
	Washington*
	West Virginia*

*State includes some form of insurance or financial responsibility requirement

in many states, those of which she knew and failed to stop or prevent). See Figure 5-1 for chart identifying full shield and partial shield states.

Other advantages of a general partnership, such as the sharing of management duties and responsibilities and the ability to raise capital by admitting new partners, exist in the LLP as well. Moreover, at least for many professionals who are accustomed to practicing in a partnership, the LLP is a comfortable and familiar structure. Additionally, if an existing general partnership converts to an LLP, few modifications need to be made to the partnership agreement in use, other than perhaps name changes necessary to comply with state statutes.

D. Disadvantages of LLPs

An LLP can be formed only by strict compliance with statute and, therefore, it may be expensive to form. An attorney will likely have to be engaged. Various forms must be filed with the secretary of state, accompanied by filing fees. Plainly, the formation of an LLP is more complex than that of a general partnership and more akin to the formation of a limited partnership.

Although the partners in an LLP are protected from liability for the wrongful acts and conduct of their partners, they continue to have unlimited personal liability for other acts of their partners in partial shield states. Thus, using our example above, if one of the partners in the Houston office signed a lease to rent new office space for the partnership, the partnership and all of the other partners in Houston, Cleveland, and Chicago would have unlimited liability for the obligations under that lease. Full shield statutes would protect all "innocent" partners, and only the partnership would be liable for the obligation. Thus, partial shield states are at a disadvantage over full shield states.

Another disadvantage of an LLP in some states is its lack of continuity. The term for existence of an LLP is one year in many states. At that time, additional forms or annual reports must be filed and fees paid to the secretary of state to renew the LLP.

Finally, because partners who direct or supervise other partners are liable for their acts of negligence or malpractice, LLPs may unwittingly discourage supervision of junior partners. If partners can avoid liability by "turning a blind eye" to junior partners and neglect necessary supervision, the public is not well served, although it is likely a court would nevertheless impose liability for failure to supervise properly. Some LLPs, recognizing that supervisory duties may lead to liability, provide additional compensation to supervisors or agree to indemnify them if they are found liable for a subordinate's misconduct.

E. Formation of LLPs

The formation of an LLP is somewhat similar to the formation of a limited partnership. States have application forms of varying extensiveness. In Delaware, for example, the Registered Limited Liability Certificate of Application need contain only the following six elements:

1. name of the limited liability partnership;
2. the addresses of its principal office in the state and the agent for service of process;
3. the number of partners the LLP will have;
4. a brief statement of the business in which the partnership engages;
5. an actual application statement reading as follows: "The partnership hereby applies for status as a registered limited liability partnership"; and
6. signature of an authorized partner.

See Figure 5-2 for the application form required in California. Filing fees are always imposed.

FIGURE 5-2
California Registration for Limited Liability Partnership

State of California
Bill Jones
Secretary of State

File #________________

This Space For Filing Use Only

REGISTERED LIMITED LIABILITY PARTNERSHIP REGISTRATION

A $70.00 filing fee must accompany this form.
IMPORTANT – Read instructions before completing this form.

1. Name of the registered limited liability partnership or foreign limited liability partnership:
(End the name with the word "Registered Limited Liability Partnership" or "Limited Liability Partnership" or one of the abbreviations "L.L.P.", "LLP", "R.L.L.P.", or "RLLP.")

2. ☐ Domestic (California) **OR** ☐ Foreign (Not in California) | 3. Jurisdiction

4. Address of the principal office: City State Zip Code

5. Name the Agent for Service of Process in this state and check the appropriate provision below:
_______________________________________ which is
[ ] an individual residing in California. Proceed to item 6.
[ ] a corporation which has filed a certificate pursuant to California Corporations Code Section 1505. Proceed to item 7.

6. If an individual, California address of the agent for service of process:
Address
City State **CA** Zip Code

7. Indicate the business in which the limited liability partnership shall engage: (check one)
☐ Practice of Architecture ☐ Practice of Public Accountancy
☐ Practice of Law ☐ Related:______________________

8. By filing this Registered Limited Liability Partnership (LLP-1) with the Secretary of State, the partnership named above is registering as a domestic registered limited liability partnership or foreign limited liability partnership. **(DO NOT ALTER)**

9. Indicate whether the limited liability partnership is complying with the alternative security provisions:
☐ Yes. Attach Alternative Security Provision (LLP-3) ☐ No

10. Future Effective Date Month Day Year

11. Other matters to be included in this registration may be set forth on separate attached pages and are made a part of this registration.

12. Total number of pages attached, if any:

13. **Declaration:** I declare that I am the person who executed this instrument, which execution is my act and deed.

_______________________________ Signature of Authorized Partner/Person

_______________________________ Type or Print Name of Authorized Partner/Person Date

14. RETURN TO:
NAME
FIRM
ADDRESS
CITY/STATE
ZIP CODE

SEC/STATE (REV. 1/99) FORM LLP-1 – FILING FEE $70
Approved by Secretary of State

Just as a new business can form as an LLP, an existing general partnership can convert into an LLP. In many instances, law, accounting, and medical practices that have existed as general partnerships are converting to the LLP form.

The name of the LLP must contain the words "Registered Limited Liability Partnership," "Limited Liability Partnership," the abbreviation "L.L.P.," or "R.L.L.P.," or the designation "LLP" or "RLLP" as the last words or letters of its name. The purpose of this requirement is to afford notice to those dealing with the entity that, at a minimum, the partners are shielded from liability for the wrongful acts and omissions of their partners. All letterhead, envelopes, business cards, signs, directory listings, brochures, and advertisements must also carry this designation to afford such notice to third parties. Many states require amendment of the application to reflect changes in the LLP.

The LLP should have a written partnership agreement. Because an LLP is a partnership, an agreement used for general partnerships can easily be modified for use in an LLP. (See Appendix D for form of general partnership agreement.)

An LLP formed in one state can operate as an LLP in another. Therefore, a law firm can operate as an LLP in Dover, Delaware; New Orleans, Louisiana; and Washington, D.C. The procedure for operating in another state is much the same as that for a limited partnership: An application must be completed and filed with the new state asking it to recognize the partnership as a foreign limited liability partnership. A certificate of good standing from the jurisdiction in which the partnership was originally formed will also generally be required so that the new state has some assurance that the organization is law-abiding. Filing fees will be required. See Figure 5-3 for the form used in North Carolina for registration of a foreign limited liability partnership.

Before filing the application in the foreign jurisdiction, carefully review that state's statutes to ensure the LLP is in fact required to qualify in the foreign state. Many states have statutes providing guidance as to what activities constitute "doing business," such as to require businesses formed in other states to qualify to do business therein, and it is possible that the LLP's activities do not constitute "doing business" within the meaning of the statute so as to necessitate a filing. For example, merely owning property, maintaining a bank account, or engaging in an isolated transaction in a state are generally not considered "doing business" such as would require a business to register with a state before it commences those activities. (See Chapter Fifteen for a further discussion on "doing business" in other states.)

One question that has arisen is whether the limitations imposed on liability in one jurisdiction will be followed by another jurisdiction in which the LLP does business. For example, if an LLP is formed in a full shield state and begins doing business in a partial shield state in which there is a breach of contract, are all partners jointly and severally liable as they would be in the partial shield state, or is there no liability imposed on the partners for the breach of contract, as would be the case in the home state that is a full shield state? Unfortunately, the answer to this question is not clear. Various state statutes and the cases interpreting them may provide guidance. At a minimum, LLPs should be scrupulous in inserting "choice of law" provisions in their contracts, providing that the law of a certain jurisdiction (namely, a full shield jurisdiction in which the LLP is organized or doing business) applies in any action relating to the contract, thus affording a cred-

FIGURE 5-3
North Carolina Foreign LLP Registration Application

State of North Carolina
Department of the Secretary of State

APPLICATION FOR REGISTRATION
Foreign Registered Limited Liability Partnership

Pursuant to §59-90 of the General Statutes of North Carolina, the undersigned hereby submits this application for registration as a Foreign Registered Limited Liability Partnership.

1. The name of the foreign limited liability partnership is: ______________________________
(The name must contain the words "Registered Limited Liability Partnership," "Limited Liability Partnership, or the abbreviation "L.L.P.," "R.L.L.P.," "LLP," or "RLLP" as the last words or letters of its name.)

2. The street address of the partnership's principal office is:

   Number and Street ______________________________

   City, State, Zip Code ______________________ County______________

3. The name of the initial registered agent is: ______________________________

4. The street address and county of the initial registered office of partnership is:

   Number and Street ______________________________

   City, State, Zip Code______________________ County______________

5. The mailing address *if different from the street address* of the initial registered office is:

   ____

6. Briefly describe the business in which the partnership is engaged:

   ____

7. Attached is a Certificate of Existence (or document of similar import) duly authenticated by the secretary of state or other official having custody of limited liability partnership records in the state or country of registration. **The Certificate of Existence must be less than six months old.**

8. The fiscal year end of the partnership______________________________

9. This registration will be effective upon filing, unless a date and/or time is specified: ______________

This the ______day of ______________, __________.

____

____
Signature

____
Type or Print Name and Title

NOTES:
Filing fee is $125. This document and one exact or conformed copy of the application must be filed with the Secretary of State.

CORPORATIONS DIVISION P.O.BOX 29622 RALEIGH, NC 27626-06222
(January 2000) *Form LLP-02*

ible argument that the full shield law governs so as to bar joint and several personal liability for contractual obligations no matter where the breach of contract occurred or the parties reside.

Just as with any business, the LLP may be subject to other requirements such as licensing laws, local tax requirements, and so forth.

F. Operation of LLPs

The operation of an LLP is nearly identical to that of a general partnership. The fiduciary duties owed by partners to each other apply. Each partner is an agent of the partnership for business purposes and can bind the partnership by entering into contracts, hiring employees, purchasing office furniture, and so forth. The partners co-manage the business. They will likely have a written partnership agreement highly similar to that of a general partnership. It will include the formula for profits and losses, indicate each partner's contribution to the partnership, set out provisions relating to the admission and withdrawal of partners, and specify the conditions which will cause dissolution of the partnership. (See Appendix D for an example of a written general partnership agreement.)

Similar to the RUPA on which they are based, state LLP statutes generally operate as default statutes in that they govern the LLP in the absence of the partners' agreement. The following features are also identical to general partnerships: the LLP agreement may be oral or in writing; LLP partners owe fiduciary duties to each other; in the absence of agreement to the contrary, profits, losses, management, and control will be shared equally regardless of capital contributions; and partners may dissociate without necessarily causing a dissolution and winding up. Finally, in most states, statements of authority and statements of denial (discussed in Chapter Three) may be filed to provide public notice regarding an LLP partner's authority to act or limitations on that authority.

Probably the most significant difference between the operation of a general partnership and that of the LLP is the requirement imposed on LLPs in several states to maintain liability insurance. This insurance is designed to protect injured parties who previously would have been able to sue numerous partners for acts of negligence or malpractice. Under LLP law, only malfeasing partners have unlimited liability for their wrongful acts, so an injured client or patient is limited to the partnership's assets (which may be depleted by distributions to partners) and to the assets of the individual partner or partners who performed the wrongful act. Because these claimants are denied a host of other defendants who may have immense resources, the LLP is often required to carry a certain amount of insurance. Some states that require insurance alternatively permit the LLP to set aside funds to satisfy any judgments against the partnership or its partners.

For example, while the California statute is relatively complex, in general, California requires a general liability policy in the amount of at least $100,000, multiplied by the number of licensed persons rendering professional services for the LLP, subject to certain minimum and maximum requirements. Alternatively, in California, LLPs can maintain at least $100,000 (again, multiplied by the number of licensed professionals) in a segregated account such as a bank escrow account. Because professionals practicing in states requiring insurance may be concerned that the partnership might not acquire sufficient insurance, individual partners often purchase their own insurance policies for additional protection. Because of the difficulties of predicting what kind of insurance and how much insurance should be carried for businesses of vastly different sizes and risks, most states do not impose insurance or financial responsibility requirements. See Figure 5-1 for identification of states requiring insurance.

If an LLP does not carry and maintain the requisite insurance, it cannot be recognized as an LLP in those states conditioning existence and maintenance of the LLP upon insurance. It will therefore be viewed as a general partnership, in which case all partners have unlimited liability for their partners' wrongful acts and misconduct.

Because LLP partners are shielded from some debts, generally they cannot receive distributions unless there are sufficient assets to pay creditors. In sum, the use of insurance and rules prohibiting distributions unless the LLP is solvent serve to protect creditors who can no longer sue numerous LLP partners for certain debts and obligations.

G. Transferability of Interest and Admission of New Members

Because the LLP is voluntary, just as is a general partnership, the principles relating to transferability of partnership interests in a general partnership apply to LLPs as well. Thus, a partner in an LLP may assign her profits to another but cannot substitute another in her place because this would violate the voluntary nature of a partnership.

In most cases, the written partnership agreement will provide that the withdrawal of one partner will not cause a dissolution. Provisions should be made for voluntary withdrawal by partners and return of their contributions and any profit.

New partners are admitted upon the consent of all existing partners or upon less than unanimous consent if so provided by the partnership agreement.

H. Dissolution and Liquidation of LLPs

Dissolution of LLPs is similar to that of general partnerships. LLPs, however, must generally renew their applications or certificates filed with the state on an annual basis. Failure to renew the application or certificate will result in the would-be LLP being viewed as a general partnership, one subject to that state's version of the RUPA.

The partnership agreement will likely provide the events that will cause a dissolution of the LLP. If terms are not provided, the RUPA provides the terms and conditions for dissociation and dissolution. Recall from Chapter Three that not every dissociation of a partner triggers a dissolution and a winding up. If no dissolution is caused, the LLP will buy out the dissociating partner's interest.

Before the LLP dissolves, it must liquidate or wind up by collecting any debts due it, satisfying all obligations, liquidating assets, and distributing the proceeds to third-party creditors and then to the partners. A certificate of withdrawal should be filed.

I. Taxation of LLPs

Only one critical feature of an LLP is different from that of a general partnership: Partners do not have unlimited liability for the negligence or misconduct of their partners and, in full shield states, have no personal liability for contractual or other obligations of the partnership. In nearly all other respects, LLPs are similar to general partnerships, and thus LLPs are treated as general partnerships for purposes of taxation. The tax forms used by general partnerships and general partners (shown in Chapter Three) are also used for LLPs and their partners. Thus, the income earned is passed through to the individual partners who pay at whatever rate is appropriate to them. The LLP itself does not pay tax but it must file the information tax form required of all partnerships. Like general and limited partnerships, an LLP may elect to be taxed as a corporation by "checking the box" on the appropriate tax form (see Figure 3-8).

J. Limited Liability Limited Partnerships

Limited liability limited partnership
A limited partnership in which the general partners have limited liability for partnership debts and obligations

A few states provide for limited partnerships to file certain statements with the secretary of state to be classified as **limited liability limited partnerships** (LLLP). The usual procedure is that the limited partnership files a statement of qualification with the secretary of state, the effect of which is that the general partners then have limited liability for partnership debts and obligations (just as they would if the entity was organized as an LLP in that state). In this limited partnership, the general partners continue to manage the business but have limited liability. The qualification must generally be approved by all general partners and a majority of limited partners. The name of the limited partnership then must include not only the required designation for a limited partnership, such as "LP," but another signal indicating it has qualified as an LLLP. Thus, the entity's name may be as complex as "Colonial Park Associates, L.P., L.L.L.P." See Del. Code Ann. tit. 6, Section 17-214; and Tex. Rev. Civ. Stat. Ann. Section 6132a-1.

Because limited partnerships can convert to LLPs, which provide limited liability to their partners, the advantage of a limited partnership qualifying as an LLLP is somewhat academic; thus, few states recognize this form of limited partnership.

Key Features of Limited Liability Partnerships

- Partners in LLPs have no liability in any state for wrongful acts of their co-partners.
- In approximately one-half of the states, LLP partners have no liability either for wrongful acts of their co-partners or for contractual obligations.
- Partners in LLPs retain liability for their own wrongful acts and those they direct or supervise.
- LLPs can be formed only by complying with state statutes that require the filing of an application with the appropriate state agency.
- The LLP agreement may be oral or written; in the absence of agreement, profits, losses, management, and control are shared equally regardless of capital contributions.
- Some states require the LLP to carry insurance or meet financial responsibility standards.
- Not every dissociation causes a termination and winding up; in many instances a dissociating member's interest will be purchased.
- LLPs have the pass-through taxation of general partnerships.

K. Role of Paralegal

The paralegal should check state statutes to determine any particular requirements as to naming an LLP and any designation it must include to notify third parties that the entity is an LLP. The paralegal should contact the secretary of state and request the appropriate forms for application to conduct business as an LLP. The paralegal should also request a federal employer identification number (see Figure 2-3). Research should be conducted to determine whether the state affords full shield or partial shield protection and whether any insurance requirements exist in the state.

Paralegals will also have a role in drafting the partnership agreement. An agreement for an LLP is nearly identical to that for a general partnership, except for a recitation that partners will not have liability for acts of misconduct of their partners and, in full shield states, that they will have no liability for any obligation of the partnership (unless they supervised, directed, participated in, or knew of the acts), a requirement that the application be properly filed and maintained, and that the requisite insurance be obtained. A standard form of general partnership agreement is shown in Appendix D. It can be modified for use by an LLP.

The paralegal should carefully monitor the term of the LLP and ensure that the LLP is renewed at the appropriate time or that annual reports are timely filed.

Docketing this date is critical. Many law firms have sophisticated computer programs for docketing dates. Calendar docketing or docketing by index cards known as *tickler* reminder cards is also sufficient. The law firm can then notify its clients of the renewal or reporting requirements a few months before the expiration date of the LLP.

Paralegals can also review the letterhead, business cards, advertisements, brochures, and other items used by the LLP to ensure that the appropriate name designation is provided.

Resource Guide

The various resources provided in the Chapter Three Resource Guide also apply to LLPs. The most important resource, of course, is the state statute recognizing the LLP and providing the conditions for its formation, operation, and governance. The LLP is such a new entity that there are few cases interpreting it. Thus, researchers must rely almost exclusively on state statutes, any administrative code provisions in the state implementing the LLP, and, if necessary, the legislative history for the statute (namely, the various versions of the LLP bill, any transcripts of committee hearings held when the legislature considered adopting the LLP in that state, and any comments made in debates regarding the LLP legislation).

Many form books have not developed specialized forms for agreements for LLPs. Thus, drafting the agreement for an LLP will require careful tailoring of a general partnership agreement to comply with the state LLP statute.

Because LLPs are becoming more and more popular for the obvious reason of protecting partners from their partners' acts of negligence, several periodical articles have been written about them. Check the *Index to Legal Periodicals* or *Current Law Index* and look up "partnerships, limited liability," "registered limited liability partnerships," "liability," or "limited" and you will be referred to articles written about LLPs.

◆ ◆ ◆

WEB RESOURCES

A number of sites provide general information about LLPs with clear and concise discussions of LLPs, comparing and contrasting them to other forms of business entities. Many of the sites listed below provide forms for partnership agreements. Only a few provide forms specifically for limited liability partnership agreements, since many professionals use a general partnership agreement as a starting point and then modify it to use for limited liability partnerships. As with all forms, exercise caution in using the form, as it will likely not be suitable for all LLPs. As with any form, you should modify it to suit your needs. Because most of the partnership agreements provided on the Internet are for general partnerships rather than for LLPs, you will need to revise many agreements. Review the Web site Disclaimer or Legal Terms sections to determine if there are any prohibitions on use or reproduction of the forms. In any event, the forms serve as useful starting places.

Of most importance is review of a state's statutes regarding limited liability partnerships. To review state statutes online, access <www.ll.georgetown.edu>, the Web site of Georgetown University Law Center. Select "State, Local & Territorial," and you will then be presented with a map of the United States. Point your cursor to the desired state, and you will then be able to select whether you wish to view that state's constitution, statutes, cases, or other legal information. By selecting "Statutes" or "Code," you will be able to search the state's statutes and find relevant statutory material. In some instances, you can search by statute number; in other instances, you can search by keyword. Some states allow you to browse various titles. Search for "Corporations" and then view the limited liability partnership statutes usually included either within or near this title.

Other useful Web sites include the following:

http://www.nass.org

This Web site of the National Association of Secretaries of State allows you to link directly to the home page for each state's secretary of state. Many states offer guides to forming LLPs with basic information, forms, checklists, and phone numbers. Point the cursor to "States" and then to your state's name and flag, and proceed to locate information on forming a limited liability partnership in your state. Forms for limited liability partnership certificates, certificates for correction, and certificates for cancellation of limited liability partnerships are offered on most state Web sites.

www.irs.gov

The Web site of the Internal Revenue Service offers a wealth of information about taxes, businesses, and provides Form 1065 and Schedule K, the tax forms used for LLPs, which can be downloaded and printed.

www.ask.com

"Ask Jeeves" is an Internet "butler" who will help you find what you need. Simply type in your question, in natural English, in the box presented, and you will be referred to numerous useful sites. For example, type in "Where can I find information about limited liability partnerships?" You will then be directed to sites offering information on limited liability partnerships and forms of agreements. "Ask.com" is often the first site many individuals access to find information on nearly any topic. Bookmark this site, and use it often.

www.tannedfeet.com

Billed as "The Entrepreneurs' Help Page," this site provides a wealth of information regarding the formation and operation of businesses, including limited liability partnerships.

www.about.com
"About.com" offers a wide variety of information relating to many topics. After you access the site, point your cursor to "Business/Careers" and then to "Small Business Information" for information on starting businesses, tax strategies, and information about types of entities, including limited liability partnerships.

www.ilrg.com
The Internet Legal Research Guide is a great source of information and provides a form for a partnership agreement in its "Legal Forms Archive."

www.law.com
"Law.Com" is a well-known site used by legal professionals. After viewing the home page, go to "Business" and then to "Resources for Business." Scroll down the page for access to business forms, including a form of partnership agreement.

www.lectlaw.com
The 'Lectric Law Library provides a vast array of information on legal topics. Access "the Rotunda" and then "Forms Room" to locate a form of partnership agreement.

www.lawsmart.com
Access the home page and enter "partnership" as a key term. You will be referred to a form of partnership agreement.

www.LegalWiz.com
This legal resource for entrepreneurs offers articles, general information about businesses, a glossary of business and legal terms, and a form of partnership agreement. Access "Legal Forms," and you will be provided with a partnership agreement form.

http://www.siccode.com/forms.php3
This Web site, entitled "SICCode.com" provides numerous business and legal forms. When you access the site, point your cursor to "free legal forms." You will be provided with hundreds of forms, including a form for a partnership agreement, which you are invited to cut and paste into your word processor.

www.findlaw.com/16forms/index.htm
The forms section of "FindLaw.com," a well-known legal Web site, offers numerous links to forms collections and forms indexes.

Discussion Questions

Fact Scenario. Peterson & Peterson, LLP is an accounting firm operating in more than 40 states. The LLP has a written agreement, but it is silent on the division of profits and losses.

1. Assume a partner in the LLP commits an act of accounting malpractice. Describe the liability of the other partners in the LLP and the partnership.
2. Assume that the partner who committed the act of malpractice was in the International Tax Group. What is the possible liability of the manager of Peterson & Peterson's International Tax Group?
3. Peterson & Peterson owes $500,000 to its primary lender. What is the potential liability of the partners throughout the 40 states in which business is conducted?
4. Assume that the partnership is engaged in business in a jurisdiction that limits LLPs to a one-year term, and the partnership failed to renew its LLP application. What is the effect of such failure?
5. How will profits of $1,000,000 be allocated in the LLP?
6. Peterson & Peterson has decided to open a bank account in Tennessee, one of the states in which it is not conducting business. Discuss any potential requirements that might be imposed on the LLP before opening the bank account.

6

Limited Liability Companies

CHAPTER OVERVIEW

Like registered limited liability partnerships, limited liability companies are a new form of business organization recognized in all states and the District of Columbia. Limited liability companies continue the trend seen in registered limited liability partnerships of combining the most attractive features of partnerships and corporations in a new enterprise.

Chapter Eight will discuss the characteristics of corporations. In brief, however, two features are notable at this juncture. First, shareholders in a corporation are shielded from liability arising out of the corporation's wrongful acts. Their stock may fall in value to nothing, but assuming no fraud or injustice, they will not be liable to any of the corporate creditors. Second, corporations are often said to be subject to *double taxation*, meaning that income earned by the corporation is taxed at corporate rates and then when this same money is distributed to shareholders as dividends, the shareholders also pay taxes at their individual tax rates on the money or distributions they receive. Thus, the same money is taxed twice.

The limited liability company provides its first benefit from corporation law: Its members are protected from liability for the company's acts and the acts of other members whether arising in tort or in contract. Its second benefit comes from partnership law: All money earned by the company is passed through directly to the members who pay tax on the money at their individual rates. The company itself does not pay tax on earnings, thus avoiding the burden of double taxation.

A. Characteristics of Limited Liability Companies

Limited liability company
Entity providing full protection for its members from all personal liability, whether arising in tort or contract; must comply with statutes

The **limited liability company** (LLC) was first recognized in 1977 by Wyoming. On occasion, the LLC is referred to as a statutory partnership association, partnership association, or limited partnership association. Limited liability company, however, is the most frequently used name for this new form of business organization. After Wyoming drafted its LLC statute from a combination of general partnership laws, limited partnership laws, and corporation laws, few states followed. In 1988, however, the Internal Revenue Service issued a ruling indicating that LLCs would be taxed as partnerships, and, by 1996, all 50 states and the District of Columbia had enacted legislation recognizing LLCs.

Like the limited partnership and the registered limited liability partnership (RLLP or LLP), the LLC is a creature of statute and can be formed only by compliance with state statutes. Its formation is similar to the formation of a corporation and it will be governed by an agreement, commonly known as the *operating agreement.* Unlike corporations, however, the LLC does not always have perpetual existence. In some states, LLCs exist for a thirty-year period. The fact that they do not have perpetual existence enables them to avoid the double taxation to which corporations are subject.

Members
Participants in a limited liability company

The LLC can be managed by its participants, called **members.** These members may be either individuals or entities, such as corporations. Some larger LLCs will appoint a management committee to manage the organization. LLC members may withdraw at will, generally upon giving some period of notice. They may transfer their financial interest in the LLC but cannot transfer their management or voting rights. The LLC will dissolve upon the death, withdrawal, or bankruptcy of any member, although the remaining members may continue to operate the business if they unanimously agree. LLC members can bring either direct or derivative actions, just as can limited partners in a limited partnership.

In most states, professionals such as lawyers, doctors, and accountants can adopt the LLC form, although the professionals retain liability for their own wrongful acts and those performed under their supervision or control. The professionals, however, are protected from personal liability for the wrongful acts of their colleagues and from all contractual obligations.

The most significant features of an LLC are that it protects its members from personal liability (while allowing them to participate fully in the management of the enterprise), and it provides pass-through taxation.

An LLC may transact business in another state. Generally, the LLC must file an application to transact business in the new state and must submit a certificate of its good standing from the state of formation. See Figure 6-1 for a sample application to transact business in another state. Transacting business in a state without proper authority may preclude the entity from bringing or defending an action in that jurisdiction until the defect is cured.

Unlike LLPs, which are a species of partnership, the LLC is an entirely new form of business structure. Because both LLPs and LLCs offer protection from personal liability and the pass-through tax status of a partnership, the two forms are highly similar. Generally, the key distinctions between the two business entities are as follows:

- LLCs can be managed by appointed managers (who need not be members of the LLC), while LLPs are generally co-managed by all of their partners.

FIGURE 6-1
Illinois Application for Admission to Transact Business

Form **LLC-45.5**
January 1999

Jesse White
Secretary of State
Department of Business Services
Limited Liability Company Division
Room 359, Howlett Building
Springfield, IL 62756
http://www.sos.state.il.us

Payment must be made by certified check, cashier's check, Illinois attorney's C.P.A.'s check or money order, payable to "Secretary of State."

Illinois
Limited Liability Company Act
Application for Admission to Transact Business

Submit in Duplicate
Must be typewritten

This space for use by Secretary of State
Date
Assigned File #
Filing Fee $400
Penalty $
Approved: $

This space for use by Secretary of State

1. Limited Liability Company name: ______________________
(Must comply with Section 1-10 of ILLCA or article 2 below applies.)

2. The assumed name, other than the true company name, under which the LLC proposes to transact business in Illinois is: ______________________
(If applicable, a form LLC-1.20, Application to Adopt an Assumed Name, is required to be completed and attached to this application.)

3. Federal Employer Identification Number (F.E.I.N.):______________________

4. Jurisdiction of Organization:______________________

5. Date of Organization:______________________

6. Period of Duration:______________________
(See #14 on back)

7. The address, including county, of the office required to be maintained in the jurisdiction of its organization, or if not required, of the principal place of business (Post office box alone and c/o are unacceptable):

____
(Number) (Street) (Suite)

____
(City/State) (ZIP Code) (County)

8. Registered agent:______________________
(First Name) (Middle Name) (Last Name)

Registered Office:______________________
(Number) (Street) (Suite #)

(P.O. Box or c/o are unacceptable) ______________ Illinois ______________
(City) (County) (ZIP Code)

9. The date on which this foreign LLC first did business in Illinois: ______________________

FIGURE 6-1 *Continued*
Illinois Application for Admission to Transact Business

LLC-45.5

10. The purpose or purposes for which the company is organized and proposes to conduct in this State: Include the business code # (IRS Form 1065).

11. The limited liability company is managed by:
    - ☐ manager(s)
    - ☐ vested in member(s)

12. The Illinois Secretary of State is hereby appointed the agent of the limited liability company for service of process under the circumstances set forth in a subsection (b) of Section 1-50 of the ILLCA.

13. **This application is accompanied by a certificate of good standing or existence, as well as a copy of the articles of organization, as amended, duly authenticated within the last thirty (30) days, by the officer of the state or country wherein the LLC is formed.**

14. **If the period of duration is a date certain and is not stated in the Articles of Organization from the domestic state, a copy of that page from the Operating Agreement stating the date must also be submitted.**

15. The undersigned affirms, under penalties of perjury, having authority to sign hereto, that this application for admission to transact business is to the best of my knowledge and belief, true, correct and complete.

Dated ______________________ , __________ .
(Month/Day) *(Year)*

____
(Signature)
(Signature must comply with Section 5-45 of ILLCA)

____
(Type or print name and title)

____
**(If applicant is a company or other entity, state name of company and indicate whether it is a member or manager of the LLC.)*

*Please refer to Sections 178.20(d) and (e) of the Administrative Rules

LLC-17.4

- LLC statutes nearly always require a written operating agreement, while the partnership agreement for an LLP may be oral or written.
- Only full shield states offer full protection from liability for LLP partners for both wrongful acts of co-partners and contractual obligations, while a hallmark of LLC statutes is full protection from personal liability for all LLC members whether the liability arises in tort or contract.
- If the parties' agreement fails to address the sharing of profits and losses, in an LLP profits and losses will be shared equally regardless of contributions (i.e., the partnership model), while, in an LLC, profits and losses are usually allocated in the same ratio as the members' unreturned contributions (i.e., the corporate model), although the Uniform Limited Liability Company Act provides for equal distributions.
- Some states allow a one-person LLC, making it attractive for sole proprietors to convert to LLCs and thereby achieve protection from personal liability; LLPs, however, because they are a form of partnership, must always have at least two partners.
- Under the Uniform Limited Liability Company Act, not-for-profit businesses may operate as LLCs, while the LLP, as a form of partnership, must be operated with the expectation of making a profit.

Because the LLC is a creative blending of the best features of partnerships and corporations, LLCs have become an increasingly popular vehicle for doing business in the United States. The Illinois Secretary of State recently noted that the LLC "offers the business community . . . the most modern option available in terms of business structure and function." In fact, due to the tremendous popularity and flexibility of LLCs, and the fact that they offer full protection from liability for their members (who may nevertheless manage the business) as well as offering single pass-through taxation, many experts predict that S corporations and limited partnerships may become relics of the past and that even general partnerships will be used only for the smallest and least formal businesses that do not wish to incur the costs associated with organizing and maintaining an LLC or corporation.

B. Governing Law

All 50 states and the District of Columbia have enacted statutes recognizing LLCs. All states provide not only protection from personal liability but also authorize partnership tax status. Because most states so recently passed their LLC laws, little case law exists interpreting the LLC statutes, and the states have differed vastly in their approaches to LLCs. Nevertheless, there has been tremendous acceptance of the LLC form. For example, up until 1990, only two states recognized LLCs, but it is now rare when a large law firm or accounting firm does not operate as an LLC (or LLP).

Due to the variations among state laws governing LLCs, in 1991 the National Conference of Commissioners on Uniform Legislation recommended that a uniform act be drafted for LLCs. The **Uniform Limited Liability Company Act (ULLCA)** was adopted in 1994 after extensive study of each state's LLC statutes. The ULLCA borrows heavily both from partnership and corporate laws, reflecting the nature of the LLC as a hybrid entity that combines the best features

ULLCA
Uniform Limited Liability Company Act, a uniform act to guide operation and management of LLCs

of partnerships with the best features of corporations. Selected provisions of the ULLCA are available at the law library.

As of this writing, only Alabama, Hawaii, South Carolina, South Dakota, Vermont, and West Virginia have adopted the ULLCA, although even these states have modified some of the "uniform" provisions. Citation to their statutes can be found in the ULLCA provisions available at the law library. The ULLCA is meant to be a "default statute," meaning that LLC members are free to vary its terms to a great extent, and only when they have failed to provide for certain items will the ULLCA provisions control.

In sum, LLCs are governed by state statutes, which vary widely from state to state. Experts predict that states will continue to adopt the ULLCA. Paralegals are free to create flexible operating agreements for an LLC inasmuch as the ULLCA operates as a default statute whose provisions generally control only when the parties fail to agree otherwise.

C. Advantages of LLCs

1. *Pass-Through Tax Status*

An LLC has sufficient characteristics of a partnership so that it is taxed as a partnership. All of the income earned by the LLC, whether distributed or not, is immediately passed through to the members, who then declare their respective portion of the profits on their individual tax returns and pay tax at the appropriate rate. This pass-through tax status offers advantages over a corporation, whose income is taxed twice: once when earned by the corporation and again when received by the corporate owners, the shareholders, as dividends. The imposition of two taxes often results in total taxes that are greater than the taxes that would be required if only one tax were imposed, as is the case with partnerships. Thus, the treatment of an LLC as a partnership for taxation purposes can be a significant advantage.

While one type of corporation, the S corporation, offers pass-through tax status (see Chapter Seventeen), it is subject to a number of restrictions. For example, the number of shareholders in an S corporation is limited to 75 individuals. An LLC has no such restrictions and can be composed of hundreds of members. Stock in an S corporation can typically be owned only by individuals, estates or certain trusts — not partnerships or other corporations — and cannot be owned by a nonresident alien. Thus, the S corporation is a poor vehicle for attracting foreign capital. In sum, the first advantage offered by an LLC is the pass-through tax status or single taxation enjoyed by partnerships.

2. *Limited Liability and Full Management*

The LLC offers limited liability to its members. While limited partners have limited liability, that limited liability hinges upon their passivity with regard to management of the business enterprise. In the event limited partners are viewed as managing and controlling the limited partnership business, they lose their limited liability status. In an LLC, by contrast, the members can be active in management *and* retain their limited liability, offering tremendous advantages for investors who wish to be active in the management of their money and yet not expose their other assets to liability. The liability of a member of an LLC is limited to the investment contributed by the member.

Although the LLP also shields its partners from liability, in about one-half of American jurisdictions, the protection from liability only relates to claims for a copartner's wrongful acts, leaving LLP partners with personal liability for contractual obligations. By contrast, the LLC affords full protection for its members from all personal liability, whether arising in tort or contract, in all states.

3. International Recognition

The LLC is similar to many investment vehicles recognized in other countries, primarily Germany, France, Switzerland, and several South American and Central American nations. Due to our increasingly global economy, the LLC is an attractive business organization for foreign investors who may already be familiar with the basic principles of LLCs. Latin American countries recognize a business similar to an LLC and referred to as a *limitada*. Similarly, the *GmbH* business entity recognized in Germany is analogous to American LLCs. On the other hand, an S corporation is limited to 75 individuals who cannot be nonresident aliens. It is thus not an appropriate vehicle for a business desiring to attract foreign investors.

D. Disadvantages of LLCs

Although there are some disadvantages of doing business as an LLC, the advantages far outweigh any disadvantages. The primary disadvantages of LLCs are as follows:

- While a member of an LLC may transfer his or her financial interest in the LLC to another, the transferee will not become a member of the LLC unless the operating agreement so provides or all other LLC members consent. This limitation may serve to hamper growth within an LLC.
- Since the LLC is such a relatively new form of business, little, if any, case law interpreting LLCs exists. In the event of disputes, therefore, little guidance can be gained from judicial interpretations of LLC laws.
- Because the LLC can only be formed by compliance with state statutes, an attorney must likely be engaged to draft the appropriate forms and documents. Additionally, filing these forms with the secretary of state will necessitate certain fees. Thus, the formation of an LLC can be slightly complex and expensive.
- Finally, to ensure the LLC would have the pass-through tax status of a partnership, a few states limit the LLC to a term, generally 30 years. Thus, in those states, the LLC may not be an appropriate form for a business contemplating activity in perpetuity. Due to the new IRS "check the box" provisions clarifying that LLCs will be treated as partnerships for tax

purposes unless they affirmatively elect to be taxed as corporations, many experts predict that state statutes will now begin eliminating any term limit for LLCs and allow them to exist perpetually.

E. Formation of LLCs

The formation of an LLC closely parallels the formation of a corporation. The document that creates the LLC, called the articles of organization, must be filed with the appropriate state authorities. Additionally, the LLC must be governed by an agreement, usually called the operating agreement.

1. *Articles of Organization*

Articles of organization
Document filed with the state that creates an LLC

An LLC is created by the filing of a document called the **articles of organization** with the appropriate state agency, usually the secretary of state. Each state recognizing the LLC has particular statutory requirements for the contents of the articles of organization. According to ULLCA Section 203(a), the articles of organization must include the following:

a. the name of the company (including any required abbreviations or signals);
b. the address of the initial designated office;
c. the name and street address of the initial agent who will receive service of process;
d. the name and address of each organizer;
e. whether the company is to be a term company, and, if so, the term specified;
f. whether the company is to be manager-managed, and, if so, the name and address of each initial manager; and
g. whether one or more of the members of the LLC have consented in writing to be liable for all or specified debts or obligations of the LLC.

The articles of organization may set forth any provisions that are permitted to be set forth in the operating agreement or any other matters not inconsistent with law. The articles must be signed by a manager of the LLC if it is to be manager-managed, a member of the LLC if it is to be a member-managed LLC, or a person organizing the LLC. The articles of organization can be amended at any time upon filing an appropriate document with the public official and paying the specified filing fee. See Figure 6-2 for form of Articles of Organization for Colorado LLCs.

In many states, after review of the articles of organization and acceptance of the required fee, the secretary of state will issue a certificate of organization for the LLC recognizing the existence of the business. Failure to comply substantially with statutory formalities may lead to LLC members being viewed as general partners with resulting personal liability. Most LLC statutes allow existing general and limited partnerships to convert to the LLC form to achieve protection from

FIGURE 6-2
Colorado LLC Articles of Organization

Mail to: Secretary of State
Corporations Section
1560 Broadway, Suite 200
Denver, CO 80202
(303) 894-2251
Fax (303) 894-2242

For office use only

MUST BE TYPED
FILING FEE: $50.00
MUST SUBMIT TWO COPIES

Please include a typed self-addressed envelope

ARTICLES OF ORGANIZATION

I/We the undersigned natural person(s) of the age of eighteen years or more, acting as organizer(s) of a limited liability company under the Colorado Limited Liability Company Act, adopt the following Articles of Organization for such limited liability company:

FIRST: *The name of the limited liability company is:* ______________________

SECOND: *Principal place of business (if known):* ______________________

____

THIRD: *The street address of the initial registered office of the limited liability company is:* ______________________

____

The mailing address (if different from above) of the initial registered office of the limited liability company is:

____

The name of its proposed registered agent in Colorado at that address is: ______________________

____

FOURTH: ____ *The management is vested in managers (check if appropriate)*

FIFTH: *The names and business addresses of the initial manager or managers or if the management is vested in the members, rather than managers, the names and addresses of the member or members are:*

NAME	*ADDRESS (include zip codes)*
______________________	______________________
______________________	______________________

SIXTH: *The name and address of each organizer is:*

NAME	*ADDRESS (include zip code)*
______________________	______________________
______________________	______________________

Signed ______________________ *Signed* ______________________

Organizer

liability by making a filing with the secretary of state. In the states that allow a one-member LLC, sole proprietors can convert to the LLC form.

2. *Operating Agreement*

Operating agreement
Agreement governing the operation of an LLC

The document containing the provisions for the operation and governance of an LLC is called an **operating agreement.** In most states it must be a written agreement although the ULLCA allows an oral agreement. The operating agreement for an LLC is highly similar to a partnership agreement for a general partnership. It must, however, be tailored to meet the specific requirements of the LLC statute in the state of formation. Due to the novelty of the LLC form and the lack of case law interpreting LLCs, the operating agreement should be carefully drafted. It is a private document and is not filed with any state agency. Moreover, because amending the operating agreement requires approval of all LLC members (unless the operating agreement provides otherwise), careful drafting is a must. The operating agreement can be flexibly written, and, while it cannot unreasonably restrict a member's right to information or records; eliminate the duties of good faith, fair dealing, and loyalty owed by and to LLC members; or reduce their duty of due care, members are free to regulate the affairs of the LLC as they wish. A form of LLC operating agreement is available from your instructor. The operating agreement should include the following minimum provisions:

Name of the LLC. As with any business name, the LLC's name cannot be deceptively similar to that of another business such that there would be a likelihood of confusion in the marketplace. A search should be conducted to ensure the name is available and a check made of the state statutes to determine what signal, such as "L.L.C.," or "L.C.," must be used in the business name. The ULLCA provides that the name include "limited liability company," or "limited company," or the abbreviation "L.L.C.," "LLC," "L.C.," or "LC." Most states and the ULLCA allow a new LLC to reserve a name during the formation period by filing an application to reserve the name. The reservation is valid for some period of time, often 90 days, during which another LLC may not file articles of organization using that name. The state will usually impose a fee to reserve the name. See Figure 6-3 for a sample form of the application to reserve, renew, or transfer name used in Illinois. The LLC can also operate under an assumed name, just as a sole proprietor or partnership can. The state simply needs to be informed of the assumed name the LLC has elected.

Names and Addresses of Members. The names and addresses of all members should be provided so that notices and information can be communicated to the members. Corporations may be members of LLCs, and they are deemed notified at the addresses provided.

Recitals. A recitation should be made confirming the intent of the members to form an LLC.

Purpose. The purpose of the LLC should be stated. The purpose clause should be broad enough so that the LLC can expand and grow without requiring amendment of the operating agreement. In most states, a general clause stating that the purpose of the LLC is to engage in any business lawful in the state is acceptable.

FIGURE 6-3
Illinois LLC Name Reservation, Renewal, or Transfer Application

Form **LLC-1.15**
January 1999

Jesse White
Secretary of State
Department of Business Services
Limited Liability Company Division
Room 359, Howlett Building
Springfield, IL 62756
http://www.sos.state.il.us

Payment may be made by business firm check payable to Secretary of State. (If check is returned for any reason this filing will be void.)

Illinois
Limited Liability Company Act
a. Application to Reserve a Name
b. Renewal of Reserved Name
c. Transfer of Reserved Name

Filing Fee: a. $300 b. $100 c. $100

Submit in Duplicate
Must be typewritten

This space for use by Secretary of State
Date
Assigned File #
Filing Fee $
Approved:

This space for use by Secretary of State

1. Limited Liability Company name to be reserved: ______________________

(The LLC name must contain the words "limited liability company", L.L.C. or LLC and cannot contain the terms corporation, corp., incorporated, inc., ltd., co., limited partnership, or L.P.)

2. Name of applicant ______________________

3. Address of applicant ______________________

4. Pursuant to the provisions of Article 1, Section 1-15 of the Illinois Limited Liability Company Act, the undersigned hereby applies for reservation of the above listed name or renewal of a previously reserved limited liability company name for a period of 90 days.

Dated ______________ *(Month & Day)*, ______ *(Year)*

______________________ *(Signature)*

______________________ *(Type or print name and title)*

______________________ *(If applicant is a company or other entity, state name of company and indicate whether it is a member or manager of the LLC)*

NOTICE OF TRANSFER OF RESERVED NAME

The undersigned ______________________ *(Name of Original Applicant)* hereby transfers to ______________________ *(Name and Address of Transferee)* the right to use the name ______________________ for LLC purposes in Illinois. This name was reserved on ______________ *(Month & Day)*, ______ *(Year)*.

The undersigned affirms, under penalties of perjury, that the facts stated herein are true.

Dated ______________ *(Month & Day)*, ______ *(Year)*

______________________ *(Signature)*

______________________ *(Type or print Name and Title)*

______________________ *(If applicant is a company or other entity, state name of company and indicate whether it is a member or manager of the LLC.)*

LLC-16.2

Address. The principal place of business of the LLC in the state should be provided so that members and others can provide communications to the LLC.

Term. A review of the pertinent state statutes is required to ensure that the LLC complies with any restrictions as to the duration of the LLC. Some states provide that LLCs can be formed for a maximum period of 30 years. Other states permit the operating agreement to establish a date beyond 30 years. Most states and the ULLCA provide that if no specific term is set forth in the operating agreement, the LLC will have perpetual existence.

Financial Provisions. The initial contributions to the LLC should be identified. As with a partnership, these contributions may be cash, services, or property. Typically, profits and losses will be shared according to the respective interests initially contributed by the members. Circumstances that will require additional contributions of capital should be set forth. The general rule is that additional contributions must be made in proportion to the initial capital contributions. This section of the operating agreement should also discuss the distribution of assets, namely, the percentage to be allocated to each member and when distributions will be made. If the agreement is silent, distributions by the LLC before its dissolution must be equal. ULLCA Section 405(a).

Member-managed LLCs
An LLC managed by its members

Manager-managed LLCs
An LLC managed by appointed managers rather than its membership

Operation of the LLC. One of the distinct advantages of an LLC is that it can be member-managed without subjecting those members to unlimited liability. The LLC can be managed by all of its members, voting in accord with their respective ownership interests in the LLC. Such LLCs are referred to as **member-managed LLCs.** If the operating agreement is silent, each member will have an equal right to manage the LLC business. For an LLC with numerous members, it may be cumbersome for the organization to be governed by all members. Therefore, some LLCs elect a managing committee or board of managers, much the same way a corporation is managed by its board of directors rather than its individual shareholders. The managers need not be members of the LLC. This feature may be helpful in family businesses when family members prefer to avoid conflict by delegating management duties to a professional. These LLCs are referred to as **manager-managed LLCs.**

If managers are to be elected, the operating agreement must indicate how often elections will be held and how notice of these election meetings will be given to the members. The members also need to decide the term for each manager, whether it be yearly or some longer term, such as three years.

The duties of the managers should be set forth. In general, managers of an LLC have the same fiduciary duties to the LLC and its members that general partners have, namely, a duty to act in good faith and in the best interests of the LLC.

If restrictions are to be imposed on managers, they should be clearly stated. For example, the operating agreement may restrict the managers from borrowing money in excess of a certain amount, selling certain assets, or making certain purchases unless a majority of the members approve or unless the managers unanimously agree. If the operating agreement is silent, the following activities will require consent of all members in any LLC: amendment of the operating agreement; amendment of the articles of organization; making of interim distributions; admission of new members; or the sale or lease of all or substantially all of the LLC's property. ULLCA Section 404(c).

Generally, managers of an LLC will not be personally liable for decisions affecting the LLC unless they have breached a certain duty, violated a law, received a personal benefit from a transaction (unless the other managers have been informed of this conflict and agree to the transaction), or acted in bad faith and with conscious disregard of the best interest of the LLC. Thus, managers of an LLC will generally not be liable for some mere error in business judgment. Liability requires that there was recklessness in acting in conscious disregard of a known risk or a risk which should have been obvious to the manager. ULLCA Section 409.

Because no one would agree to be a manager of an LLC if personal liability could be readily imposed, the LLC may agree to indemnify or reimburse the managers for any claims made against them so long as the manager was acting in good faith and in the best interest of the LLC. LLC managers are seldom, if ever, indemnified for acts of recklessness, gross negligence, or acts contrary to law.

Admission of New Members and Dissociation of Members. With regard to the admission of new members of an LLC, the ULLCA approach is that the admission of a new member requires unanimous consent of all members unless the operating agreement provides otherwise. ULLCA Section 503(a). This requirement may effectively impose a natural restriction on the size of an LLC. If an LLC has 100 members, it may be extremely difficult for these 100 individuals to agree unanimously on anything.

A member may withdraw or dissociate according to terms specified in the operating agreement or the articles of organization. If no specific provisions are set forth, a member may generally withdraw from the LLC upon giving notice to the LLC. Dissociation from an LLC is similar to dissociation from a general partnership. Nevertheless, if the withdrawal or resignation is a breach of the operating agreement, or is before the end of a specified term set forth in the operating agreement, the dissociation is wrongful, and the withdrawing member may be liable for any damages caused by such dissociation.

Transferability of Interests. A member's interest in an LLC is personal property. The operating agreement may provide that the interest is freely transferable or is transferable only upon certain conditions being met. If the operating agreement is silent on this issue, some states require that a majority of the members approve an assignment. Other states require unanimous approval of the assignment. The ULLCA provides that an LLC member may transfer his or her right to distributions but the transferee will become a member of the LLC only if the operating agreement provides or all other members consent. ULLCA Section 503. If such consent cannot be obtained, the assignee will have the right to the assignor's financial interest in the LLC but have no voting rights. Once again, this requirement may serve to restrict the size of LLCs, because it can be difficult and cumbersome to obtain the unanimous approval of a large number of people.

Dissolution. The agreement should specify the events that will trigger a dissolution of the LLC. Many operating agreements provide that any of the following events will cause a dissolution of the LLC:

1. the period fixed for duration expires;
2. the unanimous written agreement of all members;

3. the death or bankruptcy of any member, unless some percentage of the remaining members agree to continue doing business; or
4. the application to a court by a member alleging that it is not reasonably practicable to continue the business.

Generally, upon the dissolution of an LLC, it must file articles of termination or dissolution with the state in which it was formed. The articles of termination or dissolution must recite that all of the debts and obligations of the LLC have been satisfied. (See Figure 6-4 for a sample form of the articles of dissolution required in Illinois.)

Miscellaneous Provisions. Similar to a partnership agreement, the operating agreement for an LLC may contain numerous other provisions. For example, it may provide that members cannot transfer their interest in the LLC without offering it first to existing members of the LLC. It may provide for the purchase of life insurance for each member so that if a member dies, insurance proceeds are available to pay the decedent's estate for purchase of the interest of the decedent. Similarly, provisions should be made for dispute resolution, amendments to the operating agreement, meetings of the members, whether written ballots are required or voice votes are sufficient, whether members must be present in person or may vote by proxy, and any other matters pertinent to the operation and governance of the LLC.

F. Transferability of Interest

Most state statutes provide that a member's interest in an LLC, namely the right to profits or distributions, is personal property. Therefore, the interest may be transferred or assigned, similar to any item of personal property, such as a car, jewelry, or stock. Some states, however, place limitations on this right to assign one's LLC interest by requiring that a majority of other members consent to the assignment or even that there be unanimous consent. The assignment typically carries with it only the assignor's right to profits: It does not entitle the new owner to be a member of the LLC with rights to participation unless the operating agreement so provides or *all* other members consent. These restrictions on transferability of interest militate against an LLC with a large number of members because, as a practical matter, it is extremely difficult to achieve unanimous approval from a large group on even the most noncontroversial item.

G. Dissociation and Dissolution of LLCs

Under the RUPA, not every dissociation from a general partnership causes a dissolution of the partnership and that in many instances a departing or dissociating partner's interest will be purchased by the partnership. Many of the same principles apply to LLCs. Under the ULLCA, the results of a dissociation depend upon whether the LLC is one for a definite term or is "at will" (meaning the LLC has no definite term) and whether the LLC is member-managed or manager-managed.

In brief, the following rules apply under ULLCA Sections 601, 602, 603, 701, and 801:

FIGURE 6-4
Illinois LLC Articles of Dissolution Form

Form **LLC-35.15**

January 1999

Jesse White
Secretary of State
Department of Business Services
Limited Liability Company Division
Room 359, Howlett Building
Springfield, IL 62756
http://www.sos.state.il.us

Payment may be made by business firm check payable to Secretary of State. (If check is returned for any reason this filing will be void.)

Illinois
Limited Liability Company Act
ARTICLES OF DISSOLUTION

Submit in Duplicate
Must be typewritten

This space for use by Secretary of State

Date
Assigned File #
Filing Fee $100
Approved:

This space for use by Secretary of State

1. Limited Liability Company name: ______________________________

____

2. Post office address to which may be mailed a copy of any process against the limited liability company that may be served on the Secretary of State.

____

____

____

3. File number assigned by the Secretary of State: ______________________________

4. Federal Employer Identification Number (F.E.I.N.): ______________________________

5. All debts, obligations, and liabilities of the limited liability company have been paid and discharged or adequate provision has been made therefor.

6. All remaining property and assets of the limited liability company have been distributed among the members in accordance with their respective rights and interest.

7. There are no suits pending against the company in any court or that adequate provision has been made for the satisfaction of any judgment, order, or decree that may be entered against it in any pending suit.

8. The undersigned affirms, under penalties of perjury, having authority to sign hereto, that this articles of dissolution is to the best of my knowledge and belief, true, correct and complete.

Dated ______________________________ , ________ .
(Month & Day) (Year)

____
(Signature)

____
(Type or print Name and Title)

____
(If applicant is a company or other entity, state name of company and indicate whether it is a member or manager of the LLC.)

LLC-9.2

Member-Managed At-Will LLC. A dissociation of an LLC member in a member-managed at-will LLC for any reason (including voluntary withdrawal, death, or bankruptcy) will cause a dissolution and winding up unless a specified percentage of the other LLC members agree to continue doing business, in which case the dissociated member's interest must be purchased by the LLC.

Member-Managed Term LLC. A dissociation of an LLC member from a member-managed term company will cause a dissolution and winding up if the dissociation is caused by death or bankruptcy, unless a specified percentage of the other LLC members agree to continue doing business. Dissociations for reasons other than death or bankruptcy (such as voluntary withdrawal, assignment of all of one's interest in the LLC, or expulsion) will not cause a dissolution. In any of these events, however, while the LLC must purchase the dissociating member's interest, it need not do so until the end of the term set for the LLC.

Manager-Managed At-Will or Term LLC. If an at-will LLC or a term LLC is managed by managers rather than its members, only the dissociation of a member who is also a manager will cause dissolution. Even in this case, if all of the LLC members consent, the LLC may continue operating.

The purchase of a dissociated member's interest will be at the fair market value of the interest. A dissociated member may file a statement of dissociation in the office of the secretary of state indicating that the member has dissociated from the LLC.

If an event causes a dissolution (for example, a manager of a manger-managed LLC withdraws from the LLC), the LLC's business must be wound up. Assets must first be applied to discharge any obligations to creditors, including members of the LLC who are creditors. Any surplus will then be paid to the LLC members in accordance with their rights to distributions. The LLC then terminates its existence by filing articles of termination or dissolution with the secretary of state. The articles of termination or dissolution must contain the name of the LLC, the date of the dissolution, and a statement that the company's business has been wound up and its legal existence has been terminated.

H. Taxation of LLCs

As previously discussed, one of the primary advantages of an LLC is that it offers the pass-through tax status of a partnership. Corporate income is taxed twice: once when received by the corporation itself and then again when received by the corporate owners, the shareholders, as dividends.

In an LLC, all income, whether distributed or not, flows through or is "tagged" to the individual members, usually in proportion to their initial contributions and any subsequent contributions to the LLC. LLCs file the same informational tax return used by general partnerships, limited partnerships, and limited liability partnerships (see Figure 3-7). The members then declare their share of the LLC income on their individual tax returns and pay tax at whatever bracket is appropriate. Similarly, losses sustained by members of LLCs may be used to offset other income and thereby decrease tax liability.

As is the case with general partnerships, limited partnerships, and limited liability partnerships, the LLC (whether a single-member or multiple-member LLC) may elect to be taxed as a corporation at corporate tax rates by "checking the box" on its tax form (see Figure 3-8). This will allow the LLC to retain profits without requiring the LLC members to pay taxes on the retained profits they have not received. See Figure 6-5 for chart comparing LLCs with sole proprietorships, general partnerships, limited partnerships, and limited liability partnerships.

Key Features of Limited Liability Companies

- LLCs offer their members full protection from personal liability whether it arises in tort or contract.
- LLCs can be managed by their members ("member-managed") or by appointed managers ("manager-managed").
- LLCs can be formed only by compliance with state statutes, which mandate the filing of articles of organization with the state agency.
- The LLC is governed by its operating agreement, which is usually written.
- Unless the operating agreement provides otherwise, admission of a new member requires unanimous approval.
- The LLC provides the pass-through taxation of a general partnership.

FIGURE 6-5
Chart Comparing Unincorporated Business Structures

	Sole Proprietorship	*General Partnership*	*Limited Partnership*	*Limited Liability Partnership*	*Limited Liability Company*
Types of Members	Individuals only	No restrictions	No restrictions	No restrictions	No restrictions
Number of Members Required	One only	At least two	At least two, one general partner and one limited partner	At least two	One member permitted in some states and under ULLCA; at least two required in other states

FIGURE 6-5 *Continued*
Chart Comparing Unincorporated Business Structures

	Sole Proprietorship	*General Partnership*	*Limited Partnership*	*Limited Liability Partnership*	*Limited Liability Company*
Formalities of Organization	None	None	Filing of Certificate of Limited Partnership required	Filing of Application of LLP required	Filing of Articles of Organization required
Management	Managed solely by sole proprietor	Managed jointly by all general partners	Managed solely by general partners	Generally managed jointly by all LLP partners	Can be member-managed or managed by appointed managers
Liability	Unlimited personal liability	Unlimited personal liability	General partners have unlimited personal liability; limited partners liable only to extent of investment	In partial shield states, LLP partners have liability only for contractual obligations; in full shield states, no liability whether for acts arising in tort or contract	Members liable only to extent of investment (but professionals retain liability for their own negligence)
Transferability of All Ownership Rights	None; new sole proprietorship created upon transfer	No transfer unless with consent of all partners	No transfer unless with consent of all partners	No transfer unless with consent of all partners	Transferee cannot become member unless agreement provides or all LLC members consent
Ability to Do Business in Other States	Yes	Yes	Yes, if authorized by foreign state	Yes, if authorized by foreign state	Yes, if authorized by foreign state

FIGURE 6-5 *Continued*
Chart Comparing Unincorporated Business Structures

	Sole Proprietorship	*General Partnership*	*Limited Partnership*	*Limited Liability Partnership*	*Limited Liability Company*
Continuity of Life	No; terminates upon death of sole proprietor	Under RUPA, only certain dissociations cause dissolution and winding up	LP can survive withdrawal of limited partner and general partner if all consent	Only certain dissociations cause a dissolution and winding up	Only certain dissociations cause a dissolution and winding up; may be limited to certain term
Taxation	Income taxed directly to sole proprietor	Income taxed directly to all partners*	Income taxed directly to all partners*	Income taxed directly to all partners*	Income taxed directly to all members*
Right to Bring Derivative Action	No	No	Yes	No	Yes

* Under new IRS "check-the-box" regulation, may elect to be taxed as a corporation at corporate tax levels.

I. Role of Paralegal

The most critical task to be performed by a paralegal with regard to the formation and operation of an LLC is a thorough reading of the state statute authorizing LLCs. The requirements as to naming the LLC should be reviewed to ensure that any particular signal or designation of the adoption of LLC status is properly conveyed to third parties. Paralegals should contact the secretary of state to determine name availability, reserve the name (if the state permits), and request all appropriate forms for formation, operation, amendment, and dissolution of an LLC in that state.

Paralegals may also play a part in drafting the operating agreement. Because the LLC is a relatively new form of business enterprise, few prepared forms can be consulted for guidance. Paralegals should thus review various general partnership agreements and bylaws for corporations, and then tailor these to meet the needs of the LLC and the requirements of the LLC statute in that jurisdiction.

After forming an LLC, paralegals should prepare a list of procedures to follow in the future and "lessons learned" for the next LLC formation, noting useful phone numbers and the names of helpful state officials.

Paralegals should maintain the LLC's important documents in a binder, including the articles of organization and any amendments to the articles, a copy of the operating agreement, and an identification of the names and business and residence addresses of each member of the LLC.

Although the term of the LLC is relatively long, typically 30 years, appropriate care should be taken to docket or tickle the date in those states in which there is a maximum term for the LLC.

Resource Guide

The various resources discussed in Chapter Three for general partnerships and those discussed in Chapter Eight for corporations should be consulted. Most important is the state statute recognizing and governing LLCs. Because the statutes are so new, few cases, if any, interpret LLC statutes. Thus, paralegals must rely almost exclusively on the statutes themselves. As with LLPs, the legislative history surrounding the enactment of the LLC statute (such as the various versions of the bills, transcripts of committee hearings regarding adoption of the LLC, and debates on the issue) may be examined.

Because the LLC is such a new form of business organization, there is not yet a host of forms available for drafting either the articles of organization or the operating agreement. Paralegals should carefully review any periodical articles written in bar journals or other legal periodicals regarding LLCs for practical guidance on drafting the various documents required.

Am. Jur. Legal Forms 2d provides a variety of forms related to the establishment and operation of limited liability companies. Analysis of the use of the forms is also provided, together with checklists related to formation and operation of LLCs.

One attorneys' service company, Attorneys Corporation Service, Inc., offers an "LLC Kit" for less than $100 and which includes forms for articles of organization, operating agreements, minutes, subscription agreements, and other forms. The forms are also available on disk. Attorneys Corporation Service, Inc. is located at 4664 Lankershim Blvd., North Hollywood, CA 91602-1884 (telephone: (800) 462-5487). *A Guide to Limited Liability Companies* (Commerce Clearing House) is available for approximately $30 (telephone: (800) 835-5224). *The Essential Limited Liability Company Handbook: The Newest Alternative in Business* (Oasis Press) is available for approximately $20 and offers detailed information on organizing an LLC (telephone: (800) 228-2275).

WEB RESOURCES

A number of sites provide general information about LLCs with clear and concise discussions of LLCs, comparing and contrasting them to other forms of business entities. Many of the sites listed below provide forms for LLC operating agreements. As with all forms, exercise caution in using the form, inasmuch as it will likely not be suitable for all LLCs. As with any form, you should modify it to suit your needs and the statutory requirements in your state. Review the Web site Disclaimer or Legal Terms sections to determine if there are any prohibitions on use or reproduction of the forms. In any event, the forms serve as useful starting places.

Of most importance is a review of a state's statutes regarding limited liability companies. To review state statutes online, access <www.ll.georgetown.edu> the Web site of Georgetown University Law Center. Select "State, Local & Territorial," and you will then be presented with a map of the United States. Point your cursor to the desired state, and you will then be able to select whether you wish to view that state's constitution, statutes, cases, or other legal information. By selecting "Statutes" or "Code," you will be able to search the state's statutes and find relevant statutory material. In some instances, you can search by statute number; in other instances, you can search by keyword. Some states allow you to browse various titles. Search for "Corporations," and then view the LLC statutes usually included either within or near this title.

Other useful Web sites include the following:

http://www.nass.org
This Web site of the National Association of Secretaries of State allows you to link directly to the home page for each state's secretary of state. Many states offer guides to forming LLCs with basic information, forms, checklists, and phone numbers. Point your cursor to "States" and then to your state's name and flag, and proceed to locate information on forming an LLC in your state. Forms for name reservations, articles of organization, amendments to articles of organization, and certificates for cancellation or dissolution of LLCs are offered on most state Web sites.

www.irs.gov
The Web site of the Internal Revenue Service offers a wealth of information about taxes, businesses, and provides Form 1065 and Schedule K, the LLC tax forms, which can be downloaded and printed.

www.ask.com
"Ask Jeeves" is an Internet "butler" who will help you find what you need. Simply type in your question, in natural English, in the box presented, and you will be referred to numerous useful sites. For example, type in "Where can I find information about limited liability companies?" You will then be directed to sites offering information on LLCs, forms for organization and

operation, and forms of operating agreements. "Ask.com" is often the first site many individuals access to find information on nearly any topic. Bookmark this site, and use it often.

www.tannedfeet.com
Billed as "The Entrepreneurs' Help Page," this site provides a wealth of information regarding the formation and operation of businesses, including LLCs.

www.llc-usa.com
This site is dedicated to those interested in limited liability companies and offers a wealth of information about LLCs. Go to the "Resources" section for a chart comparing the LLC with other entities and other useful information. Access <www.llc-usa.com/revlist.html> for direct links to each state's department that handles LLC formation and questions.

www.about.com
"About.com" offers a wide variety of information relating to many topics. After you access the site, point your cursor to "Business/Careers" and then to "Small Business Information" for information on starting businesses, tax strategies, and information about types of entities, including LLCs.

www.LegalWiz.com
This legal resource for entrepreneurs offers articles, general information about businesses, and a glossary of business and legal terms.

Discussion Questions

Fact Scenario. Young, Taylor, and Randall, LLC, is a limited liability company engaged in the practice of law in several states. The firm has a written operating agreement, which provides that the term of the LLC will be 30 years. The agreement is silent on the issues of interim distributions of profits and admission of new members. The firm is managed by five of its most senior members.

1. Hannah Nelson, a member in the firm's Tucson's trademark group, has committed an act of malpractice. Discuss the liability of the other members in the firm in the Tucson office and in the firm's other offices throughout the nation.

2. Hannah is supervised by Ken, a more senior member. Discuss Ken's liability for Hannah's act of malpractice.

3. The firm owes $50,000 for rent for its New York office. What is the liability of members throughout the firm for this obligation?

4. The firm wishes to admit a new member in its Dallas office. How will admission of this new member be accomplished?

5. Teresa, a member in the firm's Boston office, has decided to withdraw from the firm. What effect will this withdrawal have on the continued existence of the firm?

6. Assume that one of the five managers of the LLC wishes to withdraw. What effect will this withdrawal have on the continued existence of the firm?

7. The managers of the firm wish to distribute profits to the members. How will this be accomplished, and what will each member's share be?

7

Other Unincorporated Organizations

CHAPTER OVERVIEW

With the exception of corporations, we have discussed the primary ways in which business is conducted in this country: sole proprietorships, general partnerships, limited partnerships, registered limited liability partnerships, and limited liability companies. Before turning to corporations, some other ways in which business is conducted in the United States are discussed in this chapter. All of the following organizations (with the exception of a real estate investment trust, which may operate as a corporation) are "unincorporated associations," meaning that none have applied to a state to be recognized as a corporation. Most of the following business forms are not nearly as well known as the enterprises already discussed or as well known as corporations. Nevertheless, a brief summary of these organizational structures is helpful because they are occasionally desired by clients.

A. Joint Ventures

The most common of the other unincorporated organizations is the joint venture. A **joint venture** (referred to in the past occasionally as a *joint adventure*) is usually viewed as a form or variety of partnership—specifically, a form of general partnership. It is an association of two or more persons or entities who combine their property, skill, or knowledge to carry out *a single enterprise* for profit. Upon completion of the undertaking, the joint venture dissolves. Thus, the primary distinc-

Joint venture
A partnership formed to carry out a single enterprise rather than an ongoing business

tion between a joint venture and a partnership is that a partnership is usually formed to engage in some ongoing business activity whereas the joint venture is formed to carry out a particular venture.

For example, if an entity intends to engage in real estate development and is formed to construct buildings of any variety, whether commercial or residential, single-family or multi-family units, it may be carried on as a partnership. The partners might reasonably expect that the partnership will last many years, or so long as there is construction to be done. A joint venture, on the other hand, might be formed among three individuals to build a single condominium complex. Upon the completion of that one complex, the joint venture dissolves. A joint venture can best be described as a short-term partnership. Joint ventures are generally governed by state partnership and contract law.

The parties to a joint venture may be individuals, general partnerships, limited partnerships, LLPs, LLCs, or corporations. For example, two utility corporations, one formed in the United States and one formed in China, may enter into an agreement to construct and operate a nuclear plant in China. In fact, it is becoming increasingly common to see joint ventures formed for the purpose of conducting business activities in a variety of foreign countries, including activities involving agricultural enterprises, construction ventures, and telecommunications businesses, often because many countries restrict the activity of foreign companies to own businesses or remove profit. In other instances, joint ventures may be formed when one party, such as a university, does not have sufficient resources to commercially develop an invention or discovery, and thus forms a joint venture with another party, which provides funding and capital to bring the invention to market.

The parties in the joint venture, the *joint venturers,* owe fiduciary duties to each other, just as do partners in a partnership. Other similarities between partnerships and joint ventures include the following:

1. There must be an agreement between the joint venturers to do business together. This agreement may be oral or written. If the agreement is written, it will greatly resemble a general partnership agreement. If the agreement is oral and disputes as to its terms later arise, courts generally rely upon cases dealing with general partnerships or upon general partnership principles to resolve the disputed issues.
2. No state formalities are required to form a joint venture.
3. The joint venturers share profits and losses according to their agreement. Typically, as in partnerships, the sharing of profits and losses is determined by the initial contributions to the joint venture. If there is no agreement, profits and losses are typically shared equally, as is the case with general partnerships.
4. Joint venturers have unlimited liability for the venture's debts and obligations. The ability of joint venturers to bind each other for debts is more limited, however, than in a general partnership, although the joint venturers owe fiduciary duties to each other.
5. The joint venturers share the right to manage and control the business. The amount of power or control a joint venturer has is usually determined by his or her initial contribution.

6. The joint venture is treated as a partnership for tax purposes. In fact, Section 761 of the Internal Revenue Code defines the term "partnership" to include joint ventures. Like partnerships, however, joint ventures may elect to be taxed as corporations. (See Chapter Three and Figure 3-8.) Thus, all of the income is passed through to the joint venturers who then declare their respective shares of the income (or losses) on their individual tax returns.

(A form of a Joint Venture Agreement is available from your instructor.)

B. Mining Partnerships

Certain states, such as Idaho, Montana, and Nevada, in which mining operations are conducted (including oil and gas exploration) have statutes providing for the organization of mining partnerships. Other states, such as Kentucky, Oklahoma, and Texas, recognize mining partnerships by judicial decision. As the name itself indicates, the **mining partnership** is established for the development of mining property and extracting minerals from the property.

Mining partnership
Partnership organized to develop mining property

Mining partnerships usually share the following features:

1. the partners voluntarily agree to do business together;
2. the agreement need not be express; the partnership arises from the ownership of interests in the mine and working the same;
3. the partners jointly own the partnership property, namely, mineral interests;
4. the partners share profits and losses according to their percentage of ownership interest;
5. partners may convey their interests without dissolving the partnership, and the purchaser automatically becomes a member of the partnership;
6. no member of the mining partnership can bind the partnership unless there is express authority to do so;
7. decisions are made by majority rule;
8. the partners owe fiduciary duties to each other; and
9. the mining partnership is taxed as a partnership.

Mining partnerships differ from general partnerships in that interests in the mining partnership are freely transferable with new purchasers automatically becoming members, while interests in general partnerships are not so freely transferable. Moreover, while under the UPA a general partnership dissolves upon the death or bankruptcy of any member, or the transfer of any partner's interest, the mining partnership survives such events and the heirs, bankruptcy trustee, or transferees become partners in the mining partnership upon purchase of their interest. Finally, unlike general partnerships which are characterized by general mutual agency, there is limited ability of one partner to bind another.

C. Joint Stock Companies

Joint stock company
Entity combining double taxation of corporation with unlimited personal liability for its members

Joint stock companies (or associations) are relatively uncommon in the United States. They combine a number of features of partnerships and corporations; unlike the new LLPs and LLCs, however, they combine some of the most unattractive features of these organizations, namely, the personal liability seen in partnerships combined with the double taxation of corporations. In brief, a joint stock company is the polar opposite of LLPs and LLCs, which combine protection from personal liability with single pass-through taxation.

Joint stock companies developed in England. They were formed informally, by agreement, rather than by compliance with statutory formalities. These business organizations were referred to as *joint stock* companies because the interests of the members, called the *stock,* were placed or pooled into one joint account which was then managed on behalf of the members.

Because English common law and customs were transplanted to America, these joint stock companies also became recognized in the United States. Although originally formed by mere agreement, some American jurisdictions (including Alabama, Minnesota, and New York) subject joint stock companies to compliance with statutes. Many Americans are unfamiliar with this type of organization and therefore joint stock companies are rarely encountered in modern practice. Moreover, due to the popularity of new enterprises, namely, LLPs and LLCs, these joint stock companies likely will become increasingly uncommon.

A joint stock company can be formed with few formalities. In most jurisdictions, no public filings are required. Nevertheless, in those states that govern joint stock companies by statute, certain publicly filed documents may be required. For example, in New York, a written certificate including basic information about the joint stock company, such as its name, its place of business, the number of its members, and the names and addresses of its officers must be filed with the Secretary of State and in the principal county in which the joint stock company will do business. The certificate must be filed within 60 days of transacting business in New York, and annually thereafter.

The joint stock company is governed by agreement. As in partnerships, there is no requirement for a written agreement. The members of the company, however, generally prefer that a written agreement be prepared. Additionally, many joint stock companies have numerous members and operation of the business without a written agreement is both foolish and inefficient. This agreement, usually called the **articles of association,** will contain provisions similar to those found in partnership agreements, such as provisions regarding the division of profits and losses, duration of existence, transfer of shares, management of the entity, and causes of dissolution.

Articles of association
The agreement governing operation of a joint stock association

1. *Similarities to Corporations*

The following features of the joint stock company make it similar to a corporation:

a. The members of the joint stock company are generally referred to as shareholders.

b. The shareholders are issued certificates representing their ownership interest in the entity, referred to as shares.
c. The shares owned by shareholders in a joint stock company are easily transferred, just as shares in a corporation can be easily sold to a third party.
d. The joint stock company is not governed by all of its members, as is the case in general partnerships, but rather is governed by a *board of managers* who act on behalf of the shareholders. This form of governance is the classic operation of a corporation: Its shareholders elect individuals to manage the company. In a corporation, these managers are referred to as the board of *directors*. In the joint stock company, only the board of managers manages the business; the members have no voice in management and operation of the enterprise.
e. Like a corporation, the joint stock company is capable of perpetual existence and the death of a member of a joint stock company or the transfer of a member's interest does not dissolve the company.
f. There is no mutual agency among the member-shareholders as there is among partners in a partnership. While the managers can act on behalf of the shareholders, the shareholders cannot bind one another by their acts and cannot act for the company.
g. The joint stock company is usually taxed as a corporation.

2. *Similarities to Partnerships*

The following features of the joint stock company make it similar to a partnership:

a. It is formed by agreement among the member-shareholders and usually does not require any documents to be publicly filed with the state.
b. Profits and losses are shared in proportion to ownership interests of the member-shareholders.
c. The member-shareholders have unlimited personal liability for the debts and obligations of the joint stock company. Because there is no general agency among the shareholders, however, one shareholder cannot perform some act which would render other shareholders liable. Thus, the opportunities for unlimited liability are somewhat decreased because only the board of managers can act on behalf of the shareholders and thereby commit them to some debt or obligation.

3. *Modern Application*

One can easily see why the joint stock company is an unattractive form of business enterprise: The member-shareholders have no voice in the management and governance of the enterprise, yet have unlimited liability for its debts and torts.

Lloyd's of London, the well-known insurance underwriter in existence for more than 300 years, is operated as a joint stock company. During the late 1980s and early 1990s, Lloyd's suffered record losses due to what it referred to as a "high incidence of catastrophes," such as asbestos and pollution claims for which it had provided insurance. To meet these obligations it had to ask its members, referred to as "names," for cash. Approximately 2,500 Americans were names and most were stunned to realize they faced unlimited liability for losses.

In fact, United States Supreme Court Associate Justice Stephen Breyer was a name, and the issue of his potential liability was a critical issue in his confirmation hearings. While Breyer had insurance for some of the losses he faced, he was required to resolve the debt fully before being confirmed. In some instances, however, names have been forced to use their savings to cover their liability. Some applied to a special hardship program allowing them to deed over their houses to Lloyd's upon their death. Hundreds are expected to be bankrupted by their losses. About 30 names committed suicide. While some Americans complained they were never fully informed of the risks, Lloyd's responded that it was never compulsory to join and people who joined freely had a duty to investigate fully before committing funds. An organization referred to as the American Names Association has sued Lloyd's. Most cases are expected to be resolved by private settlement agreements. Cases are now being heard by British courts after years of attempts by the American names to sue in the United States, despite agreements that required them to litigate in Great Britain.

This modern application of the principles of joint stock companies emphasizes the unfamiliarity American investors generally have with the enterprise as well as some of its most unattractive features, namely unlimited personal liability coupled with the members' lack of management or control of the enterprise.

D. Business Trusts

Business trust
An unincorporated association governed by the law of trusts in which trustees manage the business for others, called beneficiaries

The **business trust,** sometimes called the "Massachusetts business trust" due to its initial recognition in Massachusetts, is another form of unincorporated business enterprise rarely encountered any longer. A combination or hybrid of a corporation and a partnership, the business trust was developed in an attempt to achieve the limited liability status of corporations while circumventing certain laws and restrictions that earlier applied to corporations regarding acquisition and development of real estate.

Trustee
One to whom property or a business is entrusted to manage it for others

Beneficiary
One for whose benefit property or a business is managed

Statutory trust
A trust governed by state statute

Common law trust
A trust created and governed by case law

The *business trust* is created by a written trust agreement that defines the powers and duties of its managers, called **trustees,** and the interests of its equitable or beneficial owners, called **beneficiaries.** The trustees hold and manage property or carry on business activities for the benefit of the beneficiaries. Generally, the written trust agreement need not be filed with any state authority; however, some states, including Nevada and Wyoming, require certain public filings, treating the business trust somewhat similarly to a corporation. The requirements in New York with regard to public filings for joint stock companies are equally applicable to business trusts. Similarly, in Ohio, before commencing business, the business trust must file a detailed report with the secretary of state, giving specific information about the business trust. When business trusts are governed by statute (as they are in Nevada, New York, Ohio, and Wyoming, among other states), they are often referred to as **statutory trusts** to distinguish them from business trusts created pursuant to judicial decision, which are often called **common law trusts.**

1. *Similarities to Corporations*

The business trust shares the following features with corporations:

a. The equitable owners or investors, called beneficiaries, are issued trust certificates evidencing their ownership rights in the business trust. This is similar to stock certificates issued to the shareholders of a corporation.
b. Just as shares of stock in a corporation are easily transferred to another, ownership interests held by beneficiaries in the business trust can be easily transferred to third parties.
c. A corporation is not managed by its owners, the shareholders, but rather by directors elected by the shareholders. Similarly, the business trust is managed or governed by managers, the trustees. These trustees are solely responsible for the operation of the business.
d. The business trust does not dissolve upon the death of any of its beneficiaries or the transfer of their interests and may exist perpetually. Many business trusts, however, establish periods of duration.
e. There is no mutual general agency among the beneficiaries. They cannot act so as to bind one another or the business trust. The trustees, however, are agents of the beneficiaries and can thus bind the beneficiaries by their actions. The trustees owe fiduciary duties to the trust and the beneficiaries.
f. The beneficiaries, like shareholders in a corporation, usually enjoy limited liability for the debts and obligations of the business trust. If, however, they participate in management of the business, they may lose their limited liability status. If liability arises due to ordinary activities carried on by the trustees for the business trust, and no negligence or reckless disregard is shown, the trustees may be indemnified or reimbursed by the trust itself or by the beneficiaries. In some states, such as Wyoming, the trustees are held to the same standard of care as directors of a business corporation.
g. The business trust is usually taxed as a corporation.

2. *Similarities to Partnerships*

The business trust shares the following features with partnerships:

a. The business trust is formed by agreement and there are relatively few formalities involved in organizing the business trust.
b. Profits and losses are shared in accord with the beneficiaries' respective equitable ownership interests in the business trust.

(See Figure 7-1 for form of certificate of business trust used in Nevada.)

3. *Modern Application*

The business trust is unfamiliar to most American investors. It is rarely formed now that the reason for its creation, circumvention of certain restrictions on corporations as to acquisition and development of real property, no longer ex-

FIGURE 7-1
Nevada Certificate of Business Trust

DEAN HELLER
Secretary of State

101 North Carson Street, Suite 3
Carson City, Nevada 89701-4786
(775) 684 5708

Certificate of Business Trust

Office Use Only:

Important: Read attached instructions before completing form.

1. Name of Business Trust: (must include the words business trust, B.T. or BT.)	
2. Resident Agent Name and Street Address: (must be a Nevada address where process may be served)	Name Street Address ______ City ______, NEVADA ______ Zip Code
3. Resident Agent Mailing Address: (if different from address above)	Name Mailing Address ______ City ______, State ______ Zip Code
4. Names, Addresses, of Trustees: (must include the name and p.o. box or street address, either residence or business of at least one trustee) Attach additional pages if more than 1 to be listed.	Name Address ______ City ______, State ______ Zip Code
5. Purpose: (Optional–See Instructions)	
6. Other Matters: (See instructions)	Number of additional pages attached: ________
7. Names, Addresses and Signatures of Each Person Forming Business Trust: (must be signed by each person forming business trust) Attach additional pages if there are more than 2.	Name ______ Name Address ______ City, State, Zip ______ Address ______ City, State, Zip Signature ______ Signature
8. Certificate of Acceptance of Appointment of Resident Agent:	I, ______________________ hereby accept appointment as Resident Agent for the above named business trust. Signature of Resident Agent ______ Date

This form must be accompanied by appropriate fees. See attached fee schedule.

Nevada Secretary of State Form CORPART1999.01
Revised on: 07/08/99

ists. Moreover, there are numerous other ways of doing business, such as the LLP and LLC, affording more advantages to the owners than does the business trust.

E. Real Estate Investment Trusts

A **Real Estate Investment Trust** (REIT, pronounced "reet") is a vehicle for investment in real estate by numerous investors who pool their capital to acquire or provide financing for commercial real estate. After the real estate recession of the 1980s, banks became wary of loaning money to real estate developers and often did so only on terms unattractive to the developers. To remedy the situation, REITs were created to sell stock to the public, which then provides financing for real estate developers. REITs have become increasingly popular, and more than 300 REITs are traded on the major stock exchanges. In brief, a REIT is a company that buys, develops, operates, and sells real estate assets.

Real Estate Investment Trust
Business that invests in real estate on behalf of numerous investors who have limited liability for the business debts

REITs are usually formed either as trusts or corporations, although they can be formed as partnerships. REITs formed as trusts are governed by the law of trusts, meaning that they are created by a document called a declaration of trust that provides that the property is managed by a trustee or trustees for the benefits of others, called beneficiaries. The beneficiaries hold transferable certificates representing their ownership interest in the REIT.

REITs are usually managed by an investment advisor, the trustee, selected by the REIT's board of directors and pursuant to a written agreement between the REIT and the advisor. Moreover, there will be a declaration of trust. If the REIT offers securities to the public, it must register with the Securities and Exchange Commission and provide a complete prospectus to each prospective investor.

Many states specifically regulate REITs by statute. For example, Ohio requires that REITs transacting business in Ohio file a detailed report with the secretary of state before commencing business (see Figure 7-2). Similarly, in Alabama, REITs must file a declaration of trust giving certain required information about the REIT with the secretary of state. In other states, formation of a REIT is pursuant to common law rather than pursuant to specific statutes.

1. *Types of REITs*

There are four basic forms of REITs:

- *Equity REITs* purchase commercial real estate such as apartment buildings and shopping centers and derive income through rent received.
- *Mortgage REITs* do not own real estate but rather make loans enabling others to purchase real estate. The loans are secured by mortgages on the real estate, and the REIT derives revenue through interest paid on the mortgage loans.
- *Hybrid REITs* hold and invest in both mortgages and real estate assets.
- *Umbrella Partnership REITs* ("UPREITS") hold interests in partnerships that themselves own commercial real property. The REIT serves as the general partner in a limited partnership that owns and operates commercial real estate such as apartment projects.

FIGURE 7-2
Ohio Certificate for Formation of REIT

Prescribed by **J. Kenneth Blackwell**

Please obtain fee amount and mailing instructions from the **Forms Inventory List** (using the 3 digit form # located at the bottom of this form). To obtain the **Forms Inventory List** or for assistance, please call Customer Service:
Central Ohio: (614)-466-3910 Toll Free: 1-877-SOS-FILE (1-877-767-3453)

REPORT BY
REAL ESTATE INVESTMENT TRUST

TO THE SECRETARY OF STATE, COLUMBUS, OHIO

______________________________, a real estate investment trust desiring to transact real estate business in Ohio, pursuant to Section 1747.01 et seq., Revised Code of Ohio, hereby files the following report:

FIRST. Its business name is ______________________________

SECOND. It is a real estate investment trust organized in the state of ______________.

THIRD. The complete address of its principal office is

____
(street address)

______________________________ ______________ ______________
(city, township, or village) (state) (zip code)

FOURTH. If this report is being filed by a FOREIGN real estate investment trust, the complete address of its principal office in Ohio, if any, is

____
(street name and number)

______________________________, Ohio ______________
(city, village or township) (zip code)

FIFTH. It hereby designates ______________________________
as its agent within Ohio, upon whom process against the trust may be served. The complete address within Ohio of such agent is

____
(street name and number)

______________________________, Ohio ______________
(city, village or township) (zip code)

SIXTH. It hereby irrevocably consents to service of process on such designated agent and to service of process upon the Secretary of State, if without the registration of another agent with the Secretary of State, its designated agent has died, resigned, lost authority, dissolved, becomes disqualified, or has removed from this state, or if its designated agent cannot, with due diligence, be found.

SEVENTH. The names and complete addresses of its trustees are:

Name	Address

FIGURE 7-2 *Continued*
Ohio Certificate for Formation of REIT

J. Kenneth Blackwell
Secretary of State

EIGHTH. The approximate date upon which the real estate investment trust began transacting business in Ohio is

______________.
(date)

NINTH. This report ☐ is made ☐ is not made to enable the real estate investment trust to maintain an action in a court of this state.

TENTH. THERE IS HEREWITH SUBMITTED an executed copy of the trust instrument creating this real estate investment trust, including any amendments thereto, or a true and correct copy of such instrument, certified to be such by a trustee before an official authorized to administer oaths or by a public official in another state in whose office an executed copy is on file.

IN WITNESS WHEREOF, said ______________________________, has caused this report to be executed by trustee or an executive officer duly authorized in the premises on ______________
(date)

____
(Name of Real Estate Investment Trust)

Signature: ______________________
Name: ______________________
Title: ______________________

2. *Advantages of REITs*

REITs provide a number of advantages to their investors:

a. Investors are passive and hold shares in the REITs without assuming personal liability.
b. The REIT is subject to single taxation only. Profits earned and distributed to the investors are taxed to the investor shareholders as ordinary income (assuming a variety of tax and regulatory requirements are met, including having a minimum of 100 shareholder investors and distributing at least 95 percent of the taxable income to the investors). REITS use IRS Form 1120-REIT to report their income and elect to be treated as a pass-through entity. This form is used whether the REIT is operated as a corporation, a trust, or some form of unincorporated association.
c. While partners in partnerships and members in limited liability companies often have difficulty selling their interests (inasmuch as there is no

ready market for their ownership interests), investors in REITs can readily sell their shares in the REIT and achieve liquidity because the REITs are usually traded on the stock exchanges.

3. *Conclusion*

REITs are complex investment vehicles requiring a thorough grounding in accounting principles and tax, corporate, and securities law. Forming the REIT can take up to one year, and registration with the Securities and Exchange Commission is a complex and time-consuming process. Nevertheless, for mega–real estate transactions, REITs offer several advantages, primarily limited liability for the passive investors coupled with avoidance of double taxation and a high level of annual distributions.

Key Features of Other Unincorporated Organizations

- Joint ventures are a form of short-term partnership, usually formed to carry out one single venture; they are governed by partnership law.
- Mining partnerships are formed to develop mining property and are characterized by joint working of the property and sharing of profits; partners can easily convey their interests, and the transferee automatically becomes a new partner.
- Joint stock companies are governed by a board of managers rather than their members, the owners have personal liability, and they are taxed as corporations, thus combining the most undesirable features of partnerships and corporations.
- Business trusts are managed by trustees rather than the beneficial owners and are taxed as corporations, combining undesirable features of partnerships and corporations, except that the owners usually have no personal liability.
- Real estate investment trusts are formed as partnerships, trusts, or corporations to buy, develop, operate, and sell real estate assets; they offer liquidity to their owner investors because the interests are often traded on the major stock exchanges.

F. Role of Paralegal

Because the forms of business enterprises discussed in this chapter are not as familiar to those in the legal profession as other more conventional business enterprises, paralegals assisting in the formation of any of the business enterprises in this chapter will need to conduct research to learn as much as possible about these enterprises. Some are not governed by statute and, therefore, cases may need to be examined and discussed with your attorney to determine how courts have treated these organizations in a particular state.

A good starting point for drafting a joint venture agreement or a mining partnership agreement is a general partnership agreement, which should then be tailored to the laws in your state. The form used in Chapter Three to obtain information from clients (Figure 3-9) may also be used to assist in the drafting of the pertinent documents for formation and operation of these enterprises.

Resource Guide

The various resources discussed in Chapter Three for general partnerships should be reviewed. Most important is any statutory law controlling joint ventures, mining partnerships, joint stock companies, business trusts, or REITs. After determining whether statutes control any of these enterprises, cases interpreting those statutes will need careful review to see how those enterprises have been treated in your jurisdiction.

Because these types of business enterprises are not as widely used as others, there are few forms to assist you in drafting documents pertinent to these organizations. The best introduction to these types of business is likely found in an encyclopedia. If your jurisdiction has its own state-specific encyclopedia, use it. Otherwise, consult C.J.S. or Am. Jur. 2d for relevant information.

Although many of these forms of business enterprise are not widely used in the United States, they have a certain amount of historical and academic interest and, therefore, several periodical articles deal with these businesses. Consult the *Index to Periodicals* or *Current Law Index* to locate law review or other articles written on these forms of business. You should also check the index to the annotations in A.L.R. (*American Law Reports*), as there are some scholarly essays or articles relating to these somewhat unusual business enterprises.

Forms for the formation and operation of joint ventures, joint stock companies, business trusts, and REITs can be found in Am. Jur. Legal Forms 2d as well as in West's Legal Forms 2d.

◆ ◆ ◆

WEB RESOURCES

To obtain basic information about the types of business associations described in this chapter, access <www.ask.com> and type in your question (for example, "Where can I find information about joint ventures?") in the box provided. You will be directed to a number of sites. As of this date, there is little information on the Internet relating to mining partnerships, joint stock companies, or business trusts, probably because they are either of interest to such a narrow segment of the population or because they are unknown to most investors. The following sites are of interest, although you should always review a form carefully and modify it to suit a client's specific needs:

www.ilrg.com
The Internet Legal Research Guide provides a form for the formation of a joint venture.

http://legal-resource.com/forms
This site provides a form for a joint venture agreement.

www.lectlaw.com/formb.htm
The 'Lectric Law Library provides two separate forms for joint venture agreements.

www.law.cornell.edu/topics/joint_ventures.htm
This Web site of Cornell Law School provides very basic information about joint ventures.

www.reitnet.com
This site provides a comprehensive guide to REITs, with information about REITs, descriptions of types of REITs and the benefits of REITs.

http://invest-faq.com/articles/real-es-reit.htm
Access this site for articles about real estate investment trusts.

Discussion Questions

1. Tony and Barbara intend to construct two houses for sale during a sabbatical they are taking from their teaching careers. Once the houses sell, they intend to return to their teaching positions. Which of the forms of business structure discussed in this chapter is most suitable for the enterprise? Discuss and describe why the structure you selected is likely more suitable than a general partnership.
2. Assume Tony and Barbara have formed their business entity but have no agreement regarding dividing profits and losses. How will profits made on the sale of the houses be divided? Why?
3. Without Tony's knowledge, Barbara has purchased extremely expensive light fixtures for the houses. Who is liable to pay for the fixtures and why?
4. Describe two advantages a partnership has over a joint stock company and over a business trust.
5. In what way does a REIT provide liquidity for its owner investors?

8

Introduction to Corporations

CHAPTER OVERVIEW

Corporations are the first form of business enterprise examined thus far that exist alone from their members, so that the death, withdrawal, or bankruptcy of one of the owners of the corporation never affects the legal existence of the corporation. The next several chapters examine the business corporation, namely a corporation formed for profit-making purposes. Other types of corporations also exist: nonprofit corporations such as charitable and educational corporations, and professional corporations for doctors, lawyers, and accountants. For the most part, these other types of corporations will be discussed in Chapter Seventeen.

As discussed in Chapter One, although there are far fewer corporations than sole proprietorships, they account for a disproportionately high share of revenue. Nearly 800,000 new businesses are incorporated each year. The rate of failure is roughly 10 percent of the rate of incorporation. *Statistical Abstract of the United States* 553 (118th ed. 1998).

This chapter introduces the business corporation, discusses some of its most notable features, and distinguishes privately held corporations (those whose stock is not sold publicly and is usually held by a small number of friends and relatives) from publicly held corporations (those whose stock is traded publicly).

Because a corporation is truly a "person" in the view of the law, *it* pays taxes. This concept of double taxation has been referred to previously. The corporation itself pays taxes on its earnings; when those earnings are later distributed to the owners of the corporation, the shareholders, they pay taxes on certain distributions or dividends received by them. This chapter also examines some of the ways "double taxation" may be avoided or reduced.

A. Characteristics of Corporations

Corporation
A legal entity created by a state to carry out business (if a for-profit entity)

Corporations, like limited partnerships, registered limited liability partnerships, and limited liability companies, are creatures of statute and can only be formed by compliance with various statutory formalities. A corporation exists only when the state declares it to be in existence, and dissolves (or loses its status as a separate entity) only when the state officially terminates its existence. A corporation derives its existence from the state, while a partnership derives its existence from the agreement of its members. Corporations can comprise one shareholder or hundreds of thousands of shareholders.

According to legal theory, the corporation is a *person*. In fact, the root word for "incorporate" is *corpus,* Latin for "body." Thus, incorporation results in the existence of a new body or person that exists independently from its members. While a sole proprietorship dies with the death of the sole proprietor, all of the shareholders of a corporation could die tomorrow, and the corporation would continue its existence. This new person is also liable for the contracts it signs, the obligations it incurs, and the money it borrows. Because the corporation is not a *natural person* as are living and breathing individuals, but rather is an *artificial person,* it must act through its duly appointed agents: its board of directors and its officers. While the president of a corporation may actually sign his or her name to a contract, he or she is not bound by the contract. The corporation, the artificial person, the "it," is bound.

B. Governing Law

A corporation is governed by the laws of the state in which it is organized. Similarly, a corporation formed in one state and doing business in another is subject to the laws of both jurisdictions. Corporations operating in every state are often subject to a patchwork quilt of laws. For example, a corporation may be formed in California for restaurant and bar services. If that corporation decides to transact business in Utah, it will be subject to Utah's restrictions regarding the serving of alcoholic beverages. Similarly, some states allow grocery stores to sell hard liquor, wine, and beer; other states allow grocery stores to sell only wine and beer; still others prohibit the stores from selling any alcoholic beverages. For a national food chain, such as Safeway, these conflicts present complex issues of regulation and compliance with a number of laws. Moreover, states may regulate corporations formed outside their jurisdictions differently from their own domestic corporations. Such variation in treatment between domestic and foreign corporations is rarely done in actual practice, however, because to disfavor out-of-state corporations would discourage businesses from coming into the state.

RMBCA
Revised Model Business Corporation Act; act upon which individual state statutes governing corporations are based

Each of the 50 states and the District of Columbia has its own statutes governing corporations formed in or doing business in that jurisdiction. Nearly all of these state laws are based on the 1950 Model Business Corporation Act, drafted by a section of the American Bar Association. In 1984, the **Revised Model Business Corporation Act (RMBCA)** was drafted. (See Appendix F.) Since 1984, some other revisions and additions have been made to the RMBCA. Each state that has considered and adopted the Model Business Corporation Act or the RMBCA has added its own provisions and deleted others. Thus, while the laws relating to corporations are somewhat similar across the country, each particular state's statutes must be carefully analyzed to ensure compliance with a state's requirements as to formation, operation, and regulation of business corporations within its borders. See Appendix A for a citation to each state's corporations' statutes.

Delaware's General Corporation Law is also viewed as a model by many states. Moreover, many of the largest publicly traded corporations in this country have been incorporated in Delaware. Selected statutes from the Delaware General Corporation Law are found in Appendix G.

In addition to the statutes governing corporations, some states have a rich and complex body of case law interpreting those statutes. Therefore, to understand fully the requirements of any one state, both its corporation statutes and the cases interpreting those statutes must be consulted.

Various federal statutes, such as the Securities Act of 1933 and the Securities Exchange Act of 1934, also govern corporations whose stock is sold to members of the public at large. A thorough discussion of these federal statutes is found in Chapter Thirteen.

In addition to being governed by various laws, corporations are also governed by two basic documents: the ***articles of incorporation***, which provides basic information about and is needed to create the corporation; and the ***bylaws*** of the corporation, its own internal rules for operation.

C. The Corporation as a Person

Corporations, being artificial persons, enjoy many of the same rights and privileges as natural persons. Thus, many of the rights enjoyed by people under the United States Constitution apply equally to corporations. For example, corporations have certain rights of free speech guaranteed under the First Amendment, including both free commercial speech, such as that found in advertising, and free political speech to express their positions on political issues. Corporations have the right under the Fourth Amendment to be protected from unreasonable searches and seizures. However, they do not possess the right against self-incrimination applicable to individuals by the Fifth Amendment. While corporate officers and employees "taking the Fifth" cannot be compelled to testify against themselves, the corporation itself has no such Fifth Amendment privilege. Under the Fourteenth Amendment, corporations, like individuals, cannot be deprived of property without due process. Corporations may be defamed and can bring actions for libel (written defamation) and slander (oral defamation).

In one interesting and recent case, Procter & Gamble Company ("P&G") sued Amway for allegedly disseminating a rumor that P&G supported satanic cults. The rumor began in the early 1980s with allegations that P&G's famous 1851 trademark, a bearded "man in the moon," was a symbol of Satanism. The rumor has so plagued P&G that its own Web site discusses the rumor and strenuously refutes it by describing the origins of the trademark. The case filed by P&G in 1999 was dismissed by the district court. Nevertheless, it is a potent reminder that corporations can be injured by defamation and can commit defamation or trade disparagement. P&G's complaint alleged it had sustained several hundred million dollars in lost sales.

A corporation can be held civilly liable for the torts committed by its agents, officers, and employees. For example, a corporation can be liable for defamation of another or can be liable for the act of one of its employees who wrongfully restrains a customer for alleged shoplifting.

In general, corporations themselves have been found incapable of forming the intent needed to commit certain crimes; however, corporations can be held liable for the wrongful acts of their officers, agents, and employees and can be subjected to fines. The individual corporate wrongdoers may, of course, be found guilty of criminal acts such as bribery, conspiracy, or insider trading and securities fraud, and can be imprisoned or fined.

For the purposes of the confidential communications between attorneys and their clients, the corporation is viewed as a client and, thus, its attorneys must keep privileged information disclosed in confidence (so long as the communication does not involve the commission of fraud or a crime). Advice given by counsel to help a client perpetrate fraud or a crime is neither ethical nor privileged; however, advice given to the corporation after the wrongful act has been completed is privileged.

Other than some exceptions for small-claims court actions, corporations must appear in court through an attorney and cannot represent themselves in court as a natural person may do. Similarly, the corporation does not have certain other rights, such as the power to vote, the ability to adopt a child, or the rights to "life, liberty, and the pursuit of happiness."

When reading statutes that refer to "persons," review the definitions given to determine if a person subject to a certain law includes a corporation (or another association, such as a partnership).

D. Corporate Powers and Purposes

Corporate powers
List of activities enumerated by a state in which a corporation can engage

Each state's corporation statute grants certain **powers** to the corporation to enable it to conduct business. RMBCA Section 3.02 provides a list of corporate powers. Among the powers typically granted to a corporation by state law are the following:

a. to sue and be sued and to defend in the corporation's own name (rather than in the names of the officers, directors, or shareholders);
b. to make and amend bylaws for regulating the business of the corporation;
c. to purchase, acquire, own, hold, improve, sell, lease, or mortgage real or personal property;
d. to enter into contracts, incur liabilities, borrow money, issue bonds, and lend money;
e. to elect directors and appoint officers;
f. to establish pension and other benefit plans for its directors, officers, agents, and employees;

g. to make donations for the public welfare;
h. to make payments or donations that further the business of the corporation (such as those for political purposes);
i. to purchase and hold shares or other interests in other entities;
j. to be a member or manager of a partnership or other entity;
k. to have and use a corporate seal;
l. to transact any lawful business; and
m. to exist perpetually.

A state's statutes provide the maximum authority for a corporation. While a corporation can elect not to engage in all of the activities allowed by the statute, it cannot engage in any activity that is inconsistent with the statutorily enumerated list of powers. In the event its articles of incorporation or bylaws are inconsistent with the state statutes, the statutes will control.

A corporation's purposes are different from its powers. Its purposes are the goals and objectives it intends to achieve, for example, developing real estate, operating a restaurant, or providing computer services. These specific purposes may be stated in its articles of incorporation. A corporation's purposes are also provided for in the state statute. In the state statutes, however, the purposes are stated in general and broad terms, such as the following: "Corporations in this state may be organized for any lawful purpose." A corporation will use its powers to achieve its purposes.

E. Types of Corporations

There are various types of corporations. While most of these will be detailed in Chapter Seventeen, a brief introduction to the classification of corporations will be helpful to understand thoroughly the modern business corporation, the primary focus of our discussion.

1. *Domestic Corporations*

A corporation is a **domestic corporation** in the state in which it incorporated. For example, assume Standard Candy Company, Inc. was incorporated in Tennessee. In Tennessee, it is referred to as a domestic corporation.

Domestic corporation
A corporation operating in the state of its incorporation

2. *Foreign Corporations*

A corporation formed in one state and doing business in another is referred to in the second state as a **foreign corporation.** Thus, Standard Candy Company, Inc., which is authorized to do business in several states, is a domestic corporation in Tennessee and a foreign corporation in California and Minnesota. Corporations formed outside of the United States are also sometimes referred to as foreign corporations. The more appropriate term for a corporation formed in another country is **alien corporation.**

Foreign corporation
A corporation operating in a state other than its state of incorporation

Alien corporation
A corporation formed outside the United States

3. *Federal or State Corporations*

Federal or state corporation
An entity formed under the authority of a federal or state statute for some public good

Entities formed under the authority of a federal statute, a state constitution, or a state statute are also corporations. The Tennessee Valley Authority is a federal corporation formed to develop the resources of the Tennessee Valley. Many towns and cities are incorporated. These corporations are formed to meet some public or governmental need. On occasion, they are referred to as "public" corporations. This term is often misconstrued; most people use the term public corporation to indicate a corporation whose shares are sold to members of the general public (rather than held by a few friends or family members).

4. *Public Corporations*

Public corporation
A corporation whose shares are sold to the public at large

Public corporations (also called *publicly held* or *publicly traded* corporations) are corporations whose shares are sold to the public at large. These corporations may be giants in the industry — IBM, General Motors, Microsoft Corporation — or may simply be large corporations whose stock is available for purchase by the public. Both purchase and transfer of shares are easily accomplished.

5. *Privately Held Corporations*

Privately held corporation
A corporation whose shares are owned by a small group, usually family or friends

Many corporations are formed by a few family members or friends. Ownership of shares is limited to a few people and the shares are not sold to the public at large. These **privately held corporations** tend to be smaller enterprises, perhaps a retail store, a computer consulting company, or a landscaping business. Shareholders usually enter into agreements with each other providing that they will not sell their shares to any "outsiders" before offering them to the existing shareholders or to the corporation itself.

6. *Nonprofit Corporations*

Nonprofit corporation
A corporation formed not to make a profit but for public benefit, religious purposes, or the mutual benefit of its members

A **nonprofit corporation** (or "not-for-profit" corporation) is one that is not formed for the purpose of making a profit, but rather for some charitable, educational, scientific, or religious purpose, or for the mutual benefit of its members.

7. *Close Corporations*

Close corporation
A corporation whose shares are held by a small group of shareholders and that is allowed to act informally

A **close corporation** is one whose shares are held by a few people. Under most state laws, a corporation can elect to be a close corporation. A corporation permitted this status is often allowed certain flexibility with regard to corporate formalities that regular business corporations are not. For example, the shareholders in a close corporation are allowed to participate in management of the corporation yet retain their limited liability. They may also be allowed more latitude with regard to holding meetings and elections. The shareholders in a close corporation usually sign agreements restricting the transfer of shares so they cannot offer shares for sale to a third party without first offering them to another member in the close corporation or to the corporation itself. The rapid rise in popularity of the limited liability company, which affords full protection from liability for its members who may manage the company themselves or appoint managers, has caused a decrease in interest in close corporations.

8. *Professional Corporations*

A **professional corporation** is formed by an individual or group of persons practicing a certain profession, such as law, medicine, accounting, or engineering.

Professional corporation
A corporation organized by professionals, such as doctors

9. *S Corporations*

S corporations (formerly called "subchapter S corporations" after the Internal Revenue Act subchapter that allowed for their creation) are formed to minimize the drastic effect double taxation has on small business corporations. Corporations that meet certain criteria (those with no more than 75 individual shareholders who cannot be nonresident aliens) may elect to qualify as S corporations. In this event, the corporation does not pay tax on income it receives; all of the income is passed through to the shareholders who pay tax on the income at their appropriate rates. In this respect, an S corporation is similar to a partnership; however, it offers the advantages of limited liability for the shareholders. The limited liability company discussed in Chapter Five is thought to provide all of the advantages of an S corporation, without any of its limitations, particularly with regard to number of shareholders. Corporations that are not S corporations are referred to as **C corporations.** An S corporation is not truly a different type of corporation but is merely one that has elected and qualifies for pass-through taxation.

S corporation
A corporation that avoids double taxation by passing through all of its income to its shareholders

C corporation
A corporation that is not an S corporation and that is subject to double taxation

10. *Parent and Subsidiary Corporations*

A corporation that creates or forms another corporation is called a **parent corporation.** Typically, the parent will hold all or the vast majority of the stock of the corporation it has formed, the **subsidiary.** Thus, the expression "wholly owned subsidiary" refers to a corporation whose stock is owned entirely by its parent.

Parent corporation
A corporation that creates another corporation (the subsidiary)

Subsidiary corporation
A corporation created by another (the parent)

F. Advantages and Disadvantages of Incorporation

1. *Advantages*

Limited Liability. Probably the greatest advantage of selecting the corporate form for doing business is the limited liability protection the corporation offers to its shareholders, directors, and officers. Because the corporation can enter into contracts and borrow money in its own name (rather than the names of its shareholders, directors, or officers), it is responsible for meeting those obligations and debts.

Shareholders in Ford Motor Company may see their stock fall in value. In a worst case scenario, the stock may become worthless. Nevertheless, the shareholders are not liable for the corporation's debts and liabilities. Their risk is limited to their investment: Their stock may decrease in value to nothing but their personal assets are not at risk to satisfy corporate obligations. Similarly, directors and officers will not be liable for corporate obligations so long as they do not act with gross negligence or breach their duties of due care.

Because personal assets are not available to corporate creditors, these creditors will carefully scrutinize a corporation before extending credit or making loans. The creditors may require the corporation to provide financial statements to ensure the corporation has sufficient assets to meet or repay its obligations. Similarly, a creditor may require a corporation to pledge some asset as security for a loan; in the event the loan is not repaid, the creditor will then seize the asset to satisfy the obligation. In other instances where a corporation is financially weak, or it has no proven track record of financial stability, before lending money a bank or creditor may require that corporate directors, officers, or shareholders personally guarantee a loan so that if the corporation cannot repay the debt, the individual will be liable for it. Thus, in a practical sense, the concept of "limited liability" may be negated by a requirement that the corporate owners guarantee obligations. Nevertheless, the owners will have liability only for those obligations they expressly agree to accept, and they will know in advance their potential risk.

Because limited liability exists for the shareholders of a corporation, it is easy for a corporation to attract capital. Many individuals and businesses are willing to invest in an enterprise when their maximum exposure can be predetermined.

Corporate Deductions. While corporations are taxpaying entities, they are entitled to a wide range of deductions which can be used to offset corporate income. Items such as rent, insurance, and salaries can be deducted from the corporation's income before determining the amount on which the corporation will pay tax. Other typical deductions include interest expenses, utilities, legal and accounting costs, supplies, and some entertainment and travel expenses, if they are business related.

The corporation may also establish various benefit plans for employees. These not only attract quality workers, but are also used to reduce taxable income. For example, a corporation may provide life insurance for its employees. The corporation is allowed to deduct the expense of the premiums paid to maintain the insurance as a business expense and the employee is not taxed on the value of this benefit. Of course, when the employee dies, the estate may be taxed on the insurance proceeds.

Similarly, a corporation may provide a pension plan for its employees. Employees are allowed to contribute a certain amount of their salary pre-tax. The corporation may match this amount to some percentage. The corporation can deduct the amount it matches as a business expense. The employee does not pay tax on the amount contributed until he receives the money, typically when the employee is older and in a lower tax bracket.

Continuity of Existence. A corporation can endure perpetually. Thus, businesses intending to operate for extended periods should consider the corporate form. The sole proprietorship terminates on the death of the sole proprietor; a partnership may dissolve upon the death or withdrawal of a partner; and a limited liability company may be limited to a statutorily set term of existence; a corporation, however, survives the death of its shareholders and the transfer of their stock to some third party.

Transferability of Share Ownership. A person's ownership interest in a corporation is shown by a document called a **stock certificate.** The stock certificate is not what is owned; it merely represents ownership in a corporation. Shares (or stock) in a corporation are freely transferable. In many instances, unless there are restrictions on the sale of stock, selling stock to another is no more complex than endorsing a check over to another person. The back of the stock certificate generally contains information for transferring the stock to another. Stock in a publicly traded corporation is also easily acquired. A simple phone call to a broker, or an online trade, will initiate the purchase of stock. Sales of stock are often made through brokers (or online) as well. This easy transferability is in contrast to sole proprietorships, which cannot be transferred without terminating the sole proprietorship, or other forms of business entities that may dissolve upon a full transfer of an owner's interest.

Stock certificate
The document that represents ownership in a corporation

Shares can be given as gifts to another and, similar to other property, can be left to one's heirs upon death. The new owner inherits all rights of the deceased shareholder with regard to voting, distribution of dividends, and so forth.

2. *Disadvantages*

Double Taxation. The biggest disadvantage of corporations is **double taxation** of the income of the corporation. As a separate person or entity, the corporation's income is subject to taxation at certain rates applicable to corporations. The imposition of tax on the corporate enterprise itself is far different from taxation principles relating to sole proprietorships, general and limited partnerships, registered limited liability partnerships, and limited liability companies, all of which pass through all the income earned by the business to the owners who then pay tax at whatever rate is applicable to them (unless they have elected to be taxed as corporations under the new IRS "check the box" approach).

Double taxation
Concept in corporate law in which money earned by a corporation is taxed; when remainder is distributed to shareholders, they are also taxed

After paying taxes on its income, the corporation may then apportion its profits to shareholders in the form of distributions. Money received by shareholders, even $1, must be declared as income subject to taxation. Thus, the same money is taxed twice: once when the corporation receives it and then again when it is distributed to the shareholders.

The concept of double taxation is not really so peculiar. In many instances, money is taxed twice. For example, you pay tax on income earned from your employment. When you take a portion of that income and pay your landscaper or piano teacher, or purchase shoes at a retail store, that income must be reported by the recipient, who pays tax on the money received from you. Similarly, in some states, the purchase of a car is subject to sales tax. Assume a car is sold to its first owner for $20,000. Tax will be paid on the sum of $20,000. After five years, the owner may sell the car to another for $15,000. The new owner must now pay sales tax on the sum of $15,000. If the car is sold a third time for $10,000, the final owner must pay sales tax on the sum of $10,000. Thus, the same item has been subject to taxation on several occasions.

Avoiding Double Taxation. Various measures may be taken to avoid double taxation. They include the following:

S Corporations. Some corporations avoid the burden of double taxation by electing to be S corporations. There are several restrictions as to the election of S status, and it is not an option for any corporation having more than 75 individual shareholders. S corporations are discussed in Chapter Seventeen.

Small Corporations whose Shareholders are Employees. Small corporations whose stock is held by a few family members or friends all actively employed by the corporation can also reduce the burden of double taxation. While these corporations pay tax on income earned, they do not give distributions to the shareholders. If all of the shareholders are employed in the business, each will receive a merit bonus or Christmas bonus or salary increase rather than a "dividend" as a way of sharing in the corporation's profits. While the recipient of the bonus or salary must still pay tax on that money received, the distribution of salaries or bonuses is a deduction for a corporation which can be used to offset income and reduce tax liability. Naturally, this technique is not available to larger or publicly traded corporations whose stock is owned by nonemployees. There would be no justification for Texaco Inc. giving its shareholders a Christmas bonus and then deducting this as a business expense.

Section 1244 stock
Stock upon the sale of which (at a loss) receives favorable tax treatment and is taxed as an ordinary loss

Section 1244 Stock. "Small business corporations" may automatically qualify under **Section 1244** of the Internal Revenue Code for the shareholders to receive certain favorable tax treatment on the sale of their stock at a loss. The definition of a small business corporation for purposes of Section 1244 is different from that used in connection with S corporations. For an S corporation, there is a limit on the number of shareholders who hold stock. For Section 1244 purposes, "small business" relates not to how many people will be in the corporation but to the amount of money the corporation plans to raise by selling stock. The amount of all money and all property received by the corporation for stock cannot exceed $1 million.

Ordinary loss
A loss that can be used to offset ordinary income

Capital loss
A loss that can only be used to offset capital gains rather than ordinary losses

If the requirements of Section 1244 of the Internal Revenue Code are met, stock sold at a loss will automatically receive favorable tax treatment. The loss will be treated as an **ordinary loss,** rather than a "capital" loss, meaning that shareholders can use that loss to offset ordinary income, thus resulting in a lower taxable income. If stock is not qualified as Section 1244 stock, shareholders who sustain losses on the sale of stock must treat those losses as capital losses. **Capital losses** do not offset ordinary income but rather can only be used to offset **capital gains**—gains acquired through the sale of assets that have appreciated in value from the date of their original acquisition. If a shareholder has no capital gains in a year, the shareholder cannot deduct a capital loss sustained that year (although there are some carry-forward provisions that may allow the shareholder some deduction). If the stock is Section 1244 stock, a loss incurred when it is sold can be used to offset ordinary income (such as salaries) up to a maximum of $50,000 per year for individuals and $100,000 in the case of spouses filing joint returns.

Capital gains
Gains acquired through the sale of appreciated assets

Thus, Section 1244 provides certain tax benefits to shareholders in a small business. Under Section 1244, the corporation's shareholders will receive some favorable tax treatment if they sell their stock at a loss. Qualification of stock as Section 1244 stock presupposes the corporation will suffer losses. Nevertheless, it is a useful device and places shareholders on a more equal footing with sole proprietors and partners who are able to treat losses as ordinary rather than capital losses. Confirmation that the corporation desires the benefits of Section 1244 can be accomplished at a meeting of the corporation's directors. In many cases, confirmation takes place at the corporation's first organizational meeting.

Qualified Small Business Stock. Another way corporations can avoid or minimize the effect of double taxation is through the provisions of Section 1202 of the Internal Revenue Code (26 U.S.C. §1202), enacted in 1993 to allow individuals who hold **"qualified small business stock"** for more than five years to exclude one-half of any gain they realize on the sale of such stock. The remaining one-half of the gain is taxed as a capital gain.

Qualified small business stock
Stock issued by a qualified corporation that provides certain tax benefits on the gain realized on sale of the stock

A "qualified small business" must satisfy the following three elements:

- the corporation must be a C corporation (rather than a corporation that has elected S status to achieve pass-through single taxation);
- its total gross assets must be less than $50 million at the time the stock is issued; and
- at least 80 percent of the value of its assets must be used in the active conduct of qualified trades and businesses (a qualified trade or business is one in which the principal asset is not the reputation or skill of one or more of its employees).

Thus, corporations involving the performance of services in the fields of health, law, accounting, engineering, architecture, and financial services do not qualify for the favored tax treatment, because they are dependent upon the skill and reputation of the individuals involved. Additionally, other types of businesses are expressly excluded, such as banking, insurance, farming, and restaurant and hotel businesses. Other businesses, however, will qualify, and their shareholders will be able to exclude from the computation of their taxes one-half of the gain they realize on the sale of stock held for more than five years.

Limited Liability Companies. Limited liability companies, discussed in Chapter Six, avoid double taxation while providing limited liability to the members. All of the income earned by the company is passed through to the members who then pay taxes on the income received. Limited liability companies have a limited period of duration in some states. Therefore, they may not be suitable for every type of business enterprise and may not be suitable for businesses desiring to do business on a national scope.

Formalities of Organization and Operation. Forming a corporation requires strict compliance with the corporation laws of the state of incorporation. Incorporation fees are charged and preparing the documents may require the assistance of an attorney, thus necessitating attorneys' fees. Similarly, other documents filed with the state must also be accompanied by fees, such as amendments to the corporation's articles of incorporation, changes to the corporation's name, reports of mergers, or dissolution of the corporation.

Moreover, each state imposes annual filing or reporting requirements on corporations either incorporated in or doing business in that state. The documents must be timely filed and accompanied by the appropriate fee. See Figure 8-1 for Massachusetts's annual report form. After the corporation is formed, it must continue to comply with various statutory formalities, such as the requirement for an annual meeting of shareholders, elections of directors, and certain financial reporting and disclosure requirements made to shareholders.

The corporation must also file a tax return each year with the Internal Revenue Service and in the various states in which it does business. Publicly traded companies are subject to intensive reporting and disclosure requirements imposed by the Securities and Exchange Commission (see Chapter Thirteen).

These reporting and filing requirements make the corporation the most difficult business enterprise to form and maintain. Failure to comply with these various formalities may result in dissolution of the corporation by the state or in the loss of shareholders' limited liability status. (See Chapter Eleven for a discussion of "piercing the corporate veil" to allow creditors to pursue individual shareholders for corporate obligations.)

Centralized Management. While shareholders own the corporation, they do not manage it. Shareholders vote for *directors* who then manage the corporation as a board and appoint individuals called *officers* (president, vice-president, secretary, treasurer, and so forth) to manage the daily activities of the corporation. Individuals who wish to manage and operate a business personally may prefer to operate as sole proprietors, general partners, or members of limited liability partnerships or limited liability companies. Personal liability, however, may result from being a sole proprietor, general partner, or member of an LLP. While the shareholders in a corporation have some authority to control the directors (by removing them), this power to affect the corporate business is remote at best.

In a small corporation, however, for example, Mom and Pop Retail, Inc., the shareholders will not only own the corporation, they will elect themselves as directors and appoint themselves as officers, enabling shareholders to manage the business and yet still retain limited liability for the debts or obligations of the corporation. In larger, publicly traded corporations, however, the shareholders' only involvement in corporate affairs takes the form of voting for directors and for extraordinary corporate actions, such as a merger or dissolution of the corporation.

FIGURE 8-1
Massachusetts Corporation Annual Report Form

The Commonwealth of Massachusetts
William Francis Galvin
Secretary of the Commonwealth
One Ashburton Place, Boston, Massachusetts 02108-1512
Telephone: (617) 727-9640
NOTE: PLEASE TYPE OR PRINT CLEARLY! INSTRUCTIONS ON OTHER SIDE.

Fee $85.00

MASSACHUSETTS CORPORATION ANNUAL REPORT

Federal Identification No. ____________________

1. The exact name of the corporation is: ____________________
2. Location of its principal office in Massachusetts ____________________

____

NOTE: If corporation is organized wholly to do business outside Massachusetts, state location of that office also:

____

3. Name and address of the Resident Agent, if any: ____________________

____

4. Date of the end of the last fiscal year was: ____________________
5. Check here if the corporation stock is publicly traded: ☐
6. The capital stock of each class as of the end of its last fiscal year was:

CLASS OF STOCK	PAR VALUE PER SHARE STATE IF NO PAR	TOTAL AUTHORIZED BY ARTICLES OF ORGANIZATION OR AMENDMENTS Number of Shares	Total Par Value	TOTAL ISSUED AND OUTSTANDING Number of Shares
COMMON:				
PREFERRED:				

7. State the names and addresses of the officers specified below and of all the directors of the corporation, and the date on which the term of office of each expires:

OFFICERS	NAME	ADDRESS Number, Street, City or Town, State, Zip Code	EXPIRATION OF TERM
PRESIDENT			
TREASURER			
CLERK			
DIRECTORS			

I, the undersigned, ____________________, being the ____________________ of the above-named corporation, in compliance with the General Laws, Chapter 156B, hereby certify that the above information is true and correct as of the dates shown. IN WITNESS WHEREOF AND UNDER PENALTIES OF PERJURY, I hereto sign my name on this ____________________ day of ____________________,

Signature: ____________________ Title: ____________________
MUST BE ORIGINAL

Contact Person: ____________________ Contact Person Telephone #: ____________________

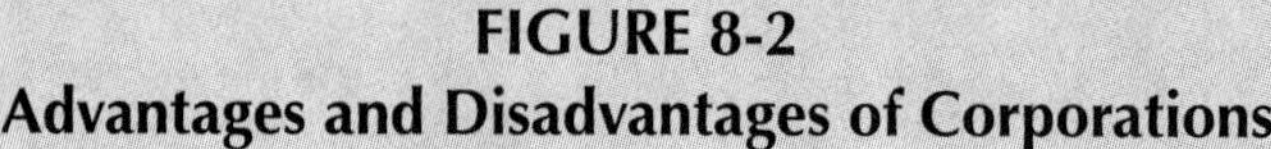

FIGURE 8-2
Advantages and Disadvantages of Corporations

Advantages	*Disadvantages*
Limited liability for directors, officers, shareholders	Double taxation
Wide range of business deductions	Formalities of organization, expense of organization and maintenance
Easy transferability of shares	Centralized management
Continuity of existence	

See Figure 8-2 for a chart summarizing the advantages and disadvantages of corporations.

Key Features of Corporations

- Corporations are persons and exist separate and apart from their owner-shareholders.
- Corporations offer limited liability for their shareholders, officers, and directors, because the corporation itself is liable for its own debts and obligations.
- Corporations can exist perpetually.
- Ownership in corporations is easily transferred.
- Corporations, as persons, are subject to double taxation: the income of a corporation is taxed, and when profits are distributed to shareholders, they also pay tax on the money received.
- Corporations can attempt to minimize double taxation by electing S status.
- The issuance of Section 1244 stock or "qualified small business stock" also provides certain tax advantages to corporate shareholders.
- Corporations can be expensive to form and maintain.
- Management of corporations is centralized in a board of directors; the owner-shareholders do not manage the typical large business corporation.

G. Role of Paralegal

More paralegals are employed in corporate law than any other field except litigation. Paralegals in this practice area engage in a variety of activities including organizing and forming corporations, assisting in maintaining corporations by preparing various resolutions and minutes of meetings, and engaging in corporate transactional work, such as mergers and acquisitions, the sale of stock, or corporate employment issues.

Generally, the attorney involved assists the client in determining which form of business enterprise best suits the client's needs. If it is determined that the corporate form should be selected, the attorney will fully explain the differences between C corporations and S corporations, Section 1244 stock, and the different types of corporations: for-profit, nonprofit, or professional.

The role of the paralegal at this stage is likely limited to fact-gathering and legal research. Inquiries regarding how many shareholders will be involved or how much stock will be issued assist in making determinations such as whether an election for S status should be made or whether stock can be issued pursuant to Section 1244 of the Internal Revenue Code. Information concerning the nature of the activities to be conducted by the enterprise will assist in determining whether the corporation will be for-profit or not-for-profit or perhaps organized as a close corporation or a professional corporation. Research can be conducted to determine any statutory limitations on the powers or purposes of corporations and to prepare to form the corporation. Forms can be gathered and information can be obtained about the costs and procedures of appointing an agent for service of process.

The explanation of these various options is handled by the attorney involved in the matter. Explaining the consequences of double taxation, limited liability, and treatment of losses as ordinary rather than capital, is the type of advice only attorneys can give. As discussed in Chapter Nine, paralegals are, however, intimately involved with the formalities of organizing and creating the corporation, once the type of corporation best fitting the client's particular needs is determined.

Resource Guide

There are five principal sources to consult to obtain further information about the advantages and disadvantages of incorporating, the types of corporations that may be formed, and the features of various types of corporations.

1. Statutes

Because corporations may be formed only in accordance with the pertinent statutory authorities, a thorough review of the statutes in your state is a must. Check the corporations code for your state and review how it is organized. Generally, definitions are given first, information about forming corporations is next, followed by laws relating to governance of the corporations, and, finally, statutes relating to the termination of corporations.

Additionally, review various federal statutes and regulations, such as Sections 1202 and 1244 of the Internal Revenue Code and other Code provisions relating to S corporations.

2. Encyclopedias

Basic information about corporations can be obtained in either of the two general encyclopedias: C.J.S. or Am. Jur. 2d. Check the index to either set and you will be instructed to review the appropriate volume and section. If your state has its own state-specific encyclopedia, consult this rather than one of the general sets. Many state-specific sets include a "table of statutes construed." This allows you to determine quickly which portion of the encyclopedia provides narrative discussion and explanation of certain state statutes. Thus, once you determine the particular statute governing an issue, you can readily locate additional information about it in the encyclopedia.

3. Specialized Texts

There are numerous texts and sets of books that provide thorough and detailed information about corporate law. Check the shelves in your law firm's library to determine what is available. Visit the nearest law school or county law library to review corporate materials. Generally, all of the corporate materials will be gathered together in one section of the law library.

One of the better known treatises in the corporate law field is *Fletcher's Cyclopedia of the Law of Private Corporations,* a multivolume set containing excellent information about corporations. A companion set, *Fletcher's Corporate Forms Annotated,* provides various forms, such as forms for resolutions by directors, forms for minutes of corporate meetings, forms for bylaws, and so forth. The word "annotated" in the name of the set indicates that you will also be sent to pertinent cases relating to the specific topic covered in a form.

4. Form Books

Because paralegals are typically involved in drafting various corporate documents, you need to be acquainted with the form books that will assist you in preparing documents. In addition to *Fletcher's Corporate Forms Annotated,* you may consult *Am. Jur. Legal Forms 2d,* a set of more than 25 volumes of forms (not all of which are related to corporations, however); *West's Legal Forms, 2d,* a set with more than 30 volumes containing forms for general law practice, including for use with corporations; or *Current Legal Forms with Tax Analysis,* an excellent multivolume set including numerous forms useful in corporate law practice.

5. Secretary of State

The office in each state charged with overseeing corporations is the secretary of state. Appendix A provides the name, address, telephone number, and Web site for the secretary of state for each state. The secretary of state can provide you with useful information regarding corporations and will also provide, generally free of charge, the various forms you will need to organize, maintain, and terminate a corporation in that state.

WEB RESOURCES

To obtain basic information about the types of corporations described in this chapter, access <www.ask.com> and type in your question (for example, "Where can I find information about S corporations?" or "Where can I find information about close corporations?") in the box provided. You will be directed to a number of sites. The following sites are of interest and provide a wide variety of general information, forms, and links to other sites.

Of most importance is the review of a state's corporations code. To review state statutes online, access <www.ll.georgetown.edu> the Web site of Georgetown University Law Center. Select "State, Local & Territorial," and you will then be presented with a map of the United States. Point your cursor to the desired state, and you will then be able to select whether you wish to view that state's constitution, statutes, cases, or other legal information. By selecting "Statutes" or "Code," you will be able to search the state's statutes and find relevant corporate statutory material. In some instances, you can search by statute number; in other instances, you can search by keyword. Some states allow you to browse various titles. Search for "Corporations" and then view the statutes within this title.

Other useful Web sites are as follows:

http://www.nass.org
This Web site of the National Association of Secretaries of State allows you to link directly to the home page for each state's secretary of state. All states offer general information about corporations together with forms, checklists, and phone numbers. Point the cursor to "States" and then to your state's name and flag, and proceed to locate information on corporations in your state. Forms for name reservations, articles of incorporation, amendments to articles of incorporation, and forms for dissolution are offered on most state Web sites.

www.irs.gov
The Web site of the Internal Revenue Service offers a wealth of information about taxes, businesses, and provides Form 1120, the corporate tax form that can be downloaded and printed.

www.ask.com
"Ask Jeeves" is an Internet "butler" who will help you find what you need. Simply type in your question, in natural English, in the box presented, and you will be referred to numerous useful sites. For example, type in "Where can I find information about corporations?" You will then be directed to sites offering information on corporations, forms for organization and operation, and forms for bylaws, minutes, resolutions, and various corporate agreements. "Ask.com" is often the first site many individuals access to find information on nearly any topic. Bookmark this site and use it often.

www.tannedfeet.com
Billed as "The Entrepreneurs' Help Page," this site provides a wealth of information regarding the formation and operation of businesses, including corporations. Access <www.tannedfeet.com/> and then go to "Legal." You will be provided with articles on taxation, choice of entity, and a list of further resources.

www.ilrg.com
The Internet Legal Research Guide provides excellent information on businesses, including corporations. Once you access the home page, scroll down to "Practice Areas" and then select "Corporations and Businesses." Alternatively, after you access "Legal," scroll to "U.S. Corporation and Business Forms, Filing Instructions," which provides you with links to each state's statutes, forms, and corporate filing information.

www.lectlaw.com
After you access the home page for The 'Lectric Law Library, scroll down to "Rotunda" and then select "Business Law Lounge" for information on businesses in general and corporations in particular.

www.law.cornell.edu
This Web site of Cornell Law School provides basic information. Access "law about" and then select "corporations" for information about corporations and links to many other useful sites.

www.law.com
This site provides a wide variety of legal information. Access "Business" and then scroll down to "Resources for Business" for forms, business news sites, and information on starting a business. Under "Business," there are links to the state corporations' commissions.

www.surfpoint.com
Surfpoint is primarily a "link exchange," sending you to hundreds of other Web sites. Access "Business" for information, business news, resources, and links to hundreds of other sites.

www.findlaw.com
In addition to sending you to cases and statutes, "FindLaw" offers a variety of business information. Access "Small Business" and then select "Small Business Guide" or "Business Tools" for general information and links to sites assisting with business formation.

www.ll.georgetown.edu
This link to Georgetown University Law Center provides excellent information on numerous legal topics. Access "By Topic" and then select "Corporations" for numerous links to government agencies, associations, and gateways to commercial and corporate law sites.

Select "Legal Sites" and then "Corporations Departments and Secretary of State Pages" to link directly to each state's secretary of state home page, which will in turn direct you to forms and general information.

Discussion Questions

1. Papa John's International Inc. has been using the slogan "Fresh Ingredients—not like Pizza Hut" in a recent advertising campaign. Pizza Hut, which uses only fresh ingredients, has sustained losses in sales ever since the ad began. Discuss whether the Pizza Hut Corporation can initiate any action in regard to the ad.
2. Discuss the primary way in which Jacobson Supplies, Inc., a corporation with three shareholders, can avoid double taxation.
3. Henderson and Henderson, Inc., a California corporation, owned by two shareholders, has had a judgment rendered against it in the amount of $100,000. The corporation has only $80,000 in its various accounts. Are the shareholders liable to pay the remainder of the judgment after the creditor has been paid the $80,000 in corporate funds?
4. Can ABC Inc., an Indiana corporation, be a general partner in a general partnership? Can ABC Inc. own stock in Henderson and Henderson, Inc.? What provision of the RMBCA governs your answers? If ABC Inc. owns stock in Henderson and Henderson, Inc., can the latter corporation elect S status?
5. Assume that Jacobs Machinery Inc. is an S corporation. May its stockholders achieve any tax advantages on the sale of their stock as "qualified small business stock"?

9

Formation of Corporations

CHAPTER OVERVIEW

Forming a corporation requires a certain amount of preparation and planning. Thought must be given to selecting the jurisdiction in which to incorporate, selecting the corporate name and ensuring it is available for the corporation, attracting capital for the enterprise, and drafting the various documents to complete the incorporation process.

This chapter discusses the activities taken prior to incorporation and those required to effect and complete the incorporation process. The people involved in the effort of organizing the corporation, promoters, may enter into contracts on behalf of the proposed corporation. They may also assist the attorney and paralegal in preparing the articles of incorporation, the document that creates a corporation. After a corporation is formed, certain formalities, such as ordering corporate supplies, must be accomplished. Finally, the new corporation needs to adopt bylaws for its governance and hold an organizational meeting to begin its business.

A. Preincorporation Activities by Promoters

1. *Duties of Promoters*

The people involved in forming a corporation and organizing its structure are referred to as **promoters.** While the term promoter may have a slightly unsavory connotation in other contexts, in the context of preincorporation activities, it refers solely to the persons who plan and create the corporation.

Promoter
One involved in organizing a corporation (also called *incorporator*)

During the process of planning and forming the corporation, the promoters are viewed as joint venturers—specifically, partners who have undertaken one particular activity, that of forming a corporation. As joint venturers, the promoters owe duties of good faith and fiduciary duties to each other and to the proposed corporation. The promoters may have a written agreement defining their rights and responsibilities, but because a joint venture can be created without a written agreement, one is not required. If, however, the parties contemplate making substantial contributions to the corporation or will be engaging in extensive activities on behalf of the corporation, the promoters should have a formal written agreement defining their rights and obligations to each other and to the proposed corporation. A form of joint venture agreement is available from your instructor.

Even without a written agreement, however, the fiduciary relationship promoters share requires them to deal in good faith. Thus, they may be liable for failing to disclose pertinent information or for secret profits obtained. For example, one promoter may be charged with the responsibility of finding a lot on which to build the corporate offices. If a promoter owns real estate and wishes to sell this to the proposed corporation, he must disclose all material information about the property. Failure to disclose that the property is subject to certain zoning and building restrictions imposing limitations on the size of the building that may be constructed or failure to disclose defects about the lot, such as drainage or access problems, would be a violation of the fiduciary duties owed by a promoter. Disclosure should be made to the other promoters and to any prospective shareholders or others who may be interested in the corporation. Similarly, full disclosure must be made if a promoter might stand to gain by a transaction (such as owning the lot next to the one he proposes the corporation buy and build upon when construction would enhance the value of his lot).

2. *Agreements by Promoters*

Preincorporation contracts
Agreements entered into by promoters on behalf of a yet-to-be formed corporation

During the course of planning the corporation and organizing it, promoters frequently enter into agreements, called **preincorporation contracts** with third parties. For example, assume Carlos, Ellen, and Amanda are the promoters for a proposed corporation that will engage in making and selling gift baskets. Carlos may be assigned the task of finding office space for the corporation, Ellen may be in charge of hiring a receptionist and a secretary, and Amanda may be responsible for ordering stationery and advertising and promotional brochures and contracting for development of a Web site for the new business. Carlos might therefore approach a landlord and offer to lease space. The landlord might engage in remodeling of the space pursuant to Carlos' instructions and may take the property off the market. Ellen may advertise for employees and hire two individuals who leave their present jobs in reliance on getting jobs at the new business. Amanda may order the stationery and brochures printed by a local company at great expense and may engage a Web site developer who begins working on the project.

Problems will arise if for some reason, such as a falling-out among the promoters, the corporation is never formed. The landlord is left with a remodeled space which has not been on the market for several weeks; the would-be employees have quit their former jobs; the printer has materials never to be used by anyone; and the Web site developer has created Web content for a site that will never be launched. The landlord, the would-be employees, the printer, and the Web site developer will want compensation for their damages. The corporation cannot be liable because it does not exist. If the promoter had obtained a promise from the third party that it will hold only the corporation liable and not the promoter, the promoter will have no liability in the event of any breach of agreement. More complex issues arise when the parties do not clearly indicate their intentions.

Courts have used a variety of theories to hold the promoters liable for their preincorporation agreements and thereby protect innocent third parties with whom the promoters have been dealing. If the promoter has signed a written agreement (such as Carlos signing a lease), the promoter is clearly bound by the terms of the agreement. If there is no signed agreement, courts generally hold the promoter has impliedly agreed to be bound. Only when there is an express intention to release the promoter from liability will the promoter be able to avoid liability for agreements he or she has entered into before the corporation is formed. In sum, in ambiguous cases, the trend is to hold promoters personally liable on contracts entered into before the corporation is formed.

In essence, this makes promoters no different from the organizers of any other form of business, who will always be liable to others who act in reliance on their actions. Promoters are thus liable, just as a sole proprietor or partners would be liable, if they enter into some agreement that causes a third party to take some action, even if the business enterprise never really gets off the ground. Some states deal with promoter liability by statute. For example, in Georgia, all persons purporting to act on behalf of a corporation with actual knowledge that there is no incorporation are jointly and severally liable for all liabilities created while so acting. Ga. Code Ann. Section 14-2-204.

When the corporation is formed, the joint venturer relationship among the promoters dissolves. The promoters may then occupy other relationships. They may be shareholders, directors, or officers of the corporation, or all three. After formation, the promoters will wish to be released from any personal obligations they may have incurred while promoters. Similarly, the corporation will wish to be the party "on the contract," so that it may complain if the roof in the leased spaces leaks, the employees are bunglers, or the stationery, brochures, and Web site contain misspellings of the corporation's name.

States use a variety of legal theories so the promoters and the now-formed corporation can accomplish their mutual goals. The corporation may **ratify** a contract, either by express ratification at a meeting of the board of directors, or by implied action; for example, moving into the leased spaces, accepting the employees' work, or using the stationery, brochures, and Web site. Ratification **"relates back"** to the date the contract was entered into, so it is as if the promoter never signed the contract, and the corporation was a party from the very date on which the contract was signed. Similarly, the contract may be *assigned* from the promoter to the corporation. The **assignment** can be made effective as of the date the contract was entered into so that, once again, it is as if the promoter never signed the contract and the corporation was always a party to it. Such an assignment is called a **nunc pro tunc** (literally "now for then") assignment, meaning that while the assignment document is executed on one date, it is effective as of a prior date. Some jurisdictions refer to assignment as **novation,** a term meaning substitution. In novation, the corporation is substituted in place of the promoter as a party to the contract in all respects.

Ratification
Approval of a transaction

Relation back
Doctrine that certain actions are viewed as having occurred on an earlier date

Assignment
Transfer of one's interest in some asset or right

Nunc pro tunc
Literally "now for then," a reference to an act or document having an effective date earlier than the date of its execution

Novation
A substitution of one party or document for another

Unless the promoter is expressly released from contractual obligations, she may remain liable under the terms of the contracts she signed. Unless misrepresentation or breach of promise by a promoter is alleged, the promoter may usually seek indemnification (or reimbursement) from the corporation for any liability incurred under the terms of a preincorporation agreement signed by a promoter on behalf of the corporation.

3. *Preincorporation Share Subscriptions*

Promoters must also undertake activities to raise capital for the corporation. A few states, including Texas, require that the corporation have a certain amount of capital before it can begin operating. Others require that each of the promoters subscribe for (or agree to purchase) at least one share of stock. Finally, from a practical standpoint, it is useful that the corporation be assured it will have a certain amount of capital at its disposal upon its formation.

Preincorporation share subscriptions
Offers to purchase shares in a corporation before its formation

Preincorporation share subscriptions, or offers to purchase stock when the corporation is later formed, are used to accomplish these goals. The preincorporation stock subscription is viewed as an offer from a potential investor to purchase stock in a corporation upon its formation. The subscription may be set forth in very simple terms, as follows:

> **I, the undersigned, hereby offer to purchase 100 shares of the common stock of Gift Baskets, Inc. at a purchase price of $25 per share, upon the incorporation of Gift Baskets, Inc. or within thirty days thereafter. The purchase price for said shares shall be payable to Gift Baskets, Inc. upon demand by its board of directors.**
>
> **Dated: January 25, 2000** **Amanda A. Carlson**

Thus, Amanda has offered to purchase 100 shares of the corporation when it is later formed. More complex share subscriptions may contain certain conditions that must be satisfied before Amanda will be required to purchase the stock; for example, a requirement that the corporation be formed on or before a certain date.

Years ago, subscriptions were revocable. Revocation led to the canny practice of presenting the subscriptions (often signed by friends and family members of the promoters) to the secretary of state as evidence the corporation could satisfy the requirement that it have a certain amount of capital before beginning business. The subscribers would then revoke their offers, leaving the corporation without the requisite capital. To eliminate this practice of having friends submit phony offers or subscriptions, many states' statutes make the share subscriptions irrevocable for a certain period of time (three months, for example, in New York and six months according to RMBCA Section 6.20). During this period of time, the subscriber cannot revoke or retract the offer to purchase stock. The offer may, however, be assigned from one person to another. Thus, Amanda Carlson could assign the offer to her sister Jane, in which case Jane would be obligated under the terms of the offer. If the corporation is formed during the period of irrevocability and accepts the offer to purchase, the subscriber or assignee is bound to pay for the stock in full. Failure to pay for the stock as agreed will leave the subscriber liable to the corporation for breach of contract.

In most jurisdictions, the corporation will accept the offers or subscriptions at its first meeting. In other jurisdictions, however, the stock subscription is viewed as automatically being accepted upon the incorporation of the corporation.

B. Selection of Jurisdiction in Which to Incorporate

A business may elect to incorporate in any of the 50 states or in the District of Columbia. Some state corporation laws are considerably more flexible than others. Some jurisdictions favor corporations formed within their boundaries by having a moderately priced and expeditious incorporation process for domestic corporations, but disfavor corporations formed outside their boundaries (foreign corporations) by subjecting them to intense regulation and high taxes and annual fees. Jurisdictions may compete with one another for the purpose of attracting corporations.

Because each state has its own corporations code, a review and comparison of all 50 states' codes would be time-consuming and costly. Thus, the first inquiry should always be "Where does the proposed corporation intend to operate its business?" If the client intends to conduct business solely in New Jersey, that state should be first choice for incorporation. To incorporate in New York when the corporation intends to do business solely in New Jersey would subject the corporation to regulation and taxation in both states. Thus, unless there is something particularly onerous in the New Jersey laws pertaining to corporations, the corporation should select New Jersey as the state of incorporation. If, however, the business will open in New Jersey but plans immediate expansion into other northeast states within 18 months, and into the Midwest within two years, then perhaps more permissive jurisdictions should be considered. Because the corporation will soon be subject to regulation and taxation in all of the states in which it conducts business, it might as well select the jurisdiction for incorporation with the most permissive corporations statutes.

1. *Delaware Incorporation*

Delaware is well-known for having liberal and permissive corporations statutes. This is no accident but rather the result of a carefully planned strategy to attract business and capital to the state of Delaware. In fact, Delaware takes great pride in referring to itself as being the "Corporation Capital of the World." Delaware collects nearly one-fourth of its annual budget in taxes and fees from corporations. More than half of the Fortune 500 companies are incorporated in Delaware. Nearly half of the corporations listed on the New York and American Stock Exchanges are incorporated there, including Marriott, Apple Computer, and Merck. Why? Because Delaware specifically designed its corporation laws (the Delaware General Corporation Law) to be the most advanced and flexible in the United States. For example, at a time when most states required corporations to have three directors, Delaware allowed corporations to exist with a single director. When most states required that corporations conduct business in the state of incorporation, Delaware allowed corporations to form in Delaware even if no business was to be conducted there. The state also allowed corporations to incorporate in Delaware yet hold their meetings anywhere they desired.

After Delaware liberalized its corporations laws, many states followed suit. Thus, there may be no true advantage to incorporating in Delaware over some of the other more permissive states, such as California and New York. Nevertheless, Delaware continues to set the standard with a modern imaging system and customer-oriented service staff. For example, Delaware offers a variety of priority filings. One can be assured of incorporation within 24 hours for up to $100, same-day incorporation for up to $200, and incorporation within two hours for $500. Moreover, Delaware accepts documents via facsimile transmission and operates until midnight. Thus, Delaware keeps one step ahead of most jurisdictions and succeeds in continuing to attract corporations to the state. All of these corporations, of course, must then pay certain fees and taxes in Delaware. These fees and taxes, however, are relatively moderate and may even be paid by credit card.

In an effort to emulate Delaware, other jurisdictions have modernized their corporations codes. For example, the District of Columbia for years had a cumbersome incorporation process, requiring three individuals to form the corporation, three individuals to serve as directors, and four persons to serve as officers. Although the District of Columbia revised its law to be more permissive, an article in *The Washington Post* flatly stated that the District was still no "Delaware on the Potomac." Similarly, Nevada has been attempting to attract business by liberalizing its corporations statutes to make them highly similar to those of Delaware and eliminating state income tax. In fact, in the last few years, incorporations in Nevada have increased 25 to 30 percent. Because California is a costly state in which to incorporate, attorneys in California have been the target of an advertising campaign to encourage them to incorporate their clients in Nevada.

2. *Factors in Selecting a Jurisdiction*

There are several factors to consider in determining where to incorporate:

a. If a corporation intends to do business in one state only, at least for the time-being, that state should be the first choice for incorporation. Incorporating in one state and doing business in another will require the corporation to pay fees and taxes and file reports in both jurisdictions. For example, in California, corporations pay a minimum franchise fee of $800 just for the privilege of doing business in California.
b. Determine whether the state disfavors foreign corporations. For example, some states prefer to award public works contracts for construction of buildings, roads, and so forth to domestic corporations. If a client intends to engage in construction work and incorporates elsewhere, this could be a serious obstacle to obtaining public works contracts.
c. States that have attracted corporations often have substantial case law to serve as a guideline as to what corporate activities are permissible. For ex-

ample, Delaware prides itself on offering over 200 years of legal precedents to assure corporations that their business decisions stand on solid legal foundations.

d. Consider the costs of formation, the annual reporting requirements, fees and taxes imposed by the state, and the comparative ease of forming and maintaining the corporation in a state.

C. The Corporate Name

The name to be used by the corporation must be given careful consideration. The name must comply with all state statutes, must not be identical or deceptively similar to another's name, and must be available for use in that state (and in any other states in which the corporation anticipates operating). Once it is determined the name is available, it should be reserved during the incorporation process.

1. *Selection*

The promoters must select a name for the new legal "person" or entity they are creating. Many state statutes require that the name of the corporation include some signal to the public that the business is a corporation and therefore personal assets may not be available to creditors. Generally, most states require that the name include the word "corporation," "company," "incorporated," or "limited," or an abbreviation of one of these words. This is also the position taken by RMBCA Section 4.01. Some states prohibit the use of "limited" in a corporate name on the basis that it signals a limited partnership or a limited liability company. Delaware allows a wide variety of signals, including "association," "club," or "society."

Other guidelines may be set forth in state statutes. For example, most states prohibit the corporation from selecting a name implying the corporation is organized for a purpose other than that stated in its articles of incorporation. Similarly, most states prohibit the corporation from using certain words in the corporate name that would imply some association with a state or federal agency. Thus, a private corporation could not use the name "Federal Mortgage Lending, Inc." as it implies some affiliation with the United States government.

Similarly, many corporation codes prohibit certain selected words such as "bank," "trust," "bond," or "insurance," without prior approval from the state commissioners of banking or insurance. Finally, various federal statutes prohibit the use of certain words such as "Olympic," or "Red Cross," as they suggest an affiliation with the well-known organizations using those names.

As is always the rule, the corporation may not select a name that is the same as or confusingly similar to that used either by another domestic corporation or that used by a foreign corporation qualified to do business in that state. In this regard, a corporation that intends to offer its goods or services nationwide at some point should give careful and deliberate thought to the corporate name. A highly descriptive name such as "Medical Supplies, Inc." is subject to two weaknesses. It is so common that it is likely already taken in at least some jurisdictions, and thus the corporation will not be able to do business under this name in all 50 states; and it is so descriptive that it will be given a very narrow scope of protection by courts, thus hindering the corporation in attempts to stop infringers from using the same or a highly similar name. In fact, the "best" names are those that are fanciful, such as "Xerox" or "Kodak." Because these names are made up, they are not only likely available worldwide but are strong names capable of being protected. Unfortunately, however, these names do not say anything about the nature of the goods or services offered under the names and require their owners to expend a great deal of money in establishing recognition of the name.

Thus, the corporation must strike a balance. With an eye toward growth, it should select a name sufficiently distinctive that it will likely be available in other states; and consideration should be given to the fact that the name must not be so unique that it conveys no information about the corporation's products and services. Corporations that anticipate operating in more than one state should check the availability of the name on a nationwide basis by consulting Thomson & Thomson at (800) 692-8833, Corsearch at (800) SEARCH-1®, or CT Corporation System's affiliate called Trademark Research Corporation at (800) 624-0909. Imagine if McDonald's could not operate as "McDonald's" in two or three states and had to operate its fast food restaurants as "Burgers To Go, Inc." in those states. It is much more cost-effective to determine name availability early in the incorporation process, rather than to devote substantial sums to developing consumer recognition of a name, only to be precluded from using the very name consumers have been trained to use when asking for the corporation's products or services.

Equally important, conducting a name availability search may help ensure the corporation does not infringe the name or trademark of another. Approval of a name by a secretary of state is no defense to a claim of trademark infringement.

Trademarks registered with the U.S. Patent and Trademark Office have nationwide protection. It is possible that the owner of a registered trademark may not conduct business in some states. In those states, the name will not appear on the records of the secretary of state. Thus, if a corporation is allowed to use a confusingly similar name by the secretary of state, such permission cannot supersede federal trademark law.

2. *Availability*

After reviewing the appropriate state statutes to assure the name complies with all pertinent laws, it must be determined if the name is available in the state of incorporation.

Incorporation matters are handled in almost all states by the secretary of state. Some states, however, designate a particular department for incorporations. For example, in Maryland, incorporations are handled by the "Assessments and Taxation Department." For ease, this text will refer to "secretary of state" when discussing the public agency responsible for corporate activity. The secretary of state in each state has the responsibility for determining whether a corporate name is available. In most jurisdictions, availability can be determined by a single telephone call to the secretary of state's office. Many states have a separate department for determining corporate name availability and will check their records while you wait on the phone. Many of the attorneys' service companies identified below will check name availability and then file the forms necessary to reserve the name to the corporation. Phone numbers, addresses, and Web sites for the secretaries of state are given in Appendix A.

When contacting the secretary of state to determine whether a corporate name is available, be sure to have at least one alternative so that if the secretary of state refuses the corporation's first choice, its second choice can be immediately checked. If a name is identical or confusingly similar to another (either a domestic corporation or a foreign corporation qualified to do business in the state), the secretary of state will refuse to allow incorporation of the corporation under that name. Thus, unless a corporate name is highly unusual or distinctive, always ensure the availability of a name before preparing and unsuccessfully filing the articles of incorporation. In some states, if the secretary of state rejects the name as being too similar to that of another, it is possible to obtain the name if the other party consents in writing and the consent is delivered to the secretary of state.

Some states, including California, now offer name availability searching on their Web sites. Access the secretary of state's home page (see Appendix A for a listing of state Web sites) and determine if online searching can be accomplished.

3. *Reservation*

If the name is available, it should be reserved for the prospective corporation during the period of time the articles of incorporation are being prepared. Some states, like Delaware, allow the proposed corporation to reserve the name by phone call and will charge a modest fee to a credit card or to the telephone bill. The more common approach, however, is to require that the **name reservation** be made in writing and accompanied by a fee. The fee will vary from state to state, with Delaware charging $10 to reserve up to three names per telephone call, to an average of approximately $25. (See Figure 9-1 for a sample name reservation form.)

Name reservation
Process of reserving a name for a corporation while its incorporation papers are being prepared

The reservation will be limited in its duration. RMBCA Section 4.02 allows for a nonrenewable 120-day period. Some states, such as Delaware, Maryland, and Massachusetts afford only a thirty-day reservation period. Other states, such as Michigan and Washington, allow reservations for six months. Still others may allow reservations for a period of one year.

During the period the reservation is in existence, the name may not be used or taken by any other corporation seeking to incorporate in that state or to qualify to do business in that state. In some states, the reservation may be renewable. Other jurisdictions have a nonrenewable reservation period, aiming to spur businesses to incorporate promptly and to clear the state's corporate rolls of unused names so they can be made available for use by others. You must be sure to docket the date the reservation expires to ensure timely filing of the incorporation papers during the period of the reservation (or to renew the reservation, if possible). The name is often reserved by the law firm or attorney incorporating the business and

FIGURE 9-1
New York Name Reservation Application

Application for Reservation of Name
Under §303 of the Business Corporation Law

NYS Department of State
DIVISION OF CORPORATIONS, STATE RECORDS and UCC
41 State Street
Albany, NY 12231-0001

PLEASE TYPE OR PRINT

APPLICANT'S NAME AND ADDRESS

NAME TO BE RESERVED

RESERVATION IS INTENDED FOR (CHECK ONE)

G New domestic corporation

G Foreign corporation intending to apply for authority to do business in New York State*

G Proposed foreign corporation, not yet incorporated, intending to apply for authority to conduct business in New York State

G Change of name of an existing domestic or an authorized foreign corporation*

G Foreign corporation intending to apply for authority to do business in New York State whose corporate name is not available for use in New York State*

G Authorized foreign corporation intending to change its fictitious name under which it does business in this state*

G Authorized foreign corporation which has changed its corporate name in its jurisdiction, such new corporate name not being available for use in New York State*

X______________________________
Signature of applicant, applicant s attorney or agent
(If attorney or agent, so specify)

____
Typed/printed name of signer

INSTRUCTIONS:

1. Upon filing this application, the name will be reserved for 60 days and a certificate of reservation will be issued.
2. The certificate of reservation must be returned with and attached to the certificate of incorporation or application for authority, amendment or with a cancellation of the reservation.
3. The name used must be the same as appears in the reservation.
4. A $20 fee payable to the Department of State must accompany this application.
5. Only names for business, transportation, cooperative and railroad corporations may be reserved under §303 of the Business Corporation Law.

***If the reservation is for an existing corporation, domestic or foreign, the corporation must be the applicant.**

DOS-234 (Rev. 10/97)

FIGURE 9-2
Illinois Reserved Name Transfer Notice

NOTICE OF TRANSFER
OF
RESERVED NAME

Date	
Filing Fee	$25.00
Approved:	

The undersigned ______________________ hereby transfers
(Name of Original Applicant)
to ______________________ the right to use the
(Name of Transferee)
name ______________________ for corporate purposes
in Illinois. This name was reserved on ______________, ______.
(Month & Day) (Year)

The undersigned affirms, under penalties of perjury, that the facts stated herein are true.

Dated ______________, ______ by ______________________
(Month & Day) (Year) (Signature of Original Applicant)

attested by ______________________ ______________________
(Type or Print Name)
If a corporation, by its President or Vice President*

* As the original applicant, I declare that this document has been examined by me and is, to the best of my knowledge and belief, true, correct and complete.

C-140.7

then transferred to its corporate owner as soon as the corporation is formed. (See Figure 9-2 for a sample notice of transfer form.)

4. *Registration*

A procedure somewhat similar to reservation of a name is **registration** of a name. Registration is used by foreign corporations to preserve the corporate name in a state in which the corporation plans to do business. For example, assume a corporation is formed in New Jersey to operate a restaurant. After a period of time, the restaurant may become well-known and the corporation may consider opening branches in the neighboring states of Pennsylvania and New York.

Name registration
Process of reserving a name in a foreign jurisdiction

During the period in which the corporation is planning its expansion, conducting market surveys, and so forth, it should register its name in Pennsylvania and New York. A name registration keeps a corporate name available for a substantial length of time, often one year. During this period, no other corporation can be formed in or qualify to do business in those states using an identical or deceptively similar name.

Name registrations are thus used by corporations considering expansion into other jurisdictions and serve to save the name during the process of planning and development. Otherwise, the corporation might establish its reputation under one name, and then be "beat out" in another state by another company operating under that name and thus be unable to capitalize on consumer recognition of the original name. Most states provide specified forms for name registration and impose filing fees therefor. (See Figure 9-3 for a sample registration of corporate name form.)

The name registration is generally effective until the end of the calendar year in which the application for registration is filed. In some states, a registration filed late in the calendar year (say after September 30) will be effective until the end of the following calendar year. Name registrations are often renewable.

Not all states permit name registration. In those states which do not, in order to preserve a name for future use a corporation might have to incorporate another corporation (a subsidiary corporation) solely for the purpose of holding the corporate name. Name reservation is not effective for this purpose because reservations are often for such short periods of time (30 to 120 days). The subsidiary will have few assets and will conduct no business. Nevertheless, it will be subject to regulation and taxation in the state of formation. Thus, this is a far more expensive and cumbersome route than name registration. It may be necessary, however, if the corporation plans to expand into other jurisdictions. Subsidiaries formed for these purposes are sometimes called **name-savers** or *nameholders*. Because corporations exist perpetually, there is no need to renew any forms when a name-saver is formed (although annual reports are required in all jurisdictions and annual taxes and fees may be imposed on the name-saver corporation). When the parent is ready to conduct business in the state, the subsidiary can be merged into the parent.

Name-saver
Corporation formed by another for purpose of reserving a corporate name in a foreign jurisdiction

In sum, a corporation planning to operate nationally must determine name availability at an early stage, reserve the name in the state in which it will incorporate, and file the papers necessary to effect incorporation during the reservation period. Thereafter, if planning national expansion, the corporation should register its name in all states that permit registration and then form a name-saver corporation in those states that do not, in order to preserve the name in other states for future use.

5. *Assumed Names*

Just as sole proprietors and general partnerships often operate under an **assumed name** (or fictitious name), corporations can also be formed under one name and then elect to operate under another. A corporation may wish each of its separate divisions to operate under its own name. Alternatively, there may be certain marketing and consumer-related issues that necessitate operation under an

Assumed name
A name under which a business operates that is not the name under which it was formed

FIGURE 9-3
Michigan Registration of Corporate Name Application

C&S 545 (10/99)

MICHIGAN DEPARTMENT OF CONSUMER & INDUSTRY SERVICES
CORPORATION, SECURITIES AND LAND DEVELOPMENT BUREAU

Date Received	**(FOR BUREAU USE ONLY)**
	This document is effective on the date filed, unless a subsequent effective date within 90 days after received date is stated in the document.

Name		
Address		
City	State	Zip Code

EXPIRATION DATE: DECEMBER 31,

Document will be returned to the name and address you enter above. If left blank document will be mailed to the registered office.

APPLICATION FOR REGISTRATION OF CORPORATE NAME
For use by Foreign Profit Corporations
(Please read information and instructions on reverse side)

Pursuant to the provisions of Act 284, Public Acts of 1972, the undersigned corporation executes the following Certificate:

1. The name of the foreign profit corporation is:

2. The mailing address of the corporation is:

3. The jurisdiction of its incorporation is: ____________________

   The date it was incorporated in that jurisdiction is: ____________________

4. The corporation is currently carrying on or doing business. The business the corporation is engaged in is:

Signed this ________ day of ________________, ________

By ______________________________
(Signature of an authorized officer or agent)

____
(Type or Print Name)

assumed name. For example, Kentucky Fried Chicken no longer operates under that name (due to consumers' distaste for the word "fried") and therefore may be operating under the name "KFC" as an assumed name. Similarly, Boston Chicken, a well-known take-out restaurant, recently ceased operating as "Boston Chicken" due to the perceived limitations of the word "chicken." It may thus be operating under the assumed name "Boston Market." (It is equally possible, however, that these corporations have actually changed their names by amending their corporate documents.)

Most states provide forms for corporations to adopt an assumed name and will charge a modest filing fee therefor. (See Figure 9-4 for an application to adopt an assumed corporate name.) In some states, the form used by sole proprietors and partnerships for fictitious names can also be used by corporations. (See Figure 2-2.) Additionally, the corporation service companies identified in the Resource Guide of this chapter can assist with filing, recording, and publication in each state and/or county that permits assumed names.

D. Articles of Incorporation

Articles of incorporation
The document that creates a corporation; also called *certificate of incorporation*

The document prepared and filed with the secretary of state creating the corporation is generally called the **articles of incorporation.** Some states, including Delaware, use the term *certificate of incorporation,* but most states and the RMBCA use the former term.

Nearly all states provide forms for the articles of incorporation. These allow for easy incorporation and can be simply completed and sent to the secretary of state with the appropriate filing fee. Other states may provide you with a list of what should be included in the articles of incorporation. Each state's corporations statutes will specify the provisions that must be included in the articles. The statutes also typically provide that other provisions may be included in the articles. As a general rule, however, you should prepare the articles of incorporation to comply with the state requirements and include no optional provisions. The articles are more difficult and costly to amend than the corporation's bylaws because amendment requires shareholder approval and filing with the secretary of state. The articles are also a public document and the corporation should be sensitive to what provisions are included in the articles. Because optional provisions can also be set forth in the bylaws, it is generally recommended that the articles comply strictly with what the state statute requires and that other optional provisions be included in the bylaws because they are comparatively easy to amend and are not open for public inspection.

1. *Elements of Articles of Incorporation*

Although there is some variation from state to state, the provisions generally required to be included in the articles of incorporation are as follows:

Name. The corporation's name must be set forth in the articles. Hopefully, it has been reserved and the articles of incorporation are filed during the reservation

FIGURE 9-4
Illinois Assumed Corporate Name Application

Form **BCA-4.15/4.20**

(Rev. Jan. 1999)

APPLICATION TO ADOPT, CHANGE OR CANCEL, AN ASSUMED CORPORATE NAME

File #

Jesse White
Secretary of State
Department of Business Services
Springfield, IL 62756
Telephone (217) 782-9520
http://www.sos.state.il.us

SUBMIT IN DUPLICATE

This space for use by Secretary of State

Date

Remit payment in check or money order, payable to "Secretary of State".

Filing Fee

Approved:

1. CORPORATE NAME: ______________________

2. State or Country of Incorporation: ______________________

3. Date incorporated *(if an Illinois corporation)* or date authorized to transact business in Illinois *(if a foreign corporation)*: ____________ *(Month & Day)*, ______ *(Year)*.

(Complete No. 4 and No. 5 if adopting or changing an assumed corporate name.)

4. The corporation intends to adopt and to transact business under the assumed corporate name of:

   ____

5. The right to use the assumed corporate name shall be effective from the date this application is filed by the Secretary of State until ____________ *(Month & Day)*, ______ *(Year)*, the first day of the corporation's anniversary month in the next year which is evenly divisible by five.

(Complete No. 6 if changing or cancelling an assumed corporate name.)

6. The corporation intends to cease transacting business under the assumed corporate name of:

   ____

7. The undersigned corporation has caused this statement to be signed by its duly authorized officers, each of whom affirms, under penalties of perjury, that the facts stated herein are true.

Dated ____________ *(Month & Day)*, ______ *(Year)* ______________________ *(Exact Name of Corporation)*

attested by ______________________ *(Signature of Secretary or Assistant Secretary)* by ______________________ *(Signature of President or Vice President)*

______________________ *(Type or Print Name and Title)* ______________________ *(Type or Print Name and Title)*

NOTE: The filing fee to adopt an assumed corporate name is $20 plus $2.50 for each month or part thereof between the date of filing this application and the date upon which the corporation may renew its use.

The fee for cancelling an assumed corporate name is $5.00.

C-148.11 The fee to change an assumed name is $25.

period so that the name is "locked up" for the corporation. Review your state statute to ensure the corporate name complies with any requirements that the name include a designation of corporate status such as "Company," "Inc.," or "Corp."

Address. The corporation must set forth its registered address in the state of incorporation so there will be a public record showing how and where the corporation may be reached. Many states require a street address rather than a mere post office box. If the corporation does not intend to do business in that state and has incorporated there only for the purpose of incorporating under a permissive and flexible corporate code, it can make arrangements with various corporate service companies to maintain a registered office in the state. For example, the following companies will, for a fee, agree to serve as the registered office or address in the state of incorporation: CT Corporation System, Corporation Service Company, and The Company Corporation. These companies provide numerous other services as well, such as assistance in reserving the corporate name, filing the articles of incorporation, serving as agent for service of process, and so forth.

Additionally, the California and Delaware Web sites (<www.ss.ca.gov/business/bpd_service_companies.htm> and <www.de.us/corp/corp.htm>) identify numerous corporate service companies.

Agent for Service of Process. In nearly all states, the corporation must designate an individual residing in the state of incorporation or a domestic corporation or qualified foreign corporation to receive service of legal process (the summons and complaint which initiate legal action). Once again, if the corporation is not actually doing business in the state of incorporation, and no individual residing in the state will agree to accept service of process, the corporation may enter into an agreement with one of the corporation service companies. For an annual fee, they will agree to accept service of process and immediately notify the corporation thereof so it can respond to the complaint and a default is not entered against the corporation. In many states, the secretary of state is also authorized to accept service of process on behalf of the corporation. In New York, the articles must designate the secretary of state as the agent and need not appoint any other. In Pennsylvania and Minnesota, the articles must identify a registered address, and process will be sent to that address. A list of attorneys' service companies is provided in the Resource Guide at the end of this chapter. Generally, changing the registered office or agent for service of process is fairly easy and does not require the complex process required for amending the articles. (See Figure 9-5 for a sample form for changing the registered agent or registered office address.) Many states require that the agent for service of process be located at the registered office.

Under RMBCA Section 14.20, failure to have a registered agent or registered address for 60 days is grounds for administrative dissolution of a corporation. The Web sites of some of the state secretaries of state permit identification of agents for service of process. Enter a company's name and you will be informed of its date of incorporation, status (active, suspended, or dissolved), and the identity of its agent who will accept service of process.

Broad purpose clause
Clause in corporate articles that states the corporation is formed to conduct any legal activity; also called *full purpose clause*

Purposes. Most states require the corporation to set forth its purposes in the articles. Most, however, also allow the corporation to use a **broad purpose** or *full*

FIGURE 9-5
Florida Statement of Change of Registered Office and/or Registered Agent

STATEMENT OF CHANGE OF REGISTERED OFFICE OR REGISTERED AGENT OR BOTH FOR CORPORATIONS

Pursuant to the provisions of sections 607.0502, 617.0502, 607.1508, or 617.1508, Florida Statutes, the undersigned corporation organized under the laws of the State of ________________________ submits the following statement in order to change its registered office or registered agent, or both, in the State of Florida.

1. The name of the corporation is:____

____

2. The mailing address of the corporation is:____

____

3. Date of incorporation/qualification: ________________ Document number:______________

4. The name and address of the current registered agent and office:

____

____

____

5. The name and address of the new registered agent and office: (P. O. Box **Not** Acceptable)

____

____

____

The street address of its registered office and the street address of the business office of its registered agent, as changed, will be identical.

Such change was authorized by resolution duly adopted by its board of directors or by an officer so authorized by the board.

____ ________________
(Signature of an officer, chairman or vice chairman of the board) (Date)

____
(Printed or typed name and title)

Having been named as registered agent and to accept service of process for the above stated corporation, I hereby accept the appointment as registered agent and agree to act in this capacity. I further agree to comply with the provisions of all statutes relative to the proper and complete performance of my duties, and I am familiar with and accept the obligation of my position as registered agent.

____
(Signature of Registered Agent) (Date)

If signing on behalf of an entity:

____
(Typed or Printed Name) (Capacity)

*** * * FILING FEE: $35.00 * * ***

CR2E045(7/97)

DIVISION OF CORPORATIONS P.O. BOX 6327 TALLAHASSEE, FL 32314 *purpose clause* rather than setting forth in detail its actual purposes. A broad purpose clause typically provides that "the purpose of the corporation is to engage in any lawful act or activity for which a corporation may be organized under the laws of this state." The advantage of using such a clause is that it does not limit the corporation to any specific activity and the corporation thus has room to grow and develop into other endeavors in the years ahead without requiring an amendment of its articles. Moreover, because the articles are open to public inspection, the corporation may not wish to set forth a detailed description of its business purposes. If a state does require that the purposes be specifically set forth, the drafter of the articles should allow room for expansion by setting forth the specific purposes and then adding a clause such as "and may transact any business or perform any act reasonably necessary to accomplish such purposes."

Ultra vires doctrine
Seldom-used legal theory that certain acts are invalid as being beyond a corporation's purposes

Years ago, when corporations were required to state their specific purposes, corporations would occasionally exceed or act beyond their stated purposes. Such acts were said to be ***ultra vires,*** literally "acts beyond the powers" of a corporation. The early view was that corporations had no capacity to act beyond their purposes; any act which exceeded such purposes was therefore null and void and either party to a contract (either the corporation or a third party) could disaffirm the contract, even if the other party had already performed its duties under the contract. Thus, the ultra vires doctrine allowed parties to avoid their contractual obligations.

Starting in approximately 1900, courts began recognizing the unfairness of the application of the ultra vires doctrine and began to refuse to apply it when one of the parties had substantially performed its duties. Later, as state statutes began allowing full purpose clauses, the ultra vires doctrine became subject to erosion. If a corporation has the power to perform any lawful act, then few acts can be challenged on the basis that they are ultra vires, or beyond the power of the corporation.

The RMBCA reflects the modern approach to the ultra vires doctrine: Neither the corporation nor any third party doing business with the corporation can escape its respective duties on the theory that the corporation lacked authority to enter into the contract or power to act. There are, however, three actions that may be taken with regard to a transaction exceeding the corporation's powers and purposes: the shareholders may sue to enjoin the transaction; the corporation can sue the directors and officers for taking the unauthorized action; and the attorney general can seek dissolution of the corporation. RMBCA Section 3.04.

Although the ultra vires doctrine is largely of historical interest, many contracts entered into by corporations include a clause reciting and warranting that the corporation has the power and authority to enter into the transaction.

Description of Stock. The corporation's shares must be fully described. If the corporation will issue more than one class or type of shares, all of the provisions relating to each must be set forth. The number of shares the corporation will issue must be provided. This number forms an upper limit on the number of shares the corporation can issue. If the corporation wishes to issue stock in an amount greater than this number, the articles will need to be amended. Thus, to eliminate this potential difficulty, the articles should provide for a large enough number to accommodate any anticipated growth. The number set forth in the articles is called the corporation's **authorized shares.** The corporation has the authority to issue only this number of shares and no more.

Authorized shares
The number of shares set forth in a corporation's articles that the corporation has authority to issue

In some states, filing fees are based upon the number of shares the corporation will issue. For example, in Delaware, a filing fee tax is based upon the number of shares the corporation will issue. For stock with no par value, the filing fee tax is one cent on the first 20,000 shares of stock issued ($200), and a half cent for the next 1,980,000 shares to be issued ($9,900). Thus, a corporation will pay a filing fee tax of $200 for shares authorized up to 20,000, making it reasonable for all corporations, even Mom and Pop-type operations, to state in their articles that they have the authority to issue up to 20,000 shares of stock.

This section of the articles must also describe any privileges, preferences, or restrictions imposed on any class of stock. If there is only one class of stock, that stock will be the "common" stock of the corporation. While common and preferred stock will be fully discussed in Chapter Ten, at this point it is sufficient to know that **common stock** is stock of a corporation having no special features or privileges, while **preferred stock** generally has some feature(s) making it more desirable than common stock.

Common stock
Stock of a corporation having no special privileges

Preferred stock
Stock of a corporation issued with desirable privileges

Par value
The minimum amount for which a corporation's stock can be sold

This section of the articles must usually state the par value of the stock, if any, or include a statement that the stock has no par value. **Par value** is the face value of each share of stock, which is generally quite low, often ten cents or $1 per share. Par value is the minimum amount for which a share of stock may be issued. Stock that has no par value may be issued for any amount per share that the directors of the corporation deem appropriate.

While these provisions may seem complex, the statement in the articles describing the stock of the corporation can be quite simple: "The corporation has the authority to issue 20,000 shares of common stock with a par value of $1 per share."

Incorporators. The name (and often the address) of each incorporator (those preparing the articles) must be provided. The incorporators must also sign the articles of incorporation. In many instances, the attorney or paralegal preparing the articles will sign as the incorporator. (See Figure 9-6 for sample forms for articles of incorporation.)

Although the elements required in each state may vary, RMBCA Section 2.02 requires the following elements to be included in the articles of incorporation:

- the corporate name (which includes a signal showing corporate status);
- the number of shares the corporation is authorized to issue;
- the street address of the corporation's initial registered office and the name of its registered agent at that office; and
- the name and address of each incorporator.

2. *Optional Provisions in Articles of Incorporation*

There may be other elements required for the articles of incorporation in certain states. For example, in Texas, the articles must include the following statement: "The corporation will not commence business until it has received for the issuance of its shares consideration of the value of a stated sum which shall be at least one thousand dollars ($1,000.00), consisting of money, labor done, or property actually received." Tex. Corps. & Ass'ns Code Section 3.02(7). Other states may require that the initial directors be identified.

FIGURE 9-6
Articles of Incorporation Forms (Delaware, Nevada, and Pennsylvania)

STATE *of* DELAWARE
CERTIFICATE *of* INCORPORATION
A STOCK CORPORATION

- **First:** The name of this Corporation is ______________________________

  ____

- **Second:** Its registered office in the State of Delaware is to be located at __________

  ______________________ Street, in the City of ______________

  County of ____________ Zip Code ________. The registered agent in

  charge thereof is ______________________________________

  ____

  ____

- **Third:** The purpose of the corporation is to engage in any lawful act or activity for which corporations may be organized under the General Corporation Law of Delaware.
- **Fourth:** The amount of the total authorized capital stock of this corporation is

  __________Dollars ($______) divided into _________ shares of ________

  __________Dollars ($______) each.

- **Fifth:** The name and mailing address of the incorporator are as follows:

  Name ______________________________________

  Mailing Address______________________________

  ____________________Zip Code__________

- **I, The Undersigned,** for the purpose of forming a corporation under the laws of the State of Delaware, do make, file and record this Certificate, and do certify that the facts herein stated are true, and I have accordingly hereunto set my hand this ________day of ____________, A.D. 19_____.

BY:______________________________
(Incorporator)

NAME:____________________________
(Type or Print)

FIGURE 9-6 *Continued*
Articles of Incorporation Forms (Delaware, Nevada, and Pennsylvania)

DEAN HELLER
Secretary of State

101 North Carson Street, Suite 3
Carson City, Nevada 89701-4786
(775) 684 5708

Articles of Incorporation
(PURSUANT TO NRS 78)

Office Use Only:

Important: Read attached instructions before completing form.

1. Name of Corporation:	
2. Resident Agent Name and Street Address: (must be a Nevada address where process may be served)	Name ______ Street Address ______ City, NEVADA ______ Zip Code
3. Shares: (No. of shares corporation authorized to issue)	Number of shares with par value: ______ Par value: ______ Number of shares without par value: ______
4. Governing Board: (Check one)	Shall be styled as ______ Directors or ______ Trustees
Names, Addresses, Number of Board of Directors/Trustees:	The First Board of Directors/Trustees shall consist of ______ members whose names and addresses are as follows: Name ______ Address ______ City, State, Zip / Name ______ Address ______ City, State, Zip
5. Purpose: (Optional-See Instructions)	The purpose of this Corporation shall be:
6. Other Matters: (See instructions)	Number of additional pages attached: ______
7. Names, Addresses and Signatures of Incorporators: (Signatures must be notarized) Attach additional pages if there are more than 2 incorporators.	Name ______ Address ______ City, State, Zip ______ Signature / Name ______ Address ______ City, State, Zip ______ Signature
Notary:	This instrument was acknowledged before me on ______, ______ by ______ Name of person As incorporator of ______ (Name of party on behalf of whom instrument executed) ______ Notary Public Signature (affix notary stamp or seal) / This instrument was acknowledged before me on ______, ______ by ______ Name of person As incorporator of ______ (Name of party on behalf of whom instrument executed) ______ Notary Public Signature (affix notary stamp or seal)
8. Certificate of Acceptance of Appointment of Resident Agent:	I, ______ hereby accept appointment as Resident Agent for the above named corporation. ______ Signature of Resident Agent ______ Date

This form must be accompanied by appropriate fees. See attached fee schedule.

Nevada Secretary of State Form CORPART1999.01
Revised on: 02/12/99

FIGURE 9-6 *Continued*
Articles of Incorporation Forms (Delaware, Nevada, and Pennsylvania)

Microfilm Number______________ Filed with the Department of State on__________

Entity Number______________

____
Secretary of the Commonwealth

ARTICLES OF INCORPORATION-FOR PROFIT
OF

____
Name of Corporation
A TYPE OF CORPORATION INDICATED BELOW

Indicate type of domestic corporation:

___ **Business-stock** (15 Pa.C.S. § 1306)

___ **Business-nonstock** (15 Pa.C.S. § 2102)

___ **Business-statutory close** (15 Pa.C.S. § 2303)

___**Cooperative** (15 Pa.C.S. § 7102)

___ **Management** (15 Pa.C.S. § 2702)

___ **Professional** (15 Pa.C.S. § 2903)

___ **Insurance** (15 Pa.C.S. § 3101)

DSCB:15-1306/2102/2303/2702/2903/3101/7102A (Rev 91)

In compliance with the requirements of the applicable provisions of 15 Pa.C.S. (relating to corporations and unincorporated associations) the undersigned, desiring to incorporate a corporation for profit hereby, state(s) that:

1. The **name** of the corporation is: ____

____

2. The (a) **address** of this corporation's initial registered office in this Commonwealth or (b) **name** of its commercial registered office provider and the county of venue is:

(a) ____
Number and Street City State Zip County

(b) c/o: ____
Name of Commercial Registered Office Provider County

For a corporation represented by a commercial registered office provider, the county in (b) shall be deemed the county in which the corporation is located for venue and official publication purposes.

3. The corporation is incorporated under the provisions of the Business Corporation Law of 1988.

4. The aggregate number of **shares** authorized is: ______________ (other provisions, if any, attach 8 1/2 x 11 sheet)

5. The name and address, including number and street, if any, of each **incorporator** is:

Name Address

______________ ______________________________

______________ ______________________________

FIGURE 9-6 *Continued*
Articles of Incorporation Forms (Delaware, Nevada, and Pennsylvania)

DSCB:15-1306/2102/2303/2702/2903/3101/7102A (Rev 91)-2

6. The **specified effective date**, if any, is:______________________________
month day year hour, if any

7. Additional provisions of the articles, if any, attach an 8 1/2 x 11 sheet.

8. **Statutory close corporation only:** Neither the corporation nor any shareholder shall make an offering of any of its shares of any class that would constitute a "public offering" within the meaning of the Securities Act of 1933 (15 U.S.C. § 77a et seq.).

9. **Cooperative corporations only:** (Complete and strike out inapplicable term) The common bond of membership among its members/shareholders is: ______________________________

IN TESTIMONY WHEREOF, the incorporator(s) has (have) signed these Articles of Incorporation this __________day of________________, ______.

____
(Signature)

____
(Signature)

Most states allow the inclusion of optional provisions. It must be remembered, however, that any additional provision included in the articles may simply create a reason for amending the articles later, a complex, time-consuming, and somewhat expensive procedure.

Among the more common optional provisions often found in articles of incorporation are the following:

a. number, names, and addresses of the initial board of directors and a statement as to how directors are to be elected or appointed;
b. the period of duration of the corporation (the articles usually provide that the corporation is to exist perpetually, although there is no reason a specific date of termination cannot be set);
c. provisions requiring greater than majority vote for certain corporate action, such as requiring two-thirds approval for a merger;
d. provisions regarding managing the business of the corporation;
e. provisions imposing personal liability on shareholders;
f. provisions eliminating or restricting the personal liability of directors in the event of a breach of duty by the directors (other than some intentional, willfully reckless, or criminal act);

g. provisions permitting the corporation to indemnify directors or officers if they incur liability (such provisions usually require that these corporate managers have acted in good faith); or
h. any provisions that may be set forth in the corporation's bylaws.

3. *Preemptive Rights*

Preemptive right
Right of shareholder to buy pro rata share of newly issued stock before it is offered to nonshareholders

The articles of incorporation may include a provision allowing preemptive rights for the shareholders. A **preemptive right** is the right of a shareholder, when new shares are being issued, to purchase as much of the newly issued stock as is needed to maintain his or her then-current ownership interest in the corporation. In essence, a preemptive right is a kind of right of first refusal. Before the corporation can sell stock to any outsiders, the current shareholders must be given the opportunity to purchase stock in an amount equal to their present percentage of ownership in the corporation.

Assume that when a corporation is formed, Chris, Sean, and Kevin purchase 37 percent, 42 percent, and 21 percent, respectively, of the stock of the corporation. The corporation has the authority to issue additional shares and wishes to do so to raise capital. If the shareholders have preemptive rights, Chris would have the opportunity to purchase 37 percent of any later stock to be issued, Sean would have the opportunity to purchase 42 percent of any later stock to be issued, and Kevin would have the right to purchase 21 percent of any newly issued stock. Only when the shareholders elect not to exercise their rights to make such purchases can the corporation offer the stock to third parties.

Thus, preemptive rights allow shareholders to maintain their proportionate interest and control in a corporation. Chris will initially have the right to purchase 37 percent of any stock to be issued so that he can maintain his 37 percent interest in the corporation. The corporation cannot flood the market with shares and thereby reduce Chris' power and control.

In most states, if preemptive rights are to be given, they must be included in the articles of incorporation. A common preemptive provision is as follows: "Shareholders shall have the right to purchase their pro rata interest in shares of any new stock that may be issued by the corporation." Failure to specify that preemptive rights exist typically means that they do not exist. The general trend is that preemptive rights are not highly favored because they tend to restrict the flexibility of a corporation that may need to issue stock quickly to raise capital. Shareholders who have preemptive rights must be given notice and an opportunity to purchase newly issued stock. This notice and waiting period may delay the corporation in raising money. Preemptive rights generally exist for shareholders only when new stock is issued for cash and not when stock is issued under employee stock option plans or other similar plans.

4. *Filing of Articles of Incorporation*

The articles of incorporation must be filed with the appropriate state agency, usually the secretary of state, in the state of incorporation. Each state's filing requirements vary slightly, and failure to comply with the state's requirements will likely result in refusal of the articles of incorporation.

In most states, the incorporator simply mails the articles of incorporation to the office of the secretary of state with an appropriate cover letter and the required filing fee. Some states, such as Florida, provide a sample cover letter. The secretary of state will then review the articles to ensure they comply with the state's requirements. The secretary of state may then return a copy of the articles to the incorporator stamped "Approved" or "Filed" along with a date or may issue a formal certificate of incorporation confirming the date of incorporation. Some states require that additional copies of the articles be provided; one copy is retained for the state's files and another is file-stamped and returned to the incorporators to verify incorporation.

Some states require that other formalities be observed. For example, in Delaware a copy of the certificate of incorporation must be recorded in the county in which the corporation's registered office of incorporation is located. Florida requires that the registered agent sign the articles, accepting the appointment as registered agent for the corporation and confirming that the agent understands her duties in connection with acting as the corporation's agent (see Figure 9-7). Pennsylvania requires that the incorporators advertise their intention to file the articles or advertise the actual filing of the articles. Proofs of publication of such advertising must be kept with the minutes of the corporation. A careful reading of the pertinent state statutes is required to ensure that any other miscellaneous formalities are completed.

In most states, and according to the RMBCA, corporate existence begins upon filing of the articles of incorporation. Some states, however, provide that corporate existence begins upon issuance of a certificate of incorporation by the secretary of state. It may be necessary to determine the date the corporation comes into existence for tax reasons or for determining when promoters' obligations for preincorporation obligations end and corporate responsibility begins.

E. Post-Incorporation Activities

Once the corporation has been formed by the filing or the acceptance of the articles of incorporation, a few basic activities must be undertaken to organize the corporation. Bylaws must be drafted, corporate supplies must be ordered, and an initial organizational meeting must be held.

1. *Bylaws*

Bylaws are rules governing the operation and management of a corporation. The bylaws are prepared by the paralegal or attorney and are then presented for adoption at the first organizational meeting of the corporation. According to RMBCA Section 206(b), the bylaws of a corporation may contain any provision for managing the business and regulating the affairs of the corporation that is not inconsistent with law or the articles of incorporation. Bylaws are adopted by either the incorporators or the initial board of directors. They are easily amended. They are not filed with any state or county office but are rather maintained by the corporation in a looseleaf binder also containing minutes of corporate meetings

Bylaws
Internal rules governing corporate procedures and operation

FIGURE 9-7
Florida Articles of Incorporation and Registered Agent Acceptance Statement

ARTICLES OF INCORPORATION

The undersigned incorporator, for the purpose of forming a corporation under the Florida Business Corporation Act, hereby adopts the following Articles of Incorporation.

ARTICLE I NAME
The name of the corporation shall be:

ARTICLE II PRINCIPAL OFFICE
The principal place of business and mailing address of this corporation shall be:

ARTICLE III SHARES
The number of shares of stock that this corporation is authorized to have outstanding at any one time is:

ARTICLE IV INITIAL REGISTERED AGENT AND STREET ADDRESS
The name and Florida street address of the initial registered agent are:

ARTICLE V INCORPORATOR
The **name and address** of the incorporator to these Articles of Incorporation are:

____________________________ ____________________________
Signature/Incorporator **Date**

(An additional article must be added if an effective date is requested.)

Having been named as registered agent and to accept service of process for the above stated corporation at the place designated in this certificate, I hereby accept the appointment as registered agent and agree to act in this capacity. I further agree to comply with the provisions of all statutes relating to the proper and complete performance of my duties, and I am familiar with and accept the obligations of my position as registered agent

____________________________ ____________________________
Signature/Registered Agent **Date**

(called the *minute book*). They are not available for public inspection as are the articles. Bylaws may be very thorough or they may be fairly simple. Most attorneys engaged in corporate law have spent some time perfecting their bylaws and have sample forms for bylaws on word processors. These bylaws can then be readily adapted for other corporate clients. Drafting bylaws, however, requires more than merely changing the name of a corporation on a predetermined set of forms. The bylaws should be carefully drafted to ensure they provide a working blueprint for the directors and officers on how to manage the corporation, and for the shareholders, with regard to their rights as owners of the corporation. In general, bylaws are more easily amended than articles inasmuch as bylaws are usually amended by the directors of the corporation, without the necessity of a meeting of the shareholders or any public filings. Thus, any provisions which might be subject to change (the date of the annual meeting, the number of days' notice before an election, a change in the fiscal year) are best set forth in the bylaws due to the relative ease of amending the bylaws.

Following are typical items usually provided in corporate bylaws:

Introductory Information. The first few sections of the bylaws will set forth the name of the corporation and the address of its principal office and any other office locations. The bylaws may designate one office as the address to which notices and communications must be provided.

Information About Directors. The bylaws should contain various provisions relating to the managers of the corporation, called the board of directors. Any specific requirements that must be met by directors (such as being residents of the state of incorporation or being shareholders in the corporation) should be set forth. Similarly, the bylaws should provide how many directors the corporation will have and when and how they will be elected, replaced, or removed from office. The bylaws should provide the directors with the authority to manage the corporation. If any limitations are desired (for example, limitations on any one director's ability to incur indebtedness), they should be specified. Authority to declare and pay distributions to shareholders should be granted to the directors. The bylaws should provide when regular meetings of the directors will be held (weekly, monthly, quarterly, and so forth), where those meetings will be held, and any minimum advance notice required to be given to the directors. Provisions should be made for calling **special meetings** of the directors (any meeting between regularly scheduled meetings) and the appropriate notice therefor. The bylaws should establish how many directors constitute a **quorum** (the minimum number of directors required to transact business), how meetings will be adjourned, how directors may resign, and any liability they may have. Because few individuals would agree to serve as directors if they believed they could be held liable for any mere error in business judgment, bylaws often contain provisions indemnifying the directors for any costs or expenses incurred in defending any lawsuit arising out of their ordinary business activities. Directors are not ordinarily indemnified against criminal acts or intentional acts of recklessness. Compensation of directors and reimbursement of their expenses should be addressed. The authority of the directors to take action without a formal meeting (that is, by unanimous written consent) should be provided.

Special meeting
A meeting held between regularly scheduled meetings

Quorum
Minimum number of persons required to transact business

Information About Officers. The bylaws should identify the corporate officers. The most typical offices are president, vice-president, secretary, and treasurer. Nevertheless, a corporation may elect to have additional officers and can create additional titles and positions. The bylaws should confirm that the officers are to be appointed by the directors to carry out whatever management functions are delegated to them by the directors, and, similarly, are removable by the directors. The manner of filling officers' vacancies should be discussed. Specific duties for each officer may be set forth as should information pertaining to their salaries and reimbursement of expenses incurred on behalf of the corporation.

Information About Shareholders. Just as the bylaws should contain all information pertaining to directors and officers of the corporation, so should they also include information relating to the owners of the corporation, the shareholders. Provisions regarding the holding and location of regular annual meetings as well as the manner for calling special meetings should be set forth. The authority of shareholders to vote in person or by proxy should also be detailed. The manner in which notice of meetings is to be provided should be specified, as well as information as to how many shareholders constitute a quorum to conduct business (typically, a quorum is a majority of shares outstanding), how elections of directors will be held, any particular provisions regarding voting, and any items which will require a **supermajority** (a vote typically of two-thirds) rather than a simple majority. Any restrictions or limitations on voting rights of any classes of stock should be set forth. If the shareholders have the authority to act outside of a meeting, for example, by unanimous written consent, this should be indicated. Shareholders should be given the authority to inspect the shareholders' list.

Supermajority
A vote greater than a simple majority, often two-thirds

Miscellaneous Information. The bylaws should also approve a form of stock certificate (typically attached to the bylaws) as well as the form for the corporate seal (often impressed upon the bylaws). Information regarding reports of the corporation may be provided. Provisions relating to inspection of corporate records, how amendment of the bylaws will be effected, the **tax year** of the corporation, which may be the **calendar year** (January 1 through December 31) or a **fiscal year** (a 12-consecutive month period), should be set forth. A tax year is an annual accounting period for keeping records and reporting income and expenses. A tax year is adopted when the corporation files its first income tax return and generally requires IRS permission to change. The bylaws should also include any information relating to banking or the issuance or transfer of shares. (A form for bylaws of a corporation is provided in Appendix H.)

Tax year
An annual accounting period for keeping records and reporting income and expenses

Calendar year
The period between January 1 and December 31

Fiscal year
Any 12-consecutive month period

2. *Corporate Supplies*

As soon as the corporation is formed, the necessary supplies for the corporation should be ordered. It is the responsibility of the law firm to order the various supplies needed to ensure the corporation has the items necessary to transact its business. The corporate supplies are usually ordered from one of the various companies the law firm generally does business with, and consist of three items: the corporate seal, the minute book (which itself includes a stock transfer ledger to record issuance and transfer of the corporation's stock), and the stock certificate book. These supplies should be ordered only after formation of the corporation has been assured, because the seal (and often the stock certificates) may display the date of incorporation.

The **seal** is a device used to impress the corporation's name on certain documents. Just as kings of England used a specific seal to attest to the validity of documents, corporations are often required to impress their seal upon certain documents to verify their authenticity. The seal may be required upon bids for government contract work, requests to open bank accounts, and various other official documents. Use of a seal is somewhat uncommon.

Seal
Device used to impress documents to verify authenticity

The **minute book** is usually a three-ringed binder divided or tabbed into different sections. In one section, the corporation may place its articles, and in another its bylaws. The minute book is best known for containing the minutes of meetings of directors and shareholders. The minutes are seldom a verbatim transcript of meetings, but are typically a summary or overview of meetings.

Minute book
Binder or book used to maintain minutes of corporate meetings and other information

The **stock certificate book** resembles a large checkbook. Rather than checks, however, it contains certificates which are completed and provided to purchasers of the corporation's stock. Each certificate is required to include certain information (the name of the corporation, the type of stock being issued, the number of shares being issued, restrictions upon transfer of the shares, if any) and must be signed by the corporate officers, typically, the president and secretary of the corporation. A rosette, or place for impressing the corporate seal, is usually found on the certificate. When the appropriate consideration for the stock has been received, the corporation will issue the certificate to the owner of the shares. A tear-off slip attached to the certificate is to be completed and maintained by the corporation to provide a ledger or accounting of those to whom stock has been issued, the date of issuance, and the number of shares issued. The reverse side of the certificate typically includes endorsement information so that an owner of the stock can transfer it to another person by merely endorsing the certificate over to the new owner. (See Figure 9-8 for a sample stock certificate.)

Stock certificate book
Book containing stock certificates to be issued to shareholders

The supplies are easily ordered from the law firm's usual supplier and will often be received within 48 hours of ordering. The cost of the supplies is generally quite reasonable, often in the range of \$50 to \$75. Often the law firm will have an account pre-established with the supplier and ordering the corporate supplies takes only a few minutes via telephone. In some instances, the corporate kit includes a form of bylaws for the corporation to use or modify to suit its purposes.

3. *Organizational Meeting*

Although a corporation is legally formed upon the filing or acceptance of its articles of incorporation, some basic organizational activities must be undertaken to complete the process and start the corporation on its way. Accomplishing these goals occurs at the corporation's first meeting, usually referred to as the **organizational meeting** and held at the attorney's office.

Organizational meeting
First corporate meeting held to launch corporation

Most states require that a corporation hold an organizational meeting. RMBCA Section 2.05(a)(1) provides that if initial directors are named in the articles of incorporation they shall call and hold an organizational meeting to complete the organization of the corporation by appointing officers, adopting bylaws,

FIGURE 9-8
Sample Stock Certificate

NUMBER

SHARES

ORGANIZED UNDER THE LAWS OF THE STATE OF ILLINOIS

SUSAN FOSTER, INC.

AUTHORIZED 1,000 COMMON SHARES OF NO PAR VALUE

This Certifies That ______________________ is the owner of ______________ Shares of the Capital Stock of the above named Corporation, fully paid, non-assessable and transferable only on the books of the Corporation by the holder hereof in person or by duly authorized Attorney upon surrender of this Certificate properly endorsed.

In Witness Whereof, the said Corporation has caused this Certificate to be signed by its duly authorized officers and its Corporate Seal to be hereunto affixed this __________ day of __________ 19______

______________________ SECRETARY

______________________ PRESIDENT

and carrying on any other business. If initial directors are not named in the articles of incorporation, the RMBCA requires that the incorporators hold the organizational meeting to elect directors and complete the organization of the corporation.

Carefully review the statutes in the state of incorporation to determine if there are any requirements for the organizational meeting. For example, must the organizational meeting be held in the state of incorporation or can it be held elsewhere? Must written notice of the organizational meeting be given? Can individuals waive their right to receive notice? If so, must the waiver be in writing?

Most attorneys prefer to hold the organizational meeting at their offices, in order to ensure the corporation, its directors, and shareholders are aware of vari-

FIGURE 9-8 *Continued*
Sample Stock Certificate

For Value Received, *hereby sell, assign and transfer*
unto
Shares
of the Capital Stock represented by the within Certificate, and do hereby irrevocably constitute and appoint
Attorney
to transfer the said Stock on the books of the within named Corporation with full power of substitution in the premises.
Dated *19*
In presence of

NOTICE: THE SIGNATURE TO THIS ASSIGNMENT MUST CORRESPOND WITH THE NAME AS WRITTEN UPON THE FACE OF THE CERTIFICATE IN EVERY PARTICULAR WITHOUT ALTERATION OR ENLARGEMENT OR ANY CHANGE WHATEVER

ous requirements imposed on them by the state and to emphasize the need to act in compliance with all statutory requirements relating to corporations in that state. The organizational meeting is usually attended by the incorporators, the initial board of directors, and any anticipated shareholders. For small corporations, the meeting may therefore be attended by a mere handful of people.

If the organizational meeting is to be held at the law firm, the attorney or paralegal may prepare an agenda for the meeting. Following are items typically discussed at the organizational meeting:

Election of Directors. If directors have not already been named in the articles of incorporation, they will be elected by the incorporators. If a "dummy" board was identified in the articles (such as the attorney, paralegal, and legal secretary), these "**dummy directors**" will resign one at a time and be replaced with the ac-

Dummy directors
Nominee directors, often a legal team, named in original articles, not intended to be permanent directors

tual initial directors. The initial board of directors will serve until the first meeting of shareholders, at which time their successors will be elected.

Appointment of Officers. The directors of the corporation will appoint the officers of the corporation. While the most typical offices are those of president, vice-president, secretary, and treasurer, large corporations may have numerous other officers.

Adoption of Bylaws. The bylaws drafted by the attorney or paralegal will be presented and adopted.

Acceptance of Preincorporation Stock Subscriptions. If parties have made offers to purchase stock upon the formation of the corporation, these offers or preincorporation share subscriptions should be accepted. The officers will be directed to issue stock certificates upon receipt of the amount offered in the subscription.

Acceptance of Preincorporation Contracts. The directors should formally consider and ratify or adopt action taken by or contracts, if any, entered into by the promoters prior to incorporation. The promoters should be expressly relieved of their liability under those contracts. The corporation will then be a party to the various contracts with the right to enforce the terms and conditions of those contracts. For example, ratification or adoption of a lease for corporate offices entered into by a promoter will allow the corporation to demand that the premises be repaired or maintained. Ratification will also allow for reimbursement of the costs, including legal fees, incurred by the incorporators in preparing and filing the articles of incorporation and drafting the bylaws.

Approval of Corporate Seal and Form of Stock Certificate. The directors should approve the form of stock certificate and the seal obtained from the corporation's supplier. A sample or specimen of the stock certificate is often attached to the minutes of the meeting. Similarly, the seal is often impressed upon the minutes of the organizational meeting to demonstrate its form.

Banking and Accounting Information. The directors should discuss where the corporation's accounts will be held and the types of accounts to be opened, as well as any restrictions on banking. For example, the directors can require that for any expenditure in excess of $10,000, two officers must sign the check rather than merely one. The accountants to be used by the corporation may be designated. The directors can establish a fiscal year for the corporation (assuming it is not set forth in the bylaws). The most common fiscal year is the calendar year (January 1 through December 31), but other possibilities may be desired for particular businesses. For example, a corporation operating a resort with its peak season in the summer may elect a fiscal year of September 1 through August 31.

S Election. The directors should discuss whether it is desirable, when feasible, for the corporation to elect to become an S corporation, meaning that the corporation itself will not pay tax; all income earned by the corporation will be passed through to the shareholders, who will pay tax on their income from the corporation. Because all shareholders must agree with the election, the directors' recommendation on this issue should be discussed with the shareholders if they are all present at the meeting or should be voted on at the first meeting of shareholders (sometimes held immediately following the organizational meeting). To obtain S status for a corporation, the filing must generally be made with the Internal Revenue Service within 75 days of incorporation. Thus, election of S status is commonly discussed at the organizational meeting held shortly after incorporation. Subchapter S corporations are discussed further in Chapter Seventeen.

Confirmation of Section 1244 Stock. As discussed in Chapter Eight, a "small business corporation" is eligible for the benefits of Section 1244 of the Internal Revenue Code, so that losses sustained on the sale of stock will be treated as ordinary losses rather than capital losses (up to certain dollar limits). While qualified corporations are not statutorily required to take affirmative action to achieve the tax benefits of Section 1244, directors or incorporators often specifically confirm at organizational meetings that it is the corporation's intent that its stock qualify under Section 1244 for the favorable tax treatment provided by that provision.

Issuance of Stock. The directors should authorize the officers to begin selling stock and should fix the consideration to be paid per share.

Other Actions Taken at Organizational Meetings. Other actions taken at organizational meetings include the following:

- Presenting the filed articles of incorporation to the attendees and placement of the articles in the corporation's minute book;
- Discussing whether the corporation will commence doing business in other states, and, if so, making plans to qualify as a foreign corporation in those other states; and
- Instructing the officers to apply for an Employee Identification Number (required by all corporations).

If the shareholders are present at the organizational meeting, they will likely vote on only two issues: the election of directors and approval of the S corporation election. If the shareholders' initial meeting immediately follows, the shareholders will likely approve the election of the directors by the incorporators and will also vote on S corporation election.

In instances involving small corporations, the incorporators, directors, officers, and shareholders may all be the same few family members or friends. In such cases, the election of directors and appointment of officers is often a mere formality requiring little or no discussion because the parties have agreed long before the meeting as to how the corporation will be managed.

After the organizational meeting, the attorney or paralegal prepares minutes of the meeting reflecting the various actions taken at the meeting. These are signed by the secretary of the corporation and placed in the minute book. Alternatively, for smaller corporations, or when it is known in advance who the directors and officers will be, the attorney or paralegal can prepare minutes prior to the meeting reflecting the standard items to be considered and then use these minutes as an agenda. The secretary of the corporation then has a form to follow in preparing future minutes of corporate meetings.

Some states do not require that an actual formal organizational meeting be held. In those states, all of the activities that would be undertaken at an actual meeting can be done by unanimous written agreement. RMBCA Section 2.05(b) allows for action by unanimous written consent of the incorporators in place of an organizational meeting. The incorporators waive their right to notice and attendance at a formal meeting and unanimously agree in writing to all of the matters which would ordinarily be discussed at the organizational meeting. The **written consent** sets forth the names of the directors to be elected, the appointment of certain individuals as officers, approval of the preincorporation share subscriptions, and the like. Each director or shareholder will sign his or her name and date the document. The consent is placed in the minute book. (See Appendix I for a form of written consent in lieu of organizational meeting.)

Written consent
Document reflecting action taken by agreement in writing rather than action taken in person at a meeting

While acting by written consent may be easier than getting all of the principals of the corporation together for a meeting, it precludes the attorney from giving advice to the principals regarding their duties and obligations to the corporation and responding to questions regarding notice of meetings, preparing minutes of meetings, and the like. Thus, even though a state statute may allow for action to be taken by unanimous written consent rather than by a formal in-person organizational meeting, many attorneys prefer that the organizational meeting be held as an opportunity to emphasize corporate responsibilities and to respond to questions.

See Figure 9-9 for an Incorporation Checklist, which can be used as a step-by-step approach for organizing corporations.

F. Defects in Incorporation Process

On occasion, a defect in the incorporation process becomes important. For example, assume that a creditor is owed $50,000 by a corporation having three individuals as the directors, officers, and shareholders. If the corporate assets are limited to $25,000, the creditor might suffer a loss of $25,000 because the corporation protects the shareholders from personal liability for corporate debts and obligations. In such a case, the creditor may begin investigating various corporate documents in an effort to defeat the shareholders' limited liability and hold them personally liable for the remaining $25,000 owed to the creditor.

Assume that the creditor obtains a copy of the articles of incorporation from the secretary of state and notices that, due to an error, the address given for the corporation's registered office in the state is incorrect. The creditor may attempt to argue that because the state statutes relating to incorporation were not complied with, the corporation has been defectively formed and the shareholders are not entitled to protection from corporate debts. Other "defects" may include failure to have the requisite number of directors, failure to adopt bylaws, or failure to impress the corporate seal on the articles. In such cases, courts typically examine the nature of the defect and then classify the corporation as *de jure* or *de facto*.

FIGURE 9-9
Incorporation Checklist

1. Select jurisdiction in which to incorporate. Consider whether business will be local in nature or whether extraterritorial expansion is planned.
2. Identify corporate name (and possible alternatives). Research required "signals" in state of incorporation.
3. Determine name availability by checking with secretary of state.
4. If business will be conducted nationally or expansion is planned, consider a full-scope nationwide name search.
5. If name is available, reserve name, and docket period of name reservation.
6. Gather the following information so articles of incorporation can be prepared:
   - Determine identity of incorporators
   - Determine principal address of corporation within the state of incorporation
   - Identify registered agent (or make arrangement with attorneys' service company to serve as registered agent)
   - Identify initial shareholders
   - Identify initial directors
   - Identify stock of company
     - Common or preferred stock (if preferred, identify preferences and special rights)
     - Number of authorized shares
     - Par value or no par value
7. Gather incorporation forms and schedule of filing fees from secretary of state.
8. Prepare articles of incorporation, have them signed and filed.
9. Order corporate kit/supplies.
10. Prepare bylaws.
11. Confirm incorporation to client, and schedule first organizational meeting. Prepare notice of meeting or waivers of notice.
12. Prepare agenda for first organizational meeting. Items should include:
    - Election of directors
    - Appointment of officers
    - Approval of bylaws
    - Ratification or adoption of preincorporation contracts or actions, including legal and incorporation fees
    - Acceptance of pre-incorporation stock subscriptions
    - Discussion of applying for status as S corporation
    - Confirmation of Section 1244 stock
    - Review of articles, seal, form of stock certificate
    - Authorization of issuance of shares
    - Authorization of application for Employee Identification Number
    - Review of miscellaneous matters, if not in bylaws (selection of fiscal year, selection of bankers and accountants, and discussion of qualifying in foreign jurisdictions)

FIGURE 9-9 *Continued*
Incorporation Checklist

13. Prepare minutes of first organizational meeting, and send to client for signature by secretary of corporation and placement in minute book.
14. Docket date for next meeting.

De jure corporation
A corporation that substantially complied with statutory requirements and is unassailable

De facto corporation
A corporation that attempted in good faith to comply with statutory requirements and can only be challenged by the state

Corporation by estoppel
Corporation that cannot be attacked by third parties because they have dealt with corporation as if it was validly organized

A **de jure corporation** (literally, one "of right") is a corporation that has substantially complied with the appropriate state statutes. For example, a mere typographical error in an address in the articles would likely be viewed as so minor that substantial compliance with the statutes is acknowledged. The corporation would be classified as de jure. The significance of achieving de jure status is that the corporation's existence and validity cannot be attacked or challenged by any party, including the state in which it was incorporated.

A corporation that fails to achieve de jure status may be classified as a **de facto corporation** (literally, one "in fact"). The significance of being classified as de facto is that the corporation cannot be attacked by any third party, such as a creditor. It may, however, be challenged by its creator, the state, which may bring an action to declare the corporation invalid. To achieve de facto status, there must be some good faith attempt by the corporation to comply with the laws of the state of incorporation and some good faith conduct of business as if a corporation existed. Some courts have held that failure to file the articles in the county in which the corporation does business (although they have been filed with the secretary of state) results in a de facto corporation.

If a corporation is neither de jure nor de facto, it can be attacked by a third party who may then recover from individual shareholders. There are, however, situations in which courts hold that the attacking party or creditor is *estopped* (or precluded) from challenging the validity of the corporation. In such cases, the corporation is said to be a **corporation by estoppel.** If creditors have dealt with the entity believing it was a corporation, they will generally be estopped from later claiming that it is not a valid corporation. Similarly, if an entity has held itself out as being a corporation *it* will later be estopped from claiming that it is not liable for debts and obligations because it is not a validly formed entity.

Various modern statutes dealing with the formation of corporations have lessened the use of the de jure and de facto doctrines. For example, RMBCA Section 2.03(b) provides that the secretary of state's filing of the articles of incorporation is "conclusive proof" that the incorporators satisfied all conditions required for incorporation (except that the state can challenge the validity of the corporation). Many states have similar statutes. These statutes preclude a third party from attacking the corporation based on defects in the formation process. Thus, there are far fewer cases today alleging that the shareholders should be liable for corporate debts due to defects in incorporation than there were years ago and the de jure/de facto doctrine is of more historical interest than practical interest.

Key Features in Forming Corporations

- Those who plan the corporation are promoters who owe fiduciary duties to each other. Agreements made by them bind them until the corporation ratifies or adopts their actions or contracts.
- Interested investors often offer or subscribe to purchase stock when the corporation is later formed. The offer is irrevocable for some period of time. The corporation usually accepts the offer at its first organizational meeting.
- Consideration should be given as to the jurisdiction in which to incorporate. The state in which the corporation will conduct business should be the favored candidate unless its statutes are inflexible and costs are high.
- The corporate name must usually include a signal showing the entity is a corporation. The name can be reserved prior to the time of incorporation.
- The document that creates a corporation is called the articles of incorporation. Its contents are dictated by state statute.
- Bylaws must be prepared for the corporation. Bylaws are the internal rules for the corporation's operation and governance.
- Corporations must hold a first meeting, called the organizational meeting, to commence the corporation's business.
- Defects in the incorporation process will not permit third parties to attack the corporation, because corporations are conclusively presumed to be validly formed upon filing of the articles.

G. Role of Paralegal

The role of the paralegal in the incorporation process is full and varied. In some instances, paralegals have nearly complete responsibility for forming the corporation. Paralegals are routinely involved in the following activities:

1. Drafting agreements to be entered into by promoters, defining their rights and obligations to each other and to the proposed corporation.
2. Preparing preincorporation share subscriptions and assignments of those subscriptions.
3. Preparing a survey of corporate statutes in various jurisdictions to ensure the corporation is incorporated in a jurisdiction beneficial to the corpo-

ration. (The survey will compare costs of incorporation, taxes, fees, requirements imposed on directors, and so forth.)

4. Assisting in selection of the name of the corporation to ensure it includes the appropriate corporate designation, if required, and then determining availability of the name.
5. Reserving the name so it is available for the corporation and docketing the date the reservation expires to ensure that the incorporation process is completed before the reservation expires.
6. Registering the name in foreign jurisdictions if the corporation intends to operate in other states.
7. Preparing the pertinent documents if the corporation will be operating under an assumed name.
8. Preparing the articles of incorporation and reviewing the state statutes to ensure the articles comply with the state's requirements.
9. Filing the articles with the secretary of state and with any county in which they must be recorded.
10. Drafting bylaws for the internal governance of the corporation.
11. Ordering the corporate supplies, namely, the stock certificates, minute book, and seal.
12. Preparing for the organizational meeting by sending out any required notices and preparing an agenda for the meeting.
13. Attending the organizational meeting and taking and preparing minutes of the meeting (or preparing the written consent action if no organizational meeting is actually held).
14. Preparing the appropriate forms for election of S corporation status (where applicable).
15. Applying to the Internal Revenue Service for an employer identification number (see Figure 2-3 for IRS Form SS-4). An employer identification number is a nine-digit number assigned to sole proprietorships that will pay wages to one or more employees and to all partnerships and corporations. (See Chapter Two, Role of Paralegal.)

Resource Guide

There are eight resources that will be of assistance to paralegals in forming and organizing corporations.

1. State Statutes

Because corporate existence is regulated by law in every state, the most critical resource is the corporations code for the state of incorporation. It will set forth the elements required to be included in the articles of incorporation and will also provide for adoption of bylaws and the organizational meeting. Use the general index to your state's annotated codes to review the topics you need, for example, "articles of incorporation," "bylaws," "directors," and so forth. Check the pocket part (or any supplement) to the code to ensure there have been no recent modifications or revisions of the statutes in your state.

To prepare a survey of the relative advantages and disadvantages of incorporating in various jurisdictions, use the volumes of the *Martindale-Hubbell Law Directory* which contain brief overviews of the laws of all 50 states (usually referred to as the "Law Digest Volumes"), and then compare and contrast the requirements for corporations in various states.

You may also need to review various federal statutes, for example, those pertaining to Section 1244 stock, Section 1202 qualified small business stock, or S corporation elections.

2. Encyclopedias

Use either of the general encyclopedias, C.J.S. or Am. Jur. 2d, to obtain introductory information about corporations. If your state has an encyclopedia devoted solely to the law of your state, use it to review the requirements for forming corporations in your state. Remember to use the Table of Statutes Construed found in most state encyclopedias, which will direct you to the portion of the encyclopedia discussing specific corporate (or other) statutes.

3. Specialized Texts

Browse your law library section containing books on corporations to locate texts and treatises devoted solely to corporate law. If your law firm has a treatise devoted to incorporation in your state, this should be consulted initially because it will have the most detailed and specific information relating to the formation of corporations in your jurisdiction. You may wish to review the very thorough and multivolume work *Fletcher's Cyclopedia of the Law of Private Corporations.*

4. Form Books

Because so many of a paralegal's activities in organizing a corporation relate to the preparation of various documents, form books will be an invaluable guide in drafting requests for name reservations, articles of incorporation, preincorporation share subscriptions, bylaws, and so forth. If a treatise exists relating to forming corporations in your state, it will likely also include forms to be used in the incorporation process. Alternatively, you can consult some of the "general" form books (form books containing sample forms acceptable in most jurisdictions, rather than state-specific forms). Some of the better known form books are the following:

a. *Fletcher's Corporate Forms Annotated* provides excellent forms and drafting tips.
b. *Am. Jur. Legal Forms 2d* includes practice-oriented forms for nearly all aspects of corporate organization, maintenance, and dissolution. *Am. Jur. Legal Forms 2d* is a particularly useful guide because it provides: introductory explanations of the proper use of certain forms and provisions; cautionary notes regarding forms; drafting tips, guides, and checklists; tax notes; practice comments; and annotations sending you to cases and annotations (or essays) in *American Law Reports.* Forms for almost all aspects of corporation practice are provided, including forms for articles of incorporation, corporate management, preincorporation documents, bylaws, mergers, dissolutions, and other useful documents and forms. The form book is updated by pocket parts providing revised forms and references to more recent cases and annotations. Customer assistance on use of the set is available by calling (800) 527-0430.
c. *West's Legal Forms 2d* also offers excellent basic forms that can then be modified to suit the particular needs of a client. The forms are easy to use and clearly presented.

d. *Current Legal Forms with Tax Analysis* by Rabkin and Johnson also offers a wide variety of forms used in corporate law practice.
e. *Corporation Forms* by Marvin Hyman takes the reader through the life of a corporation. Any phase of corporate life for which a form may be needed, whether for a large corporation or a small corporation, is included. The forms are introduced by text to guide readers as to the use of the forms. The text often contains cautionary notes and warnings about particular items.
f. *Nichols Cyclopedia of Legal Forms Annotated* also offers a useful variety of forms for organizing, maintaining, and dissolving corporations.

It is also possible that attorneys in a firm have attended various seminars and continuing education programs on corporations. The materials distributed at such seminars usually include forms and practice tips. Check the shelves of the firm's law library or ask the law librarian if any such seminar materials exist.

5. Secretary of State

Using Appendix A, call the office of your secretary of state and ask that various forms be sent to you. Most secretaries of state will provide a sample package of forms which you can photocopy and keep in the office to use in the future. A fee schedule is usually also enclosed. Most states provide these forms free of charge. Alternatively, access the Web site for the secretary of state and download the forms.

6. Law Office Forms

If your law office engages in corporate law practice, it is highly likely that a variety of forms, letters, and other documents have already been drafted for use in the office. Check with one of the attorneys, the office administrator, the law librarian, or a secretary. The forms may be available on the word processor. You can simply retrieve the standard form used in your office and then modify it to fit the client's particular needs. Some law firms attempt to collect forms from all jurisdictions and keep these in alphabetically arranged binders or folders. If your office does not have such a collection, offer to contact the secretary of state in each state and obtain the basic forms for each state and compile them in such a binder for future use in the office.

7. WESTLAW

West Group's computer-assisted research source provides access to corporate records from the states and the District of Columbia. The name of record of a company, its address, and the states in which it transacts business can be quickly determined. To search all available states at once, access the ALLCORP database.

8. Service Companies

The various attorneys' service companies can provide information, forms, and fees relating to incorporation. Some of them will handle all details of the incorporation process or will agree to handle only certain activities, such as reserving the name. The Company Corporation advertises that it is headquartered in Delaware with a computer network linked directly to the Delaware Secretary of State to assure filing of the certificate of incorporation in eight minutes. Attorneys Corporation Service offers same-day incorporation and name availability services. CT Corporation Service acts as the registered agent for more than 250,000 corporations. Of the Fortune 1,000 companies, approximately 80 percent are represented by CT Corporation System. Many service companies also provide corporate kits, some of which include "canned" or prepared bylaws and minutes for an organizational meeting. These minutes and bylaws may also be available on diskette. Generally, these service companies can also provide other related forms such as S corporation election forms, forms for obtaining a federal tax identification number, or forms for nonprofit corporations. Some of the service companies offer packages of forms including forms for minutes for annual and special meetings, employment agreements, notices, and proxies.

Some of the better known attorneys service or corporations service companies are:

Attorneys Corporation Service, Inc.
4664 Lankershim Blvd.
North Hollywood, CA 91602-1884
phone: (800) 462-5487

CT Corporation System
111 8th Avenue
New York, NY 10011
phone: (800) 624-0909

The Corporation Trust Company
Corporation Trust Center
1209 Orange Street
Wilmington, DE 19801
phone: (302) 658-7581

Corporation Service Company
1013 Centre Road
Wilmington, DE 19805
phone: (800) 927-9800
www.incspot.com

The Company Corporation
1013 Centre Rd.
Wilmington, DE 19805
phone: (800) 542-2677
www.corporate.com

Corpex Banknote Company, Inc.
1440 Fifth Avenue
Bayshore, NY 11706-9807
phone: (800) 221-8181

CorpAmerica, Inc.
30 Old Rudnick Lane
Dover, Delaware 19901
phone: (800) 622-6414
www.corpAmerica.com

Business Incorporators, Inc.
1019 Cypress Road
Wilmington, DE 19801
phone: (800) 695-6596

◆ ◆ ◆

WEB RESOURCES

Because nearly all states have posted their forms relating to incorporations on their Web sites, the most important Web resources are the home pages of the various secretaries of state. See Appendix A for the specific Web address for each of the state's secretaries of state. Other alternatives follow. Remember that forms provided are anonymous and should serve as a model only. Revise forms to suit the client's needs. Check Web site "Disclaimer" and "Legal Conditions" sections to determine whether the forms are available for use.

www.nass.org
This Web site of the National Association of Secretaries of State will provide you with links to each of the secretaries of state. After you access the home page of the Association, select "States." You will then be given an alphabetical list of all 50 states and the District of Columbia (together with their state flags). Point your cursor at the state you wish, and you will be immediately linked to the home page for that state's secretary of state. In most instances, you will immediately see entries for "Corporations" or "Business." Select the relevant entry, and you will be given basic information about forming a corporation in that state, instructions for filing, addresses and phone numbers, fee schedules, and forms that you can either download or request to be mailed to you. In some instances, you can check name availability on the Web site. For example, California and North Carolina allow one to check the state database to make a preliminary determination of name availability. In California, another database may be used to obtain basic information about a corporation, such as its date of incorporation, its status (active, suspended, or dissolved), and its agent for service of process.

www.ll.georgetown.edu
This Web site for Georgetown University Law Center provides access to a wealth of legal information. Select "State, Local & Territorial," and you will then be presented of a map of the United States. Point your cursor to the desired state, and you will then be able to select whether you wish to view that state's constitution, statutes, or other legal information. By selecting "Statutes" or "Code" you will be able to search the state's statutes and find relevant corporate statutory material.

www.ss.ca.gov/business/bpd_service_companies.htm
This Web site of the State of California lists numerous companies and individuals that will serve as registered agents for service of process.

www.state.de.us/corp/corp.htm
This Web site of the State of Delaware lists more than 70 companies that will serve as registered agents for service of process.

www.legalwiz.com
When you access this site, select "Legal Sites" and then "Corporate Department and Secretary of State Pages" for links to each state's secretary of state.

www.findlaw.com/16/forms/index.html
When you access this Forms Collection and Forms Index at the FindLaw Web site, select "Corporate and Business Forms" under the listing for "Government Forms" for a directory of state corporate and business forms.

www.state.sc.us/states
The Web site of the Secretary of State of South Carolina also provides direct links to the secretaries of state of the other states.

www.about.com
After you access this site, select "Business/Careers" and then "More Links." Scroll down the page to "Business Information," and then select "State Government Resources" for links to corporate and business information from each state.

http://legal-resource.com/forms
This Web site provides a form for articles of incorporation, assignments, corporate bylaws, and minutes for the first meeting of the board of directors of a corporation.

www.siccode.com/forms.php3
Access "Free Legal Forms" for a variety of business and corporate forms, including one for assignment of a contract that can be modified to reflect assignment of a promoter's rights under a preincorporation contract to a corporation (as well as a form for consent to an assignment of contract), a form for minutes confirming that the tax benefits of Section 1244 of the Internal Revenue Code will be elected by the shareholders, and various forms for minutes and waivers of notice of meetings.

www.lectlaw.com
When you access this site, select "Rotunda," then "Forms Room," and then "Business and General Forms" for forms for assignments, articles of incorporation, bylaws, and minutes of organizational meeting of incorporators (and waiver of the meeting).

Discussion Questions

1. Pam, a promoter of a corporation to be formed for catering services, has been shopping around for commercial cooking and baking equipment. Pam sees some excellent equipment at W & T Restaurant Supply Co. and orders $10,000 worth of equipment and supplies for the corporation. Due to a falling out among the individuals involved, the corporation is never formed. W & T specially ordered the equipment and has sent a bill for it to Pam's home. Can W & T recover the cost of the equipment from Pam?

2. Discuss whether the following are acceptable corporate names under most state statutes.

- Tanning Salon & Spa
- Federal Bank Check Cashing Co.
- Limited Reserve Winery
- Fast Photo Gallery Inc.

3. Galloway Enterprises, Inc. incorporated in Georgia last year. Since then, the company has experienced great success and is considering branching out into

neighboring states within the next year. What should the corporation do at this time?

4. Helen and Jim Hays plan to form a corporation to offer music lessons in a small studio near their home in Virginia. Should a state-by-state survey be conducted to determine the best state in which they should incorporate their business? Why or why not?

5. Susan subscribed for 100 shares of stock in her brother's corporation. The corporation was incorporated and at its first organizational meeting accepted Susan's subscription. Susan does not have the money to pay for the stock and has discovered that there was a defect in the incorporation papers in that the corporation did not indicate a par value for its stock although the state statute requires a par value to be identified. Susan has refused to pay for the stock she subscribed for on the basis that the corporation was defectively formed. Is the defect a valid defense for Susan? Discuss fully. Use the RMBCA approach.

6. Would a provision identifying the place of the annual shareholders' meeting for a corporation be better placed in the corporation's articles or bylaws? Why?

10

Corporate Finances

CHAPTER OVERVIEW

At the beginning of a corporation's existence, it obtains capital from investors who give money to the corporation in return for part ownership of the corporation, in the form of shares of the corporation, or stock. After the corporation is established, it may engage in a variety of methods to obtain additional infusions of capital. The corporation may issue bonds, documents evidencing the corporation's debt, to an investor (the bondholder) who has loaned money to the corporation. Stocks and bonds, collectively referred to as securities, are vehicles used by corporations desiring to raise capital. Capital is also derived from the operation of the corporation's business.

Corporations are often said to be subject to double taxation, meaning the corporation pays tax on the income it earns and then the shareholders pay taxes when corporate profit is distributed to them in the form of distributions.

This chapter explores the various types of securities issued by corporations, and the rights and privileges thereof, as well as aspects of taxation of corporations.

A. Introduction to Securities

Security
A share, participation, or other interest in property or an enterprise of the issuer or an obligation of the issuer

Equity security
A security representing ownership interest in an enterprise (often called a *share*)

According to the Uniform Commercial Code, which promotes uniformity in various commercial and contractual relationships, a **security** is a share, participation, or other interest in property or an enterprise of the issuer or an obligation of the issuer. UCC Section 8-102(1). Thus, viewing the corporation as the issuer, securities fall into two classes: those that show a person's ownership interest in the corporation and those that show an obligation of the corporation. The term **equity securities** refers to shares of a corporation that are sold to investors called share-

Equity capital
Capital received by a corporation in return for issuance of stock

Debt security
A security representing an obligation of the corporate issuer (often called a *bond*)

Bondholder
One to whom a debt is owed by a corporation

Debt capital
Money received by a corporation in return for issuing debt securities

Dividend
A distribution of corporate profits

holders or stockholders (the terms are synonymous). The capital received by a corporation in return for issuance of equity securities is called **equity capital.** The term **debt securities** refers to documents issued by a corporation, usually called *bonds,* representing the corporation's debt to an investor, who is typically called a **bondholder.** The capital received by a corporation in return for issuance of a debt security is known as **debt capital.**

While the terms stocks and bonds are often referred to in the same breath, these two types of securities are vastly different from each other. A shareholder who owns equity securities (shares) in a corporation is an insider, an owner of the corporation who will likely be entitled to vote on various corporate issues, may receive distributions of corporate profits (called **dividends**), and may receive assets of the corporation upon its liquidation and dissolution. A bondholder, on the other hand, is an outsider, not a corporate owner, and is thus not entitled to vote, receive dividends, or share in the distribution of net assets upon liquidation and dissolution. The bondholder is, however, entitled to be repaid the amount borrowed by the corporation at the agreed-upon time and under the agreed-upon terms.

Issuance of each type of security by a corporation offers certain advantages and disadvantages. The issuance of shares offers a corporation the advantage of receiving needed capital that need not be repaid because the shareholder expects to make money either by receiving dividends or from increasing value of the stock. Each new share of stock issued, however, dilutes the power of the current shareholders. The issuance of bonds offers the advantage of receiving needed capital without any loss of power to current shareholders. Moreover, the corporation can deduct interest paid to the bondholder as a corporate expense. Nevertheless, the bond must be repaid at some time as must interest on it, whether the corporation is having a profitable year or not.

According to statistics, the number of bonds issued has been decreasing in the past 20 years while the number of stocks listed has been dramatically increasing, reflecting a trend of corporations to raise money through the issuance of stock rather than bonds. See *U.S. Statistical Abstract* 552 (118th ed. 1998).

	1980	*1990*	*1995*
Shares Listed (in billions)	33.7	90.7	207.1
Bonds	3,057	2,912	1,965

Similarly, the percentage of American families owning stock continues to increase, from 32 percent in 1989 to 40 percent in 1995. *Id.* at 532. The majority of stock sold on the national exchanges, however, is not held by individual investors but by institutional investors. For example, approximately 55 percent of the stock of Texaco Inc. is held by institutional investors such as TIAA-CREF, Barclay's, and the California Public Employees' Retirement System.

Most experts believe that stocks have a greater potential for return than bonds; however, stocks also carry a greater risk of loss and can fluctuate wildly in value. Bonds, on the other hand, are far more stable because the investor can predict in advance the expected return. Thus, many investors attempt to diversify their portfolios by allocating their assets into a mix of both stocks and bonds.

Common stock
Ordinary stock of a corporation having no special privileges

Shareholders of **common stock** (the ordinary stock of the corporation) expect reasonable growth. Common stock is not particularly safe, however, as it may plunge in value with little or no warning and because the corporation has no obligation to return the amount invested to the shareholder. Shareholders of **preferred stock** (stock that has some right, privilege, or preference over another type of stock) expect steady income and a reasonably safe investment. Bondholders expect no growth (because the bond amount is fixed) but will receive steady income in the form of regular payments of interest and principal. A bond is the safest form of investment in a corporation.

Preferred stock
Stock in a corporation that carries certain rights and privileges

Corporations will issue a mix of equity and debt securities depending on market conditions and risk evaluation. Investors may be unwilling to lend money to a corporation engaged in a high-risk venture. Such a corporation may rely nearly exclusively on equity financing, or the sale of shares, to raise needed capital.

The public sale of corporate securities, whether stock or bonds, is subject to regulation by applicable state laws, as well as the Federal Securities Act of 1933 and Securities Exchange Act of 1934 (see Chapter Thirteen). All of these laws are designed to protect the public from fraud and unfair business practices. Many small issuances of stock, such as those in which the total amount of the offering does not exceed $1 million, are exempt from such regulation.

B. Equity Securities

1. *Introduction*

The corporation's equity securities are identified in the articles of incorporation, which set forth the number of shares the corporation is authorized to issue. This number should be determined after giving careful consideration to the corporation's anticipated needs for capital (and investigating whether the state assesses different fees depending on the number of shares authorized by the articles). The number of shares authorized to be sold should be large enough to accommodate growth because once the corporation has issued the number specified, no further shares can be issued until the articles of incorporation are amended. Because amendment usually requires shareholder approval and always requires state approval and filing fees, failure to allow a sufficient number of authorized shares will delay the corporation from obtaining needed capital until it can hold a shareholders' meeting and file the appropriate documents to amend the articles.

The shares identified in the articles are referred to as **authorized shares** of the corporation. Those who wish to purchase shares will give the appropriate consideration for the shares (cash, property, services already performed, contracts for services to be performed, or other securities of the corporation) and the corporation will issue or deliver the shares to the investor. Shares that have been issued are referred to as **outstanding shares.** Thus, shareholders of a corporation hold authorized, issued, and outstanding shares. Large corporations can have significant numbers of outstanding shares. For example, in early 2000, General Mills had more than 300 million outstanding shares.

Authorized shares
The number of shares the corporation has the authority to issue according to its articles

Outstanding shares
Shares issued by a corporation and held by investors

Shares are issued and outstanding unless they are reacquired, redeemed, converted, or canceled by the corporation. Stock reacquired by the corporation (often because the shareholder exercised a right to compel the corporation to

Treasury stock
Stock reacquired by a corporation and which is not outstanding

repurchase or redeem the stock) is called **treasury stock.** Treasury shares are not considered outstanding because they are not held by investors but rather by the corporation itself. Thus, they are not entitled to voting rights or to share in dividends. Moreover, they are not entitled to receive any distribution of the corporation's net assets upon liquidation.

The decision to issue shares is made by the board of directors acting in the best interest of the corporation. Not only does the number of shares authorized by the articles act as a ceiling on the number of shares that can be issued, the directors must also observe any preemptive rights given to shareholders by the articles that allow the existing shareholders to purchase their respective ownership proportion of newly issued stock before it can be issued to others.

The articles may authorize more than one type or class of shares. For example, shares may be issued having certain rights or preferences over other types of stock. This stock is usually referred to as *preferred stock.*

The articles of incorporation *must* authorize one or more classes of shares that together have unlimited voting rights and one or more classes of shares that together are entitled to receive the net assets of the corporation upon dissolution under RMBCA Section 6.01(b). Most state statutes are similar. This provision ensures that the corporation will have shareholders who can vote on corporate action and receive the net assets of the corporation in the event it liquidates.

An equity security holder has three ownership interests in a corporation: the right to vote (usually one vote per share); the right to receive distributions, if declared by the board in its discretion and if the corporation is solvent; and the right to receive net assets on liquidation of the corporation once creditors have been satisfied.

2. *Par Value and No Par Value Stock*

The initial issuance of stock is dependent upon the initial capital needs of the corporation. For example, if the business requires $100,000 and ten initial investors wish to invest equally, they can each be issued $10,000 worth of stock. The directors commonly establish the price for the shares. They will be guided by the best interest of the corporation and by market conditions. If the price per share is too high, for example, $10,000 per share, few investors will be able to pay this amount. Thus, in the present example, it may be better to issue each investor 200 shares at a price of $50 per share rather than to issue one share for $10,000 because the division into more shares enhances the ability to sell the stock at a later date. A stockholder may be unable to locate a buyer who wishes to invest $10,000, but may readily be able to find a few buyers willing to invest $50 per share. If the price per share is too low, it will dilute the interest of the then-existing shareholders by reducing the value of their shares.

In addition to the directors' duty to establish the value of the stock while acting in the corporation's best interest, there is another limitation relating to the amount for which stock can be issued. The **par value** of the stock as set forth in the articles of incorporation is the minimum amount for which stock can be issued. Thus, if the par value is $10, the stock can be issued for $10 or any amount in excess of this, but cannot be issued for an amount less than $10. This explains why par value is traditionally set at such a low amount (often $1 or even ten cents): it gives directors the flexibility to issue shares for a small amount of money

Par value
The lowest price for which stock can be sold

if they need to raise capital but there is little market for the shares. Par value is not equivalent to market value. In fact, because par value is usually so low, corporations hope that market value is far in excess of par value.

Some states, however, allow directors to issue stock for less than the par value if the directors determine this is in the best interest of the corporation. In general, shares issued for less than the par value are referred to as **watered stock** (or sometimes *discount* or *bonus stock*). Shares without a par value set forth in the articles, referred to as **no par value shares,** can be sold for whatever price the directors fix so long as this price is reasonable.

Watered stock
Stock sold for less than its par value (also called *discount* or *bonus* stock)

No par value stock
Stock with no stated par value and which can be sold according to the directors' discretion

In most states, corporations have the option of stating a par value for the stock in the articles of incorporation or stating that there will be no par value. The RMBCA typifies the modern trend in not requiring any par value to be stated. In those states that do not require that a par value be specified in the articles, statutes often provide that par value is deemed to be a certain amount, for example, $1; this is solely for the purpose of determining filing fees, annual fees, and taxes.

Because of the elimination of the concept of par value, under the RMBCA there is no minimum price at which shares must be issued. The shares will be issued for whatever consideration is determined by the board of directors. The only limitation on the directors' discretion is that shares issued at approximately the same time must be issued for approximately the same consideration unless there is a valid business reason for the price differential. RMBCA Section 6.21(c) provides that before the corporation issues shares, the board must determine that the consideration is adequate.

Some general corporate accounting principles are also affected by issuance of par value shares and no par value shares. If shares with a par value of $15 are in fact sold for $15 each, the amount received by the corporation is placed in an account referred to as **stated capital.** Any amount received for shares over and above the par value amount is called **capital surplus** and is placed in a capital surplus account. If the stock has no par value, the directors can sell the stock at any price they determine and then in their discretion allocate the proceeds received to the stated capital account and to the capital surplus account. For example, if no par value stock is issued for $25 per share, the directors can allocate $5 to stated capital and $20 to capital surplus. The advantage of a large capital surplus account is that most state statutes permit corporations to repurchase their own shares only if there is sufficient money in the capital surplus account to make the purchase. The existence of no par value stock gives the directors the flexibility to create a large capital surplus account for this purpose (and also for the distribution of dividends in some instances). Because the RMBCA has eliminated the concept of par value, the concept of stated capital is likewise eradicated and the corporation may allocate the consideration received as the directors deem appropriate.

Stated capital
Amount received by a corporation when stock is sold at its par value

Capital surplus
Amount received by a corporation in excess of a stock's par value

3. *Consideration for Shares*

To ensure that corporations were adequately capitalized, the older view required that the consideration given for shares generally be in cash. **Promissory notes** (agreements promising to pay a certain sum in the future) and agreements to provide services in the future were generally unacceptable. According to RMBCA Section 6.21(b) and most modern statutes, shares may be issued for consideration consisting of any tangible or intangible property or benefit to the

Promissory note
An agreement to pay or repay money in the future

corporation, including cash, promissory notes, services performed, contracts for services to be performed, or other securities of the corporation. This very flexible standard allows for almost anything to be exchanged for shares so long as there is some benefit to the corporation. Naturally, a corporation cannot issue all of its stock for future services or promissory notes inasmuch as the corporation needs a certain amount of cash to meet its needs. To ensure the individual will pay the note or perform the services, the corporation may place the shares in an escrow account or otherwise restrict their transfer until the investor has complied. If intangible property or services are given as consideration, the board will appraise or determine the value of such contributions and issue stock accordingly. Some states continue to require that the consideration be in the form of cash, property, or already performed services.

Just as stock can be watered by issuance for less cash than par value, it can also be watered if the corporation does not receive adequate property or services in return for stock issued. While some jurisdictions have determined that the holder of watered stock enjoys no rights with respect to the watered stock and can be subject to liability for the difference between what was paid and par value, most jurisdictions are adopting the modern approach found in the RMBCA. Once the board determines what consideration should be paid for the stock, that determination is deemed conclusive as far as adequacy is concerned. RMBCA Section 6.21(c). Moreover, when the corporation receives the consideration for which the board of directors authorized the issuance of shares, the shares are "fully paid and nonassessable." RMBCA Section 6.21(d). Thus, under the modern view, the recipient of watered stock has simply gotten a good deal on the stock and can participate in voting and other issues just as other shareholders can without being liable to the corporation for any additional sums (assuming no fraud or misrepresentation by the purchaser of the stock exists).

4. *Stock Certificates*

Uncertificated shares
Stock issued without actual stock certificates

Corporations can issue stock without physically delivering a certificate to the shareholder. Shares issued without the formality of stock certificates are called **uncertificated shares.** The ownership of such shares is recorded in the corporate books. Owners of uncertificated stock have the same rights as owners of stock evidenced by paper certificates. The issuance of uncertificated stock simply reduces the burden on a corporation engaged in rapid trading of its stock. In fact, in today's volatile and modern stock market, many investors never possess actual stock certificates. In some instances, purchasers request certificates when stock is bought as a gift, for example, for a graduation or birthday present.

When actual certificates are used, their content and form is controlled by state statute. RMBCA Section 6.25 provides that share certificates must provide the following information:

a. the name of the issuing organization and the state law under which it is organized;
b. the name of the person to whom the share is issued; and
c. the number and class of shares (and the designation of the series, if any).

Within a reasonable amount of time after uncertificated shares are issued, the corporation must send the shareholder a written statement including the information required to be set forth on certificates.

The share certificate must be signed (either manually or by facsimile signature or autopen) by two officers of the corporation, generally the president and the secretary. The seal may be impressed on the face of the certificate although this is not required. Issuance of new certificates in a small corporation is typically performed by the corporate secretary or treasurer. In large corporations, however, this task would be daunting and is therefore often performed by a **transfer agent,** usually a bank or other institution that has a supply of blank certificates with facsimile signatures of the officers. The transfer agent also records transfer of shares and may act as the corporate **registrar,** and maintain the list of shareholders.

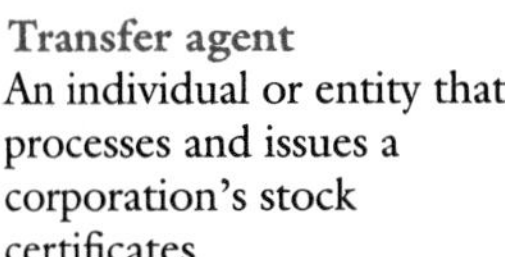

Transfer agent
An individual or entity that processes and issues a corporation's stock certificates

Registrar
An individual or entity that maintains a corporation's list of shareholders

If corporations issue only one class of stock, the content of the certificate will be as described above. If more than one class of stock is authorized by the articles of incorporation, the preferences and limitations and rights of each class must be stated on the certificate. Alternatively, and as is more common, the certificate may state that the corporation will furnish this information without charge to any shareholder upon written request.

Because the certificate is not what is owned but merely represents ownership of an interest in a corporation, the loss, theft, or destruction of a stock certificate is not critical. When the shareholder provides an affidavit to the corporation stating that the certificate is lost and cannot be found, or has been stolen or destroyed, the corporation or its transfer agent will cancel the original certificate and issue a duplicate.

On occasion, shareholders own fractions of shares. This generally occurs when the corporation declares a share dividend. For example, if the corporation declares a dividend of 1 share for every 100 owned, the owner of 150 shares would be entitled to receive 1½ shares. If the state corporations code allows fractional shares, the corporation may issue a certificate for a fraction of a share. The owner of this fractional share will be entitled to fractional voting right, dividends, and to participate in the assets of the corporation upon liquidation. The RMBCA authorizes the payment of cash to a shareholder for the value of fractional shares. RMBCA Section 6.04(a).

Alternatively, and in the discretion of the board of directors, the corporation can issue scrip rather than a stock certificate for the fractional share. **Scrip** is a document or certificate evidencing ownership of a fractional share. The certificate must be conspicuously labeled "scrip." When the shareholder has accumulated sufficient scrip to total one share, the scrip may be surrendered to the corporation for a certificate evidencing one full share. Scrip is transferable but generally does not carry voting, dividend, or liquidation rights. Scrip is often issued with the requirement that it be exchanged for a full share within some specified period of time or it will be void.

Scrip
A document or certificate showing ownership of a fractional share

5. *Classes of Stock*

Most corporations issue only one type of stock, generally referred to as common stock. A corporation may, however, if its articles so provide, authorize the issuance of more than one class of stock. These additional classes generally have some benefit or preference over the common stock and are therefore called preferred stock. The preferences may be in the form of cumulative dividends or the right to convert the preferred stock to common stock. While the RMBCA provides various ways in which one class of stock will have privileges or preferences over others, the enumeration of these preferences is not meant to be exclusive and the directors are free to create other benefits or preferences. Thus, corporations have great flexibility in their financial structuring.

The holders of preferred stock have generally elected a more conservative approach to investing. Because dividends are almost always paid on preferred stock, this type of security provides a reasonably certain cash flow.

Common Stock. If the corporation does not specify in its articles of incorporation the type of stock to be issued and only one class of stock is authorized, it will be common stock. The common shareholders are owners of the corporation. Their interests, however, are often referred to as **residual interests,** meaning that they are entitled to the remains of the corporation after all other groups have been satisfied, namely, creditors, bondholders, and preferred shareholders. RMBCA Section 6.22 provides that an individual who purchases shares from a corporation is not liable to the corporation or to its creditors except to pay the consideration required for issuance of the shares.

Residual interests
The interests of common stockholders, who are entitled to assets remaining after others have been satisfied

The holders of common stock usually enjoy the following rights:

Voting Rights. Each outstanding share of common stock is typically entitled to one vote and fractional shares are entitled to corresponding fractional votes. RMBCA Section 7.21(a). It is possible to have different classes of common stock, each having different voting rights. For example, Common A shareholders may be entitled to two votes per share, Common B shareholders to one vote per share, and Common C shareholders may have nonvoting stock (nonvoting stock is useful in obtaining capital for the corporation without a corresponding loss of power or control by existing shareholders). While classes A, B, and C may have different rights from one another, every shareholder within the Common A class must be treated the same, every shareholder within the Common B class must be treated the same, and so forth. Some corporations issue **"supervoting" stock.** For example, Marriott International once had a class of a stock with ten votes per share.

Supervoting stock
Stock that carries more than one vote per share

Distribution Rights. There is no requirement that a corporation ever pay distributions or dividends to its shareholders. Dividends, whether in the form of cash, property, or other shares of the corporation, are paid within the discretion of the board, assuming profits permit. If an individual owns 18 percent of the Common A stock, she will be entitled to 18 percent of whatever distribution is declared by the board of directors for Common A shareholders. Thus, common shareholders receive distributions in the same proportion that their share ownership bears to the total number of common shares issued and outstanding.

While common shareholders *may* receive distributions, there is no guarantee that they will. Furthermore, they will receive distributions only if the corporation is solvent (able to pay its debts as they come due or if assets exceed liabilities) and only after the preferred shareholders have received their distributions.

Liquidation
The wrapping up of a business and its affairs

Liquidation Rights. Upon **liquidation** of the corporation (the wrapping up of its affairs and business before termination of the corporate existence), the corporation must satisfy its creditors and bondholders. The shareholders are then entitled to their proportionate share of the corporation's net assets. Once again, however, the common shareholders are "junior," in that they receive net assets only after the preferred shareholders have been satisfied.

Other Rights. In addition to the typical rights of common shareholders described above, common shareholders may also have preemptive rights (usually only when provided by the articles of incorporation) which allow them the first opportunity to purchase newly issued shares before they are offered to others. Common shareholders may also have cumulative voting rights (see Chapter 11) which allow them, in an election for directors, to multiply the number of shares owned by the number of directors being elected and to cast these as they like. These preemptive rights or cumulative voting rights are usually mandated by statute or provided for in the articles of incorporation.

Preferred Stock. A class of stock that has some sort of right or preference over another class is preferred stock. The preference may be in receipt of dividends, receipt of net assets upon liquidation, or some other preference devised by the board of directors. In many instances, shareholders pay more initially for preferred stock than for common stock because of the preferences attached to it. The creation of preferred stock must be authorized by the articles of incorporation. Preferred stock can be used by a corporation to attract investors with a more conservative approach who desire steady returns on investments.

In other instances, preferences may be given to certain shareholders to even the playing field. For example, assume that Jessica and Patti intend to operate a golf course. Patti may have minimal funds to contribute, for example, $20,000, but may have experience in the business and agrees to manage the course. Jessica has no experience but is able to invest $80,000. If each is issued common stock according to her investment, Jessica, as the controlling shareholder, will always be able to make the business decisions. To provide some comfort to each investor, the corporation may issue 20,000 common shares to each woman so they have equal voting rights. To compensate Jessica for her added investment, the corporation can issue her $60,000 worth of nonvoting preferred stock with a fixed dividend and the right to receive net assets before Patti in the event of a liquidation of the business. All of the terms, limitations, preferences, and rights of each class of shares must be set forth in the articles and on the share certificate (unless the corporation agrees to furnish this information without charge upon written request).

The RMBCA does not use the terms "common" or "preferred" but merely states that the articles of incorporation may authorize one or more classes of stock that have special or preferential rights over other classes as to voting, distributions, or other matters. Although the RMBCA does not expressly use the terms common or preferred to describe stock, those terms are typically used in common parlance and in many state filing forms.

Preferred stock generally has the following features:

Voting Rights. Preferred stock may or may not have voting rights. The articles of incorporation will set forth any limitations or restrictions on the preferred shareholders' rights to vote. Preferred stock may also have contingent voting rights, meaning that the owners of preferred stock can vote upon the occurrence of certain events, such as failure of the directors to declare a dividend for some period of time.

Cumulative distributions
Distributions that add up and must be paid once a corporation has funds to do so

Distribution Rights. A common feature of preferred stock designed to attract investors is a preference in distributions. In many cases, these are **cumulative distributions,** meaning that if the distribution is not paid during any given year, it simply adds up, and the corporation is required to pay these cumulative distributions to the preferred stockholders before distributions are paid to common stockholders. This cumulative dividend is generally built into the stock itself. For example, the articles (as well as the certificate itself) may provide that each share of preferred stock is entitled to a $5 annual cumulative dividend. Assume a preferred stockholder owns 100 shares of stock. Each year the stockholder is entitled to a distribution of $500. If the corporation does not have sufficient profits to pay this dividend for three years, the distribution continues to accumulate. In year four, the corporation must pay the preferred stockholder $2,000 ($500 for four years) before any distributions can be made to common shareholders.

Noncumulative distribution
A distribution that does not accumulate and is lost if it cannot be paid

A **noncumulative distribution** means that the distribution does not accumulate. If the corporation has insufficient profits to pay a distribution to our shareholder for three years, the shareholder simply loses his right to the distribution. In year four, the corporation must pay the preferred stockholder $500 (one year's worth of distributions) before distributions are made to other shareholders.

These distributions, especially the cumulative distributions, allow preferred shareholders to predict their income from their stock holdings with some amount of certainty. Nevertheless, while these provisions lend certainty, they can also be viewed as restrictive. If the corporation has a record year and the directors declare significant distributions to the common shareholders, the preferred shareholders may actually receive less than the common shareholders inasmuch as their rights are limited to the agreed-upon and stated distribution fixed by the articles and the stock certificate.

The distribution preference can be expressed in terms of dollars ("each share of preferred stock is entitled to receive $10 per share each year before any distributions can be made to any other shareholders") or in terms of ownership interest ("each share of preferred stock is entitled to receive 10 percent of the preferred stock's par value [or stated value] each year before any distributions can be made to any other shareholders").

Participating preferred stock
Stock that has the right to participate in other distributions as well as those "built into" the stock

Preferred stock can also be **participating preferred,** meaning that the preferred shareholder also has the right to participate in other distributions, if any, declared by the board of directors in addition to the preference. Participating preferred dividends thus allow the preferred shareholders to share with the common shareholders when the corporation has had an exceptional year and large distributions of the corporation's profits are made. Preferred shareholders would receive their cumulative or noncumulative distribution and would then share in the other distribution made by the corporation. Participating preferred dividends are somewhat rare and are usually paid to the preferred shareholders after the common shareholders have received their distribution of the corporation's earnings.

Liquidation Rights. The holders of preferred stock may be entitled to a stated distribution upon liquidation of the corporation. For example, the articles may provide that upon liquidation, the preferred stockholders are entitled to be paid $85 per share of preferred stock together with interest thereon at 7 percent per year, before any other shareholders may receive assets in liquidation. Similarly, the articles may provide that the liquidation preference is some percentage of par value, for example, "full par value plus 30 percent." After the preferred shareholders have been fully satisfied in the agreed-upon amount, they may also share with the common shareholders in receiving net assets upon liquidation.

Conversion Rights. Preferred shareholders may be given the **right to convert** their preferred shares into shares of some other class or series, usually common shares, either at an agreed-upon price or an agreed-upon ratio. For example, the articles and share certificates may provide that preferred shares with a par value of $50 may be convertible into common stock shares with a par value of $50. If the preferred shareholders elect to exercise this right, the preferred shares are surrendered to the transfer agent of the corporation and are canceled, and new common shares are issued. Naturally, the articles of incorporation must authorize a sufficient number of shares to accommodate this right of conversion and the corporation must have an adequate number of authorized but unissued shares to allow the preferred shareholders to exercise their conversion rights.

Conversion right
Right to convert preferred stock into some other form of equity security, usually common stock

Conversion rights may be subject to some contingency. For example, they may be exercisable only after some specified period of time or only in the event the corporation has not paid a dividend for two or more consecutive years. Conversion rights that are noncontingent offer tremendous advantages to preferred shareholders. They may safely and accurately predict their income and have the advantage of this more conservative investment, and yet they may be able to convert their preferred shares to common shares if the common shares are doing extraordinarily well.

Redemption Rights. Preferred stock may be issued with **redemption rights** (sometimes referred to as a **call**) by which the corporation has the power to reacquire the shares from the shareholders, or to call them back. The right of redemption may be exercised by the board of directors when the distributions required to be given to shareholders of cumulative preferred stock become too much of a financial burden on the corporation, and the corporation desires to stem the flow of cash paid each year to the preferred stockholders. The amount to be paid when the corporation redeems the shares (typically, a percentage of the par value of the stock together with any accrued and unpaid distributions) is governed by the articles of incorporation. The articles should contain all other terms relating to the redemption, such as when it may be exercised, the period of notice required to be given to the shareholder, and whether the redemption will be partial (and relate only to some of the stock owned by the preferred shareholder) or will be total, in which case all of the stock owned by the preferred shareholder can be called back by the corporation.

Redemption rights
Right to compel a stockholder or a corporation to sell or buy stock back

Call
Right by corporation to reacquire its stock from a shareholder

To ensure sufficient funds to repurchase the redeemable preferred stock, the corporation will usually establish a separate account, called the **sinking fund,** into which the corporation, over time, deposits funds for redemption purposes, for "retiring the stock." The sinking fund cannot be used for other purposes such as the payment of expenses or distributions.

Sinking fund
An account kept for redemption of stock

Rights of redemption may also be given to the preferred shareholder. In this case, the shareholder has the right to compel the corporation to redeem the

Put
Right by shareholder to require corporation to redeem or repurchase shares

shares, if it has sufficient funds in the sinking fund to do so, upon the terms and conditions provided in the articles of incorporation. This particular right of redemption is referred to as a **put** and offers a preferred shareholder the advantage of having a ready buyer if the shareholder cannot sell the stock on the market.

When a corporation reacquires shares through redemption (either through the corporation's call for the stock or the shareholder's put), it will usually cancel the shares and restore them to the status of authorized but unissued shares. The effect is as if the original issuance of stock to the shareholder had never taken place. This is the RMBCA approach. RMBCA Section 6.31(a). These shares can thereafter be reissued. The transfer agent is responsible for recording the cancellation of the shares.

RMBCA Section 6.31(b) provides that if the articles of incorporation prohibit the reissue of acquired shares, the number of authorized shares is reduced by the number of shares acquired. In such a case, the directors must file a statement with the secretary of state setting forth the name of the corporation, the reduction in the number of authorized shares (itemized by class and series), and the total number of authorized shares (itemized by class and series) remaining after reduction. The statement is treated as an amendment to the articles of incorporation without the necessity of shareholder approval. (See Figure 10-1 for a statement of cancellation of non-reissuable shares.)

In brief, the RMBCA approach is that shares reacquired by a corporation automatically "bump up" the number of shares the corporation can thereafter issue unless the articles prohibit such reissue, in which case the reacquired shares are canceled by reducing the number of shares that the corporation's articles authorize it to issue.

As an alternative either to cancelling the shares and reissuing them or cancelling the shares and not reissuing them, in some states, the corporation can place the reacquired shares in its treasury. These treasury shares are viewed as authorized and issued, but not outstanding. Thus, they do not carry any rights to voting or distributions. The RMBCA has eliminated the concept of treasury shares and merely provides that a corporation can acquire its own shares, which then constitute authorized but unissued shares. RMBCA Section 6.31(a).

Other Rights. Just as common shareholders may have preemptive rights (rights of first refusal to newly issued stock) or cumulative voting rights in elections for directors, so also may the preferred shareholders have these rights. (See Figure 10-2 for Equity Securities Glossary and Figure 10-3 for chart comparing common and preferred stock.)

Series of Stock. Stock of a corporation may be issued in various classes, for example, common and preferred. If more than one class of stock is issued, the terms, preferences, limitations, and rights of each class must be stated in the articles of incorporation and on the face of the stock certificates (or the certificates must indicate that the terms, preferences, limitations, and rights will be provided by the corporation without charge upon written request).

If only one class of stock is issued, that class will be common stock. It must have full voting rights and full rights to share the net assets upon liquidation. If, after incorporation, the corporation wishes to create another class of stock, it must amend its articles, an expensive and time-consuming process that requires

FIGURE 10-1
Illinois Statement of Cancellation of Non-Reissuable Shares

Form **BCA-9.05** (Rev. Jan. 1999)	**STATEMENT OF CANCELLATION of NON-REISSUABLE SHARES**	File #
Jesse White Secretary of State Department of Business Services Springfield, IL 62756 Telephone (217) 782-1831 http://www.sos.state.il.us		**SUBMIT IN DUPLICATE** **This space for use by Secretary of State** Date Filing Fee $ 5.00 Approved:
Remit payment in check or money order, payable to "Secretary of State."		

1. CORPORATE NAME: ______________________________

2. **The corporation has acquired and cancelled its own shares, and the articles of incorporation prohibit the re-issuance of such shares.**

3. Number of shares cancelled and redemption or purchase price:

Class	Series	Par Value	Number of Shares Cancelled	Redemption or Purchase Price	Date of Cancellation

	BEFORE CANCELLATION				AFTER CANCELLATION			
	Class	Series	Par	Number	Class	Series	Par	Number
4. Number of authorized shares:								
5. Number of issued shares:								
6. Paid-in capital:	$ ____				$ ____			

7. The undersigned corporation has caused this statement to be signed by its duly authorized officers, each of whom affirms, under penalties of perjury, that the facts stated herein are true. (All signatures must be in **BLACK INK**.)

Dated ______________________ , ________ ______________________________
(Month & Day) *(Year)* *(Exact Name of Corporation)*

attested by ______________________________ by ______________________________
(Signature of Secretary or Assistant Secretary) *(Signature of President or Vice President)*

______________________________ ______________________________
(Type or Print Name and Title) *(Type or Print Name and Title)*

FIGURE 10-2
Equity Securities Glossary

Authorized Shares Shares authorized for sale in the corporation's articles of incorporation

Common Stock Shares of a corporation that have rights to vote, receive distributions (if declared by directors of a solvent corporation), and receive a proportionate share of net assets upon liquidation of the corporation

Convertible Preferred Stock Preferred stock that can be converted or changed into common stock of the corporation

Cumulative Preferred Stock Preferred stock of the corporation that has a built-in dividend which, if not paid due to the corporation's financial status, will cumulate until it can be paid and which will be paid prior to distributions to common shareholders

Equity Securities Ownership interests in a corporation

Issued Shares Shares sold to shareholders

No Par Value Shares Shares without a stated minimum face value and which can be issued for a price set by the board of directors

Outstanding Shares Shares held by shareholders that are authorized and issued

Participating Preferred Stock Preferred stock whose owners are entitled to receive dividends for preferred shareholders and then also share or participate in dividends after their distribution to common shareholders

Par Value The lowest amount for which a share of stock can be sold

Par Value Shares Shares that cannot be sold for less than the minimum amount set forth in the articles of incorporation

Preferred Stock Shares of a corporation that have some right, privilege, limitation, or preference over other shares of the corporation, usually as to dividends or receipt of net assets upon liquidation

Redeemable Preferred Stock Preferred stock that can be required to be resold to the corporation, either upon the corporation's call for such, or upon the shareholder's demand (or put)

Sinking Fund A reserve account dedicated to redemption of stock

Stock/Shares Units into which the proprietary interests in the corporation are divided

Treasury Shares Shares reacquired by the corporation, usually by redemption, which are viewed as authorized and issued, but not outstanding

Watered Stock Shares issued for less than par value

FIGURE 10-3
Comparison of Common and Preferred Stock

	Common Stock	*Preferred Stock*
Voting Rights	Usually one vote per share	Voting rights may or may not exist; articles will specify.
Distribution Rights	No right to distributions; distributions declared in discretion of board and corporation must be solvent	Distributions may be cumulative, meaning that if profits do not permit a distribution, right to distribution carries over till corporation can pay it. Shareholders may have participating preferred stock, meaning that they receive regularly declared dividends in addition to their cumulative or noncumulative distribution.
Liquidation Rights	Shareholders receive assets after distribution to creditors and then preferred shareholders.	Shareholders receive assets after creditors and before common shareholders; distribution may be guaranteed or specified in articles.
Conversion Rights	No conversion rights	Shareholders may have right to convert their preferred shares into some other type of shares (usually common).
Redemption Rights	No redemption rights	Shareholders may be forced to sell their stock back to corporation or to compel corporation to purchase their stock at agreed-upon price.

shareholder approval and public filings and hinders and delays a corporation needing to raise capital promptly.

To avoid the necessity of amending the articles, the board of directors can create a series of shares if the authority to do so is provided in the articles of incorporation. RMBCA Section 6.02 allows the board of directors to issue shares that vary from other shares *within the same class* if the board determines the rights, preferences, and limitations on such stock prior to actual issuance. This approach also allows the directors to tailor stock to suit then-prevailing market conditions quickly without requiring shareholder approval.

Each group of stock within a series will have rights and preferences different from each other group in the series. Similarly, each class of stock will have rights and preferences different from other classes. There is little substantial difference between shares issued in classes (common and preferred) and shares issued in series (Series A, Series B, and Series C) except that the rights of the classes must be set forth in the articles (or the articles must be amended to set forth the specific rights and preferences of each class), while stock can be issued in a series without the ne-

Series stock
Stock issued within one class including rights different from others and which can be issued without requiring amendment of a corporation's articles; often called *blank stock*

cessity of amending the articles, so long as the articles preauthorize the issuance of the series stock. For this reason, the allowance of **series stock** by the articles of incorporation is sometimes referred to as a "blank check" given to the directors permitting them to establish a series and to fix its rights and preferences. The stock is then referred to as *blank stock*. While the articles need not be amended to allow the creation of a series, prior to actual issuance of the stock the directors must file a statement with the secretary of state containing basic information about the new series, such as its rights, limitations, and preferences. No shareholder approval is needed for the statement, which becomes an amendment to the articles of incorporation. Once the directors determine the relative rights of the series stock and file the statement, they may then issue the stock.

Thus, corporations may have several different classes of stock—Common A, Common B, and Common C, as well as Preferred A and Preferred B—and may create series of stock within a class—Common A, Series A and Series B—with each group having certain rights, limitations, and preferences that make it different from any other type.

Share subscription
Agreement to purchase stock

Share Subscriptions and Options. A **share subscription** is simply an agreement whereby a party offers to purchase stock in a corporation. These subscriptions can be entered into prior to the corporation's existence (preincorporation share subscriptions, discussed in Chapter Nine) or after incorporation. Similarly, one can become a shareholder in a corporation by acquiring stock from another.

Option
Agreement by corporation granting a right to purchase shares at a specified price at a specified time

RMBCA Section 6.24 provides that a corporation may issue options, rights, or warrants for the purchase of its shares. An **option** is an agreement whereby the corporation gives a party the right to purchase a specified number of shares from the corporation at a specified price during a specified time period. Options are often given to key employees of the corporation. If the option price is fixed at $30 per share and the corporation's stock is being traded on the market for $60 per share, an option would allow its holder to purchase a specified number of the shares at $30 per share, thus giving the option holder a tremendous savings. The option holder, of course, may allow the option to expire without exercising it. A **right** is a short-term option. A **warrant** is a long-term option, usually with an option period longer than one year. Options and warrants are usually transferable but they do not have voting rights or distribution rights. Some corporations publicly trade warrants on the national exchanges.

Right
A short-term option

Warrant
A long-term option, often longer than one year

In one interesting transaction in early 2000, a start-up communication corporation bought 14½ acres from the city of Oakland, California for the company's new headquarters, paying $6 million in cash and awarding the city warrants for 100 shares of its stock. If the company goes public and the city exercises its warrants, the city could make a great deal of money. Stock options are more fully discussed in Chapter Eighteen.

C. Debt Securities

1. *Introduction*

In addition to issuing stock in order to raise capital, corporations are also empowered to borrow money. Money may be borrowed from banks or from members of the public. A *debt security* is the instrument that evidences the corporation's debt to another. The party who has loaned money to the corporation is called the **debt security holder.** The debt security holder is not an owner of the corporation, as is the case with a shareholder (or equity security holder), and therefore enjoys no rights of ownership such as voting rights or rights to distributions. The debt security holder is a creditor of the corporation and is entitled to be repaid the principal amount of the debt at the appropriate time and with the stated interest. Debt security holders, moreover, enjoy greater security than shareholders, inasmuch as they are entitled to be repaid the debt before any distribution of net assets can be made to any shareholders, whether preferred or common.

Debt security holder
One to whom a corporate obligation or debt is owed

A corporation usually raises capital through a mix of equity financing (issuing shares) and debt financing (borrowing money). One consideration is tax consequences. Interest paid by a corporation on money it has borrowed is tax deductible while distributions made to its shareholders are not deductible as a corporate expense.

There are a variety of debt securities, ranging from simple unsecured promissory notes to more complex secured bonds that include a number of features to attract lenders. Corporate debt can be unsecured or secured. If a debt is **unsecured,** the creditor has no right to any corporate asset upon default by the corporation, and will simply have to sue the corporation to receive repayment of the debt. Such an unsecured obligation is often called a **debenture.** If debt is **secured,** the creditor will have rights to some specified corporate property (trademarks, real estate, accounts receivable) in the event of a default in payment by the corporation. Thus, the creditor enjoys the security of knowing that if the corporation does not pay its debt as promised, the creditor will be able to reach some corporate asset pledged as collateral for its promise to repay money borrowed. Such a secured obligation is often called a *bond*. Many people use the term "bond" loosely to refer to any debt owed by a corporation, whether or not secured.

Unsecured debt
Debt for which no collateral is pledged

Debenture
An unsecured debt

Secured debt
Money borrowed by a corporation backed by collateral that can be seized in the event of nonpayment (often called a *bond*)

Creditors, of course, much prefer that a debt be secured. They may, however, be willing to lend money on an unsecured basis if the interest to be paid to them is higher than the standard rate. Higher interest will compensate them for the risk of making a loan unsecured by any real estate or personal property. The terms and conditions on which money is borrowed by a private corporation can vary greatly and may be fiercely negotiated by both parties. The issuance of bonds by a public company, however, is on stated, published terms, and investors either accept the terms or decide against the investment inasmuch as no negotiation is possible.

Corporations often secure money through loans from banks. The loans may be secured or unsecured. If unsecured, the bank may insist that corporate managers personally guarantee repayment of the loan. In the event the corporation does not repay the loan, the corporate managers' personal funds may be seized. If the bank loan is secured, the corporation's real estate, personal property, intellectual property (such as trademarks, copyrights, or patents), or accounts receivable (money owed to the corporation) may serve as security or collateral for the loan. In the event of a default, the collateral pledged can be seized by the lender. One type of bank loan is a **line of credit,** which is a form of pre-authorized loan, up to a certain maximum amount, which the corporation can borrow from on a variable basis, as its monthly capital needs fluctuate.

Line of credit
A type of pre-authorized loan that a business draws against as needed

2. *Unsecured Debt*

Promissory note
A document evidencing one's promise to pay money

Corporations may borrow money without pledging any property as collateral or security for the debt. Often, the corporation's obligation is set forth in a simple document called a **promissory note,** by which the corporation merely promises to repay money borrowed at a specified time and with specified interest. Figure 10-4 shows a form of unsecured promissory note.

Demand note
A type of promissory note; payment of which can be demanded at any time

Confession of judgment
Clause within a promissory note authorizing immediate court judgment in the event of nonpayment

The promissory note may be modified to include a variety of other terms, such as providing for installment payments of principal, interest, or both, or providing that in the event the debtor misses any payment, the creditor can declare the entire balance to be immediately payable. The note can also be a **demand note,** meaning that no specific time is stated for repayment and the creditor has the right to demand repayment by the corporation at any time. Some notes contain a provision referred to as a **confession of judgment,** which allows the creditor to obtain an immediate judgment in court against the debtor in the event of a default. In this case, the corporation agrees that an immediate judgment may be taken against it in the event of its default, without the necessity of a trial. Because such a provision does not allow the debtor corporation to assert any defenses as to why it has not repaid the debt, some states prohibit confessions of judgment.

In the event of a default by the corporation, the creditor will sue the corporation. The creditor will not be entitled to seize any specific corporate property upon default. If the sum remains unpaid, and the corporation liquidates, the unsecured creditors will be paid before net assets are distributed to any shareholders but after payment of secured creditors.

FIGURE 10-4
Unsecured Promissory Note

$20,000 January 1, 2000

For value received, the undersigned, Simmons Corp., a corporation organized and existing under the laws of the State of California, promises to pay to Paul J. Higgins at 2725 Delaney Circle, Los Angeles, California, the sum of Twenty Thousand Dollars ($20,000) with interest from January 1, 2000 until paid, at the rate of six percent (6%) per annum, payable on December 31, 2003. Should suit be commenced or an attorney employed to enforce the terms of this note, Simmons Corp. agrees to pay such additional sum as the court might order reasonable as attorneys' fees. Principal and interest payable in lawful money of the United States.

Simmons Corp.

By: ______________________

Title: ______________________

3. *Secured Debt*

When the corporation's obligation to repay money is secured, upon corporate default in repayment the creditor can seize some specific corporate asset that has been pledged as collateral to ensure the corporation will repay its loan. The property may be sold and the proceeds used to repay the lender or bondholder.

The document evidencing the corporation's obligation to repay is called a *bond*. It will specify the principal amount due, the interest required, the date of repayment (often called the **maturity date**), and the property pledged to secure repayment of the loan. Some bonds are represented by coupons which are clipped or cut and sent by the creditor to the corporation for payment. Thus, the expression "clipping coupons" you may have heard refers to a creditor making demand on a corporation to make its periodic payments of its debt.

Maturity date
The date repayment of a debt is due

In some instances, the property pledged by the corporation is real estate, for example, a parcel of land. In the event of a default, the creditor has the right to sell the property to satisfy the debt. The document evidencing the corporation's obligations and identifying the real estate as the collateral is called a **mortgage note** or *mortgage bond*. This mortgage does not differ significantly from any other type of mortgage. For example, if an individual purchases a house for $150,000 and pays $30,000 down, the remainder of the purchase price, $120,000, must be borrowed from a bank. The bank will lend this money only on the condition that if the home buyer does not make the required monthly payments, the bank can take back, or foreclose on, the house in order to ensure repayment of the $120,000 borrowed by the home buyer. In a corporate scenario, the corporation will usually be obligated to keep the property in good condition, to insure it, to pay the taxes due thereon, and to keep it free and clear of other encumbrances.

Mortgage note
Document by which real estate is pledged as collateral to secure payment of a debt (also called "mortgage bond")

Real property pledged must not be over-secured by the corporation. For example, if the corporation borrows $100,000 from Bank of America and executes a mortgage pledging a parcel of property with a value of $110,000, the corporation may be able thereafter to pledge the same real estate parcel for another loan in the amount of $10,000. Thereafter, the property cannot be subject to any other mortgages because there is not enough value in the property to satisfy any other creditor. To ensure the corporation does not over-secure or over-collateralize its property, the mortgage will be recorded with the county recorder where the real estate is located. This recordation provides potential creditors notice of previous mortgages placed on the property.

Rather than pledging real estate as collateral for repayment of a debt, the corporation can pledge personal property such as machinery, equipment, inventory, or accounts receivable. Trademarks, patents, and copyrights can also be pledged as security for a loan. When personal property forms the security for the loan, a document called a **security agreement** will be executed by the corporation. The creditor will then file a **financing statement** with the secretary of state or county recorder to provide notice of the security interest claimed in the property. (See Figure 19-2 for a copy of the Uniform Commercial Code Financing Statement, Form UCC-1.) The financing statement will specify and itemize the specific personal property pledged by the corporation. Banks and other lenders usually conduct "UCC searches" before extending credit to ensure the borrower has not already pledged security interests in its personal property. Obtaining information about financing statements on file with the secretary of state is easily ac-

Security agreement
Document by which personal property is pledged as collateral to secure payment of a debt

Financing statement
Document filed with a secretary of state to provide notice of a security interest

complished by filing a simple request for information (see Figure 10-5). In some states, the information is available online, at no cost, at the home page of the state's secretary of state. Records can usually be searched either by the debtor's or creditor's name.

4. *Trust Indentures*

If a corporation issues numerous bonds to the public at once (rather than simply executing bonds sporadically), the corporation may appoint a trustee to act on behalf of the various creditors. The trustee is usually an institutional lender or commercial bank. In the event of a default by the corporation, the trustee will represent the interests of all of the creditors in seizing the property securing the corporation's debt. The trustee's rights and responsibilities and the terms of the securities, the obligations of the corporate issuer, and the rights of creditors are set forth in an agreement called a **trust indenture.** The use of a trustee is an advantage to both the corporation and the creditor. In the event of a default, the corporation will have the advantage of dealing with only one party, the trustee, rather than with numerous creditors, and the creditors have the advantage of having a representative act for them, rather than having to pursue their claims individually. In many cases the trustee is the trust department of a bank or other financial institution.

Trust indenture
Agreement entered into when numerous bonds are issued at once, specifying corporation's and lenders' rights

In 1939, Congress passed the Trust Indenture Act (15 U.S.C. Section 77aaa, et seq.) to regulate the public offering of notes, bonds, and debentures in excess of $10 million. The Act requires a corporate issuer to prepare and file a registration statement with the Securities and Exchange Commission in order to provide information about the proposed issuance. Additionally, trustees must be qualified and file a separate statement signifying the trustee's compliance with various eligibility and standard of conduct rules.

5. *Common Features of Debt Securities*

Because investors can always place their money in banks and receive interest thereon, the corporation may introduce various features or provisions in its debt securities to induce investors to loan money to the corporation rather than simply placing it in a bank account. While higher rates of interest may be offered than those paid by banks, other features can also be offered to make the debt security attractive to an investor.

Redemption Terms. Most creditors do not want a debtor to pay off a debt prior to the stated maturity date. The profit made by a creditor is in the interest paid rather than in the repayment of the principal amount borrowed. Therefore, the corporation may include favorable **redemption terms** in the debt security and may agree not to redeem the debt security before its stated maturity date, not to redeem the debt during some specified period, or to pay a penalty or premium to the creditor if the debt is redeemed prior to its date of maturity. Generally, this prepayment penalty will decline as the loan matures. This assures the debt security holder that it will receive the bargained-for interest. Otherwise, if the debt

Redemption terms
Terms relating to a borrower's right to pay off or redeem a debt prior to its maturity date

FIGURE 10-5
California UCC-3 Request for Information

STATE OF CALIFORNIA
SECRETARY OF STATE
UNIFORM COMMERCIAL CODE DIVISION
REQUEST FOR INFORMATION - FORM UCC3

SoS 10-24-94

Filing Officer please provide the following type(s) of information concerning the debtor named below:
(For personal name, show LAST NAME, FIRST NAME)

DEBTOR NAME:
SSN/FTN: ***(optional)***

ADDRESS:
CITY: **STATE:** **ZIP:** **COUNTRY:**

**** PLEASE CHECK AT LEAST ONE REQUEST TYPE BELOW ****

____**CERTIFICATE** A list of active filings containing the information stated above.

____**COPIES** If copies are requested **at the same time** as a CERTIFICATE, copies of all filings appearing on the CERTIFICATE will be provided, unless otherwise noted.

If only copies are requested, up to 10 file numbers may be listed below. **Copies are not certified unless requested. An additional fee is required in that case.**

Special Instructions: ____________________

(This section applies if only COPIES are requested)

FILE NUMBER	TYPE OF DOCUMENT	FILE DATE	QUANTITY/INSTRUCTIONS

SIGNATURE OF REQUESTOR: ____________________ Date: ________

This Space Reserved for Use by the Filing Office

RETURN INFORMATION TO

NAME:

ADDRESS:
CITY: **STATE:** **ZIP:**

COUNTRY:

was negotiated at a 5 percent rate of interest, and the rate fell to 3 percent, the corporation would redeem the debt and renegotiate another loan at the then-prevailing rate of 3 percent thereby depriving the first creditor of the interest it planned on receiving over the life of the loan. The corporation may create a sinking fund to use for purposes of redeeming or retiring debt.

Conversion term
Right of a lender to convert a debt security to an equity security

Conversion Terms. Debt securities may be convertible into equity securities, or shares of the corporation. Such a feature would allow the creditor to trade in debt for shares evidencing ownership in the corporation. It may be that the corporation is doing extremely well and the debtor would love to buy stock but does not have sufficient liquid assets (cash) to do so. A right of conversion thus allows the creditor to purchase stock without using actual cash; the purchase price is funded by turning in the debenture (unsecured debt) or bond (secured debt). If conversion rights are to be allowed, the bond must set forth the number of shares into which it can be converted, the procedure for conversion, and any other terms, limitations, or conditions relating to the conversion. See Figure 10-6 for a glossary detailing the types of debt securities.

FIGURE 10-6
Debt Securities Glossary

Bonds Debts secured by some type of collateral that can be reached by a creditor in the event a corporation defaults in repayment of its debt

Convertible Debt Security Debt security that can be converted or changed into equity security (shares) of the corporation

Debentures Debts unsecured by any collateral which, in the event of a default, must be recovered through a lawsuit by the creditor

Debt Securities Documents which evidence a corporation's debt to a party who is a creditor of the corporation and who therefore has no voting rights or rights to participate in distributions

Mortgage Bonds/Notes Documents executed by a corporation pledging corporate real estate as collateral or security for repayment of a debt

Redeemable Debt Security Debt security that can be paid off or redeemed prior to its stated date of maturity

Security Agreement Document executed by a corporation pledging corporate personal property as collateral or security for repayment of a debt

Subordinated Debt Security Debt junior in order of payment to another debt having priority over it

Priority and Subordination Rights. A corporation may borrow money over a period of time and the debtors will know their place in the payment line in the event the corporation defaults in repaying its debts. They may receive payment before (or have **priority** over) some creditors, and may be paid after (or be **subordinate** to) others. A corporation can entice a creditor to loan it money by inserting a clause into the debenture or bond stating that the debt cannot be subordinated to any other debt. The debt security holder thus knows its debt must be paid first. Alternatively, the debenture or bond may state that the debt is subordinate to any future borrowing by the corporation. Typically, a creditor would agree to accept such a disadvantageous position only in return for favorable interest rates, redemption terms, or conversion terms.

Priority
Process of making one obligation senior to others

Subordination
Process of making one obligation junior to others

In some instances, a creditor may be willing to lend money to a corporation only if its debt has priority over all others. This will pose problems if various debt security holders already occupy first, second, and third places in the payment line. The corporation may need to approach these debt security holders and ask them to agree to occupy second, third, and fourth places, by subordinating their debt so the corporation can secure needed financing. The debt security holders may agree to do this if it appears the corporation is struggling financially and this influx of new capital is crucial for the corporation's continued existence. The existing debt security holders may also bargain for more favorable interest rates, redemption terms, or conversion terms in return for subordinating their debts to the new creditor.

Voting Rights. Some jurisdictions, including Delaware and New York, authorize the articles of incorporation to allow debt security holders to vote on certain issues, such as election of directors, amendment of the articles of incorporation, and mergers, although this is not a common approach. In Delaware, if bondholders are to vote, such must be provided for in the certificate of incorporation. If the certificate so provides, the bondholders are deemed to be stockholders for purposes of voting and inspection of records. Del. Code. Ann. tit. 8, Section 221. (See Figure 10-7 for comparison of equity securities and debt securities.)

D. Taxation of Corporations

Because a corporation is viewed as a separate entity created under the authority of the state, it must pay taxes just as other persons do. Corporations are subject to federal taxation and may be subject to state and local taxation as well. The taxation of a corporation is accomplished by corporate tax rates different from those for natural persons. The taxation of a corporation is a significant feature of corporate existence and distinguishes the corporation from other forms of business enterprise (sole proprietorships, general partnerships, limited partnerships, limited liability partnerships, limited liability companies, and joint ventures) in which enterprises money earned is simply passed through to the individuals involved, who pay tax at the rate established by the Internal Revenue Code for individuals (unless they elect to be taxed as corporations under the Internal Revenue Code "check the box" approach).

FIGURE 10-7
Comparison of Equity and Debt Securities

Equity Securities ("Stock")	*Debt Securities ("Bonds")*
Shareholder is an owner of the corporation and is entitled to vote and receive distributions, if earnings permit	Bondholder is an outside creditor of the corporation and is entitled to timely repayment of the debt
Issuance of shares produces cash for the corporation	Issuance of bonds produces cash for the corporation
Issuance of shares dilutes power of existing shareholders but costs the corporation nothing	Issuance of bonds does not dilute power of existing shareholders but bonds must be repaid
If corporation is insolvent, no distributions will be paid to any shareholder	Bondholder may be entitled to periodic payments of interest and principal whether or not the corporation is solvent
Corporation may not deduct distributions paid to shareholders (and distributions are taxed to the shareholder recipients)	Corporation may deduct interest paid to bondholders and reduce taxable income
In event of liquidation, shareholders receive assets after outside creditors/bondholders	In event of liquidation, bondholders receive assets before shareholders

Double taxation
Taxation of corporate income at two levels, once when earned by corporation and then again when distributed to shareholders

As described in Chapter Eight, corporations are subject to **double taxation**. Corporations pay tax at specified corporate tax rates on income; then when net profits are distributed to shareholders, the shareholders pay income tax on distributions received at the applicable individual tax rates. Figure 10-8 displays the most current available tax rates for individuals and corporations. Figure 10-9 shows Internal Revenue Service Form 1120, the U.S. Corporation Income Tax Return, which must be filed by all corporations. S corporations file Form 1120S. If a corporation's gross receipts are under $500,000 and it meets certain other criteria, it may file Form 1120-A, a short form corporate tax return.

Subsidiary corporations (those formed by other corporations, called parents) are subject to triple taxation: the subsidiary pays tax on the income it earns; it then distributes that income to its parent as a distribution. The parent pays tax on the distribution it has received, then distributes dividends to its shareholders, who pay taxes on the distributions they received from the parent.

Statistics show that corporate income subject to tax has steadily risen in the past years as have cash dividends paid on common stock. See *Statistical Abstract of the United States* 532, 544 (118th ed. 1998). The following table shows corporate income and cash dividends in billions of dollars. Clearly, increased corpo-

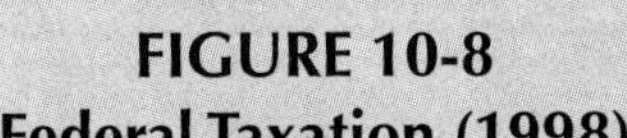

FIGURE 10-8
Federal Taxation (1998)

Taxable Income Taxpayers Filing Jointly	*Taxable Income Taxpayer Filing Singly*	*Tax Rate*
$0-$42,350	$0-$25,350	15%
$42,351-$102,300	$25,351-$61,400	28%
$102,301-$155,950	$61,401-$128,100	31%
$155,951-$278,450	$128,101-$278,450	36%
More than $278,450	More than $278,450	39.6%

Taxable Income Corporations	*Tax Rate*
$0-$50,000	15%
$50,001-$75,000	25%
$75,001-$100,000	34%
$100,001-$335,000	39%
$335,001-$10,000,000	34%
$10,000,001-$15,000,000	35%
$15,000,001-$18,333,330	38%
$18,333,331 and up	35%

If a corporation has taxable income between $100,000 and $15,000,000, the amount of the tax is increased by the lesser of 5 percent or $11,750. If a corporation has taxable income in excess of $15,000,000, the amount of tax is increased by an additional amount of the lesser of 3 percent of such excess or $100,000.
Source: *Information Please Almanac,* 45, 46 (49th ed. 1996)

rate revenue leads to increased revenue for federal and state governments. When the profits are passed along to the shareholders in the form of cash dividends, which they also pay tax on, federal and state government revenues increase again.

	1980	*1990*	*1995*
Corporate Income	$247	$366	$565
Cash Dividends	$53.1	$103.2	$147.0

Until the late 1980s, some relief against double taxation was provided for dividends received by small-time corporate shareholders: the first $100 received by a shareholder (or $200 if shareholders filed jointly), was excluded from taxation. The current tax scheme, however, requires individuals to report dividends even if only 51 cents are received in any tax year. Corporations are, however, entitled to deductions for various expenses, such as rent, salaries, interest, contribu-

FIGURE 10-9
IRS Form 1120

Form **1120**
Department of the Treasury
Internal Revenue Service

U.S. Corporation Income Tax Return

For calendar year 1999 or tax year beginning ____, 1999, ending ____, __
▶ Instructions are separate. See page 1 for Paperwork Reduction Act Notice.

OMB No. 1545-0123

1999

A Check if a:
1 Consolidated return (attach Form 851) ☐
2 Personal holding co. (attach Sch. PH) ☐
3 Personal service corp. (as defined in Temporary Regs. sec. 1.441-4T—see instructions) ☐

Use IRS label. Otherwise, print or type.

Name

Number, street, and room or suite no. (If a P.O. box, see page 5 of instructions.)

City or town, state, and ZIP code

B Employer identification number

C Date incorporated

D Total assets (see page 6 of instructions)

$

E Check applicable boxes: (1) ☐ Initial return (2) ☐ Final return (3) ☐ Change of address

Income				
	1a	Gross receipts or sales ____ b Less returns and allowances ____ c Bal ▶	1c	
	2	Cost of goods sold (Schedule A, line 8)	2	
	3	Gross profit. Subtract line 2 from line 1c	3	
	4	Dividends (Schedule C, line 19)	4	
	5	Interest	5	
	6	Gross rents	6	
	7	Gross royalties	7	
	8	Capital gain net income (attach Schedule D (Form 1120))	8	
	9	Net gain or (loss) from Form 4797, Part II, line 18 (attach Form 4797)	9	
	10	Other income (see page 7 of instructions—attach schedule)	10	
	11	**Total income.** Add lines 3 through 10 ▶	11	

tions to employee benefit plans, group life insurance, and other employee benefits. Corporations are also free to elect their own tax year, which need not be a calendar year but may rather be responsive to the particular seasonal needs of a corporation. Moreover, some relief is provided by the fact that shareholders pay taxes only on distributions actually received by them. If shareholders receive share dividends rather than cash or property as a form of distribution, they need not pay tax on the shares upon receipt but rather when the share is later sold. (See discussion in Chapter Twelve.)

Just as the tax rate for individuals is graduated, the tax rate for corporations is graduated as well. This means that the corporation does not simply calculate its income and plug this entire number into a chart. Rather, the first $50,000 is subject to tax at the rate of 15 percent, the next $25,000 is subject to tax at the rate of 25 percent, and so forth.

Large publicly held corporations simply accept double taxation as a cost of doing business. Smaller corporations, however, may minimize double taxation through the use of various means, such as S corporation status (in which all income earned by the corporation is passed through to the shareholders who pay at their individual rates) or close corporations (in which the shareholders receive bonuses or salary increases which, though they may be taxable to the shareholder, are deductible to the corporation as expenses).

Similarly, the corporation can elect to obtain funds through debt financing rather than equity financing because interest paid to creditors is a deductible corporate expense. To ensure the corporation does not encumber itself by issuing only debt securities, the Internal Revenue Service has devised the theory of **thin incorporation.** This doctrine discourages the corporation from issuing too many debt securities. If debt is deemed excessive by the Internal Revenue Service, meaning the corporation has a high "debt to equity ratio," the Internal Revenue Service may characterize interest payments on debts as dividends on equity securities, which are then subject to taxes. A number of authorities suggest that the debt to equity ratio not exceed 4:1 or perhaps even 3:1.

Thin incorporation
A corporation whose debts are disproportionately high to its equity

To discourage corporations from simply holding on to profits and not distributing them (thereby reducing the impact of double taxation), the Internal Revenue Service has also devised certain penalties that give corporations a strong incentive to distribute profits to shareholders rather than hoarding them. The Internal Revenue Service, of course, wishes to see corporate profits distributed to shareholders so that the shareholders will pay tax on distributions received. According to Internal Revenue Code Sections 531-535 (26 U.S.C. Sections 531-535), C corporations that accumulate earnings beyond the reasonable needs of the business in order to avoid having shareholders pay income taxes on earnings that should have been distributed to them are subject to an **accumulated earnings tax** in the amount of 39.6 percent of the accumulated taxable amount, although certain credits and adjustments are allowed. By imposing this penalty on corporations that retain earnings, the IRS incentivizes corporations to distribute income.

Accumulated earnings tax
Tax penalty imposed on corporations that retain earnings beyond reasonable business needs

As discussed briefly in Chapter Eight and more thoroughly in Chapter Seventeen, corporations may elect status as an S corporation to alleviate the burdens of double taxation. S corporation status, however, is restricted to corporations with 75 or fewer individual shareholders who cannot be nonresident aliens. Due to the increasingly global nature of our economy, S election may be replaced by election of the limited liability company which has no maximum number of shareholders (and who may be foreign nationals) and retains limited liability for its members, yet has the pass-through tax status of a partnership (see Chapter Six).

A corporation may also be subject to the **alternative minimum tax,** an extra tax required in addition to the "regular" income tax the corporation will be required to pay. In essence, the alternative minimum tax rules set a minimum threshold amount for taxes. If the corporation's income exceeds this amount, it need not pay the alternative minimum tax. If the regular tax liability is less than the minimum threshold amount, then the corporation must make up the difference by paying the alternative minimum tax. See IRS Form 4626 and its instructions on calculating the alternative minimum tax.

Alternative minimum tax
Tax penalty imposed on corporations to ensure that a certain minimum threshold amount of tax is paid

Beginning in 1998, the corporate alternative minimum tax was repealed for small corporations if their average annual gross receipts for the three-year period before 1999 did not exceed \$7.5 million (or \$5 million if the corporation had only one prior tax year). A corporation will continue to be exempt from the alternative minimum tax so long as its average gross receipts for the prior three years does not exceed \$7.5 million.

When the corporation files its first federal tax return, it will select its method of accounting. If the corporation later wishes to change its method of accounting, it must obtain IRS approval. As discussed briefly in Chapter Three, under the *cash method* of accounting, one includes all items of income received during the year in calculating gross income for that year, and one deducts expenses in the year in which the expenses are actually paid. Most individuals and many small businesses with no inventory use the cash method of accounting. Under the *accrual method* of accounting, income is reported in the year that it is earned (regardless of when it is actually received), and expenses are deducted in the year they are incurred (regardless of when they are actually paid).

With regard to state income taxes, the general rule is that corporations transacting business within any state are subject to that state's income tax, if any. Corporations may also be subject to local taxes or franchise taxes imposed by the state merely as a condition for being permitted to do business there. All states except Nevada, South Dakota, Texas, Washington, and Wyoming impose a tax on corporate net income. Delaware does not impose state income tax on corporations unless they are engaged in business in Delaware.

Key Features of Corporate Finances

- To raise money, corporations will issue stock (equity securities), which show ownership interest in the corporation or bonds (debt securities), which are loans to the corporation.
- Shares issued by a corporation must be authorized by the articles.
- The par value of a share is the lowest price for which it can be sold.
- If stock has no par value, it can be sold for whatever amount the directors determine is in the best interest of the corporation.
- Corporations may have more than one class of stock.
- "Common" stock is ordinary stock of the corporation and usually has voting rights, distribution rights, and liquidation rights (distribution and liquidation rights are exercised after preferred stockholders exercise their rights).
- "Preferred" stock has some sort of right or preference other classes do not have, often as to cumulating dividends, conversion (changing preferred stock to common stock), or redemption [acquisition of the stock by the corporation, either at the corporation's demand (a "call") or the shareholder's demand (a "put")].
- Debt securities may be unsecured, in which case, in the event of a default, the creditor simply sues to recover the amount lent to the corporation.
- Debt securities may be secured by real estate (a "mortgage bond" or "note") or personal property (a "security agreement"); in the event of a default the creditor can recover the property pledged as security or collateral.
- Debt securities may have favorable redemption terms (so the corporation does not pay off the debt early) or conversion terms (so they can be converted into equity securities or shares).
- Corporations are said to be subject to "double taxation": the corporation pays tax on money it earns, and shareholders then pay tax on distributions made to them. Interest paid on bonds is a deductible expense for a corporation.

E. Role of Paralegal

While advice given to corporations regarding the relative advantages and disadvantages of issuing equity securities and debt securities (and the taxation thereof) is the purview of the attorney advising the client, there are a number of activities in which the paralegal will be involved.

Any issuance of stock (including conversion of preferred stock for common stock or conversion of debt securities to equity securities) must be authorized by the articles of incorporation. The paralegal will monitor the issuance of stock to ensure an appropriate number of shares are authorized to accommodate any such transaction. If the authorized number of shares is not sufficient to permit such conversion, the paralegal will need to prepare the appropriate documents to call a shareholders' meeting and amend the articles of incorporation accordingly.

The paralegal will prepare notices of the shareholders' meeting to permit the corporation to amend its articles to allow for the issuance of different classes of shares. Articles of amendment must also be prepared and filed with the secretary of state.

If different series of shares are authorized by the articles, the paralegal will prepare the requisite statement to be submitted to the secretary of state.

The paralegal can assist the corporation in its bookkeeping activities to ensure interest payments are timely made, funds are accumulated for the sinking fund, and share certificates contain the appropriate information regarding preferences and limitations of different classes of stock.

The paralegal can assist the corporation in preparing notices of redemption of stock and notices of redemption of bonds.

Resource Guide

The controlling resources regarding the issuance of equity and debt securities are the pertinent statutes of the state of incorporation. These statutes will contain provisions regarding requirements for the form of the share certificate, the authority of the board to authorize blank stock (stock in series), the appropriate consideration to be received for shares, the reacquisition by a corporation of its own shares and the treatment thereof, the issuance of fractional shares and share options, and so forth. The Internal Revenue Code should also be consulted for information relating to taxation of corporations and allowable deductions.

Form books may also be helpful in drafting a variety of forms relating to the issuance of equity and debt securities (including resolutions calling for redemption of shares), forms for simple unsecured obligations such as promissory notes, forms providing for common provisions found in debt securities (such as provisions relating to conversion, redemption, priority, and subordination), and forms providing that the notice (*legend*) to be contained on share certificates will allow the holder to receive information about the securities issued by the corporation upon written request and without any charge therefor. Am. Jur. Legal Forms 2d provides a variety of useful forms and checklists.

Various treatises and the encyclopedias C.J.S. and Am. Jur. 2d will also provide explanations of the differences among securities issued by corporations and the process of such issuance. (See Chapter Nine for specific identifications of form books, treatises, and encyclopedias).

◆ ◆ ◆

WEB RESOURCES

The most important Web resources are state and federal statutes relating to issuance of stock and taxation of corporations.

www.ll.georgetown.edu
When you access this site for Georgetown University Law Center, select "State, Local & Territorial." You will be presented with a map of the United States. Point your cursor to the state in which you are interested and you will be provided with links to a variety of legal sources relating to that state. Select "Statutes" or "Codes" and you will be linked to the state's statutes. In some states, searching can be done by either keywords or by section number. In other states, searching is accomplished exclusively by keywords.

www4.law.cornell.edu/usccode
This excellent site allows searching by keyword or by section number. You can review all fifty titles of the U.S. Code or look up statutes by their popular names. All of the tax statutes are located in Title 26, entitled "Internal Revenue Code."

www.irs.gov
This Web site of the Internal Revenue Service allows you to locate more than 700 tax forms and instructions. In many cases, the instructions provided for a corresponding form are clearly and articulately presented. You may look up forms by number, by keyword, or by scanning a list of all forms.

Because nearly all states have posted their forms relating to corporations and UCC filings on their Web sites, important Web resources are the home pages of the various secretaries of state. See Appendix A for the specific Web address for each of the state's secretaries of state. Other alternatives follow.

www.nass.org
This Web site of the National Association of Secretaries of State will provide you with links to each of the secretaries of state. After you access the home page of the Association, select "States." You will then be given an alphabetical list of all 50 states and the District of Columbia (together with their state flags). Point your cursor at the state you wish, and you will be immediately linked to the home page for that state's secretary of state. In most instances, you will immediately see entries for "Corporations," "Business," or "UCC." Select the relevant entry, and you will be given basic information on the use of various state forms (including state tax forms), instructions for filing forms, addresses and phone numbers, fee schedules, and forms that you can

either download or request to be mailed to you. Basic and introductory tax information is often provided. In some instances, you can check UCC debtor information on the Web site. For example, California and North Carolina allow one to check the state database to locate information about security statements filed claiming liens in debtors' property. If you need to determine the number of authorized shares of a company or what preferences it has identified in its articles, you can file a written request and pay a fee to the secretary of state and the information will be sent to you.

www.legalwiz.com
When you access this site, select "Legal Sites" and then "Corporate Department and Secretary of State Pages" for links to each state's secretary of state.

www.about.com
When you access this site, type "State Government Resources" into the search box, and you will be given links for each state, providing information on various taxes and license requirements.

www.freeedgar.com
This Securities and Exchange Commission site allows electronic access to documents filed with the SEC since 1994. Companies that offer their securities publicly are required to file various documents with the SEC giving information about the authorized number of shares, descriptions of preferences, and authority given to directors to create series stock. Similarly, information relating to bond issuances is provided.

www.companylink.com
This site provides news, research, and contacts for more than 65,000 companies. Enter either the company's name or stock ticker symbol, and you will be provided with basic information about the company.

www.hoovers.com
When you access this site, covering most large companies, select the "Main Directory." Then select "Company Directory A-Z" for capsule descriptions of companies, their addresses, company officials, competitors, and other valuable information.

www.ilrg.com
Select "Forms Index" and then "Legal Forms Archive" for a form for a promissory note.

http://legal-resource.com/forms/d.cgi [IDNUMBER]
This site offers a variety of useful forms including forms for installment and promissory notes.

http:www.siccode.com/forms.php3
This site offers numerous forms for promissory notes, a form for a security agreement, and forms for guarantees.

Discussion Questions

Fact Scenario. ABC Inc., is a Florida corporation, whose articles authorize the issuance of 50,000 shares and which has issued 45,000 shares. The corporation's articles specify that there will be two classes of stock, one of which will have cumulative distribution rights. Bonds were issued last June, which provided favorable redemption terms for the bondholders.

1. ABC needs to raise funds as soon as possible. Moreover, it needs to offset certain corporate income with deductions. What strategy should the company employ to raise money? Why? Is there any risk to ABC in the approach you suggest?
2. One of ABC's shareholders, Marcy, is the holder of 100 shares of stock with cumulative distribution rights. The corporation has not made a distribution for the previous two years because it was unable to pay its debts as they came due. This year, a distribution will be made. What are Marcy's rights?
3. Describe the tax consequences to ABC and to Marcy arising out of the distribution that will be made this year. What is this concept called?
4. Assume that ABC has not paid a dividend for three years, not because of financial difficulties, but because it simply desires to retain all of its earnings for a "rainy day." What risk does ABC run in adopting such a strategy?
5. ABC issued bonds in June with a three-year maturity date. Six months after issuance, the corporation would like to redeem the bonds so it does not have to continue paying interest on the bonds. Discuss the implications to ABC and to the bondholders.

11

Corporate Management

CHAPTER OVERVIEW

A corporation is owned by its shareholders. Although they own the corporation, however, shareholders play little, if any, role in the day-to-day operation of a large corporation. Shareholders' activities are generally limited to electing and removing directors and to taking part in extraordinary corporate actions, such as amendment of the articles of incorporation and other fundamental changes to the corporate structure, including approval of mergers and dissolutions. These limited activities take the form of voting at shareholders' meetings.

Because shareholders do not manage the corporation, their liability is limited. While their stock may decline in value, they are not liable for debts and obligations of the corporation. One exception to this rule of limited liability exists when shareholders do not respect the corporate entity and commingle its funds with theirs or fail to follow corporate formalities, such as failing to hold elections, meetings, and so forth. In such cases, it is said that the veil of limited liability will be "pierced" to prevent fraud and injustice by holding shareholders liable for corporate debts and obligations.

A corporation is governed by its directors functioning as a board. The directors have responsibility for all policy-making decisions required for operation of the corporation. The board of directors is elected by the shareholders. The directors have fiduciary duties to the shareholders and to the corporation. The directors are not guarantors of a corporation's success, however, and are usually required to act with reasonable diligence as a similar person would exercise in similar circumstances. They can be personally liable if injury to the corporation is a result of their breach of duty. Directors also have a duty of loyalty to the corporation. They cannot engage in competitive activities or, without full disclosure, personally gain from a corporate transaction.

A corporation's officers are appointed and removed by the board. The most commonly seen officers are president, vice-president, secretary, and treasurer. The board of directors delegates power and authority to the officers to execute the policies determined by the board. Like directors, officers are also fiduciaries and are subject to the same standard of conduct as directors.

This chapter will address the three groups of people involved in corporate management and governance: shareholders, directors, and officers.

A. Shareholders' Rights and Responsibilities

1. *Introduction*

Shareholder
An owner of a corporation; also called *stockholder*

The owners of a corporation are called **shareholders** (or *stockholders,* a synonymous term). Not all shareholders are individuals. In fact, it is becoming increasingly common for ownership in major corporations to be held by institutions such as banks, trusts, mutual funds, and insurance companies.

Although they own the corporation, shareholders do not own any specific corporate assets such as cars, real estate, or trademarks. Moreover, these owners do not manage the enterprise they own. The business of a corporation is managed by the officers acting on the board's instructions and subject to its oversight. Shareholder participation in management is somewhat indirect and generally takes the form of voting. Shareholders do not vote on day-to-day activities but rather are restricted to voting to elect directors and on fundamental changes to the corporation, including amendment of the articles of incorporation, mergers, dissolutions, and other similar structural changes to the corporation. These rights to vote take place at two types of meetings: annual and special. Alternatively, some states allow shareholders to take action without a meeting if they unanimously consent in writing to the action to be taken. Such unanimous written consent is impracticable for all but the smallest corporations. Shareholders' rights, responsibilities, liabilities, and duties are governed by state statutes and the articles of incorporation.

2. *Rights to Information*

Shareholders have the right to be informed of the affairs of the corporation. At common law, their right to inspect records and books, including the list of shareholders, bylaws, minutes of meetings, and so forth, was qualified by the requirement that the inspection be in good faith. Examples of bad faith or improper purposes were examination of the list of shareholders for personal business reasons (such as to solicit customers for the shareholder's own business), appropriation of trade secrets to sell to competitors, or pursuing political goals. Most states have enacted statutes specifically authorizing inspection by shareholders of books and records. Some of these statutes provide an absolute right to inspect most records. This is the RMBCA approach. RMBCA Section 16.02. Others, such as Delaware, provide that the inspection must be for a "proper purpose." Nevertheless, if a shareholder secures information used to injure the corporation, the corporation may be entitled to damages. Many statutes provide that a shareholder may inspect corporate books and records so long as the inspection is for a purpose "reasonably related" to one's interest as a shareholder. Other states allow inspection of the list of shareholders for any reason whatsoever, while inspection of accounts and minutes of directors' meetings is subject to the requirement that it be done in good faith. Still other states impose a waiting period on the shareholders: Inspection is not permitted unless the shareholder owns a specified number of shares (often 5 percent) or has owned shares for a specified period of time. These limitations ensure corporations are not overburdened with demands from shareholders who may only own one share.

While the corporation is usually free to require that the inspection be done upon prior notice and during reasonable business hours, the articles of incorporation cannot contravene the state statutes. If the corporation wrongfully refuses inspection, it may be subjected to monetary penalties and a court may grant a request by a shareholder for an injunction requiring inspection.

3. *Voting Rights*

Shareholders exercise their limited role in the conduct and operation of the corporation primarily through voting, either for election or removal of directors or relating to some structural change in the corporation. The articles of incorporation can grant, deny, or limit voting rights. For example, one class of shares may have nonvoting stock. There are different types of voting: straight voting, cumulative voting, class voting, contingent voting, and disproportionate voting.

Straight Voting. Generally, and unless the articles of incorporation provide otherwise, each share of record is entitled to one vote for each director's position to be filled or for each issue being considered. This is referred to as **straight voting** and is the most common type of voting exercised by shareholders. Some jurisdictions allow fractional shares to exercise fractional voting rights. For example, due to a share dividend, a shareholder may have 100½ shares of stock. Under straight voting, the shareholder would be entitled to 100½ votes.

Straight voting
Voting in which each share of record has one vote

Cumulative Voting. **Cumulative voting** may be provided in the articles of incorporation or mandated by a state's statutes. Cumulative voting applies *only* to the election of directors and not to any other corporate issues, such as voting for mergers, dissolutions, or amendments to the articles of incorporation. Cumulative voting is a particular type of voting designed to allow some representation of minority shareholders on the board of directors. If cumulative voting rights exist, each share is multiplied by the number of vacancies to be filled. For example, if Andrews owns 100 shares of OmniWorld, Inc. and five directors are being elected, cumulative voting would allow Andrews 500 votes to cast however he likes, while straight voting would allow him only 100 votes.

Cumulative voting
Method of voting in election for directors in which each share carries as many votes as there are directors being elected

To maximize the advantage of cumulative voting, minority shareholders tend to "dump" all their votes on one candidate rather than spread the votes among the board and thereby dilute the impact of cumulative voting. For example, assume OmniWorld, Inc. has 1,000 shares outstanding. Its articles provide for cumulative voting. Further assume that the minority shareholders, Andrews and Baker, together own 400 shares, while the majority shareholders, Carter, Dowell, and Edwards together own 600 shares. Three directors are being elected. The candidates are Taylor, Tyler, and Tuttle (candidates the majority shareholders would like to see elected), and O'Brien, whom the minority shareholders would like to elect. If straight voting exists, the majority shareholders will always be able to elect the directors. Under cumulative voting, the minority shareholders, Andrews and Baker, can elect one person to the board who they hope will represent their interests. If voting cumulatively, Andrews and Baker will have 1,200 shares to vote (400 shares multiplied by three vacancies to be filled). The majority shareholders will have 1,800 shares to vote (600 shares multiplied by three vacancies to be filled). If Andrews and Baker dump all 1,200 of their votes on their candidate, O'Brien will be elected. While the majority shareholders have 1,800 votes, these votes must be divided somehow between their three choices for candidates. No matter which way the majority shareholders divide up their votes, they will elect two directors and the minority shareholders will be able to elect O'Brien if they cast all their votes for O'Brien. (See Figure 11-1.) Cumulative voting generally requires cohesion and agreement among minority shareholders in order to take advantage of the benefits of cumulative voting.

In some states, such as California, cumulative voting is mandatory and cannot be denied by the articles of incorporation, the bylaws, or any other corporate document, except that corporations listed on the national exchanges can eliminate cumulative voting. In other states, and according to RMBCA Section 7.28(b), it is permissive, meaning that the articles of incorporation may provide for cumulative voting. If not provided for in the articles of incorporation, cumulative voting does not exist. In many instances, shareholders wishing to assure election of a representative to the board will examine the shareholder voting list (often kept at the office of the registrar) to identify and locate shareholders with whom they can band together to exercise their voting power.

The impact of cumulative voting can be diluted by decreasing the number of directorships (if only one director is being elected, Andrews and Baker have a total of 400 votes rather than the 1,200 votes they would have if three directors are being elected) or by staggering the board so that not all directors are elected at the same time. The United States Senate is a prototypical stagger system: All senators have a term of six years yet only one-third of the group stands for election every two years. If a nine-member board is staggered or classified into three groups of three directors, rather than having 3,600 votes (400 × 9) to cast were all directors elected at one time, Andrews and Baker would have a total of 1,200 votes (400 × 3) because only three directors are elected every two years. Because a stagger system so severely dilutes the impact of cumulative voting, a stagger system is often not permitted in states where cumulative voting is mandated by statute.

Similarly, to ensure that majority shareholders do not defeat the effect of cumulative voting by immediately removing a director elected by minority share-

FIGURE 11-1
Cumulative Voting

Ballot	*Majority Shareholders*			*Minority Shareholders*	
	Taylor	*Tyler*	*Tuttle*	*O'Brien*	
1	1,300	400	100	1,200	Elected: Taylor, Tyler & O'Brien
2	601	600	599	1,200	Elected: Taylor, Tyler & O'Brien
3	1,500	200	100	1,200	Elected: Taylor, Tyler & O'Brien

holders, states and corporations mandating cumulative voting usually permit removal of a director only upon cumulative voting as well.

Class Voting. If one or more classes or series of shares exist, classes may vote as a separate unit or block. For example, Common A and Common B shareholders may be one group or class for purposes of voting on amendment of the articles of incorporation while Common C and Common D shareholders are a group or class for voting on other issues, such as election of directors for their own group of shareholders.

Class voting
Voting by a class of stock as a separate unit

Contingent Voting. Some shares vote only upon occurrence of a certain contingency or event. For example, the articles of incorporation might provide that Preferred A shareholders can vote for directors only in those years in which dividends are not distributed.

Contingent voting
Voting rights that exist only upon the occurrence of some event

Disproportionate Voting. **Disproportionate voting** exists when one class has voting power disproportionate to that of another. For example, if Common A shareholders had two votes per share and Common B shareholders had one vote per share, disproportionate voting would exist.

Disproportionate voting
Voting rights held by a class that is disproportionate to voting rights of other classes

Nonvoting Stock. **Nonvoting shares** may be authorized and issued so long as full voting rights reside in at least one class of shares.

Nonvoting stock
Stock that carries no voting rights

4. *Shareholder Meetings*

Shareholders have a limited right to participate in the management and operation of the corporation. Typically, this right takes the form of voting. Voting occurs at two types of shareholder meetings: annual and special.

Annual Meetings. Most state statutes require that corporations hold **annual meetings** of shareholders. RMBCA Section 7.01 provides that a corporation shall hold a meeting of shareholders annually. Shareholders may apply to a court to order a meeting if one has not been held within six months of the end of the corporation's fiscal year or 15 months of the last annual meeting. RMBCA Section 7.03. These statutes reflect the legislative policy that because shareholders are not involved in the day-to-day operation of the corporation, they must be provided with some minimum of information about the corporation.

Annual meeting
Yearly meeting of shareholders

The time and date of annual meetings is usually provided in the corporate bylaws. For example, a typical bylaw provision might specify that "annual meetings of shareholders shall be held the first Monday of May of each calendar year." The key action taken at the annual meeting is the election of directors. Other action also may be taken, such as reports of management, amendment of the articles of incorporation, or appointment of the corporation's accountants.

Most corporations hold their annual meetings in the spring (April, May, or June) because this allows sufficient time for corporate accounting and payment of taxes to be accomplished. Financial reports then discussed at the meeting are current and complete.

Special Meetings. **Special meetings** are shareholder meetings held between annual meetings. Shareholders must have some mechanism to call meetings between the annual meetings to investigate fraud, abuse, or mismanagement. For

Special meeting
A meeting held between regular or annual meetings

example, if a corporation's annual meeting is in April, and the shareholders discover embezzlement in June, they should not have to wait until the next annual meeting in April to discuss this critical matter. A special meeting allows the shareholders to meet between the annual meetings to discuss and consider matters of interest.

Most state statutes provide the terms and conditions upon which special meetings may be called. RMBCA Section 7.02 is typical of most statutes. It provides that the board of directors of a corporation may call a special meeting or that shareholders owning 10 percent or more of the outstanding stock may demand that the corporation call a special meeting. Additionally, any person authorized to do so in the corporation's articles of incorporation or its bylaws may call a special meeting. The demand is made upon the secretary of the corporation. In general, only such transactions as are described in the notice of the special meeting may be considered.

Place of Meetings. The bylaws may designate the location of annual or special meetings. Alternatively, and as is more common, the bylaws may provide that the directors can determine the location of meetings. If no location is specified in the bylaws, the meetings will take place at the corporation's principal office.

Many larger corporations tend to rotate their meetings to allow shareholders across the country to attend. Thus, one year's meeting may be held in Atlanta, while the next year's meeting is held in Dallas, followed by an annual meeting in San Francisco. Older statutes required that all meetings be held in the state of incorporation. Modern statutes usually permit meetings to be held in any location, provided proper notice is given.

Notice of Meetings. All jurisdictions require that shareholders receive notice of all meetings. The pertinent state statutes must be reviewed to ensure the notice requirements are followed. Notice requirements can be very detailed and should be scrutinized carefully to avoid having a meeting declared invalid. In general, small corporations tend to act informally and will often provide notice by telephone, if permitted by statute and the corporate bylaws. Larger corporations act in a more formal manner and provide written notices to all shareholders entitled to receive notice. Generally, either the corporate secretary or the registrar prepares and sends notices.

Shareholders Entitled to Notice. Generally, unless the articles of incorporation require otherwise, the corporation is only required to give notice to shareholders entitled to vote at a meeting. Thus, if the holders of Preferred A stock have nonvoting shares, they will not be entitled to notice of a meeting to elect directors.

Record date
A date selected in advance of a meeting or event

Record holder
The owner of stock as of a specified date

To determine the particular shareholders who will receive notice, the corporate bylaws will usually provide a **record date** (some date selected in advance of a meeting) and any persons owning shares on that record date will be entitled to notice of the meeting. Many bylaws provide that the record date will be 30 days before the meeting; any shareholders whose names are "on the books" on that date will be entitled to receive notice. These shareholders are sometimes called the *holders of record* or **record holders.** If the bylaws do not fix or provide for fixing a record date, RMBCA Section 7.05 states that the record date will be the day before the first notice is delivered to shareholders. In no event can the record date be more than 70 days before the meeting. RMBCA Section 7.07(b).

Because the record date is set in advance of the meeting, a shareholder might be entitled to receive notice and to vote even though she no longer owns any shares in the corporation at the time of the meeting. For example, assume the bylaws of Hunter Development Corp. fix the date of the annual meeting as May 1 of each year. The bylaws also provide that any person who owns shares 30 days prior to any meeting is entitled to notice of and to vote at the meeting. If Francie Hoffman owns 100 shares on April 1, she will be entitled to receive notice and to vote. If Francie sells her shares to her sister on April 4, Francie will still receive notice of the meeting and be eligible to vote at the meeting.

To determine the shareholders entitled to receive notice, it is as if the corporation takes a snapshot of its list of shareholders *on that given date*. Those individuals whose names are on the list receive notice and they may vote. Shareholders who buy stock in the corporation after the record date and before the meeting date, in this case between April 1 and May 1, are simply out of luck.

This notice prerequisite is similar to that underlying voter registration. One must be "on the books" by a certain date before an election to vote. An individual who moves to a new county may simply miss the cut-off date for registration and be unable to vote in the next election. The rules relating to record dates likewise exist for the orderly administration of corporate matters.

Contents of Notice. Shareholders are entitled to receive notice of annual and special meetings. RMBCA Section 7.05(a) provides that the notice shall specify the date, time, and place of each meeting. The notice must be given no fewer than ten nor more than 60 days before the meeting date. These time limits provide protection to shareholders by ensuring that they get adequate advance notice so they can make arrangements to attend, but not so much advance notice that they forget about the meeting.

Notice of a special meeting must describe the purpose for which the meeting is called. Some jurisdictions require that all notices for all meetings describe the purpose for which the meeting is called, but the RMBCA rule is similar to that in most jurisdictions in providing that only notices for special meetings must specify the purpose. Erring on the side of caution, most corporations specify the purposes of all meetings, whether annual or special.

Delivery of Notice. According to RMBCA Section 1.41(c), written notice by a corporation to its shareholders is effective when mailed (if mailed prepaid and correctly addressed) or when transmitted electronically to the shareholder in a manner authorized by the shareholder. Alternatively, notice may be delivered in person, or by telephone or voice mail, in which case it is effective when received.

Defective Notice. If the corporation fails to meet its obligations with regard to sending appropriate notice to the appropriate shareholders within the specified period, the meeting is invalid and can be attacked by any shareholder who failed to receive proper notice. Because rescheduling the meeting, preparing new notices, and transporting the directors and officers to another meeting can be expensive, there are two alternatives corporations can use to save an otherwise invalid meeting. First, a shareholder may sign a written waiver of notice, expressly waiving the right to receive notice. This waiver is effective whether signed before or after the meeting. Second, a shareholder may consent in writing to action taken at the meeting. A shareholder's attendance at a meeting is deemed a waiver of notice unless the shareholder objects to the holding of the meeting as it commences. RMBCA Section 7.06. See Figure 11-2 for a typical notice of an annual shareholders' meeting.

As a precautionary matter, many corporations instruct the corporate secretary to prepare an affidavit or certificate of mailing to verify that all notices were properly and timely delivered. Such a certificate is similar in effect to the document signed by process servers who verify in writing that a summons and complaint were properly served upon a defendant and which protects against defendants' claims that they never received the documents. In nearly all cases, a corporation's certificate of mailing will be presumptive evidence that notices were properly prepared and delivered.

Annual report
Report describing corporate performance during the preceding year

Annual Reports. When the corporation sends out the notice of the annual shareholders' meeting, it usually includes a formal **annual report,** often a professional and glossy magazine-style presentation explaining the company's perfor-

FIGURE 11-2
Notice of Annual Meeting of Shareholders

Notice is hereby given that the Annual Meeting of Shareholders of FTB, Inc. will be held in Room Three, Fifth Floor, 5 World Trade Center, New York, New York 10048, on May 16, 2000 at 9:00 A.M., Eastern Standard Time, for the following purposes:

1. To elect five (5) directors to serve until the next annual meeting or until their successors shall have been elected and qualified;
2. To ratify the appointment of PriceWaterhouseCoopers as the Company's independent accountants for the next fiscal year;
3. To act upon a shareholder proposal with respect to the distribution of quarterly reports; and
4. To transact such other business as may properly come before the meeting or any adjournment thereof.

Only shareholders of record at the close of business on April 15, 2000 are entitled to notice of and to vote at the meeting or any adjournments thereof.

April 15, 2000
New York, New York

By order of the Board of Directors
William V. Curtis,
Secretary

mance. Typical sections include a letter from the board's chair, financial reviews (summarizing sales, profit, income, cash flow, liabilities, and shareholders' equity), charts showing stock performance, brief biographies and pictures of the board members, and other information of interest to the shareholders. As part of the continuing trend utilizing technology, many companies now post these reports on their Web sites and provide CDs with audio messages from the board of directors.

Shareholder Lists. After the record date has been determined, the corporation will prepare an alphabetical list of shareholders entitled to receive notice. The list must be arranged by voting groups and provide the address of each shareholder as well as the number of shares held by each shareholder. The list must be made available for inspection by any shareholder beginning two business days after notice of the meeting is given and must remain open for inspection during any meeting. The list will be available at the corporation's principal office or at a place identified in the meeting notice (for larger corporations, possibly the office of the registrar). Shareholders (or their agents or attorneys) have the right to inspect and copy the list upon written demand. RMBCA Section 7.20.

The rationale for making the list available to all shareholders is to encourage discussion among shareholders. Additionally, shareholders may wish to band together and agree to vote as a group to achieve certain goals.

Quorum. No action can be taken at any shareholder meeting unless a certain minimum number of shareholders, a **quorum,** is present. RMBCA Section 7.25 provides that unless the articles specify otherwise, a quorum is a majority of votes entitled to be cast on a given matter. Thus, if 100 shares are entitled to vote on the election of directors, holders representing at least 51 of those shares (a majority of 100) must be present in order for the meeting to be held. If fewer than 51 shares are present at the meeting, the meeting cannot be held and will have to be rescheduled. This will cause great expense to the corporation because it will be required to provide new notices to all shareholders, reserve a location for another meeting, make arrangements for management to attend the new meeting, and so forth.

Quorum
The minimum number of shareholders or directors required to be present before action can be taken

Many states allow corporations to modify the requirements for a quorum by providing such in the articles of incorporation, so long as the quorum is not so low as to be unfair. Most states allow such modification so long as a quorum is not less than one-third of the shares entitled to vote. In such a case, if 100 shares were outstanding and entitled to vote on an issue, 34 shares (one-third of 100) must be present for the meeting to go forward.

Quorum requirements prevent small factions of shareholders from controlling all shareholder action. For example, if a corporation had 100 outstanding shares entitled to vote, and the quorum was one-eighth, a shareholder owning only 13 shares could control a meeting and its outcome. The typical provision that a majority of outstanding shares constitutes a quorum ensures that action is not taken unless some reasonable and fair number of shareholders have the opportunity to consider the matter.

Once a quorum is established, it cannot be destroyed by a group of shareholders who walk out of a meeting (perhaps for the purpose of preventing action being taken on a certain matter). Once a share is represented at a meeting, it is deemed present for quorum purposes for the remainder of the meeting and any adjournment thereof. RMBCA Section 7.25(b).

Proxies. Most states allow shareholders to vote by proxy if they are unable or do not wish to attend a meeting. A **proxy** is a written authorization instructing another person to vote one's shares on one's behalf. The closest analogy to a proxy is an absentee ballot: Voters who are unable to be present for voting on election day may vote by absentee ballot. Similarly, shareholders who cannot attend shareholder meetings may vote by proxy.

Proxy
Written authorization from one directing another to vote his shares

The proxy creates an agent-principal relationship between the parties. The shareholder, as the principal, authorizes another, the agent, to vote his or her shares. The proxy may be specific and authorize the agent (or **proxy holder**) to vote a certain way on specific issues. If such specific instructions are given, the proxy holder must so vote. This type of proxy is referred to as a **limited proxy.** Alternatively, the proxy may authorize the proxy holder to cast the shareholder's votes in the proxy holder's discretion on any issue properly arising at the meeting. This type of proxy is referred to as a **general proxy.** See Figure 11-3 for an example of a general proxy.

Proxy holder
The person who exercises the rights of a shareholder who has granted a proxy

Limited proxy
A proxy given with specific instructions

General proxy
Proxy given in which proxy holder can exercise discretion in voting

The Securities Exchange Act of 1934 regulates the form and content of proxies for corporations whose stock is traded on an exchange or "over the counter" if the company has at least 500 shareholders and assets of at least $5 million. Among other requirements, SEC regulations ensure that the name of each nominee is listed on the proxy form.

Proxies may generally be revoked by the shareholder at any time before they are voted. If the proxy does not state its duration, it will automatically expire 11 months after it is received by the corporation. RMBCA Section 7.22(c). This provision ensures that shareholders grant new proxies for each annual shareholders'

FIGURE 11-3
General Proxy

I hereby appoint Edward L. Goodman or Virginia Nelson Andrews my agent with full power to vote and act for me at their discretion upon any business, including the election of directors at any meeting of the shareholders of FTB, Inc. or any adjournment thereof, held during the term of this proxy at which I am not present in person.

This proxy shall be valid for one year unless sooner revoked by me by delivering to the secretary of the corporation a written revocation of this proxy.

All previous proxies are hereby revoked.

____________________ Date

____________________ Signature

meeting. One type of proxy that is irrevocable is that granted to an individual who has purchased the shareholder's shares or has agreed to do so. Thus, in the event a shareholder sells shares after the record date and grants the new owner a proxy, this proxy cannot be revoked. Proxies are revoked by delivering a written revocation of proxy to the secretary of the corporation or by attending the meeting and voting in person.

Proxies are most often used and needed for large corporations with numerous shareholders. For example, assume General Motors has 800,000 shareholders. There is no stadium or facility that can accommodate such a large group. Thus, most shareholders vote by proxy rather than voting in person at the meeting.

Proxies may be solicited by corporate management to elect management's slate of directors. In some cases, insurgent shareholders will also solicit shareholders for proxies to elect candidates favored by the insurgents or for changes in corporate policy desired by them. This fight for control of the company is a ***proxy fight*** or **proxy contest.** The costs of a proxy contest can be significant and the question often arises as to who should pay for the expenses. Generally, if management has acted in good faith and is successful in the proxy contest, the corporation will pay the costs and expenses associated with the proxy contest, at least if it involves policy issues rather than director personnel issues. Some cases have allowed reimbursement to insurgents of reasonable expenses if they succeed with regard to proxy contests on policy issues. In one recent proxy solicitation, TIAA-CREF, a large institutional investor in Furr's/Bishop's Inc., a struggling cafeteria company, argued to other shareholders that the then-present board had not provided tangible growth and convinced 80 percent of the company's shareholders to replace the entire nine-member board with a seven-member board proposed by TIAA-CREFF.

Proxy contest
A fight for control of a company (also called ***proxy fight***)

The proxy form or card is generally distributed with the notice of the meeting. Many corporations distribute additional notices with the proxy card which stress the importance of voting by proxy. See Figure 11-4 for a model notice.

FIGURE 11-4
Important Notice

No matter how many shares you own, please sign, date, and mail your proxy now, especially if you do not plan to attend the meeting. A majority is required by law. Therefore, it is important that you vote so that your corporation will not have to bear the expense of another solicitation of proxies. You may revoke your proxy at any time prior to its exercise by delivering to the secretary of the corporation a written revocation of proxy or by attending the meeting and voting in person.

FTB, Inc.

Conducting the Meeting. At the meeting, items on the agenda are presented in the form of resolutions which the shareholders then vote upon. Most states provide that approval by a majority vote is required to take action. (Some matters, however, such as amending the articles of incorporation or mergers, may require the affirmative vote of a supermajority, perhaps two-thirds approval.)

For example, assume FTB, Inc. has 100,000 voting shares outstanding. For any business to be conducted, a quorum, or majority of shares, must be present. In this case, a quorum would be 50,001. Assume 60,000 shares are actually present (either in person or by proxy). When the shareholders vote on ratifying PriceWaterhouseCoopers as the independent accountants for the corporation, a majority of those 60,000 votes, or 30,001, is needed to approve the appointment of PriceWaterhouseCoopers. If fewer than 50,001 shares are present, a quorum does not exist and the meeting must be rescheduled and re-noticed. In many corporations, sufficient proxies are received before the actual meeting so that results are known in advance and the meeting is a formality.

Under RMBCA Section 7.25(c), a measure (other than election of directors) passes when the votes for it exceed the votes against it, regardless of abstentions. This allows a measure to pass without receiving a majority vote. For example, if 100 voting shares are outstanding, at least 51 must be present for a quorum to exist. If 51 shares are present and corporate statutes require a majority vote to take action, at least 26 of those shares must approve a certain action. Under the RMBCA approach, however, the measure could pass with less than 26 votes if 20 shares voted in favor, 19 shares voted against the action, and 12 shares abstained. In Delaware and other states, directors may be elected by plurality while any other matters may pass only upon receiving a majority vote of the shares present.

Plurality
The number of votes received by one in an election when the candidate does not have a majority of votes

For elections, the distinction between majority votes and **plurality** votes is as follows: in an election in which two candidates are running for director, he who receives the greatest number of votes is said to have a majority. If, however, there are more than two candidates, the person who receives the greatest number of votes has a plurality, but that person does not have a majority unless he receives more than one-half of all votes cast. For example, if Amanda and Ted are vying for a director's position (100 shares are voting) and Amanda gets 60 votes and Ted gets 40, Amanda received a majority of the votes. If, however, Mike is also running, and Amanda receives 45 votes, Ted receives 30 votes, and Mike receives 25 votes, Amanda has won by a plurality. She cannot win by majority vote unless she receives at least 51 votes.

Most statutes do not address the actual method of voting. For a small corporation with few shareholders, a voice vote or a show of hands may be acceptable, assuming the shareholders own equal shares. If shareholders own differing numbers of shares, a written ballot will lend certainty. Some corporations use election judges or inspectors to determine that a quorum is present, that proxies have been counted, and measures have been approved. RMBCA Section 7.29 provides that if a corporation's shares are listed on a national securities exchange, it must use election inspectors or judges. In many instances, the **election judges** are employees of the corporation's registrar or transfer agent. In other instances, they are officers or employees of the corporation.

Election judge
Neutral party who oversees election and voting processes

Shareholder Voting Agreement. As discussed above, there are several types of voting. Straight voting (one vote per share) is the most common. Cumulative voting may exist in elections for directors. Similarly, shareholders may enter into voting agreements or form voting trusts in order to maximize their voting power.

A *voting agreement,* sometimes called a **pooling agreement,** is an agreement among shareholders that specifies the manner in which they will vote. Shareholders may agree to cast their votes in a certain way on various matters or to pool their shares and cast them as they agree by majority agreement on a case-by-case basis. Such an agreement allows shareholders to band together to seek control. There is little, if any, state regulation of voting agreements. RMBCA Section 7.31 simply provides that two or more shareholders may agree upon the manner in which they will vote their shares by signing an agreement for that purpose. The RMBCA also states that the agreement is specifically enforceable, meaning that a court can order a shareholder to act as previously agreed upon in the written voting agreement.

Pooling agreement
An agreement among shareholders specifying how they will vote (also called a *voting agreement*)

A **voting trust** is an agreement by which shareholders transfer their rights to vote to a trustee who is instructed to vote their shares on their behalf according to the terms of a written trust agreement. The shareholders surrender their shares to the trustee who then becomes the record holder of the shares for purposes of receiving notice and voting. Most states regulate the formation and operation of voting trusts. RMBCA Section 7.30 specifies the manner of creating a voting trust. Failure to follow the statutory requirements usually voids the trust. The terms of the trust may allow the trustee to exercise his or her independent judgment when voting or may require the trustee to obtain a consensus of a certain percentage of the beneficial owners of the shares.

Voting trust
Agreement by which shareholders transfer their rights to a trustee to vote their shares

Under RMBCA Section 7.30(a), a voting trust agreement must be delivered to the corporation. Thus, the corporation may know in advance how the shares subject to the trust will be voted. On the other hand, a pooling agreement is a private agreement between its parties, and the corporation will generally have no knowledge of its existence or terms. Moreover, while voting trusts are generally limited to some specified period of duration, often ten years, pooling agreements can last indefinitely.

When the shareholders relinquish their stock certificates in a voting trust situation, they will receive **voting trust certificates,** which are freely transferable, although the new owner will be bound by the terms of the trust agreement. The shareholders retain their rights to dividends and other rights, and the trustee is substituted for the shareholders only for the purposes of receiving notices of meetings and voting at those meetings. In the pooling agreement situation, new purchasers may or may not take shares subject to the terms of the agreement; the agreement itself will address this matter.

Voting trust certificate
Document showing ownership in a corporation, which evidences that the shares are subject to a voting trust

Shares that are subject to any type of voting agreement must generally be marked with a **legend** indicating that they are subject to the terms of a restrictive agreement. Typically, the legend provides either the terms of the agreement or states that the agreement will be provided upon request. The legend usually warns that any transaction whereby shares are attempted to be transferred in violation of the agreement is not sufficient to transfer ownership, and the purported new owner will not be recognized for any purpose.

Legend
A notation marked on a share of stock indicating the stock is subject to some restriction or limitation

A trustee appointed under a voting trust agreement is subject to fiduciary duties and is usually compensated a fee for services rendered. Typically, the trust agreement provides that the trustee is not liable for errors in business judgment and will be indemnified for acts of ordinary negligence but will be liable for acts of gross negligence or recklessness. There may be more than one trustee appointed. If so, a mechanism should be established to resolve disputes that may arise among trustees.

While a voting trust agreement is more expensive and complex than a pooling agreement and will usually involve payment of a fee to the trustee, it lends more certainty in that the shareholders will not have any power to "go back on their word" and vote contrary to terms of the trust inasmuch as they have no power to vote their shares. With a pooling agreement, a rogue shareholder could decide to breach the agreement and vote contrary to its terms. While other shareholders can sue for breach of contract and apply to a court to compel the shareholder to vote according to the agreement, a voting trust eliminates the possibility of such events even occurring.

Minutes of Meeting. The corporation's secretary usually has the responsibility for taking **minutes** of the shareholders' meetings. There is no one statutorily required format for minutes. Some law firms provide their smaller corporate clients with "canned" or prepared minutes, allowing the secretary to merely fill in the blanks and indicate action taken at a meeting. Larger corporations tend to keep more detailed minutes. Similarly, statutes seldom address the actual manner of conducting the meeting. Many larger corporations follow *Robert's Rules of Order*.

Minutes
Written record of events occurring at a meeting

To provide protection against later challenges, the minutes should include a variety of recitals: that notice was properly given to all shareholders entitled to receive notice or that the shareholders properly waived notice, that a quorum was present, that a measure passed by sufficient vote, and so forth. The minutes reflect action taken at the meeting and provide an overview rather than a verbatim transcript of what was uttered at the meeting. See Figure 11-5 for sample minutes of a shareholders' meeting.

5. *Shareholder Action Without a Meeting*

RMBCA Section 7.04 and state statutes allow shareholders to take action without formally meeting. This allows business to be conducted without the expense of holding meetings. Action can be taken without a meeting if all shareholders entitled to vote on the issue consent to the proposed action in writing. The corporate secretary prepares a document called a "**written consent action**" or a "unanimous consent by shareholders in lieu of meeting" and distributes it to the shareholders for signature. Alternatively, rather than being required to obtain all signatures on one document, the secretary can prepare separate documents and send one to each shareholder. Once signed by the last shareholder, the measure is effective.

Written consent action
Action taken without the necessity of a meeting; generally, must be unanimous

Although the majority of states and the RMBCA approach require that the consent be unanimous, a growing number of states, including Delaware, allow for written consent by the minimum number of shares that would be required to take such action at a meeting. The rationale for demanding unanimous consent is that in the absence of a meeting, there is no opportunity for open discussion. Thus, without such discussion, *all* shareholders should be in agreement with the action proposed to be taken. See Figure 11-6 illustrating a form of written consent action.

FIGURE 11-5
Minutes of Annual Meeting of Shareholders

An annual meeting of the shareholders of Tech Management Team, Inc., a Delaware corporation, was held on May 1, 2000 at 10:00 A.M., in the Spanish Ballroom of the Four Seasons Olympic Hotel, 411 University Street, Seattle, Washington for the purpose of electing directors of the corporation, voting on the approval of Price Waterhouse as independent auditors of the corporation, and to transact such other business properly before the meeting.

Daniel J. Sullivan, Chief Executive Officer, acted as Chairman and Diana Hendrix acted as Secretary.

At 10:00 A.M. the Chairman called the meeting to order.

The secretary announced that the meeting was called pursuant to Del. Code Ann. tit. 8, Section 211 (b) and Article VII of the bylaws of the corporation.

The secretary announced that the meeting was held pursuant to notice properly given as required under the laws of the State of Delaware and the bylaws of the corporation, or that notice had been waived by those entitled to receive notice under the bylaws. Copies of any written waivers executed by those persons entitled to receive notice will be attached to the minutes of this meeting by the secretary.

The secretary announced that an alphabetical list of the names of shareholders and the number of shares held by each was available for inspection by any person in attendance at the meeting.

The secretary announced that a quorum was present at the meeting.

All of the directors of the corporation were present at the meeting. The following other persons were present: James K. Eckmann, Chief Financial Officer of the corporation, Susan M. Blakely, representative of the corporation's registrar and transfer agent, Citigroup Inc. and Harry S. Hunter, election judge appointed by the corporation's registrar and transfer agent, Citigroup Inc.

The reports of the President and Chief Financial Officer were presented to the shareholders and were placed in the corporate minute book.

The Chairman then called for the election of directors of the corporation.

Upon motion duly made, seconded, and carried, the following persons were elected to the board of directors of the corporation, to serve as directors until their successors are elected at the next annual meeting of shareholders of the corporation and qualify:

Lisa Black
Christopher Wagner
Kenneth Lyons
William Booher
Patricia E. Moore

The Chairman then called for the approval of PriceWaterhouseCoopers as independent auditors of the corporation.

Upon motion duly made, seconded, and carried, PriceWaterhouseCoopers was appointed as independent auditors of the corporation upon the terms and conditions set forth in the Notice of this Annual Meeting of Shareholders and placed in the minute book.

There being no further business before the meeting, on motion duly made, seconded, and unanimously carried, it was adjourned.

Date: ______________________ ______________________
Diana Hendrix, Secretary

FIGURE 11-6
Written Consent in Lieu of Shareholders' Meeting

The undersigned, constituting a majority of the shareholders of FTB, Inc., a Delaware corporation, and acting pursuant to Del. Code Ann. tit. 8, Section 228 (a) and Article VIII of the bylaws of the corporation, hereby take the following action as if present at a meeting duly called pursuant to proper notice.

RESOLVED, that Article I of the Certificate of Incorporation shall be amended to read as follows: The name of the corporation is FTB Access Link, Co.

RESOLVED, that Article III of the Certificate of Incorporation be amended to read as follows: The aggregate number of shares that the corporation shall have authority to issue is 100,000 shares of common stock.

The officers and directors of the corporation are authorized to take all appropriate action to effect these Resolutions.

Date: ______________________ ______________________
Signature

Date: ______________________ ______________________
Signature

Date: ______________________ ______________________
Signature

Date: ______________________ ______________________
Signature

Action by written consent is impractical for large corporations with numerous shareholders. It is instead designed to simplify corporate formalities for smaller corporations when it may be difficult for shareholders to get together for meetings.

6. *Modern Trends*

Modern technology is having a significant effect on shareholder meetings and action. Many large corporations, including AT&T and Cisco Systems, Inc., now offer proxy statements and annual reports electronically over the Internet. Shareholders can also now vote telephonically (by calling a toll-free number, identifying themselves by entering a control number located on a voting instruction card sent to them, and then following recorded instructions) or by accessing a

Web site and voting. The method of voting electronically via the Internet is often called "e-proxy." In fact, in 1998, more than one thousand companies permitted their shareholders to vote online.

The statutes of some states, including California, Delaware, and New York, specifically permit shareholders of companies incorporated in those states to authorize others to act as proxies by transmission of a telegram, cablegram, or other means of electronic transmission, thus explicitly recognizing e-proxies. One company in particular, ProxyVote.com (<www.proxyvote.com>), is active in serving as a monitor for e-proxies cast in various shareholder matters.

These advances not only help the corporation reduce printing and postage costs, but due to their ease, greatly enhance shareholder participation in corporate governance. Moreover, shareholders are increasingly using the Internet to discuss the merits of various corporate activities. For example, when USA Networks Inc. was considering a merger with Lycos Inc., USA executives routinely reviewed chat room conversations. When those conversations revealed a high level of shareholder concern over the proposed merger, USA killed the deal. The Internet is thus able to unite investors who once met only at annual meetings, if then. While previously individual investors often threw away their notices of meetings and proxy cards, or forgot to vote, the ease of voting telephonically or through the use of e-proxies promotes shareholder involvement and activism.

Releases by the Securities and Exchange Commission provide guidance for companies that wish to use e-proxies, generally requiring companies to do the following: provide timely and adequate notice of the availability of electronic documents; allow effective and easy access to the documents; and be able to demonstrate that the documents were actually delivered.

Additionally, experts predict that corporations will eventually hold "cybermeetings," with shareholders all over the country and around the world participating via the Internet. Holding meetings online would clearly save companies and shareholders time and money and further expand shareholder involvement inasmuch as shareholders could ask pertinent questions and then cast their votes electronically.

Legally, the barrier to holding shareholder meetings online is the question whether online involvement constitutes "attendance." Most state statutes impose requirements that shareholders can attend meetings either in person or by proxy. Thus, there is a question whether viewing the meeting on a screen constitutes attendance. Some modifications to state statutes and corporate bylaws may be necessary before cybermeetings can be effective. Confidentiality and security of meeting proceedings are also issues, and corporations will have to find a way to ensure that outside "hackers" do not access an online meeting and cast phony votes.

At present, some companies, including Intel Corp., Ford Motor Company, and Gateway 2000 Inc., broadcast their annual shareholder meetings live as well as videotape those meetings to permit later viewing of those meetings via the Internet.

All of these efforts, from posting reports online, to allowing voting telephonically and via the Internet, to the eventual holding of meetings online, serve to promote the laudable goal of shareholder participation in matters of corporate governance.

7. *Preemptive Rights*

A shareholder may have preemptive rights. As discussed in Chapter Nine, a preemptive right gives a shareholder the right to purchase as many newly issued shares as will maintain the shareholder's proportionate ownership interest in the corporation. Shareholders with preemptive rights are given this opportunity before newly issued shares can be offered to others for purchase. Because preemptive rights can delay the corporation from obtaining needed funds by issuing shares under any terms and conditions the board desires, preemptive rights generally do not exist unless specifically provided for in the articles of incorporation.

8. *Dividends*

Shareholders may have the right to receive dividends. As discussed in Chapter Twelve, directors are usually under no obligation to pay dividends. Dividends may be declared in the discretion of the board of directors from time to time. If preferred shareholders have cumulative dividends, dividends must be paid to them first for the current year and any previous years' arrearages before they can be distributed to other shareholders. Only a solvent corporation may distribute dividends. Thus, shareholders generally have no absolute right to receive dividends.

9. *Right to Transfer Shares and Shareholder Agreements*

Because shareholders own an interest in the corporation, they can transfer this property to others upon the terms they negotiate. Some shareholders, however, enter into agreements with other shareholders or the corporation restricting the transfer of their shares and generally requiring that shareholders who wish to sell their stock must first offer it to the corporation and/or to the other shareholders. If the corporation and the other shareholders decline to purchase the shares, they may then be sold to an "outsider." Such a provision not only restricts the intrusion of outsiders but also provides a ready market for a shareholder who wishes to sell his or her shares. Such restrictions are permitted by RMBCA Section 6.27.

Buy-sell agreement Agreement among shareholders regarding their rights to purchase and sell stock in a corporation and usually imposing some restrictions on those rights

These shareholder agreements, often called **buy-sell agreements,** preserve present ownership interests and prevent the admission of new shareholders who might disturb the relationships among small groups of shareholders, who are frequently family or friends. Agreements cannot absolutely restrict or prohibit shareholders from transferring their shares because one of the key attributes of owning property is the ability to sell it. Nevertheless, some restrictions on transferring stock are acceptable.

The least restrictive agreements generally offer the corporation or its shareholders the right to purchase another shareholder's stock before it can be sold to an outsider. Such a provision does not obligate the corporation or its shareholders to purchase the stock but merely gives them a right of first refusal to do so.

The right of first refusal is usually triggered by the receipt of a valid offer made by a third party to a shareholder to purchase her shares. The shareholder then notifies the corporation and the shareholders of the terms of the offer and the corporation and the shareholders have the right to purchase the stock on the same terms as offered by the offeror. The agreement may provide that the corporation has the right of first refusal to purchase the shares and, if it declines to do so, then the existing shareholders have the right to purchase the stock. If numerous shareholders exist, they may purchase the selling shareholder's stock according to their proportionate ownership interests. Thus, a shareholder who owns 24 percent of the outstanding stock may purchase 24 percent of the stock to be sold.

The agreement may be drafted to allow for either partial or complete purchase of the selling shareholder's stock. For example, if the existing shareholders are allowed to purchase some of the offered stock, each may purchase a few shares. The shareholder can then sell the remaining shares to the offeror (who may not wish to purchase a small block). Other agreements require the corporation or its shareholders to buy all of the stock. If they do not agree to purchase all of the stock, it can be sold to the outsider.

Other provisions may require the corporation to purchase the stock of a shareholder who dies. This ensures that the shareholder's heirs do not try to come in and begin running the corporation. Typically, the purchase is funded by life insurance policies. The corporation will purchase life insurance policies on its shareholders and upon the death of a shareholder use the proceeds of the policy to purchase the stock from the deceased shareholder's estate. The estate must sell upon the terms agreed upon by the shareholder. Many corporations include formulas or procedures for determining the value of stock. The agreement can also provide for installment payments. Some agreements are funded by cross-purchase insurance policies. In this case, each shareholder purchases life insurance on the life of every other shareholder. In the event of that shareholder's death, each shareholder receives a fund of money that can be used to purchase the decedent's shares.

Other events that may trigger a forced sale of shares may be a shareholder's retirement, bankruptcy, or disability.

To ensure that shareholders do not violate the terms of a shareholder agreement and sell their shares without complying with the agreement, their share certificates must be conspicuously marked with a notice stating that the transfer of the shares represented by the certificate is subject to restriction. RMBCA Section 6.27. This notation is called a *legend condition*. The terms of the restriction may be set forth on the certificate or the certificate may simply indicate where the agreement containing the restriction can be inspected. Agreements entered into by shareholders will require that the shareholders surrender their certificates so the legend condition can be marked thereon. See Appendix J for a sample buy-sell agreement.

When shares are transferred, the appropriate entry indicating the name, address, and number of shares owned by the new shareholder is made in the stock ledger book. Until the corporation is notified, the record owner of the shares will continue to receive notice of meetings and will be entitled to vote and receive dividends, if declared.

Shareholder buy-sell agreements are further discussed in Chapter Seventeen.

10. *Shareholder Actions*

Among the other rights shareholders of a corporation possess is the right to institute litigation either against the corporation or on its behalf. There are two principal types of actions instituted by shareholders of a corporation: direct actions, for injury caused directly to the shareholder by the corporation, and derivative actions, for injury sustained by the corporation that the corporation fails to redress. You may recall from Chapter Four that limited partners and LLC members can also institute direct and derivative actions.

Direct action
Action initiated to address direct harm done to the complainant

Direct Actions. A **direct action** is one brought by a shareholder who has been injured by some act of the corporation. In such instances, shareholders bring suit against the corporation in much the same way they would bring suit against any party causing them injury. The shareholder is the plaintiff who asserts his grievance, or *cause of action,* in a complaint filed against the corporation. Reasons for shareholders instituting direct action might be a refusal to distribute a dividend to a shareholder when every other member of the shareholder's class received a dividend; denial of voting rights to a particular shareholder; or refusal to allow inspection of the shareholder list by a shareholder.

Class action
Action brought on behalf of a large group of people who are similarly situated (often called *representative action*)

If numerous shareholders are similarly situated (for example, if an entire class of shareholders, those 100 individuals owning Common B stock, are wrongfully denied their voting rights), one or more of the shareholders can institute a **class action** on behalf of the other shareholders. *Class actions,* sometimes called *representative actions,* promote judicial economy in that similar claims are adjudicated at the same time rather than having the 100 shareholders institute 100 separate lawsuits.

Derivative action
Action initiated to enforce a right owned by another

Derivative Actions. A derivative suit is brought by one or more shareholders to enforce a right or cause of action owned by the corporation but which it will not enforce. In brief, the shareholder sues the corporation to compel it to enforce corporate rights. The shareholder is the plaintiff and both the corporation and the wrongdoer are the defendants. The shareholder is not suing for injury done to herself; the action "derives" from the shareholder's ownership interest in the corporation which will not sue the wrongdoer.

For example, assume that FTB, Inc. has loaned $100,000 to the wife of its director, Dan Donoghue. The time to repay the loan has expired but FTB, Inc. will not sue Mrs. Donoghue, due to Dan's powerful presence on the board. A shareholder could institute a derivative suit on behalf of the corporation to recover the $100,000 from Mrs. Donoghue. If the shareholder prevails, the shareholder does not receive the $100,000 because that sum is properly owned by the corporation. The shareholder will, however, be entitled to reimbursement for the costs and expenses of bringing the action. Presumably, the shareholder will receive some indirect or ultimate benefit by the corporation having an additional $100,000 in assets. In fact, the corporation might then be able to pay a dividend to the shareholders.

Derivative actions involve various procedural complexities, such as requiring that the shareholder make a formal written demand on the corporation before instituting the derivative action and requiring that the shareholder had owned stock at the time the wrong occurred (or acquired the stock from one who was a shareholder when the wrong occurred). This latter requirement helps assure that the shareholder is genuinely aggrieved and has not purchased stock for the sole purpose of suing the corporation in hopes of a generous settlement. Under RMBCA Section 7.46, a court can order a plaintiff to pay any defendant's reasonable expenses (including counsel fees) if the proceeding was commenced for an improper purpose or without reasonable cause.

Modern Shareholder Suits. Shareholder lawsuits showed a dramatic increase in the 1990s. In many instances, shareholders sued on the basis that their company overstated profits, with shareholders viewing quarterly earnings statements and forecasts as to expected performance as representations on which they could rely. When earnings do not meet such projections, shareholders have sued. For example, in 1998, the day after a company announced it was restating its revenues downward from $8.3 million to $1.4 million, 23 class actions alleging securities fraud were filed.

In an effort to reduce such suits, Congress enacted the Securities Litigation Reform Act (15 U.S.C. Sections 78u-4, et seq.) in late 1995 to make it harder for such shareholder suits to succeed. Its advocates had convincingly argued that the law was necessary to combat the increasingly familiar practice of initiating shareholder suits the moment stock losses occurred. While the number of suits continues to increase, perhaps due to increasing numbers of investors in the stock market (235 companies having been named as defendants in federal class actions in 1998, the highest number ever), more than one-half of the suits are dismissed nearly immediately.

The 1995 Reform Act requires plaintiffs to state in specific detail any allegations of misrepresentation regarding stock sales rather than merely generally alleging misconduct and then using discovery to obtain specificity and perhaps uncover claims. The Act also eliminated joint and several liability for various securities violations. This rule had previously resulted in peripheral defendants with "deep pockets," often attorneys, auditors, and underwriters, being liable for an entire judgment. Under the Act, liability will be apportioned such that each party is liable only for the portion of the judgment that corresponds to its actual assigned allocation of fault. Only those who knowingly commit violations remain jointly and severally liable.

Moreover, the Act allows control of litigation to be assumed by the largest investor, the **"lead plaintiff,"** who is most capable of adequately representing the interests of the class. There is a rebuttable presumption that the party with the largest financial interest in the relief sought by the class is the most adequate plaintiff. To eliminate "professional plaintiffs," a person may be a lead plaintiff in no more than five securities class actions during any three-year period. The largest class action securities action settlement to date occurred in December 1999 with the payment of $2.8 billion to shareholders of Cendant Corporation arising out of overstated financial results. In ad`dition to the payment by the corporation to its shareholders, the accounting firm of Ernst & Young agreed to pay $335 million to settle accounting malpractice charges against the firm arising from its auditing of Cendant's financial statements.

Lead plaintiff
The largest investor in a class action alleging corporate misconduct

11. *Miscellaneous Rights of Shareholders*

In addition to the foregoing, shareholders enjoy other rights. Most of these take the form of voting. While the primary activity engaged in by shareholders is electing directors, shareholders can also vote on removing directors and on certain extraordinary corporate activities such as mergers, amending the articles of incorporation, and voluntary dissolution of the corporation. Additionally, in specific cases, shareholders have the right to have their shares appraised and purchased from them if they disagree with certain extraordinary matters such as mergers.

12. *Shareholders' Responsibilities*

Generally, shareholders have only one responsibility: to pay for the stock issued to them. RMBCA Section 6.22(a). Once the stock is paid for, shareholders are not liable to the corporation or to its creditors for debts and obligations. Because the corporation is viewed as a separate person under the law, *it* is responsible for its own debts. While the shareholder's stock may plummet in value to zero, a shareholder generally has no liability for corporate obligations. In fact, this limited liability is often viewed as the principal purpose for incorporating.

13. *Piercing the Corporate Veil*

While the general rule is that shareholders are not personally liable for a corporation's debts and obligations, there are exceptions to this rule. Shareholders can certainly agree to accept personal responsibility for corporate obligations. For example, a newly formed small corporation operating a restaurant will not have a proven track record upon which the food, equipment, and beverage suppliers can rely. Therefore, before extending credit to the corporation, the suppliers may require that individual shareholders personally guarantee the corporation's obligation to pay for provisions supplied to it. While corporate law does not impose personal liability on the shareholders, the shareholders, by contract, may agree to accept such liability. Similarly, banks and other lenders may require personal guarantees from shareholders of smaller corporations who are active in managing the business.

Piercing the veil
Holding individual shareholders liable for corporate obligations

Alter ego
Doctrine alleging separate corporate existence has been ignored by shareholders

Because the corporation typically shields its shareholders from liability, it is said that there is a "veil" between it and the shareholders such that creditors cannot "**pierce the veil**" to hold individual shareholders liable for corporate obligations. Nevertheless, courts will pierce the veil whenever it is necessary "to prevent fraud or injustice." While this standard gives courts great flexibility in determining the circumstances under which liability can be imposed on shareholders, in actual practice, piercing-the-veil cases tend to share a common element: The shareholders have not acted as if the corporation is a separate entity; rather they view the corporation as their mere **alter ego** or business conduit. The most frequent examples seen in piercing cases involve commingling of assets, lack of corporate formalities, and under-capitalization.

Commingling of Assets. The corporation is a separate person. Therefore, it has its own bank accounts, funds, and books. In some small corporations, cash flow may be tight or unpredictable. When bills arrive, the corporation's bank account may be low on funds. In this situation, shareholders may be likely to "loan" money to the corporation to help it meet its obligations. Similarly, when shareholders need funds, they may "borrow" from the corporation's accounts. This transferring of money back and forth is called **commingling of funds.** It does not matter whether each party dutifully repays the money, either with or without interest. Just as an individual cannot legally dip into another person's wallet when he is short of funds, the shareholders and corporation cannot dip into each other's accounts. These situations differ from permissible loans made by a shareholder to the corporation or by the corporation to the shareholder (which should be formally documented). If the shareholders disregard the fact that the corporation is a separate entity, a court may do so as well. This lack of respect for the separateness of the corporate entity may result in liability being imposed on the shareholders.

Commingling of funds Combining funds owned by different individuals or entities

Lack of Formalities. Sometimes all of the energy and time of those involved in a corporation is focused on making a success of the business. The individuals involved may devote themselves to making the business work and neglect the fact that corporations are subject to various requirements, such as annual shareholders' meetings, regular action by the board of directors, and so forth. In some instances, individuals have formed corporations, and then never held a meeting, never elected directors, and never issued stock. When shareholders do not treat the corporation as a separate entity, there is little reason why courts should. Thus, clients should be adequately counseled to observe corporate formalities. The first counseling session should occur at the corporation's organizational meeting. "Canned" or prepared forms for notices, waivers, and minutes can be provided to clients, and the dates for annual meetings can be docketed, all to help ensure that clients observe required corporate formalities.

Inadequate Capitalization. Another situation in which courts may pierce the veil of limited liability to hold individual shareholders responsible for corporate obligations exists when the corporation is so inadequately capitalized or routinely drains its funds to pay distributions to its shareholders that it could not expect to meet its responsibilities. Failure to ensure that the corporation has sufficient funds to meet its needs works an injustice on creditors and others dealing with the corporation.

Creditors can readily determine if commingling of assets, lack of formalities, or under-capitalization has occurred. Once the creditor has sued the corporation and discovered that it does not have sufficient assets to pay its debt, the creditor will begin scrutinizing the corporate structure to determine if other defendants may be available to assist in repaying the debt. Through the discovery process, the creditor may examine various corporate records. Requesting the books of account from the corporation, its minute books, stock transfer ledger, and other records will reveal whether funds have been transferred back and forth, whether meetings and elections have been held, and whether the corporation was operating on a sound fiscal footing. If it is believed that the corporate form has been disregarded by the shareholders, the creditor will amend its complaint to add the individual shareholders as defendants.

Most jurisdictions allow one-person corporations. Even these one-person corporations, however, must be established on a sound fiscal foundation and must operate on a corporate basis rather than a personal basis. They too must observe corporate formalities.

Piercing-the-veil cases tend to be brought more frequently against smaller corporations than larger ones. Larger corporations rely upon advice of counsel and accountants to ensure they do not disregard the corporate entity. Smaller corporations have few shareholders, all of whom may be active in managing the business and are often so busy that they ignore corporate formalities and the separateness of the corporate books and accounts. If the corporation has adequate assets, of course, the veil will never need to be pierced. It is only when a creditor cannot obtain full payment of a debt from the corporation that the creditor will ask a court to pierce the corporate veil and impose personal liability on individual shareholders.

B. Directors' Rights and Responsibilities

1. *Introduction*

Directors
Those who manage a corporation

Corporations are managed or governed by individuals called **directors.** These directors function as a body rather than as individuals. Their duties and powers derive from state statutes, the articles of incorporation, and the corporate bylaws. Directors have full authority and responsibility for determining corporate policy. Directors exercise this authority in their regular and special meetings. Directors each have one vote, and generally a simple majority is required to take action. Most states allow directors to take action without a meeting if they act by unanimous written consent. Directors owe duties of due care and good faith to the corporation. Generally, directors are not liable for a mere error in judgment unless their action (or lack thereof) is clearly and grossly negligent.

2. *Number and Qualifications of Directors*

While some states continue to require at least three directors, the more modern approach, that of the RMBCA, is to require only one director. Approximately one-half of the states, including Delaware, require only one director. Corporations having more than one director typically have an odd number (five, seven, or nine) to minimize the possibility of a deadlock. While the older statutes required that directors be residents of the state of incorporation, the modern view is that directors need not be residents of the state of incorporation or shareholders of the corporation, unless the articles or bylaws so require. RMBCA Section 8.02. While the articles or bylaws can set minimum and maximum age standards and residency requirements, the trend is to avoid such limitations.

To ensure that directors have the legal capacity to enter into contracts, they should have attained the age of majority, namely 18 years of age. Statutes do not set a maximum age. They also set no maximum number of directors. Having an unusually large board, however, makes management difficult and cumbersome. Directors can usually increase or decrease the size of the board by amending the bylaws (or articles, if provisions establishing the size of the board are contained therein), but the corporation can never have fewer directors than required by the state statute.

Directors cannot sit on the boards of competing corporations. Because directors owe fiduciary duties and duties of loyalty to the corporation, a director cannot fulfill those duties if he or she is also on the board of directors of a competitor.

3. *Functions of Directors*

Although directors are elected and removable by shareholders, directors are not puppets of the shareholders. Once elected, their duties are owed to the corporation to promote its welfare. Under RMBCA Section 8.01, directors are charged with exercising all corporate powers and managing the entire business affairs of a corporation. While directors may delegate some of their duties to officers or committees, certain duties, such as authorizing dividends, filling vacancies on the board, and amending bylaws, cannot be so delegated.

Directors are generally responsible for taking the following actions:

a. authorizing distributions;
b. adopting, amending, and repealing bylaws;
c. appointing, supervising, and removing officers;
d. determining financial matters, such as issuing stock, reacquiring stock, obtaining loans, and issuing bonds;
e. determining products and services to be offered and the prices for them;
f. determining wages and employee benefits and compensation, including their own benefits and compensation;
g. initiating extraordinary matters such as mergers or the purchase or sale of corporate assets; and
h. exercising responsibility for corporate operations.

4. *Election, Term, Vacancies, and Removal of Directors*

Election. The initial directors may be named in the articles of incorporation. If not, the initial board will be elected at the corporation's first organizational meeting. Those directors will serve until the corporation's first annual meeting. The directors will then be elected at the first annual meeting and at every annual meeting thereafter, unless their terms are staggered.

Directors are elected by a plurality of votes. For example, assume Omni-World, Inc., a corporation, has 1,000 shares outstanding, 600 of which are represented at a meeting called to elect a director. Three individuals are running for one vacancy on the board of directors. If Candidate A receives 290 votes, Candidate B receives 220 votes, and Candidate C receives 90 votes, Candidate A will be the winner by a plurality of votes, even though Candidate A did not receive a vote of the majority (in this case, a majority vote would be 301, or one-half of the number present plus one).

Staggered system
Method of corporate governance in which not all directors are elected at the same time or election

Term. The articles or bylaws may provide that not all of the directors are to be elected each year. This arrangement is referred to as a **staggered system** because the directors do not all face election at the same time; their terms are divided into groupings or are staggered. The most common staggered system for boards of directors is a total of nine directors, divided into three groups, with the members of a group standing for election each year. Each director will have a three-year term; however, those terms will not all be served concurrently. In essence, the U.S. Senate is a staggered system, with all senators having a six-year term but only one-third standing for election every two years. Staggered boards provide some continuity of expertise for corporations inasmuch as the entire board of directors will not be replaced at one time. RMBCA Section 8.06 provides that there cannot be a staggered board unless there are at least nine directors. Such provisions, and others relating to maximum terms, are fairly common. Because a staggered system will reduce the impact of cumulative voting, it is generally not allowed when cumulative voting exists. For example, if a shareholder has 100 votes and nine directors are being elected, under cumulative voting, the shareholder will have 900 votes to cast; if the board is staggered, however, and only three directors will be elected each time, the shareholder has only 300 votes to cast.

If the articles authorize dividing the shares into classes, the articles may also authorize the election of all or some directors by one or more classes. Thus, if there are three classes of stock, Common A shareholders might elect three directors, Common B shareholders might elect three directors, and Common C shareholders might elect three directors. Such an arrangement may well promote minority representation on the board because Common A shareholders might own only a small percentage of the corporation's stock (the articles having specified that the corporation can issue only a certain number of shares of Common A stock), but will be guaranteed they can elect one-third of the board.

Vacancies. If a vacancy occurs in the board of directors due to resignation, retirement, or death, of if a new position is created pursuant to amendment of the corporate articles or bylaws, the vacancy will be filled either by the shareholders or the remaining directors. Most statutes provide that the remaining directors may fill such a vacancy. If numerous vacancies exist, perhaps due to the simultaneous deaths of directors in an accident, if the remaining directors do not constitute a quorum, they may nevertheless fill vacancies by a majority vote of all directors remaining in office. RMBCA Section 8.10(a)(3). The new director elected to fill the vacancy usually "steps into the shoes" of his or her predecessor and serves for the remainder of the predecessor's term. Directors may resign at any time, by providing written notice to the corporation.

Removal. At common law, directors, once elected by the shareholders, could be removed from their positions only "for cause." The "cause" was typically fraud or dishonesty. The modern approach provided in most state statutes now allows shareholders to remove directors either with or without cause. The theory underlying the modern policy is that the shareholders own the corporation and they thus have the right at any time to determine who should manage it. This allows the shareholders greater flexibility because it is often difficult to prove fraud or dishonesty. Thus, if the shareholders elect directors in April, they can remove some or even all of those directors at any time thereafter without waiting for the next annual meeting.

Shareholders representing 10 percent of the ownership of the corporation can require that a meeting be held by demanding that the corporate secretary call a special meeting. The notice of the meeting must state its purpose, for example, to consider removal of a director. Generally, a director can be removed only by majority vote of the shareholders that were entitled to elect him. Thus, if director Smith is elected by Common A shareholders, only Common A shareholders can remove Smith. When cumulative voting is authorized, a director cannot be removed if the number of votes sufficient to elect him under cumulative voting is voted against removal. Thus, if 100 shares would have been sufficient to elect a director under cumulative voting, then the director cannot be removed if 100 shares vote against removal. This ensures that the interests of minority shareholders who cumulatively vote are not circumvented by removal of a director by majority vote immediately after election.

In the event that shareholders cannot muster sufficient votes to remove a director who is also a majority shareholder (because the director has sufficient votes to block his own removal), shareholders can apply to court for removal. In this case, removal by the court is dependent upon proof of the director's fraudulent or dishonest conduct, gross abuse of authority, or a showing that removal is in the best interest of the corporation. RMBCA Section 8.09.

5. *Directors' Meetings*

The management of the corporation is accomplished by the directors acting at meetings (or by unanimous written consent). Few statutes give guidance regarding the notice and conduct of directors' meetings. Thus, most directors' meetings are governed by the bylaws of the corporation. Just as there are two types of shareholder meetings (annual and special), there are two types of directors' meetings, regular and special.

Regular Meetings. Most boards meet at regularly scheduled intervals, whether once a week, once a month, or once a quarter. These scheduled meetings are called regular meetings and the board conducts its business and manages the corporation at these meetings. Although there is no requirement to do so, many corporations also hold annual board of directors' meetings immediately following the shareholders' annual meeting. New officers are often appointed at this annual meeting.

Special Meetings. A special meeting is any meeting held between regular meetings. Special meetings are typically called to discuss matters that cannot wait until the next regular meeting. Provisions relating to who is authorized to call a special meeting (generally, the chair of the board) will be found in the bylaws.

Place of Meetings. The place of the meeting, whether regular or special, may be specified in the bylaws or may be determined by the directors. Meetings need not be held in the state of incorporation and generally can be held anywhere. If no specific location is provided in the bylaws, at the end of each regular meeting, the board should specify the location of the next regular meeting.

Notice of Meetings. Generally, directors are not entitled to notice of regular meetings. Because it is their duty to manage the corporation, they are expected to know when the board regularly meets. Thus, providing notice of a regular meeting is as unneeded as a phone call from an employer to an employee each morning reminding the employee to come to work.

RMBCA Section 8.22(b) provides that unless the articles or bylaws provide otherwise, special meetings require two days' advance notice of the date, time, and place of the meeting. Other statutes merely require that reasonable advance notice be given of special meetings. The notice typically need not state the purpose of the special meeting.

Waiver of Notice. Directors can give up or waive their right to receive notice of any meeting either before or after the meeting. The waiver must be in writing and filed with the minutes or other corporate records. See Figure 11-7 for a sample waiver of notice by director. A director's attendance at a meeting constitutes a waiver, unless the director attends the meeting for the purpose of objecting to the meeting. Such an objection must be made at the beginning of any meeting.

The stringent and detailed provisions relating to notice for shareholders are somewhat relaxed with regard to notice for directors. The rationale is generally that because the directors manage the corporation, they have access to information relating to the corporation's affairs and need little protection. Shareholders, on the other hand, participate in corporate affairs only by voting, and are therefore entitled to greater protection to ensure their limited rights of participation are safeguarded.

Quorum. Directors cannot take action at any meeting unless a quorum is present. Generally, a quorum consists of a majority of the number of directors as fixed in the articles or bylaws. While the articles or bylaws may provide that a greater

FIGURE 11-7
Waiver of Notice of Meeting by Director

The undersigned, a director of FTB, Inc., a Delaware corporation, hereby waives notice of and consents to the holding of a special meeting of the board of directors of FTB, Inc., held on September 30, 2000 at 1024 Fifteenth Street, N. W., Washington, D.C. 20005 at 10:00 A.M. for the purpose of selecting officers for FTB, Inc.

Date: ____________________ ____________________

Signature

number than a majority is needed for a quorum, they may not provide that a quorum consists of fewer than one-third of the prescribed number of directors. RMBCA Section 8.24.

Assume the bylaws of a corporation prescribe that there shall be nine directors. Unless other provisions exist, a quorum will be five directors (regardless of board vacancies). Once five board members are present, action may be taken.

These quorum requirements are typically relaxed with regard to filling vacancies. If the number of directors remaining in office is insufficient to constitute a quorum, the directors may fill a vacancy by the affirmative vote of those directors remaining.

Proxies. Generally, directors cannot act or vote by proxy. Directors have a fiduciary duty to the corporation and under this duty are required to act personally.

Conducting the Meeting. Action is taken by directors at meetings by majority vote, unless the articles or bylaws require approval by a greater number of directors. Assuming a nine-member board, once a quorum is established, in this case five, action may be taken by a majority of those present (in this case three). Each director is entitled to one vote on each issue presented at the meeting. Because the number of directors is manageable, a showing of hands or a voice vote is usually acceptable. If the vote is not unanimous, each director's respective vote should be reflected in the minutes of the meeting so that if liability arises with respect to action taken by the board, it can be readily determined which directors, if any, violated their duties to the corporation.

The modern statutes recognize the difficulty of gathering a quorum for a meeting, and, therefore, most states (and the RMBCA) permit directors to be present at meetings through conference calls or any other means by which the parties may simultaneously hear each other. These statutes would therefore likely permit directors' meetings via the Internet. Many large corporations already use videoconferencing to conduct directors' meetings and such is expressly permitted by statute in California. Cal. Corp. Code Section 307(b).

Minutes. Minutes of directors' meetings are usually taken and signed by the corporate secretary. There is no required format for minutes but they should reflect the action taken on each matter or resolution presented and should recite that notice was properly given, or that directors have signed appropriate waivers of notice (which are then placed in the minute book), that a quorum was present, and detail any other pertinent matters. See Figure 11-8 for typical minutes of directors' meeting.

6. *Directors' Action Without a Meeting*

Recognizing the difficulty of getting directors together for a meeting, nearly all states permit directors to take action without a meeting if they unanimously consent in writing. Written consents are popular both for large corporations whose directors may reside in different places and for small corporations which may not take the time to have formal meetings for each action taken. This is a now a very common method of taking board action. The procedure and

FIGURE 11-8
Minutes of Regular Meeting of Board of Directors

A regular meeting of the Board of Directors of FTB, Inc., a Delaware corporation, was held on Tuesday, June 1, 2000 at 9:00 A.M. at the principal offices of the corporation located at 1024 Fifteenth Street, N.W., Washington D.C. 20005.

The following persons, constituting all of the Directors of the corporation were present at the meeting: Lisa Black, Christopher Wagner, Kenneth Lyons, William Booher, and Patricia E. Moore.

The Chairman of the Board of the corporation, Frederick G. Tellam, presided as Chairman of the meeting, and Diana Hendrix acted as its Secretary.

The Chairman called the meeting to order and stated that a quorum of directors was present for the meeting.

The Secretary announced that the meeting was called pursuant to Article IX of the Bylaws.

The Secretary read the minutes of the last regular meeting of the Board of Directors. The minutes were approved and placed in the corporate minute book.

A discussion was had on the proposed lease for the corporation's offices in Maryland, the corporation's financial status, including the need for additional sums for operating expenses, and dividends to be paid on the outstanding common shares of the Corporation.

After motions duly made, seconded and carried, the following resolutions were unanimously adopted by the Board of Directors:

> RESOLVED, that the proposed lease between the corporation and Josephine LaPointe for the premises located at 511 State Street, Baltimore, Maryland is commercially reasonable and in the best interests of the corporation and the lease is approved.
>
> RESOLVED, that the Treasurer of the Corporation is authorized to borrow on behalf of the corporation from one or more banks or other lending institutions such amount as the Treasurer determines necessary to meet the operating needs of the Corporation, and on such terms as the Treasurer may determine, but in no event may the Treasurer borrow more than the sum of $300,000 in total.
>
> RESOLVED, the corporation shall pay a cash dividend from its capital surplus to those persons identified as owners of its common shares on its books as of June 1, 2000 in the amount of $1.50 per share. The payment date for said dividend shall be July 1, 2000.

The officers were instructed to take appropriate action to effect the purposes of these resolutions.

There being no further business before the meeting, on motion duly made, seconded, and unanimously carried, it was adjourned.

Date: ____________________

____

Diana Hendrix, Secretary

format of the written consent action for directors is nearly identical to that for shareholders. A document expressing the action to be taken is circulated to all directors for signature. Alternatively, the directors can sign counterparts or separate documents that are then compiled and placed in the minute book. See Figure 11-9 for a sample action by written consent of directors.

FIGURE 11-9
Action by Written Consent of Directors

The undersigned, constituting all of the Directors of FTB, Inc. (the "Corporation") hereby take the following actions by written consent pursuant to Del. Code Ann. tit. 8, Section 141(f) and Article IV of the bylaws of the Corporation as if present at a meeting duly called pursuant to notice.

> RESOLVED, the directors approve the hiring of Celia G. Spiritos as General Counsel for the Corporation, to perform such duties and at a salary as determined by the President of the Corporation.
> RESOLVED, the Certificate of Incorporation shall be amended to change the name of the Corporation to FTB Access Link, Co. and to increase the aggregate number of common shares which may be issued by the Corporation to 100,000, said actions to be voted on by the shareholders of the Corporation pursuant to a special meeting to be called therefor by the President of the Corporation.

The officers of the Corporation are hereby authorized to take appropriate action to effect the purposes of these resolutions.

Date: ____________________ ____________________
Lisa Black

Date: ____________________ ____________________
Christopher Wagner

Date: ____________________ ____________________
Kenneth Lyons

Date: ____________________ ____________________
William Booher

Date: ____________________ ____________________
Patricia E. Moore

7. *Compensation of Directors*

The older view was that directors were not required to be compensated merely for serving as directors. Directors were typically shareholders who, having a substantial financial stake in the corporation's affairs, would be amply rewarded through dividends and growth of the corporation. Most statutes now allow for compensation of directors pursuant to the articles or bylaws, or pursuant to action by shareholders or even by the board itself. The RMBCA provides that directors may fix their own compensation unless the articles or bylaws provide otherwise. RMBCA Section 8.11. The safeguard against directors establishing inappropri-

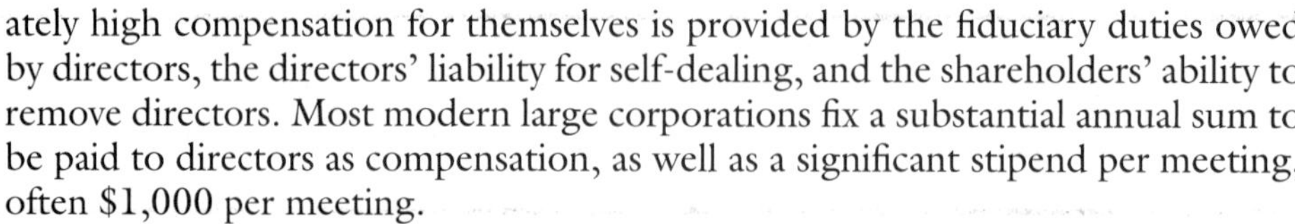

ately high compensation for themselves is provided by the fiduciary duties owed by directors, the directors' liability for self-dealing, and the shareholders' ability to remove directors. Most modern large corporations fix a substantial annual sum to be paid to directors as compensation, as well as a significant stipend per meeting, often $1,000 per meeting.

8. *Rights of Directors to Information*

In order to fulfill their duties to the corporation, directors have the right to inspect corporate records and books. The right of inspection extends to having copies made of various documents, and to have the reasonable assistance of experts, such as accountants and attorneys. If directors use these rights of inspection for an improper purpose, such as obtaining the list of corporate clients and customers to sell to a competitor, they may be liable for breach of their fiduciary duties to the corporation.

9. *Duties and Liability of Directors*

The general standard of conduct for directors is set forth in RMBCA Section 8.30, which provides that a director must discharge his or her duties:

a. in good faith;
b. with the care that a person in a like position would exercise under similar circumstances; and
c. in a manner reasonably believed to be in the best interests of the corporation.

Directors owe fiduciary duties, duties of the utmost good faith, to the corporation. This fiduciary responsibility includes a duty of loyalty to the corporation. Directors can be liable not only for affirmative actions causing injury to the corporation but also for failure to take appropriate action when required.

Conflicts of Interest. A director of a corporation may have other business involvements that lead to a conflict of interest. For example, a director may own stock in another corporation desiring to transact business with the corporation of which he is a director. Similarly, a director may own certain property (real estate, inventory, trademarks) that the corporation wishes to acquire. Such situations pose an inherent conflict; the director is bound to exercise due care for the corporation of which he is a director and yet will want to gain personally from the transaction.

The older approach took a dim view of such transactions between the corporation and a director and generally made the transaction voidable at the option of the corporation. This older approach has been substantially relaxed by modern statutes. Delaware law provides that a transaction in which a director is interested is acceptable if any of the following are true:

- the material facts of the transaction and the director's interest were disclosed to or known by the board and the board of directors approves or ratifies the transaction by majority vote (without the interested director's participation in the vote); or

- the material facts of the transaction and the director's interest were disclosed to or known by shareholders entitled to vote on the transaction and they approve or ratify the transaction; or
- the transaction was fair to the corporation. Del. Code Ann. tit. 8, Section 144.

Interested directors may be counted in determining the presence of a quorum at a meeting considering the transaction.

Business Judgment Rule. Courts are somewhat reluctant to impose liability too readily on directors for fear no one would agree to serve as a director if such a spectre was likely and because courts recognize that they should not use the advantage of hindsight to second-guess decisions made by directors. Thus, many jurisdictions recognize the **business judgment rule,** which immunizes directors from liability for decisions made by the board so long as the board had a reasonable basis for its decision and acted in good faith. Directors are therefore not placed in the untenable position of being guarantors of the corporation's success. Thus, if mistakes are made or errors in judgment occur, directors are generally not liable unless they failed to act with reasonable care. In essence, a presumption exists that the board acted with sound business judgment, and so long as some rational business purpose can be found for board action or inaction, the directors will be protected from liability. Delaware has taken this approach a step further by providing that the shareholders can state in the articles of incorporation that directors will only be liable for conduct that involves illegality, a breach of the duty of loyalty, personal financial benefit, or intentional misconduct. Del. Code Ann. tit. 8, Section 102(b) (7).

Business judgment rule
Rule immunizing directors and officers for action taken so long as they acted in good faith

Reliance on Others. In discharging their duties and making decisions, directors are entitled to rely on information, opinions, reports, and advice of corporate officers, attorneys, accountants, or other professionals, including financial statements and data prepared by committees. Generally, this reliance must be reasonable, and directors cannot bury their heads in the sand when they have actual knowledge or should make inquiries that would make reliance unreasonable. Moreover, directors have a duty of reasonable inquiry and a duty to become informed to ensure reliance is reasonable. Thus, directors may likely rely on appraisals of property performed by competent and professional appraisers; reliance, however, on advice from a neighbor's son taking a real estate class would not be "reasonable."

Extent of Liability and Defenses. If directors violate their duties, they may be personally liable for the injury caused to the corporation by their breach. For example, directors may be personally liable for the payment of distributions to shareholders in violation of the articles of incorporation or state statutes. Directors may also be liable for acts of corporate officers or other agents of the corporation if the officers or agents were improperly supervised or were obviously incapable of fulfilling their functions.

In one case in mid-1999, a corporation was found liable for the deaths of three employees when a former employee went on a workplace rampage. The jury found that the company's vice-president and the company were negligent in failing to prevent the assault because they had actual knowledge of the employee's previous acts of violence and threats. In view of such knowledge, the corporation had a duty to provide adequate security for its employees. The judgment was nearly $8 million. In another case in mid-1999, three former officials at agricultural giant Archer Daniels Midland Inc. were fined and sentenced to prison terms for their roles in an illegal price-fixing conspiracy.

It is generally not a defense to liability that a director was a "marquee" director, elected only to lend prestige to the board of directors. Once a person accepts the position of director, he or she is subject to the duty of due care. Similarly, directors cannot generally assert that they are not liable because they did not attend board meetings and were not informed of the board's activities. Board members have a duty to be informed of corporate activities. Particularly with the advent of technology enabling meetings to be held by conference call or video conference, failure to attend meetings will not protect directors from liability. Advanced age, poor health, and inexperience are typically not defenses to liability. Once directors realize they cannot perform their duties because of age, infirmity, or inexperience, they should act in the best interests of the corporation by resigning.

Modern Practice: Insurance, Statutory Limitations, and Indemnification. Fearing litigation, many prospective directors and officers refuse to serve unless the corporation procures **director and officer liability insurance (D & O insurance)** to insure against claims of breach of duty by directors and officers. In most instances, such insurance provides for attorneys' fees and costs incurred in defending directors and officers against claims made for breaches of duty. Moreover, most policies will pay the amount of a judgment rendered against the directors or officer if the director or officer acted in good faith. Willful, reckless, illegal acts are rarely insured. The cost of D & O insurance is very high and for some matters, such as patent infringement protection, is nearly prohibitively expensive.

D & O insurance
Insurance procured to protect directors and officers from claims and lawsuits

Due to rising insurance costs, and the increased litigation against directors and officers, many states have enacted statutes limiting the exposure of directors. California and Delaware statutes are typical of many. They state that the certificate of incorporation may include a provision eliminating or limiting the personal liability of a director to the corporation or to its shareholders (but not to third parties). The limitation is not available for breach of the director's duty of loyalty, for acts or omissions not in good faith or which involve intentional misconduct or a knowing violation of the law, for any transaction from which the director derived an improper benefit, or, in California, for acts or omissions that constitute an unexcused pattern of inattention that amounts to abdication of the director's duty to the corporation or its shareholders. Cal. Corp. Code Section 204 (10); Del. Code Ann. tit. 8, Section 102(b)(7). Other states have adopted different approaches, such as imposing a ceiling for damages against directors.

Indemnification
Reimbursing another for injury sustained by the other; "holding one harmless" from allegations against the person

Corporations may agree to **indemnify** or reimburse directors or officers from liability and expenses incurred in defending a lawsuit brought against them. Generally, corporations will indemnify corporate management only if the directors and officers acted in good faith and in a manner reasonably believed to be in the corporation's best interests. RMBCA Section 8.52 provides that, unless limited by the articles of incorporation, a corporation must indemnify reasonable expenses incurred by a director who was successful in defending an action brought against her due to alleged acts or omissions as a director. On the other hand, RMBCA Section 8.51(d) prohibits a corporation from indemnifying a director if she is adjudged liable to the corporation in an action brought by the corporation or on its behalf or in connection with any proceeding in which a director is adjudged liable for receiving an improper benefit.

10. Delegation of Authority

The board of directors has the authority to delegate some of its functions to officers or to various committees. Any such committee generally must have at least one member of the board serving on it. These committees assist the board by carrying out ordinary corporate activities. RMBCA Section 8.25 ensures that committees exercise only limited authority by prohibiting them from taking certain actions such as authorizing distributions, amending the articles or bylaws, authorizing the issuance of shares, or approving a plan of merger. The delegation of certain duties to officers or committees does not relieve directors of their responsibilities and duties inasmuch as they are expected to select and supervise carefully those to whom duties have been delegated.

11. Governance Guidelines

Perhaps in response to increased shareholder activism and lawsuits, the past several years have witnessed a trend in the adoption by public companies of formal written guidelines dealing with corporate governance. General Motors Company took the lead in 1994, and many large companies are following. In many instances, the guidelines are drafted by institutional investors who have issued statements called **governance guidelines,** on how they want their investees to operate. Both TIAA-CREF and the California Public Employees' Retirement System have issued such statements to the corporations in which they invest heavily. While the investors cannot force the corporations to implement the guidelines, the guidelines have spurred many companies to enact guidelines of their own. A recent survey of corporate board practices by the American Society of Corporate Secretaries found that nearly half of the survey respondents reported they had either adopted guidelines or were seriously considering doing so.

Governance guidelines
Formal written policies relating to management of corporations

Some of the guidelines suggested by institutional investors call for the following:

- Clear definitions of director relationships in order to determine when directors are independent rather than subject to a conflict of interest involving other companies or family members;
- Diversity in boards of directors;
- Periodic reviews by corporations of their processes and structures to provide a "check up" as to how well the corporation is operating;

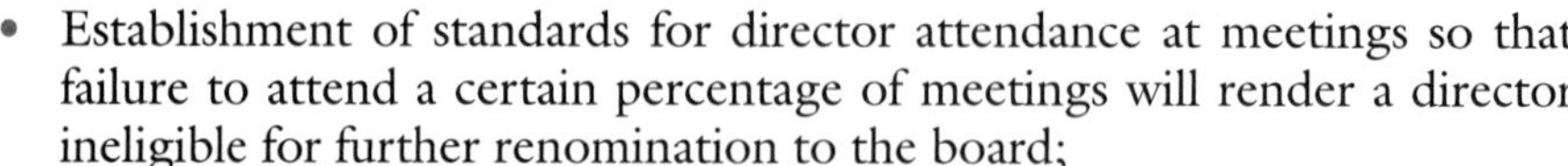

- Establishment of standards for director attendance at meetings so that failure to attend a certain percentage of meetings will render a director ineligible for further renomination to the board;
- Performance reviews of individual board members and of the boards themselves;
- Mandatory retirement age for directors; and
- Mandatory stock ownership by directors to ensure directors' interests are closely aligned with those of shareholders (with some guidelines setting actual targets, for example, requiring directors to own stock worth five times their annual compensation).

The adoption of governance guidelines is a direct result of investor pressure to improve board functioning and another sign of the continuing shift of increasing power to shareholders.

C. Rights and Duties of Officers

1. *Introduction*

Officers
Individuals appointed by directors to carry out various corporate activities

The traditional **officers** of a corporation are president, vice president, secretary, and treasurer. A corporation may have fewer officers or may have more officers, if needed. The officers carry out day-to-day corporate activities and are selected, supervised, and removed by the board of directors. Officers are usually subject to the same standards of care as directors and, like directors, are fiduciaries of the corporation.

2. *Qualifications, Appointment, and Tenure*

Some statutes require that the president or chief executive officer be a director. Most statutes, however, impose no qualifications or restrictions on those who can serve as officers.

Officers are typically selected or appointed by the board of directors, although some jurisdictions allow the shareholders to elect officers. See Figure 11-10 for a sample resolution appointing officers. It is often said that officers serve "at the pleasure of the board," meaning the directors have the authority to remove officers at any time, either with or without cause. RMBCA Section 8.43(b). Some officers, however, serve pursuant to an employment contract. In such case, removal of an officer contrary to the terms of the contract subjects the corporation to damages caused by the breach. In some instances, boards have removed officers and continued to pay them their contractually stipulated salary, much the same way some coaches of professional teams are "bought out of" their contracts. An officer may generally resign at any time by simply delivering notice of the resignation to the board of directors. Directors fill vacancies in offices. Some senior officers may be allowed by the board of directors to appoint other inferior officers or assistant officers.

FIGURE 11-10
Resolution Appointing Officers

RESOLVED, the following persons are appointed to serve in the following corporate offices, at the pleasure of the Board of Directors, at the annual salary set forth next to their names.

President: Francis Fisher	$100,000
Vice President: Timothy J. Mislock	$85,000
Secretary: Nicola Pellegrini	$75,000
Treasurer: James Crittenden	$75,000

Each officer shall have the duties specified in the bylaws and as may be designated by the Board of Directors of the Corporation.

3. *Officers' Functions*

The range of functions performed by the officers is extremely broad. In general, officers perform whatever functions are delegated to them by the directors. In large corporations, the board of directors may establish a policy or goal and then charge the officers with achieving the objective. For example, the board of a large corporation engaged in the manufacture of cars may determine that the corporation should introduce a new sports car into the market. The officers may be told, in effect, "Make it happen." The officers would then engage engineers, commission market studies, approve advertising, and perform all other tasks so that the board's goal is met.

RMBCA Section 8.41 provides that officers have the authority and shall perform the duties set forth in the bylaws or the duties prescribed by the directors. See the bylaws in Appendix H defining the duties and responsibilities of corporate officers. Typically, the only functions statutorily imposed on officers are that one of the officers shall have the responsibility for preparing minutes of the meetings of directors' and shareholders' meetings and authenticating records for the corporation (for example, verifying that a copy of the bylaws is true and correct).

4. *Titles of Officers*

The RMBCA does not require any specific officers. The corporation's bylaws may describe the officers desired, or the board of directors may appoint officers as needed. The most typical officers are president, vice president, secretary, and treasurer. A corporation is not limited by these titles, however, and is free to create other officer positions with other titles. For example, a large corporation may have a treasurer, a chief financial officer, and a comptroller, each of whom has specific duties relating to the financial affairs of the corporation. Many corporations create officer positions by adding to the title "assistant" or "executive," such as assistant secretary, executive vice president, and so forth. Under the modern approach, and that taken by the RMBCA, one person may simultaneously hold more than one corporate office. Some states, however, prohibit the same person from acting as president and secretary, generally because those are the two officers whose signatures are usually required when stock certificates are issued.

President. The president of a corporation generally presides at directors' and shareholders' meetings and performs all duties assigned by the board of directors. Often, the president acts as general manager of the corporation.

Vice President. The vice president acts in the place of the president in his absence and assists the president. Some large corporations will have numerous vice presidents, with various titles such as senior vice president, vice president of marketing, vice president of design, vice president of human resources, administrative vice president, and the like.

Secretary. The corporation's secretary usually has the responsibility for taking minutes of meetings of directors and shareholders and ensuring the minute book is kept in proper condition. The corporate secretary may prepare and furnish other reports, correspondence, and notices.

Treasurer. The treasurer is the fiscal officer of the corporation and has responsibility for receiving, maintaining, and disbursing corporate funds.

Chief executive officer
Individual who supervises other officers

Chair
Individual who presides at corporate meetings

Chief financial officer
Individual with primary responsibility for all financial matters

Other Officers. Many corporations appoint a **chief executive officer** (the CEO) who will supervise all of the other officers, preside over meetings of directors and shareholders, and have primary responsibility for managing the corporation. A **chairman** of the board, if appointed, is a board member who presides at directors' meetings and performs such duties as may be assigned by the board. A **chief financial officer** keeps all financial records and has responsibility for receiving money on behalf of the corporation, depositing money as directed by the board, disbursing money as directed, and preparing various reports relating to the financial affairs of the corporation.

5. *Authority of Officers*

Because the authority given officers comes from the board of directors, officers are agents of the corporation. As agents, officers may have authority to bind the corporation. This authority may be actual, apparent, or inherent. In many instances, however, either the corporation or a third party may try to avoid various obligations by asserting that the corporate officer did not have the authority to bind the corporation when he purported to act on behalf of the corporation.

Actual authority
Express authority or direction given by one to another

Actual Authority. **Actual** (or *express*) **authority** arises from statutes, the articles of incorporation, or the bylaws, all of which may specify the activities to be undertaken by the officers. Additionally, specific direction given to an officer by the board of directors (acting in a meeting or by unanimous written consent), such as an instruction given to the treasurer to pay certain bills, is a form of actual authority. Officers also have the authority to take any actions needed to accomplish these specific instructions. Moreover, a course of conduct acquiesced in by the board is generally sufficient to show that a transaction is authorized. Thus, even a particular transaction not expressly approved by the board yet typical of those performed on numerous prior occasions will bind the corporation to the act of the officer.

Apparent Authority. If an agent acts beyond the scope of her authority but the impression created in the mind of a third party is that the agent does have authority to bind the corporation, the corporation may be bound by the agent's (officer's) actions. In such cases, the corporation has manifested to third parties that the agent may act on its behalf and will therefore be bound by the action taken. For example, if the corporation's president informs a job applicant that his annual salary will be $30,000, and yet the board does not approve the salary, the corporation may be bound to pay the new employee $30,000 inasmuch as the employee reasonably relied on an officer of the corporation who had the apparent authority to speak for and bind the corporation. It was reasonable for the candidate to assume the president had the authority to make this decision. On the other hand, it would be unreasonable to assume that an assistant secretary has the sole authority to approve some extraordinary action, such as a merger or a sale of all of the corporation's assets.

Apparent authority
Authority that one believes another to possess due to the other's conduct or position

Inherent Authority. Officers also have the **inherent authority** to carry out their duties. For example, the president has the inherent authority to bind the corporation for matters in the usual course of day-to-day business. In any event, a corporation may ratify any acts beyond an officer's authority. Ratification "relates back" to the date of the original transaction so that the corporation is bound from the day the transaction was entered into. Ratification may be express (provided by a resolution of the board) or implied (by the corporation's acceptance of the benefits of the transaction).

Inherent authority
Authority that naturally flows from one's position

6. *Officers' Standard of Conduct, Liability, and Indemnification*

Officers are usually subject to the same duties of care and fiduciary duties imposed on directors. Like directors, they are protected by the business judgment rule and, therefore, liability is usually founded on acts (or omissions) of clear and gross abuse or negligence. Officers are entitled to rely on advice and reports given by others, so long as that reliance is reasonable.

The standard of conduct required of directors and of officers under the RMBCA is nearly identical. Both are required to discharge their duties in good faith, with the care that a person would exercise under similar circumstances, and in a manner reasonably believed to be in the best interest of the corporation. So long as directors and officers perform their duties in compliance with these requirements, they will not be liable for any action taken by them as a director or officer. RMBCA Sections 8.30 and 8.42.

The various provisions relating to indemnification of directors for liability and litigation costs and expenses apply equally to officers. Similarly, the corporation may purchase and maintain insurance on behalf of any officer or other agent to insure against liability asserted against or incurred by the officer or other agent.

Key Features of Corporate Management

- Corporations involve three groups of people: shareholders (the owners of the corporation); directors (the managers of the corporation); and officers (appointees of the directors).
- While shareholders own the corporation, they do not manage it, and their participation primarily takes the form of voting to elect (or remove) directors and extraordinary actions.
- There are two types of shareholder meetings: annual meetings (at which directors are elected); and special meetings (those held between annual meetings).
- Shareholders often vote by proxy (written instruction to another).
- Shareholders may enter into agreements to pool their votes or otherwise concentrate their voting power.
- Shareholders can initiate action against the corporation; direct actions allege direct harm to a shareholder while derivative actions allege the corporation has sustained harm and has failed to enforce its own cause of action.
- While shareholders ordinarily have no liability for corporate obligations, they can be liable if they disregard the corporate entity by commingling assets, failing to observe corporate formalities, or undercapitalizing the corporation.
- Directors manage the corporation and are elected by shareholders; they meet in regular meetings or special meetings.
- Directors and shareholders can act without a formal meeting if they unanimously consent in writing to take certain actions.
- Directors have fiduciary duties to their corporation but will usually be protected from liability under the business judgment rule so long as there is some reasonable business purpose for their actions, and they did not act illegally or with gross negligence.
- Directors may rely on others if such reliance is reasonable.
- Officers are appointed by directors to carry out whatever functions are assigned to them by the directors.
- Unless they have valid employment contracts, officers serve at the discretion of the board of directors.
- Officers are subject to the same fiduciary duties as directors.

D. Role of Paralegal

Paralegals are extensively involved in all phases of maintaining the corporation. There are a number of reasons to ensure that all corporate paperwork is up to date and accurate:

1. The documentation of corporate action provides directors and shareholders with notice of corporate decisions. Shareholders and directors may later be precluded from complaining about certain action if they are viewed as having acquiesced to it.
2. Corporate records demonstrate that the corporation is in compliance with state statutes, its articles of incorporation, and its bylaws.
3. Records reflecting basic formalities will help protect against piercing of the corporate veil, which would render shareholders personally liable for corporate obligations.
4. Various banks, creditors, or vendors may require that the corporation provide resolutions and minutes to demonstrate that it has the authority to take certain action, such as borrowing money or entering into contracts.

In some instances, paralegals have nearly complete responsibility for preparing notices, minutes, resolutions, and written consents. Paralegals are routinely involved in the following activities:

1. Maintaining a tickler system for annual meetings for all corporate clients and sending reminders to directors or officers of annual meeting requirements.
2. Preparing and sending out notices for annual and special shareholders' meetings and special meetings of the board of directors.
3. Preparing affidavits verifying the mailing of notices of shareholders' meetings.
4. Assisting in preparation of annual reports.
5. Preparing agendas for meetings of shareholders and directors.
6. Preparing minutes for meetings of shareholders and directors.
7. Preparing waivers of notice of meetings of shareholders and directors.
8. Preparing and ensuring execution of written consent actions by shareholders or directors when acting by written consent in lieu of meeting.
9. Maintaining the corporate minute book. For easy reference, the first sheet in the minute book should identify all the particulars of the corporation: its state and date of incorporation, tax identification number, date of annual meeting, number of directors required, and whether action may be taken by written consent. Minutes should be carefully organized and kept chronologically with the minutes of the most recent meeting on top.

Resource Guide

There are four sources that will assist paralegals in maintaining the corporate structure.

1. State Statutes

Pertinent state statutes are the most critical resources used in activities related to corporate governance. The state statutes specify when meetings must be held, how many days' notice must be given in advance of any meeting, whether the corporation can act by written consent as an alternative to holding a meeting, requirements for directors and officers, whether cumulative voting is allowed, whether a staggered board of directors is permissible, and so forth. Because the statutes control the articles and bylaws, in case of any inconsistency among the articles, bylaws, or state statutes, the statutes will prevail.

2. State-specific Texts

Because the various requirements imposed on corporations will vary from state to state, general texts may provide little practical value. Browse the library to see if there are books or practice sets relating to your jurisdiction's requirements for corporations. Many of these texts also contain forms and practice guides for drafting minutes, resolutions, and other documents.

3. Form Books

Because of the demand for compliance with statutory requirements and the need for corporate recordkeeping, most paralegals will devote considerable time to drafting documents. Form books are of great assistance in providing alternative formats and suggestions for preparing various notices, resolutions, minutes, and other documents. While the following texts are not state-specific, the forms provided can be easily modified to comply with requirements imposed by your jurisdiction: *Fletcher's Corporate Forms Annotated; Am. Jur. Legal Forms 2d;* and *Current Legal Forms with Tax Analysis.*

4. Law Office Forms

The corporate practitioners in your office will likely have compiled various forms for corporate clients. These forms may be available on your word processor so you will be able to modify easily the standard forms used by your office. Alternatively, the corporation's own minute book may have forms it has previously used that you can modify to serve your present purpose.

◆ ◆ ◆

WEB RESOURCES

The most important Web resources are state statutes relating to shareholders' and directors' meetings, voting, notice of meetings, proxies, record dates, directors' and officers' duties to their corporations, and indemnification of directors and officers. Other valuable Web resources are the various forms posted on several Web sites. As always, exercise discretion in using forms. Check the site's "Disclaimer" and "Legal Terms" sections to determine if there are any restrictions on your use of the forms.

www.ll.georgetown.edu

When you access this site for Georgetown University Law Center, select "State, Local & Territorial." You will be presented with a map of the United States. Point your cursor to the state in which you are interested, and you will be provided with links to a variety of legal sources relating to that state. Select "Statutes" or "Codes," and you will be linked to the state's statutes. In some states, searching can be done by either keywords or by section number. In other states, searching is accomplished exclusively by keywords.

www.findlaw.com/16/forms/index.html
When you access this Forms Collection and Forms Index at the FindLaw Web site, you will be presented with links to numerous other sites offering forms.

http://legal-resource.com/forms
This Web site provides forms for minutes of annual meetings of shareholders, minutes for directors' meetings, forms for waivers of notice of shareholders' and directors' meetings, and a form for a shareholder's agreement.

www.siccode.com/forms.php3
Access "Free Legal Forms" for a variety of business and corporate forms, including forms for notices of meetings of shareholders and directors, forms for minutes of annual and special shareholders' meetings, forms for minutes of directors' meeting, forms for waivers of notice, forms for resignations of officers and directors, a general proxy, an indemnification agreement, and a form for a certificate verifying votes at a meeting.

www.lectlaw.com
When you access this site, select "Rotunda," then "Forms Room," and then "Business and General Forms" for forms for a shareholder's agreement, a proxy, and a waiver of notice of a special meeting of shareholders.

http://legal-resource.com/forms/d.cgi[IDNUMBER]
This site includes forms for a buy-sell agreement, shareholder's agreement, proxy, and minutes of various meetings.

http://www.jefren.comDOWNLOAD.HTML
While this site offers many forms for various fees, some forms are available at no cost, including a voting trust agreement and voting trust certificate.

Discussion Questions

Fact Scenario. Red Net, Inc. is a corporation engaged in computer consulting services. It has 450,000 outstanding shares. Its annual meeting is May 1, and the corporate bylaws provide that the record date for determining shareholders entitled to notice of the meeting and to vote is 30 days prior to the annual meeting date. The corporation's bylaws authorize seven directors.

1. How many shares constitute a quorum? Assume the corporation has a bare quorum at its annual meeting. How many shareholders need to vote affirmatively to approve Arthur Andersen as the corporation's auditors?

2. What is the record date for the meeting?

3. Assume that Emily did not receive notice of the annual meeting. What can the corporation do to save itself from the expense of noticing and holding another meeting?

4. Two of the directors of the corporation have resigned. What is a quorum for a directors' meeting?

5. The shareholders are unhappy with the voting record of one of the directors and would like to remove him. How can they accomplish this?

6. The directors recently decided to purchase certain software that is extremely expensive, approximately $150,000. The directors hired a qualified consultant to evaluate available software and followed the consultant's recommendations. The software has not performed as expected, and the corporation must now pay an additional $200,000 for purchase and implementation of the correct software. Do the directors have any liability for this expense? Discuss fully.

7. Assume that Owen, a shareholder, was denied a dividend when all others in his class received one. What type of action should Owen initiate? What if 500 other shareholders in his class were denied the dividend (and 100 received the dividend). What type of action should the shareholders take?

12

Corporate Dividends

CHAPTER OVERVIEW

Shareholders not only hope and expect that the stock they own will increase in value, they also hope and sometimes expect that the corporation will pay distributions to them based on their proportionate ownership of the corporation. These distributions are generally called dividends, and may be paid in the form of cash, property, or the corporation's own shares or those of a subsidiary. The distribution will be allocated to shareholders in direct proportion to their respective ownership interest or shares in the corporation.

Dividends are generally declared by the board of directors in its discretion from time to time. There is no rule requiring that corporations make distributions to shareholders. Directors who fail to do so, however, when corporate profits permit, may find themselves out of a job at the next election. Large publicly traded corporations tend to declare distributions every calendar quarter.

Shareholders may also participate in the growth of the corporation by stock splits (divisions of outstanding shares), which tend to encourage trading and ultimately result in an increase in the value of one's shares.

A. Introduction to Dividends

Distribution
Used strictly to refer to payments to shareholders that are not a sharing of profits; used loosely to refer to any type of payment to shareholders

Dividend
Used strictly to refer to a distribution of a corporation's profits to its shareholders; used loosely to refer to any kind of payment made to shareholders

A **distribution** is a direct or indirect transfer of money or other property (except a corporation's own shares) to or for the benefit of shareholders of a corporation. RMBCA Section 1.40(6). More traditional terminology has been to use the term **dividend** to refer to a distribution of a corporation's profits to its shareholders, and to use the term *distribution* to refer to other payments to shareholders, such as payments made when the corporation liquidates. Many jurisdictions, however, refer to any type of payment whatsoever to a shareholder as a distribution, whether it is a distribution of profit or some other type of distribution, such as a distribution of net assets in liquidation.

Cash dividends
Cash distribution made by corporation

There are three types of dividends: those paid in cash, those paid in property, and those paid in shares. **Cash dividends** (typically sent in the form of a check made payable to the shareholder) are the most common type of dividend and are probably the most welcome. If corporate profits permit, the board of directors will declare a cash dividend and fix a certain amount per share. For example, the directors may declare a dividend to all shareholders of the corporation in the amount of $1 per share. An individual owning 100 shares would receive $100, while an individual owning 50 shares would receive $50. All shareholders within a given class or series must be treated uniformly. Thus, all shareholders owning Common A stock must be treated the same, although they may be treated differently from shareholders owning Common B stock.

Property dividend
Distribution of some form of property by a corporation

Property dividends, distributions that do not consist of cash or other shares of the corporation, are the least common dividend declared. The property may consist of a sample of products of the corporation, such as shampoos, lotions, and creams, or may consist of discount coupons to be used at retail stores or restaurants owned by the corporation. While some corporations distribute property dividends, these are not particularly desirable to shareholders who may not wish to receive an assortment of the corporation's products. Distribution of such products causes unique problems. If the directors determine that for each 100 shares of stock owned, shareholders will receive $10 worth of products, it may be difficult and burdensome to calculate properly and deliver appropriate amounts of a product to a large number of shareholders, each of whom owns varying amounts of stock. A property dividend may also consist of shares in another or subsidiary corporation.

Share dividend
Distribution by a corporation of its own shares

Share dividends are distributions of the corporation's own shares (rather than those of another or subsidiary corporation) made in proportion to the shareholders' respective ownership interests in the corporation. For example, the directors may declare a share dividend in the amount of one share of common stock for every ten shares outstanding. Shareholder Smith, who owns ten shares, would receive one share. Shareholder Jones, who owns 20 shares, would receive two shares, and so forth. Thus, while the raw number of shares owned by a shareholder will increase, the shareholder's proportionate ownership or control are not affected inasmuch as every other shareholder within the class or series will be treated the same. Using our example, it is readily seen that before the share dividend, Jones had twice as much power and control as Smith. After the dividend, Jones still has twice as much power and control as Smith.

Share dividends often result in fractional shares. If Shareholder Daley owns 25 shares, Daley will be entitled to receive 2½ shares of the corporation's stock. As discussed in Chapter Ten, the corporation may issue a stock certificate representing the fractional share or may issue scrip (which may be repurchased by the corporation or must be surrendered to the corporation for a complete share within some time period or it will become void). Rather than issuing fractional shares, some corporations will pay the cash value of the fractional share to the shareholder.

Liquidation dividend
Distributions made to shareholders when corporation liquidates (also called *dissolution dividends*)

The distributions made to shareholders when the business is liquidated are often referred to as **liquidation dividends** or *dissolution dividends.* These one-time distributions are discussed in Chapter Sixteen.

B. Restrictions Relating to Dividends

Each state's corporations code will specify the manner by which a corporation distributes dividends as well as the sources from which dividends may be paid. Because the end result of a dividend is that assets of the corporation are transferred to others, the shareholders, certain restrictions exist governing the distribution of dividends. In general, these restrictions operate to protect creditors and ensure that a financially unhealthy corporation does not take its few profits and distribute them to its owners rather than paying the claims of creditors. Additionally, these restrictions ensure the continued operations of the corporation and provide management with sufficient funds to conduct and expand the business.

1. *Solvency*

Solvency
State of being able to pay debts as they come due

RMBCA Section 6.40 and most state statutes provide that a corporation cannot pay a dividend if to do so would render the corporation insolvent, that is, unable to pay its debts as they come due in the ordinary course of business or if payment of dividends would be contrary to the articles of incorporation. Moreover, a dividend can be made only if, after giving it effect, the corporation's assets will exceed its liabilities and the amount that would be required to be paid to satisfy the rights of preferred shareholders (whose rights are superior to those receiving the dividend) in the event of a liquidation. For example, assume ABC Inc. has total assets of $200,000 and total liabilities of $150,000. If preferred shareholders would receive $20,000 in the event the corporation were to liquidate, ABC has $30,000 available for dividends to be paid ($200,000 minus $150,000 minus $20,000).

The primary purpose of these limitations is to protect the rights of third party creditors. Some states, such as California, permit the corporation to estimate its expected earnings and expenses for the next year in order to determine if payment of a dividend is allowable. Cal. Corp. Code Section 500(b)(2). The requirement that a corporation be solvent to distribute a dividend does not restrict a stock dividend because stock dividends do not involve the transfer of cash and are mere paper transactions. Thus, in most states, even an insolvent corporation may distribute share dividends because they do not harm creditors.

2. *Legally Available Funds*

Some state statutes mandate that dividends can be made only from certain corporate accounts. In general, dividends can usually only be paid from retained earnings and surplus.

Retained earnings
Undistributed net profits

Retained Earnings. All states allow corporations to pay dividends out of **retained earnings,** the undistributed net profits accumulated by the corporation.

Surplus
Value of assets greater than stated capital

Surplus. Some states allow dividends to be paid out of any kind of **surplus** account, whether earned surplus or unearned surplus. Other jurisdictions limit the payment of dividends to earned surplus accounts only. *Surplus* is the value of the amount of the corporation's net assets greater than the corporation's stated capital. **Earned surplus** is total corporate profits earned during preceding accounting periods, including net profits, income, and gains. **Unearned surplus** is surplus other than earned surplus, usually capital surplus. **Capital surplus** is the amount received by the corporation for stock in excess of its par value, together with the consideration received by the corporation from the issuance of shares without par value. The RMBCA approach is that dividends can be paid from any source, so long as the corporation is solvent and its assets exceed its liabilities (plus amounts payable as preferences in the event of a liquidation). RMBCA Section 6.40(c).

Earned surplus
Total corporate profits

Unearned surplus
Surplus other than earned surplus, usually capital surplus

Capital surplus
Amount received by corporation for stock in excess of its par value plus amount received for stock with no par value

3. *Tests for Distribution*

In addition to regulation of the sources of funds that can be used for the payment of dividends, several tests have been formulated to determine whether payment of a dividend is proper.

Balance Sheet Test. Under the **balance sheet test,** dividends may be paid only when, *after* giving effect to the distribution of the dividend, the corporation's assets exceed its liabilities and the stated capital of the corporation. The corporation's balance sheet shows its assets in one column or on one side of a ledger. On the other side is a listing of the corporation's liabilities and the shareholders' equity. **Shareholders' equity** is the net worth of the corporation, the amount by which assets exceed liabilities. (Some jurisdictions define shareholders' equity as the sum of stated capital and any surplus accounts.) Thus, assets are equal to the sum of liabilities and shareholders' equity.

Balance sheet test
Test to determine if dividends can be paid in which equity exceeds liabilities

Shareholders' equity
Net worth of corporation; amount by which assets exceed liabilities

When an amount is entered on one side of the ledger, an amount must be entered on the other side as well so that there is always a "balance." For example, if a dividend is paid in cash in the amount of $100,000, both the cash account and the surplus account will be reduced by the sum of $100,000. If the corporation borrows $50,000, the sum of $50,000 will be entered on one side of the balance sheet as an "asset" and will also be entered on the other side of the balance sheet as a "liability."

Equity Insolvency Test. As previously discussed, all jurisdictions preclude the payment of a cash or property dividend that would render the corporation insolvent. The distribution of share dividends is not subject to the equity insolvency test because they do not involve the transfer of cash or property to shareholders. Thus, even an insolvent corporation may make a dividend of its own shares.

Modern Test. The RMBCA and a number of jurisdictions have eliminated the concepts of stated capital, capital surplus, and earned surplus. The test set forth in RMBCA Section 6.40(c) requires that after distribution of the dividend, assets must exceed liabilities plus the total amount that would have to be paid if the corporation were to be dissolved at the time of distribution to satisfy the preferential rights of shareholders whose rights are superior to the shares receiving a distribution. In effect, this latter condition treats the preferential distribution rights of senior shareholders as a liability for determining the amount available for dividend distributions.

4. *Contractual Limitations*

To induce bankers or bondholders to lend it money, the corporation may contractually agree to limit the payment of dividends or may agree to retain a certain level of funds in a specific account, such as earned surplus. This helps assure creditors that the corporate debtor will have sufficient funds from which to repay the debt. If such a restriction exists, the amount held in reserve cannot be used in determining the amount available for dividend distributions.

5. *Preferences*

Articles of incorporation for corporations with complex financial structures may create preferences with regard to dividends. These must be honored. Nevertheless, even preferred dividends are payable only when the corporation is solvent and only out of legally available funds. If the corporation decides to issue a total of $1 million as cash dividends, preferred shareholders are entitled to receive their dividends first. If the dividends are cumulative, the corporation must pay the current dividend as well as any arrearages to the preferred shareholders before any distribution can be made to other shareholders.

6. *Classes of Shares*

To ensure that one class of stock does not subsume another, shares of one class cannot generally be used as dividends for another class unless the articles of incorporation permit or if the shareholders of the class from which the distribution is to be made approve the transaction. Thus, share dividends are typically paid to shareholders in shares of the same class as are already owned.

C. Effect of Illegal Dividends

Illegal dividends
Distributions paid when corporation is insolvent or from unauthorized accounts

If directors pay dividends while the corporation is insolvent, or from unauthorized accounts, the distribution is referred to as an **illegal dividend.** The effect of an illegal dividend on a shareholder often depends upon whether the dividend was made when the corporation was insolvent or whether it was made from an improper source or fund. Shareholders who receive dividends while the corporation is insolvent must generally return the dividend, on the basis that the transfer of the corporation's assets to the shareholder is a fraud on creditors and these shareholders can be sued for the return of the dividend. Shareholders who receive dividends from unauthorized accounts must, however, generally return them only if it can be proven they knew the dividend was illegal when received. They are liable for the amount received illegally, with interest, or the fair market value of any property received, with interest.

Directors who vote for or assent to a dividend contrary to any restrictions are generally liable, jointly and severally, for the amount of the dividend in excess of that which was legally permissible. Cal. Corp. Code Section 316; Del. Code Ann. tit. 8, Section 174. If shareholders knowingly receive illegal dividends, directors are often entitled to reimbursement from the shareholders. As a defense, directors are generally permitted to rely upon the corporation's books of account and financial statements, reports of officers, accountants, counsel, or other experts.

D. Procedure for Declaring and Paying Dividends

The decision to declare a dividend is made by the board of directors, either by majority vote at a meeting or by unanimous written consent action taken without a meeting. The decision is recorded in the minutes or the written consent as a resolution. (See Figure 12-1 for resolution authorizing dividend.)

For cash and property dividends, the directors will establish a record date for determining shareholders' eligibility to receive dividends. In many instances, the rules relating to establishing a record date for a dividend distribution are the same as those for establishing a record date for meetings. Those shareholders who own stock on the record date fixed by the board of directors will be entitled to dividends. If no record date is set, those individuals who were shareholders on the date the directors declared the dividend will be entitled to receive the dividend.

For share dividends, the directors will also typically establish a record date and those individuals who owned shares on the record date are entitled to the share dividend. A payment date will also be established. On this date, the corporation will issue stock certificates reflecting the dividend received.

For all dividends, the dividend will be paid to the individual who was the shareholder of record on the record date, even if the shareholder sells his or her stock by the time the actual payment is made. A shareholder or share without the

FIGURE 12-1
Resolution Authorizing Dividend

The Board of Directors of the Corporation next considered the issue of declaring and distributing a cash dividend to the common shareholders of the Corporation. After reviewing the report furnished to the Corporation by its independent auditors and after receiving reports from the Chief Financial Officer on the financial condition of the Corporation and its anticipated business needs and revenue for the next 12 months, and on motion duly made, seconded, and unanimously carried:

RESOLVED, that a dividend of One Dollar ($1.00) per share be and hereby is declared payable to the holders of record of the common stock of the Corporation shown by the records of the Corporation on December 1, 2000, and said dividend shall be paid to said shareholders on or before January 1, 2001. The Treasurer of the Corporation is hereby directed and authorized to take appropriate action to effect the purpose of this Resolution.

right to receive a declared dividend is called **ex-dividend** and once the dividend is declared, many newspaper financial sections will note the stock is ex-dividend, a situation which often causes the price per share to drop slightly.

Ex-dividend
Status of a shareholder without the right to receive a declared dividend

The corporation must accurately account for share dividends. For example, assume that a corporation declares a one share per 100 common stock dividend and the stock has a par value of $1. Ten shareholders each own 100 shares. Thus, the corporation will be issuing each shareholder one new share. If the corporation had simply sold the shares to others, it would have received the fair market value for the shares, which we will assume is $40 per share. Thus, the corporation would have received $400. It would have then placed $10 (the total par value of the stock) in stated capital and $390 in capital surplus (see Chapter Ten). When the corporation distributes the shares as dividends rather than selling them outright to others, the corporation must likewise make the proper allocation and deduct $400 from surplus and then transfer $10 to stated capital and $390 to capital surplus.

To distribute share dividends, the corporation must have sufficient authorized and unissued stock to distribute. If the articles of incorporation do not authorize a sufficient number of shares they must be amended to increase the number of shares the corporation is authorized to issue. Alternatively, the corporation can use treasury stock as the source for share dividends.

If shareholders cannot be located, their dividends will *escheat* (or revert) to the state of their last known residence.

E. Right to Dividends

The general rule is that shareholders receive dividends when and if declared by the board of directors acting in its discretion. Thus, the determination to distribute dividends is a discretionary decision subject to the business judgment of the directors. The directors may properly decide that dividends should not be paid so the corporation can build up a "war chest" to acquire another corporation, for purposes of growth and expansion, or for the purpose of investing its profits. The mere fact that the corporation has sufficient funds from which to pay a dividend does not entitle the shareholders to a dividend. Courts are reluctant to interfere with the management of corporations, and, therefore, unless the shareholders can clearly prove bad faith or an abuse of discretion by the directors, the directors cannot be compelled to pay dividends. If such bad faith or abuse of discretion is shown, a court may issue an order compelling the directors to declare a dividend. As a practical matter, however, directors who fail to declare dividends when profits permit may well find themselves out of a job.

The articles of incorporation may provide for a fixed dividend to one class or series of shares. In such a case, the directors will be required to declare and pay the agreed-upon dividend when legally available funds exist. If the dividends are cumulative, any arrearages must be paid for prior years in which the corporation did not pay dividends (often because it did not have the funds to do so) before any dividends can be paid to other, usually common, shareholders.

Although directors are under no obligation to declare dividends, once they have legally declared a cash or property dividend, this decision is irrevocable and the dividend becomes a debt owing from the corporation to the shareholders, who can then enforce the debt just like any other debt. These shareholders are viewed as being on the same footing as other general unsecured creditors of the corporation. RMBCA Section 6.40(f). If, however, the declaration is illegal in that the corporation intends to pay the dividend out of unauthorized funds, the declaration is likely revocable. The declaration of a stock dividend is revocable until it is actually issued.

F. Tax Considerations

Because a corporation is a person, it pays taxes on its net profits at the applicable corporate rates. The tax disadvantage referred to as double taxation means that when corporate profits are distributed as dividends, the shareholders receiving those dividends pay tax on the same money or property for which taxes have already been paid by the corporation.

1. *Cash Dividends*

Shareholders of C corporations must declare and pay taxes on cash dividends received. Until a few years ago, for the purpose of affording some tax relief to small investors the first $100 of dividends received (or $200 if shareholders filed jointly) was exempt from tax. Now, however, all cash dividends must be declared for tax purposes. Thus, even a cash dividend of $0.89 will be subject to taxation at the individual's appropriate tax rate. Corporations that distribute more than $10 to any shareholder in any year must report the dividend on an informational return so the Internal Revenue Service can verify the shareholder declared and paid the appropriate taxes. This is similar to information tax returns filed by general partnerships, limited liability partnerships, and limited liability companies, used by the Internal Revenue Service to verify that partners and members have declared and paid taxes on their share of partnership or company profits.

2. *Property Dividends*

As to property dividends, for example, the distribution of corporate products such as cosmetics, candy, or tobacco products, shareholders receiving such property dividends must declare and pay tax on the fair market value of the property received. This is another disadvantage of property dividends: A shareholder may receive products she has no use for and yet be required to pay taxes on the unwelcome distribution.

3. *Share Dividends*

The tax ramifications of stock dividends are quite different from those of cash or property dividends. Tax is not paid when the stock dividend is received but rather when it is sold. The reason taxes are not paid when a share dividend is issued is that such a dividend is not viewed as a true distribution of value because each shareholder in a class will be treated uniformly and each will have the same proportion of ownership interest after the distribution as before. Moreover, the corporation still has the same assets after distribution of the share dividend as it did before.

Computation of the taxes due at the time of eventual sale of the shares can be confusing. For example, assume a shareholder originally purchased 1,000 shares of stock at $10 per share, for a total original investment of $10,000. If a one-for-fifty share dividend is received, the shareholder will now own 1,020 shares for an investment of $10,000, or will have a cost or *basis* per share of $98.04 ($10,000 divided by 1,020). This is the figure that will be used to compute capital gains taxes when the shares are ultimately sold. The situation becomes even more complicated over time because the shareholder may purchase additional shares in the future at varying prices each time and thus the basis will continually adjust.

4. *Encouraging Dividends*

To encourage corporations to pay dividends (which eventually provides the federal government with tax revenue), a "federal accumulated earnings tax" will be imposed on a corporation's accumulated taxable income in excess of that reasonably needed for the business. 26 U.S.C. Sections 531-535. (See discussion in Chapter Ten, Section D.) Corporations are thus penalized for having accumulated earnings and given an incentive to declare and pay dividends. In some cases, shareholders have sued directors for negligence in allowing the corporation to be subjected to the federal accumulated earnings tax; personal liability has been imposed on directors for the loss.

5. *Avoiding Double Taxation*

Small corporations whose shareholders are employed by or are actively involved in the business can avoid the burden of double taxation by distributing corporate profits to the shareholder-employees as bonuses, salaries, or consulting fees rather than dividends. In such a case, the bonus, salary, or fee received by the shareholder-employee is still taxable to the recipient but the corporation's payment is a deductible business expense, thus reducing taxation of the money at the corporate level. While this is feasible for smaller corporations, a corporation whose stock is publicly owned cannot justify a "salary" for its hundreds of thousands of shareholders. Thus, double taxation is simply a feature of the corporate landscape for such corporations.

G. Stock Splits

A **stock split** (or *share split*) occurs when an outstanding share is divided into a larger number of shares. The result is to decrease the price per share. Stock splits resemble share dividends in that each involves the issuance to shareholders of a certain number of shares based on the shares presently held. The tax treatment for stock splits is also the same as that for stock dividends. The most common sce-

Stock split
Division of outstanding shares (also called a *share split*)

nario involves a two-for-one split, in which case a shareholder owning 100 shares would own 200 shares after declaration of the split.

Dividing the par value of stock is the most common means to achieve a stock split. For example, assume shareholder Robert Martinez owns 100 shares of stock with a par value of $1, for a total value of $100. If the directors declare a two-for-one split, shareholder Martinez now owns 200 shares of stock with a par value of 50 cents each, for a total value of $100. This change in par value will necessitate an amendment to the corporation's articles of incorporation. Similarly, an amendment to the articles of incorporation may be required to increase the number of shares authorized to be issued in order to accommodate the split. Although the most common stock split is two-for-one, three-for-one, four-for-one, and other splits are also valid.

A stock split is accomplished by directors' resolution, either by majority vote at a meeting or by unanimous written consent action. If an amendment to the articles will be required as a result of the split, shareholder approval is typically required (see Chapter Fourteen). RMBCA Section 10.02(4), however, allows the directors to increase the number of issued and unissued authorized shares without shareholder approval if the corporation only has one class of shares. New certificates will be issued to shareholders reflecting the additional shares created by the split. Moreover, because the RMBCA has eliminated the concept of par value, there is no distinction between a share dividend and a stock split, and both transactions are referred to simply as "share dividends" which may be authorized by the board.

Because the par value of each share is decreased, the shares may be more attractive to investors. If enough investors buy stock at this new reduced and "on sale" price, the value of the stock may creep up and achieve its pre-split price. Shareholders may then realize a doubling in profits. For example, stock may traditionally trade at approximately $50 per share. If the price per share reaches $80 per share, trading may level off as investors fear to buy stock at the top of its peak only to see it perhaps decline to its historic trading price. Moreover, many investors buying stock in **round lots** of hundreds may be reluctant to purchase such expensive stock. Thus, to stimulate trading, a corporation may declare a stock split whereby the stock is now $40 per share. Assuming the corporation is stable, investors will view the reduced trading price as a bargain and may invest heavily. When the stock reaches its pre-split price of $80 per share, shareholder Martinez will have doubled his money: before the split, he owned 100 shares at a value of $80 per share, for a total of $8,000; after the split, when the price increases, Martinez will own 200 shares at $80 per share, for a total of $16,000. A stock split, however, is no guarantee that the stock will rise in price after the split.

Round lot
Group of 100 shares

The opposite of a stock split is a **reverse stock split,** sometimes called a *split down,* in which the corporation reduces rather than increases the number of outstanding shares. For example, a ten-for-one reverse split would have the effect of requiring that each group of ten shares be exchanged or surrendered to the corporation in return for the issuance of one new share. Thus, the result of any reverse stock split is fewer outstanding shares in a corporation.

Reverse stock split
Reduction of outstanding shares (also called a *split down*)

Reverse stock splits are often used by a corporation to eliminate smaller shareholders. If a corporation is allowed by state law to require that fractional shares be sold to the corporation, the board may declare a reverse stock split in the amount of 1,000 to one, requiring that each 1,000 shares of stock be exchanged for one share. In many cases, this results in fractional shares which the corporation then repurchases as a means to eliminate shareholders. Reverse stock splits may require amendment of the articles of incorporation to provide for a much lower number of authorized shares than was originally authorized. This reduction in authorized shares then compels the directors to repurchase outstanding shares in order to be in compliance with the articles. Because shareholders are generally opposed to owning fewer shares of stock (even though their proportionate ownership interest remains the same), they may vote against the amendment, and, therefore, reverse stock splits are somewhat rare. Some companies reverse split their stock in the hope that the higher trading price per share will lend prestige to the company.

H. Purchase by a Corporation of its Own Shares

A corporation may acquire all or some of its own outstanding shares from shareholders if state corporations statutes and the articles of incorporation so permit and if the corporation is solvent or would not be rendered insolvent by the transaction. The corporation may wish to redeem or reacquire its shares for a variety of reasons, including a desire to decrease supply of the stock and thereby increase price, a desire to thwart shareholders from selling the shares to outside parties, a desire to improve its equity-debt ratio, or a desire to increase earnings per share by reducing the total number of outstanding shares. The corporation may be required to repurchase the shares pursuant to an agreement with a shareholder.

The repurchase need not be all of a class and may be part of a class (a partial redemption). In such cases, the shares selected for redemption by the corporation are typically chosen on a lottery basis so as to prevent discrimination against shareholders. For example, if the board elects only to reacquire shares held by the directors and immediately thereafter the stock falls dramatically in price, the directors may be liable for fraud or breach of fiduciary duty.

Exchange
Exchange of cash for shares

A repurchase of stock is sometimes referred to as an **exchange** because the corporation is exchanging cash for shares. This first type of exchange is to be distinguished from a *share exchange* in which a target corporation's shareholders exchange their shares for shares in the acquiring corporation. (See Chapter Fourteen for further discussion of share exchanges.) The repurchase is generally treated as a distribution to shareholders. Assume there are ten shareholders of the corporation, each owning 100 shares of stock. If the corporation redeems ten shares from each of them, and pays $20 per share, when the transaction is completed the shareholders will each own 90 shares of stock and the corporation will have transferred or distributed the sum of $200 to each shareholder. The corporation is poorer, having exchanged its hard-earned cash for shares, and the shareholders are richer. Thus, it can readily be seen that a distribution has occurred even though it was not as immediate and direct as a distribution of cash or property. Because a repurchase of stock by the corporation is a distribution, the same limitations that apply to the distribution of dividends apply equally to the repurchase by a corporation of its own shares, namely, limitations as to solvency and limitations as to the legally available funds for such repurchase. RMBCA Sections 6.31 and 6.40.

In the previous example, the shareholders' proportionate interest in the corporation remained the same: both before and after the transaction each owned one-tenth of the corporation's outstanding shares. If the repurchase relates only to part of a class, however, and is done on a random basis, the proportionate interests of the remaining shareholders will be changed after the redemption inasmuch as some shareholders will own less stock than before while others will own the same amount of shares as before the transaction. Those whose shares were not purchased will own a greater proportionate interest in the corporation because other shareholders now own fewer shares.

The acquisition by a corporation of its shares is to be distinguished from the situation in which shareholders (usually preferred shareholders) are issued shares with a right of redemption (the right to compel the corporation to repurchase the shares). In such a case, the various limitations applicable to the distribution of dividends do not apply.

When the corporation reacquires the previously outstanding shares, it may cancel them and thereby return them to the status of authorized but unissued shares or it may hold them as treasury shares. If shares are canceled, the corporation must usually file a statement of cancellation with the secretary of state providing information about the number of authorized shares and the number of issued shares before and then after cancellation (see Figure 10-1).

Key Features of Corporate Dividends

- A dividend is a distribution of a corporation's profits to its shareholders.
- Dividends may be in the form of cash (the most common form of dividend), property (the least common form of dividend), or shares of the corporation. A share dividend does not increase a shareholder's power or control because every shareholder in a class will be treated uniformly.
- To distribute a dividend, a corporation must be solvent, meaning that it is able to pay its debts as they come due.
- Most state statutes mandate that dividends can be paid only from certain funds, usually retained earnings and surplus.
- Dividends must be uniform within a class but can vary from class to class.
- The decision to declare a dividend is made by the board of directors, who will set a record date for determining the shareholders entitled to a dividend.
- Generally, shareholders have no absolute right to receive dividends, and they are declared in the discretion of the board.
- Shareholders who receive cash must pay taxes on the amount received.
- Shareholders who receive a property dividend must pay tax on the fair market value of the property received.
- Shareholders who receive share dividends do not pay tax at the time the dividend is received but at the time the share is sold.

I. Role of Paralegal

The decision to distribute dividends originates with the board of directors of a corporation. Usually, this decision is made by the board after consultation with its financial advisors. Thus, the attorney and paralegal do not generally come into play until after this decision has been made. There are, however, many activities the paralegal will be involved in to assist the corporation. These include the following:

1. *Corporate Records*

The paralegal may need to assist the corporation in preparing minutes of the board meeting authorizing the distribution. This authorization will be in the form of a resolution. It should state a record date to determine the shareholders who will be entitled to the dividend. Alternatively, the decision of the board may be reflected by a resolution adopted by unanimous written consent, the drafting of which may be done by the paralegal. To enhance protection for the board of directors, the resolution may recite that the board is acting in the best interest of the corporation and has based its decision on reports and recommendations from the corporate officers and its accountants and auditors.

2. *Amending Articles*

If the dividend is to be paid in the form of shares, the paralegal must ensure that the articles of incorporation authorize a sufficient number of shares to accommodate the distribution. If the authorized number of shares is not sufficiently large, the paralegal will need to work with the corporation in calling a meeting of shareholders to amend the articles and then prepare the necessary articles of amendment before the dividend can be declared. If the amendment is one that does not require shareholder approval, namely, an amendment to accommodate a stock split, no shareholder meeting need be held, although articles of amendment must still be prepared and filed.

3. *Honoring of Preferences*

The paralegal should carefully scrutinize the articles of incorporation and the pertinent state statutes to ensure that the corporation's distribution complies with any provisions in its articles or any statutes permitting distributions only when the corporation's assets exceed its liabilities plus the dissolution preferences of senior or preferred shareholders.

4. *Statement of Cancellation*

If the corporation repurchases (and then cancels) its own shares from shareholders, a statement of cancellation must usually be prepared and filed with the secretary of state. (See Figure 10-1 for a sample statement of cancellation.) This statement will inform the secretary of state of the number of authorized and issued shares before cancellation and the changes in the number of authorized shares and issued shares after the cancellation.

5. *Authorization of Bonuses*

If the corporation is small and the shareholders are all active in managing the business, dividends per se will not be declared. The corporation will rather distribute salaries and bonuses to the employees. The employees thus share in the profits of the enterprise and the corporation is able to deduct the payments as a business expense. In such cases, the paralegal will prepare minutes of meetings or unanimous written consent actions with the appropriate resolutions authorizing payment of the various bonuses.

Resource Guide

The distribution of dividends is governed nearly exclusively by the corporation's articles of incorporation and state statutes. The statutes will provide restrictions applicable to all corporations, namely restrictions relating to solvency and the funds that may be used for the distribution of dividends. The articles will provide for repurchase by the corporation of its own shares and will state whether any preferences exist in the distribution of dividends.

General information relating to dividends is provided in both general encyclopedias, C.J.S. and Am. Jur. 2d, as well as in state-specific encyclopedias, which offer the advantage of discussing applicable state statutes. Additionally, a thorough discussion of the process, manner, and effect of dividend distributions can be found in any of the numerous treatises on corporate law. These treatises will generally be gathered together in the same section of the law library. Form books will be helpful in drafting minutes of meetings and written consent actions authorizing the payment of dividends. (See Chapter Nine for specific identifications of encyclopedias, treatises, and form books.)

◆ ◆ ◆

WEB RESOURCES

The most important Web resources are state statutes relating to the procedure for declaring dividends and the funds from which they may legally be paid. The only forms needed will be forms for the minutes of the meeting of the board of directors declaring the dividend (or a unanimous written consent by the directors if they act without a meeting). For sites posting such minutes, see Web Resources for Chapter Eleven. To locate your state's statutes on the Web, try the following:

www.ll.georgetown.edu
When you access this site for Georgetown University Law Center, select "State, Local & Territorial." You will be presented with a map of the United States. Point your cursor to the state in which you are interested, and you will be provided with links to a variety of legal sources relating to that state. Select "Statutes" or "Codes," and you will be linked to the state's statutes. In some states, searching can be done by either keywords or by section number. In other states, searching is accomplished exclusively by keywords.

Discussion Questions

Fact Scenario. Jackson & Jackson, Inc. is a corporation engaged in franchising restaurants. There are nine people on the board of directors, and the corporation has two classes of stock, Common A and Common B.

1. The corporation has had a profitable year and would like to issue cash dividends to half of its Common A shareholders and share dividends to the remaining half of the Common A shareholders. May it do so?
2. Can the Common A shareholders receive a property dividend while the Common B shareholders receive cash dividends? Discuss.
3. Assume that the corporation continually has trouble meeting its monthly expenses, and each month a loan is advanced from a bank that has issued a line of credit to the corporation. May the corporation declare a cash dividend? May it declare a share dividend? Assume that the Common B shareholders have cumulative dividends. Will they receive their dividends? Discuss.
4. Assume that the corporation is insolvent. At the most recent board meeting, at which all nine directors were present, six of them voted to declare a cash dividend for all shareholders. Three board members voted against the resolution. What is the effect of the dividend as to the shareholders who receive it, the directors who voted for it, and the directors who voted against it?
5. Last year, Shelby, a Common A shareholder, received $25 as a dividend. Greg, a Common B shareholder, received four additional Common B shares as a dividend. What are the tax consequences for Shelby and Greg?
6. Assume that Shelby has 150 shares of stock, and the corporation has declared a two-for-one stock split for the Common A stock. How many shares will Shelby own after the split?
7. The corporation has had three consecutive profitable years and yet has distributed no dividends. What can the shareholders do, if anything? What risk does the corporation run by not distributing dividends?

13

Securities Regulation and the Stock Exchanges

CHAPTER OVERVIEW

Investors in corporations are protected not only by state statutes relating to the formation, operation, and management of corporations but also by various federal and state laws mandating disclosure requirements for the issuance of corporate securities.

The Securities Act of 1933 imposes requirements on corporations issuing stocks and bonds to the public. These requirements relate to disclosure of certain matters through registration of documents with the Securities and Exchange Commission. The 1933 Act focuses on the original issuance of securities to the public. The Securities Exchange Act of 1934 is concerned primarily with the trading of stock, specifically the buying and selling of securities subsequent to their original issuance. Each state also regulates the issuance and sale of securities within its borders through laws called blue sky laws.

In addition to examining the various federal and state statutes designed for investor protection, this chapter also reviews the process by which stocks are publicly traded on the national exchanges and the effect of the Internet on stock trading.

A. Introduction to Investor Protection

Although public corporations represent a small percentage of all businesses in the United States, their economic impact on the country is significant. Approximately 25 percent of all adults in the United States own stock in a public corporation. Many nightly news broadcasts open with a report on the day's stock market activities. Newspapers devote special sections to financial and business news, carefully noting rising and falling stocks and commenting on the stock market in general.

For many years, corporations desiring to sell stock to the public simply distributed securities by having agents sell stock on commission. The stock market crash of October 29, 1929 and the subsequent Great Depression provided the impetus for a public examination of the practices of selling securities. After reports of speculative and unscrupulous trading practices, the public clamored for action. Congress responded in 1931 by examining and investigating trade practices and by passing the Securities Act of 1933, also referred to as the "truth in securities" law. The following year, in 1934, Congress enacted the Securities Exchange Act, which created the **Securities and Exchange Commission (SEC),** an independent federal agency charged with regulation of securities and the administration of the 1933 and 1934 Acts. The SEC is composed of five commissioners appointed by the president for five-year terms, with no more than three from any one political party. It was initially chaired by Joseph P. Kennedy, Sr. Over time, the SEC has expanded its role, promoting harsher penalties for insider trading and addressing the issue of increasing numbers of corporate takeovers. The SEC does not actually approve the securities being issued by a corporation; it rather requires disclosure of material information for consumer protection. The 1933 Act focuses on the initial sale of securities while the 1934 Act deals mostly with the resale of securities.

SEC
Securities and Exchange Commission; federal agency charged with regulation of securities

B. Going Public

When a corporation decides to sell its shares to members of the public at large, the decision is referred to as **going public.** This decision is made by the directors acting in the best interest of the corporation. The first offering of the corporation's stock to the public is referred to as the **initial public offering** (IPO). Going public will raise capital for the corporation and will result in prominent exposure for the corporation and its business. The downside of going public is that the influx of new shareholders will result in a loss of control and power by the then-current shareholders. The costs of going public and complying with the various regulations imposed on corporations selling their stock publicly are significant. Additionally, the corporation's financial history and that of its managers will be open for inspection and discussion by the public.

Going public
Sale of shares to the public at large

Initial public offering
The first offering of stock to the public (an *IPO*)

A corporation selling securities to the public for the first time does not usually offer the securities through any of the stock markets. The process of issuing securities from the corporation to the ultimate shareholder is called an **underwriting.** Once the corporation has made the decision to go public it will enter into an agreement with an investment bank or securities firm, called the **underwriter.**

Underwriting
Process of issuing stock to the public

Underwriter
A securities firm that assists a corporation in offering stock to the public

Some underwriters specialize in certain industries. The nationally known underwriters, such as Merrill Lynch & Co., Inc. and The Goldman Sachs Group, generally do not display interest in a company unless its sales or value exceed a certain amount, often as high as $50 million.

There are different types of agreements the corporation and the underwriter may enter into:

- **Firm Commitment Agreement.** With a firm commitment, the underwriter agrees to purchase the entire issue from the corporation and then reoffers to sell the stock to others. If the underwriter cannot sell the stock to others, it will pay the agreed-upon issue price to the corporation. In a firm commitment, the underwriter has guaranteed the sale of the stock and has assumed all risk for it. To spread the risk, the underwriter may form a **syndicate,** a group of investment banks who will participate in selling the issue. Alternatively, the underwriter may enter into agreements with other securities firms (referred to as **dealers**) by which the dealers buy the securities for resale to their customers. For example, assume the directors of Pearson Corp. enter into arrangements with Merrill Lynch to underwrite two million of its shares at $20 per share. Merrill Lynch may buy the stock and enter into arrangements for the dealers to purchase portions of the shares for resale to customers of the dealers at a profit, perhaps for $22 per share. In this way, the underwriter makes $2 per share. On the other hand, if Merrill Lynch cannot enter into such arrangements with dealers, it is simply stuck and must buy all the stock from Pearson Corp.

Firm commitment agreement
Agreement by underwriter to purchase all stock from corporation at a set price and resell it to others

Syndicate
Group of investors, usually banks, that participate in selling an issue of stock

Dealers
Securities firms that buy stock for resale to their customers

- **Best Efforts Agreement.** Under a best efforts agreement, the underwriter agrees to use its best efforts to sell the securities but does not guarantee the amount of capital that will be raised by the offering.
- **All-or-Nothing Agreement.** Under an all-or-nothing agreement, which is relatively rare, the underwriter agrees to use its best efforts to sell the entire issue by a certain date. All proceeds from sales are placed in an escrow account. If the entire issue is not sold by the agreed-upon date, the money received from buyers is returned to them and the offering is canceled.

Best efforts agreement
Agreement by underwriter to use its best efforts to sell a corporation's securities

All-or-nothing agreement
Agreement by underwriter to use best efforts to sell all of a corporation's securities by a fixed date; if issue is not sold by date, offering is canceled

C. Securities Act of 1933

1. *Introduction*

The securities to be issued by the corporation are usually in the form of equity securities (*stock* representing ownership interest in the corporation) or debt securities (*bonds* representing money owed by a corporation to a creditor). Securities can take other forms, however, such as specific property items, ranging from orange trees to liquor, cosmetics to investment contracts in condominiums. The generally accepted test used to determine if a "security" is being issued is whether the person is investing money in a common enterprise and is reasonably led to expect profits primarily from the managerial or entrepreneurial efforts of others. *SEC v. W.J. Howey Co.,* 328 U.S. 293, 299 (1946). If so, a security is being offered and, unless exemptions exist, the issuer must comply with the **1933 Act.** The 1933 Act imposes registration requirements and anti-fraud provisions on the initial or primary distribution of securities.

1933 Act
Act requiring registration before issuance of securities through interstate commerce

2. *Registration Requirements*

The 1933 Act (15 U.S.C. Section 77a, et seq.) provides that no security may be offered or sold through the mails or any instrumentalities of interstate commerce (telephone, facsimile, Internet, and so forth) without compliance with certain registration requirements unless either the security or the transaction is exempt. The SEC does not evaluate the merits of offerings but rather declares registration statements "effective" if companies satisfy SEC disclosure rules.

Registration statement
Statement filed with SEC prior to issuance of securities to public

Prospectus
Primary part of registration statement

The form of **registration statement** provided by the SEC is Form S-1. The SEC has adopted regulations requiring the use of "plain English" in the registration form so that it is clear and understandable to the average investor. Since 1993, registration forms must be filed electronically with the SEC through its database called "EDGAR" (Electronic Data Gathering and Retrieval). The main part (or Part I) of the registration statement is called the **prospectus.** It is this document that must be provided to any investors. The prospectus describes the securities being sold, provides background information about the issuing corporation and its directors and officers, and describes the investment so that investors can fully evaluate the potential risks involved in purchasing the security. Part II of the registration statement includes "additional information" about the company and the offering.

The registration statement must include the following:

a. a description of the security offered for sale;
b. a description of the issuer's business;
c. a description of the management of the issuer;
d. a financial statement audited by an independent certified public accountant; and
e. a description of any pending litigation involving the issuer.

The statement is filed electronically in triplicate with the SEC and becomes a matter of public record. It is subject to a twenty-day waiting period, sometimes called the "cooling off period," before it becomes effective, although the SEC may accelerate this period if requested. The SEC may also delay the effective date if the statement is incomplete or inaccurate and often requests additional information or clarifications. A filing fee must accompany the registration statement. The filing fee is one-fiftieth of 1 percent of the maximum price at which the securities are to be offered, but in no event less than $100.

Tombstone ad
Announcement in newspaper that securities are being issued by a corporation

Red herring prospectus
Preliminary form of prospectus describing stock to be sold

During the twenty-day waiting period, certain activities may occur. For example, oral offers between interested investors and the issuer corporation may take place although actual sales cannot occur. Limited advertising may also take place in the form of **tombstone ads,** called such because of the black border surrounding the advertisement. Tombstone ads generally merely announce that securities are being issued by a corporation; they are not considered prospectuses and thus need not comply with the 1933 Act's registration requirements, but they must include certain basic information about the issuer. (See Figure 13-1 for a sample tombstone ad.) The issuer corporation may also distribute a form of preliminary prospectus called the **red herring prospectus,** so named for the notation (or *legend*) printed in red ink informing investors that the registration statement has been filed but has not yet become effective. The primary purpose of the red

FIGURE 13-1
Sample Tombstone Advertisement

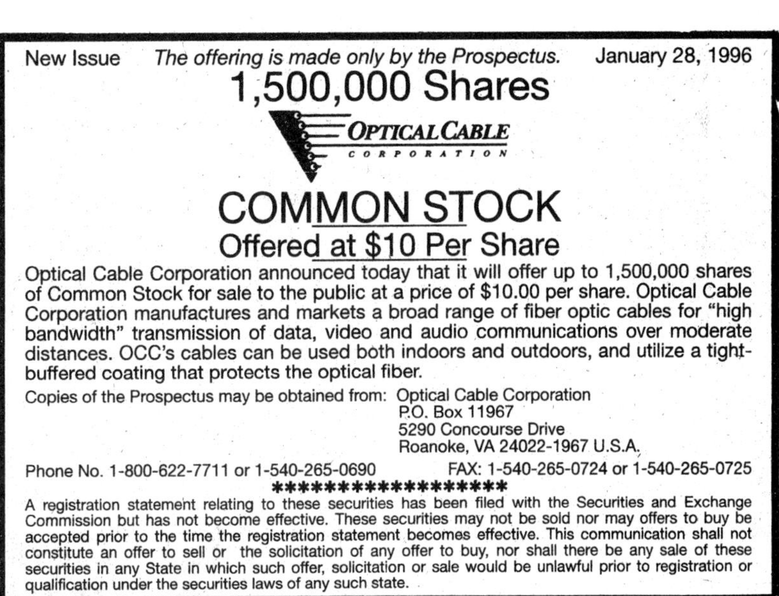

herring is to stimulate interest in the company. No price is noted in the red herring. After the effective date of the registration statement, the corporation may commence full-scale sales and promotional efforts and will issue a final prospectus to interested parties. The underwriters and dealers are paid from the proceeds of the issue.

3. *Exemptions from Registration*

The exhaustive coverage of the 1933 Act's requirements are moderated by a number of exemptions to the Act. Certain securities, small issues offerings, intrastate offerings, and private offerings are exempt from the complex disclosure and registration requirements of the Act. All offerings, however, are subject to the anti-fraud provisions of the Act.

Securities Exemptions. The Act provides that certain classes of **securities are exempt** from the registration requirements of the Act. Among them are: securities issued by the United States or state governments and banks; securities of charitable organizations; securities issued by savings and loan associations and farmers' cooperative associations; insurance policies and annuities; securities issued only

Exempt securities
Securities that are exempt from registration requirements of 1933 Act

within a single state; and certain short-term commercial paper financing. These exemptions are found in Sections 3 and 4 of the 1933 Act.

Small issues exemptions
Issuances exempt from registration requirements of 1933 Act due to small size of issuance or sophistication of investors, or both

Small Issues Exemptions. Section 3(b) of the 1933 Act exempts certain "small issues" from registration requirements when the total amount of the offering does not exceed $5 million. The SEC has adopted Regulation A detailing the requirements for qualifying for this exemption.

Under Regulation A, the securities offered in any twelve-month period must not exceed $5 million. The issuer must file both notice of the issue and an offering circular with the SEC. The documents are filed with the SEC's regional office and are less complex than full registration. For example, the financial statements provided under Regulation A need not be audited. Purchasers must be provided with an offering circular that is similar to a prospectus.

Under the SEC's Regulation D, other offerings are exempt from the SEC registration requirements.

Under Regulation D, three separate rules provide exemptions:

(1) Rule 504 permits an issuer to sell securities in any twelve-month period for a total price up to $1 million without furnishing any information to investors. A Form D notice must be filed with the SEC within 15 days after the first sale of any securities. General advertising may not be used to sell the securities.

(2) Rule 505 exempts from registration offerings of less than $5 million to less than 35 nonaccredited investors during a twelve-month period. A Form D notice must be filed with the SEC within 15 days after the first sale. General advertising may not be used to sell the securities.

Accredited investor
An investor with a certain net worth who is presumed to be financially sophisticated

An **accredited investor** is an individual with a net worth in excess of $1 million or yearly income in excess of $200,000 ($300,000 jointly with a spouse), banks, savings and loans, principals of the issuers, and other similarly sophisticated investors. Accredited investors are presumed to be sufficiently knowledgeable that they require less protection than the typical investor. There are no restrictions on the number of accredited investors to whom the issuer may sell securities under Rule 505.

(3) Rule 506 exempts offers and sales in an unlimited amount in any twelve-month period to less than 35 nonaccredited investors, but only if the issuer reasonably believes that the nonaccredited investors have a certain level of knowledge and experience in financial and business matters such that they are capable of evaluating the risks and merits of the transaction. Unlike Rule 505, the nonaccredited investors must have a certain level of knowledge and expertise in financial and business matters to qualify for the Rule 506 exemption. Securities can be sold to an unlimited number of accredited investors under Rule 506.

Intrastate offering
Offering of stock solely within one state

Intrastate Offerings. Intrastate offerings are also exempt from the registration and disclosure requirements of the 1933 Act. This exemption applies only if the following conditions are met:

(1) the issuer corporation must be incorporated in the state in which it is making the offering;

(2) the offering must be made only to residents of the state of incorporation (and no resale to an out-of-state resident may take place during the nine months after the sale); and
(3) the issuer corporation must conduct a significant amount of its business in the state (typically, 80 percent of the issuer's assets must be located in the state and 80 percent of its gross revenue must be generated in the state).

There is no limit on the size of the offering or the number of purchasers.

Private Placement Offerings. Nonpublic offerings can be made in an unlimited amount so long as the offering is not generally advertised and the investors are believed to have sufficient knowledge of financial matters that they are capable of evaluating the risks in the transaction. This exemption is often referred to as the "private placement" exemption and the securities are offered through a **private placement offering** (PPO) or *private placement memorandum* (PPM).

Private placement offering
A private, nonpublic offering of stock (also called a *private placement memorandum*)

This exemption is often viewed as the most important one for corporations wishing to raise capital and yet avoid the rigorous disclosure and registration requirements of the 1933 Act. There is no specific fixed limit either on the amount of money that can be raised through the private placement offering or on the number of people who can be involved, so long as the investors meet the requirement of being sufficiently sophisticated that they understand the risks inherent in the investment.

4. *Anti-Fraud Provisions of 1933 Act*

Although a security or transaction may be exempt from the registration requirements of the 1933 Act, the anti-fraud provisions of the Act apply to *any* offer or sale of securities. These provisions apply if the mails or interstate commerce instrumentalities are used in the offer or sale of securities and protect investors from fraud, deceit, material misrepresentations and omissions, half-truths, and so forth.

5. *Penalties for Violations of 1933 Act*

Any person damaged by inaccurate or misleading material statements in a registration statement has a cause of action against any person who signed the registration statement, any director of the corporate issuer, accountants and experts involved in the preparation of the statement, and underwriters. Because a host of individuals will be involved in the preparation of the registration statement, and not all of them will have access to all pertinent information, individuals are not liable if they can prove they conducted **due diligence** in preparing the statement; that is, they conducted a reasonable investigation and had reasonable grounds to believe the statement was true and accurate. Thus, attorneys, paralegals, and accountants who assist in preparing the registration statement have a duty to make a reasonable investigation of the issuer's records, contracts, and so forth. This investigation is often referred to as due diligence work and is time-consuming and expensive for the issuer corporation. If a violation of the Act is

Due diligence
Investigation of records and data

proven, the plaintiff may recover damages for the loss in value of the investment. Alternatively, the purchaser can rescind the transaction and receive a return of the money invested (with interest). Criminal liability may also be imposed.

D. Securities Exchange Act of 1934

1. *Introduction*

1934 Act
Act governing resale of securities after their initial issuance

While the 1933 Act is concerned with the initial offering of securities, the focus of the **Securities Exchange Act of 1934** (15 U.S.C. Section 78a et seq.) is on the resale of securities after their original issuance and on various reporting requirements imposed on issuers. The 1934 Act provides for the regulation and registration of those involved in the sale of securities such as brokers, dealers, and exchanges. The Act also authorizes the SEC to investigate fraud, manipulation, and other undesirable trading practices in the market. The 1934 Act requires registration of certain securities with the SEC, requires periodic reporting by issuers, and regulates the use of proxies.

Section 12 companies
Companies that trade on national exchanges or those with significant assets that are required to register securities and file other reports with SEC (also called *reporting companies*)

Under Section 12 of the 1934 Act, only certain companies are required to register their securities with the SEC. These companies are those whose securities are traded on a national securities exchange, such as the New York Stock Exchange, or those companies having assets of $10 million or more and 500 or more shareholders. These companies are often called **Section 12 companies,** *registered companies,* or *reporting companies.* Companies such as McDonald's, Coca Cola Company, General Motors, and Federal Express are Section 12 companies subject to compliance with the 1934 Act, which primarily involves periodic reporting to the SEC.

2. *Registration Requirements*

The registration statement required under the 1934 Act is substantially similar to that required under the 1933 Act. The statement, called an application, is filed with the appropriate exchange and with the SEC. It includes information about the corporation, the securities offered, the financial structure of the business, material contracts, profit-and-loss statements, and so forth. Registration is generally effective 30 days after filing the application. The registration under the 1933 Act is done prior to offering securities for sale. The registration under the 1934 Act is primarily for reporting purposes.

3. *Periodic Reporting Requirements*

Section 12 companies must file a variety of reports with the SEC. These include periodic reports of any changes to the original application statements, annual reports, and quarterly reports. Falsification of reports can result in the imposition of criminal penalties.

Form 8-K
Form filed with SEC to report changes in a Section 12 company

The SEC furnishes the forms necessary to comply with the periodic reporting requirements. **Form 8-K** is used to report any significant changes such as mergers that have occurred since the filing of the application. The 8-K report must be filed with the SEC within ten days after the end of the month in which the material change occurred. The **10-K form** is used for annual reporting and must be filed with the SEC within 90 days after the end of the corporation's fiscal year. **Form 10-Q** is used for the quarterly report and must be filed with the SEC within 45 days after the close of each of the first three quarters of the corporation's fiscal year. The fourth quarterly report is subsumed into the annual report on form 10-K.

Form 10-K
Annual report filed with SEC by Section 12 company

Form 10-Q
Quarterly report filed with SEC by Section 12 company

4. *Insider Trading: Rule 10b-5*

Section 10(b) of the 1934 Act makes it unlawful for any person to use any manipulative or deceptive device in connection with the purchase or sale of any security. To implement this section, the SEC adopted **Rule 10b-5,** often referred to as the *anti-fraud rule,* which provides:

Rule 10b-5
SEC rule prohibiting insider trading

> **It shall be unlawful for any person, directly or indirectly, by the use of any means or instrumentality of interstate commerce, or of the mails, or of any facility of any national securities exchange,**
> **(1) to employ any device, scheme, or artifice to defraud,**
> **(2) to make any untrue statement of a material fact or to omit to state a material fact necessary in order to make the statements made, in the light of the circumstances under which they were made, not misleading, or**
> **(3) to engage in any act, practice, or course of business which operates or would operate as a fraud or deceit upon any person, in connection with the purchase or sale of any security.**

This rule has been used by the SEC and courts to prevent a variety of unscrupulous practices, most notably, **insider trading.** The prohibitions against insider trading are meant to ensure that all investors are on an equal footing. Corporate **insiders,** such as directors and officers are in a position to know critical matters affecting the corporation and the value of its stock, such as plans to merge, technological advances and discoveries, and adverse financial conditions. If these insiders purchase stock, knowing the stock is about to soar in value due to a recent discovery, they receive a benefit from their position not available to other investors. Similarly, if the insiders sell their stock, knowing that a future public announcement of a lawsuit against the company will cause the stock to fall, they abuse their position to the detriment of others. Insider trading allegations are common in shareholder lawsuits. Nearly three-fourths of cases involving high-tech companies include allegations of insider trading.

Insider trading
Trading in stock by corporate insiders with information unknown by public at large

Insider
Corporate officers and directors and others with knowledge of corporate matters

Rule 10b-5 applies to purchases and sales, applies to nearly all securities, and applies whether or not those securities have been registered under either the 1933 Act or the 1934 Act. Thus, the prohibitions against insider trading apply in virtually every instance of the trading of securities, whether those securities are traded on one of the national exchanges, such as the New York Stock Exchange, or whether they are traded over the counter, or traded privately. Liability may result from affirmative misrepresentations of a material fact or nondisclosure of a material fact.

Material fact
A fact that influences conduct

A **material fact** is one that would have influenced the injured party's conduct. Some examples of facts held to be material are a significant drop in corporate profits, management's decision to pay a dividend, an agreement for the sale of corporate assets, and critical discoveries. In one well-known case, *SEC v. Texas Gulf Sulphur Co.*, 401 F.2d 833 (8th Cir. 1968), a company discovered significant mineral deposits. The news was leaked to the media and the company then downplayed the discovery with a misleading press release. During this period, various officers, directors, and employees of the company purchased stock. When the announcement of the mineral deposit was eventually made public, the value of the stock increased, and the insiders received a windfall in the value of their stock. The company was sued by the SEC as well as by individuals who sold their stock after reading the press release, believing the corporation had not made a significant discovery. The court held that all of the transactions by the corporate insiders were in violation of Rule 10b-5.

Tippee
One who receives a tip from a corporate insider

Tipper
Corporate insider who gives a tip to another

To discourage fraud and manipulative devices, Rule 10b-5 applies not only to corporate insiders but also to individuals who acquire inside information as a result of an insider's breach of fiduciary or good-faith duty. Thus, **tippees** (those who receive tips from insiders) as well as **tippers** (those insiders giving tips) can be held liable. Consequently, corporate insiders cannot avoid liability by having a relative or friend purchase or sell stock for them. Both the insider tipper and the relative and friend tippees have violated Rule 10b-5. Even sub-tippees of tippees have been held liable.

Rule 10b-5 applies only to actual purchases or sales of securities. For example, if the corporation releases an untrue and pessimistic annual report when the financial situation is actually quite strong, a current shareholder may decide to "hold firm" and not purchase any additional stock until the corporation's financial picture has improved. Although the damage seems clear, the United States Supreme Court has held that nonpurchasers and nonsellers do not have standing to bring an action under Rule 10b-5. Despite criticism of this rule, many scholars believe that allowing individuals to claim "I would have purchased [or sold] stock but for the company's misconduct" would open the floodgate to litigation and enormous liability that might be speculative at best.

5. *Remedies and Penalties for Violation of 1934 Act*

Rescission
Cancellation of a transaction

Purchasers or sellers of stock traded in violation of Rule 10b-5 have a wide array of remedies available to them. One remedy is **rescission:** Defrauded purchasers can cancel the transaction and defrauded sellers can get their stock back. Another remedy is to compel those who benefited from the transaction to disgorge their profits, and, in some cases, pay three times the amount of the profit gained or loss avoided as a result of the violation of Rule 10b-5. The most common remedy is to allow the defrauded party to recover "out-of-pocket" damages, namely, the difference between what the victim purchased or sold the stock for and its actual worth at the time of the deception. Additionally, the SEC itself may institute action against the insiders, tippees, or tippers.

Bounty payment
Payment by SEC for information relating to securities fraud

Recently enacted federal statutes also provide the SEC with authority to award **"bounty payments"** to persons who provide information relating to violations of the 1934 Act. Stricter criminal penalties for violations have also been enacted. Jail terms have been increased to ten years from five years and fines have increased to $1 million for individuals and $2.5 million for firms. Many of these remedies and penalties were prompted by the insider-trading scandals of the 1980s, involving well-known Wall Street traders such as Michael Milken and Ivan Boesky. These penalties do not affect any other actions that can be taken by the SEC or by private investors.

The stock markets and the NASD are self-regulatory organizations, meaning they regulate themselves and try to prevent fraud by member firms and investigate complaints made. To determine whether inside trading is occurring, the NYSE monitors unusual stock activity and transactions, using a computer system called "Stock Watch," designed to search for odd trading patterns. The computer then alerts NYSE regulatory personnel so an investigation can be conducted. If a trade or transaction raises a red flag, investigation of the owner of the stock is begun by cross-referencing his or her name with employees of the corporation, the underwriter, or the law firm assisting in the issuance to determine if a match has occurred, in that the trader is a relative of an insider, went to the same college, lives in the same neighborhood, and so forth. In this way, the NYSE attempts to keep its own house in order and monitor for insider trading. The NSYE then refers the matter to the SEC for further investigation and possible fines and jail terms.

Because insider trading is so serious and causes lack of public confidence in the stock market, some companies now appoint their own compliance officers to clear or approve trades by inside company executives who may have access to nonpublic information.

In the year ending September 20, 1998, the SEC initiated 49 insider trading cases, the great majority of which followed or preceded mergers or other acquisitions. While the insider trading scandal of the 1980s involved high-level insiders, current cases mainly involve young brokerage firm professionals. Some recent cases have involved **front running,** a practice in which floor brokers trade for themselves before trading on behalf of their clients.

Front running
Trading by floor brokers for their own account before trading on behalf of clients

6. *Short Swing Profits: Section 16(b)*

Section 16(b) of the 1934 Act requires officers, directors, and shareholders owning 10 percent or more of the beneficial stock of any class of stock of a Section 12 company to report their ownership and trading in their corporation's stock to the SEC. These individuals must report their ownership interest to the SEC and file additional reports within ten days of the end of a calendar month if there has been a change in their stock ownership during the month. Section 16 provides that any profits realized from the purchase or sale of any stock in a company by these officers, directors, or ten-percent shareholders in any six-month period shall be recaptured by the corporation. It is irrelevant whether the insider has actually used insider information; any such profits made in such a short time frame (the **"short-swing" profit**) must be returned to the corporation. Thus, Section 16(b) imposes liability without regard to fraud or intent. The profits obtained through this *short-swing trading* must be disgorged to the corporation even if innocently obtained.

Short-swing profits
Profits made by certain corporate insiders within six months and which must be disgorged

7. *Proxy Regulation*

Section 14 of the Securities Exchange Act of 1934 also regulates the solicitation of proxies from shareholders of Section 12 companies. The intent of Section 14 is to protect shareholders from abuse by corporate management, which might mislead shareholders. The 1934 Act thus requires that any solicitation of proxies must be accompanied by a written proxy statement containing specified information such as information about the management of the corporation, compensation of managers, the background of nominees, and any other matters being voted upon. Thus, shareholders are given sufficient information from which to make an informed decision.

To ensure that shareholders do not issue a blank check to management, the form of the proxy card itself is regulated. It must indicate whether the proxy is being solicited on behalf of management and must clearly and impartially identify each matter to be acted upon. A form of proxy that provides for the election of directors must set forth the names of all nominees and provide authority for the shareholder to withhold a vote for any nominee.

Preliminary copies of the proxy statement and form of proxy must be provided to the SEC at least ten days before they are sent to shareholders. In general, anyone who solicits a proxy must fully and truthfully disclose any matters pertinent to the proxy or to the matters to be voted upon. Remedies for violation include injunctions preventing solicitation or voting of the proxies as well as the imposition of monetary fines.

E. State Securities Regulation

A company selling securities must comply with federal and state securities laws. Each one of the states has its own statutes regulating the issuance of securities within its jurisdictional borders. Many of these state statutes pre-date the federal securities laws. According to *Hall v. Geiger-Jones Co.*, 242 U.S. 539, 550 (1917), these regulations were intended to prevent "speculative schemes which have no more basis than so many feet of 'blue sky.'" As a result, state laws regulating the issuance of securities are referred to as **blue sky laws.** The best-known loose-leaf service containing each state's laws, recent topics, and digests of cases relating thereto is the *Blue Sky Law Reports,* published by Commerce Clearing House. The state blue sky laws exist concurrently with the federal statutes relating to issuance and sale of securities. Therefore, a corporation wishing to go public may need to comply not only with the federal securities laws but with a variety of state laws as well. Securities that are offered and sold only to persons residing in one state are exempt from federal registration, 15 U.S.C. Section 77c(a)(11), and need only comply with the pertinent state's regulations.

Blue sky laws
State laws regulating issuance of securities within a state

Provisions of state blue sky laws differ widely among states. Generally, however, there are three common elements:

- *Prohibition of fraud.* Most state blue sky laws contain anti-fraud provisions highly similar to or patterned after the anti-fraud provisions of Rule 10b-5. These provisions prohibit fraud in the sale of securities.

- *Broker and Dealer Registration.* Many states regulate securities by regulating the persons involved in the offer and sale of securities, namely, brokers, dealers, salespersons, and so forth.
- *Registration Requirements.* Most states combine securities registration requirements with other provisions to require disclosure of pertinent information by registration. Unless a valid exemption applies, the issuer must register or qualify the securities with the state corporations commissioner. Some states require that certain information be provided in an application to register the securities before the securities may be sold in the state.

The actual process of registering securities in the states varies greatly. Some states follow a **registration by coordination** scheme: If the securities have been registered under federal law, they may be issued in the state without further requirements. Some states have adopted a **registration by qualification** scheme: The issuer must provide comprehensive information to the state, similar to the registration statement required under the 1933 Act. The state corporations commissioner will carefully review the statement and securities being offered, generally because there has been no federal registration of the securities. Still other states allow **registration by filing:** If a registration statement has been filed under the 1933 Act and the issuer had been engaged in business in the United States for some period of time, the issuer provides a simple notification to the state that it will be offering securities in the state. Attached to this is a copy of the latest prospectus filed with the SEC. Generally, if an issuer has filed a registration statement with the SEC, the process of state registration is somewhat simpler than if the issuer is selling securities in the state for the first time without having filed a federal registration statement.

Registration by coordination
Allowance of sale of stock within state because issuance has been federally registered

Registration by qualification
Requirement by state that issuer file information statement with state prior to issuance of stock

Registration by filing
Notice provided to state that issuer has filed federal registration statement and will be offering securities within state

The National Conference of Commissioners on Uniform State Laws has approved the Uniform Securities Act. The provisions of this uniform act have been adopted, at least to some degree, in at least 40 states and the District of Columbia.

As is true of federal registration requirements, there are numerous exemptions from state blue sky laws. Some of the exemptions relate to the type of security being offered while others relate to smaller issues, exempting them from the state registration requirements.

F. The Securities Markets

1. *Introduction*

A **stock exchange** is a marketplace where securities, principally stocks and bonds, are traded. There are two types of markets: primary and secondary. The **primary market** is the underwriting process described above, used when a corporation makes its initial issue of securities to the public. The new issuer rarely places its securities for sale on a market. Rather, it reaches an agreement with a securities firm, the underwriter, which either buys the stock itself for resale to customers or enters into arrangements with others, dealers, for the dealers to sell the

Stock exchange
Marketplace where securities are traded

Primary market
Marketplace for initial trading of securities through the underwriting process

Secondary market
Marketplace for trading of securities to the public through the nationally known exchanges

stock to customers. The **secondary markets** are composed of the principal stock markets, namely the New York Stock Exchange (NYSE) and the American Stock Exchange (AMEX); the over-the-counter market; and the National Association of Securities Dealers Automated Quotations (NASDAQ) stock market. These secondary markets effect the trading of securities of established companies.

Corporations engaged in new issues principally use the primary market, while stockholders and investors trade anonymously on the secondary markets, typically called the stock exchanges.

Listing
Process of qualifying to sell stocks at a marketplace or exchange

Not all stocks are **"listed"** or available for purchase on the stock markets. Only those corporations that have met various criteria of the exchange and are well-established list their stock for sale through the exchanges. For example, the NYSE requires that a stock already be widely held before it can be listed. Generally, there must be at least 1.1 million shares held by members of the public with a total market value of $60 million and there must be at least 2,000 holders of 100 shares or more. The NYSE also requires that the company have earned, pre-tax, at least $2.5 million during its most recent year and at least $2 million during each of the previous two years. These requirements are intended to promote continuous trading and orderly price movements. By their very nature, these requirements exclude start-up companies from listing on the NYSE. Moreover, there are significant initial and annual fees imposed by the NYSE. Initial fees are $36,800 plus an additional fee based on the number of shares issued. Annual fees are also calculated based on the number of shares issued, subject to a minimum annual fee of $16,170 and a maximum annual fee of $500,000. Companies that no longer meet the stringent requirements of the NYSE may have their trading suspended by the exchange, or the exchange may impose additional criteria for continued trading, or the stock may be delisted.

Big board
Reference to the New York Stock Exchange

Blue chip company
Reference to nationally known and well-established company

In New York City, 24 brokers originally met under a buttonwood tree on Wall Street. In 1792, they organized the New York Stock Exchange. The NYSE is the oldest and most prestigious exchange in the country. It has the strictest rules and is often referred to as the **"big board."** More than 3,000 stocks are traded on the NYSE. A listing on the NYSE is a signal that the corporation has joined the elite corporations in this country, that it has become nationally known, and that its earnings are stable. These corporations are often said to offer **blue chip** stock and they are nationally known — General Motors, Coca Cola Company, IBM, and so forth. Many companies send out announcements or clearly state in their advertising "now trading on the New York Stock Exchange." Companies which have not yet achieved such status may trade on the American Stock Exchange, formerly called the "Curb Exchange" because of its origin on the streets of New York City. The listing criteria for AMEX are easier to meet than those for the NYSE and many of its stocks trade for $25 per share or less. AMEX lists over 700 companies and is the world's second-largest auction marketplace. Listing requirements for AMEX include pre-tax income of $750,000 in the most recent year, a market value of at least $3 million, at least 800 shareholders, and a minimum stock price of $3.00. AMEX has 661 seats or memberships. While the following discussion of stock trading focuses on the NYSE, the process is substantially similar on AMEX. As corporations grow, they may advance from the AMEX to the NYSE.

There are also a number of regional exchanges, such as the Pacific Coast Exchange. The stocks traded on these exchanges are often of smaller companies of primarily local rather than national interest, although many stocks traded on the NYSE are also traded on the regional exchanges. Exchanges operate in Baltimore,

Boston, Chicago, Cincinnati, Detroit, Honolulu, Los Angeles, Philadelphia, Pittsburgh, Salt Lake City, San Francisco, and Washington, D.C. A complex computer network routes orders for stock with the exchange then offering the most favorable price.

The New York Stock Exchange is located in the heart of the financial district at the corner of Wall Street and Broad Street in New York City. All share transactions occur in a 36,000 square foot room in the NYSE building, called the **trading floor,** the *floor*, or *the floor of the Exchange*. Not just anyone may simply walk in and purchase or sell stock. Only members of the Exchange have the privilege of trading on the floor. To become a member, an individual or firm must purchase a membership, called a **seat,** on the Exchange. As the number of seats is restricted, the seats themselves are valuable. The NYSE has 1,366 members and 600 member organizations (brokerage firms or corporations). The highest price paid for a membership was $2,600,000, paid on March 1, 1999. Additionally, each new member must meet various standards and be approved by the Exchange's board of governors. Many brokerage firms have more than one membership or seat on the Exchange.

Trading floor
Location of NYSE where trading of securities occurs

Seat
Membership on an exchange allowing privilege of trading

Non–U.S. issuers are playing an increasingly significant role in the NYSE. As of July 1999, 382 non–U.S. companies were listed on the NYSE, more than triple the number just five years earlier.

2. *Trading on the New York Stock Exchange*

A Typical Transaction. The floor of the NYSE consists of a series of 17 desks, called **posts,** at which specific securities are traded. Members interested in the securities being traded at a certain post collect around the post. All buying and selling takes place around these posts. Numerous computer screens display information about the stocks traded at the post and a stock ticker operates. The ticker is a teletype machine printing nearly 900 characters each minute on a one-inch-wide paper tape called the ticker tape. The ticker records and prints stock transactions by identifying the issuing corporation, the number of shares involved, and the purchase or sale price of the stock. Most of this information is now displayed on computer screens and there are far fewer actual tickers in operation, perhaps only a few hundred, compared to the thousands that were in operation prior to the advent of the computer in the Exchange in the 1960s.

Posts
Locations on trading floor of NYSE where trading occurs

Assume you wish to purchase 100 shares in General Motors on March 10. On that date, GM stock is selling for $110 per share. Thus, to buy 100 shares you will need $11,000 in cash plus commissions. If you have this amount on deposit with your stockbroker, you simply call the broker and place your order by instructing the broker to buy 100 shares of GM **"at the market,"** meaning that you will pay the price in effect at the time your order reaches the floor. Alternatively, you can give your broker a **limit order,** instructing the broker that the purchase is to be effected only at $110 per share or less.

At market
Expression meaning one will buy stock at whatever price is in effect when purchase occurs

Limit order
Instructions to broker to buy or sell at a certain price

An order for 100 shares is referred to as a **round lot,** and this is the standard trading unit. Any purchase or sale involving less than 100 shares is called an **odd lot.** The stock quotations printed in the newspaper are for round lots.

Round lot
Group of 100 shares

Odd lot
Group of less than 100 shares

Before the introduction of computers, your order would have been called in from your broker to either another broker in New York or to the broker's own New York office. The order would then be transmitted by telephone to the floor of the Exchange where a floor broker would receive the order and walk to the GM post. Near the GM post is a **specialist** handling GM transactions who generally acts like an auctioneer. Other brokers may also surround the GM post, with instructions from their customers to either buy or sell GM stock.

Specialist
A person assigned to handling securities for one company

Bid price
Price at which specialist will buy stock

Asked price
Price at which specialist will sell stock

The current bid-and-asked prices are displayed for view. The **bid price** is the price at which the specialist will buy the stock; the **asked price** is the price at which the specialist will sell the stock. The asked price is almost always higher than the bid price. Assume the quotations are "110 bid, 111¼ asked." The broker may indicate that she wishes to buy 100 shares of GM at the market. One of the other brokers surrounding the GM post may have an instruction to sell 100 shares of GM at the market. Your broker and the other broker may consummate the transaction immediately, either at the bid price, the asked price, or some other negotiated price. A reporter records the pertinent information (names of brokers for buyer and seller, price, and quantity) which is relayed to the ticker for viewing by others.

If your broker does not meet another broker at the post who can match your order, the specialist will complete the transaction, usually at the asked price. The specialist's stock will come from one of two sources: the specialist either has his own inventory of stock from which to complete orders or the order will be filled by the specialist matching your order to a limit order on the specialist's books. All of this takes some time and the price of the stock may fluctuate slightly during this period.

Closing
Settlement of transaction

Upon completion of the transaction you are the owner of 100 shares of GM. The actual **closing** (or *settlement*) of the transaction requires three business days, per NYSE rules. At that time, the broker pays for the shares from your account and you become entitled to a certificate for your 100 GM shares. If you do not have an account with a broker, you must pay on the third business day after the purchase. The broker will sell the stock if you do not pay. Rather than providing you with a stock certificate, your broker may simply record your ownership in the broker's books and give you periodic statements relating to the value of the stock. Securities registered in the name of the broker and held by it for safekeeping are said to be registered in the **"street name."** This practice facilitates easy trading for the owner.

Street name
Registration of stock in the name of a broker and held for safekeeping

The NYSE now uses a computerized system called Designated Order Turnaround (DOT). Many experts believe that DOT is responsible for the tremendous growth in trading over the years. For example, in the 1960s a typical day involved trading of approximately 10 million shares. By the late 1990s, this volume had increased to approximately 600 million shares traded per day, a volume that could not have been accomplished before computerization. Enhancements to the system to allow larger orders resulted in SuperDOT.

SuperDOT allows brokers to transmit orders electronically to the posts (without the need for a floor broker). Your purchase order is simply matched against someone else's selling order or against the specialist's own inventory. If the order is a **small order,** meaning less than 2,099 shares, it will be filled automatically by computer. SuperDOT can handle smaller orders in about a minute, meaning that there will be less fluctuation in the price of the stock and you will be likelier to pay what you expected. SuperDOT accounts for roughly 80 percent of all orders executed on the trading floor of the NYSE. Thus, only about 20 percent of all orders involve face-to-face negotiations between brokers and specialists. Typically, only larger orders are handled manually by the specialist.

Small order
Order involving less than 2,099 shares

To protect against market plunges, in 1988 the NYSE initiated a series of curbs on trading, often called **collars,** which limit or halt trading when the market moves up or down by more than a certain amount in a trading day. Intended to prevent panic in the marketplace, these mechanisms are also known as *circuit breakers* because they cut off automated trading when certain triggers are met. For example, trading is suspended for one hour if prices drop 10 percent, two hours if prices drop 20 percent, and the remainder of the day if there is a 30 percent drop. The percentage drops reflect decreases in the Dow Jones Industrial Average of 1,100 points, 2,250 points, and 3,350 points, respectively. Trading begins each day with no curbs in place.

Collars
Automatic halts to trading (also called *curbs* or *circuit breakers*)

Limit Orders. When you give an order to your broker to purchase or sell shares, you may limit the broker's authority by specifying that the purchase price be "$110 or lower" or the sales price be "$112 or higher." These instructions are called limit orders. Assume you have instructed your broker to buy 100 shares of GM at "110 or lower." If the market price for GM is 113 (namely, three **points** — or dollars — higher than you specified), the broker knows that the seller will not sell at 110 when the market price is 113. The broker cannot wait idly by the post all day hoping the market price will decrease three points. The broker thus gives the limit order to the specialist who records it in a book (or on computer). If GM stock falls three points to 110, the specialist will execute, in order received, all transactions for GM at 110. Because the orders are handled in the priority in which they are received, it is possible that the stock price may rise before your order is filled, leaving you without the stock you wished to purchase.

Points
Dollars

Some limit orders may be **day orders,** meaning that the broker is to buy 100 shares of GM at 110 or lower, but in any event the transaction must be completed by the close of that trading day. If the order cannot be filled by the end of the day, it expires. Alternatively, the order can be "**Good Till Canceled,**" meaning that the order remains open until it is specifically canceled. Nevertheless, brokers must reconfirm Good Till Canceled orders every six months. Another variety of limit order is the **stop order,** which is an automatic order to sell or buy when the stock reaches a certain price. For example, assume you purchased your 100 shares of GM stock for $110 per share. You may be fearful of a decline and thus may instruct your broker to sell all of the stock if it hits $107. This enables you to cut your losses at a known figure. On other occasions, you may believe that once a stock increases to a certain point, or breaks through its traditional trading price, it is likely to continue to increase. In that event, you instruct your broker to buy 100 additional shares of GM stock as soon as it reaches $114.

Day order
Order that must be filled within a day

Good till canceled order
Order that stays open until it is specifically canceled

Stop order
Automatic order to sell or buy when stock reaches a stated price

Margin Rules. A broker or bank is permitted to lend a customer up to one-half of the cost of the securities being traded. The customer opens a margin account with a broker authorizing purchases of stock and pledges the securities themselves for repayment of the debt. In the event of a default, the broker thus owns sufficient securities for repayment.

Although the NYSE rules provide that payment for stock must be made on the third business day after the purchase, federal law requires only that payment be made no later than seven business days after the purchase. The NYSE rules are stricter than the federal law to ensure the broker is not in violation of federal law. Moreover, extending the date for payment is another form of extending credit;

Trading on margin
Purchasing stock without paying purchase price in full

ever since the stock market crash in 1929, there has been concern about **trading on margin,** namely, trading speculatively, without paying the actual cash amount of the purchase.

The margin and credit rules exist to provide some stability to the market. For example, assume you purchase $1,000 worth of GM stock by paying $500 cash and borrowing the remainder on margin from your broker. If the stock declines in value to $600, the broker will become concerned that soon the stock will not be worth enough to cover the $500 debt owed. The broker then makes a **margin call,** meaning that the broker demands additional collateral. If the collateral is not given, the broker will sell the shares to ensure she is repaid the $500 advanced to you. NYSE rules actually compel margin calls when the value of the collateral drops to a level that does not exceed more than 25 percent. In this case, 25 percent of the loan amount of $500 is $125, or a total of $625. Once the stock drops below $625, the broker *must* make a margin call.

Margin call
Demand for additional collateral by broker for purchase of stock in which stock was not paid for in full

Before the stock market crash of 1929, customers were often allowed to purchase stock by paying only 10 percent of the price in cash, and the remainder on margin. When the market began to decline, few investors had sufficient resources to meet the margin calls. Many people believe this turned a decline into a crash. Margin rules exist to prevent such occurrences in the future.

Block trade
Trade involving at least 10,000 shares of stock

Block Trades. **Block trades** involve a trade of at least 10,000 shares of stock or a transaction with a value of at least $200,000. They have become increasingly common over the years. In the mid 1960s, there were only approximately 2,000 block trades per year. By the late 1990s, there were nearly three and one-half million yearly block trades, representing nearly half of all of the activity on the NYSE. Because block trades can be so complex, they are generally put together "upstairs" from the floor by large institutional firms, often called **block positioners.** The block positioners attempt to assemble a group of institutional investors to purchase the block and may purchase part of the block themselves. Technological advances enable the block positioners to solicit nearly instantaneously hundreds of investors to determine if they wish to participate in acquiring the block.

Block positioners
Institutional firms that assemble groups of investors to purchase blocks of stock

The Specialist's Function. The 38 firms designated as specialists by the NYSE are far more than mere functionaries assisting in the purchase and sale of stock. One of their primary duties is to even out fluctuations in the market. By federal law, they are charged with maintaining a fair and orderly market, as far as possible. For example, there may be times when there are no buyers for GM stock. If the only people interested in GM stock are sellers, the price of the stock would be expected to decline. When such a fluctuation occurs, the specialists are expected to buy GM stock to ensure orderly trading. Similarly, if a stock continues rising, the specialist is expected to sell some of his inventory. Specialists typically have large inventories of stock, often acquired in the past at advantageous prices. Similarly, if specialists buy stock when it declines and then resell at a higher price when the stock later rises, they may realize significant profits. Specialists also earn commissions on the execution of each limit order placed with them by brokers.

Although there are 38 firms functioning as specialists, approximately 450 individuals actually perform as specialists. Each individual specialist (or "spec") handles approximately six issues. Very big companies often have a spec devoted solely to them. Specialists are called **downstairs brokers** because they deal only with members having seats on the NYSE rather than members of the general public. The brokerage firms dealing with the general public are called **upstairs brokers**

Downstairs broker
Specialists dealing with NYSE members

Upstairs broker
Brokerage firms dealing with general public

because their location was originally physically above the floor, although now the brokers are arranged in 1,500 trading booths along the perimeter of the trading floor.

3. *Other Trading Systems*

Within the last 20 years, alternatives to auction trading on the NYSE and the AMEX have arisen. The best known alternatives are the over-the-counter market and NASDAQ.

The Over-the-Counter Market. There is no physical place or location for the **over-the-counter (OTC) market** as it is essentially a computerized trading network. There is no floor where stocks are traded. Rather, brokers and dealers communicate via computer or telephone to buy and sell securities for their customers. A stock or bond traded "over the counter" is simply one that is not traded on a securities exchange.

A **broker** is an individual or firm acting upon instructions from a customer. The broker is thus the agent for the customer, who is the principal, much the same way that a real estate broker acts as an agent to assist a customer in buying or selling a house. A **dealer** is an institutional securities firm that trades on its own behalf. Some securities firms act as both brokers and dealers. Dealers involved in the OTC market are organized into a self-regulating group, the National Association of Securities Dealers (NASD), which plans to offer its stock via a private placement memorandum.

OTC market
Sale of stock "over the counter" and through computerized trading systems, rather than through a securities exchange

Broker
Securities firm or individual that acts on behalf of a customer

Dealer
An institutional securities firm trading on its own behalf rather than for a customer

NASDAQ. NASD has created a computerized trading system called NASDAQ, which stands for National Association of Securities Dealers Automated Quotations. Established in 1971, NASDAQ was the world's first electronic exchange, trading securities through computers rather than at a specific location. Thus, in a sense, all stock traded through NASDAQ is over the counter. The NASDAQ system allows users to obtain current price quotations from all dealers for all securities traded in the system.

In 1990, NASDAQ formally changed its name to "The NASDAQ Stock Market." That same year it created its Over-the-Counter Bulletin Board to give investors information on and access to securities not listed on NASDAQ, such as pink sheet and penny stocks (discussed below). NASDAQ trading information is broadcast to more than 500 computers worldwide, allowing NASDAQ participants equal access to the market through simultaneous access to quotes and orders.

The NASDAQ Stock Market has two tiers, each with its own listing requirements. To trade on NASDAQ's "National Market," a company's tangible net assets must be $6 million, its pretax income must be $1 million, and it must have at least 400 shareholders. NASDAQ's second tier, known as the "SmallCap Market," has more lenient listing requirements, requiring tangible net assets of $4 million, pretax income of $750,000, and 300 shareholders.

More than 5,400 companies trade their stocks on NASDAQ, and it is considered "tech heavy," in that it has attracted many of the emerging e-commerce, Internet-based, and computer consulting companies. While NASDAQ has a larger dollar volume and trades more shares than any other U.S. market, the companies listed on the NYSE have a higher market capitalization. By the late 1990s, NASDAQ's daily share volume was 802 million, and over several days the world witnessed more than one billion shares changing hands. In its heaviest day of trading, on March 1, 2000, more than 2.230 billion shares were traded. In fact, by 1995, the volume of trading on NASDAQ exceeded that on the NYSE.

In 1998, an acquisition transaction by NASD and the AMEX occurred by which NASD became the parent company of the AMEX. Based in Washington, D.C., NASDAQ is the second largest stock market in the United States and lists more companies and initial public offerings than any other exchange. The dealers who trade on the NASDAQ market are called **market makers.**

Market maker
Dealers trading on NASDAQ

Stocks listed on the NYSE, AMEX, and NASDAQ are not required to be traded there. For example, the NASDAQ system engages in trading of stocks listed on the NYSE, such as General Motors.

Pink Sheet and Penny Stocks. Companies who do not meet the criteria required to list their stock on the NYSE, AMEX, or NASDAQ are traded on the **pink sheets,** a reference to the fact that quotes for these stocks historically were shown on pink paper. Many companies list in the pink sheets as a primary step to listing on NASDAQ. Similarly, in 1998, when a company was delisted from NASDAQ due to its failure to remain in compliance with NASDAQ's net tangible assets requirement, it sought approval to have its stock traded in the pink sheets. **Penny stocks** are those with a price of $5 per share or less. Penny stocks are also known as Over-the-Counter Bulletin Board Stocks, because they do not have a high enough value to trade on NASDAQ.

Pink sheet stocks
Stocks of companies that are not traded on NYSE, AMEX, or NASDAQ

Penny stocks
Stocks with a price of less than $5 per share; also known as Over-the-Counter Bulletin Board Stocks

Electronic Communications Networks. **Electronic communications networks (ECNs)** are private electronic trading systems maintained separately from the public markets such as the NYSE and NASDAQ. The first ECN was "Instinet," created by Reuters for trading by institutions that desired to buy and sell large blocks of stock. ECNs are powerful communications networks, allowing quick and inexpensive trading 24 hours each day. By promoting fast matching of buyers and sellers, investors are protected from market fluctuations. As of late 1999, there were more than ten ECNs in existence, threatening the trading hegemony of the NYSE, AMEX, and NASDAQ.

ECN
Electronic Communication Network; a private electronic trading system

The SEC has determined that ECNs can register as stock exchanges. Archipelago, a Chicago-based ECN, has applied for such registration. When Archipelago itself does not offer the best price for a stock, it automatically routes the order electronically to the best price location, allowing investors instant, one-stop shopping for the entire marketplace.

Both the NYSE and NASDAQ have determined they should become for-profit entities that offer shares to the public. Some experts believe these determinations reflect the fact that the NYSE and NASDAQ need to raise money to invest in new technology to fend off the threat of increased investor trading through ECNs. Similarly, in late 1999, the NYSE announced it was developing an electronic trading system to handle small orders, allowing customers to place an order without going through the floor of the exchange. Under the new system, orders of 1,000 shares or less will be handled electronically, skirting the floor.

Even in the event the NYSE and NASDAQ "go public," as announced, their internal regulatory functions will likely remain separate and apart from the for-profit entities, and the NYSE and NASDAQ will remain charged with enforcing SEC rules and monitoring activities of their own members.

4. *Understanding the Newspaper Reports of Stock Trading*

The financial section of major daily newspapers provides detailed information about stocks traded on the NYSE, AMEX, and NASDAQ. To the uninitiated, however, the numerous symbols, fractions, and figures are nearly incomprehensible. Most newspapers publish either a daily or weekly guide describing the meaning of various abbreviations and symbols.

The trading section of the newspaper will likely be divided into different categories: Market Indicators, reporting the Dow Jones Industrial Average, Standard & Poor's Averages, New York Stock Exchange Index, the AMEX Index, and the NASDAQ Index; information relating to the roughly 2,100 most actively traded NYSE stocks, the 250 most actively traded AMEX stocks, and the 1,900 most actively traded NASDAQ stocks, all in alphabetical order; prices of selected bonds offered on the NYSE; averages for various foreign exchanges; and dividends declared that day. "Up-Down Volume" is also given, showing how many shares advanced and how many shares declined on the NYSE, the AMEX, and the NASDAQ.

A typical listing would show the following:

52 Week						*Sales*				
Hi	*Low*	*Stock*	*Div*	*Yld*	*PE*	*100s*	*High*	*Lo*	*Last*	*Chg.*
35¼	26⅛	CirCty	1.82	5.2	ˉ15	5141	35	34⅝	34⅞	+¼

The interpretation of such an entry is as follows:

Hi-Low: High-Low numbers are the highest and lowest prices paid for the stock during the last 52 weeks.

Stock: Stocks are listed alphabetically, by the company's name. The entry above is for the retailer Circuit City.

Div: The "Div" figure represents the current annual dividend rate paid on the stock, based on the latest quarterly or semiannual dividend declaration.

Yld: The yield figure represents the current annual dividend rate divided by the closing price of the stock, expressed as a percentage.

PE: The figure given represents the closing price of the stock divided by the company's earnings per share for the latest twelve-month period reported.

Sales 100s: Day's volume, in hundreds of shares.

High-Lo: Highest and lowest prices of the stock during the day.

Last: The price at which the stock was trading when the exchange closed for the day.

Chg.: The loss or gain for the day, compared with the previous session's closing price.

Additionally, a variety of footnote abbreviations may be used. For example, "a" indicates an extra dividend paid in addition to a regular dividend; "d" indicates a new 52 week low; "n" indicates stock newly issued within the past 52 weeks; "pf" indicates preferred stock; "r" indicates a cash dividend declared or paid within the preceding 12 months; and "s" indicates a stock split or stock dividend.

While the preceding discussion shows stock traded in eighths, in 1997 the SEC allowed the exchanges to quote prices in sixteenths as well. Both the NYSE and NASDAQ are in the process of converting their systems to show trading in dollars and cents rather than fractions, and the conversion is expected to occur in 2001. At the time of this writing, the SEC planned to allow quoting of stocks in increments of five cents. The conversion to decimals will make it easier for investors to compare prices and will harmonize U.S. policy with that of foreign markets, which trade in decimals.

The smaller the fractional unit, the more active trading is expected to be. For example, if a \$30 stock is rising, the next bid must be \$30⅛ (\$30.12½). If the stock is priced in sixteenths, the next highest bid can be \$30 1/16 (\$30.06¼). If the stock can increase by a nickel, the next highest bid can be \$30.05, allowing you to buy at a more advantageous price. The smallest amount by which stock prices normally change is called a **tick.** Under an SEC pilot program, ticks of a penny will be tested (using our example, you could buy stock at \$30.01) and many expect penny ticks to be widely available by 2001.

Tick
The smallest amount by which stock prices change

Every stock traded on any stock exchange or on NASDAQ is identified by a short symbol, called the ticker symbol. The NYSE uses some one-letter symbols, such as "F" for Ford Motor Company, "K" for Kellogg, and "T" for AT&T. The chairman of the NYSE has announced publicly that he is reserving the symbols "M" for Microsoft and "I" for Intel in hopes of convincing them to move from NASDAQ to the NYSE.

G. Trading in Cyberspace

As in nearly every aspect of modern life, the advent of the Internet and electronic communications is playing a part in the trading of stocks. Some of the more interesting developments of the past few years are as follows:

- In October 1999, the SEC worked jointly with eBay, the online auction service, to stop consumers from auctioning stock on the eBay Web site. Because the Securities Act of 1933 requires that if securities are to be offered to the public, they must be registered with the SEC or must be exempt from registration, an offer on the Web violates the Act.
- As discussed previously, electronic communications networks (ECNs) are changing the face of trading in that they promote nearly instantaneous trading 24 hours per day. In view of the threat of increased trading via ECNs, both the NYSE and NASDAQ are stepping up development of similar electronic trading systems.
- The phenomenon of **day trading** emerged in the late 1990s. Day trading involves numerous trades in the course of a day with the intent of profiting from very small increases in stock prices. A day trader usually completes all transactions in a day and ends the day owning no stock whatsoever. It is estimated that there are about 4,000 to 5,000 full-time

Day trading
Trading involving numerous electronic trades in the course of a day

professional day traders who execute roughly 35 trades each day. Day traders typically operate from one of 70 or 80 day trading firms that maintain offices and powerful computers for the day traders to use, upon payment of a fee.

- **Online trading** is distinguishable from day trading in that an online trader usually trades a few times each day or a few times each month, from home (rather than a professional office), using an online trading brokerage company, which charges a small fee per trade.

Online trading
Trading from home computers a few times each day or month

- A hotly debated issue is whether NASD Rule 2310(a), called the "**suitability rule,**" applies to day trading firms that maintain the offices and computers used by professional day traders. The suitability rule requires that in recommending a purchase or sale of stock to a customer, a broker must have reasonable grounds for believing the recommendation is suitable for the customer. Typically, a broker satisfies this duty by obtaining information from his or her customers about their financial status and investment goals. In late 1999, the SEC acknowledged that determining whether day trading firms were "recommending" investments by offering computers and research information to their day trading customers in an online environment was extremely difficult and urged further study and dialog about the applicability of the suitability rule to online trading.

Suitability rule
Rule requiring that in recommending purchase or sale of stock a broker must have reason for believing transaction is suitable for customer

- The proliferation of false and misleading information disseminated in chat rooms also causes concern to the SEC, which has recommended that a study be conducted to analyze the effect of chat room discussions on corporate stock prices. Many experts believe, however, that the SEC will be unable to enact rules relating to chat room discussions about company rumors and news unless fraud is being committed, likening chat room discussions to informal discussions one has with one's hair stylist or neighbor about stock prices. Nevertheless, in late 1999, the SEC engaged in an enforcement action when an individual posted a phony press release on the Internet, purportedly announcing a strategic alliance between two companies that caused the stock price of one to increase $8.50 per share. Similarly, in early 2000, the SEC charged the creator of the "Tokyo Joe" investment advice Web site for misleading investors by not disclosing he was selling stocks at the same time he was urging investors to buy those stocks and for exaggerating the results of his advice. At about the same time, three law students agreed to settle charges of fraudulently scheming to manipulate stock prices via Internet advice. In sum, publication of false information can be prohibited, but regulation of opinions and free speech in chat rooms is far more problematic.
- In 1998, Spring Street Brewing Co., became the first U.S. company to conduct an IPO over the Internet. The offering was pursuant to Regulation A, which provides an exemption from SEC registration for smaller issuances (those up to $5 million). Due to the impact of state blue sky laws (each state's laws being theoretically implicated by national dissemination of an offer over the Internet), IPOs via the Internet are likely to be restricted to those involving qualified or sophisticated purchasers. California has enacted legislation allowing the sale of securities over the Web

if the issue is a small one and the purchasers are qualified, meaning that they possess a certain level of financial sophistication, shown by requirements as to their annual income.

- To level the investor playing field, the SEC recently enacted rules (Regulation FD) requiring companies to issue a press release, file a notice with the SEC, or open up conference calls to the public at the same time they discuss any "material" company information with analysts or institutional investors. Previously, company managers had private telephone calls with analysts, discussing company performance issues. The analysts then related this information about the company to their institutional investors. Allowing the public in on the calls or broadcasts now places individual investors on the same footing as institutional investors who have been a party to what is called **selective disclosure** by the company. SEC enforcement of full and fair disclosure will assist small investors.
- The SEC is becoming increasingly concerned about the practice of **cybersmearing,** a form of electronic stock market manipulation in which false information is published on the Internet in an attempt to manipulate the market price of stock. In an early-2000 case, a California judge entered a temporary restraining order to halt the practice and required a full and complete retraction of false statements.

Selective disclosure
Practice of disclosure of company information only to analysts rather than to public at large

Cybersmearing
Disseminating false information about a company in an attempt to manipulate stock prices

H. Stock Market Indexes

Indexes
Averages that track movements of stock

Bull market
Rising market

Bear market
Declining market

Nearly every news report during the course of a day will report the Dow Jones Industrial Average or the Standard & Poor's 500 Index. These averages attempt to show the trend of prices of stocks and bonds by reporting on certain selected stocks traded on the NYSE or other exchanges, enabling investors to determine if the market is a **bull** (rising) or a **bear** (declining) market. If you have difficulty remembering which is a rising market and which is a declining market, remember the way in which these animals attack their victims: a bull uses its horns to toss a victim *up* into the air while a bear typically knocks its victim *down* to the ground.

1. *Dow Jones Average*

Dow Jones & Company is a publishing firm. It computes averages every hour of every day of trading. The Dow Jones Average is actually made up of four different averages: the averages of 30 selected industrial companies (including Du Pont, IBM, McDonald's, and United Technologies), 20 transportation stocks, (including Delta Airlines, Federal Express, and Consolidated Rail), 15 utilities stocks (including Consolidated Edison and Pacific Gas and Electric), and then a composite average of these 65 stocks. The theory is that a view of certain selected industrial, transportation, and utility companies will provide information about trends in the market in general. The snapshot of the market revealed by the average may be somewhat limited, however, inasmuch as the companies selected for review tend to be the "blue chip" companies.

Companies can be dropped from the Dow Jones averages and other companies can be added. For example, on November 1, 1999, Home Depot, Intel, Microsoft Corporation, and SBC Communications were added, replacing Union Carbide, Goodyear Tire & Rubber, Sears, and Chevron. Intel and Microsoft are the first NASDAQ stocks included in the more than 100-year old average. The new components have an average market value of $236 billion, compared with $21 billion of the four companies dropped. Some experts predict that the NYSE will double its efforts to woo Intel and Microsoft to the NYSE.

In a highly unusual event, in February 2000, a tech equipment maker called Aeroflex Inc. became the first company to leave the NYSE since 1939 and list its shares on NASDAQ.

Dow Jones began to publish an industrial average in the late 1800s. It used the stock of 12 companies, totaled their trading prices, and divided by 12. This "average" was announced to the public as an indicator of market trends as a whole.

The Dow Jones Industrial Average is the one most often relied upon by investors. The Industrial Average reports only the averages of the 30 selected industrial stocks. The Average is computed by adding the prices of the stocks in the average and then dividing by a constant called the "divisor," currently set at about 0.35. Its advances and declines are given in points, meaning dollars. For example, assume that the industrial average on the close of trading one day is 850.42. If, at the close of trading the next day, the industrial average is 853.55, the average has risen 3.13 points, or $3.13.

The Dow is one of the few market indicators that is price weighted, meaning that high-priced stocks such as IBM have more of an effect on the average than lower-priced ones.

One investment strategy is called investing in "**Dogs of the Dow.**" Investors select the ten (or five or one) Dow Jones Industrial stocks with the lowest price-earnings ratio and the highest dividend yield and buy equal amounts of stock in each. These stocks are referred to as "dogs" only because they are the least expensive Dow Jones stocks relative to others. At the end of the year, the investor adjusts the portfolio to select the current "dogs" of the Dow. According to experts, in the last 20 years, this strategy has lost in only three years.

Dogs of the Dow
Investment strategy involving investing in certain DJI stocks

2. *Other Indexes*

There are a variety of other indexes used to report trends in the market. Among them are Standard & Poor's Index and the NYSE Composite Index. None of these other indexes has achieved the notoriety of the Dow Jones Average, perhaps because of its long-standing tradition.

Standard & Poor's Corporation is an investment advisory and research firm. It publishes the *Standard & Poor's 500 Index,* a report reflecting stock prices for 500 companies traded on the NYSE. These 500 companies are comprised of 400 industrial firms, 40 public utilities, 40 financial institutions, and 20 transportation companies. Because the Standard & Poor's Index considers a wider array of companies, and more of today's dominant high-tech companies, some experts believe it is more reliable than the narrow Dow Jones Industrial Average of merely 30 industrial companies.

Standard & Poor's analysts calculate the 500 Index every five minutes of every trading day. They compare current stock prices with average prices of stock during a base period of 1941-1943, when the base was ten, meaning that current prices of stock are set forth in tenths of the average prices during the 1941-1943 base period. Thus, an announcement that the Standard & Poor's 500 Index is 130 means that the current selected stock prices average 13 times higher than in the period 1941-1943. About one-fourth of the 500 companies tracked by Standard & Poor's are high-tech. While the Dow average is price weighted, the Standard & Poor's is weighted by market capitalization, meaning it is influenced most strongly by companies whose total value is the greatest.

The NYSE Composite functions nearly identically to that of Standard & Poor's. It is based on 1,632 companies trading on the NYSE. Its base period is December 31, 1965, when the base was 50.

The NASDAQ Composite indexes or averages all of the over-the-counter stocks traded on the NASDAQ.

Stock Market Trivia

- The average price of a share traded on the NYSE in 1998 was $43.10.
- The tradition of pricing stocks in fractions with 8 or 16 as the denominator derives from Spanish trading in the 1500s when Spanish silver could be cut into "pieces of eight," and gold doubloons could be cut into 16 pieces.
- Originally, a Chinese gong was used to signal the beginning and ending of the trading each day on the floor of the NYSE. It is considered an honor to be invited to ring the opening or closing bell of the exchange.
- The longest listed company on any U.S. exchange is ConEdison, listed on the NYSE in 1824.
- Small investors own about one-half of the shares in U.S. publicly traded companies.
- In 1998, underwriters spent more than $50 million on placing tombstone ads for companies going public, primarily to promote their own involvement in the issuance, according to some experts.
- As a signal of the growing power of individual investors, as of late 1999, nearly $10 billion worth of stock transactions were occurring weekly through the brokerage company Charles Schwab's Web site.
- The largest volume of trading on the NYSE involved 1.2 billion shares in the late 1990s.
- The largest volume of trading on NASDAQ (as of the publication of this text) occurred on March 1, 2000, when more than 2.230 billion shares changed hands.

I. Glossary of Financial Terms

This section provides a brief description of various other terms often encountered in the financial section of the newspaper.

Arbitrageur: One who buys different stocks and bonds in different markets at the same time, taking advantage of price differences.

Derivative: A financial instrument that does not itself constitute ownership but is rather a promise to convey ownership in the future. Options and futures, discussed below, are examples of derivatives.

Futures Contract: An agreement between two parties to exchange a specified quantity of an asset (often an agricultural commodity such as wheat, corn, coffee beans, orange juice, and so forth) at a specified price at some designated future date. For example, a buyer may agree to pay $3.10 per bushel for 500 bushels of corn next November 18. The buyer must put up a certain sum of money at the time the agreement is entered into, often 10 percent. The buyer hopes the actual price on November 18 is higher than $3.10 per bushel so that a profit will be realized. Options are often traded on an exchange, such as the Chicago Board Options Exchange.

Junk Bonds: Bonds below investment grade as established by various investment rating services.

Money Market Funds: A money market fund is a mutual fund investing only in short-term and nearly risk-free investments. The funds invest in commercial paper, short-term certificates of deposit, and so forth. Depositors are usually allowed to write checks on the amount they have deposited into the fund. The arrangement is highly similar to a bank account, although it is uninsured.

Mutual Funds: An open-end investment company which invests, reinvests, holds, and trades in the securities of other issuers for an unlimited number of persons wishing to invest in the fund. Basically, a mutual fund is a pool of money from numerous investors invested in various companies and managed by an investment professional. The money may be invested in stocks or bonds, and the fund will charge fees to manage the money invested. The term "open end" refers to the fact that there is no fixed capitalization of the investment company. As it grows in size, it will hold increasingly larger numbers of shares. A *load* (or *front-end load*) is an additional charge imposed on an investor in a mutual fund. A *no load fund* is a fund usually sold without a broker; the investor must locate the investment herself and will not pay the extra charge associated with a load.

Options: Publicly traded securities, of two types.

Call Options: The right to buy a certain stock or a certain commodity at a fixed price for a limited period, perhaps several months.

Put Options: The right to sell certain stock or a certain commodity at a fixed price for a limited period, perhaps several months.

Like futures, options are traded on various exchanges, including AMEX, the Chicago Board Options Exchange, and the Philadelphia Stock Exchange. If the options are not exercised prior to their stated expiration date, the options expire and are worthless.

Key Features in Securities Regulation and Trading

- Securities (stocks and bonds) may not be offered for sale using any means of interstate commerce unless they are either registered with the SEC or exempt from registration.
- Two key federal statutes govern the issuance of securities: the Securities Act of 1933, governing initial issuance, and the Securities Exchange Act of 1934, governing resale of securities and reporting by public companies.
- Registration with the SEC is accomplished by electronically filing a statement with the SEC providing information about the issuer and the issue.
- Certain securities need not be registered, and small issue offerings and private offerings need not be registered.
- The 1934 Act imposes periodic reporting requirements on any company whose stock is listed on an exchange or that has assets exceeding a certain amount. The reports are intended to provide information to the public about the company.
- The 1934 Act prohibits inside trading, namely the trading of stock by a company insider who has access to information not available to the public, and requires insiders to disgorge short-swing profits, those profits made by certain insiders on the purchase or sale of stock within a six-month period.
- The individual states regulate the sale of securities through their state laws, called "blue sky laws."
- Stock can be traded on an exchange, such as the NYSE or AMEX, which involve auction bidding and selling at a physical location or through automated systems, such as that of NASDAQ.
- The movement of stocks is tracked by various measures and indexes, including the Dow Jones Industrial Average and Standard and Poor's 500 Index. These averages and indices are viewed as providing a snapshot as to market trends.

J. Role of Paralegal

Paralegals in the securities arena are often experts who have gained tremendous information and experience in a very complex field of law. Some of these paralegals are called "blue sky specialists" and others are called "securities paralegals." Because this area of the law is so technical and because exposure is increased (attorneys practicing in this field typically pay higher premiums for malpractice insurance), a highly skilled securities paralegal can make as much as $90,000 per year in cities such as Washington, D.C., or New York.

Due to the ramifications of leaks, any staff having access to information relating to the trading of corporate clients will be expected to maintain the highest level of confidentiality. Many law firms not only have strict policies prohibiting divulging any privileged information but also require attorneys, paralegals, and staff members to sign confidentiality agreements and agreements promising not to trade in any client's securities.

The decision to "go public" will be made by the board of directors of a corporation acting in concert with the officers, accountants, attorneys, and other advisors. Once the decision has been made, there are a number of activities calling for the paralegal's involvement.

1. Drafting minutes of meetings and resolutions confirming the decision to offer securities publicly.
2. Drafting registration statements.
3. Assisting in "due diligence" work such as verifying information provided by the corporate issuer, preparing and compiling results of questionnaires for officers, directors, and principal shareholders.
4. Researching exemptions from requirements of the 1933 Act.
5. Researching provisions of state blue sky laws and exemptions thereto; obtaining state registration and notification forms.
6. Coordinating exhibits to registration statements, including financial statements, profit-and-loss statements, and so forth.
7. Drafting and filing dealer and/or broker registration forms with NASD, the SEC, and state corporations commissions.
8. Assisting in the preparation of private placement offerings/memoranda.
9. Reviewing copy for tombstone ads and any press releases.
10. Proofreading the registration statement, prospectus, and so forth.
11. Docketing dates for periodic filing requirements (annual, quarterly, and periodic report of changes in issuer's statement) for Section 12 companies and preparing such reports.

Resource Guide

Because the field of securities regulation is controlled almost entirely by statute, the most critical resources are the various federal and state statutes and any rules interpreting those statutes. Loose-leaf services provide a wealth of practical information and your law firm itself may have binders of regulations, forms, and other resources. Resources include:

1. Federal Statutes

a. Securities Act of 1933, 15 U.S.C. Section 77a, et seq.
b. Securities Exchange Act of 1934, 15 U.S.C. Section 78a, et seq.

2. SEC Rules

a. Rules under the Securities Act of 1933 (including Regulation A for small issues exemption, Regulation C for registration, and Regulation D for limited offerings). 17 C.F.R. Section 230.100 et seq.
b. Rules under the Securities Exchange Act of 1934, including Rule 10b-5 relating to manipulation and deception, Rule 14 relating to solicitation of proxies, and Rule 16a relating to short swing profits by directors, officers, and principal shareholders. 17 C.F.R. Section 240.0-1 et seq.

3. State Statutes

Review your state's corporations code and any administrative regulations in your state relating to registration of securities to be offered in the state. Most indexes refer to these under the heading "Blue Sky Laws." Contact your state corporations commissioner to ask for forms, filing fees, and other information (see Appendix A for phone numbers and Web sites).

4. Services and Periodicals

A number of loose-leaf services publish the pertinent statutes, rules, forms, and digests or summaries of cases relating to securities registration. Commerce Clearing House, BNA, and Prentice-Hall are some of the principal publishers of these services, which consist of sets of binders updated by new page inserts as new materials are developed or provided.

a. *Securities and Exchange Commission Decisions and Reports* (1934 to date). This set reports decisions of the SEC.
b. *Securities and Exchange Commission Releases.* This set reports announcements and decisions by the SEC.
c. *Securities & Federal Corporate Law Report* (Clark Boardman). This set reports decisions and new developments in the field of securities regulation.
d. *Securities Law Review.* This periodical publishes articles relating to securities issues, registration, and fraud. Articles on particular topics can be located by using the Index to Legal Periodicals.
e. *Securities Regulation & Law Report.* This loose-leaf service published by BNA reports cases and new topics and developments in securities regulation.
f. *Securities Regulation Guide* (Prentice-Hall).
g. *Federal Securities Law Reporter* (Commerce Clearing House).
h. *Blue Sky Law Reports* (Commerce Clearing House). This set reports the regulations, statutes, and cases dealing with registration of securities in the individual states.

5. Law Firm Resources

Few law firms do securities work on an intermittent basis. The firms that provide securities advice and assistance to their clients tend to have practice departments performing only securities work. Most of these firms have extensive collections of books, treatises, journals, and loose-leaf services. Additionally, they have a wide array of the forms needed for securities registration and exemptions. There may be a set of blue sky binders compiled for the firm, with one binder for each state, containing all of the pertinent statutes, regulations, forms, filing fees, and phone numbers.

6. Agency Names and Addresses

The following addresses may be helpful in obtaining forms and information.

Securities and Exchange Commission
450 5th St., N.W.
Washington, D.C. 20549
telephone: (202) 942-0100
SEC Information Line:
(202) 942-8945
www.sec.gov

New York Stock Exchange
11 Wall Street
New York, NY 10005
telephone: (212) 656-3000

American Stock Exchange
86 Trinity Place
New York, NY 10006
telephone: (212) 306-1000

National Association of Securities Dealers Automated Quotations
1735 K Street, N.W. - Fourth Floor
Washington, D.C. 20006-1500
telephone: (202) 496-2500

National Association of Securities Dealers
1735 K Street, N.W.
Washington, D.C. 20006
telephone: (202) 728-8000

7. SEC Filings

There are several approaches that can be used to obtain copies of a company's filings with the SEC.

a. Service Providers. Several companies will obtain copies of a given company's SEC filings and send them to you via facsimile or express mail within a day or two. One of the better known providers is CCH Washington Service Bureau (telephone: (800) 289-1057).

b. LEXIS or WESTLAW. SEC filings can be obtained on LEXIS or WESTLAW, which each have an "SEC-Online" database including full-text 10-Ks, 10-Qs, annual reports and proxy statements. Both include a database called EDGAR which provides the full-text of SEC filings since 1993. There is a three to ten business-day delay for full-text filings.

WEB RESOURCES

The most important Web resources are federal and state statutes relating to registration of securities and fraud in the trading and sale of securities.

www4.law.cornell.edu/usccode
This excellent site allows searching by keyword or by section number. You can review all fifty titles of the U.S. Code or look up statutes by their popular names. The Securities Act of 1933 and the Securities Exchange Act of 1934 are located in Title 15, entitled "Commerce and Trade."

www.ll.georgetown.edu
When you access this site for Georgetown University Law Center, select "State, Local & Territorial." You will be presented with a map of the United States. Point your cursor to the state in which you are interested, and you will be provided with links to a variety of legal sources relating to that state. Select "Statutes" or "Codes," and you will be linked to the state's statutes. In some states, searching can be done by either keywords or by section number. In other states, searching is accomplished exclusively by keywords.

Because many states have posted their forms relating to registration of securities on their Web sites, important Web resources are the home pages of the various secretaries of state. See Appendix A for the specific Web address for each of the state's secretaries of state. Other alternatives follow.

www.nass.org
This Web site of the National Association of Secretaries of State will provide you with links to each of the secretaries of state. After you access the home page of the Association, select "States." You will then be given an alphabetical list of all 50 states and the District of Columbia (together with their state flags). Point your cursor at the state you wish, and you will be immediately linked to the home page for that state's secretary of state. In most instances, you will immediately see entries for "Corporations" or "Securities." Select the relevant entry, and you will be given basic information on registration of securities in that state.

www.legalwiz.com
When you access this site, select "Legal Sites" and then "Corporate Department and Secretary of State Pages" for links to each state's secretary of state.

www.sec.gov
This Web site of the Securities and Exchange Commission is a gateway to small business information, current SEC rules, enforcement actions, and, most importantly, EDGAR, the database of registration statements and periodic reports. The site also provides Form S-1 (for initial registration of securities) as well as forms for the periodic and annual reporting required of Section 12 companies. Additionally, one can review the statements

filed by companies that offer their stock on the exchanges or whose assets exceed certain minimums. Generally, one can locate the forms and information by name of the company, type of document or form, or date of the issuance or report. A great deal of financial information is provided, including explanations of Rules 504, 505, and 506 relating to exemptions from registration requirements, all of it at no cost. Not all documents filed with the SEC will be available on EDGAR; most filings after May 1996 are available. Filings are posted to the site about 24 hours after submission to the SEC.

www.freedgar.com
This commercial site allows free unlimited access to SEC EDGAR filings. Searching can be done by company name or stock ticker symbol. Companies can also be tracked by a "watchlist" that notifies you by e-mail when any company designated by you submits an electronic filing to the SEC.

http://edgarscan.pwc.global.com
PriceWaterhouseCoopers' site offers "EdgarScan," an interface to the documents filed with the SEC, allowing you to go directly to specific sections of the filings.

http://www.law.uc.edu/CCL/intro.html
This site offers "The Securities Lawyer's Deskbook," including the full text of the basic federal securities laws and regulations as well as forms required by the SEC to comply with those regulations.

www.companylink.com
This site provides news, research, and contacts for more than 65,000 companies. Enter either the company's name or stock ticker symbol, and you will be provided with basic information about the company.

www.hoovers.com
When you access this site, covering most large companies, select the "Main Directory." Then select "Company Directory A-Z" for capsule descriptions of companies, their addresses, company officials, competitors, and other valuable information.

The Web sites of the various exchanges provide excellent information about the process of trading, glossaries of financial terms, and facts and statistics. Many of the sites offer interesting photos and simulations of floor trading or over-the-counter trading. Check the following sites:

www.nyse.com
Web site for the New York Stock Exchange

www.amex.com
Web site for the American Stock Exchange

www.nasdaq.com
Web site for NASDAQ

www.dowjones.com
Web site for Dow Jones

A number of sites offer basic investing and trading information for consumers. Try the following:

http://invest-faq.com
This excellent site offers a wealth of information about investing, the stock exchanges, trading basics, facts, and trivia.

www.fool.com
The Web site of "The Motley Fool" provides a list of the current "Dogs of the Dow" as well as a wide variety of investing and trading information.

http://www.e-analytics.com
This Web site offers information about how companies raise capital, basic primers on stocks and bonds, comprehensive information on the Dow Jones Indexes, and basic information about the stock market.

Discussion Questions

Fact Scenario. TechTalk, Inc. is a New York corporation that has achieved a great deal of success in the e-commerce field. It has decided to "go public" and offer approximately $35 million worth of stock nationally. It has tangible net assets of $7 million, 500 shareholders, and pretax income of $14 million.

1. What type of arrangement with an underwriter is the most advantageous for TechTalk and why?
2. On what exchange or market is TechTalk most likely to list its shares?
3. What regulatory filings must TechTalk make before it sells its securities to the public?
4. Can TechTalk qualify for any exemptions to any federal regulatory requirements? Why or why not?
5. Approximately six months after the IPO, TechTalk was approached by a larger corporation to consider a merger of the two companies. Hannah Stone, a director of TechTalk, informed her two sisters and mother of the possible merger. All purchased stock at $35 per share. When the merger was publicly announced, TechTalk's stock soared to $52 per share. Have any federal rules been violated? Which ones? By which individuals?
6. The merger was completed in March. In June, Keith O'Brien, a vice president of the company, bought stock at $54 per share. Four months later, Keith sold the stock for $61 per share. Keith did not use any inside information, and there was no fraud involved in the transaction. Has Keith violated any federal laws? Which ones? What penalty may be imposed?

14

Changes in the Corporate Structure and Corporate Combinations

CHAPTER OVERVIEW

Perhaps the most fundamental feature of corporate operation is that while the shareholders own the corporation, they do not manage it. Their participation in the corporation primarily takes the form of voting, chiefly voting on the election of the directors who will manage the corporation. There are, however, some matters that are viewed as effecting such significant change to the structure of the corporation that shareholder approval is required. These matters are often referred to as extraordinary matters and consist of the amending of the articles of incorporation, mergers, consolidations, share exchanges, sales of corporate assets, and dissolution of the corporation.

Corporations can amend their articles of incorporation to add or delete provisions or to modify existing provisions. Because the articles created the corporation and are available for public inspection by any potential shareholder, amending the articles requires shareholder approval. A procedure somewhat similar to amending the articles is restating the articles of incorporation. A restatement is a clean-up of previous amendments to articles so there is one easily readable complete document. Because no changes are made to the articles, restating the articles can be done without shareholder approval. Amending the corporate bylaws is typically accomplished by the directors, without shareholder participation.

Corporations can gain control of other corporations through a variety of means: mergers, consolidations, share exchanges, purchase of assets, or purchase of stock.

Mergers and consolidations are combinations of corporations that result in one corporate entity. The new entity, the survivor, takes over all assets and liabilities of any corporations merged or consolidated into it. A share exchange occurs when an acquiring corporation compels a target corporation to exchange all of its shares for cash or for shares of the acquiring corporation. Mergers, consolidations, and share exchanges must be approved by the board of directors and the shareholders of the corporations involved. Shareholders who dissent from the transaction are usually given appraisal rights, namely, the right to have their stock appraised and bought from them for cash.

One corporation can acquire all or substantially all of another's tangible and intangible assets. The acquiring corporation need not obtain shareholder approval inasmuch as the acquisition is viewed as within the board's ordinary powers. The selling corporation, however, must have approval of its board of directors and its shareholders. Dissenting shareholders will be afforded appraisal rights. As an alternative to acquiring a corporation's assets, a corporation can acquire another corporation's stock. While most stock acquisitions are negotiated arrangements, some are not. These nonconsensual takeovers are "hostile" and call into play a wide variety of defensive strategies used by the target to avoid takeover by the aggressor.

A. Amending the Articles of Incorporation

1. *Reasons for Amending Articles*

According to most state statutes and RMBCA Section 10.01, a corporation may amend its articles at any time to add or change a provision that was permitted or required in the original articles or to delete any provision not required to be included in the articles of incorporation. Thus, amendments can be used to add preemptive rights for shareholders, create new classes of shares, change the par value of the stock, and so forth. The most common reasons for amending the articles are changing the corporation's name and increasing the number of shares the corporation is authorized to issue. Some statutes identify a list of acceptable amendments, but the more modern practice is that followed by the RMBCA: If a provision could have been stated in the original articles, it can be included in the amended articles.

Although the articles set forth the basic structure of the corporation, no shareholder has a vested right in the articles, such that his or her individual approval is required before an amendment can be accomplished. In general, majority vote rules. The original articles may, however, set forth certain restrictions on future amendments by requiring approval in excess of that mandated by the state statute, for example, a provision requiring 80 percent shareholder approval to create a new class of stock.

If the corporation has included provisions in its articles that were not required — for example, a provision setting the date for the annual shareholders' meeting — any desired change will require amending the articles. Thus, the better practice is to draft articles that strictly comply with the pertinent state statutes, but go no further, because each additional provision may require amendment in the future.

2. *Procedure for Amending Articles*

The most common procedure for amending the articles (or "charter" or "certificate," if so called by the state) is discussion of the proposed amendment by the board of directors and then adoption by the board of a resolution setting forth the text of the proposed amendment and directing that it be submitted for shareholder approval. The board may act at a meeting by majority vote, or may act by written consent, which most states require to be unanimous.

Some states and the RMBCA allow the directors to make certain amendments to the articles without shareholder approval. In general, these are amendments that do not affect the basic rights of shareholders. For example, RMBCA Section 10.02 provides that the board, acting alone, can adopt the following amendments: extending the duration of the corporation; deleting the names and addresses of the initial directors; deleting the name and address of the initial agent for service of process if a statement of change has been filed with the secretary of state; changing each issued and unissued authorized share of an outstanding class into a greater number of whole shares, if the corporation has only shares of that class outstanding (in other words, increasing the number of authorized shares to accommodate a stock split); or changing the corporate name by substituting the words "corporation" or "incorporated" or the abbreviations "inc.," "co.," or "corp.," for a similar word or abbreviation or by adding, deleting, or changing a geographic attribute for the name.

A few states permit a specified percentage of shareholders to propose an amendment to the articles. If no shares have yet been issued, the directors or incorporators can amend the articles by themselves. The more typical procedure, however, is that described: the board of directors will adopt a resolution setting forth the amendment and a meeting of shareholders will be held to vote on the amendment. (See Figure 14-1 for a sample resolution.) An amendment merely changing the corporation's agent for service of process can usually be effected by

FIGURE 14-1
Resolution to Amend Articles

RESOLVED, that Article 1 of the Articles of Incorporation for the Company be amended to read as follows: The name of the corporation is Taylor Visions, Inc.

RESOLVED, that Article 4 of the Articles of Incorporation be deleted in its entirety.

RESOLVED, that Article 6 of the Articles of Incorporation for the Company be added as follows: The holders of shares of the Company shall have preemptive rights to purchase shares issued by the Company from time to time in the respective ratio which the number of shares held by each holder at the time of any issue bears to the total number of shares outstanding at the time of any issue.

the directors without shareholder approval by filing a simple form with the secretary of state.

The amendment may be voted upon by the shareholders at their annual meeting or at a special meeting. The notice of the special meeting must state the purpose of the meeting and must set forth the text or a summary of the proposed amendment. Appropriate notice of any meeting must be given to all shareholders, even those not entitled to vote. If a class of shareholders has nonvoting stock, and a proposed amendment would affect their rights (for example, by cancelling their preemptive rights), those shareholders must also be allowed to vote on the amendment.

The Model Business Corporation Act required a two-thirds approval by the shareholders to amend the articles. That provision has been revised to require a simple majority (50 percent plus one). RMBCA Section 10.03(e). Similarly, most states require a simple majority vote. A few states, however, still require two-thirds approval by shareholders. The original articles, of course, may have provided that amendments to the articles can only be accomplished by a certain percentage, for example, 75 percent; in such a case, these greater than majority requirements must be met. If shareholders are allowed to act by written consent, this procedure may also be used to effect an amendment to the articles of incorporation.

3. *Articles of Amendment*

Articles of amendment
Document filed with state that amends articles of incorporation

After the amendment has been approved by the shareholders, the corporation must prepare and file **articles of amendment** with the secretary of state. Almost all states provide forms for articles of amendment. Most states also require that the amendment recite that the original articles were amended pursuant to state statute and that the requisite shareholder vote was received, or that shareholder approval was not needed. (See Figure 14-2 for sample articles of amendment.)

Rather than require that the entire articles be redrafted, most states allow corporations to simply set forth the text of the new amendment. The articles are then filed with the secretary of state together with the requisite filing fee. After examination of the articles of amendment, the secretary of state will issue a certificate of amendment, or return a copy of the articles of amendment stamped "approved." Any requirements relating to the original articles must also be complied with when amending articles. For example, if the original articles were required to be published or filed with a county clerk, the amended articles must be also. If the amendment changes the corporation's name or authorized number of shares, new stock certificates and a new corporate seal should be obtained.

A minority of states, and the RMBCA, allow shareholders who dissented from amending the articles to have their shares bought by the corporation at the fair market value. This right to dissent and have one's shares appraised and bought out is generally triggered only by an amendment that seriously impairs or adversely affects one's shares, such as an amendment abolishing some preferential right, preemptive rights, or a right to vote. The RMBCA approach is to allow appraisal rights only when an amendment reduces the number of shares of a shareholder to a fraction of a share, and the corporation will have the obligation or

FIGURE 14-2
Washington Articles of Amendment

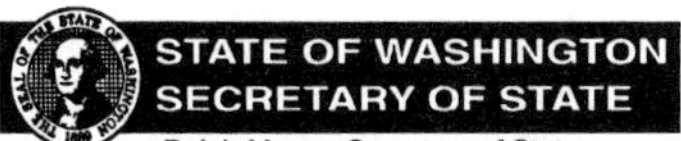
STATE OF WASHINGTON
SECRETARY OF STATE
Ralph Munro, Secretary of State

- Please PRINT or TYPE in black ink
- Sign, date and return original AND ONE COPY to:

CORPORATIONS DIVISION
505 E. UNION • PO BOX 40234
OLYMPIA, WA 98504-0234

- BE SURE TO INCLUDE FILING FEE. Checks should be made payable to "Secretary of State"

ARTICLES OF AMENDMENT
WASHINGTON
PROFIT CORPORATION
(Per Chapter 23B.10 RCW)

FEE: $30

EXPEDITED (24-HOUR) SERVICE AVAILABLE – $20 PER ENTITY INCLUDE FEE AND WRITE "EXPEDITE" IN BOLD LETTERS ON OUTSIDE OF ENVELOPE

FOR OFFICE USE ONLY
FILED: / /

FOR OFFICE USE ONLY

IMPORTANT! Person to contact about this filing	Daytime Phone Number (with area code)

AMENDMENT TO ARTICLES OF INCORPORATION

NAME OF CORPORATION *(As currently recorded with the Office of the Secretary of State)*

UBI NUMBER	CORPORATION NUMBER *(If known)*	AMENDMENTS TO ARTICLES OF INCORPORATION WERE ADOPTED ON Date: ______

EFFECTIVE DATE OF ARTICLES OF AMENDMENT *(Specified effective date may be up to 30 days AFTER receipt of the document by the Secretary of State)*
☐ Specific Date: ______ ☐ Upon filing by the Secretary of State

ARTICLES OF AMENDMENT WERE ADOPTED BY *(Please check ONE of the following)*
☐ Incorporators. Shareholders action was not required
☐ Board of Directors. Shareholders action was not required
☐ Duly approved shareholder action in accordance with Chapter 23B.10 RCW

AMENDMENTS TO THE ARTICLES OF INCORPORATION ARE AS FOLLOWS
If amendment provides for an exchange, reclassification, or cancellation of issued shares, provisions for implementing the amendment must be included. If necessary, attach additional amendments or information.

FOR OFFICE USE ONLY

SIGNATURE OF OFFICER
This document is hereby executed under penalties of perjury, and is, to the best of my knowledge, true and correct.

Signature of Officer *Printed Name* *Date*

FOR OFFICE USE ONLY

INFORMATION AND ASSISTANCE – 360/753-7115 (TDD – 360/753-1485)

005-002 (8/97)

right to repurchase the fractional share from the shareholder. RMBCA Section 13.02(a)(4).

If the only change to the articles is a change of corporate name, consider whether the same result can be accomplished by allowing the corporation to do business under a fictitious business name. The cumbersome and somewhat expensive amendment procedure may be avoided by simply filing a fictitious business name statement with the secretary of state or local county clerk. The fictitious business name will allow the corporation to use a name different from the one it was incorporated under without necessitating a formal amendment to the articles of incorporation. Additionally, corporate name changes should be undertaken with all of the precautions used when selecting the original corporate name: a trade name search should be conducted to ensure the name is not confusingly similar to another, a check with the secretary of state should be conducted to ensure the name is available, and, if available, the name should be reserved during the amendment process.

An amendment to a corporation's articles does not affect the rights of any third parties. For example, the fact that a corporation changes its name does not release the corporation from a debt owed to a creditor who originally contracted with the differently named corporation. The corporate debtor remains the same — only its name has changed.

Finally, if the corporation is doing business in any other jurisdictions, their state statutes should be reviewed to determine whether an amendment to the articles triggers any filing requirements in the other jurisdictions.

B. Restating the Articles of Incorporation

Over a period of time, a corporation may amend its articles several times. If each document filed with the secretary of state contains only the amending language rather than setting forth all of the articles, the articles may become difficult to read. For example, if a corporation filed its original articles in 1980, and thereafter amended them three times, anyone attempting to review the articles would need to compare all four documents. Therefore, almost all states allow a corporation to restate its articles by combining the original articles with any later amendments into one clean document that supersedes all of the previous documents.

Restated articles
Articles compiled into one readable form with no changes made

Because the **restated articles** of incorporation do not include any changes, but are rather a composite of previously approved amendments, shareholder approval is not necessary to restate articles of incorporation (unless a change to the articles is being made at the same time, in which case, the required procedure for amendments must be followed). The directors will approve a restatement either by majority vote at a meeting or by written consent, and then the entire text of the articles, including any changes, additions, or deletions made since filing of the original articles, will be prepared and filed with the secretary of state accompanied by a filing fee.

C. Amending the Bylaws of the Corporation

Changes in the corporation's bylaws are easily accomplished. Generally, unless state statute, the articles, or the bylaws themselves require shareholder participation, the bylaws may be amended solely by the directors. If shareholder approval is required, a simple majority vote is generally sufficient. The bylaws may be amended to change the date of the annual meeting of shareholders, to change the duties of the corporate treasurer, to add an officer, and so forth.

In most states, amendment of the bylaws is performed by the directors acting at a meeting or acting by written consent. The minutes of the meeting or written consent action setting forth the change should be placed in the minute book. The section of the minute book containing the bylaws should also reflect the change. Either an entire new set of bylaws should be prepared and marked "Bylaws — Amended as of __________" or the new bylaw provision should be prepared on a separate piece of paper marked "Amendment to Bylaw No. __________, amended as of __________" and inserted at the end of the bylaws.

Because the original bylaws did not require filing with the secretary of state, the amended bylaws need not be filed with the secretary of state.

D. Corporate Combinations

Corporations may take control of other corporations or increase their size by a variety of means. One corporation may be merged into another, with all of the merged corporation's assets and property transferred to the survivor corporation. A corporation may purchase the assets of another corporation. One corporation may acquire sufficient stock in another corporation that it can assume control. The corporations involved in these transactions are usually called **constituents.**

Constituent
Party involved in a merger or other similar transaction

The reasons why such combinations take place are as varied as the means to accomplish the combination. A corporation may wish to acquire some special process or technology owned by another corporation; to diversify and expand its product line; or to rid itself of a competitor. These goals can be accomplished by merger, consolidation, a share exchange, acquisition of assets, or acquisition of stock. Because all of these combinations affect significant rights of shareholders, all are subject, to varying degrees, to the requirement of shareholder approval.

In tax terminology, mergers, consolidations, and share exchanges are called **reorganizations.** The various types of reorganizations have different names and different tax consequences. For example, the IRS calls mergers and consolidations *Type A Reorganizations.* An exchange of shares is referred to as a *Type B Reorganization,* and an acquisition of substantially all of the assets of another corporation in exchange for shares of the aggressor is called a *Type C Reorganization.* The Internal Revenue Code provides varying tax treatment for these different types of reorganizations.

Reorganization
Terminology used by IRS to classify various corporate combinations

1. *Mergers and Consolidations*

Merger
Combination of two or more corporations into one corporate entity

Mergers. State statutes permit the combination of two or more corporations into one corporate entity. This combination is called a **merger.** Because the merger process is controlled by statute, mergers are often referred to as *statutory mergers.* In the classic merger scenario, Corporation A combines with Corporation B. At the conclusion of the combination, one of the corporations (assume Corporation A) will cease to exist. The survivor, Corporation B, will acquire everything previously owned by Corporation A: its assets, its contracts, its rights, its debts, its obligations, and its shareholders. In the example given, Corporation A is referred to as the *merged corporation* or the **extinguished corporation.** Corporation B is called the **survivor.** Mergers can take place between two or more domestic corporations or between domestic and foreign corporations, so long as the laws of each corporation's state of incorporation are followed. Most state statutes prohibit mergers between corporations and other business entities, such as partnerships and limited liability companies. A merger between such different business entities is called a **cross-species merger** (or *interspecies merger*).

Extinguished corporation
Corporation that does not survive a merger

Survivor
Corporation that survives a merger

Cross-species merger
Merger between corporation and some other business entity (also called an *interspecies merger*)

Varieties of Mergers. There are several variations on the classic merger: the upstream merger, the downstream merger, the triangular merger, and the reverse triangular merger. Upstream and downstream mergers involve mergers between parent corporations and their subsidiaries. A corporation owned or formed by another corporation is called a **subsidiary.** The creator corporation is called the *parent.* On occasion, the parent may wish to merge the subsidiary back into itself, perhaps to eliminate the costs and paperwork involved in maintaining two corporations. If the parent owns at least 90 percent of the stock of the subsidiary, most states allow the merger to take place without approval of the shareholders of either the parent or the subsidiary. This type of merger is called a **short-form merger.** When the subsidiary merges into the parent and the parent is the survivor, it is called an **upstream merger.** When the parent merges into the subsidiary and the subsidiary is the survivor, it is called a **downstream merger.**

Subsidiary
Corporation formed by another, called the *parent*

Short-form merger
Merger of a subsidiary into a parent

Upstream merger
Merger between parent and subsidiary in which parent is survivor

Downstream merger
Merger between parent and subsidiary in which subsidiary is survivor

A **triangular merger** involves three parties or constituent corporations: a parent, its subsidiary, and a target corporation. The subsidiary merges with the target corporation and is the survivor, although the parent still owns that new entity. Rather than directly acquiring the target itself, the parent may wish to keep the subsidiary separate from it for diversification purposes or to protect itself from either the subsidiary's or the newly acquired target's liabilities. In a classic merger, the parent would be liable for the extinguished corporation's debts. In a triangular merger, the subsidiary remains liable for its own and the target's debts. In many instances, a parent creates a subsidiary for the sole purpose of accomplishing a triangular merger. The subsidiary is thus formed for the target to merge into it. The target is then extinguished, and the subsidiary survives separate and apart from its parent.

Triangular merger
Merger involving three parties in which target merges into parent's subsidiary and target is extinguished

A **reverse triangular merger** is substantially similar to a triangular merger, except that rather than the target being merged into the subsidiary, the subsidiary is merged into the target. The target then becomes the new subsidiary of the parent. This transaction may be used when the target's leases and other contracts cannot be assigned or transferred to another party; the target remains a party to the leases or other contracts and yet the parent reaps their benefits.

Reverse triangular merger
Merger involving three parties in which subsidiary merges into target and is extinguished and target become new subsidiary

Consolidations. A **consolidation** is closely similar to a merger. In this transaction, however, two or more corporations combine together and form an entirely new corporation, a different legal entity from either of the two constituent corporations involved. At the end of the consolidation, all of the combining constituent corporations cease to exist. The newly formed corporation acquires everything previously owed by the constituents: their assets, contracts, rights, liabilities, and shareholders. In a classic consolidation scenario, Corporation A combines with Corporation B to form Corporation X.

Consolidation Combination of two or more corporations into one new entity

The result of a consolidation can be effected by merger. For example, a parent may create a subsidiary corporation. The parent, subsidiary, and target enter into an agreement to merge whereby they agree that the parent and the target will merge into the newly formed subsidiary which was created for the express purpose of surviving the transaction. Because the effect of a consolidation can be achieved through such a merger, the RMBCA and some states no longer recognize consolidations. See Figure 14-3 for diagrams showing varieties of mergers and a consolidation.

Procedures for Effecting Mergers and Consolidations. Mergers and consolidations may be completed in various ways. The following issues may arise.

Director and Shareholder Approval. The procedures for accomplishing mergers and consolidations are the same. Any references in this section to mergers also include consolidations. The first step in the merger process is negotiation between or among the constituent corporations involved. These preliminary negotiations usually lead to a **letter of intent,** a letter-form document setting forth the basic understanding and intent of the parties. The letter of intent will eventually be replaced with a formal, definitive agreement; however, the letter is sufficiently detailed to outline the key terms of the transaction. (See Appendix K for a form of a letter of intent.) The negotiation process itself can be complex and take several months.

Letter of intent Initial document setting forth basic understanding of parties to a transaction

The constituent corporations must then prepare a **plan of merger.** The content of the plan of merger is generally regulated by statute. For example, RMBCA Section 11.01(b) provides that the plan of merger must set forth the following:

Plan of merger Document setting forth particulars as to planned merger

1. the name of each corporation planning to merge and the name of the surviving corporation;
2. the terms and conditions of the merger; and
3. the manner and basis of converting the shares of each corporation into shares or other securities of the survivor.

The plan of merger may include other provisions as well, such as amendments that will be required to be made to the survivor's articles of incorporation (perhaps a name change, creation of a new class of stock, and so forth).

The plan of merger is then submitted to the board of directors of each constituent corporation for its approval. After adopting the plan of merger, the boards of the constituent corporations must submit the plan for shareholder approval. The boards of directors must recommend the plan of merger (unless, because of conflict of interest or other circumstances, the board determines it should make no recommendation), and the shareholders entitled to vote must then ap-

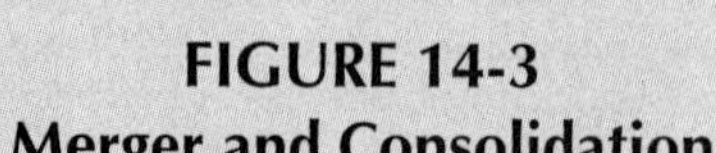

FIGURE 14-3
Merger and Consolidation

Merger

ABC + XYZ = ABC

Upstream Merger

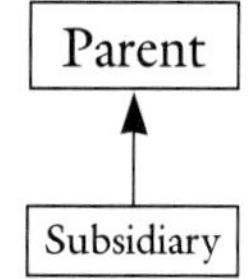

Parent + Subsidiary = Parent

Downstream Merger

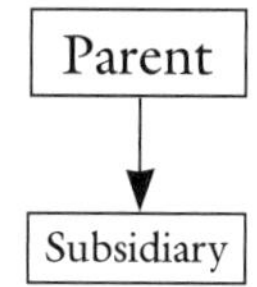

Parent + Subsidiary = Subsidiary

Triangular Merger

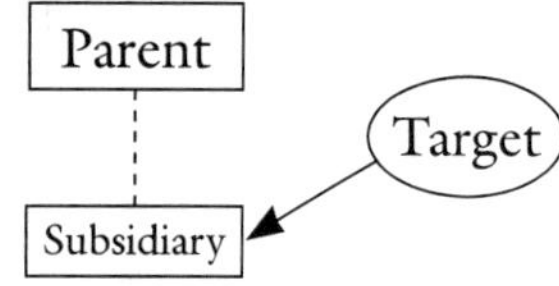

Target merges into parent's subsidiary and target is extinguished

Reverse Triangular Merger

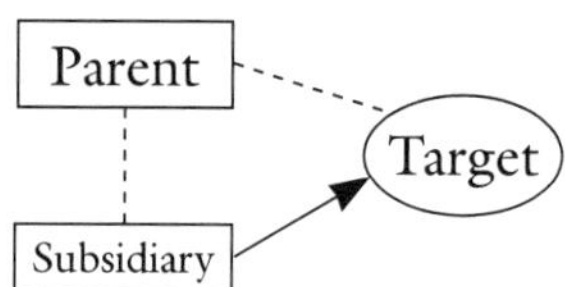

Subsidiary merges into target and subsidiary is extinguished and target becomes new subsidiary of parent

CONSOLIDATION

ABC + XYZ = LMN

prove the plan. Unless this activity takes place at or near the time of the annual meeting, the corporations will likely call special meetings of shareholders for approval, the notice of which must specify that the purpose of the special meeting is to consider the plan of merger. The notice must include a copy or summary of the plan of merger. The more modern approach and that of the RMBCA is to require a simple majority approval by the shareholders; many states, however, require two-thirds approval. Some states permit nonvoting shares of stock to vote on the merger. All shareholders, however, must receive notice of the meeting, whether or not they are entitled to vote. RMBCA Section 11.03(d). Furthermore, the notice must state whether the shareholders will have appraisal rights (discussed below). If so, shareholders must be provided copies of the statutes relating to appraisal rights.

Approval by shareholders of all constituent corporations is required due to the dramatic impact a merger (or consolidation) has upon the shareholders. The corporation owned by the shareholders of the merging corporation will be extinguished; such an extraordinary matter should be approved by the owners of that corporation. The corporation owned by the shareholders of the survivor corporation will likely be taking on debts, liabilities, and other obligations of the extinguished corporation. Additionally, share ownership in the survivor will be affected because the survivor must take in shareholders of the extinguished corporation and issue them shares of the survivor. This issuance of shares to the newcomers may cause a shift in power and control among the shareholders of the survivor. Thus, their approval is required.

Exceptions to Requirement of Shareholder Approval. There are generally two exceptions to the requirement that shareholders of all constituent corporations must approve a merger. First, a merger between a parent and subsidiary need not be approved by the shareholders of *either* corporation if the parent owns at least 90 percent of the outstanding stock of its subsidiary. RMBCA Section 11.04. This is the short-form merger discussed above. Shareholder approval is simply not needed; if the parent owns 90 percent or more of the subsidiary's stock and it desires that the subsidiary be extinguished, the parent has the necessary votes to make that happen. Voting by the subsidiary's shareholders would be a superfluous exercise. Similarly, voting by the parent's shareholders is not needed because the recapture of the subsidiary by the parent does not materially affect their share ownership.

The second exception provides that a merger need not be approved by the shareholders of the *survivor* corporation if the number of the survivor's voting shares outstanding after the merger (plus the number issued as a result of the merger) will not exceed by more than 20 percent the total number of voting shares of the survivor outstanding before the merger. This type of merger, often called a **small-scale merger,** does not dramatically affect the power and control of the shareholders of the survivor. Very little of the survivor's outstanding stock will be issued to any incoming shareholders; therefore, the survivor's shareholders need not approve the transaction.

Small-scale merger
Merger involving little transfer of survivor's stock to incoming shareholders

The RMBCA provides other instances in which shareholders of the *survivor* corporation are not required to vote on the merger: if the survivor's articles will not be changed as a result of the merger, or if each shareholder of the survivor will have as many shares with the same rights after the merger as before. RMBCA Section 11.03. All of these exceptions to the requirement of shareholder approval rest upon the same premise: shareholder approval of a merger is not needed when either the merger cannot be prevented or when the transaction has little impact upon the shareholders.

Rights of Dissenting Shareholders. It is possible that some shareholders are adamantly opposed to a merger; they may have philosophic or moral objections

Dissenting shareholders Shareholders who vote against merger or some other transaction

Appraisal right Right of dissenting shareholder to have shares purchased at their fair market value

to one or more of the constituents involved. Therefore, all states allow these **dissenting shareholders** the right to have their shares appraised and to receive the fair value of their shares as of the date of the merger in cash. This right is called the **appraisal right,** and it is a dissenting shareholder's exclusive remedy if she is opposed to a merger.

Dissenting shareholders must follow a fairly complex procedure in order to be entitled to appraisal rights. Generally, the shareholder must deliver a written notice of intent to demand payment for his or her shares. This notice must be delivered to the corporation before the vote on the merger is held and the shareholder must not vote in favor of the merger. Within ten days after the shareholders' meeting authorizing the merger, the corporation must deliver a written dissenters' notice to any shareholder who previously provided written notice of an intent to demand payment. The corporation must include a form for the dissenter to use to demand payment. The shareholder must return the form by a certain date; however, the shareholder must be given not less than 40 and not more than 60 days, per RMBCA Section 13.22. The corporation must estimate the fair value of the shares. The ultimate payment made to the shareholder must equal or exceed this estimate. Shareholders then surrender their certificates. Assuming compliance with these elaborate requirements have been met, the corporation will pay each dissenter the fair value of her shares, as of the time immediately before effectuation of the merger transaction, together with accrued interest. The payment will be accompanied by financial statements of the corporation. Any appreciation or depreciation of the stock in anticipation of the transaction will be excluded. If the dissenting shareholder objects to the corporation's valuation of the shares, the corporation will institute a judicial proceeding to determine the fair value of the shares. Unless the dissenting shareholder strictly and timely complies with the various statutory requirements, the corporation has no duty to pay the value of the shares.

Some states and the RMBCA allow partial appraisal rights so that a shareholder may dissent regarding some shares owned and be cashed out with respect to those shares, and remain a shareholder as to the remainder of the shares. Appraisal rights are not permitted in short-form mergers between a parent and subsidiary because the dissenting shareholder's vote was not necessary to approve the transaction. Similarly, there are no appraisal rights in small-scale mergers. A few states, including Delaware, do not allow dissent and appraisal rights if the shares are listed on a national exchange or if there are more than 2,000 shareholders of a class of shares. The basis for this exception is that if the shares are listed on a national exchange or if there are at least 2,000 shareholders, there should be ready and available buyers for the dissenter's shares. Similarly, RMBCA Section 13.02(b) provides that appraisal rights are not available if the shareholders' stock is traded on a national exchange or if there are at least 2,000 shareholders, and the outstanding shares have a market value of at least $20 million.

Articles of merger Document filed with state to effect merger

Articles of Merger. After the merger has been approved by the requisite shareholder vote, **articles of merger** must be prepared and filed with the secretary of state. The articles must set forth or attach the plan of merger and a statement regarding the approval of the plan of merger by the shareholders, including the number of votes for and against the merger. If shareholder approval was not required, the articles of merger must so state. See Figure 14-4 for form for cer-

FIGURE 14-4
Virginia Articles of Merger or Share Exchange

SCC720
(01/00)

GUIDE FOR ARTICLES OF MERGER OR SHARE EXCHANGE

ARTICLES OF (MERGER) (SHARE EXCHANGE) OF

_____ *(Names of corporations)* _____

The undersigned corporation(s), pursuant to Title 13.1, Chapter 9, Article 12 of the Code of Virginia, hereby execute(s) the following articles of (merger or share exchange) and set(s) forth:

ONE

(Set forth the plan of merger or share exchange.)

TWO

(State the reason why shareholder approval of the plan of merger was not required. See §13.1-718.G and 13.1-719) **OR**

(If shareholder approval of one or more of the corporations is required, with respect to each such corporation, set forth either A or B, below, whichever is applicable.)

(A.) The plan of (merger or share exchange) was adopted by unanimous consent of the shareholders. **OR**

(B.) The plan of (merger or share exchange) was submitted to the shareholders by the board of directors in accordance with the provisions of Chapter 9 of Title 13.1 of the Code of Virginia, and:

The designation, number of outstanding shares, and number of votes entitled to be cast by each voting group entitled to vote separately on the plan of (merger or share exchange) were:

Designation	No. of Outstanding Shares	No. of Votes
______	______	______
______	______	______

(i.) The total number of votes cast for and against the plan by each voting group entitled to vote separately on the plan were:

Voting Group	Total No. of Votes Cast **FOR** the Plan	Total No. of Votes Cast **AGAINST** the Plan
______	______	______
______	______	______

OR

(continued on the back)

FIGURE 14-4 *Continued*
Virginia Articles of Merger or Share Exchange

(ii.) The total number of undisputed votes cast for the plan separately by each voting group was:

Voting Group	Total No. of Undisputed Votes Cast **FOR** the Plan
____________	____________
____________	____________

and the number cast for the plan by each voting group was sufficient for approval by that voting group.

The undersigned *(chairman or vice-chairman of the board of directors, president, or any other of its officers authorized to act on behalf of the corporation [USE APPROPRIATE TERM])* declares that the facts herein stated are true as of______________, 20____.

______*(Name of corporation)*______

By: ______*(Signature)*______

______*(Printed name and corporate title)*___

(The articles must be similarly executed by each corporation that is a party to the merger.)

NOTE

If shareholder approval is required, the plan must be approved by each voting group entitled to vote on the plan by MORE THAN 2/3 of all votes entitled to be cast by that voting group unless the Act or the board of directors requires a greater vote or unless the articles of incorporation provide for a greater or lesser vote, but not less than a majority of all votes cast at a meeting at which a quorum exists (See § 13.1-718).

INSTRUCTIONS

1. The articles should be typewritten on white, opaque paper 8 1/2" by 11" in size. A minimum of a 1" margin must be provided on the left, top and bottom margins and 1/2" on the right margin. Use only one side of a page.

2. The Certificate of Merger cannot be issued unless the corporation has paid all fees and taxes assessed by the Commission.

3. The articles must be executed in the name of the corporation by the chairman or any vice-chairman of the board of directors, the president, or any other of its officers authorized to act on behalf of the corporation.

SEND THE ARTICLES ALONG WITH THE $25 FILING FEE PLUS ANY ADDITIONAL CHARTER FEE AMOUNT REQUIRED BY ANY INCREASE IN THE NUMBER OF AUTHORIZED SHARES OF THE SURVIVING CORPORATION TO THE CLERK OF THE STATE CORPORATION COMMISSION, P. O. BOX 1197, RICHMOND, VA 23218-1197. (Street address: 1300 East Main Street, Richmond, VA 23219.) PLEASE MAKE CHECK PAYABLE TO THE STATE CORPORATION COMMISSION. (804) 371-9733.

tificates or articles of merger. Some states require that the plan of merger be certified as approved and then filed with the secretary of state. A filing fee is required. Additionally, just as the original articles of incorporation and amended articles of incorporation may need to be published or filed with a county recorder, so may the articles of merger. New stock certificates and a new seal may need to be ordered.

The articles of incorporation of the survivor are deemed amended in accordance with the plan of merger; thus, there is often no requirement for the survivor to file a separate amendment of its articles of incorporation although most corporations do so to ensure their articles are current and can be read without reference to other documents. The secretary of state will examine the articles of merger, ensure that all taxes and fees have been paid, and then issue a certificate of merger. Many states allow a corporation to specify a later effective date for the merger so that simultaneous transactions may be completed in other states.

Upon the effective date of the merger, the merged corporation ceases to exist and the survivor takes over all of the extinguished corporation's assets, properties, personnel, shareholders, debts, obligations, and liabilities. The shareholders of the extinguished corporation, unless they have dissented and exercised their appraisal rights, will be issued shares of the survivor in return for their shares in the extinguished corporation.

Merger Trivia

- ◆ U.S. companies are five times more likely to acquire a foreign company than foreign companies are to acquire U.S. companies.
- ◆ Since 1995, the number of businesses seeking to merge has increased by 50 percent each year.
- ◆ The value of assets involved in mergers has increased eightfold since 1995.
- ◆ Corporations providing business services are the most likely to be involved in mergers, followed by those engaged in banking, and then those involved in communications. Pharmaceutical industries are increasingly engaged in mergers.
- ◆ The merger of Time Warner Inc. and America Online Inc., announced in early 2000, involves $165 billion.
- ◆ Foreign acquisitions of U.S. companies peaked in 1990 and have been steadily declining since that time.

2. *Share Exchanges*

Another way in which a corporation can gain control of another corporation is a share exchange. In a **share exchange,** both corporations may continue to exist; the target's shareholders exchange some or all of their shares for shares in the

Share exchange
Exchange of some or all of target's shares for shares in acquiring corporation

acquiring corporation (in which case the target becomes the subsidiary of the acquiring corporation), for cash, or for shares in some other corporation. The acquiring corporation is in an identical position to that of the survivor of a merger. Because a share exchange is so similar in its effect to a merger, all of the procedural formalities of a merger must be complied with, namely, approval of a plan of exchange by directors and shareholders of both the acquiring and the target corporations, provision of appraisal rights to dissenting shareholders, and filing of articles or a certificate of share exchange with the secretary of state.

Asset purchase
Purchase of assets of an entity, terms of which are found in *asset purchase agreement*

3. *Purchase of Assets*

A corporation may gain control of another or combine with another by purchasing all or substantially all of its assets, both tangible and intangible. The selling corporation may be paid for its assets in cash or in stock of the acquiring corporation. At the end of the transaction, the acquiring corporation owns additional assets, and the selling corporation is a mere shell, owning nothing other than the cash or shares it has recently received. After it has paid its liabilities and distributed the proceeds of the sale to its shareholders, it may dissolve.

An asset purchase also affords a corporation the opportunity to buy assets of an unincorporated entity, such as a partnership or a limited liability company. Because state statutes relating to mergers, consolidations, and share exchanges often refer to constituent *corporations,* a corporation cannot merge with a partnership or other noncorporate entity in those states. A corporation can, however, purchase the assets of a partnership or other noncorporate entity.

Because there is no change in the status of the legal entity of the acquiring corporation and it is simply buying additional assets, it need not secure the approval of its shareholders. The transaction is viewed as within the purview of the directors, who have the sole authority to manage the business affairs of the corporation. The selling corporation, however, is undergoing significant change and is disposing of all or substantially all of its assets, thereby impairing its ability to carry out its business. Therefore, the selling corporation must have approval by its board of directors and its shareholders and, in most states, must offer appraisal rights to its dissenting shareholders. A purchase of assets may therefore be more advantageous than a merger to an acquiring corporation; the purchase of another corporation's assets does not require shareholder approval, and, in most cases, the seller retains liabilities, having sold only its assets. Moreover, no public filings or amendments to articles are necessitated by the asset transaction.

A mere mortgage or pledge by a corporation of its assets as security to ensure or guarantee repayment of a loan is not viewed as a sale of assets. Thus, there is no need for shareholder approval. When the borrowing corporation repays the loan, the mortgage or pledge of the assets will be released and the corporation may continue its ordinary business.

A sale of assets in the ordinary course of a corporation's business does not require shareholder approval. For example, a real estate company may sell all of its inventory of properties without requiring shareholder approval because this is exactly the type of business activity the corporation should be conducting. Shareholder approval is required, however, if there is a sale, lease, exchange, or disposition of all or substantially all of a corporation's assets *not* within the ordinary course of business. Additionally, shareholder approval is not required if the assets of a subsidiary are being transferred to the parent corporation when the parent owns all of the shares of the subsidiary. Because the subsidiary cannot stop the sale, seeking approval would be futile and superfluous.

The procedure for effecting the purchase and sale of assets closely parallels the procedure for effecting mergers and consolidations. After a period of initial negotiation and a letter of intent setting forth the basic terms of the transaction (see Appendix K), the board of directors of the selling corporation recommends the transaction and then directs that it be voted upon by the shareholders, either at an annual meeting or a special meeting. All shareholders, even nonvoting shareholders, are entitled to notice of the meeting, which must state that the purpose of the meeting is to consider the sale of the corporation's assets. A description of the transaction must accompany the notice. The approval requirement is a simple majority under RMBCA Section 12.02(e) and in some states, and a two-thirds approval in other states. Most states require appraisal rights for dissenting shareholders. An *asset purchase agreement* will be prepared and signed by both parties. This agreement will identify the parties, list the assets being sold, disclose any pending claims or litigation involving the seller, provide for the method and terms of payment, specify a date and place for closing, and include provisions in the event of either party's default. A complete form of an asset purchase agreement is available from your instructor.

In an asset purchase, the acquiring corporation, in effect, "goes shopping," picking and choosing the assets it desires. It seldom, if ever, agrees to assume any liability of the target corporation, which will retain responsibility for its obligations and liabilities.

The sale of all or substantially all of a corporation's assets may trigger certain requirements of Article 6 of the Uniform Commercial Code relating to **bulk transfers,** the sale or transfer of the major portion of a company's business outside the scope of its ordinary course of business. To protect creditors of the selling corporation, the bulk sales provisions require that creditors of the selling corporation be given notice of the intended transfer. Failure to comply with the bulk sales requirements may invalidate the transfer as to creditors who did not receive proper notice. The pertinent state statutes should be consulted to determine if the selling corporation must comply with its state's bulk sales requirements.

Bulk transfer
Sale of all or substantially all of one's assets

4. *De Facto Merger Doctrine*

As noted, there are a variety of ways in which one corporation can gain control over another: it can merge another corporation into it; it can create a subsidiary to acquire a target; it can consolidate with another corporation and create a new legal entity; it can negotiate with a target corporation to exchange its shares for cash or other shares; it can purchase all or substantially all of the assets of another corporation. The determination as to which particular transaction should be selected depends on a variety of factors, including liability, shareholder approval issues, and taxation. For example, the net effect of an asset acquisition is strikingly similar to that of a merger, yet while a merger requires shareholder approval of both corporations involved, a corporation acquiring another's assets need not obtain its own shareholders' approval.

To ensure that shareholders are fully protected, the courts have developed what is called the **de facto merger doctrine.** The doctrine requires that corpora-

De facto merger doctrine
Legal principle that if a transaction has the effect of a merger, it must follow procedural requirements of a merger

tions comply with all of the formalities of a merger — board approval, shareholder approval, and appraisal rights for dissenters — if a transaction has the effect of a merger, no matter what the parties involved choose to call it. Thus, courts will carefully scrutinize transactions to ensure that shareholders have the ability to vote upon matters that dramatically affect their share ownership or may result in the assumption of liabilities. In brief, the doctrine allows courts to treat an acquisition as a merger if it is a merger "in fact," although it may not be a merger in name.

5. *Purchase of Stock*

Stock purchase
Purchase of shares of a corporation, terms of which are found in *stock purchase agreement*

A **stock purchase** is highly similar to an asset acquisition; however, in this transaction, the acquiring corporation (or acquiring individual) purchases all or substantially all of another corporation's stock rather than its assets. The target corporation usually becomes a subsidiary of the acquiring corporation or may merge into it. The acquiring corporation will be responsible for the debts and liabilities of the corporation whose stock is being acquired.

Many stock acquisition transactions involve negotiations between the management of the constituent corporations. The board of directors of the acquiring corporation seldom needs approval of its shareholders because the board is acting in the ordinary scope of business activities in determining that purchasing the stock is in the acquiring corporation's best interest. The management of the corporation whose stock is being acquired will pass a resolution recommending that the shareholders sell their stock to the acquiring corporation. Of course, the shareholders are free to decide whether or not to sell their stock. Stock acquisitions can be difficult to effect when there are numerous shareholders.

Ultimately, a stock purchase agreement will be negotiated and executed, at which time the acquiring corporation will become the owner of the outstanding shares of the other corporation. Because it owns the outstanding shares, it now controls the destiny of the target and may decide to dissolve the target, allow the target to function as a subsidiary, or merge with the target.

Tender offer
Public offer made by bidder to acquire shares in a target corporation

Rather than dealing with management of the corporation whose stock is being purchased, the acquiring corporation may deal directly with the shareholders of the target corporation in seeking to acquire their shares. A public offer made by the acquiring corporation to the shareholders of the target corporation is referred to as a **tender offer,** so called because the acquiring corporation is asking the shareholders to surrender, or tender, their shares to it. The price the acquiring corporation or individual will pay is higher than the stock's current market value. This increased price induces the shareholders to sell. If the target's stock is currently selling at $36 per share, and the acquiring corporation states it will pay $45 per share, it may be very difficult for shareholders to resist this inducement. The tender offer can be made contingent upon the acquisition of a specified number of shares by a specified date. For example, the acquiring corporation's tender offer can provide that it is willing to purchase 350,000 shares of the common stock of ABC, Inc. at $45 per share, if the purchases can be effected by December 15. If the requisite 350,000 shares are not tendered by December 15, the acquiring corporation has no obligation to purchase any of the shares.

The management of the target corporation may or may not know of the aggressor's plans. If it does, the transaction is usually consensual and the corporations will prepare and execute a stock acquisition agreement providing the terms and conditions of the transaction. If the target's management is unaware of the tender offer until it is made public, the acquisition is likely a *hostile* one, and the target may elect to defend itself aggressively from acquisition.

Federal securities laws strictly regulate tender offers. The Securities Exchange Act of 1934 provides that any person who purchases stock in a Section 12 company, and thereby owns more than 5 percent of a class of stock, must file an information statement with the SEC.

6. *Hostile Takeovers*

Introduction. Not all combinations of corporations are consensual. While many transactions involve months and perhaps even years of planning and negotiating by the constituents, some combinations occur without the consent of the acquired, or target, corporation. Because these combinations are not consensual, they are usually referred to as **hostile takeovers.**

Hostile takeover
Transaction pursued by bidder without support of target's management

Despite the media attention given to hostile takeovers in the past ten years, they still remain the exception rather than the rule. In most proposed combinations, after a period of negotiations the management of the constituent companies either ultimately disagree upon the transaction, in which case, it usually dies, or they eventually come to mutually agreeable terms. The boards of directors of the corporations involved then recommend the combination to the shareholders. In the hostile takeover, however, the aggressor or bidder goes over the head of the target's management and courts the shareholders directly. Often, such large amounts of cash are offered to the shareholders for their stock that they simply cannot resist the offer.

One corporation may wish to acquire another to expand its business operations, to acquire new technology and operations, or to eliminate competition. In some instances, the aggressor may set its sights on a target that should be operating more profitably but is not, perhaps due to poor management. The aggressor may believe that a takeover of the company and a replacement of management will result in increased profits. In those instances, management of the target naturally feels threatened and may develop a variety of defenses to ward off the takeover.

Not all takeovers involve large aggressors pitted against weak targets. In many instances, contests involve bids by smaller corporations or even individuals to take over corporations whose assets exceed their own.

Regulation of takeovers is accomplished through Section 13(d) of the Securities Exchange Act of 1934 regulating the reporting of acquisitions of stock that result in ownership of more than 5 percent of a class of stock, Section 14(d) of the 1934 Act regulating the making of tender offers, and the **Williams Act,** passed in 1968, which is basically a series of refinements to Sections 13 and 14 of the 1934 Act that apply to Section 12 companies. The intent of the Williams Act is to impose some structure and rules for tender offers and eliminate fraud by requiring certain disclosures by both aggressors and targets. It protects shareholders from

Williams Act
Statute regulating tender offers and takeovers

their own management as well as from the other corporation. Additionally, many states have enacted legislation regulating takeovers of their domestic corporations, generally to attempt to limit takeovers of locally based corporations that contribute significantly to the state's economy.

Preparing for the Takeover. Assume that both the aggressor and the target are publicly traded corporations. The aggressor's first step may be to build up a war chest of cash to finance the acquisition. It may borrow money or even sell some of its assets to acquire cash. The aggressor may collect information about the target, its management, and its operations in order to confirm that a takeover of the target is a sound decision. Some of this information is publicly available and on file with the SEC. Additional information may be acquired through private investigators or other sources, perhaps even rumor "on the street," the "street" being Wall Street.

The aggressor must then evaluate whether it wishes to attempt a consensual acquisition and deal with the target's management or whether it should appeal directly to the target's shareholders. Each technique has advantages and disadvantages. An approach to the target's management may yield significant accurate information about the target so that the aggressor does not pay too much for acquiring the target. On the other hand, if the target's management believes it is threatened, it may take immediate steps to thwart the transaction. An approach directly to the shareholders may result in overpaying for their stock, yet it has the distinct advantage of surprise, which may preclude the target's management from taking action to defend itself.

Assume the aggressor decides to proceed by surprise. It will usually begin purchasing the target's stock on the open market. To conceal its intent, the aggressor may place orders for the target's stock with different brokers in different cities using different names. Because a purchase of more than 5 percent of a class of stock requires disclosure and filings with the SEC, the aggressor often purchases up to 4.9 percent of the target's outstanding shares. This is called the **foothold** or *toehold*. An acute target will notice that its stock is being actively traded and that the increased trading is causing its stock to rise in value. The target may thus suspect an aggressor is planning a takeover, but it might not know the identity of the aggressor at this time. The target may begin adopting defensive strategies to ward off the anticipated aggressor.

Foothold
Acquisition of up to 4.9 percent of a target's stock (also called a *toehold*)

The Tender Offer. Rather than purchase shares anonymously on the open market, the aggressor may publicly announce a cash offer for as much of the target's stock as it needs to acquire all or majority control, in this case, 45.2 percent of the target's stock (45.2 percent + 4.9 percent = 50.1 percent). This is a tender offer. Because it would result in the aggressor owning more than 5 percent of a class of stock, the aggressor must comply with reporting and disclosure requirements of Section 14(d) of the 1934 Act. The aggressor must file the appropriate statement with the SEC (and provide a copy to the target), identifying itself, the source of the money being used to purchase the target's stock, how much of the target's stock it owns, and any plans it has for the target (such as liquidating it, selling its assets, merging it with another corporation, and so forth) in the event the tender offer is successful. The aggressor may continue to purchase stock during the tender offer period. Announcement of the tender offer is often done by advertisement or press release and is said to put the target "into play." The SEC has never defined the term tender offer, but it is usually referred to as a means by which one seeks to acquire control of a corporation by offering to buy a substantial portion of its shares at a pre-established price.

The tender offer is a public announcement specifying the identity of the bidder, price at which the aggressor will purchase the stock, the amount of stock it wishes to purchase, the date by which the shares must be tendered by the target's shareholders, and the identification of the place where the shares are to be tendered. For example, the aggressor may offer to buy 45.2 percent of the target's stock, at $43 per share, the offer to expire in 45 business days. The federal statute governing takeovers, the Williams Act, requires that the tender offer remain open for at least 20 business days. Shareholders must be given a right to withdraw their tenders, and all shareholders must be treated equally.

If the aggressor acquires 45.2 percent of the stock, it will have sufficient power to replace the majority of the target's board of directors and thereby effectively control the target corporation. If insufficient shares are tendered to give the aggressor 45.2 percent of the target's stock, the aggressor will return all the tendered shares and may decide not to proceed. At this point, the aggressor has invested only the amount of its toehold and some costs in attempting the takeover.

During the tender offer period, another aggressor corporation may enter the fray and offer to buy the toehold from the first aggressor. The first aggressor may sell this to the second at a substantial profit. The second aggressor will then proceed with the takeover.

Setting the price for the tender offer is highly complex. The aggressor needs to make the offer high enough to induce shareholders to tender their shares yet not so high as to be excessive and wasteful. Many tender offers range from 30 percent to 50 percent above the market price of the stock.

Tender offers can be partial in nature, in which case the bidder attempts to acquire only a majority interest in the corporation, or they can be full, in which case the bidder offers to buy all of the outstanding shares of the corporation. The bidder may offer cash only or a combination of cash and its own shares.

Oversubscription
Situation in which bidder acquires more stock than it offered to buy in its tender offer

If the shares tendered exceed the amount specified in the tender offer, the offer is **oversubscribed.** To avoid a stampede by shareholders to sell their stock without adequate time for reflection, the Williams Act requires that an oversubscribed tender offer must be effected on a pro rata basis rather than a "first come, first served" basis. Thus, the aggressor cannot simply elect to purchase the first shares tendered to it. For example, if the aggressor needs to purchase 10 million shares, and 12 million shares are actually tendered, it cannot buy the first 10 million tendered; it must purchase 10,000,000/12,000,000 (or 5/6) of each tender. Alternatively, the aggressor can elect to purchase all 12 million shares tendered.

During the period the tender offer is open, the aggressor cannot negotiate with individual shareholders or make purchases other than according to the tender offer. Once the tender offer period expires, however, it can negotiate privately with shareholders in attempts to acquire more shares.

Risk arbitrage
Speculation in target's stock

When a tender offer is made and the target is put into play, other investors may begin trading in the target's shares. For example, as soon as the tender offer is announced, speculators may begin buying the target's stock so that they can then tender the stock to the aggressor and make an immediate profit. This behavior is called **risk arbitrage,** and while it is hugely speculative, it can also be hugely lucrative. The danger to the risk arbitrageurs (the *arbs*), of course, is that insufficient shares will be tendered or some other force may make the aggressor's bid unsuccessful, leaving the risk arbitrageur holding stock that it paid dearly for in a target that is still weak and poorly managed.

Post-Tender Offer Transactions. If the aggressor abandons its takeover bid, much of the stock of the target may be in the hands of the risk arbitrageurs or other speculators who recently bought stock in the target only to make a profit and not for any desire to control the target, improve its management, or make it more profitable. Thus, if the tender offer is unsuccessful, either the aggressor or some other third party may deal directly with the risk arbitrageurs and other speculators to purchase the target's stock from them. This practice is called a **street sweep,** once again, the reference being to Wall Street. The SEC has proposed rules to prohibit street sweeps on the basis they are inherently unfair to small shareholders, who are not offered the opportunity to sell their shares inasmuch as typically only the arbs and speculators are approached to sell the target's stock.

Street sweep
Purchase of stock from speculators after an unsuccessful tender offer

If the tender offer is successful and the aggressor acquires a controlling interest in the target, the aggressor usually thereafter attempts to gain even more stock, with the ideal being ownership of 100 percent of the target's outstanding stock. No matter how attractive the offer is, however, some individual shareholders will refuse to sell their shares. To obtain 100 percent ownership, the aggressor will proceed with a **mop up** or *back end* **transaction,** essentially a merger, to obtain total ownership of the target's stock. Because there are so few shareholders left, they are powerless to stop a merger initiated by the target with its controlling shares of stock. While these holdouts may have appraisal rights as dissenters, often the appraisal right is not as attractive as the tender offer, thus encouraging shareholders to accept promptly the terms of the tender offer rather than being forced to sell their shares at a less attractive price later.

Mop up transaction
Attempt by bidder to secure 100 percent ownership in target after tender offer is complete (also called a *back end transaction*)

Proxy Fights. As an alternative to a hostile takeover, an aggressor corporation may solicit the target's shareholders with a proposal that they vote for the aggressor's management team. This is the **proxy fight;** both management and the aggressor will be attempting to obtain proxies from shareholders for election of their own directors. If the aggressor is successful, it effectively obtains control of the target through controlling the majority of the board. Once it has control of the board, it may negotiate a consensual merger. In general, it is more difficult to obtain control of a corporation through a proxy fight than through a tender offer, primarily because it is difficult to induce shareholders to vote out management. Shareholders would much rather be induced with the profit they can make by tendering their shares at above-market prices to the aggressor.

Proxy fight
Competition between corporate management and an aggressor to take over board of directors

Defensive Strategies. Corporations have developed a number of strategies to avoid being taken over. These **takeover defenses** may be developed even before a tender offer is made, to discourage a takeover bid in the first place, or may be adopted after a tender offer has been made, in an attempt by the target to defeat the aggressor. In general, the response of the target's management to the takeover bid is subject to the duty of due care. Directors of the target often set up takeover committees to evaluate the relative merits of the takeover to ensure that the board fulfills its duties. Thus, actions by the target's directors that are directed only to perpetuating their own status, rewarding themselves, and entrenching their positions may be breaches of fiduciary duty.

Takeover defenses
Strategies implemented by target to thwart a takeover

Many state statutes also operate to discourage takeovers. For example, Del. Code Ann. tit. 8, Section 203 imposes a moratorium for three years on combinations or mergers between the target and anyone who acquires 15 percent or more of the corporation's stock, unless the board of directors of the target had approved the transaction or the bidder owns more than 85 percent of the target's stock. Thus, once a bidder acquires 15 percent of a target's stock, it generally cannot engage in any back-end merger for three years.

Pre-Tender Offer Defenses. Provisions instituted before a takeover bid are generally designed to make the target less attractive to would-be aggressors. These provisions are usually called **shark repellents** or *porcupine provisions.* Among them are the following:

Shark repellents
Anti-takeover measures implemented before a takeover bid (also called *porcupine provisions*)

- A staggered board of directors may be introduced together with a provision that directors can only be removed "for cause." This approach means that it may take the aggressor several years to acquire control of the target's board. Of course, if the bidder acquires all or nearly all of the outstanding shares, it can amend the articles to "unstagger" the board.
- The corporation may grant directors, officers, and key employees **golden parachutes** requiring that these individuals, if ousted, are to be compensated in some extraordinary amount. The golden parachutes may make the takeover too expensive for the aggressor, as these contractual requirements must be satisfied by the aggressor before installing its own key people. Severance contracts for lower-level employees are sometimes called **tin parachutes** (or even *lead parachutes*).

Golden parachute
Highly favorable financial packages awarded to senior managers in event of a takeover or their retirement

Tin parachute
Financial packages awarded to junior managers in event of a takeover or their retirement; less favorable than golden parachutes

- The target may make itself unattractive by selling off certain assets or divisions, or distributing a huge cash dividend to its shareholders. Thus, the aggressor will be forced to acquire a cash-poor target with few desirable assets.
- The target may adopt a **poison pill** defense, also known as a *shareholder rights plan.* This defense is extremely popular and has been adopted by more than 90 percent of Fortune 500 companies. The poison pill defense is implemented as part of an anti-takeover program and is triggered by a tender offer made by a bidder. Once the tender offer is announced or an acquisition reaches certain limits, the target's shareholders are automatically given additional rights, including increased voting rights, the right to acquire additional shares or bonds of the target at bargain prices, or the right to turn in shares for cash if the takeover is successful. These rights granted to the shareholders make acquisition of control by a bidder far more difficult and nearly prohibitively expensive.

  Because aggressors might seize control of a board of directors and then deactivate the poison pill to avoid the shareholders' rights, targets have adopted the following variations or refinements to poison pill defenses.

  - A **dead-hand poison pill** is one that can only be deactivated by the directors who established it (or their designated successors). The dead-hand pill is also called a *continuing director plan.* In many instances directors eliminate the dead-hand by redeeming the purchase rights from shareholders by paying them a small fee. The dead-hand pill protects the target's current board be-

Poison pill
An anti-takeover measure triggered by a tender offer at which time the target's shareholders are given additional rights (also called *shareholder rights plan*)

Dead-hand poison pill
Poison pill that can only be deactivated by the directors who established it (also called a *continuing director plan*)

cause it can only be deactivated by those who continue after a takeover. Some states, notably Delaware, have held that dead-hand pills are invalid because they result in two different classes of directors: those who can deactivate the dead-hand and those who cannot. Moreover, dead-hand pills wrest too much control from shareholders.

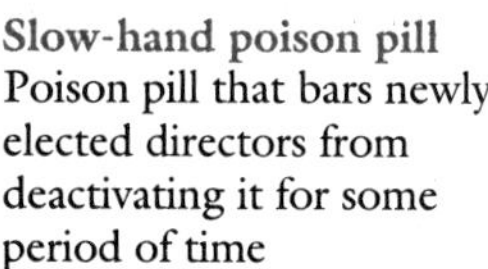

Slow-hand poison pill Poison pill that bars newly elected directors from deactivating it for some period of time

No-hand poison pill Poison pill that cannot be removed by any director if control of the board changes hands

Chewable poison pill Poison pill that is of short duration and is triggered only when a bidder buys significant numbers of shares

- A **slow-hand poison pill** is one that bars newly elected directors from deactivating or redeeming the pill for some limited period of time, often six months. Some states have also held slow-hand pills invalid on the basis that they impermissibly interfere with directors' abilities to manage the corporation.
- A **no-hand poison pill** provides that no director can remove the pill if control of the board changes hands.
- A **chewable poison pill** is one that is more palatable to shareholders and is one of short duration (often five years rather than the usual ten year term of a standard poison pill), is triggered only when a significant number of shares are purchased by a bidder (often 20 percent rather than the trigger threshold of 10 percent or 15 percent for most poison pills), and allows a takeover to proceed if it is fully financed and all cash, even if the incumbent board opposes it. Chewable poison pills are a recent innovation that appeal to shareholders.

In sum, poison pills are favored devices used to fend off takeovers, but there is some concern that they are used by an incumbent board to preserve power rather than for the best interests of the shareholders and the corporation. Thus, the enforceability of dead-hand, slow-hand, and no-hand poison pills is subject to much debate and uncertainty. In general, if poison pills and other defensive measures are adopted in good faith and are reasonable in relation to the threat by the bidder, they are acceptable and do not constitute breaches of the directors' fiduciary duties.

Post-Tender Offer Defenses. Once the cash tender offer has been made, the target may implement a variety of defenses in an attempt to thwart the aggressor. Some of these defenses are as follows:

- The target may attempt to find another more compatible corporation with which to merge. The third party is called the *white knight* because its function is to save the target from the enemy aggressor, often called the *black knight*.
- The target may turn the tables and make a tender offer to acquire the aggressor. This is the *Pac-Man* defense, because its effect is to eat up the opposition.
- The target may begin selling off some of its most valuable assets to make itself less attractive to the aggressor. This is the *crown jewel* defense.
- The target may engage in a *scorched earth* battle by selling off its crown jewels, loading the target up with debt, or through an immediate and sudden departure of all of the target's management, in an effort to avoid capture.
- The target may use the *Jonestown* defense and effectively commit suicide by going into liquidation.

- The target may quickly purchase another corporation engaged in a business substantially similar to the aggressor's business, thereby creating antitrust problems for the aggressor.
- The management of the target may enter into a so-called *suicide pact,* whereby managers agree that if any one of them is fired or demoted after a takeover, they will all resign. Such an en masse walkout leaves the aggressor without any stability or continuity in management.
- The target may attempt a *self-tender,* a purchase of its own shares on the open market or from its own shareholders so as to prevent the aggressor from acquiring control. Such a self-tender is subject to various SEC rules imposing disclosure requirements on the target much the same way that disclosure is required of an aggressor.

Most experts advise that companies keep a watchful eye on potential adversaries to avoid being taken over. Some measures recommended include early warning programs to detect stock purchases made in a company, working with corporate counsel to implement anti-takeover measures, and identification and monitoring of companies that might target a company. While such measures might not absolutely prevent a takeover, they may discourage a bidder from bypassing the board of directors and appealing directly to the shareholders through a tender offer.

Takeover Terminology. You may already have noticed that much of the terminology used in describing hostile takeovers and the defenses thereto has war-like connotations. First, the aggressor builds up a war chest to acquire the target. The target institutes a number of defensive strategies to avoid being captured, including adopting poison pill defenses, suicide pacts, and scorched earth tactics. A number of other colorful terms are also used in the jargon of hostile takeovers. Among them are the following:

Bear hug: An approach by the aggressor to the target after the aggressor has acquired its toehold. The aggressor meets with the target's management and makes clear that if the target does not cooperate in the transaction, the aggressor will pursue a hostile takeover.

Blitz: A "lightning," no-notice strike against a target sufficiently forceful that the target is so overwhelmed it cannot adopt any defenses.

Greenmail: A kind of legal corporate blackmail, in which an aggressor threatens to take over a target, and then sells the toehold back to the target at an inflated price. The target thus "buys" peace from the aggressor who has made money at *not* being successful at its takeover attempt. To discourage greenmail, high taxes are imposed on greenmail money.

Killer bees: Attorneys, advisors, and public relations teams retained by the target to fight off the takeover.

Midnight raid: A raid by an aggressor after the afternoon closing of the New York Stock Exchange and concluded before the resumption of trading in the morning by securing firm commitments from large institutional shareholders of the target to sell sufficient stock so that the aggressor can obtain control of the target before it is even aware a raid has begun.

Nuclear war: A hostile takeover involving numerous large publicly traded companies.

Preemptive strike: An extremely attractive offer made by an aggressor with the intent of obtaining immediate control of a target.

Saturday night special: A raid by an aggressor made over a weekend so that the target has difficulty marshaling its management forces. Some experts recommend that companies identify and establish a permanent takeover team, even before a tender offer is made, specifically to ward off a Saturday night special.

Standstill agreement: An agreement by an aggressor not to purchase any more shares of the target for some specified period of time, perhaps several years. The standstill agreement is usually part of the peace pact entered into between an aggressor and the target when the aggressor accepts greenmail to stay away from the target.

Stock watch: An early warning system employed by corporations to detect fluctuations in the market that might warn them of action by aggressors.

Strike team: The aggressor's legal counsel, investment advisors, public relations teams, and so forth.

7. *Leveraged Buy-Outs*

Leveraged buy-out
Purchase of a corporation's stock by its managers in order to take it private

A corporation may decide to "go private" through a relatively new transaction called the **leveraged buy-out** (or LBO). To avoid a takeover by an aggressor, management of a target may offer to purchase all of its publicly held shares from its own shareholders. Because of the enormous amount of cash required to buy out all of the existing shareholders, management typically borrows most of the funds, pledging various corporate assets as security or collateral for repayment of the debts. In some instances, a new entity may be created by management and investors. This new entity borrows the money needed for the buy-out and uses the funds to purchase all of the outstanding shares.

In some transactions, after the buy-out is complete and management (and perhaps other investors) owns all of the stock of the corporation, unneeded assets are sold to reduce the corporation's debt. Then the corporation will "go public" by offering shares at a price higher than management paid for the shares when it went private. If successful, this technique results in great profits for management as well as reduction of the corporation's debt. In other instances, the debt taken on by the corporation to finance the buy-out of all shareholders is so crippling the corporation does not survive.

Some companies buy back their own stock on the open market, primarily to increase demand for the shares in order to push the stock price up. Simultaneously, a stock buyback strategy increases earnings per share because it reduces the number of shares outstanding in the marketplace.

8. *Governmental Regulation*

Hart-Scott-Rodino Act
Federal statute requiring notification to government before mergers involving certain amounts or parties

The federal government has the authority to review mergers and acquisitions under the Clayton Act (15 U.S.C. Section 18) to ensure that such transactions do not impair competition and result in monopolies. Specifically, the **Hart-Scott-Rodino Antitrust Improvements Act** of 1976 ("HSR") requires that parties to certain merger transactions file notification with the government and wait for a certain period before closing a transaction. The waiting period, 30 days, allows the government to review the transaction and take action, if needed, to protect competition. The waiting period can be shortened upon request.

Generally, although there are several exceptions, if either party to the proposed transaction has total annual net sales or total assets of at least $100 million and the other party has annual net sales or total assets of at least $10 million and, as a result of the transaction, the acquiring party will hold more than $15 million of the acquired party's stock or assets, each party must complete a premerger notification form providing certain information about the parties and the transaction and file it with either the Federal Trade Commission or the Department of Justice, depending upon the industries involved. The filing fee is $45,000, regardless of the size of the transaction (although legislation is pending as of this writing to implement a sliding-scale fee depending on the size of the transaction involved). If the government does not object to the transaction or request additional information, the parties may proceed once the waiting period expires.

In its Annual Report to Congress for 1998, the FTC reported that the United States is in the "midst of a merger wave of unprecedented proportions." During fiscal year 1998, the number of premerger transactions reported to the FTC increased 28 percent over 1997 transactions and constituted a 200 percent increase over 1991 filings. Despite the increased number of mergers, government challenges remain few. For example, in 1999, the FTC challenged only 30 of nearly 4,700 transactions. The Department of Justice challenged just 51 transactions. When a transaction is challenged, the parties often enter into consent agreements, agreeing to divest certain assets, or they may restructure the transaction or even abandon it. Fines for HSR violations can run up to $11,000 per day.

Key Features of Corporate Changes and Combinations

- Significant changes to a corporation typically require shareholder approval.
- A corporation may amend its articles at any time by resolution by the directors followed by shareholder approval (either by majority or two-thirds vote). Articles of amendment must be filed with the state agency.
- A corporation may restate its articles to create one composite document superseding prior amendments; shareholder approval is unnecessary because nothing new is being added to the articles.
- Amending corporate bylaws is typically handled by directors without shareholder approval inasmuch as the bylaws regulate only the internal affairs of the corporation.
- A merger is the combination of two or more corporations into one corporate entity. The survivor succeeds to all of the business, debts, liabilities, and assets of the extinguished corporation. Shareholders of both corporations must approve the transaction.

- A consolidation is the combination of two or more corporations and the formation of an entirely new entity that succeeds to all of the business, debts, liabilities, and assets of the consolidating corporations. Shareholders of both corporations must approve the transaction.
- Shareholders who dissent from a merger or consolidation have the right to have their shares appraised and purchased from them at fair value.
- In a share exchange, the target's shareholders exchange their shares for cash or shares in the acquiring corporation.
- As an alternative to a merger, one corporation can purchase all or substantially all of another's assets. Liabilities are generally not purchased.
- One corporation can purchase a majority or all of another corporation's stock as a means of gaining control of a corporation. If the acquisition is consensual, all directors and shareholders will vote. In a hostile acquisition or takeover, the bidder bypasses the target's management and appeals directly to the shareholders.
- Hostile takeovers are regulated by the Securities Exchange Act of 1934. Once a bidder or aggressor acquires 5 percent of another corporation's stock, it must file a Section 13(d) statement with the SEC providing information about the proposed takeover.
- If a bidder makes a public offer offering to purchase more than 5 percent of a corporation's stock, a Section 14(d) statement must be filed with the SEC providing information about the offer and offeror. Such a public offer is called a tender offer.
- Corporations may enact a variety of defenses to ward off a takeover. Some are put into place even before the attempted takeover. One of the most popular defenses is a poison pill or shareholder rights plan, by which shareholders are given extra voting rights or rights to purchase more shares at fire sale prices once a tender offer is announced. Other defenses are implemented after a tender offer has been made.

E. Role of Paralegal

There are numerous tasks for paralegals engaged in changes to corporations or working in the field of mergers and acquisitions. The work is fast-paced, stressful, challenging, and document-intensive. Some of the typical tasks paralegals are involved in include:

1. Drafting minutes of directors' meetings or written consent actions authorizing amendment of the articles of incorporation, restatement of the articles of incorporation, or amendment of the bylaws.
2. Drafting notices of shareholders' meetings called to consider and vote upon amendments of the articles of incorporation; preparing the minutes of shareholders' meetings.
3. Preparing and filing articles of amendment and restated articles.
4. Preparing amended bylaws.

5. Drafting the minutes of directors' meetings or written consent actions authorizing and recommending mergers, consolidations, share exchanges, acquisition of assets, and acquisitions of stock; researching exceptions to the requirement of shareholder approval for such structural changes; preparing notices for shareholders' meetings called to consider and vote upon such transactions; preparing minutes of meetings at which shareholders voted on structural changes.
6. Reviewing and analyzing the plan of merger, plan of consolidation, plan of share exchange, or agreement for asset or stock purchase. Preparing a list of "to do" items and collecting various documents and records needed for the closing of the transaction, for example, reviewing pleadings for any litigation involving the acquired corporation, its directors, officers, or key employees.
7. Preparing and filing articles of merger, consolidation, or share exchange.
8. Preparing various documents needed to complete transactions, including assignments of various assets, trademarks, and copyrights; deeds for the transfer of real estate; notices for the SEC; new stock certificates to be issued to shareholders of extinguished corporations; notices relating to appraisal rights, and so forth.
9. Assembling documents for execution by the appropriate parties.
10. Arranging for the closing transaction, ensuring staff is available to assist in photocopying or faxing, ensuring a notary public is available to notarize signatures, if needed.
11. Preparing and compiling the closing binders so they contain all documents pertinent to the transaction, including the letter of intent, corporate authorizations, the plan or agreement, and all exhibits to such documents.
12. Conducting post-closing checks to ensure all documents have been signed by all appropriate parties, necessary filings have been effected with the secretary of state, recording of assignments or deeds has been accomplished with the appropriate local or federal agencies, and all documents required to be delivered by the other parties have been received.
13. Ordering new corporate supplies such as stock certificates and the corporate seal.

Resource Guide

1. Statutes

As always, the first and most critical resources to be consulted are the pertinent statutes: Sections 13(d) and 14(d) of the Securities Exchange Act of 1934, the Williams Act, and any state statutes relating to changes in corporate structure or combinations of corporations.

2. State Sources

Contact your secretary of state to obtain forms and filing fee information for the filing of articles of amendment, restated articles of incorporation, articles of merger, articles of consolidation, and certificate of share exchange.

3. Form Books

General form books will provide forms for resolutions and for minutes of meetings discussing and approving corporate changes such as amending or restating the articles of incorporation, mergers, and other corporate combinations. Forms for articles of amendment, restated articles, and articles of merger will also be provided. See Chapter Nine for specific identification of form books.

4. Texts and Articles

There are numerous texts and articles devoted to changes in corporate structure, with special emphasis on mergers and acquisitions. Many sources, such as C.J.S. and Am. Jur. 2d, tend to provide background and general information only, rather than practical advice and guidance. Texts can be located either through a manual or electronic card catalog at a law library. Articles can be located through *The Index to Legal Periodicals.*

5. Law Office or Department Resources

Similar to securities work, law firms tend to be either deeply involved in merger and acquisition work or not at all. The law firms routinely engaged as counsel to provide advice and assistance for mergers and acquisitions generally have extensive collections of books, journals, and other resources. Similarly, if you work in the legal department of a corporation, there will likely be a variety of books and treatises. Review closing binders for previous similar transactions to get acquainted with the type of documents you may be expected to prepare and to gain an overview of the organization of the closing binders you will likely compile.

After you have engaged in any combination transaction, prepare a memorandum for your own files of "lessons learned." This will be useful to you in the next transaction. Maintain copies of any checklists, agendas, or other documents that will be of assistance to you in the future. Perhaps the most useful skill for paralegals involved in the field of corporate changes and combinations is organization. Take copious notes at meetings, note telephone numbers and names of federal and state officials who were of assistance in providing information and forms, keep copies of documents, prepare a step-by-step manual for your use in the future or for training new paralegals in the department.

WEB RESOURCES

The most important Web resources are the state and federal statutes relating to amending and restating articles and corporate changes, such as mergers and consolidations.

www.ll.georgetown.edu

When you access this site for Georgetown University Law Center, select "State, Local & Territorial." You will be presented with a map of the United States. Point your cursor to the state in which you are interested, and you will be provided with links to a variety of legal sources relating to that state. Select "Statutes" or "Codes" and you will be linked to the state's statutes. In some states, searching can be done by either keywords or by section number. In other states, searching is accomplished exclusively by keywords.

Because many states have posted their forms relating to amending and restating articles and forms for articles of merger, consolidation, and share exchange on their Web sites, important Web resources are the home pages of the various secretaries of state. See Appendix A for the specific Web address for each of the state's secretaries of state. Other alternatives follow.

www.nass.org
This Web site of the National Association of Secretaries of State will provide you with links to each of the secretaries of state. After you access the home page of the Association, select "States." You will then be given an alphabetical list of all 50 states and the District of Columbia (together with their state flags). Point your cursor at the state you wish, and you will be immediately linked to the home page for that state's secretary of state. In most instances, you will immediately see entries for "Corporations" or "Securities." Select the relevant entry and you will be directed to the pertinent forms, nearly all of which can be downloaded and printed. Fee schedules are also included on the sites.

www.legalwiz.com
When you access this site, select "Legal Sites" and then "Corporate Department and Secretary of State Pages" for links to each state's secretary of state.

www4.law.cornell.edu/usccode
This excellent site allows searching of federal statutes by keyword or by section number. You can review all 50 titles of the U.S. Code or look up statutes by their popular names. The Securities Exchange Act of 1934, relating to the acquisition of stock and tender offers, is located in Title 15, entitled "Commerce and Trade," as is the Hart-Scott-Rodino Act.

http://www.law.uc.edu/CCL/intro.html
This site offers "The Securities Lawyer's Deskbook," including the full text of the basic federal securities laws and regulations as well as forms required by the SEC to comply with those regulations.

www.sec.gov
This Web site of the Securities and Exchange Commission is a gateway to small business information, current SEC rules, enforcement actions, and, most importantly, EDGAR, the database of registration statements and periodic reports. Additionally, one can review the Section 13(d) and 14(d) statements filed by companies that have acquired 5 percent or more of the stock of another corporation or that have made tender offers for stock of other companies. Generally, one can locate the forms and information by name of the company, type of document or form, or date of the issuance or report. A great deal of financial information is provided, all of it at no cost. Not all documents filed with the SEC will be available on EDGAR; most filings after May 1996 are available. Filings are posted to the site about 24 hours after submission to the SEC.

www.freedgar.com
This commercial site allows free unlimited access to SEC EDGAR filings. Searching can be done by company name or stock ticker symbol. Companies can also be tracked by a "watchlist" that notifies you by e-mail when any company designated by you submits an electronic filing to the SEC.

http://edgarscan.pwc.global.com
PriceWaterhouseCoopers' site offers "EdgarScan," an interface to the documents filed with the SEC, allowing you to go directly to specific sections of the filings.

www.companylink.com
This site provides news, research, and contacts for more than 65,000 companies. Enter either the company's name or stock ticker symbol, and you will be provided with basic information about the company.

www.hoovers.com
When you access this site, covering most large companies, select the "Main Directory." Then select "Company Directory A-Z" for capsule descriptions of companies, their addresses, company officials, competitors, and other valuable information.

For forms for resolutions and minutes of meetings authorizing amending articles and bylaws, restating articles, and mergers, consolidations, and share exchanges, see the following sites, which are described in more thorough detail in Chapter Nine:

www.siccode.com/forms.php3

http://legal-resource.com/forms/d.cgi[IDNUMBER]
This site also includes a form for a stock purchase agreement.

Discussion Questions

Fact Scenario. Harris Brothers Manufacturing Corp. ("Harris") is a Delaware corporation formed in 1980 and whose stock is publicly traded on NASDAQ. It has recently changed its focus from the manufacturing of machinery to the manufacture of components for wireless communications devices. Its stock has been trading at $50 per share, and there are one million outstanding shares.

1. Harris would like to change its name to reflect the change in the focus of the company's business. How can this be effected?

2. Assume that the name change is the fifth change to the corporation's articles of incorporation. What would you suggest so that the articles are more readily comprehensible to readers?

3. Harris has been approached by Jacobson Wire Inc. ("Jacobson"), one of its biggest competitors, to merge into Jacobson, which will survive the transaction. What will happen to Harris' debts, assets, and shareholders? Which shareholders of which corporation may vote on the transaction? What if shareholders are opposed to the transaction?

4. Assume that due to increased trading in its stock, Harris has begun to suspect that it is a potential target of a takeover. Discuss some defensive tactics Harris can adopt to attempt to ward off the bidder.

5. Blakely Enterprises, Inc. has decided to make a tender offer for all of the stock of Harris. What SEC requirements are imposed on Blakely with regard to this offer?

6. Assume that Blakely Enterprises, Inc. is purchasing Harris' stock on the open market and has purchased 48,000 shares. What SEC requirements are imposed on Blakely with regard to this purchase?

15

Qualification of Foreign Corporations

CHAPTER OVERVIEW

Corporations may be formed in one state and yet do business in others. You have seen that many large corporations have elected to incorporate in Delaware due to its moderate fees and taxes and permissive statutes. Most of these corporations transact business in several other states.

In order for a foreign corporation to lawfully conduct business in a state other than the state of incorporation, it must "qualify" or become authorized to do business there. In general, most states require that the foreign corporation file an application to transact business, appoint an agent for service of process, and pay the appropriate filing fees and taxes. The corporation will then receive permission from the secretary of state to conduct business. Failure to qualify may result in fines being imposed on the corporation or a refusal to allow the corporation to sue or defend itself in that state. When the corporation ceases to conduct business in a state, it should formally withdraw from doing business as a foreign corporation.

A. Basis for Qualification

A corporation incorporated in a state is a **domestic corporation** in that state. Because recognition of corporate status is granted only by each state's secretary of state, the corporation has no legal existence beyond the borders of the state in which it was incorporated. To conduct intrastate business (business conducted wholly within the borders of a single state) in other states, the corporation must

Domestic corporation
Corporation doing business in the state in which it was formed

be granted authority; it must qualify to do business in those states. A corporation doing business in states other than its state of incorporation is a **foreign corporation** to those states.

Foreign corporation Corporation doing business in a state other than the state in which it was formed

The qualification requirement imposed on foreign corporations provides a way for states to protect their citizens. Requiring qualification ensures that citizens have some basic information about the corporation (by reviewing its articles of incorporation filed in its state of incorporation) and are able to sue the corporation and serve its registered agent in the state.

The decision to conduct business in other states begins with the board of directors. Upon seeing the need for expansion into other states, the board will pass a resolution (or act by written consent) authorizing the officers to take any needed action so the corporation can transact business in another state or states. Hopefully, the decision to expand into other jurisdictions has been carefully thought out, and the corporation's name has been registered in the foreign state so it is available to the corporation for use (see Figure 15-1) or the corporation has incorporated a subsidiary to serve as a "name saver" for the same purpose.

Just as corporations must qualify to do business in states other than their state of incorporation, so also must limited partnerships, limited liability partnerships, and limited liability companies. (See discussion in Chapters Four, Five, and Six.) Most states provide the pertinent forms for qualifications for these entities.

B. Transacting Business

Transacting business Generally, statutory list of activities in which a corporation can engage in a foreign state without being required to qualify to do business therein

Generally, most state statutes provide that a foreign corporation cannot "**transact business**" within the state until it obtains a certificate of authority from the secretary of state. The critical question, and one that has resulted in much litigation, is what particular activities are considered transacting business such that qualification is required? What if a Minnesota corporation has its annual shareholders' meeting in California? Is that transacting business? What if the Minnesota corporation wishes to sue an individual who has moved from Minnesota to Wisconsin? Must the corporation qualify to do business in order to institute the litigation in Wisconsin?

To reduce litigation over this issue, many states have enacted statutes enumerating certain activities that may be engaged in by a foreign corporation without having to qualify in the state. RMBCA Section 15.01(b) states that the following activities do not constitute transacting business:

1. maintaining, defending, or settling any proceeding;
2. holding meetings of the board of directors or shareholders or carrying on other activities concerning internal corporate affairs;
3. maintaining bank accounts;
4. maintaining offices or agencies for the transfer, exchange, and registration of the corporation's own securities or maintaining trustees or depositories with respect to those securities;
5. selling through independent contractors;
6. soliciting or obtaining orders, whether by mail or through employees or agents or otherwise, if the orders require acceptance outside the state before they become contracts;

FIGURE 15-1
Illinois Foreign Corporation Name Application

Form **BCA-4.25**
(Rev. Jan 1999)

APPLICATION FOR REGISTRATION, RENEWAL OR CANCELLATION OF FOREIGN CORPORATION NAME

File #

Jesse White
Secretary of State
Department of Business Services
Springfield, IL 62756
Telephone (217) 782-9520
http://www.sos.state.il.us

SUBMIT IN DUPLICATE

This space for use by Secretary of State

Date

Filing Fee $

Approved:

Payment must be made by certified check, cashier's check or a money order, payable to "Secretary of State."

1. CORPORATE NAME: ______________________
2. STATE OR COUNTRY OF INCORPORATION: ______________________
3. Date of incorporation: ______________________
4. Business in which the corporation is engaged: ______________________
5. Post office address of the corporation to which the Secretary of State may mail notices:
6. The corporation desires to register its corporate name pursuant to Section 4.25, and it is not transacting business in the State of Illinois at this time.
7. Attached to this application is a certificate setting forth that the corporation is in good standing under the laws of the state or country wherein it is organized, executed by the proper officer of the state or country wherein it is organized, which certificate shall not be more than ninety (90) days old.
8. Check the appropriate box:
   - ☐ The fee for registration is $50.
   - ☐ The fee for renewal is $50.
   - ☐ The fee for cancellation is $25.
9. Such registration or renewal of registration shall be effective from the date of filing by the Secretary of State until the first day of the twelfth month following such date.
10. The cancellation shall be effective upon filing with the Secretary of State.
11. The undersigned corporation has caused this statement to be signed by its duly authorized officers, each of whom affirms, under penalties of perjury, that the facts stated herein are true.

Dated ______________ (Month & Day), ______ (Year) ______________________ (Exact Name of Corporation)

attested by ______________________ (Signature of Secretary or Assistant Secretary) by ______________________ (Signature of President or Vice President)

______________________ (Type or Print Name and Title) ______________________ (Type or Print Name and Title)

C-197.5

7. creating or acquiring indebtedness, mortgages, and security interests in property securing the debts;
8. securing or collecting debts or enforcing mortgages and security interests in property securing the debts;
9. owning, without more, real or personal property;
10. conducting an isolated transaction that is completed within 30 days and that is not one in the course of repeated transactions of a like nature; and
11. transacting business in interstate commerce.

This list is not exhaustive, and other activities may also not constitute "transacting business" such that qualification would be necessary.

Some states have similar lists, while others provide no statutory guidance whatsoever. In such instances, case law from the state will need to be analyzed to determine what sorts of activities have been considered in the past to be "transacting business." Because qualifying is a rather straightforward procedure, any doubts regarding the issue should be resolved in favor of qualification. Qualification will, however, subject the corporation to service of process in that state as well as to various reporting requirements, fees, and taxes.

C. Procedures in Qualification

Qualifying to transact business
Process of seeking permission from foreign jurisdiction to do business therein

All states have statutes setting forth the requirements for **qualification** of foreign corporations. Most states have forms available from the secretary of state's office. The requirements vary slightly from state to state; however, most states require that detailed information be contained in an application by a foreign corporation for authority to transact business. The name of the foreign corporation must comply with the statutes of the state in which it seeks authority to transact business. Thus, it may need to include a corporate signal such as "Inc." or "Corp." Moreover, the name cannot be the same as or confusingly similar to that of a domestic corporation of the state or another foreign corporation already authorized to do business in the state. If the name is not available, the corporation may have to operate under an assumed or fictitious name. To reduce the chances of such an unwelcome possibility, the corporation should register its name in any states in which it intends to do business in the future or set up a "name saver" subsidiary in those states so its name will be available for future use. (See Chapter Nine for discussion of name registration and name savers.) Alternatively, the corporation may be able to secure approval from the other corporation to use a similar name.

Identification of the state under whose law the foreign corporation is incorporated is also necessary. This information is required so potential investors can conduct investigation of the foreign corporation. Moreover, the date of incorporation and period of duration, the street addresses of the foreign corporation's principal office and its registered office in the state in which it is qualifying and the name of the registered agent at that office are also required. A qualified foreign corporation must maintain a registered office in each state in which it transacts business. The registered agent may be an individual who resides in the state or a domestic corporation or another qualified foreign corporation. The function of the registered agent is to receive service of process. Most statutes provide that if there is no registered agent or no registered agent can be readily found, the secretary of state of the foreign state will receive service of process on behalf of the foreign corporation. Many corporation service companies provide their services to corporations to act as registered agents for foreign corporations. CT Corporation System acts as the registered agent for more than 240,000 corporations. A list of service companies is provided at the end of Chapter Nine and this chapter.

The names and usual business addresses of the corporation's current officers and directors must be provided. This information can be used by potential investors to investigate the backgrounds of the principals of the corporation before investing in the corporation.

Other states may impose additional requirements, such as requiring a description of the business the foreign corporation proposes doing in the state, an identification of the value of the assets of the corporation and its liabilities, or description of its stock.

The application must usually be accompanied by a **certificate of good standing** issued by the secretary of state of the state of incorporation. This is obtained from the state of incorporation upon request and payment of a fee. The secretary of state will check various state records to ensure the corporation is in *good standing*, meaning that it has paid its taxes and complied with any reporting requirements. This certificate will be presented to the foreign state as a method of assuring it that the foreign corporation will comply with the foreign state's tax and reporting requirements. (See Figure 15-2 for the application for certificate of authority to transact business in Delaware.) Some states require that the qualifying corporation provide a certified copy of its articles of incorporation from its state of incorporation.

Certificate of good standing
Document issued by state of incorporation verifying corporation is in compliance with state requirements

Upon filing with the secretary of state, the application will be examined to ensure it complies with the statutory requirements and that the requisite filing fee has been paid. The secretary of state will then issue a certificate of authority. The foreign corporation may then transact business so long as it adheres to the requirements of the foreign state.

D. Effects of Qualifying

There are four primary effects on foreign corporations that have qualified to do business in another state.

1. The foreign corporation will be subject to any restrictions imposed on domestic corporations. For example, a corporation formed in New Jersey and operating a gambling casino will be precluded from operating casinos in Nebraska, inasmuch as Nebraska does not permit its own domestic corporations to operate for gambling purposes. The corporation is now subject to various restrictions in its state of incorporation as well as any foreign state in which it has qualified to do business. Its internal affairs, however, such as amending its bylaws, giving notice of meetings, and other similar matters, are governed by the state of incorporation.

2. The foreign corporation will be subject to service of process in the new state. Service of process upon the registered agent in the foreign state is as effective as service of process upon the corporation's agent in its own state of incorporation.

FIGURE 15-2
Delaware Foreign Corporation Certificate

STATE *of* DELAWARE
FOREIGN CORPORATION CERTIFICATE

- **The Undersigned,** a corporation duly organized and existing under the laws of the State of ____________________, in accordance with the provisions of Section 371 of Title 8 of the Delaware Code, does hereby certify:

- **First:** That ____ is a corporation duly organized and existing under the laws of the State of ____________ and is filing herewith a certificate evidencing its corporate existence.

- **Second:** That the name and address of its Registered Agent in said State of Delaware upon whom service of process may be had is __________________________________ ____.

- **Third:** That the assets of said corporation are $______________ and the liabilities thereof are $______________. The assets and liabilities indicated are as of a date within six months prior to the filing date of this Certificate.

- **Fourth:** That the business which it proposes to do in the State of Delaware is as follows: ____ ____.

- **Fifth:** That the business which it proposes to do in the state of Delaware is the business it is authorized to do in the jurisdiction of its incorporation.

- **In Witness Whereof,** said corporation has caused this Certificate to be signed on its behalf and its corporate seal affixed this ______ day of _____________, 20_______.

BY: ________________________________
(Authorized Officer)

NAME: ________________________________
(Type or Print)

3. The corporation must pay various taxes to the state which has permitted it to transact business within its borders. Some states assess an annual license or franchise fee for the privilege of doing business. These fees vary from state to state. Similarly, foreign corporations will be required to pay any other taxes imposed on domestic corporations in that state, such as income taxes.

4. The corporation must file annual reports with the state. The annual report is generally a fairly simple form sent to the corporation by the secretary of state and usually requires the following information: the name of the corporation; the address of its registered office in that state and the name of its registered agent at that address; the address of the corporation's principal office; the names and addresses of its directors and officers; a statement of the number of shares the corporation has the authority to issue, itemized by class (namely, common and preferred); a statement of the number of shares already issued; and a statement of the amount of paid-in capital of the corporation. To determine the amount of taxes or fees the corporation will pay, the annual report usually requires statements regarding the value of all of the property owned by the corporation and the value of property owned by the corporation and located in that particular state; the gross amount of business transacted by the corporation and the gross amount of business transacted in that particular state. The reporting requirements are usually identical for domestic and foreign corporations.

E. Effects of Failure to Qualify

Although they vary from state to state, sanctions are imposed on corporations that have transacted business without first having qualified to do so. RMBCA Section 15.02 provides the following penalties for transacting business in a foreign jurisdiction without authority:

1. the foreign corporation may not maintain a proceeding in any court in the foreign state until it obtains a certificate of authority; and
2. monetary penalties will be imposed for each day the corporation was not properly qualified (not to exceed a stated amount).

Some states, adopting a harsher approach, provide that any acts performed by the unqualified corporation are void, that its contracts are unenforceable, that it cannot bring or defend an action, that fines may be imposed directly on corporate directors and officers as well as fines for each day the corporation was in violation of the state statutes, and that the attorney general of the state can enjoin the corporation from conducting any further business. Moreover, the corporation will be liable for any back taxes or fees it should have paid during the period in which it was transacting business in the state as well as penalties thereon.

The more permissive approach and that adopted by the RMBCA is to refuse an unqualified corporation to maintain legal action. It may, however, defend itself in any legal action, and its failure to qualify will not impair the validity of its acts or the contracts it entered into during the period of nonqualification. Most states allow a corporation that has failed to qualify to cure the defect by subsequent qualification, even during a lawsuit. Nevertheless, various penalties may still be imposed on the corporation.

Thus, whenever there is a doubt regarding whether a corporation should qualify to do business in another state, it may be wise to resolve the doubt in favor of qualification, particularly if not qualifying subjects the corporation to the risk of excessive fines, being precluded from defending itself, or having its contracts declared invalid.

F. Effect of Changes to Domestic Corporation

Just as domestic corporations must inform the secretary of state of a change of corporate name, a merger, or a change in purposes, so also must a corporation qualified to transact business in a state inform that state of such changes.

Generally, when a corporation amends its articles of incorporation in its state of incorporation it must also file a certified copy of the amended articles in any state in which it transacts business as a foreign corporation. RMBCA Section 15.04 requires that a foreign corporation obtain an amended certificate of authority if it changes its name, its period of duration, or the state in which it is incorporated. (See Figure 15-3 for the Illinois application for amended certificate to transact business.) A corporation that wishes merely to change its registered agent and/or registered office address usually files a separate and less complex form. Filing fees will be imposed for either of these forms. Additionally, there may be certain time limits with which the foreign corporation must comply. For example, in Illinois, an application for amended certificate of authority to transact business in Illinois must be filed within 90 days after the corporation has changed its name, duration, or purpose.

If the foreign corporation merges with another and is the surviving entity, it must generally file a copy of the articles of merger with the secretary of state of the foreign jurisdiction.

G. Withdrawal of Foreign Qualification

Withdrawal
Process of canceling authority to do business in a foreign state

When a corporation ceases doing business in a state in which it has qualified as a foreign corporation, it should file an application for **withdrawal.** This will ensure that the corporation is no longer subject to service of process, taxes, or annual reporting requirements in the state.

The application for withdrawal form is usually provided by the secretary of state. It generally includes the corporation's name and state of incorporation and specifies that the corporation surrenders authority to transact business in the state and revokes the authority of its registered agent to receive service of process. (See Figure 15-4 for a sample form for application for certificate of withdrawal.) The secretary of state is then authorized to receive any later process. The corporation must provide an address so that the secretary of state can forward any process for any action filed against the corporation. Many states and the RMBCA also require a commitment to notify the secretary of state of any later change in the mailing address. Finally, some states require that certain financial information be

FIGURE 15-3
Illinois Application for Amended Certificate to Transact Business

Form **BCA-13.40**
(Rev. Jan. 1999)

APPLICATION FOR AMENDED CERTIFICATE OF AUTHORITY TO TRANSACT BUSINESS IN ILLINOIS

File #

Jesse White
Secretary of State
Department of Business Services
Springfield, IL 62756
Telephone (217) 782-1837
http://www.sos.state.il.us

Remit payment in check or money order, payable to "Secretary of State."

SUBMIT IN DUPLICATE

This space for use by Secretary of State
Date
Filing Fee $ 25.00
Approved:

1. (a) CORPORATE NAME: ______

   (b) **If changed,** NEW CORPORATE NAME: ______

   (c) (Complete only if the new corporate name is not available in this state.)
   ASSUMED CORPORATE NAME: ______
   (By electing this assumed name, the corporation hereby agrees NOT to use its corporate name in the transaction of business in Illinois. Form BCA 4.15 is attached.)

2. (a) State or Country of Incorporation: ______

   (b) If changed, Period of Duration: ______

3. If changed, Purpose or Purposes proposed to be pursued in transacting business in this State:
   (If not sufficient space to cover this point, use reverse side or add one or more sheets of this size.)

4. **This application is accompanied by a copy of the articles of Amendment to the Articles of Incorporation, if any, as evidence of any change of name, duration or purpose reported herein, such copy being duly authenticated by the proper officer of the state or country wherein the corporation is incorporated, which certification is not more than ninety (90) days old. The filing fee for the certified copy of the Articles of Amendment is $25 unless the amendment acts as a restatement of the Articles of Incorporation, in which case the filing fee is $100. In the event the statutory change was effected in a merger, a certified copy of the merger is required, plus applicable fee.**

5. The undersigned corporation has caused this statement to be signed by its duly authorized officers, each of whom affirms, under penalties of perjury, that the facts stated herein are true. (All signatures must be in **BLACK INK**.)

Dated ______ , ______ ______
(Month/Day) *(Year)* *(Exact Name of Corporation)*

attested by ______ by ______
(Signature of Secretary or Assistant Secretary) *(Signature of President or Vice President)*

______ ______
(Type or Print Name and Title) *(Type or Print Name and Title)*

C-196.8

FIGURE 15-4
Louisiana Application for Withdrawal of a Foreign Corporation

W. Fox McKeithen Secretary of State	APPLICATION FOR WITHDRAWAL OF A FOREIGN CORPORATION FROM THE STATE OF LOUISIANA (R.S. 12:312)	
	Foreign Corporation Enclose $100.00 filing fee Make remittance payable to Secretary of State *Do not send cash*	Return to: Corporations Division P.O. Box 94125 Baton Rouge, LA 70804-9125 Phone (504)925-4704

STATE OF_______________________________

PARISH/COUNTY OF_______________________

____ a corporation
Corporation Name

organized under the laws of the state of ________________________, county of __________________

is no longer transacting business in the State of Louisiana, effective the ________________________ day of

_________________, 19 ________, and surrenders its authority to transact business in the State of Louisiana; revokes the authority of its registered agent to accept service of process, and consents that service of process in any action or proceeding based on any cause of action arising out of or resulting from or connected with any business transacted by it in this State during the time the corporation was authorized to transact business in this state, be made on the corporation by service thereof on the Secretary of State, or on a person in his office designated to receive service of process on corporations; such service, if made on the Secretary of State shall be mailed to:

____

Dated at ______________________________ on the _________ day of _____________, 19______.

____
To be signed by any officer

On this ___________ day of ___________________, 19 _____, personally came and appeared before me

____ who being by me duly sworn, declared that he/she is the

____ of ________________________________

that he/she executed the foregoing document as ____ of the corporation, and that the statements therein contained are true.

____
Notary Date

338 Rev. 7/97 (See instructions on back)

provided, such as a statement of the number of shares that have been issued and a statement of the amount of paid-in capital of the corporation.

Upon receipt of the application for withdrawal and the filing fee therefor, the secretary of state will check to make sure all taxes and fees have been paid and will then issue a certificate of withdrawal. The corporation is then no longer authorized to transact business in the state and no longer subject to any of its laws or requirements.

H. Revocation of Qualification by State

In some instances, a state in which a foreign corporation has qualified to transact business may revoke that authority or qualification. Typically, revocation of the certificate of authority of a foreign corporation is triggered by some unlawful act by the corporation or failure to comply with the state's laws and requirements. The most common reasons for revocation are failure to file annual reports, failure to pay taxes, failure to have a registered agent or to inform the secretary of state of a change in the registered agent, filing a document with the secretary of state that is false, or dissolution or disappearance of the corporation as a result of merger. Some states, such as Illinois, will revoke the certificate of authority if the foreign corporation has not conducted business in the state for one year and has no tangible property there.

Most states provide a delinquency notice to the corporation before revoking the authority of the corporation to transact business in the state. The corporation is usually given some stated period (typically 30 to 90 days) to correct its default. If the default is not corrected, the secretary of state will issue a certificate of revocation that recites the grounds for revocation and the corporation will no longer have any authority to conduct business in the state.

In many states, a corporation may seek to be reinstated, especially if authority to transact business in the foreign jurisdiction was revoked due to failure to file an annual report, pay taxes, or some other similar administrative reason. Reinstatement is an easier process than seeking to requalify to transact business in the foreign jurisdiction.

Key Features of Foreign Qualification

- Corporations that intend to transact business in other states must "qualify" or be approved by the foreign jurisdiction prior to commencing business in those states.
- Not all activities are considered to be "transacting business" such that a corporation must qualify in the foreign state. Some activities are considered relatively peripheral or isolated and thus do not require qualification.

- To qualify, the corporation must complete the foreign state's form and pay a filing fee. The corporation must have an agent for service of process in the foreign jurisdiction. Qualification will result in the corporation being amenable to service of process in the foreign state and will require the corporation to file annual reports and pay various taxes and fees to the foreign jurisdiction.
- If a corporation transacts business without qualifying, it is usually forbidden from instituting action in that state's courts and is usually subject to monetary fines and penalties. A few states take a harsher approach and provide that acts engaged in while the corporation was not qualified are void and that it cannot defend itself in court.
- When a corporation makes changes in its state of incorporation, it should conduct research to determine if foreign jurisdictions in which it operates must be notified of those changes.
- Once a corporation ceases doing business in the foreign jurisdiction, it should withdraw its qualification.

I. Role of Paralegal

Once the determination has been made by corporate management to expand into other states, the paralegal's involvement will begin. An application for name registration or an application for name reservation should be filed after determining availability of the corporate name in the new jurisdiction. The expiration dates for the name registration or name reservation should be calendared so that the application for qualification will be filed on time.

The paralegal should review the appropriate state statutes to determine the process of qualifying to transact business as a foreign corporation. Particular attention should be given to the state's definition of "transacting business." The secretary of state's office should be contacted so that appropriate forms can be gathered.

Almost all of the activities needed to qualify a foreign corporation to transact business in another state can be handled by the paralegal. The paralegal should make arrangements for an agent for service of process on the corporation. An attorneys' service may be used as the agent (see list following). The paralegal should obtain a certificate of good standing from the secretary of state in the state of incorporation as well as a certified copy of the articles of incorporation. The application for authority to transact business should be completed. Upon receipt of the certificate of authority granted by the secretary of state, the paralegal should calendar the dates for payment of taxes and annual reporting. If the corporation is engaged in business in several states, a separate file should be maintained for each state, together with a master list identifying all states in which the corporation is qualified to do business, the date such qualification became effective, and the dates for any reporting requirements or tax payments.

If amendments are made to the articles, an amended application should be timely filed. Similarly, changes in the address of the principal office or registered agent should be reported to the secretary of state on the appropriate forms. Finally, if the corporation ceases to do business in the state, the paralegal can prepare and file the application for withdrawal of qualification.

If the law office or corporate counsel's office do not have complete sets of forms for qualifying in all states, contact the secretary of state for each state and order the forms so they will be available for use in the future.

Resource Guide

There are five resources that will be of assistance to paralegals involved in qualifying corporations to do business in other jurisdictions.

1. State Statutes

Because qualification of foreign corporations is regulated slightly differently by each state, the most critical resource is the corporations code for the state in which the corporation intends to qualify to do business. The code will set forth the definition of "transacting business" and enumerate any activities not considered "transacting business" (or annotations will direct you to cases interpreting the meaning of the phrase). The statutes will also identify the documents required to be completed by a corporation intending to qualify to do business in the state.

If the state corporations code is not readily available, check *Martindale-Hubbell Law Directory* for brief overviews of the corporate statutes of all 50 states and the District of Columbia. The state statutes for all states should be maintained at the largest law library in your area (either at the courthouse or at a law school library).

2. Secretary of State

Using Appendix A, call the office of the secretary of state of the foreign jurisdiction and ask that all forms relating to qualification of foreign corporations be sent to you (the application form, amendment of application form, change of registered agent/registered office form, withdrawal of certificate of authority form) together with the current fee schedule. Copy these forms (so long as they are not copyrighted) so they are available for use by your office in the future. Most states provide these forms free of charge.

3. Law Office Forms

Check the forms already available at your office. If the forms are available, contact the secretary of state simply to verify the filing fee and whether the form is still current (most forms have numbers and dates on them).

4. WESTLAW

WESTLAW provides access to corporate records from all states and the District of Columbia. Access the ALLCORP database to determine the states in which a corporation conducts business.

5. Service Companies

The various corporation service companies can effect qualification of corporations in other jurisdictions. Because the process is fairly straightforward, however, it may be more cost-effective to complete the process yourself.

The following service companies can assist in qualification procedures:

Attorneys Corporation Service, Inc.
4664 North Lankershim Blvd.
North Hollywood, CA 91602-1884
phone: (800) 462-5487

CT Corporation System
1633 Broadway
New York, NY 10019
phone: (800) 624-0909

The Company Corporation
1013 Centre Road
Wilmington, DE 19805
phone: (800) 542-2677
www.corporate.com

[Note: CT Corporation System offers a pamphlet articulately presenting information on the topic of qualifying to do business in other states. Ask for the booklet entitled *What Constitutes Doing Business.*]

◆ ◆ ◆

WEB RESOURCES

The most important resources relating to qualification of foreign corporations are the various state statutes, especially the statutes that enumerate the activities that constitute "transacting business" such that a foreign corporation must qualify in that state.

www.ll.georgetown.edu
When you access this site for Georgetown University Law Center, select "State, Local & Territorial." You will be presented with a map of the United States. Point your cursor to the state in which you are interested, and you will be provided with links to a variety of legal sources relating to that state. Select "Statutes" or "Codes," and you will be linked to the state's statutes. In some states, searching can be done by either keywords or by section number. In other states, searching is accomplished exclusively by keywords.

Because nearly all states have posted their forms relating to name reservations and qualification of foreign corporations on their Web sites, important Web resources are the home pages of the various secretaries of state. See Appendix A for the specific Web address for each of the state's secretaries of state. Other alternatives follow.

www.nass.org
This Web site of the National Association of Secretaries of State will provide you with links to each of the secretaries of state. After you access the home page of the Association, select "States." You will then be given an alphabetical list of all 50 states and the District of Columbia (together with their state flags). Point your cursor at the state you wish, and you will be immediately

linked to the home page for that state's secretary of state. In most instances, you will immediately see entries for "Corporations" or "Securities." Select the relevant entry, and you will be directed to the pertinent forms, nearly all of which can be downloaded and printed. Fee schedules are also included on the sites. In some states, you can check name availability for the foreign corporation on the Web site. For example, California and North Carolina allow one to check the state database to make a preliminary determination of name availability.

www.legalwiz.com
When you access this site, select "Legal Sites" and then "Corporate Department and Secretary of State Pages" for links to each state's secretary of state.

www.ss.ca.gov/business/bpd_service_comapnies.htm
This Web site of the State of California identifies numerous companies and individuals that will serve as registered agents for service of process in California.

www.state.de.us/corp.htm
This Web site of the State of Delaware identifies more than 70 companies that will serve as registered agents for service of process.

The following sites can be used to review forms for directors' resolutions and minutes of meetings authorizing qualification in foreign states:

http://legal-resource.com/forms

www.siccode.com/forms.php3

www.lectlaw.com

Discussion Questions

Fact Scenario. Lowell Home Decorating, Inc. ("Lowell") is a corporation organized in Georgia, which is engaged in the business of interior decorating and design.

1. Lowell intends to branch out and begin offering its services throughout Florida and Mississippi within the next two years. What should Lowell do now to plan for this expansion?

2. At present, Lowell has taken on one decorating job in South Carolina for a friend of the president of the company. The job is a small one and will be complete within ten days. Is this "transacting business" within the meaning of the RMBCA?

3. The secretary of state in Florida has informed Lowell that its name is not available in Florida. What options should Lowell consider?

4. Assume that Lowell amended its articles of incorporation in Georgia to add a class of preferred stock. What filings, if any, might be required in the other states in which Lowell has qualified to transact business?

5. The decorating service has not been successful in Mississippi. What should Lowell do?

6. Lowell has amended its bylaws to provide for a staggered board of directors. Assume that a state in which Lowell is qualified does not permit a staggered board. Whose law controls?

16

Termination of Corporate Existence

CHAPTER OVERVIEW

Just as a corporation can only be created by strict compliance with state statutes, it can only be terminated or dissolved in accordance with state statutes. There are two types of dissolution: voluntary dissolution, initiated by the directors, or occasionally, the shareholders, and involuntary dissolution, initiated by the state, shareholders, or creditors. Dissolution ends the corporation's life as a legal "person."

Before allowing a corporation to dissolve, a state must be assured that all of the business of the corporation has been completed, that creditors have been paid, and that shareholders have received any assets remaining after payment of creditors. This process of wrapping up the business affairs of the corporation is called liquidation. When dissolution is voluntary, corporate management will oversee the liquidation process; when dissolution is involuntary, a court will oversee the liquidation process.

The corporation's existence is formally ended with the filing and acceptance of articles of dissolution with the state of incorporation.

A. Dissolution

1. *Introduction*

Corporations may dissolve for any number of reasons. It is possible that the term of duration specified in the articles of incorporation has expired. Absent a specified period of duration, however, a corporation will continue in existence until it is expressly dissolved. Termination of the corporation's existence as a legal entity is referred to as **dissolution.** Dissolution may be caused for a variety of business reasons: the corporation may be unprofitable or even insolvent; its business activities may have ended; it may have merged into another corporation; or its assets may have been acquired by another corporation.

Dissolution
Termination of the legal status of an entity

Dissolution can be initiated by the corporation itself, namely, its directors or shareholders, in which case the dissolution is **voluntary,** or it may be dissolved against its will, by the state, its shareholders, or creditors, in which case the dissolution is referred to as **involuntary.**

Voluntary dissolution
Dissolution initiated by a corporation's directors or shareholders

Involuntary dissolution
Dissolution against the will of a corporation, initiated by state, shareholders, or creditors (also called *judicial dissolution*)

In some states, the corporation is dissolved upon receipt of the requisite vote by the directors and shareholders or upon entry of a judgment by a court, if the dissolution is judicial. In other states, such as California, the corporation is not deemed dissolved until the secretary of state accepts and approves articles of dissolution.

2. *Voluntary Dissolution*

A corporation may be dissolved at any time after it is formed, even before shares have been issued to any shareholders. In this case, if no directors have been named, the incorporators who formed the corporation will dissolve it. Otherwise, the initial directors will dissolve the corporation. In most cases, however, a corporation dissolves after it has named directors, appointed officers, issued shares, and conducted business. Once shares have been issued, shareholders must approve the decision to dissolve because shareholders are the actual owners of the corporation. A voluntary decision to dissolve the corporation may originate with the directors or with the shareholders.

Typically, the decision to dissolve is initiated by the directors. As the ultimate managers of the corporation, they are in the best position to know whether dissolution is called for or whether the corporation should continue its operations. The directors will propose dissolution and this will be approved at a directors' meeting, by majority vote, or by written consent, which usually must be unanimous.

The directors will recommend dissolution to the shareholders and must call a special meeting of shareholders to vote on the proposed dissolution (unless the matter can be considered at an annual meeting). Notice of the special meeting must generally be given to all shareholders, whether or not they ordinarily have voting rights. The notice must state that the purpose of the meeting is to consider dissolution.

The more modern approach, followed in Delaware and by the RMBCA, is to require a simple majority vote of shareholders in order to approve dissolution (unless the corporation's articles require a greater vote). Many states, however, require two-thirds approval by shareholders. Some states allow all shareholders to vote; others allow only shareholders holding voting stock to vote on the dissolution. Shareholders are seldom given any right to dissent and have their shares appraised; they will share in any assets remaining after creditors have been satisfied.

In many states, the next step in the dissolution process is for the corporation to file a notice with the secretary of state indicating its intent to dissolve. The RMBCA does not require this public notice but simply provides that after dissolution is authorized, the corporation may proceed to dissolve by filing articles of dissolution with the secretary of state. Some states require that all creditors of the corporation also receive a notice stating the corporation's intent to dissolve. Alternatively, many jurisdictions allow the notice of intent to be published in a legal newspaper in the county in which the corporation's principal office is located. The purpose of these notices is to inform the public and the corporation's creditors that the corporation is dissolving; this allows corporate creditors and other claimants to submit claims for debts owed to them. (See Figure 16-1 for Statement of Intent to Dissolve.)

Some jurisdictions refer to the notice of intent to dissolve as the *certificate of dissolution*. The more common approach requires the filing of two documents with the secretary of state: the **notice of intent to dissolve** and the *articles of dissolution* (called the **certificate of dissolution** in some states). The confusion in the names of the documents is relatively minor: the corporation must generally notify the state of its intent to dissolve by some form of written statement and then must file a document that will actually effect the dissolution, whether the document is called articles of dissolution or certificate of dissolution. During the time between the filing of the two documents, the corporation will wind up its business affairs so that the final document can recite that no debts remain unpaid. It will not carry on any ordinary business activities, except those appropriate to winding up and liquidation.

Notice of intent to dissolve
Document filed with state indicating corporation's intent to dissolve

Certificate of dissolution
Final document filed with state effecting termination of an entity (more commonly called *articles of dissolution*)

Some states allow shareholders to initiate the decision to dissolve. In most instances, when dissolution originates with the shareholders unanimous approval is required. The shareholders can act by unanimous written consent. The requirement for unanimous consent is based upon the fact that because shareholders do not manage the corporation, they are not likely to be in the best position to evaluate whether dissolution is wise. On the other hand, if *all* of the owners of the corporation agree that it should be dissolved, there is no logical reason it should not be.

Articles of Dissolution. After dissolution has been approved by both the directors and the shareholders, articles of dissolution are prepared and filed with the secretary of state in the state of incorporation. Most states provide forms for the articles of dissolution. (See Figure 16-2 for sample articles of dissolution.) The articles must generally set forth the following items:

1. the name of the corporation;
2. the date dissolution was authorized;
3. that the dissolution was approved by the requisite shareholder vote (or that the corporation has not issued shares and therefore it is being dissolved by the incorporators);
4. that all debts, obligations, and liabilities of the corporation have been paid or discharged or adequate provision has been made therefor; and
5. that the corporate assets have been distributed to the persons entitled thereto.

The articles of dissolution are filed in the office of secretary of state with the appropriate filing fee. The secretary of state will usually require that the corporation submit appropriate documentation showing it does not owe any outstanding taxes to the state. Most states supply forms for tax clearance. Failure to provide the tax clearance form will result in rejection of the articles of dissolution. Additionally, the corporation must notify the Internal Revenue Service that it is

FIGURE 16-1
Maine Statement of Intent to Dissolve

Filing Fee $20.00

DOMESTIC
BUSINESS CORPORATION

STATE OF MAINE

STATEMENT OF INTENT TO DISSOLVE

(Written Consent of All Shareholders)

____
(Name of Corporation)

____________________ Deputy Secretary of State
A True Copy When Attested By Signature ____________________ Deputy Secretary of State

Pursuant to 13-A MRSA §1102, the undersigned corporation intends to dissolve the corporation.

FIRST: The names and respective addresses of its officers and directors are:

Title	Name	Address
President	____________	____________
Treasurer	____________	____________
Secretary	____________	____________
Clerk	____________	____________
Directors:	____________	____________
	____________	____________
	____________	____________

SECOND: Exhibit A attached hereto is a copy of the written consent signed by all shareholders of the corporation, or signed in their names by their duly authorized attorneys.

THIRD: All required Annual Reports have been filed with the Secretary of State. (Note: If the dissolution process is completed on or before June 1st, then the Annual Report covering the previous calendar year is not required.)

FOURTH: The undersigned corporation understands that the filing of this document ***DOES NOT*** complete the dissolution process. You must ***ALSO FILE*** Articles of Dissolution.

FIFTH: The address of the registered office of the corporation in the State of Maine is ____________________

____
(street, city, state and zip code)

FIGURE 16-1 *Continued*
Maine Statement of Intent to Dissolve

DATED ____________________

*By ______________________________________
(signature)

____
(type or print name and capacity)

*By ______________________________________
(signature)

____
(type or print name and capacity)

MUST BE COMPLETED FOR VOTE OF SHAREHOLDERS
I certify that I have custody of the minutes showing the above action by the shareholders.
______________________________________ (signature of clerk, secretary or asst. secretary)

Notice of the filing of this statement shall be mailed to each known creditor of the corporation and to the State Tax Assessor pursuant to 13-A MRSA §1106.2.

---

*This document **MUST** be signed by (1) the **Clerk** **OR** (2) the **President** or a vice-president ***and*** the **Secretary** or an assistant secretary, or such other officer as the bylaws may designate as a 2nd certifying officer **OR** (3) if there are no such officers, then a majority of the **Directors** or such directors as may be designated by a majority of directors then in office **OR** (4) if there are no such directors, then the **Holders**, or such of them as may be designated by the holders, **of record of a *majority* of all outstanding shares** entitled to vote thereon **OR** (5) the **Holders of all of the outstanding shares** of the corporation.

SUBMIT COMPLETED FORMS TO: CORPORATE EXAMINING SECTION, SECRETARY OF STATE,
101 STATE HOUSE STATION, AUGUSTA, ME 04333-0101
TEL. (207) 287-4195

FORM NO. MBCA-11 Rev. 96

FIGURE 16-2
Sample Articles of Dissolution

ARTICLES OF DISSOLUTION

Pursuant to section 607.1403, Florida Statutes, this Florida profit corporation submits the following articles of dissolution:

FIRST: The name of the corporation is:____

____

SECOND: The date dissolution was authorized:___________________________________

THIRD: Adoption of Dissolution (CHECK ONE)

☐ Dissolution was approved by the shareholders. The number of votes cast for dissolution was sufficient for approval.

☐ Dissolution was approved by vote of the shareholders through voting groups.

The following statement must be separately provided for each voting group entitled to vote separately on the plan to dissolve:

The number of votes cast for dissolution was sufficient for approval by

____
(voting group)

Signed this ________ day of __________________________, ________.

Signature ____
(By the Chairman or Vice Chairman of the Board, President, or other officer)

____
(Typed or printed name)

____
(Title)

dissolving and make arrangements to pay federal taxes. The corporation should also withdraw its authority to transact business in any states in which it has qualified to do business (see Figure 15-4). Once the secretary of state reviews and approves the articles, the corporation ceases to exist.

Revocation of Dissolution. Almost all states allow corporations to revoke the decision to dissolve. Generally, the revocation of dissolution must be authorized in the same manner as was the dissolution. Typically, approval by the board and then the requisite vote of shareholders is needed. The corporation then files articles of revocation of dissolution (see Figure 16-3), usually within some specific time period after the dissolution. RMBCA Section 14.04 provides that a corporation may revoke its decision to dissolve within 120 days of the effective date of the dissolution. The RMBCA also provides that the revocation relates back to the date of dissolution so that it is as if the dissolution had never occurred. Many states permit a revocation only if the corporation has not begun to distribute its assets.

3. *Involuntary Dissolution*

State statutes allow for the dissolution of corporations even when dissolution is not desired by the board of directors. This is referred to as an involuntary dissolution or, because the dissolution proceeding is brought before a court, an involuntary dissolution is also called a **judicial dissolution.** A corporation can be forced to dissolve against its will by the state, its shareholders, or unsatisfied creditors.

Judicial dissolution
Dissolution brought before a court (also called *involuntary dissolution*)

Actions by the State. Corporations exist only by virtue of the authority of the state of incorporation. Because a state always has the power and authority to ensure compliance with its laws, a corporation can be dissolved by its creator, the state of incorporation. An action for involuntary dissolution is usually brought in the name of the state attorney general, the individual in each state charged with enforcing the laws of the state.

Generally, the grounds for dissolution by the state include the following:

1. failing to pay taxes or file annual reports, failing to have a registered agent for some period of time (often 60 days), continuing to operate after the corporation's period of duration expires, or failing to notify the state that its registered agent or office has changed (grounds of this nature are often called *technical*—or *administrative*—*defaults*);
2. procuring the articles of incorporation through fraud; or
3. exceeding or abusing the authority given to the corporation by the state.

Many states provide notice to the corporation of technical defaults and give the corporation an opportunity to cure the defaults. A number of states also allow a corporation to petition for reinstatement within a certain period of time after it has been dissolved on technical grounds. The corporation must cure the default. If the corporation is reinstated, it is as if the dissolution never occurred. If the prior name of the corporation is no longer available, it must select a new name

FIGURE 16-3
Illinois Articles of Revocation of Dissolution

Form **BCA-12.25** (Rev. Jan. 1999)	**ARTICLES OF REVOCATION OF DISSOLUTION**	File #
Jesse White Secretary of State Department of Business Services Springfield, IL 62756 Telephone (217) 782-2353 http://www.sos.state.il.us		*SUBMIT IN DUPLICATE* **This space for use by Secretary of State** Date
Remit payment in check or money order, payable to "Secretary of State."		Filing Fee $ 5.00 Approved:

1. Corporate name: ______________________________

2. The Certificate of Dissolution was issued on ______________ (Month & Day), ______ (Year).

3. The corporation has not begun to distribute its assets and has not commenced a proceeding for court supervision of its winding-up.

4. A resolution revoking the dissolution was adopted on ______________ (Month & Day), ______ (Year)

   ☐ By a majority of the incorporators, no shares having been issued and no directors having been named in the articles of incorporation nor elected by the incorporators, as of the time this action was taken.

   ☐ By a majority of the Board of Directors.

5. The undersigned corporation has caused these Articles of Revocation of Dissolution to be signed in its name by its duly authorized officers, each of whom affirms, under penalties of perjury, that the facts stated herein are true. (All signatures must be in BLACK INK.)

If the action was taken by the Board of Directors, sign as follows below.

Dated ______________ (Month & Day), ______ (Year) ______________________ (Exact Name of Corporation)

attested by ______________________ (Signature of Secretary or Assistant Secretary) by ______________________ (Signature of President or Vice President)

______________________ (Type or Print Name and Title) ______________________ (Type or Print Name and Title)

If the action was taken by the incorporators, a majority of them must sign.

Dated ______________ (Month & Day), ______ (Year) ______________________ (Corporation Name)

By ______________________ ______________________

______________________ ______________________

______________________ ______________________

C-153.8

and file an amendment to its original articles of incorporation. (See Figure 16-4 for an application for reinstatement.) Generally, if the grounds for dissolution were not technical, a corporation may not be reinstated.

The RMBCA takes a modern approach to involuntary dissolution by the state. Rather than instituting a court action, the state petitions for dissolution of the corporation based on technical defaults in an administrative proceeding brought by the secretary of state. RMBCA Section 14.20 and many states refer to this proceeding as **administrative dissolution.** The most common grounds for administrative dissolution are failure to pay taxes when due, failure to file the corporation's annual report, or failure to have a registered office or agent for some period of time, often 60 days. The corporation is given notice of the grounds for dissolution and an opportunity to cure the defect. If the defect is not corrected, the secretary of state will sign and file a certificate of dissolution. **Reinstatement** is allowed within two years after the effective date of dissolution based on technical defaults. After reinstatement, the corporation may continue doing business as if the administrative dissolution had never occurred.

Administrative dissolution
A dissolution initiated for technical or administrative defaults, such as failing to file reports or pay taxes

Reinstatement
Process of reviving a corporation dissolved for administrative reasons

Dissolutions on the basis of procuring the articles through fraud or by exceeding or abusing the state's authority are instituted in court by the state attorney general and are referred to as *judicial dissolutions* by RMBCA Section 14.30. Generally, reinstatement is not available after a judicial dissolution.

Action by the Shareholders. If directors act fraudulently or waste corporate assets, it may be nearly impossible for a voluntary dissolution to occur. The negligent directors will not pass a resolution to dissolve a corporation they are in the process of looting, and, if the directors own stock in the corporation, unanimous shareholder consent is impossible, because acting in their capacity as shareholders, the directors will not vote for dissolution.

In situations such as these, a shareholder can institute a legal action and request that a court dissolve the corporation. To prevail, the shareholder must generally establish:

1. the directors are deadlocked in managing the business affairs of the corporation and irreparable injury is being threatened to the corporation to the detriment of the shareholders;
2. corporate management has acted in an illegal, oppressive, or fraudulent manner;
3. the shareholders are deadlocked and have failed to elect directors at two successive annual meetings;
4. the corporate assets are being wasted or misapplied; or
5. the corporation has failed to conduct business for some statutorily specified period of time.

Because dissolution is such a drastic remedy, RMBCA Section 14.34 and many state statutes provide that if a shareholder proves one of the grounds specified above, as an alternative to dissolution, the corporation or another shareholder may elect to purchase all of the shares owned by the complaining shareholder at their fair market value. Such a remedy is available only if the corporation's stock is not publicly traded. Shareholders of corporations whose stock is publicly traded are adequately protected, because they can always sell their shares on the open market.

FIGURE 16-4
Illinois Application for Reinstatement

Form **BCA-12.45/ 13.60** (Rev. Jan. 1999)	**APPLICATION FOR REINSTATEMENT of DOMESTIC OR FOREIGN CORPORATIONS**	File #
Jesse White Secretary of State Department of Business Services Springfield, IL 62756 http://www.sos.state.il.us	This space for use by Secretary of State	***SUBMIT IN DUPLICATE!***
Payment must be made by certified check, cashier's check, Illinois attorney's check, Illinois C.P.A.'s check or money order, payable to "Secretary of State."		**This space for use by Secretary of State** Date Filing Fee $ 100.00 Approved:

1. (a) Corporate name as of the date of issuance of the certificate of dissolution or revocation:
   ____
   ____

   (b) Corporate name as changed: ______________________________
   ______________________________ *(Note 1)*

   (c) If a foreign corporation having a certificate of authority under an assumed corporate name restriction, the assumed corporate name: ______________________________
   ______________________________ *(Note 2)*

2. State of incorporation: ______________________________

3. Date that the certificate of dissolution or revocation was issued: ______________________________

4. Name and address of the Illinois registered agent and the Illinois registered office, upon reinstatement: *(Note 3)* NOTICE! Completion of item #4 does not constitute a registered agent or office change. See note #3 on back of this form.

   Registered Agent ______________________________
   First Name *Middle Name* *Last Name*

   Registered Office ______________________________
   Number *Street* *Suite # (A P.O. Box alone is not acceptable)*

   ____
   City *ZIP Code* *County*

5. This application is accompanied by all delinquent report forms together with the filing fees, franchise taxes, license fee and penalties required.

6. The undersigned corporation has caused this statement to be signed by its duly authorized officers, each of whom affirms, under penalties of perjury, that the facts stated herein are true. (All signatures must be in **BLACK INK**.)

   Dated ____________________, __________ ______________________________
   (Month & Day) *(Year)* *(Exact Name of Corporation)*

   attested by ______________________________ by ______________________________
   (Signature of Secretary or Assistant Secretary) *(Signature of President or Vice President)*

   ______________________________ ______________________________
   (Type or Print Name and Title) *(Type or Print Name and Title)*

While the election to purchase a complaining shareholder's shares in lieu of dissolution requires a fairly elaborate procedure, it affords a method of protecting a disputing shareholder and yet continuing the corporation for those who wish to see it continue in existence.

Action by a Creditor. A creditor of the corporation may institute a proceeding for judicial dissolution of a corporation. Typically, the creditor must establish that the corporation is insolvent and that the creditor has either received a judgment against the corporation for the claim or the corporation has acknowledged that the claim is owed. Because creditors' claims must be paid before assets are distributed to shareholders upon dissolution, the creditor may believe it is in his best interest to force a dissolution and thereby collect some amount of the claim rather than no amount at all if the corporation is refusing to satisfy the debt.

If a court determines that there are grounds for dissolution shown by the state, the shareholders, or the creditors, it will enter a decree of dissolution specifying the effective date of the dissolution. The decree will be provided to the secretary of state by the clerk of the court and the secretary of state will then file the decree in its records. The court will then order winding up and liquidation of the corporation's business and affairs.

B. Liquidation

1. *Introduction*

Before a corporation can terminate its existence, it must conduct the process of liquidation, sometimes called *winding up*. **Liquidation** involves the following activities:

Liquidating
Process of collecting assets, paying debts, and distributing remains to business owners (also called *winding up*)

a. collecting assets;
b. disposing of properties that will not be distributed to shareholders;
c. discharging liabilities or making provisions for discharging liabilities; and
d. distributing the remaining property to the shareholders according to their respective interests. (RMBCA Section 14.05)

Once a corporation has filed its notice of intent to dissolve, it continues business only for the purpose of liquidating and cannot conduct ordinary or additional business. A state will not allow a corporation to end its legal existence unless liquidation has been accomplished. Thus, the corporation must wind up its business affairs before a certificate of dissolution will be issued.

2. *Nonjudicial Liquidation*

Nonjudicial liquidation
Process of winding up by corporate managers

When dissolution is voluntary (initiated by the directors with shareholder approval or unanimously agreed to by the shareholders), the officers and directors will liquidate the corporation. Contracts will be completed, creditors will be notified to submit their claims, and assets will be collected. State statutes do not generally impose any specific time limit within which the liquidation must be completed.

Judicial liquidation
Process of winding up by court appointee

3. *Judicial Liquidation*

A dissolution initiated by the state, shareholders, or creditors is often caused by the directors' failure to manage the corporation properly, failure to pay taxes, fraud, or waste of the corporate assets. Because a court therefore cannot place confidence in corporate management to conduct liquidation properly, the court generally appoints a **receiver** whose function is to receive the assets of the corporation and distribute them to the shareholders. Some jurisdictions refer to the individual or company appointed to oversee the winding up process as the *court-appointed liquidator.* The receiver will be compensated for services rendered in effecting an orderly liquidation.

Receiver
One appointed by a court to oversee liquidation (also called *liquidator*)

4. *Claims Against the Corporation*

Known claim
A claim known by an entity

Unknown claim
Claim that has not yet been made against an entity

There are two types of claims that must be discharged or resolved by a dissolving corporation: **known claims** (those claims, debts, and obligations the corporation knows about), and **unknown claims** (claims that have not yet been made against the corporation, for example, damages for injuries recently sustained by an employee at the corporation's workplace).

Corporations cannot use dissolutions to avoid contractual obligations. For example, if the corporation is a party to a long-term employment contract, it must satisfy the obligations thereunder, at least as to money to be paid to the employee, unless the terms of the contract contemplate dissolution and excuse performance by the corporation in the event of a dissolution.

The RMBCA provides an orderly process for disposing of claims against the corporation. As to known claims, the corporation is required to notify the claimants in writing of the dissolution, inform the creditor or claimant where to submit the claim, provide at least 120 days for the creditor to make the claim, and inform the creditor the claim will be barred if not timely submitted to the corporation. If the creditor does not submit the claim in a timely fashion, the claim will be barred. If a claim is submitted and the corporation rejects it, the claimant must institute legal action within 90 days of rejection of the claim to enforce the claim or it will be barred. RMBCA Section 14.06.

To ensure that unknown claims are also discharged, RMBCA Section 14.07 provides that the corporation may place in a newspaper of general circulation a notice of its intent to dissolve stating that the claim will be barred unless an action to enforce the claim is brought within five years of publication of the notice. If the corporation's assets have been distributed before the claim is made, shareholders may be liable, but only to the extent of assets distributed to them. A shareholder's liability cannot exceed the amount distributed to him or her. If the corporation was dissolved because of a merger or consolidation, a creditor is usually able to enforce a claim against the surviving corporation. In many states, the articles of dissolution must recite that no debt remains unpaid or that the corporation's debts and liabilities have been adequately provided for by their assumption by certain individuals or companies whose addresses are provided.

C. Distributions to Shareholders

After all debts have been discharged and any expenses of liquidation have been paid, and assuming any assets remain, the shareholders are entitled to receive a distribution, generally called a **liquidation distribution.** Corporate assets are typically converted to "liquid" form, namely cash, and the shareholders will receive cash payments. Alternatively, they may receive assets. If preferences exist, those must be honored. Shareholders participate in the distribution in accordance with their ownership interests; if a shareholder owns 23 percent of the common stock of a corporation, the shareholder will be entitled to receive 23 percent of any liquidation distribution made to common shareholders.

Liquidation distribution
Distribution of cash to shareholders in liquidation process

Shareholders are not entitled to appraisal rights arising out of a dissolution inasmuch as all shareholders are equally affected by a dissolution. Their sole right is to receive a distribution, if sufficient assets remain after payment of liquidation costs and creditors' claims.

D. Directors' Duties to Minority Shareholders

In corporations in which directors hold large amounts of stock, it may be possible for the directors to force a dissolution over the wishes of minority shareholders. For example, assume a corporation has five directors, three of whom own stock in the corporation in a total amount of 52 percent. The remaining 48 percent of the stock is held by 100 individuals. The three powerful directors could compel a dissolution: because they constitute a majority of the board, they can pass a directors' resolution recommending dissolution; because they own more than a majority of the outstanding stock, as shareholders their affirmative vote is sufficient to approve a dissolution. If the corporation's business is extremely profitable, these three directors-shareholders may decide to force a voluntary dissolution, pay off the 100 individual shareholders, and re-form a corporation by themselves to do the same business and thereby keep all of the profits. This type of dissolution is called a **freeze-out** or *squeeze-out.*

Freeze-out
Action by majority shareholders to force a dissolution against wishes of minority (also called *squeeze-out*)

Because a freeze-out is patently inequitable to the minority shareholders, courts will prevent or enjoin dissolutions that have the effect of oppressing minority shareholders.

Key Features of Corporate Dissolution and Liquidation

- Corporations can dissolve voluntarily (usually by action of the directors, which is then approved by shareholders) or involuntarily (by action by the state, shareholders, or creditors).
- Dissolution refers to termination of the corporate entity, while liquidation refers to termination of the corporation's business and affairs.
- If dissolution is voluntary, articles of dissolution will be filed with the state.

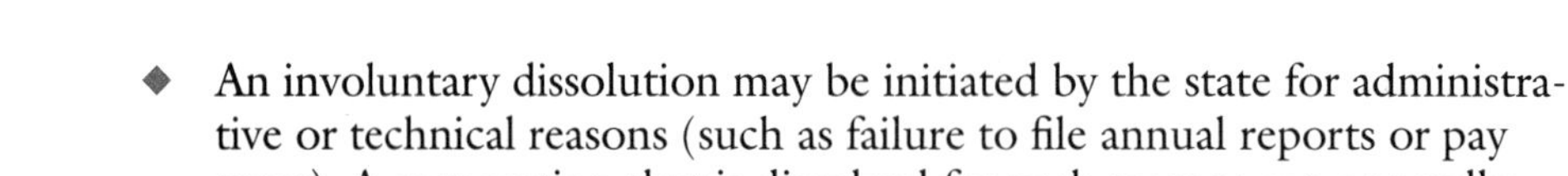

- An involuntary dissolution may be initiated by the state for administrative or technical reasons (such as failure to file annual reports or pay taxes). A corporation that is dissolved for such reasons can generally apply to be reinstated.
- An involuntary dissolution may be initiated by the state if the corporation exceeds state authority or procured its articles through fraud. Reinstatement is generally not permissible in such an event.
- Shareholders may initiate a dissolution, often because of director or shareholder deadlock, waste of assets, or fraud by directors. In lieu of ordering a dissolution, a court can allow the complaining shareholder's shares to be purchased.
- Creditors can initiate a dissolution if the corporation is insolvent, and their claim is undisputed. The court will order winding up and liquidation so the creditor may be paid the money owed to it.
- If dissolution is voluntary, corporate management will oversee liquidation; if dissolution is involuntary, the court will supervise liquidation.
- Corporations must generally notify known claimants and instruct them to submit their claims against the corporation within a certain period of time or be barred thereafter. As to unknown claims, corporations generally publish a notice in a newspaper, and claimants can enforce the claim within five years thereafter.
- Corporations cannot dissolve unless known claims have been paid and unknown liabilities provided for.
- During liquidation, the expenses of liquidation will be paid, creditors will be paid, and then remaining assets will be distributed to shareholders on a pro rata basis in accordance with any preferences.

E. Role of Paralegal

The decision to dissolve is generally made by corporate management with the advice of attorneys and accountants. The effective date of the dissolution may trigger various tax consequences. Therefore, the corporation's accountants are often directly involved in the dissolution process.

Paralegals play a direct role in dissolutions and may be involved in the following:

1. Drafting resolutions contained in the minutes of board of directors' meetings (or written consent actions) recommending dissolution.
2. Preparing notice of the shareholders' meeting to vote on dissolution.
3. Preparing minutes of the meeting of shareholders approving dissolution.
4. Preparing and filing the notice of intent to dissolve with the secretary of state.
5. Reviewing corporate documents to prepare a list of known claims.
6. Preparing notices to be sent to individual creditors notifying them of the corporation's intended dissolution and the process for submitting claims against the corporation.

7. Arranging for publication of notices of intent to dissolve in newspapers so creditors can make claims against the corporation.
8. Obtaining the tax clearance certificate.
9. Preparing and filing the articles of dissolution.
10. Assisting in the distribution of assets by preparing deeds, assignments, and other instruments to transfer title from the corporation to the shareholders.

Resource Guide

1. State Statutes

The process of dissolution is controlled strictly by state statute. Therefore, the most critical resources are the state statutes relating to dissolution and any cases interpreting them. These statutes will specify the grounds for dissolution and the required vote for shareholder approval and will outline the timing and sequence of liquidation and the filing of the articles of dissolution. (See Appendix A for citation to each state's corporations statutes.)

2. Secretary of State

Most states provide the pertinent forms for the dissolution process, including forms for the statement of intent to dissolve and for the articles of dissolution. Contact your secretary of state to request these forms. (See Appendix A listing phone numbers for all states' secretaries of state.)

3. Encyclopedias, Texts, Treatises, and Periodicals

Your office may have a variety of treatises and other sources discussing dissolution and liquidation. In most texts, for example C.J.S. and Am. Jur. 2d, the discussions provide a general overview of the process and effect of dissolution and liquidation and will not provide specific practice pointers.

4. Form Books

The form books identified in Chapter Nine will provide a variety of forms to assist you in drafting directors' resolutions recommending dissolution, notices for shareholders' meetings to consider and vote upon dissolution, minutes of shareholders' meetings approving dissolution, and notices for individual creditors.

5. Office Resources

Try to locate a file in your office in which a corporation was previously dissolved. The file will not only contain copies of completed forms but will likely provide an overview and timeline for the dissolution and liquidation process. Previous letters to the corporation and to its creditors and shareholders will provide a sequence of events.

WEB RESOURCES

The most important resources relating to dissolution of corporations are the various state statutes. Following is a site allowing access to state statutes.

www.ll.georgetown.edu
When you access this site for Georgetown University Law Center, select "State, Local & Territorial." You will be presented with a map of the United States. Point your cursor to the state in which you are interested, and you will be provided with links to a variety of legal sources relating to that state. Select "Statutes" or "Codes," and you will be linked to the state's statutes. In some states, searching can be done by either keywords or by section number. In other states, searching is accomplished exclusively by keywords.

Because nearly all states have posted their forms relating to dissolution on their Web sites, important Web resources are the home pages of the various secretaries of state. See Appendix A for the specific Web address for each of the state's secretaries of state. Other alternatives follow.

www.nass.org
This Web site of the National Association of Secretaries of State will provide you with links to each of the secretaries of state. After you access the home page of the Association, select "States." You will then be given an alphabetical list of all 50 states and the District of Columbia (together with their state flags). Point your cursor at the state you wish, and you will be immediately linked to the home page for that state's secretary of state. In most instances, you will immediately see entries for "Corporations" or "Securities." Select the relevant entry and you will be directed to the pertinent forms, nearly all of which can be downloaded and printed. Fee schedules are also included on the sites.

www.legalwiz.com
When you access this site, select "Legal Sites" and then "Corporate Department and Secretary of State Pages" for links to each state's secretary of state.

The following sites can be used to review forms for directors' resolutions and minutes of meetings authorizing dissolution:

http://legal-resource.com/forms

www.siccode.com/forms.php3

www.lectlaw.com

Discussion Questions

Fact Scenario. Young & Young Inc. ("Young"), a New York corporation, has experienced a steady decline in its business. It has been sued by several creditors who have obtained judgments in varying amounts against the corporation. A number of shareholders believe the directors have looted the corporation's accounts. Young has not paid its taxes in New York this year.

1. What can the creditors do to protect their interests?

2. What can the shareholders do to protect their interests? What alternatives exist to a court-ordered dissolution of Young?

3. If a court orders dissolution of Young, who will liquidate the corporation? Why?

4. Assume the state initiates a dissolution action against Young for failure to pay New York taxes. If Young wishes to continue doing business thereafter, what should it do?

5. Assume that Young has been judicially dissolved. Two years after liquidation, a creditor, Simmons, makes a claim for $50,000 owed to her. The claim was known at the time of liquidation, and prior to dissolution Simmons was given instruction to present the claim. Will Simmons be able to collect the claim? What if the claim was unknown at the time of dissolution?

6. Assume that after payment of liquidation expenses and creditors' claims, Young has $50,000 in cash. How should this be distributed among Julie, who owns 40 percent of the outstanding stock of the corporation; Al, who owns 25 percent of the stock; and Tina, who owns 35 percent of the stock? What if an unknown claim is made for $1000 after dissolution? How will it be satisfied?

17

◆ ◆ ◆

Corporate Variations

◆ ◆ ◆

CHAPTER OVERVIEW

The major portion of this text has been devoted to the business corporation, the most common corporation in the United States. Its distinguishing characteristic is its status as a legal person, which gives rise to double taxation and the protection of its owners from personal liability. Formed for a profit-making purpose, the business corporation is well-suited to the needs of many entrepreneurs. However, other forms of corporations respond to specialized purposes, goals, and groups. This chapter will examine those other types of corporations.

The close corporation is a corporation whose stock is not publicly traded and is generally held by a small group of family or friends. In most instances, these shareholders are involved in the management of the business of the corporation. Failure to adhere strictly to some corporate formalities, such as holding meetings and elections, will generally not result in piercing the corporate veil to hold individual shareholders liable for corporate liabilities.

A nonprofit or not-for-profit corporation is one formed for a purpose other than to earn a profit. It may be formed for educational, scientific, charitable, or even social reasons. The selection of the corporate form provides protection from liability for the nonprofit's members as well as significant tax benefits to the corporation itself.

A subsidiary corporation is one formed by another corporation, called the parent. The parent may create subsidiaries to operate different business divisions, to hold certain assets, and so forth. The parent usually owns all or the majority of the stock of the subsidiary. Nevertheless, the parent will not be liable for the subsidiary's debts unless the parent controls and directs the subsidiary.

For many years, individuals were not allowed to incorporate their professional practices. The authority now given to most professionals to incorporate provides them with significant corporate benefits and tax advantages.

Finally, to avoid double taxation, qualified corporations may elect to be "S" corporations. If a corporation meets the statutory requirements for S status, none of the income earned by the corporation itself is taxable; all of the taxable income is passed through to the individual shareholders in the corporation who then declare and pay taxes on this income.

A. Close Corporations

1. *Introduction to Close Corporations*

In a large or publicly held corporation, the rationale for the separation of ownership and management is readily apparent. The corporation is best managed by a dedicated core of professional managers, the board of directors, because it cannot readily be managed by thousands of shareholders who have little or no interest in the corporation other than their wish that it make money.

In smaller corporations, this division of ownership and management is a dilemma. A small group of family members or friends who have formed a corporation naturally want to manage it themselves. The very limited participation available to shareholders through voting will not be acceptable to a small group of investors who desire hands-on exposure to the business operations of a corporation in which they have invested their capital and themselves. Recognizing the need for some relaxation of the general corporate rules restricting shareholder participation in the management of the corporation, many states (including Delaware, California, Illinois, Maryland, and New York), have adopted special statutes to address the needs of these smaller owner-managed corporations, typically called *closely held* (or *close*) *corporations,* or **statutory close corporations.** In other states, there are no statutes designed solely for close corporations; in those states, close corporations are required to adhere to all of the statutes relating to corporations in general, except when judicial decisions have liberalized those statutes. The American Bar Association has approved a Model Statutory Close Corporation Supplement (MSCCS) to the RMBCA designed to be adopted in states to govern the formation and operation of close corporations.

Close corporation
Corporation whose shares are held by a small group that is active in managing the corporation (also called *statutory close corporation*)

In brief, participants in a close corporation act as general partners yet they have selected the corporate form of business enterprise for protection from personal liability and for certain tax advantages.

The increasing acceptance of limited liability partnerships and limited liability companies, now recognized in all states, may result in fewer close corporations being formed than in the past. The limited liability company, discussed in Chapter Six, can be managed by its members, who are protected from personal liability as are shareholders in a close corporation. A limited liability company, moreover, has no restrictions on the number of people who may be involved in the enterprise, as does a close corporation. Additionally, a limited liability company offers the "pass through" tax status of a partnership and thereby avoids the burden of double taxation. Finally, in a limited liability company, members can be allocated profits and losses in an amount disproportionate to their contributions, while in a close corporation, shareholders will receive profit in accordance with their investment. Thus, limited liability companies (and limited liability partnerships) offer all of the advantages of close corporations and none of the disadvantages.

2. *Characteristics of Close Corporations*

Close corporations share a number of features in common, whether or not they are incorporated under statutes that expressly recognize this corporate form. The most common characteristics of a close corporation are as follows:

a. There is a limitation on the number of shareholders in a close corporation. Some states and the MSCCS permit up to 50 shareholders, while other states restrict the number of shareholders to 25 or 30.
b. The shareholders typically enter into agreements restricting the transfer of shares. Thus, there is no readily available outside market for the shares of a close corporation.
c. All or most of the shareholders participate in the management of the corporation.

Because there are typically agreements restricting the free transfer of shares in a close corporation, the possibility of attracting outside investors is reduced. Few investors, other than family members or friends, wish to be involved in a corporation whose stock is subject to restrictions on its sale.

3. *Formation of Close Corporations*

A corporation may initially incorporate as a close corporation. Alternatively, a corporation that has been in existence may amend its articles of incorporation to elect close corporation status. In Delaware, amendments to the articles of incorporation for business corporations require only a simple majority; an amendment electing close corporation status, however, must be approved by two-thirds of the shareholders. Other states require unanimous approval to amend the articles to elect status as a close corporation.

A close corporation is formed in the same way as any corporation: by filing of articles of incorporation. The articles of incorporation for a close corporation must generally recite that the corporation is being formed as a close corporation. Additionally, some states require a recitation of the various restrictions to which close corporations are generally subject. For example, the articles of incorporation form provided in Delaware (see Figure 17-1) contains four elements not found in the form used for incorporation of other entities:

a. The title of the document provides public notice of the type of corporation being incorporated by specifying "State of Delaware—Certificate of Incorporation—A Close Corporation";
b. The articles confirm that all of the corporation's issued stock, exclusive of treasury stock, will be held by less than 30 shareholders of record (stock held jointly by a husband and wife is treated as being held by one shareholder);
c. The articles recite that all of the issued stock of all classes will be subject to restrictions on their transfer; and
d. The articles confirm that there will be no "public offering" of any class of stock within the meaning of the Securities Act of 1933.

When the articles of incorporation are filed with the secretary of state, they will be reviewed for compliance with the pertinent state statutes and will be approved. Any other requirement imposed for the formation of corporations, such as publication of the articles in newspapers or recording of the articles with county clerks, must generally be followed. Additionally, the MSCCS and most states re-

FIGURE 17-1
Delaware Close Corporation Certificate of Incorporation

STATE *of* DELAWARE
CERTIFICATE *of* INCORPORATION
A CLOSE CORPORATION
of

____

- **First:** The name of this Corporation is ______________________________ ____.
- **Second:** Its Registered Office in the State of Delaware is to be located at __________ ______________________Street, in the City of ______________ County of ______________Zip Code _______. The registered agent in charge thereof is ______________________________________ ____ ____
- **Third:** The nature of business and the objects and purposes proposed to be transacted, promoted and carried on , are to engage in any lawful act of activity for which corporations may be organized under the General corporation Law of Delaware.
- **Fourth:** The amount of the total authorized capital stock of this corporation is ____________Dollars ($_______) divided into __________ shares of __________ ____________Dollars ($_______) each.
- **Fifth:** The name and mailing address of the incorporator are as follows:
  Name ______________________________________
  Mailing Address______________________________
  ______________________Zip Code____________
- **Sixth:** All of the corporation's issued stock, exclusive of treasury shares, shall be held of record by not more than thirty (30) persons.
- **Seventh:** All of the issued stock of all classes shall be subject to one or more of the restrictions on transfer permitted by Section 202 of the General Corporation Law.
- **Eighth:** The corporation shall make no offering of any of its stock of any class which would constitute a "public offering" within the meaning of the United States Securities Act of 1933, as it may be amended from time to time.
- **I, The Undersigned,** for the purpose of forming a corporation under the laws of the State of Delaware, do make, file and record this Certificate, and do certify that the facts herein stated are true, and I have accordingly hereunto set my hand this _________ day of ______________, A.D. 20______.

BY: ______________________________
(Incorporator)

NAME: ______________________________
(Type or Print)

quire that the close corporation's stock certificates contain a legend alerting potential purchasers that the corporation is a close corporation whose transfer of shares is subject to certain restrictions.

A close corporation may be terminated by an amendment to its articles of incorporation, approved by two-thirds shareholders' vote, ending its status as a close corporation. Status as a close corporation will automatically terminate if any of the conditions required of a close corporation is breached, for example, admission of shareholders in excess of the maximum number allowed. Alternatively, the close corporation may terminate as would any other corporation: by voluntary or involuntary dissolution.

4. *Restrictions on Transfer of Shares*

Perhaps the most significant characteristic of a close corporation is an agreement among shareholders to restrict or limit their ability to transfer (or **alienate**) their ownership interests in the corporation.

Alienation
Transfer of property

Because the close corporation almost always involves a group of individuals well known to each other either through family ties or friendship, the group will be reluctant to allow "outsiders" in who might change the dynamics of the organization. Therefore, shareholders in close corporations enter into agreements whereby they agree to certain restrictions placed on their ability to sell their shares. In states with separate statutes for close corporations and under the MSCCS, restrictions on transfer are imposed by statute. Generally, transfers to the corporation, other shareholders, family members, or to executors upon the death of a shareholder are permissible and are subject to no restrictions. Transfers to "outsiders," however, are restricted and can only be effected after the corporation has been offered the shares and refused to purchase them. These restrictions may be a disadvantage for an individual requiring certain and ready liquidity of her investments, and, therefore, in such a case, the close corporation may not be a suitable investment vehicle.

There are several reasons why restrictions on the transfer of shares in close corporations exist. The shareholders, who are almost always friends or relatives, may desire continuity in management and may not wish to answer to outsiders. The restrictions also help ensure that a corporation maintain S status so that it is not subject to double taxation. (See Section E below.) Finally, restrictions on transfer prohibit a "palace coup" by a faction of shareholders who combine together to oust other shareholders.

Restrictions on the transfer of shares may be placed in the articles of incorporation, the bylaws, or in a private agreement among the shareholders or between the shareholders and the corporation. The private agreements are generally called **buy-sell agreements.** See Appendix J for a sample buy-sell agreement.

Buy-sell agreement
Agreement among shareholders regarding transfer of shares

The restrictions placed on the transferability or alienability of shares may vary. Although some courts have upheld absolute prohibitions against the transfer of shares, this is a minority view inasmuch as one of the characteristics of property ownership is the right to transfer it. Therefore, absolute bars to transfer are often invalidated on the basis that they are inherently at odds with the rights of a property owner.

Right of first refusal
Agreement to allow another to purchase something before it is sold to a third party

The most common restriction on the transfer of shares is a **right of first refusal.** The shareholders enter into an agreement, either with each other or with the corporation, whereby they agree that before they can sell their shares to any outsider, either the corporation or the shareholders, or both, shall have the right to purchase the shares on the same terms as any third party who has made an offer for the shares. Only if the corporation and other shareholders decline to purchase the shares may they then be sold to the outsider. Any transfer of the shares in violation of such an agreement is ineffective.

If the corporation or other shareholders elect not to purchase the shares within some time period specified in the agreement, the shareholder may then sell them to the third party. Many agreements anticipate the possibility of phony or rigged offers by requiring that any offer be bona fide and that it be submitted for review by the corporation or other shareholders.

Many close corporations also take great care in providing for the disposition of the shares of a deceased shareholder. Agreements often provide that upon the death of a shareholder the decedent's shares will be immediately transferred to the corporation, which is then obligated to pay the fair value of the shares to the shareholder's estate. Placing a value on shares that do not have a public market can be difficult. Therefore, appraisers are often used. Alternatively, a pre-established formula can be used.

Cross-purchase agreement
Agreement under which each shareholder insures the life of each other shareholder

There are two types of agreements for the sale of a shareholder's interest upon the death or disability of the shareholder. A **cross-purchase agreement** provides for the purchase of the shareholder's interest from him or his estate by the remaining shareholders. Under a cross-purchase agreement, each shareholder takes out a life/disability policy on the life of each of the other shareholders. Upon a shareholder's death or disability, each shareholder then has funds from the insurance policy to purchase a portion of the deceased or disabled shareholder's shares.

Entity purchase agreement
Agreement under which entity purchases insurance on life of each member or shareholder (also called *stock redemption agreement*)

The other type of agreement is generally referred to as an **entity purchase agreement,** or *stock redemption agreement.* In this case, the corporate entity itself is the beneficiary under the terms of an insurance policy, and in the event of the death or disability of a shareholder, the entity receives the insurance proceeds and then purchases the deceased or disabled shareholder's interest. Such an agreement is often preferable when there are more than two or three shareholders, because the number of policies required to fund such an agreement will be less than the number required to fund a cross-purchase agreement. Under an entity purchase or stock redemption agreement, the corporation simply pays the premiums for and owns a single policy on the life of each shareholder.

Some corporations employ mandatory buy-sell provisions that flatly require the corporation to purchase the shares of a shareholder who dies or wishes to withdraw. Such provisions provide certainty for both parties: the individual shareholders know that the shares can be disposed of and the corporation knows that it need never worry about outsiders. Many agreements allow the corporation to pay the purchase price for the shares in installments, with appropriate interest.

5. *Operation of Close Corporations*

Shareholders are almost always active in managing the close corporation and are often employees of the corporation as well. Management and governance tends to be less formal than in larger or non-close corporations. In fact, many statutes expressly allow the shareholders to enter into an agreement to regulate the management and business affairs of the corporation. Under MSCCS Section 20, such an agreement is effective even if it eliminates a board of directors, restricts the discretion or powers of the board, or its effect is to treat the corporation as a partnership. Bylaws are not required if sufficient provisions are provided in the articles of incorporation or the agreement among shareholders. Annual meetings need not be held unless one or more shareholders request a meeting in writing. Delaware's statutes governing close corporations are similar to the MSCCS, although Delaware allows an agreement providing management to be performed by shareholders to be approved by a majority vote of the shareholders, while the MSCCS and many states require unanimous approval of such a provision.

If the shareholders agree to eliminate the board, this decision must generally be unanimous. The management and control of the corporation is then conducted by the shareholders. The shareholders may appoint one or more shareholders as **designated directors** to sign documents on behalf of the corporation. If shareholders act like directors in managing the corporation, they will be subject to the liabilities and fiduciary duties of directors.

Designated director
Shareholder appointed in a close corporation to operate its affairs when there is no board of directors

Dissatisfied creditors of close corporations often try to pierce the corporate veil to hold shareholders liable for corporate obligations. Because piercing the veil can occur when a corporation fails to follow statutory formalities required of corporations, it would seem that the close corporation (which may not have directors, bylaws, or annual meetings) is particularly vulnerable to attack on this ground. Most statutes anticipate this potential problem by providing that the failure of a close corporation to observe the usual corporate formalities is not a ground for imposing personal liability on the shareholders for liabilities of the corporation. While a court can pierce the veil of a close corporation if circumstances warrant, a court cannot pierce the veil merely on the basis that the corporation is a close one, functioning like a partnership and not observing the usual corporate formalities.

Because close corporations typically involve small groups of individuals familiar to one another, and because almost all of the individuals are actively involved in managing the business, the close corporation provides many opportunities for dissension and in-fighting. For example, majority shareholders may reduce the compensation of minority shareholders, remove them from positions of authority, and so forth. The minority shareholder may petition for judicial relief from oppressive conduct and breach of fiduciary duties. The most dramatic remedy is for a shareholder to initiate an action for involuntary dissolution, based on waste of corporate assets, fraud, or oppression.

Another common scenario in close corporations is deadlock among directors or shareholders that results in corporate paralysis. Courts can fashion several alternatives to remedy a deadlock. A court may appoint a custodian or provisional director until deadlocked issues are resolved and the corporation's business may again be conducted for the advantage of the shareholders. A court may appoint an individual to manage corporate business to protect the interests of shareholders or may order a forced buy-out of shares of oppressed minority shareholders. The most drastic remedy is a court-ordered involuntary dissolution.

B. Nonprofit Corporations

1. *Introduction*

Nonprofit corporation
Corporation formed for a purpose other than to earn profit (also called (*not-for-profit corporation*)

Nonprofit (or *not-for-profit*) **corporations** are not formed to earn a profit and do not distribute any part of their income or profit to their members, directors, or officers. These corporations are often formed for some charitable, scientific, religious, or educational purpose, or for the mutual benefit of the members of the corporation. Most states have specific statutes governing formation, operation, and termination of nonprofit corporations in their jurisdictions. Merely incorporating in a state as a nonprofit corporation does not automatically qualify the corporation for exemption from federal taxes. The corporation must file a separate application with the Internal Revenue Service for tax-exempt status.

Some states, such as Florida, provide a laundry list of all of the purposes for which nonprofit corporations may be organized. Fla. Stat. Ann. Section 617.0301 provides in pertinent part as follows:

> Corporations may be organized under this act for any lawful purpose or purposes not for pecuniary profit and not specifically prohibited to corporations under other laws of this state. Such purposes include, without limitation, charitable, benevolent, eleemosynary, educational, historical, civic, patriotic, political, religious, social, fraternal, literary, cultural, athletic, scientific, agricultural, horticultural, animal husbandry, and professional, commercial, industrial, or trade association purposes.

Religious corporation
Corporation formed for religious purposes

Public benefit corporation
Corporation formed primarily for charitable purposes

Mutual benefit corporation
Corporation formed for the benefit of its members

Other states classify their nonprofit corporations into separate categories based on the purpose of the corporation. For example, California and many other states recognize three types of nonprofit corporations: those formed primarily for **religious** purposes; those organized primarily for charitable purposes, such as those promoting science, health, education, or the arts (called "**public benefit corporations**"); and those organized for other than religious, charitable, civic, or social welfare purposes, such as country clubs, homeowners' associations, and professional associations (called "**mutual benefit corporations**").

2. *Formation of Nonprofit Corporations*

Nonprofit corporations are formed in the same manner as other corporations: by the filing of articles of incorporation. The contents of the articles will be specified in the pertinent state statutes and most states provide forms for articles of incorporation for nonprofit corporations. (See Figure 17-2 for sample articles of incorporation for a nonprofit corporation.)

The name of the corporation may be subject to various requirements. Some states do not permit a nonprofit corporation's name to contain a corporate designation such as "incorporated," "company," or "limited." Other states, such as Florida, prohibit "company" or "co." but allow "corporation" or "incorporated" or their abbreviations. Some statutes specify that designations such as "association," "club," "group," and so forth be used.

FIGURE 17-2
Montana Articles of Incorporation for Nonprofit Corporation

STATE OF MONTANA

ARTICLES *of* INCORPORATION
for DOMESTIC NONPROFIT
CORPORATION
(35-2-213, MCA)

Prepare, sign and submit an ORIGINAL AND COPY with fee.
This is the minimum information required.

(This space for use by the Secretary of State only)

Form: DN-1
Filing Fee: $20.00

MAIL: **MIKE COONEY**
Secretary of State
P.O. Box 202801
Helena, MT 59620-2801
PHONE: ☎(406)444-3665
FAX: (406)444-3976
WEB SITE: ***www.state.mt.us/sos***

☐ **Priority Filing Add $20.00**

▸ *Executed by the undersigned person for the purpose of forming a Montana nonprofit corporation.*

▸ **FIRST:** The name of the Nonprofit Corporation is ____________________

____________________.

▸ **SECOND:** The name and address of the registered office/agent in Montana:

Name ____________________

Street Address ____________________

Mailing Address ____________________

City ____________________, MONTANA Zip Code __________

Signature of Agent **(Required)** ____________________

▸ **THIRD:** The name and address of the incorporator is as follows:

Name ____________________

Address ____________________

____________________, ________ Zip Code __________

▸ **FOURTH:** The Nonprofit Corporation ☐ **WILL** ☐ **WILL NOT** have members.

▸ **FIFTH:** This Nonprofit Corporation is a (check one):
☐ Public Benefit Corporation
☐ Mutual Benefit Corporation
☐ Religious Corporation

▸ **SIXTH:** Upon dissolution, the assets shall be distributed in the following manner:

____

____
Signature of Incorporator Date

s:\forms\dn-1
Revised:08/23/99

Many states prohibit the use of general purpose clauses and require that the purposes of the nonprofit corporation be expressly stated in the articles. A registered agent must be designated and a registered address must be given. Some states require that the corporation provide how its assets will be distributed upon dissolution. Other states, such as California, require a recitation by public benefit and religious corporations that "no substantial part of the activities of this corporation shall consist of carrying on propaganda, or otherwise attempting to influence legislation, and the corporation shall not participate or intervene in any political campaign (including the publishing or distribution of statements) on behalf of any candidate for public office." Mutual benefit corporations formed for political purposes are, of course, not subject to any such restrictions.

The articles are submitted to the secretary of state with the appropriate filing fee. Other formalities required in the state, such as publishing the articles in a newspaper, must be followed as well. The corporation is formed upon filing of the articles.

3. *Operation and Governance of Nonprofit Corporations*

In many ways, nonprofit corporations function similarly to business corporations. A board of directors will be elected, bylaws will be adopted, the directors will manage and control the affairs of the corporation at regular meetings or by unanimous written consent, and the directors must perform their duties in good faith and with the care of ordinarily prudent and diligent persons. In most states, the state attorney general has the authority to take a public benefit corporation to court to ensure it is being operated in the public interest, while disputes regarding mutual benefit corporations are typically resolved by their members.

Membership
What is offered by nonprofit corporations to their "owners" rather than stock

In some important respects, however, the nonprofit corporation is far different from a business corporation. For example, **membership** in the nonprofit corporation is what is offered, if anything. Stock is not sold. Generally, an individual or business is entitled to only one membership. Thus, there are no issues of majority shareholders oppressing minority shareholders. Members of public benefit or religious corporations do not usually vote unless the articles or bylaws so provide.

A nonprofit corporation may have no members, one class of members, or more than one class of members. For example, you may refer to yourself as a member of a church but it is unlikely that the church has issued a formal membership to you. On the other hand, you may be a registered "parishioner," entitling you to vote on limited church issues. You may also be a member of a homeowners' association. Generally, one membership accompanies each parcel of real estate sold. As a member of a homeowners' association, you may have specific rights to written notice of meetings, to vote either personally or by proxy at those meetings, and to inspect the books of the association. Membership or registration in a church seldom confers such rights.

There may be different classes of members. For example, in a nonprofit country club, there may be "A" memberships, which are expensive and carry certain rights and privileges, and there may be "B" memberships, offered at lower prices and which may carry certain restrictions on use of the club facilities and on voting. The rights and privileges of each class must be set forth in the articles or bylaws. If memberships are issued, the corporation may issue a certificate of membership. Members are liable for dues, assessments, or fees, but are not liable for any liability or obligation of the corporation.

Although the nonprofit corporation is formed for some purpose other than making a profit, it is possible that the corporation may invest and manage wisely and thereby earn a profit. The earning of profit will not affect the corporation's nonprofit status. The corporation, however, cannot pay any dividend or take any part of its income or profit and distribute it to its members, directors, or officers. Generally, any profits made should be devoted to the purposes of the corporation: providing medical assistance to the needy, scholarships for underprivileged students, grants for scientific research, and so forth. Alternatively, the corporation may improve its offices, hire more skilled employees, and purchase new equipment. While the nonprofit corporation is allowed to compensate its directors, officers, and employees, one which extravagantly compensates its personnel and provides plush accommodations and yet expends little, if any, of its income accomplishing its proclaimed purposes may be dissolved by the state, or may lose its federal tax-exempt status.

Upon dissolution, and after payment to its creditors, a nonprofit corporation may make a payment or distribution to its members. While this one-time distribution is commonly seen when mutual benefit corporations (homeowners' associations, country clubs, and so forth) are involved, upon dissolution of a public benefit or religious organization, a distribution is usually made to a like-minded group or association rather than the members.

Nonprofit corporations may generally be dissolved in the same manner as business corporations: voluntarily by the directors or members, or involuntarily by the state, the members, or creditors. Nonprofit corporations formed in one state may transact business in others so long as they properly qualify to do so (see Chapter Fifteen).

4. *Exemption from Taxation for Nonprofit Corporations*

After the nonprofit corporation is formed, it should apply for federal tax-exempt status. Because the provisions of the Internal Revenue Code relating to most nonprofit corporations are set forth in Section 501(c)(3) of Title 26, nonprofit corporations which have tax-exempt status are often referred to as **501(c)(3) corporations.** Section 501(c)(3) specifies the purposes that qualify a corporation for an exemption from paying federal taxes.

501(c)(3) corporation Term used to refer to tax-exempt nonprofit corporations, after Section 501(c)(3) of the Internal Revenue Code

Tax-exempt status is a privilege that must be applied for, rather than an automatic right conferred upon a nonprofit corporation. The IRS identifies 27 types of tax-exempt organizations in its publication IRS No. 557, *Tax Exempt Status for Your Organization.* After the application is filed, the IRS will issue a ruling or determination letter recognizing the organization's tax-exempt status. Generally, a nonprofit corporation will be granted tax-exempt status if it is organized and operated exclusively for charitable, religious, literary, scientific, educational, or other similar purposes.

Generally, contributions made to a public benefit corporation (The Heart Fund, The Sudden Infant Death Research Foundation, and the like) are tax deductible. Similarly, contributions made to religious organizations generally result in a tax deduction for the donor. On the other hand, memberships in mutual benefit associations are generally not deductible unless they qualify as valid business expenses. Thus, membership dues paid to Riverbend Country Club or Oak View Homeowners' Association may not be deductible, while membership in the National Capital Area Paralegal Association may well be tax deductible.

Nonprofit corporations generally pay no state income taxes. Certain annual fees and reports, however, are usually required by the state of incorporation.

C. Parent and Subsidiary Corporations

1. *Introduction*

Parent
A corporation that forms another

Subsidiary
A corporation formed by another

One corporation may form another. The creator corporation is called the **parent,** and the corporation it creates is called a **subsidiary.** A corporation may create subsidiaries for a variety of reasons: it may wish each of its different business activities to be carried out by a separate corporation; it may wish certain subsidiaries to hold title to certain assets and then license their use to the parent; it may form subsidiaries to do business in other jurisdictions, and so forth.

2. *Formation and Characteristics of Subsidiary Corporations*

A subsidiary corporation is formed like any other corporation: by filing articles of incorporation that comply with the state of incorporation. No special provisions are required in the articles and the articles need not recite that the corporation being formed is a subsidiary of another. A close review of the signature block on the articles of incorporation may reveal, however, that rather than an individual signing as an incorporator, an individual has signed as president or vice president of a corporate incorporator. In general, however, the creation of a subsidiary corporation does not differ in any significant respect from the creation of any other corporation; the only difference is that the incorporator may be another corporation.

Affiliates
Corporations with common parents (also called *brother-sister* corporations)

If a parent (*P*) creates several different subsidiaries (*A, B, C,* and *D*), the subsidiaries *A, B, C,* and *D* are sometimes referred to as brother-sister corporations (because they share the same parent) or as **affiliates** with respect to their relationships to each other.

Wholly owned subsidiary
A corporation the stock of which is entirely owned by the parent

The distinguishing characteristic of a parent-subsidiary relationship is that the parent will either own all of the subsidiary's stock or will own the majority of it, such that it can elect the directors of the subsidiary and thereby control its business activities. A subsidiary whose stock is issued only to the parent is called a **wholly owned subsidiary.**

In general, all of the rules and policies governing other business corporations also apply to parents and subsidiaries. They are each managed by elected directors who owe fiduciary duties to the respective shareholders, their operation parallels that of other business corporations, and dissolution may be either voluntary or involuntary. When the parent owns all of the stock of the subsidiary, however, decisions such as whether to merge or sell assets will be made solely by the directors of the parent inasmuch as it is the only shareholder of the subsidiary. Once the parent has made certain decisions with respect to the subsidiary, the subsidiary may be powerless to stop them.

The existence of a subsidiary may subject the parent to additional taxation. For example, the subsidiary will pay taxes on the income it earns. When the income is then distributed as a dividend to its sole shareholder, the parent has received additional corporate income on which it pays taxes. If the parent distributes cash dividends to its shareholders, they will pay taxes on the distribution they have received. Rather than double taxation, this is triple taxation. The same money has been subject to taxation three times: when received by the subsidiary, when received by the parent, and when received by the parent's shareholders.

3. *Liability of Parent for Subsidiary's Debts*

In general, the primary issue giving rise to litigation involving parents and subsidiaries is whether, and under what circumstances, the parent may be liable for a subsidiary's debt. For example, assume P Corp. has incorporated Sub Corp. and is its sole shareholder. If Sub Corp. enters into a contract to purchase certain items from a creditor and then cannot pay for those items, the creditor may allege that the parent is liable for the subsidiary's debts. Absent some condition calling for "piercing the corporate veil," shareholders are not liable for their corporation's debts. Should a corporate parent nonetheless be liable for a subsidiary's debts solely on the basis that it is the only shareholder of the subsidiary?

The parent and subsidiary are typically viewed as separate legal entities and each remains liable for its own debts. Just because the parent is the sole or majority shareholder of the subsidiary, does not mean the parent will be liable for the subsidiary's debts. There are, however, a number of instances in which courts have pierced the veil between a parent and subsidiary to impose liability upon the parent for the subsidiary's obligations. The factors that result in the veil being pierced between a parent and subsidiary are closely parallel to those that result in the veil being pierced between a corporation and its individual shareholders. Generally, the parent will not be liable for its subsidiary's debts if:

a. the respective bank accounts, records, financial information, and business transactions are kept separate from each other;
b. the corporations have separate employees, directors, officers, and meetings;
c. the subsidiary has been sufficiently capitalized so that it can meet the normal business obligations that would be expected to arise;
d. the respective corporations are held out to the public as separate enterprises (thus, the common announcement by a parent that another corporation is a wholly owned subsidiary provides public notice of the separate nature of the entities); and/or
e. the policies of the subsidiary are directed to its own interests rather than solely to the interests of the parent.

In determining whether to impose liability upon a parent for its subsidiary's debts, all of the factors above are considered. The court will conduct a balancing test to determine if sufficient separateness of the two entities has been maintained. If the parent treats the subsidiary's accounts as its own, commingles funds, shares personnel or business departments, files consolidated financial statements or tax returns with the subsidiary, pays the subsidiary's salaries and expenses, and controls and dominates the subsidiary to the extent that it is a mere instrumentality, agent, or puppet of the parent, courts will reason that if the parent does not respect the separate nature of the subsidiary, there is no need for a creditor to do so. Similarly, looting of the subsidiary's profits by distributing dividends to the sole shareholder, the parent, such that the subsidiary has insufficient assets to meet its obligations, is viewed as an injustice to or fraud on creditors, in which case the parent may be liable for the subsidiary's obligations.

D. Professional Corporations

1. *Introduction*

Until relatively recently, professionals, including doctors, lawyers, accountants, and architects, were not permitted to incorporate their professional practices. Because a distinctive characteristic of a corporation is that it protects its owners from liability, a fear existed that professionals would use the corporate form to shield themselves from claims, leaving victims of professional negligence without sufficient redress. The absolute bar against incorporation of the professions also resulted in professionals being unable to take advantage of other benefits of incorporation, such as possible tax advantages and benefit plans available to other individuals or businesses wishing to incorporate.

Approximately 30 years ago, in response to demands by professionals that they be allowed to incorporate their practices, many states began enacting statutes permitting professional practices to operate as corporations. In the late 1970s, the Model Professional Corporation Act was adopted to serve as a model for states enacting statutes dealing with professionals.

Professional corporation The incorporation of the practice of a professional, including a doctor or lawyer (also called *professional association*)

All states now allow the incorporation of professional practices, primarily by separate acts enacted for **professional corporations** (or *professional associations,* as they are called in some states), although in some states, the statutes relating to professionals are included within the state's general corporation laws. The definition of a "professional" differs greatly from state to state. Many states identify specific professions that may incorporate, with the more modern approach including an ever-increasing variety of professionals, such as physical and occupational therapists, marriage counselors, registered nurses, and acupuncturists. Other states, following the Model Professional Corporation Act, do not enumerate the particular professions that may incorporate but rather limit the formation of professional corporations to those individuals who must be licensed by the state to provide a certain service.

An individual who incorporates his professional practice becomes an employee of the corporation. The corporation may then establish certain benefit plans for its employee.

The distinguishing characteristics of a professional corporation are that share ownership is limited to the licensed professionals and that professionals retain liability for their own acts of malpractice and the acts of others under their authority and control. Thus, while perhaps the most important feature of corporate existence, limited liability, is unavailable to the professional, other advantages of the corporate form, namely fringe benefit plans available to employees, may make the selection of the corporate form attractive to a professional. Professional corporations are subject to the same tax treatment as business corporations and they may have perpetual existence.

The emergence of the new business entity, the limited liability partnership (sometimes called the registered limited liability partnership), may result in a decrease in the number of professional corporations. The LLP, discussed in Chapter Five, is an ideal business enterprise for professionals because it protects its members from acts of negligence of their co-partners. The LLP is taxed as a partnership and all taxable income earned by the partnership is passed through to the individual partners who pay tax thereon at their appropriate rates. Similarly, as discussed in Chapter Six, limited liability companies, recognized in all jurisdictions, can be formed by professionals in most states, although the professionals retain liability for their own wrongful acts and those performed under their supervision or control. LLCs are also taxed as partnerships, namely, with pass-through taxation.

2. *Formation, Operation, and Liability of Professional Corporations*

A professional corporation is formed by filing articles of incorporation. A professional corporation may be formed by an individual professional or by a group composed of professionals. For example, if Gail Wagner is an attorney practicing in the firm of Reed, Markey, and Maguire, Gail may incorporate herself. Alternatively, the law firm itself may incorporate and then issue shares in the professional corporation of Reed, Markey, and Maguire to its attorneys, including Gail.

The articles must usually specify the particular service to be rendered by the corporation (medical services, accounting services, and so forth) and typically recite that the corporation is organized for the sole and specific purpose of rendering those services. Most states also require that the name of the corporation include some signal to provide notice to the public that the professional has adopted the corporate form. The most typical signals required are "professional corporation," "professional association," or "service corporation," or their initials, "P. C.," "P. A.," or "S. C." The appropriate signal must usually be displayed on all letterhead and business stationery of the professional, as well as on any signs, literature, or nameplates. Because the name of the corporation is often the name of the individual professional, for example, "Howard A. Ross, P. C.," individuals may use a name similar or identical to that of another professional if it is their personal name. Thus, while states prohibit a corporation from using a name likely to cause confusion with another, the names of professional corporations may duplicate each other because some professionals share the same names.

The articles of incorporation must specify the number of shares the corporation is authorized to issue. Share ownership is generally restricted to the licensed professionals. In the example given above, the law firm Reed, Markey, and

Maguire could issue shares only to its licensed attorneys, not to their spouses, the office administrator, or office support staff. Most statutes typically require that the directors and officers of the corporation be licensed as well so that management of the corporation is not conducted by lay persons. Other states require that a certain percentage of directors and officers (usually at least one-half) be licensed professionals. If nonlicensed professionals may serve as directors or officers, they are usually prohibited from making decisions on professional matters. Most statutes impose express restrictions on the transfer of shares in the professional corporation. The shares of a professional who dies, or who loses a license to practice the profession, or who wishes to leave the group must be transferred to another qualified shareholder or to the corporation itself. Thus, professional corporations should be sure to use shareholders' agreements (or "buy-sell" agreements) for that purpose. The share certificates must also include a notice that the corporation is a professional corporation and that its shares are subject to restrictions on their transfer. The articles of incorporation must identify a registered office and an agent for service of process. Most states will supply forms for articles of incorporation for a professional corporation (see Figure 17-3).

The licensed professional retains liability for her own wrongful acts or those performed under her supervision and control. Thus, attorneys are generally liable for mistakes made by their secretaries and paralegals. The attorney is liable for acts of malpractice, such as failing to file a document on time, even if the filing was the responsibility of the secretary or clerk. In some states, and under the Model Professional Corporation Act, the professional is liable only for her own acts of negligence and not for those of other professionals in the group. In such cases, of course, the corporation itself is liable for the negligent act. Using our example, Gail Wagner would therefore be liable for missing a statute of limitations, but in some states she would not share any liability if Thomas Barnes, another attorney in the office, committed an act of negligence. In these states, a professional corporation is similar to an LLP or LLC with regard to liability. In other states, however, liability is imposed jointly and severally so that liability may be imposed on Gail Wagner for Thomas Barnes' negligence. An LLP and LLC, however, provide protection from the negligent acts or omissions of one's colleagues. Still, in actual practice a claim is usually made against the law firm employing the attorney, the group employing the doctor, and so forth, as these entities generally have more extensive assets than the individuals and often maintain professional liability insurance.

The Model Professional Corporation Act approach is similar to that of the LLP and LLC: any individual who renders professional services as an employee of a professional corporation is liable for a negligent or wrongful act or omission in which he personally participates to the same extent as if he rendered the services as a sole practitioner; however, the individual is not liable for the conduct of other employees of the corporation, unless he is at fault in appointing, supervising, or cooperating with them.

Professional corporations engage in many of the same activities as business corporations: they may amend their articles, merge with another corporation, and dissolve, either voluntarily or involuntarily. A professional corporation may usually operate in another state upon filing the appropriate documents to qualify to conduct business in the other state.

FIGURE 17-3
Michigan Professional Service Corporation Articles of Incorporation

C&S 501 (Rev. 10/99)

MICHIGAN DEPARTMENT OF CONSUMER & INDUSTRY SERVICES
CORPORATION, SECURITIES AND LAND DEVELOPMENT BUREAU

Date Received	**(FOR BUREAU USE ONLY)**
	This document is effective on the date filed, unless a subsequent effective date within 90 days after received date is stated in the document.

Name		
Address		
City	State	Zip Code

EFFECTIVE DATE:

Document will be returned to the name and address you enter above.
If left blank document will be mailed to the registered office.

ARTICLES OF INCORPORATION
For use by Domestic Profit Professional Service Corporations
(Please read information and instructions on the last page)

Pursuant to the provisions of Act 192, Public Acts of 1962 as amended, the undersigned corporation executes the following Articles:

ARTICLE I

The name of the corporation is:

ARTICLE II

This corporation is organized for the sole and specific purpose of rendering the following professional service(s):

ARTICLE III

The total authorized shares:

1. Common Shares ______________________

   Preferred Shares ______________________

2. A statement of all or any of the relative rights, preferences and limitations of the shares of each class is as follows:

FIGURE 17-3 *Continued*
Michigan Professional Service Corporation Articles of Incorporation

ARTICLE IV

1. The address of the registered office is:

_______________________________ , Michigan __________
(Street Address) (City) (ZIP Code)

2. The mailing address of the registered office if different than above:

_______________________________ , Michigan __________
(Street address or P.O. Box) (City) (ZIP Code)

3. The name of the resident agent at the registered office is: __________________

ARTICLE V

The name(s) and address(es) of the incorporator(s) is (are) as follows:

Name Residence or Business Address

____

____

____

____

____

ARTICLE VI (Optional. Delete if not applicable)

When a compromise or arrangement or a plan of reorganization of this corporation is proposed between this corporation and its creditors or any class of them or between this corporation and its shareholders or any class of them, a court of equity jurisdiction within the state, on application of this corporation or of a creditor or shareholder thereof, or on application of a receiver appointed for the corporation, may order a meeting of the creditors or class of creditors or of the shareholders or class of shareholders to be affected by the proposed compromise or arrangement or reorganization, to be summoned in such manner as the court directs. If a majority in number representing 3/4 in value of the creditors or class of creditors, or of the shareholders or class of shareholders to be affected by the proposed compromise or arrangement or a reorganization, agree to a compromise or arrangement or a reorganization of this corporation as a consequence of the compromise or arrangement, the compromise or arrangement and the reorganization, if sanctioned by the court to which the application has been made, shall be binding on all the creditors or class of creditors, or on all the shareholders or class of shareholders and also on this corporation.

ARTICLE VII (Optional. Delete if not applicable)

Any action required or permitted by the Act to be taken at an annual or special meeting of shareholders may be taken without a meeting, without prior notice, and without a vote, if consents in writing, setting forth the action so taken, are signed by the holders of outstanding shares having not less than the minimum number of votes that would be necessary to authorize or take the action at a meeting at which all shares entitled to vote on the action were present and voted. The written consents shall bear the date of signature of each shareholder who signs the consent. No written consents shall be effective to take the corporate action referred to unless, within 60 days after the record date for determining shareholders entitled to express consent to or to dissent from a proposal without a meeting, written consents dated not more than 10 days before the record date and signed by a sufficient number of shareholders to take the action are delivered to the corporation. Delivery shall be to the corporation's registered office, its principal place of business, or an officer or agent of the corporation having custody of the minutes of the proceedings of its shareholders. Delivery made to a corporation's registered office shall be by hand or by certified or registered mail, return receipt requested.

Prompt notice of the taking of the corporate action without a meeting by less than unanimous written consent shall be given to shareholders who would have been entitled to notice of the shareholder meeting if the action had been taken at a meeting and who have not consented in writing.

FIGURE 17-3 *Continued*
Michigan Professional Service Corporation Articles of Incorporation

ARTICLE VIII

This corporation fully complies with the Professional Service Corporation Act. All shareholders are duly licensed or otherwise legally authorized to render one or more of the professional service(s) for which this corporation is organized, unless otherwise provided in Section 4 of the Act.

Use space below for additional Articles or for continuation of previous Articles. Please identify any Article being continued or added. Attach additional pages if needed.

I, (We), the incorporator(s) sign my (our) name(s) this ________ day of ____________________, ______.

______________________________ ______________________________

______________________________ ______________________________

______________________________ ______________________________

______________________________ ______________________________

______________________________ ______________________________

FIGURE 17-3 *Continued*
Michigan Professional Service Corporation Articles of Incorporation

C&S 501

Name of person or organization remitting fees:

____

____

Preparer's name and business telephone number:

____

____

INFORMATION AND INSTRUCTIONS

1. The Articles of Incorporation cannot be filed until this form, or a comparable document, is submitted.

2. Submit one original of this document. Upon filing, the document will be added to the records of the Corporation, Securities and Land Development Bureau. The original will be returned to your registered office address, unless you enter a different address in the box on the front of this document.

   Since the document will be maintained on optical disk media, it is important that the filing be legible. Documents with poor black and white contrast, or otherwise illegible, will be rejected.

3. This document is to be used pursuant to the provisions of Act 192, P.A. of 1962, by one or more persons for the purpose of forming a domestic profit professional service corporation.

4. Article I - The corporate name shall contain the words "Professional Corporation" or the abbreviation "P.C."

5. Article II - State the specific professional service(s) for which the corporation is organized.

6. Article III - Indicate the total number of shares which the corporation has authority to issue. If there is more than one class or series of shares, state the relative rights, preferences and limitations of the shares of each class in Article III(2).

7. Article IV - A post office box may not be designated as the address of the registered office.

8. Article V - The Act requires one or more incorporators who, except as otherwise provided or prohibited, must be licensed to perform at least one of the services for which the corporation is organized. The address(es) should include a street number and name (or other designation), city and state.

9. Act 192, P.A. of 1962, as amended provides if the professional corporation renders a professional service that is included within the public health code, Act No 368 of the Public Acts of 1978, being sections 333.1101 to 333.25211 of the Michigan Compiled Laws, then all shareholders of the corporation shall be licensed or legally authorized in this state to render the same professional service.

10. The duration of the corporation should be stated in the Articles only if not perpetual.

11. This document is effective on the date endorsed "filed" by the Bureau. A later effective date, no more than 90 days after the date of delivery, may be stated as an additional article.

12. The Articles must be signed in ink by each incorporator. The names of the incorporators as set out in Article V should correspond with the signatures.

13. **FEES:** Make remittance payable to the State of Michigan. Include corporation name on check or money order.

NONREFUNDABLE FEE $10.00
ORGANIZATION FEE: first 60,000 authorized shares or portion thereof $50.00
TOTAL MINIMUM FEE $60.00
ADDITIONAL ORGANIZATION FEE FOR AUTHORIZED SHARES OVER 60,000:
each additional 20,000 authorized shares or portion thereof $30.00
maximum fee for first 10,000,000 authorized shares $5,000.00
each additional 20,000 authorized shares or portion thereof in excess of 10,000,000 shares $30.00
maximum fee for authorized shares in excess of 10,000,000 shares $200,000.00

To submit by mail:
Michigan Department of Consumer & Industry Services
Corporation, Securities and Land Development Bureau
Corporation Division
7150 Harris Drive
P.O. Box 30054
Lansing, MI 48909

To submit in person:
6546 Mercantile Way
Lansing, MI
Telephone: (517) 241-6400

Fees may be paid by VISA or Mastercard when delivered in person to our office.

To submit electronically: (517) 334-8048

*To use this service complete a MICH-ELF application to provide your VISA or Mastercard number. Include your assigned Filer number on your transmission. To obtain an application for a filer number, contact (517) 241-6420 or visit our WEB site at http://www.cis.state.mi.us/corp/.

E. S Corporations

1. *Introduction*

An **S corporation** is not truly a different form of corporation but is rather an existing corporation qualifying for special tax treatment. Any business corporation that is not an S corporation is simply referred to as a "C" corporation. Small corporations will nearly always give serious consideration to electing status as an S corporation. According to subchapter S of the Internal Revenue Code (26 U.S.C. Sections 1361–1364), a "small business corporation" may elect not to have its income taxed at the corporate level, but to have the income passed through to the shareholders who then pay tax at their appropriate rates. Tax must be paid on income whether or not it is distributed. Thus, if the corporation decides to retain $50,000 in an emergency account, the individual shareholders must declare and pay tax on this sum as if they had received it personally. Losses sustained by the corporation can be used by the shareholders to offset other income and thereby decrease taxes. The requirement that the corporation be "small" refers to the number of its shareholders, not the size of the business or its amount of revenue. Thus, a corporation with a handful of shareholders could elect S status, even if revenue is in the millions of dollars. Electing S status avoids double taxation (taxation of the corporate income and then taxation of individual shareholders when income is distributed to them) by eliminating payment of federal taxes by the corporation. In brief, tax-wise, the S corporation is treated like a sole proprietorship, partnership, limited liability partnership, or limited liability company.

S corporation
Corporation whose income is not taxed at corporate level but is passed through to its shareholders who pay tax at their rates

2. *Formation, Operation, and Termination of S Corporations*

To elect to be treated and exist as an S corporation, a corporation must file Forms 2553 and 1120S with the Internal Revenue Service (see Figures 17-4 and 17-5). The election permits the income of the S corporation to be taxed to the shareholders of the corporation, whether or not that income is distributed.

A corporation may make the election to be treated as an S corporation only if it meets all of the following tests:

a. it is a domestic corporation rather than one formed in a foreign country;
b. it has no more than 75 shareholders (a husband and wife are treated as one shareholder);
c. it has only individuals, estates, or certain trusts (rather than other corporations or partnerships) as shareholders;
d. it has no nonresident alien shareholders;
e. it generally has a calendar year as its tax year;
f. it has only one class of stock;
g. it is not a bank, insurance company, or domestic international sales corporation; and
h. all shareholders consent to the election.

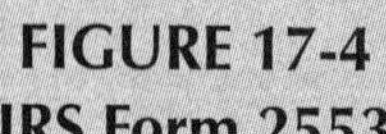

FIGURE 17-4
IRS Form 2553

Form **2553** (Rev. July 1999) Department of the Treasury Internal Revenue Service

Election by a Small Business Corporation
(Under section 1362 of the Internal Revenue Code)
▶ **See Parts II and III on back and the separate instructions.**
▶ **The corporation may either send or fax this form to the IRS. See page 1 of the instructions.**

OMB No. 1545-0146

Notes: 1. *This election to be an S corporation can be accepted only if all the tests are met under* ***Who may elect*** *on page 1 of the instructions; all signatures in Parts I and III are originals (no photocopies); and the exact name and address of the corporation and other required form information are provided.*

2. *Do not file* ***Form 1120S,*** *U.S. Income Tax Return for an S Corporation, for any tax year before the year the election takes effect.*

3. *If the corporation was in existence before the effective date of this election, see* ***Taxes an S corporation may owe*** *on page 1 of the instructions.*

Part I Election Information

Please Type or Print	Name of corporation (see instructions)	**A** Employer identification number
	Number, street, and room or suite no. (If a P.O. box, see instructions.)	**B** Date incorporated
	City or town, state, and ZIP code	**C** State of incorporation

D Election is to be effective for tax year beginning (month, day, year) . . . . ▶ / /

E Name and title of officer or legal representative who the IRS may call for more information

F Telephone number of officer or legal representative ( )

G If the corporation changed its name or address after applying for the EIN shown in **A** above, check this box . . . . ▶ ☐

H If this election takes effect for the first tax year the corporation exists, enter month, day, and year of the **earliest** of the following: (1) date the corporation first had shareholders, (2) date the corporation first had assets, or (3) date the corporation began doing business . . . . ▶ / /

I Selected tax year: Annual return will be filed for tax year ending (month and day) ▶

If the tax year ends on any date other than December 31, except for an automatic 52-53-week tax year ending with reference to the month of December, you **must** complete Part II on the back. If the date you enter is the ending date of an automatic 52-53-week tax year, write "52-53-week year" to the right of the date. See Temporary Regulations section 1.441-2T(e)(3).

J Name and address of each shareholder; shareholder's spouse having a community property interest in the corporation's stock; and each tenant in common, joint tenant, and tenant by the entirety. (A husband and wife (and their estates) are counted as one shareholder in determining the number of shareholders without regard to the manner in which the stock is owned.)	**K** Shareholders' Consent Statement. Under penalties of perjury, we declare that we consent to the election of the above-named corporation to be an S corporation under section 1362(a) and that we have examined this consent statement, including accompanying schedules and statements, and to the best of our knowledge and belief, it is true, correct, and complete. We understand our consent is binding and may not be withdrawn after the corporation has made a valid election. (Shareholders sign and date below.)		**L** Stock owned		**M** Social security number or employer identification number (see instructions)	**N** Shareholder's tax year ends (month and day)
	Signature	Date	Number of shares	Dates acquired		

Under penalties of perjury, I declare that I have examined this election, including accompanying schedules and statements, and to the best of my knowledge and belief, it is true, correct, and complete.

Signature of officer ▶ Title ▶ **Date** ▶

For Paperwork Reduction Act Notice, see page 2 of the instructions. Cat. No. 18629R Form **2553** (Rev. 7-99)

FIGURE 17-5
IRS Form 1120S

Form **1120S** | **U.S. Income Tax Return for an S Corporation** | OMB No. 1545-0130

Department of the Treasury
Internal Revenue Service

▶ **Do not file this form unless the corporation has timely filed Form 2553 to elect to be an S corporation.**
▶ **See separate instructions.**

1999

For calendar year 1999, or tax year beginning , 1999, and ending ,

A Effective date of election as an S corporation	Use IRS label. Otherwise, please print or type.	Name	C Employer identification number
B Business code no. (see pages 26–28)		Number, street, and room or suite no. (If a P.O. box, see page 10 of the instructions.)	D Date incorporated
		City or town, state, and ZIP code	E Total assets (see page 10) $

F Check applicable boxes: (1) ☐ Initial return (2) ☐ Final return (3) ☐ Change in address (4) ☐ Amended return
G Enter number of shareholders in the corporation at end of the tax year . . . . ▶

Caution: *Include **only** trade or business income and expenses on lines 1a through 21. See page 10 of the instructions for more information.*

Section	Line	Description	Box	Amount
Income	1a	Gross receipts or sales ____ b Less returns and allowances ____ c Bal ▶	1c	
	2	Cost of goods sold (Schedule A, line 8)	2	
	3	Gross profit. Subtract line 2 from line 1c	3	
	4	Net gain (loss) from Form 4797, Part II, line 18 *(attach Form 4797)*	4	
	5	Other income (loss) *(attach schedule)*	5	
	6	**Total income (loss).** Combine lines 3 through 5 ▶	6	
Deductions (see page 11 of the instructions for limitations)	7	Compensation of officers	7	
	8	Salaries and wages (less employment credits)	8	
	9	Repairs and maintenance	9	
	10	Bad debts	10	
	11	Rents	11	
	12	Taxes and licenses	12	
	13	Interest	13	
	14a	Depreciation *(if required, attach Form 4562)* 14a		
	b	Depreciation claimed on Schedule A and elsewhere on return 14b		
	c	Subtract line 14b from line 14a	14c	
	15	Depletion **(Do not deduct oil and gas depletion.)**	15	
	16	Advertising	16	
	17	Pension, profit-sharing, etc., plans	17	
	18	Employee benefit programs	18	
	19	Other deductions *(attach schedule)*	19	
	20	**Total deductions.** Add the amounts shown in the far right column for lines 7 through 19 ▶	20	
	21	Ordinary income (loss) from trade or business activities. Subtract line 20 from line 6	21	
Tax and Payments	22	**Tax: a** Excess net passive income tax *(attach schedule)* 22a		
	b	Tax from Schedule D (Form 1120S) 22b		
	c	Add lines 22a and 22b (see page 14 of the instructions for additional taxes)	22c	
	23	**Payments: a** 1999 estimated tax payments and amount applied from 1998 return 23a		
	b	Tax deposited with Form 7004 23b		
	c	Credit for Federal tax paid on fuels *(attach Form 4136)* 23c		
	d	Add lines 23a through 23c	23d	
	24	Estimated tax penalty. Check if Form 2220 is attached ▶☐	24	
	25	**Tax due.** If the total of lines 22c and 24 is larger than line 23d, enter amount owed. See page 4 of the instructions for depository method of payment ▶	25	
	26	**Overpayment.** If line 23d is larger than the total of lines 22c and 24, enter amount overpaid ▶	26	
	27	Enter amount of line 26 you want: **Credited to 2000 estimated tax ▶** **Refunded ▶**	27	

Please Sign Here

Under penalties of perjury, I declare that I have examined this return, including accompanying schedules and statements, and to the best of my knowledge and belief, it is true, correct, and complete. Declaration of preparer (other than taxpayer) is based on all information of which preparer has any knowledge.

▶ Signature of officer | Date | ▶ Title

Paid Preparer's Use Only

Preparer's signature ▶	Date	Check if self-employed ▶ ☐	Preparer's SSN or PTIN
Firm's name (or yours if self-employed) and address ▶		EIN ▶	
		ZIP code ▶	

For Paperwork Reduction Act Notice, see the separate instructions. Cat. No. 11510H Form **1120S** (1999)

The S corporation election is not mentioned or addressed in the corporation's articles of incorporation and the state of incorporation has no interest in whether its domestic corporations elect S status. The S election is made with the Internal Revenue Service after incorporation. Individual shareholders will sign consent statements to make the election. These will be filed with Form 2553. Alternatively, all of the shareholders' consents may be combined in one document. Within approximately 60 days after submission of Form 2553 to the Internal Revenue Service, the corporation will be informed of the acceptance or rejection of the S election.

The S election must be made within a specified time period: S status must be elected on or before the fifteenth day of the third month of the corporation's tax year for which the S status is to be effective. For example, a corporation with a calendar tax year could elect S status until March 15, 2000 and its 2000 income would be passed through to the shareholders rather than being taxed at the corporate level.

Because the number of shareholders involved in an S corporation is relatively small, these shareholders are nearly always active in managing the business. Additionally, to ensure that stock is not transferred to others (which could jeopardize the corporation's S status), most shareholders in S corporations enter into agreements restricting the transfer of their shares so that shares are not transferred to a seventy-sixth shareholder, a nonresident alien, or a corporation—any of which transfers would result in automatic termination of S status. S election may be made by a close corporation, assuming the requirements for S status are met. A corporation that is not an S corporation is called a "C corporation."

S status may be particularly helpful during the first few years of a corporation's existence, when it may sustain losses. These losses may be passed through to the shareholders who may then use them to offset other income, thereby decreasing their tax liability. S status may also be desirable when individual shareholders' tax rates are lower than the applicable corporate tax rates.

Although S corporations do not pay federal income tax, they must report their annual income to the Internal Revenue Service using Form 1120S. Attached to Form 1120S is Schedule K, which discloses each shareholder's portion of corporate income and losses. The individual shareholders report their income (whether distributed or not) or losses on Schedule E, a form attached to their individual 1040 tax forms. Thus, a shareholder owning 14 percent of the stock of an S corporation declares and pays tax on 14 percent of the income earned and declares 14 percent of any losses sustained.

S corporation status remains in effect until formally revoked by a majority of the shareholders. Additionally, S status will automatically terminate if the corporation no longer meets the requirements for small business corporations, for example, a transfer occurs that results in a seventy-sixth shareholder, or preferences are granted to one class of stock and not another.

The emergence and popularity of the limited liability company (see Chapter Six)—which also protects its members from liability, is member-managed, has no limitations on the number of members (who need not be individuals and can be nonresident aliens), all while allowing pass-through of income—may make the S corporation a relic of the past. The LLC avoids the restrictions imposed on S corporations while maintaining pass-through tax status. Therefore, it is an increasingly popular investment vehicle.

Key Features
of Other Forms of Corporations

- A close corporation is a smaller corporation owned and operated by a group of family and/or friends. There is usually a limit of 50 shareholders who enter into agreements restricting the transfer of shares. Close corporations are generally allowed less formality in operation than ordinary C corporations.
- A nonprofit (or not-for-profit corporation) is one formed not to earn a profit but for some charitable or religious purpose or for the mutual benefit of its members. Stock is not sold. Memberships are often granted to the members of the nonprofit corporation. If nonprofits apply for and are granted tax-exempt status, they need not pay federal taxes. Contributions made to charitable or religious nonprofits are generally tax deductible, while contributions made to a mutual benefit nonprofit are deductible only if they are valid business expenses.
- A subsidiary corporation is one formed by another, the parent. The parent either owns all of the stock of the subsidiary or the vast majority of it. A parent will be liable for a subsidiary's debts only if it dominates and controls the subsidiary such that they do not operate as two separate corporations.
- A professional corporation is formed by a group of professionals, such as doctors or lawyers. The professionals retain liability for their own acts of negligence and for those performed under their supervision and authority. The corporate form has been selected for certain tax advantages and benefit plans available to corporations.
- An S corporation is not a different type of corporation but is a corporation that has qualified for special tax treatment such that all of its income is not taxed at the corporate level but is passed through to the shareholders who pay tax at their appropriate brackets. An S corporation is limited to 75 shareholders who must all be individuals.

F. Role of Paralegal

Paralegals are involved in a variety of activities when both forming and maintaining the status of close corporations, nonprofit corporations, parent and subsidiary corporations, professional corporations, and S corporations. Typical tasks conducted by paralegals include the following:

1. Preparing and filing the articles of incorporation to create close corporations, nonprofit corporations, subsidiary corporations, or professional corporations.

2. Researching state statutes to determine special requirements for the names of nonprofit and professional corporations and special provisions required for the articles of close corporations, nonprofit, and professional corporations.
3. Preparing shareholders' statements of consent to election of S corporation status.
4. Drafting agreements among shareholders of a close corporation or an S corporation imposing restrictions on transfer of stock and ensuring that stock certificates include a legend condition stating that the transfer of shares is subject to restriction.
5. Preparing Internal Revenue Service Form 2553 to elect S corporation status.
6. Applying for tax-exempt status for nonprofit corporations.
7. Preparing notices of meetings and minutes of the meetings of board of directors and of shareholders for all varieties of corporations.
8. Conducting annual reviews, often called legal audits, of close corporations, professional corporations, and S corporations to ensure compliance with statutory requirements, including reviewing stationery, share certificates, signs, literature, and other materials to ensure that the corporate name is correctly displayed, that share certificates bear proper legends, that the number of shareholders in close and S corporations does not exceed the statutory maximum, and ensuring that shareholders, directors, and officers in professional corporations are duly licensed.

Resource Guide

1. Statutes

As always, the primary resource guide governing close, nonprofit, parent-subsidiary, professional, and S corporations are the relevant statutes. S corporations are governed by the Internal Revenue Code, Title 26, and, like the remaining corporations, are also governed by the statutes of the state of incorporation and any foreign jurisdiction in which they have qualified to transact business. Many states have special statutory supplements containing their statutes for close, nonprofit, and professional corporations. Other states simply integrate provisions relating to these corporations into the state's business corporation code.

2. State and Federal Officials

Forms for articles of incorporation for close corporations, nonprofit corporations, and professional corporations can usually be obtained by calling the secretary of state and requesting the forms. Phone numbers for the secretaries of state are provided in Appendix A. Creating a subsidiary corporation is accomplished by completing the state's usual form for articles of incorporation.

Information on S corporations is included in IRS Publication 589, *Tax Information on S Corporations,* which may be obtained by calling the IRS. Form 2553 (needed to elect S status), IRS Form 1120S (the annual information tax report filed by S corporations), Schedule K (identifying shareholders' pro rata income and losses), and Schedule E (used by individual shareholders to report corporate income and losses) can be obtained from the IRS by calling (800) TAX-FORM.

3. Texts and Treatises

The two general encyclopedias, C.J.S. and Am. Jur. 2d, offer clear and introductory information about close, nonprofit, parent-subsidiary, professional, and S corporations. If your state has a local encyclopedia, use it for background information and to direct you to the pertinent statutes and cases dealing with these corporate varieties.

Use the card catalog at your local law library to locate books devoted to these corporate varieties. Similarly, the *Index to Legal Periodicals* will refer you to published articles discussing these corporations.

Your law firm or legal department may have collected a variety of texts and forms for you to consult. If your office or department does not have the pertinent forms, contact the secretary of state and request forms for close corporations, nonprofit corporations, and professional corporations. Prepare form files for these forms. Similarly, keep copies of the pertinent IRS forms needed. Don't forget how helpful other people in your office or department may be. Send out an E-mail message or memo asking for forms, assistance, and so forth. Many attorneys have voluminous form files and are just waiting to be asked to share them.

4. Form Books

The form books identified in Chapter Nine will assist in preparing minutes of meetings, shareholder resolutions, and other documents needed by the corporations discussed in this chapter, such as forms for incorporating professional corporations, making the election to be treated as an S corporation, and other related documents.

◆ ◆ ◆

WEB RESOURCES

The most important resources relating to other forms of corporations and S corporations are the various state and federal statutes. The following is a site allowing access to statutes.

www.ll.georgetown.edu

When you access this site for Georgetown University Law Center, select "State, Local & Territorial." You will be presented with a map of the United States. Point your cursor to the state in which you are interested, and you will be provided with links to a variety of legal sources relating to that state. Select "Statutes" or "Codes," and you will be linked to the state's statutes. In some states, searching can be done by either keywords or by section number. In other states, searching is accomplished exclusively by keywords. Alternatively, when you access the site, select "Federal," and you will be directed to federal statutes. Statutes relating to S corporations are located in Title 26 of the Internal Revenue Code.

Because nearly all states have posted their forms relating to creation and dissolution of close corporations, professional corporations, and nonprofit corporations on their Web sites, important Web resources are the home pages of the various secretaries of state. See Appendix A for the specific Web address for each of the state's secretaries of state. Other alternatives follow.

www.nass.org
This Web site of the National Association of Secretaries of State will provide you with links to each of the secretaries of state. After you access the home page of the Association, select "States." You will then be given an alphabetical list of all 50 states and the District of Columbia (together with their state flags). Point your cursor at the state you wish and you will be immediately linked to the home page for that state's secretary of state. In most instances, you will immediately see entries for "Corporations" or "Securities." Select the relevant entry, and you will be directed to the pertinent forms, nearly all of which can be downloaded and printed. Fee schedules are also included on the sites.

www.legalwiz.com
When you access this site, select "Legal Sites" and then "Corporate Department and Secretary of State Pages" for links to each state's secretary of state.

www4.law.cornell.edu/usccode
This excellent site allows searching of federal statutes by keyword, by section number, or popular name. You can review all 50 titles of the U.S. Code or look up statutes by their popular names. All of the tax statutes are located in Title 26, entitled "Internal Revenue Code."

www.irs.gov
This Web site of the Internal Revenue Service allows you to locate more than 700 tax forms and instructions, including all forms relating to S corporations. In many cases, the instructions provided for a corresponding form are clearly and articulately presented. You may look up forms by number, by keyword, or by scanning a list of all forms.

The following site can be used to review forms for shareholders' agreements used in close or in S corporations:

http://legal-resource.com/forms

To locate other forms, access <http://www.findlaw.com/16forms/index.html> for a list of numerous other sites where various legal forms can be found.

Discussion Questions

1. Francis Associates, Inc. has 82 shareholders. It would like to avoid double taxation. May it elect to be taxed as an S corporation? Why or why not?
2. Adams Consulting, Inc. is a close corporation with 15 shareholders. It wishes to ensure that upon the death of any shareholder there are sufficient funds

to purchase a shareholder's stock so that it is not inherited by "outsiders." What type of agreement/policy would best serve the corporation's needs? Why?

3. Susan Miller has incorporated her law practice.
   a. What name should the corporation be given?
   b. Is incorporation an effective way for Ms. Miller to avoid liability for acts of legal malpractice?
   c. May Ms. Miller grant shares of stock in her corporation to her receptionist? Why or why not?
   d. May Ms. Miller deduct dues she pays to Northwood Country Club as a corporate business expense?

4. The Murphy Heart Association, Inc. was organized as a nonprofit corporation dedicated to educating the public about cardiovascular health.
   a. May the corporation sell its shares to the public?
   b. Due to careful investing in the stock market, the Association made $350,00 last year. Will it lose its nonprofit status due to the fact that it has earned a profit?
   c. If the Association dissolves, how should money in its accounts be distributed?
   d. Is a contribution made by you to the Association tax deductible?

5. Peterson, Inc. formed Sanders, Inc. and owns all of the stock of Sanders, Inc. Sanders, Inc. owes $100,000 to a bank. Will Peterson, Inc. be liable to pay this debt? Discuss fully.

6. What advantages does a limited liability company offer over an S corporation?

18

Employee Compensation and Employment Agreements

CHAPTER OVERVIEW

To attract and retain quality employees, employers need to be creative in compensating employees. While a fixed salary is the most common form of compensation, numerous other benefits can be offered to employees to motivate them to remain with the company. These additional benefits may take the form of commissions, bonuses, stock options, insurance, retirement plans, and other fringe benefits. Some retirement plans provide tax advantages to both employers and employees. Plans may be qualified or nonqualified. Qualified plans are those complying with various Internal Revenue Code provisions. Contributions to the plan made by employers may be deductible as business expenses; similarly, the money contributed to the plan is not taxed to the employees. Nonqualified plans do not provide the same tax advantages to the employer as do qualified plans.

Unless an employment agreement exists, employment is deemed to be "at will," meaning that it can be terminated by either the employer or employee at any time for any reason. To recruit skilled personnel, an employer may offer an employee an employment contract. The contract not only provides job security for the employee but usually protects valuable proprietary information of the company as well. Employment agreements are formal contracts, typically in writing, specifying the terms and conditions of employment. They may be used for employees with special skills and talents as well as for senior executives. Most employment contracts include a variety of restrictive covenants or contractual prohibitions designed to prevent uniquely skilled employees from working for competitors, misappropriating proprietary information, or misusing valuable trade secrets.

A. Employee Compensation

1. *Introduction*

In addition to paying fixed salaries or hourly wages, corporations and other businesses can provide a variety of additional forms of compensation to their employees. Generally, these non-cash forms of compensation are referred to as **fringe benefits.** In recognition of the increasing importance of these forms of compensation, they are more commonly referred to as *benefits* today. The benefits may include insurance, stock options, and various profit-sharing and retirement plans. The employee compensation plans may provide tax advantages for the employer as well as play a primary role in attracting and retaining skilled employees. Moreover, the benefits provided are generally not taxed as "income" to the employees.

Fringe benefits
Benefits provided to employees in addition to salary (often called *benefits*)

A few general principles apply to any form of fringe benefit provided to employees:

a. it should be reasonable in amount;
b. it should be based upon services rendered to the employer;
c. it should not be subject to any claim of *self-dealing* on the part of corporate management, for example, extraordinary benefits awarded by corporate managers to themselves; and
d. benefits must be provided fairly and evenly without discrimination in favor of highly compensated employees.

Although employers may elect to provide a variety of benefits, three are mandated by federal law: unemployment insurance, workers' compensation insurance, and Social Security disability insurance, all of which are government programs designed to provide an employee's income when the employee cannot work.

2. *Insurance Benefits*

Health Insurance. Health insurance is of ever-increasing importance to employees. Health insurance covers costs and expenses incurred by an employee resulting from sickness or physical injury. While employers traditionally offer healthcare insurance, they are not required by federal law to do so. The corporate employer will pay the insurance **premium,** the amount paid to the insurance company to provide the insurance. Employees typically pay part of the premium as well in the form of some amount deducted from their paychecks. There may be some restrictions on coverage, for example, a requirement that the employee be employed for a certain period of time before insurance is provided, a provision that health insurance is available only to full-time employees, or a provision refusing coverage for illnesses or conditions that existed before the commencement of the employee's employment.

Premium
Amount paid to insurer to provide coverage

Premiums paid by the corporation are deductible business expenses. Employees are not taxed on the premiums paid by the corporation to the insurance company for this employee benefit.

COBRA
Federal law requiring insurance continuation after employee departs employment

Under the 1986 federal law, Consolidated Omnibus Budget Reconciliation Act (**COBRA**), employers are required to offer former employees the option to continue group healthcare insurance for 18 months after termination. The former employee pays all costs but is provided with insurance for this period of time until, presumably, other employment offering insurance is found.

Accident and Disability Insurance. **Accident insurance** covers the insured for expenses arising out of an accident which causes physical injury. If the insured is unable to work, **disability insurance** provides a certain income stream to the insured for some stated period of time or for as long as the disability lasts. While Social Security disability insurance exists, the amount provided is usually less than the employee's income, so disability insurance fills in the income gap.

Accident insurance Insurance designed to protect insured who cannot work due to accident

Disability insurance Insurance designed to protect insured who cannot work due to disability

Premiums paid by the corporation for accident and disability insurance are tax deductible. While employees need not pay tax on the value of this benefit provided to them, a payment made to the insured to compensate for lost wages is generally taxable income to the employee because it is a mere replacement for taxable wages.

Life Insurance. Corporations may purchase life insurance policies for employees. For key persons in the corporation, an additional policy may be purchased naming the corporation (rather than the employee's heirs) as the beneficiary. Upon the death of the employee, the corporation will receive a lump-sum payment to compensate it for the loss of this critical employee and perhaps to fund the repurchase of the employee's stock from his heirs.

Some policies are split-dollar plans. In **split-dollar insurance,** the corporation and the employee each pay a portion of the premium for insurance on the life of the employee. The corporation is a named beneficiary of the policy to the extent of any premiums it has paid and the employee's heirs are the beneficiaries of the remainder of the proceeds of the policy. Upon the employee's death, the corporation will be reimbursed the amount it has paid for the premium over the years, and the employee's heirs receive the major part of the proceeds of the policy. The corporation thus recovers all the money it has paid, the beneficiaries receive most of the proceeds, and the employee's cost of the premiums was shared with the employer.

Split-dollar insurance Insurance for which employer and employee each pay part of premium

Corporations may purchase group term life insurance for the life of each employee for a policy amount up to $50,000 without causing employees any taxable income. Premiums paid by the employer are tax deductible and the insurance proceeds ultimately received by the beneficiaries are tax free. If the corporation purchases a policy that will pay more than $50,000, the premium paid for the amount of insurance in excess of $50,000 will be considered income to the employee upon which tax must be paid.

Death Benefits. A corporation can agree to make a cash payment to an employee's heirs upon his or her death. This one-time lump-sum payment is deductible to the corporation as a business expense. Proceeds received by the beneficiaries in excess of $5,000 are taxable income.

3. *Retirement Plans*

Introduction. Employers may establish retirement plans for their employees so that upon retirement, employees will have funds in addition to those provided by Social Security benefits. The most significant legislation regulating these retirement plans is the **Employee Retirement Income Security Act (ERISA)** enacted in 1974. There is no requirement imposed upon employers to establish a retirement plan. Once a plan exists, however, ERISA governs its management. Certain retirement plans, however, such as those offered by the United States government or nonprofit corporations, are exempt from the provisions of ERISA. While retirement or pension plans need not include all workers, they cannot be structured to benefit only senior executives.

ERISA
Federal law governing retirement plans

Retirement plans are referred to as qualified or nonqualified. A **qualified plan** is one that meets certain requirements of the Internal Revenue Code and is thus eligible for special tax treatment. Employers typically submit the proposed qualified plan to obtain a determination letter indicating that the plan has been reviewed by the IRS and that it satisfies the requirements imposed on qualified plans. Alternatively, to save time and money, an employer may adopt a **master plan** (or *prototype plan*) that has been prequalified by the IRS and is sold by pension plan specialists to employers desiring qualified plans. A **nonqualified plan** is not subject to the extensive regulation governing a qualified plan; it does not provide the same tax advantages as a qualified plan and is typically a private agreement between the employer and its key personnel.

Qualified plan
Retirement plan meeting IRS requirements and which is eligible for favorable tax treatment

Master plan
Retirement plan prequalified by IRS (also called *prototype plan*)

Nonqualified plan
Usually a private agreement between employer and employee that does not meet requirements needed to achieve favorable tax treatment

The tax advantages of a qualified plan are as follows:

1. Contributions made by the employer are deductible as business expenses just as wages would be.
2. The interest earned on funds paid into the plan is not taxable. Therefore, the funds grow more quickly than if a portion was being siphoned off for taxes.
3. The employee does not pay any tax on the funds contributed until they are actually received, generally, upon retirement, when the employee is in a lower tax bracket.
4. Retirement plan funds do not go through probate and therefore pass free of estate taxes.

Qualified Retirement Plans. Qualified plans are generally classified as defined benefit plans or defined contribution plans. Both of these types of qualified plans share a variety of features in common. Most important, qualified plans receive the favorable tax treatment described above. The social justification for depriving the government of tax revenue until some later date is that the plans assist individuals in providing for their retirement, thereby supplementing Social Security.

The plan itself is a written document containing the terms and conditions of the employer's retirement program. The plan is usually described in a booklet or pamphlet given to employees. The employer providing the plan is referred to as the **sponsor.** The sponsor of a qualified retirement plan may be a corporation, a partnership, or a sole proprietor. The people for whom the plan is designed, namely, employees, are called the **plan participants.** The plan is managed by the **plan administrator,** who owes fiduciary duties to the sponsor and the plan par-

Sponsor
Party providing a retirement plan

Plan participant
One for whom a retirement plan is designed

Plan administrator
Party who manages retirement plan

ticipants and is responsible for accounting for all contributions made to the plan and all distributions made from the plan. The plan administrator is usually entitled to a fee for these services. Contributions to the plan may be made by the plan sponsor, plan participants, or both. Plans in which both the employer and employee contribute are referred to as **contributory plans.** Plans funded solely by the employer are called **noncontributory plans.** Certain limits are imposed on the amounts that may be contributed. A corporate sponsor may contribute either cash or shares of its own stock.

Contributory plan
Retirement plan funded by both employer and employee

Noncontributory plan
Retirement plan funded solely by employer

Employees are generally eligible to participate in the plan when they reach age 21 or have completed one year of employment, whichever is later. The time at which an employee is entitled to receive the benefits of the plan (referred to as **vesting** of the benefits) is mandated by ERISA. Once the benefits have vested, the employee has an absolute right to them. At this point, the employee's incentive to remain with the employer may decrease. Therefore, employers often prefer to impose the longest vesting periods they can. The employee's right to the benefits derived from her own contribution is nonforfeitable under any circumstance.

Vesting
The time at which an employee's rights occur or when employee is entitled to benefits of retirement plan

The Internal Revenue Code provides two alternate schemes for vesting. The plan may provide that benefits do not vest until five years of service have been completed. At that time, the benefits are 100 percent vested and nonforfeitable. Alternatively, the plan may provide for three to seven years vesting. After three years of service, the employee has a nonforfeitable right to 20 percent of the employer's contribution. This amount increases 20 percent for each year of completed service, until year seven, when the nonforfeitable percentage is 100 percent. The plan may, of course, allow immediate vesting and then impose a certain waiting requirement, such as requiring employees to complete two years of service before they may participate in the plan. As soon as they participate, however, all benefits derived from their contributions are 100 percent nonforfeitable.

A plan cannot be "**top heavy**" or "discriminate" by favoring more highly compensated employees over lower-paid employees. A plan is top heavy if more than 60 percent of the plan is in the accounts of senior or key employees. Another requirement imposed is that the employer must physically set aside or "fund" the money for the plan. Typically, the employer contributes funds to a trust or other entity that invests the funds for the employees' benefit. The plan may generally be terminated only for circumstances not within the employer's control, such as dissolution of the corporate employer.

Top-heavy plan
A retirement plan that discriminates in favor of senior employees

Defined Benefit Plans. **Defined benefit plans** are those which set a pre-established benefit that will be paid to employees, usually monthly, after they leave the company. The amount of the employer's contribution is set in stone. The retirement plan provided by the military is a prototype of a defined benefit plan. Military members know that after 20 years of service, they will receive 50 percent of their base pay. Employee participants in a defined benefit plan can predetermine exactly how much money will be available to them upon retirement. Pension plans are a type of defined benefit plan.

Defined benefit plan
Retirement plan that fixes a pre-established benefit that will be paid to employees

A pension plan provides for the payment of benefits to employees after their retirement. Typically, pension plans contemplate payments for the employee's lifetime, post-retirement. The amount required to be contributed by the employer to achieve the desired payment goal is calculated by actuaries using mathematical models based on employees' ages and lengths of service. Thus, establishing and maintaining a defined benefit plan can be costly and complex. Because the employer's annual contributions are mandated, a pension plan may impose some hardship on a company going through a difficult financial period inasmuch as the employer is required to contribute an established amount regardless of its profits. Contributions to the pension plan are held in trust.

Defined contribution plan
Retirement plan that specifies the contribution that will be made to it

Defined Contribution Plans. Rather than guaranteeing a specified total retirement payout to an employee, a **defined contribution plan** simply specifies the amount the employer will place into the plan account each year on behalf of the participant. If the plan trustee does not invest wisely, less money will be available to the plan participants upon their retirement than if the investments succeeded. For example, the employer could agree to contribute $100 per month (per employee) to the company's pension plan. The size of monthly payments the employee receives after retirement will vary depending on how the sum was invested.

There are many types of defined contribution plans, including profit-sharing plans, money-purchase pension plans, and 401(k) plans, the most popular of all defined contribution plans. Most small businesses adopt defined contribution plans rather than defined benefit plans, and the use of defined benefit plans decreased by 14 percent between 1975 and 1995. The disadvantage to most defined contribution plans for the employer is that the employer's contribution is fixed, requiring a contribution even in years without profit.

Typically, defined contribution plans establish a certain percentage amount that the employer is required to contribute. This amount is usually based on the participant's annual compensation. For example, the plan might specify that the employer will contribute 5 percent of each eligible employee's salary per year. Employees generally have some choices as to where the funds are invested. Interest earned on funds invested is credited to the participant's account and is not taxable until received, thus deferring taxes for the employee. Additionally, employees may borrow a portion of the funds in their account to meet certain expenses. The employee may also contribute to the plan, usually up to some specified percentage of annual salary. The employee's contribution is vested as of the date of any contribution; employer's contributions are vested in accordance with the ERISA requirements. The employer's contributions are tax deductible up to a specified amount. This type of plan is often referred to as a **money-purchase pension plan.** In money-purchase pension plans, the employer's commitment to contribute a specified percentage of an employee's salary is fixed, allowing employees to calculate how much money will be in the plan upon their retirement.

Money-purchase pension plan
Retirement plan by which employer contributes a certain percentage of employee's salary each year

Profit-sharing plan
Retirement plan funded by employer's profits

Another common type of defined contribution plan is a **profit-sharing plan.** As the name indicates, money contributed to the plan is funded by the employer's profits, usually a percentage of profits from the previous fiscal year. Amounts contributed by the employer are divided among employee accounts, usually in proportion to employee compensation. The fact that contributions hinge on the company's performance may motivate employees to work hard and may help to establish a team or collegial atmosphere. The percentage to be contributed annually does not have to be established in advance and usually varies from year to year. The board of directors usually has the discretion to fix the annual contribution. In fact, in lean years, the company may not make any contribution at all. This is a significant advantage to a company inasmuch as other plans mandate yearly contributions, regardless of the employer's profitability. The tax deduction available to the corporate employer in a profit-sharing plan is more limited than for other defined contribution plans. Thus, the amount contributed by an employer in a profit-sharing plan may be somewhat less than that contributed under other defined contribution plans, such as the money-purchase pension plan. The risk under a profit-sharing plan is that the benefit may not be adequate at retirement.

Stock bonus plans are similar to profit-sharing plans. The employer's contribution may be in the form of stock, allowing participants to become shareholders of the corporation without requiring a substantial cash outlay on the part of the corporate employer. The corporation will have the discretion to establish its annual contribution to the plan. If the stock is publicly traded, the employee may usually opt for a cash contribution rather than stock. Corporations whose stock is publicly traded often purchase their own stock on the securities market for their employees.

Stock bonus plan
Plan in which employer contributes stock

A unique plan entitled the **employee stock ownership plan** (ESOP) is also designed to give ownership rights in a corporation to the employees. In this plan, the employer contributes funds (from its profits or money it has borrowed) to a trust it has established. The money is then used to purchase stock in the corporation. The employer's contributions to the trust are tax deductible. The stock may be purchased from shareholders wishing to sell stock or may be from the corporation's authorized but unissued shares. Shares in the trust are then allocated to individual employee accounts. Employees must be 100 percent vested within five to seven years. When an employee leaves the company, she receives her stock, which the company must buy back from her at its fair market value.

Employee stock ownership plan
Plan in which employer contributes funds it has borrowed to a trust and which money is then used to buy stock in the corporation for employees

The ESOP offers a unique advantage to an employer who can borrow money from a bank to fund its contribution rather than using cash on hand. The money is then lent by the corporation to the fund or trust. The corporation has cash in its accounts and the employees own stock in the company. ESOPs have been used in defending hostile takeovers by distributing sufficient amounts of stock to employees such that the aggressor has difficulty in obtaining stock in the target.

Companies can mix and match plans. For example, a company could establish a money-purchase pension plan and then add a somewhat limited profit-sharing plan. Defined contribution plans can be combined with defined benefit plans to create **target benefit plans,** usually to increase the amount of tax deductible contributions that may be made by the employer.

Target benefit plan
Combination of defined contribution and defined benefit plans

401(k) Plans. A **401(k) plan,** so called because it is authorized by Internal Revenue Code Section 401(k), offers advantages to small and mid-sized corporations because most contributions are made by the employees rather than the employer. 401(k)s allow employees to save and invest for their own retirement. Employees contribute an annual amount to the 401(k) account, usually a percentage of their annual compensation. Employee contributions are capped at a maximum amount ($10,500 at present). This is deducted from wages by the employer prior to receipt by the employee without being taxed. The amount may be matched by the employer or the employer may make some lesser contribution; for example, it may match an employee's contribution dollar-for-dollar, ten cents on the dollar, or in a fixed amount of *X* percent of the employee's annual salary, regardless of what the employee contributes. A 401(k) plan provides retirement funds for employees; however, it also reduces their present salaries. Additionally, while it defers federal income tax for employees, the amount contributed is still subject to social security taxes.

401(k) plan
Retirement plan funded by employee's nontaxable contributions

The funds contributed are usually invested in various mutual funds or stocks pre-established by the plan sponsor, the employer, but selected by the employee. The money earned in the 401(k) each year is not subject to tax. Taxes are paid when the money is withdrawn, presumably when the employee has reached age 59½ and is in a lower tax bracket. Contributions attributable to the employer may not be withdrawn without penalty by an employee unless the employee retires, leaves the company's service, becomes disabled, reaches age 59½, or suffers some hardship. An employee who leaves one place of employment can usually "roll over" funds in the 401(k) account to the new employer's plan. Thus, 401(k)s are highly portable. Participants must begin taking distributions by age 70½.

Keogh plan
Retirement plan for self-employed individuals

Keogh Plans. The significant tax advantages provided by qualified employee benefit plans were not available to the self-employed or to sole proprietors until passage of the Keogh Act, named for New York Congressman Eugene Keogh. Self-employed individuals or sole proprietors may establish accounts for retirement purposes called **Keogh plans.** Contributions made to the Keogh plan are then deducted from the person's taxable income. Maximum contributions (generally, $30,000) and deductions are specified by the Keogh Act. The money is invested with a bank or financial institution. Interest earned on the amount invested is not subject to taxation until withdrawal. Tax penalties are imposed on funds withdrawn before the participant reaches age 59½. Withdrawals must begin before age 70½. Taxes are imposed when the money is distributed.

Individual retirement account
Retirement plans funded by employees not covered by company-sponsored retirement plans (*IRAs*)

Individual Retirement Accounts. Some individuals are employed by companies that have not established any qualified retirement plan. These individuals may plan for their retirement by creating **individual retirement accounts** (IRAs) with banks or other financial institutions. They make periodic contributions to the IRA, which are then deducted from their taxable income. At one point, Congress allowed any individual (even those covered by qualified plans established by their employers) to establish IRAs and make a tax deductible contribution up to $2,000 per year. Since the mid 1980s, deductions are permitted for IRA contributions only by those persons not covered by other plans, and, thus, IRAs are less popular than they once were. Moreover, deductibility of contributions decreases the greater one's income is until it is phased out completely once one's gross income is $40,000. Money withdrawn from the IRA account before the individual reaches the age of 55½ is subject to tax penalties and money must be withdrawn once the IRA owner reaches age 70½. The main difference between an IRA and a Keogh plan is the contribution limit.

SEP-IRA
Plan allowing self-employed individual to contribute to his/her retirement

SEP-IRAs. A **Simplified Employee Pension (SEP)** is a written plan that allows a self-employed individual to make contributions to his or her own retirement (and those of his or her employees if there are employees) without getting involved in the more complex Keogh plan. Under a SEP, contributions are made to an individual retirement account (thus, the name SEP-IRA). Contributions cannot be more than 15 percent of the individual's compensation or $30,000 each year, whichever is less. Contributions made to the SEP-IRA are tax deductible. Distributions are subject to the same rules as IRAs, discussed above.

SIMPLE-IRA
Plan in which both employer (a small employer) and employee contribute

SIMPLE-IRAs. A **Savings Incentive Match Plan for Employees** (SIMPLE plan) is a written agreement between employers (who must have fewer than 100 employees) and their employees. Both employer and employee must contribute to the plan. A SIMPLE-IRA, considered to be a "starter plan" for small employers, is subject to the same rules as an IRA except for a higher contribution limit. The plan is usually structured as a type of IRA into which employees contribute up to $6000 of their income annually, compared with $2000 contributable under ordinary IRAs.

Roth IRAs. A **Roth IRA** (named for its sponsor, Sen. William Roth of Delaware) was created in 1998 to allow taxpayers to save money for use in retirement. Unlike ordinary IRAs, contributions to a Roth IRA are never deductible; however distributions taken after age 59½ are free of tax. Withdrawals are not taxed at all at this time, because tax has already been paid on the money before its deposit into the Roth IRA. Moreover, earnings on the money in the Roth IRA are not taxed. Roths are only available to individuals with certain income levels. If an individual's gross income is greater than $110,000 (or $160,000 for married couples filing jointly), a Roth is unavailable. Unlike traditional IRAs, the money need never be withdrawn from a Roth IRA. Thus, the money in the account can be passed on to one's heirs. Traditional IRAs can be converted to Roth IRAs.

Roth IRA
Retirement plan in which contributions are not deductible but distributions (after a certain age) are

Nonqualified Plans. Employers may establish plans that do not comply with all of the regulations imposed on qualified plans. These *nonqualified plans,* however, do not achieve the same tax advantages as do qualified plans. Nonqualified plans may be established by a corporation wishing to reward its top executives yet not include other employees whereas a qualified plan cannot be top heavy or discriminate. Alternatively, the employer may wish to reward employees in excess of the limits imposed on qualified plans. Nonqualified plans are often in the form of private agreements between the employer and its key executives. Regulation and paperwork are minimal.

4. *Incentive Stock Option Plans*

A corporation may also award cash or property bonuses as incentives for meeting certain production goals or sales quotas. Bonuses consisting of shares of the corporation or of its subsidiary may also be used to compensate employees. Share bonuses do not affect the corporation's cash flow; however, they do dilute the proportionate power and control of existing shareholders. Stock option plans are also utilized by corporations to motivate and reward workers. Under a **stock option** plan, employees are granted the right to purchase the corporation's shares for fixed prices at certain times, regardless of the market price of the stock at the time the option may be exercised. An option would typically be exercised when the option price is lower than the market price of the stock. For example, if Martin Shelby, an employee of ABC, Inc., has an option to buy 100 shares of ABC, Inc. at $20 per share when the market price is $50 per share, Martin would likely exercise his option and realize an immediate benefit of $3,000 (the difference in the option price and market price multiplied by 100, the number of shares purchased). If the option price is higher than the market price, the employee will generally not exercise his or her rights to purchase the stock. If the employee exercises the option and purchases shares which later increase in value, the employee will profit from this increase. Stock option plans also enhance employer-employee relations because the employees realize that the better they perform, the more the company's shares will be worth, and they will be direct beneficiaries of any such

Stock option
Right to purchase fixed number of shares at a certain date at a fixed price

increases. Employees thus share in the company's growth and success and become owners of the corporation.

Incentive stock option plan
Stock option plan that is qualified under IRS regulations, allowing for favorable tax treatment

Incentive stock option plans may be qualified under various Internal Revenue Code provisions and thereby receive advantageous tax treatment. The Internal Revenue Code imposes various requirements on qualified incentive stock option plans, including provisions relating to the terms of the option plan, the option price, the employees covered under the plan, and the amount of stock that may be subject to the option. An employee is not taxed upon receipt of the stock purchased through a qualified incentive option plan. Tax will be paid later, when the stock is ultimately sold, at which time the employee may be in a lower tax bracket. If the employee holds the stock for one year from the date of exercise, appreciation in value is taxed as a long-term capital gain. A **nonqualified stock option** does not qualify for such preferential tax treatment. In an NSO, employees pay no tax when the option is granted but rather pay ordinary income tax on the difference (the "**spread**") between the grant price and the stock's value at the time the option is exercised by purchase of the stock. Careful consideration should be given to the awarding of stock to ensure that this issuance of securities is in compliance with, or exempt from, the applicable federal and state securities regulations.

Nonqualified stock option
Stock option that does not qualify for favorable tax treatment

Spread
Difference between stock price at which option is granted and stock price when option is exercised or purchased

Stock options have become increasingly popular in recent years. Not only are they used by publicly traded companies but they are often used by smaller start-ups that are strapped for cash. In such situations, stock options assist in recruiting and retaining employees. They are the norm in high-tech companies, which typically grant them to all workers, not just senior employees as is the case in some companies. During the past two or three years, the media has devoted significant attention to the cadres of young employees granted options in high-tech companies who become instant millionaires when the companies go public, and their stock soars.

Options usually are granted with a vesting period, meaning that the employee cannot exercise the option for some period of time, often two or three years. Such a vesting period helps the company retain valuable employees. Generally, employees who voluntarily resign or who are terminated for cause lose their unvested options. Once options vest, the employee has a right to exercise the option, even if employment is terminated (although exercise must often occur within some specified time period after termination, and the employee may be required to sell the stock back to the employer at its fair value, if the stock is not traded publicly).

Strike price
Price at which option was granted

Once options vest, employees can exercise the option, buy the stock at the **strike price** (the price at which the option was granted), and then sell on the open market for more than the strike price (although minimum holding periods must be met in order to receive favorable tax treatment). Alternatively, they can exercise the option, buy the stock at the strike price, and then hold the stock in the hope it continues to increase in value.

You may recall from Chapter Ten that in early 2000, the city of Oakland, California, accepted $6 million in cash in addition to stock warrants (long-term options) for the sale of a parcel of land to a start-up communications corporation. If the company goes public, the city can exercise the warrants and perhaps make a great deal of money, putting a new twist on the practice of the awarding of stock options by emerging companies that are strapped for cash.

The stock options described herein are different from the option contracts traded on AMEX, the Chicago Board Options Exchange, and the Philadelphia Stock Exchange, discussed in Chapter Thirteen.

5. *Other Fringe Benefits*

In addition to providing insurance and retirement benefits, employers can provide numerous other fringe benefits or perquisites **(perks)**. Thus, employers may compensate their employees in the form of licensing fees (for doctors, lawyers, and so forth), country club dues, health club memberships, reimbursement of legal fees or group legal services plans, car leases, cell phones, pagers, interest-free loans, discounts on company products or services, tuition plans for employees wishing to return to school, and numerous other benefits. Some corporations have undertaken to pay or reimburse employees for some or all of the taxes imposed on the employee. The tax reimbursement payment itself is taxable income, which the corporation pays taxes on, and so forth, with a continual "pyramiding effect."

Perks
Perquisites or fringe benefits provided by employers

Some directors receive payments, called **honoraria,** for attending directors' meetings. These payments may range from $100 per meeting to more than $1,000 per meeting for larger publicly traded corporations.

Honoraria
Payments given for appearing at an event or meeting

6. *Reimbursement of Expenses*

Employees are typically reimbursed by the employer for expenses incurred on behalf of the employer. For example, transportation costs and food and lodging expenses are generally reimbursed by employers. Some employers establish a certain daily allowance for traveling employees. This *per diem* may be as high as $150. If the employee does not use $150 per day in lodging or other expenses, the employee retains the excess tax-free. Most companies have various forms and procedures in place for claiming and receiving expense reimbursement. Other companies issue credit cards to employees for business expenses. The bill may go directly to the employer for payment or to the employee who pays it and then seeks reimbursement from the company.

B. Employment Agreements

1. *Introduction*

Most individuals in the United States are **employed at will,** meaning they can be fired at any time at the will of the employer, for a valid reason, such as incompetence, or for no reason at all. Similarly, the employee can terminate the employment at any time, leaving the employer for another opportunity. The employment at will doctrine has been modified by statute in some states and by court decisions to ensure that employees are not terminated for exercising certain rights and privileges, such as their rights to engage in free speech, unionization activities, or to complain about unfair or unsafe working conditions.

Employment at will
Employment relationship that either party can terminate for any reason or no reason

Wrongful discharge
Termination of employee for improper reason

Recent years have witnessed an explosion in cases brought by employees whose employment has been terminated. The cases, usually referred to as **wrongful discharge** or *termination* cases, have often resulted in significant damages being imposed on employers for improper termination. Similarly, corporate downsizing has resulted in increased litigation between employers and employees.

Employees may have several options to pursue: claims based on age, religious, gender, or racial discrimination may be filed with administrative agencies such as the Equal Employment Opportunity Commission or a similar state agency, or they may be brought in federal district court alleging violation of constitutionally protected rights. Other issues, such as termination in retaliation for an employee's complaints about smoke in the workplace, may be initiated in state court, especially if the state or local jurisdiction has enacted laws requiring smoke-free work environments. These employees may be protected under the "**whistle-blower**" doctrine, meaning they cannot be punished or terminated for raising valid safety complaints or revealing unlawful conduct by the employer.

Whistle blower
One who discloses improper conduct of his/her superior

Employee handbooks or manuals often include provisions relating to termination of employees or provisions that employees will be terminated only for cause. Some courts have held that such provisions constitute implied contracts and that employees terminated contrary to the terms of the handbook or manual, or perhaps contrary to an unstated office policy, may sue the employer for breach of contract.

While most employees are hired at will pursuant to a simple oral agreement, certain employees who bring needed skills and expertise to the employer may be subject to a formal written employment contract specifying the terms and conditions of their employment. The employment contract benefits both parties: the employer can be assured of having the employee's skills for a certain time period (and may afterward bar him from working for competitors) and the employee receives job security and potential advancement in the company. Employment contracts are used not only for top-level and highly compensated employees, but also for other employees who possess special skills, such as researchers or scientists, volume-producing salespeople, or computer wizards.

Generally, an employee may terminate his employment before the term specified in the written agreement without incurring any liability. Courts are reluctant to force people to work in places against their will, classifying such a situation as a type of involuntary servitude. Other provisions in the agreement, however, such as prohibitions against the employee working for a competitor for a certain period of time, or using the employer's trade secrets, will remain binding on the employee. If the employer terminates the employment before the specified time, it may be required to continue paying the employee pursuant to the contract, unless the employer can show the employee breached some term or condition of the employment.

2. *Terms of Employment Agreements*

Introduction. Most employment agreements or contracts are drafted by the employer's attorney. Some employment agreements are relatively simple and straightforward, containing only the basic elements, while others may be fiercely negotiated and contain complex provisions for compensation, benefits, and protection of the employer's proprietary information.

While each agreement should be fashioned to fit the particular needs of the parties, typical employment agreements contain certain standard provisions, such as those specifying each party's duties and obligations, compensation of the employee, the term of the agreement, termination of the agreement, and various restrictive covenants prohibiting the employee from working for competitors or using the employer's trade secrets. Inherent in every employment agreement is a covenant of good faith and fair dealing imposed on all parties to the agreement.

Recitals. The employment agreement usually begins with an identification of the parties, their names and addresses, and a recital that it is the intent of the parties to enter into an employment agreement. If the employee has adopted the corporate form, as a lawyer or accountant might, the individual as well as the corporate employee should be a party to the agreement, so that in the event of breach, the employer is not limited to pursuing only the corporation.

Duties of Parties. Each party's duties and responsibilities should be set forth clearly. This section should be as specific as possible so each party knows what is expected and, in the event of breach of the agreement, a party will be able to prove that the other party failed to perform certain identifiable duties. The hours the employee is expected to work, the location of the workplace, and a description of duties should be included. The employee's title should be specified.

Some employment contracts include specific duties, such as those requiring an employee to achieve certain sales volumes, produce a certain product, or develop a computer program for corporate accounting purposes. In other instances, the duties of the employee may necessarily be general in nature. For example, an individual hired to be the chief executive officer of a company will have a myriad of duties, most of which cannot be specifically described. Thus, provisions for such an employee might be somewhat vague, imposing a duty of good faith on the employee to act at all times in the employer's best interests, to work full-time, to devote her best efforts and attention to company business, and to perform tasks typically expected of those in such positions. Most employment contracts provide a catchall provision permitting the employer to specify additional reasonable duties from time to time. This type of provision allows flexibility so that if the nature of the position changes or the parties realize that other tasks should be performed, these needs can be accommodated.

The employer may be required to provide a safe, well-ventilated, private work space for the employee. Additionally, the employer may be required generally to provide such assistance needed by the employee to perform his duties, such as support personnel, supplies, or access to corporate information.

Any restrictions to be placed on the employee should be set forth in this section. For example, the employee may be restricted to soliciting sales in certain territories, may be subject to a dollar limit in spending money for supplies, or may be prohibited from entering into contracts without the prior approval of more senior employees or the board of directors.

Compensation of Employee. The employment agreement should clearly set forth any compensation to which the employee is entitled, whether in terms of salary or benefits. Because the matter of compensation is often the most critical issue for both an employer and employee, this section of the agreement should be carefully drafted.

The simplest form of compensation is a fixed annual salary. The times for payment should be specified (biweekly, monthly, and so forth). Annual increases can be based on a fixed percentage, may be tied to annual cost-of-living increases, or may be based on company profits. Incentives may be added so that if the employee achieves certain goals or sales, compensation increases proportionately.

Some executives of large publicly traded corporations receive staggering compensation. In early 1996, *Time Magazine* reported that for boosting the stock of the Disney Company 25 percent and orchestrating the second largest merger in United States history with Capital Cities/ABC, Michael Eisner, Disney's chief executive officer, earned a $14.8 million compensation package — an increase of 40 percent over his prior year's pay. Campbell Soup's chairman saw a raise of 150 percent as Campbell's stock increased nearly 40 percent. While early twentieth-century financier J.P. Morgan believed that a corporation's chief executive officer should never make more than 20 times the salary of a company's average employee, the ratio in Fortune 500 companies is now approaching 185:1.

Commission
Payment based on sales generated

Some employees, primarily those in sales, are compensated on a **commission** basis, meaning they receive a fixed percentage based upon the amount of goods or services sold by them. Managers may be awarded a certain commission on profits earned by their departments or divisions. The commission may vary and increase as certain sales levels are achieved. Because total sales or profits cannot be determined until the end of an employer's fiscal year, the employee may be entitled to a **draw,** or advance payment, against anticipated compensation. If the employee draws more during the course of the year than that to which she is ultimately entitled, the employee may be required to repay the employer. Alternatively, the overpayment can be credited against the next year's draw. Most employers carefully monitor profits, however, and may periodically reduce draws to ensure employees are not "negative" at the end of the year.

Draw
An advance payment against future salary or commission

Compensation based on "sales" or "profits" should expressly specify whether these sales or profits are total sales, net sales, net sales adjusted for discounts and bad checks, and so forth. Clear definition of terms will prevent later misunderstandings. In general, however, any ambiguity in an employment agreement is construed against the employer because the employer is viewed as being in a stronger bargaining position than the employee.

The compensation section of the employment agreement should also specify any benefits to be provided to the employee, including bonuses, insurance, vacation, retirement plans and benefits, fringe benefits, stock options, reimbursement of expenses, and any other form of compensation to which the employee is entitled, such as discounts on the company's products or services, right to retain and use frequent-flier mileage earned traveling on behalf of the employer, interest free loans, and so forth.

Term of the Agreement. The beginning and ending date of the employment agreement should be provided. If renewal of the agreement will be permitted, the terms and conditions for exercising the right to renew should be specified. For example, the right to renew may be granted to either the employer or employee, may be made mutual, or may occur automatically unless one of the parties objects.

If no term of employment is specified, the arrangement between the parties will likely be viewed as one at will, in which case either party can terminate the agreement at any time, with or without cause.

Termination of the Agreement. The employment agreement should provide for termination of the agreement prior to the specified term in the event of default, breach, or other stated reasons. Generally, either party may terminate the agreement in the event of breach or default by the other party or "upon cause." Breach of duties will be easier to prove if those duties have been expressly stated in the agreement. Some employers specify that the agreement will terminate if the employee dies, becomes permanently disabled or otherwise unable to perform his duties, is convicted of a crime, fails to achieve certain sales or production goals, the business becomes insolvent or is sold or merged, and so forth.

Senior executives may be entitled to a severance package, a golden parachute, if the company terminates their employment before the agreed-upon date. These severance benefits are often tied to the employee's agreement not to compete with the employer or divulge trade secrets.

Restrictive Covenants and Protection of Intellectual Property. Although an employer cannot generally force an employee to work for the employer, the employer may be able to enforce certain prohibitions or restrictions, called **restrictive covenants,** on an employee even after the employee leaves the company. Most of these restrictions are imposed to protect valuable knowledge, skill, and know-how the employer has accumulated over the years. For example, Coca Cola Company would lose a distinct competitive advantage if its marketing chief quit and then went to work for PepsiCo Company and disclosed Coca Cola's future marketing plans and advertising strategies. Therefore, most employers will impose certain restrictions on employees with special skills and knowledge. These restrictions must serve a valid purpose and must be reasonable and fair. Courts dislike covenants unfairly restricting the right of persons to work. Using our example, it would be grossly unfair if Coca Cola's advertising manager was unable to work in the advertising field at any time after termination of her employment with Coca Cola. If such a restriction was allowed, the employee would forfeit all of his or her accumulated knowledge and skills and be forced to enter another industry. Thus, a balance must be struck between the rights of employers to protect their valuable and proprietary information and the right of employees to move and work freely.

Restrictive covenants Agreements imposing certain restrictions or prohibitions on employees

Employers will also want to own inventions or unique processes discovered by the employee while on company time. Finally, employers will want to protect their trade secrets and customer lists from disclosure to competitors. Such restrictions are generally valid and enforceable by the employer if they serve the legitimate need of the employer for protection, are limited in scope, and do not impose an undue hardship on the employee.

Covenants Not to Compete. The most common restrictive covenant is an agreement by the employee not to compete with the employer. This restriction is designed to prevent employees from leaving one company with valuable information and know-how and then going directly to a competitor. Because covenants not to compete are disfavored and are viewed as restraints upon trade, many states have enacted statutes specifically dealing with such covenants and outlining the circumstances for their validity and enforcement.

Covenant not to compete Agreement by employee not to compete against employer

In general, covenants not to compete can only be imposed on employees with special skills and talents. A mass restriction imposed by McDonald's Corporation prohibiting all of its food handlers from working for other fast-food franchisors or restaurants after termination of their employment with McDonald's serves no legitimate public purpose and no legitimate business need of McDonald's. On the other hand, if a company has carefully recruited top personnel, trained them, and invested money and time in teaching them the employer's methods and processes, it would be inequitable for a competitor to reap the advantage of this investment of years of training.

Courts have developed several guidelines to assist in balancing the legitimate business needs of the employer with the employee's right to pursue his livelihood. Generally, covenants not to compete must be limited in duration and must be limited in scope. An employer cannot forever prohibit a former employee from working for a competitor; however, a reasonable restriction of one or two years may be enforceable. Similarly, a blanket prohibition forbidding the employee from working anywhere in the world is grossly overbroad. Therefore, the prohibition should be limited in its geographic scope. For example, an employee may be prohibited from working within 50 miles of any of the former employer's plants or within the territorial limits of a certain city or county.

The covenant not to compete should be carefully drafted to ensure the employee does not find a loophole enabling her to circumvent the restriction. For example, if the covenant merely precludes employment with a competitor, the employee could establish her own business or could serve as a consultant for a competitor. The provision should be drafted to afford the employer with the protection it needs. (See Figure 18-1 for a sample non-competition provision.)

In a late-1999 case, the Southern District of New York refused to enforce a covenant that would have prevented a Web site content manager from working for a competitor company for one year. The judge ruled that in the Internet environment, a one-year restriction was "several generations, if not an eternity."

FIGURE 18-1
Covenant Not to Compete

For one year after termination of Employee's employment with Employer, for any reason or cause whatsoever, other than material breach of this Agreement by Employer, Employee agrees that he will not directly, or indirectly, as owner, shareholder, partner, joint venturer, consultant, agent, principal, licensor, officer, director, or in any capacity whatsoever, engage in, become financially interested in, be employed by, or have any connection with any cable television business or operation in Cook County, Illinois. This limitation will only apply for one year from the date of termination or expiration of the Agreement and will only apply in the County of Cook, Illinois. In addition, for two years Employee shall not contact any party who is a customer of Employer during the term of this Agreement in Cook County, Illinois, in any manner which could be detrimental to the interests of Employer or solicit for employment or employ any employee of Employer during the term of this Agreement without the prior written consent of Employer.

In some states, notably California, covenants not to compete are invalid as constituting a restraint against trade (unless they are procured in the course of the sale of a business). Cal. Bus. & Prof. Code Section 16600. In late 1999, a San Francisco Superior Court ordered Aetna Inc., an insurance company, to pay $1.2 million to an employee who was fired after she refused to sign a non-compete covenant. The court held that Aetna knew the covenant not to compete violated the California statute. Aetna attempted to require all of its employees to agree not to compete against Aetna for six months after leaving.

These new cases demonstrate that the area of non-compete covenants must be carefully researched, and any covenants must be carefully drafted to ensure they comply with state laws.

Finally, courts generally will not enforce a covenant not to compete if the employee has left employment due to the employer's breach of the employment agreement. Otherwise, an employer could hire uniquely talented individuals, have them sign covenants not to compete, refuse to pay them, and still reap the benefits of precluding them for working for others.

In the event of any doubt or ambiguity, the covenant not to compete will be construed against the employer and in favor of the employee. Courts will, however, often use injunctions to enforce covenants not to compete, prohibiting the employee from working for a certain employer or within a certain geographical area. In the event the restriction is overly broad, some courts have revised the covenant to make it fit the parties' intentions rather than strike the entire covenant, a procedure called **"blue-penciling."**

Blue-penciling
Procedure of correcting non-compete clauses to make them legal

Inventions, Intellectual Property, and Work Product. Employees may be hired to develop new products or computer programs for the employer. Similarly, the employee may develop a new slogan or a corporate logo for the company. These types of property are referred to as **intellectual property** because they are property rights capable of being owned, sold, exploited, and transferred, but are neither real property nor tangible personal property.

Intellectual property
Products of human creative thought and effort

Work made-for-hire doctrine
Legal doctrine that work created by employee is owned by employer

Generally, under the **work made-for-hire doctrine,** works, processes, and systems developed or prepared by an employee within the scope of his employment are owned by the employer and not the employee. Employers hiring inventors, scientists, engineers, artists, and other individuals who may develop or create such work products will want to ensure and confirm that the employer owns all of the rights to the intellectual property created by the employee. The employment agreement should therefore provide that any inventions, designs, or other intellectual property developed by the employee while working for the employer are the property of the employer. Additional provisions should specify that the employee will cooperate in signing any applications filed with the United States Patent and Trademark Office or United States Copyright Office or any other documents to reflect the employer's ownership rights. Most agreements include a provision for extra protection specifying that, if for some reason the intellectual property is not viewed by a court as being owned by the employer, by virtue of the employment contract the employee thereby irrevocably and immediately assigns any interest he may have in the property to the employer. The employer will then have the rights to further exploit the intellectual property, to license it to others and collect royalties thereon, or to sell it to some third party. Most agreements also require the employee to warrant and represent that his work is original and does not infringe on anyone else's rights. This protects the employer from

FIGURE 18-2
Ownership of Work

Employee agrees that all inventions, improvements, data, processes, systems, and discoveries (hereinafter called "Proprietary Information") that are conceived of or made by Employee, whether alone or with others, while employed by Employer are the sole property of Employer.

Employee agrees that if any of the Proprietary Information described in this Agreement is protectable by copyright and is deemed in any way to fall within the definition of "work made for hire," as such term is defined in 17 U.S.C. Section 101, such work shall be considered a "work made for hire," and by virtue of this Agreement, the copyright of which shall be owned solely, completely, and exclusively by Employer, free and clear from any claims of any nature relating to Employee's contributions and other efforts. Employer shall have the right to copyright the work in its name as author and proprietor thereof.

Employee intends that Employer shall have full ownership of any of the aforesaid items with no rights of ownership in Employee. Employee agrees that in the event any of the items described herein are determined by a court not to be work for hire under federal copyright laws, this Agreement shall operate as an irrevocable assignment by Employee to Employer of the copyright in the aforementioned items. Under this irrevocable assignment, Employee hereby assigns to Employer the sole and exclusive right, title, interest in and to the aforementioned items, without further consideration, and agrees to assist Employer in registering and enforcing the copyrights and other rights relating to the aforementioned items.

It is Employee's specific intention to assign all right, title, and interest whatsoever in any and all copyright right in the aforesaid items, in any media, and for any purpose, to Employer. To that end, Employee agrees to execute and deliver all appropriate documents requested by Employer in connection therewith.

some later claim that the work infringes some other party's interests. (See Figure 18-2 for a model provision relating to an employer's ownership of work product.)

Employers generally attempt to draft provisions relating to ownership of intellectual property sufficiently broadly that the employer owns all rights to inventions, designs, or processes, as well as any later enhancements or modifications to those work products. The parties may, of course, negotiate so that while the employer owns the intellectual property, the employee may receive a royalty based upon sales of any product incorporating the employee's contributions.

Many disputes have arisen over inventions and processes developed by employees. If employees develop the work on their own time, for example, in the evenings and weekends at home, and do not use any information, skills, or supplies acquired through the employer, they may individually own the rights in any such intellectual property.

The rights of independent contractors may differ from the rights of employees, especially with regard to **copyrights,** namely rights in literary, artistic, musical, dramatic, sculptural or architectural works, or in sound recordings and motion pictures. Generally, as discussed, works that are developed by employees in the course and scope of their employment are owned by employers under the work made for hire doctrine. The work made for hire doctrine is found in the United States Copyright Act, at 17 U.S.C. Section 101. That section provides that if an employer hires an independent contractor to create special types of commissioned or ordered works (such as motion pictures, translations, texts, supplementary works, tests, and atlases) and the parties agree in writing that it is to be a work for hire, the employer will be the owner of the work. If the work is not a specially commissioned item of the type identified in the statute, and the parties have not agreed in writing that the employer will be the owner, the creator retains ownership rights in the work. The parties are always free to agree in writing that the commissioning party owns the work and the creator can assign his or her rights in the work to the commissioning party.

Copyright
Right in original literary, artistic, dramatic, and other works

Because work prepared by an employee within the scope of her employment is a work made for hire belonging to the employer, the creator will often attempt to argue that she was not an employee, but rather an **independent contractor,** and thus retains ownership of the work created. In determining whether an individual is an employee or an independent contractor, courts consider a variety of factors: control by the employer over the work itself, for example, control as to how the work is done, whether it is done at the employer's location, and whether the employer provides equipment or other means to create the work; control by the employer over the individual, for example, control over the individual's schedule in creating the work; and the status of the employer, for example, whether the employer provides the individual with benefits and/or withholds tax from the individual's payment. In general, the more control an employer exercises over the work and the individual, the more likely it is that an employer-employee relationship has been created.

Independent contractor
One who provides work or services for another but is not an employee; one who controls and directs one's own work

Independent contractors are not eligible for benefits provided to employees, and employers need not pay payroll taxes for independent contractors. Thus, the IRS and the Department of Labor carefully scrutinize employers' classifications of workers to ensure true employees are not improperly classified as independent contractors.

Trade Secrets. Many companies have invested time, money, and effort in developing new products or systems. Similarly, data about customers, their preferences, credit ratings, and so forth may be extremely valuable to a company. This type of information may qualify as a trade secret. According to Section 1(4) of the Uniform Trade Secrets Act, a **trade secret** is defined as information, including a formula, pattern, compilation, program, device, method, technique, or process that derives independent commercial value from not being generally known or ascertainable and is the subject of reasonable efforts to keep it secret. Trade secrets need not be complex to be protectable and they can endure forever if properly protected.

Trade secret
Information providing a competitive edge to its owner

Perhaps one of the most famous trade secrets is the recipe and process for Coca Cola. Maintaining the confidentiality of the recipe allows the Coca Cola Company a competitive edge in the marketplace. If another company was able to market an identical product, Coca Cola's unique and identifiable product would be lost. A variety of other information can also qualify as a trade secret, such as sales data, marketing plans, market studies, customer lists, or virtually any concrete information that gives the owner a competitive advantage over others who do not know it or use it. To qualify as a trade secret, the owner must generally have made some effort to protect the information and prevent it from becoming disclosed.

To retain the confidentiality of such trade secrets, employers will include provisions in employment contracts prohibiting employees from disclosing confidential information or trade secrets. The covenant not to disclose the trade secret can bind the employee not only during employment but afterward as well, perhaps indefinitely. Because it can be difficult to prove damages arising out of misappropriation of a trade secret, many agreements provide for fixed, or liquidated, damages upon disclosure of trade secrets.

A matter cannot be a trade secret if it is in the public domain (a matter of public knowledge) or was already known to the employee or independently developed by the employee. (See Figure 18-3 for typical nondisclosure provisions.)

Intellectual property and trade secrets are discussed further in Chapter Nineteen.

Manner of Resolving Disputes. The employment agreement should provide for the resolution of disputes, for example, by arbitration or litigation. A clause

FIGURE 18-3
Covenant of Nondisclosure of Trade Secrets

Employee acknowledges and agrees that Employer's subscriber lists, customer lists, maps, diagrams, computer programs, financial information, terms of contracts with clients and customers, pricing information, marketing information, and sales techniques (hereinafter referred to as the "Confidential Information") are valuable trade secrets of Employer and that any disclosure or unauthorized use thereof will cause irreparable harm to Employer. In consideration of Employer's employment of Employee, Employee agrees to treat the Confidential Information in confidence and to use the Confidential Information for the sole purpose of performing his or her obligations under this Employment Agreement, not to disclose or divulge the Confidential Information outside of Employer, not to copy the Confidential Information or any portion thereof, and to return the Confidential Information and any material relating thereto to Employer upon the expiration or termination of this Agreement for any reason whatsoever.

This Agreement shall not bind Employee to maintain the confidentiality of any Confidential Information which has been widely published, patented, or which has become part of the public domain and no longer constitutes a trade secret of Employer, or any information which Employee can demonstrate was known to him or her prior to the date of disclosure or which was legally acquired from an independent, legitimate source.

The restrictions and obligations of this Section shall survive any expiration, termination, or cancellation of the Agreement and shall bind Employee, his or her successors, heirs, and assignees.

may be included that the prevailing party is entitled to recover attorneys' fees and costs from the losing party.

Miscellaneous Provisions. A variety of other provisions should be included in a well-drafted employment agreement, including the following:

- a provision specifying which state's law governs the contract;
- provisions for amending the agreement;
- a warranty by the employee that entering into the agreement does not violate any other agreement to which he or she may be a party;
- a provision stating that the agreement supersedes any prior agreements between the parties and constitutes their entire agreement with respect to the employment;
- a provision relating to how notices should be delivered, for example, whether by mail, facsimile, or registered mail;
- a provision making the agreement binding upon successors and assignees of the parties; and
- a provision providing that in the event any part of the agreement is held invalid, such invalidity will not affect the remainder of the agreement.

The agreement should then be signed and dated by each party.

Key Features of Employee Compensation and Employee Agreements

- Employers often provide benefits in addition to salary to attract and retain valuable employees. Among these benefits are insurance (health, disability, and life) and retirement plans.
- Retirement plans can be qualified (meaning they qualify for favorable tax treatment) or nonqualified (meaning they do not qualify for favorable tax treatment).
- Retirement plans can be "defined benefit plans," meaning that a preestablished benefit is set that will be paid to employees when they retire, or they can be "defined contribution plans," meaning that the employer must place a specified amount of money into the plan. Profit sharing plans and 401(k) plans are examples of defined contribution plans.
- Employers can grant employees stock options or the right to buy shares in the company at a fixed price at some later time. As a company grows in value, stock options can be extremely profitable.
- Employment is generally "at will," meaning that either the employer or employee is free to terminate the relationship at any time for any reason or no reason.
- Employment agreements are often used for more senior or key employees.

- In most states, an employer may restrict an employee from competing against the employer upon termination of employment if the restriction is limited in scope, duration, and geographical area.
- Under the "work made-for-hire doctrine," employers own the work product created by their employees. To be safe, many employers use agreements confirming such ownership rights. Employers should use such agreements for their independent contractors because works created by them are owned by the independent contractor unless the work is a special type, and the parties have agreed in writing that the commissioning party will own the work.

C. Role of Paralegal

The area of employment law is becoming increasingly more complex. A number of law firms and attorneys specialize in advising clients on various retirement, pension, and profit-sharing plans. These law firms and attorneys generally use paralegals to assist in drafting qualified plans, conducting research regarding requirements for the plan, and preparing the explanation of benefits for employees. Similarly, many corporations with in-house legal, personnel, and human resources departments rely on paralegals to assist in drafting various employee compensation plans and additional documents.

Paralegals also conduct research to determine a state's statutory treatment of restrictive covenants. With increased advances in the technological and communications fields, the validity of covenants not to compete, ownership of intellectual property, and protection of trade secrets has been much litigated. Due to recent changes and developments both by legislatures and courts, paralegals will need to be alert to recent developments in the field of restrictive covenants.

Paralegals are commonly involved in the following tasks:

1. Conducting research regarding the statutory requirements for various employee compensation plans, both qualified and nonqualified.
2. Drafting qualified plans and supplementary materials.
3. Preparing and submitting determination letters to the IRS for approval of the plan.
4. Preparing employee handbooks or manuals setting forth the terms and conditions of employment and describing any retirement plans and other fringe benefits.
5. Assisting in legal audits to ensure plans are not top-heavy, do not impose illegal vesting periods, or do not exclude eligible employees.
6. Preparing descriptions of the plans for employees.
7. Drafting minutes of directors' meetings adopting resolutions that approve compensation plans.
8. Conducting research regarding permissible terms and conditions of employment agreements, especially with regard to restrictive covenants.
9. Collecting information from clients regarding desired terms and conditions in preparation for drafting employment agreements.

10. Preparing worksheets or questionnaires for the employer to complete setting forth employee duties, the term of agreement, whether restrictive covenants are needed, renewal of the agreement, and benefits to which an employee is entitled.
11. Drafting the employment agreement.
12. Preparing resolutions for the board of directors to approve hiring of key personnel and the terms and conditions of employment.
13. Ensuring the employment agreement is signed by all parties.
14. Docketing dates for termination and renewal of employment contracts.
15. Assisting in a legal audit to advise the client as to any need for restrictive covenants for certain employees and for protection of intellectual property.

Resource Guide

1. Statutes and Cases

As always, the most critical resource is the law governing employee compensation and contractual agreements. Various federal statutes, such as ERISA and the Internal Revenue Code, must be reviewed to ensure compliance by compensation plans. State statutes and court decisions should be reviewed to determine any limitations imposed on employment agreements, such as prohibitions or limitations on the use of restrictive covenants. If the employer conducts business in several states, it may be necessary to prepare a survey of the various state laws relating to the validity and enforcement of restrictive covenants. If the employee will be creating certain intellectual property for the employer, the United States Copyright Act should be scrutinized to make sure the employer owns rights under the work made for hire doctrine.

2. Texts and Encyclopedias

There are a variety of texts and treatises dealing with employment law. Browse the shelves of the local law library or your office's law library to locate pertinent materials. The general encyclopedias, C.J.S. and Am. Jur. 2d, will provide general overviews of employment compensation and permissible conditions of employment agreements. If your state has a local encyclopedia, consult this initially because it will provide state-specific information relating to the use of restrictive covenants in employment agreements. If you know the section number of the statute in your state dealing with the permissibility of restrictive covenants, use the table of statutes construed in the encyclopedia to locate the section discussing the pertinent statutes.

3. Form Books

There are numerous sources containing forms to assist you in drafting employment agreements and descriptions of employee compensation plans. The general form books are *Am. Jur. Legal Forms 2d, West's Legal Forms 2d,* and *Current Legal Forms with Tax Analysis.* These will include long-form employment agreements, short-form employment agreements, various provisions to be inserted into employment agreements, and some analysis of the use and preparation of employment agreements.

4. Law Office or Department Forms

It is likely that your office or legal department has a variety of forms, worksheets, checklists, letters, and other documents relating to employee compensation and employment agreements. Check with attorneys and paralegals who have experience in the field of employment law or general corporate work and ask whether they have any pertinent materials or forms you can review to get started. The law librarian may be a source of assistance as well. Send out a message over E-mail or route a memo through the office explaining what you need. You will likely be deluged with information, forms, documents, and materials.

5. *Internal Revenue Service Pamphlets*

The Internal Revenue Service provides a number of publications useful in explaining rules for fringe benefit plans and various business expenses. The publications may be obtained by contacting your local Internal Revenue Service Center. Useful publications include:

- IRS Publication 334, *Tax Guide for Small Business,* which provides the basic rules relating to fringe benefits for employees.
- IRS Publication 535, *Business Expenses,* which sets forth the rules relating to qualified benefit plans.
- IRS Publication 463, *Travel, Entertainment, Gift and Car Expenses.*
- IRS Publication 1542, *Per Diem Rules.*

◆ ◆ ◆

WEB RESOURCES

The most important resources relating to compensation for employees, benefit plans, and employment agreements are the various state and federal statutes. The following are sites allowing access to statutes.

www.ll.georgetown.edu

When you access this site for Georgetown University Law Center, select "State, Local & Territorial." You will be presented with a map of the United States. Point your cursor to the state in which you are interested, and you will be provided with links to a variety of legal sources relating to that state. Select "Statutes" or "Codes," and you will be linked to the state's statutes. In some states, searching can be done by either keywords or by section number. In other states, searching is accomplished exclusively by keywords. Alternatively, when you access the site, select "Federal," and you will be directed to federal statutes where you can review statutes relating to tax treatment for qualified and nonqualified plans.

www4.law.cornell.edu/usccode

This excellent site allows searching of federal statutes by keyword or section number. You can review all 50 titles of the U.S. Code or look up statutes by their popular names.

Information about intellectual property can be located through various government Web sites. For information about patents and trademarks, access the site of the U.S. Patent and Trademark Office at <www.uspto.gov>.

For information about copyrights and the work made-for-hire doctrine, access the site of the U.S. Copyright Office at <www.loc.gov/copyright>.

To obtain basic information about various employee benefit plans, access any of the following sites:

- **http://www.toolkit.cch/com/text/p05_4660.asp** (information about profit-sharing plans)
- **http://www.nceo.org/library/esops.html** (information about ESOPs)
- **www.401kforum.com** (information about 401(k) plans)
- **http://invest-faq.com/articles/ret-plan** (information about Keogh plans and 401(k) plans)
- **http://www.irs.gov/forms_pubs** (information about IRAs and Keogh plans)
- **http://sbinformation.about.com/business/sbinformation/library/weekly/aa052598.htm** (information about IRAs, 401(k)s, Keogh plans)

Alternatively, access "Ask Jeeves" at <www.ask.com> and type in "Where can I find information about [stock options] [Keogh plans] [401(k) plans]?" to find other sites discussing such plans and benefits.

For forms related to employee benefit plans, access <http://www.jefren.com/DOWNLOAD.HTML> for forms for a stock option plan and stock appreciation rights plan.

To locate employment agreements and independent contractor agreements, access the following sites:

- **www.siccode.com/forms.php3** (for employment agreements, assignment of copyright, and independent contractor agreement)
- **www.lectlaw.com/formb.htm** (for employment agreements, consulting agreements, and independent contractor agreements)
- **www.morebusiness.com/templates_worksheets/samples** (for confidentiality agreement and employment agreements)
- **www.legal-resource.com/forms/d.cgi/[IDNUMBER]** (for employment agreement and employee non-disclosure agreements)

Discussion Questions

Fact Scenario. Grayson Associates, Inc. is an engineering consulting firm with more than 100 employees, some of whom have extremely specialized engineering skills. The corporation has four shareholders, all of whom also serve as directors and officers.

1. Because the company has more than 100 employees, is it required to offer its employees a retirement plan? Discuss.

2. May the company offer a pension plan that provides significantly better benefits to its 15 most senior employees? Discuss.

3. Anna Murphy recently left the company to take a year off to be with her

family. Is the company required to continue any insurance afforded to Anna while she was with the company?

4. The company has determined that it will contribute a certain amount of its profits to employee accounts each year. If the company made no profit this year, must it contribute to the plan? Must the amount contributed be the same each year? Discuss.

5. The company plans to "go public" with an IPO next year. The company has therefore provided employees with the right to purchase 1000 shares of the company's stock at $3.00 per share six months after the IPO or four years after the date of grant, whichever is sooner. Assume the company goes public, and the stock begins trading at $15.00 per share. Six months later the stock is trading at $30 per share. Discuss the employees' rights, and identify the right they have been provided.

6. The company has entered into employment agreements with its ten most senior executives, providing that upon termination of their employment, they cannot compete with the company by providing any engineering services to any competitor of the company for four years, within 500 miles of any company office. Is this covenant enforceable? Discuss.

7. Assume the employment contract requires the employees to maintain the secrecy of the company's customer list for ten years. Is such a covenant valid?

8. While working on a company project, Daniel, one of the company's employees, wrote a computer program to assist in engineering analysis. Who owns the rights to the computer program?

19

Special Topics in Business Law

CHAPTER OVERVIEW

This chapter discusses some of the ethical dilemmas facing attorneys and paralegals as well as the increased need for attention to ethics in the marketplace. While there are no perfect answers for every question that may arise, even recognizing that certain ethical concerns must be addressed represents a step forward.

This chapter also discusses the interplay between corporate law and other practice areas, such as the sale of goods, franchising, leasing, intellectual property, and antitrust and unfair competition law. Corporate law is not practiced in a vacuum. Skilled attorneys and paralegals need to be familiar with a variety of other principles, including those relating to contracts, torts, real property, and crimes.

Finally, the roles and relationships of outside counsel and the corporation's own inside counsel are discussed. Until relatively recently, in-house legal departments were skeleton crews, working on only the most basic legal issues. In an effort to contain legal costs, many corporations have increased the size and quality of their inside legal departments. They now perform many of the legal tasks formerly conducted exclusively by private practitioners. The types of tasks performed by internal and outside counsel and their delicate relationship to each other will be discussed.

A. Ethics

1. *Introduction*

With the extensive media attention given to the insider trading scandals of the 1980s, the jail terms imposed on Wall Street traders Ivan Boesky and Michael Milken, the fast-paced world and jargon of hostile takeovers, movies such as *Wall Street* and *Boiler Room* promoting the philosophy of "greed is good," and reported stock disparagement occurring in Internet chat rooms, one may be tempted to think that the world of business is populated by unethical financiers and investors motivated solely by self-interest. In reality, consumers are likely simply more aware of the need for businesses to act responsibly, as witnessed by the increasing number of lawsuits alleging the sale of unsafe and untested products, the Federal Trade Commission's investigations of fraud on the Internet, and the Securities and Exchange Commission's review of online trading.

The basic ethical question faced by businesspeople is how to balance the need to act responsibly with the duty to earn profits for the owners of a business. There is no one perfect answer to this question, just as there is no text that will provide guidance for every ethical dilemma that may arise in business situations. Your own ethical convictions will serve as the basis for your decision-making. Be alert to more than just the immediate consequences of business activities. Consider whether the action serves the business owners at the expense of the community and whether there is a win-win situation that benefits both the business owners and society.

2. *Business Ethics*

Ethics
Study of right and wrong

Ethics is the study of standards of right and wrong. Ethics is not merely some remote philosophical concept existing in a vacuum. Ethical questions arise in your life every day. What if a salesperson undercharges you for an item? Are requests for reimbursement of various expenses padded? Do you tell a client that a document has been prepared and will be sent shortly when you have not yet begun working on the project? These issues and numerous other issues of basic morality arise each day and constantly challenge us to make ethical decisions.

Business ethics
Study of standards of right and wrong in the business environment

If ethics is the study of standards of right and wrong, **business ethics** is the study of standards of right and wrong in the business environment. While laws are designed to preserve order, ethics deal with the propriety of relationships between people. Laws and ethics are not necessarily synonymous. An action can be both illegal and unethical; for example, insider trading. An act may be legal but not ethical, such as a decision by a board of directors to award themselves bonuses in a lean year. Finally, an act may be illegal but ethical, such as the inadvertent submission of a tax return without a signature. Thus, the fact that some action is legal does not necessarily mean that it is ethical, moral, or right. Our laws are limited and cannot be relied upon to provide answers to all of our ethical questions. Personal ethical convictions must complement the law.

Additionally, ethics may have a cultural component. In many countries, gifts to officials are customary signs of respect and are an accepted part of business transactions. In the United States, however, a gift given in certain circumstances may be viewed as a bribe or an attempt to exert improper influence. Thus, some questions of ethics may be resolved differently in different cultures.

3. *Ethical Approaches*

We have all debated whether "the end justifies the means," or whether a good result can be justified by dishonest methods. For example, if a prosecutor knows a defendant is guilty of the crime charged, is the prosecutor justified in withholding evidence from the defense? Was *Les Miserables'* Jean Valjean justified in stealing a single loaf of bread to prevent his nephew's starvation?

Many religions adhere to the philosophy that ethical standards are absolute rather than relative and that a wrongful act can never be justified. This philosophy takes an absolute view of the duties imposed by religious strictures such that there is a reason, for instance, they are called the Ten Commandments rather than the Ten Suggestions.

In addition to setting forth absolute rules and duties, religions also advocate mercy and compassion. There may be a conflict between the absolute duty to do right and the concept of compassion. For example, a corporation may be experiencing severe financial difficulties. Unless the corporation merges with a stronger corporation, the corporation will be forced to lay off 10 percent of its work force. The area in which the corporation is located is economically depressed. If workers are laid off, it is unlikely they will be able to find jobs and many may have to apply for public assistance or move. Would a corporate executive be justified in verbally painting a rosier picture of the corporation to the prospective buyer to make the corporation more attractive? Which precept controls: the absolute duty to avoid wrongful acts, including any form of misrepresentation, or the duty to be compassionate to one's employees and shareholders who will genuinely suffer if the merger does not take place?

Many ethical dilemmas are like the one above. There may no bright line defining and delineating good from bad, but rather only shades of gray delineating good from better and bad from worse.

Under other ethical approaches, an action is judged not by absolute rules and duties, but rather by outcome: If the action benefits the majority of people, it is right, even if a minority is adversely affected. This ethical approach is exemplified by traditional cost-benefit analysis. For example, if survival of the corporation depends on a 10 percent reduction in workforce, the benefit to the corporation (survival) outweighs the cost of the action (the misery and unhappiness of 10 percent of the workers). The movie *Class Action* revealed risk analysis conducted by a company that decided it was cheaper to pay damages in lawsuits for injuries and death rather than to fix a known defect in a car. The drawback to this approach to ethical questions is that it treats human beings as fungibles, items that can be easily substituted for each other, like pennies. Human beings are complex individuals, however, with needs and desires. Simply looking at a group of people as "cost ineffective" denies them their humanity.

Another approach to ethical questions is demonstrated by basic capitalist theory: Left alone, the marketplace will naturally produce social good. This philosophy argues that consumers' needs will dictate the marketplace. Consumers will only buy products that are useful and will only pay a certain price for them. Businesses that provide quality goods at lower prices will thrive and those that do not will fail. The competitive business environment will naturally work for the good of consumers and society by encouraging lower prices. Nevertheless, capitalist theory also has some drawbacks. For example, a product may be useful to consumers and offered at a competitive price. The consumers "win" by possessing a useful product at a lower price. The company "wins" by selling numerous units of its goods and making a profit. But what if a necessary byproduct of producing the goods is toxic waste? Society itself bears the burden of this ill. Thus, profit cannot be the sole determinant in whether a product is good for society.

4. *Making Decisions*

Making business decisions requires a constant interplay and balancing of ethical issues, legal concerns, and the need for a company to make a profit in order to survive and serve the needs of its owners and community. You have seen that just because something is legal, it is not necessarily ethical. Similarly, you have seen that just because profit is made, a result is not always for the good of society. This delicate balance between ethics, law, and profit confronts business owners daily. There may be a need to sacrifice or compromise one of these elements for the good of the others. For example, a company may be willing to accept less profit to achieve some socially useful goal or to ensure that its actions are legal. Similarly, a company may be willing to bend the rules (namely, sacrifice ethics) so long as its actions are legal and produce revenue for the good of the business and its owners.

Decisions made by businesspeople thus involve an evaluation of whether an anticipated action is ethical, whether it is legal, and whether it is profitable. There are no perfect rules or answers for the dilemmas confronting business owners. In each instance, an analysis of these three factors will be combined with the decision-maker's own ethical standards to produce a decision.

5. *Legal Duties*

In the business arena, a number of court decisions and statutes have combined to create a blueprint for ethical decision-making. These concepts have been discussed throughout the text, but are examined here briefly insofar as they relate to ethical issues.

Fiduciary Duties. Partners owe fiduciary, or good-faith, duties to each other. Similarly, corporate directors and officers owe fiduciary duties to the corporate enterprise. These fiduciary duties require corporate managers to act in the best interests of the corporation and with the highest degree of good faith. Thus, some ethical conflicts may be resolved by determining which course of action is supported by the trust and confidence reposed in corporate management.

Duty of Due Care. Corporate officers and directors are required to act with due care, and with a duty of inquiry, as ordinarily prudent persons would exercise in like circumstances. Thus, corporate managers must inform themselves of all aspects relating to decision-making. Management cannot look solely to the bottom line and ignore the legality of an action. Any reasonably diligent person acting with due care would examine whether certain actions are legal and whether the consequences of those actions will produce harm to society and perhaps harm to the corporation (which may ultimately be held liable for acts of wrongdoing).

Duty of Loyalty and Prohibition Against Self-Dealing. Partners and corporate managers are required to devote their time, skill, and energy to the business enterprise. They cannot engage in activities that are competitive with those of the business and cannot undertake actions that benefit themselves personally at the expense of their partners, the business, or its owners. Instituting unreasonable compensation packages for managers, buying property or stock back from insiders at a price higher than market value, and structuring mergers and benefit plans to benefit senior executives, are all examples of breaches of the duty of loyalty. Corporate managers or partners cannot put their own interests above the interests of those to whom they owe fiduciary duties.

Covenants of Good Faith and Fair Dealing. Whether expressed or not, every contract includes an **implied covenant of good faith and fair dealing.** Thus, whether or not an employee has been promised specific benefits, a court would likely determine that an employer who arbitrarily changed the employee's title, belittled him in meetings, refused to provide support staff assistance and supplies to the employee, and moved the employee into a cramped office, would likely have breached the covenant of good faith inherent in an employment agreement, even if these actions did not amount to a technical breach of any specific terms and conditions of a written agreement.

Implied covenant of good faith and fair dealing An implied condition in every contract requiring each party to deal fairly with the other

The covenant of good faith and fair dealing applies not only to contracts made between the corporation and its internal staff, but also to agreements between the corporation and third parties. Thus, in a merger, a corporation is required to disclose any matter that would be deemed material or relevant to the other party, even if specific disclosure was not called for by the merger agreement. Each party to a contract must act so as not to deprive the other party of receiving that for which it has bargained.

Fiduciary duties, duties of due care, duties of loyalty, and covenants of good faith assist businesspeople in making ethical decisions. By examining case law, decision-makers can review court interpretations of these duties in order to arrive at an ethical and legal decision that still produces profit for the business enterprise and its owners.

6. *Ethical Codes*

Some companies set forth their ethical standards in written codes or publications. These codes may specify the mission of the company and may describe the standard of conduct expected in the workplace. (See Figure 19-1 for ethical code.) The publication may be posted in various prominent places throughout the company offices and provided to each employee upon commencement of employment. These codes provide a solid foundation for employer-employee relations and foster an atmosphere of trust and confidence. Nevertheless, a set of written policies and guidelines can never cover every ethical dilemma that may arise and can never substitute for individual standards of right and wrong. Moreover, the benefits of a formal code will be illusory if managers' actions are in contradiction to the written policy. Employees are quick to observe that a standard is not truly "Do as the code says" but "Do as we do."

The American Bar Association has promulgated a code of ethics for attorneys. Most states, using the ABA code as a model, have adopted their own codes of ethics for attorneys in their jurisdictions. These codes relate to duties owed to clients, courts, and adversaries. The bar associations of most states have set up ethics "hot lines" to respond to questions dealing with ethics. While legal advice will not be given, callers are generally referred to provisions in their state's code of ethics and pertinent case law.

FIGURE 19-1
Ethical Business Code

ABC Inc.'s customers have played an important role in our continuous growth and success. In order to avoid any conflict of interest between our suppliers and our employees and to maintain all business relationships on a professional basis, ABC has established the following business practices:

- ABC expects all of its employees to provide a quality product or service and to act professionally at all times.
- All work performed by ABC employees must be of the highest quality possible. All work must be performed competently, professionally, and courteously.
- No ABC employee may ask for or receive anything of value from a customer. Gifts from a customer such as tickets to athletic or entertainment events or any type of personal item are not permitted by ABC.
- If any ABC employee is offered or accepts any item of value from a customer, the employee is to report it to the appropriate ABC manager.
- Occasional meals during visits to a customer's facilities or during business meetings are acceptable, although ABC employees are required to report such activities to the appropriate ABC manager.
- Violations of these practices may constitute grounds for ABC to take appropriate disciplinary action against the employee, including a warning, probation, suspension without pay, or termination of employment.

Moreover, the two major paralegal associations have each prepared ethical codes. Affirmation of Professional Responsibility is the product of the National Federation of Paralegal Associations. The National Association of Legal Assistants' code is called Code of Ethics and Professional Responsibility. These ethical codes may provide guidelines for ethical dilemmas.

Many states are considering ethics codes for paralegals that will discipline paralegals for ethical violations. At the present time, most state guidelines are designed to instruct and educate attorneys on how to use paralegals ethically. The attorneys remain responsible for supervision of paralegals and are disciplined in the event of ethical violations by their paralegals.

Many law firms are drafting their own codes for paralegals. These codes usually include guidelines regarding the disclosure of client confidences and conflict-of-interest clearance checks to ensure that paralegals who switch law firms do not work on matters involving clients of their former firms. In one recent Arizona case, a paralegal switched jobs during litigation and went to work for a law firm representing the plaintiffs in a case in which the paralegal had formerly assisted in the original clients' defense. The Arizona appellate court agreed with the trial court that the entire law firm should be disqualified from representing the plaintiffs.

In some states, paralegal associations are establishing codes of ethics and disciplinary committees that can hold hearings and take action against paralegals violating ethical standards. Discipline can range from counseling to revocation of the paralegal's membership in the association.

B. Common Interdisciplinary Issues

1. *Introduction*

In corporate or business practice, a number of issues commonly arise that are not strictly corporate law matters, but are intertwined with other areas of law, primarily commercial, contractual, real property, intellectual property, and antitrust law. These issues deal with the purchase and sale of goods, franchise relationships, leases, intellectual property and anticompetitive and deceptive practices.

2. *Commercial Transactions and the Sale of Goods*

Until relatively recently, state statutes regarding sales varied significantly from state to state, hindering interstate transactions. To remedy this problem, the National Conference of Commissioners on Uniform State Laws developed the **Uniform Commercial Code (UCC)**, which governs contracts of sale. Adopted in every state but Louisiana, the UCC provides a national framework for commercial transactions governing merchants of goods, whether the merchants are sole proprietors, partnerships, or corporations. Many states have made revisions to the UCC in adopting it.

UCC
Uniform Commercial Code, which governs commercial transactions

While there is some variation among states, the UCC serves as the standard reference for laws governing the sale of goods. The UCC covers more than just an actual sale. It governs payment methods, banking, warranties relating to the goods, leases, the extension of credit for the purchase of goods, and nearly all aspects of commercial transactions.

The best known portion of the UCC is Article 2, entitled Sales, relating to "transactions in goods" (as opposed to transactions relating to real property or intellectual property). Common law and statutory principles relating to contracts, such as offer, acceptance, consideration, and so forth, are not superseded by the UCC. If the UCC does not cover a certain issue, general state law will control.

The UCC provides a national approach to the interpretation of contracts for the sale of goods. For example, the UCC provides that if a contract was unfair and overreaching when made, it can be set aside as "unconscionable." In determining unconscionability, courts will consider the express terms of the contract as well as what is ordinary and customary in the relevant trade or industry. For example, some contracts contain clauses of *adhesion,* clauses that dramatically and unfairly prejudice one party's rights, yet must be accepted if the affected party, usually in a weaker bargaining position, wants to make the deal. In general, adhesion contracts or clauses are unenforceable.

The UCC also covers which party to a contract must bear the risk of loss of the goods due to damage in shipment or actual loss of the goods. While parties may mutually determine which one of them will bear the risk of loss, if they fail to agree the UCC provides specific rules, depending on whether the goods are transported by a common carrier, whether the goods must be delivered to a particular destination, or whether the goods can be "delivered" even without actual movement, as is the case when the buyer picks up the goods.

The UCC provides remedies for both the buyer and seller in the event of the other party's breach of contract. The Code discusses return of the goods, resale of the goods to some third party, or rejection of non-conforming goods.

Perhaps one of the most significant sections of UCC Article 2 relates to warranties on the sale of goods. For centuries, the maxim governing the sale of goods was ***caveat emptor,*** literally, "Let the buyer beware." Sellers historically had little liability for defective goods. The UCC, however, provides a detailed and consumer-oriented approach in establishing a series of warranties included in nearly every sale. For example, UCC Section 2-314 provides that in every sale of goods, there is an implied warranty that the goods are "merchantable," that the goods are reasonably fit for their intended purposes. Thus, consumers have a right to expect that televisions will provide clear pictures and sound, that coffeemakers will brew coffee, and that watches will accurately tell time.

Caveat emptor
Latin expression meaning, "let the buyer beware"

While sellers may attempt to disclaim warranties — for example, by selling goods "as is" or by expressly stating that no warranties are made with respect to an item sold — courts disfavor such disclaimers. To protect consumers, the UCC requires that disclaimers be set forth in clear and conspicuous writing. Thus, a disclaimer "in fine print" is likely ineffective.

Article 9 of the UCC covers **secured transactions,** namely, transactions in which certain property is pledged as collateral to secure the repayment of a debt. For example, you may wish to borrow $100 from a friend. The friend, having some concerns about your ability to repay the debt, may require that you surrender your watch as "collateral" for the loan. When you repay the loan, your watch will be returned to you. If you do not repay the loan, your friend has a watch that can be used or sold to defray the bad debt. In this sense, your friend has "security" for repayment of the debt. She holds a **security interest** in the watch and is referred to as the **secured party.** In most instances, the secured property, the watch, will be retained by the borrower or purchaser and surrendered to the lender or seller only upon default.

Secured transaction
Transaction in which property is pledged as collateral for a debt

Security interest
The interest the creditor has in collateral pledged for a debt

Secured party
The creditor in a secured transaction

The lender will want to be assured that you do not pledge the watch as collateral to numerous other lenders, so that in the event of a default of the loan, there is sufficient collateral to satisfy the debt and creditors are not left fighting among themselves.

Article 9 regulates these secured transactions. Generally, to enforce a security interest, there must be a writing, the **security agreement,** granting a security interest in favor of the lender. To protect, or *perfect,* her rights against some other party, the lender must prepare and file a **financing statement** (usually called a *UCC-1*) with the secretary of state. The financing statement identifies the debtor, the creditor, and the collateral, and provides a public record so that later lenders have a means of assuring that the property has not been "over-collateralized," or pledged to satisfy more debt than it is worth. Because these UCC filings are a matter of public record, it is easy to determine whether security interests have been claimed in certain property. (See Figure 19-2 for a UCC-1 form.) Data on outstanding UCC filings and liens can be located on WESTLAW, using the UCC database. The Web sites for many states allow online searching for information relating to UCC filings. (See Appendix A for Web addresses for each state.)

Security agreement
Agreement setting forth parties' rights in a secured transaction

Financing statement
Document filed with state to provide notice of a security interest (also called a *UCC-1*)

FIGURE 19-2
Delaware UCC-1 Form (Financing Statement)

State of Delaware
UNIFORM COMMERCIAL CODE - FINANCING STATEMENT - FORM UCC - 1

This FINANCING STATEMENT is presented to a Filing Officer for filing pursuant to the Uniform Commercial Code.

If to be filed with Recorder of Deeds indicate Tax Parcel No.(s) __________
No. of additional sheets presented. __________

PARTIES	PARTIES
Debtor (or Assignor) (last name first if individual) and mailing address:	Secured Party (ies) (last name first if individual) and address:
Debtor (or Assignor) (last name first if individual) and mailing address:	Assignee (if any) of Secured Party(ies) and address of Assignee:

This statement is filed without the Debtor's signature to perfect a security interest in collateral (check X in applicable box(es))
- ❑ Already subject to a security interest in another jurisdiction when it was brought into this State.
- ❑ Already subject to a security interest in another jurisdiction when the Debtor's location changed into this State.
- ❑ Which is proceeds of the original collateral described below in which a security interest is perfected.
- ❑ Acquired after a change of name, identity or corporate structure of Debtor.
- ❑ As to which the filing has lapsed.

By: __________
Signature of Secured Party(ies) *Title*
(Required only if item is checked)

Special Types of Parties (check X in applicable box(es))
- ❑ The terms "Debtor" and "Secured Party" means "Lessee" and "Lessor", respectively.
- ❑ The terms "Debtor" and "Secured Party" means "Consignee" and "Consignor", respectively.
- ❑ Debtor is a Transmitting Utility.
- ❑ Debtor acting in representative capacity (e.g., as trustee).

Filed With:

Prepared By (Name and Address):

❑ Check to request Continuation Statement notice for additional fee.

This Financing Statement covers the following types (or items) of property: Check only if applicable: ❑ Products of collateral are also covered.

If the collateral is crops, the crops are growing or to be grown on the following described real estate:

If the collateral is (a) goods that are or are to become fixtures; (b) timber to be cut; or (c) minerals or the like (including oil and gas) or accounts resulting from the sale thereof at the wellhead or minehead, the description of the real estate concerned is: (check X in applicable box(es))

❑ Fixtures ❑ Timber ❑ Minerals or accounts resulting from sale thereof at wellhead or minehead

And this Financing Statment is to be filed in the real estate records where a mortgage on such real estate would be recorded. If the Debtor does not have an interest of record, the name of a record owner is:

By: __________
Signature of Debtor (or Assignor) *Title*

By: __________
Signature of Debtor (or Assignor) *Title*

THIS SPACE FOR USE OF FILING OFFICER
(DATE, TIME, NUMBER, FILING OFFICER)

Just as the secretary of state accepts articles of incorporation, he will accept UCC-1 forms and requests for information. A filing fee is generally charged. In Delaware, the fee varies depending on how quickly the creditor would like to assure filing of the financing statement. The secured party may pay additional fees to assure same-day filing or even filing within two hours of receipt.

When the debt is paid in full, the secured party will release the security interest in the property by filing an additional form verifying that the debt has been paid and that the creditor therefore releases any interest it may have in the secured property. (See Figure 19-3 for a UCC-3 form, used in terminating a security interest.) Paralegals often conduct UCC-1 searches when corporations are merging or acquiring the assets of another entity to ensure that the assets purchased are free and clear of outstanding security interests. In many states, searching can be done online, through the home page of the secretary of state.

In August 1999, the National Conference of Commissioners on Uniform State Laws passed a model law, called the Uniform Computer Information Transaction Act, to regulate electronic commerce, namely the purchase and sale of goods, including software, online. The Act has already been subject to much debate and dissension, and attorneys general from nearly half of the states oppose it, many on the basis that it favors the Internet industry to the detriment of consumers. Due to the vigorous debate over the Act, few experts expect passage in all states.

Effective October 2000, electronic signatures have the same force and effect as their pen and ink counterparts. Consumers can elect whether to use an electronic signature (usually consisting of a keystroke on an "I agree" button) or handwritten signature for most documents. Nevertheless, certain documents, such as those canceling basic services such as heat and water, must be provided to consumers in conventional print form.

3. *Franchising*

Franchise
License granted by one party to another to use the first party's system and trademarks

Franchise agreement
Agreement setting forth parties' rights in a franchise relationship

A **franchise** is a license granted by one party to another enabling the latter to use the licensor's proprietary system and trademarks in selling goods and services. Arguably, the best-known example of franchising in the United States is McDonald's restaurants. An individual or entity wishing to offer McDonald's products will enter into an agreement with McDonald's, called a **franchise agreement,** whereby a certain initial franchise fee will be paid for the privilege of using McDonald's recipes, systems, trademarks, logos, and so forth.

The franchisee can operate his own business and yet enjoy the proven track record of McDonald's, the franchisor. While 15 states have separate statutory provisions governing franchises, the remainder of the states follow regulations established by the Federal Trade Commission (FTC). The FTC has promulgated regulations requiring certain disclosures by franchisors to franchisees. For example, the franchisor must disclose the anticipated costs in establishing the franchise, the number of other franchisees in the system, any litigation pending against the franchisor, and the number and circumstances of termination of other franchisees.

A franchise relationship is a contractual relationship. The rights and duties of the parties are governed by their franchise agreement. The FTC, however, requires that certain items and information be disclosed to the potential franchisee. These disclosures are set forth in a document called the **franchise offering circular,** which must be provided to every potential franchisee.

Franchise offering circular
Document provided to prospective franchisee providing information on the franchised business and franchisor

Typically, the franchisee pays a certain initial franchise fee for the privilege of operating the franchise, whether it is a McDonald's, a Taco Bell, or a Midas Muffler Repair Shop. Additionally, franchisees are generally required to pay stated

FIGURE 19-3
Florida UCC-3 Form

State of Florida

UNIFORM COMMERCIAL CODE | **STATEMENT OF CHANGE** | FORM UCC-3 (REV.1993)

This Statement of Change is presented to a filing officer pursuant to the Uniform Commercial Code:

1. Debtor (Last Name First if an individual)		1a. Date of Birth or FEI#
1b. Mailing Address	1c. City, State	1d. Zip Code
2. Additional Debtor or Trade Name (Last Name First if an individual)		2a. Date of Birth or FEI#
2b. Mailing Address	2c. City, State	2d. Zip Code
3. Secured Party (Last Name First if an individual)		
3a. Mailing Address	3b. City, State	3c. Zip Code
4. Additional Secured Party (Last Name First if an individual)		
4a. Mailing Address	4b. City, State	4c. Zip Code

5. This Statement refers to original Financing Statement bearing file number: ______________________ filed on ______________

6. A. ☐ Continuation -	The original Financing Statement between the Debtor and Secured Party bearing the file number shown above is continued.
B. ☐ Release -	The Secured Party releases the collateral described in Block 7 below from the Financing Statement bearing the file number shown above. RELEASE DOES NOT TERMINATE LIEN AGAINST A DEBTOR.
C. ☐ Full Assignment -	All of the Secured Party's rights under the Financing Statement have been assigned to the assignee whose name and address is shown in Block 7 below.
D. ☐ Partial Assignment -	Some of Secured Party's rights under the Financing Statement have been assigned to the assignee whose name and address in shown in Block 7. A description of the collateral subject to the assignment is also shown in Block 7.
E. ☐ Amendment -	The Financing Statement bearing the file number shown above is amended as set forth in Block 7. (See instructions for signature requirements)
F. ☐ Termination -	The Secured Party no longer claims an interest under the Financing Statement bearing the file number shown above.
G. ☐ Other -	

7. Description of collateral released or assigned, Assignee name and address, or amendment. Use additional sheet(s) if necessary.

	This space for use of Filing Officer
8. Signature(s) of Debtor(s): (only if amendment - see instructions)	
9. Signature(s) of Secured party (ies):	
10. Number of Additional Sheets Presented ______________	
11. Return Copy to: Name Address Address City, State, Zip	

STANDARD FORM - FORM UCC-3 Approved by Secretary of State, State of Florida royalties to the franchisor based on their sales. Thus, the better the franchisee does, the better the franchisor does. The franchisor, however, must provide certain support and training to franchisees. Many franchisors collect money from franchisees to fund national advertising campaigns to benefit all franchisees in the system or to promote a new product or service.

Because of the potential for abuse, the law is replete with complex franchise litigation cases. For example, what if you expend a significant amount of money for a McDonald's franchise and then McDonald's itself establishes its own restaurant half a block away from yours and undersells your products? What if you have expended a great deal of money to purchase a Baskin-Robbins franchise and then the franchisor begins offering its ice cream products in ordinary grocery stores, thus competing with you? What if Taco Bell franchisees are required by the terms of their franchise agreement to purchase salsa only from the franchisor and then the franchisor increases the price of the salsa so high that it drives the franchisee out of business?

From the franchisor's perspective, what if the franchisee refuses to follow the recipe for Kentucky Fried Chicken and independently begins offering new products? What if the franchisee refuses to follow the franchisor's requirements as to appearance and sanitation of the business so that the franchisor begins suffering a loss of its reputation as a clean and healthy restaurant?

Just as the general trend in other contracts is away from caveat emptor, and toward a wider recognition of rights of consumers, the general trend in franchising is to ensure that franchisees obtain the benefit of that for which they have paid and bargained. Nevertheless, the needs of franchisees are balanced with the need of franchisors to impose quality controls and standards on their franchisees to ensure that consumers who order a hamburger in Des Moines receive the same product and quality they would if ordering the product in Jacksonville.

4. *Leases*

Many businesses either rent office space from another party or perhaps rent to others their own excess space. Just as for centuries the guiding principle in contract law was caveat emptor, the general principle in real property law was that only the landlord had rights, not the tenant.

In the past several years, a number of cases and statutes have taken a more aggressive posture in protecting tenants, on the basis that they are in an inferior bargaining position to the landlord. Thus, over the past generation, a number of compelling cases have changed the landscape of landlord-tenant law. In general, while the earlier view was that the tenant took the premises as she found them, and accepted any risk or deterioration, modern law has fashioned a number of principles to ensure that tenants are not subject to unconscionable contracts.

Landlord
Owner of premises (also called *lessor*)

Tenant
One who uses or rents a landlord's property (also called *lessee*)

The owner of premises is called the **landlord** or *lessor*. The party who uses the real property and pays a sum therefor is called the **tenant** or *lessee*. The agreement whereby the tenant agrees to occupy the premises may be oral or written and may be for a specified term or at will, meaning that either party has the right to terminate the lease upon notice to the other. Whether the lease or rental agreement is oral or written, each party must abide by its terms, as is the case with any contract. Moreover, the law may impose additional obligations on the landlord. For example, if a state statute requires that landlords can only institute an eviction action against tenants after providing 30 days' notice, the landlord cannot circumvent that law by requiring otherwise. Similarly, a landlord cannot require the tenant to assume the burden of the landlord's statutory duties. The landlord cannot, therefore, require the tenant to release the landlord from a duty to install a fire detection system; such an **exculpatory clause** is unconscionable and is unenforceable.

Exculpatory clause
A clause attempting to excuse oneself from one's own negligence or fault

The landlord-tenant relationship is subject to a number of rights, duties, and responsibilities. For example, the landlord must deliver physical possession of the premises to the tenant. The landlord cannot allow a former tenant to occupy the space and inform the incoming tenant that it is his responsibility to take possession.

Tenants have a **right of quiet enjoyment,** meaning they have a right to use and enjoy the premises for that purpose for which they are designed. If the landlord permits raucous parties, routinely explodes fireworks in the parking lot, or allows other tenants to destroy the premises, a tenant may have the right to terminate the lease based on the fact that the right to quiet enjoyment of the premises has been breached by the landlord.

Right of quiet enjoyment
Provision inherent in all leases allowing tenant to use and enjoy rented premises

Landlords cannot evict tenants without prior notice. Even in the event the tenant has failed to pay rent, the landlord must provide the tenant with notice and an opportunity to cure the default. Similarly, the landlord is generally precluded from **constructive eviction** of the tenant, by turning off heat, water, or other essential services. The tenant should be provided with an opportunity to defend any default in the terms of the lease. It is possible the tenant has withheld rent due to a leak in the roof that has caused the tenant to incur expenses for repair or to cease operating its business. Similarly, landlords are generally prohibited from **retaliatory eviction,** or evicting tenants who have exercised certain statutory rights, such as complaining to the local health department about the condition of the premises.

Constructive eviction
Impairment of tenant's rights that is so significant the tenant might as well have been physically evicted

Retaliatory eviction
Eviction of tenant by landlord in retaliation for tenant's lawful exercise of rights

The tenant may be restricted as to use of the premises. In some commercial leases, business tenants often negotiate for written covenants by the landlord that a similar business will not be allowed to lease premises in the building or space. Thus, for example, if a tenant operates a yogurt shop in a shopping center, she will want to make sure that the landlord does not lease other spaces in the center to some competitive business, such as another yogurt shop or possibly even an ice cream store or deli.

Generally, tenants have a duty to maintain the leased premises in good condition; however, tenants are not required to repair defective plumbing, wiring, and so forth. Additionally, tenants may not alter the premises without the landlord's approval, even if the tenant believes the alteration, such as removal of a wall, is an improvement. A concomitant duty is imposed on the landlord: the landlord is generally required to maintain the premises in good condition, including repairing leaky pipes, replacing broken appliances, and so forth, but has no duty to improve the premises. Landlords must maintain common areas, such as parking lots, hallways, and elevators, in good condition.

A tenant cannot typically be charged with ordinary wear and tear of the premises. In previous years, a common practice of landlords was to retain all or a significant portion of security deposits for such items as cleaning or painting the premises after the tenant vacated. Many modern statutes attempt to control this practice by requiring that the landlord bear the cost of ordinary wear and tear and return the security deposit within a certain time period unless the landlord provides the former tenant with an itemized list of the repairs needed. Cases instituted in small claims courts dealing with disputes over retention of security deposits are plentiful, revealing that this remains an area of much dissension.

A common conflict in landlord-tenant relations relates to the withholding of rent by a tenant due to some alleged breach of the lease or misconduct by the landlord. Many states have enacted laws dealing with this issue because it has given rise to so much litigation. Generally, tenants may withhold rent in an amount equivalent to the sum by which the premises have decreased in value due to any defect, such as a leaky roof or faulty plumbing. Rent withholding, sometimes called a **rent strike,** is a complex and hotly debated matter. Some statutes require and many attorneys advise that rather than merely withholding rent, tenants deposit the rent into a special account to be released to the landlord upon resolution of the dispute. This gesture shows the tenant's good faith and demonstrates that the tenant is not merely avoiding payment obligations.

Rent strike
Withholding of rent

The amount charged for rent of the premises is subject to agreement of the parties. A landlord who sets the rent excessively high will not be successful in attracting tenants as they will simply shop for better bargains. Thus, courts rarely interfere with the agreement of the parties dealing with the amount of rent to be paid. Rent need not always be paid in cash. The parties are free to work out other arrangements, such as providing space rent-free to the tenant in return for the tenant's agreement to manage the building, providing one year's free rent in exchange for an advantageously long rental term, and so forth. The parties may agree that the rent will increase periodically. The increase may be established in advance or may be based on increases in the consumer price index or other relevant statistics. If there is no written lease agreement and the tenant rents at will, the landlord may increase the rent upon appropriate notice, usually one month.

Generally, the landlord may assign or transfer his interest in the leased premises. A tenant, however, seldom has the right to transfer his rights without prior approval of the landlord. An **assignment** of a lease is a transfer of all of the renter's interest in the space to another. A **sublease,** however, is a transfer of the premises for a period less than the term of the lease agreement. Because landlords have the right to interview and screen candidates to ensure they have a proven track record as reliable tenants, to allow a tenant to transfer the space to another without the approval of the owner of the premises would jeopardize the valuable property rights the owner has in the premises. While landlords may use valid criteria in screening applicants, such as rent history, employment information, and references, landlords are prohibited from discriminating against tenants due to their religion, race, gender, and so forth.

Assignment
A transfer of all of lessee's interest to another

Sublease
Transfer by lessee of less than all of its rights to another

With regard to liability to third persons, the tenant is liable for reasonably foreseeable injuries proximately caused by her. For example, if a tenant fails to shovel snow at the doorstep of her store premises, or fails to adequately warn customers of the condition, the tenant may be liable. Landlords are liable to third parties on the same basis. While landlords may not be liable for totally unpredictable events, such as the shooting of a tenant by a deranged individual, the landlord will be liable for acts which reasonably could have been foreseen. To illustrate, if a particular locale has been the scene of a number of rapes, and the landlord has notice of the rapes and has been provided a description of the suspected rapist, the landlord may be liable for damages for a resulting rape of a tenant if the landlord failed to disclose this pertinent and known information to tenants. Similarly, the landlord may be liable for injury to tenants or third parties caused by defective conditions on the premises such as potholes or inadequate lighting. While not a guarantor of safety and well-being, a landlord is charged with maintaining the premises. Additionally, if the landlord has knowledge of information that would be viewed as material to tenants, the landlord has an affirmative duty to disclose that information.

Courts may fashion a variety of remedies for breach of lease agreements. If the tenant is not provided with what it bargained for, the court may allow the tenant to set off rent previously paid or terminate its obligations under the lease. In the event of a breach by the tenant, the landlord must usually initiate an eviction action (called an **unlawful detainer** action) in court. Evidence will be presented and the court will render a decision. If the court determines that eviction is necessary, a certain period of time is generally given to the tenant to remove himself from the premises. If the tenant fails to vacate the premises, after a period of notice, the local sheriff will forcefully evict the tenant by placing the tenant's personal possessions in the street, physically removing the tenant from the premises, and changing the locks on the doors. If a tenant vacates the premises prior to the agreed-upon term, the tenant will remain liable for the rent owed under the lease. The landlord, however, has an affirmative duty to mitigate these damages by making a good-faith effort to lease the premises to a third party.

Unlawful detainer
Action brought by landlord to evict a tenant

5. *Intellectual Property*

Introduction. As discussed in Chapter Eighteen, businesses desire to own all work products produced by their employees. Moreover, some companies own valuable products, including software, which can be licensed to other parties. The products of human creativity are called **intellectual property,** to distinguish them from items of real property (real estate) and personal property (tangible items, such as jewelry, stock, and cars). Intellectual property comprises four types of property rights: trademarks, copyrights, patents, and trade secrets.

Intellectual property
Products of human creative thought, including trademarks, copyrights, patents, and trade secrets

Trademarks. A **trademark** is any word, name, symbol, or device used by a person to identify and distinguish his or her goods and to indicate the source of those goods. 15 U.S.C. Section 1127. Technically, the term *trademark* is used to identify one's product (such as the use of NIKE® in connection with shoes), while the term **service mark** is used to identify one's services (such as HILTON® for lodging services). Many companies use both trademarks and service marks, such as the use of STARBUCKS® in connection with products, such as coffee and mugs, and in connection with restaurant services. In common usage, however, the term trademark is often used to refer to marks identifying products or services.

Trademark
A logo, symbol, word, or device used to identify and distinguish goods

Service mark
A logo, symbol, word, or device used to identify and distinguish services

Trademarks can consist of slogans (such as YOU DESERVE A BREAK TODAY®), designs (such as the famous GOLDEN ARCHES® used by McDonald's Corporation), sounds (such as Tarzan's distinctive yell), and even fragrances and colors.

While the use of the word "device" in the definition of a trademark is broad enough to encompass a variety of items, there are some exclusions from trademark protection, including marks that are merely descriptive, marks that are confusingly similar to others' marks, marks that are scandalous or immoral, and marks that are primarily merely surnames. Moreover, some marks are stronger than others: marks that are coined (such as XEROX®) are the strongest and most protectable, followed by marks that involve the arbitrary use of a word for a product or service (such as APPLE® for computers), and then marks that are suggestive (such as CIRCUIT CITY® for electronic goods). Marks that merely describe a product cannot be registered with the U.S. Patent and Trademark Office (PTO) unless they have achieved **secondary meaning** such that upon encountering the mark, consumers immediately associate it with the source or offeror of the goods. Secondary meaning can also be achieved through five years of continuous use of a mark. Words that are generic (such as BREAD for bread) cannot function as trademarks.

Secondary meaning
Achieving wide renown

Trademarks provide guarantees of quality and consistency so that a consumer purchasing a latte at a Starbucks in Miami knows it will be of the same quality as one purchased at a Starbucks in San Francisco.

Rights in trademarks arise from use of the mark. Federal registration of a mark is not required to acquire trademark rights; however, registration with the PTO does afford a number of advantages to an owner, including the right to bring an action for infringement in federal court. Only marks in use in interstate commerce can be registered with the PTO. If a mark is in use exclusively intrastate, for example, solely in Denver, it may be registered with the state of Colorado. A mark in use in such a local area will have prior rights over any later user who uses a confusingly similar mark in the area of use or a reasonable area of geographic expansion. A federal registration, however, affords nationwide priority so that its owner can preclude a later user from use of a confusingly similar mark anywhere in the United States. Marks used without being subject to federal registration are often called **common law marks.**

Common law mark
A trademark in use without benefit of federal registration

If a mark qualifies for federal registration, an application should be filed with the PTO. Additionally, if one has a bona fide intent to use a mark in interstate commerce, one can file an application for federal registration. The PTO registration process is fairly lengthy, and generally takes about one year. The filing fee is presently $325. After registration, the owner of the mark will be required to periodically confirm use of the mark to the PTO and to renew registration of the mark. Once a mark is registered, its owner may use the federal registration symbol ®. Use of the symbol is not required, but is advisable because it affords notice to others of the owner's rights. The statutes governing federal registration and trademark infringement are found at 15 U.S.C. Section 1051, et seq.

The standard for determining infringement of a mark is whether the two marks are likely to be confused. Courts examine a variety of factors to determine if marks are confusingly similar, including their appearance, connotation, whether consumers have actually been confused, and whether the marks and goods are used in the same channels of trade.

Properly protected, trademarks can last forever and afford their owners significant competitive advantages. With sufficient advertising, marks can become so well known that just a bar or two of music or a combination of colors is sufficient for consumers to identify a mark. It has been estimated that the average person in the United States encounters approximately 1,500 trademarks each day, making trademarks among the most visible items of intellectual property.

Companies must therefore actively protect and monitor their marks to ensure they continue to identify the company's products and services.

Copyrights. **Copyright** is a form of protection provided to the authors of original works of authorship, including literary, dramatic, musical, artistic, and other works. Like trademarks, copyright requires no federal registration. Copyright rights arise from the time a work is created in fixed form, whether or not registration is sought with the Copyright Office.

Copyright
Form of protection provided to authors of original works of authorship in literary, artistic, and other works

The scope of copyright protection is quite broad. The copyrightability of "literary" works affords protection to more than serious works of literature. Even advertising and marketing materials are protectable as literary works. Computer programs are also protectable as literary works, because they are expressed in words and numbers. Copyright is available for original works — no judgment is made as to their artistic merit or quality. Nevertheless, certain works are not protectable under copyright law, including slogans, titles, lists of ingredients, ideas, processes, and methods, although the expression of ideas, processes, and methods is protectable. Thus, having a great idea for a new sitcom is not protectable. Once you write a script, however, that expression of your idea is protected by copyright.

Copyright owners have the exclusive right to reproduce, distribute, display, and perform the copyrighted work, and to create derivative works (such as sequels) based on the work. Only the author of the work can rightfully claim copyright. There is, however, an exception to this rule: in the case of **"works made for hire,"** the employer or commissioning party is viewed as the author of the work. Under 17 U.S.C. Section 101, a work made for hire is one prepared by an employee in the scope and course of employment or a work specially ordered or commissioned for use as part of a motion picture, a translation, or other types of special works, if the parties agree in writing that the work shall be considered a work made for hire and will be owned by the commissioning party. Thus, the copyright in all work produced by employees is owned by the employer, whether or not the parties have agreed to or discussed ownership rights.

Work made for hire
A work created by employee which is presumptively owned by employer (or a specially commissioned work that the parties have agreed in writing will be owned by the commissioning party)

No publication of a work or registration or other action in the Copyright Office is required to secure copyright. Copyright is secured automatically when the work is created in a fixed form. Thus, typing the sitcom script on paper or into a word processor "fixes" the work. While registration is not required to secure copyright, it does afford enhanced protection for a work, and registration is required for works of U.S. origin before an infringement suit may be filed in court.

Registration with the Copyright Office is a very straightforward and inexpensive process. An application is filed with a $30 filing fee, and unless the work is uncopyrightable, a registration will issue in about four months. Use of the copyright notice (© plus the year of first publication and the owner's name) is not required, although it does afford notice to the public that the work is protected by copyright. Copyright protection endures for the life of the author plus 70 years after the author's death. For works made for hire, however, the term of protection is 95 years from publication or 120 years from creation, whichever is shorter. There is no provision for state registration of copyright and copyright is exclusively governed by federal law (17 U.S.C. Section 101, et seq.).

Patent
Grant by the federal government to exclude others from making, selling, or using an invention

Patents. A **patent** is a grant by the federal government to exclude others from making, using, or selling another's invention. There are three types of patents: **utility patents** protect any new and useful process, machine, or composition of matter, or improvements thereto (and are broad enough to cover inventions such as the disposable razor, the airplane, and genetically altered mice); **design patents** protect new, original, and ornamental designs for useful articles, such as furniture

Utility patent
Patent for a new and useful process or machine

Design patent
Patent for new, original, and ornamental designs

Plant patent
Patent for new and distinct asexually reproduced plants

and containers; and **plant patents** cover new and distinct asexually reproduced plant varieties, such as a new variety of rose or grass.

Patents are governed exclusively by federal law (35 U.S.C. Section 100, et seq.). There is no such thing as a common law patent, and a patent is only enforceable if it has been issued by the federal government, specifically the PTO.

Patent law requires that the invention must be novel, useful, and nonobvious. An insignificant improvement to an invention is obvious and would therefore be unpatentable. An invention already in use by another would not be novel and would not qualify for patent protection. Additionally, laws of nature, physical phenomena, and abstract ideas are not patentable subject matter, although business methods that produce a useful and tangible result are patentable. Thus, Amazon.com has received a patent for its "one click" shopping method.

To obtain a patent, the inventor must file an application with the PTO. The process is expensive and time-consuming. Filing fees are presently $760 ($385 for small entities), and the application process can take from one to two years. Protection lasts for 20 years from the date of filing of an application for utility and plant patents and 14 years from the date of issuance of a design patent. Additionally, maintenance fees are due during the term of protection for a utility patent, at 3½, 7½, and 11½ years after the date of grant.

If a patent is infringed (by unauthorized making, using, or selling of the invention), an action may be brought in federal court. The patentee is not required to mark the invention with the word "Patent" and the number of the patent, although marking is highly recommended, inasmuch as a patentee may not recover damages from an infringer unless the infringer was notified of the infringement and continued to infringe thereafter. Marking gives notice of one's patent rights.

Trade secret
Any valuable information that, if known by a competitor, would afford the competitor a benefit

Trade Secrets. A **trade secret** is any valuable information that, if known to a competitor, would afford the competitor some benefit or advantage. Trade secrets need not be complex and can consist of customer lists, recipes, financial projections, methods of doing business, and marketing plans. Nearly any type of information can qualify as a trade secret so long as it affords its owner a competitive edge, and the owner has taken reasonable methods to protect the information. Such methods would include limiting access to confidential material, marking materials with legends such as "confidential," and monitoring use of the material.

There is no federal registration of trade secrets, and they are governed nearly exclusively by state statutes and case law. If property protected, trade secrets can last forever.

Use of Intellectual Property. Companies need to be aware of the value of their intellectual property assets. Names and slogans can be protected as trademarks; marketing materials and software can be protected under copyright law; and customer lists and valuable information about the business can be protected as trade secrets. Once companies understand the full range of materials that can be protected, they will be in a better position to use those assets to increase revenue, either by licensing or selling the property to others. Intellectual property must be actively monitored to be protected. Courts are reluctant to protect intellectual property assets in cases in which owners have routinely allowed infringing uses. Thus, companies must be vigilant about monitoring and protecting intellectual property assets, particularly in the electronic age, when valuable trade secret information or copyrighted material can be disseminated to thousands with a single keystroke.

6. *Antitrust Law*

Antitrust law
Field of law protecting against monopolies

The free enterprise system presumes that competition is healthy: companies that offer competing products will attempt to attain greater market share by decreasing the price of the product offered or increasing its attractiveness to the consumer, or both. The ultimate winner in such a system is the consumer. Conversely, if one company is allowed to dominate an entire business or industry, such as airline transportation, there would be no incentive to improve the service offered or to decrease the price, because the supplier, the airline carrier, would have a captive audience with no choice to go elsewhere with business patronage. The one airline carrier could then charge whatever prices it wanted, and would fail to remain competitive by developing better systems and products because it would know that consumers have no option but to continue using its services. Such a situation is referred to as a *monopoly* (literally, "single sale"), or an exclusive privilege or advantage to offer a product or service.

A number of laws have been enacted to avoid monopoly situations and to encourage suppliers to offer ever-better products and services at even more competitive prices. The body of law regulating competition in the business arena to foster competition is antitrust law. The first efforts to regulate business occurred in the late 1800s when Congress passed the Sherman Act to rein in railroad companies that had been organized as trusts and dominated the transportation field. The Sherman Act, sometimes called the Sherman Antitrust Act, was aimed at *trust-busting*, or breaking up monopolistic companies. It prohibits agreements that restrain trade, as well as monopolization or attempts to monopolize. The primary focus of the Sherman Act is to preclude agreements between businesses to fix prices, lower supply of goods, divide the market into specific regions (with each business having complete unrestricted control over its designated territory), or reduce competition in the marketplace. These types of activities undertaken by "equal" rivals are referred to as **horizontal restraints** and are considered the most serious of antitrust violations. Thus, criminal penalties are often imposed for horizontal restraints. Agreements restraining trade between buyers and sellers are **vertical restraints,** and would include, for example, an agreement between Hanes' Hosiery and the Nordstrom Company by which Hanes would agree to provide Nordstrom with its products only if Nordstrom agreed not to offer the goods in its stores at a price below that specified by Hanes.

Horizontal restraint
Activities engaged in by equal competitors to restrain trade

Vertical restraint
Activities engaged in between buyers and sellers to restrain trade

The Sherman Act also prohibits refusals to deal, or group boycotts by which two or more companies refuse to do business with another person or company, generally in an attempt to drive that company out of the marketplace.

The Clayton Act and the Federal Trade Commission Act were passed in the early 1900s to prohibit specific monopolistic acts and practices not covered by the Sherman Act. The Clayton Act prohibits **price discrimination,** namely, the practice of imposing different prices for the same goods on different purchasers. Also precluded are **exclusive-dealing contracts,** agreements for the sale of goods in which the purchaser is required to agree not to use or deal in competitors' products. Thus, the sellers of Hunt's tomato sauce could not preclude your local grocery from also offering Contadina products, S & W sauces, or even a house brand

Price discrimination
Practice of charging different prices for the same goods

Exclusive-dealing contracts
Agreements requiring a purchaser not to use a competitor's product

Tying arrangement
Linking the sale of one product to another

product. Similarly, tying arrangements are precluded. A **tying arrangement** occurs when a seller conditions the sale of one product on the purchase of another. For example, if McDonald's were allowed to condition its sale of a franchise upon an agreement that franchisees would order all cups and paper products only from McDonald's and no other supplier, McDonald's would have tied the sale of the franchise to the purchase of the paper products. While McDonald's may lawfully insist that its franchisee use paper goods of a certain quality that clearly display McDonald's trademarks and logos, there is nothing so inherently special about paper products that they could not be ordered from some other supplier at a lower price. Thus, while McDonald's may offer the paper products to its franchisees, it cannot insist that such products be purchased as a condition of obtaining or retaining the franchise. On the other hand, if the products are special or proprietary, for example, a special recipe that gives a product its unique taste, such as the seasoning for KFC's chicken, the franchisor *may* lawfully require that the franchisee purchase this product only from it.

Horizontal merger
Mergers between competitors

Mergers between companies will be carefully scrutinized by the Department of Justice to ensure that the effect of a merger will not create a monopoly or adversely affect competition in the marketplace. Mergers between rival firms are called **horizontal mergers.** In 1992, the Department of Justice and the FTC jointly issued Horizontal Merger Guidelines to clarify the factors considered in their review of mergers. If the effect of a horizontal merger is an entity that has a disproportionate market share, the merger will be prohibited by the Justice Department. For example, a merger between Alcoa, with nearly 30 percent of the market share for aluminum products, and a rival in the aluminum industry, with less than 5 percent market share, was prohibited on the basis that even though Alcoa would have less than 50 percent of the market share for aluminum products after the merger, the effect would decrease competition. Because Alcoa was a leader in the industry, the practice of buying out or merging with its smallest rivals would eventually give Alcoa a monopoly or near monopoly on aluminum goods.

Vertical mergers
Mergers between companies in a buyer-seller relationship

Vertical mergers involve companies in a buyer-seller relationship. For example, a merger between McDonald's and Kimberly-Clark may be prohibited on the basis that McDonald's control of the paper products giant would impact or "foreclose" Burger King's ability to purchase paper products. In one case, Du Pont was prohibited from purchasing a large block of the stock of General Motors on the basis that this would foreclose producers of other fabrics and finishes from selling their products to General Motors, which presumably would use Du Pont's fabrics and finishes in its car seats and interiors.

Product extension
Expansion of product offerings by a company

Diversification
Offering of new product or service by a company

Some mergers occur because a company wants to diversify or offer a new service or product. Rather than start from scratch, a company might simply acquire a firm already established in the relevant industry. **Product extension** occurs when a company wishes to expand by offering a new product somewhat related to its previous products. For example, if a company engaged in the business of selling cosmetics acquired a company offering bath products, this would be a mere extension of its business. **Diversification** occurs when a company merges with another company whose products and services are totally unrelated to its own. Thus, the acquisition of a publishing company by McDonald's Corporation would be a diversification of McDonald's business. Mergers resulting in diversification are rarely prohibited because they do not greatly affect market concentration; however, a product extension that might lead to decreased competition may be prohibited.

Not every industry is subject to antitrust regulation. A number of industries are exempt from antitrust law, including insurance, labor unions, agricultural cooperatives, and a variety of other businesses and activities, most notably baseball. Baseball has been exempt from antitrust laws since 1922, when it was classified as an activity not in interstate commerce. There has been significant debate about this exemption over the past several years, especially since the baseball strike of 1994-1995, and because other professional sports are subject to antitrust law. Additionally, some industries are subject to oversight and control by administrative agencies having the primary authority to regulate them, such as the authority of the Federal Communications Commission to regulate the communications industry.

The Department of Justice and the Federal Trade Commission are charged with regulating and enforcing antitrust law. They can act prospectively by preventing anticompetitive activities (by enjoining certain practices or mergers), and can act retrospectively by correcting practices (by requiring companies to divest themselves of certain business divisions and by punishing violators). The Justice Department can punish violations of the Sherman Act through either civil or criminal actions. The Justice Department can ask a court for the remedy of **divestiture,** requiring a company to relinquish some of its operations, or the remedy of **dissolution,** which would terminate the existence of the offending company. A private party injured by anticompetitive acts or practices may also sue for treble damages or may seek injunctive relief to prevent antitrust violations that would result in irreparable harm. In one late-1999 case, LePage, Inc., a maker of transparent tape, was awarded more than $22 million (which was automatically trebled to more than $68 million) against 3M Company (the maker of Scotch and Highland brand adhesive tapes) in an antitrust suit that had alleged that 3M drove LePage out of the market for transparent tape. LePage proved that retailers offering its tape were forced to dump LePage's in order to obtain generous rebates from 3M.

Divestiture
Relinquishing certain assets or companies

Dissolution
Termination of a business entity

As discussed herein and in Chapter Fourteen, the federal government has the authority to review mergers and acquisitions to ensure that such transactions do not impair competition in the marketplace. Under the **Hart-Scott-Rodino Antitrust Improvements Act** (15 U.S.C. Section 18a), parties to certain merger transactions must notify the federal government and wait for 30 days before closing a transaction. The transaction or the parties in question must involve a certain amount of money before the Act applies. When the government receives the notice, it will review the transaction for its anticompetitive effect. If the government does not object to the transaction, it may proceed. In cases in which the government objects, companies may divest themselves of certain assets, restructure the transaction, or abandon the transaction.

Hart-Scott-Rodino
Federal act requiring premerger notification to the federal government so it can investigate anticompetitive effect of proposed transaction

7. *Unfair Competition*

Unfair competition
Legal field attempting to protect consumers from unfair and deceptive commercial practices

The law of **unfair competition** seeks to ensure that individuals are protected against unfair and deceptive commercial practices. In general, the most common types of unfair competition are as follows:

- **Passing off (or palming off).** Passing off occurs when one party attempts to sell his goods as those of another, such as placing the REEBOK® trademark on shoes of an inferior quality, leading consumers to believe that REEBOK® is the source of the goods.
- **Misappropriation.** Misappropriation occurs when one party takes or appropriates another's property, for example, the pirating of a news story created by another party at great expense and cost.
- **Right of publicity.** The right of publicity protects a person's identity, voice, likeness, or persona from unauthorized commercial exploitation, such as would occur by using a celebrity look-alike or voice to advertise a product without permission.
- **False advertising.** Making false statements about one's own or another's goods or services is false advertising, unless the statements are vague; are opinions; or are **puffery,** statements no reasonable person would believe (such as "our KEEBLER® cookies are made by elves"). Advertisements that purport to be objectively certifiable or statistical (such as "nine out of ten doctors recommend our product") must be supported by evidence.

Puffery
Commercial boasting; statements no reasonable person would believe

- **Product disparagement (or trade libel).** Making false statements about another's goods or services is actionable as product disparagement.
- **Dilution.** Tarnishing another's trademark by using it in an unsavory manner or causing it to lose its distinctiveness is actionable as dilution.
- **Infringement of trade dress.** Adopting the overall image and appearance of another's distinctive product, packaging, or image (such as establishing another restaurant with menus, logos, uniforms, decor, and products confusingly similar to those of Taco Bell) is actionable as trade dress infringement.

Parties found liable for acts of unfair competition can be enjoined from further deceptive practices and can be liable for damages as well.

C. Transactional and Business Law Practice

1. *Introduction*

In general, the practice of law is divided into two types: civil law and criminal law. Criminal law relates to the defense and prosecution of individuals and companies for alleged violations of federal law or a state's penal code. Civil law is typically any practice of law that is not criminal law, and would thus include family law, securities regulation, taxation, corporate law, wills and estates, torts, and so forth. Even within civil law, there are two primary divisions: litigation and transactional work. Litigation involves civil actions filed in court, whether for medical malpractice, personal injury, or breach of contract. Transactional law is generally viewed as being non-litigation work relating to business organizations including: the formation of partnerships, corporations, and other business organizations; counseling clients with regard to mergers and acquisitions; and providing general advice to business clients on matters like establishment of retirement plans or termination of employees, or guiding a client through dissolution of the entity.

Thus, advising business organizations is generally referred to as **transactional law.** Because much of the legal work involves corporations, the field is specifically referred to as *corporate law.* While most corporate attorneys and paralegals work in law firms, called **private practice,** a growing number of them work in the legal departments of corporations or business organizations, and are typically referred to as being **in-house.** This portion of this chapter will examine the types of tasks and activities involved in the corporate field, both in private practice and in-house.

Transactional law
Field of law that is not litigation; generally, advising business entities

Private practice
Working in a law firm

In-house
Working in the legal department of a business or corporation

2. *Private Corporate Law Practice*

Small Firm Practice. While some sole practitioners and small law firms may provide general advice and assistance to sole proprietors, partnerships, and corporations, these business clients tend to be smaller and in the emerging development stage. The sole practitioner or small law firm will generally be involved in other practice areas rather than focusing solely on the corporate field. Once a business achieves a certain size, whether in terms of employees or revenues, it will generally require a larger law firm with several legal professionals offering special skills and experience to handle its more complex needs.

Sole practitioners may give general advice to business clients, assist them in obtaining fictitious business names and various business licenses, draft partnership agreements, and form and dissolve corporations. The relationship between a new business and its counsel is intimate and challenging. The client generally needs a wealth of information on topics as diverse as naming the enterprise, making arrangements for contributions to Social Security, the procedures for calling and conducting meetings, drafting resolutions, terminating employees, entering into contracts, and so forth. The sheer variety of the tasks makes it a challenging field. Similarly, there is satisfaction and excitement in playing a part in a client's growth and success.

Paralegals working for sole practitioners and small law firms typically share in both this challenge and excitement. Because these newly emerging companies are generally cost-conscious, the teaming of an attorney and a paralegal offers great advantages to the client. The attorney provides legal advice and opinions and the paralegal executes that advice by preparing agreements, drafting documents, and performing other tasks such as checking name availability, reserving names, and qualifying the corporation to conduct business in other states.

Paralegals generally have a great amount of client contact in solo or small practices. There will be no "hoarding" of the client by senior attorneys anxious to be the client's sole contact in the firm and no hiding of the paralegal's role by having all of the paralegal's work prepared exclusively for the attorney's signature. Small practices encourage paralegals to get to know the client. It can be tremendously satisfying to accomplish specific tasks and receive sincere appreciation from the client and the attorney.

Large Firm Practice. Larger law firms often have specialized departments devoted solely to the corporate field; the attorneys and paralegals in this department work exclusively on corporate matters. Thus, within a relatively short time, paralegals can become extremely proficient in corporate law. Even within corporate departments, there may be sub-specialties, such as specific practice groups focusing on formation of businesses, mergers, takeovers and acquisitions, issuance and regulation of securities, or employee benefit issues. Others in the litigation department may work with the corporate department if a business client is involved in litigation.

While larger law firms may represent some of the nationally known corporate giants, the paralegal may have little, if any, contact with these clients. Attorneys may jealously safeguard their relationships with their corporate clients and, while paralegals may be intimately involved in the work itself, they may have little direct participation with or exposure to the clients themselves.

The relationship between larger corporate clients and law firms is often facilitated through the attorney employed directly by the corporate client, typically called the *in-house counsel.* Matters may arise for which the in-house corporate counsel may need advice. In that event, the in-house counsel often calls the private "outside" counsel to assist in some specific task. Some law firms with specialized practices may provide specific representation for corporate clients, such as **boutique law firms** that represent corporations exclusively with regard to intellectual property matters or firms representing the client only in connection with labor and employment issues. Thus, the in-house counsel may have relationships with numerous outside counsel at different firms, each of whom handles specific matters on behalf of the corporation.

Boutique law firms
Firms that specialize in a particular practice field

Practice Diversity and Needed Skills. Corporate law practice is diverse and challenging. There are crossovers with many different areas of law: when the corporation leases its office space, real property issues are involved; the purchase and sale of goods and services necessitates familiarity with contract law and the UCC; corporations entering into employment agreements with specially skilled employees require guidance in both contract and intellectual property law. If the corporate client is involved in a particular type of enterprise, the practitioner may need knowledge of specific regulations, such as those imposed by the Federal Trade Commission and state law regulating franchise relationships, the intricate tax treatment and advantages relating to employee benefits, or statutes and regulations relating to unfair competition. Because laws can change so frequently, simply learning legal concepts will not be sufficient. The corporate practitioner will need to stay current in the field by becoming knowledgeable about new laws, cases, and regulations that may affect the corporation.

Additionally, successful corporate practitioners may need experience in nonlegal areas of expertise such as accounting and finance. Strong interpersonal skills are also needed. The practitioner may have contact with numerous other attorneys representing the client as well as the in-house counsel and a variety of corporate officers and directors, each of whom has a different style and approach to problems. A great deal of time may be spent on the phone responding to questions, relaying information, and assisting in negotiations. Successful business entrepreneurs are highly demanding and know that "time is money." They therefore expect the legal team to return phone calls promptly, be available at a moment's notice, and be willing to switch approaches and arrive at creative solutions to ensure a transaction is accomplished. Oftentimes, transactions must occur within a certain time period so that particular tax advantages can be secured. These constraints require corporate practitioners to be highly organized and efficient so that time-sensitive deadlines are met.

Increased Competition and Pressure. The legal field has become highly competitive. While years ago clients formed strong relationships with their attorneys and would change attorneys only in the event of a major mistake or misunderstanding, many corporate clients are now lured away by other law firms offering lower rates, more responsive service, and creative fee arrangements. Moreover, a corporate client may be acquired by another corporation and its legal business is then transferred to the law firm representing the acquiring corporation.

Many law firms have high expectations for "business development," meaning the ability to attract new clients. Attorneys who provide this role as **rainmaker** may be more highly compensated than the "drones" who sit at their desks and merely churn out documents. Thus, there is competition not only between law firms but within law firms. Corporate clients may demand unique fee arrangements. Some clients will negotiate with the law firm on prices for photocopying and faxing. Some corporate clients will put the law firm on an annual retainer, meaning a fixed sum is set for providing legal services for the client. The client will pay a certain sum of money to the law firm per year, in return for which it can seek unlimited legal advice. Because of the possibility of abuse by both parties, these arrangements are not quite as popular as they once were and must be carefully structured.

Rainmaker
One who generates business for a law firm

A newer trend in corporate representation is the **success fee.** In this type of arrangement, the corporate client agrees to pay for legal services for a transaction either by the hour or in a fixed amount. If the law firm can achieve certain goals for the client, such as closing the transaction before a certain date, negotiating a monetary savings for the client, or producing a certain result, the client may pay an additional success fee to the law firm. This motivates the law firm to act as efficiently and aggressively as possible; every dollar or day saved for the client also represents dollars for the law firm.

Success fee
Fee paid to legal team based on success or closing of a transaction on specified terms or dates

Thus, corporate practice has become increasingly more stressful. Nevertheless, the fast pace, challenging legal problems, and need for creativity and flexibility make the practice area an exciting and stimulating one. There will always be businesses; they will always need legal assistance.

3. *In-House Corporate Practice*

Growth of In-House Legal Departments. Years ago, corporations generally sent all of their legal work to outside counsel. In-house counsel, if they existed, functioned more as managers or gatekeepers, keeping track of the corporation's legal matters and communicating with the outside counsel. Only the most basic of legal tasks were accomplished by inside counsel, such as preparing minutes of meetings, forming new corporate subsidiaries, and the like. Within the past ten years, however, many corporations came to realize how expensive their outside legal bills had become. In a concerted effort to reduce costs, many corporations began increasing the size of their in-house legal departments. In many instances, these corporations made offers to the attorneys in private practice who had been working with the corporation and had become familiar with the corporation's needs and demands. It has therefore become relatively common for attorneys and paralegals to work with corporate clients for a few years and then go in-house with the corporate client. Such arrangements can be extremely helpful for the corporate client. It continues working with the same legal team, a known commodity having intimate knowledge of the corporation's business needs and structure and, rather than paying $250 per hour for advice, the corporation pays annual salaries to the team members and obtains the advantage of having them on-site every day to assist the corporation.

The arrangement can be simultaneously disadvantageous to the law firm. The firm may have invested several years in training the attorney and paralegal; once they become productive, knowledgeable, and efficient, they are spirited away from the firm. Additionally, because more legal work will be done in-house, the corporate client may have a substantially decreased need for the firm's services. Thus, some law firms may attempt to minimize contact between corporate clients and attorneys and paralegals so that relationships cannot be formed that might lead to the luring away of legal talent by the corporate client.

Rather than looting the outside law firm for legal talent, the chief legal counsel in-house may hire additional attorneys. These attorneys work with the outside counsel on a variety of matters until they have been essentially trained and taught by the outside counsel to handle these matters independently. The corporation then relies exclusively on its inside legal department, consulting the outside counsel only if complex or novel problems arise.

For many years, in-house legal work was considered relatively staid and predictable. As challenging and exciting issues occurred, they were generally turned over to outside counsel. Moreover, pay was significantly lower in-house than in private practice. As a result, in-house positions were generally not the first choice for recent law school graduates who knew that more money could be made in private practice. The changing nature of the legal profession, however, has dramatically changed these facts as well. As corporate clients have become more conscious of their legal budgets, they expect more from their in-house counsel. Corporations began making a priority of upgrading and staffing their legal departments to cut back on the enormous sums spent on outside counsel. Thus, in-house counsel today face the same challenging and demanding tasks as private practitioners. Moreover, rather than billing by the hour, with the attendant pressure to keep one's billable hours high, the in-house legal staff can devote themselves wholeheartedly to an issue without worrying about billing, costs, and so forth. Many attorneys and paralegals find being freed from their time sheets extremely liberating and more conducive to their role as counselors. While the salaries at larger law firms typically remain higher than those for in-house counsel, pay has increased for inside counsel in order to attract and retain quality legal talent. Additionally, the in-house counsel receives some distinct advantages for any reduction in salary: the work day is slightly more predictable; the killer hours expected at the largest law firms are not as frequently encountered; the high stress and competitive atmosphere of the law firm is often reduced; pressure to bring in clients is nonexistent; the atmosphere may be more secure and stable than that of a law firm; the in-house legal staff often play an integral role in corporate management and policy; and in-house legal staff may have the opportunity to become part owners of the company through stock options and so forth. All of these factors combine to make in-house positions considerably more attractive than they were several years ago.

A number of studies have confirmed that businesses in the United States have reduced spending on outside counsel and have expanded their in-house legal departments. A 1995 Price-Waterhouse survey revealed that while corporations held total legal spending relatively steady, they increased spending on in-house legal counsel by nearly 5 percent. Forty-three percent of the respondents stated they had increased in-house legal staffing and 37 percent anticipated future increases. See *National Paralegal Reporter*, Summer 1996, vol. 20, no. 4.

In-House Legal Departments. Some major corporations have immense legal departments with more than 100 attorneys. These legal departments somewhat resemble large firms in that there may be an intellectual property section, a tax section, a contracts group, an employment and labor practice group, and a litigation team. The most senior attorney is usually called the **general counsel.** His tasks include not only representation of the corporation, his employer, but management of the legal department itself. The general counsel's advice may be sought on many issues other than solely legal ones, such as how to deal with a difficult employee, sensitivity training for all corporate employees, and negotiating with the company's insurance carrier. Many in-house counsel are also officers of the corporation. Some serve pursuant to formal written employment contracts with specified terms. All are salaried.

General counsel
The most senior lawyer in-house

In-house counsel generally report directly to the corporation's board of directors or one of its committees. Counsel generally attend directors' meetings in order to assist in taking minutes and to be available to answer any legal questions that arise in the course of the meeting. Therefore, the in-house counsel are generally conversant with the corporation's most sensitive and private issues and enjoy close contact with the corporation's decision-makers. As a result, some counsel eventually become members of the board of directors or even the chief executive officer of the corporation.

This closeness to the corporation is both a benefit and a burden. The benefit, of course, is having detailed knowledge of the corporation's workings and the confidence of the corporation's management team. The burden flows from this same closeness. For example, while outside counsel never relish being the bearer of bad news — such as telling the corporate client that a certain planned activity is unlawful or subject to substantial risk — giving this advice is what outside counsel are paid for, and they are seldom reticent in expressing their opinions in the strongest terms possible. Inside counsel, however, are often part of the corporate management team, and therefore may be reluctant to have to put the brakes on a transaction that is viewed as highly favored by the corporation and its management. Therefore, in-house counsel often ask for a second opinion from outside counsel on such issues. Similarly, knowing that inside counsel identify so strongly with the corporation, many third parties, such as accountants and insurance companies, often require opinions on sensitive issues from outside counsel rather than inside counsel.

Delegating Work to Outside Counsel. If inside legal staffs do increasingly more diverse and complex legal tasks, what is left for outside counsel? The assumption of greater legal work by in-house counsel has led to greater specialization in private practice. The in-house legal staff may have neither the experience nor the time to devote to certain tasks. This work may be delegated to outside counsel. Additionally, there are four situations that typically call for direct involvement of outside counsel.

Large-scale Litigation. Complex litigation requires the sophistication, personnel, and experience of outside counsel. Large-scale litigation can involve hundreds of thousands of documents, numerous depositions, and an avalanche of written materials. Most of these written materials must be coded, indexed, and organized for easy retrieval and reference. Many large law firms have litigation teams experienced in the paper war often encountered in complex litigation. Moreover, in-house counsel will seldom have sufficient time to devote to such cases because ordinary corporate tasks, negotiations, and transactions are still occurring. Thus, outside counsel are typically relied upon to handle large-scale litigation on behalf of the corporation.

Internal Conflicts. Conflicts of interest or even the appearance of impropriety may prevent in-house counsel from performing certain legal tasks. For example, involvement in the termination of employment of senior executives may create a conflict. The departure of some senior executive may work in favor of in-house counsel, who may assume some of the departed employee's functions. Thus, outside counsel will become involved to ensure that such sensitive issues are handled fairly and impartially. An outside counsel's ethical duties are owed to the corporation itself rather than to the in-house attorney who referred the issue to him or her. Similarly, lawsuits or claims by shareholders should be referred to outside counsel. Because in-house counsel are employees of the corporation and often enjoy close relationships with directors and officers, they may not have the confidence of shareholders that they will act on behalf of the corporation's owners rather than in a manner benefiting management or that will result in increased value of their own stock. Additionally, management may not wish that in-house counsel be privy to certain matters, such as compensation packages offered to certain executives. Thus, outside counsel may draft and negotiate employment contracts for senior managers.

Efficiency. Crisis issues typically require the involvement of outside counsel. To be cost-effective, the in-house legal department should staff only as many attorneys, paralegals, and support staff as are needed to handle the corporation's routine business. Thus, when a crisis arises requiring immediate and intense attention, in-house counsel may not have sufficient time to devote to these issues as well as perform ordinary work on behalf of the corporation. In such cases, the matter will be turned over to outside counsel for resolution.

Expertise. Highly specialized issues that fall outside the ordinary legal work performed by the in-house staff must be referred to outside counsel. Such matters might include complex employment issues, patent infringement cases, proxy fights, and so forth.

More importantly, outside counsel often act as a sounding board for in-house counsel. Many decisions in-house legal counsel are called upon to make are sensitive and complex. In such cases, just as attorneys in private practice will discuss the issue with other attorneys in the firm, in-house counsel will wish to seek the opinion of private practitioners. In many instances, the approach is quite informal. In-house counsel may call the outside counsel, explain the issue, summarize his conclusion, and then simply ask, "Am I missing anything?" Outside counsel is often then asked to prepare a confirming letter to the corporation. This provides the in-house counsel with an objective view and reassurance that his view is appropriate.

Some outside counsel, if asked what tasks they perform at the request of inside counsel, may cynically reply, "I do what in-house counsel doesn't want to do." While this may be a bit of an oversimplification, in many instances there is some truth to this statement. Additionally, there may be some friction between the two counsel. Typically, attorneys in private practice are not grilled by their business clients as to the wisdom and effectiveness of their legal conclusions. They become accustomed to being unchallenged. Because inside counsel are also skilled attorneys, however, they may well propose alternate solutions to a problem, insist upon certain tactics or strategy, or refuse to follow outside counsel's recommendations. In such cases, outside counsel often protect themselves by preparing correspondence or memoranda reflecting the dispute and their conclusions. In some instances, outside counsel may need to resign from the case, inasmuch as "he who won't be counseled, can't be helped."

In sum, while the working relationship between private practitioners and inside counsel can be delicate, there is plenty of work to go around and there is always a need for talented corporate attorneys and paralegals.

Key Features of Special Topics in Business Law

- Businesses should be conducted not only in accordance with the law, but also in accordance with ethical principles.
- Representing businesses involves an interplay with other areas of law, including the following:

  1. Contract law, specifically relating to the purchase and sale of goods, governed by the Uniform Commercial Code;
  2. Franchise law, in which an entity grants the right to operate a franchise to another under the owner's marks and using the owner's business methods and procedures;
  3. Real estate law, specifically the leasing of property for or by the business;
  4. Intellectual property law, by which a company uses its assets to achieve its unique identity, including trademarks (names and logos), copyrights (written materials, including software), patents (inventions), and trade secrets (confidential competitive information);
  5. Antitrust law, which plays a part in business combinations and mergers; and
  6. Unfair competition law, which attempts to ensure that the marketplace is free from deceptive practices.

- Business or corporate law is practiced in law firms and in-house in companies.

D. Role of Paralegal

Just as the need to reduce legal costs led corporations to increase the size and quality of their in-house legal staffs, the same consideration has led to increased utilization of paralegals in the corporate field, both in private practice and in the legal departments of corporations and other businesses. Paralegals routinely perform tasks that would have previously been done by associate attorneys in private practice. To remain competitive, law firms must provide corporate clients with the best services at the best price. Paralegals are an integral component in this objective. Similarly, in-house legal departments often believe they can get "more bang for the buck" by hiring two or more paralegals rather than one overpriced and under-experienced attorney. Thus, the corporate field remains an attractive area for paralegals.

With regard to ethical issues, paralegals should be alert to potential conflicts and ethical concerns. At a minimum, these concerns should be pointed out to the attorney. A better practice may be to set forth your concerns in a written memorandum, provide it to the attorney, place a copy in the file, and then retain a copy in your own files. Almost all state bar associations have ethics hot lines offering information and guidance on ethical issues. Be sure to contact your state bar association if ethical concerns arise during the course of your work.

The role of paralegals is rich and varied in the areas of law that cross over with the corporate field. Paralegals are routinely involved in the following activities:

- Conducting legal research regarding the Uniform Commercial Code; drafting agreements for the purchase and sale of goods; preparing and filing UCC-1 forms to perfect security interests and UCC-3 forms to release security interests.
- Drafting franchise offering circulars and franchise agreements; preparing state registrations for franchise clients; reviewing franchisees' advertising materials for compliance with the franchisor's requirements; drafting notices of default; and preparing agreements relating to franchise agreements, including assignments of leases, noncompetition agreements, and the like.
- Conducting legal research regarding required lease terms; preparing lease agreements, assignments of leases, and notices of default; docketing dates for termination and renewal of lease agreements; assisting in the representation of clients in actions to enforce terms of leases.
- Preparing trademark and copyright applications and assisting in preparing patent applications; drafting trade secret policies; monitoring the use of clients' and competitors' trademarks and advertising materials.
- Conducting research regarding applicability of the Sherman, Clayton, Hart-Scott-Rodino, and Federal Trade Commission Acts; assisting in the preparation of briefs and memoranda regarding antitrust matters.

Resource Guide

1. Ethics Codes

For ethics issues, the primary resource guide is the applicable code of ethics. The state bar association can provide you with a copy of the state's ethics code. Most of these state codes are based upon the American Bar Association's Model Rules of Professional Conduct (set forth in the Martindale-Hubbell Law Directory). Call directory assistance in your state's capital for the number of the state bar association. You will be directed to the ethics division, which may send you a copy of the code of ethics and provide you with miscellaneous and related information.

The ethics hot line maintained at the offices of most state bar associations can give you immediate guidance and assistance with regard to ethical issues and concerns.

The two major national paralegal associations have each drafted ethical codes for paralegals. The National Federation of Paralegal Associations' code is called Affirmation of Professional Responsibility. The National Association of Legal Assistants' code is called the Code of Ethics and Professional Responsibility. Additionally, the National Association of Legal Assistants has drafted Model Standards and Guidelines for Utilization of Legal Assistants. These codes can be obtained directly from the two associations:

National Federation of Paralegal Associations
Post Office Box 33108
Kansas City, Missouri 64114
Telephone: (816) 941-4000

National Association of Legal Assistants
1516 S. Boston, Suite 200
Tulsa, Oklahoma 74119
Telephone: (918) 587-6828

One excellent resource is the book *Ethics for the Legal Assistant* (3d ed.) by Deborah K. Orlick (Marien Hill Publishing, (818) 981-3573).

2. Form Books

Because most of the tasks conducted by paralegals in the practice areas related to corporate law involve the drafting of documents, the form books described in Chapter Nine provide an excellent guide to preparing and drafting many agreements and other documents.

a. Sale of Goods. The most critical resource for understanding the sale of goods is the Uniform Commercial Code, particularly your state's version of it. Locate your state's annotated statutes. Using the index, look up "commercial," "sales," or other related terms. You will be referred to the UCC or the variation of it that your state (except Louisiana) has adopted. After being provided with the pertinent statutes, you will be directed to cases interpreting those statutes.

The secretary of state of your state can likely provide you with UCC-1 and UCC-3 forms and fee schedules for the filing requirements of UCC-1 Financing Statements. A number of specialized texts provide information relating to the UCC, including the following:

- James J. White & Robert S. Summers, *Uniform Commercial Code* (3d student ed. 1988);
- *Uniform Commercial Code Law Journal;* and
- *Uniform Commercial Code Reporting Service* (Callaghan).

WESTLAW's UCC Filings, Liens and Judgments database provides information on outstanding UCC filings in all 50 states and the District of Columbia. Records can be searched by the debtor's name, the secured party's name, or by the state document or instrument number.

Capitol Services, Inc. of Austin, Texas ((800) 345-4647) also conducts UCC searches and effects UCC filings. Most of the attorneys' service companies identified in Chapter Nine also assist in locating UCC documents and making UCC filings. For example, CT Corporation System offers an electronic desktop system called CT Advantage that allows you to quickly and efficiently perform search and filing tasks from your own desk. CT Corporation System can be contacted at (800) 624-0909.

b. Franchise Law. The content and format of franchise offering circulars and franchise agreements is dictated by the Federal Trade Commission. Therefore, the most important resource in franchise law is the FTC regulations themselves. Additionally, the *Franchise Law Journal* publishes numerous articles on franchise law and related topics. Perhaps the most practical resource is a loose-leaf set of binders published by Commerce Clearing House entitled *Business Franchise Guide.* This set provides the FTC regulations, explains the nature and purpose of the regulations, contains suggested language for drafting franchise agreements, refers to pertinent cases, and provides the relevant information regarding the 15 states which have specific statutes amplifying the FTC requirements. Any franchise law practitioner will have this loose-leaf set handy at all times.

c. Real Property. In addition to numerous journals relating to real property law, such as the *Real Estate Law Journal,* specialized texts and treatises may exist. Additionally, the American Law Institute publishes the Restatement (Second) of Property which provides a clear and straightforward explanation of real property law principles. Browse the section of the law library dealing with real property related materials and texts.

Landlord and tenant issues will generally be governed by your state's statutes. These statutes will set forth the required terms in a lease, the content for notices of default, how notices must be served on a tenant, and how many days' notice a tenant must receive. These statutes will be annotated, meaning that after reading the statute you will be directed to cases interpreting the statute.

Forms for leases and related documents can be located in the form books described in Chapter Nine.

d. Intellectual Property. The U.S. Trademark Act is found at 15 U.S.C. Section 1051, et seq.; the U.S. Copyright Act is found at 17 U.S.C. Section 101, et seq., and the U.S. Patent Act is found at 35 U.S.C. Section 100, et seq. Statutes relating to trade secrets can be found in state codes.

There are a number of excellent treatises in the field of intellectual property, including the following:

- J. Thomas McCarthy, *McCarthy on Trademarks and Unfair Competition* (5th ed. 1997);

- Melville B. Nimmer & David Nimmer, *Nimmer on Copyright* (1978);
- Paul Goldstein, *Copyright* (2d ed. 2000);
- Donald S. Chisum, *Chisum on Patents* (1995); and
- Ernest Bainbridge Lipscomb III, *Walker on Patents* (3d ed. 1984).

e. Antitrust. The Sherman Act is located at 15 U.S.C. (or U.S.C.A. or U.S.C.S.) Sections 1-7. The Clayton Act is found at 15 U.S.C. Section 12, et seq. The Hart-Scott-Rodino Antitrust Improvements Act is located at 15 U.S.C. Section 18a. There are hundreds of cases interpreting each of these acts. The statutes and the cases construing them are the most significant resource in antitrust law.

Additionally, there are a number of excellent treatises, loose-leaf materials, and journals, including:

- Phillip E. Areeda & Donald F. Turner, *Antitrust Law* (1980);
- the loose-leaf service published by the Bureau of National Affairs entitled *Antitrust and Trade Regulation Reporter;* and
- *Antitrust Law Journal.*

f. Unfair Competition. Statutes relating to unfair competition can be found at 15 U.S.C. Section 1125 (often referred to as a "national unfair competition statute") and 15 U.S.C. Section 43(c) (relating to dilution), as well as in various state codes. An excellent analysis of unfair competition is found in the multivolume treatise by J. Thomas McCarthy, *McCarthy on Trademarks and Unfair Competition* (5th ed. 1997).

3. Numerous journals and magazines publish articles on paralegals. The national paralegal associations each publish journals. The following journals typically publish excellent articles on topics of interest to paralegals, including practice tips, information on salaries, and specific articles on working in the corporate practice area: *Legal Assistant Today, Facts and Findings* (published by the National Association of Legal Assistants), *Journal of Paralegal Education and Practice, California Paralegal Magazine, Legal Assistant Management Association,* and *National Paralegal Reporter* (published by the National Federation of Paralegal Associations).

◆ ◆ ◆

WEB RESOURCES

The following sources provide information about ethics:

www.law.cornell.edu/ethics/listing.htm
This site provides state-by-state collections of information about ethics.

www.legalethics.com
This site offers up-to-date information about ethical activity in cyberspace, as well as a list of ethics resources at www.legalethics.com/ethicsites.htm.

www.abanet.org/cpr/ethicopinions.html
The Web site of the American Bar Association offers summaries of its ethics opinions.

The most important resources relating to commercial transactions, franchising, leases, trade secrets, and unfair competition are the various state statutes. The most important resources for information relating to trademarks, copyrights, patents, and antitrust are federal statutes. The following are sites allowing access to statutes.

www.ll.georgetown.edu
When you access this site for Georgetown University Law Center, select "State, Local & Territorial." You will be presented with a map of the United States. Point your cursor to the state in which you are interested, and you will be provided with links to a variety of legal sources relating to that state. Select "Statutes" or "Codes," and you will be linked to the state's statutes. In some states, searching can be done by either keywords or by section number. In other states, searching is accomplished exclusively by keywords. Alternatively, when you access the site, select "Federal" and you will be directed to federal statutes.

www4.law.cornell.edu/usccode
This excellent site allows searching of federal statutes by keyword or section number. You can review all 50 titles of the U.S. Code or look up statutes by their popular names. The laws relating to antitrust are found at 15 U.S.C. Sections 1-7 and 12, et seq.; the laws relating to trademarks are found at 15 U.S.C. Section 1051, et seq.; copyright laws are found at 17 U.S.C. Section 101, et seq.; and patent laws are found at 35 U.S.C. Section 100, et seq.

Information about intellectual property can be located through various government Web sites. For information about patents and trademarks, access the site of the U.S. Patent and Trademark Office at <www.uspto.gov>. Fee schedules and forms are provided, and some searching may be done of the PTO databases to check for already issued patents, and pending and issued trademark registrations. For information about copyrights and the work made-for-hire doctrine, access the site of the U.S. Copyright Office at <www.loc.gov/copyright>. A variety of informational circulars are offered, as well as basic information and fee schedules.

The following sites provide useful information about the UCC and other uniform acts:

http://www.nccusl.org
This home page for the National Conference of Commissioners on Uniform State Laws provides current drafts of uniform acts.

http://www.law.cornell.edu/ucc/ucc.table.html
This site provides the text of the UCC.

http://www.law.cornell.edu/uniform/ucc.html
This site links to individual state versions of the UCC.

http://www.law.upenn.edu/bll/ulc/ulc.htm
This site provides the text of drafts of various uniform and model acts.

The UCC forms are usually located at the Web site of each state's secretary of state. Use the Web site addresses given in Appendix A, or access <www.nass.org>, select "States," and then point your cursor to your state. You will be linked to the home page for your secretary of state. Look for "UCC" or "Uniform Commercial Code" for information and forms for filing and releasing security interests.

Information about franchising and false advertising as well as other deceptive trade practices can be found at the Web site of the Federal Trade Commission at <www.ftc.gov>.

For various forms and agreements, try the following sites:

http://legal-resource.com/forms/d.cgi/[IDNUMBER]
This site offers a non-disclosure agreement for trade secrets as well as forms for leases.

www.lectlaw.com/formb.htm
This site offers forms for an assignment of copyright, contracts for the sale of goods, bills of sale, and forms for leases.

www.siccode.com/forms.php3
This site offers a form for an assignment of trademarks, forms related to the sale of goods, and lease forms.

The following site is also of interest:

http://www.aclaa.org
This Web site for the American Corporation Legal Assistants Association, an organization of corporate in-house legal assistants, offers excellent information about continuing legal education, keeps members informed of new issues in the field of corporate law, and provides a variety of other useful information for in-house corporate legal assistants.

Alternatively, access "Ask Jeeves" at <www.ask.com> and type in "Where can I find information about [franchising], [antitrust], [false advertising]?" to find other sites discussing such topics.

Discussion Questions

1. The attorney you work for has made a revision to a court document already signed by a client. The purpose of the revision was merely to correct a typo. The attorney has asked you to photocopy the client's signature and place it on the revised document. Discuss.

2. Why should a company-wide stock option plan drafted by the in-house legal team be reviewed by outside legal counsel?

3. There is an ambiguity in the lease prepared for your company by the landlord. Two interpretations of the ambiguous clause are equally plausible. Which interpretation will a court likely favor? Why?

4. The representatives of Shell Oil and Texaco Oil have met to determine that the prices of gasoline in your area will increase by 5 cents per gallon each month for the next three months. Have any federal laws been violated? Discuss.

5. Your law firm's client is acquiring another business. Why should you conduct UCC searches and searches of the PTO databases on behalf of the client?

6. Your law firm's client is using a Woody Allen look-alike to promote sales of its famous New York-style pizza. Discuss.

7. Your law firm's client, ABC, has observed the following advertisement used by its chief competitor: "We use only fresh ingredients in our prepared dinners — unlike ABC." Discuss under what circumstances such a statement would be actionable.

8. What if ABC's competitor used the slogan "The finest ingredients on the earth" for its prepared dinners? Is such a statement actionable?

APPENDIX

Secretaries of State and State Corporations Statutes

The following are the references to each state's business corporations statutes and the addresses of each state's secretary of state. Web sites for each secretary of state are also given. All states have Web sites for their secretaries of state, and all sites offer basic information about corporations. All Web sites, except that for South Carolina, provide forms for downloading; all Web sites, except that for the District of Columbia, provide fee schedules; and nearly half of all states offer searching for corporate and UCC data through their Web sites. An easy way to locate individual state Web sites is to access the home page of the National Association of Secretaries of State at <www.nass.org>. Go to "States," and you will be presented with a link to each state's secretary of state.

ALABAMA

Ala. Code Sections 10-2B-1.01, et seq.

Secretary of State
P.O. Box 5616
Montgomery, AL 36103-5616
(334) 242-5324
http://www.sos.state.al.us/

ALASKA

Alaska Stat. Sections 10.06.005, et seq.

Division of Banking, Securities and Corporations
State Office Building, Ninth Floor
P.O. Box 110808
Juneau, AK 99801-0808
(907) 465-2530
http://www.commerce.state.ak.us/corps.htm

ARIZONA

Ariz. Rev. Stat. Ann. Sections 10-001, et seq.

Secretary of State
Corporations Division
1300 West Washington
Phoenix, AZ 85007-2996
(602) 542-4258 or (800) 345-5819
http://www.cc.state.az.us/ *or* www.sosaz.com

ARKANSAS

Ark. Code Ann. Sections 4-27-101, et seq.

Secretary of State Aegon Building, Suite 310
510 Woodlane
Little Rock, AR 72291
(501) 682-3409 or (888) 233-0325
http://www.sos.state.ar.us/

California

Cal. Corp. Code Sections 1, et seq.

Secretary of State
1500 11th Street, Third Floor
Sacramento, CA 95814-5701
(916) 653-2121 or (916) 653-7315
http://www.ss.ca.gov

Colorado

Colo. Rev. Stat. Sections 7-101-101, et seq.

Secretary of State
1560 Broadway, Suite 200
Denver, CO 80202
(303) 894-2200
http://www.sos.state.co.us

Connecticut

Conn. Gen. Stat. Sections 33-600, et seq.

Secretary of State
30 Trinity Street
Hartford, CT 06106
(860) 509-6000
http://www.sots.state.ct.us/

Delaware

Del. Code Ann. tit. 8, Sections 101, et seq.

Secretary of State
401 Federal Street, Suite 4
Dover, DE 19901
(302) 739-3073
http://www.state.de.us/sos/corp.htm

District of Columbia

D.C. Code Ann. Sections 29-301, et seq.

Department of Consumer and Regulatory Affairs (Corporate Division)
One Judiciary Square
441 Fourth Street, N.W., Suite 1130
Washington, D.C. 20001
(202) 727-6248 or (202) 727-6303
http://sss.ci.washington.dc.us/ *or* http://www.dcra.org

Florida

Fla. Stat. Ann. Sections 607.0101, et seq.

Secretary of State
Division of Corporations
P.O. Box 6327
Tallahassee, FL 32314
(850) 414-5500 or (850) 488-9000
http://www.dos.state.fl.us/

Georgia

Ga. Code Ann. Sections 14-2-101

Secretary of State
315 West Tower
2 Martin Luther King, Jr. Drive
Atlanta, GA 30334
(404) 656-2817
http://www.sos.state.ga.us/

Hawaii

Haw. Rev. Stat. Sections 415-1, et seq.

Commerce and Consumer Affairs Division
Business Registration Division
1010 Richards Street
P.O. Box 40
Honolulu, HI 96813-2920
(808) 586-2744
http://www.state.hi.us/ *or*
http://www.hawaii.gov/dcca/html

Idaho

Idaho Code Sections 30-1-101, et seq.

Secretary of State
700 West Jefferson, Room 203
P.O. Box 83720
Boise, ID 83720-0080
(208) 334-2300 or (208) 334-2301
http://www.idsos.state.id.us/

Illinois

Ill. Comp. Stat. 5/1.01, et seq.

Secretary of State
213 State Capitol Building
Springfield, IL 62706
(217) 782-2201 or (800) 252-8980
http://www.sos.state.il.us

Indiana

Ind. Code Sections 23-1-17-1, et seq.

Secretary of State
Business Services
302 W. Washington
Room E-018
Indianapolis, IN 46204
(317) 232-6576
http://www.state.in.us/

Iowa

Iowa Code Sections 490.101, et seq.

Business Services Division
Office of the Secretary of State
1305 E. Walnut
2nd Floor, Hoover Building
Des Moines, IA 50319
(515) 281-5204
http://www.sos.state.ia.us/

Kansas

Kan. Stat. Ann. Sections 17-6001, et seq.

Secretary of State
Corporation Division
First Floor, Memorial Hall
120 S.W. 10th Avenue
Topeka, KS 66612-1594
(785) 296-4564
http://www.kssos.org/

Kentucky

Ky. Rev. Stat. Ann. Sections 271B.1-010, et seq.

Secretary of State
Capitol Building, Suite 152
700 Capitol Avenue
Frankfort, KY 40601-3493
(502) 564-3490
http://www.sos.state.ky.us/

Louisiana

La. Rev. Stat. Ann. Sections 12:1, et seq.

Secretary of State
P.O. Box 94125
Baton Rouge, LA 70804-9125
(225) 925-4704
http://www.sec.state.la.us/

Maine

Me. Rev. Stat. Ann. tit. 13A, Sections 101, et seq.

Secretary of State
Corporations Elections and Commissions Bureau
148 State House Station
Augusta, ME 04333-0148
(207) 626-8400
http://www.state.me.us/

Maryland

Md. Code Ann., Corps. & Ass'ns Sections 1-101, et seq.

Assessments and Taxation Department
301 West Preston Street, Room 809
Baltimore, MD 21201
(410) 225-1340 or (410) 767-1184
http://www.dat.state.md.us/

Massachusetts

Mass. Gen. L. ch. 156, Sections 1, et seq.

Secretary of the Commonwealth
Corporations Division
One Ashburton Place, 17th Floor
Boston, MA 02108
(617) 727-9640
http://www.state.ma.us/sec

Michigan

Mich. Stat. Ann. Sections 450.1101, et seq.

Commerce Department—Corporation, Securities and Land Development Bureau
P.O. Box 30054
Lansing, MI 48909-7554
(517) 241-6420 or (517) 241-6400
http://www.commerce.state.mi.us/corp/corpinfo.htm *or*
http://www.cis.state.mi.us/corp

Minnesota

Minn. Stat. Sections 302A.001

Secretary of State
180 State Office Building
100 Constitution Avenue
St. Paul, MN 55155-1299
(612) 296-2803
http://www.state.mn.us

Mississippi

Miss. Code Ann. Sections 79-4-1.01, et seq.

Secretary of State
P.O. Box 136
Jackson, MS 39205-0136
(601) 359-1350
http://www.sos.state.ms.us/

Missouri

Mo. Rev. Stat. Sections 351.010, et seq.

Corporations Division
P.O. Box 778
Jefferson City, MO 65102
(573) 751-4153
http://www.mosl.sos.state.mo.us/

MONTANA

Mont. Code Ann. Sections 35-1-112, et seq.

Secretary of State
P.O. Box 202801
Helena, MT 59620-2801
(406) 444-2034
http://www.state.mt.us/isd/index.htm *or*
http://www.state.mt.us/sos/biz.htm

NEBRASKA

Neb. Rev. Stat. Sections 21-2001, et seq.

Secretary of State
State Capitol, Room 1305
P.O. Box 94608
Lincoln, NE 68509-4608
(402) 471-4079
http://www.nol.org/home/sos/htm/services.htm

NEVADA

Nev. Rev. Stat. Sections 78.010, et seq.

Secretary of State
Capitol Complex
101 N. Carson Street, Suite 3
Carson City, NV 89710-4786
(775) 684-5708
http://www.sos.state.nv.us/

NEW HAMPSHIRE

N.H. Rev. Stat. Ann. Sections 293-A:1.01, et seq.

Secretary of State
State House, Room 204
Concord, NH 03301
(603) 271-3244
http://www.state.nh.us/sos

NEW JERSEY

N.J. Stat. Ann. Sections 14A:1-1, et seq.

Secretary of State
225 West State Street, CN 300
Trenton, NJ 08608-1001
(609) 530-6400 or (609) 292-9292
http://www.state.nj.us/treasury/taxation/corppart.htm *or*
http://www.state.nj.us/state/index.htm

NEW MEXICO

N.M. Stat. Ann. Sections 53-11-1, et seq.

Office of the New Mexico Secretary of State
State Capitol, North Annex, Suite 300
Santa Fe, NM 85703
(505) 827-3600 or (800) 477-3632
http://www.state.nm.us/scc/scchome.html *or*
http://web.state.nm.us/

NEW YORK

N.Y. Bus. Corp. Law Sections 101, et seq.

Secretary of State
Division of Corporations, State Records and Uniform Commercial Code
41 State Street
Albany, NY 12231-0001
(518) 473-2492
http://www.dos.state.ny.us/corp/corpwww.html *or*
http://www.dos.state.ny.us/

NORTH CAROLINA

N.C. Gen. Stat. Sections 55-1-01

Secretary of State
P.O. Box 29622
Raleigh, NC 27626-0622
(919) 733-4201
http://www.secstate.state.nc.us/

NORTH DAKOTA

N.D. Cent. Code Sections 10-19.1-01

Secretary of State
State Capitol
600 East Boulevard Avenue, Dept. 108
Bismarck, ND 58505-0500
(701) 328-4284
http://www.state.nd.us/sec

OHIO

Ohio Rev. Code Ann. Sections 1701.01, et seq.

Secretary of State
30 East Broad Street, 14th Floor
Columbus, OH 43266-0418
(614) 466-3910 or 1-877-SOS-FILE
http://www.state.oh.us/sos/body.htm

Oklahoma

Okla. Stat. Ann. tit. 18, Sections 1001, et seq.

Secretary of State
101 State Capitol
2300 North Lincoln Boulevard, Room 101
Oklahoma City, OK 73105-4897
(405) 521-3911
http://www.state.ok.us/~sos

Oregon

Or. Rev. Stat. Sections 60.001, et seq.

Secretary of State
Corporations Division
151 Public Service Building
255 Capitol Street, NE, Suite 151
Salem, OR 97310
(503) 986-2200
http://www.sos.state.or.us/

Pennsylvania

Pa. Stat. Ann. tit. 19, Sections 1.1, et seq.

Secretary of State
Corporations Bureau
302 North Office Building
Harrisburg, PA 17120
(717) 787-6458
http://www.dos.state.pa.us/

Rhode Island

R.I. Gen. Laws Sections 7-1.1-1, et seq.

Secretary of State
State House Room 220
Providence, RI 02903
(401) 222-2357
http://www.sec.state.ri.us

South Carolina

S.C. Code Ann. Sections 33-1-101, et seq.

Secretary of State
P.O. Box 11350
Columbia, SC 29211
(803) 734-2170 or (803) 734-2158
http://www.scsos.com/

South Dakota

S.D. Codified Laws Sections 47-1-1, et seq.

Secretary of State
State Capitol, Suite 204
500 East Capitol Avenue
Pierre, SD 57501-5070
(605) 773-4845
http://www.state.sd.us/sos *or*
http://www.state.sd.us/state/executive/sos/sos.htm

Tennessee

Tenn. Code Ann. Sections 48-11-101, et seq.

Secretary of State
Suite 1800
James K. Polk Building
Nashville, TN 37243-0305
(615) 741-2286
http://www.state.tn.us/sos/soshmpg.htm *or*
http://www.state.tn.us/sos/service.htm

Texas

Tex. Corps. & Ass'ns Code Ann. Sections 1.01, et seq.

Secretary of State
P.O. Box 13697
Austin, TX 78711
(512) 463-5555 or (900) 740-2662
http://www.sos.state.tx.us/about/aboutcorp.htm

Utah

Utah Code Ann. Sections 16-10a-101

Commerce Department
160 East 300 South
Second Floor, Box 146705
Salt Lake City, UT 84114-6705
(801) 530-4849
http://www.commerce.state.ut.us/

Vermont

Vt. Stat. Ann. tit. 11A, Sections 1.01, et seq.

Secretary of State
Heritage I Building
81 River Street, Drawer 09
Montpelier, VT 05609-1104
(802) 828-2386
http://www.sec.state.vt.us/

Virginia

Va. Code Ann. Sections 13-1-601, et seq.

State Corporation Commission
Tyler Building
1300 East Main Street
Richmond, VA 23218
(804) 371-9967 or (800) 552-7945
http://www.state.va.us/

Washington

Wash. Rev. Code Ann. Sections 23B.01.010, et seq.

Secretary of State
Corporations Division
505 East Union, Second Floor
P.O. Box 40234
Olympia, WA 98504-0234
(360) 753-75115
http://www.secstate.wa.gov/

West Virginia

W. Va. Code Sections 31-1-1, et seq.

Secretary of State
State Capitol Complex
Building 1, Suite 157K
1900 Kanawha Boulevard East
Charleston, WV 25305-0770
(304) 558-8000
http://www.state.wv.us/

Wisconsin

Wis. Stat. Ann. Sections 180.0101, et seq.

Secretary of State
P.O. Box 7846
Madison, WI 53707
(608) 261-7577
http://www.wdfi.org

Wyoming

Wyo. Stat. Ann. Sections 17-16-101, et seq.

Secretary of State
State Capitol
Cheyenne, WY 82002-0020
(307) 777-7378
http://soswy.state.wy.us/

APPENDIX

B

Uniform Partnership Act

UNIFORM PARTNERSHIP ACT
Table of Jurisdictions Wherein Act Has Been Adopted

Jurisdiction	*Laws*	*Effective Date*	*Statutory Citation*
Alaska	1917, c. 69	5-3-1917	AS 32.05.010 to 32.05.860.
Arkansas	1941, Act 263	3-26-1941	A.C.A. §§ 4-42-101 to 4-42-706.
Delaware	1947, c. 229	4-8-1947	6 Del. C. §§ 1501 to 1553.
Georgia	1984, p. 1439	4-1-1985	O.C.G.A. §§ 14-8-1 to 14-8-61.
Hawaii	1972, c. 17	1-1-1973	HRS §§ 425-101 to 425-143, 425-191.
Illinois	1917, p. 625	7-1-1917	S.H.A. 805 ILCS 205/1 to 205/52.
Indiana	1949, c. 114	1-1-1950	West's A.I.C. 23-4-1-1 to 23-4-1-43.
Kentucky	1954, c. 38	3-24-1954	KRS 362.150 to 362.360.
Maine	1973, c. 377	10-3-1973	31 M.R.S.A. §§ 281 to 323.
Massachusetts	1922, c. 486	1-1-1923	M.G.L.A. c. 108A, §§ 1 to 49.
Michigan	1917, No. 72	4-17-1917	M.C.L.A. §§ 449.1 to 449.48.
Mississippi	1976, c. 407	4-1-1977	Code 1972, §§ 79-12-1 to 79-12-119.
Missouri	1949, p. 506	8-9-1949	V.A.M.S. §§ 358.010 to 358.520.
Nevada	1931, c. 74	7-1-1931	N.R.S. 87.010 to 87.560.
New Hampshire	1973, c. 378	8-29-1973	RSA 304-A:1 to 304-A:55.
New Jersey	1919, c. 212	4-15-1919	N.J.S.A. 42:1-1 to 42:1-49.
New York	1919, c. 408	10-1-1919	McKinney's Partnership Law, §§ 1 to 74, 121-1500 to 121-1504.
North Carolina	1941, c. 374	3-15-1941	G.S. §§ 59-31 to 59-73.
Ohio	1949, p. 329	9-14-1949	R.C. §§ 1775.01 to 1775.42, 1775.61 to 1775.65.
Pennsylvania	1915, P.L. 18	7-1-1915	15 Pa.C.S.A. §§ 8301 to 8365.
Rhode Island	1957, c. 74	10-1-1957	Gen.Laws 1956, §§ 7-12-12 to 7-12-59.
South Carolina	1950, p. 1841	2-13-1950	Code 1976, §§ 33-41-10 to 33-41-1220.
South Dakota	1923, c. 296	3-12-1923	SDCL 48-1-1 to 48-5-56.
Tennessee	1917, c. 140	7-1-1917	West's Tenn. Code §§ 61-1-101 to 61-1-148.
Utah	1921, c. 89	5-10-1921	U.C.A. 1953, 48-1-1 to 48-1-48.
Wisconsin	1915, c. 358	7-6-1915	W.S.A. 178.01 to 178.53.

Part I. Preliminary Provisions

§1. *Name of Act*

This act may be cited as Uniform Partnership Act.

§2. *Definition of Terms*

In this act, "Court" includes every court and judge having jurisdiction in the case.

"Business" includes every trade, occupation, or profession.

"Person" includes individuals, partnerships, corporations, and other associations.

"Bankrupt" includes bankrupt under the Federal Bankruptcy Act or insolvent under any state insolvent act.

"Conveyance" includes every assignment, lease, mortgage, or encumbrance.

"Real property" includes land and any interest or estate in land.

§3. *Interpretation of Knowledge and Notice*

(1) A person has "knowledge" of a fact within the meaning of this act not only when he has actual knowledge thereof, but also when he has knowledge of such other facts as in the circumstances shows bad faith.

(2) A person has "notice" of a fact within the meaning of this act when the person who claims the benefit of the notice:

(a) States the fact to such person, or

(b) Delivers through the mail, or by other means of communication, a written statement of the fact to such person or to a proper person at his place of business or residence.

§4. *Rules of Construction*

(1) The rule that statutes in derogation of the common law are to be strictly construed shall have no application to this act.

(2) The law of estoppel shall apply under this act.

(3) The law of agency shall apply under this act.

(4) This act shall be so interpreted and construed as to effect its general purpose to make uniform the law of those states which enact it.

(5) This act shall not be construed so as to impair the obligations of any contract existing when the act goes into effect, nor to affect any action or proceedings begun or right accrued before this act takes effect.

§5. Rules for Cases Not Provided for in This Act

In any case not provided for in this act the rules of law and equity, including the law merchant, shall govern.

Part II. Nature of Partnership

§6. Partnership Defined

(1) A partnership is an association of two or more persons to carry on as co-owners a business for profit.

(2) But any association formed under any other statute of this state, or any statute adopted by authority, other than the authority of this state, is not a partnership under this act, unless such association would have been a partnership in this state prior to the adoption of this act; but this act shall apply to limited partnerships except in so far as the statutes relating to such partnerships are inconsistent herewith.

§7. Rules for Determining the Existence of a Partnership

In determining whether a partnership exists, these rules shall apply:

(1) Except as provided by section 16 persons who are not partners as to each other are not partners as to third persons.

(2) Joint tenancy, tenancy in common, tenancy by the entireties, joint property, common property, or part ownership does not of itself establish a partnership, whether such co-owners do or do not share any profits made by the use of the property.

(3) The sharing of gross returns does not of itself establish a partnership, whether or not the persons sharing them have a joint or common right or interest in any property from which the returns are derived.

(4) The receipt by a person of a share of the profits of a business is prima facie evidence that he is a partner in the business, but no such inference shall be drawn if such profits were received in payment:

(a) As a debt by installments or otherwise,

(b) As wages of an employee or rent to a landlord,

(c) As an annuity to a widow or representative of a deceased partner,

(d) As interest on a loan, though the amount of payment vary with the profits of the business,

(e) As the consideration for the sale of a good-will of a business or other property by installments or otherwise.

§8. Partnership Property

(1) All property originally brought into the partnership stock or subsequently acquired by purchase or otherwise, on account of the partnership, is partnership property.

(2) Unless the contrary intention appears, property acquired with partnership funds is partnership property.

(3) Any estate in real property may be acquired in the partnership name. Title so acquired can be conveyed only in the partnership name.

(4) A conveyance to a partnership in the partnership name, though without words of inheritance, passes the entire estate of the grantor unless a contrary intent appears.

Part III. Relations of Partners to Persons Dealing with the Partnership

§9. Partner Agent of Partnership as to Partnership Business

(1) Every partner is an agent of the partnership for the purpose of its business, and the act of every partner, including the execution in the partnership name of any instrument, for apparently carrying on in the usual way the business of the partnership of which he is a member binds the partnership, unless the partner so acting has in fact no authority to act for the partnership in the particular matter, and the person with whom he is dealing has knowledge of the fact that he has no such authority.

(2) An act of a partner which is not apparently for the carrying on of the business of the partnership in the usual way does not bind the partnership unless authorized by the other partners.

(3) Unless authorized by the other partners or unless they have abandoned the business, one or more but less than all the partners have no authority to:

(a) Assign the partnership property in trust for creditors or on the assignee's promise to pay the debts of the partnership,

(b) Dispose of the good-will of the business,

(c) Do any other act which would make it impossible to carry on the ordinary business of a partnership,

(d) Confess a judgment,

(e) Submit a partnership claim or liability to arbitration or reference.

(4) No act of a partner in contravention of a restriction on authority shall bind the partnership to persons having knowledge of the restriction.

§10. Conveyance of Real Property of the Partnership

(1) Where title to real property is in the partnership name, any partner may convey title to such property by a conveyance executed in the partnership name; but the partnership may recover such property unless the partner's act binds the partnership under the provisions of paragraph (1) of section 9, or unless such property has been conveyed by the grantee or a person claiming through such grantee to a holder for value without knowledge that the partner, in making the conveyance, has exceeded his authority.

(2) Where title to real property is in the name of the partnership, a conveyance executed by a partner, in his own name, passes the equitable interest of the partnership, provided the act is one within the authority of the partner under the provisions of paragraph (1) of section 9.

(3) Where title to real property is in the name of one or more but not all the partners, and the record does not disclose the right of the partnership, the partners in whose name the title stands may convey title to such property, but the partnership may recover such property if the partners' act does not bind the partnership under the provisions of paragraph (1) of section 9, unless the purchaser or his assignee, is a holder for value, without knowledge.

(4) Where the title to real property is in the name of one or more or all the partners, or in a third person in trust for the

partnership, a conveyance executed by a partner in the partnership name, or in his own name, passes the equitable interest of the partnership, provided the act is one within the authority of the partner under the provisions of paragraph (1) of section 9.

(5) Where the title to real property is in the names of all the partners a conveyance executed by all the partners passes all their rights in such property.

§11. *Partnership Bound by Admission of Partner*

An admission or representation made by any partner concerning partnership affairs within the scope of his authority as conferred by this act is evidence against the partnership.

§12. *Partnership Charged with Knowledge of or Notice to Partner*

Notice to any partner of any matter relating to partnership affairs, and the knowledge of the partner acting in the particular matter, acquired while a partner or then present to his mind, and the knowledge of any other partner who reasonably could and should have communicated it to the acting partner, operate as notice to or knowledge of the partnership, except in the case of a fraud on the partnership committed by or with the consent of that partner.

§13. *Partnership Bound by Partner's Wrongful Act*

Where, by any wrongful act or omission of any partner acting in the ordinary course of the business of the partnership or with the authority of his co-partners, loss or injury is caused to any person, not being a partner in the partnership, or any penalty is incurred, the partnership is liable therefor to the same extent as the partner so acting or omitting to act.

§14. *Partnership Bound by Partner's Breach of Trust*

The partnership is bound to make good the loss:

(a) Where one partner acting within the scope of his apparent authority receives money or property of a third person and misapplies it; and

(b) Where the partnership in the course of its business receives money or property of a third person and the money or property so received is misapplied by any partner while it is in the custody of the partnership.

§15. *Nature of Partner's Liability*

All partners are liable

(a) Jointly and severally for everything chargeable to the partnership under sections 13 and 14.

(b) Jointly for all other debts and obligations of the partnership; but any partner may enter into a separate obligation to perform a partnership contract.

§16. *Partner by Estoppel*

(1) When a person, by words spoken or written or by conduct, represents himself, or consents to another representing him to any one, as a partner in an existing partnership or with one or more persons not actual partners, he is liable to any such person to whom such representation has been made, who has, on the faith of such representation, given credit to the actual or apparent partnership, and if he has made such representation or consented to its being made in a public manner he is liable to such person, whether the representation has or has not been made or communicated to such person so giving credit by or with the knowledge of the apparent partner making the representation or consenting to its being made.

(a) When a partnership liability results, he is liable as though he were an actual member of the partnership.

(b) When no partnership liability results, he is liable jointly with the other persons, if any, so consenting to the contract or representation as to incur liability, otherwise separately.

(2) When a person has been thus represented to be a partner in an existing partnership, or with one or more persons not actual partners, he is an agent of the persons consenting to such representation to bind them to the same extent and in the same manner as though he were a partner in fact, with respect to persons who rely upon the representation. Where all the members of the existing partnership consent to the representation, a partnership act or obligation results; but in all other cases it is the joint act or obligation of the person acting and the persons consenting to the representation.

§17. *Liability of Incoming Partner*

A person admitted as a partner into an existing partnership is liable for all the obligations of the partnership arising before his admission as though he had been a partner when such obligations were incurred, except that this liability shall be satisfied only out of partnership property.

Part IV. Relations of Partners to One Another

§18. *Rules Determining Rights and Duties of Partners*

The rights and duties of the partners in relation to the partnership shall be determined, subject to any agreement between them, by the following rules:

(a) Each partner shall be repaid his contributions, whether by way of capital or advances to the partnership property and share equally in the profits and surplus remaining after all liabilities, including those to partners, are satisfied; and must contribute towards the losses, whether of capital or otherwise, sustained by the partnership according to his share in the profits.

(b) The partnership must indemnify every partner in respect of payments made and personal liabilities reasonably incurred by him in the ordinary and proper conduct of its business, or for the preservation of its business or property.

(c) A partner, who in aid of the partnership makes any payment or advance beyond the amount of capital which he agreed to contribute, shall be paid interest from the date of the payment or advance.

(d) A partner shall receive interest on the capital contributed by him only from the date when repayment should be made.

(e) All partners have equal rights in the management and conduct of the partnership business.

(f) No partner is entitled to remuneration for acting in the partnership business, except that a surviving partner is entitled to reasonable compensation for his services in winding up the partnership affairs.

(g) No person can become a member of a partnership without the consent of all the partners.

(h) Any difference arising as to ordinary matters connected with the partnership business may be decided by a majority of the partners; but no act in contravention of any agreement between the partners may be done rightfully without the consent of all the partners.

§19. *Partnership Books*

The partnership books shall be kept, subject to any agreement between the partners, at the principal place of business of the partnership, and every partner shall at all times have access to and may inspect and copy any of them.

§20. *Duty of Partners to Render Information*

Partners shall render on demand true and full information of all things affecting the partnership to any partner or the legal representation of any deceased partner or partner under legal disability.

§21. *Partner Accountable as a Fiduciary*

(1) Every partner must account to the partnership for any benefit, and hold as trustee for it any profits derived by him without the consent of the other partners from any transaction connected with the formation, conduct, or liquidation of the partnership or from any use by him of its property.

(2) This section applies also to the representatives of a deceased partner engaged in the liquidation of the affairs of the partnership as the personal representatives of the last surviving partner.

§22. *Right to an Account*

Any partner shall have the right to a formal account as to partnership affairs:

(a) If he is wrongfully excluded from the partnership business or possession of its property by his co-partners,

(b) If the right exists under the terms of any agreement,

(c) As provided by section 21,

(d) Whenever other circumstances render it just and reasonable.

§23. *Continuation of Partnership Beyond Fixed Term*

(1) When a partnership for a fixed term or particular undertaking is continued after the termination of such term or particular undertaking without any express agreement, the rights and duties of the partners remain the same as they were at such termination, so far as is consistent with a partnership at will.

(2) A continuation of the business by the partners or such of them as habitually acted therein during the term, without any settlement or liquidation of the partnership affairs, is prima facie evidence of a continuation of the partnership.

Part V. Property Rights of a Partner

§24. *Extent of Property Rights of a Partner*

The property rights of a partner are (1) his rights in specific partnership property, (2) his interest in the partnership, and (3) his right to participate in the management.

§25. *Nature of a Partner's Right in Specific Partnership Property*

(1) A partner is co-owner with his partners of specific partnership property holding as a tenant in partnership.

(2) The incidents of this tenancy are such that:

(a) A partner, subject to the provisions of this act and to any agreement between the partners, has an equal right with his partners to possess specific partnership property for partnership purposes; but he has no right to possess such property for any other purpose without the consent of his partners.

(b) A partner's right in specific partnership property is not assignable except in connection with the assignment of rights of all the partners in the same property.

(c) A partner's right in specific partnership property is not subject to attachment or execution, except on a claim against the partnership. When partnership property is attached for a partnership debt the partners, or any of them, or the representatives of a deceased partner, cannot claim any right under the homestead or exemption laws.

(d) On the death of a partner his right in specific partnership property vests in the surviving partner or partners, except where the deceased was the last surviving partner, when his right in such property vests in his legal representative. Such surviving partner or partners, or the legal representative of the last surviving partner, has no right to possess the partnership property for any but a partnership purpose.

(e) A partner's right in specific partnership property is not subject to dower, curtesy, or allowances to widows, heirs, or next of kin.

§26. *Nature of Partner's Interest in the Partnership*

A partner's interest in the partnership is his share of the profits and surplus, and the same is personal property.

§27. *Assignment of Partner's Interest*

(1) A conveyance by a partner of his interest in the partnership does not of itself dissolve the partnership, nor, as against the other partners in the absence of agreement, entitle the assignee, during the continuance of the partnership, to interfere in the management or administration of the partnership business or affairs, or to require any information or account of partnership transactions, or to inspect the partnership books; but it merely entitles the assignee to receive in accordance with his contract the profits to which the assigning partner would otherwise be entitled.

(2) In case of a dissolution of the partnership, the assignee is entitled to receive his assignor's interest and may require an account from the date only of the last account agreed to by all the partners.

§28. Partner's Interest Subject to Charging Order

(1) On due application to a competent court by any judgment creditor of a partner, the court which entered the judgment, order, or decree, or any other court, may charge the interest of the debtor partner with payment of the unsatisfied amount of such judgment debt with interest thereon; and may then or later appoint a receiver of his share of the profits, and of any other money due or to fall due to him in respect of the partnership, and make all other orders, directions, accounts and inquiries which the debtor partner might have made, or which the circumstances of the case may require.

(2) The interest charged may be redeemed at any time before foreclosure, or in case of a sale being directed by the court may be purchased without thereby causing a dissolution:

(a) With separate property, by any one or more of the partners, or

(b) With partnership property, by any one or more of the partners with the consent of all the partners whose interests are not so charged or sold.

(3) Nothing in this act shall be held to deprive a partner of his right, if any, under the exemption laws, as regards his interest in the partnership.

PART VI. DISSOLUTION AND WINDING UP

§29. Dissolution Defined

The dissolution of a partnership is the change in the relation of the partners caused by any partner ceasing to be associated in the carrying on as distinguished from the winding up of the business.

§30. Partnership Not Terminated by Dissolution

On dissolution the partnership is not terminated, but continues until the winding up of partnership affairs is completed.

§31. Causes of Dissolution

Dissolution is caused:

(1) Without violation of the agreement between the partners,

(a) By the termination of the definite term or particular undertaking specified in the agreement,

(b) By the express will of any partner when no definite term or particular undertaking is specified,

(c) By the express will of all the partners who have not assigned their interests or suffered them to be charged for their separate debts, either before or after the termination of any specified term or particular undertaking,

(d) By the expulsion of any partner from the business bona fide in accordance with such a power conferred by the agreement between the partners;

(2) In contravention of the agreement between the partners, where the circumstances do not permit a dissolution under any other provision of this section, by the express will of any partner at any time;

(3) By any event which makes it unlawful for the business of the partnership to be carried on or for the members to carry it on in partnership;

(4) By the death of any partner;

(5) By the bankruptcy of any partner or the partnership;

(6) By decree of court under section 32.

§32. Dissolution by Decree of Court

(1) On application by or for a partner the court shall decree a dissolution whenever:

(a) A partner has been declared a lunatic in any judicial proceeding or is shown to be of unsound mind,

(b) A partner becomes in any other way incapable of performing his part of the partnership contract,

(c) A partner has been guilty of such conduct as tends to affect prejudicially the carrying on of the business,

(d) A partner willfully or persistently commits a breach of the partnership agreement, or otherwise so conducts himself in matters relating to the partnership business that it is not reasonably practicable to carry on the business in partnership with him,

(e) The business of the partnership can only be carried on at a loss,

(f) Other circumstances render a dissolution equitable.

(2) On the application of the purchaser of a partner's interest under sections 28 or 29 [should read 27 or 28];

(a) After the termination of the specified term or particular undertaking,

(b) At any time if the partnership was a partnership at will when the interest was assigned or when the charging order was issued.

§33. General Effect of Dissolution on Authority of Partner

Except so far as may be necessary to wind up partnership affairs or to complete transactions begun but not then finished, dissolution terminates all authority of any partner to act for the partnership,

(1) With respect to the partners,

(a) When the dissolution is not by the act, bankruptcy or death of a partner; or

(b) When the dissolution is by such act, bankruptcy or death of a partner, in cases where section 34 so requires.

(2) With respect to persons not partners, as declared in section 35.

§34. Rights of Partner to Contribution From Co-partners After Dissolution

Where the dissolution is caused by the act, death or bankruptcy of a partner, each partner is liable to his co-partners for his share of any liability created by any partner acting for the partnership as if the partnership had not been dissolved unless

(a) The dissolution being by act of any partner, the partner acting for the partnership had knowledge of the dissolution, or

(b) The dissolution being by the death or bankruptcy of a partner, the partner acting for the partnership had knowledge or notice of the death or bankruptcy.

§35. Power of Partner to Bind Partnership to Third Persons After Dissolution

(1) After dissolution a partner can bind the partnership except as provided in Paragraph (3).

(a) By any act appropriate for winding up partnership affairs or completing transactions unfinished at dissolution;

(b) By any transaction which would bind the partnership if dissolution had not taken place, provided the other party to the transaction

(I) Had extended credit to the partnership prior to dissolution and had no knowledge or notice of the dissolution; or

(II) Though he had not so extended credit, had nevertheless known of the partnership prior to dissolution, and, having no knowledge or notice of dissolution, the fact of dissolution had not been advertised in a newspaper of general circulation in the place (or in each place if more than one) at which the partnership business was regularly carried on.

(2) The liability of a partner under Paragraph (1b) shall be satisfied out of partnership assets alone when such partner had been prior to dissolution

(a) Unknown as a partner to the person with whom the contract is made; and

(b) So far unknown and inactive in partnership affairs that the business reputation of the partnership could not be said to have been in any degree due to his connection with it.

(3) The partnership is in no case bound by any act of a partner after dissolution

(a) Where the partnership is dissolved because it is unlawful to carry on the business, unless the act is appropriate for winding up partnership affairs; or

(b) Where the partner has become bankrupt; or

(c) Where the partner has no authority to wind up partnership affairs; except by a transaction with one who

(I) Had extended credit to the partnership prior to dissolution and had no knowledge or notice of his want of authority; or

(II) Had not extended credit to the partnership prior to dissolution, and, having no knowledge or notice of his want of authority, the fact of his want of authority has not been advertised in the manner provided for advertising the fact of dissolution in Paragraph (1bII).

(4) Nothing in this section shall affect the liability under Section 16 of any person who after dissolution represents himself or consents to another representing him as a partner in a partnership engaged in carrying on business.

§36. *Effect of Dissolution on Partner's Existing Liability*

(1) The dissolution of the partnership does not of itself discharge the existing liability of any partner.

(2) A partner is discharged from any existing liability upon dissolution of the partnership by an agreement to that effect between himself, the partnership creditor and the person or partnership continuing the business; and such agreement may be inferred from the course of dealing between the creditor having knowledge of the dissolution and the person or partnership continuing the business.

(3) Where a person agrees to assume the existing obligations of a dissolved partnership, the partners whose obligations have been assumed shall be discharged from any liability to any creditor of the partnership who, knowing of the agreement, consents to a material alteration in the nature or time of payment of such obligations.

(4) The individual property of a deceased partner shall be liable for all obligations of the partnership incurred while he was a partner but subject to the prior payment of his separate debts.

§37. *Right to Wind Up*

Unless otherwise agreed the partners who have not wrongfully dissolved the partnership or the legal representative of the last surviving partner, not bankrupt, has the right to wind up the partnership affairs; provided, however, that any partner, his legal representative or his assignee, upon cause shown, may obtain winding up by the court.

§38. *Rights of Partners to Application of Partnership Property*

(1) When dissolution is caused in any way, except in contravention of the partnership agreement, each partner, as against his co-partners and all persons claiming through them in respect of their interests in the partnership, unless otherwise agreed, may have the partnership property applied to discharge its liabilities, and the surplus applied to pay in cash the net amount owing to the respective partners. But if dissolution is caused by expulsion of a partner, bona fide under the partnership agreement and if the expelled partner is discharged from all partnership liabilities, either by payment or agreement under section 36(2), he shall receive in cash only the net amount due him from the partnership.

(2) When dissolution is caused in contravention of the partnership agreement the rights of the partners shall be as follows:

(a) Each partner who has not caused dissolution wrongfully shall have,

I. All the rights specified in paragraph (1) of this section, and

II. The right, as against each partner who has caused the dissolution wrongfully, to damages for breach of the agreement.

(b) The partners who have not caused the dissolution wrongfully, if they all desire to continue the business in the same name, either by themselves or jointly with others, may do so, during the agreed term for the partnership and for that purpose may possess the partnership property, provided they secure the payment by bond approved by the court, or pay to any partner who has caused the dissolution wrongfully, the value of his interest in the partnership at the dissolution, less any damages recoverable under clause (2aII) of this section, and in like manner indemnify him against all present or future partnership liabilities.

(c) A partner who has caused the dissolution wrongfully shall have:

I. If the business is not continued under the provisions of paragraph (2b) all the rights of a partner under paragraph (1), subject to clause (2aII), of this section,

II. If the business is continued under paragraph (2b) of this section the right as against his co-partners and all claiming through them in respect of their interests in the partnership, to have the value of his interest in the partnership, less any damages caused to his co-partners by the dissolution, ascertained and paid to him in cash, or the payment secured by bond approved by the court, and to be released from all existing liabilities of the partnership; but in ascertaining the value of the partner's interest the value of the good-will of the business shall not be considered.

§39. *Rights Where Partnership is Dissolved for Fraud or Misrepresentation*

Where a partnership contract is rescinded on the ground of the fraud or misrepresentation of one of the parties thereto, the party entitled to rescind is, without prejudice to any other right, entitled,

(a) To a lien on, or a right of retention of, the surplus of the partnership property after satisfying the partnership liabilities to third persons for any sum of money paid by him for the purchase of an interest in the partnership and for any capital or advances contributed by him; and

(b) To stand, after all liabilities to third persons have been satisfied, in the place of the creditors of the partnership for any payments made by him in respect of the partnership liabilities; and

(c) To be indemnified by the person guilty of the fraud or making the representation against all debts and liabilities of the partnership.

§40. *Rules for Distribution*

In settling accounts between the partners after dissolution, the following rules shall be observed, subject to any agreement to the contrary:

(a) The assets of the partnership are:

I. The partnership property,

II. The contributions of the partners necessary for the payment of all the liabilities specified in clause (b) of this paragraph.

(b) The liabilities of the partnership shall rank in order of payment, as follows:

I. Those owing to creditors other than partners,

II. Those owing to partners other than for capital and profits,

III. Those owing to partners in respect of capital,

IV. Those owing to partners in respect of profits.

(c) The assets shall be applied in the order of their declaration in clause (a) of this paragraph to the satisfaction of the liabilities.

(d) The partners shall contribute, as provided by section 18(a) the amount necessary to satisfy the liabilities; but if any, but not all, of the partners are insolvent, or, not being subject to process, refuse to contribute, the other partners shall contribute their share of the liabilities, and, in the relative proportions in which they share the profits, the additional amount necessary to pay the liabilities.

(e) An assignee for the benefit of creditors or any person appointed by the court shall have the right to enforce the contributions specified in clause (d) of this paragraph.

(f) Any partner or his legal representative shall have the right to enforce the contributions specified in clause (d) of this paragraph, to the extent of the amount which he has paid in excess of his share of the liability.

(g) The individual property of a deceased partner shall be liable for the contributions specified in clause (d) of this paragraph.

(h) When partnership property and the individual properties of the partners are in possession of a court for distribution, partnership creditors shall have priority on partnership property and separate creditors on individual property, saving the rights of lien or secured creditors as heretofore.

(i) Where a partner has become bankrupt or his estate is insolvent the claims against his separate property shall rank in the following order:

I. Those owing to separate creditors,

II. Those owing to partnership creditors,

III. Those owing to partners by way of contribution.

§41. *Liability of Persons Continuing the Business in Certain Cases*

(1) When any new partner is admitted into an existing partnership, or when any partner retires and assigns (or the representative of the deceased partner assigns) his rights in partnership property to two or more of the partners, or to one or more of the partners and one or more third persons, if the business is continued without liquidation of the partnership affairs, creditors of the first or dissolved partnership are also creditors of the partnership so continuing the business.

(2) When all but one partner retire and assign (or the representative of a deceased partner assigns) their rights in partnership property to the remaining partner, who continues the business without liquidation of partnership affairs, either alone or with others, creditors of the dissolved partnership are also creditors of the person or partnership so continuing the business.

(3) When any partner retires or dies and the business of the dissolved partnership is continued as set forth in paragraphs (1) and (2) of this section, with the consent of the retired partners or the representative of the deceased partner, but without any assignment of his right in partnership property, rights of creditors of the dissolved partnership and of the creditors of the person or partnership continuing the business shall be as if such assignment had been made.

(4) When all the partners or their representatives assign their rights in partnership property to one or more third persons who promise to pay the debts and who continue the business of the dissolved partnership, creditors of the dissolved partnership are also creditors of the person or partnership continuing the business.

(5) When any partner wrongfully causes a dissolution and the remaining partners continue the business under the provisions of section 38(2b), either alone or with others, and without liquidation of the partnership affairs, creditors of the dissolved partnership are also creditors of the person or partnership continuing the business.

(6) When a partner is expelled and the remaining partners continue the business either alone or with others, without liquidation of the partnership affairs, creditors of the dissolved partnership are also creditors of the person or partnership continuing the business.

(7) The liability of a third person becoming a partner in the partnership continuing the business, under this section, to the creditors of the dissolved partnership shall be satisfied out of partnership property only.

(8) When the business of a partnership after dissolution is continued under any conditions set forth in this section the creditors of the dissolved partnership, as against the separate creditors of the retiring or deceased partner or the representative of the deceased partner, have a prior right to any claim of the retired partner or the representative of the deceased partner against the person or partnership continuing the business, on account of the retired or deceased partner's interest in the dissolved partnership or on account of any consideration promised for such interest or for his right in partnership property.

(9) Nothing in this section shall be held to modify any right of creditors to set aside any assignment on the ground of fraud.

(10) The use by the person or partnership continuing the business of the partnership name, or the name of a deceased partner as part thereof, shall not of itself make the individual property of the deceased partner liable for any debts contracted by such person or partnership.

§42. *Rights of Retiring or Estate of Deceased Partner When the Business Is Continued*

When any partner retires or dies, and the business is continued under any of the conditions set forth in section 41(1, 2, 3, 5, 6), or section 38(2b) without any settlement of accounts as between him or his estate and the person or partnership continuing the business, unless otherwise agreed, he or his legal representative as against such person or partnership may have the value of his interest at the date of dissolution ascertained, and shall receive as an ordinary creditor an amount equal to the value of his interest in the dissolved partnership with interest, or, at his option or at the option of his legal representative, in lieu of interest, the profits attributable to the use of his right in the property of the dissolved partnership; provided that the creditors of the dissolved partnership as against the separate creditors, or the representative of the retired or deceased partner, shall have priority on any claim arising under this section, as provided by section 41(8) of this act.

§43. *Accrual of Actions*

The right to an account of his interest shall accrue to any partner, or his legal representative, as against the winding up partners or the surviving partners or the person or partnership continuing the business, at the date of dissolution, in the absence of any agreement to the contrary.

Part VII. Miscellaneous Provisions

§44. *When Act Takes Effect*

This act shall take effect on the ______________________ day of ______________________________________ one thousand nine hundred and ____________________________________.

§45. *Legislation Repealed*

All acts or parts of acts inconsistent with this act are hereby repealed.

APPENDIX

Revised Uniform Partnership Act

REVISED UNIFORM PARTNERSHIP ACT (1997)
Table of Jurisdictions Wherein Act Has Been Adopted

Jurisdiction	*Laws*	*Effective Date*	*Statutory Citation*
Alabama	1996, No. 96-528	1-1-1997	Code 1975, §§ 10-8A-101 to 10-8A-1109.
Arizona	1996, c. 226	7-20-1996	A.R.S. §§ 29-1001 to 29-1111.
California	1996, c. 1003	1-1-1997	West's Ann. Cal. Corp. Code, §§ 16100 to 16962.
Colorado	1997 H.B. 97-1237	1-1-1998	West's C.R.S.A. §§ 7-64-101 to 7-64-1206.
Connecticut	1995, P.A. 95-341	7-1-1997	C.G.S.A. §§ 34-300 to 34-434.
District of Columbia	1997, D.C. Law No. 11-234	4-9-1997	D.C. Code 1981, §§ 41-151.1 to 41-162.3.
Florida	1995, c. 95-242	1-1-1996	West's F.S.A. §§ 620.81001 to 620.91.
Idaho	1998, c. 65	1-1-2001	I.C. §§ 53-3-101 to 53-3-1205.
Iowa	1998, S.F. 2311	1-1-1999	I.C.A. §§ 486A.101 to 486A.1302.
Kansas	1998, c. 93	1-1-1999	K.S.A. §§ 56a-101 to 56a-1305.
Maryland	1997, c. 654	7-1-1998	Code, Corporations and Associations, §§ 9A-101 to 9A-1205.
Minnesota	1997, c. 174	1-1-1999	M.S.A. §§ 323A.1-01 to 323A.12-03.
Montana	1993, c. 238	10-1-1993	MCA §§ 35-10-101 to 35-10-710.
Nebraska	1997, L.B. 523	1-1-1998	R.R.S. 1943, §§ 67-401 to 67-467.
New Mexico	1996, c. 53	7-1-1997	NMSA 1978 §§ 54-1-47, 54-1A-101 to 54-1A-1206.
North Dakota	1995, c. 430	1-1-1996	NDCC 45-13-01 to 45-21-08.
Oklahoma	1997, c. 399	11-1-1997	54 Okl.St.Ann. §§ 1-100 to 1-1207.
Oregon	1997, c. 775	1-1-1998	ORS 67.005 to 67.815
Texas	1993, c. 917	1-1-1994	Vernon's Ann. Civ.St. art. 6132b-1.01 to 6132b-11.04.
Vermont	1998, No. 149	1-1-1999	11 V.S.A. §§ 3201 to 3313.
Virginia	1996, c. 292		Code 1950, §§ 50-73.79 to 50-73.149.
Washington	1998, c. 103	1-1-1999	West's RCWA 25.05.005 to 25.05.907.
West Virginia	1995, c. 250	90 days from 3-19-1995	Code, 47B-1-1 to 47B-11-5.
Wyoming	1993, c. 194	1-1-1994	W.S.1977, §§ 17-21-101 to 17-21-1003.

Article 1. General Provisions

§101. Definitions.

In this [Act]:

(1) "Business" includes every trade, occupation, and profession.

(2) "Debtor in bankruptcy" means a person who is the subject of:

(i) an order for relief under Title 11 of the United States Code or a comparable order under a successor statute of general application; or

(ii) a comparable order under federal, state, or foreign law governing insolvency.

(3) "Distribution" means a transfer of money or other property from a partnership to a partner in the partner's capacity as a partner or to the partner's transferee.

(4) "Foreign limited liability partnership" means a partnership that:

(i) is formed under laws other than the laws of this State; and

(ii) has the status of a limited liability partnership under those laws.

(5) "Limited liability partnership" means a partnership that has filed a statement of qualification under Section 1001 and does not have a similar statement in effect in any other jurisdiction.

(6) "Partnership" means an association of two or more persons to carry on as co-owners a business for profit formed under Section 202, predecessor law, or comparable law of another jurisdiction.

(7) "Partnership agreement" means the agreement, whether written, oral, or implied, among the partners concerning the partnership, including amendments to the partnership agreement.

(8) "Partnership at will" means a partnership in which the partners have not agreed to remain partners until the expiration of a definite term or the completion of a particular undertaking.

(9) "Partnership interest" or "partner's interest in the partnership" means all of a partner's interests in the partnership, including the partner's transferable interest and all management and other rights.

(10) "Person" means an individual, corporation, business trust, estate, trust, partnership, association, joint venture, government, governmental subdivision, agency, or instrumentality, or any other legal or commercial entity.

(11) "Property" means all property, real, personal, or mixed, tangible or intangible, or any interest therein.

(12) "State" means a State of the United States, the District of Columbia, the Commonwealth of Puerto Rico, or any territory or insular possession subject to the jurisdiction of the United States.

(13) "Statement" means a statement of partnership authority under Section 303, a statement of denial under Section 304, a statement of dissociation under Section 704, a statement of dissolution under Section 805, a statement of merger under Section 907, a statement of qualification under Section 1001, a statement of foreign qualification under Section 1102, or an amendment or cancellation of any of the foregoing.

(14) "Transfer" includes an assignment, conveyance, lease, mortgage, deed, and encumbrance.

§102. *Knowledge and Notice.*

(a) A person knows a fact if the person has actual knowledge of it.

(b) A person has notice of a fact if the person:

(1) knows of it;

(2) has received a notification of it; or

(3) has reason to know it exists from all of the facts known to the person at the time in question.

(c) A person notifies or gives a notification to another by taking steps reasonably required to inform the other person in ordinary course, whether or not the other person learns of it.

(d) A person receives a notification when the notification:

(1) comes to the person's attention; or

(2) is duly delivered at the person's place of business or at any other place held out by the person as a place for receiving communications.

(e) Except as otherwise provided in subsection (f), a person other than an individual knows, has notice, or receives a notification of a fact for purposes of a particular transaction when the individual conducting the transaction knows, has notice, or receives a notification of the fact, or in any event when the fact would have been brought to the individual's attention if the person had exercised reasonable diligence. The person exercises reasonable diligence if it maintains reasonable routines for communicating significant information to the individual conducting the transaction and there is reasonable compliance with the routines. Reasonable diligence does not require an individual acting for the person to communicate information unless the communication is part of the individual's regular duties or the individual has reason to know of the transaction and that the transaction would be materially affected by the information.

(f) A partner's knowledge, notice, or receipt of a notification of a fact relating to the partnership is effective immediately as knowledge by, notice to, or receipt of a notification by the partnership, except in the case of a fraud on the partnership committed by or with the consent of that partner.

§103. *Effect of Partnership Agreement; Nonwaivable Provisions.*

(a) Except as otherwise provided in subsection (b), relations among the partners and between the partners and the partnership are governed by the partnership agreement. To the extent the partnership agreement does not otherwise provide, this [Act] governs relations among the partners and between the partners and the partnership.

(b) The partnership agreement may not:

(1) vary the rights and duties under Section 105 except to eliminate the duty to provide copies of statements to all of the partners;

(2) unreasonably restrict the right of access to books and records under Section 403(b);

(3) eliminate the duty of loyalty under Section 404(b) or 603(b)(3), but:

(i) the partnership agreement may identify specific types or categories of activities that do not violate the duty of loyalty, if not manifestly unreasonable; or

(ii) all of the partners or a number or percentage specified in the partnership agreement may authorize or ratify, after full disclosure of all material facts, a specific act or transaction that otherwise would violate the duty of loyalty;

(4) unreasonably reduce the duty of care under Section 404(c) or 603(b)(3);

(5) eliminate the obligation of good faith and fair dealing under Section 404(d), but the partnership agreement may prescribe the standards by which the performance of the obligation is to be measured, if the standards are not manifestly unreasonable;

(6) vary the power to dissociate as a partner under Section 602(a), except to require the notice under Section 601(1) to be in writing;

(7) vary the right of a court to expel a partner in the events specified in Section 601(5);

(8) vary the requirement to wind up the partnership business in cases specified in Section 801(4), (5), or (6); or

(9) restrict rights of third parties under this [Act].

§104. Supplemental Principles of Law.

(a) Unless displaced by particular provisions of this [Act], the principles of law and equity supplement this [Act].

(b) If an obligation to pay interest arises under this [Act] and the rate is not specified, the rate is that specified in [applicable statute].

§105. Execution, Filing, and Recording of Statements.

(a) A statement may be filed in the office of [the Secretary of State]. A certified copy of a statement that is filed in an office in another state may be filed in the office of [the Secretary of State]. Either filing has the effect provided in this [Act] with respect to partnership property located in or transactions that occur in this State.

(b) A certified copy of a statement that has been filed in the office of the [Secretary of State] and recorded in the office for recording transfers of real property has the effect provided for recorded statements in this [Act]. A recorded statement that is not a certified copy of a statement filed in the office of the [Secretary of State] does not have the effect provided for recorded statements in this [Act].

(c) A statement filed by a partnership must be executed by at least two partners. Other statements must be executed by a partner or other person authorized by this [Act]. An individual who executes a statement as, or on behalf of, a partner or other person named as a partner in a statement shall personally declare under penalty of perjury that the contents of the statement are accurate.

(d) A person authorized by this [Act] to file a statement may amend or cancel the statement by filing an amendment or cancellation that names the partnership, identifies the statement, and states the substance of the amendment or cancellation.

(e) A person who files a statement pursuant to this section shall promptly send a copy of the statement to every nonfiling partner and to any other person named as a partner in the statement. Failure to send a copy of a statement to a partner or other person does not limit the effectiveness of the statement as to a person not a partner.

(f) The [Secretary of State] may collect a fee for filing or providing a certified copy of a statement. The [officer responsible for] recording transfers of real property may collect a fee for recording a statement.

§106. Governing Law.

(a) Except as otherwise provided in subsection (b), the law of the jurisdiction in which a partnership has its chief executive office governs relations among the partners and between the partners and the partnership.

(b) The law of this State governs relations among the partners and between the partners and the partnership and the liability of partners for an obligation of a limited liability partnership.

§107. Partnership Subject to Amendment or Repeal of [Act].

A partnership governed by this [Act] is subject to any amendment to or repeal of this [Act].

Article 2. Nature of Partnership

§201. Partnership as Entity.

(a) A partnership is an entity distinct from its partners.

(b) A limited liability partnership continues to be the same entity that existed before the filing of a statement of qualification under Section 1001.

§202. Formation of Partnership.

(a) Except as otherwise provided in subsection (b), the association of two or more persons to carry on as co-owners a business for profit forms a partnership, whether or not the persons intend to form a partnership.

(b) An association formed under a statute other than this [Act], a predecessor statute, or a comparable statute of another jurisdiction is not a partnership under this [Act].

(c) In determining whether a partnership is formed, the following rules apply:

(1) Joint tenancy, tenancy in common, tenancy by the entireties, joint property, common property, or part ownership does not by itself establish a partnership, even if the co-owners share profits made by the use of the property.

(2) The sharing of gross returns does not by itself establish a partnership, even if the persons sharing them have a joint or common right or interest in property from which the returns are derived.

(3) A person who receives a share of the profits of a business is presumed to be a partner in the business, unless the profits were received in payment:

(i) of a debt by installments or otherwise;

(ii) for services as an independent contractor or of wages or other compensation to an employee;

(iii) of rent;

(iv) of an annuity or other retirement benefit to a beneficiary, representative, or designee of a deceased or retired partner;

(v) of interest or other charge on a loan, even if the amount of payment varies with the profits of the business, including a direct or indirect present or future ownership of the collateral, or rights to income, proceeds, or increase in value derived from the collateral; or

(vi) for the sale of the goodwill of a business or other property by installments or otherwise.

§203. *Partnership Property.*

Property acquired by a partnership is property of the partnership and not of the partners individually.

§204. *When Property Is Partnership Property.*

(a) Property is partnership property if acquired in the name of:

(1) the partnership; or

(2) one or more partners with an indication in the instrument transferring title to the property of the person's capacity as a partner or of the existence of a partnership but without an indication of the name of the partnership.

(b) Property is acquired in the name of the partnership by a transfer to:

(1) the partnership in its name; or

(2) one or more partners in their capacity as partners in the partnership, if the name of the partnership is indicated in the instrument transferring title to the property.

(c) Property is presumed to be partnership property if purchased with partnership assets, even if not acquired in the name of the partnership or of one or more partners with an indication in the instrument transferring title to the property of the person's capacity as a partner or of the existence of a partnership.

(d) Property acquired in the name of one or more of the partners, without an indication in the instrument transferring title to the property of the person's capacity as a partner or of the existence of a partnership and without use of partnership assets, is presumed to be separate property, even if used for partnership purposes.

ARTICLE 3. RELATIONS OF PARTNERS TO PERSONS DEALING WITH PARTNERSHIP

§301. *Partner Agent of Partnership.*

Subject to the effect of a statement of partnership authority under Section 303:

(1) Each partner is an agent of the partnership for the purpose of its business. An act of a partner, including the execution of an instrument in the partnership name, for apparently carrying on in the ordinary course the partnership business or business of the kind carried on by the partnership binds the partnership, unless the partner had no authority to act for the partnership in the particular matter and the person with whom the partner was dealing knew or had received a notification that the partner lacked authority.

(2) An act of a partner which is not apparently for carrying on in the ordinary course the partnership business or business of the kind carried on by the partnership binds the partnership only if the act was authorized by the other partners.

§302. *Transfer of Partnership Property.*

(a) Partnership property may be transferred as follows:

(1) Subject to the effect of a statement of partnership authority under Section 303, partnership property held in the name of the partnership may be transferred by an instrument of transfer executed by a partner in the partnership name.

(2) Partnership property held in the name of one or more partners with an indication in the instrument transferring the property to them of their capacity as partners or of the existence of a partnership, but without an indication of the name of the partnership, may be transferred by an instrument of transfer executed by the persons in whose name the property is held.

(3) Partnership property held in the name of one or more persons other than the partnership, without an indication in the instrument transferring the property to them of their capacity as partners or of the existence of a partnership, may be transferred by an instrument of transfer executed by the persons in whose name the property is held.

(b) A partnership may recover partnership property from a transferee only if it proves that execution of the instrument of initial transfer did not bind the partnership under Section 301 and:

(1) as to a subsequent transferee who gave value for property transferred under subsection (a)(1) or (2), proves that the subsequent transferee knew or had received a notification that the person who executed the instrument of initial transfer lacked authority to bind the partnership; or

(2) as to a transferee who gave value for property transferred under subsection (a)(3), proves that the transferee knew or had received a notification that the property was partnership property and that the person who executed the instrument of initial transfer lacked authority to bind the partnership.

(c) A partnership may not recover partnership property from a subsequent transferee if the partnership would not have been entitled to recover the property, under subsection (b), from any earlier transferee of the property.

(d) If a person holds all of the partners' interests in the partnership, all of the partnership property vests in that person. The person may execute a document in the name of the partnership to evidence vesting of the property in that person and may file or record the document.

§303. *Statement of Partnership Authority.*

(a) A partnership may file a statement of partnership authority, which:

(1) must include:

(i) the name of the partnership;

(ii) the street address of its chief executive office and of one office in this State, if there is one;

(iii) the names and mailing addresses of all of the partners or of an agent appointed and maintained by the partnership for the purpose of subsection (b); and

(iv) the names of the partners authorized to execute an instrument transferring real property held in the name of the partnership; and

(2) may state the authority, or limitations on the authority, of some or all of the partners to enter into other

transactions on behalf of the partnership and any other matter.

(b) If a statement of partnership authority names an agent, the agent shall maintain a list of the names and mailing addresses of all of the partners and make it available to any person on request for good cause shown.

(c) If a filed statement of partnership authority is executed pursuant to Section 105(c) and states the name of the partnership but does not contain all of the other information required by subsection (a), the statement nevertheless operates with respect to a person not a partner as provided in subsections (d) and (e).

(d) Except as otherwise provided in subsection (g), a filed statement of partnership authority supplements the authority of a partner to enter into transactions on behalf of the partnership as follows:

(1) Except for transfers of real property, a grant of authority contained in a filed statement of partnership authority is conclusive in favor of a person who gives value without knowledge to the contrary, so long as and to the extent that a limitation on that authority is not then contained in another filed statement. A filed cancellation of a limitation on authority revives the previous grant of authority.

(2) A grant of authority to transfer real property held in the name of the partnership contained in a certified copy of a filed statement of partnership authority recorded in the office for recording transfers of that real property is conclusive in favor of a person who gives value without knowledge to the contrary, so long as and to the extent that a certified copy of a filed statement containing a limitation on that authority is not then of record in the office for recording transfers of that real property. The recording in the office for recording transfers of that real property of a certified copy of a filed cancellation of a limitation on authority revives the previous grant of authority.

(e) A person not a partner is deemed to know of a limitation on the authority of a partner to transfer real property held in the name of the partnership if a certified copy of the filed statement containing the limitation on authority is of record in the office for recording transfers of that real property.

(f) Except as otherwise provided in subsections (d) and (e) and Sections 704 and 805, a person not a partner is not deemed to know of a limitation on the authority of a partner merely because the limitation is contained in a filed statement.

(g) Unless earlier canceled, a filed statement of partnership authority is canceled by operation of law five years after the date on which the statement, or the most recent amendment, was filed with the [Secretary of State].

§304. *Statement of Denial.*

A partner or other person named as a partner in a filed statement of partnership authority or in a list maintained by an agent pursuant to Section 303(b) may file a statement of denial stating the name of the partnership and the fact that is being denied, which may include denial of a person's authority or status as a partner. A statement of denial is a limitation on authority as provided in Section 303(d) and (e).

§305. *Partnership Liable for Partner's Actionable Conduct.*

(a) A partnership is liable for loss or injury caused to a person, or for a penalty incurred, as a result of a wrongful act or omission, or other actionable conduct, of a partner acting in the ordinary course of business of the partnership or with authority of the partnership.

(b) If, in the course of the partnership's business or while acting with authority of the partnership, a partner receives or causes the partnership to receive money or property of a person not a partner, and the money or property is misapplied by a partner, the partnership is liable for the loss.

§306. *Partner's Liability.*

(a) Except as otherwise provided in subsection (b), all partners are liable jointly and severally for all obligations of the partnership unless otherwise agreed by the claimant or provided by law.

(b) A person admitted as a partner into an existing partnership is not personally liable for any partnership obligation incurred before the person's admission as a partner.

(c) An obligation of a partnership incurred while the partnership is a limited liability partnership, whether arising in contract, tort, or otherwise, is solely the obligation of the partnership. A partner is not personally liable, directly or indirectly, by way of contribution or otherwise, for such a partnership obligation solely by reason of being or so acting as a partner. This subsection applies notwithstanding anything inconsistent in the partnership agreement that existed immediately before the vote required to become a limited liability partnership under Section 1001(b).

§307. *Actions By and Against Partnership and Partners.*

(a) A partnership may sue and be sued in the name of the partnership.

(b) An action may be brought against the partnership and, to the extent not inconsistent with Section 306, any or all of the partners in the same action or in separate actions.

(c) A judgment against a partnership is not by itself a judgment against a partner. A judgment against a partnership may not be satisfied from a partner's assets unless there is also a judgment against the partner.

(d) A judgment creditor of a partner may not levy execution against the assets of the partner to satisfy a judgment based on a claim against the partnership unless the partner is personally liable for the claim under Section 306 and:

(1) a judgment based on the same claim has been obtained against the partnership and a writ of execution on the judgment has been returned unsatisfied in whole or in part;

(2) the partnership is a debtor in bankruptcy;

(3) the partner has agreed that the creditor need not exhaust partnership assets;

(4) a court grants permission to the judgment creditor to levy execution against the assets of a partner based on a finding that partnership assets subject to execution are clearly insufficient to satisfy the judgment, that exhaustion of partnership assets is excessively burdensome, or that the grant of permission is an appropriate exercise of the court's equitable powers; or

(5) liability is imposed on the partner by law or contract independent of the existence of the partnership.

(e) This section applies to any partnership liability or obligation resulting from a representation by a partner or purported partner under Section 308.

§308. Liability of Purported Partner.

(a) If a person, by words or conduct, purports to be a partner, or consents to being represented by another as a partner, in a partnership or with one or more persons not partners, the purported partner is liable to a person to whom the representation is made, if that person, relying on the representation, enters into a transaction with the actual or purported partnership. If the representation, either by the purported partner or by a person with the purported partner's consent, is made in a public manner, the purported partner is liable to a person who relies upon the purported partnership even if the purported partner is not aware of being held out as a partner to the claimant. If partnership liability results, the purported partner is liable with respect to that liability as if the purported partner were a partner. If no partnership liability results, the purported partner is liable with respect to that liability jointly and severally with any other person consenting to the representation.

(b) If a person is thus represented to be a partner in an existing partnership, or with one or more persons not partners, the purported partner is an agent of persons consenting to the representation to bind them to the same extent and in the same manner as if the purported partner were a partner, with respect to persons who enter into transactions in reliance upon the representation. If all of the partners of the existing partnership consent to the representation, a partnership act or obligation results. If fewer than all of the partners of the existing partnership consent to the representation, the person acting and the partners consenting to the representation are jointly and severally liable.

(c) A person is not liable as a partner merely because the person is named by another in a statement of partnership authority.

(d) A person does not continue to be liable as a partner merely because of a failure to file a statement of dissociation or to amend a statement of partnership authority to indicate the partner's dissociation from the partnership.

(e) Except as otherwise provided in subsections (a) and (b), persons who are not partners as to each other are not liable as partners to other persons.

ARTICLE 4. RELATIONS OF PARTNERS TO EACH OTHER AND TO PARTNERSHIP

§401. Partner's Rights and Duties.

(a) Each partner is deemed to have an account that is:

(1) credited with an amount equal to the money plus the value of any other property, net of the amount of any liabilities, the partner contributes to the partnership and the partner's share of the partnership profits; and

(2) charged with an amount equal to the money plus the value of any other property, net of the amount of any liabilities, distributed by the partnership to the partner and the partner's share of the partnership losses.

(b) Each partner is entitled to an equal share of the partnership profits and is chargeable with a share of the partnership losses in proportion to the partner's share of the profits.

(c) A partnership shall reimburse a partner for payments made and indemnify a partner for liabilities incurred by the partner in the ordinary course of the business of the partnership or for the preservation of its business or property.

(d) A partnership shall reimburse a partner for an advance to the partnership beyond the amount of capital the partner agreed to contribute.

(e) A payment or advance made by a partner which gives rise to a partnership obligation under subsection (c) or (d) constitutes a loan to the partnership which accrues interest from the date of the payment or advance.

(f) Each partner has equal rights in the management and conduct of the partnership business.

(g) A partner may use or possess partnership property only on behalf of the partnership.

(h) A partner is not entitled to remuneration for services performed for the partnership, except for reasonable compensation for services rendered in winding up the business of the partnership.

(i) A person may become a partner only with the consent of all of the partners.

(j) A difference arising as to a matter in the ordinary course of business of a partnership may be decided by a majority of the partners. An act outside the ordinary course of business of a partnership and an amendment to the partnership agreement may be undertaken only with the consent of all of the partners.

(k) This section does not affect the obligations of a partnership to other persons under Section 301.

§402. Distributions in Kind.

A partner has no right to receive, and may not be required to accept, a distribution in kind.

§403. Partner's Rights and Duties With Respect to Information.

(a) A partnership shall keep its books and records, if any, at its chief executive office.

(b) A partnership shall provide partners and their agents and attorneys access to its books and records. It shall provide former partners and their agents and attorneys access to books and records pertaining to the period during which they were partners. The right of access provides the opportunity to inspect and copy books and records during ordinary business hours. A partnership may impose a reasonable charge, covering the costs of labor and material, for copies of documents furnished.

(c) Each partner and the partnership shall furnish to a partner, and to the legal representative of a deceased partner or partner under legal disability:

(1) without demand, any information concerning the partnership's business and affairs reasonably required for the proper exercise of the partner's rights and duties under the partnership agreement or this [Act]; and

(2) on demand, any other information concerning the partnership's business and affairs, except to the extent the demand or the information demanded is unreasonable or otherwise improper under the circumstances.

§404. *General Standards of Partner's Conduct.*

(a) The only fiduciary duties a partner owes to the partnership and the other partners are the duty of loyalty and the duty of care set forth in subsections (b) and (c).

(b) A partner's duty of loyalty to the partnership and the other partners is limited to the following:

(1) to account to the partnership and hold as trustee for it any property, profit, or benefit derived by the partner in the conduct and winding up of the partnership business or derived from a use by the partner of partnership property, including the appropriation of a partnership opportunity;

(2) to refrain from dealing with the partnership in the conduct or winding up of the partnership business as or on behalf of a party having an interest adverse to the partnership; and

(3) to refrain from competing with the partnership in the conduct of the partnership business before the dissolution of the partnership.

(c) A partner's duty of care to the partnership and the other partners in the conduct and winding up of the partnership business is limited to refraining from engaging in grossly negligent or reckless conduct, intentional misconduct, or a knowing violation of law.

(d) A partner shall discharge the duties to the partnership and the other partners under this [Act] or under the partnership agreement and exercise any rights consistently with the obligation of good faith and fair dealing.

(e) A partner does not violate a duty or obligation under this [Act] or under the partnership agreement merely because the partner's conduct furthers the partner's own interest.

(f) A partner may lend money to and transact other business with the partnership, and as to each loan or transaction, the rights and obligations of a partner are the same as those of a person who is not a partner, subject to other applicable law.

(g) This section applies to a person winding up the partnership business as the personal or legal representative of the last surviving partner as if the person were a partner.

§405. *Actions by Partnership and Partners.*

(a) A partnership may maintain an action against a partner for a breach of the partnership agreement, or for the violation of a duty to the partnership, causing harm to the partnership.

(b) A partner may maintain an action against the partnership or another partner for legal or equitable relief, with or without an accounting as to partnership business, to:

(1) enforce the partner's rights under the partnership agreement;

(2) enforce the partner's rights under this [Act], including:

(i) the partner's rights under Sections 401, 403, or 404;

(ii) the partner's right on dissociation to have the partner's interest in the partnership purchased pursuant to Section 701 or enforce any other right under Article 6 or 7; or

(iii) the partner's right to compel a dissolution and winding up of the partnership business under Section 801 or enforce any other right under Article 8; or

(3) enforce the rights and otherwise protect the interests of the partner, including rights and interests arising independently of the partnership relationship.

(c) The accrual of, and any time limitation on, a right of action for a remedy under this section is governed by other law. A right to an accounting upon a dissolution and winding up does not revive a claim barred by law.

§406. *Continuation of Partnership Beyond Definite Term or Particular Undertaking.*

(a) If a partnership for a definite term or particular undertaking is continued, without an express agreement, after the expiration of the term or completion of the undertaking, the rights and duties of the partners remain the same as they were at the expiration or completion, so far as is consistent with a partnership at will.

(b) If the partners, or those of them who habitually acted in the business during the term or undertaking, continue the business without any settlement or liquidation of the partnership, they are presumed to have agreed that the partnership will continue.

Article 5. Transferees and Creditors of Partner

§501. *Partner Not Co-owner of Partnership Property.*

A partner is not a co-owner of partnership property and has no interest in partnership property which can be transferred, either voluntarily or involuntarily.

§502. *Partner's Transferable Interest in Partnership.*

The only transferable interest of a partner in the partnership is the partner's share of the profits and losses of the partnership and the partner's right to receive distributions. The interest is personal property.

§503. *Transfer of Partner's Transferable Interest.*

(a) A transfer, in whole or in part, of a partner's transferable interest in the partnership:

(1) is permissible;

(2) does not by itself cause the partner's dissociation or a dissolution and winding up of the partnership business; and

(3) does not, as against the other partners or the partnership, entitle the transferee, during the continuance of the partnership, to participate in the management or conduct of the partnership business, to require access to information concerning or an account of partnership transactions, or to inspect or copy the partnership books or records.

(b) A transferee of a partner's transferable interest in the partnership has a right:

(1) to receive, in accordance with the transfer, distributions to which the transferor would otherwise be entitled;

(2) to receive upon the dissolution and winding up of the partnership business, in accordance with the transfer, the net amount otherwise distributable to the transferor; and

(3) to seek under Section 801(6) a judicial determination that it is equitable to wind up the partnership business.

(c) In a dissolution and winding up, a transferee is entitled to an account of partnership transactions only from the date of the latest account agreed to by all of the partners.

(d) Upon transfer, the transferor retains the rights and duties of a partner other than the interest in distributions transferred.

(e) A partnership need not give effect to a transferee's rights under this section until it has notice of the transfer.

(f) A transfer of a partner's transferable interest in the partnership in violation of a restriction on transfer contained in the partnership agreement is ineffective as to a person having notice of the restriction at the time of transfer.

§504. *Partner's Transferable Interest Subject to Charging Order.*

(a) On application by a judgment creditor of a partner or of a partner's transferee, a court having jurisdiction may charge the transferrable interest of the judgment debtor to satisfy the judgment. The court may appoint a receiver of the share of the distributions due or to become due to the judgment debtor in respect of the partnership and make all other orders, directions, accounts, and inquiries the judgment debtor might have made or which the circumstances of the case may require.

(b) A charging order constitutes a lien on the judgment debtor's transferable interest in the partnership. The court may order a foreclosure of the interest subject to the charging order at any time. The purchaser at the foreclosure sale has the rights of a transferee.

(c) At any time before foreclosure, an interest charged may be redeemed:

(1) by the judgment debtor;

(2) with property other than partnership property, by one or more of the other partners; or

(3) with partnership property, by one or more of the other partners with the consent of all of the partners whose interests are not so charged.

(d) This [Act] does not deprive a partner of a right under exemption laws with respect to the partner's interest in the partnership.

(e) This section provides the exclusive remedy by which a judgment creditor of a partner or partner's transferee may satisfy a judgment out of the judgment debtor's transferable interest in the partnership.

Article 6. Partner's Dissociation

§601. *Events Causing Partner's Dissociation.*

A partner is dissociated from a partnership upon the occurrence of any of the following events:

(1) the partnership's having notice of the partner's express will to withdraw as a partner [upon the date of notice] or on a later date specified by the partner;

(2) an event agreed to in the partnership agreement as causing the partner's dissociation;

(3) the partner's expulsion pursuant to the partnership agreement;

(4) the partner's expulsion by the unanimous vote of the other partners if:

(i) it is unlawful to carry on the partnership business with that partner;

(ii) there has been a transfer of all or substantially all of that partner's transferable interest in the partnership, other than a transfer for security purposes, or a court order charging the partner's interest, which has not been foreclosed;

(iii) within 90 days after the partnership notifies a corporate partner that it will be expelled because it has filed a certificate of dissolution or the equivalent, its charter has been revoked, or its right to conduct business has been suspended by the jurisdiction of its incorporation, there is no revocation of the certificate of dissolution or no reinstatement of its charter or its right to conduct business; or

(iv) a partnership that is a partner has been dissolved and its business is being wound up;

(5) on application by the partnership or another partner, the partner's expulsion by judicial determination because:

(i) the partner engaged in wrongful conduct that adversely and materially affected the partnership business;

(ii) the partner willfully or persistently committed a material breach of the partnership agreement or of a duty owed to the partnership or the other partners under Section 404; or

(iii) the partner engaged in conduct relating to the partnership business which makes it not reasonably practicable to carry on the business in partnership with the partner;

(6) the partner's:

(i) becoming a debtor in bankruptcy;

(ii) executing an assignment for the benefit of creditors;

(iii) seeking, consenting to, or acquiescing in the appointment of a trustee, receiver, or liquidator of that partner or of all or substantially all of that partner's property; or

(iv) failing, within 90 days after the appointment, to have vacated or stayed the appointment of a trustee, receiver, or liquidator of the partner or of all or substantially all of the partner's property obtained without the partner's consent or acquiescence, or failing within 90 days after the expiration of a stay to have the appointment vacated;

(7) in the case of a partner who is an individual:

(i) the partner's death;

(ii) the appointment of a guardian or general conservator for the partner; or

(iii) a judicial determination that the partner has otherwise become incapable of performing the partner's duties under the partnership agreement;

(8) in the case of a partner that is a trust or is acting as a partner by virtue of being a trustee of a trust, distribution of the trust's entire transferable interest in the partnership, but not merely by reason of the substitution of a successor trustee;

(9) in the case of a partner that is an estate or is acting as a partner by virtue of being a personal representative of an estate, distribution of the estate's entire transferable interest in the partnership, but not merely by reason of the substitution of a successor personal representative; or

(10) termination of a partner who is not an individual, partnership, corporation, trust, or estate.

§602. *Partner's Power to Dissociate; Wrongful Dissociation*

(a) A partner has the power to dissociate at any time, rightfully or wrongfully, by express will pursuant to Section 601(1).

(b) A partner's dissociation is wrongful only if:

(1) it is in breach of an express provision of the partnership agreement; or

(2) in the case of a partnership for a definite term or particular undertaking, before the expiration of the term or the completion of the undertaking:

(i) the partner withdraws by express will, unless the withdrawal follows within 90 days after another partner's dissociation by death or otherwise under Section 601(6) through (10) or wrongful dissociation under this subsection;

(ii) the partner is expelled by judicial determination under Section 601(5); or

(iii) the partner is dissociated by becoming a debtor in bankruptcy; or

(iv) in the case of a partner who is not an individual, trust other than a business trust, or estate, the partner is expelled or otherwise dissociated because it willfully dissolved or terminated.

(c) A partner who wrongfully dissociates is liable to the partnership and to the other partners for damages caused by the dissociation. The liability is in addition to any other obligation of the partner to the partnership or to the other partners.

§603. *Effect of Partner's Dissociation.*

(a) If a partner's dissociation results in a dissolution and winding up of the partnership business, [Article] 8 applies; otherwise, [Article] 7 applies.

(b) Upon a partner's dissociation:

(1) the partner's right to participate in the management and conduct of the partnership business terminates, except as otherwise provided in Section 803;

(2) the partner's duty of loyalty under Section 404(b)(3) terminates; and

(3) the partner's duty of loyalty under Section 404(b)(1) and (2) and duty of care under Section 404(c) continue only with regard to matters arising or events occurring before the partner's dissociation, unless the partner participates in winding up the partnership's business pursuant to Section 803.

Article 7. Partner's Dissociation When Business Not Wound Up

§701. *Purchase of Dissociated Partner's Interest.*

(a) If a partner is dissociated from a partnership without resulting in a dissolution and winding up of the partnership business under Section 801, the partnership shall cause the dissociated partner's interest in the partnership to be purchased for a buyout price determined pursuant to subsection (b).

(b) The buyout price of a dissociated partner's interest is the amount that would have been distributable to the dissociating partner under Section 807(b) if, on the date of dissociation, the assets of the partnership were sold at a price equal to the greater of the liquidation value or the value based on a sale of the entire business as a going concern without the dissociated partner and the partnership were wound up as of that date. Interest must be paid from the date of dissociation to the date of payment.

(c) Damages for wrongful dissociation under Section 602(b), and all other amounts owing, whether or not presently due, from the dissociated partner to the partnership, must be offset against the buyout price. Interest must be paid from the date the amount owed becomes due to the date of payment.

(d) A partnership shall indemnify a dissociated partner whose interest is being purchased against all partnership liabilities, whether incurred before or after the dissociation, except liabilities incurred by an act of the dissociated partner under Section 702.

(e) If no agreement for the purchase of a dissociated partner's interest is reached within 120 days after a written demand for payment, the partnership shall pay, or cause to be paid, in cash to the dissociated partner the amount the partnership estimates to be the buyout price and accrued interest, reduced by any offsets and accrued interest under subsection (c).

(f) If a deferred payment is authorized under subsection (h), the partnership may tender a written offer to pay the amount it estimates to be the buyout price and accrued interest, reduced by any offsets under subsection (c), stating the time of payment, the amount and type of security for payment, and the other terms and conditions of the obligation.

(g) The payment or tender required by subsection (e) or (f) must be accompanied by the following:

(1) a statement of partnership assets and liabilities as of the date of dissociation;

(2) the latest available partnership balance sheet and income statement, if any;

(3) an explanation of how the estimated amount of the payment was calculated; and

(4) written notice that the payment is in full satisfaction of the obligation to purchase unless, within 120 days after the written notice, the dissociated partner commences an action to determine the buyout price, any offsets under subsection (c), or other terms of the obligation to purchase.

(h) A partner who wrongfully dissociates before the expiration of a definite term or the completion of a particular undertaking is not entitled to payment of any portion of the buyout price until the expiration of the term or completion of the undertaking, unless the partner establishes to the satisfaction of the court that earlier payment will not cause undue hardship to the business of the partnership. A deferred payment must be adequately secured and bear interest.

(i) A dissociated partner may maintain an action against the partnership, pursuant to Section 405(b)(2)(ii), to determine the buyout price of that partner's interest, any offsets under subsection (c), or other terms of the obligation to purchase. The action must be commenced within 120 days after the partnership has tendered payment or an offer to pay or within one year after written demand for payment if no payment or offer to pay is tendered. The court shall determine the buyout price of the dissociated partner's interest, any offset due under subsection (c), and accrued interest, and enter judgment for any additional payment or refund. If deferred payment is authorized under subsection (h), the court shall also determine the security for payment and other terms of the obligation to purchase. The court may assess reasonable attorney's fees and the fees and expenses of appraisers or other experts for a party to the action, in amounts the court finds equitable, against a party that the court finds acted arbitrarily, vexatiously, or not in good faith. The finding may be based on the partnership's failure to tender payment or an offer to pay or to comply with subsection (g).

§702. *Dissociated Partner's Power to Bind and Liability to Partnership.*

(a) For two years after a partner dissociates without resulting in a dissolution and winding up of the partnership business, the partnership, including a surviving partnership under [Article] 9, is bound by an act of the dissociated partner which would have bound the partnership under Section 301 before dissociation only if at the time of entering into the transaction the other party:

(1) reasonably believed that the dissociated partner was then a partner;

(2) did not have notice of the partner's dissociation; and

(3) is not deemed to have had knowledge under Section 303(e) or notice under Section 704(c).

(b) A dissociated partner is liable to the partnership for any damage caused to the partnership arising from an obligation incurred by the dissociated partner after dissociation for which the partnership is liable under subsection (a).

§703. *Dissociated Partner's Liability to Other Persons.*

(a) A partner's dissociation does not of itself discharge the partner's liability for a partnership obligation incurred before dissociation. A dissociated partner is not liable for a partnership obligation incurred after dissociation, except as otherwise provided in subsection (b).

(b) A partner who dissociates without resulting in a dissolution and winding up of the partnership business is liable as a partner to the other party in a transaction entered into by the partnership, or a surviving partnership under [Article] 9, within two years after the partner's dissociation, only if at the time of entering into the transaction the other party:

(1) reasonably believed that the dissociated partner was then a partner;

(2) did not have notice of the partner's dissociation; and

(3) is not deemed to have had knowledge under Section 303(e) or notice under Section 704(c).

(c) By agreement with the partnership creditor and the partners continuing the business, a dissociated partner may be released from liability for a partnership obligation.

(d) A dissociated partner is released from liability for a partnership obligation if a partnership creditor, with notice of the partner's dissociation but without the partner's consent, agrees to a material alteration in the nature or time of payment of a partnership obligation.

§704. *Statement of Dissociation.*

(a) A dissociated partner or the partnership may file a statement of dissociation stating the name of the partnership and that the partner is dissociated from the partnership.

(b) A statement of dissociation is a limitation on the authority of a dissociated partner for the purposes of Section 303(d) and (e).

(c) For the purposes of Sections 702(a)(3) and 703(b)(3), a person not a partner is deemed to have notice of the dissociation 90 days after the statement of dissociation is filed.

§705. *Continued Use of Partnership Name.*

Continued use of a partnership name, or a dissociated partner's name as part thereof, by partners continuing the business does not of itself make the dissociated partner liable for an obligation of the partners or the partnership continuing the business.

Article 8. Winding Up Partnership Business

§801. *Events Causing Dissolution and Winding up of Partnership Business.*

A partnership is dissolved, and its business must be wound up, only upon the occurrence of any of the following events:

(1) in a partnership at will, the partnership's having notice from a partner, other than a partner who is dissociated under Section 601(2) through (10), of that partner's express will to withdraw as a partner [as of the time of the notice], or on a later date specified by the partner;

(2) in a partnership for a definite term or particular undertaking:

(i) within 90 days after a partner's dissociation by death or otherwise under Section 601(6) through (10) or wrongful dissociation under Section 602(b), the express will of at least half of the remaining partners to wind up the partnership business, for which purpose a partner's rightful dissociation pursuant to Section 602(b)(2)(i) constitutes the expression of that partner's will to wind up the partnership business;

(ii) the express will of all of the partners to wind up the partnership business; or

(iii) the expiration of the term or the completion of the undertaking;

(3) an event agreed to in the partnership agreement resulting in the winding up of the partnership business;

(4) an event that makes it unlawful for all or substantially all of the business of the partnership to be continued, but a cure of illegality within 90 days after notice to the partnership of the event is effective retroactively to the date of the event for purposes of this section;

(5) on application by a partner, a judicial determination that:

(i) the economic purpose of the partnership is likely to be unreasonably frustrated;

(ii) another partner has engaged in conduct relating to the partnership business which makes it not reasonably practicable to carry on the business in partnership with that partner; or

(iii) it is not otherwise reasonably practicable to carry on the partnership business in conformity with the partnership agreement; or

(6) on application by a transferee of a partner's transferable interest, a judicial determination that it is equitable to wind up the partnership business:

(i) after the expiration of the term or completion of the undertaking, if the partnership was for a definite term or particular undertaking at the time of the transfer or entry of the charging order that gave rise to the transfer; or

(ii) at any time, if the partnership was a partnership at will at the time of the transfer or entry of the charging order that gave rise to the transfer.

§802. *Partnership Continues After Dissolution.*

(a) Subject to subsection (b), a partnership continues after dissolution only for the purpose of winding up its business. The partnership is terminated when the winding up of its business is completed.

(b) At any time after the dissolution of a partnership and before the winding up of its business is completed, all of the partners, including any dissociating partner other than a wrongfully dissociating partner, may waive the right to have the partnership's business wound up and the partnership terminated. In that event:

(1) the partnership resumes carrying on its business as if dissolution had never occurred, and any liability incurred by the partnership or a partner after the dissolution and before the waiver is determined as if dissolution had never occurred; and

(2) the rights of a third party accruing under Section 804(1) or arising out of conduct in reliance on the dissolution before the third party knew or received a notification of the waiver may not be adversely affected.

§803. *Right to Wind up Partnership Business.*

(a) After dissolution, a partner who has not wrongfully dissociated may participate in winding up the partnership's business, but on application of any partner, partner's legal representative, or transferee, the [designate the appropriate court], for good cause shown, may order judicial supervision of the winding up.

(b) The legal representative of the last surviving partner may wind up a partnership's business.

(c) A person winding up a partnership's business may preserve the partnership business or property as a going concern for a reasonable time, prosecute and defend actions and proceedings, whether civil, criminal, or administrative, settle and close the partnership's business, dispose of and transfer the partnership's property, discharge the partnership's liabilities, distribute the assets of the partnership pursuant to Section 807, settle disputes by mediation or arbitration, and perform other necessary acts.

§804. *Partner's Power to Bind Partnership After Dissolution.*

Subject to Section 805, a partnership is bound by a partner's act after dissolution that:

(1) is appropriate for winding up the partnership business; or

(2) would have bound the partnership under Section 301 before dissolution, if the other party to the transaction did not have notice of the dissolution.

§805. *Statement of Dissolution.*

(a) After dissolution, a partner who has not wrongfully dissociated may file a statement of dissolution stating the name of the partnership and that the partnership has dissolved and is winding up its business.

(b) A statement of dissolution cancels a filed statement of partnership authority for the purposes of Section 303(d) and is a limitation on authority for the purposes of Section 303(e).

(c) For the purposes of Sections 301 and 804, a person not a partner is deemed to have notice of the dissolution and the limitation on the partners' authority as a result of the statement of dissolution 90 days after it is filed.

(d) After filing and, if appropriate, recording a statement of dissolution, a dissolved partnership may file and, if appropriate, record a statement of partnership authority which will operate with respect to a person not a partner as provided in Section 303(d) and (e) in any transaction, whether or not the transaction is appropriate for winding up the partnership business.

§806. *Partner's Liability to Other Partners After Dissolution.*

(a) Except as otherwise provided in subsection (b) and Section 306, after dissolution a partner is liable to the other partners for the partner's share of any partnership liability incurred under Section 804.

(b) A partner who, with knowledge of the dissolution, incurs a partnership liability under Section 804(2) by an act that is not appropriate for winding up the partnership business is liable to the partnership for any damage caused to the partnership arising from the liability.

§807. *Settlement of Accounts and Contributions Among Partners.*

(a) In winding up a partnership's business, the assets of the partnership, including the contributions of the partners required by this section, must be applied to discharge its obligations to creditors, including, to the extent permitted by law, partners who are creditors. Any surplus must be applied to pay in cash the net amount distributable to partners in accordance with their right to distributions under subsection (b).

(b) Each partner is entitled to a settlement of all partnership accounts upon winding up the partnership business. In settling accounts among the partners, the profits and losses that result from the liquidation of the partnership assets must be credited and charged to the partners' accounts. The partnership shall make a distribution to a partner in an amount equal to any excess of the credits over the charges in the partner's account. A partner shall contribute to the partnership an amount equal to any excess of the charges over the credits in the partner's account but excluding from the calculation charges attributable to an obligation for which the partner is not personally liable under Section 306.

(c) If a partner fails to contribute the full amount required under subsection (b), all of the other partners shall contribute, in the proportions in which those partners share partnership losses, the additional amount necessary to satisfy the partnership obligations for which they are personally liable under Section 306. A partner or partner's legal representative may recover from the other partners any contributions the partner makes to the extent the amount contributed exceeds that partner's share of the partnership obligations for which the partner is personally liable under Section 306.

(d) After the settlement of accounts, each partner shall contribute, in the proportion in which the partner shares partnership losses, the amount necessary to satisfy partnership obligations that were not known at the time of the settlement and for which the partner is personally liable under Section 306.

(e) The estate of a deceased partner is liable for the partner's obligation to contribute to the partnership.

(f) An assignee for the benefit of creditors of a partnership or a partner, or a person appointed by a court to represent creditors of a partnership or a partner, may enforce a partner's obligation to contribute to the partnership.

ARTICLE 9. CONVERSIONS AND MERGERS

§901. *Definitions.*

In this [article]:

(1) "General partner" means a partner in a partnership and a general partner in a limited partnership.

(2) "Limited partner" means a limited partner in a limited partnership.

(3) "Limited partnership" means a limited partnership created under the [State Limited Partnership Act], predecessor law, or comparable law of another jurisdiction.

(4) "Partner" includes both a general partner and a limited partner.

§902. *Conversion of Partnership to Limited Partnership.*

(a) A partnership may be converted to a limited partnership pursuant to this section.

(b) The terms and conditions of a conversion of a partnership to a limited partnership must be approved by all of the partners or by a number or percentage specified for conversion in the partnership agreement.

(c) After the conversion is approved by the partners, the partnership shall file a certificate of limited partnership in the jurisdiction in which the limited partnership is to be formed. The certificate must include:

(1) a statement that the partnership was converted to a limited partnership from a partnership;

(2) its former name; and

(3) a statement of the number of votes cast by the partners for and against the conversion and, if the vote is less than unanimous, the number or percentage required to approve the conversion under the partnership agreement.

(d) The conversion takes effect when the certificate of limited partnership is filed or at any later date specified in the certificate.

(e) A general partner who becomes a limited partner as a result of the conversion remains liable as a general partner for an obligation incurred by the partnership before the conversion takes effect. If the other party to a transaction with the limited partnership reasonably believes when entering the transaction that the limited partner is a general partner, the limited partner is liable for an obligation incurred by the limited partnership within 90 days after the conversion takes effect. The limited partner's liability for all other obligations of the limited partnership incurred after the conversion takes effect is that of a limited partner as provided in the [State Limited Partnership Act].

§903. *Conversion of Limited Partnership to Partnership.*

(a) A limited partnership may be converted to a partnership pursuant to this section.

(b) Notwithstanding a provision to the contrary in a limited partnership agreement, the terms and conditions of a conversion of a limited partnership to a partnership must be approved by all of the partners.

(c) After the conversion is approved by the partners, the limited partnership shall cancel its certificate of limited partnership.

(d) The conversion takes effect when the certificate of limited partnership is canceled.

(e) A limited partner who becomes a general partner as a result of the conversion remains liable only as a limited partner for an obligation incurred by the limited partnership before the conversion takes effect. Except as otherwise provided in Section 306, the partner is liable as a general partner for an obligation of the partnership incurred after the conversion takes effect.

§904. *Effect of Conversion; Entity Unchanged.*

(a) A partnership or limited partnership that has been converted pursuant to this [article] is for all purposes the same entity that existed before the conversion.

(b) When a conversion takes effect:

(1) all property owned by the converting partnership or limited partnership remains vested in the converted entity;

(2) all obligations of the converting partnership or limited partnership continue as obligations of the converted entity; and

(3) an action or proceeding pending against the converting partnership or limited partnership may be continued as if the conversion had not occurred.

§905. *Merger of Partnerships.*

(a) Pursuant to a plan of merger approved as provided in subsection (c), a partnership may be merged with one or more partnerships or limited partnerships.

(b) The plan of merger must set forth:

(1) the name of each partnership or limited partnership that is a party to the merger;

(2) the name of the surviving entity into which the other partnerships or limited partnerships will merge;

(3) whether the surviving entity is a partnership or a limited partnership and the status of each partner;

(4) the terms and conditions of the merger;

(5) the manner and basis of converting the interests of each party to the merger into interests or obligations of the surviving entity, or into money or other property in whole or part; and

(6) the street address of the surviving entity's chief executive office.

(c) The plan of merger must be approved:

(1) in the case of a partnership that is a party to the merger, by all of the partners, or a number or percentage specified for merger in the partnership agreement; and

(2) in the case of a limited partnership that is a party to the merger, by the vote required for approval of a merger by the law of the State or foreign jurisdiction in which the limited partnership is organized and, in the absence of such a specifically applicable law, by all of the partners, notwithstanding a provision to the contrary in the partnership agreement.

(d) After a plan of merger is approved and before the merger takes effect, the plan may be amended or abandoned as provided in the plan.

(e) The merger takes effect on the later of:

(1) the approval of the plan of merger by all parties to the merger, as provided in subsection (c);

(2) the filing of all documents required by law to be filed as a condition to the effectiveness of the merger; or

(3) any effective date specified in the plan of merger.

§906. *Effect of Merger.*

(a) When a merger takes effect:

(1) the separate existence of every partnership or limited partnership that is a party to the merger, other than the surviving entity, ceases;

(2) all property owned by each of the merged partnerships or limited partnerships vests in the surviving entity;

(3) all obligations of every partnership or limited partnership that is a party to the merger become the obligations of the surviving entity; and

(4) an action or proceeding pending against a partnership or limited partnership that is a party to the merger may be continued as if the merger had not occurred, or the surviving entity may be substituted as a party to the action or proceeding.

(b) The [Secretary of State] of this State is the agent for service of process in an action or proceeding against a surviving foreign partnership or limited partnership to enforce an obligation of a domestic partnership or limited partnership that is a party to a merger. The surviving entity shall promptly notify the [Secretary of State] of the mailing address of its chief executive office and of any change of address. Upon receipt of process, the [Secretary of State] shall mail a copy of the process to the surviving foreign partnership or limited partnership.

(c) A partner of the surviving partnership or limited partnership is liable for:

(1) all obligations of a party to the merger for which the partner was personally liable before the merger;

(2) all other obligations of the surviving entity incurred before the merger by a party to the merger, but those obligations may be satisfied only out of property of the entity; and

(3) except as otherwise provided in Section 306, all obligations of the surviving entity incurred after the merger takes effect, but those obligations may be satisfied only out of property of the entity if the partner is a limited partner.

(d) If the obligations incurred before the merger by a party to the merger are not satisfied out of the property of the surviving partnership or limited partnership, the general partners of that party immediately before the effective date of the merger shall contribute the amount necessary to satisfy that party's obligations to the surviving entity, in the manner provided in Section 807 or in the [Limited Partnership Act] of the jurisdiction in which the party was formed, as the case may be, as if the merged party were dissolved.

(e) A partner of a party to a merger who does not become a partner of the surviving partnership or limited partnership is dissociated from the entity, of which that partner was a partner, as of the date the merger takes effect. The surviving entity shall cause the partner's interest in the entity to be purchased under Section 701 or another statute specifically applicable to that partner's interest with respect to a merger. The surviving entity is bound under Section 702 by an act of a general partner dissociated under this subsection, and the partner is liable under Section 703 for transactions entered into by the surviving entity after the merger takes effect.

§907. *Statement of Merger.*

(a) After a merger, the surviving partnership or limited partnership may file a statement that one or more partnerships or limited partnerships have merged into the surviving entity.

(b) A statement of merger must contain:

(1) the name of each partnership or limited partnership that is a party to the merger;

(2) the name of the surviving entity into which the other partnerships or limited partnership were merged;

(3) the street address of the surviving entity's chief executive office and of an office in this State, if any; and

(4) whether the surviving entity is a partnership or a limited partnership.

(c) Except as otherwise provided in subsection (d), for the purposes of Section 302, property of the surviving partnership or limited partnership which before the merger was held in the name of another party to the merger is property held in the name of the surviving entity upon filing a statement of merger.

(d) For the purposes of Section 302, real property of the surviving partnership or limited partnership which before the merger was held in the name of another party to the merger is property held in the name of the surviving entity upon recording a certified copy of the statement of merger in the office for recording transfers of that real property.

(e) A filed and, if appropriate, recorded statement of merger, executed and declared to be accurate pursuant to Section 105(c), stating the name of a partnership or limited partnership that is a party to the merger in whose name property was held before the merger and the name of the surviving entity, but not containing all of the other information required by subsection (b), operates with respect to the partnerships or limited partnerships named to the extent provided in subsections (c) and (d).

§908. Nonexclusive.

This [article] is not exclusive. Partnerships or limited partnerships may be converted or merged in any other manner provided by law.

ARTICLE 10. LIMITED LIABILITY PARTNERSHIP

§1001. Statement of Qualification.

(a) A partnership may become a limited liability partnership pursuant to this section.

(b) The term and conditions on which a partnership becomes a limited liability partnership must be approved by the vote necessary to amend the partnership agreement except, in the case of a partnership agreement that expressly considers contribution obligations, the vote necessary to amend those provisions.

(c) After the approval required by subsection (b), a partnership may become a limited liability partnership by filing a statement of qualification. The statement must contain:

(1) the name of the partnership;

(2) the street address of the partnership's chief executive office and, if different, the street address of an office in this State, if any;

(3) if there is no office in this State, the name and street address of the partnership's agent for service of process who must be an individual resident of this State or any other person authorized to do business in this State;

(4) a statement that the partnership elects to be a limited liability partnership; and

(5) a deferred effective date, if any.

(d) The status of a partnership as a limited liability partnership is effective on the later of the filing of the statement or a date specified in the statement. The status remains effective, regardless of changes in the partnership, until it is canceled pursuant to Section 105(d) or revoked pursuant to Section 1003.

(e) The status of a partnership as a limited liability partnership and the liability of its partners is not affected by errors or later changes in the information required to be contained in the statement of qualification under subsection (c).

(f) The filing of a statement of qualification establishes that a partnership has satisfied all conditions precedent to the qualification of the partnership as a limited liability partnership.

(g) An amendment or cancellation of a statement of qualification is effective when it is filed or on a deferred effective date specified in the amendment or cancellation.

§1002. Name.

The name of a limited liability partnership must end with "Registered Limited Liability Partnership," "Limited Liability Partnership," "R.L.L.P.," "L.L.P.," "RLLP," or "LLP."

§1003. Annual Report.

(a) A limited liability partnership, and a foreign limited liability partnership authorized to transact business in this State, shall file an annual report in the office of the [Secretary of State] which contains:

(1) the name of the limited liability partnership and the State or other jurisdiction under whose laws the foreign limited liability partnership is formed;

(2) the current street address of the partnership's chief executive office and, if different, the current street address of an office in this State, if any; and

(3) if there is no current office in this State, the name and street address of the partnership's current agent for service of process who must be an individual resident of this State or any other person authorized to do business in this State.

(b) An annual report must be filed between [January 1 and April 1] of each year following the calendar year in which a partnership files a statement of qualification or a foreign partnership becomes authorized to transact business in this State.

(c) The [Secretary of State] may administratively revoke the statement of qualification of a partnership that fails to file an annual report when due or to pay the required filing fee. The [Secretary of State] shall provide the partnership at least 60 days' written notice of intent to revoke the statement. The notice must be mailed to the partnership at its chief executive office set forth in the last filed statement of qualification or annual report. The notice must specify the annual report that has not been filed, the fee that has not been paid, and the effective date of the revocation. The revocation is not effective if the annual report is filed and the fee is paid before the effective date of the revocation.

(d) A revocation under subsection (c) only affects a partnership's status as a limited liability partnership and is not an event of dissolution of the partnership.

(e) A partnership whose statement of qualification has been administratively revoked may apply to the [Secretary of State] for reinstatement within two years after the effective date of the revocation. The application must state:

(1) the name of the partnership and the effective date of the revocation; and

(2) that the ground for revocation either did not exist or has been corrected.

(f) A reinstatement under subsection (e) relates back to and takes effect as of the effective date of the revocation, and the partnership's status as a limited liability partnership continues as if the revocation had never occurred.

ARTICLE 11. FOREIGN LIMITED LIABILITY PARTNERSHIP

§1101. Law Governing Foreign Limited Liability Partnership.

(a) The laws under which a foreign limited liability partnership is formed govern relations among the partners and between the partners and the partnership and the liability of partners for obligations of the partnership.

(b) A foreign limited liability partnership may not be denied a statement of foreign qualification by reason of any difference between the laws under which the partnership was formed and the laws of this State.

(c) A statement of foreign qualification does not authorize a foreign limited liability partnership to engage in any business or exercise any power that a partnership may not engage in or exercise in this State as a limited liability partnership.

§1102. Statement of Foreign Qualification.

(a) Before transacting business in this State, a foreign limited liability partnership must file a statement of foreign qualification. The statement must contain:

(1) the name of the foreign limited liability partnership which satisfies the requirements of the State or other jurisdiction under whose laws it is formed and ends with "Registered Limited Liability Partnership," "Limited Liability Partnership," "R.L.L.P.," "L.L.P.," "RLLP," or "LLP";

(2) the street address of the partnership's chief executive office and, if different, the street address of an office in this State, if any;

(3) if there is no office in this State, the name and street address of the partnership's agent for service of process who must be an individual resident of this State or any other person authorized to do business in this State; and

(4) a deferred effective date, if any.

(b) The status of a partnership as a foreign limited liability partnership is effective on the later of the filing of the statement of foreign qualification or a date specified in the statement. The status remains effective, regardless of changes in the partnership, until it is canceled pursuant to Section 105(d) or revoked pursuant to Section 1003.

(c) An amendment or cancellation of a statement of foreign qualification is effective when it is filed or on a deferred effective date specified in the amendment or cancellation.

§1103. Effect of Failure to Qualify.

(a) A foreign limited liability partnership transacting business in this State may not maintain an action or proceeding in this State unless it has in effect a statement of foreign qualification.

(b) The failure of a foreign limited liability partnership to have in effect a statement of foreign qualification does not impair the validity of a contract or act of the foreign limited liability partnership or preclude it from defending an action or proceeding in this State.

(c) Limitations on personal liability of partners are not waived solely by transacting business in this State without a statement of foreign qualification.

(d) If a foreign limited liability partnership transacts business in this State without a statement of foreign qualification, the [Secretary of State] is its agent for service of process with respect to [claims for relief] arising out of the transaction of business in this State.

§1104. Activities Not Constituting Transacting Business.

(a) Activities of a foreign limited liability partnership which do not constitute transacting business within the meaning of this [article] include:

(1) maintaining, defending, or settling an action or proceeding;

(2) holding meetings of its partners or carrying on any other activity concerning its internal affairs;

(3) maintaining bank accounts;

(4) maintaining offices or agencies for the transfer, exchange, and registration of the partnership's own securities or maintaining trustees or depositories with respect to those securities;

(5) selling through independent contractors;

(6) soliciting or obtaining orders, whether by mail or through employees or agents or otherwise, if the orders require acceptance outside this State before they become contracts;

(7) creating or acquiring indebtedness, mortgages, or security interests in real or personal property;

(8) securing or collecting debts or foreclosing mortgages or other security interests in property securing the debts, and holding, protecting, and maintaining property so acquired;

(9) conducting an isolated transaction that is completed within 30 days and is not one in the course of similar transactions of like nature; and

(10) transacting business in interstate commerce.

(b) For purposes of this [article], the ownership in this State of income-producing real property or tangible personal property, other than property excluded under subsection (a), constitutes transacting business in this State.

(c) This section does not apply in determining the contacts or activities that may subject a foreign limited liability partnership to service of process, taxation, or regulation under any other law of this State.

§1105. Action by [Attorney General].

The [Attorney General] may maintain an action to restrain a foreign limited liability partnership from transacting business in this State in violation of this [article].

ARTICLE 12. MISCELLANEOUS PROVISIONS

§1201. Uniformity of Application and Construction.

This [Act] shall be applied and construed to effectuate its general purpose to make uniform the law with respect to the subject of this [Act] among States enacting it.

§1202. Short Title.

This [Act] may be cited as the Uniform Partnership Act (1994).

§1203. Severability Clause.

If any provision of this [Act] or its application to any person or circumstance is held invalid, the invalidity does not affect other provisions or applications of this [Act] which can be given effect without the invalid provision or application, and to this end the provisions of this [Act] are severable.

§1204. Effective Date.

This [Act] takes effect. . . .

§1205. Repeals.

Effective January 1, 199____, the following acts and parts of acts are repealed: [the State Partnership Act as amended and in effect immediately before the effective date of this Act].

§1206. Applicability.

(a) Before January 1, 199____, this [Act] governs only a partnership formed:

(1) after the effective date of this [Act], unless that partnership is continuing the business of a dissolved partnership under [Section 41 of the prior Uniform Partnership Act]; and

(2) before the effective date of this [Act], that elects, as provided by subsection (c), to be governed by this [Act].

(b) After January 1, 199____, this [Act] governs all partnerships.

(c) Before January 1, 199____, a partnership voluntarily may elect, in the manner provided in its partnership agreement or by law for amending the partnership agreement, to be governed by this [Act]. The provisions of this [Act] relating to the liability of the partnership's partners to third parties apply to limit those partners' liability to a third party who had done business with the partnership within one year preceding the partnership's election to be governed by this [Act], only if the third party knows or has received a notification of the partnership's election to be governed by this [Act].

§1207. Savings Clause.

This [Act] does not affect an action or proceeding commenced or right accrued before this [Act] takes effect.

APPENDIX

General Partnership Agreement

GENERAL PARTNERSHIP AGREEMENT

THIS AGREEMENT is entered into this ____________ day of ___________________________, 20__________, by and among Christopher Walter (Walter), an individual residing at ___________________________________, Timothy Mislock, (Mislock), an individual residing at ______________________, and Erin Murphy (Murphy), an individual residing at _______________________________________. Walter, Mislock, and Murphy are hereinafter sometimes referred to individually as "Partner" and collectively as "Partners."

RECITALS

WHEREAS the Partners desire to form a partnership for the purpose of ______________________________ and have decided that it is in their best commercial interests to do so.

NOW, THEREFORE, for good and valuable consideration, the receipt and sufficiency of which are hereby acknowledged, the parties hereto agree as follows:

1. *Formation and Purpose of the Partnership.* The Partners hereby form a general partnership (the Partnership) under the laws of the State of ______________________________ for the purpose of ___________________________________, and the carrying on of any and all activities necessary and incident thereto.

2. *Partnership Name and Address.* The name of the Partnership is "WMM Enterprises" and its principal place of business shall be located at ______________________________, in the City of ___________________________________, State of ______________________________, and at such other places as may be mutually agreed upon by the Partners.

3. *Term.* The Partnership shall commence on __________________________________ and shall continue until dissolved by mutual agreement of the Partners or as provided in Paragraph 13 below.

4. *Capital Contributions.*

(a) Initial Capital Contributions. Each Partner shall contribute the following amounts:

Name	*Amount*
Walter	$____________
Mislock	$____________
Murphy	$____________

The contributions shall be made to the Partnership on or before ___________________________, 20________, or this Agreement shall be void and of no effect.

(b) Additional Capital Contributions. At such time or times as the Partners mutually agree that additional capital is necessary to operate the business of the Partnership, the Partners shall contribute additional capital in accordance with their respective partnership interests at the relevant time and in accordance with the agreed amount of the additional capital contribution and the method of payment thereof determined by the Partners. In the event that a Partner fails to make an additional capital contribution required to be made under this Agreement within the time period prescribed, such Partner shall be deemed to be a "Defaulting Partner" and a non-defaulting Partner shall be entitled to make the contribution on behalf of the Defaulting Partner and such contribution shall be a personal debt due and owing to the non-defaulting Partner from the Defaulting Partner(s) with interest at the rate of ______________ percent (________%) per annum until paid. No money or assets may be distributed by the Partnership to a Defaulting Partner unless and until the Defaulting Partner shall have paid in full the amount owed to the non-defaulting Partner(s), together with interest. Accordingly, all distributions from the Partnership which would have been made to the Defaulting Partner shall instead be made to the non-defaulting Partner(s) until the personal debt of the Defaulting Partner to the non-defaulting Partner(s) is paid in full.

(c) Return of Capital Contribution. No interest shall be paid on any Partner's capital contribution. No Partner has a right to receive a return of all or any part of his or her capital contribution except as expressly provided in this Agreement or in the event of liquidation or dissolution of the Partnership, and then only to the extent of the net assets of the Partnership available for distribution.

5. *Interests of Partners in Partnership.* Each Partner shall own a _____________ percent (_________%) interest in the Partnership. Any change in the partnership interest of any Partner shall be reflected in writing and signed by all Partners.

6. *Profits and Losses.* Partners shall share in the profits and losses of the Partnership in accordance with their respective partnership interests.

7. *Voting.* The Partners shall be vested with voting rights in the Partnership equal to their respective partnership interests. Except as otherwise agreed by the Partners, actions of the Partnership shall require majority action of the outstanding partnership interests.

8. *Management.* The management and operation of the business and affairs of the Partnership shall be conducted by the Partners or by such person or persons as are designated by the Partners to perform such functions on behalf of the Partnership. Walter shall be the Managing Partner and shall be entitled to enter into contracts and agreements on behalf of the Partnership for the conduct of partnership operations in the ordinary course of business. Persons dealing with the Partnership shall be entitled to rely on the power and authority of Walter.

Notwithstanding the foregoing, nothing herein is intended to grant Walter the authority to make all decisions regarding the business of the Partnership. The authority vested in Walter pertains only to the right to bind the Partnership, without the consent or approval of any other Partner, for contracts or obligations in the ordinary course of business which are necessary, appropriate, or incidental to the performance of the Partnership's business.

Walter shall not undertake any of the following business activities without the majority vote of the Partners:

(a) borrow money in excess of _____________ Dollars ($_____________);
(b) purchase or sell any real estate;
(c) enter into any agreement which requires the Partnership to make any payment of more than $________ per year;
(d) compromise any claim or institute any litigation or other proceeding on behalf of the Partnership; or
(e) sell all or substantially all of the partnership's assets.

9. *Duties of Partners.* Each of the Partners shall give his or her undivided time and attention to the business and affairs of the Partnership and shall use his or her best efforts to promote the interests of the Partnership. Partners shall have fiduciary duties to each other and to the Partnership.

10. *Books of Account.* Books of account of the transactions of the Partnership shall be kept at the principal place of business of the Partnership and shall be available at all reasonable times for inspection by any Partner. Financial statements shall be prepared on a quarterly basis and shall include a statement of cash flow. The financial statements shall be prepared by independent certified public accountants selected by the Partners. The tax and accounting year of the partnership shall be the calendar year. Any Partner, at his or her sole expense, may cause the books of the Partnership to be audited at any time. No later than thirty (30) days after the close of the fiscal year, an annual accounting shall be prepared by the Partnership's independent certified public accountants.

11. *Bank Accounts.* The funds of the Partnership shall be kept in such bank accounts or in such manner designated by the Partners. Checks drawn on partnership funds in any account shall be signed by Walter or such person or persons as the Partnership shall designate from time to time.

12. *Withdrawals, Distributions, and Expenses.*

(a) Withdrawal. Each Partner shall be permitted to draw from the funds of the Partnership _____________ Dollars ($_________) per _____________ for the Partner's living expenses. The sums so drawn shall be charged to the Partner and at the annual accounting shall be charged against that Partner's share of the profits. If the Partner's share of the profits is insufficient to equal the sum drawn, the Partner must pay the amount of the deficiency within ten (10) days notice from the Partnership and said deficiency shall draw interest at the rate of _____________ percent (_________%) per year until paid.

(b) Distributions. So far as is practicable, the net cash flow, if any, of the Partnership (after allocation of an amount agreed upon by the Partners for working capital obligations and contingencies) shall be distributed among the Partners in accordance with their respective partnership interests at least annually or on a more frequent basis as decided by the Partners.

(c) Expenses. Partners who have incurred expenses on behalf of the Partnership in the ordinary course of Partnership business shall be reimbursed therefor upon submission to the Partnership of appropriate evidence of such expenses, as determined in the sole discretion of the Partners.

13. *Dissolution.* The Partnership shall be dissolved upon the agreement of all Partners or the sale or other disposition of all or substantially all of its assets. Upon dissolution of the Partnership, the Partners shall proceed with reasonable promptness to liquidate the assets of the Partnership. Thereafter, the assets of the Partnership shall be used and distributed in the following order: first, to pay or provide for the payment of all Partnership liabilities and liquidating expenses; and second, to distribute to the Partners, in accordance with their respective partnership interests, the remaining assets of the Partnership.

14. *Change of Partners.* Any change of Partners shall be done only in the manner set forth in this Paragraph and any attempt to transfer otherwise shall be null and void.

(a) Withdrawal of Partner. Any Partner may withdraw from the Partnership by giving to each of the other Partners and the Partnership at least thirty (30) days' prior written notice of the Partner's intent to withdraw. On withdrawal of a Partner, that Partner's partnership interest shall be determined by appraisal of the value of the Partnership, and the withdrawing Partner shall be repaid his or her capital contributions within ______________ days of the appraisal of the Partnership's value. After deduction for any draw or indebtedness, the withdrawing Partner shall receive cash payments in ______________ equal installments, commencing immediately after the end of the fiscal year for the Partner's interest in the Partnership's profits.

(b) Bankruptcy, Death, or Permanent Disability. The bankruptcy, death, or permanent disability of a Partner shall not result in the dissolution of the Partnership unless required by law. The death of a Partner, the filing of any petition by any Partner under the federal Bankruptcy Act, or the permanent disability of a Partner due to sickness or injury shall immediately terminate all right, title, and interest of that Partner in the Partnership. The deceased, bankrupt, or permanently disabled Partner's share of the Partnership shall be established based on the Partner's date of death or permanent disability or date of filing of any petition under the federal Bankruptcy Act, and, after deduction for any draw or any indebtedness of the Partner, the Partner's estate, trustee in bankruptcy, or the permanently disabled Partner shall be paid a cash payment representing the Partner's capital contribution to the Partnership, the Partner's share of the net profits or losses for the current fiscal year to the date of death or permanent disability or of such filing of such petition, and the Partner's share of the current Partnership business as of the date of death or permanent disability or the date of filing of such petition

(c) New Partner. New partners may be added to the Partnership by invitation from the then-existing Partners or by purchase of a withdrawing, deceased, bankrupt, or permanently disabled Partner's interest.

An invitation to a new Partner may be extended on a vote of existing Partners representing ______________ percent (_________%) of the outstanding interests in the Partnership. When a Partner's interest is to be sold to a third party by a Partner leaving the Partnership, a vote on the acceptability of the proposed new partner shall be made by a vote of existing Partners representing ______________ percent (_________%) of the outstanding interests of the Partnership. A new partner must execute an Amendment to this Agreement agreeing to the terms and conditions of this Agreement. In the event a proposed new partner is not found acceptable as herein provided, the Partnership shall purchase the departing Partner's interest at the price and upon the terms offered by the third party and the Partnership may resell the interest to a candidate acceptable to the Partners.

15. *Miscellaneous Provisions.*

(a) Valuation. Any valuation or appraisal of the Partnership or any Partner's interest therein shall be conducted by an independent appraiser selected by Partners representing a majority of the outstanding interests of the Partnership.

(b) Notices. All notices required by law or this Agreement shall be in writing and may be delivered to the Partners personally or may be deposited in the United States mail, postage prepaid, addressed to the Partners at their addresses identified in this Agreement.

(c) Disputes. Any dispute arising under the terms of this Agreement that cannot be resolved amicably by the parties shall be submitted to binding arbitration in accordance with the rules of the American Arbitration Association.

(d) Amendments to Agreement. No change or modification of this Agreement shall be valid or binding upon the Partners, nor shall any waiver of any term or provision hereof be deemed a waiver of such term or provision unless such change, modification, or waiver shall be in writing and signed by all of the Partners.

(e) Time of Performance. Whenever performance by a Partner or the Partnership is required under this Agreement, time shall be of the essence.

(f) Counterparts. This Agreement may be executed in one or more counterparts, but all such counterparts shall constitute one and the same Agreement.

(g) Severability. In the event any provision of this Agreement is invalid or unenforceable, then such provision shall be deemed severable from this Agreement.

(h) Applicable law. This Agreement shall be governed under the laws of the State of ________________________.

IN WITNESS WHEREOF, the Partners have executed this Agreement at ________________________ as of the day and year given herein.

Name: _________ Address: __________________

Name: _________ Address: __________________

Name: _________ Address: __________________

APPENDIX

E

Revised Uniform Limited Partnership Act

TABLE OF JURISDICTIONS
Wherein Act Has Been Adopted

Jurisdiction	*Laws*	*Effective Date*	*Statutory Citation*
Alabama	1997, 1st Sp. Sess. 97-921	10-1-1998	Code 1975, §§ 10-9B-101 to 10-9B-1206.
Alaska	1992, c. 128	7-1-1993	AS 32.11.010 to 32.11.990.
Arizona	1982, c. 192	4-22-1982[1]	A.R.S. §§ 29-301 to 29-376.
Arkansas	1979, No. 657	7-1-1979	A.C.A. §§ 4-43-101 to 4-43-1110.
California	1983, c. 1223	7-1-1984	West's Ann.Cal.Corp.Code, §§ 15611 to 15723.
Colorado[2]	1981, c. 77	11-1-1981	West's C.R.S.A. §§ 7-62-101 to 7-62-1201.
Connecticut	1979, P.A. 440	6-14-1979[1]	C.G.S.A. §§ 34-9 to 34-38r.
Delaware	L.1982, c. 420	7-21-1982[1]	6 Del.C. §§ 17-101 to 17-1111.
Dist. of Columbia	1987, D.C.Law 7-49		D.C.Code 1981 §§ 41-401 to 41-499.25.
Florida	1986, c. 86-263	1-1-1987	West's F.S.A. §§ 620.101 to 620.186.
Georgia[2]	1988, pp. 1016, 1018		O.C.G.A. §§ 14-9-100 to 14-9-1204.
Hawaii	1989, Act 288	1-1-1990	HRS §§ 425D-101 to 425D-1109.
Idaho	1982, c. 106		I.C. §§ 53-201 to 53-268.
Illinois	1986, P.A. 84-1412	7-1-1987	S.H.A. 805 ILCS 210/100 to 210/1205.
Indiana	1988, P.L. 147	7-1-1988	West's A.I.C. 23-16-1-1 to 23-16-12-6.
Iowa	1982, c. 1103	7-1-1982	I.C.A. §§ 487.101 to 487.1106.
Kansas	1983, c. 88	1-1-1984	K.S.A. 56-1a101 to 56-1a609.
Kentucky	1988, c. 284	4-9-1988	KRS 362.401 to 362.527.
Maine	1991, c. 552	1-1-1992	31 MRSA §§ 401 to 530.
Maryland	1981, c. 801	7-1-1982	Code, Corporations and Associations, §§ 10-101 to 10-1105.
Massachusetts	1982, c. 202	7-1-1982	M.G.L.A. c. 109, §§ 1 to 62.
Michigan	1982, P.A. 213	1-1-1983	M.C.L.A. §§ 449.1101 to 449.2108.
Minnesota[2]	1980, c. 582	4-16-1980[1]	M.S.A. §§ 322A.01 to 322A.88.

Jurisdiction	*Laws*	*Effective Date*	*Statutory Citation*
Mississippi	1987, c. 488	1-1-1988	Code 1972, §§ 79-14-101 to 79-14-1107.
Missouri	1985, H.B. 512, 650	1-1-1987	V.A.M.S. §§ 359.011 to 359.691.
Montana	1981, c. 522		MCA §§ 35-12-501 to 35-12-1404.
Nebraska	1981, LB 272	1-1-1982	R.R.S. 1943, §§ 67-233 to 67-296.
Nevada	1985, c. 445	1-1-1987	N.R.S. 88.315 to 88.645.
New Hampshire	1987, c. 349	1-1-1988	RSA 304-B:1 to 304-B:64.
New Jersey	1983, c. 489	1-1-1985	N.J.S.A. 42:2A-1 to 42:2A-73.
New Mexico	1988, c. 90	9-1-1988	NMSA 1978, §§ 54-2-1 to 54-2-63.
New York[2]	1990, c. 950	4-1-1991	McKinney's Partnership Law, §§ 121-101 to 121-1300.
North Carolina	L.1985 (Reg.Sess. 1986), c. 989	10-1-1986	G.S. §§ 59-101 to 59-1106.
North Dakota	1985, c. 504		NDCC 45-10.1-01 to 45-10.1-62, 45-12-01.
Ohio	1984, H.B. 607	4-1-1985	R.C. §§ 1782.01 to 1782.63.
Oklahoma[2]	1984, c. 50	11-1-1984	54 Okl.St.Ann. §§ 301 to 365.
Oregon	1985, c. 677	7-1-1986	ORS 70.005 to 70.490.
Pennsylvania	1988, Act 177	10-1-1989	15 Pa.C.S.A. §§ 8501 to 8594.
Rhode Island	1985, c. 390	1-1-1986	Gen.Laws 1956, §§ 7-13-1 to 7-13-65.
South Carolina	1984, No. 491	6-27-1984	Code 1976, §§ 33-42-10 to 33-42-2020.
South Dakota	SL 1986, c. 391	7-1-1986	SDCL 48-7-101 to 48-7-1105.
Tennessee	1988, c. 922	1-1-1989	T.C.A. §§ 61-2-101 to 61-2-1208.
Texas	1987, c. 49	9-1-1987	Vernon's Ann. Texas Civ. St. art. 6132a-1.
Utah	1990, c. 233	7-1-1990	U.C.A. 1953, 48-2a-101 to 48-2a-1107.
Vermont	1998, no. 149	1-1-1999	11 V.S.A. §§ 3401 to 3503.
Virginia	1985, c. 607	1-1-1987	Code 1950, §§ 50-73.1 to 50-73.78.
Washington	1981, c. 51	1-1-1982	West's RCWA 25.10.010 to 25.10.690.
West Virginia	1981, c. 208	1-1-1982	Code, 47-9-1 to 47-9-63.
Wisconsin	1983-85, Act 173	9-1-1984	W.S.A. 179.01 to 179.94.
Wyoming	1979, c. 153	7-1-1979	W.S. 1977 §§ 17-14-201 to 17-14-1104.

Louisiana limited partnerships are governed by La. Rev. Stat. Ann. § 9:3401 et seq.

[1]Date of approval.

[2]Enacted Revised Limited Partnership Act of 1976 without repealing the 1916 Limited Partnership Act.

Article 1. General Provisions

§101. *Definitions*

As used in this [Act], unless the context otherwise requires:

(1) "Certificate of limited partnership" means the certificate referred to in Section 201, and the certificate as amended or restated.

(2) "Contribution" means any cash, property, services rendered, or a promissory note or other binding obligation to contribute cash or property or to perform services, which a partner contributes to a limited partnership in his capacity as a partner.

(3) "Event of withdrawal of a general partner" means an event that causes a person to cease to be a general partner as provided in Section 402.

(4) "Foreign limited partnership" means a partnership formed under the laws of any state other than this State and having as partners one or more general partners and one or more limited partners.

(5) "General partner" means a person who has been admitted to a limited partnership as a general partner in accordance with the partnership agreement and named in the certificate of limited partnership as a general partner.

(6) "Limited partner" means a person who has been admitted to a limited partnership as a limited partner in accordance with the partnership agreement.

(7) "Limited partnership" and "domestic limited partnership" mean a partnership formed by two or more persons under the laws of this State and having one or more general partners and one or more limited partners.

(8) "Partner" means a limited or general partner.

(9) "Partnership agreement" means any valid agreement, written or oral, of the partners as to the affairs of a limited partnership and the conduct of its business.

(10) "Partnership interest" means a partner's share of the profits and losses of a limited partnership and the right to receive distributions of partnership assets.

(11) "Person" means a natural person, partnership, limited partnership (domestic or foreign), trust, estate, association, or corporation.

(12) "State" means a state, territory, or possession of the United States, the District of Columbia, or the Commonwealth of Puerto Rico.

§102. *Name*

The name of each limited partnership as set forth in its certificate of limited partnership:

(1) shall contain without abbreviation the words "limited partnership";

(2) may not contain the name of a limited partner unless (i) it is also the name of a general partner or the corporate name of a corporate general partner, or (ii) the business of the limited partnership had been carried on under that name before the admission of that limited partner;

(3) may not be the same as, or deceptively similar to, the

name of any corporation or limited partnership organized under the laws of this State or licensed or registered as a foreign corporation or limited partnership in this State; and

(4) may not contain the following words [here insert prohibited words].

§103. Reservation of Name

(a) The exclusive right to the use of a name may be reserved by:

(1) any person intending to organize a limited partnership under this [Act] and to adopt that name;

(2) any domestic limited partnership or any foreign limited partnership registered in this State which, in either case, intends to adopt that name;

(3) any foreign limited partnership intending to register in this State and adopt that name; and

(4) any person intending to organize a foreign limited partnership and intending to have it register in this State and adopt that name.

(b) The reservation shall be made by filing with the Secretary of State an application, executed by the applicant, to reserve a specified name. If the Secretary of State finds that the name is available for use by a domestic or foreign limited partnership, he [or she] shall reserve the name for the exclusive use of the applicant for a period of 120 days. Once having so reserved a name, the same applicant may not again reserve the same name until more than 60 days after the expiration of the last 120-day period for which that applicant reserved that name. The right to the exclusive use of a reserved name may be transferred to any other person by filing in the office of the Secretary of State a notice of the transfer, executed by the applicant for whom the name was reserved and specifying the name and address of the transferee.

§104. Specified Office and Agent

Each limited partnership shall continuously maintain in this State:

(1) an office, which may but need not be a place of its business in this State, at which shall be kept the records required by Section 105 to be maintained; and

(2) an agent for service of process on the limited partnership, which agent must be an individual resident of this State, a domestic corporation, or a foreign corporation authorized to do business in this State.

§105. Records to Be Kept

(a) Each limited partnership shall keep at the office referred to in Section 104(1) the following:

(1) a current list of the full name and last known business address of each partner, separately identifying the general partners (in alphabetical order) and the limited partners (in alphabetical order);

(2) a copy of the certificate of limited partnership and all certificates of amendment thereto, together with executed copies of any powers of attorney pursuant to which any certificate has been executed;

(3) copies of the limited partnership's federal, state and local income tax returns and reports, if any, for the three most recent years;

(4) copies of any then effective written partnership agreements and of any financial statements of the limited partnership for the three most recent years; and

(5) unless contained in a written partnership agreement, a writing setting out:

(i) the amount of cash and a description and statement of the agreed value of the other property or services contributed by each partner and which each partner has agreed to contribute;

(ii) the times at which or events on the happening of which any additional contributions agreed to be made by each partner are to be made;

(iii) any right of a partner to receive, or of a general partner to make, distributions to a partner which include a return of all or any part of the partner's contribution; and

(iv) any events upon the happening of which the limited partnership is to be dissolved and its affairs wound up.

(b) Records kept under this section are subject to inspection and copying at the reasonable request and at the expense of any partner during ordinary business hours.

§106. Nature of Business

A limited partnership may carry on any business that a partnership without limited partners may carry on except [here designate prohibited activities].

§107. Business Transactions of Partner With Partnership

Except as provided in the partnership agreement, a partner may lend money to and transact other business with the limited partnership and, subject to other applicable law, has the same rights and obligations with respect thereto as a person who is not a partner.

Article 2. Formation; Certificate of Limited Partnership

§201. Certificate of Limited Partnership

(a) In order to form a limited partnership, a certificate of limited partnership must be executed and filed in the office of the Secretary of State. The certificate shall set forth:

(1) the name of the limited partnership;

(2) the address of the office and the name and address of the agent for service of process required to be maintained by Section 104;

(3) the name and the business address of each general partner;

(4) the latest date upon which the limited partnership is to dissolve; and

(5) any other matters the general partners determine to include therein.

(b) A limited partnership is formed at the time of the filing of the certificate of limited partnership in the office of the Secretary of State or at any later time specified in the certificate of limited partnership if, in either case, there has been substantial compliance with the requirements of this section.

§202. Amendment to Certificate

(a) A certificate of limited partnership is amended by filing a certificate of amendment thereto in the office of the Secretary of State. The certificate shall set forth:

(1) the name of the limited partnership;

(2) the date of filing the certificate; and

(3) the amendment to the certificate.

(b) Within 30 days after the happening of any of the following events, an amendment to a certificate of limited partnership reflecting the occurrence of the event or events shall be filed:

(1) the admission of a new general partner;

(2) the withdrawal of a general partner; or

(3) the continuation of the business under Section 801 after an event of withdrawal of a general partner.

(c) A general partner who becomes aware that any statement in a certificate of limited partnership was false when made or that any arrangements or other facts described have changed, making the certificate inaccurate in any respect, shall promptly amend the certificate.

(d) A certificate of limited partnership may be amended at any time for any other proper purpose the general partners determine.

(e) No person has any liability because an amendment to a certificate of limited partnership has not been filed to reflect the occurrence of any event referred to in subsection (b) of this section if the amendment is filed within the 30-day period specified in subsection (b).

(f) A restated certificate of limited partnership may be executed and filed in the same manner as a certificate of amendment.

§203. Cancellation of Certificate

A certificate of limited partnership shall be cancelled upon the dissolution and the commencement of winding up of the partnership or at any other time there are no limited partners. A certificate of cancellation shall be filed in the office of the Secretary of State and set forth:

(1) the name of the limited partnership;

(2) the date of filing of its certificate of limited partnership;

(3) the reason for filing the certificate of cancellation;

(4) the effective date (which shall be a date certain) of cancellation if it is not to be effective upon the filing of the certificate; and

(5) any other information the general partners filing the certificate determine.

§204. Execution of Certificates

(a) Each certificate required by this Article to be filed in the office of the Secretary of State shall be executed in the following manner:

(1) an original certificate of limited partnership must be signed by all general partners;

(2) a certificate of amendment must be signed by at least one general partner and by each other general partner designated in the certificate as a new general partner; and

(3) a certificate of cancellation must be signed by all general partners.

(b) Any person may sign a certificate by an attorney-in-fact, but a power of attorney to sign a certificate relating to the admission of a general partner must specifically describe the admission.

(c) The execution of a certificate by a general partner constitutes an affirmation under the penalties of perjury that the facts stated therein are true.

§205. Execution by Judicial Act

If a person required by Section 204 to execute any certificate fails or refuses to do so, any other person who is adversely affected by the failure or refusal may petition [designate the appropriate court] to direct the execution of the certificate. If the court finds that it is proper for the certificate to be executed and that any person so designated has failed or refused to execute the certificate, it shall order the Secretary of State to record an appropriate certificate.

§206. Filing in Office of Secretary of State

(a) Town signed copies of the certificate of limited partnership and of any certificates of amendment or cancellation (or of any judicial decree of amendment or cancellation) shall be delivered to the Secretary of State. A person who executes a certificate as an agent or fiduciary need not exhibit evidence of his [or her] authority as a prerequisite to filing. Unless the Secretary of State finds that any certificate does not conform to law, upon receipt of all filing fees required by law he [or she] shall:

(1) endorse on each duplicate original the word "Filed" and the day, month, and year of the filing thereof;

(2) file one duplicate original in his [or her] office; and

(3) return the other duplicate original to the person who filed it or his [or her] representative.

(b) Upon the filing of a certificate of amendment (or judicial decree of amendment) in the office of the Secretary of State, the certificate of limited partnership shall be amended as set forth therein, and upon the effective date of a certificate of cancellation (or a judicial decree thereof), the certificate of limited partnership is cancelled.

§207. Liability for False Statement in Certificate

If any certificate of limited partnership or certificate of amendment or cancellation contains a false statement, one who suffers loss by reliance on the statement may recover damages for the loss from:

(1) any person who executes the certificate, or causes another to execute it on his behalf, and knew, and any general partner who knew or should have known, the statement to be false at the time the certificate was executed; and

(2) any general partner who thereafter knows or should have known that any agreement or other fact described in the certificate has changed, making the statement inaccurate in any respect within a sufficient time before the statement was relied upon reasonably to have enabled that general partner to cancel or amend the certificate, or to file a petition for its [judicial] cancellation or amendment.

§208. Scope of Notice

The fact that a certificate of limited partnership is on file in the office of the Secretary of State is notice that the partnership is a limited partnership and the persons designated therein as general partners are general partners, but it is not notice of any other fact.

§209. Delivery of Certificates to Limited Partners

Upon the return by the Secretary of State pursuant to Section 206 of a certificate marked "Filed," the general partners shall promptly deliver or mail a copy of the certificate of limited partnership and each certificate of amendment or cancellation to each limited partner unless the partnership agreement provides otherwise.

ARTICLE 3. LIMITED PARTNERS

§301. Admission of Limited Partners

(a) A person becomes a limited partner:

(1) at the time the limited partnership is formed; or

(2) at any later time specified in the records of the limited partnership for becoming a limited partner.

(b) After the filing of a limited partnership's original certificate of limited partnership, a person may be admitted as an additional limited partner:

(1) in the case of a person acquiring a partnership interest directly from the limited partnership, upon compliance with the partnership agreement or, if the partnership agreement does not so provide, upon the written consent of all partners; and

(2) in the case of an assignee of a partnership interest of a partner who has the power, as provided in Section 704, to grant the assignee the right to become a limited partner, upon the exercise of that power and compliance with any conditions limiting the grant or exercise of the power.

§302. Voting

Subject to Section 303, the partnership agreement may grant to all or a specified group of the limited partners the right to vote (on a per capita or other basis) upon any matter.

§303. Liability to Third Parties

(a) Except as provided in subsection (d), a limited partner is not liable for the obligations of a limited partnership unless he [or she] is also a general partner or, in addition to the exercise of his [or her] rights and powers as a limited partner, he [or she] participates in the control of the business. However, if the limited partner participates in the control of the business, he [or she] is liable only to persons who transact business with the limited partnership reasonably believing, based upon the limited partner's conduct, that the limited partner is a general partner.

(b) A limited partner does not participate in the control of the business within the meaning of subsection (a) solely by doing one or more of the following:

(1) being a contractor for or an agent or employee of the limited partnership or of a general partner or being an officer, director, or shareholder of a general partner that is a corporation;

(2) consulting with and advising a general partner with respect to the business of the limited partnership;

(3) acting as surety for the limited partnership or guaranteeing or assuming one or more specific obligations of the limited partnership;

(4) taking any action required or permitted by law to bring or pursue a derivative action in the right of the limited partnership;

(5) requesting or attending a meeting of partners;

(6) proposing, approving, or disapproving, by voting or otherwise, one or more of the following matters:

(i) the dissolution and winding up of the limited partnership;

(ii) the sale, exchange, lease, mortgage, pledge, or other transfer of all or substantially all of the assets of the limited partnership;

(iii) the incurrence of indebtedness by the limited partnership other than in the ordinary course of its business;

(iv) a change in the nature of the business;

(v) the admission or removal of a general partner;

(vi) the admission or removal of a limited partner;

(vii) a transaction involving an actual or potential conflict of interest between a general partner and the limited partnership or the limited partners;

(viii) an amendment to the partnership agreement or certificate of limited partnership; or

(ix) matters related to the business of the limited partnership not otherwise enumerated in this subsection (b), which the partnership agreement states in writing may be subject to the approval or disapproval of limited partners;

(7) winding up the limited partnership pursuant to Section 803; or

(8) exercising any right or power permitted to limited partners under this [Act] and not specifically enumerated in this subsection (b).

(c) The enumeration in subsection (b) does not mean that the possession or exercise of any other powers by a limited partner constitutes participation by him [or her] in the business of the limited partnership.

(d) A limited partner who knowingly permits his [or her] name to be used in the name of the limited partnership, except under circumstances permitted by Section 102(2), is liable to creditors who extend credit to the limited partnership without actual knowledge that the limited partner is not a general partner.

§304. Person Erroneously Believing Himself [or Herself] Limited Partner

(a) Except as provided in subsection (b), a person who makes a contribution to a business enterprise and erroneously but in good faith believes that he [or she] has become a limited partner in the enterprise is not a general partner in the enterprise and is not bound by its obligations by reason of making the contribution, receiving distributions from the enterprise, or exercising any rights of a limited partner, if, on ascertaining the mistake, he [or she]:

(1) causes an appropriate certificate of limited partnership or a certificate of amendment to be executed and filed; or

(2) withdraws from future equity participation in the enterprise by executing and filing in the office of the Secretary of State a certificate declaring withdrawal under this section.

(b) A person who makes a contribution of the kind described in subsection (a) is liable as a general partner to any third party who transacts business with the enterprise (i) before the person withdraws and an appropriate certificate is filed to show withdrawal, or (ii) before an appropriate certificate is filed to show that he [or she] is not a general partner, but in either case only if the third party actually believed in good faith that the person was a general partner at the time of the transaction.

§305. Information

Each limited partner has the right to:

(1) inspect and copy any of the partnership records required to be maintained by Section 105; and

(2) obtain from the general partners from time to time upon reasonable demand (i) true and full information regarding the state of the business and financial condition of the limited partnership, (ii) promptly after becoming available, a copy of the limited partnership's federal, state, and local income tax returns for each year, and (iii) other information regarding the affairs of the limited partnership as is just and reasonable.

Article 4. General Partners

§401. Admission of Additional General Partners

After the filing of a limited partnership's original certificate of limited partnership, additional general partners may be admitted as provided in writing in the partnership agreement or, if the partnership agreement does not provide in writing for the admission of additional general partners, with the written consent of all partners.

§402. Events of Withdrawal

Except as approved by the specific written consent of all partners at the time, a person ceases to be a general partner of a limited partnership upon the happening of any of the following events:

(1) the general partner withdraws from the limited partnership as provided in Section 602;

(2) the general partner ceases to be a member of the limited partnership as provided in Section 702;

(3) the general partner is removed as a general partner in accordance with the partnership agreement;

(4) unless otherwise provided in writing in the partnership agreement, the general partner: (i) makes an assignment for the benefit of creditors; (ii) files a voluntary petition in bankruptcy; (iii) is adjudicated a bankrupt or insolvent; (iv) files a petition or answer seeking for himself [or herself] any reorganization, arrangement, composition, readjustment, liquidation, dissolution, or similar relief under any statute, law, or regulation; (v) files an answer or other pleading admitting or failing to contest the material allegations of a petition filed against him [or her] in any proceeding of this nature; or (vi) seeks, consents to, or acquiesces in the appointment of a trustee, receiver, or liquidator of the general partner or of all or any substantial part of his [or her] properties;

(5) unless otherwise provided in writing in the partnership agreement, [120] days after the commencement of any proceeding against the general partner seeking reorganization, arrangement, composition, readjustment, liquidation, dissolution, or similar relief under any statute, law, or regulation, the proceeding has not been dismissed, or if within [90] days after the appointment without his [or her] consent or acquiescence of a trustee, receiver, or liquidator of the general partner or of all or any substantial part of his [or her] properties, the appointment is not vacated or stayed or within [90] days after the expiration of any such stay, the appointment is not vacated;

(6) in the case of a general partner who is a natural person,

(i) his [or her] death; or

(ii) the entry of an order by a court of competent jurisdiction adjudicating him [or her] incompetent to manage his [or her] person or his [or her] estate;

(7) in the case of a general partner who is acting as a general partner by virtue of being a trustee of a trust, the termination of the trust (but not merely the substitution of a new trustee);

(8) in the case of a general partner that is a separate partnership, the dissolution and commencement of winding up of the separate partnership;

(9) in the case of a general partner that is a corporation, the filing of a certificate of dissolution, or its equivalent, for the corporation or the revocation of its charter; or

(10) in the case of an estate, the distribution by the fiduciary of the estate's entire interest in the partnership.

§403. General Powers and Liabilities

(a) Except as provided in this [Act] or in the partnership agreement, a general partner of a limited partnership has the rights and powers and is subject to the restrictions of a partner in a partnership without limited partners.

(b) Except as provided in this [Act], a general partner of a limited partnership has the liabilities of a partner in a partnership without limited partners to persons other than the partnership and the other partners. Except as provided in this [Act] or in the partnership agreement, a general partner of a limited partnership has the liabilities of a partner in a partnership without limited partners to the partnership and to the other partners.

§404. Contributions by General Partner

A general partner of a limited partnership may make contributions to the partnership and share in the profits and losses of, and in distributions from, the limited partnership as a general partner. A general partner also may make contributions to and

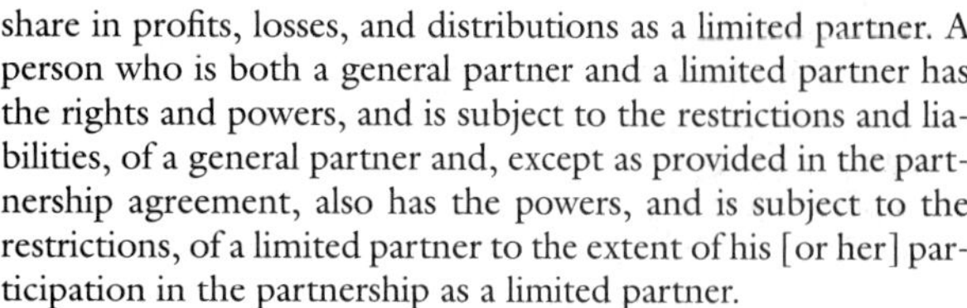

share in profits, losses, and distributions as a limited partner. A person who is both a general partner and a limited partner has the rights and powers, and is subject to the restrictions and liabilities, of a general partner and, except as provided in the partnership agreement, also has the powers, and is subject to the restrictions, of a limited partner to the extent of his [or her] participation in the partnership as a limited partner.

§405. Voting

The partnership agreement may grant to all or certain identified general partners the right to vote (on a per capita or any other basis), separately or with all or any class of the limited partners, on any matter.

ARTICLE 5. FINANCE

§501. Form of Contribution

The contribution of a partner may be in cash, property, or services rendered, or a promissory note or other obligation to contribute cash or property or to perform services.

§502. Liability for Contribution

(a) A promise by a limited partner to contribute to the limited partnership is not enforceable unless set out in a writing signed by the limited partner.

(b) Except as provided in the partnership agreement, a partner is obligated to the limited partnership to perform any enforceable promise to contribute cash or property or to perform services, even if he [or she] is unable to perform because of death, disability, or any other reason. If a partner does not make the required contribution of property or services, he [or she] is obligated at the option of the limited partnership to contribute cash equal to that portion of the value, as stated in the partnership records required to be kept pursuant to Section 105, of the stated contribution which has not been made.

(c) Unless otherwise provided in the partnership agreement, the obligation of a partner to make a contribution or return money or other property paid or distributed in violation of this [Act] may be compromised only by consent of all partners. Notwithstanding the compromise, a creditor of a limited partnership who extends credit, or, otherwise acts in reliance on that obligation after the partner signs a writing which reflects the obligation and before the amendment or cancellation thereof to reflect the compromise may enforce the original obligation.

§503. Sharing of Profits and Losses

The profits and losses of a limited partnership shall be allocated among the partners, and among classes of partners, in the manner provided in writing in the partnership agreement. If the partnership agreement does not so provide in writing, profits and losses shall be allocated on the basis of the value, as stated in the partnership records required to be kept pursuant to Section 105, of the contributions made by each partner to the extent they have been received by the partnership and have not been returned.

§504. Sharing of Distributions

Distributions of cash or other assets of a limited partnership shall be allocated among the partners and among classes of partners in the manner provided in writing in the partnership agreement. If the partnership agreement does not so provide in writing, distributions shall be made on the basis of the value, as stated in the partnership records required to be kept pursuant to Section 105, of the contributions made by each partner to the extent they have been received by the partnership and have not been returned.

ARTICLE 6. DISTRIBUTIONS AND WITHDRAWAL

§601. Interim Distributions

Except as provided in this Article, a partner is entitled to receive distributions from a limited partnership before his [or her] withdrawal from the limited partnership and before the dissolution and winding up thereof to the extent and at the times or upon the happening of the events specified in the partnership agreement.

§602. Withdrawal of General Partner

A general partner may withdraw from a limited partnership at any time by giving written notice to the other partners, but if the withdrawal violates the partnership agreement, the limited partnership may recover from the withdrawing general partner damages for breach of the partnership agreement and offset the damages against the amount otherwise distributable to him [or her].

§603. Withdrawal of Limited Partner

A limited partner may withdraw from a limited partnership at the time or upon the happening of events specified in writing in the partnership agreement. If the agreement does not specify in writing the time or the events upon the happening of which a limited partner may withdraw or a definite time for the dissolution and winding up of the limited partnership, a limited partner may withdraw upon not less than six months' prior written notice to each general partner at his [other] address on the books of the limited partnership at its office in this State.

§604. Distribution Upon Withdrawal

Except as provided in this Article, upon withdrawal any withdrawing partner is entitled to receive any distribution to which he [or she] is entitled under the partnership agreement and, if not otherwise provided in the agreement, he [or she] is entitled to receive, within a reasonable time after withdrawal, the fair value of his [or her] interest in the limited partnership as of the date of withdrawal based upon his [or her] right to share in distributions from the limited partnership.

§605. Distribution in Kind

Except as provided in writing in the partnership agreement, a partner, regardless of the nature of his [or her] contribution, has no right to demand and receive any distribution from a limited partnership in any form other than cash. Except as provided in writing in the partnership agreement, a partner may not be compelled to accept a distribution of any asset in kind from a limited partnership to the extent that the percentage of the asset distributed to him [or her] exceeds a percentage of that asset which is equal to the percentage in which he [or she] shares in distributions from the limited partnership.

§606. Right to Distribution

At the time a partner becomes entitled to receive a distribution, he [or she] has the status of, and is entitled to all remedies available to, a creditor of the limited partnership with respect to the distribution.

§607. Limitations on Distribution

A partner may not receive a distribution from a limited partnership to the extent that, after giving effect to the distribution, all liabilities of the limited partnership, other than liabilities to partners on account of their partnership interests, exceed the fair value of the partnership assets.

§608. Liability Upon Return of Contribution

(a) If a partner has received the return of any part of his [or her] contribution without violation of the partnership agreement or this [Act], he [or she] is liable to the limited partnership for a period of one year thereafter for the amount of the returned contribution, but only to the extent necessary to discharge the limited partnership's liabilities to creditors who extended credit to the limited partnership during the period the contribution was held by the partnership.

(b) If a partner has received the return of any part of his [or her] contribution in violation of the partnership agreement or this [Act], he [or she] is liable to the limited partnership for a period of six years thereafter for the amount of the contribution wrongfully returned.

(c) A partner receives a return of his [or her] contribution to the extent that a distribution to him [or her] reduces his [or her] share of the fair value of the net assets of the limited partnership below the value, as set forth in the partnership records required to be kept pursuant to Section 105, of his contribution which has not been distributed to him [or her].

ARTICLE 7. ASSIGNMENT OF PARTNERSHIP INTERESTS

§701. Nature of Partnership Interest

A partnership interest is personal property.

§702. Assignment of Partnership Interest

Except as provided in the partnership agreement, a partnership interest is assignable in whole or in part. An assignment of a partnership interest does not dissolve a limited partnership or entitle the assignee to become or to exercise any rights of a partner. An assignment entitles the assignee to receive, to the extent assigned, only the distribution to which the assignor would be entitled. Except as provided in the partnership agreement, a partner ceases to be a partner upon assignment of all his [or her] partnership interest.

§703. Rights of Creditor

On application to a court of competent jurisdiction by any judgment creditor of a partner, the court may charge the partnership interest of the partner with payment of the unsatisfied amount of the judgment with interest. To the extent so charged, the judgment creditor has only the rights of an assignee of the partnership interest. This [Act] does not deprive any partner of the benefit of any exemption laws applicable to his [or her] partnership interest.

§704. Right of Assignee to Become Limited Partner

(a) An assignee of a partnership interest, including an assignee of a general partner, may become a limited partner if and to the extent that (i) the assignor gives the assignee that right in accordance with authority described in the partnership agreement, or (ii) all other partners consent.

(b) An assignee who has become a limited partner has, to the extent assigned, the rights and powers, and is subject to the restrictions and liabilities, of a limited partner under the partnership agreement and this [Act]. An assignee who becomes a limited partner also is liable for the obligations of his [or her] assignor to make and return contributions as provided in Articles 5 and 6. However, the assignee is not obligated for liabilities unknown to the assignee at the time he [or she] became a limited partner.

(c) If an assignee of a partnership interest becomes a limited partner, the assignor is not released from his [or her] liability to the limited partnership under Sections 207 and 502.

§705. Power of Estate of Deceased or Incompetent Partner

If a partner who is an individual dies or a court of competent jurisdiction adjudges him [or her] to be incompetent to manage his [or her] person or his [or her] property, the partner's executor, administrator, guardian, conservator, or other legal representative may exercise all of the partner's rights for the purpose of settling his [or her] estate or administering his [or her] property, including any power the partner had to give an assignee the right to become a limited partner. If a partner is a corporation, trust, or other entity and is dissolved or terminated, the powers of that partner may be exercised by its legal representative or successor.

ARTICLE 8. DISSOLUTION

§801. Nonjudicial Dissolution

A limited partnership is dissolved and its affairs shall be wound up upon the happening of the first to occur of the following:

(1) at the time specified in the certificate of limited partnership;

(2) upon the happening of events specified in writing in the partnership agreement;

(3) written consent of all partners;

(4) an event of withdrawal of a general partner unless at the time there is at least one other general partner and the written provisions of the partnership agreement permit the business of the limited partnership to be carried on by the remaining general partner and that partner does so, but the limited partnership is not dissolved and is not required to be wound up by reason of any event of withdrawal if, within 90 days after the withdrawal, all partners agree in writing to continue the business of the limited partnership and to the appointment of one or more additional general partners if necessary or desired; or

(5) entry of a decree of judicial dissolution under Section 802.

§802. *Judicial Dissolution*

On application by or for a partner the [designate the appropriate court] court may decree dissolution of a limited partnership whenever it is not reasonably practicable to carry on the business in conformity with the partnership agreement.

§803. *Winding Up*

Except as provided in the partnership agreement, the general partners who have not wrongfully dissolved a limited partnership or, if none, the limited partners, may wind up the limited partnership's affairs; but the [designate the appropriate court] court may wind up the limited partnership's affairs upon application of any partner, his [or her] legal representative, or assignee.

§804. *Distribution of Assets*

Upon the winding up of a limited partnership, the assets shall be distributed as follows:

(1) to creditors, including partners who are creditors, to the extent permitted by law, in satisfaction of liabilities of the limited partnership other than liabilities for distributions to partners under Section 601 or 604;

(2) except as provided in the partnership agreement, to partners and former partners in satisfaction of liabilities for distributions under Section 601 or 604; and

(3) except as provided in the partnership agreement, to partners first for the return of their contributions and secondly respecting their partnership interests, in the proportions in which the partners share in distributions.

Article 9. Foreign Limited Partnerships

§901. *Law Governing*

Subject to the Constitution of this State, (i) the laws of the state under which a foreign limited partnership is organized govern its organization and internal affairs and the liability of its limited partners, and (ii) a foreign limited partnership may not be denied registration by reason of any difference between those laws and the laws of this State.

§902. *Registration*

Before transacting business in this State, a foreign limited partnership shall register with the Secretary of State. In order to register, a foreign limited partnership shall submit to the Secretary of State, in duplicate, an application for registration as a foreign limited partnership, signed and sworn to by a general partner and setting forth:

(1) the name of the foreign limited partnership and, if different, the name under which it proposes to register and transact business in this State;

(2) the State and date of its formation;

(3) the name and address of any agent for service of process on the foreign limited partnership whom the foreign limited partnership elects to appoint; the agent must be an individual resident of this State, a domestic corporation, or a foreign corporation having a place of business in, and authorized to do business in, this State;

(4) a statement that the Secretary of State is appointed the agent of the foreign limited partnership for service of process if no agent has been appointed under paragraph (3) or, if appointed, the agent's authority has been revoked or if the agent cannot be found or served with the exercise of reasonable diligence;

(5) the address of the office required to be maintained in the state of its organization by the laws of that state or, if not so required, of the principal office of the foreign limited partnership;

(6) the name and business address of each general partner; and

(7) the address of the office at which is kept a list of the names and addresses of the limited partners and their capital contributions, together with an undertaking by the foreign limited partnership to keep those records until the foreign limited partnership's registration in this State is cancelled or withdrawn.

§903. *Issuance of Registration*

(a) If the Secretary of State finds that an application for registration conforms to law and all requisite fees have been paid, he [or she] shall:

(1) endorse on the application the word "Filed", and the month, day, and year of the filing thereof;

(2) file in his [or her] office a duplicate original of the application; and

(3) issue a certificate of registration to transact business in this State.

(b) The certificate of registration, together with a duplicate original of the application, shall be returned to the person who filed the application or his [or her] representative.

§904. *Name*

A foreign limited partnership may register with the Secretary of State under any name, whether or not it is the name under which it is registered in its state of organization, that includes without abbreviation the words "limited partnership" and that could be registered by a domestic limited partnership.

§905. *Changes and Amendments*

If any statement in the application for registration of a foreign limited partnership was false when made or any arrangements or other facts described have changed, making the application inaccurate in any respect, the foreign limited partnership shall promptly file in the office of the Secretary of State a certificate, signed and sworn to by a general partner, correcting such statement.

§906. *Cancellation of Registration*

A foreign limited partnership may cancel its registration by filing with the Secretary of State a certificate of cancellation signed and sworn to by a general partner. A cancellation does not terminate the authority of the Secretary of State to accept service of process on the foreign limited partnership with respect to [claims for relief] [causes of action] arising out of the transactions of business in this State.

§907. *Transaction of Business Without Registration*

(a) A foreign limited partnership transacting business in this State may not maintain any action, suit, or proceeding in any court of this State until it has registered in this State.

(b) The failure of a foreign limited partnership to register in this State does not impair the validity of any contract or act of the foreign limited partnership or prevent the foreign limited partnership from defending any action, suit, or proceeding in any court of this State.

(c) A limited partner of a foreign limited partnership is not liable as a general partner of the foreign limited partnership solely by reason of having transacted business in this State without registration.

(d) A foreign limited partnership, by transacting business in this State without registration, appoints the Secretary of State as its agent for service of process with respect to [claims for relief] [causes of action] arising out of the transaction of business in this State.

§908. *Action by [Appropriate Official]*

The [designate the appropriate official] may bring an action to restrain a foreign limited partnership from transacting business in this State in violation of this Article.

Article 10. Derivative Actions

§1001. *Right of Action*

A limited partner may bring an action in the right of a limited partnership to recover a judgment in its favor if general partners with authority to do so have refused to bring the action or if an effort to cause those general partners to bring the action is not likely to succeed.

§1002. *Proper Plaintiff*

In a derivative action, the plaintiff must be a partner at the time of bringing the action and (i) must have been a partner at the time of the transaction of which he [or she] complains or (ii) his [or her] status as a partner must have devolved upon him [or her] by operation of law or pursuant to the terms of the partnership agreement from a person who was a partner at the time of the transaction.

§1003. *Pleading*

In a derivative action, the complaint shall set forth with particularity the effort of the plaintiff to secure initiation of the action by a general partner or the reasons for not making the effort.

§1004. *Expenses*

If a derivative action is successful, in whole or in part, or if anything is received by the plaintiff as a result of a judgment, compromise, or settlement of an action or claim, the court may award the plaintiff reasonable expenses, including reasonable attorney's fees, and shall direct him [or her] to remit to the limited partnership the remainder of those proceeds received by him [or her].

Article 11. Miscellaneous

§1101. *Construction and Application*

This [Act] shall be so applied and construed to effectuate its general purpose to make uniform the law with respect to the subject of this [Act] among states enacting it.

§1102. *Short Title*

This [Act] may be cited as the Uniform Limited Partnership Act.

§1103. *Severability*

If any provision of this [Act] or its application to any person or circumstances is held invalid, the invalidity does not affect other provisions or applications of the [Act] which can be given effect without the invalid provision or application, and to this end the provisions of this [Act] are severable.

§1104. *Effective Date, Extended Effective Date and Repeal*

Except as set forth below, the effective date of this [Act] is ______________ and the following acts [list existing limited partnership acts] are hereby repealed:

(1) The existing provisions for execution and filing of certificates of limited partnerships and amendments thereunder and cancellations thereof continue in effect until [specify time required to create central filing system] the extended effective date, and Sections 102, 103, 104, 105, 201, 202, 203, 204 and 206 are not effective until the extended effective date.

(2) Section 402, specifying the conditions under which a general partner ceases to be a member of a limited partnership, is not effective until the extended effective date, and the applicable provisions of existing law continue to govern until the extended effective date.

(3) Sections 501, 502 and 608 apply only to contributions and distributions made after the effective date of this [Act].

(4) Section 704 applies only to assignments made after the effective date of this [Act].

(5) Article 9, dealing with registration of foreign limited partnerships, is not effective until the extended effective date.

(6) Unless otherwise agreed by the partners, the applicable provisions of existing law governing allocation of profits and losses (rather than the provisions of Section 503), distributions to a withdrawing partner (rather than the provisions of Section 604), and distributions of assets upon the winding up of a limited partnership (rather than the provisions of Section 804) govern limited partnerships formed before the effective date of this [Act].

§1105. *Rules for Cases Not Provided for in This [Act]*

In any case not provided for in this [Act] the provisions of the Uniform Partnership Act govern.

§1106. *Savings Clause*

The repeal of any statutory provision by this [Act] does not impair, or otherwise affect, the organization or the continued existence of a limited partnership existing at the effective date of this [Act], nor does the repeal of any existing statutory provision by this [Act] impair any contract or affect any right accrued before the effective date of this [Act].

APPENDIX

Revised Model Business Corporation Act

Subchapter B. Issuance of Shares

§6.20. Subscription for Shares Before Incorporation
§6.21. Issuance of Shares
§6.22. Liability of Shareholders
§6.23. Share Dividends
§6.24. Share Options
§6.25. Form and Content of Certificates
§6.26. Shares Without Certificates
§6.27. Restriction on Transfer of Shares and Other Securities
§6.28. Expense of Issue

Subchapter C. Subsequent Acquisition of Shares by Shareholders and Corporation

§6.30. Shareholders' Preemptive Rights
§6.31. Corporation's Acquisition of Its Own Shares

Subchapter D. Distributions

§6.40. Distributions to Shareholders

Chapter 7. Shareholders

Subchapter A. Meetings

§7.01. Annual Meeting
§7.02. Special Meeting
§7.03. Court-ordered Meeting
§7.04. Action Without Meeting
§7.05. Notice of Meeting
§7.06. Waiver of Notice
§7.07. Record Date
§7.08. Conduct of the Meeting

Subchapter B. Voting

§7.20. Shareholders' List for Meeting
§7.21. Voting Entitlement of Shares
§7.22. Proxies
§7.23. Shares Held by Nominees
§7.24. Corporation's Acceptance of Votes
§7.25. Quorum and Voting Requirements for Voting Groups
§7.26. Action by Single and Multiple Voting Groups
§7.27. Greater Quorum or Voting Requirements
§7.28. Voting for Directors; Cumulative Voting
§7.29. Inspectors of Election

Subchapter C. Voting Trusts and Agreements

§7.30. Voting Trusts
§7.31. Voting Agreements
§7.31. Shareholder Agreements

Subchapter D. Derivative Proceedings

§7.40. Subchapter Definitions
§7.41. Standing
§7.42. Demand
§7.43. Stay of Proceedings
§7.44. Dismissal
§7.45. Discontinuance or Settlement
§7.46. Payment of Expenses
§7.47. Applicability to Foreign Corporations

Chapter 8. Directors and Officers

Subchapter A. Board of Directors

§8.01. Requirement for and Duties of Board of Directors
§8.02. Qualifications of Directors
§8.03. Number and Election of Directors
§8.04. Election of Directors by Certain Classes of Shareholders
§8.05. Terms of Directors Generally
§8.06. Staggered Terms for Directors
§8.07. Resignation of Directors
§8.08. Removal of Directors by Shareholders
§8.09. Removal of Directors by Judicial Proceeding
§8.10. Vacancy on Board
§8.11. Compensation of Directors

Subchapter B. Meetings and Action of the Board

§8.20. Meetings
§8.21. Action Without Meeting
§8.22. Notice of Meeting
§8.23. Waiver of Notice
§8.24. Quorum and Voting
§8.25. Committees

Subchapter C. Standards of Conduct

§8.30. Standards of Conduct for Directors
§8.31. Standards of Liability for Directors
§8.32. [Reserved]
§8.33. Directors' Liability for Unlawful Distributions

Subchapter D. Officers

§8.40. Required Officers
§8.41. Duties of Officers
§8.42. Standards of Conduct for Officers
§8.43. Resignation and Removal of Officers
§8.44. Contract Rights of Officers

Subchapter E. Indemnification

§8.50. Subchapter Definitions
§8.51. Permissible Indemnification
§8.52. Mandatory Indemnification
§8.53. Advance for Expenses
§8.54. Court-Ordered Indemnification and Advance for Expenses
§8.55. Determination and Authorization of Indemnification
§8.56. Officers
§8.57. Insurance
§8.58. Variation by Corporate Action; Application of Subchapter
§8.59. Exclusivity of Subchapter

Subchapter F. Directors' Conflicting Interest Transactions

§8.60. Subchapter Definitions
§8.61. Judicial Action

Chapter 1. General Provisions

Subchapter A. Short Title and Reservation of Power

§1.01. Short Title

This Act shall be known and may be cited as the "[name of state] Business Corporation Act."

§1.02. Reservation of Power to Amend or Repeal

The [name of state legislature] has power to amend or repeal all or part of this Act at any time and all domestic and foreign corporations subject to this Act are governed by the amendment or repeal.

Subchapter B. Filing Documents

§1.20. Filing Requirements

(a) A document must satisfy the requirements of this section, and of any other section that adds to or varies from these requirements, to be entitled to filing by the secretary of state.

(b) This Act must require or permit filing the document in the office of the secretary of state.

(c) The document must contain the information required by this Act. It may contain other information as well.

(d) The document must be typewritten or printed or, if electronically transmitted, it must be in a format that can be retrieved or reproduced in typewritten or printed form.

(e) The document must be in the English language. A corporate name need not be in English if written in English letters or Arabic or Roman numerals, and the certificate of existence required of foreign corporations need not be in English if accompanied by a reasonably authenticated English translation.

(f) The document must be executed:

(1) by the chairman of the board of directors of a domestic or foreign corporation, by its president, or by another of its officers;

(2) if directors have not been selected or the corporation has not been formed, by an incorporator; or

(3) if the corporation is in the hands of a receiver, trustee, or other court-appointed fiduciary, by that fiduciary.

(g) The person executing the document shall sign it and state beneath or opposite his signature the name and the capacity in which he signs. The document may but need not contain a corporate seal, attestation acknowledgment, or verification.

(h) If the secretary of state has prescribed a mandatory form for the document under section 1.21, the document must be in or on the prescribed form.

(i) The document must be delivered to the office of the secretary of state for filing. Delivery may be made by electronic transmission if and to the extent permitted by the secretary of state. If it is filed in typewritten or printed form and not transmitted electronically, the secretary of state may require one exact or conformed copy to be delivered with the document (except as provided in sections 5.03 and 15.09).

(j) When the document is delivered to the office of the secretary of state for filing, the correct filing fee, and any franchise tax, license fee, or penalty required to be paid therewith by this Act or other law must be paid or provision for payment made in a manner permitted by the secretary of state.

§1.21. Forms

(a) The secretary of state may prescribe and furnish on request forms for: (1) an application for a certificate of existence, (2) a foreign corporation's application for a certificate of authority to transact business in this state, (3) a foreign corporation's application for a certificate of withdrawal, and (4) the annual report. If the secretary of state so requires, use of these forms is mandatory.

(b) The secretary of state may prescribe and furnish on request forms for other documents required or permitted to be filed by this Act but their use is not mandatory.

§1.22. Filing, Service, and Copying Fees

(a) The secretary of state shall collect the following fees when the documents described in this subsection are delivered to him for filing:

§1.23. Effective Time and Date of Document

(a) Except as provided in subsection (b) and section 1.24(c), a document accepted for filing is effective:

(1) at the date and time of filing, as evidenced by such means as the secretary of state may use for the purpose of recording the date and time of filing; or

(2) at the time specified in the document as its effective time on the date it is filed.

(b) A document may specify a delayed effective time and date, and if it does so the document becomes effective at the time and date specified. If a delayed effective date but no time is specified, the document is effective at the close of business on that date. A delayed effective date for a document may not be later than the 90th day after the date it is filed.

	Document	
(1)	Articles of incorporation	$_________.
(2)	Application for use of indistinguishable name	$_________.
(3)	Application for reserved name	$_________.
(4)	Notice of transfer of reserved name	$_________.
(5)	Application for registered name	$_________.
(6)	Application for renewal of registered name	$_________.
(7)	Corporation's statement of change of registered agent or registered office or both	$_________.
(8)	Agent's statement of change of registered office for each affected corporation not to exceed a total of	$_________.
(9)	Agent's statement of resignation	No fee.
(10)	Amendment of articles of incorporation	$_________.
(11)	Restatement of articles of incorporation with amendment of articles	$_________.
(12)	Articles of merger or share exchange	$_________.
(13)	Articles of dissolution	$_________.
(14)	Articles of revocation of dissolution	$_________.
(15)	Certificate of administrative dissolution	No fee.
(16)	Application for reinstatement following administrative dissolution	$_________.
(17)	Certificate of reinstatement	No fee.
(18)	Certificate of judicial dissolution	No fee.
(19)	Application for certificate of authority	$_________.
(20)	Application for amended certificate of authority	$_________.
(21)	Application for certificate of withdrawal	$_________.
(22)	Certificate of revocation of authority to transact business	No fee.
(23)	Annual report	$_________.
(24)	Articles of correction	$_________.
(25)	Application for certificate of existence or authorization	$_________.
(26)	Any other document required or permitted to be filed by this Act	$_________.

(b) The secretary of state shall collect a fee of $_________ each time process is served on him under this Act. The party to a proceeding causing service of process is entitled to recover this fee as costs if he prevails in the proceeding.

(c) The secretary of state shall collect the following fees for copying and certifying the copy of any filed document relating to a domestic or foreign corporation:

(1) $_________ a page for copying; and
(2) $_________ for the certificate.

§1.24. Correcting Filed Document

(a) A domestic or foreign corporation may correct a document filed by the secretary of state if (1) the document contains an inaccuracy, or (2) the document was defectively executed, attested, sealed, verified, or acknowledged, or (3) the electronic transmission was defective.

(b) A document is corrected:

(1) by preparing articles of correction that (i) describe the document (including its filing date) or attach a copy of it to the articles, (ii) specify the inaccuracy or defect to be corrected, and (iii) correct the inaccuracy or defect; and

(2) by delivering the articles to the secretary of state for filing.

(c) Articles of correction are effective on the effective date of the document they correct except as to persons relying on the uncorrected document and adversely affected by the correction. As to those persons, articles of correction are effective when filed.

§1.25. Filing Duty of Secretary of State

(a) If a document delivered to the office of the secretary of state for filing satisfies the requirements of section 1.20, the secretary of state shall file it.

(b) The secretary of state files a document by recording it as filed on the date and time of receipt. After filing a document, except as provided in sections 5.03 and 15.10, the secretary of state shall deliver to the domestic or foreign corporation or its representative a copy of the document with an acknowledgment of the date and time of filing.

(c) If the secretary of state refuses to file a document, he shall return it to the domestic or foreign corporation or its representative within five days after the document was delivered, together with a brief, written explanation of the reason for his refusal.

(d) The secretary of state's duty to file documents under this section is ministerial. His filing or refusing to file a document does not:

(1) affect the validity or invalidity of the document in whole or part;

(2) relate to the correctness or incorrectness of information contained in the document;

(3) create a presumption that the document is valid or invalid or that information contained in the document is correct or incorrect.

§1.26. Appeal from Secretary of State's Refusal to File Document

(a) If the secretary of state refuses to file a document delivered to his office for filing, the domestic or foreign corporation may appeal the refusal within 30 days after the return of the document to the [name or describe] court [of the county where the corporation's principal office (or, if none in this state, its registered office) is or will be located] [of county]. The appeal is commenced by petitioning the court to compel filing the document and by attaching to the petition the document and the secretary of state's explanation of his refusal to file.

(b) The court may summarily order the secretary of state to file the document or take other action the court considers appropriate.

(c) The court's final decision may be appealed as in other civil proceedings.

§1.27. *Evidentiary Effect of Copy of Filed Document*

A certificate from the secretary of state delivered with a copy of a document filed by the secretary of state is conclusive evidence that the original document is on file with the secretary of state.

§1.28. *Certificate of Existence*

(a) Anyone may apply to the secretary of state to furnish a certificate of existence for a domestic corporation or a certificate of authorization for a foreign corporation.

(b) A certificate of existence or authorization sets forth:

(1) the domestic corporation's corporate name or the foreign corporation's corporate name used in this state;

(2) that (i) the domestic corporation is duly incorporated under the law of this state, the date of its incorporation, and the period of its duration if less than perpetual; or (ii) that the foreign corporation is authorized to transact business in this state;

(3) that all fees, taxes, and penalties owed to this state have been paid, if (i) payment is reflected in the records of the secretary of state and (ii) nonpayment affects the existence or authorization of the domestic or foreign corporation;

(4) that its most recent annual report required by section 16.22 has been delivered to the secretary of state;

(5) that articles of dissolution have not been filed; and

(6) other facts of record in the office of the secretary of state that may be requested by the applicant.

(c) Subject to any qualification stated in the certificate, a certificate of existence or authorization issued by the secretary of state may be relied upon as conclusive evidence that the domestic or foreign corporation is in existence or is authorized to transact business in this state.

§1.29. *Penalty for Signing False Document*

(a) A person commits an offense if he signs a document he knows is false in any material respect with intent that the document be delivered to the secretary of state for filing.

(b) An offense under this section is a [________] misdemeanor [punishable by a fine of not to exceed [$________].

Subchapter C. Secretary of State

§1.30. *Powers*

The secretary of state has the power reasonably necessary to perform the duties required of him by this Act.

Subchapter D. Definitions

§1.40. *Act Definitions*

In this Act:

(1) "Articles of incorporation" include amended and restated articles of incorporation and articles of merger.

(2) "Authorized shares" means the shares of all classes a domestic or foreign corporation is authorized to issue.

(3) "Conspicuous" means so written that a reasonable person against whom the writing is to operate should have noticed it. For example, printing in italics or boldface or contrasting color, or typing in capitals or underlined, is conspicuous.

(4) "Corporation" or "domestic corporation" means a corporation for profit, which is not a foreign corporation, incorporated under or subject to the provisions of this Act.

(5) "Deliver" or "delivery" means any method of delivery used in conventional commercial practice, including delivery by hand, mail, commercial delivery, and electronic transmission.

(6) "Distribution" means a direct or indirect transfer of money or other property (except its own shares) or incurrence of indebtedness by a corporation to or for the benefit of its shareholders in respect of any of its shares. A distribution may be in the form of a declaration or payment of a dividend; a purchase, redemption, or other acquisition of shares; a distribution of indebtedness; or otherwise.

(7) "Effective date of notice" is defined in section 1.41.

(7a) "Electronic transmission" or "electronically transmitted" means any process of communications not directly involving the physical transfer of paper that is suitable for the retention, retrieval, and reproduction of information by the recipient.

(8) "Employee" includes an officer but not a director. A director may accept duties that make him also an employee.

(9) "Entity" includes corporation and foreign corporation; not-for-profit corporation; profit and not-for-profit unincorporated association; business trust, estate, partnership, trust, and two or more persons having a joint or common economic interest; and state, United States, and foreign government.

(10) "Foreign corporation" means a corporation for profit incorporated under a law other than the law of this state.

(11) "Governmental subdivision" includes authority, county, district, and municipality.

(12) "Includes" denotes a partial definition.

(13) "Individual" includes the estate of an incompetent or deceased individual.

(14) "Means" denotes an exhaustive definition.

(15) "Notice" is defined in section 1.41.

(16) "Person" includes individual and entity.

(17) "Principal office" means the office (in or out of this state) so designated in the annual report where the principal executive offices of a domestic or foreign corporation are located.

(18) "Proceeding" includes civil suit and criminal, administrative, and investigatory action.

(19) "Record date" means the date established under chapter 6 or 7 on which a corporation determines the identity of its shareholders and their shareholdings for purposes of this Act. The determinations shall be made as of the close of business on the record date unless another time for doing so is specified when the record date is fixed.

(20) "Secretary" means the corporate officer to whom the board of directors has delegated responsibility under section 8.40(c) for custody of the minutes of the meetings of the board of directors and of the shareholders and for authenticating records of the corporation.

(21) "Shares" means the units into which the proprietary interests in a corporation are divided.

(22) "Shareholder" means the person in whose name shares are registered in the records of a corporation or the beneficial owner of shares to the extent of the rights granted by a nominee certificate on file with a corporation.

(22A) "Sign" or "signature" includes any manual, facsimile, conformed, or electronic signature.

(23) "State," when referring to a part of the United States, includes a state and commonwealth (and their agencies and governmental subdivisions) and a territory and insular possession (and their agencies and governmental subdivisions) of the United States.

(24) "Subscriber" means a person who subscribes for shares in a corporation, whether before or after incorporation.

(25) "United States" includes district, authority, bureau, commission, department, and any other agency of the United States.

(26) "Voting group" means all shares of one or more classes or series that under the articles of incorporation or this Act are entitled to vote and be counted together collectively on a matter at a meeting of shareholders. All shares entitled by the articles of incorporation or this Act to vote generally on the matter are for that purpose a single voting group.

§1.41. Notice

(a) Notice under this Act must be in writing unless oral notice is reasonable under the circumstances. Notice by electronic transmission is written notice.

(b) Notice may be communicated in person; by mail or other method of delivery; or by telephone, voice mail, or other electronic means. If these forms of personal notice are impracticable, notice may be communicated by a newspaper of general circulation in the area where published; or by radio, television, or other form of public broadcast communication.

(c) Written notice by a domestic or foreign corporation to its shareholder, if in a comprehensible form, is effective (i) upon deposit in the United States mail, if mailed postpaid and correctly addressed to the shareholder's address shown in the corporation's current record of shareholders, or (ii) when electronically transmitted to the shareholder in a manner authorized by the shareholder.

(d) Written notice to a domestic or foreign corporation (authorized to transact business in this state) may be addressed to its registered agent at its registered office or to the corporation or its secretary at its principal office shown in its most recent annual report or, in the case of a foreign corporation that has not yet delivered an annual report, in its application for a certificate of authority.

(e) Except as provided in subsection (c), written notice, if in a comprehensible form, is effective at the earliest of the following:

(1) when received;

(2) five days after its deposit in the United States Mail, if mailed postpaid and correctly addressed;

(3) on the date shown on the return receipt, if sent by registered or certified mail, return receipt requested, and the receipt is signed by or on behalf of the addressee.

(f) Oral notice is effective when communicated if communicated in a comprehensible manner.

(g) If this Act prescribes notice requirements for particular circumstances, those requirements govern. If articles of incorporation or bylaws prescribe notice requirements, not inconsistent with this section or other provisions of this Act, those requirements govern.

§1.42. Number of Shareholders

(a) For purposes of this Act, the following identified as a shareholder in a corporation's current record of shareholders constitutes one shareholder:

(1) three or fewer coowners;

(2) a corporation, partnership, trust, estate, or other entity;

(3) the trustees, guardians, custodians, or other fiduciaries of a single trust, estate, or account.

(b) For purposes of this Act, shareholdings registered in substantially similar names constitute one shareholder if it is reasonable to believe that the names represent the same person.

Chapter 2. Incorporation

§2.01. Incorporators

One or more persons may act as the incorporator or incorporators of a corporation by delivering articles of incorporation to the secretary of state for filing.

§2.02. Articles of Incorporation

(a) The articles of incorporation must set forth:

(1) a corporate name for the corporation that satisfies the requirements of section 4.01;

(2) the number of shares the corporation is authorized to issue;

(3) the street address of the corporation's initial registered office and the name of its initial registered agent at that office; and

(4) the name and address of each incorporator.

(b) The articles of incorporation may set forth:

(1) the names and addresses of the individuals who are to serve as the initial directors;

(2) provisions not inconsistent with law regarding:

(i) the purpose or purposes for which the corporation is organized;

(ii) managing the business and regulating the affairs of the corporation;

(iii) defining, limiting, and regulating the powers of the corporation, its board of directors, and shareholders;

(iv) a par value for authorized shares or classes of shares;

(v) the imposition of personal liability on shareholders for the debts of the corporation to a specified extent and upon specified conditions;

(3) any provision that under this Act is required or permitted to be set forth in the bylaws;

(4) a provision eliminating or limiting the liability of a director to the corporation or its shareholders for money damages for any action taken, or any failure to take any action, as a director, except liability for (A) the amount of a financial benefit received by a director to which he is not entitled; (B) an intentional infliction of harm on the corporation or the shareholders; (C) a violation of section 8.33; or (D) an intentional violation of criminal law; and

(5) a provision permitting or making obligatory indemnification of a director for liability (as defined in section 8.50(5)) to any person for any action taken, or any failure to take any action, as a director, except liability for (A) receipt of a financial benefit to which he is not entitled, (B) an intentional infliction of harm on the corporation or its shareholders, (C) a violation of section 8.33, or (D) an intentional violation of criminal law.

(c) The articles of incorporation need not set forth any of the corporate powers enumerated in this Act.

§2.03. *Incorporation*

(a) Unless a delayed effective date is specified, the corporate existence begins when the articles of incorporation are filed.

(b) The secretary of state's filing of the articles of incorporation is conclusive proof that the incorporators satisfied all conditions precedent to incorporation except in a proceeding by the state to cancel or revoke the incorporation or involuntarily dissolve the corporation.

§2.04. *Liability for Preincorporation Transactions*

All persons purporting to act as or on behalf of a corporation, knowing there was no incorporation under this Act, are jointly and severally liable for all liabilities created while so acting.

§2.05. *Organization of Corporation*

(a) After incorporation:

(1) if initial directors are named in the articles of incorporation, the initial directors shall hold an organizational meeting, at the call of a majority of the directors, to complete the organization of the corporation by appointing officers, adopting bylaws, and carrying on any other business brought before the meeting;

(2) if initial directors are not named in the articles, the incorporator or incorporators shall hold an organizational meeting at the call of a majority of the incorporators:

(i) to elect directors and complete the organization of the corporation; or

(ii) to elect a board of directors who shall complete the organization of the corporation.

(b) Action required or permitted by this Act to be taken by incorporators at an organizational meeting may be taken without a meeting if the action taken is evidenced by one or more written consents describing the action taken and signed by each incorporator.

(c) An organizational meeting may be held in or out of this state.

§2.06. *Bylaws*

(a) The incorporators or board of directors of a corporation shall adopt initial bylaws for the corporation.

(b) The bylaws of a corporation may contain any provision for managing the business and regulating the affairs of the corporation that is not inconsistent with law or the articles of incorporation.

§2.07. *Emergency Bylaws*

(a) Unless the articles of incorporation provide otherwise, the board of directors of a corporation may adopt bylaws to be effective only in an emergency defined in subsection (d). The emergency bylaws, which are subject to amendment or repeal by the shareholders, may make all provisions necessary for managing the corporation during the emergency, including:

(1) procedures for calling a meeting of the board of directors;

(2) quorum requirements for the meeting; and

(3) designation of additional or substitute directors.

(b) All provisions of the regular bylaws consistent with the emergency bylaws remain effective during the emergency. The emergency bylaws are not effective after the emergency ends.

(c) Corporate action taken in good faith in accordance with the emergency bylaws:

(1) binds the corporation; and

(2) may not be used to impose liability on a corporate director, officer, employee, or agent.

(d) An emergency exists for purposes of this section if a quorum of the corporation's directors cannot readily be assembled because of some catastrophic event.

Chapter 3. Purposes and Powers

§3.01. *Purposes*

(a) Every corporation incorporated under this Act has the purpose of engaging in any lawful business unless a more limited purpose is set forth in the articles of incorporation.

(b) A corporation engaging in a business that is subject to regulation under another statute of this state may incorporate under this Act only if permitted by, and subject to all limitations of, the other statute.

§3.02. General Powers

Unless its articles of incorporation provide otherwise, every corporation has perpetual duration and succession in its corporate name and has the same powers as an individual to do all things necessary or convenient to carry out its business and affairs, including without limitation power:

(1) to sue and be sued, complain and defend in its corporate name;

(2) to have a corporate seal, which may be altered at will, and to use it, or a facsimile of it, by impressing or affixing it or in any other manner reproducing it;

(3) to make and amend bylaws, not inconsistent with its articles of incorporation or with the laws of this state, for managing the business and regulating the affairs of the corporation;

(4) to purchase, receive, lease, or otherwise acquire, and own, hold, improve, use, and otherwise deal with, real or personal property, or any legal or equitable interest in property, wherever located;

(5) to sell, convey, mortgage, pledge, lease, exchange, and otherwise dispose of all or any part of its property;

(6) to purchase, receive, subscribe for, or otherwise acquire; own, hold, vote, use, sell, mortgage, lend, pledge, or otherwise dispose of; and deal in and with shares or other interests in, or obligations of, any other entity;

(7) to make contracts and guarantees, incur liabilities, borrow money, issue its notes, bonds, and other obligations (which may be convertible into or include the option to purchase other securities of the corporation), and secure any of its obligations by mortgage or pledge of any of its property, franchises, or income;

(8) to lend money, invest and reinvest its funds, and receive and hold real and personal property as security for repayment;

(9) to be a promoter, partner, member, associate, or manager of any partnership, joint venture, trust, or other entity;

(10) to conduct its business, locate offices, and exercise the powers granted by this Act within or without this state;

(11) to elect directors and appoint officers, employees, and agents of the corporation, define their duties, fix their compensation, and lend them money and credit;

(12) to pay pensions and establish pension plans, pension trusts, profit sharing plans, share bonus plans, share option plans, and benefit or incentive plans for any or all of its current or former directors, officers, employees, and agents;

(13) to make donations for the public welfare or for charitable, scientific, or educational purposes;

(14) to transact any lawful business that will aid governmental policy;

(15) to make payments or donations, or do any other act, not inconsistent with law, that furthers the business and affairs of the corporation.

§3.03. Emergency Powers

(a) In anticipation of or during an emergency defined in subsection (d), the board of directors of a corporation may:

(1) modify lines of succession to accommodate the incapacity of any director, officer, employee, or agent; and

(2) relocate the principal office, designate alternative principal offices or regional offices, or authorize the officers to do so.

(b) During an emergency defined in subsection (d), unless emergency bylaws provide otherwise:

(1) notice of a meeting of the board of directors need be given only to those directors whom it is practicable to reach and may be given in any practicable manner, including by publication and radio; and

(2) one or more officers of the corporation present at a meeting of the board of directors may be deemed to be directors for the meeting, in order of rank and within the same rank in order of seniority, as necessary to achieve a quorum.

(c) Corporate action taken in good faith during an emergency under this section to further the ordinary business affairs of the corporation:

(1) binds the corporation; and

(2) may not be used to impose liability on a corporate director, officer, employee, or agent.

(d) An emergency exists for purposes of this section if a quorum of the corporation's directors cannot readily be assembled because of some catastrophic event.

§3.04. Ultra Vires

(a) Except as provided in subsection (b), the validity of corporate action may not be challenged on the ground that the corporation lacks or lacked power to act.

(b) A corporation's power to act may be challenged:

(1) in a proceeding by a shareholder against the corporation to enjoin the act;

(2) in a proceeding by the corporation, directly, derivatively, or through a receiver, trustee, or other legal representative, against an incumbent or former director, officer, employee, or agent of the corporation; or

(3) in a proceeding by the Attorney General under section 14.30.

(c) In a shareholder's proceeding under subsection (b)(1) to enjoin an unauthorized corporate act, the court may enjoin or set aside the act, if equitable and if all affected persons are parties to the proceeding, and may award damages for loss (other than anticipated profits) suffered by the corporation or another party because of enjoining the unauthorized act.

Chapter 4. Name

§4.01. Corporate Name

(a) A corporate name:

(1) must contain the word "corporation," "incorporated," "company," or "limited," or the abbreviation "corp.," "inc.," "co.," or "ltd.," or words or abbreviations of like import in another language; and

(2) may not contain language stating or implying that the corporation is organized for a purpose other than that permitted by section 3.01 and its articles of incorporation. . . .

§4.02. *Reserved Name*

(a) A person may reserve the exclusive use of a corporate name, including a fictitious name for a foreign corporation whose corporate name is not available, by delivering an application to the secretary of state for filing. The application must set forth the name and address of the applicant and the name proposed to be reserved. If the secretary of state finds that the corporate name applied for is available, he shall reserve the name for the applicant's exclusive use for a nonrenewable 120-day period.

(b) The owner of a reserved corporate name may transfer the reservation to another person by delivering to the secretary of state a signed notice of the transfer that states the name and address of the transferee.

§4.03. *Registered Name*

(a) A foreign corporation may register its corporate name, or its corporate name with any addition required by section 15.06, if the name is distinguishable upon the records of the secretary of state from the corporate names that are not available under section 4.01(b)(3).

(b) A foreign corporation registers its corporate name, or its corporate name with any addition required by section 15.06, by delivering to the secretary of state for filing an application:

(1) setting forth its corporate name, or its corporate name with any addition required by section 15.06, the state or country and date of its incorporation, and a brief description of the nature of the business in which it is engaged; and

(2) accompanied by a certificate of existence (or a document of similar import) from the state or country of incorporation.

(c) The name is registered for the applicant's exclusive use upon the effective date of the application.

(d) A foreign corporation whose registration is effective may renew it for successive years by delivering to the secretary of state for filing a renewal application, which complies with the requirements of subsection (b), between October 1 and December 31 of the preceding year. The renewal application when filed renews the registration for the following calendar year.

(e) A foreign corporation whose registration is effective may thereafter qualify as a foreign corporation under the registered name or consent in writing to the use of that name by a corporation thereafter incorporated under this Act or by another foreign corporation thereafter authorized to transact business in this state. The registration terminates when the domestic corporation is incorporated or the foreign corporation qualifies or consents to the qualification of another foreign corporation under the registered name.

Chapter 5. Office and Agent

§5.01. *Registered Office and Registered Agent*

Each corporation must continuously maintain in this state:

(1) a registered office that may be the same as any of its places of business; and

(2) a registered agent, who may be:

(i) an individual who resides in this state and whose business office is identical with the registered office;

(ii) a domestic corporation or not-for-profit domestic corporation whose business office is identical with the registered office; or

(iii) a foreign corporation or not-for-profit foreign corporation authorized to transact business in this state whose business office is identical with the registered office.

§5.02. *Change of Registered Office or Registered Agent*

(a) A corporation may change its registered office or registered agent by delivering to the secretary of state for filing a statement of change that sets forth:

(1) the name of the corporation;

(2) the street address of its current registered office;

(3) if the current registered office is to be changed, the street address of the new registered office;

(4) the name of its current registered agent;

(5) if the current registered agent is to be changed, the name of the new registered agent and the new agent's written consent (either on the statement or attached to it) to the appointment; and

(6) that after the change or changes are made, the street addresses of its registered office and the business office of its registered agent will be identical.

(b) If a registered agent changes the street address of his business office, he may change the street address of the registered office of any corporation for which he is the registered agent by notifying the corporation in writing of the change and signing (either manually or in facsimile) and delivering to the secretary of state for filing a statement that complies with the requirements of subsection (a) and recites that the corporation has been notified of the change.

§5.03. *Resignation of Registered Agent*

(a) A registered agent may resign his agency appointment by signing and delivering to the secretary of state for filing the signed original and two exact or conformed copies of a statement of resignation. The statement may include a statement that the registered office is also discontinued.

(b) After filing the statement the secretary of state shall mail one copy to the registered office (if not discontinued) and the other copy to the corporation at its principal office.

(c) The agency appointment is terminated, and the registered office discontinued if so provided, on the 31st day after the date on which the statement was filed.

§5.04. *Service on Corporation*

(a) A corporation's registered agent is the corporation's agent for service of process, notice, or demand required or permitted by law to be served on the corporation.

(b) If a corporation has no registered agent, or the agent cannot with reasonable diligence be served, the corporation may be served by registered or certified mail, return receipt requested, addressed to the secretary of the corporation at its principal office. Service is perfected under this subsection at the earliest of:

(1) the date the corporation receives the mail;

(2) the date shown on the return receipt, if signed on behalf of the corporation; or

(3) five days after its deposit in the United States Mail, as evidenced by the postmark, if mailed postpaid and correctly addressed.

(c) This section does not prescribe the only means, or necessarily the required means, of serving a corporation.

CHAPTER 6. SHARES AND DISTRIBUTIONS

SUBCHAPTER A. SHARES

§6.01. Authorized Shares

(a) The articles of incorporation must prescribe the classes of shares and the number of shares of each class that the corporation is authorized to issue. If more than one class of shares is authorized, the articles of incorporation must prescribe a distinguishing designation for each class, and, prior to the issuance of shares of a class, the preferences, limitations, and relative rights of that class must be described in the articles of incorporation. All shares of a class must have preferences, limitations, and relative rights identical with those of other shares of the same class except to the extent otherwise permitted by section 6.02.

(b) The articles of incorporation must authorize (1) one or more classes of shares that together have unlimited voting rights, and (2) one or more classes of shares (which may be the same class or classes as those with voting rights) that together are entitled to receive the net assets of the corporation upon dissolution.

(c) The articles of incorporation may authorize one or more classes of shares that:

(1) have special, conditional, or limited voting rights, or no right to vote, except to the extent prohibited by this Act;

(2) are redeemable or convertible as specified in the articles of incorporation (i) at the option of the corporation, the shareholder, or another person or upon the occurrence of a designated event; (ii) for cash, indebtedness, securities, or other property; (iii) in a designated amount or in an amount determined in accordance with a designated formula or by reference to extrinsic data or events;

(3) entitle the holders to distributions calculated in any manner, including dividends that may be cumulative, noncumulative, or partially cumulative;

(4) have preference over any other class of shares with respect to distributions, including dividends and distributions upon the dissolution of the corporation.

(d) The description of the designations, preferences, limitations, and relative rights of share classes in subsection (c) is not exhaustive.

§6.02. Terms of Class or Series Determined by Board of Directors

(a) If the articles of incorporation so provide, the board of directors may determine, in whole or part, the preferences, limitations, and relative rights (within the limits set forth in section 6.01) of (1) any class of shares before the issuance of any shares of that class or (2) one or more series within a class before the issuance of any shares of that series.

(b) Each series of a class must be given a distinguishing designation.

(c) All shares of a series must have preferences, limitations, and relative rights identical with those of other shares of the same series and, except to the extent otherwise provided in the description of the series, with those of other series of the same class.

(d) Before issuing any shares of a class or series created under this section, the corporation must deliver to the secretary of state for filing articles of amendment, which are effective without shareholder action, that set forth:

(1) the name of the corporation;

(2) the text of the amendment determining the terms of the class or series of shares;

(3) the date it was adopted; and

(4) a statement that the amendment was duly adopted by the board of directors.

§6.03. Issued and Outstanding Shares

(a) A corporation may issue the number of shares of each class or series authorized by the articles of incorporation. Shares that are issued are outstanding shares until they are reacquired, redeemed, converted, or canceled.

(b) The reacquisition, redemption, or conversion of outstanding shares is subject to the limitations of subsection (c) of this section and to section 6.40.

(c) At all times that shares of the corporation are outstanding, one or more shares that together have unlimited voting rights and one or more shares that together are entitled to receive the net assets of the corporation upon dissolution must be outstanding.

§6.04. Fractional Shares

(a) A corporation may:

(1) issue fractions of a share or pay in money the value of fractions of a share;

(2) arrange for disposition of fractional shares by the shareholders;

(3) issue scrip in registered or bearer form entitling the holder to receive a full share upon surrendering enough scrip to equal a full share.

(b) Each certificate representing scrip must be conspicuously labeled "scrip" and must contain the information required by section 6.25(b).

(c) The holder of a fractional share is entitled to exercise the rights of a shareholder, including the right to vote, to receive dividends, and to participate in the assets of the corporation upon liquidation. The holder of scrip is not entitled to any of these rights unless the scrip provides for them.

(d) The board of directors may authorize the issuance of scrip subject to any condition considered desirable, including:

(1) that the scrip will become void if not exchanged for full shares before a specified date; and

(2) that the shares for which the scrip is exchangeable may be sold and the proceeds paid to the scripholders.

SUBCHAPTER B. ISSUANCE OF SHARES

§6.20. *Subscription for Shares Before Incorporation*

(a) A subscription for shares entered into before incorporation is irrevocable for six months unless the subscription agreement provides a longer or shorter period or all the subscribers agree to revocation.

(b) The board of directors may determine the payment terms of subscriptions for shares that were entered into before incorporation, unless the subscription agreement specifies them. A call for payment by the board of directors must be uniform so far as practicable as to all shares of the same class or series, unless the subscription agreement specifies otherwise.

(c) Shares issued pursuant to subscriptions entered into before incorporation are fully paid and nonassessable when the corporation receives the consideration specified in the subscription agreement.

(d) If a subscriber defaults in payment of money or property under a subscription agreement entered into before incorporation, the corporation may collect the amount owed as any other debt. Alternatively, unless the subscription agreement provides otherwise, the corporation may rescind the agreement and may sell the shares if the debt remains unpaid more than 20 days after the corporation sends written demand for payment to the subscriber.

(e) A subscription agreement entered into after incorporation is a contract between the subscriber and the corporation subject to section 6.21.

§6.21. *Issuance of Shares*

(a) The powers granted in this section to the board of directors may be reserved to the shareholders by the articles of incorporation.

(b) The board of directors may authorize shares to be issued for consideration consisting of any tangible or intangible property or benefit to the corporation, including cash, promissory notes, services performed, contracts for services to be performed, or other securities of the corporation.

(c) Before the corporation issues shares, the board of directors must determine that the consideration received or to be received for shares to be issued is adequate. That determination by the board of directors is conclusive insofar as the adequacy of consideration for the issuance of shares relates to whether the shares are validly issued, fully paid, and nonassessable.

(d) When the corporation receives the consideration for which the board of directors authorized the issuance of shares, the shares issued therefore are fully paid and nonassessable.

(e) The corporation may place in escrow shares issued for a contract for future services or benefits or a promissory note, or make other arrangements to restrict the transfer of the shares, and may credit distributions in respect of the shares against their purchase price, until the services are performed, the note is paid, or the benefits received. If the services are not performed, the note is not paid, or the benefits are not received, the shares escrowed or restricted and the distributions credited may be cancelled in whole or part.

§6.22. *Liability of Shareholders*

(a) A purchaser from a corporation of its own shares is not liable to the corporation or its creditors with respect to the shares except to pay the consideration for which the shares were authorized to be issued (section 6.21) or specified in the subscription agreement (section 6.20).

(b) Unless otherwise provided in the articles of incorporation, a shareholder of a corporation is not personally liable for the acts or debts of the corporation except that he may become personally liable by reason of his own acts or conduct.

§6.23. *Share Dividends*

(a) Unless the articles of incorporation provide otherwise, shares may be issued pro rata and without consideration to the corporation's shareholders or to the shareholders of one or more classes or series. An issuance of shares under this subsection is a share dividend.

(b) Shares of one class or series may not be issued as a share dividend in respect of shares of another class or series unless (1) the articles of incorporation so authorize, (2) a majority of the votes entitled to be cast by the class or series to be issued approve the issue, or (3) there are no outstanding shares of the class or series to be issued.

(c) If the board of directors does not fix the record date for determining shareholders entitled to a share dividend, it is the date the board of directors authorizes the share dividend.

§6.24. *Share Options*

A corporation may issue rights, options, or warrants for the purchase of shares of the corporation. The board of directors shall determine the terms upon which the rights, options, or warrants are issued, their form and content, and the consideration for which the shares are to be issued.

§6.25. *Form and Content of Certificates*

(a) Shares may but need not be represented by certificates. Unless this Act or another statute expressly provides otherwise, the rights and obligations of shareholders are identical whether or not their shares are represented by certificates.

(b) At a minimum each share certificate must state on its face:

(1) the name of the issuing corporation and that it is organized under the law of this state;

(2) the name of the person to whom issued; and

(3) the number and class of shares and the designation of the series, if any, the certificate represents.

(c) If the issuing corporation is authorized to issue different classes of shares or different series within a class, the designations, relative rights, preferences, and limitations applicable to each class and the variations in rights, preferences, and limitations determined for each series (and the authority of the board of directors to determine variations for future series) must be summarized on the front or back of each certificate. Alternatively, each certificate may state conspicuously on its front or back that the corporation will furnish the shareholder this information on request in writing and without charge.

(d) Each share certificate (1) must be signed (either manually or in facsimile) by two officers designated in the bylaws or by the board of directors and (2) may bear the corporate seal or its facsimile.

(e) If the person who signed (either manually or in facsimile) a share certificate no longer holds office when the certificate is issued, the certificate is nevertheless valid.

§6.26. *Shares Without Certificates*

(a) Unless the articles of incorporation or bylaws provide otherwise, the board of directors of a corporation may authorize the issue of some or all of the shares of any or all of its classes or series without certificates. The authorization does not affect shares already represented by certificates until they are surrendered to the corporation.

(b) Within a reasonable time after the issue or transfer of shares without certificates, the corporation shall send the shareholder a written statement of the information required on certificates by section 6.25(b) and (c), and, if applicable, section 6.27.

§6.27. *Restriction on Transfer of Shares and Other Securities*

(a) The articles of incorporation, bylaws, an agreement among shareholders, or an agreement between shareholders and the corporation may impose restrictions on the transfer or registration of transfer of shares of the corporation. A restriction does not affect shares issued before the restriction was adopted unless the holders of the shares are parties to the restriction agreement or voted in favor of the restriction.

(b) A restriction on the transfer or registration of transfer of shares is valid and enforceable against the holder or a transferee of the holder if the restriction is authorized by this section and its existence is noted conspicuously on the front or back of the certificate or is contained in the information statement required by section 6.26(b). Unless so noted, a restriction is not enforceable against a person without knowledge of the restriction.

(c) A restriction on the transfer or registration of transfer of shares is authorized:

(1) to maintain the corporation's status when it is dependent on the number or identity of its shareholders;

(2) to preserve exemptions under federal or state securities law;

(3) for any other reasonable purpose.

(d) A restriction on the transfer or registration of transfer of shares may:

(1) obligate the shareholder first to offer the corporation or other persons (separately, consecutively, or simultaneously) an opportunity to acquire the restricted shares;

(2) obligate the corporation or other persons (separately, consecutively, or simultaneously) to acquire the restricted shares;

(3) require the corporation, the holders of any class of its shares, or another person to approve the transfer of the restricted shares, if the requirement is not manifestly unreasonable;

(4) prohibit the transfer of the restricted shares to designated persons or classes of persons, if the prohibition is not manifestly unreasonable.

(e) For purposes of this section, "shares" includes a security convertible into or carrying a right to subscribe for or acquire shares.

§6.28. *Expense of Issue*

A corporation may pay the expenses of selling or underwriting its shares, and of organizing or reorganizing the corporation, from the consideration received for shares.

SUBCHAPTER C. SUBSEQUENT ACQUISITION OF SHARES BY SHAREHOLDERS AND CORPORATION

§6.30. *Shareholders' Preemptive Rights*

(a) The shareholders of a corporation do not have a preemptive right to acquire the corporation's unissued shares except to the extent the articles of incorporation so provide.

(b) A statement included in the articles of incorporation that "the corporation elects to have preemptive rights" (or words of similar import) means that the following principles apply except to the extent the articles of incorporation expressly provide otherwise:

(1) The shareholders of the corporation have a preemptive right, granted on uniform terms and conditions prescribed by the board of directors to provide a fair and reasonable opportunity to exercise the right, to acquire proportional amounts of the corporation's unissued shares upon the decision of the board of directors to issue them.

(2) A shareholder may waive his preemptive right. A waiver evidenced by a writing is irrevocable even though it is not supported by consideration.

(3) There is no preemptive right with respect to:

(i) shares issued as compensation to directors, officers, agents, or employees of the corporation, its subsidiaries or affiliates;

(ii) shares issued to satisfy conversion or option rights created to provide compensation to directors, officers, agents, or employees of the corporation, its subsidiaries or affiliates;

(iii) shares authorized in articles of incorporation that are issued within six months from the effective date of incorporation;

(iv) shares sold otherwise than for money.

(4) Holders of shares of any class without general voting rights but with preferential rights to distributions or assets have no preemptive rights with respect to shares of any class.

(5) Holders of shares of any class with general voting rights but without preferential rights to distributions or assets have no preemptive rights with respect to shares of any class with preferential rights to distributions or assets unless the shares with preferential rights are convertible into or

carry a right to subscribe for or acquire shares without preferential rights.

(6) Shares subject to preemptive rights that are not acquired by shareholders may be issued to any person for a period of one year after being offered to shareholders at a consideration set by the board of directors that is not lower than the consideration set for the exercise of preemptive rights. An offer at a lower consideration or after the expiration of one year is subject to the shareholders' preemptive rights.

(c) For purposes of this section, "shares" includes a security convertible into or carrying a right to subscribe for or acquire shares.

§6.31. *Corporation's Acquisition of Its Own Shares*

(a) A corporation may acquire its own shares and shares so acquired constitute authorized but unissued shares.

(b) If the articles of incorporation prohibit the reissue of acquired shares, the number of authorized shares is reduced by the number of shares acquired, effective upon amendment of the articles of incorporation.

(c) The board of directors may adopt articles of amendment under this section without shareholder action and deliver them to the secretary of state for filing. The articles must set forth:

(1) the name of the corporation;

(2) the reduction in the number of authorized shares, itemized by class and series; and

(3) the total number of authorized shares, itemized by class and series, remaining after reduction of the shares.

Subchapter D. Distributions

§6.40. *Distributions to Shareholders*

(a) A board of directors may authorize and the corporation may make distributions to its shareholders subject to restriction by the articles of incorporation and the limitation in subsection (c).

(b) If the board of directors does not fix the record date for determining shareholders entitled to a distribution (other than one involving a purchase, redemption, or other acquisition of the corporation's shares), it is the date the board of directors authorizes the distribution.

(c) No distribution may be made if, after giving it effect:

(1) the corporation would not be able to pay its debts as they become due in the usual course of business; or

(2) the corporation's total assets would be less than the sum of its total liabilities plus (unless the articles of incorporation permit otherwise) the amount that would be needed, if the corporation were to be dissolved at the time of the distribution, to satisfy the preferential rights upon dissolution of shareholders whose preferential rights are superior to those receiving the distribution.

(d) The board of directors may base a determination that a distribution is not prohibited under subsection (c) either on financial statements prepared on the basis of accounting practices and principles that are reasonable in the circumstances or on a fair valuation or other method that is reasonable in the circumstances.

(e) Except as provided in subsection (g), the effect of a distribution under subsection (c) is measured:

(1) in the case of distribution by purchase, redemption, or other acquisition of the corporation's shares, as of the earlier of (i) the date money or other property is transferred or debt incurred by the corporation or (ii) the date the shareholder ceases to be a shareholder with respect to the acquired shares;

(2) in the case of any other distribution of indebtedness, as of the date the indebtedness is distributed; and

(3) in all other cases, as of (i) the date the distribution is authorized if the payment occurs within 120 days after the date of authorization or (ii) the date the payment is made if it occurs more than 120 days after the date of authorization.

(f) A corporation's indebtedness to a shareholder incurred by reason of a distribution made in accordance with this section is at parity with the corporation's indebtedness to its general, unsecured creditors except to the extent subordinated by agreement.

(g) Indebtedness of a corporation, including indebtedness issued as a distribution, is not considered a liability for purposes of determinations under subsection (c) if its terms provide that payment of principal and interest are made only if and to the extent that payment of a distribution to shareholders could then be made under this section. If the indebtedness is issued as a distribution, each payment of principal or interest is treated as a distribution, the effect of which is measured on the date the payment is actually made.

Chapter 7. Shareholders

Subchapter A. Meetings

§7.01. *Annual Meeting*

(a) A corporation shall hold a meeting of shareholders annually at a time stated in or fixed in accordance with the bylaws.

(b) Annual shareholders' meetings may be held in or out of this state at the place stated in or fixed in accordance with the bylaws. If no place is stated in or fixed in accordance with the bylaws, annual meetings shall be held at the corporation's principal office.

(c) The failure to hold an annual meeting at the time stated in or fixed in accordance with a corporation's bylaws does not affect the validity of any corporate action.

§7.02. *Special Meeting*

(a) A corporation shall hold a special meeting of shareholders:

(1) on call of its board of directors or the person or persons authorized to do so by the articles of incorporation or bylaws; or

(2) if shareholders having at least 10 percent of all the votes entitled to be cast on an issue proposed to be considered at the proposed special meeting sign, date, and deliver to the corporation one or more written demands for the meeting describing the purpose or purposes for which it is to be held, provided that the articles of incorporation may

fix a lower percentage or a higher percentage not exceeding 25 percent of all the votes entitled to be cast on any issue proposed to be considered. Unless otherwise provided in the articles of incorporation, a written demand for a special meeting may be revoked by a writing to that effect received by the corporation prior to the receipt by the corporation of demands sufficient in number to require the holding of a special meeting.

(b) If not otherwise fixed under section 7.03 or 7.07, the record date for determining shareholders entitled to demand a special meeting is the date the first shareholder signs the demand.

(c) Special shareholders' meetings may be held in or out of this state at the place stated in or fixed in accordance with the bylaws. If no place is stated or fixed in accordance with the bylaws, special meetings shall be held at the corporation's principal office.

(d) Only business within the purpose or purposes described in the meeting notice required by section 7.05(c) may be conducted at a special shareholders' meeting.

§7.03. *Court-Ordered Meeting*

(a) The [name or describe] court of the county where a corporation's principal office (or, if none in this state, its registered office) is located may summarily order a meeting to be held:

(1) on application of any shareholder of the corporation entitled to participate in an annual meeting if an annual meeting was not held within the earlier of 6 months after the end of the corporation's fiscal year or 15 months after its last annual meeting; or

(2) on application of a shareholder who signed a demand for a special meeting valid under section 7.02, if:

(i) notice of the special meeting was not given within 30 days after the date the demand was delivered to the corporation's secretary; or

(ii) the special meeting was not held in accordance with the notice.

(b) The court may fix the time and place of the meeting, determine the shares entitled to participate in the meeting, specify a record date for determining shareholders entitled to notice of and to vote at the meeting, prescribe the form and content of the meeting notice, fix the quorum required for specific matters to be considered at the meeting (or direct that the votes represented at the meeting constitute a quorum for action on those matters), and enter other orders necessary to accomplish the purpose or purposes of the meeting.

§7.04. *Action Without Meeting*

(a) Action required or permitted by this Act to be taken at a shareholders' meeting may be taken without a meeting if the action is taken by all the shareholders entitled to vote on the action. The action must be evidenced by one or more written consents bearing the date of signature and describing the action taken, signed by all the shareholders entitled to vote on the action, and delivered to the corporation for inclusion in the minutes or filing with the corporate records.

(b) If not otherwise fixed under section 7.03 or 7.07, the record date for determining shareholders entitled to take action without a meeting is the date the first shareholder signs the consent under subsection (a). No written consent shall be effective to take the corporate action referred to therein unless, within 60 days of the earliest date appearing on a consent delivered to the corporation in the manner required by this section, written consents signed by all shareholders entitled to vote on the action are received by the corporation. A written consent may be revoked by a writing to that effect received by the corporation prior to the receipt by the corporation of unrevoked written consents sufficient in number to take corporate action.

(c) A consent signed under this section has the effect of a meeting vote and may be described as such in any document.

(d) If this Act requires that notice of proposed action be given to nonvoting shareholders and the action is to be taken by unanimous consent of the voting shareholders, the corporation must give its nonvoting shareholders written notice of the proposed action at least 10 days before the action is taken. The notice must contain or be accompanied by the same material that, under this Act, would have been required to be sent to nonvoting shareholders in a notice of meeting at which the proposed action would have been submitted to the shareholders for action.

§7.05. *Notice of Meeting*

(a) A corporation shall notify shareholders of the date, time, and place of each annual and special shareholders' meeting no fewer than 10 nor more than 60 days before the meeting date. Unless this Act or the articles of incorporation require otherwise, the corporation is required to give notice only to shareholders entitled to vote at the meeting.

(b) Unless this Act or the articles of incorporation require otherwise, notice of an annual meeting need not include a description of the purpose or purposes for which the meeting is called.

(c) Notice of a special meeting must include a description of the purpose or purposes for which the meeting is called.

(d) If not otherwise fixed under section 7.03 or 7.07, the record date for determining shareholders entitled to notice of and to vote at an annual or special shareholders' meeting is the day before the first notice is delivered to shareholders.

(e) Unless the bylaws require otherwise, if an annual or special shareholders' meeting is adjourned to a different date, time, or place, notice need not be given of the new date, time, or place if the new date, time, or place is announced at the meeting before adjournment. If a new record date for the adjourned meeting is or must be fixed under section 7.07, however, notice of the adjourned meeting must be given under this section to persons who are shareholders as of the new record date.

§7.06. *Waiver of Notice*

(a) A shareholder may waive any notice required by this Act, the articles of incorporation, or bylaws before or after the date and time stated in the notice. The waiver must be in writing, be signed by the shareholder entitled to the notice, and be delivered to the corporation for inclusion in the minutes or filing with the corporate records.

(b) A shareholder's attendance at a meeting:

(1) waives objection to lack of notice or defective notice of the meeting, unless the shareholder at the beginning of the meeting objects to holding the meeting or transacting business at the meeting;

(2) waives objection to consideration of a particular matter at the meeting that is not within the purpose or purposes described in the meeting notice, unless the shareholder objects to considering the matter when it is presented.

§7.07. Record Date

(a) The bylaws may fix or provide the manner of fixing the record date for one or more voting groups in order to determine the shareholders entitled to notice of a shareholders' meeting, to demand a special meeting, to vote, or to take any other action. If the bylaws do not fix or provide for fixing a record date, the board of directors of the corporation may fix a future date as the record date.

(b) A record date fixed under this section may not be more than 70 days before the meeting or action requiring a determination of shareholders.

(c) A determination of shareholders entitled to notice of or to vote at a shareholders' meeting is effective for any adjournment of the meeting unless the board of directors fixes a new record date, which it must do if the meeting is adjourned to a date more than 120 days after the date fixed for the original meeting.

(d) If a court orders a meeting adjourned to a date more than 120 days after the date fixed for the original meeting, it may provide that the original record date continues in effect or it may fix a new record date.

§7.08. Conduct of the Meeting

(a) At each meeting of shareholders, a chair shall preside. The chair shall be appointed as provided in the bylaws or, in the absence of such provision, by the board.

(b) The chair, unless the bylaws provide otherwise, shall determine the order of business and shall establish rules for the conduct of the meeting.

(c) The rules adopted for, and the conduct of, the meeting shall be fair to shareholders.

(d) The chair of the meeting shall announce at the meeting when the polls close for each matter voted upon. If no announcement is made, the polls shall be deemed to have closed upon the final adjournment of the meeting. After the polls close, no ballots, proxies or votes nor any revocations or changes thereto may be accepted.

SUBCHAPTER B. VOTING

§7.20. Shareholders' List for Meeting

(a) After fixing a record date for a meeting, a corporation shall prepare an alphabetical list of the names of all its shareholders who are entitled to notice of a shareholders' meeting. The list must be arranged by voting group (and within each voting group by class or series of shares) and show the address of and number of shares held by each shareholder.

(b) The shareholders' list must be available for inspection by any shareholder, beginning two business days after notice of the meeting is given for which the list was prepared and continuing through the meeting, at the corporation's principal office or at a place identified in the meeting notice in the city where the meeting will be held. A shareholder, his agent, or attorney is entitled on written demand to inspect and, subject to the requirements of section 16.02(c), to copy the list, during regular business hours and at his expense, during the period it is available for inspection.

(c) The corporation shall make the shareholders' list available at the meeting, and any shareholder, his agent, or attorney is entitled to inspect the list at any time during the meeting or any adjournment.

(d) If the corporation refuses to allow a shareholder, his agent, or attorney to inspect the shareholders' list before or at the meeting (or copy the list as permitted by subsection (b)), the [name or describe] court of the county where a corporation's principal office (or, if none in this state, its registered office) is located, on application of the shareholder, may summarily order the inspection or copying at the corporation's expense and may postpone the meeting for which the list was prepared until the inspection or copying is complete.

(e) Refusal or failure to prepare or make available the shareholders' list does not affect the validity of action taken at the meeting.

§7.21. Voting Entitlement of Shares

(a) Except as provided in subsections (b) and (c) or unless the articles of incorporation provide otherwise, each outstanding share, regardless of class, is entitled to one vote on each matter voted on at a shareholders' meeting. Only shares are entitled to vote.

(b) Absent special circumstances, the shares of a corporation are not entitled to vote if they are owned, directly or indirectly, by a second corporation, domestic or foreign, and the first corporation owns, directly or indirectly, a majority of the shares entitled to vote for directors of the second corporation.

(c) Subsection (b) does not limit the power of a corporation to vote any shares, including its own shares, held by it in a fiduciary capacity.

(d) Redeemable shares are not entitled to vote after notice of redemption is mailed to the holders and a sum sufficient to redeem the shares has been deposited with a bank, trust company, or other financial institution under an irrevocable obligation to pay the holders the redemption price on surrender of the shares.

§7.22. Proxies

(a) A shareholder may vote his shares in person or by proxy.

(b) A shareholder or his agent or attorney-in-fact may appoint a proxy to vote or otherwise act for the shareholder by signing an appointment form, or by an electronic trans-

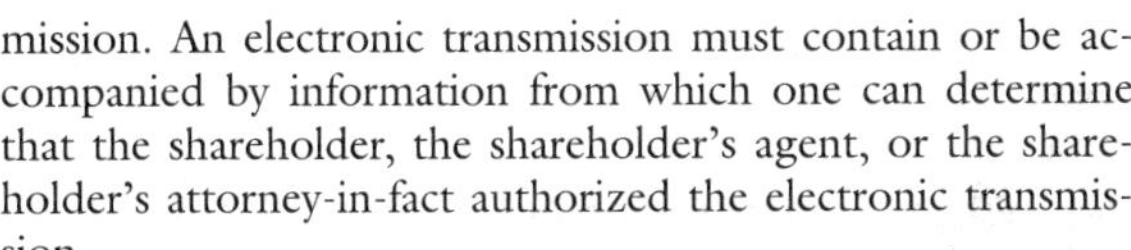

mission. An electronic transmission must contain or be accompanied by information from which one can determine that the shareholder, the shareholder's agent, or the shareholder's attorney-in-fact authorized the electronic transmission.

(c) An appointment of a proxy is effective when a signed appointment form or an electronic transmission of the appointment is received by the inspector of election or the officer or agent of the corporation authorized to tabulate votes. An appointment is valid for 11 months unless a longer period is expressly provided in the appointment.

(d) An appointment of a proxy is revocable unless the appointment form or electronic transmission conspicuously states that it is irrevocable and the appointment is coupled with an interest. Appointments coupled with an interest include the appointment of:

(1) a pledgee;

(2) a person who purchased or agreed to purchase the shares;

(3) a creditor of the corporation who extended it credit under terms requiring the appointment;

(4) an employee of the corporation whose employment contract requires the appointment; or

(5) a party to a voting agreement created under section 7.31.

(e) The death or incapacity of the shareholder appointing a proxy does not affect the right of the corporation to accept the proxy's authority unless notice of the death or incapacity is received by the secretary or other officer or agent authorized to tabulate votes before the proxy exercises his authority under the appointment.

(f) An appointment made irrevocable under subsection (d) is revoked when the interest with which it is coupled is extinguished.

(g) A transferee for value of shares subject to an irrevocable appointment may revoke the appointment if he did not know of its existence when he acquired the shares and the existence of the irrevocable appointment was not noted conspicuously on the certificate representing the shares or on the information statement for shares without certificates.

(h) Subject to section 7.24 and to any express limitation on the proxy's authority stated in the appointment form or electronic transmission, a corporation is entitled to accept the proxy's vote or other action as that of the shareholder making the appointment.

§7.23. *Shares Held by Nominees*

(a) A corporation may establish a procedure by which the beneficial owner of shares that are registered in the name of a nominee is recognized by the corporation as the shareholder. The extent of this recognition may be determined in the procedure.

(b) The procedure may set forth:

(1) the types of nominees to which it applies;

(2) the rights or privileges that the corporation recognizes in a beneficial owner;

(3) the manner in which the procedure is selected by the nominee;

(4) the information that must be provided when the procedure is selected;

(5) the period for which selection of the procedure is effective; and

(6) other aspects of the rights and duties created.

§7.24. *Corporation's Acceptance of Votes*

(a) If the name signed on a vote, consent, waiver, or proxy appointment corresponds to the name of a shareholder, the corporation if acting in good faith is entitled to accept the vote, consent, waiver, or proxy appointment and give it effect as the act of the shareholder.

(b) If the name signed on a vote, consent, waiver, or proxy appointment does not correspond to the name of its shareholder, the corporation if acting in good faith is nevertheless entitled to accept the vote, consent, waiver, or proxy appointment and give it effect as the act of the shareholder if:

(1) the shareholder is an entity and the name signed purports to be that of an officer or agent of the entity;

(2) the name signed purports to be that of an administrator, executor, guardian, or conservator representing the shareholder and, if the corporation requests, evidence of fiduciary status acceptable to the corporation has been presented with respect to the vote, consent, waiver, or proxy appointment;

(3) the name signed purports to be that of a receiver or trustee in bankruptcy of the shareholder and, if the corporation requests, evidence of this status acceptable to the corporation has been presented with respect to the vote, consent, waiver, or proxy appointment;

(4) the name signed purports to be that of a pledgee, beneficial owner, or attorney-in-fact of the shareholder and, if the corporation requests, evidence acceptable to the corporation of the signatory's authority to sign for the shareholder has been presented with respect to the vote, consent, waiver, or proxy appointment;

(5) two or more persons are the shareholder as cotenants or fiduciaries and the name signed purports to be the name of at least one of the coowners and the person signing appears to be acting on behalf of all the coowners.

(c) The corporation is entitled to reject a vote, consent, waiver, or proxy appointment if the secretary or other officer or agent authorized to tabulate votes, acting in good faith, has reasonable basis for doubt about the validity of the signature on it or about the signatory's authority to sign for the shareholder.

(d) The corporation and its officer or agent who accepts or rejects a vote, consent, waiver, or proxy appointment in good faith and in accordance with the standards of this section or section 7.22(b) are not liable in damages to the shareholder for the consequences of the acceptance or rejection.

(e) Corporate action based on the acceptance or rejection of a vote, consent, waiver, or proxy appointment under this section or section 7.22(b) is valid unless a court of competent jurisdiction determines otherwise.

§7.25. *Quorum and Voting Requirements for Voting Groups*

(a) Shares entitled to vote as a separate voting group may take action on a matter at a meeting only if a quorum of those shares exists with respect to that matter. Unless the articles of incorporation or this Act provide otherwise, a majority of the votes entitled to be cast on the matter by the voting group constitutes a quorum of that voting group for action on that matter.

(b) Once a share is represented for any purpose at a meeting, it is deemed present for quorum purposes for the remainder of the meeting and for any adjournment of that meeting unless a new record date is or must be set for that adjourned meeting.

(c) If a quorum exists, action on a matter (other than the election of directors) by a voting group is approved if the votes cast within the voting group favoring the action exceed the votes cast opposing the action, unless the articles of incorporation or this Act require a greater number of affirmative votes.

(d) An amendment of articles of incorporation adding, changing, or deleting a quorum or voting requirement for a voting group greater than specified in subsection (a) or (c) is governed by section 7.27.

(e) The election of directors is governed by section 7.28.

§7.26. *Action by Single and Multiple Voting Groups*

(a) If the articles of incorporation or this Act provide for voting by a single voting group on a matter, action on that matter is taken when voted upon by that voting group as provided in section 7.25.

(b) If the articles of incorporation or this Act provide for voting by two or more voting groups on a matter, action on that matter is taken only when voted upon by each of those voting groups counted separately as provided in section 7.25. Action may be taken by one voting group on a matter even though no action is taken by another voting group entitled to vote on the matter.

§7.27. *Greater Quorum or Voting Requirements*

(a) The articles of incorporation may provide for a greater quorum or voting requirement for shareholders (or voting groups of shareholders) than is provided for by this Act.

(b) An amendment to the articles of incorporation that adds, changes, or deletes a greater quorum or voting requirement must meet the same quorum requirement and be adopted by the same vote and voting groups required to take action under the quorum and voting requirements then in effect or proposed to be adopted, whichever is greater.

§7.28. *Voting for Directors; Cumulative Voting*

(a) Unless otherwise provided in the articles of incorporation, directors are elected by a plurality of the votes cast by the shares entitled to vote in the election at a meeting at which a quorum is present.

(b) Shareholders do not have a right to cumulate their votes for directors unless the articles of incorporation so provide.

(c) A statement included in the articles of incorporation that "[all] [a designated voting group of] shareholders are entitled to cumulate their votes for directors" (or words of similar import) means that the shareholders designated are entitled to multiply the number of votes they are entitled to cast by the number of directors for whom they are entitled to vote and cast the product for a single candidate or distribute the product among two or more candidates.

(d) Shares otherwise entitled to vote cumulatively may not be voted cumulatively at a particular meeting unless:

(1) the meeting notice or proxy statement accompanying the notice states conspicuously that cumulative voting is authorized; or

(2) a shareholder who has the right to cumulate his votes gives notice to the corporation not less than 48 hours before the time set for the meeting of his intent to cumulate his votes during the meeting, and if one shareholder gives this notice all other shareholders in the same voting group participating in the election are entitled to cumulate their votes without giving further notice.

§7.29. *Inspectors of Election*

(a) A corporation having any shares listed on a national securities exchange or regularly traded in a market maintained by one or more members of a national or affiliated securities association shall, and any other corporation may, appoint one or more inspectors to act at a meeting of shareholders and make a written report of the inspectors' determinations. Each inspector shall take and sign an oath faithfully to execute the duties of inspector with strict impartiality and according to the best of the inspector's ability.

(b) The inspectors shall

(1) ascertain the number of shares outstanding and the voting power of each;

(2) determine the shares represented at a meeting;

(3) determine the validity of proxies and ballots;

(4) count all votes; and

(5) determine the result.

(c) An inspector may be an officer or employee of the corporation.

Subchapter C. Voting Trusts and Agreements

§7.30. *Voting Trusts*

(a) One or more shareholders may create a voting trust, conferring on a trustee the right to vote or otherwise act for them, by signing an agreement setting out the provisions of the trust (which may include anything consistent with its purpose) and transferring their shares to the trustee. When a voting trust agreement is signed, the trustee shall prepare a list of the names and addresses of all owners of beneficial interests in the trust, together with the number and class of shares each transferred to the trust, and deliver copies of the list and agreement to the corporation's principal office.

(b) A voting trust becomes effective on the date the first shares subject to the trust are registered in the trustee's name. A voting trust is valid for not more than 10 years after its effective date unless extended under subsection (c).

(c) All or some of the parties to a voting trust may extend it for additional terms of not more than 10 years each by signing an extension agreement and obtaining the voting trustee's written consent to the extension. An extension is valid for 10 years from the date the first shareholder signs the extension agreement. The voting trustee must deliver copies of the extension agreement and list of beneficial owners to the corporation's principal office. An extension agreement binds only those parties signing it.

§7.31. *Voting Agreements*

(a) Two or more shareholders may provide for the manner in which they will vote their shares by signing an agreement for that purpose. A voting agreement created under this section is not subject to the provisions of section 7.30.

(b) A voting agreement created under this section is specifically enforceable.

§7.32. *Shareholder Agreements*

(a) An agreement among the shareholders of a corporation that complies with this section is effective among the shareholders and the corporation even though it is inconsistent with one or more other provisions of this Act in that it:

(1) eliminates the board of directors or restricts the discretion or powers of the board of directors;

(2) governs the authorization or making of distributions whether or not in proportion to ownership of shares, subject to the limitations in section 6.40;

(3) establishes who shall be directors or officers of the corporation, or their terms of office or manner of selection or removal;

(4) governs, in general or in regard to specific matters, the exercise or division of voting power by or between the shareholders and directors or by or among any of them, including use of weighted voting rights or director proxies;

(5) establishes the terms and conditions of any agreement for the transfer or use of property or the provision of services between the corporation and any shareholder, director, officer or employee of the corporation or among any of them;

(6) transfers to one or more shareholders or other persons all or part of the authority to exercise the corporate powers or to manage the business and affairs of the corporation, including the resolution of any issue about which there exists a deadlock among directors or shareholders;

(7) requires dissolution of the corporation at the request of one or more of the shareholders or upon the occurrence of a specified event or contingency; or

(8) otherwise governs the exercise of the corporate powers or the management of the business and affairs of the corporation or the relationship among the shareholders, the directors and the corporation, or among any of them, and is not contrary to public policy.

(b) An agreement authorized by this section shall be:

(1) set forth (A) in the articles of incorporation or bylaws and approved by all persons who are shareholders at the time of the agreement or (B) in a written agreement that is signed by all persons who are shareholders at the time of the agreement and is made known to the corporation;

(2) subject to amendment only by all persons who are shareholders at the time of the amendment, unless the agreement provides otherwise; and

(3) valid for 10 years, unless the agreement provides otherwise.

(c) The existence of an agreement authorized by this section shall be noted conspicuously on the front or back of each certificate for outstanding shares or on the information statement required by section 6.26(b). If at the time of the agreement the corporation has shares outstanding represented by certificates, the corporation shall recall the outstanding certificates and issue substitute certificates that comply with this subsection. The failure to note the existence of the agreement on the certificate or information statement shall not affect the validity of the agreement or any action taken pursuant to it. Any purchaser of shares who, at the time of purchase, did not have knowledge of the existence of the agreement shall be entitled to rescission of the purchase. A purchaser shall be deemed to have knowledge of the existence of the agreement if its existence is noted on the certificate or information statement for the shares in compliance with this subsection and, if the shares are not represented by a certificate, the information statement is delivered to the purchaser at or prior to the time of purchase of the shares. An action to enforce the right of rescission authorized by this subsection must be commenced within the earlier of 90 days after discovery of the existence of the agreement or two years after the time of purchase of the shares.

(d) An agreement authorized by this section shall cease to be effective when shares of the corporation are listed on a national securities exchange or regularly traded in a market maintained by one or more members of a national or affiliated securities association. If the agreement ceases to be effective for any reason, the board of directors may, if the agreement is contained or referred to in the corporation's articles of incorporation or bylaws, adopt an amendment to the articles of incorporation or bylaws, without shareholder action, to delete the agreement and any references to it.

(e) An agreement authorized by this section that limits the discretion or powers of the board of directors shall relieve the directors of, and impose upon the person or persons in whom such discretion or powers are vested, liability for acts or omissions imposed by law on directors to the extent that the discretion or powers of the directors are limited by the agreement.

(f) The existence or performance of an agreement authorized by this section shall not be a ground for imposing personal liability on any shareholder for the acts or debts of the corporation even if the agreement or its performance treats the corporation as if it were a partnership or results in failure to observe the corporate formalities otherwise applicable to the matters governed by the agreement.

(g) Incorporators or subscribers for shares may act as shareholders with respect to an agreement authorized by this section if no shares have been issued when the agreement is made.

Subchapter D. Derivative Proceedings

§7.40. *Subchapter Definitions*

In this subchapter:

(1) "Derivative proceeding" means a civil suit in the right of a domestic corporation or, to the extent provided in section 7.47, in the right of a foreign corporation.

(2) "Shareholder" includes a beneficial owner whose shares are held in a voting trust or held by a nominee on the beneficial owner's behalf.

§7.41. Standing

A shareholder may not commence or maintain a derivative proceeding unless the shareholder:

(1) was a shareholder of the corporation at the time of the act or omission complained of or became a shareholder through transfer by operation of law from one who was a shareholder at that time; and

(2) fairly and adequately represents the interests of the corporation in enforcing the right of the corporation.

§7.42. Demand

No shareholder may commence a derivative proceeding until:

(1) a written demand has been made upon the corporation to take suitable action; and

(2) 90 days have expired from the date the demand was made unless the shareholder has earlier been notified that the demand has been rejected by the corporation or unless irreparable injury to the corporation would result by waiting for the expiration of the 90 day period.

§7.43. Stay of Proceedings

If the corporation commences an inquiry into the allegations made in the demand or complaint, the court may stay any derivative proceeding for such period as the court deems appropriate.

§7.44. Dismissal

(a) A derivative proceeding shall be dismissed by the court on motion by the corporation if one of the groups specified in subsections (b) or (f) has determined in good faith after conducting a reasonable inquiry upon which its conclusions are based that the maintenance of the derivative proceeding is not in the best interests of the corporation.

(b) Unless a panel is appointed pursuant to subsection (f), the determination in subsection (a) shall be made by:

(1) a majority vote of independent directors present at a meeting of the board of directors if the independent directors constitute a quorum; or

(2) a majority vote of a committee consisting of two or more independent directors appointed by majority vote of independent directors present at a meeting of the board of directors, whether or not such independent directors constituted a quorum.

(c) None of the following shall by itself cause a director to be considered not independent for purposes of this section:

(1) the nomination or election of the director by persons who are defendants in the derivative proceeding or against whom action is demanded;

(2) the naming of the director as a defendant in the derivative proceeding or as a person against whom action is demanded; or

(3) the approval by the director of the act being challenged in the derivative proceeding or demand if the act resulted in no personal benefit to the director.

(d) If a derivative proceeding is commenced after a determination has been made rejecting a demand by a shareholder, the complaint shall allege with particularity facts establishing either (1) that a majority of the board of directors did not consist of independent directors at the time the determination was made or (2) that the requirements of subsection (a) have not been met.

(e) If a majority of the board of directors does not consist of independent directors at the time the determination is made, the corporation shall have the burden of proving that the requirements of subsection (a) have been met. If a majority of the board of directors consists of independent directors at the time the determination is made, the plaintiff shall have the burden of proving that the requirements of subsection (a) have not been met.

(f) The court may appoint a panel of one or more independent persons upon motion by the corporation to make a determination whether the maintenance of the derivative proceeding is in the best interests of the corporation. In such case, the plaintiff shall have the burden of proving that the requirements of subsection (a) have not been met.

§7.45. Discontinuance or Settlement

A derivative proceeding may not be discontinued or settled without the court's approval. If the court determines that a proposed discontinuance or settlement will substantially affect the interests of the corporation's shareholders or a class of shareholders, the court shall direct that notice be given to the shareholders affected.

§7.46. Payment of Expenses

On termination of the derivative proceeding the court may:

(1) order the corporation to pay the plaintiff's reasonable expenses (including counsel fees) incurred in the proceeding if it finds that the proceeding has resulted in a substantial benefit to the corporation;

(2) order the plaintiff to pay any defendant's reasonable expenses (including counsel fees) incurred in defending the proceeding if it finds that the proceeding was commenced or maintained without reasonable cause or for an improper purpose; or

(3) order a party to pay an opposing party's reasonable expenses (including counsel fees) incurred because of the filing of a pleading, motion or other paper, if it finds that the pleading, motion or other paper was not well grounded in fact, after reasonable inquiry, or warranted by existing law or a good faith argument for the extension, modification or reversal of existing law and was interposed for an improper purpose, such as to harass or to cause unnecessary delay or needless increase in the cost of litigation.

§7.47. Applicability to Foreign Corporations

In any derivative proceeding in the right of a foreign corporation, the matters covered by this subchapter shall be governed by the laws of the jurisdiction of incorporation of the foreign corporation except for sections 7.43, 7.45, and 7.46.

CHAPTER 8. DIRECTORS AND OFFICERS

SUBCHAPTER A. BOARD OF DIRECTORS

§8.01. Requirements for and Duties of Board of Directors

(a) Except as provided in section 7.32, each corporation must have a board of directors.

(b) All corporate powers shall be exercised by or under the authority of, and the business and affairs of the corporation managed under the direction of, its board of directors, subject to any limitation set forth in the articles of incorporation or in an agreement authorized under section 7.32.

§8.02. Qualifications of Directors

The articles of incorporation or bylaws may prescribe qualifications for directors. A director need not be a resident of this state or a shareholder of the corporation unless the articles of incorporation or bylaws so prescribe.

§8.03. Number and Election of Directors

(a) A board of directors must consist of one or more individuals, with the number specified in or fixed in accordance with the articles of incorporation or bylaws.

(b) If a board of directors has power to fix or change the number of directors, the board may increase or decrease by 30 percent or less the number of directors last approved by the shareholders, but only the shareholders may increase or decrease by more than 30 percent the number of directors last approved by the shareholders.

(c) The articles of incorporation or bylaws may establish a variable range for the size of the board of directors by fixing a minimum and maximum number of directors. If a variable range is established, the number of directors may be fixed or changed from time to time, within the minimum and maximum, by the shareholders or the board of directors. After shares are issued, only the shareholders may change the range for the size of the board or change from a fixed to a variable-range size board or vice versa.

(d) Directors are elected at the first annual shareholders' meeting and at each annual meeting thereafter unless their terms are staggered under section 8.06.

§8.04. Election of Directors by Certain Classes of Shareholders

If the articles of incorporation authorize dividing the shares into classes, the articles may also authorize the election of all or a specified number of directors by the holders of one or more authorized classes of shares. A class (or classes) of shares entitled to elect one or more directors is a separate voting group for purposes of the election of directors.

§8.05. Terms of Directors Generally

(a) The terms of the initial directors of a corporation expire at the first shareholders' meeting at which directors are elected.

(b) The terms of all other directors expire at the next annual shareholders' meeting following their election unless their terms are staggered under section 8.06.

(c) A decrease in the number of directors does not shorten an incumbent director's term.

(d) The term of a director elected to fill a vacancy expires at the next shareholders' meeting at which directors are elected.

(e) Despite the expiration of a director's term, he continues to serve until his successor is elected and qualifies or until there is a decrease in the number of directors.

§8.06. Staggered Terms for Directors

If there are nine or more directors, the articles of incorporation may provide for staggering their terms by dividing the total number of directors into two or three groups, with each group containing one half or one-third of the total, as near as may be. In that event, the terms of directors in the first group expire at the first annual shareholders' meeting after their election, the terms of the second group expire at the second annual shareholders' meeting after their election, and the terms of the third group, if any, expire at the third annual shareholders' meeting after their election. At each annual shareholders' meeting held thereafter, directors shall be chosen for a term of two years or three years, as the case may be, to succeed those whose terms expire.

§8.07. Resignation of Directors

(a) A director may resign at any time by delivering written notice to the board of directors, its chairman, or to the corporation.

(b) A resignation is effective when the notice is delivered unless the notice specifies a later effective date.

§8.08. Removal of Directors by Shareholders

(a) The shareholders may remove one or more directors with or without cause unless the articles of incorporation provide that directors may be removed only for cause.

(b) If a director is elected by a voting group of shareholders, only the shareholders of that voting group may participate in the vote to remove him.

(c) If cumulative voting is authorized, a director may not be removed if the number of votes sufficient to elect him under cumulative voting is voted against his removal. If cumulative voting is not authorized, a director may be removed only if the number of votes cast to remove him exceeds the number of votes cast not to remove him.

(d) A director may be removed by the shareholders only at a meeting called for the purpose of removing him and the meeting notice must state that the purpose, or one of the purposes, of the meeting is removal of the director.

§8.09. Removal of Directors by Judicial Proceeding

(a) The [name or describe] court of the county where a corporation's principal office (or, if none in this state, its registered office) is located may remove a director of the corporation from office in a proceeding commenced either by the corporation or by its shareholders holding at least 10 percent of the outstanding shares of any class if the court finds that (1) the director engaged in fraudulent or dishonest conduct, or gross abuse of authority or discretion, with respect to the corporation and (2) removal is in the best interest of the corporation.

(b) The court that removes a director may bar the director from reelection for a period prescribed by the court.

(c) If shareholders commence a proceeding under subsection (a), they shall make the corporation a party defendant.

§8.10. *Vacancy on Board*

(a) Unless the articles of incorporation provide otherwise, if a vacancy occurs on a board of directors, including a vacancy resulting from an increase in the number of directors:

(1) the shareholders may fill the vacancy;

(2) the board of directors may fill the vacancy; or

(3) if the directors remaining in office constitute fewer than a quorum of the board, they may fill the vacancy by the affirmative vote of a majority of all the directors remaining in office.

(b) If the vacant office was held by a director elected by a voting group of shareholders, only the holders of shares of that voting group are entitled to vote to fill the vacancy if it is filled by the shareholders.

(c) A vacancy that will occur at a specific later date (by reason of a resignation effective at a later date under section 8.07(b) or otherwise) may be filled before the vacancy occurs but the new director may not take office until the vacancy occurs.

§8.11. *Compensation of Directors*

Unless the articles of incorporation or bylaws provide otherwise, the board of directors may fix the compensation of directors.

Subchapter B. Meetings and Action of the Board

§8.20. *Meetings*

(a) The board of directors may hold regular or special meetings in or out of this state.

(b) Unless the articles of incorporation or bylaws provide otherwise, the board of directors may permit any or all directors to participate in a regular or special meeting by, or conduct the meeting through the use of, any means of communication by which all directors participating may simultaneously hear each other during the meeting. A director participating in a meeting by this means is deemed to be present in person at the meeting.

§8.21. *Action Without Meeting*

(a) Unless the articles of incorporation or bylaws provide otherwise, action required or permitted by this Act to be taken at a board of directors' meeting may be taken without a meeting if the action is taken by all members of the board. The action must be evidenced by one or more written consents describing the action taken, signed by each director, and included in the minutes or filed with the corporate records reflecting the action taken.

(b) Action taken under this section is effective when the last director signs the consent, unless the consent specifies a different effective date.

(c) A consent signed under this section has the effect of a meeting vote and may be described as such in any document.

§8.22. *Notice of Meeting*

(a) Unless the articles of incorporation or bylaws provide otherwise, regular meetings of the board of directors may be held without notice of the date, time, place, or purpose of the meeting.

(b) Unless the articles of incorporation or bylaws provide for a longer or shorter period, special meetings of the board of directors must be preceded by at least two days' notice of the date, time, and place of the meeting. The notice need not describe the purpose of the special meeting unless required by the articles of incorporation or bylaws.

§8.23. *Waiver of Notice*

(a) A director may waive any notice required by this Act, the articles of incorporation, or bylaws before or after the date and time stated in the notice. Except as provided by subsection (b), the waiver must be in writing, signed by the director entitled to the notice, and filed with the minutes or corporate records.

(b) A director's attendance at or participation in a meeting waives any required notice to him of the meeting unless the director at the beginning of the meeting (or promptly upon his arrival) objects to holding the meeting or transacting business at the meeting and does not thereafter vote for or assent to action taken at the meeting.

§8.24. *Quorum and Voting*

(a) Unless the articles of incorporation or bylaws require a greater number or unless otherwise specifically provided in this Act, a quorum of a board of directors consists of:

(1) a majority of the fixed number of directors if the corporation has a fixed board size; or

(2) a majority of the number of directors prescribed, or if no number is prescribed the number in office immediately before the meeting begins, if the corporation has a variable-range size board.

(b) The articles of incorporation or bylaws may authorize a quorum of a board of directors to consist of no fewer than one-third of the fixed or prescribed number of directors determined under subsection (a).

(c) If a quorum is present when a vote is taken, the affirmative vote of a majority of directors present is the act of the board of directors unless the articles of incorporation or bylaws require the vote of a greater number of directors.

(d) A director who is present at a meeting of the board of directors or a committee of the board of directors when corporate action is taken is deemed to have assented to the action taken unless: (1) he objects at the beginning of the meeting (or promptly upon his arrival) to holding it or transacting business at the meeting; (2) his dissent or abstention from the action taken is entered in the minutes of the meeting; or (3) he delivers written notice of his dissent or abstention to the presiding officer of the meeting before its adjournment or to the corporation immediately after adjournment of the meeting. The right of dissent or abstention is not available to a director who votes in favor of the action taken.

§8.25. Committees

(a) Unless the articles of incorporation or bylaws provide otherwise, a board of directors may create one or more committees and appoint members of the board of directors to serve on them. Each committee must have two or more members, who serve at the pleasure of the board of directors.

(b) The creation of a committee and appointment of members to it must be approved by the greater of (1) a majority of all the directors in office when the action is taken or (2) the number of directors required by the articles of incorporation or bylaws to take action under section 8.24.

(c) Sections 8.20 through 8.24, which govern meetings, action without meetings, notice and waiver of notice, and quorum and voting requirements of the board of directors, apply to committees and their members as well.

(d) To the extent specified by the board of directors or in the articles of incorporation or bylaws, each committee may exercise the authority of the board of directors under section 8.01.

(e) A committee may not, however:

(1) authorize distributions;

(2) approve or propose to shareholders action that this Act requires be approved by shareholders;

(3) fill vacancies on the board of directors or on any of its committees;

(4) amend articles of incorporation pursuant to section 10.02;

(5) adopt, amend, or repeal bylaws;

(6) approve a plan of merger not requiring shareholder approval;

(7) authorize or approve reacquisition of shares, except according to a formula or method prescribed by the board of directors; or

(8) authorize or approve the issuance or sale or contract for sale of shares, or determine the designation and relative rights, preferences, and limitations of a class or series of shares, except that the board of directors may authorize a committee (or a senior executive officer of the corporation) to do so within limits specifically prescribed by the board of directors.

(f) The creation of, delegation of authority to, or action by a committee does not alone constitute compliance by a director with the standards of conduct described in section 8.30.

Subchapter C. Standards of Conduct

§8.30. Standards of Conduct for Directors

(a) Each member of the board of directors, when discharging the duties of a director, shall act: (1) in good faith, and (2) in a manner the director reasonably believes to be in the best interests of the corporation.

(b) The members of the board of directors or a committee of the board, when becoming informed in connection with their decision-making function or devoting attention to their oversight function, shall discharge their duties with the care that a person in a like position would reasonably believe appropriate under similar circumstances.

(c) In discharging board or committee duties a director, who does not have knowledge that makes reliance unwarranted, is entitled to rely on the performance by any of the persons specified in subsection (e)(1) or subsection (e)(3) to whom the board may have delegated, formally or informally by course of conduct, the authority or duty to perform one or more of the board's functions that are delegable under applicable law.

(d) In discharging board or committee duties a director, who does not have knowledge that makes reliance unwarranted, is entitled to rely on information, opinions, reports or statements, including financial statements and other financial data, prepared or presented by any of the persons specified in subsection (e).

(e) A director is entitled to rely, in accordance with subsection (c) or (d), on:

(1) one or more officers or employees of the corporation whom the director reasonably believes to be reliable and competent in the functions performed or the information, opinions, reports or statements provided;

(2) legal counsel, public accountants, or other persons retained by the corporation as to matters, involving skills or expertise the director reasonably believes are matters (1) within the particular person's professional or expert competence or (ii) as to which the particular person merits confidence; or

(3) a committee of the board of directors of which the director is not a member if the director reasonably believes the committee merits confidence.

§8.31. Standards of Liability for Directors

(a) A director shall not be liable to the corporation or its shareholders for any decision to take or not to take action, or any failure to take any action, as a director, unless the party asserting liability in a proceeding establishes that:

(1) any provision in the articles of incorporation authorized by section 2.02(b)(4) or the protection afforded by section 8.61 for action taken in compliance with section 8.62 or 8.63, if interposed as a bar to the proceeding by the director, does not preclude liability; and

(2) the challenged conduct consisted or was the result of:

(i) action not in good faith; or

(ii) a decision

(A) which the director did not reasonably believe to be in the best interests of the corporation, or

(B) as to which the director was not informed to an extent the director reasonably believed appropriate in the circumstances; or

(iii) a lack of objectivity due to the director's familial, financial or business relationship with, or a lack of independence due to the director's domination or control by, another person having a material interest in the challenged conduct

(A) which relationship or which domination or control could reasonably be expected to have affected the director's judgment respecting the challenged conduct in a manner adverse to the corporation, and

(B) after a reasonable expectation to such effect has been established, the director shall not have established that the challenged conduct was reasonably believed by the director to be in the best interests of the corporation; or

(iv) a sustained failure of the director to devote attention to ongoing oversight of the business and affairs of the corporation, or a failure to devote timely attention, by making (or causing to be made) appropriate inquiry, when particular facts and circumstances of significant concern materialize that would alert a reasonably attentive director to the need therefor; or

(v) receipt of a financial benefit to which the director was not entitled or other breach of the director's duties to deal fairly with the corporation and its shareholders that is actionable under applicable law.

(b) The party seeking to hold the director liable:

(1) for money damages, shall also have the burden of establishing that:

(i) harm to the corporation or its shareholders has been suffered, and

(ii) the harm suffered was proximately caused by the director's challenged conduct; or

(2) for other money payment under a legal remedy, such as compensation for the unauthorized use of corporate assets, shall also have whatever persuasion burden may be called for to establish that the payment sought is appropriate in the circumstances; or

(3) for other money payment under an equitable remedy, such as profit recovery by or disgorgement to the corporation, shall also have whatever persuasion burden may be called for to establish that the equitable remedy sought is appropriate in the circumstances.

(c) Nothing contained in this section shall (1) in any instance where fairness is at issue, such as consideration of the fairness of a transaction to the corporation under section 8.61(b)(3), alter the burden of proving the fact or lack of fairness otherwise applicable, (2) alter the fact or lack of liability of a director under another section of this Act, such as the provisions governing the consequences of an unlawful distribution under section 8.33 or a transactional interest under section 8.61, or (3) affect any rights to which the corporation or a shareholder may be entitled under another statute of this state or the United States.

§8.33. *Directors' Liability for Unlawful Distributions*

(a) A director who votes for or assents to a distribution in excess of what may be authorized and made pursuant to section 6.40(a) is personally liable to the corporation for the amount of the distribution that exceeds what could have been distributed without violating section 6.40(a) if the party asserting liability establishes that when taking the action the director did not comply with section 8.30.

(b) A director held liable under subsection (a) for an unlawful distribution is entitled to:

(1) contribution from every other director who could be held liable under subsection (a) for the unlawful distribution; and

(2) recoupment from each shareholder of the pro-rata portion of the amount of the unlawful distribution the shareholder accepted, knowing the distribution was made in voilation of section 6.40(a).

(c) A proceeding to enforce:

(1) the liability of a director under subsection (a) is barred unless it is commenced within two years after the date on which the effect of the distribution was measured under section 6.40(e) or (g) or as of which the violation of section 6.40(a) occurred as the consequence of disregard of a restriction in the articles of incorporation; or

(2) contribution or recoupment under subsection (b) is barred unless it is commenced within one year after the liability of the claimant has been finally adjudicated under subsection (a).

Subchapter D. Officers

§8.40. *Required Officers*

(a) A corporation has the officers described in its bylaws or appointed by the board of directors in accordance with the bylaws.

(b) A duly appointed officer may appoint one or more officers or assistant officers if authorized by the bylaws or the board of directors.

(c) The bylaws or the board of directors shall delegate to one of the officers responsibility for preparing minutes of the directors' and shareholders' meetings and for authenticating records of the corporation.

(d) The same individual may simultaneously hold more than one office in a corporation.

§8.41. *Duties of Officers*

Each officer has the authority and shall perform the duties set forth in the bylaws or, to the extent consistent with the bylaws, the duties prescribed by the board of directors or by direction of an officer authorized by the board of directors to prescribe the duties of other officers.

§8.42. *Standards of Conduct for Officers*

(a) An officer, when performing in such capacity, shall act:

(1) in good faith;

(2) with the care that a person in a like position would reasonably exercise under similar circumstances; and

(3) in a manner the officer reasonably believes to be in the best interest of the corporation.

(b) In discharging those duties an officer, who does not have knowledge that makes reliance unwarranted, is entitled to rely on:

(1) the performance of properly delegated responsibilities by one or more employees of the corporation whom the officer reasonably believes to be reliable and competent in performing the responsibilities delegated; or

(2) information, opinions, reports or statements, including financial statements and other financial data, pre-

pared or presented by one or more employees of the corporation whom the officer reasonably believes, to be reliable and competent in the matters presented or by legal counsel, public accountants, or other persons retained by the corporation as to matters involving skills or expertise the officer reasonably believes are matters (i) within the particular person's professional or expert competence or (ii) as to which the particular person merits confidence.

(c) An officer shall not be liable to the corporation or its shareholders for any decision to take or not to take action, or any failure to take any action, as an officer, if the duties of the office are performed in compliance with this section. Whether an officer who does not comply with this section shall have liability will depend in such instance on applicable law, including those principles §8.31 that have relevance.

§8.43. *Resignation and Removal of Officers*

(a) An officer may resign at any time by delivering notice to the corporation. A resignation is effective when the notice is delivered unless the notice specifies a later effective date. If a resignation is made effective at a later date and the corporation accepts the future effective date, its board of directors may fill the pending vacancy before the effective date if the board of directors provides that the successor does not take office until the effective date.

(b) A board of directors may remove any officer at any time with or without cause.

§8.44. *Contract Rights of Officers*

(a) The appointment of an officer does not itself create contract rights.

(b) An officer's removal does not affect the officer's contract rights, if any, with the corporation. An officer's resignation does not affect the corporation's contract rights, if any, with the officer.

Subchapter E. Indemnification

§8.50. *Subchapter Definitions*

In this subchapter:

(1) "Corporation" includes any domestic or foreign predecessor entity of a corporation in a merger.

(2) "Director" or "officer" means an individual who is or was a director or officer, respectively, of a corporation or who, while a director or officer of the corporation, is or was serving at the corporation's request as a director, officer, partner, trustee, employee, or agent of another domestic or foreign corporation, partnership, joint venture, trust, employee benefit plan, or other entity. A director or officer is considered to be serving an employee benefit plan at the corporation's request if his duties to the corporation also impose duties on, or otherwise involve services by, him to the plan or to participants in or beneficiaries of the plan. "Director" or "officer" includes, unless the context requires otherwise, the estate or personal representative of a director or officer.

(3) "Disinterested director" means a director who, at the time of a vote referred to in section 8.53(c) or a vote or selection referred to in section 8.55(b) or (c), is not (i) a party to the proceeding, or (ii) an individual having a familial, financial, professional, or employment relationship with the director whose indemnification or advance for expenses is the subject of the decision being made, which relationship would, in the circumstances, reasonably be expected to exert an influence on the director's judgment when voting on the decision being made.

(4) "Expenses" includes counsel fees.

(5) "Liability" means the obligation to pay a judgment, settlement, penalty, fine (including an excise tax assessed with respect to an employee benefit plan), or reasonable expenses incurred with respect to a proceeding.

(6) "Official capacity" means: (i) when used with respect to a director, the office of director in a corporation; and (ii) when used with respect to an officer, as contemplated in section 8.56, the office in a corporation held by the officer. "Official capacity" does not include service for any other domestic or foreign corporation or any partnership, joint venture, trust, employee benefit plan, or other entity.

(7) "Party" means an individual who was, is, or is threatened to be made, a defendant or respondent in a proceeding.

(8) "Proceeding" means any threatened, pending, or completed action, suit, or proceeding, whether civil, criminal, administrative, arbitrative, or investigative and whether formal or informal.

§8.51. *Permissible Indemnification*

(a) Except as otherwise provided in this section, a corporation may indemnify an individual who is a party to a proceeding because he is a director against liability incurred in the proceeding if:

(1)(i) he conducted himself in good faith; and

(ii) he reasonably believed:

(A) in the case of conduct in his official capacity, that his conduct was in the best interests of the corporation; and

(B) in all other cases, that his conduct was at least not opposed to the best interests of the corporation; and

(iii) in the case of any criminal proceeding, he had no reasonable cause to believe his conduct was unlawful; or

(2) he engaged in conduct for which broader indemnification has been made permissible or obligatory under a provision of the articles of incorporation (as authorized by section 2.02(b)(5)).

(b) A director's conduct with respect to an employee benefit plan for a purpose he reasonably believed to be in the interests of the participants in, and the beneficiaries of, the plan is conduct that satisfies the requirement of subsection (a)(1)(ii)(B).

(c) The termination of a proceeding by judgment, order, settlement, or conviction, or upon a plea of nolo contendere or its equivalent, is not, of itself, determinative that the director did not meet the relevant standard of conduct described in this section.

(d) Unless ordered by a court under section 8.54(a) (3), a corporation may not indemnify a director:

(1) in connection with a proceeding by or in the right of the corporation, except for reasonable expenses incurred

in connection with the proceeding if it is determined that the director has met the relevant standard of conduct under subsection (a); or

(2) in connection with any proceeding with respect to conduct for which he was adjudged liable on the basis that he received a financial benefit to which he was not entitled, whether or not involving action in his official capacity.

§8.52. Mandatory Indemnification

A corporation shall indemnify a director who was wholly successful, on the merits or otherwise, in the defense of any proceeding to which he was a party because he was a director of the corporation against reasonable expenses incurred by him in connection with the proceeding.

§8.53. Advance for Expenses

(a) A corporation may, before final disposition of a proceeding, advance funds to pay for or reimburse the reasonable expenses incurred by a director who is a party to a proceeding because he is a director if he delivers to the corporation:

(1) a written affirmation of his good faith belief that he has met the relevant standard of conduct described in section 8.51 or that the proceeding involves conduct for which liability has been eliminated under a provision of the articles of incorporation as authorized by section 2.02(b)(4); and

(2) his written undertaking to repay any funds advanced if he is not entitled to mandatory indemnification under section 8.52 and it is ultimately determined under section 8.54 or section 8.55 that he has not met the relevant standard of conduct described in section 8.51.

(b) The undertaking required by subsection (a) (2) must be an unlimited general obligation of the director but need not be secured and may be accepted without reference to financial ability of the director to make repayment.

(c) Authorization under this section shall be made:

(1) by the board of directors:

(i) if there are two or more disinterested directors, by a majority vote of all the disinterested directors (a majority of whom shall for such purpose constitute a quorum) or by a majority of the members of a committee of two or more disinterested directors appointed by such a vote; or

(ii) if there are fewer than two disinterested directors, by the vote necessary for action by the board in accordance with section 8.24(c), in which authorization directors who do not qualify as disinterested directors may participate; or

(2) by the shareholders, but shares owned by or voted under the control of a director who at the time does not qualify as a disinterested director may not be voted on the authorization.

§8.54. Court-Ordered Indemnification and Advance for Expenses

(a) A director who is a party to a proceeding because he is a director may apply for indemnification or an advance for expenses to the court conducting the proceeding or to another court of competent jurisdiction. After receipt of an application and after giving any notice it considers necessary, the court shall:

(1) order indemnification if the court determines that the director is entitled to mandatory indemnification under section 8.52;

(2) order indemnification or advance for expenses if the court determines that the director is entitled to indemnification or advance for expenses pursuant to a provision authorized by section 8.58(a); or

(3) order indemnification or advance for expenses if the court determines, in view of all the relevant circumstances, that it is fair and reasonable

(i) to indemnify the director, or

(ii) to advance expenses to the director, even if he has not met the relevant standard of conduct set forth in section 8.51(a), failed to comply with section 8.53 or was adjudged liable in a proceeding referred to in subsection 8.51(d)(1) or (d)(2), but if he was adjudged so liable his indemnification shall be limited to reasonable expenses incurred in connection with the proceeding.

(b) If the court determines that the director is entitled to indemnification under subsection (a)(1) or to indemnification or advance for expenses under subsection (a)(2), it shall also order the corporation to pay the director's reasonable expenses incurred in connection with obtaining court-ordered indemnification or advance for expenses. If the court determines that the director is entitled to indemnification or advance for expenses under subsection (a)(3), it may also order the corporation to pay the director's reasonable expenses to obtain court-ordered indemnification or advance for expenses.

§8.55. Determination and Authorization of Indemnification

(a) A corporation may not indemnify a director under section 8.51 unless authorized for a specific proceeding after a determination has been made that indemnification of the director is permissible because he has met the relevant standard of conduct set forth in section 8.51.

(b) The determination shall be made:

(1) If there are two or more disinterested directors, by the board of directors by a majority vote of all the disinterested directors (a majority of whom shall for such purpose constitute a quorum), or by a majority of the members of a committee of two or more disinterested directors appointed by such a vote;

(2) by special legal counsel:

(i) selected in the manner prescribed in subdivision (1); or

(ii) if there are fewer than two disinterested directors, selected by the board of directors (in which selection directors who do not qualify as disinterested directors may participate); or

(3) by the shareholders, but shares owned by or voted under the control of a director who at the time does not qualify as a disinterested director may not be voted on the determination.

(c) Authorization of indemnification shall be made in the same manner as the determination that indemnification is permissible, except that if there are fewer than two disinterested directors or if the determination is made by special legal counsel, authorization of indemnification shall be made by those entitled under subsection (b)(2)(ii) to select special legal counsel.

§8.56. *Officers*

(a) A corporation may indemnify and advance expenses under this subchapter to an officer of the corporation who is a party to a proceeding because he is an officer of the corporation

(1) to the same extent as a director; and

(2) if he is an officer but not a director, to such further extent as may be provided by the articles of incorporation, the bylaws, a resolution of the board of directors, or contract except for (A) liability in connection with a proceeding by or in the right of the corporation other than for reasonable expenses incurred in connection with the proceeding or (B) liability arising out of conduct that constitutes (i) receipt by him of a financial benefit to which he is not entitled, (ii) an intentional infliction of harm on the corporation or the shareholders, or (iii) an intentional violation of criminal law.

(b) The provisions of subsection (a)(2) shall apply to an officer who is also a director if the basis on which he is made a party to the proceeding is an act or omission solely as an officer.

(c) An officer of a corporation who is not a director is entitled to mandatory indemnification under section 8.52, and may apply to a court under section 8.54 for indemnification or an advance for expenses, in each case to the same extent to which a director may be entitled to indemnification or advance for expenses under those provisions.

§8.57. *Insurance*

A corporation may purchase and maintain insurance on behalf of an individual who is a director or officer of the corporation, or who, while a director or officer of the corporation, serves at the corporation's request as a director, officer, partner, trustee, employee, or agent of another domestic or foreign corporation, partnership, joint venture, trust, employee benefit plan, or other entity, against liability asserted against or incurred by him in that capacity or arising from his status as a director or officer, whether or not the corporation would have power to indemnify or advance expenses to him against the same liability under this subchapter.

§8.58. *Variation by Corporate Action; Application of Subchapter*

(a) A corporation may, by a provision in its articles of incorporation or bylaws or in a resolution adopted or a contract approved by its board of directors of shareholders, obligate itself in advance of the act or omission giving rise to a proceeding to provide indemnification in accordance with section 8.51 or advance funds to pay for or reimburse expenses in accordance with section 8.53. Any such obligatory provision shall be deemed to satisfy the requirements for authorization referred to in section 8.53(c) and in section 8.55(c). Any such provision that obligates the corporation to provide indemnification to the fullest extent permitted by law shall be deemed to obligate the corporation to advance funds to pay for or reimburse expenses in accordance with section 8.53 to the fullest extent permitted by law, unless the provision specifically provides otherwise.

(b) Any provision pursuant to subsection (a) shall not obligate the corporation to indemnify or advance expenses to a director of a predecessor of the corporation, pertaining to conduct with respect to the predecessor, unless otherwise specifically provided. Any provision for indemnification or advance for expenses in the articles of incorporation, bylaws, or a resolution of the board of directors or shareholders of a predecessor of the corporation in a merger or in a contract to which the predecessor is a party, existing at the time the merger takes effect, shall be governed by section 11.06(a)(3).

(c) A corporation may, by a provision in its articles of incorporation, limit any of the rights to indemnification or advance for expenses created by or pursuant to this subchapter.

(d) This subchapter does not limit a corporation's power to pay or reimburse expenses incurred by a director or an officer in connection with his appearance as a witness in a proceeding at a time when he is not a party.

(e) This subchapter does not limit a corporation's power to indemnify, advance expenses to or provide or maintain insurance on behalf of an employee or agent.

§8.59. *Exclusivity of Subchapter*

A corporation may provide indemnification or advance expenses to a director or an officer only as permitted by this subchapter.

Subchapter F. Directors' Conflicting Interest Transactions

§8.60. *Subchapter Definitions*

In this subchapter:

(1) "Conflicting interest" with respect to a corporation means the interest a director of the corporation has respecting a transaction effected or proposed to be effected by the corporation (or by a subsidiary of the corporation or any other entity in which the corporation has a controlling interest) if:

(i) whether or not the transaction is brought before the board of directors of the corporation for action, the director knows at the time of commitment that he or a related person is a party to the transaction or has a beneficial financial interest in or so closely linked to the transaction and of such financial significance to the director or a related person that the interest would reasonably be expected to exert an influence on the director's judgment if he were called upon to vote on the transaction; or

(ii) the transaction is brought (or is of such character and significance to the corporation that it would in the normal course be brought) before the board of directors of the corporation for action, and the director knows at the time of commitment that any of the following persons is either a party to the transaction or has a beneficial financial interest in or so closely linked to the transaction and of such financial significance to the person that the interest would reasonably be expected to exert an influence on the director's judgment if he were called upon to vote on the transaction:

(A) an entity (other than the corporation) of which the director is a director, general partner, agent, or employee;

(B) a person that controls one or more of the entities specified in subclause (A) or an entity that is controlled by, or is under common control with, one or more of the entities specified in subclause (A); or

(C) an individual who is a general partner, principal, or employer of the director.

(2) "Director's conflicting interest transaction" with respect to a corporation means a transaction effected or proposed to be effected by the corporation (or by a subsidiary of the corporation or any other entity in which the corporation has a controlling interest) respecting which a director of the corporation has a conflicting interest.

(3) "Related person" of a director means (i) the spouse (or a parent or sibling thereof) of the director, or a child, grandchild, sibling, parent (or spouse of any thereof) of the director, or an individual having the same home as the director, or a trust or estate of which an individual specified in this clause (i) is a substantial beneficiary; or (ii) a trust, estate, incompetent, conservatee, or minor of which the director is a fiduciary.

(4) "Required disclosure" means disclosure by the director who has a conflicting interest of (i) the existence and nature of his conflicting interest, and (ii) all facts known to him respecting the subject matter of the transaction that an ordinarily prudent person would reasonably believe to be material to a judgment about whether or not to proceed with the transaction.

(5) "Time of commitment" respecting a transaction means the time when the transaction is consummated or, if made pursuant to contract, the time when the corporation (or its subsidiary or the entity in which it has a controlling interest) becomes contractually obligated so that its unilateral withdrawal from the transaction would entail significant loss, liability, or other damage.

§8.61. Judicial Action

(a) A transaction effected or proposed to be effected by a corporation (or by a subsidiary of the corporation or any other entity in which the corporation has a controlling interest) that is not a director's conflicting interest transaction may not be enjoined, set aside, or give rise to an award of damages or other sanctions, in a proceeding by a shareholder or by or in the right of the corporation, because a director of the corporation, or any person with whom or which he has a personal, economic, or other association, has an interest in the transaction.

(b) A director's conflicting interest transaction may not be enjoined, set aside, or give rise to an award of damages or other sanctions, in a proceeding by a shareholder or by or in the right of the corporation, because the director, or any person with whom or which he has a personal, economic, or other association, has an interest in the transaction, if:

(1) directors' action respecting the transaction was at any time taken in compliance with section 8.62;

(2) shareholders' action respecting the transaction was at any time taken in compliance with section 8.63; or

(3) the transaction, judged according to the circumstances at the time of commitment, is established to have been fair to the corporation.

§8.62. Directors' Action

(a) Directors' action respecting a transaction is effective for purposes of section 8.61(b)(1) if the transaction received the affirmative vote of a majority (but no fewer than two) of those qualified directors on the board of directors or on a duly empowered committee of the board who voted on the transaction after either required disclosure to them (to the extent the information was not known by them) or compliance with subsection (b); provided that action by a committee is so effective only if (1) all its members are qualified directors, and (2) its members are either all the qualified directors on the board or are appointed by the affirmative vote of a majority of the qualified directors on the board.

(b) If a director has a conflicting interest respecting a transaction, but neither he nor a related person of the director specified in section 8.60(3)(i) is a party to the transaction, and if the director has a duty under law or professional canon, or a duty of confidentiality to another person, respecting information relating to the transaction such that the director may not make the disclosure described in section 8.60(4)(ii), then disclosure is sufficient for purposes of subsection (a) if the director (1) discloses to the directors voting on the transaction the existence and nature of his conflicting interest and informs them of the character and limitations imposed by that duty before their vote on the transaction, and (2) plays no part, directly or indirectly, in their deliberations or vote.

(c) A majority (but no fewer than two) of all the qualified directors on the board of directors, or on the committee, constitutes a quorum for purposes of action that complies with this section. Directors' action that otherwise complies with this section is not affected by the presence or vote of a director who is not a qualified director.

(d) For purposes of this section, "qualified director" means, with respect to a director's conflicting interest transaction, any director who does not have either (1) a conflicting interest respecting the transaction, or (2) a familial, financial, professional, or employment relationship with a second director who does have a conflicting interest respecting the transaction, which relationship would, in the circumstances, reasonably be expected to exert an influence on the first director's judgment when voting on the transaction.

§8.63. Shareholders' Action

(a) Shareholders' action respecting a transaction is effective for purposes of section 8.61(b)(2) if a majority of the votes entitled to be cast by the holders of all qualified shares were cast in favor of the transaction after (1) notice to shareholders describing the director's conflicting interest transaction, (2) provision of the information referred to in subsection (d), and (3) required disclosure to the shareholders who voted on the transaction (to the extent the information was not known by them).

(b) For purposes of this section, "qualified shares"

means any shares entitled to vote with respect to the director's conflicting interest transaction except shares that, to the knowledge, before the vote, of the secretary (or other officer or agent of the corporation authorized to tabulate votes), are beneficially owned (or the voting of which is controlled) by a director who has a conflicting interest respecting the transaction or by a related person of the director, or both.

(c) A majority of the votes entitled to be cast by the holders of all qualified shares constitutes a quorum for purposes of action that complies with this section. Subject to the provisions of subsections (d) and (e), shareholders' action that otherwise complies with this section is not affected by the presence of holders, or the voting, of shares that are not qualified shares.

(d) For purposes of compliance with subsection (a), a director who has a conflicting interest respecting the transaction shall, before the shareholders' vote, inform the secretary (or other officer or agent of the corporation authorized to tabulate votes) of the number, and the identity of persons holding or controlling the vote, of all shares that the director knows are beneficially owned (or the voting of which is controlled) by the director or by a related person of the director, or both.

(e) If a shareholders' vote does not comply with subsection (a) solely because of a failure of a director to comply with subsection (d), and if the director establishes that his failure did not determine and was not intended by him to influence the outcome of the vote, the court may, with or without further proceedings respecting section 8.61(b)(3), take such action respecting the transaction and the director, and give such effect, if any, to the shareholders' vote, as it considers appropriate in the circumstances.

Chapter 10. Amendment of Articles of Incorporation and Bylaws

Subchapter A. Amendment of Articles of Incorporation

§10.01. Authority to Amend

(a) A corporation may amend its articles of incorporation at any time to add or change a provision that is required or permitted in the articles of incorporation or to delete a provision not required in the articles of incorporation. Whether a provision is required or permitted in the articles of incorporation is determined as of the effective date of the amendment.

(b) A shareholder of the corporation does not have a vested property right resulting from any provision in the articles of incorporation, including provisions relating to management, control, capital structure, dividend entitlement, or purpose or duration of the corporation.

§10.02. Amendment by Board of Directors

Unless the articles of incorporation provide otherwise, a corporation's board of directors may adopt one or more amendments to the corporation's articles of incorporation without shareholder action:

(1) to extend the duration of the corporation if it was incorporated at a time when limited duration was required by law;

(2) to delete the names and addresses of the initial directors;

(3) to delete the name and address of the initial registered agent or registered office, if a statement of change is on file with the secretary of state;

(4) to change each issued and unissued authorized share of an outstanding class into a greater number of whole shares if the corporation has only shares of that class outstanding;

(5) to change the corporate name by substituting the word "corporation," "incorporated," "company," "limited," or the abbreviation "corp.," "inc.," "co.," or "ltd.," for a similar word or abbreviation in the name, or by adding, deleting, or changing a geographical attribution for the name; or

(6) to make any other change expressly permitted by this Act to be made without shareholder action.

§10.03. Amendment by Board of Directors and Shareholders

(a) A corporation's board of directors may propose one or more amendments to the articles of incorporation for submission to the shareholders.

(b) For the amendment to be adopted:

(1) the board of directors must recommend the amendment to the shareholders unless the board of directors determines that because of conflict of interest or other special circumstances it should make no recommendation and communicates the basis for its determination to the shareholders with the amendment; and

(2) the shareholders entitled to vote on the amendment must approve the amendment as provided in subsection (e).

(c) The board of directors may condition its submission of the proposed amendment on any basis.

(d) The corporation shall notify each shareholder, whether or not entitled to vote, of the proposed shareholders' meeting in accordance with section 7.05. The notice of meeting must also state that the purpose, or one of the purposes, of the meeting is to consider the proposed amendment and contain or be accompanied by a copy or summary of the amendment.

(e) Unless this Act, the articles of incorporation, or the board of directors (acting pursuant to subsection (c)) require a greater vote or a vote by voting groups, the amendment to be adopted must be approved by:

(1) a majority of the votes entitled to be cast on the amendment by any voting group with respect to which the amendment would create dissenters' rights; and

(2) the votes required by sections 7.25 and 7.26 by every other voting group entitled to vote on the amendment.

§10.04. Voting on Amendments by Voting Groups

(a) The holders of the outstanding shares of a class are entitled to vote as a separate voting group (if shareholder voting is otherwise required by this Act) on a proposed amendment if the amendment would:

(1) increase or decrease the aggregate number of authorized shares of the class;

(2) effect an exchange or reclassification of all or part of the shares of the class into shares of another class;

(3) effect an exchange or reclassification, or create the right of exchange, of all or part of the shares of another class into shares of the class;

(4) change the designation, rights, preferences, or limitations of all or part of the shares of the class;

(5) change the shares of all or part of the class into a different number of shares of the same class;

(6) create a new class of shares having rights or preferences with respect to distributions or to dissolution that are prior, superior, or substantially equal to the shares of the class;

(7) increase the rights, preferences, or number of authorized shares of any class that, after giving effect to the amendment, have rights or preferences with respect to distributions or to dissolution that are prior, superior, or substantially equal to the shares of the class;

(8) limit or deny an existing preemptive right of all or part of the shares of the class; or

(9) cancel or otherwise affect rights to distributions or dividends that have accumulated but not yet been declared on all or part of the shares of the class.

(b) If a proposed amendment would affect a series of a class of shares in one or more of the ways described in subsection (a), the shares of that series are entitled to vote as a separate voting group on the proposed amendment.

(c) If a proposed amendment that entitles two or more series of shares to vote as separate voting groups under this section would affect those two or more series in the same or a substantially similar way, the shares of all the series so affected must vote together as a single voting group on the proposed amendment.

(d) A class or series of shares is entitled to the voting rights granted by this section although the articles of incorporation provide that the shares are nonvoting shares.

§10.05. Amendment Before Issuance of Shares

If a corporation has not yet issued shares, its incorporators or board of directors may adopt one or more amendments to the corporation's articles of incorporation.

§10.06. Articles of Amendment

A corporation amending its articles of incorporation shall deliver to the secretary of state for filing articles of amendment setting forth:

(1) the name of the corporation;

(2) the text of each amendment adopted;

(3) if an amendment provides for an exchange, reclassification, or cancellation of issued shares, provisions for implementing the amendment if not contained in the amendment itself;

(4) the date of each amendment's adoption;

(5) if an amendment was adopted by the incorporators or board of directors without shareholder action, a statement to that effect and that shareholder action was not required;

(6) if an amendment was approved by the shareholders:

(i) the designation, number of outstanding shares, number of votes entitled to be cast by each voting group entitled to vote separately on the amendment, and number of votes of each voting group indisputably represented at the meeting;

(ii) either the total number of votes cast for and against the amendment by each voting group entitled to vote separately on the amendment or the total number of undisputed votes cast for the amendment by each voting group and a statement that the number cast for the amendment by each voting group was sufficient for approval by that voting group.

§10.07. Restated Articles of Incorporation

(a) A corporation's board of directors may restate its articles of incorporation at any time with or without shareholder action.

(b) The restatement may include one or more amendments to the articles. If the restatement includes an amendment requiring shareholder approval, it must be adopted as provided in section 10.03.

(c) If the board of directors submits a restatement for shareholder action, the corporation shall notify each shareholder, whether or not entitled to vote, of the proposed shareholders' meeting in accordance with section 7.05. The notice must also state that the purpose, or one of the purposes, of the meeting is to consider the proposed restatement and contain or be accompanied by a copy of the restatement that identifies any amendment or other change it would make in the articles.

(d) A corporation restating its articles of incorporation shall deliver to the secretary of state for filing articles of restatement setting forth the name of the corporation and the text of the restated articles of incorporation together with a certificate setting forth:

(1) whether the restatement contains an amendment to the articles requiring shareholder approval and, if it does not, that the board of directors adopted the restatement; or

(2) if the restatement contains an amendment to the articles requiring shareholder approval, the information required by section 10.06.

(e) Duly adopted restated articles of incorporation supersede the original articles of incorporation and all amendments to them.

(f) The secretary of state may certify restated articles of incorporation, as the articles of incorporation currently in effect, without including the certification information required by subsection (d).

§10.08. Amendment Pursuant to Reorganization

(a) A corporation's articles of incorporation may be amended without action by the board of directors or shareholders to carry out a plan of reorganization ordered or decreed by a court of competent jurisdiction under federal statute if the articles of incorporation after amendment contain only provisions required or permitted by section 2.02.

(b) The individual or individuals designated by the court shall deliver to the secretary of state for filing articles of amendment setting forth:

(1) the name of the corporation;

(2) the text of each amendment approved by the court;

(3) the date of the court's order or decree approving the articles of amendment;

(4) the title of the reorganization proceeding in which the order or decree was entered; and

(5) a statement that the court had jurisdiction of the proceeding under federal statute.

(c) Shareholders of a corporation undergoing reorganization do not have dissenters' rights except as and to the extent provided in the reorganization plan.

(d) This section does not apply after entry of a final decree in the reorganization proceeding even though the court retains jurisdiction of the proceeding for limited purposes unrelated to consummation of the reorganization plan.

§10.09. *Effect of Amendment*

An amendment to articles of incorporation does not affect a cause of action existing against or in favor of the corporation, a proceeding to which the corporation is a party, or the existing rights of persons other than shareholders of the corporation. An amendment changing a corporation's name does not abate a proceeding brought by or against the corporation in its former name.

Subchapter B. Amendment of Bylaws

§10.20. *Amendment by Board of Directors or Shareholders*

(a) A corporation's board of directors may amend or repeal the corporation's bylaws unless:

(1) the articles of incorporation or this Act reserve this power exclusively to the shareholders in whole or part; or

(2) the shareholders in amending or repealing a particular bylaw provide expressly that the board of directors may not amend or repeal that bylaw.

(b) A corporation's shareholders may amend or repeal the corporation's bylaws even though the bylaws may also be amended or repealed by its board of directors.

§10.21. *Bylaw Increasing Quorum or Voting Requirement for Shareholders*

(a) If authorized by the articles of incorporation, the shareholders may adopt or amend a bylaw that fixes a greater quorum or voting requirement for shareholders (or voting groups of shareholders) than is required by this Act. The adoption or amendment of a bylaw that adds, changes, or deletes a greater quorum or voting requirement for shareholders must meet the same quorum requirement and be adopted by the same vote and voting groups required to take action under the quorum and voting requirement then in effect or proposed to be adopted, whichever is greater.

(b) A bylaw that fixes a greater quorum or voting requirement for shareholders under subsection (a) may not be adopted, amended, or repealed by the board of directors.

§10.22. *Bylaw Increasing Quorum or Voting Requirement for Directors*

(a) A bylaw that fixes a greater quorum or voting requirement for the board of directors may be amended or repealed:

(1) if originally adopted by the shareholders, only by the shareholders;

(2) if originally adopted by the board of directors, either by the shareholders or by the board of directors.

(b) A bylaw adopted or amended by the shareholders that fixes a greater quorum or voting requirement for the board of directors may provide that it may be amended or repealed only by a specified vote of either the shareholders or the board of directors.

(c) Action by the board of directors under subsection (a)(2) to adopt or amend a bylaw that changes the quorum or voting requirement for the board of directors must meet the same quorum requirement and be adopted by the same vote required to take action under the quorum and voting requirement then in effect or proposed to be adopted, whichever is greater.

Chapter 11. Merger and Share Exchange

§11.01. *Merger*

(a) One or more corporations may merge into another corporation if the board of directors of each corporation adopts and its shareholders (if required by section 11.03) approve a plan of merger.

(b) The plan of merger must set forth:

(1) the name of each corporation planning to merge and the name of the surviving corporation into which each other corporation plans to merge;

(2) the terms and conditions of the merger; and

(3) the manner and basis of converting the shares of each corporation into shares, obligations, or other securities of the surviving or any other corporation or into cash or other property in whole or part.

(c) The plan of merger may set forth:

(1) amendments to the articles of incorporation of the surviving corporation; and

(2) other provisions relating to the merger.

§11.02. *Share Exchange*

(a) A corporation may acquire all of the outstanding shares of one or more classes or series of another corporation if the board of directors of each corporation adopts and its shareholders (if required by section 11.03) approve the exchange.

(b) The plan of exchange must set forth:

(1) the name of the corporation whose shares will be acquired and the name of the acquiring corporation;

(2) the terms and conditions of the exchange;

(3) the manner and basis of exchanging the shares to be acquired for shares, obligations, or other securities of the acquiring or any other corporation or for cash or other property in whole or part.

(c) The plan of exchange may set forth other provisions relating to the exchange.

(d) This section does not limit the power of a corporation to acquire all or part of the shares of one or more classes or series of another corporation through a voluntary exchange or otherwise.

§11.03. Action on Plan

(a) After adopting a plan of merger or share exchange, the board of directors of each corporation party to the merger, and the board of directors of the corporation whose shares will be acquired in the share exchange, shall submit the plan of merger (except as provided in subsection (g)) or share exchange for approval by its shareholders.

(b) For a plan of merger or share exchange to be approved:

(1) the board of directors must recommend the plan of merger or share exchange to the shareholders, unless the board of directors determines that because of conflict of interest or other special circumstances it should make no recommendation and communicates the basis for its determination to the shareholders with the plan; and

(2) the shareholders entitled to vote must approve the plan.

(c) The board of directors may condition its submission of the proposed merger or share exchange on any basis.

(d) The corporation shall notify each shareholder, whether or not entitled to vote, of the proposed shareholders' meeting in accordance with section 7.05. The notice must also state that the purpose, or one of the purposes, of the meeting is to consider the plan of merger or share exchange and contain or be accompanied by a copy or summary of the plan.

(e) Unless the Act, the articles of incorporation, or the board of directors (acting pursuant to subsection (c)) require a greater vote or a vote by voting groups, the plan of merger or share exchange to be authorized must be approved by each voting group entitled to vote separately on the plan by a majority of all the votes entitled to be cast on the plan by that voting group.

(f) Separate voting by voting groups is required:

(1) on a plan of merger if the plan contains a provision that, if contained in a proposed amendment to articles of incorporation, would require action by one or more separate voting groups on the proposed amendment under section 10.04;

(2) on a plan of share exchange by each class or series of shares included in the exchange, with each class or series constituting a separate voting group.

(g) Action by the shareholders of the surviving corporation on a plan of merger is not required if:

(1) the articles of incorporation of the surviving corporation will not differ (except for amendments enumerated in section 10.02) from its articles before the merger;

(2) each shareholder of the surviving corporation whose shares were outstanding immediately before the effective date of the merger will hold the same number of shares, with identical designations, preferences, limitations, and relative rights, immediately after;

(3) the number of voting shares outstanding immediately after the merger, plus the number of voting shares issuable as a result of the merger (either by the conversion of securities issued pursuant to the merger or the exercise of rights and warrants issued pursuant to the merger), will not exceed by more than 20 percent the total number of voting shares of the surviving corporation outstanding immediately before the merger; and

(4) the number of participating shares outstanding immediately after the merger, plus the number of participating shares issuable as a result of the merger (either by the conversion of securities issued pursuant to the merger or the exercise of rights and warrants issued pursuant to the merger), will not exceed by more than 20 percent the total number of participating shares outstanding immediately before the merger.

(h) As used in subsection (g):

(1) "Participating shares" means shares that entitle their holders to participate without limitation in distributions.

(2) "Voting shares" means shares that entitle their holders to vote unconditionally in elections of directors.

(i) After a merger or share exchange is authorized, and at any time before articles of merger or share exchange are filed, the planned merger or share exchange may be abandoned (subject to any contractual rights), without further shareholder action, in accordance with the procedure set forth in the plan of merger or share exchange or, if none is set forth, in the manner determined by the board of directors.

§11.04. Merger of Subsidiary

(a) A parent corporation owning at least 90 percent of the outstanding shares of each class of a subsidiary corporation may merge the subsidiary into itself without approval of the shareholders of the parent or subsidiary.

(b) The board of directors of the parent shall adopt a plan of merger that sets forth:

(1) the names of the parent and subsidiary; and

(2) the manner and basis of converting the shares of the subsidiary into shares, obligations, or other securities of the parent or any other corporation or into cash or other property in whole or part.

(c) The parent shall mail a copy or summary of the plan of merger to each shareholder of the subsidiary who does not waive the mailing requirement in writing.

(d) The parent may not deliver articles of merger to the secretary of state for filing until at least 30 days after the date it mailed a copy of the plan of merger to each shareholder of the subsidiary who did not waive the mailing requirement.

(e) Articles of merger under this section may not contain amendments to the articles of incorporation of the parent corporation (except for amendments enumerated in section 10.02).

§11.05. Articles of Merger or Share Exchange

(a) After a plan of merger or share exchange is approved by the shareholders, or adopted by the board of directors if shareholder approval is not required, the surviving or acquiring corporation shall deliver to the secretary of state for filing articles of merger or share exchange setting forth:

(1) the plan of merger or share exchange;

(2) if shareholder approval was not required, a statement to that effect;

(3) if approval of the shareholders of one or more cor-

porations party to the merger or share exchange was required:

(i) the designation, number of outstanding shares, and number of votes entitled to be cast by each voting group entitled to vote separately on the plan as to each corporation; and

(ii) either the total number of votes cast for and against the plan by each voting group entitled to vote separately on the plan or the total number of undisputed votes cast for the plan separately by each voting group and a statement that the number cast for the plan by each voting group was sufficient for approval by that voting group.

(b) A merger or share exchange takes effect upon the effective date of the articles of merger or share exchange.

§11.06. *Effect of Merger or Share Exchange*

(a) When a merger takes effect:

(1) every other corporation party to the merger merges into the surviving corporation and the separate existence of every corporation except the surviving corporation ceases;

(2) the title to all real estate and other property owned by each corporation party to the merger is vested in the surviving corporation without reversion or impairment;

(3) the surviving corporation has all liabilities of each corporation party to the merger;

(4) a proceeding pending against any corporation party to the merger may be continued as if the merger did not occur or the surviving corporation may be substituted in the proceeding for the corporation whose existence ceased;

(5) the articles of incorporation of the surviving corporation are amended to the extent provided in the plan of merger; and

(6) the shares of each corporation party to the merger that are to be converted into shares, obligations, or other securities of the surviving or any other corporation or into cash or other property are converted, and the former holders of the shares are entitled only to the rights provided in the articles of merger or to their rights under chapter 13.

(b) When a share exchange takes effect, the shares of each acquired corporation are exchanged as provided in the plan, and the former holders of the shares are entitled only to the exchange rights provided in the articles of share exchange or to their rights under chapter 13.

§11.07. *Merger or Share Exchange with Foreign Corporation*

(a) One or more foreign corporations may merge or enter into a share exchange with one or more domestic corporations if:

(1) in a merger, the merger is permitted by the law of the state or country under whose law each foreign corporation is incorporated and each foreign corporation complies with that law in effecting the merger;

(2) in a share exchange, the corporation whose shares will be acquired is a domestic corporation, whether or not a share exchange is permitted by the law of the state or country under whose law the acquiring corporation is incorporated;

(3) the foreign corporation complies with section 11.05 if it is the surviving corporation of the merger or acquiring corporation of the share exchange; and

(4) each domestic corporation complies with the applicable provisions of sections 11.01 through 11.04 and, if it is the surviving corporation of the merger or acquiring corporation of the share exchange, with section 11.05.

(b) Upon the merger or share exchange taking effect, the surviving foreign corporation of a merger and the acquiring foreign corporation of a share exchange is deemed:

(1) to appoint the secretary of state as its agent for service of process in a proceeding to enforce any obligation or the rights of dissenting shareholders of each domestic corporation party to the merger or share exchange; and

(2) to agree that it will promptly pay to the dissenting shareholders of each domestic corporation party to the merger or share exchange the amount, if any, to which they are entitled under chapter 13.

(c) This section does not limit the power of a foreign corporation to acquire all or part of the shares of one or more classes or series of a domestic corporation through a voluntary exchange or otherwise.

Chapter 12. Sale of Assets

§12.01. *Sale of Assets in Regular Course of Business and Mortgage of Assets*

(a) A corporation may, on the terms and conditions and for the consideration determined by the board of directors:

(1) sell, lease, exchange, or otherwise dispose of all, or substantially all, of its property in the usual and regular course of business;

(2) mortgage, pledge, dedicate to the repayment of indebtedness (whether with or without recourse), or otherwise encumber any or all of its property whether or not in the usual and regular course of business; or

(3) transfer any or all of its property to a corporation all the shares of which are owned by the corporation.

(b) Unless the articles of incorporation require it, approval by the shareholders of a transaction described in subsection (a) is not required.

§12.02. *Sale of Assets Other Than in Regular Course of Business*

(a) A corporation may sell, lease, exchange, or otherwise dispose of all, or substantially all, of its property (with or without the good will), otherwise than in the usual and regular course of business, on the terms and conditions and for the consideration determined by the corporation's board of directors, if the board of directors proposes and its shareholders approve the proposed transaction.

(b) For a transaction to be authorized:

(1) the board of directors must recommend the proposed transaction to the shareholders unless the board of directors determines that because of conflict of interest or

other special circumstances it should make no recommendation and communicates the basis for its determination to the shareholders with the submission of the proposed transaction; and

(2) the shareholders entitled to vote must approve the transaction.

(c) The board of directors may condition its submission of the proposed transaction on any basis.

(d) The corporation shall notify each shareholder, whether or not entitled to vote, of the proposed shareholders' meeting in accordance with section 7.05. The notice must also state that the purpose, or one of the purposes, of the meeting is to consider the sale, lease, exchange, or other disposition of all, or substantially all, the property of the corporation and contain or be accompanied by a description of the transaction.

(e) Unless the articles of incorporation or the board of directors (acting pursuant to subsection (c)) require a greater vote or a vote by voting groups, the transaction to be authorized must be approved by a majority of all the votes entitled to be cast on the transaction.

(f) After a sale, lease, exchange, or other disposition of property is authorized, the transaction may be abandoned (subject to any contractual rights) without further shareholder action.

(g) A transaction that constitutes a distribution is governed by section 6.40 and not by this section.

Chapter 13. Dissenters' Rights

Subchapter A.

§13.01. Definitions

In this chapter:

(1) "Affiliate" means a person that directly or indirectly through one or more intermediaries controls, is controlled by, or is under common control with another person or is a senior executive thereof. For purposes of section 13.02(b)(4), a person is deemed to be an affiliate of its senior executives.

(2) "Beneficial shareholder" means a person who is the beneficial owner of shares held in a voting trust or by a nominee on the beneficial owner's behalf.

(3) "Corporation" means the issuer of the shares held by a shareholder demanding appraisal and, for matters covered in sections 13.22–13.31, includes the surviving entity in a merger.

(4) "Fair value" means the value of the corporation's shares determined:

(i) immediately before the effectuation of the corporate action to which the shareholder objects;

(ii) using customary and current valuation concepts and techniques generally employed for similar businesses in the context of the transaction requiring appraisal; and

(iii) without discounting for lack of marketability or minority status except, if appropriate, for amendments to the articles pursuant to section 13.02(a)(5).

(5) "Interest" means interest from the effective date of the corporate action until the date of payment, at the rate of interest on judgments in this state on the effective date of the corporate action.

(6) "Preferred shares" means a class or series of shares whose holders have preferences over any other class or series with respect to distributions.

(7) "Record shareholder" means the person in whose name shares are registered in the records of the corporation or the beneficial owner of shares to the extent of the rights granted by a nominee certificate on file with the corporation.

(8) "Senior executive" means the chief executive officer, chief operating officer, chief financial officer, and anyone in charge of a principal business unit or function.

(9) "Shareholder" means both the record shareholder and a beneficial shareholder.

§13.02. Right to Appraisal

(a) A shareholder is entitled to appraisal rights, and to obtain payment of the fair value of that shareholder's shares, in the event of any of the following corporate actions:

(1) consummation of a merger to which the corporation is a party (i) if shareholder approval is required for the merger by section 11.04 and the shareholder is entitled to vote on the merger, except that appraisal rights shall not be available to any shareholder of the corporation with respect to shares of any class or series that remain outstanding after consummation of the merger, or (ii) if the corporation is a subsidiary and the merger is governed by section 11.05;

(2) consummation of a share exchange to which the corporation is a party as the corporation whose shares will be acquired if the shareholder is entitled to vote on the exchange, except that appraisal rights shall not be available to any shareholder of the corporation with respect to any class or series of shares of the corporation that is not exchanged;

(3) consummation of a disposition of assets pursuant to section 12.02 if the shareholder is entitled to vote on the disposition;

(4) an amendment of the articles of incorporation with respect to a class or series of shares that reduces the number of shares of a class or series owned by the shareholder to a fraction of a share if the corporation has the obligation or right to repurchase the fractional share so created; or

(5) any other amendment to the articles of incorporation, merger, share exchange or disposition of assets to the extent provided by the articles of incorporation, bylaws or a resolution of the board of directors.

(b) Notwithstanding subsection (a), the availability of appraisal rights under subsections (a)(1), (2), (3) and (4) shall be limited in accordance with the following provisions:

(1) Appraisal rights shall not be available for the holders of shares of any class or series of shares which is:

(i) listed on the New York Stock Exchange or the American Stock Exchange or designated as a national market system security on an interdealer quotation system by the National Association of Securities Dealers, Inc.; or

(ii) not so listed or designated, but has at least 2,000 shareholders and the outstanding shares of such class or series has a market value of at least $20 million (exclusive of the value of such shares held by its subsidiaries, senior executives, directors and beneficial shareholders owning more than 10 percent of such shares).

(2) The applicability of subsection (b)(1) shall be determined as of:

(i) the record date fixed to determine the shareholders entitled to receive notice of, and to vote at, the meeting of shareholders to act upon the corporate action requiring appraisal rights; or

(ii) the day before the effective date of such corporate action if there is no meeting of shareholders.

(3) Subsection (b)(1) shall not be applicable and appraisal rights shall be available pursuant to subsection (a) for the holders of any class or series of shares who are required by the terms of the corporate action requiring appraisal rights to accept for such shares anything other than cash or shares of any class or any series of shares of any corporation, or any other proprietary interest of any other entity, that satisfies the standards set forth in subsection (b)(1) at the time the corporate action becomes effective.

(4) Subsection (b)(1) shall not be applicable and appraisal rights shall be available pursuant to subsection (a) for the holders of any class or series of shares where:

(i) any of the shares or assets of the corporation are being acquired or converted, whether by merger, share exchange or otherwise, pursuant to the corporate action by a person, or by an affiliate of a person, who:

(A) is, or at any time in the one-year period immediately preceding approval by the board of directors of the corporate action requiring appraisal rights was, the beneficial owner of 20 percent or more of the voting power of the corporation, excluding any shares acquired pursuant to an offer for all shares having voting power if such offer was made within one year prior to the corporate action requiring appraisal rights for consideration of the same kind and of a value equal to or less than that paid in connection with the corporate action; or

(B) directly or indirectly has, or at any time in the one-year period immediately preceding approval by the board of directors of the corporation of the corporate action requiring appraisal rights had, the power, contractually or otherwise, to cause the appointment or election of 25 percent or more of the directors to the board of directors of the corporations; or

(ii) any of the shares or assets of the corporation are being acquired or converted, whether by merger, share exchange or otherwise, pursuant to such corporate action by a person, or by an affiliate of a person, who is, or at any time in the one-year period immediately preceding approval by the board of directors of the corporate action requiring appraisal rights was, a senior executive or director of the corporation or a senior executive of any affiliate thereof, and that senior executive or director will receive, as a result of the corporate action, a financial benefit not generally available to other shareholders as such, other than:

(A) employment, consulting, retirement or similar benefits established separately and not as part of or in contemplation of the corporate action; or

(B) employment, consulting, retirement or similar benefits established in contemplation of, or as part of, the corporate action that are not more favorable than those existing before the corporate action or, if more favorable, that have been approved on behalf of the corporation in the same manner as is provided in section 8.62; or

(C) in the case of a director of the corporation who will, in the corporate action, become a director of the acquiring entity in the corporate action or one of its affiliates, rights and benefits as a director that are provided on the same basis as those afforded by the acquiring entity generally to other directors of such entity or such affiliate.

(5) For the purposes of a paragraph (4) only, the term "beneficial owner" means any person who, directly or indirectly, through any contract, arrangement, or understanding, other than a revocable proxy, has or shares the power to vote, or to direct the voting of, shares, provided that member of a national securities exchange shall not be deemed to be a beneficial owner of securities held directly or indirectly by it on behalf of another person solely because such member is the record holder of such securities if the member is precluded by the rules of such exchange from voting without instruction or contested matters or matters that may affect substantially the rights or privileges of the holders of the securities to be voted. When two or more persons agree to act together for the purpose of voting their shares of the corporation, each member of the group formed thereby shall be deemed to have acquired beneficial ownership, as of the date of such agreement, of all voting shares of the corporation beneficially owned by any member of the group.

(c) Notwithstanding any other provision of section 13.02, the articles of incorporation as originally filed or any amendment thereto may limit or eliminate appraisal rights for any class or series of preferred shares, but, any such limitation or elimination contained in an amendment to the articles of incorporation that limits or eliminates appraisal rights for any of such shares that are outstanding immediately prior to the effective date of such amendment or that the corporation is or may be required to issue or sell thereafter pursuant to any conversion, exchange or other right existing immediately before the effective date of such amendment shall not apply to any corporate action that becomes effective within one year of that date if such action would otherwise afford appraisal rights.

(d) A shareholder entitled to appraisal rights under this chapter may not challenge a completed corporate action for which appraisal rights are available unless such corporate action:

(i) was not effectuated in accordance with the applicable provisions of chapters 10, 11 or 12 or the corporation's articles of incorporation, bylaws or board of directors' resolution authorizing the corporate action; or

(ii) was procured as a result of fraud or material misrepresentation.

§13.03. Assertion of Rights by Nominees and Beneficial Owners

(a) A record shareholder may assert appraisal rights as to fewer than all the shares registered in the record shareholder's name but owned by a beneficial shareholder only if the record shareholder objects with respect to all shares of the class or series owned by the beneficial shareholder and notifies the corporation in writing of the name and address of each beneficial shareholder on whose behalf appraisal rights are being asserted. The rights of a record shareholder who asserts appraisal rights for only part of the shares held of record in the record shareholder's name under this subsection shall be determined as if the shares as to which the record shareholder objects and the record shareholder's other shares were registered in the names of different record shareholders.

(b) A beneficial shareholder may assert appraisal rights as to shares of any class or series held on behalf of the shareholder only if such shareholder:

(1) submits to the corporation the record shareholder's written consent to the assertion of such rights no later than the date referred to in section 13.22(b)(2)(ii); and

(2) does so with respect to all shares of the class or series that are beneficially owned by the beneficial shareholder.

SUBCHAPTER B. PROCEDURE FOR EXERCISE OF APPRAISAL RIGHTS

§13.20. Notice of Appraisal Rights

(a) If proposed corporate action described in section 13.02(a) is to be submitted to a vote at a shareholders' meeting, the meeting notice must state that the corporation has concluded that shareholders are, are not or may be entitled to assert appraisal rights under this chapter. If the corporation concludes that appraisal rights are or may be available, a copy of this chapter must accompany the meeting notice sent to those record shareholders entitled to exercise appraisal rights.

(b) In a merger pursuant to section 11.05, the parent corporation must notify in writing all record shareholders of the subsidiary who are entitled to assert appraisal rights that the corporate action became effective. Such notice must be sent within ten days after the corporate action became effective and include the materials described in section 13.22.

§13.21. Notice of Intent to Demand Payment

(a) If proposed corporate action requiring appraisal rights under section 13.02 is submitted to a vote at a shareholders' meeting, a shareholder who wishes to assert appraisal rights with respect to any class or series of shares:

(1) must deliver to the corporation before the vote is taken written notice of the shareholder's intent to demand payment if the proposed action is effectuated; and

(2) must not vote, or cause or permit to be voted, any shares of such class or series in favor of the proposed action.

(b) A shareholder who does not satisfy the requirements of subsection (a) is not entitled to payment under this chapter.

§13.22. Appraisal Notice and Form

(a) If proposed corporate action requiring appraisal rights under section 13.02(a) becomes effective, the corporation must deliver a written appraisal notice and form required by subsection (b)(1) to all shareholders who satisfied the requirements of section 13.21. In the case of a merger under section 11.05, the parent must deliver a written appraisal notice and form to all record shareholders who may be entitled to assert appraisal rights.

(b) The appraisal notice must be sent no earlier than the date the corporate action became effective and no later than ten days after such date and must:

(1) supply a form that specified the date of the first announcement to shareholders of the principal terms of the proposed corporate action and requires the shareholder asserting the appraisal rights to certify (i) whether or not beneficial ownership of those shares for which appraisal rights are asserted was acquired before that date and (ii) that the shareholder did not vote for the transaction;

(2) state:

(i) where the form must be sent and where certificates for certificated shares must be deposited and the date by which those certificates must be deposited, which date may not be earlier than the date for receiving the required form under subsection (2)(ii);

(ii) a date by which the corporation must receive the form which date may not be fewer than 40 nor more than 60 days after the date the subsection (a) appraisal notice and form are sent, and state that the shareholder shall have waived the right to demand appraisal with respect to the shares unless the form is received by the corporation by such specified date;

(iii) the corporation's estimate of the fair value of the shares;

(iv) that, if requested in writing, the corporation will provide, to the shareholder so requesting, within ten days after the date specified in subsection (2)(ii) the number of shareholders who return the forms by the specified date and the total number of shares owned by them; and

(v) the date by which the notice to withdraw under section 13.23 must be received, which date must be within 20 days after the date specified in subsection (2)(ii); and

(3) be accompanied by a copy of this chapter.

§13.23. Perfection of Rights; Right to Withdraw

(a) A shareholder who receives notice pursuant to section 13.22 and who wishes to exercise appraisal rights must certify on the form sent by the corporation whether the beneficial owner of such shares acquired beneficial ownership of the shares before the date required to be set forth in the notice pursuant to section 13.22(b)(1). If a shareholder fails to make this certification, the corporation may elect to treat the shareholder's shares as after-acquired shares under section

13.25. In addition, a shareholder who wishes to exercise appraisal rights must execute and return the form and, in the case of certificated shares, deposit the shareholder's certificates in accordance with the terms of the notice by the date referred to in the notice pursuant to section 13.22(b)(2)(ii). Once a shareholder deposits that shareholder's certificates or, in the case of uncertificated shares, returns the executed forms, that shareholder loses all rights as a shareholder, unless the shareholder withdraws pursuant to subsection (b).

(b) A shareholder who has complied with subsection (a) may nevertheless decline to exercise appraisal rights and withdraw from the appraisal process by so notifying the corporation in writing by the date set forth in the appraisal notice pursuant to section 13.22(b)(2)(v). A shareholder who fails to so withdraw from the appraisal process may not thereafter withdraw without the corporation's written consent.

(c) A shareholder who does not execute and return the form and, in the case of certificated shares, deposit that shareholder's share certificates where required, each by the date set forth in the notice described in section 13.22(b), shall not be entitled to payment under this chapter.

§13.24. Payment

(a) Except as provided in section 13.25, within 30 days after the form required by section 13.22(b)(2)(ii) is due, the corporation shall pay in cash to those shareholders who complied with section 13.23(a) the amount the corporation estimates to be the fair value of the shares, plus interest.

(b) The payment to each shareholder pursuant to subsection (a) must be accompanied by:

(1) financial statements of the corporation that issued the shares to be appraised, consisting of a balance sheet as of the end of a fiscal year ending not more than 16 months before the date of payment, an income statement for that year, a statement of changes in shareholders' equity for that year, and the latest available interim financial statements, if any;

(2) a statement of the corporation's estimate of the fair value of the shares, which estimate must equal or exceed the corporation's estimate given pursuant to section 13.22(b)(2)(iii);

(3) a statement that shareholders described in subsection (a) have the right to demand further payment under section 13.26 and that if any such shareholder does not do so within the time period specified therein, such shareholder shall be deemed to have accepted such payment in full satisfaction of the corporation's obligations under this chapter.

§13.25. After-Acquired Shares

(a) A corporation may elect to withhold payment required by section 13.24 from any shareholder who did not certify that beneficial ownership of all of the shareholder's shares for which appraisal rights are asserted was acquired before the date set forth in the appraisal notice sent pursuant to section 13.22(b)(1).

(b) If the corporation elected to withhold payment under subsection (a), it must, within 30 days after the form required by section 13.22(b)(2)(ii) is due, notify all shareholders who are described in subsection (a):

(1) of the information required by section 13.24(b)(1);

(2) of the corporation's estimate of fair value pursuant to section 13.24(b)(2);

(3) that they may accept the corporation's estimate of fair value, plus interest, in full satisfaction of their demands or demand appraisal under section 13.26;

(4) that those shareholders who wish to accept such offer must so notify the corporation of their acceptance of the corporation's offer within 30 days after receiving the offer; and

(5) that those shareholders who do not satisfy the requirements for demanding appraisal under section 13.26 shall be deemed to have accepted the corporation's offer.

(c) Within ten days after receiving the shareholder's acceptance pursuant to subsection (b), the corporation must pay in cash the amount it offered under subsection (b)(2) to each shareholder who agreed to accept the corporation's offer in full satisfaction of the shareholder's demand.

(d) Within 40 days after sending the notice described in subsection (b), the corporation must pay in cash the amount it offered to pay under subsection (b)(2) to each shareholder described in subsection (b)(5).

§13.26. Procedure if Shareholder Dissatisfied with Payment or Offer

(a) A shareholder pursuant to section 13.24 who is dissatisfied with the amount of the payment must notify the corporation in writing of that shareholder's estimate of the fair value of the shares and demand payment of that estimate plus interest (less any payment under section 13.24). A shareholder offered payment under section 13.25 who is dissatisfied with that offer must reject the offer and demand payment of the sharesholder's stated estimate of the fair value of the shares plus interest.

(b) A shareholder who fails to notify the corporation in writing of that shareholder's demand to be paid the shareholder's stated estimate of the fair value plus interest under subsection (a) within 30 days after receiving the corporation's payment or offer of payment under section 13.24 or section 13.25, respectively, waives the right to demand payment under this section and shall be entitled only to the payment made or offered pursuant to those respective sections.

Subchapter C. Judicial Appraisal of Shares

§13.30. Court Action

(a) If a shareholder makes demand for payment under section 13.26 which remains unsettled, the corporation shall commence a proceeding within 60 days after receiving the payment demand and petition the court to determine the fair value of the shares and accrued interest. If the corporation does not commence the proceeding within the 60-day period, it shall pay in cash to each shareholder the amount the shareholder demanded pursuant to section 13.26 plus interest.

(b) The corporation shall commence the proceeding in the appropriate court of the county where the corporation's principal office (or, if none, its registered office) in this state is located. If the corporation is a foreign corporation without a registered office in this state, it shall commence the proceeding in the county in this state where the principal office or registered office of the domestic corporation merged with the foreign corporation was located at the time of the transaction.

(c) The corporation shall make all shareholders (whether or not residents of this state) whose demands remain unsettled parties to the proceeding as in an action against their shares, and all parties must be served with a copy of the petition. Nonresidents may be served by registered or certified mail or by publication as provided by law.

(d) The jurisdiction of the court in which the proceeding is commenced under subsection (b) is plenary and exclusive. The court may appoint one or more persons as appraisers to receive evidence and recommend a decision on the question of fair value. The appraisers shall have the powers described in the order appointing them, or in any amendment to it. The shareholders demanding appraisal rights are entitled to the same discovery rights as parties in other civil proceedings. There shall be no right to a jury trial.

(e) Each shareholder made a party to the proceeding is entitled to judgment (i) for the amount, if any, by which the court finds the fair value of the shareholder's shares, plus interest, exceeds the amount paid by the corporation or (ii) for the fair value, plus interest, of the shareholder's shares for which the corporation elected to withhold payment under section 13.25.

§13.31. *Court Costs and Counsel Fees*

(a) The court in an appraisal proceeding commenced under section 13.30 shall determine all costs of the proceeding, including the reasonable compensation and expenses of appraisers appointed by the court. The court shall assess the costs against the corporation, except that the court may assess costs against all or some of the shareholders demanding appraisal, in amounts the court finds equitable, to the extent the court finds such shareholders acted arbitrarily vexatiously, or not in good faith with respect to the rights provided by this chapter.

(b) The court in an appraisal proceeding may also assess the fees and expenses of counsel and experts for the respective parties, in amounts the court finds equitable:

(1) against the corporation and in favor of any or all shareholders demanding appraisal if the court finds the corporation did not substantially comply with the requirements of sections 13.20, 13.22, 13.24 or 13.25; or

(2) against either the corporation or a shareholder demanding appraisal, in favor of any other party, if the court finds that the party against whom the fees and expenses are assessed acted arbitrarily vexatiously, or not in good faith with respect to the rights provided by this chapter.

(c) If the court in an appraisal proceeding finds that the services of counsel for any shareholder were of substantial benefit to other shareholders similarly situated, and that the fees for those services should not be assessed against the corporation, the court may award to such counsel reasonable fees to be paid out of the amounts awarded the shareholders who were benefitted.

(d) To the extent the corporation fails to make a required payment pursuant to sections 13.24, 13.25, or 13.26, the shareholder may sue directly for the amount owned and, to the extent successful, shall be entitled to recover from the corporation all costs and expenses of the suit, including counsel fees.

Chapter 14. Dissolution

Subchapter A. Voluntary Dissolution

§14.01. *Dissolution by Incorporators or Initial Directors*

A majority of the incorporators or initial directors of a corporation that has not issued shares or has not commenced business may dissolve the corporation by delivering to the secretary of state for filing articles of dissolution that set forth:

(1) the name of the corporation;

(2) the date of its incorporation;

(3) either (i) that none of the corporation's shares has been issued or (ii) that the corporation has not commenced business;

(4) that no debt of the corporation remains unpaid;

(5) that the net assets of the corporation remaining after winding up have been distributed to the shareholders, if shares were issued; and

(6) that a majority of the incorporators or initial directors authorized the dissolution.

§14.02. *Dissolution by Board of Directors and Shareholders*

(a) A corporation's board of directors may propose dissolution for submission to the shareholders.

(b) For a proposal to dissolve to be adopted:

(1) the board of directors must recommend dissolution to the shareholders unless the board of directors determines that because of conflict of interest or other special circumstances it should make no recommendation and communicates the basis for its determination to the shareholders; and

(2) the shareholders entitled to vote must approve the proposal to dissolve as provided in subsection (e).

(c) The board of directors may condition its submission of the proposal for dissolution on any basis.

(d) The corporation shall notify each shareholder, whether or not entitled to vote, of the proposed shareholders' meeting in accordance with section 7.05. The notice must also state that the purpose, or one of the purposes, of the meeting is to consider dissolving the corporation.

(e) Unless the articles of incorporation or the board of directors (acting pursuant to subsection (c)) require a greater vote or a vote by voting groups, the proposal to dissolve to be adopted must be approved by a majority of all the votes entitled to be cast on that proposal.

§14.03. *Articles of Dissolution*

(a) At any time after dissolution is authorized, the corporation may dissolve by delivering to the secretary of state for filing articles of dissolution setting forth:

(1) the name of the corporation;

(2) the date dissolution was authorized;

(3) if dissolution was approved by the shareholders:

(i) the number of votes entitled to be cast on the proposal to dissolve; and

(ii) either the total number of votes cast for and against dissolution or the total number of undisputed votes cast for dissolution and a statement that the number cast for dissolution was sufficient for approval.

(4) If voting by voting groups was required, the information required by subparagraph (3) must be separately provided for each voting group entitled to vote separately on the plan to dissolve.

(b) A corporation is dissolved upon the effective date of its articles of dissolution.

§14.04. *Revocation of Dissolution*

(a) A corporation may revoke its dissolution within 120 days of its effective date.

(b) Revocation of dissolution must be authorized in the same manner as the dissolution was authorized unless that authorization permitted revocation by action of the board of directors alone, in which event the board of directors may revoke the dissolution without shareholder action.

(c) After the revocation of dissolution is authorized, the corporation may revoke the dissolution by delivering to the secretary of state for filing articles of revocation of dissolution, together with a copy of its articles of dissolution, that set forth:

(1) the name of the corporation;

(2) the effective date of the dissolution that was revoked;

(3) the date that the revocation of dissolution was authorized;

(4) if the corporation's board of directors (or incorporators) revoked the dissolution, a statement to that effect;

(5) if the corporation's board of directors revoked a dissolution authorized by the shareholders, a statement that revocation was permitted by action by the board of directors alone pursuant to that authorization; and

(6) if shareholder action was required to revoke the dissolution, the information required by section 14.03(a)(3) or (4).

(d) Revocation of dissolution is effective upon the effective date of the articles of revocation of dissolution.

(e) When the revocation of dissolution is effective, it relates back to and takes effect as of the effective date of the dissolution and the corporation resumes carrying on its business as if dissolution had never occurred.

§14.05. *Effect of Dissolution*

(a) A dissolved corporation continues its corporate existence but may not carry on any business except that appropriate to wind up and liquidate its business and affairs, including:

(1) collecting its assets;

(2) disposing of its properties that will not be distributed in kind to its shareholders;

(3) discharging or making provision for discharging its liabilities;

(4) distributing its remaining property among its shareholders according to their interests; and

(5) doing every other act necessary to wind up and liquidate its business and affairs.

(b) Dissolution of a corporation does not:

(1) transfer title to the corporation's property;

(2) prevent transfer of its shares or securities, although the authorization to dissolve may provide for closing the corporation's share transfer records;

(3) subject its directors or officers to standards of conduct different from those prescribed in chapter 8;

(4) change quorum or voting requirements for its board of directors or shareholders; change provisions for selection, resignation, or removal of its directors or officers or both; or change provisions for amending its bylaws;

(5) prevent commencement of a proceeding by or against the corporation in its corporate name;

(6) abate or suspend a proceeding pending by or against the corporation on the effective date of dissolution; or

(7) terminate the authority of the registered agent of the corporation.

§14.06. *Known Claims Against Dissolved Corporation*

(a) A dissolved corporation may dispose of the known claims against it by following the procedure described in this section.

(b) The dissolved corporation shall notify its known claimants in writing of the dissolution at any time after its effective date. The written notice must:

(1) describe information that must be included in a claim;

(2) provide a mailing address where a claim may be sent;

(3) state the deadline, which may not be fewer than 120 days from the effective date of the written notice, by which the dissolved corporation must receive the claim; and

(4) state that the claim will be barred if not received by the deadline.

(c) A claim against the dissolved corporation is barred:

(1) if a claimant who was given written notice under subsection (b) does not deliver the claim to the dissolved corporation by the deadline;

(2) if a claimant whose claim was rejected by the dissolved corporation does not commence a proceeding to enforce the claim within 90 days from the effective date of the rejection notice.

(d) For purposes of this section, "claim" does not include a contingent liability or a claim based on an event occurring after the effective date of dissolution.

§14.07. *Unknown Claims Against Dissolved Corporation*

(a) A dissolved corporation may also publish notice of its dissolution and request that persons with claims against the corporation present them in accordance with the notice.

(b) The notice must:

(1) be published one time in a newspaper of general circulation in the county where the dissolved corporation's principal office (or, if none in this state, its registered office) is or was last located;

(2) describe the information that must be included in a claim and provide a mailing address where the claim may be sent; and

(3) state that a claim against the corporation will be barred unless a proceeding to enforce the claim is commenced within five years after the publication of the notice.

(c) If the dissolved corporation publishes a newspaper notice in accordance with subsection (b), the claim of each of the following claimants is barred unless the claimant commences a proceeding to enforce the claim against the dissolved corporation within five years after the publication date of the newspaper notice:

(1) a claimant who did not receive written notice under section 14.06;

(2) a claimant whose claim was timely sent to the dissolved corporation but not acted on;

(3) a claimant whose claim is contingent or based on an event occurring after the effective date of dissolution.

(d) A claim may be enforced under this section:

(1) against the dissolved corporation, to the extent of its undistributed assets; or

(2) if the assets have been distributed in liquidation, against a shareholder of the dissolved corporation to the extent of his pro rata share of the claim or the corporate assets distributed to him in liquidation, whichever is less, but a shareholder's total liability for all claims under this section may not exceed the total amount of assets distributed to him.

Subchapter B. Administrative Dissolution

§14.20. *Grounds for Administrative Dissolution*

The secretary of state may commence a proceeding under section 14.21 to administratively dissolve a corporation if:

(1) the corporation does not pay within 60 days after they are due any franchise taxes or penalties imposed by this Act or other law;

(2) the corporation does not deliver its annual report to the secretary of state within 60 days after it is due;

(3) the corporation is without a registered agent or registered office in this state for 60 days or more;

(4) the corporation does not notify the secretary of state within 60 days that its registered agent or registered office has been changed, that its registered agent has resigned, or that its registered office has been discontinued; or

(5) the corporation's period of duration stated in its articles of incorporation expires.

§14.21. *Procedure for and Effect of Administrative Dissolution*

(a) If the secretary of state determines that one or more grounds exist under section 14.20 for dissolving a corporation, he shall serve the corporation with written notice of his determination under section 5.04.

(b) If the corporation does not correct each ground for dissolution or demonstrate to the reasonable satisfaction of the secretary of state that each ground determined by the secretary of state does not exist within 60 days after service of the notice is perfected under section 5.04, the secretary of state shall administratively dissolve the corporation by signing a certificate of dissolution that recites the ground or grounds for dissolution and its effective date. The secretary of state shall file the original of the certificate and serve a copy on the corporation under section 5.04.

(c) A corporation administratively dissolved continues its corporate existence but may not carry on any business except that necessary to wind up and liquidate its business and affairs under section 14.05 and notify claimants under sections 14.06 and 14.07.

(d) The administrative dissolution of a corporation does not terminate the authority of its registered agent.

§14.22. *Reinstatement Following Administrative Dissolution*

(a) A corporation administratively dissolved under section 14.21 may apply to the secretary of state for reinstatement within two years after the effective date of dissolution. The application must:

(1) recite the name of the corporation and the effective date of its administrative dissolution;

(2) state that the ground or grounds for dissolution either did not exist or have been eliminated;

(3) state that the corporation's name satisfies the requirements of section 4.01; and

(4) contain a certificate from the [taxing authority] reciting that all taxes owed by the corporation have been paid.

(b) If the secretary of state determines that the application contains the information required by subsection (a) and that the information is correct, he shall cancel the certificate of dissolution and prepare a certificate of reinstatement that recites his determination and the effective date of reinstatement, file the original of the certificate, and serve a copy on the corporation under section 5.04.

(c) When the reinstatement is effective, it relates back to and takes effect as of the effective date of the administrative dissolution and the corporation resumes carrying on its business as if the administrative dissolution had never occurred.

§14.23. *Appeal from Denial of Reinstatement*

(a) If the secretary of state denies a corporation's application for reinstatement following administrative dissolution, he shall serve the corporation under section 5.04 with a written notice that explains the reason or reasons for denial.

(b) The corporation may appeal the denial of reinstatement to the [name or describe] court within 30 days after service of the notice of denial is perfected. The corporation appeals by petitioning the court to set aside the dissolution and attaching to the petition copies of the secretary of state's certificate of dissolution, the corporation's application for reinstatement, and the secretary of state's notice of denial.

(c) The court may summarily order the secretary of state to reinstate the dissolved corporation or may take other action the court considers appropriate.

(d) The court's final decision may be appealed as in other civil proceedings.

Subchapter C. Judicial Dissolution

§14.30. Grounds for Judicial Dissolution

The [name or describe court or courts] may dissolve a corporation:

(1) in a proceeding by the attorney general if it is established that:

(i) the corporation obtained its articles of incorporation through fraud; or

(ii) the corporation has continued to exceed or abuse the authority conferred upon it by law;

(2) in a proceeding by a shareholder if it is established that:

(i) the directors are deadlocked in the management of the corporate affairs, the shareholders are unable to break the deadlock, and irreparable injury to the corporation is threatened or being suffered, or the business and affairs of the corporation can no longer be conducted to the advantage of the shareholders generally, because of the deadlock;

(ii) the directors or those in control of the corporation have acted, are acting, or will act in a manner that is illegal, oppressive, or fraudulent;

(iii) the shareholders are deadlocked in voting power and have failed, for a period that includes at least two consecutive annual meeting dates, to elect successors to directors whose terms have expired; or

(iv) the corporate assets are being misapplied or wasted;

(3) in a proceeding by a creditor if it is established that:

(i) the creditor's claim has been reduced to judgment, the execution on the judgment returned unsatisfied, and the corporation is insolvent; or

(ii) the corporation has admitted in writing that the creditor's claim is due and owing and the corporation is insolvent; or

(4) in a proceeding by the corporation to have its voluntary dissolution continued under court supervision.

§14.31. Procedure for Judicial Dissolution

(a) Venue for a proceeding by the attorney general to dissolve a corporation lies in [name the county or counties]. Venue for a proceeding brought by any other party named in section 14.30 lies in the county where a corporation's principal office (or, if none in this state, its registered office) is or was last located.

(b) It is not necessary to make shareholders parties to a proceeding to dissolve a corporation unless relief is sought against them individually.

(c) A court in a proceeding brought to dissolve a corporation may issue injunctions, appoint a receiver or custodian pendente lite with all powers and duties the court directs, take other action required to preserve the corporate assets wherever located, and carry on the business of the corporation until a full hearing can be held.

(d) Within 10 days of the commencement of a proceeding under section 14.30(2) to dissolve a corporation that has no shares listed on a national securities exchange or regularly traded in a market maintained by one or more members of a national securities exchange, the corporation must send to all shareholders, other than the petitioner, a notice stating that the shareholders are entitled to avoid the dissolution of the corporation by electing to purchase the petitioner's shares under section 14.34 and accompanied by a copy of section 14.34.

§14.32. Receivership or Custodianship

(a) A court in a judicial proceeding brought to dissolve a corporation may appoint one or more receivers to wind up and liquidate, or one or more custodians to manage, the business and affairs of the corporation. The court shall hold a hearing, after notifying all parties to the proceeding and any interested persons designated by the court, before appointing a receiver or custodian. The court appointing a receiver or custodian has exclusive jurisdiction over the corporation and all of its property wherever located.

(b) The court may appoint an individual or a domestic or foreign corporation (authorized to transact business in this state) as a receiver or custodian. The court may require the receiver or custodian to post bond, with or without sureties, in an amount the court directs.

(c) The court shall describe the powers and duties of the receiver or custodian in its appointing order, which may be amended from time to time. Among other powers:

(1) the receiver (i) may dispose of all or any part of the assets of the corporation wherever located, at a public or private sale, if authorized by the court; and (ii) may sue and defend in his own name as receiver of the corporation in all courts of this state;

(2) the custodian may exercise all of the powers of the corporation, through or in place of its board of directors or officers, to the extent necessary to manage the affairs of the corporation in the best interests of its shareholders and creditors.

(d) The court during a receivership may redesignate the receiver a custodian, and during a custodianship may redesignate the custodian a receiver, if doing so is in the best interests of the corporation, its shareholders, and creditors.

(e) The court from time to time during the receivership or custodianship may order compensation paid and expense disbursements or reimbursements made to the receiver or custodian and his counsel from the assets of the corporation or proceeds from the sale of the assets.

§14.33. Decree of Dissolution

(a) If after a hearing the court determines that one or more grounds for judicial dissolution described in section 14.30 exist, it may enter a decree dissolving the corporation and specifying the effective date of the dissolution, and the clerk of the court shall deliver a certified copy of the decree to the secretary of state, who shall file it.

(b) After entering the decree of dissolution, the court shall direct the winding up and liquidation of the corporation's business and affairs in accordance with section 14.05 and the notification of claimants in accordance with sections 14.06 and 14.07.

§14.34. Election to Purchase in Lieu of Dissolution

(a) In a proceeding under section 14.30(2) to dissolve a corporation that has no shares listed on a national securities exchange or regularly traded in a market maintained by one or more members of a national or affiliated securities association, the corporation may elect or, if it fails to elect, one or more shareholders may elect to purchase all shares owned by the petitioning shareholder at the fair value of the shares. An election pursuant to this section shall be irrevocable unless the court determines that it is equitable to set aside or modify the election.

(b) An election to purchase pursuant to this section may be filed with the court at any time within 90 days after the filing of the petition under section 14.30(2) or at such later time as the court in its discretion may allow. If the election to purchase is filed by one or more shareholders, the corporation shall, within 10 days thereafter, give written notice to all shareholders, other than the petitioner. The notice must state the name and number of shares owned by the petitioner and the name and number of shares owned by each electing shareholder and must advise the recipients of their right to join in the election to purchase shares in accordance with this section. Shareholders who wish to participate must file notice of their intention to join in the purchase no later than 30 days after the effective date of the notice to them. All shareholders who have filed an election or notice of their intention to participate in the election to purchase thereby become parties to the proceeding and shall participate in the purchase in proportion to their ownership of shares as of the date the first election was filed, unless they otherwise agree or the court otherwise directs. After an election has been filed by the corporation or one or more shareholders, the proceeding under section 14.30(2) may not be discontinued or settled, nor may the petitioning shareholder sell or otherwise dispose of his shares, unless the court determines that it would be equitable to the corporation and the shareholders, other than the petitioner, to permit such discontinuance, settlement, sale, or other disposition.

(c) If, within 60 days of the filing of the first election, the parties reach agreement as to the fair value and terms of purchase of the petitioner's shares, the court shall enter an order directing the purchase of petitioner's shares upon the terms and conditions agreed to by the parties.

(d) If the parties are unable to reach an agreement as provided for in subsection (c), the court, upon application of any party, shall stay the section 14.30(2) proceedings and determine the fair value of the petitioner's shares as of the day before the date on which the petition under section 14.30(2) was filed or as of such other date as the court deems appropriate under the circumstances.

(e) Upon determining the fair value of the shares, the court shall enter an order directing the purchase upon such terms and conditions as the court deems appropriate, which may include payment of the purchase price in installments, where necessary in the interests of equity, provision for security to assure payment of the purchase price and any additional costs, fees, and expenses as may have been awarded, and, if the shares are to be purchased by shareholders, the allocation of shares among them. In allocating petitioner's shares among holders of different classes of shares, the court should attempt to preserve the existing distribution of voting rights among holders of different classes insofar as practicable and may direct that holders of a specific class or classes shall not participate in the purchase. Interest may be allowed at the rate and from the date determined by the court to be equitable, but if the court finds that the refusal of the petitioning shareholder to accept an offer of payment was arbitrary or otherwise not in good faith, no interest shall be allowed. If the court finds that the petitioning shareholder had probable grounds for relief under paragraphs (ii) or (iv) of section 14.30(2), it may award to the petitioning shareholder reasonable fees and expenses of counsel and of any experts employed by him.

(f) Upon entry of an order under subsections (c) or (e), the court shall dismiss the petition to dissolve the corporation under section 14.30, and the petitioning shareholder shall no longer have any rights or status as a shareholder of the corporation, except the right to receive the amounts awarded to him by the order of the court which shall be enforceable in the same manner as any other judgment.

(g) The purchase ordered pursuant to subsection (e), shall be made within 10 days after the date the order becomes final unless before that time the corporation files with the court a notice of its intention to adopt articles of dissolution pursuant to sections 14.02 and 14.03, which articles must then be adopted and filed within 50 days thereafter. Upon filing of such articles of dissolution, the corporation shall be dissolved in accordance with the provisions of sections 14.05 through 07, and the order entered pursuant to subsection (e) shall no longer be of any force or effect, except that the court may award the petitioning shareholder reasonable fees and expenses in accordance with the provisions of the last sentence of subsection (e) and the petitioner may continue to pursue any claims previously asserted on behalf of the corporation.

(h) Any payment by the corporation pursuant to an order under subsection (c) or (e), other than an award of fees and expenses pursuant to subsection (e), subject to the provisions of section 6.40.

Miscellaneous

§14.40. Deposit with State Treasurer

Assets of a dissolved corporation that should be transferred to a creditor, claimant, or shareholder of the corporation who cannot be found or who is not competent to receive them shall be reduced to cash and deposited with the state treasurer or other appropriate state official for safekeeping. When the creditor, claimant, or shareholder furnishes satisfactory proof of entitlement to the amount deposited, the state treasurer or other appropriate state official shall pay him or his representative that amount.

Chapter 15. Foreign Corporations

Subchapter A. Certificate of Authority

§15.01. Authority to Transact Business Required

(a) A foreign corporation may not transact business in this state until it obtains a certificate of authority from the secretary of state.

(b) The following activities, among others, do not constitute transacting business within the meaning of subsection (a):

(1) maintaining, defending, or settling any proceeding;

(2) holding meetings of the board of directors or shareholders or carrying on other activities concerning internal corporate affairs;

(3) maintaining bank accounts;

(4) maintaining offices or agencies for the transfer, exchange, and registration of the corporation's own securities or maintaining trustees or depositaries with respect to those securities;

(5) selling through independent contractors;

(6) soliciting or obtaining orders, whether by mail or through employees or agents or otherwise, if the orders require acceptance outside this state before they become contracts;

(7) creating or acquiring indebtedness, mortgages, and security interests in real or personal property;

(8) securing or collecting debts or enforcing mortgages and security interests in property securing the debts;

(9) owning, without more, real or personal property;

(10) conducting an isolated transaction that is completed within 30 days and that is not one in the course of repeated transactions of a like nature;

(11) transacting business in interstate commerce.

(c) The list of activities in subsection (b) is not exhaustive.

§15.02. Consequences of Transacting Business Without Authority

(a) A foreign corporation transacting business in this state without a certificate of authority may not maintain a proceeding in any court in this state until it obtains a certificate of authority.

(b) The successor to a foreign corporation that transacted business in this state without a certificate of authority and the assignee of a cause of action arising out of that business may not maintain a proceeding based on that cause of action in any court in this state until the foreign corporation or its successor obtains a certificate of authority.

(c) A court may stay a proceeding commenced by a foreign corporation, its successor, or assignee until it determines whether the foreign corporation or its successor requires a certificate of authority. If it so determines, the court may further stay the proceeding until the foreign corporation or its successor obtains the certificate.

(d) A foreign corporation is liable for a civil penalty of $__________ for each day, but not to exceed a total of $__________ for each year, it transacts business in this state without a certificate of authority. The attorney general may collect all penalties due under this subsection.

(e) Notwithstanding subsections (a) and (b), the failure of a foreign corporation to obtain a certificate of authority does not impair the validity of its corporate acts or prevent it from defending any proceeding in this state.

§15.03. Application for Certificate of Authority

(a) A foreign corporation may apply for a certificate of authority to transact business in this state by delivering an application to the secretary of state for filing. The application must set forth:

(1) the name of the foreign corporation or, if its name is unavailable for use in this state, a corporate name that satisfies the requirements of section 15.06;

(2) the name of the state or country under whose law it is incorporated;

(3) its date of incorporation and period of duration;

(4) the street address of its principal office;

(5) the address of its registered office in this state and the name of its registered agent at that office; and

(6) the names and usual business addresses of its current directors and officers.

(b) The foreign corporation shall deliver with the completed application a certificate of existence (or a document of similar import) duly authenticated by the secretary of state or other official having custody of corporate records in the state or country under whose law it is incorporated.

§15.04. Amended Certificate of Authority

(a) A foreign corporation authorized to transact business in this state must obtain an amended certificate of authority from the secretary of state if it changes:

(1) its corporate name;

(2) the period of its duration; or

(3) the state or country of its incorporation.

(b) The requirements of section 15.03 for obtaining an original certificate of authority apply to obtaining an amended certificate under this section.

§15.05. Effect of Certificate of Authority

(a) A certificate of authority authorizes the foreign corporation to which it is issued to transact business in this state subject, however, to the right of the state to revoke the certificate as provided in this Act.

(b) A foreign corporation with a valid certificate of authority has the same but no greater rights and has the same but no greater privileges as, and except as otherwise provided by this Act is subject to the same duties, restrictions, penalties, and liabilities now or later imposed on, a domestic corporation of like character.

(c) This Act does not authorize this state to regulate the organization or internal affairs of a foreign corporation authorized to transact business in this state.

§15.06. Corporate Name of Foreign Corporation

(a) If the corporate name of a foreign corporation does not satisfy the requirements of section 4.01, the foreign corporation to obtain or maintain a certificate of authority to transact business in this state:

(1) may add the word "corporation," "incorporated," "company," or "limited," or the abbreviation "corp.," "inc.," "co.," or "ltd.," to its corporate name for use in this state; or

(2) may use a fictitious name to transact business in this state if its real name is unavailable and it delivers to the secretary of state for filing a copy of the resolution of its board of directors, certified by its secretary, adopting the fictitious name.

(b) Except as authorized by subsections (c) and (d), the corporate name (including a fictitious name) of a foreign corporation must be distinguishable upon the records of the secretary of state from:

(1) the corporate name of a corporation incorporated or authorized to transact business in this state;

(2) a corporate name reserved or registered under section 4.02 or 4.03;

(3) the fictitious name of another foreign corporation authorized to transact business in this state; and

(4) the corporate name of a not-for-profit corporation incorporated or authorized to transact business in this state.

(c) A foreign corporation may apply to the secretary of state for authorization to use in this state the name of another corporation (incorporated or authorized to transact business in this state) that is not distinguishable upon his records from the name applied for. The secretary of state shall authorize use of the name applied for if:

(1) the other corporation consents to the use in writing and submits an undertaking in form satisfactory to the secretary of state to change its name to a name that is distinguishable upon the records of the secretary of state from the name of the applying corporation; or

(2) the applicant delivers to the secretary of state a certified copy of a final judgment of a court of competent jurisdiction establishing the applicant's right to use the name applied for in this state.

(d) A foreign corporation may use in this state the name (including the fictitious name) of another domestic or foreign corporation that is used in this state if the other corporation is incorporated or authorized to transact business in this state and the foreign corporation:

(1) has merged with the other corporation;

(2) has been formed by reorganization of the other corporation; or

(3) has acquired all or substantially all of the assets, including the corporate name, of the other corporation.

(e) If a foreign corporation authorized to transact business in this state changes its corporate name to one that does not satisfy the requirements of section 4.01, it may not transact business in this state under the changed name until it adopts a name satisfying the requirements of section 4.01 and obtains an amended certificate of authority under section 15.04.

§15.07. *Registered Office and Registered Agent of Foreign Corporation*

Each foreign corporation authorized to transact business in this state must continuously maintain in this state:

(1) a registered office that may be the same as any of its places of business; and

(2) a registered agent, who may be:

(i) an individual who resides in this state and whose business office is identical with the registered office;

(ii) a domestic corporation or not-for-profit domestic corporation whose business office is identical with the registered office; or

(iii) a foreign corporation or foreign not-for-profit corporation authorized to transact business in this state whose business office is identical with the registered office.

§15.08. *Change of Registered Office or Registered Agent of Foreign Corporation*

(a) A foreign corporation authorized to transact business in this state may change its registered office or registered agent by delivering to the secretary of state for filing a statement of change that sets forth:

(1) its name;

(2) the street address of its current registered office;

(3) if the current registered office is to be changed, the street address of its new registered office;

(4) the name of its current registered agent;

(5) if the current registered agent is to be changed, the name of its new registered agent and the new agent's written consent (either on the statement or attached to it) to the appointment; and

(6) that after the change or changes are made, the street addresses of its registered office and the business office of its registered agent will be identical.

(b) If a registered agent changes the street address of his business office, he may change the street address of the registered office of any foreign corporation for which he is the registered agent by notifying the corporation in writing of the change and signing (either manually or in facsimile) and delivering to the secretary of state for filing a statement of change that complies with the requirements of subsection (a) and recites that the corporation has been notified of the change.

§15.09. *Resignation of Registered Agent of Foreign Corporation*

(a) The registered agent of a foreign corporation may resign his agency appointment by signing and delivering to the secretary of state for filing the original and two exact or conformed copies of a statement of resignation. The statement of resignation may include a statement that the registered office is also discontinued.

(b) After filing the statement, the secretary of state shall attach the filing receipt to one copy and mail the copy and receipt to the registered office if not discontinued. The secretary of state shall mail the other copy to the foreign corporation at its principal office address shown in its most recent annual report.

(c) The agency appointment is terminated, and the registered office discontinued if so provided, on the 31st day after the date on which the statement was filed.

§15.10. Service on Foreign Corporation

(a) The registered agent of a foreign corporation authorized to transact business in this state is the corporation's agent for service of process, notice, or demand required or permitted by law to be served on the foreign corporation.

(b) A foreign corporation may be served by registered or certified mail, return receipt requested, addressed to the secretary of the foreign corporation at its principal office shown in its application for a certificate of authority or in its most recent annual report if the foreign corporation:

(1) has no registered agent or its registered agent cannot with reasonable diligence be served;

(2) has withdrawn from transacting business in this state under section 15.20; or

(3) has had its certificate of authority revoked under section 15.31.

(c) Service is perfected under subsection (b) at the earliest of:

(1) the date the foreign corporation receives the mail;

(2) the date shown on the return receipt, if signed on behalf of the foreign corporation; or

(3) five days after its deposit in the United States Mail, as evidenced by the postmark, if mailed postpaid and correctly addressed.

(d) This section does not prescribe the only means, or necessarily the required means, of serving a foreign corporation.

SUBCHAPTER B. WITHDRAWAL

§15.20. Withdrawal of Foreign Corporation

(a) A foreign corporation authorized to transact business in this state may not withdraw from this state until it obtains a certificate of withdrawal from the secretary of state.

(b) A foreign corporation authorized to transact business in this state may apply for a certificate of withdrawal by delivering an application to the secretary of state for filing. The application must set forth:

(1) the name of the foreign corporation and the name of the state or country under whose law it is incorporated;

(2) that it is not transacting business in this state and that it surrenders its authority to transact business in this state;

(3) that it revokes the authority of its registered agent to accept service on its behalf and appoints the secretary of state as its agent for service of process in any proceeding based on a cause of action arising during the time it was authorized to transact business in this state;

(4) a mailing address to which the secretary of state may mail a copy of any process served on him under subdivision (3); and

(5) a commitment to notify the secretary of state in the future of any change in its mailing address.

(c) After the withdrawal of the corporation is effective, service of process on the secretary of state under this section is service on the foreign corporation. Upon receipt of process, the secretary of state shall mail a copy of the process to the foreign corporation at the mailing address set forth under subsection (b).

SUBCHAPTER C. REVOCATION OF CERTIFICATE OF AUTHORITY

§15.30. Grounds for Revocation

The secretary of state may commune a proceeding under section 15.31 to revoke the certificate of authority of a foreign corporation authorized to transact business in this state if:

(1) the foreign corporation does not deliver its annual report to the secretary of state within 60 days after it is due;

(2) the foreign corporation does not pay within 60 days after they are due any franchise taxes or penalties imposed by this Act or other law;

(3) the foreign corporation is without a registered agent or registered office in this state for 60 days or more;

(4) the foreign corporation does not inform the secretary of state under section 15.08 or 15.09 that its registered agent or registered office has changed, that its registered agent has resigned, or that its registered office has been discontinued within 60 days of the change, resignation, or discontinuance;

(5) an incorporator, director, officer, or agent of the foreign corporation signed a document he knew was false in any material respect with intent that the document be delivered to the secretary of state for filing;

(6) the secretary of state receives a duly authenticated certificate from the secretary of state or other official having custody of corporate records in the state or country under whose law the foreign corporation is incorporated stating that it has been dissolved or disappeared as the result of a merger.

§15.31. Procedure for and Effect of Revocation

(a) If the secretary of state determines that one or more grounds exist under section 15.30 for revocation of a certificate of authority, he shall serve the foreign corporation with written notice of his determination under section 15.10.

(b) If the foreign corporation does not correct each ground for revocation or demonstrate to the reasonable satisfaction of the secretary of state that each ground determined by the secretary of state does not exist within 60 days after service of the notice is perfected under section 15.10, the secretary of state may revoke the foreign corporation's certificate of authority by signing a certificate of revocation that recites the ground or grounds for revocation and its effective date. The secretary of state shall file the original of the certificate and serve a copy on the foreign corporation under section 15.10.

(c) The authority of a foreign corporation to transact business in this state ceases on the date shown on the certificate revoking its certificate of authority.

(d) The secretary of state's revocation of a foreign corporation's certificate of authority appoints the secretary of state the foreign corporation's agent for service of process in any proceeding based on a cause of action which arose during the time the foreign corporation was authorized to transact business in this state. Service of process on the secretary of state under this subsection is service on the foreign corporation. Upon receipt of process, the secretary of state shall mail a copy of the process to the secretary of the foreign corporation at its principal office shown on its most recent annual report or in any subsequent communication received from the corporation stating the current mailing address of its principal office or, if none are on file, in its application for a certificate of authority.

(e) Revocation of a foreign corporation's certificate of authority does not terminate the authority of the registered agent of the corporation.

§15.32. Appeal from Revocation

(a) A foreign corporation may appeal the secretary of state's revocation of its certificate of authority to the [name or describe] court within 30 days after service of the certificate of revocation is perfected under section 15.10. The foreign corporation appeals by petitioning the court to set aside the revocation and attaching to the petition copies of its certificate of authority and the secretary of state's certificate of revocation.

(b) The court may summarily order the secretary of state to reinstate the certificate of authority or may take any other action the court considers appropriate.

(c) The court's final decision may be appealed as in other civil proceedings.

Chapter 16. Records and Reports

Subchapter A. Records

§16.01. Corporate Records

(a) A corporation shall keep as permanent records minutes of all meetings of its shareholders and board of directors, a record of all actions taken by the shareholders or board of directors without a meeting, and a record of all actions taken by a committee of the board of directors in place of the board of directors on behalf of the corporation.

(b) A corporation shall maintain appropriate accounting records.

(c) A corporation or its agent shall maintain a record of its shareholders, in a form that permits preparation of a list of the names and addresses of all shareholders, in alphabetical order by class of shares showing the number and class of shares held by each.

(d) A corporation shall maintain its records in written form or in another form capable of conversion into written form within a reasonable time.

(e) A corporation shall keep a copy of the following records at its principal office:

(1) its articles or restated articles of incorporation and all amendments to them currently in effect;

(2) its bylaws or restated bylaws and all amendments to them currently in effect;

(3) resolutions adopted by its board of directors creating one or more classes or series of shares, and fixing their relative rights, preferences, and limitations, if shares issued pursuant to those resolutions are outstanding;

(4) the minutes of all shareholders' meetings, and records of all action taken by shareholders without a meeting, for the past three years;

(5) all written communications to shareholders generally within the past three years, including the financial statements furnished for the past three years under section 16.20;

(6) a list of the names and business addresses of its current directors and officers; and

(7) its most recent annual report delivered to the secretary of state under section 16.22.

§16.02. Inspection of Records by Shareholders

(a) A shareholder of a corporation is entitled to inspect and copy, during regular business hours at the corporation's principal office, any of the records of the corporation described in section 16.01 (e) if he gives the corporation written notice of his demand at least five business days before the date on which he wishes to inspect and copy.

(b) A shareholder of a corporation is entitled to inspect and copy, during regular business hours at a reasonable location specified by the corporation, any of the following records of the corporation if the shareholder meets the requirements of subsection (c) and gives the corporation written notice of his demand at least five business days before the date on which he wishes to inspect and copy:

(1) excerpts from minutes of any meeting of the board of directors, records of any action of a committee of the board of directors while acting in place of the board of directors on behalf of the corporation, minutes of any meeting of the shareholders, and records of action taken by the shareholders or board of directors without a meeting, to the extent not subject to inspection under section 16.02(a);

(2) accounting records of the corporation; and

(3) the record of shareholders.

(c) A shareholder may inspect and copy the records described in subsection (b) only if:

(1) his demand is made in good faith and for a proper purpose;

(2) he describes with reasonable particularity his purpose and the records he desires to inspect; and

(3) the records are directly connected with his purpose.

(d) The right of inspection granted by this section may not be abolished or limited by a corporation's articles of incorporation or bylaws.

(e) This section does not affect:

(1) the right of a shareholder to inspect records under section 7.20 or, if the shareholder is in litigation with the corporation, to the same extent as any other litigant;

(2) the power of a court, independently of this Act, to compel the production of corporate records for examination.

(f) For purposes of this section, "shareholder" includes a beneficial owner whose shares are held in a voting trust or by a nominee on his behalf.

§16.03. Scope of Inspection Right

(a) A shareholder's agent or attorney has the same inspection and copying rights as the shareholder represented.

(b) The right to copy records under section 16.02 includes, if reasonable, the right to receive copies made by xerographic or other means, including copies through an electronic transmission if available and so requested by the shareholder.

(c) The corporation may comply at its expense with a shareholder's demand to inspect the record of shareholders under section 16.02(b)(3) by providing the shareholder with a list of its shareholders that was compiled no earlier than the date of the shareholder's demand.

(d) The corporation may impose a reasonable charge, covering the costs of labor and material, for copies of any documents provided to the shareholder. The charge may not exceed the estimated cost of production, reproduction, or transmission of the records.

§16.04. Court-Ordered Inspection

(a) If a corporation does not allow a shareholder who complies with section 16.02(a) to inspect and copy any records required by that subsection to be available for inspection, the [name or describe court] of the county where the corporation's principal office (or, if none in this state, its registered office) is located may summarily order inspection and copying of the records demanded at the corporation's expense upon application of the shareholder.

(b) If a corporation does not within a reasonable time allow a shareholder to inspect and copy any other record, the shareholder who complies with section 16.02(b) and (c) may apply to the [name or describe court] in the county where the corporation's principal office (or, if none in this state, its registered office) is located for an order to permit inspection and copying of the records demanded. The court shall dispose of an application under this subsection on an expedited basis.

(c) If the court orders inspection and copying of the records demanded, it shall also order the corporation to pay the shareholder's costs (including reasonable counsel fees) incurred to obtain the order unless the corporation proves that it refused inspection in good faith because it had a reasonable basis for doubt about the right of the shareholder to inspect the records demanded.

(d) If the court orders inspection and copying of the records demanded, it may impose reasonable restrictions on the use or distribution of the records by the demanding shareholder.

SUBCHAPTER B. REPORTS

§16.20. Financial Statements for Shareholders

(a) A corporation shall furnish its shareholders annual financial statements, which may be consolidated or combined statements of the corporation and one or more of its subsidiaries, as appropriate, that include a balance sheet as of the end of the fiscal year, an income statement for that year, and a statement of changes in shareholders' equity for the year unless that information appears elsewhere in the financial statements. If financial statements are prepared for the corporation on the basis of generally accepted accounting principles, the annual financial statements must also be prepared on that basis.

(b) If the annual financial statements are reported upon by a public accountant, his report must accompany them. If not, the statements must be accompanied by a statement of the president or the person responsible for the corporation's accounting records:

(1) stating his reasonable belief whether the statements were prepared on the basis of generally accepted accounting principles and, if not, describing the basis of preparation; and

(2) describing any respects in which the statements were not prepared on a basis of accounting consistent with the statements prepared for the preceding year.

(c) A corporation shall mail the annual financial statements to each shareholder within 120 days after the close of each fiscal year. Thereafter, on written request from a shareholder who was not mailed the statements, the corporation shall mail him the latest financial statements.

§16.21. Other Reports to Shareholders

(a) If a corporation indemnifies or advances expenses to a director under section 8.51, 8.52, 8.53, or 8.54 in connection with a proceeding by or in the right of the corporation, the corporation shall report the indemnification or advance in writing to the shareholders with or before the notice of the next shareholders' meeting.

(b) If a corporation issues or authorizes the issuance of shares for promissory notes or for promises to render services in the future, the corporation shall report in writing to the shareholders the number of shares authorized or issued, and the consideration received by the corporation, with or before the notice of the next shareholders' meeting.

§16.22. Annual Report for Secretary of State

(a) Each domestic corporation, and each foreign corporation authorized to transact business in this state, shall deliver to the secretary of state for filing an annual report that sets forth:

(1) the name of the corporation and the state or county under whose law it is incorporated;

(2) the address of its registered office and the name of its registered agent at that office in this state;

(3) the address of its principal office;

(4) the names and business addresses of its directors and principal officers;

(5) a brief description of the nature of its business;

(6) the total number of authorized shares, itemized by class and series, if any, within each class; and

(7) the total number of issued and outstanding shares, itemized by class and series, if any, within each class.

(b) Information in the annual report must be current as of the date the annual report is executed on behalf of the corporation.

(c) The first annual report must be delivered to the secretary of state between January 1 and April 1 of the year following the calendar year in which a domestic corporation was incorporated or a foreign corporation was authorized to transact business. Subsequent annual reports must be delivered to the secretary of state between January 1 and April 1 of the following calendar years.

(d) If an annual report does not contain the information required by this section, the secretary of state shall promptly notify the reporting domestic or foreign corporation in writing and return the report to it for correction. If the report is corrected to contain the information required by this section and delivered to the secretary of state within 30 days after the effective date of notice, it is deemed to be timely filed.

Chapter 17. Transition Provisions

§17.01. Application to Existing Domestic Corporations

This Act applies to all domestic corporations in existence on its effective date that were incorporated under any general statute of this state providing for incorporation of corporations for profit if power to amend or repeal the statute under which the corporation was incorporated was reserved.

§17.02. Application to Qualified Foreign Corporations

A foreign corporation authorized to transact business in this state on the effective date of this Act is subject to this Act but is not required to obtain a new certificate of authority to transact business under this Act.

§17.03. Saving Provisions

(a) Except as provided in subsection (b), the repeal of a statute by this Act does not affect:

(1) the operation of the statute or any action taken under it before its repeal;

(2) any ratification, right, remedy, privilege, obligation, or liability acquired, accrued, or incurred under the statute before its repeal;

(3) any violation of the statute, or any penalty, forfeiture, or punishment incurred because of the violation, before its repeal;

(4) any proceeding, reorganization, or dissolution commenced under the statute before its repeal, and the proceeding, reorganization, or dissolution may be completed in accordance with the statute as if it had not been repealed.

(b) If a penalty or punishment imposed for violation of a statute repealed by this Act is reduced by this Act, the penalty or punishment if not already imposed shall be imposed in accordance with this Act.

§17.04. Severability

If any provision of this Act or its application to any person or circumstance is held invalid by a court of competent jurisdiction, the invalidity does not affect other provisions or applications of the Act that can be given effect without the invalid provision or application, and to this end the provisions of the Act are severable.

§17.05. Repeal

The following laws and parts of laws are repealed: [to be inserted].

§17.06. Effective Date

This Act takes effect ______________________________.

APPENDIX

G

Selected Delaware Statutes

§101. Incorporators; How Corporation Formed; Purposes

(a) Any person, partnership, association or corporation, singly or jointly with others, and without regard to his or their residence, domicile or state of incorporation, may incorporate or organize a corporation under this chapter by filing with the Secretary of State a certificate of incorporation which shall be executed, acknowledged, filed and recorded in accordance with section 103 of this title.

(b) A corporation may be incorporated or organized under this chapter to conduct or promote any lawful business or purposes, except as may otherwise be provided by the constitution or other law of this State.

(c) Corporations for constructing, maintaining and operating public utilities, whether in or outside of this State, may be organized under this chapter, but corporations for constructing, maintaining and operating public utilities within this State shall be subject to, in addition to the provisions of this chapter, the special provisions and requirements of Title 26 applicable to such corporations.

§102. Contents of Certificate of Incorporation

(a) The certificate of incorporation shall set forth—

(1) The name of the corporation which (i) shall contain one of the words "association", "company", "corpora-

tion", "club", "foundation", "fund", "incorporated", "institute", "society", "union", "syndicate", or "limited", or one of the abbreviations "co.", "corp.", "inc.", "ltd.", or words or abbreviations of like import in other languages (provided they are written in Roman characters or letters); provided, however, that the Division of Corporations in the Department of State may waive such requirement (unless it determines that such name is, or might otherwise appear to be, that of a natural person) if such corporation executes, acknowledges and files with the Secretary of State in accordance with §103 of this title a certificate stating that its total assets, as defined in subsection (ii) of §503 of this title, are not less than 10 million dollars, (ii) shall be such as to distinguish it upon the records in the office of the Secretary of State from the names of other corporations or limited partnerships organized, reserved or registered as a foreign corporation or foreign limited partnership under the laws of this State except with the written consent of such other foreign corporation or domestic or foreign limited partnership, executed, acknowledged, and filed with the Secretary of State in accordance with section 103 of this title and (iii) shall not contain the word "bank", or any variation thereof, except for the name of a bank reporting to and under the supervision of the State Bank Commissioner of this State, or a subsidiary of a bank or savings association (as those terms are defined in the Federal Deposit Insurance Act, as amended, at 12 U.S.C. §1813), or a corporation regulated under the Bank Holding Company Act of 1956, as amended, 12 U.S.C. §1841 et seq., or the Home Owners' Loan Act, as amended, 12 U.S.C. §1461 et seq., provided, however, that this section shall not be consumed to prevent the use of the word "bank", or any variation thereof, in a context clearly not purporting to refer to a banking business or otherwise likely to mislead the public about the nature of the business of the corporation or to lead to a pattern and practice of abuse that might cause harm to the interests of the public or the State as determined by the Division of Corporations in the Department of State;

(2) The address (which shall include the street, number, city and county) of the corporation's registered office in this State, and the name of its registered agent at such address;

(3) The nature of the business or purposes to be conducted or promoted. It shall be sufficient to state, either alone or with other businesses or purposes, that the purpose of the corporation is to engage in any lawful act or activity for which corporations may be organized under the General Corporation Law of Delaware, and by such statement all lawful acts and activities shall be within the purposes of the corporation, except for express limitations, if any;

(4) If the corporation is to be authorized to issue only 1 class of stock, the total number of shares of stock which the corporation shall have authority to issue and the par value of each of such shares, or a statement that all such shares are to be without par value. If the corporation is to be authorized to issue more than one class of stock, the certificate of incorporation shall set forth the total number of shares of all classes of stock which the corporation shall have authority to issue and the number of shares of each class, and shall specify each class the shares of which are to be without par value and each class the shares of which are to have par value and the par value of the shares of each such class. The certificate of incorporation shall also set forth a statement of the designations and the powers, preferences and rights, and the qualifications, limitations or restrictions thereof, which are permitted by §151 of this Title in respect of any class or classes of stock or any series of any class of stock of the corporation and the fixing of which by the certificate of incorporation is desired, and an express grant of such authority as it may then be desired to grant to the board of directors to fix by resolution or resolutions any thereof that may be desired but which shall not be fixed by the certificate of incorporation. The foregoing provisions of this paragraph shall not apply to corporations which are not to have authority to issue capital stock. In the case of such corporations, the fact that they are not to have authority to issue capital stock shall be stated in the certificate of incorporation. The conditions of membership of such corporations shall likewise be stated in the certificate of incorporation or the certificate may provide that the conditions of membership shall be stated in the bylaws;

(5) The name and mailing address of the incorporator or incorporators;

(6) If the powers of the incorporator or incorporators are to terminate upon the filing of the certificate of incorporation, the names and mailing addresses of the persons who are to serve as directors until the first annual meeting of stockholders or until their successors are elected and qualify.

(b) In addition to the matters required to be set forth in the certificate of incorporation by subsection (a) of this section, the certificate of incorporation may also contain any or all of the following matters:

(1) Any provision for the management of the business and for the conduct of the affairs of the corporation, and any provision creating, defining, limiting and regulating the powers of the corporation, the directors, and the stockholders, or any class of the stockholders, or the members of a non-stock corporation; if such provisions are not contrary to the laws of this State. Any provision which is required or permitted by any section of this chapter to be stated in the by-laws may instead be stated in the certificate of incorporation;

(2) The following provisions, in haec verba, viz.—

"Whenever a compromise or arrangement is proposed between this corporation and its creditors or any class of them and/or between this corporation and its stockholders or any class of them, any court of equitable jurisdiction within the State of Delaware may, on the application in a summary way of this corporation or of any creditor or stockholder thereof or on the application of any receiver or receivers appointed for this corporation under the provisions of section 291 of Title 8 of the Delaware

Code or on the application of trustees in dissolution or of any receiver or receivers appointed for this corporation under the provisions of section 279 of Title 8 of the Delaware Code order a meeting of the creditors or class of creditors, and/or of the stockholders or class of stockholders of this corporation, as the case may be, to be summoned in such manner as the said court directs. If a majority in number representing three-fourths in value of the creditors or class of creditors, and/or of the stockholders or class of stockholders of this corporation, as the case may be, agree to any compromise or arrangement and to any reorganization of this corporation as consequence of such compromise or arrangement, the said compromise or arrangement and the said reorganization shall, if sanctioned by the court to which the said application has been made, be binding on all the creditors or class of creditors, and/or on all the stockholders or class of stockholders, of this corporation, as the case may be, and also on this corporation;"

(3) Such provisions as may be desired granting to the holders of the stock of the corporation, or the holders of any class or series of a class thereof, the preemptive right to subscribe to any or all additional issues of stock of the corporation of any or all classes or series thereof, or to any securities of the corporation convertible into such stock. No stockholder shall have any preemptive right to subscribe to an additional issue of stock or to any security convertible into such stock unless, and except to the extent that, such right is expressly granted to him in the certificate of incorporation. All such rights in existence on July 3, 1967, shall remain in existence unaffected by this paragraph (3) unless and until changed or terminated by appropriate action which expressly provides for such change or termination;

(4) Provisions requiring for any corporate action, the vote of a larger portion of the stock or of any class or series thereof, or of any other securities having voting power, or a larger number of the directors, than is required by this chapter;

(5) A provision limiting the duration of the corporation's existence to a specified date; otherwise, the corporation shall have perpetual existence;

(6) A provision imposing personal liability for the debts of the corporation on its stockholders or members to a specified extent and upon specified conditions; otherwise, the stockholders or members of a corporation shall not be personally liable for the payment of the corporation's debts except as they may be liable by reason of their own conduct or acts;

(7) A provision eliminating or limiting the personal liability of a director to the corporation or its stockholders for monetary damages for breach of fiduciary duty as a director, provided that such provision shall not eliminate or limit the liability of a director: (i) For any breach of the director's duty of loyalty to the corporation or its stockholders; (ii) for acts or omissions not in good faith or which involve intentional misconduct or a knowing violation of law; (iii) under §174 of this title; or (iv) for any transaction from which the director derived an improper personal benefit. No such provision shall eliminate or limit the liability of a director for any act or omission occurring prior to the date when such provision becomes effective. All references in this paragraph to a director shall also be deemed to refer (x) to a member of the governing body of a corporation which is not authorized to issue capital stock, and (y) to such other person or persons, if any, who, pursuant to a provision of the certificate of incorporation in accordance with §141(a) of this title, exercise or perform any of the powers or duties otherwise conferred or imposed upon the board of directors by this title.

(c) It shall not be necessary to set forth in the certificate of incorporation any of the powers conferred on corporations by this chapter.

§103. Execution, Acknowledgment, Filing, Recording and Effective Date of Original Certificate of Incorporation and Other Instruments; Exceptions

(a) Whenever any instrument is to be filed with the Secretary of State or in accordance with this section or chapter, such instrument shall be executed as follows:

(1) The certificate of incorporation, and any other instrument to be filed before the election of the initial board of directors if the initial directors were not named in the certificate of incorporation, shall be signed by the incorporator or incorporators.

(2) All other instruments shall be signed—

(a) By any authorized officer of the corporation; or

(b) If it shall appear from the instrument that there are no such officers, then by a majority of the directors or by such directors as may be designated by the board; or

(c) If it shall appear from the instrument that there are no such officers or directors, then by the holders of record, or such of them as may be designated by the holders of record, of a majority of all outstanding shares of stock; or

(d) By the holders of record of all outstanding shares of stock.

(b) Whenever any provision of this chapter requires any instrument to be acknowledged, such requirement is satisfied by either:

(1) The formal acknowledgement by the person or one of the persons signing the instrument that it is such person's act and deed or the act and deed of the corporation, as the case may be, and that the facts stated therein are true. Such acknowledgement shall be made before a person who is authorized by the law of the place of execution to take acknowledgements of deeds. If such person has a seal of office he shall affix it to the instrument.

(2) The signature, without more, of the person or persons signing the instrument, in which case such signature or signatures shall constitute the affirmation or acknowledgement of the signatory, under penalties of perjury, that the instrument is such person's act and deed or the act and deed of the corporation, as the case may be, and that the facts stated therein are true.

(c) Whenever any provision of this chapter requires any instrument to be filed with the Secretary of State or in accordance with this section or chapter, such requirement means that:

(1) The original signed instrument shall be delivered to the office of the Secretary of State.

(2) All taxes and fees authorized by law to be collected by the Secretary of State in connection with the filing of the instrument shall be tendered to the Secretary of State.

(3) Upon delivery of the instrument, and upon tender of the required taxes and fees, the Secretary of State shall certify that the instrument has been filed in the Secretary of State's office by endorsing upon the original signed instrument the word "Filed", and the date and hour of its filing. This endorsement is the "filing date" of the instrument, and is conclusive of the date and time of its filing in the absence of actual fraud. The Secretary of State shall thereupon file and index the endorsed instrument.

(4) The Secretary of State, acting as agent for the recorders of each of the counties, shall collect and deposit it in a separate account established exclusively for that purpose a county assessment fee with respect to each filed instrument, and shall thereafter weekly remit from such account to the recorder of each of the said counties the amount or amounts of such fees as provided for in paragraph (c)(5) of this section or as elsewhere provided by law. Said fees shall be for the purposes of defraying certain costs incurred by the counties in merging the information and images of such filed documents with the document information systems of each of the recorder's ofices in the counties, and in retrieving, maintaining and displaying such information and images in the offices of the recorders and at remote locations in each of such counties. In consideration for its acting as the agent for the recorders with respect to the collection and payment of the county assessment fees, the Secretary of State shall retain and pay over to the general fund of the State an administrative charge of one percent of the total fees collected.

(5) The assessment fee to the counties shall be $24 for each one-page instrument filed with the Secretary of State in accordance with this section and $9 for each additional page for instruments with more than one page. The recorder's office to receive the assessment fee shall be the recorder's office in the county in which the corporation's registered office in this State is, or is to be, located, except that an assessment fee shall not be charged for either a certificate of dissolution qualifying for treatment under §391(a)(5)(b) . . . [short-form dissolution], or a document filed in accordance with subchapter XV of this title.

(6) The Secretary of State shall enter such information from each instrument as he deems appropriate into the Delaware Corporation Information System or any system which is a successor thereto in the office of the Secretary of State, and such information shall be permanently maintained. A copy of each instrument shall be permanently maintained on optical disk or by other suitable medium.

(d) Any instrument filed in accordance with subsection (c) of this section shall be effective upon its filing date. Any instrument may provide that it is not to become effective until a specified time subsequent to the time it is filed, but such time shall not be later than a time on the 90th day after the date of its filing.

(e) If another section of this chapter specifically prescribes a manner of executing, acknowledging, filing or recording a specified instrument or a time when such instrument shall become effective which differs from the corresponding provisions of this section, then the provisions of such other section shall govern.

(f) Whenever any instrument authorized to be filed with the Secretary of State under any provision of this title has been so filed and is an inaccurate record of the corporate action therein referred to, or was defectively or erroneously executed, sealed or acknowledged, such instrument may be corrected by filing with the Secretary of State a certificate of correction of such instrument which shall be executed, acknowledged and filed in accordance with this section. The certificate of correction shall specify the inaccuracy or defect to be corrected and shall set forth the portion of the instrument in corrected form. In lieu of filing a certificate of correction the instrument may be corrected by filing with the Secretary of State a corrected instrument which shall be executed, acknowledged and filed in accordance with this section. The corrected instrument shall be specifically designated as such in its heading, shall specify the inaccuracy or defect to be corrected, and shall set forth the entire instrument in corrected form. An instrument corrected in accordance with this section shall be effective as of the date the original instrument was filed, except as to those persons who are substantially and adversely affected by the correction and as to those persons the instrument as corrected shall be effective from the filing date.

(g) Notwithstanding that any instrument authorized to be filed with the Secretary of State under any provision of this title is when filed inaccurately, defectively or erroneously executed, sealed or acknowledged, or otherwise defective in any respect, the Secretary of State shall have no liability to any person for the preclearance for filing, the acceptance for filing, or the filing and indexing of such instrument by the Secretary of State.

(h) Any signature on any instrument authorized to be filed with the Secretary of State under any provision of this title may be a facsimile, a conformed signature, or an electronically transmitted signature.

§104. Certificate of Incorporation; Definition

The term "certificate of incorporation," as used in this chapter, unless the context requires otherwise, includes not only the original certificate of incorporation filed to create a corporation but also all other certificates, agreements of merger or consolidation, plans of reorganization, or other instruments, howsoever designated, which are filed pursuant to §§102, 133-136, 151, 241-243, 245, 251-258, 263-264, 303, or any other section of this title, and which have the effect of amending or supplementing in some respect a corporation's original certificate of incorporation.

§105. Certificate of Incorporation and Other Certificates; Evidence

A copy of a certificate of incorporation, or a restated certificate of incorporation, or of any other certificate which has been filed in the office of the Secretary of State as required by any provision of this title shall, when duly certified by the Secretary of State, be received in all courts, public offices, and official bodies as prima facie evidence of:

(a) due execution, acknowledgment, and filing of the instrument;

(b) observance and performance of all acts and conditions necessary to have been observed and performed precedent to the instrument becoming effective; and of

(c) any other facts required or permitted by law to be stated in the instrument.

§106. Commencement of Corporate Existence

Upon the filing with the Secretary of State of the certificate of incorporation, executed and acknowledged in accordance with section 103, the incorporator or incorporators who signed the certificate, and such incorporator's or incorporators' successors and assigns, shall, from the date of such filing, be and constitute a body corporate, by the name set forth in the certificate, subject to the provisions of section 103(d) of this title and subject to dissolution or other termination of its existence as provided in this chapter.

§107. Powers of Incorporators

If the persons who are to serve as directors until the first annual meeting of stockholders have not been named in the certificate of incorporation, the incorporator or incorporators, until the directors are elected, shall manage the affairs of the corporation and may do whatever is necessary and proper to perfect the organization of the corporation, including the adoption of the original by-laws of the corporation and the election of directors.

§108. Organization Meeting of Incorporators or Directors Named in Certificate of Incorporation

(a) After the filing of the certificate of incorporation an organization meeting of the incorporator or incorporators, or of the board of directors if the initial directors were named in the certificate of incorporation, shall be held, either within or without this State, at the call of a majority of the incorporators or directors, as the case may be, for the purposes of adopting by-laws, electing directors (if the meeting is of the incorporators) to serve or hold office until the first annual meeting of stockholders or until their successors are elected and qualify, electing officers if the meeting is of the directors, doing any other or further acts to perfect the organization of the corporation, and transacting such other business as may come before the meeting.

(b) The persons calling the meeting shall give to each other incorporator or director, as the case may be, at least 2 days written notice thereof by any usual means of communication, which notice shall state the time, place and purposes of the meeting as fixed by the persons calling it. Notice of the meeting need not be given to anyone who attends the meeting or who signs a waiver of notice either before or after the meeting.

(c) Any action permitted to be taken at the organization meeting of the incorporators or directors, as the case may be, may be taken without a meeting if each incorporator or director, where there is more than one, or sole incorporator or director where there is only one, signs an instrument which states the action so taken.

§109. By-Laws

(a) The original or other by-laws of a corporation may be adopted, amended, or repealed by the incorporators, by the initial directors if they were named in the certificate of incorporation, or, before a corporation has received any payment for any of its stock, by its board of directors. After a corporation has received any payment for any of its stock, the power to adopt, amend or repeal by-laws shall be in the stockholders entitled to vote, or, in the case of a nonstock corporation, in its members entitled to vote; provided, however, any corporation may, in its certificate of incorporation, confer the power to adopt, amend, or repeal by-laws upon the directors or, in the case of a non-stock corporation, upon its governing body by whatever name designated. The fact that such power has been so conferred upon the directors or governing body, as the case may be, shall not divest the stockholders or members of the power, nor limit their power to adopt, amend or repeal by-laws.

(b) The by-laws may contain any provision, not inconsistent with law or with the certificate of incorporation, relating to the business of the corporation, the conduct of its affairs, and its rights or powers or the rights or powers of its stockholders, directors, officers or employees.

§110. Emergency By-Laws and Other Powers in Emergency

The board of directors of any corporation may adopt emergency by-laws, subject to repeal or change by action of the stockholders, which shall notwithstanding any different provision elsewhere in this chapter or in Chapters 3 and 5 of Title 26, or in Chapter 7 of Title 5, or in the certificate of incorporation or by-laws, be operative during any emergency resulting from an attack on the United States or on a locality in which the corporation conducts its business or customarily holds meetings of its board of directors or its stockholders, or during any nuclear or atomic disaster, or during the existence of any catastrophe, or other similar emergency condition, as a result of which a quorum of the board of directors or a standing committee thereof cannot readily be convened for action. The emergency by-laws may make any provision that may be practical and necessary for the circumstances of the emergency.

§121. General Powers

(a) In addition to the powers enumerated in Section 122 of this title, every corporation, its officers, directors, and stockholders shall possess and may exercise all the powers and privileges granted by this chapter or by any other law or by its certificate of incorporation, together with any powers incidental thereto, so far as such powers and privileges are necessary or convenient to the conduct, promotion or attainment of the business or purposes set forth in its certificate of incorporation.

(b) Every corporation shall be governed by the provisions and be subject to the restrictions and liabilities contained in this chapter.

§122. Specific Powers

Every corporation created under this chapter shall have power to:

(1) Have perpetual succession by its corporate name, unless a limited period of duration is stated in its certificate of incorporation;

(2) Sue and be sued in all courts and participate, as a party or otherwise, in any judicial, administrative, arbitrative or other proceeding, in its corporate name;

(3) Have a corporate seal, which may be altered at pleasure, and use the same by causing it or a facsimile thereof, to be impressed or affixed or in any other manner reproduced;

(4) Purchase, receive, take by grant, gift, devise, bequest or otherwise lease, or otherwise acquire, own, hold, improve, employ, use and otherwise deal in and with real or personal property, or any interest therein, wherever situated, and to sell, convey, lease, exchange, transfer or otherwise dispose of, or mortgage or pledge, all or any of its property and assets, or any interest therein, wherever situated;

(5) Appoint such officers and agents as the business of the corporation requires and to pay or otherwise provide for them suitable compensation;

(6) Adopt, amend and repeal by-laws;

(7) Wind up and dissolve itself in the manner provided in this chapter;

(8) Conduct its business, carry on its operations, and have offices and exercise its powers within or without this State;

(9) Make donations for the public welfare or for charitable, scientific or educational purposes, and in time of war or other national emergency in aid thereof;

(10) Be an incorporator, promoter, or manager of other corporations of any type or kind;

(11) Participate with others in any corporation, partnership, limited partnership, joint venture, or other association of any kind, or in any transaction, undertaking or arrangement which the participating corporation would have power to conduct by itself, whether or not such participation involves sharing or delegation of control with or to others;

(12) Transact any lawful business which the corporation's board of directors shall find to be in aid of governmental authority;

(13) Make contracts, including contracts of guaranty and suretyship, incur liabilities, borrow money at such rates of interest as the corporation may determine, issue its notes, bonds and other obligations, and secure any of its obligations by mortgage, pledge or other encumbrance of all or any of its property, franchises and income, and make contracts of guaranty and suretyship which are necessary or convenient to the conduct, promotion or attainment of the business of (a) a corporation all of the outstanding stock of which is owned, directly or indirectly, by the contracting corporation, or (b) a corporation which owns, directly or indirectly, all of the outstanding stock of the contracting corporation, or (c) a corporation all of the outstanding stock of which is owned, directly or indirectly, by a corporation which owns, directly or indirectly, all of the outstanding stock of the contracting corporation, which contracts of guaranty and suretyship shall be deemed to be necessary or convenient to the conduct, promotion or attainment of the business of the contracting corporation, and make other contracts of guaranty and suretyship which are necessary or convenient to the conduct, promotion or attainment of the business of the contracting corporation;

(14) Lend money for its corporate purposes, invest and reinvest its funds, and take, hold and deal with real and personal property as security for the payment of funds so loaned or invested;

(15) Pay pensions and establish and carry out pension, profit sharing, stock option, stock purchase, stock bonus, retirement, benefit, incentive and compensation plans, trusts and provisions for any or all of its directors, officers, and employees, and for any or all of the directors, officers, and employees of its subsidiaries;

(16) Provide insurance for its benefit on the life of any of its directors, officers, or employees, or on the life of any stockholder for the purpose of acquiring at his death shares of its stock owned by such stockholder.

§123. Powers Respecting Securities of Other Corporations or Entities

Any corporation organized under the laws of this State may guarantee, purchase, take, receive, subscribe for or otherwise acquire; own, hold, use or otherwise employ; sell, lease, exchange, transfer, or otherwise dispose of; mortgage, lend, pledge or otherwise deal in and with, bonds and other obligations of, or shares or other securities or interests in, or issued by, any other domestic or foreign corporation, partnership, association, or individual, or by any government or agency or instrumentality thereof. A corporation while owner of any such securities may exercise all the rights, powers and privileges of ownership, including the right to vote.

§124. Lack of Corporate Capacity or Power; Effect; Ultra Vires

No act of a corporation and no conveyance or transfer of real or personal property to or by a corporation shall be invalid by reason of the fact that the corporation was without capacity or power to do such act or to make or receive such conveyance or transfer, but such lack of capacity or power may be asserted:

(1) In a proceeding by a stockholder against the corporation to enjoin the doing of any act or acts or the transfer of real or personal property by or to the corporation. If the unauthorized acts or transfer sought to be enjoined are being, or are to be, performed or made pursuant to any contract to which the corporation is a party, the court may, if all of the parties to the contract are parties to the proceeding and if it deems the same to be equitable, set aside and enjoin the performance of such contract, and in so doing may allow to the corporation or to the other parties to the contract, as the case may be, such compensation as may be equitable for the loss or damage sustained by any of them which may result from the action of the court in setting aside and enjoining the performance of such contract, but anticipated profits to be derived from the performance of the contract shall not be awarded by the court as a loss or damage sustained.

(2) In a proceeding by the corporation, whether acting directly or through a receiver, trustee, or other legal representative, or through stockholders in a representative suit, against an incumbent or former officer or director of the corporation, for loss or damage due to such incumbent or former officer's or director's unauthorized act.

(3) In a proceeding by the Attorney General to dissolve the corporation, or to enjoin the corporation from the transaction of unauthorized business.

§131. Registered Office in State; Principal Office or Place of Business in State

(a) Every corporation shall have and maintain in this State a registered office which may, but need not be, the same as its place of business.

(b) Whenever the term "corporation's principal office or place of business in this State" or "principal office or place of business of the corporation in this State", or other term of like import, is or has been used in a corporation's certificate of incorporation, or in any other document, or in any statute, it shall be deemed to mean and refer to, unless the context indicates otherwise, the corporation's registered office required by this section; and it shall not be necessary for any corporation to amend its certificate of incorporation or any other document to comply with this section.

§132. Registered Agent in State; Resident Agent

(a) Every corporation shall have and maintain in this State a registered agent, which agent may be any of (i) the corporation itself, (ii) an individual resident in this State, (iii) a domestic corporation (other than the corporation itself), a domestic limited partnership, a domestic limited liability company or a domestic business trust or (iv) a foreign corporation, a foreign limited partnership or a foreign limited liability company authorized to transact business in this State, in each case, having a business office identical with the office of such registered agent which generally is open during normal business hours to accept service of process and otherwise perform the functions of a registered agent.

(b) Whenever the term "resident agent" or "resident agent in charge of a corporation's principal office or place of business in this State", or other term of like import which refers to a corporation's agent required by statute to be located in this State, is or has been used in a corporation's certificate of incorporation, or in any other document, or in any statute, it shall be deemed to mean and refer to, unless the context indicates otherwise, the corporation's registered agent required by this section; and it shall not be necessary for any corporation to amend its certificate of incorporation or any other document to comply with this section.

§133. Change of Location of Registered Office; Change of Registered Agent

Any corporation may, by resolution of its board of directors, change the location of its registered office in this State to any other place in this State. By like resolution, the registered agent of a corporation may be changed to any other person or corporation including itself. In either such case, the resolution shall be as detailed in its statement as is required by section 102(a)(2) of this title. Upon the adoption of such a resolution, a certificate certifying the change shall be executed, acknowledged, and filed in accordance with section 103 of this title; and a certified copy shall be recorded in the office of the Recorder for the county in which the new office is located; and, if such new office is located in a county other than that in which the former office was located, a certified copy of such certificate shall also be recorded in the office of the Recorder for the county in which such former office was located.

§134. Change of Address or Name of Registered Agent

(a) A registered agent may change the address of the registered office of the corporation or corporations for which he is registered agent to another address in this State by filing with the Secretary of State a certificate, executed and acknowledged by such registered agent, setting forth the names of all the corporations represented by such registered agent, and the address at which such registered agent has maintained the registered office for each of such corporations, and further certifying to the new address to which each such registered office will be changed on a given day, and at which new address such registered agent will thereafter maintain the registered office for each of the corporations recited in the certificate. Upon the filing of such certificate, the Secretary of State shall furnish a certified copy of the same under his hand and seal of office, and the certified copy shall be recorded in the office of the Recorder of the county where the registered office of the corporation is located in this State, and thereafter, or until further change of address, as authorized by law, the registered office in this State of each of the corporations recited in the certificate shall be located at the new address of the registered agent thereof as given in the certificate. If the location of such office shall be changed from one county to another county, a certified copy of such certificate shall also be recorded in the office of the Recorder for the county in which such office was formerly located.

(b) In the event of a change of name of any person or corporation acting as registered agent in this State, such registered agent shall file with the Secretary of State a certificate, executed and acknowledged by such registered agent, setting forth the new name of such registered agent, the name of such registered agent before it was changed, the names of all the corporations represented by such registered agent, and the address at which such registered agent has maintained the registered office for each of such corporations. Upon the filing of such certificate, the Secretary of State shall furnish a certified copy of the same under his hand and seal of office, and the certified copy shall be recorded in the office of the recorder of the county where the registered office of each of the corporations recited in the certificate is located in this State.

§135. Resignation of Registered Agent Coupled With Appointment of Successor

The registered agent of one or more corporations may resign and appoint a successor registered agent by filing a certificate with the Secretary of State, stating the name and address of the successor agent, in accordance with section 102(a)(2) of this title. There shall be attached to such certificate a statement of each affected corporation ratifying and approving such change of registered agent. Each such statement shall be executed and acknowledged in accordance with section 103 of this title. Upon such filing, the successor registered agent shall become the registered agent of such corporations as have ratified and approved such substitution and the successor registered agent's address, as stated in such certificate, shall become the address of each such corporation's registered office in this State. The Secretary of State shall then issue his certificate that the successor registered agent has become the registered agent of the corporations so ratifying and approving such change, and setting out the names of such corporations. The certificate of the Secretary of State shall be recorded in accordance with section 103 of this title, and the Recorder shall forthwith make a note of the change of registered office and registered agent on the margin of the record of the certificates of incorporation of those corporations which have ratified and approved such change. If the location of such office shall be changed from one county to another county, a certified copy of such certificate shall also be recorded in the office of the Recorder for the county in which such office will thereafter be located.

§136. Resignation of Registered Agent Not Coupled With Appointment of Successor

(a) The registered agent of one or more corporations may resign without appointing a successor by filing a certificate with the Secretary of State; but such resignation shall not become effective until 60 days after the certificate is filed. There shall be attached to such certificate an affidavit of such registered agent, if an individual, or of the president, a vice president or the secretary thereof, if a corporation, that at least 30 days prior to the date of the filing of said certificate, due notice was sent by certified or registered mail to the corporation for which such registered agent was acting, at the principal office thereof outside the State, if known to such registered agent or, if not, to the last known address of the attorney or other individual at whose request such registered agent was appointed for such corporation, of the resignation of such registered agent.

(b) Upon the filing of such certificate of resignation with the Secretary of State, the Secretary of State shall then notify the Recorder for the county in which the certificate of incorporation of such corporation is recorded of the resignation of its registered agent as set forth in such certificate and the Recorder shall forthwith make a note of the resignation of such registered agent on the margin of the record of the certificate of incorporation of such corporation.

(c) After receipt of the notice of the resignation of its registered agent, provided for in subsection (a) of this section, the corporation for which such registered agent was acting shall obtain and designate a new registered agent to take the place of the registered agent so resigning in the same manner as provided in section 133 of this title for change of registered agent. If such corporation being a corporation of this State, fails to obtain and designate a new registered agent as aforesaid prior to the expiration of the period of 60 days after the filing by the registered agent of the certificate of resignation, the Secretary of State shall declare the charter of such corporation forfeited. If such corporation, being a foreign corporation, fails to obtain and designate a new registered agent as aforesaid prior to the expiration of the period of 60 days after the filing by the registered agent of the certificate of resignation, the Secretary of State shall forfeit its authority to do business in this State.

(d) After the resignation of the registered agent shall have become effective as provided in this section and if no new registered agent shall have been obtained and designated in the time and manner aforesaid, service of legal process against the corporation for which the resigned registered agent had been acting shall thereafter be upon the Secretary of State in accordance with section 321 of this title.

§141. Board of Directors; Powers; Number, Qualifications, Terms and Quorum; Committees; Classes of Directors; Reliance Upon Books; Action Without Meeting; Removal

(a) The business and affairs of every corporation organized under this chapter shall be managed by or under the direction of a board of directors, except as may be otherwise provided in this chapter or in its certificate of incorporation. If any such provision is made in the certificate of incorporation, the powers and duties conferred or imposed upon the board of directors by this chapter shall be exercised or performed to such extent and by such person or persons as shall be provided in the certificate of incorporation.

(b) The board of directors of a corporation shall consist of one or more members. The number of directors shall be fixed by, or in the manner provided in, the by-laws, unless the certificate of incorporation fixes the number of directors, in which case a change in the number of directors shall be made only by amendment of the certificate. Directors need not be stockholders unless so required by the certificate of incorporation or the by-laws. The certificate of incorporation or by-laws may prescribe other qualifications for directors. Each director shall hold office until such director's successor is elected and qualified or until such director's earlier resignation or removal. Any director may resign at any time upon written notice to the corporation. A majority of the total number of directors shall constitute a quorum for the transaction of business unless the certificate of incorporation or the by-laws require a greater number. Unless the certificate of incorporation provides otherwise, the bylaws may provide that a number less than a majority shall constitute a quorum which in no case shall be less than one-third of the total number of directors except that when a board of one director is authorized under the provisions of this section, then one director shall constitute a quorum. The vote of the majority of the directors present at a meeting at which a quorum is present shall be the act of the board of directors unless the certificate of incorporation or the by-laws shall require a vote of a greater number.

(c)(1) All corporations incorporated prior to July 1, 1996, shall be governed by subsection (1) of this section, provided that any such corporation may by a resolution adopted by a majority of the whole board elect to be governed by subsection (2) of this section, in which case subsection (1) of this section shall not apply to such corporation. All corporations incorporated on or after July 1, 1996, shall be governed by subsection (2) of this section. The board of directors may, by resolution passed by a majority of the whole board, designate one or more committees, each committee to consist of one or more of the directors of the corporation. The board may designate one or more directors as alternate members of any committee, who may replace any absent or disqualified member at any meeting of the committee. The by-laws may provide that in the absence or disqualification of a member of a committee, the member or members thereof present at any meeting and not disqualified from voting, whether or not he or they constitute a quorum, may unanimously appoint another member of the board of directors to act at the meeting in the place of any such absent or disqualified member. Any such committee, to the extent provided in the resolution of the board of directors, or in the by-laws of the corporation, shall have and may exercise all the powers and authority of the board of directors in the management of the business and affairs of the corporation, and may authorize the seal of the corporation to be affixed to all papers which may require it; but no such committee shall have the power or authority in reference to amending the certificate of incorporation (except that a committee may, to the extent authorized in the resolution or resolutions providing for the issuance of shares of stock adopted by the board of directors as provided in Section 151(a) of of this title, fix the designations and any of the preferences or rights of such shares relating to dividends, redemption, dissolution, any distribution of assets of the corporation or the conversion into, or the exchange of such shares for, shares of any other class or classes or any other series of the same or any other class or classes of stock of the corporation or fix the number of shares of any series of stock or authorize the increase or decrease of the shares of any series), adopting an agreement of merger or consolidation under Sections 251, 252, 254, 255, 256, 257, 258, 263 or 264 of this title, recommending to the stockholders the sale, lease or exchange of all or substantially all of the corporation's property and assets, recommending to the stockholders a dissolution of the corporation or a revocation of a dissolution, or amending the by-laws of the corporation; and, unless the resolution, by-laws, or certificate of incorporation expressly so provide, no such committee shall have the power or authority to declare a dividend, to authorize the issuance of stock, or to adopt a certificate of ownership and merger pursuant to Section 253 of this title.

(2) The board of directors may designate 1 or more committees, each committee to consist of 1 or more of the directors of the corporation. The board may designate one or more directors as alternate members of any committee, who may replace any absent or disqualified member at any meeting of the committee. The bylaws may provide that in the absence or disqualification of a member of a committee, the member or members present at any meeting and not disqualified from voting, whether or not such member or members constitute a quorum, may unanimously appoint another member of the board of directors to act at the meeting in the place of any such absent or disqualified member. Any such committee, to the extent provided in the resolution of the board of directors, or in the bylaws of the corporation, shall have and may exercise all the powers and authority of the board of directors in the management of the business and affairs of the corporation, and may authorize the seal of the corporation to be affixed to all papers which may require it; but no such committee shall have the power or authority in reference to the following matters: (i) approving or adopting, or recommending to the stockholders, any action or matter expressly required by this chapter to be submitted to stockholders for approval or (ii) adopting, amending or repealing any bylaw of the corporation.

(d) The directors of any corporation organized under this chapter may, by the certificate of incorporation or by an initial by-law, or by a by-law adopted by a vote of the stockholders, be divided into one, two or three classes; the term of office of those of the first class to expire at the annual meeting next ensuing; of the second class one year thereafter; of the third class two years thereafter; and at each annual election held after such classification and election, directors shall be chosen for a full term, as the case may be, to succeed those whose terms expire. The certificate of incorporation may confer upon holders of any class or series of stock the right to elect one or more directors who shall serve for such term, and have such voting powers as shall be stated in the certificate of incorporation. The terms of office and voting powers of the directors elected in the manner so provided in the certificate of incorporation may be greater than or less than those of any other director or class of directors. If the certificate of incorporation provides that directors elected by the holders of a class or series of stock shall have more or less than 1 vote per director on any matter, every reference in this chapter to a majority or other proportion of directors shall refer to a majority or other proportion of the votes of such directors.

(e) A member of the board of directors, or a member of any committee designated by the board of directors, shall, in the performance of his duties, be fully protected in relying in good faith upon the records of the corporation and upon such information, opinions, reports or statements presented to the corporation by any of the corporation's officers or employees, or committees of the board of directors, or by any other person as to matters the member reasonably believes are within such other person's professional or expert competence and who has been selected with reasonable care by or on behalf of the corporation.

(f) Unless otherwise restricted by the certificate of incorporation or by-laws, any action required or permitted to be taken at any meeting of the board of directors, or of any committee thereof may be taken without a meeting if all members of the board or committee, as the case may be, consent thereto in writing, and the writing or writings are filed with the minutes of proceedings of the board, or committee.

(g) Unless otherwise restricted by the certificate of incorporation or by-laws, the board of directors of any corporation organized under this chapter may hold its meetings, and have an office or offices, outside of this State.

(h) Unless otherwise restricted by the certificate of incorporation or by-laws, the board of directors shall have the authority to fix the compensation of directors.

(i) Unless otherwise restricted by the certificate of incorporation or by-laws, members of the board of directors of any corporation, or any committee designated by such board, may participate in a meeting of such board, or committee by means of conference telephone or similar communications equipment by means of which all persons participating in the meeting can hear each other, and participation in a meeting pursuant to this subsection shall constitute presence in person at such meeting.

(j) The certificate of incorporation of any corporation organized under this chapter which is not authorized to issue capital stock may provide that less than one-third of the members of the governing body may constitute a quorum thereof and may otherwise provide that the business and affairs of the corporation shall be managed in a manner different from that provided in this section. Except as may be otherwise provided by the certificate of incorporation, the provisions of this section shall apply to such a corporation, and when so applied, all references to the board of directors, to members thereof, and to stockholders shall be deemed to refer to the governing body of the corporation, the members thereof and the members of the corporation, respectively.

(k) Any director or the entire board of directors may be removed, with or without cause, by the holders of a majority of the shares then entitled to vote at an election of directors, except as follows:

(i) Unless the certificate of incorporation otherwise provides, in the case of a corporation whose board is classified as provided in subsection (d) of this section, shareholders may effect such removal only for cause; or

(ii) In the case of a corporation having cumulative voting, if less than the entire board is to be removed, no director may be removed without cause if the votes cast against his removal would be sufficient to elect him if then cumulatively voted at an election of the entire board of directors, or, if there be classes of directors, at an election of the class of directors of which he is a part.

Whenever the holders of any class or series are entitled to elect one or more directors by the provisions of the certificate of incorporation, the provisions of this subsection shall apply, in respect to the removal without cause of a director or directors so elected, to the vote of the holders of the outstanding shares of that class or series and not to the vote of the outstanding shares as a whole.

§142. Officers; Titles; Duties; Selection; Term; Failure to Elect; Vacancies

(a) Every corporation organized under this chapter shall have such officers with such titles and duties as shall be stated in the by-laws or in a resolution of the board of directors which is not inconsistent with the by-laws and as may be necessary to enable it to sign instruments and stock certificates which comply with sections 103(a)(2) and 158 of this chapter. One of the officers shall have the duty to record the proceedings of the meetings of the stockholders and directors in a book to be kept for that purpose. Any number of offices may be held by the same person unless the certificate of incorporation or by-laws otherwise provide.

(b) Officers shall be chosen in such manner and shall hold their offices for such terms as are prescribed by the by-laws or determined by the board of directors or other governing body. Each officer shall hold his office until his successor is elected and qualified or until his earlier resignation or removal. Any officer may resign at any time upon written notice to the corporation.

(c) The corporation may secure the fidelity of any or all of its officers or agents by bond or otherwise.

(d) A failure to elect officers shall not dissolve or otherwise affect the corporation.

(e) Any vacancy occurring in any office of the corporation by death, resignation, removal or otherwise, shall be filled as the by-laws provide. In the absence of such provision, the vacancy shall be filled by the board of directors or other governing body.

§143. Loans to Employees and Officers; Guaranty of Obligations of Employees and Officers

Any corporation may lend money to, or guarantee any obligation of, or otherwise assist any officer or other employee of the corporation or of its subsidiary, including any officer or employee who is a director of the corporation or its subsidiary, whenever, in the judgment of the directors, such loan, guaranty or assistance may reasonably be expected to benefit the corporation. The loan, guaranty or other assistance may be with or without interest, and may be unsecured, or secured in such manner as the board of directors shall approve, including, without limitation, a pledge of shares of stock of the corporation. Nothing in this section contained shall be deemed to deny, limit or restrict the powers of guaranty or warranty of any corporation at common law or under any statute.

§144. Interested Directors; Quorum

(a) No contract or transaction between a corporation and one or more of its directors or officers, or between a corporation and any other corporation, partnership, association, or other organization in which one or more of its directors or officers are directors or officers, or have a financial interest, shall be void or voidable solely for this reason, or solely because the director or officer is present at or participates in the meeting of the board or committee thereof which authorizes the contract or transaction, or solely because any such director's or officer's votes are counted for such purpose, if:

(1) The material facts as to the director's or officer's relationship or interest and as to the contract or transaction are disclosed or are known to the board of directors or the committee, and the board or committee in good faith authorizes the contract or transaction by the affirmative votes of a majority of the disinterested directors, even though the disinterested directors be less than a quorum; or

(2) The material facts as to the director's or officer's relationship or interest and as to the contract or transaction are disclosed or are known to the shareholders entitled to vote thereon, and the contract or transaction is specifically approved in good faith by vote of the shareholders; or

(3) The contract or transaction is fair as to the corporation as of the time it is authorized, approved or ratified, by the board of directors, a committee thereof, or the shareholders.

(b) Common or interested directors may be counted in determining the presence of a quorum at a meeting of the board of directors or of a committee which authorizes the contract or transaction.

§145. Indemnification of Officers, Directors, Employees and Agents; Insurance

(a) A corporation shall have power to indemnify any person who was or is a party or is threatened to be made a party to any threatened, pending or completed action, suit or proceeding, whether civil, criminal, administrative or investigative (other than an action by or in the right of the corporation) by reason of the fact that such person is or was a director, officer, employee or agent of the corporation, or is or was serving at the request of the corporation as a director, officer, employee or agent of another corporation, partnership, joint venture, trust or other enterprise, against expenses (including attorneys' fees), judgments, fines and amounts paid in settlement actually and reasonably incurred by him in connection with such action, suit or proceeding if such person acted in good faith and in a manner such person reasonably believed to be in or not opposed to the best interests of the corporation, and, with respect to any criminal action or proceeding, had no reasonable cause to believe his conduct was unlawful. The termination of any action, suit or proceeding by judgment, order, settlement, conviction, or upon a plea of *nolo contendere* or its equivalent, shall not, of itself, create a presumption that the person did not act in good faith and in a manner which such person reasonably believed to be in or not opposed to the best interests of the corporation, and, with respect to any criminal action or proceeding, had reasonable cause to believe that such person's conduct was unlawful.

(b) A corporation shall have the power to indemnify any person who was or is a party or is threatened to be made a party to any threatened, pending or completed action or suit by or in the right of the corporation to procure a judgment in its favor by reason of the fact that such person is or was a director, officer, employee or agent of the corporation, or is or was serving at the request of the corporation as a director, officer, employee or agent of another corporation, partnership, joint venture, trust or other enterprise against expenses (including attorneys' fees) actually and reasonably incurred by such person in connection with the defense or settlement of such action or suit if such person acted in good faith and in a manner such person reasonably believed to be in or not opposed to the best interests of the corporation and except that no indemnification shall be made in respect of any claim, issue or matter as to which such person shall have been adjudged to be liable to the corporation unless and only to the extent that the Court of Chancery or the court in which such action or suit was brought shall determine upon application that, despite the adjudication of liability but in view of all the circumstances of the case, such person is fairly and reasonably entitled to indemnity for such expenses which the Court of Chancery or such other court shall deem proper.

(c) To the extent that a director, officer, employee or agent of a corporation has been successful on the merits or otherwise in defense of any action, suit or proceeding referred to in subsections (a) and (b), or in defense of any claim, issue or matter therein, such person shall be indemnified against expenses (including attorneys' fees) actually and reasonably incurred by such person in connection therewith.

(d) Any indemnification under subsections (a) and (b) (unless ordered by a court) shall be made by the corporation only as authorized in the specific case upon a determination that indemnification of the director, officer, employee or agent is proper in the circumstances because such person has met the applicable standard of conduct set forth in subsections (a) and (b) of this Section. Such determination shall be made, with respect to a person who is a director or officer at the time of such determination, (1) by a majority vote of the directors who are not parties to such action, suit or proceeding, even though less than a quorum, or (2) by a committee of such directors designated by majority vote of such directors, even though less than a quorum, or (3) if there are no such directors, or if such directors direct, by independent legal counsel in a written opinion, or (4) by the stockholders.

(e) Expenses (including attorneys' fees) incurred by an officer or director in defending any civil, criminal, administrative or investigative action, suit or proceeding may be paid by the corporation in advance of the final disposition of such action, suit or proceeding upon receipt of an undertaking by or on behalf of such director or officer to repay such amount if it shall ultimately be determined that such person is not entitled to be indemnified by the corporation as authorized in this Section. Such expenses (including attorneys' fees) incurred by former directors and officers or other employees and agents may be so paid upon such terms and conditions, if any, as the corporation deems appropriate.

(f) The indemnification and advancement of expenses provided by, or granted pursuant to, the other subsections of this section shall not be deemed exclusive of any other rights to which those seeking indemnification or advancement of expenses may be entitled under any by-law, agreement, vote of stockholders or disinterested directors or otherwise, both as to action in such person's official capacity and as to action in another capacity while holding such office.

(g) A corporation shall have power to purchase and maintain insurance on behalf of any person who is or was a director, officer, employee or agent of the corporation, or is or was serving at the request of the corporation as a director, officer, employee or agent of another corporation, partnership, joint venture, trust or other enterprise against any liability asserted against such person and incurred by such person in any such capacity, or arising out of such person's status as such, whether or not the corporation would have the power to indemnify such person against such liability under the provisions of this section.

(h) For purposes of this Section, references to "the corporation" shall include, in addition to the resulting corporation, any constituent corporation (including any constituent of a constituent) absorbed in a consolidation or merger which, if its separate existence had continued, would have had power and authority to indemnify its directors, officers, and employees or agents, so that any person who is or was a director, officer, employee or agent of such constituent corporation, or is or was serving at the request of such constituent corporation as a director, officer, employee or agent of another corporation, partnership, joint venture, trust or other enterprise, shall stand in the same position under the provisions of this Section with respect to the resulting or surviving corporation as such person would have with respect to such constituent corporation if its separate existence had continued.

(i) For purposes of this Section, references to "other enterprises" shall include employee benefit plans; references to "fines" shall include any excise taxes assessed on a person with respect to an employee benefit plan; and references to "serving at the request of the corporation" shall include any service as a director, officer, employee or agent of the corporation which imposes duties on, or involves services by, such director, officer, employee, or agent with respect to an employee benefit plan, its participants, or beneficiaries; and a person who acted in good faith and in a manner such person reasonably believed to be in the interest of the participants and beneficiaries of an employee benefit plan shall be deemed to have acted in a manner "not opposed to the best interests of the corporation" as referred to in this Section.

(j) The indemnification and advancement of expenses provided by, or granted pursuant to, this section shall, unless otherwise provided when authorized or ratified, continue as to a person who has ceased to be a director, officer, employee or agent and shall inure to the benefit of the heirs, executors and administrators of such a person.

(k) The Court of Chancery is hereby vested with exclusive jurisdiction to hear and determine all actions for advancement of expenses or indemnification brought under this section or under any bylaw, agreement, vote of stockholders or disinterested directors, or otherwise. The Court of Chancery may summarily determine a corporation's obligation to advance expenses (including attorneys' fees).

§151. Classes and Series of Stock; Rights, etc.

(a) Every corporation may issue one or more classes of stock or one or more series of stock within any class thereof, any or all of which classes may be of stock with par value or stock without par value and which classes or series may have such voting powers, full or limited, or no voting powers, and such designations, preferences and relative, participating, optional or other special rights, and qualifications, limitations or restrictions thereof, as shall be stated and expressed in the certificate of incorporation or of any amendment thereto, or in the resolution or resolutions providing for the issue of such stock adopted by the board of directors pursuant to authority expressly vested in it by the provisions of its certificate of incorporation. Any of the voting powers, designations, preferences, rights and qualifications, limitations or restrictions of any such class or series of stock may be made dependent upon facts ascertainable outside the certificate of incorporation or of any amendment thereto, or outside the resolution or resolutions providing for the issue of such stock adopted by the board of directors pursuant to authority expressly vested in it by its certificate of incorporation, provided that the manner in which such facts shall operate upon the voting powers, designations, preferences, rights and qualifications, limitations or restrictions of such class or series of stock is clearly and expressly set forth in the certificate of incorporation or in the resolution or resolutions providing for the issue of such stock adopted by the board of directors. The term "facts" as used in this subsection, includes, but is not limited to, the occurrence of any event, including a determination or action by any person or body, including the corporation. The power to increase or decrease or otherwise adjust the capital stock as provided in this chapter shall apply to all or any such classes of stock.

(b) The stock of any class or series may be made subject to redemption by the corporation at its option or at the option of the holders of such stock or upon the happening of a specified event; provided, however, that immediately following any such redemption the corporation shall have outstanding 1 or more shares of 1 or more classes or series of stock which share, or shares together, shall have full voting powers. Notwithstanding the limitation stated in the foregoing proviso:

(1) Any stock of a regulated investment company registered under the Investment Company Act of 1940, as heretofore or hereafter amended, may be made subject to redemption by the corporation at its option or at the option of the holders of such stock.

(2) Any stock of a corporation which holds (directly or indirectly) a license or franchise from a governmental agency to conduct its business or is a member of a national securities exchange, which license, franchise or membership is conditioned upon some or all of the holders of its stock possessing prescribed qualifications, may be made subject to redemption by the corporation to the extent necessary to prevent the loss of such license, franchise or membership or to reinstate it.

Any stock which may be made redeemable under this section may be redeemed for cash, property or rights, including securities of the same or another corporation, at such time or times, price or prices, or rate or rates, and with such adjustments, as shall be stated in the certificate of incorporation or in the resolution or resolutions providing for the issue of such stock adopted by the board of directors pursuant to subsection (a) of this section.

(c) The holders of preferred or special stock of any class or of any series thereof shall be entitled to receive dividends at such rates, on such conditions and at such times as shall be stated in the certificate of incorporation or in the resolution or resolutions providing for the issue of such stock adopted by the board of directors as hereinabove provided, payable in preference to, or in such relation to, the dividends payable on any other class or classes or of any other series of stock, and cumulative or non-cumulative as shall be so stated and expressed. When dividends upon the preferred and special stocks, if any, to the extent of the preference to which such stocks are entitled, shall have been paid or declared and set apart for payment, a dividend on the remaining class or classes or series of stock may then be paid out of the remaining assets of the corporation available for dividends as elsewhere in this chapter provided.

(d) The holders of the preferred or special stock of any class or of any series thereof shall be entitled to such rights upon the dissolution of, or upon any distribution of the assets of, the corporation as shall be stated in the certificate of incorporation or in the resolution or resolutions providing for the issue of such stock adopted by the board of directors as hereinabove provided.

(e) Any stock of any class or of any series thereof may be made convertible into, or exchangeable for, at the option of either the holder or the corporation or upon the happening of a specified event, shares of any other class or classes or any other series of the same or any other class or classes of stock of the corporation, at such price or prices or at such rate or rates of exchange and with such adjustments as shall be stated in the certificate of incorporation or in the resolution or resolutions providing for the issue of such stock adopted by the board of directors as hereinabove provided.

(f) If any corporation shall be authorized to issue more than one class of stock or more than one series of any class, the powers, designations, preferences and relative, participating, optional or other special rights of each class of stock or series thereof and the qualifications, limitations or restrictions of such preferences and/or rights shall be set forth in full or summarized on the face or back of the certificate which the corporation shall issue to represent such class or series of stock, provided that, except as otherwise provided in section 202 of this title, in lieu of the foregoing requirements, there may be set forth on the face or back of the certificate which the corporation shall issue to represent such class or series of stock, a statement that the corporation will furnish without charge to each stockholder who so requests the powers, designations, preferences and relative, participating optional or other special rights of each class of stock or series thereof and the qualifications, limitations or restrictions of such preferences and/or rights. Within a reasonable time after the issuance or transfer of uncertificated stock, the corporation shall send to the registered owner thereof a written notice containing the information required to be set forth or stated on certificates pursuant to this Section or Sections 156, 202(a) or 218(a) or with respect to this Section a statement that the corporation will furnish without charge to each stockholder who so requests the powers, designations, preferences and relative participating, optional or other special rights of each class of stock or series thereof and the qualifications, limitations or restrictions of such preferences and/or rights. Except as otherwise expressly provided by law, the rights and obligations of the holders of uncertificated stock and the rights and obligations of the holders of certificates representing stock of the same class and series shall be identical.

(g) When any corporation desires to issue any shares of stock of any class or of any series of any class of which the powers, designations, preferences and relative, participating, optional or other rights, if any, or the qualifications, limitations or restrictions thereof, if any, shall not have been set forth in the certificate of incorporation or in any amendment thereto but shall be provided for in a resolution or resolutions adopted by the board of directors pursuant to authority expressly vested in it by the certificate of incorporation or any amendment thereto, a certificate of designations setting forth a copy of such resolution or resolutions and the number of shares of stock of such class or series as to which the resolution or resolutions apply shall be executed, acknowledged, filed, recorded and shall become effective, in accordance with §103 of this Title. Unless otherwise provided in any such resolution or resolutions, the number of shares of stock of any such series to which such resolution or resolutions apply may be increased (but not above the total number of authorized shares of the class) or decreased (but not below the number of shares thereof then outstanding) by a certificate likewise executed, acknowledged and filed setting forth a statement that a specified increase or decrease therein had been authorized and directed by a resolution or resolutions likewise adopted by the board of directors. In case the number of such shares shall be decreased the number of shares so specified in the certificate shall resume the status which they had prior to the adoption of the first resolution or resolutions. When no shares of any such class or series are outstanding, either because none were issued or because no issued shares of any such class or series remain outstanding, a certificate setting forth a resolution or resolutions adopted by the board of directors that none of the authorized shares of such class or series are outstanding, and that none will be issued subject to the certificate of designations previously filed with respect to such class or series, may be executed, acknowledged and filed in accordance with §103 of this Title and, when such certificate becomes effective, it shall have the effect of eliminating from the certificate of incorporation all matters set forth in the certificate of designations with respect to such class or series of stock. Unless otherwise provided in the certificate of incorporation, if no shares of stock have been issued of a class or series of stock established by a resolution of the board of directors, the voting powers, designations, preferences and relative, participating, optional or other rights, if any, or the qualifications, limitations or restrictions thereof, may be amended by a resolution or resolutions adopted by the board of directors. A certificate which (1) states that no shares of the class or series have been issued, (2) sets forth a copy of the resolution or resolutions and (3) if the designation of the class or series is being changed, indicates the original designation and the new designation, shall be executed, acknowledged and filed and shall become effective, in accordance with §103 of this title. When any certificate filed under this subsection becomes effective, it shall have the effect of amending the certificate of incorporation; except that neither the filing of such certificate nor the filing of a restated certificate of incorporation pursuant to §245 of this title shall prohibit the board of directors from subsequently adopting such resolutions as authorized by this subsection.

§152. Issuance of Stock; Lawful Consideration; Fully Paid Stock

The consideration, as determined pursuant to subsections (a) and (b) of Section 153 of this title, for subscriptions to, or the purchase of, the capital stock to be issued by a corporation shall be paid in such form and in such manner as the board of directors shall determine. In the absence of actual fraud in the transaction, the judgment of the directors as to the value of such consideration shall be conclusive. The capital stock so issued shall be deemed to be fully paid and nonassessable stock, if: (1) the entire amount of such consideration has been received by the corporation in the form of cash, services rendered, personal property, real property, leases of real property, or a combination thereof; or (2) not less than the amount of the consideration determined to be capital pursuant to Section 154 of this title has been received by the corporation in such form and the corporation has received a binding obligation of the subscriber or purchaser to pay the balance of the subscription or purchase price; provided, however, nothing contained herein shall prevent the board of directors from issuing partly paid shares under Section 156 of this title.

§153. Consideration for Stock

(a) Shares of stock with par value may be issued for such consideration, having a value not less than the par value thereof, as is determined from time to time by the board of directors, or by the stockholders if the certificate of incorporation so provides.

(b) Shares of stock without par value may be issued for such consideration as is determined from time to time by the board of directors, or by the stockholders if the certificate of incorporation so provides.

(c) Treasury shares may be disposed of by the corporation for such consideration as may be determined from time to time by the board of directors, or by the stockholders if the certificate of incorporation so provides.

(d) If the certificate of incorporation reserves to the stockholders the right to determine the consideration for the issue of any shares, the stockholders shall, unless the certificate requires a greater vote, do so by a vote of a majority of the outstanding stock entitled to vote thereon.

§154. Determination of Amount of Capital; Capital, Surplus and Net Assets Defined

Any corporation may, by resolution of its board of directors, determine that only a part of the consideration which shall be received by the corporation for any of the shares of its capital stock which it shall issue from time to time shall be capital; but, in case any of the shares issued shall be shares having a par value, the amount of the part of such consideration so determined to be capital shall be in excess of the aggregate par value of the shares issued for such consideration having a par value, unless all the shares issued shall be shares having a par value, in which case the amount of the part of such consideration so determined to be capital need be only equal to the aggregate par value of such shares. In each such case the board of directors shall specify in dollars the part of such consideration which shall be capital. If the board of directors shall not have determined (1) at the time of issue of any shares of the capital stock of the corporation issued for cash or (2) within 60 days after the issue of any shares of the capital stock of the corporation issued for property other than cash what part of the consideration for such shares shall be capital, the capital of the corporation in respect of such shares shall be an amount equal to the aggregate par value of such shares having a par value, plus the amount of the consideration for such shares without par value. The amount of the consideration so determined to be capital in respect of any shares without par value shall be the stated capital of such shares. The capital of the corporation may be increased from time to time by resolution of the board of directors directing that a portion of the net assets of the corporation in excess of the amount so determined to be capital be transferred to the capital account. The board of directors may direct that the portion of such net assets so transferred shall be treated as capital in respect of any shares of the corporation of any designated class or classes. The excess, if any, at any given time, of the net assets of the corporation over the amount so determined to be capital shall be surplus. Net assets means the amount by which total assets exceed total liabilities. Capital and surplus are not liabilities for this purpose.

§155. Fractions of Shares

A corporation may, but shall not be required to, issue fractions of a share. If it does not issue fractions of a share, it shall (1) arrange for the disposition of fractional interests by those entitled thereto, (2) pay in cash the fair value of fractions of a share as of the time when those entitled to receive such fractions are determined or (3) issue scrip or warrants in registered form (either represented by a certificate or uncertificated) or in bearer form (represented by a certificate) which shall entitle the holder to receive a full share upon the surrender of such scrip or warrants aggregating a full share. A certificate for a fractional share or an uncertificated fractional share shall, but scrip or warrants shall not unless otherwise provided therein, entitle the holder to exercise voting rights, to receive dividends thereon and to participate in any of the assets of the corporation in the event of liquidation. The board of directors may cause scrip or warrants to be issued subject to the conditions that they shall become void if not exchanged for certificates representing the full shares or uncertificated full shares before a specified date, or subject to the conditions that the shares for which scrip or warrants are exchangeable may be sold by the corporation and the proceeds thereof distributed to the holders of scrip or warrants, or subject to any other conditions which the board of directors may impose.

§156. Partly Paid Shares

Any corporation may issue the whole or any part of its shares as partly paid and subject to call for the remainder of the consideration to be paid therefor. Upon the face or back of each stock certificate issued to represent any such partly paid shares, or upon the books and records of the corporation in the case of uncertificated partly paid shares, the total amount of the consideration to be paid therefor and the amount paid thereon shall be stated. Upon the declaration of any dividend on fully paid shares, the corporation shall declare a dividend upon partly paid shares of the same class, but only upon the basis of the percentage of the consideration actually paid thereon.

§157. Rights and Options Respecting Stock

Subject to any provisions in the certificate of incorporation, every corporation may create and issue, whether or not in connection with the issue and sale of any shares of stock or other securities of the corporation, rights or options entitling the holders thereof to purchase from the corporation any shares of its capital stock of any class or classes, such rights or options to be evidenced by or in such instrument or instruments as shall be approved by the board of directors. The terms upon which, including the time or times, which may be limited or unlimited in duration, at or within which, and the price or prices at which any such shares may be purchased from the corporation upon the exercise of any such right or option, shall be such as shall be stated in the certificate of incorporation, or in a resolution adopted by the board of directors providing for the creation and issue of such rights or options, and, in every case, shall be set forth or incorporated by reference in the instrument or instruments evidencing such rights or options. In the absence of actual fraud in the transaction, the judgment of the directors as to the consideration for the issuance of such rights or options and the sufficiency thereof shall be conclusive. In case the shares of stock of the corporation to be issued upon the exercise of such rights or options shall be shares having a par value, the price or prices so to be received therefor shall not be less than the par value thereof. In case the shares of stock so to be issued shall be shares of stock without par value, the consideration therefor shall be determined in the manner provided in section 153 of this title.

§158. Stock Certificates; Uncertificated Shares

The shares of a corporation shall be represented by certificates, provided that the board of directors of the corporation may provide by resolution or resolutions that some or all of any or all classes or series of its stock shall be uncertificated shares. Any such resolution shall not apply to shares represented by a certificate until such certificate is surrendered to the corporation. Notwithstanding the adoption of such a resolution by the board of directors, every holder of stock represented by certificates and upon request every holder of uncertificated shares shall be entitled to have a certificate signed by, or in the name of the corporation by the chairperson or vice-chairperson of the board of directors, or the president or vice-president, and by the treasurer or an assistant treasurer, or the secretary or an assistant secretary of such corporation representing the number of shares registered in certificate form. Any or all the signatures on the certificate may be a facsimile. In case any officer, transfer agent or registrar who has signed or whose facsimile signature has been placed upon a certificate shall have ceased to be such officer, transfer agent or registrar before such certificate is issued, it may be issued by the corporation with the same effect as if such person were such officer, transfer agent or registrar at the date of issue.

§159. Shares of Stock; Personal Property, Transfer and Taxation

The shares of stock in every corporation shall be deemed personal property and transferable as provided in Article 8 of Subtitle I of Title 6. No stock or bonds issued by any corporation organized under this chapter shall be taxed by this State when the same shall be owned by non-residents of this State, or by foreign corporations. Whenever any transfer of shares shall be made for collateral security, and not absolutely, it shall be so expressed in the entry of transfer if, when the certificates are presented to the corporation for transfer or uncertificated shares are requested to be transferred, both the transferor and transferee request the corporation to do so.

§160. Corporation's Powers Respecting Ownership, Voting, etc., of Its Own Stock; Rights of Stock Called for Redemption

(a) Every corporation may purchase, redeem, receive, take or otherwise acquire, own and hold, sell, lend, exchange, transfer or otherwise dispose of, pledge, use and otherwise deal in and with its own shares; provided, however, that no corporation shall —

1. Purchase or redeem its own shares of capital stock for cash or other property when the capital of the corporation is impaired or when such purchase or redemption would cause any impairment of the capital of the corporation, except that a corporation may purchase or redeem out of capital any of its own shares which are entitled upon any distribution of its assets, whether by dividend or in liquidation, to a preference over another class or series of its stock or, if no shares entitled to such a preference are outstanding, any of its own shares, if such shares will be retired upon their acquisition and the capital of the corporation reduced in accordance with Sections 243 and 244 of this title. Nothing in this subsection shall invalidate or otherwise affect a note, debenture or other obligation of a corporation given by it as consideration for its acquisition by purchase, redemption or exchange of its shares of stock if at the time such note, debenture or obligation was delivered by the corporation its capital was not then impaired or did not thereby become impaired;

2. Purchase, for more than the price at which they may then be redeemed, any of its shares which are redeemable at the option of the corporation; or,

3. Redeem any of its shares unless their redemption is authorized by Section 151(b) of this title and then only in accordance with such Section and the certificate of incorporation.

(b) Nothing in this section limits or affects a corporation's right to resell any of its shares theretofore purchased or redeemed out of surplus and which have not been retired, for such consideration as shall be fixed by the board of directors.

(c) Shares of its own capital stock belonging to the corporation or to another corporation, if a majority of the shares entitled to vote in the election of directors of such other corporation is held, directly or indirectly, by the corporation, shall neither be entitled to vote nor be counted for quorum purposes. Nothing in this section shall be construed as limiting the right of any corporation to vote stock, including but not limited to its own stock, held by it in a fiduciary capacity.

(d) Shares which have been called for redemption shall not be deemed to be outstanding shares for the purpose of voting or determining the total number of shares entitled to vote on any matter on and after the date on which written notice of redemption has been sent to holders thereof and a sum sufficient to redeem such shares has been irrevocably deposited or set aside to pay the redemption price to the holders of the shares upon surrender of certificates therefor.

§161. Issuance of Additional Stock; When and by Whom

The directors may, at any time and from time to time, if all of the shares of capital stock which the corporation is authorized by its certificate of incorporation to issue have not been issued, subscribed for, or otherwise committed to be issued, issue or take subscriptions for additional shares of its capital stock up to the amount authorized in its certificate of incorporation.

§162. Liability of Stockholder or Subscriber for Stock Not Paid in Full

(a) When the whole of the consideration payable for shares of a corporation has not been paid in, and the assets shall be insufficient to satisfy the claims of its creditors, each holder of or subscriber for such shares shall be bound to pay on each share held or subscribed for by such holder or subscriber the sum necessary to complete the amount of the unpaid balance of the consideration for which such shares were issued or to be issued by the corporation.

(b) The amounts which shall be payable as provided in subsection (a) of this section may be recovered as provided in section 325 of this title, after a writ of execution against the corporation has been returned unsatisfied as provided in that section.

(c) Any person becoming an assignee or transferee of shares or of a subscription for shares in good faith and without knowledge or notice that the full consideration therefor has not been paid shall not be personally liable for any unpaid portion of such consideration, but the transferor shall remain liable therefor.

(d) No person holding shares in any corporation as collateral security shall be personally liable as a stockholder but the person pledging such shares shall be considered the holder thereof and shall be so liable. No executor, administrator, guardian, trustee or other fiduciary shall be personally liable as a stockholder, but the estate or funds held by such executor, administrator, guardian, trustee or other fiduciary in such fiduciary capacity shall be liable.

(e) No liability under this section or under section 325 of this title shall be asserted more than six years after the issuance of the stock or the date of the subscription upon which the assessment is sought.

(f) In any action by a receiver or trustee of an insolvent corporation or by a judgment creditor to obtain an assessment under this section, any stockholder or subscriber for stock of the insolvent corporation may appear and contest the claim or claims of such receiver or trustee.

§163. Payment for Stock Not Paid in Full

The capital stock of a corporation shall be paid for in such amounts and at such times as the directors may require. The directors may, from time to time, demand payment, in respect of each share of stock not fully paid, of such sum of money as the necessities of the business may, in the judgment of the board of directors, require, not exceeding in the whole the balance remaining unpaid on said stock, and such sum so demanded shall be paid to the corporation at such times and by such installments as the directors shall direct. The directors shall give written notice of the time and place of such payments, which notice shall be mailed at least 30 days before the time for such payment, to each holder of or subscriber for stock which is not fully paid at such holder's or subscriber's last known post-office address.

§164. Failure to Pay for Stock; Remedies

When any stockholder fails to pay any installment or call upon such stockholder's stock which may have been properly demanded by the directors, at the time when such payment is due, the directors may collect the amount of any such installment or call or any balance thereof remaining unpaid, from the said stockholder by an action at law, or they shall sell at public sale such part of the shares of such delinquent stockholder as will pay all demands then due from such stockholder with interest and all incidental expenses, and shall transfer the shares so sold to the purchaser, who shall be entitled to a certificate therefor. Notice of the time and place of such sale and of the sum due on each share shall be given by advertisement at least one week before the sale, in a newspaper of the county in this State where such corporation's registered office is located, and such notice shall be mailed by the corporation to such delinquent stockholder at such stockholder's last known post-office address, at least 20 days before such sale. If no bidder can be had to pay the amount due on the stock, and if the amount is not collected by an action at law, which may be brought within the county where the corporation has its registered office, within one year from the date of the bringing of such action at law, the said stock and the amount previously paid in by the delinquent stockholder on the stock shall be forfeited to the corporation.

§165. Revocability of Preincorporation Subscriptions

Unless otherwise provided by the terms of the subscription, a subscription for stock of a corporation to be formed shall be irrevocable, except with the consent of all other subscribers or the corporation, for a period of 6 months from its date.

§166. Formalities Required of Stock Subscriptions

A subscription for stock of a corporation, whether made before or after the formation of a corporation, shall not be enforceable against a subscriber, unless in writing and signed by the subscriber or by such subscriber's agent.

§169. Situs of Ownership of Stock

For all purposes of title, action, attachment, garnishment and jurisdiction of all courts held in this State, but not for the purpose of taxation, the situs of the ownership of the capital stock of all corporations existing under the laws of this State, whether organized under this chapter or otherwise, shall be regarded as in this State.

§170. Dividends; Payment; Wasting Asset Corporations

(a) The directors of every corporation, subject to any restrictions contained in its certificate of incorporation, may declare and pay dividends upon the shares of its capital stock, or to its members if the corporation is a nonstock corporation organized for profit, either (1) out of its surplus, as defined in and computed in accordance with Sections 154 and 244 of this title, or (2) in case there shall be no such surplus, out of its net profits for the fiscal year in which the dividend is declared and/or the preceding fiscal year. If the capital of the corporation, computed in accordance with Sections 154 and 244 of this title, shall have been diminished by depreciation in the value of its property, or by losses, or otherwise, to an amount less than the aggregate amount of the capital represented by the issued and outstanding stock of all classes having a preference upon the distribution of assets, the directors of such corporation shall not declare and pay out of such net profits any dividends upon any shares of any classes of its capital stock until the deficiency in the amount of capital represented by the issued and outstanding stock of all classes having a preference upon the distribution of assets shall have been repaired. Nothing in this subsection shall invalidate or otherwise affect a note, debenture or other obligation of the corporation paid by it as a dividend on shares of its stock, or any payment made thereon, if at the time such note, debenture or obligation was delivered by the corporation, the corporation had either surplus or net profits as provided in clause (1) or (2) of this subsection from which the dividend could lawfully have been paid.

(b) Subject to any restrictions contained in its certificate of incorporation, the directors of any corporation engaged in the exploitation of wasting assets (including but not limited to a corporation engaged in the exploitation of natural resources or other wasting assets, including patents, or engaged primarily in the liquidation of specific assets) may determine the net profits derived from the exploitation of such wasting assets or the net proceeds derived from such liquidation without taking into consideration the depletion of such assets resulting from lapse of time, consumption, liquidation or exploitation of such assets.

§171. Special Purpose Reserves

The directors of a corporation may set apart out of any of the funds of the corporation available for dividends a reserve or reserves for any proper purpose and may abolish any such reserve.

§172. Liability of Directors as to Dividends or Stock Redemption

A member of the board of directors, or a member of any committee designated by the board of directors, shall be fully protected in relying in good faith upon the records of the corporation and upon such information, opinions, reports or statements presented to the corporation by any of its officers or employees, or committees of the board of directors, or by any other person as to matters the director reasonably believes are within such other person's professional or expert competence and who has been selected with reasonable care by or on behalf of the corporation, as to the value and amount of the assets, liabilities and/or net profits of the corporation, or any other facts pertinent to the existence and amount of surplus or other funds from which dividends might properly be declared and paid, or with which the corporation's stock might properly be purchased or redeemed.

§173. Declaration and Payment of Dividends

No corporation shall pay dividends except in accordance with this chapter. Dividends may be paid in cash, in property, or in shares of the corporation's capital stock. If the dividend is to be paid in shares of the corporation's theretofore unissued capital stock the board of directors shall, by resolution, direct that there be designated as capital in respect of such shares an amount which is not less than the aggregate par value of par value shares being declared as a dividend and, in the case of shares without par value being declared as a dividend, such amount as shall be determined by the board of directors. No such designation as capital shall be necessary if shares are being distributed by a corporation pursuant to a split-up or division of its stock rather than as payment of a dividend declared payable in stock of the corporation.

§174. Liability of Directors for Unlawful Payment of Dividend or Unlawful Stock Purchase or Redemption; Exoneration From Liability; Contribution Among Directors; Subrogation

(a) In case of any willful or negligent violation of the provisions of sections 160 or 173 of this title, the directors under whose administration the same may happen shall be jointly and severally liable, at any time within six years after paying such unlawful dividend or after such unlawful stock purchase or redemption, to the corporation, and to its creditors in the event of its dissolution or insolvency, to the full amount of the dividend unlawfully paid, or to the full amount unlawfully paid for the purchase or redemption of the corporation's stock, with interest from the time such liability accrued. Any director who may have been absent when the same was done, or who may have dissented from the act or resolution by which the same was done, may be exonerated from such liability by causing his or her dissent to be entered on the books containing the minutes of the proceedings of the directors at the time the same was done, or immediately after such director has notice of the same.

(b) Any director against whom a claim is successfully asserted under this section shall be entitled to contribution from the other directors who voted for or concurred in the unlawful dividend, stock purchase or stock redemption.

(c) Any director against whom a claim is successfully asserted under this section shall be entitled, to the extent of the amount paid by such director as a result of such claim, to be subrogated to the rights of the corporation against stockholders who received the dividend on, or assets for the sale or redemption of, their stock with knowledge of facts indicating that such dividend, stock purchase or redemption was unlawful under this chapter, in proportion to the amounts received by such stockholders respectively.

§201. Transfer of Stock, Stock Certificate and Uncertificated Stock

Except as otherwise provided in this Chapter, the transfer of stock and the certificates of stock which represent the stock or uncertificated stock shall be governed by Article 8 of Subtitle I of Title 6. To the extent that any provision of this Chapter is inconsistent with any provision of subtitle I of Title 6, the provisions of this Chapter shall be controlling.

§202. Restriction on Transfer of Securities

(a) A written restriction on the transfer or registration of transfer of a security of a corporation, if permitted by this Section and noted conspicuously on the certificate representing the security or, in the case of uncertificated shares, contained in the notice sent pursuant to Section 151(f) of this Title, may be enforced against the holder of the restricted security or any successor or transferee of the holder including an executor, administrator, trustee, guardian or other fiduciary entrusted with like responsibility for the person or estate of the holder. Unless noted conspicuously on the certificate representing the security or, in the case of uncertificated shares, contained in the notice sent pursuant to Section 151(f) of this Title, a restriction, even though permitted by this Section, is ineffective except against a person with actual knowledge of the restriction.

(b) A restriction on the transfer or registration of transfer of securities of a corporation may be imposed either by the certificate of incorporation or by the by-laws or by an agreement among any number of security holders or among such holders and the corporation. No restriction so imposed shall be binding with respect to securities issued prior to the adoption of the restriction unless the holders of the securities are parties to an agreement or voted in favor of the restriction.

(c) A restriction on the transfer of securities of a corporation is permitted by this section if it:

(1) Obligates the holder of the restricted securities to offer to the corporation or to any other holders of securities of the corporation or to any other person or to any combination of the foregoing, a prior opportunity, to be exercised within a reasonable time, to acquire the restricted securities; or

(2) Obligates the corporation or any holder of securities of the corporation or any other person or any combination of the foregoing, to purchase the securities which are the subject of an agreement respecting the purchase and sale of the restricted securities; or

(3) Requires the corporation or the holders of any class of securities of the corporation to consent to any proposed transfer of the restricted securities or to approve the proposed transferee of the restricted securities; or

(4) Prohibits the transfer of the restricted securities to designated persons or classes of persons, and such designation is not manifestly unreasonable.

(d) Any restriction on the transfer of the shares of a corporation for the purpose of maintaining its status as an elect-

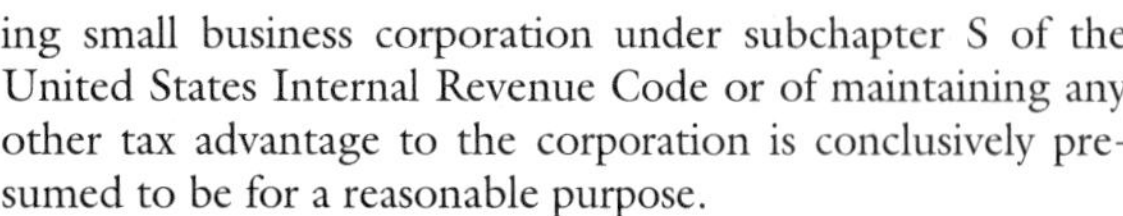

ing small business corporation under subchapter S of the United States Internal Revenue Code or of maintaining any other tax advantage to the corporation is conclusively presumed to be for a reasonable purpose.

(e) Any other lawful restriction on transfer or registration of transfer of securities is permitted by this section.

§211. Meetings of Stockholders

(a) Meetings of stockholders may be held at such place, either within or without this State, as may be designated by or in the manner provided in the by-laws or, if not so designated, at the registered office of the corporation in this State.

(b) Unless directors are elected by written consent in lieu of an annual meeting as permitted by this subsection, an annual meeting of stockholders shall be held for the election of directors on a date and at a time designated by or in the manner provided in the by-laws. Stockholders may, unless the certificate of incorporation otherwise provides, act by written consent to elect directors; provided, however, that, if such consent is less than unanimous, such action by written consent may be in lieu of holding an annual meeting only if all of the directorships to which directors could be elected at an annual meeting held at the effective time such action are vacant and are filled by such action. Any other proper business may be transacted at the annual meeting.

(c) A failure to hold the annual meeting at the designated time or to elect a sufficient number of directors to conduct the business of the corporation shall not affect otherwise valid corporate acts or work a forfeiture or dissolution of the corporation except as may be otherwise specifically provided in this chapter. If the annual meeting for election of directors is not held on the date designated therefor or action by written consent to elect directors in lieu of an annual meeting has not been taken, the directors shall cause the meeting to be held as soon as is convenient. If there be a failure to hold the annual meeting or to take action by written consent to elect directors in lieu of an annual meeting for a period of 30 days after the date designated for the annual meeting, or if no date has been designated, for a period of 13 months after the latest to occur of the organization of the corporation, its last annual meeting or the last action by written consent to elect directors in lieu of an annual meeting, the Court of Chancery may summarily order a meeting to be held upon the application of any stockholder or director. The shares of stock represented at such meeting, either in person or by proxy, and entitled to vote thereat, shall constitute a quorum for the purpose of such meeting, notwithstanding any provision of the certificate of incorporation or by-laws to the contrary. The Court of Chancery may issue such orders as may be appropriate, including, without limitation, orders designating the time and place of such meeting, the record date for determination of stockholders entitled to vote, and the form of notice of such meeting.

(d) Special meetings of the stockholders may be called by the board of directors or by such person or persons as may be authorized by the certificate of incorporation or by the by-laws.

(e) All elections of directors shall be by written ballot, unless otherwise provided in the certificate of incorporation.

§212. Voting Rights of Stockholders; Proxies; Limitations

(a) Unless otherwise provided in the certificate of incorporation and subject to the provisions of section 213 of this title, each stockholder shall be entitled to one vote for each share of capital stock held by such stockholder. If the certificate of incorporation provides for more or less than one vote for any share, on any matter, every reference in this chapter to a majority or other proportion of stock shall refer to such majority or other proportion of the votes of such stock.

(b) Each stockholder entitled to vote at a meeting of stockholders or to express consent or dissent to corporate action in writing without a meeting may authorize another person or persons to act for him by proxy, but no such proxy shall be voted or acted upon after three years from its date, unless the proxy provides for a longer period.

(c) Without limiting the manner in which a stockholder may authorize another person or persons to act for him as proxy pursuant to subsection (b) of this section, the following shall constitute a valid means by which a stockholder may grant such authority.

(1) A stockholder may execute a writing authorizing another person or persons to act for such stockholder as proxy. Execution may be accomplished by the stockholder or such stockholder's authorized officer, director, employee or agent signing such writing or causing such person's signature to be affixed to such writing by any reasonable means including, but not limited to, by facsimile signature.

(2) A stockholder may authorize another person or persons to act for such stockholder as proxy by transmitting or authorizing the transmission of a telegram, cablegram, or other means of electronic transmission to the person who will be the holder of the proxy or to a proxy solicitation firm, proxy support service organization or like agent duly authorized by the person who will be the holder of the proxy to receive such transmission, provided that any such telegram, cablegram or other means of electronic transmission must either set forth or be submitted with information from which it can be determined that the telegram, cablegram or other electronic transmission was authorized by the stockholder. If it is determined that such telegrams, cablegrams or other electronic transmissions are valid, the inspectors or, if there are no inspectors, such other persons making that determination shall specify the information upon which they relied.

(d) Any copy, facsimile telecommunication or other reliable reproduction of the writing or transmission created pursuant to subsection (c) of this section may be substituted or used in lieu of the original writing or transmission for any and all purposes for which the original writing or transmission could be used, provided that such copy, facsimile telecommunication or other reproduction shall be a complete reproduction of the entire original writing or transmission.

(e) A duly executed proxy shall be irrevocable if it states that it is irrevocable and if, and only as long as, it is coupled with an interest sufficient in law to support an irrevocable power. A proxy may be made irrevocable regardless of whether the interest with which it is coupled is an interest in the stock itself or an interest in the corporation generally.

§213. Fixing Date for Determination of Stockholders of Record

(a) In order that the corporation may determine the stockholders entitled to notice of or to vote at any meeting of stockholders or any adjournment thereof, the board of directors may fix a record date, which record date shall not precede the date upon which the resolution fixing the record date is adopted by the board of directors, and which record date shall not be more than sixty nor less than ten days before the date of such meeting. If no record date is fixed by the board of directors, the record date for determining stockholders entitled to notice of or to vote at a meeting of stockholders shall be at the close of business on the day next preceding the day on which notice is given, or, if notice is waived, at the close of business on the day next preceding the day on which the meeting is held. A determination of stockholders of record entitled to notice of or to vote at a meeting of stockholders shall apply to any adjournment of the meeting; provided, however, that the board of directors may fix a new record date for the adjourned meeting.

(b) In order that the corporation may determine the stockholders entitled to consent to corporate action in writing without a meeting, the board of directors may fix a record date, which record date shall not precede the date upon which the resolution fixing the record date is adopted by the board of directors, and which date shall not be more than ten days after the date upon which the resolution fixing the record date is adopted by the board of directors. If no record date has been fixed by the board of directors, the record date for determining stockholders entitled to consent to corporate action in writing without a meeting, when no prior action by the board of directors is required by this chapter, shall be the first date on which a signed written consent setting forth the action taken or proposed to be taken is delivered to the corporation by delivery to its registered office in this State, its principal place of business, or an officer or agent of the corporation having custody of the book in which proceedings of meetings of stockholders are recorded. Delivery made to a corporation's registered office shall be by hand or by certified or registered mail, return receipt requested. If no record date has been fixed by the board of directors and prior action by the board of directors is required by this chapter, the record date for determining stockholders entitled to consent to corporate action in writing without a meeting shall be at the close of business on the day on which the board of directors adopts the resolution taking such prior action.

(c) In order that the corporation may determine the stockholders entitled to receive payment of any dividend or other distribution or allotment of any rights or the stockholders entitled to exercise any rights in respect of any change, conversion or exchange of stock, or for the purpose of any other lawful action, the board of directors may fix a record date, which record date shall not precede the date upon which the resolution fixing the record date is adopted, and which record date shall be not more than sixty days prior to such action. If no record date is fixed, the record date for determining stockholders for any such purpose shall be at the close of business on the day on which the board of directors adopts the resolution relating thereto.

§214. Cumulative Voting

The certificate of incorporation of any corporation may provide that at all elections of directors of the corporation, or at elections held under specified circumstances, each holder of stock or of any class or classes or of a series or series thereof shall be entitled to as many votes as shall equal the number of votes which (except for such provision as to cumulative voting) such holder would be entitled to cast for the election of directors with respect to such holder's shares of stock multiplied by the number of directors to be elected by such holder, and that such holder may cast all of such votes for a single director or may distribute them among the number to be voted for, or for any two or more of them as such holder may see fit.

§216. Quorum and Required Vote for Stock Corporations

Subject to this chapter in respect of the vote that shall be required for a specific action, the certificate of incorporation or by-laws of any corporation authorized to issue stock may specify the number of shares and/or the amount of other securities having voting power the holders of which shall be present or represented by proxy at any meeting in order to constitute a quorum for, and the votes that shall be necessary for, the transaction of any business, but in no event shall a quorum consist of less than one-third of the shares entitled to vote at the meeting, except that, where a separate vote by a class or series or classes or series is required, a quorum shall consist of no less than one-third of the shares of such class or series or classes or series. In the absence of such specification in the certificate of incorporation or by-laws of the corporation:

(i) A majority of the shares entitled to vote, present in person or represented by proxy, shall constitute a quorum at a meeting of stockholders;

(ii) In all matters other than the election of directors, the affirmative vote of the majority of shares present in person or represented by proxy at the meeting and entitled to vote on the subject matter shall be the act of the stockholders;

(iii) Directors shall be elected by a plurality of the votes of the shares present in person or represented by proxy at the meeting and entitled to vote on the election of directors; and

(iv) Where a separate vote by a class or classes is required, a majority of the outstanding shares of such class or series or classes or series, present in person or represented by proxy, shall constitute a quorum entitled to take action with respect to that vote on that matter and the affirmative vote of the majority of shares of such class or series or classes or series present in person or represented by proxy at the meeting shall be the act of such class or series or classes or series.

§217. Voting Rights of Fiduciaries, Pledgors and Joint Owners of Stock

(a) Persons holding stock in a fiduciary capacity shall be entitled to vote the shares so held. Persons whose stock is pledged shall be entitled to vote, unless in the transfer by the pledgor on the books of the corporation he has expressly empowered the pledgee to vote thereon, in which case only the pledgee, or such pledgee's proxy, may represent such stock and vote thereon.

(b) If shares or other securities having voting power stand of record in the names of two or more persons, whether fiduciaries, members of a partnership, joint tenants, tenants in common, tenants by the entirety or otherwise, or if two or more persons have the same fiduciary relationship respecting the same shares, unless the secretary of the corporation is given written notice to the contrary and is furnished with a copy of the instrument or order appointing them or creating the relationship wherein it is so provided, their acts with respect to voting shall have the following effect:

(1) If only one votes, such person's act binds all;

(2) If more than one vote, the act of the majority so voting binds all;

(3) If more than one vote, but the vote is evenly split on any particular matter, each faction may vote the securities in question proportionally, or any person voting the shares, or a beneficiary, if any, may apply to the Court of Chancery or such other court as may have jurisdiction to appoint an additional person to act with the persons so voting the shares, which shall then be voted as determined by a majority of such persons and the person appointed by the Court. If the instrument so filed shows that any such tenancy is held in unequal interests, a majority or even-split for the purpose of this subsection shall be a majority or even-split in interest.

§218. Voting Trusts and Other Voting Agreements

(a) One stockholder or 2 or more stockholders may by agreement in writing deposit capital stock of an original issue with or transfer capital stock to any person or persons, or corporation or corporations authorized to act as trustee, for the purpose of vesting in such person or persons, corporation or corporations, who may be designated voting trustee, or voting trustees, the right to vote thereon for any period of time determined by such agreement, upon the terms and conditions stated in such agreement. The agreement may contain any other lawful provisions not inconsistent with such purpose. After the filing of a copy of the agreement in the registered office of the corporation in this State, which copy shall be open to the inspection of any stockholder of the corporation or any beneficiary of the trust under the agreement daily during business hours, certificates of stock or uncertificated stock shall be issued to the voting trustee or trustees to represent any stock of an original issue so deposited with such voting trustee or trustees, and any certificates of stock or uncertificated stock so transferred to the voting trustee or trustees shall be surrendered and cancelled and new certificates or uncertificated stock shall be issued therefore to the voting trustee or trustees. In the certificate so issued, if any, it shall be stated that it is issued pursuant to such agreement, and that fact shall also be stated in the stock ledger of the corporation. The voting trustee or trustees may vote the stock so issued or transferred during the period specified in the agreement. Stock standing in the name of the voting trustee or trustees may be voted either in person or by proxy, and in voting the stock, the voting trustee or trustees shall incur no responsibility as stockholder, trustee or otherwise, except for their own individual malfeasance. In any case where two or more persons are designated as voting trustees, and the right and method of voting any stock standing in their names at any meeting of the corporation are not fixed by the agreement appointing the trustees, the right to vote the stock and the manner of voting it at the meeting shall be determined by a majority of the trustees, or if they be equally divided as to the right and manner of voting the stock in any particular case, the vote of the stock in such case shall be divided equally among the trustees.

(b) Any amendment to a voting trust agreement shall be made by a written agreement, a copy of which shall be filed in the registered office of the corporation in this State.

(c) An agreement between two or more stockholders, if in writing and signed by the parties thereto, may provide that in exercising any voting rights, the shares held by them shall be voted as provided by the agreement, or as the parties may agree, or as determined in accordance with a procedure agreed upon by them.

(d) This section shall not be deemed to invalidate any voting or other agreement among stockholders or any irrevocable proxy which is not otherwise illegal.

§219. List of Stockholders Entitled to Vote; Penalty for Refusal to Produce; Stock Ledger

(a) The officer who has charge of the stock ledger of a corporation shall prepare and make, at least ten days before every meeting of stockholders, a complete list of the stockholders entitled to vote at the meeting, arranged in alphabetical order, and showing the address of each stockholder and the number of shares registered in the name of each stockholder. Such list shall be open to the examination of any stockholder, for any purpose germane to the meeting, during ordinary business hours, for a period of at least ten days prior to the meeting, either at a place within the city where the meeting is to be held, which place shall be specified in the notice of the meeting, or, if not so specified, at the place where the meeting is to be held. The list shall also be produced and kept at the time and place of the meeting during the whole time thereof, and may be inspected by any stockholder who is present.

(b) Upon the willful neglect or refusal of the directors to produce such a list at any meeting for the election of directors, they shall be ineligible for election to any office at such meeting.

(c) The stock ledger shall be the only evidence as to who are the stockholders entitled to examine the stock ledger, the list required by this section or the books of the corporation, or to vote in person or by proxy at any meeting of stockholders.

§220. Inspection of Books and Records

(a) As used in this section, "stockholder" means a stockholder of record in a stock corporation. . . .

(b) Any stockholder, in person or by attorney or other agent, shall, upon written demand under oath stating the purpose thereof, have the right during the usual hours for business to inspect for any proper purpose the corporation's stock ledger, a list of its stockholders, and its other books and records, and to make copies or extracts therefrom. A proper purpose shall mean a purpose reasonably related to such person's interest as a stockholder. In every instance where an attorney or other agent shall be the person who seeks the right to inspection, the demand under oath shall be accompanied by a power of attorney or such other writing which authorizes the attorney or other agent to so act on behalf of the stockholder. The demand under oath shall be directed to the corporation at its registered office in this State or at its principal place of business.

(c) If the corporation, or an officer or agent thereof, refuses to permit an inspection sought by a stockholder or attorney or other agent acting for the stockholder pursuant to sub-section (b) or does not reply to the demand within five business days after the demand has been made, the stockholder may apply to the Court of Chancery for an order to compel such inspection. The Court of Chancery is hereby vested with exclusive jurisdiction to determine whether or not the person seeking inspection is entitled to the inspection sought. The Court may summarily order the corporation to permit the stockholder to inspect the corporation's stock ledger, an existing list of stockholders, and its other books and records, and to make copies or extracts therefrom; or the Court may order the corporation to furnish to the stockholder a list of its stockholders as of a specific date on condition that the stockholder first pay to the corporation the reasonable cost of obtaining and furnishing such list and on such other conditions as the Court deems appropriate. Where the stockholder seeks to inspect the corporation's books and records, other than its stock ledger or list of stockholders, such stockholder shall first establish (1) that such stockholder has complied with the provisions of this section respecting the form and manner of making demand for inspection of such document; and (2) that the inspection such stockholder seeks is for a proper purpose. Where the stockholder seeks to inspect the corporation's stock ledger or list of stockholders and such stockholder has complied with the provisions of this section respecting the form and manner of making demand for inspection of such documents, the burden of proof shall be upon the corporation to establish that the inspection he seeks is for an improper purpose. The court may, in its discretion, prescribe any limitations or conditions with reference to the inspection, or award such other or further relief as the court may deem just and proper. The court may order books, documents and records, pertinent extracts therefrom, or duly authenticated copies thereof, to be brought within this State and kept in this State upon such terms and conditions as the order may prescribe.

(d) Any director shall have the right to examine the corporation's stock ledger, a list of its stockholders and its other books and records for a purpose reasonably related to his position as a director. The Court of Chancery is hereby vested with the exclusive jurisdiction to determine whether a director is entitled to the inspection sought. The court may summarily order the corporation to permit the director to inspect any and all books and records, the stock ledger and the stock list and to make copies or extracts therefrom. The court may, in its discretion, prescribe any limitations or conditions with reference to the inspection, or award such other and further relief as the court may deem just and proper.

§221. Voting, Inspection and Other Rights of Bondholders and Debenture Holders

Every corporation may in its certificate of incorporation confer upon the holders of any bonds, debentures or other obligations issued or to be issued by the corporation the power to vote in respect to the corporate affairs and management of the corporation to the extent and in the manner provided in the certificate of incorporation and may confer upon such holders of bonds, debentures or other obligations the same right of inspection of its books, accounts and other records, and also any other rights, which the stockholders of the corporation have or may have by reason of this chapter or of its certificate of incorporation. If the certificate of incorporation so provides, such holders of bonds, debentures or other obligations shall be deemed to be stockholders, and their bonds, debentures or other obligations shall be deemed to be shares of stock, for the purpose of any provision of this chapter which requires the vote of stockholders as a prerequisite to any corporate action and the certificate of incorporation may divest the holders of capital stock, in whole or in part, of their right to vote on any corporate matter whatsoever, except as set forth in §242(b)(2) of this chapter.

§222. Notice of Meetings and Adjourned Meetings

(a) Whenever stockholders are required or permitted to take any action at a meeting, a written notice of the meeting shall be given which shall state the place, date and hour of the meeting, and, in the case of a special meeting, the purpose or purposes for which the meeting is called.

(b) Unless otherwise provided in this chapter, the written notice of any meeting shall be given not less than ten nor more than sixty days before the date of the meeting to each stockholder entitled to vote at such meeting. If mailed, notice is given when deposited in the United States mail, postage prepaid, directed to the stockholder at such stockholder's address as it appears on the records of the corporation. An affidavit of the secretary or an assistant secretary or of the transfer agent of the corporation that the notice has been given shall, in the absence of fraud, be prima facie evidence of the facts stated therein.

(c) When a meeting is adjourned to another time or place, unless the by-laws otherwise require, notice need not be given of the adjourned meeting if the time and place thereof are announced at the meeting at which the adjournment is taken. At the adjourned meeting the corporation may transact any business which might have been transacted at the original meeting. If the adjournment is for more than thirty days, or if after the adjournment a new record date is fixed for the adjourned meeting, a notice of the adjourned meeting shall be given to each stockholder of record entitled to vote at the meeting.

§223. Vacancies and Newly Created Directorships

(a) Unless otherwise provided in the certificate of incorporation or by-laws: (1) vacancies and newly created directorships resulting from any increase in the authorized number of directors elected by all of the stockholders having the right to vote as a single class may be filled by a majority of the directors then in office, although less than a quorum, or by a sole remaining director; (2) whenever the holders of any class or classes of stock or series thereof are entitled to elect one or more directors by the provisions of the certificate of incorporation, vacancies and newly created directorships of such class or classes or series may be filled by a majority of the directors elected by such class or classes or series thereof then in office, or by a sole remaining director so elected.

If at any time, by reason of death or resignation or other cause, a corporation should have no directors in office, then any officer or any stockholder or an executor, administrator, trustee or guardian of a stockholder, or other fiduciary entrusted with like responsibility for the person or estate of a stockholder, may call a special meeting of stockholders in accordance with the provisions of the certificate of incorporation or the by-laws, or may apply to the Court of Chancery for a decree summarily ordering an election as provided in section 211 of this title.

(b) In the case of a corporation the directors of which are divided into classes, any directors chosen under subsection (a) of this section shall hold office until the next election of the class for which such directors shall have been chosen, and until their successors shall be elected and qualified.

(c) If, at the time of filling any vacancy or any newly created directorship, the directors then in office shall constitute less than a majority of the whole board (as constituted immediately prior to any such increase), the Court of Chancery may, upon application of any stockholder or stockholders holding at least ten percent of the total number of the shares at the time outstanding having the right to vote for such directors, summarily order an election to be held to fill any such vacancies or newly created directorships, or to replace the directors chosen by the directors then in office as aforesaid, which election shall be governed by the provisions of section 211 of this title as far as applicable.

(d) Unless otherwise provided in the certificate of incorporation or by-laws, when one or more directors shall resign from the board, effective at a future date, a majority of the directors then in office, including those who have so resigned, shall have power to fill such vacancy or vacancies, the vote thereon to take effect when such resignation or resignations shall become effective, and each director so chosen shall hold office as provided in this section in the filling of other vacancies.

§224. Form of Records

Any records maintained by a corporation in the regular course of its business, including its stock ledger, books of account, and minute books, may be kept on, or be in the form of, punch cards, magnetic tape, photographs, microphotographs, or any other information storage device, provided that the records so kept can be converted into clearly legible written form within a reasonable time. Any corporation shall so convert any records so kept upon the request of any person entitled to inspect the same. Where records are kept in such manner, a clearly legible written form produced from the cards, tapes, photographs, microphotographs or other information storage device shall be admissible in evidence and shall be accepted for all other purposes, to the same extent as an original written record of the same information would have been, when said written form accurately portrays the record.

§226. Appointment of Custodian or Receiver of Corporation on Deadlock or for Other Cause

(a) The Court of Chancery, upon application of any stockholder, may appoint one or more persons to be custodians, and, if the corporation is insolvent, to be receivers, of and for any corporation when:

(1) At any meeting held for the election of directors the stockholders are so divided that they have failed to elect successors to directors whose terms have expired or would have expired upon qualification of their successors; or

(2) The business of the corporation is suffering or is threatened with irreparable injury because the directors are so divided respecting the management of the affairs of the corporation that the required vote for action by the board of directors cannot be obtained and the stockholders are unable to terminate this division; or

(3) The corporation has abandoned its business and has failed within a reasonable time to take steps to dissolve, liquidate or distribute its assets.

(b) A custodian appointed under this section shall have all the powers and title of a receiver appointed under section 291 of this title, but the authority of the custodian is to continue the business of the corporation and not to liquidate its affairs and distribute its assets, except when the Court shall otherwise order and except in cases arising under subparagraph (a)(3) of this section or section 352(a)(2) of this title.

§228. Consent of Stockholders in Lieu of Meeting

(a) Unless otherwise provided in the certificate of incorporation, any action required by this chapter to be taken at any annual or special meeting of stockholders of a corporation, or any action which may be taken at any annual or special meeting of such stockholders, may be taken without a meeting, without prior notice and without a vote, if a consent or consents in writing, setting forth the action so taken, shall be signed by the holders of outstanding stock having not less than the minimum number of votes that would be necessary to authorize or take such action at a meeting at which all shares entitled to vote thereon were present and voted and shall be delivered to the corporation by delivery to its registered office in this State, its principal place of business, or an officer or agent of the corporation having custody of the book in which proceedings of meetings of stockholders are recorded. Delivery made to a corporation's registered office shall be by hand or by certified or registered mail, return receipt requested.

(b) Unless otherwise provided in the certificate of incorporation, any action required by this chapter to be taken at a meeting of the members of a non-stock corporation, or any action which may be taken at any meeting of the members of a non-stock corporation, may be taken without a meeting, without prior notice and without a vote, if a consent or consents in writing, setting forth the action so taken, shall be signed by members having not less than the minimum number of votes that would be necessary to authorize or take such action at a meeting at which all members having a right to vote thereon were present and voted and shall be delivered to the corporation by delivery to its registered office in this State, its principal place of business, or an officer or agent of the corporation having custody of the book in which proceedings of meetings of members are recorded. Delivery made to a corporation's registered office shall be by hand or by certified or registered mail, return receipt requested.

(c) Every written consent shall bear the date of signature of each stockholder or member who signs the consent and no written consent shall be effective to take the corporate action referred to therein unless, within sixty days of the earliest dated consent delivered in the manner required by this Section to the corporation, written consents signed by a sufficient number of holders or members to take action are delivered to the corporation by delivery to its registered office in this State, its principal place of business or an officer or agent of the corporation having custody of the book in which proceedings of meetings of stockholders or members are recorded. Delivery made to a corporation's registered office shall be by hand or by certified or registered mail, return receipt requested.

(d) Prompt notice of the taking of the corporate action without a meeting by less than unanimous written consent shall be given to those stockholders or members, as the case may be, who have not consented in writing and who, if the action had been taken at a meeting, would have been entitled to notice of the meeting if the record date for such meeting had been the date that written consents signed by a sufficient number of holders or members to take the action were delivered to the corporation as provided in subsection (c) of this section. In the event that the action which is consented to is such as would have required the filing of a certificate under any other section of this title, if such action had been voted on by stockholders or by members at a meeting thereof, the certificate filed under such other section shall state, in lieu of any statement required by such section concerning any vote of stockholders or members, that written consent has been given in accordance with the provisions of this section, and that written notice has been given as provided in this section.

§229. Waiver of Notice

Whenever notice is required to be given under any provision of this chapter or of the certificate of incorporation or by-laws, a written waiver thereof, signed by the person entitled to notice, whether before or after the time stated therein, shall be deemed equivalent to notice. Attendance of a person at a meeting shall constitute a waiver of notice of such meeting, except when the person attends a meeting for the express purpose of objecting, at the beginning of the meeting, to the transaction of any business because the meeting is not lawfully called or convened. Neither the business to be transacted at, nor the purpose of, any regular or special meeting of the stockholders, directors, or members of a committee of directors need be specified in any written waiver of notice unless so required by the certificate of incorporation or the by-laws.

§230. Exception to Requirements of Notice

(a) Whenever notice is required to be given, under any provision of this chapter or of the certificate of incorporation or by-laws of any corporation, to any person with whom communication is unlawful, the giving of such notice to such person shall not be required and there shall be no duty to apply to any governmental authority or agency for a license or permit to give such notice to such person. Any action or meeting which shall be taken or held without notice to any such person with whom communication is unlawful shall have the same force and effect as if such notice had been duly given. In the event that the action taken by the corporation is such as to require the filing of a certificate under any of the other sections of this title, the certificate shall state, if such is the fact and if notice is required, that notice was given to all persons entitled to receive notice except such persons with whom communication is unlawful.

(b) Whenever notice is required to be given, under any provision of this chapter or the certificate of incorporation or by-laws of any corporation, to any stockholder or, if the corporation is a nonstock corporation, to any member, to whom (i) notice of two consecutive annual meetings, and all notices of meetings or of the taking of action by written consent without a meeting to such person during the period between such two consecutive annual meetings, or (ii) all, and at least two, payments (if sent by first-class mail) of dividends or interest on securities during a 12-month period, have been mailed addressed to such person at his address as shown on the records of the corporation and have been returned undeliverable, the giving of such notice to such person shall not be required. Any action or meeting which shall be taken or held without notice to such person shall have the same force and effect as if such notice had been duly given. If any such person shall deliver to the corporation a written notice setting forth his then current address, the requirement that notice be given to such person shall be reinstated. In the event that the action taken by the corporation is such as to require the filing of a certificate under any of the other sections of this Title, the certificate need not state that notice was not given to persons to whom notice was not required to be given pursuant to this subsection.

§231. Voting Procedures and Inspectors of Elections

(a) The corporation shall, in advance of any meeting of stockholders, appoint 1 or more inspectors to act at the meeting and make a written report thereof. The corporation may designate 1 or more persons as alternate inspectors to replace any inspector who fails to act. If no inspector or alternate is able to act at a meeting of stockholders, the person presiding at the meeting shall appoint 1 or more inspectors to act at the meeting. Each inspector, before entering upon the discharge of the duties of inspector, shall take and sign an oath faithfully to execute the duties of inspector with strict impartiality and according to the best of such inspector's ability.

(b) The inspectors shall:

(1) Ascertain the number of shares outstanding and the voting power of each;

(2) Determine the shares represented at a meeting and the validity of proxies and ballots;

(3) Count all votes and ballots;

(4) Determine and retain for a reasonable period a record of the disposition of any challenges made to any determination by the inspectors; and

(5) Certify their determination of the number of shares represented at the meeting, and their count of all votes and ballots.

The inspectors may appoint or retain other persons or entities to assist the inspectors in the performance of the duties of the inspectors.

(c) The date and time of the opening and the closing of the polls for each matter upon which the stockholders will vote at a meeting shall be announced at the meeting. No ballot, proxies or votes, nor any revocations thereof or changes thereto, shall be accepted by the inspectors after the closing of the polls unless the Court of Chancery upon application by a stockholder shall determine otherwise.

(d) In determining the validity and counting of proxies and ballots, the inspectors shall be limited to an examination of the proxies, any envelopes submitted with those proxies, any information provided in accordance with §212(c)(2) of this title, ballots and the regular books and records of the corporation, except that the inspectors may consider other reliable information for the limited purpose of reconciling proxies and ballots submitted by or on behalf of banks, brokers, their nominees or similar persons which represent more votes than the holder of a proxy is authorized by the record owner to cast or more votes than the stockholder holds of record. If the inspectors consider other reliable information for the limited purpose permitted herein, the inspectors at the time they make their certification pursuant to subsection (b)(5) of this section shall specify the precise information considered by them including the person or persons from whom they obtained the information, when the information was obtained, the means by which the information was obtained and the basis for the inspectors' belief that such information is accurate and reliable.

(e) Unless otherwise provided in the certificate of incorporation or bylaws, this section shall not apply to a corporation that does not have a class of voting stock that is:

(1) Listed on a national securities exchange;

(2) Authorized for quotation on an interdealer quotation system of a registered national securities association; or

(3) Held of record by more than 2,000 stockholders.

§241. Amendment of Certificate of Incorporation Before Receipt of Payment for Stock

(a) Before a corporation has received any payment for any of its stock, it may amend its certificate of incorporation at any time or times, in any and as many respects as may be desired, so long as its certificate of incorporation as amended would contain only such provisions as it would be lawful and proper to insert in an original certificate of incorporation filed at the time of filing the amendment.

(b) The amendment of a certificate of incorporation authorized by this section shall be adopted by a majority of the incorporators, if directors were not named in the original certificate of incorporation or have not yet been elected, or, if directors were named in the original certificate of incorporation or have been elected and have qualified, by a majority of the directors. A certificate setting forth the amendment and certifying that the corporation has not received any payment for any of its stock and that the amendment has been duly adopted in accordance with the provisions of this section shall be executed, acknowledged, filed and recorded in accordance with section 103 of this title. Upon such filing, the corporation's certificate of incorporation shall be deemed to be amended accordingly as of the date on which the original certificate of incorporation became effective except as to those persons who are substantially and adversely affected by the amendment and as to those persons the amendment shall be effective from the filing date.

§242. Amendment of Certificate of Incorporation After Receipt of Payment for Stock

(a) After a corporation has received payment for any of its capital stock, it may amend its certificate of incorporation, from time to time, in any and as many respects as may be desired, so long as its certificate of incorporation as amended would contain only such provisions as it would be lawful and proper to insert in an original certificate of incorporation filed at the time of the filing of the amendment; and, if a change in stock or the rights of stockholders, or an exchange, reclassification or cancellation of stock or rights of stockholders is to be made, such provisions as may be necessary to effect such change, exchange, reclassification or cancellation. In particular, and without limitation upon such general power of amendment, a corporation may amend its certificate of incorporation, from time to time, so as:

(1) To change its corporate name; or

(2) To change, substitute, enlarge or diminish the nature of its business or its corporate powers and purposes; or

(3) To increase or decrease its authorized capital stock or to reclassify the same, by changing the number, par value, designations, preferences, or relative, participating, optional, or other special rights of the shares, or the qualifications, limitations or restrictions of such rights, or by changing shares with par value into shares without par value, or shares without par value into shares with par value either with or without increasing or decreasing the number of shares or by subdividing or combining the outstanding shares of any class or series of a class of shares into a greater or lesser number of outstanding shares; or

(4) To cancel or otherwise affect the right of the holders of the shares of any class to receive dividends which have accrued but have not been declared; or

(5) To create new classes of stock having rights and preferences either prior and superior or subordinate and inferior to the stock of any class then authorized, whether issued or unissued; or

(6) To change the period of its duration.

Any or all such changes or alterations may be effected by one certificate of amendment.

(b) Every amendment authorized by subsection (a) of this section shall be made and effected in the following manner —

(1) If the corporation has capital stock, its board of directors shall adopt a resolution setting forth the amendment proposed, declaring its advisability, and either calling a special meeting of the stockholders entitled to vote in respect thereof for the consideration of such amendment or directing that the amendment proposed be considered at the next annual meeting of the stockholders. Such special or annual meeting shall be called and held upon notice in accordance with section 222 of this title. The notice shall set forth such amendment in full or a brief summary of the changes to be effected thereby, as the directors shall deem advisable. At the meeting a vote of the stockholders entitled to vote thereon shall be taken for and against the proposed amendment. If a majority of the outstanding stock entitled to vote thereon, and a majority of the outstanding stock of each class entitled to vote thereon as a class has been voted in favor of the amendment, a certificate setting forth the amendment and certifying that such amendment has been duly adopted in accordance with the provisions of this section shall be executed, acknowledged, and filed, and shall become effective in accordance with section 103 of this title.

(2) The holders of the outstanding shares of a class shall be entitled to vote as a class upon a proposed amendment, whether or not entitled to vote thereon by the provisions of the certificate of incorporation, if the amendment would increase or decrease the aggregate number of authorized shares of such class, increase or decrease the par value of the shares of such class, or alter or change the powers, preferences or special rights of the shares of such class so as to affect them adversely. If any proposed amendment would alter or change the powers, preferences, or special rights of one or more series of any class so as to affect them adversely, but shall not so affect the entire class, then only the shares of the series so affected by the amendment shall be considered a separate class for the purposes of this paragraph. The number of authorized shares of any such class or classes of stock may be increased or decreased (but not below the number of shares thereof then outstanding) by the affirmative vote of the holders of a majority of the stock of the corporation entitled to vote irrespective of the provision of this paragraph (b)(2), if so provided in the original certificate of incorporation, in any amendment thereto which created such class or classes of stock or which was adopted prior to the issuance of any shares of such class or classes of stock, or in any amendment thereto which was authorized by a resolution or resolutions adopted by the affirmative vote of the holders of a majority of such class or classes of stock.

(3) If the corporation has no capital stock, then the governing body thereof shall adopt a resolution setting forth the amendment proposed and declaring its advisability. If at a subsequent meeting, held, on notice stating the purpose thereof, not earlier than 15 days and not later than 60 days from the meeting at which such resolution has been passed, a majority of all the members of the governing body, shall vote in favor of such amendment, a certificate thereof shall be executed, acknowledged, filed, recorded, and shall become effective in accordance with section 103 of this title. The certificate of incorporation of any such corporation without capital stock may contain a provision requiring any amendment thereto to be approved by a specified number or percentage of the members or of any specified class of members of such corporation in which event only one meeting of the governing body thereof shall be necessary, and such proposed amendment shall be submitted to the members or to any specified class of members of such corporation without capital stock in the same manner, so far as applicable, as is provided in this section for an amendment to the certificate of incorporation of a stock corporation; and in the event of the adoption thereof, a certificate evidencing such amendment shall be executed, filed, acknowledged, recorded and shall become effective in accordance with section 103 of this title.

(4) Whenever the certificate of incorporation shall require for action by the board of directors, by the holders of any class or series of shares or by the holders of any other securities having voting power the vote of a greater number or proportion than is required by any section of this title, the provision of the certificate of incorporation requiring such greater vote shall not be altered, amended or repealed except by such greater vote.

(c) The resolution authorizing a proposed amendment to the certificate of incorporation may provide that at any time prior to the effectiveness of the filing of the amendment with the Secretary of State, notwithstanding authorization of the proposed amendment by the stockholders of the corporation or by the members of a nonstock corporation, the board of directors or governing body may abandon such proposed amendment without further action by the stockholders or members.

§243. Retirement of Stock

(a) A corporation, by resolution of its board of directors, may retire any shares of its capital stock that are issued but are not outstanding.

(b) Whenever any shares of the capital stock of a corporation are retired, they shall resume the status of authorized and unissued shares of the class or series to which they belong unless the certificate of incorporation otherwise provides. If the certificate of incorporation prohibits the reissuance of such shares, or prohibits the reissuance of such shares as a part of a specific series only, a certificate stating that reissuance of the shares (as part of the class or series) is prohibited identifying the shares and reciting their retirement shall be executed, acknowledged and filed and shall become effective in accordance with §103 of this title. When such certificate becomes effective, it shall have the effect of amending the certificate of incorporation so as to reduce accordingly the number of authorized shares of the class or series to with such shares belong or, if such retired shares constitute all of the authorized shares of the class or series to which they belong, of eliminating from the certificate of incorporation all reference to such class or series of stock.

(c) If the capital of the corporation will be reduced by or in connection with the retirement of shares, the reduction of capital shall be effected pursuant to Section 244 of this title.

§244. Reduction of Capital

(a) A corporation, by resolution of its board of directors, may reduce its capital in any of the following ways:

1. By reducing or eliminating the capital represented by shares of capital stock which have been retired;

2. By applying to an otherwise authorized purchase or redemption of outstanding shares of its capital stock some or all of the capital represented by the shares being purchased or redeemed, or any capital that has not been allocated to any particular class of its capital stock;

3. By applying to an otherwise authorized conversion or exchange of outstanding shares of its capital stock some or all of the capital represented by the shares being converted or exchanged, or some or all of any capital that has not been allocated to any particular class of its capital stock, or both, to the extent that such capital in the aggregate exceeds the total aggregate par value or the stated capital of any previously unissued shares issuable upon such conversion or exchange; or,

4. By transferring to surplus (i) some or all of the capital not represented by any particular class of its capital stock; (ii) some or all of the capital represented by issued shares of its par value capital stock, which capital is in excess of the aggregate par value of such shares; or (iii) some of the capital represented by issued shares of its capital stock without par value.

(b) Notwithstanding the other provisions of this section, no reduction of capital shall be made or effected unless the assets of the corporation remaining after such reduction shall be sufficient to pay any debts of the corporation for which payment has not been otherwise provided. No reduction of capital shall release any liability of any stockholder whose shares have not been fully paid.

§245. Restated Certificate of Incorporation

(a) A corporation may, whenever desired, integrate into a single instrument all of the provisions of its certificate of incorporation which are then in effect and operative as a result of there having theretofore been filed with the Secretary of State one or more certificates or other instruments pursuant to any of the sections referred to in §104 of this title, and it may at the same time also further amend its certificate of incorporation by adopting a restated certificate of incorporation.

(b) If the restated certificate of incorporation merely restates and integrates but does not further amend the certificate of incorporation, as theretofore amended or supplemented by any instrument that was filed pursuant to any of the sections mentioned in §104 of this title, it may be adopted by the board of directors without a vote of the stockholders, or it may be proposed by the directors and submitted by them to the stockholders for adoption, in which case the procedure and vote required by §242 of this title for amendment of the certificate of incorporation shall be applicable. If the restated certificate of incorporation restates and integrates and also further amends in any respect the certificate of incorporation, as theretofore amended or supplemented, it shall be proposed by the directors and adopted by the stockholders in the manner and by the vote prescribed by §242 of this title "or, if the corporation has not received any payment for any of its stock, in the manner and by the vote prescribed by §241 of this title."

(c) A restated certificate of incorporation shall be specifically designated as such in its heading. It shall state, either in its heading or in an introductory paragraph, the corporation's present name, and, if it has been changed, the name under which it was originally incorporated, and the date of filing of its original certificate of incorporation with the Secretary of State. A restated certificate shall also state that it was duly adopted in accordance with the provisions of this section. If it was adopted by the board of directors without a vote of the stockholders (unless it was adopted pursuant to the provisions of section 241 of this title), it shall state that it only restates and integrates and does not further amend the provisions of the corporation's certificate of incorporation as theretofore amended or supplemented, and that there is no discrepancy between those provisions and the provisions of the restated certificate. A restated certificate of incorporation may omit (a) such provisions of the original certificate of incorporation which named the incorporator or incorporators, the initial board of directors and the original subscribers for shares, and (b) such provisions contained in any amendment to the certificate of incorporation as were necessary to effect a change, exchange, reclassification or cancellation of stock, if such change, exchange, reclassification or cancellation has become effective. Any such omissions shall not be deemed a further amendment.

(d) A restated certificate of incorporation shall be executed, acknowledged, filed and recorded in accordance with §103 of this title. Upon its filing with the Secretary of State, the original certificate of incorporation, as theretofore amended or supplemented, shall be superseded; thenceforth, the restated certificate of incorporation, including any further amendments or changes made thereby, shall be the certificate of incorporation of the corporation, but the original date of incorporation shall remain unchanged.

(e) Any amendment or change effected in connection with the restatement and integration of the certificate of incorporation shall be subject to any other provision of this chapter, not inconsistent with this section, which would apply if a separate certificate of amendment were filed to effect such amendment or change.

§251. Merger or Consolidation of Domestic Corporations

(a) Any two or more corporations existing under the laws of this State may merge into a single corporation, which may be any one of the constituent corporations or may consolidate into a new corporation formed by the consolidation, pursuant to an agreement of merger or consolidation, as the case may be, complying and approved in accordance with this section.

(b) The board of directors of each corporation which desires to merge or consolidate shall adopt a resolution approving an agreement of merger or consolidation. The agreement shall state: (1) the terms and conditions of the merger or consolidation; (2) the mode of carrying the same into effect; (3) in the case of a merger, such amendments or changes in the certificate of incorporation of the surviving corporation as are desired to be effected by the merger, or, if no such amendments or changes are desired, a statement that the certificate of incorporation of the surviving corporation shall be its certificate of incorporation; (4) in the case of a consolidation, that the certificate of incorporation of the resulting corporation shall be as is set forth in an attachment to the agreement; (5) the manner of converting the shares of each of the constituent corporations into shares or other securities of the corporation surviving or resulting from the merger or consolidation, and, if any shares of any of the constituent corporations are not to be converted solely into shares or other securities of the surviving or resulting corporation, the cash, property, rights or securities of any other corporation or entity which the holders of such shares are to receive in exchange for, or upon conversion of such shares and the surrender of any certificates evidencing them, which cash, property, rights or securities of any other corporation or entity may be in addition to or in lieu of shares or other securities of the surviving or resulting corporation; and (6) such other details or provisions as are deemed desirable, including, without limiting the generality of the foregoing, a provision for the payment of cash in lieu of the issuance or recognition of fractional shares, interests or rights, or for any other arrangement with respect thereto, consistent with the provisions of Section 155 of this title. The agreement so adopted shall be executed and acknowledged in accordance with Section 103 of this title. Any of the terms of the agreement of merger or consolidation may be made dependent upon facts ascertainable outside of such agreement, provided that the manner in which such facts shall operate upon the terms of the agreement is clearly and expressly set forth in the agreement of merger or consolidation. The term "facts," as used in the preceding sentence, includes, but is not limited to, the occurrence of any event, including a determination or action by any person or body, including the corporation.

(c) The agreement required by subsection (b) shall be submitted to the stockholders of each constituent corporation at an annual or special meeting for the purpose of acting on the agreement. The terms of the agreement may require that the agreement be submitted to the stockholders whether or not the board of directors determines at any time subsequent to declaring its advisability that the agreement is no longer advisable and recommends that the stockholders reject it. Due notice of the time, place and purpose of the meeting shall be mailed to each holder of stock, whether voting or nonvoting, of the corporation at his address as it appears on the records of the corporation, at least 20 days prior to the date of the meeting. The notice shall contain a copy of the agreement or a brief summary thereof, as the directors shall deem advisable. At the meeting, the agreement shall be considered and a vote taken for its adoption or rejection. If a majority of the outstanding stock of the corporation entitled to vote thereon shall be voted for the adoption of the agreement, that fact shall be certified on the agreement by the secretary or assistant secretary of the corporation. If the agreement shall be so adopted and certified by each constituent corporation, it shall then be filed and shall become effective, in accordance with Section 103 of this title. In lieu of filing the agreement of merger or consolidation required by this Section, the surviving or resulting corporation may file a certificate of merger or consolidation, executed in accordance with Section 103 of this title, which states: (1) The name and state of incorporation of each of the constituent corporations; (2) that an agreement of merger or consolidation has been approved, adopted, certified, executed and acknowledged by each of the constituent corporations in accordance with this section; (3) the name of the surviving or resulting corporation; (4) in the case of a merger, such amendments or changes in the certificate of incorporation of the surviving corporation as are desired to be effected by the merger, or, if no such amendments or changes are desired, a statement that the certificate of incorporation of the surviving corporation shall be its certificate of incorporation; (5) in the case of a consolidation, that the certificate of incorporation of the resulting corporation shall be as set forth in an attachment to the certificate; (6) that the executed agreement of consolidation or merger is on file at an office of the surviving corporation, stating the address thereof; and (7) that a copy of the agreement of consolidation or merger will be furnished by the surviving corporation, on request and without cost, to any stockholder of any constituent corporation.

(d) Any agreement of merger or consolidation may contain a provision that at any time prior to the time that an agreement (or a certificate in lieu thereof) filed with the Secretary of State becomes effective in accordance with §103 of this title, the agreement may be terminated by the board of directors of any constituent corporation notwithstanding approval of the agreement by the stockholders of all or any of the constituent corporations; in the event the agreement of merger or consolidation is terminated after the filing of the agreement (or a certificate in lieu thereof) with the Secretary of State but before the agreement (or a certificate in lieu thereof) has become effective, a certificate of termination or merger or consolidation shall be filed in accordance with §103 of this title. Any agreement of merger or consolidation may contain a provision that the boards of directors of the constituent corporations may amend the agreement at any time prior to the time that the agreement (or a certificate in lieu thereof) filed with the Secretary of State becomes effective in accordance with §103 of this title, provided that an amendment made subsequent to the adoption of the agreement by the stockholders of any constituent corporation shall not (1) alter or change the amount or kind of shares, securities, cash, property and/or rights to be received in exchange for or on conversion of all or any of the shares of any class or series thereof of such constituent corporation, (2) alter or change any term of the certificate of incorporation of the surviving corporation to be effected by the merger or consolidation, or (3) alter or change any of the terms and conditions of the agreement if such alteration or change would adversely affect the holders of any class or series thereof of such constituent corporation; in the event the agreement of merger or consolidation is amended after the filing thereof with the Secretary of State but before the agreement has become effective, a certificate of amendment of merger or consolidation shall be filed in accordance with §103 of this title.

(e) In the case of a merger, the certificate of incorporation of the surviving corporation shall automatically be amended to the extent, if any, that changes in the certificate of incorporation are set forth in the agreement of merger.

(f) Notwithstanding the requirements of subsection (c), unless required by its certificate of incorporation, no vote of stockholders of a constituent corporation surviving a merger shall be necessary to authorize a merger if (1) the agreement of merger does not amend in any respect the certificate of incorporation of such constituent corporation, (2) each share of stock of such constituent corporation outstanding immediately prior to the effective date of the merger is to be an identical outstanding or treasury share of the surviving corporation after the effective date of the merger, and (3) either no shares of common stock of the surviving corporation and no shares, securities or obligations convertible into such stock are to be issued or delivered under the plan of merger, or the authorized unissued shares or the treasury shares of common stock of the surviving corporation to be issued or delivered under the plan of merger plus those initially issuable upon conversion of any other shares, securities or obligations to be issued or delivered under such plan do not exceed 20 percent of the shares of common stock of such constituent corporation outstanding immediately prior to the effective date of the merger. No vote of stockholders of a constituent corporation shall be necessary to authorize a merger or consolidation if no shares of the stock of such corporation shall have been issued prior to the adoption by the board of directors of the resolution approving the agreement of merger or consolidation. If an agreement of merger is adopted by the constituent corporation surviving the merger, by action of its board of directors and without any vote of its stockholders pursuant to this subsection, the secretary or assistant secretary of that corporation shall certify on the agreement that the agreement has been adopted pursuant to this subsection and, (i) if it has been adopted pursuant to the first sentence of this subsection, that the conditions specified in that sentence have been satisfied, or (ii) if it has been adopted pursuant to the second sentence of this subsection, that no shares of stock of such corporation were issued prior to the adoption by the board of directors of the resolution approving the agreement of merger or consolidation. . . .

§252. Merger or Consolidation of Domestic and Foreign Corporations; Service of Process Upon Surviving or Resulting Corporation

(a) Any 1 or more corporations of this State may merge or consolidate with 1 or more other corporations of any other state or states of the United States, or of the District of Columbia if the laws of the other state or states, or of the District permit a corporation of such jurisdiction to merge or consolidate with a corporation of another jurisdiction. The constituent corporations may merge into a single corporation, which may be any 1 of the constituent corporations, or they may consolidate into a new corporation formed by the consolidation, which may be a corporation of the state of incorporation of any 1 of the constituent corporations, pursuant to an agreement of merger or consolidation, as the case may be, complying and approved in accordance with this section. In addition, any 1 or more corporations existing under the laws of this State may merge or consolidate with 1 or more corporations organized under the laws of any jurisdiction other than 1 of the United States if the laws under which the other corporation or corporations are organized permit a corporation of such jurisdiction to merge or consolidate with a corporation of another jurisdiction.

(b) All the constituent corporations shall enter into an agreement of merger or consolidation. The agreement shall state: (1) The terms and conditions of the merger or consolidation; (2) the mode of carrying the same into effect; (3) the manner of converting the shares of each of the constituent corporations into shares or other securities of the corporation surviving or resulting from the merger or consolidation and, if any shares of any of the constituent corporations are not to be converted solely into shares or other securities of the surviving or resulting corporation, the cash, property, rights or securities of any other corporation or entity which the holders of such shares are to receive in exchange for, or upon conversion of, such shares and the surrender of any certificates evidencing them, which cash, property, rights or securities of any other corporation or entity may be in addition to or in lieu of the shares or other securities of the surviving or resulting corporation; (4) such other details or provisions as are deemed desirable, including, without limiting the generality of the foregoing, a provision for the payment of cash in lieu of the issuance or recognition of fractional shares of the surviving or resulting corporation or of any other corporation the securities of which are to be received in the merger or consolidation, or for some other arrangement with respect thereto consistent with §155 of this title; and (5) such other provisions or facts as shall be required to be set forth in certificates of incorporation by the laws of the state which are stated in the agreement to be the laws that shall govern the surviving or resulting corporation and that can be stated in the case of a merger or consolidation. Any of the terms of the agreement of merger or consolidation may be made dependent upon facts ascertainable outside of such agreement, provided that the manner in which such facts shall operate upon the terms of the agreement is clearly and expressly set forth in the agreement of merger or consolidation.

(c) The agreement shall be adopted, approved, certified, executed and acknowledged by each of the constituent corporations in accordance with the laws under which it is formed, and, in the case of a Delaware corporation, in the same manner as is provided in §251 of this title. The agreement shall be filed and recorded and shall become effective for all purposes of the laws of this State when and as provided in §251 of this title with respect to the merger or consolidation of corporations of this State. In lieu of filing and recording the agreement of merger or consolidation, the surviving or resulting corporation may file a certificate of merger or consolidation, executed in accordance with §103 of this title, which states: (1) The name and state or jurisdiction of incorporation of each of the constituent corporations; (2) That an agreement of merger or consolidation has been approved, adopted, certified, executed and acknowledged by each of the constituent corporations in accordance with this subsection; (3) the name of the surviving or resulting corporation; (4) in the case of a merger, such amendments or changes in the certificate of incorporation of the surviving corporation as are desired to be effected by the merger, or, if no such amendments or changes are desired, a statement that the certificate of incorporation of the surviving corporation shall be its certificate of incorporation; (5) in the case of a consolidation, that the certificate of incorporation of the resulting corporation shall be as is set forth in an attachment to the certificate; (6) That the executed agreement of consolidation or merger is on file at the principal place of business of the surviving corporation and the address thereof; (7) That a copy of the agreement of consolidation or merger will be furnished by the surviving corporation, on request and without cost, to any stockholder of any constituent corporation; (8) if the corporation surviving or resulting from the merger or consolidation is to be a corporation of this State, the authorized capital stock of each constituent corporation which is not a corporation of this State; and (9) The agreement, if any, required by subsection (d) of this section.

(d) If the corporation surviving or resulting from the merger or consolidation is to be governed by the laws of the District of Columbia or any state or jurisdiction other than this State, it shall agree that it may be served with process in this State in any proceeding for enforcement of any obligation of any constituent corporation of this State, as well as for enforcement of any obligation of the surviving or resulting corporation arising from the merger or consolidation, including any suit or other proceeding to enforce the right of any stockholders as determined in appraisal proceedings pursuant to §262 of this title, and shall irrevocably appoint the Secretary of State as its agent to accept service of process in any such suit or other proceedings and shall specify the address to which a copy of such process shall be mailed by the Secretary of State. In the event of such service upon the Secretary of State in accordance with this subsection, the Secretary of State shall forthwith notify such surviving or resulting corporation thereof by letter, certified mail, return receipt requested, directed to such surviving or resulting corporation at its address so specified, unless such surviving or resulting corporation shall have designated in writing to the Secretary of State a different address for such purpose, in which case it shall be mailed to the last address so designated. Such letter shall enclose a copy of the process and any other papers served on the Secretary of State pursuant to this subsection. It shall be the duty of the plaintiff in the event of such service to serve process and any other papers in duplicate, to notify the Secretary of State that service is being effected pursuant to this subsection and to pay the Secretary of State the sum of $50 for the use of the State, which sum shall be taxed as part of the costs in the proceeding, if the plaintiff shall prevail therein. The Secretary of State shall maintain an alphabetical record of any such service setting forth the name of the plaintiff and the defendant, the title, docket number and nature of the proceeding in which process has been served upon him, the fact that service has been effected pursuant to this subsection, the return date thereof, and the day and hour service was made. The Secretary of State shall not be required to retain such information longer than 5 years from his receipt of the service of process.

(e) The provisions of subsection (d) of section 251 of this title shall apply to any merger or consolidation under this section; the provisions of subsection (e) of section 251 shall apply to a merger under this section in which the surviving corporation is a corporation of this State; the provisions of subsection (f) of section 251 shall apply to any merger under this section.

§253. MERGER OF PARENT CORPORATION AND SUBSIDIARY OR SUBSIDIARIES

(a) In any case in which at least 90% of the outstanding shares of each class of the stock of a corporation or corporations (other than a corporation which has in its certificate of incorporation the provision required by subsection (g)(7)(i) of Section 251 of this title) is owned by another corporation and one of such corporations is a corporation of this State and the other or others are corporations of this State, or any other state or states, or of the District of Columbia and the laws of the other state or states, or of the District permit a corporation of such jurisdiction to merge with a corporation of another jurisdiction, the corporation having such stock ownership may either merge such other corporation or corporations into itself and assume all of its or their obligations, or merge itself, or itself and one or more of such other corporations, into one of such other corporations by executing, acknowledging and filing, in accordance with Section 103 of this title, a certificate of such ownership and merger setting forth a copy of the resolution of its board of directors to so merge and the date of the adoption thereof; provided, however, that in case the parent corporation shall not own all the outstanding stock of all the subsidiary corporations, parties to a merger as aforesaid, the resolution of the board of directors of the parent corporation shall state the terms and conditions of the merger, including the securities, cash, property, or rights to be issued, paid, delivered or granted by the surviving corporation upon surrender of each share of the subsidiary corporation or corporations not owned by the parent corporation. Any of the terms of the resolution of the board of directors to so merge may be made dependent upon facts ascertainable outside of such resolution, provided that the manner in which such facts shall operate upon the terms of the resolution is clearly and expressly set forth in the resolution. The term "facts", as used in the preceding sentence, includes, but is not limited to, the occurrence of any event, including a determination or action by any person or body, including the corporation. If the parent corporation be not the surviving corporation, the resolution shall include provision for the pro rata issuance of stock of the surviving corporation to the holders of the stock of the parent corporation on surrender of any certificates therefor, and the certificate of ownership and merger shall state that the proposed merger has been approved by a majority of the outstanding stock of the parent corporation entitled to vote thereon at a meeting duly called and held after 20 days' notice of the purpose of the meeting mailed to each such stockholder at his address as it appears on the records of the corporation if the parent corporation is a corporation of this State or state that the proposed merger has been adopted, approved, certified, executed and acknowledged by the parent corporation in accordance with the laws under which it is organized if the parent corporation is not a corporation of this State. If the surviving corporation exists under the laws of the District of Columbia or any state or jurisdiction other than this State, the provisions of Section 252(d) of this title shall also apply to a merger under this section.

(b) If the surviving corporation is a Delaware corporation, it may change its corporate name by the inclusion of a provision to that effect in the resolution of merger adopted by the directors of the parent corporation and set forth in the certificate of ownership and merger, and upon the effective date of the merger, the name of the corporation shall be so changed.

(c) The provisions of Section 251(d) of this title shall apply to a merger under this section, and the provisions of Section 251(e) shall apply to a merger under this section in which the surviving corporation is the subsidiary corporation and is a corporation of this State. References to "agreement of merger" in Sections 251(d) and 251(e) of this title shall mean for purposes of this Section 253(c) the resolution of merger adopted by the board of directors of the parent corporation. Any merger which effects any changes other than those authorized by this section or made applicable by this subsection shall be accomplished under the provisions of Section 251 or Section 252 of this title. The provisions of Section 262 of this title shall not apply to any merger effected under this section, except as provided in subsection (d) of this section.

(d) In the event all of the stock of a subsidiary Delaware corporation party to a merger effected under this Section is not owned by the parent corporation immediately prior to the merger, the stockholders of the subsidiary Delaware corporation party to the merger shall have appraisal rights as set forth in Section 262 of this Title.

(e) A merger may be effected under this section although one or more of the corporations parties to the merger is a corporation organized under the laws of a jurisdiction other than one of the United States; provided that the laws of such jurisdiction permit a corporation of such jurisdiction to merge with a corporation of another jurisdiction.

§259. Status, Rights, Liabilities, etc., of Constituent and Surviving or Resulting Corporations Following Merger or Consolidation

(a) When any merger or consolidation shall have become effective under this chapter, for all purposes of the laws of this State the separate existence of all the constituent corporations, or of all such constituent corporations except the one into which the other or others of such constituent corporations have been merged, as the case may be, shall cease and the constituent corporations shall become a new corporation, or be merged into one of such corporations, as the case may be, possessing all the rights, privileges, powers and franchises as well of a public as of a private nature, and being subject to all the restrictions, disabilities and duties of each of such corporations so merged or consolidated; and all and singular, the rights, privileges, powers and franchises of each of said corporations, and all property, real, personal and mixed, and all debts due to any of said constituent corporations on whatever account, as well for stock subscriptions as all other things in action or belonging to each of such corporations shall be vested in the corporation surviving or resulting from such merger or consolidation; and all property, rights, privileges, powers and franchises, and all and every other interest shall be thereafter as effectually the property of the surviving or resulting corporation as they were of the several and respective constituent corporations, and the title to any real estate vested by deed or otherwise, under the laws of this State, in any of such constituent corporations, shall not revert or be in any way impaired by reason of this chapter; but all rights of creditors and all liens upon any property of any of said constituent corporations shall be preserved unimpaired, and all debts, liabilities and duties of the respective constituent corporations shall thenceforth attach to said surviving or resulting corporation, and may be enforced against it to the same extent as if said debts, liabilities and duties had been incurred or contracted by it.

(b) In the case of a merger of banks or trust companies, without any order or action on the part of any court or otherwise, all appointments, designations, and nominations, and all other rights and interests as trustee, executor, administrator, registrar of stocks and bonds, guardian of estates, assignee, receiver, trustee of estates of persons mentally ill and in every other fiduciary capacity, shall be automatically vested in the corporation resulting from or surviving such merger; provided, however, that any party in interest shall have the right to apply to an appropriate court or tribunal for a determination as to whether the surviving corporation shall continue to serve in the same fiduciary capacity as the merged corporation, or whether a new and different fiduciary should be appointed.

§260. Powers of Corporation Surviving or Resulting From Merger or Consolidation; Issuance of Stock, Bonds or Other Indebtedness

When two or more corporations are merged or consolidated, the corporation surviving or resulting from the merger may issue bonds or other obligations, negotiable or otherwise, and with or without coupons or interest certificates thereto attached, to an amount sufficient with its capital stock to provide for all the payments it will be required to make, or obligations it will be required to assume, in order to effect the merger or consolidation. For the purpose of securing the payment of any such bonds and obligations, it shall be lawful for the surviving or resulting corporation to mortgage its corporate franchise, rights, privileges and property, real, personal or mixed. The surviving or resulting corporation may issue certificates of its capital stock or uncertificated stock if authorized to do so and other securities to the stockholders of the constituent corporations in exchange or payment for the original shares, in such amount as shall be necessary in accordance with the terms of the agreement of merger or consolidation in order to effect such merger or consolidation in the manner and on the terms specified in the agreement.

§261. Effect of Merger Upon Pending Actions

Any action or proceeding, whether civil, criminal or administrative, pending by or against any corporation which is a party to a merger or consolidation shall be prosecuted as if such merger or consolidation had not taken place, or the corporation surviving or resulting from such merger or consolidation may be substituted in such action or proceeding.

§262. Appraisal Rights

(a) Any stockholder of a corporation of this State who holds shares of stock on the date of the making of a demand pursuant to subsection (d) of this section with respect to such shares, who continuously holds such shares through the effective date of the merger or consolidation, who has otherwise complied with subsection (d) of this section and who has neither voted in favor of the merger or consolidation nor consented thereto in writing pursuant to §228 of this title shall be entitled to an appraisal by the Court of Chancery of the fair value of his shares of stock under the circumstances described in subsections (b) and (c) of this section. As used in this section, the word "stockholder" means a holder of record of stock in a stock corporation and also a member of record of a nonstock corporation; the words "stock" and "share" mean and include what is ordinarily meant by those words and also membership or membership interest of a member of a nonstock corporation; and the words "depository receipt" mean a receipt or other instrument issued by a depository representing an interest in one or more shares, or fractions thereof, solely of stock of a corporation, which stock is deposited with the depository.

(b) Appraisal rights shall be available for the shares of any class or series of stock of a constituent corporation in a merger or consolidation to be effected pursuant to §251 (other than a merger effected pursuant to subsection (g) of §251), §252, §254, §257, §258, §263 or §264 of this title:

(1) Provided, however, that no appraisal rights under this section shall be available for the shares of any class or series of stock which stock, or depository receipts in respect thereof, at the record date fixed to determine the stockholders entitled to receive notice of and to vote at the meeting of stockholders to act upon the agreement of merger or consolidation, were either (i) listed on a national securities exchange or designated as a national market system security or an interdealer quotation system by the National Association of Securities Dealers, Inc. or (ii) held of record by more than 2,000 stockholders; and further provided that no appraisal rights shall be available for any shares of stock of the constituent corporation surviving a merger if the merger did not require for its approval the vote of the stockholders of the surviving corporation as provided in subsection (f) of §251 of this title.

(2) Notwithstanding paragraph (1) of this subsection, appraisal rights under this section shall be available for the shares of any class or series of stock of a constituent corporation if the holders thereof are required by the terms of an agreement of merger or consolidation pursuant to §§251, 252, 254, 257, 258, 263 and 264 of this title to accept for such stock anything except: a. Shares of stock of the corporation surviving or resulting from such merger or consolidation or depository receipts in respect thereof; b. Shares of stock of any other corporation or depository receipts in respect thereof which shares of stock (or depository receipts in respect thereof) or depository receipts at the effective date of the merger or consolidation will be either listed on a national securities exchange or designated as a national market system security as an interdealer quotation system by the National Association of Securities Dealers, Inc. or held of record by more than 2,000 stockholders; c. Cash in lieu of fractional shares of the corporations described in the foregoing subparagraphs a. and b. of this paragraph; or d. Any combination of the shares of stock,

depository receipts and cash in lieu of fractional shares or fractional depository receipts described in the foregoing subparagraphs a., and b. and c. of this paragraph.

(3) In the event all of the stock of a subsidiary Delaware corporation party to a merger effected under §253 of this title is not owned by the parent corporation immediately prior to the merger, appraisal rights shall be available for the shares of the subsidiary Delaware corporation.

(c) Any corporation may provide in its certificate of incorporation that appraisal rights under this Section shall be available for the shares of any class or series of its stock as a result of an amendment to its certificate of incorporation, any merger or consolidation in which the corporation is a constituent corporation or the sale of all or substantially all of the assets of the corporation. If the certificate of incorporation contains such a provision, the procedures of this Section, including those set forth in subsections (d) and (e) of this section, shall apply as nearly as is practicable.

(d) Appraisal rights shall be perfected as follows:

(1) If a proposed merger or consolidation for which appraisal rights are provided under this Section is to be submitted for approval at a meeting of stockholders, the corporation, not less than 20 days prior to the meeting, shall notify each of its stockholders who was such on the record date for such meeting with respect to shares for which appraisal rights are available pursuant to subsections (b) or (c) hereof that appraisal rights are available for any or all of the shares of the constituent corporations, and shall include in such notice a copy of this Section. Each stockholder electing to demand the appraisal of such stockholder's shares shall deliver to the corporation, before the taking of the vote on the merger or consolidation, a written demand for appraisal of such stockholder's shares. Such demand will be sufficient if it reasonably informs the corporation of the identity of the stockholder and that the stockholder intends thereby to demand the appraisal of such stockholder's shares. A proxy or vote against the merger or consolidation shall not constitute such a demand. A stockholder electing to take such action must do so by a separate written demand as herein provided. Within 10 days after the effective date of such merger or consolidation, the surviving or resulting corporation shall notify each stockholder of each constituent corporation who has complied with this subsection and has not voted in favor of or consented to the merger or consolidation of the date that the merger or consolidation has become effective; or

(2) If the merger or consolidation was approved pursuant to §228 or §253 of this title, each constituent corporation, either before the effective date of the merger or consolidation or within ten days thereafter, shall notify each of the holders of any class or series of stock of such constituent corporation who are entitled to appraisal rights of the approval of the merger or consolidation and that appraisal rights are available for any or all shares of such class or series of stock of such constituent corporation, and shall include in such notice a copy of this section; provided that, if the notice is given on or after the effective date of the merger or consolidation, such notice shall be given by the surviving or resulting corporation to all such holders of any class or series to stock of a constituent corporation that are entitled to appraisal rights. Such notice may, and, if given on or after the effective date of the merger or consolidation, shall, also notify such stockholders of the effective date of the merger or consolidation. Any stockholder entitled to appraisal rights may, within twenty days after the date of mailing of such notice, demand in writing from the surviving or resulting corporation the appraisal of such holder's shares. Such demand will be sufficient if it reasonably informs the corporation of the identity of the stockholder and that the stockholder intends thereby to demand the appraisal of such holder's shares. If such notice did not notify stockholders of the effective date of the merger or consolidation, either (i) each such constituent corporation shall send a second notice before the effective date of the merger or consolidation notifying each of the holders of any class or series of stock of such constituent corporation that are entitled to appraisal rights of the effective date of the merger or consolidation or (ii) the surviving or resulting corporation shall send such a second notice to all such holders on or within 10 days after such effective date; provided, however, that if such second notice is sent more than 20 days following the sending of the first notice, such second notice need only be sent to each stockholder who is entitled to appraisal rights and who has demanded appraisal of such holder's shares in accordance with this subsection. An affidavit of the secretary or assistant secretary or of the transfer agent of the corporation that is required to give either notice that such notice has been given shall, in the absence of fraud, be prima facie evidence of the facts stated therein. For purposes of determining the stockholders entitled to receive either notice, each constituent corporation may fix, in advance, a record date that shall be not more than 10 days prior to the date the notice is given; provided that, if the notice is given on or after the effective date of the merger or consolidation, the record date shall be such effective date. If no record date is fixed and the notice is given prior to the effective date, the record date shall be the close of business on the day next preceding the day on which the notice is given.

(e) Within 120 days after the effective date of the merger or consolidation, the surviving or resulting corporation or any stockholder who has complied with subsections (a) and (d) hereof and who is otherwise entitled to appraisal rights, may file a petition in the Court of Chancery demanding a determination of the value of the stock of all such stockholders. Notwithstanding the foregoing, at any time within 60 days after the effective date of the merger or consolidation, any stockholder shall have the right to withdraw his demand for appraisal and to accept the terms offered upon the merger or consolidation. Within 120 days after the effective date of the merger or consolidation, any stockholder who has complied with the requirements of subsections (a) and (d) hereof, upon written request, shall be entitled to receive from the corporation surviving the merger or resulting from the consolidation a statement setting forth the aggregate number of shares not voted in favor of the merger or consolidation and with respect to which demands for appraisal have been received and the aggregate number of holders of such shares. Such written statement shall be mailed to the stockholder within 10 days after such stockholder's written request for such a statement is received by the surviving or resulting corporation or within 10 days after expiration of the period for delivery of demands for appraisal under subsection (d) hereof, whichever is later.

(f) Upon the filing of any such petition by a stockholder, service of a copy thereof shall be made upon the surviving or resulting corporation, which shall within 20 days after such service file in the office of the Register in Chancery in which the petition was filed a duly verified list containing the names and addresses of all stockholders who have demanded payment for their shares and with whom agreements as to the value of their shares have not been reached by the surviving or resulting corporation. If the petition shall be filed by the surviving or resulting corporation, the petition shall be accompanied by such a duly verified list. The Register in Chancery, if so ordered by the Court, shall give notice of the time and place fixed for the hearing of such petition by registered or certified mail to the surviving or resulting corporation and to the stockholders shown on the list at the addresses therein stated. Such notice shall also be given by one or more publications at least one week before the day of the hearing, in a newspaper of general circulation published in the City of Wilmington, Delaware or such publication as the Court deems advisable. The forms of the notices by mail and by publication shall be approved by the Court, and the costs thereof shall be borne by the surviving or resulting corporation.

(g) At the hearing on such petition, the Court shall determine the stockholders who have complied with this section and who have become entitled to appraisal rights. The Court may require the stockholders who have demanded an appraisal for their shares and who hold stock represented by certificates to submit their certificates of stock to the Register in Chancery for notation thereon of the pendency of the appraisal proceedings; and if any stockholder fails to comply with such direction, the Court may dismiss the proceedings as to such stockholder.

(h) After determining the stockholders entitled to an appraisal, the Court shall appraise the shares, determining their fair value exclusive of any element of value arising from the accomplishment or expectation of the merger or consolidation, together with a fair rate of interest, if any, to be paid upon the amount determined to be the fair value. In determining such fair value, the Court shall take into account all relevant factors. In determining the fair rate of interest, the Court may consider all relevant factors, including the rate of interest which the surviving or resulting corporation would have had to pay to borrow money during the pendency of the proceeding. Upon application by the surviving or resulting corporation or by any stockholder entitled to participate in the appraisal proceeding, the Court may, in its discretion, permit discovery or other pretrial proceedings and may proceed to trial upon the appraisal prior to the final determination of the stockholder entitled to an appraisal. Any stockholder whose name appears on the list filed by the surviving or resulting corporation pursuant to subsection (f) of this section and who has submitted such stockholder's certificates of stock to the Register in Chancery, if such is required, may participate fully in all proceedings until it is finally determined that such stockholder is not entitled to appraisal rights under this Section.

(i) The Court shall direct the payment of the fair value of the shares, together with interest, if any, by the surviving or resulting corporation to the stockholders entitled thereto. Interest may be simple or compound, as the Court may direct. Payment shall be so made to each such stockholder, in the case of holders of uncertificated stock forthwith, and in the case of holders of shares represented by certificates upon the surrender to the corporation of the certificates representing such stock. The Court's decree may be enforced as other decrees in the Court of Chancery may be enforced, whether such surviving or resulting corporation be a corporation of this State or of any state.

(j) The costs of the proceeding may be determined by the Court and taxed upon the parties as the Court deems equitable in the circumstances. Upon application of a stockholder, the Court may order all or a portion of the expenses incurred by any stockholder in connection with the appraisal proceeding, including, without limitation, reasonable attorney's fees and the fees and expenses of experts, to be charged pro rata against the value of all of the shares entitled to an appraisal.

(k) From and after the effective date of the merger or consolidation, no stockholder who has demanded his appraisal rights as provided in subsection (d) of this section shall be entitled to vote such stock for any purpose or to receive payment of dividends or other distributions on the stock (except dividends or other distributions payable to stockholders of record at a date which is prior to the effective date of the merger or consolidation); provided, however, that if no petition for an appraisal shall be filed within the time provided in subsection (e) of this Section, or if such stockholder shall deliver to the surviving or resulting corporation a written withdrawal of such stockholder's demand for an appraisal and an acceptance of the merger or consolidation, either within 60 days after the effective date of the merger or consolidation as provided in subsection (e) of this section or thereafter with the written approval of the corporation, then the right of such stockholder to an appraisal shall cease. Notwithstanding the foregoing, no appraisal proceeding in the Court of Chancery shall be dismissed as to any stockholder without the approval of the Court, and such approval may be conditioned upon such terms as the Court deems just.

(l) The shares of the surviving or resulting corporation to which the shares of such objecting stockholders would have been converted had they assented to the merger or consolidation shall have the status of authorized and unissued shares of the surviving or resulting corporation.

§263. Merger or Consolidation of Domestic Corporation and Limited Partnership

(a) Any 1 or more corporations of this State may merge or consolidate with 1 or more limited partnerships, of this State or of any other state or states of the United States, or the District of Columbia, unless the laws of such other state or states or the District of Columbia forbid such merger or consolidation. Such corporation or corporations and such 1 or more limited partnerships may merge with or into a corporation, which may be any 1 of such corporations, or they may merge with or into a limited partnership, which may be any 1 of such limited partnerships, or they may consolidate into a new corporation or limited partnership formed by the consolidation, which shall be a corporation or limited partnership of this State or any other state of the United States, or the District of Columbia, which permits such merger or consolidation, pursuant to an agreement of merger or consolidation, as the case may be, complying and approved in accordance with this section.

(b) Each such corporation and limited partnership shall enter into a written agreement of merger or consolidation. The agreement shall state: (1) The terms and conditions of the merger or consolidation; (2) the mode carrying the same into effect; (3) the manner of converting the shares of stock of each such corporation and the partnership interests of each such limited partnership into shares, partnership interests or other securities of the entity surviving or resulting from such merger or consolidation, and if any shares of any such corporation or any partnership interests of any such limited partnership are not to be converted solely into shares, partnership interests or other securities of the entity surviving or resulting from such merger or consolidation, the cash, property, rights or securities of any other corporation or entity which the holders of such shares or partnership interests are to receive in exchange for, or upon conversion of such shares or partnership interests and the surrender of any certificates evidencing them, which cash, property, rights or securities of any other corporation or entity may be in addition to or in lieu of shares, partnership interests or other securities of the entity surviving or resulting from such merger or consolidation; and (4) such other details or provisions as are deemed desirable, including, without limiting the generality of the foregoing, a provision for the payment of cash in lieu of the issuance of fractional shares or interests of the surviving or resulting corporation or limited partnership. Any of the terms of the agreement of merger or consolidation may be made dependent upon facts ascertainable outside of such agreement, provided that the manner in which such facts shall operate upon the terms of the agreement is clearly and expressly set forth in the agreement of merger or consolidation. The term "facts," as used in the preceding sentence, includes, but is not limited to, the occurrence of any event, including a determination or action by any person or body, including the corporation.

(c) The agreement required by subsection (b) of this section shall be adopted, approved, certified, executed and acknowledged by each of the corporations in the same manner as is provided in §251 of this title and, in the case of the limited partnerships, in accordance with their limited partnership agreements and in accordance with the laws of the state under which they are formed, as the case may be. The agreement shall be filed and shall become effective for all purposes of the laws of this State when and as provided in §251 of this title with respect to the merger or consolidation of corporations of this State. In lieu of filing the agreement of merger or consolidation, the surviving or resulting corporation or limited partnership may file a certificate of merger or consolidation, executed in accordance with §103 of this title, if the surviving or resulting entity is a corporation, or by a general partner, if the surviving or resulting entity is a limited partnership, which states: (1) The name and state of domicile of each of the constituent entities; (2) that an agreement of merger or consolidation has been approved, adopted, certified, executed and acknowledged by each of the constituent entities in accordance with this subsection; (3) the name of the surviving or resulting corporation or limited partnership; (4) in the case of a merger in which a corporation is the surviving entity, such amendments or changes in the certificate of incorporation of the surviving corporation as are desired to be effected by the merger, or, if no such amendments or changes are desired, a statement that the certificate of incorporation of the surviving corporation shall be its certificate of incorporation; (5) in the case of a consolidation in which a corporation is the resulting entity, that the certificate of incorporation of the resulting corporation shall be as is set forth in an attachment to the certificate; (6) that the executed agreement of consolidation or merger is on file at an office of the surviving corporation or limited partnership and the address thereof; (7) that a copy of the agreement of consolidation or merger will be furnished by the surviving or resulting entity, on request and without cost, to any stockholder of any constituent corporation or any partner of any constituent limited partnership; and (8) the agreement, if any, required by subsection (d) of this section.

(d) If the entity surviving or resulting from the merger or consolidation is to be governed by the laws of the District of Columbia or any state other than this State, it shall agree that it may be served with process in this State in any proceeding for enforcement of any obligation of any constituent corporation or limited partnership of this State, as well as for enforcement of any obligation of the surviving or resulting corporation or limited partnership arising from the merger or consolidation, including any suit or other proceeding to enforce the right of any stockholders as determined in appraisal proceedings pursuant to §262 of this title, and shall irrevocably appoint the Secretary of State as its agent to accept service of process in any such suit or other proceedings and shall specify the address to which a copy of such process shall be mailed by the Secretary of State. In the event of such service upon the Secretary of State in accordance with this subsection, the Secretary of State shall forthwith notify such surviving or resulting corporation or limited partnership thereof by letter, certified mail, return receipt requested, directed to such surviving or resulting corporation or limited partnership at its address so specified, unless such surviving or resulting corporation or limited partnership shall have designated in writing to the Secretary of State a different address for such purpose, in which case it shall be mailed to the last address so designated. Such letter shall enclose a copy of the process and any other papers served on the Secretary of State pursuant to this subsection. It shall be the duty of the plaintiff in the event of such service to serve process and any other papers in duplicate, to notify the Secretary of State that service is being effected pursuant to this subsection and to pay the Secretary of State the sum of $50 for the use of the State, which sum shall be taxed as part of the costs in the proceeding, if the plaintiff shall prevail therein. The Secretary of State shall maintain an alphabetical record of any such service setting forth the name of the plaintiff and the defendant, the title, docket number and nature of the proceeding in which process has been served upon the Secretary of State, the fact that service has been effected pursuant to this subsection, the return date thereof, and the day and hour service was made. The Secretary of State shall not be required to retain such information longer than 5 years from receipt of the service of process.

(e) Sections 251(c) (second sentence) and (d)–(f), 259–261 and 328 of this title shall, insofar as they are applicable, apply to mergers or consolidations between corporations and limited partnerships.

§264. Merger or Consolidation of Domestic Corporation and Limited Liability Company

(a) Any one or more corporations of this State may merge or consolidate with one or more limited liability companies, of this State or of any other state or states of the United States, or of the District of Columbia, unless the laws of such other state or states or the District of Columbia forbid such merger or consolidation. Such corporation or corporations and such one or more limited liability companies may merge with or into a corporation, which may be any one of such corporations, or they may merge with or into a limited liability company, which may be any one of such limited liability companies, or they may consolidate into a new corporation or limited liability company formed by the consolidation, which shall be a corporation or limited liability company of this State or any other state of the United States, or the District of Columbia, which permits such merger or consolidation, pursuant to an agreement of merger or consolidation, as the case may be, complying and approved in accordance with this section.

(b) Each such corporation and limited liability company shall enter into a written agreement of merger or consolidation. The agreement shall state: (1) the terms and conditions of the merger or consolidation; (2) the mode of carrying the same into effect; (3) the manner of converting the shares of stock of each such corporation and the limited liability company interests of each such limited liability company into shares, limited liability company interests or other securities of the entity surviving or resulting from such merger or consolidation, and if any shares of any such corporation or any limited liability company interests of any such limited liability company are not to be converted solely into shares, limited liability company interests or other securities of the entity surviving or resulting from such merger or consolidation, the cash, property, rights or securities of any other corporation or entity which the holders of such shares or limited liability company interests are to receive in exchange for, or upon conversion of such shares or limited liability company interests and the surrender of any certificates evidencing them, which cash, property, rights or securities of any other corporation or entity may be in addition to or in lieu of shares, limited liability company interests or other securities of the entity surviving or resulting from such merger or consolidation; and (4) such other details or provisions as are deemed desirable, including, without limiting the generality of the foregoing, a provision for the payment of cash in lieu of the issuance of fractional shares or interests of the surviving or resulting corporation or limited liability company. Any of the terms of the agreement of merger or consolidation may be made dependent upon facts ascertainable outside of such agreement, provided that the manner in which such facts shall operate upon the terms of the agreement is clearly and expressly set forth in the agreement of merger or consolidation. The term "facts" as used in the preceding sentence, includes, but is not limited to, the occurrence of any event, including a determination or action by any person or body, including the corporation.

(c) The agreement required by subsection (b) shall be adopted, approved, certified, executed and acknowledged by each of the corporations in the same manner as is provided in §251 of this title and, in the case of the limited liability companies, in accordance with their limited liability company agreements and in accordance with the laws of the state under which they are formed, as the case may be. The agreement shall be filed and shall become effective for all purposes of the laws of this State when and as provided in §251 of this title with respect to the merger or consolidation of corporations of this State. In lieu of filing the agreement of merger or consolidation, the surviving or resulting corporation or limited liability company may file a certificate of merger or consolidation, executed in accordance with §103 of this title, if the surviving or resulting entity is a corporation, or by an authorized person, if the surviving or resulting entity is a limited liability company, which states: (1) the name and state of domicile of each of the constituent entities; (2) that an agreement of merger or consolidation has been approved, adopted, certified, executed and acknowledged by each of the constituent entities in accordance with this subsection; (3) the name of the surviving or resulting corporation or limited liability company; (4) in the case of a merger in which a corporation is the surviving entity, such amendments or changes in the certificate of incorporation of the surviving corporation as are desired to be effected by the merger, or, if no such amendments or changes are desired, a statement that the certificate of incorporation of the surviving corporation shall be its certificate of incorporation; (5) in the case of a consolidation in which a corporation is the resulting entity, that the certificate of incorporation of the resulting corporation shall be as is set forth in an attachment to the certificate; (6) that the executed agreement of consolidation or merger is on file at the principal place of business of the surviving corporation or limited liability company and the address thereof; (7) that a copy of the agreement of consolidation or merger will be furnished by the surviving or resulting entity, on request and without cost, to any stockholder of any constituent corporation or any member of any constituent limited liability company; and (8) the agreement, if any, required by subsection (d) of this section.

(d) If the entity surviving or resulting from the merger or consolidation is to be governed by the laws of the District of Columbia or any state other than this State, it shall agree that it may be served with process in this State in any proceeding for enforcement of any obligation of any constituent corporation or limited liability company of this State, as well as for enforcement of any obligation of the surviving or resulting corporation or limited liability company arising from the merger or consolidation, including any suit or other proceeding to enforce the right of any stockholders as determined in appraisal proceedings pursuant to the provisions of §262 of this title, and shall irrevocably appoint the Secretary of State as its agent to accept service of process in any such suit or other proceedings and shall specify the address to which a copy of such process shall be mailed by the Secretary of State. In the event of such service upon the Secretary of State in accordance with this subsection, the Secretary of State shall forthwith notify such surviving or resulting corporation or limited liability company thereof by letter, certified mail, return receipt requested, directed to such surviving or resulting corporation or limited liability company at its address so specified, unless such surviving or resulting corporation or limited liability company shall have designated in writing to the Secretary of State a different address for such purpose, in which case it shall be mailed to the last address so designated. Such letter shall enclose a copy of the process and any other papers served on the Secretary of State pursuant to this subsection. It shall be the duty of the plaintiff in the event of such service to serve process and any other papers in duplicate, to notify the Secretary of State that service is being effected pursuant to this subsection and to pay the Secretary of State the sum of $50 for the use of the State, which sum shall be taxed as part of the costs in the proceeding, if the plaintiff shall prevail therein. The Secretary of State shall maintain an alphabetical record of any such service setting forth the name of the plaintiff and the defendant, the title, docket number and nature of the proceeding in which process has been served upon him, the fact that service has been effected pursuant to this subsection, the return date thereof, and the day and hour service was made. The Secretary of State shall not be required to retain such information longer than 5 years from receipt of the service of process.

(e) Sections 251(c) (second sentence) and (d)–(f), 259–261 and 328 of this title shall, insofar as they are applicable, apply to mergers or consolidations between corporations and limited liability companies.

§271. Sale, Lease or Exchange of Assets; Consideration; Procedure

(a) Every corporation may at any meeting of its board of directors or governing body sell, lease or exchange all or substantially all of its property and assets, including its goodwill and its corporate franchises, upon such terms and conditions and for such consideration, which may consist in whole or in part of money or other property, including shares of stock in, and/or other securities of, any other corporation or corporations, as its board of directors or governing body deems expedient and for the best interests of the corporation, when and as authorized by a resolution adopted by the holders of a majority of the outstanding stock of the corporation entitled to vote thereon or, if the corporation is a nonstock corporation, by a majority of the members having the right to vote for the election of the members of the governing body, at a meeting duly called upon at least 20 days' notice. The notice of the meeting shall state that such a resolution will be considered.

(b) Notwithstanding authorization or consent to a proposed sale, lease or exchange of a corporation's property and assets by the stockholders or members, the board of directors or governing body may abandon such proposed sale, lease or exchange without further action by the stockholders or members, subject to the rights, if any, of third parties under any contract relating thereto.

§272. Mortgage or Pledge of Assets

The authorization or consent of stockholders to the mortgage or pledge of a corporation's property and assets shall not be necessary, except to the extent that the certificate of incorporation otherwise provides.

§274. Dissolution Before the Issuance of Shares or Beginning of Business; Procedure

If a corporation has not issued shares or has not commenced the business for which the corporation was organized, a majority of the incorporators, or, if directors were named in the certificate of incorporation or have been elected, a majority of the directors, may surrender all of the corporation's rights and franchises by filing in the office of the Secretary of State a certificate, executed and acknowledged by a majority of the incorporators or directors, stating that no shares of stock have been issued or that the business or activity for which the corporation was organized has not been begun; that no part of the capital of the corporation has been paid, or, if some capital has been paid, that the amount actually paid in for the corporation's shares, less any part thereof disbursed for necessary expenses, has been returned to those entitled thereto; that if the corporation has begun business but it has not issued shares all debts of the corporation have been paid; that if the corporation has not begun business but has issued stock certificates all issued stock certificates, if any, have been surrendered and cancelled; and that all rights and franchises of the corporation are surrendered. Upon such certificate becoming effective in accordance with section 103 of this title, the corporation shall be dissolved.

§275. Dissolution; Procedure

(a) If it should be deemed advisable in the judgment of the board of directors of any corporation that it should be dissolved, the board, after the adoption of a resolution to that effect by a majority of the whole board at any meeting called for that purpose, shall cause notice to be mailed to each stockholder entitled to vote thereon of the adoption of the resolution and of a meeting of stockholders to take action upon the resolution.

(b) At the meeting a vote shall be taken upon the proposed dissolution. If a majority of the outstanding stock of the corporation entitled to vote thereon shall vote for the proposed dissolution, a certification of dissolution shall be filed with the Secretary of State pursuant to subsection (d) of this Section.

(c) Dissolution of a corporation may also be authorized without action of the directors if all the stockholders entitled to vote thereon shall consent in writing and a certificate of dissolution shall be filed with the Secretary of State pursuant to subsection (d) of this Section.

(d) If dissolution is authorized in accordance with this Section, a certificate of dissolution shall be executed, acknowledged and filed, and shall become effective, in accordance with §103 of this Title. Such certificate of dissolution shall set forth:

(i) the name of the corporation;

(ii) the date dissolution was authorized;

(iii) that the dissolution has been authorized by the board of directors and stockholders of the corporation, in accordance with subsections (a) and (b) of this Section, or that the dissolution has been authorized by all of the stockholders of the corporation entitled to vote on a dissolution, in accordance with subsection (c) of this section; and

(iv) the names and addresses of the directors and officers of the corporation.

(e) The resolution authorizing a proposed dissolution may provide that notwithstanding authorization or consent to the proposed dissolution by the stockholders, or the members of a nonstock corporation pursuant to §276 of this title, the board of directors or governing body may abandon such proposed dissolution without further action by the stockholders or members.

(f) Upon a certificate of dissolution becoming effective in accordance with §103 of this title, the corporation shall be dissolved.

§277. Payment of Franchise Taxes Before Dissolution

No corporation shall be dissolved under this chapter until all franchise taxes due to or assessable by the State have been paid by the corporation.

§278. Continuation of Corporation After Dissolution for Purposes of Suit and Winding Up Affairs

All corporations, whether they expire by their own limitation or are otherwise dissolved, shall nevertheless be continued, for the term of three years from such expiration or dissolution or for such longer period as the Court of Chancery shall in its discretion direct, bodies corporate for the purpose of prosecuting and defending suits, whether civil, criminal or administrative, by or against them, and of enabling them gradually to settle and close their business, to dispose of and convey their property, to discharge their liabilities, and to distribute to their stockholders any remaining assets, but not for the purpose of continuing the business for which the corporation was organized. With respect to any action, suit or proceeding begun by or against the corporation either prior to or within 3 years after the date of its expiration or dissolution the action shall not abate by reason of the dissolution of the corporation; the corporation shall, solely for the purpose of such action, suit or proceeding, be continued as a body corporate beyond the 3-year period and until any judgments, orders or decrees therein shall be fully executed, without the necessity for any special direction to that effect by the Court of Chancery.

§279. Trustees or Receivers for Dissolved Corporations; Appointment; Powers; Duties

When any corporation organized under this chapter shall be dissolved in any manner whatever, the Court of Chancery, on application of any creditor, stockholder or director of the corporation, or any other person who shows good cause therefor, at any time, may either appoint one or more of the directors of the corporation to be trustees, or appoint one or more persons to be receivers, of and for the corporation, to take charge of the corporation's property, and to collect the debts and property due and belonging to the corporation, with power to prosecute and defend, in the name of the corporation, or otherwise, all such suits as may be necessary or proper for the purposes aforesaid, and to appoint an agent or agents under them, and to do all other acts which might be done by the corporation, if in being, that may be necessary for the final settlement of the unfinished business of the corporation. The powers of the trustees or receivers may be continued as long as the Court of Chancery shall think necessary for the purposes aforesaid.

§280. Notice to Claimants; Filing of Claims

(a)(1) After a corporation has been dissolved in accordance with the procedures set forth in this chapter, the corporation or any successor entity may give notice of the dissolution requiring all persons having a claim against the corporation other than a claim against the corporation in a pending action, suit or proceeding to which the corporation is a party to present their claims against the corporation in accordance with such notice. Such notice shall state:

(a) that all claims must be presented in writing and must contain sufficient information reasonably to inform the corporation or successor entity of the identity of the claimant and the substance of the claim;

(b) the mailing address to which a claim must be sent;

(c) the date by which a claim must be received by the corporation or successor entity, which date shall be no earlier than 60 days from the date thereof; and

(d) That such claim will be barred if not received by the date referred to in subparagraph c. of this subsection; and

(e) That the corporation or a successor entity may make distributions to other claimants and the corporation's stockholders or persons interested as having been such without further notice to the claimant; and

(f) The aggregate amount, on an annual basis, of all distributions made by the corporation to its stockholders for each of the 3 years prior to the date the corporation dissolved.

Such notice shall also be published at least once a week for two consecutive weeks in a newspaper of general circulation in the county in which the office of the corporation's last registered agent in this State is located and in the corporation's principal place of business and, in the case of a corporation having $10,000,000 or more in total assets at the time of its dissolution, at least once in all editions of a daily newspaper with a national circulation. On or before the date of the first publication of such notice, the corporation or successor entity shall mail a copy of such notice by certified or registered mail, return receipt requested, to each known claimant of the corporation including persons with claims asserted against the corporation in a pending action, suit or proceeding to which the corporation is a party.

(2) Any claim against the corporation required to be presented pursuant to this subsection is barred if a claimant who was given actual notice under this subsection does not present the claim to the dissolved corporation or successor entity by the date referred to in subparagraph (1)c. of this subsection.

(3) A corporation or successor entity may reject, in whole or in part, any claim made by a claimant pursuant to this subsection by mailing notice of such rejection by certified mail return receipt requested to the claimant within 90 days after receipt of such claim and, in all events, at least 150 days before the expiration of the period described in §278 of this title; provided, however, that in the case of a claim filed pursuant to §295 of this title against a corporation or successor entity for which a receiver or trustee has been appointed by the Court of Chancery the time period shall be as provided in §296 of this title, and the 30-day appeal period provided for in §296 shall be applicable. A notice sent by a corporation or successor entity pursuant to this subsection shall state that any claim rejected therein will be barred if an action, suit or proceeding with respect to the claim is not commenced within 120 days of the date thereof, and shall be accompanied by a copy of §§278–283 of this title; and, in the case of a notice sent by a court-appointed receiver or trustee and as to which a claim has been filed pursuant to §295, copies of §295 of this title and §296 of this title.

(4) A claim against a corporation is barred if a claimant whose claim is rejected pursuant to paragraph (3) of this subsection does not commence ac action, suit or proceeding with respect to the claim no later than 120 days after the mailing of the rejection notice.

(b)(1) A corporation or successor entity electing to follow the procedures described in subsection (a) of this section shall also give notice of the dissolution of the corporation to persons with contractual claims contingent upon the occurrence or nonoccurrence of future events or otherwise conditional or unmatured, and request that such persons present such claims in accordance with the terms of such notice. Provided, however, that as used in this section and in §281 of this title, the term "contractual claims" shall not include any implied warranty as to any product manufactured, sold, distributed or handled by the dissolved corporation. Such notice shall be in substantially the form, and sent and published in the same manner, as described in subsection (a)(1) of this section.

(2) The corporation or successor entity shall offer any claimant on a contract whose claim is contingent, conditional or unmatured, such security as the corporation or successor entity determines is sufficient to provide compensation to the claimant if the claim matures. The corporation or successor entity shall mail such offer to the claimant by certified mail return receipt requested, within 90 days of receipt of such claim and, in all events, at least 150 days before the expiration of the period described in §278 of this title. If the claimant offered such security does not deliver in writing to the corporation or successor entity a notice rejecting the offer within 120 days after receipt of such offer for security, the claimant shall be deemed to have accepted such security as the sole source from which to satisfy his claim against the corporation.

(c)(1) A corporation or successor entity which has given notice in accordance with subsection (a) of this section shall petition the Court of Chancery to determine the amount and form of security that will be reasonably likely to be sufficient to provide compensation for any claim against the corporation which is the subject of a pending action, suit or proceeding to which the corporation is a party other than a claim barred pursuant to subsection (a) of this section.

(2) A corporation or successor entity which has given notice in accordance with subsections (a) and (b) of this section shall petition the Court of Chancery to determine the amount and form of security that will be sufficient to provide compensation to any claimant who has rejected the offer for security made pursuant to subsection (b)(2) of this section.

(3) A corporation or successor entity which has given notice in accordance with subsection (a) of this section shall petition the Court of Chancery to determine the amount and form of security which will be reasonably likely to be sufficient to provide compensation for claims that have not been made known to the corporation or that have not arisen but that, based on facts known to the corporation or successor entity, are likely to arise or become known to the corporation or successor entity within 5 years after the date of dissolution or such longer period of time as the Court of Chancery may determine not to exceed 10 years after the date of dissolution. The Court of Chancery may appoint a guardian ad litem in respect of any such proceeding brought under this subsection. The reasonable fees and expenses of such guardian, including all reasonable expert witness fees, shall be paid by the petitioner in such proceeding.

(d) The giving of any notice or making of any offer pursuant to the provisions of this section shall not revive any claim then barred or constitute acknowledgment by the corporation or successor entity that any person to whom such notice is sent is a proper claimant and shall not operate as a waiver of any defense or counterclaim in respect of any claim asserted by any person to whom such notice is sent.

(e) As used in this section, the term "successor entity" shall include any trust, receivership or other legal entity governed by the laws of this State to which the remaining assets and liabilities of a dissolved corporation are transferred and which exists solely for the purposes of prosecuting and defending suits, by or against the dissolved corporation, enabling the dissolved corporation to settle and close the business of the dissolved corporation, to dispose of and convey the property of the dissolved corporation, to discharge the liabilities of the dissolved corporation, and to distribute to the dissolved corporation's stockholders any remaining assets, but not for the purpose of continuing the business for which the dissolved corporation was organized.

(f) The time periods and notice requirements of this section shall, in the case of a corporation or successor entity for which a receiver or trustee has been appointed by the Court of Chancery, be subject to variation by, or in the manner provided in, the Rules of the Court of Chancery.

§281. Payment and Distribution to Claimants and Stockholders

(a) A dissolved corporation or successor entity which has followed the procedures described in §280 of this title (i) shall pay the claims made and not rejected in accordance with §280(a) of this title, (ii) shall post the security offered and not rejected pursuant to §280(b)(2) of this title, (iii) shall post any security ordered by the Court of Chancery in any proceeding under §280(c) of this title and (iv) shall pay or make provision for all other claims that are mature, known and uncontested or that have been finally determined to be owing by the corporation or such successor entity. Such claims or obligations shall be paid in full and any such provision for payment shall be made in full if there are sufficient assets. If there are insufficient assets, such claims and obligations shall be paid or provided for according to their priority, and, among claims of equal priority, ratably to the extent of funds legally available therefor. Any remaining funds shall be distributed to the stockholders of the dissolved corporation; provided, however, that such distribution shall not be made before the expiration of 150 days from the date of the last notice of rejections given pursuant to §280(a)(2) of this title. In the absence of actual fraud, the judgment of the directors of the dissolved corporation or the governing persons of such successor entity as to the provision made for the payment of all obligations under (iv) above shall be conclusive.

(b) A dissolved corporation or successor entity which has not followed the procedures described in §280 of this title shall, prior to the expiration of the period described in §278 of this title, adopt a plan of distribution pursuant to which the dissolved corporation or successor entity (i) shall pay or make reasonable provision to pay all claims and obligations, including all contingent, conditional, or unmatured contractual claims known to the corporation or such successor entity, (ii) shall make such provision as will be reasonably likely to be sufficient to provide compensation for any claim against the corporation which is the subject of a pending action, suit or proceeding to which the corporation is a party, and (iii) shall make such provision as will be reasonably likely to be sufficient to provide compensation for claims that have not been made known to the corporation or that have not arisen but that, based on facts known to the corporation or successor entity, are likely to arise or to become known to the corporation or successor entity within 10 years after the day of dissolution. The plan of distribution shall provide that such claims shall be paid in full and any such provision for payment made shall be made in full if there are sufficient assets. If there are insufficient assets, such plan shall provide that such claims and obligations shall be paid or provided for according to their priority and, among claims of equal priority, ratably to the extent of assets legally available therefor. Any remaining assets shall be distributed to the stockholders of the dissolved corporation.

(c) Directors of a dissolved corporation or governing persons of a successor entity which has complied with subsections (a) or (b) of this section shall not be personally liable to the claimants of the dissolved corporation.

(d) As used in this section, the term "successor entity" has the meaning set forth in §280(e) of this title.

(e) The term "priority", as used in this section, does not refer either to the order of payments set forth in subsection (a) (1)–(4) of this section or to the relative times at which any claims mature or are reduced to judgment.

§282. Liability of Stockholders of Dissolved Corporations

(a) A stockholder of a dissolved corporation the assets of which were distributed pursuant to §281(a) or (b) of this title shall not be liable for any claim against the corporation in an amount in excess of such stockholder's pro rata share of the claim or the amount so distributed to such stockholder, whichever is less.

(b) A stockholder of a dissolved corporation the assets of which were distributed pursuant to §281(a) of this title shall not be liable for any claim against the corporation on which an action, suit or proceeding is not begun prior to the expiration of the period described in §278 of this title.

(c) The aggregate liability of any stockholder of a dissolved corporation for claims against the dissolved corporation shall not exceed the amount distributed to such stockholder in dissolution.

§283. Jurisdiction of the Court

The Court of the Chancery shall have jurisdiction of any application prescribed in this subchapter and of all questions arising in the proceedings thereon, and may make such orders and decrees and issue injunctions therein as justice and equity shall require.

§284. Revocation or Forfeiture of Charter; Proceedings

(a) The Court of Chancery shall have jurisdiction to revoke or forfeit the charter of any corporation for abuse, misuse or nonuse of its corporate powers, privileges or franchises. The Attorney General shall, upon the Attorney General's own motion or upon the relation of a proper party, proceed for this purpose by complaint in the County in which the registered office of the corporation is located.

(b) The Court of Chancery shall have power, by appointment of receivers or otherwise, to administer and wind up the affairs of any corporation whose charter shall be revoked or forfeited by any court under any section of this title or otherwise, and to make such orders and decrees with respect thereto as shall be just and equitable respecting its affairs and assets and the rights of its stockholders and creditors.

(c) No proceeding shall be instituted under this section for non-use of any corporation's powers, privileges or franchises during the first two years after its incorporation.

§285. Dissolution or Forfeiture of Charter by Decree of Court; Filing

Whenever any corporation is dissolved or its charter forfeited by decree or judgment of the Court of Chancery, the decree or judgment shall be forthwith filed by the Register in Chancery of the county in which the decree or judgment was entered, in the office of the Secretary of State, and a note thereof shall be made by the Secretary of State on the corporation's charter or certificate of incorporation and on the index thereof.

§325. Actions Against Officers, Directors or Stockholders to Enforce Liability of Corporation; Unsatisfied Judgment Against Corporation

(a) When the officers, directors or stockholders of any corporation shall be liable by the provisions of this chapter to pay the debts of the corporation, or any part thereof, any person to whom they are liable may have an action, at law or in equity, against any one or more of them, and the complaint shall state the claim against the corporation, and the ground on which the plaintiff expects to charge the defendants personally.

(b) No suit shall be brought against any officer, director, or stockholder for any debt of a corporation of which such person is an officer, director or stockholder, until judgment be obtained therefor against the corporation and execution thereon returned unsatisfied.

§327. Stockholder's Derivative Action; Allegation of Stock Ownership

In any derivative suit instituted by a stockholder of a corporation, it shall be averred in the complaint that the plaintiff was a stockholder of the corporation at the time of the transaction of which such stockholder complains or that such stockholder's stock thereafter devolved upon such stockholder by operation of law.

§328. Liability of Corporation, etc., Impairment by Certain Transactions

The liability of a corporation of this State, or the stockholders, directors or officers thereof, or the rights or remedies of the creditors thereof, or of persons doing or transacting business with the corporation, shall not in any way be lessened or impaired by the sale of its assets, or by the increase or decrease in the capital stock of the corporation, or by its merger or consolidation with one or more corporations or by any change or amendment in its certificate of incorporation.

§329. Defective Organization of Corporation as Defense

(a) No corporation of this State and no person sued by any such corporation shall be permitted to assert the want of legal organization as a defense to any claim.

(b) This section shall not be construed to prevent judicial inquiry into the regularity or validity of the organization of a corporation, or its lawful possession of any corporate power it may assert in any other suit or proceeding where its corporate existence or the power to exercise the corporate rights it asserts is challenged, and evidence tending to sustain the challenge shall be admissible in any such suit or proceeding.

APPENDIX

Corporate Bylaws

BYLAWS OF ______________________________

ARTICLE I — OFFICES

Section 1. *Registered Office:* The registered office of the Corporation in the State of ____________________ shall be ____________________, County of ____________________, ____________________. The registered agent of the Corporation at such address shall be ____________________.
Section 2. *Other Offices:* The corporation may also have offices at such other places, both within and without the State of ____________________, as the Board of Directors may from time to time determine or the business of the Corporation may require.

ARTICLE II — MEETINGS OF SHAREHOLDERS

Section 1. *Place of Meetings:* Meetings of shareholders shall be held at the principal office of the Corporation or at such place as may be determined from time to time by the Board of Directors.
Section 2. *Annual Meetings:* The Corporation shall hold annual meetings of shareholders commencing with the year __________, on such date and at such time as shall be determined from time to time by the Board of Directors, at which meeting shareholders shall elect a Board of Directors and transact such other business as may properly be brought before the meeting.

Section 3. *Special Meetings:* Special meetings of the shareholders, for any purpose or purposes, may be called at any time by the President of the Corporation, or the Board of Directors, or shareholders holding at least ________________________ percent (____%) of the issued and outstanding voting stock of the Corporation.

Business transacted at any special meeting shall be confined to the purpose or purposes set forth in the notice of the special meeting.

Section 4. *Notice of Meetings:* Whenever shareholders are required or permitted to take any action at a meeting, a written notice of the meeting shall be provided to each shareholder of record entitled to vote at or entitled to notice of the meeting, which shall state the place, date, and hour of the meeting, and, in the case of a special meeting, the purpose or purposes for which the meeting is called.

Unless otherwise provided by law, written notice of any meeting shall be given not less than ten nor more than sixty days before the date of the meeting to each shareholder entitled to vote at such meeting.

Section 5. *Quorum at Meetings:* Shareholders may take action on a matter at a meeting only if a quorum exists with respect to that matter. Except as otherwise provided by law, a majority of the outstanding shares of the Corporation entitled to vote, represented in person or by proxy, shall constitute a quorum at a meeting of shareholders. Once a share is represented for any purpose at a meeting (other than solely to object to the holding of the meeting), it is deemed present for quorum purposes for the remainder of the meeting and the shareholders present at a duly organized meeting may continue to transact business until adjournment, notwithstanding the withdrawal of sufficient shareholders to leave less than a quorum.

The holders of a majority of the outstanding shares represented at a meeting, whether or not a quorum is present, may adjourn the meeting from time to time.

Section 6. *Proxies:* Each shareholder entitled to vote at a meeting of shareholders or to express consent or dissent to corporate action in writing without a meeting may authorize another person or persons to vote for him or her by proxy, but no such proxy shall be voted or acted upon one year from its date, unless the proxy provides for a longer period.

A duly executed proxy shall be irrevocable if it states that it is irrevocable and if, and only so long as, it is coupled with an interest sufficient in law to support an irrevocable power.

Except as otherwise provided herein or by law, every proxy is revocable at the pleasure of the shareholder executing it by communicating such revocation, in writing, to the Secretary of the Corporation.

Section 7. *Voting at Meetings:* If a quorum exists, action on a matter (other than the election of directors) is approved if the votes cast favoring the action exceed the votes cast opposing the action. Directors shall be elected by a plurality of the votes cast by the shares entitled to vote in the election (provided a quorum exists).

Unless otherwise provided by law or in the Corporation's Articles of Incorporation, and subject to the other provisions of these Bylaws, each shareholder shall be entitled to one vote on each matter, in person or by proxy, for each share of the Corporation's capital stock that has voting power and that is held by such shareholder. Voting need not be by written ballot.

Section 8. *List of Shareholders:* The officer of the Corporation who has charge of the stock ledger of the Corporation shall prepare and make, at least ten days before any meeting of shareholders, a complete list of the shareholders entitled to vote at the meeting, arranged alphabetically, and showing the address of each shareholder and the number of shares held by each shareholder. The list shall be open to the examination of any shareholder for any purpose germane to the meeting, during ordinary business hours, for a period of at least ten days before the meeting, either at a place in the city where the meeting is to be held, which place must be specified in the notice of the meeting, or at the place where the meeting is to be held. The list shall also be produced and kept available at the time and place of the meeting, for the entire duration of the meeting, and may be inspected by any shareholder present at the meeting.

Section 9. *Consent in Lieu of Meetings:* Any action required to be taken or which may be taken at any meeting of shareholders, whether annual or special, may be taken without a meeting, without prior notice, and without a vote, if a consent in writing, setting forth the action so taken, shall be signed by the holders of outstanding shares having not less than the minimum number of votes that would be necessary to take such action at a meeting at which all shareholders entitled to vote were present and voted.

The action must be evidenced by one or more written consents, describing the action taken, signed and dated by the shareholders entitled to take action without a meeting, and delivered to the Corporation at its registered office or to the officer having charge of the Corporation's minute book.

No consent shall be effective to take the corporate action referred to in the consent unless the number of consents required to take action are delivered to the Corporation or to the officer having charge of its minute book within sixty days of the delivery of the earliest-dated consent.

Prompt notice of the taking of the corporate action without a meeting by less than unanimous vote shall be given to those shareholders who have not consented in writing.

Section 10. *Conference Call:* One or more shareholders may participate in a meeting of shareholders by means of conference telephone, videoconferencing, or similar communications equipment by means of which all persons participating in the meeting can hear each other. Participation in this manner shall constitute presence in person at such meeting.

Section 11. *Annual Statement:* The President and the Board of Directors shall present at each annual meeting a full and complete statement of the business and affairs of the corporation for the preceding year.

ARTICLE III — DIRECTORS

Section 1. *Powers of Directors:* The business and affairs of the Corporation shall be managed by or under the direction of the Board of Directors, which may exercise all such powers of the Corporation and do all lawful acts and things, subject to any limitations set forth in these Bylaws or the Articles of Incorporation for the Corporation.

Section 2. *Number, Qualification, and Election:* The number of directors which shall constitute the whole board shall be not fewer than ____________________ nor more than ____________________. Each director shall be at least 18 years of age. The directors need not be residents of the state of incorporation. Directors need not be shareholders in the Corporation. The directors shall be elected by the shareholders at the annual meeting of shareholders by the vote of shareholders holding of record in the aggregate at least a plurality of the shares of stock of the Corporation present in person or by proxy and entitled to vote at the annual meeting of shareholders. Each director shall be elected for a term of ____ year[s], and until his or her successor shall be elected and shall qualify or until his or her earlier resignation or removal.

Section 3. *Nomination of Directors:* The Board of Directors shall nominate candidates to stand for election as directors; and other candidates may also be nominated by any shareholder of the Corporation, provided such nomination[s] is submitted in writing to the Corporation's Secretary no later than _____ days prior to the meeting of shareholders at which such directors are to be elected, together with the identity of the nominator and the number of shares of the stock of the Corporation owned by the nominator.

Section 4. *Vacancies:* Except as otherwise provided by law, any vacancy in the Board of Directors occurring by reason of an increase in the authorized number of directors or by reason of the death, withdrawal, removal, disqualification, inability to act, or resignation of a director shall be filled by the majority of directors then in office. The successor shall serve the unexpired portion of the term of his or her predecessor. Any director may resign at any time by giving written notice to the Board or the Secretary.

Section 5. *Meetings:*

a. Regular Meetings: Regular meetings of the Board of Directors shall be held without notice and at such time and at such place as determined by the Board.

b. Special Meetings: Special meetings of the Board may be called by the Chairperson or the President on _____ days' notice to each director, either personally or by telephone, express delivery service, telegram, or facsimile transmission, and on _____ days' notice by mail (effective upon deposit of such notice in the mail). The notice need not specify the purpose of a special meeting.

Section 6. *Quorum and Voting at Meetings:* A majority of the total number of authorized directors shall constitute a quorum for transaction of business. The act of a majority of directors present at any meeting at which a quorum is present shall be the act of the Board of Directors, except as provided by law, the Articles of Incorporation, or these Bylaws. Each director present shall have one vote, irrespective of the number of shares of stock, if any, he or she may hold.

Section 7. *Committees of Directors:* The Board of Directors, by resolution, may create one or more committees, each consisting of one or more Directors. Each such committee shall serve at the pleasure of the Board. All provisions of the law of the State of _____________ and these Bylaws relating to meetings, action without meetings, notice, and waiver of notice, quorum, and voting requirements of the Board of Directors shall apply to such committees and their members.

Section 8. *Consent in Lieu of Meetings:* Any action required or permitted to be taken at any meeting of the Board of Directors or of any committee thereof, may be taken without a meeting if all members of the Board or committee, as the case may be, consent thereto in writing, such writing or writings to be filed with the minutes of proceedings of the Board or committee.

Section 9. *Conference Call:* One or more directors may participate in meetings of the Board or a committee of the Board by any communication, including videoconference, by means of which all participating directors can simultaneously hear each other during the meeting. Participation in this manner shall constitute presence in person at such meeting.

Section 10. *Compensation:* The Board of Directors shall have the authority to fix the compensation of Directors. A fixed sum and expenses of attendance may be allowed for attendance at each regular or special meeting of the Board. No such payment shall

preclude any director from serving the Corporation in any other capacity and receiving compensation therefor.
Section 11. *Removal of Directors:* Any director or the entire Board of Directors may be removed, with or without cause, by the holders of a majority of the shares then entitled to vote at an election of directors.

ARTICLE IV — OFFICERS

Section 1. *Positions:* The officers of the Corporation shall be a Chairperson, a President, a Secretary, and a Treasurer, and such other officers as the Board may from time to time appoint, including one or more Vice Presidents and such other officers as it deems advisable. Any number of offices may be held by the same person, except that the President and the Secretary may not be the same person. Each such officer shall exercise such powers and perform such duties as shall be set forth herein and such other powers and duties as may be specified from time to time by the Board of Directors. The officers of the Corporation shall be elected by the Board of Directors. Each of the Chairperson, President, and/or any Vice Presidents may execute bonds, mortgages, and other documents under the seal of the Corporation, except where required or permitted by law to be otherwise executed and except where execution thereof shall be expressly delegated by the Board to some other officer or agent of the Corporation.
Section 2. *Chairperson:* The Chairperson shall have overall responsibility and authority for management and operations of the Corporation, shall preside at all meetings of the Board of Directors and shareholders, and shall ensure that all orders and resolutions of the Board of Directors and shareholders are effected.
Section 3. *President:* The President shall be the chief operating officer of the Corporation and shall have full responsibility and authority for management of the day-to-day operations of the Corporation. The President shall be an ex-officio member of all committees and shall have the general powers and duties of management and supervision usually vested in the office of president of a corporation.
Section 4. *Secretary:* The Secretary shall attend all meetings of the Board and all meetings of the shareholders and shall act as clerk thereof, and record all the votes of the Corporation and the minutes of all its transactions in a book to be kept for that purpose, and shall perform like duties for all committees of the Board of Directors when required. The Secretary shall give, or cause to be given, notice of all meetings of the shareholders and special meetings of the Board of Directors, and shall perform such other duties as may be prescribed by the Board of Directors or President, and under whose supervision the Secretary shall be. The Secretary shall maintain the records, minutes, and seal of the Corporation and may attest any instruments signed by any other officer of the Corporation.
Section 5. *Treasurer:* The Treasurer shall be the chief financial officer of the Corporation, shall have responsibility for the custody of the corporate funds and securities, shall keep full and accurate records and accounts of receipts and disbursements in books belonging to the Corporation, and shall keep the monies of the Corporation in a separate account in the name of the Corporation. The Treasurer shall provide to the President and directors, at the regular meetings of the Board, or whenever requested by the Board, an account of all financial transactions and of the financial condition of the Corporation.
Section 6. *Term of Office:* The officers of the Corporation shall hold office until

their successors are chosen and have qualified or until their earlier resignation or removal. Any officer or agent elected or appointed by the Board may be removed at any time, with or without cause, by the affirmative vote of a majority of the Board of Directors. Any vacancy occurring in any office as a result of death, resignation, removal, or otherwise, shall be filled for the unexpired portion of the term by a majority vote of the Board of Directors.

Section 7. *Compensation:* The compensation of officers of the Corporation shall be fixed by the Board of Directors.

ARTICLE V — CAPITAL STOCK

Section 1. *Stock Certificates:* The shares of the Corporation shall be represented by certificates, provided that the Board of Directors may provide by resolution that some or all of any or all classes or series of the stock of the Corporation shall be uncertificated shares. Notwithstanding the adoption of such a resolution by the Board of Directors, every holder of stock represented by certificates and, upon request, every holder of uncertificated shares, shall be entitled to have a certificate signed in the name of the Corporation, by the Chairperson, President or any Vice President, and by the Treasurer or Secretary. Any or all of the signatures on the certificate may be by facsimile. The stock certificates of the Corporation shall be numbered and registered in the share ledger and transfer books of the Corporation as they are issued and shall bear the corporate seal.

Section 2. *Lost Certificates:* The Corporation may issue a new certificate of stock in place of any certificate theretofor issued and alleged to have been lost, stolen, or destroyed, and the Corporation may require the owner of the lost, stolen, or destroyed certificate, or his or her legal representative, to make an affidavit of that fact, and the Corporation may require indemnity against any claim that may be made against the Corporation on account of the alleged loss, theft, or destruction of any such certificate or the issuance of such new certificate.

Section 3. *Transfers:* Transfers of shares shall be made on the books of the Corporation upon surrender and cancellation of the certificates therefor, endorsed by the person named in the certificate or by his or her legal representative. No transfer shall be made which is inconsistent with any provision of law, the Articles of Incorporation for the Corporation, or these Bylaws.

Section 4. *Record Date:* In order that the Corporation may determine the shareholders entitled to notice of or to vote at any meeting of shareholders, or any adjournment thereof, or to take action without a meeting, or to receive payment of any dividend or other distribution, or to exercise any rights in respect of any change, conversion, or exchange of stock, or for the purpose of any other lawful action, the Board of Directors may fix a record date, which record date shall not precede the date upon which the resolution fixing the record date is adopted by the Board of Directors and shall not be less than ten nor more than fifty days before the meeting or action requiring a determination of shareholders.

If no record date is fixed by the Board of Directors:

a. for determining shareholders entitled to notice of or to vote at a meeting, the record date shall be at the close of business on the day next preceding the day on which notice is given, or, if notice is waived, at the close of business on the day next preceding the day on which the meeting is held or other action taken;

b. for determining shareholders entitled to consent to corporate action without a meeting, the record date shall be the day on which the first written consent is delivered to the Corporation is accordance with these bylaws; and

c. for determining shareholders for another purpose, the record date shall be at the close of business on the day on which the Board of Directors adopts the resolution relating thereto.

ARTICLE VI — DIVIDENDS

Section 1. *Dividends:* The Board of Directors may declare and pay dividends upon the outstanding shares of the Corporation, from time to time and to such extent as the Board deems advisable, in the manner and upon the terms and conditions provided by law and the Articles of Incorporation of the Corporation.

Section 2. *Reserves:* The Directors may set apart, out of the funds of the Corporation available for dividends, said sum as the directors, from time to time, in their absolute discretion, think proper as a reserve fund for any proper purpose. The directors may abolish any such reserve in the manner it was created.

ARTICLE VII — GENERAL PROVISIONS

Section 1. *Insurance and Indemnity:* The Corporation may purchase and maintain insurance on behalf of any person who is or was a director, officer, agent, or employee of the Corporation against liability asserted against or incurred by such person in such capacity or arising from such person's status as such.

Subject to applicable statute, any person made or threatened to be made a party to any action, suit, or proceeding, by reason of the fact that he or she, his or her testator or intestate representative, is or was a director, officer, agent, or employee of the Corporation, may be indemnified by the Corporation against the reasonable expenses, including attorneys' fees, actually and necessarily incurred by him or her in connection with such an action, suit, or proceeding.

No indemnification shall be made by the Corporation if judgment or other final determination establishes that the potential indemnitee's acts were committed in bad faith or were the result of active or deliberate fraud or dishonesty or clear and gross negligence.

Section 2. *Corporate Records:* Any shareholder of record, in person or by attorney or other agent, shall, upon written demand under oath stating the purpose thereof, have the right during the usual hours for business to inspect for any proper purpose the Corporation's stock ledger, a list of its shareholders, and its other books and records, and to make copies or extracts therefrom. A proper purpose shall mean a purpose reasonably related to such person's interest as a shareholder. In every instance in which an attorney or other agent shall be the person seeking the right to inspection, the demand under oath shall be accompanied by a power of attorney or such other writing authorizing the attorney or other agent to so act on behalf of the shareholder. The demand under oath shall be directed to the Corporation at its registered office or its principal place of business.

Section 3. *Fiscal Year:* The fiscal year of the Corporation shall be the calendar year.

Section 4. *Seal:* The corporate seal shall be in such form as the Board of Directors shall approve. The seal may be used by causing it or a facsimile thereof to be impressed, affixed, or otherwise reproduced.

Section 5. *Execution of Instruments:* All contracts, checks, drafts, or demands for money and notes and other instruments or rights of any nature of the Corporation shall be signed by such officer or officers as the Board of Directors may from time to time designate.

Section 6. *Notice:* Whenever written notice is required to be given to any person, it may be given to such person, either personally or by sending a copy thereof through the United States mail, or by telegram, or facsimile, charges prepaid, to his or her address appearing on the books of the Corporation, or supplied by him or her to the Corporation for the purpose of notice. If the notice is sent by mail or by telegraph, it shall be deemed to have been given to the person entitled thereto when deposited in the United States mail or with a telegraph office for transmission to such person. If the notice is sent by facsimile, it shall be deemed to have been given at the date and time shown on a written confirmation of the transmission of such facsimile communication. Such notice shall specify the place, day, and hour of the meeting, and, in the case of a special meeting of shareholders, the purpose of and general nature of the business to be transacted at such special meeting.

Section 7. *Waiver of Notice:* Whenever any written notice is required by law, or by the Articles of Incorporation or by these Bylaws, a waiver thereof in writing, signed by the person or persons entitled to such notice, whether before or after the time stated therein, shall be deemed equivalent to the giving of such notice. Except in the case of a special meeting of shareholders, neither the business to be conducted at nor the purpose of the meeting need be specified in the waiver of notice of the meeting. Attendance of a person either in person or by proxy, at any meeting, shall constitute a waiver of notice of such meeting, except where a person attends a meeting for the express purpose of objecting to the transaction of any business because the meeting was not lawfully convened or called.

Section 8. *Amendments:* The Board of Directors shall have the power to make, adopt, alter, amend, and repeal from time to time the Bylaws of the Corporation except that the adoption, amendment, or repeal of any Bylaw regulating the election of directors shall be subject to the vote of shareholders entitled to cast at least a majority of the votes which all shareholders are entitled to cast at any regular or special meeting of the shareholders, duly convened after notice to the shareholders of that purpose.

The foregoing Bylaws were adopted by the Board of Directors on ____________.

____

Secretary

APPENDIX

I

Written Consent in Lieu of the Organizational Meeting

WRITTEN CONSENT IN LIEU OF THE ORGANIZATIONAL MEETING OF THE BOARD OF DIRECTORS OF

____

(A Delaware Corporation)

Pursuant to Section 141 of the Delaware General Corporation Law, the undersigned, constituting all ______________ (______________) of the initial director(s) of ______________________, a corporation organized and existing under the laws of the State of Delaware (the "Corporation"), do/does hereby consent in writing to the adoption of the following resolutions, such resolutions to have effect as if adopted at a duly held meeting of the directors of the Corporation:

RESOLVED, that the Charter issued to the Corporation by the Division of Corporation of the Delaware Department of State be filed in the minute book of the Corporation.

RESOLVED, that the Bylaws attached to this Consent are hereby adopted as the Bylaws of the Corporation.

RESOLVED, that the corporate seal, an impression of which is affixed in the margin hereof, is adopted as the corporate seal of the Corporation.

RESOLVED, that the form of stock certificate, a copy of which is attached to this Consent, is hereby adopted as the certificate for the common stock of the Corporation.

RESOLVED, that the following persons are hereby elected to the offices set forth after their respective names, to assume the duties and responsibilities fixed by the Bylaws, each such officer to hold office until a successor is chosen and qualifies in that officer's stead, or until that officer's earlier resignation or removal:

Name	*Office*
______________________	President
______________________	Vice-President
______________________	Treasurer
______________________	Secretary

RESOLVED, that any officer of the Corporation is hereby authorized to open such bank accounts as may be necessary or appropriate to conduct the business of the Corporation with such banks or financial institutions as that officer deems necessary; and

FURTHER RESOLVED, that the corporate banking resolutions of any such bank or financial institution are hereby incorporated by reference and are adopted as if fully set forth herein.

RESOLVED, that the Corporation elect to be treated as an S corporation for income tax purposes, subject to the receipt of written consent to such election by each shareholder; and

FURTHER RESOLVED, that upon receipt of written consent of said election by each shareholder, the President is hereby authorized and directed to take any and all action necessary or desirable to comply with all of the requirements of the Internal Revenue Service for making said election.

RESOLVED, that the Corporation hereby confirms that all shares of the common stock of the Corporation issued upon acceptance of the following subscription offers shall be treated as Section 1244 stock; and

RESOLVED, that the officers of the Corporation are authorized and directed to perform such actions and execute such documents as they shall deem necessary or appropriate to enable the Corporation to carry out its business in such jurisdictions as its activities make such qualification necessary or appropriate.

WHEREAS, the following person(s) has/have offered the amounts set forth next to his/her/their name(s) below in consideration of the issuance of the number of shares of the common stock, one cent ($0.10) par value per share, of the Corporation set forth below;

RESOLVED, that in consideration of the amounts indicated below, an aggregate of ____________ (_______) shares of the common stock of the Corporation be and hereby is issued to the person(s) listed below, and that upon receipt from [each] such person of the amount set forth opposite the person's name, the President and Secretary are hereby authorized and directed to issue to such person a certificate representing the number of shares set forth opposite that person's name, as follows:

Name	*Shares*	*Consideration*
________________	________________	$________________
________________	________________	$________________
________________	________________	$________________

RESOLVED, that the [accrual/cash] method of accounting shall be the basis on which the Corporation computes its income and keeps its books; and

FURTHER RESOLVED, that the fiscal year of the Corporation shall be the twelve-month period ending ____.

RESOLVED, that any officer of the Corporation be and hereby is authorized to pay all expenses incurred in connection with the organization of the Corporation and to reimburse the incorporators or directors for any amounts expended by them on behalf of the Corporation prior date hereof; and

FURTHER RESOLVED, that the Secretary of the Corporation be and hereby is authorized and directed to procure all corporate books, including books of account and stock books, required by the statutes of the State of Delaware or necessary or appropriate in connection with the business of the Corporation, and to apply in the name and on behalf of the Corporation on Form SS-4 for a Federal Employer Identification Number.

RESOLVED, that any officer of the Corporation be and hereby is authorized to take such actions and execute such documents as may be necessary, appropriate, or convenient to carry out the foregoing resolutions.

Dated as of ______________, 20_____.

____
Name

____
Name

____
Name

CONSENT

I, ___________, hereby consent to my election as Director of ____________________, by __________________, the Sole Incorporator of the Corporation.

______________________	______________________
Date of Execution	Name

WAIVER OF SOLE INCORPORATOR OF ________________________

I, ________________, being the Sole Incorporator named in the Certificate of Incorporation of ________________ (the "Corporation"), which Articles of Incorporation were received and filed with the Delaware Secretary of State on ________________, 20___, hereby waive all right, title, and interest in and to any stock or property of the Corporation and any right in the management thereof.

________________________	________________________
Date of Execution	Sole Incorporator

APPENDIX

J

Shareholders' Buy-Sell Agreement

SHAREHOLDERS' BUY-SELL AGREEMENT

THIS AGREEMENT is made this __________ day of ______________________, 20_______, by and among Celia G. Spiritos, James Hays, and Mary Jo Stanton (hereinafter referred to individually as a "Shareholder" and collectively as "the Shareholders") and SHS Corporation (the "Corporation"), a corporation organized under the laws of the State of ______________________.

RECITALS

WHEREAS, all of the issued and outstanding shares of the stock of the Corporation are owned by the Shareholders in the following percentages as of the date of this Agreement:

Shareholder	*Shares Owned*
Celia G. Spiritos	____________________
James Hays	____________________
Mary Jo Stanton	____________________

WHEREAS, the parties desire to restrict the transfer, encumbrance, pledge, or assignment of the shares of the Corporation;

WHEREAS, the parties desire to provide for the purchase and sale of shares of the Corporation under specified conditions; and

WHEREAS, the parties desire to provide for continuity and harmony in the management and affairs of the Corporation and for the orderly operation of its business.

NOW, THEREFORE, for good and valuable consideration, the receipt and sufficiency of which are hereby acknowledged, the parties hereto agree as follows:

1. Stock Subject to This Agreement.

All of the shares of the Corporation, which are owned by the Shareholders and which represent all of the issued and outstanding shares of the Corporation as of the date of this Agreement, shall be subject to the terms of this Agreement. Any additional shares of the Corporation, of whatever class, which from time to time shall be issued by the Corporation, shall become subject to the terms of this Agreement.

2. Restrictive Legend on Stock Certificates.

The certificates evidencing shares of the Corporation which are or hereafter become subject to the terms of this Agreement shall include the following restrictive legend which shall be displayed prominently on each certificate:

> The shares represented by this certificate are issued and held subject to a Shareholders' Buy-Sell Agreement made the ________ day of __________________, 20______, to which this Corporation is subject. A copy of the Agreement is on file at the principal business office of the Corporation. Any assignment or transfer of any nature of any shares represented by this certificate shall be void and without any effect, unless undertaken and effected in compliance with the terms of the Agreement.

3. Stock Transfer Restrictions.

(a) No Shareholder shall have the right or power to sell, assign, transfer, pledge, or otherwise dispose of (hereinafter collectively referred to as a "transfer") all or any portion of his or her shares of the Corporation, or any interest therein, except in accordance with the terms and conditions of this Agreement.

(b) Notwithstanding the foregoing provision, this Agreement shall not apply to a transfer of shares in the Corporation to the Corporation, a transfer to all of the Shareholders on a pro rata basis for equal consideration, or to shares acquired by way of merger.

4. Permitted Transfers.

(a) An interest in shares of the Corporation that is not exempt under Paragraph 3(b) above can only be transferred if the Shareholder desiring to make a transfer (the "offering Shareholder") first makes an offer to the remaining Shareholders to sell all of his or her shares to the remaining Shareholders. The offer by the offering Shareholder must be in writing, must state the offeror's name and address and all terms and conditions of the offer, and must be delivered to the remaining Shareholders pursuant to Paragraph 8 of this Agreement.

(b) Within sixty (60) days of receipt of the offer, the remaining Shareholders shall provide notice to the offering Shareholder of their determination whether to purchase the offered shares. If no written notice shall be given within the sixty (60) day period, the offer to purchase shall be deemed rejected. The remaining Shareholders may make a counteroffer to the offering Shareholder.

(c) If an offer to purchase is accepted by more than one of the remaining Shareholders, the shares of the offering Shareholder shall be allocated among the remaining Shareholders according to their pro rata interest in the Corporation.

(d) If the offer to purchase is rejected by the remaining Shareholders, the offering Shareholder shall be entitled, for a period of sixty (60) days after thc rejection of the offer to sell all of his or her shares to a third person in accordance with the terms of the original offer made to the remaining Shareholders. As a prerequisite to ownership rights to shares being transferred to a third person, such third person must execute a counterpart of this Agreement, agreeing to be bound by all of its terms.

(e) If the remaining Shareholders accept the offer to purchase, certificates for the shares shall be delivered to the purchasing Shareholder(s) and the purchasing Shareholder(s) shall comply with the terms of the offer within thirty (30) days after the notice of acceptance of the offer.

(f) Any attempt to transfer any interest in shares of the Corporation in violation of this Paragraph 4 shall be ineffective and the Corporation shall refuse to register the shares in question in the name of the purported transferee.

5. <u>Buy-Out Rights</u>.

(a) Buy-Out Price. For purposes of this Agreement, the term "Buy-Out Price" shall mean the sum of One Thousand Dollars ($1,000) multiplied by the number of shares sold by the selling Shareholder or his or her successor in interest. The Buy-Out Price may be modified by the Shareholders at any time, by unanimous written consent, and the Shareholders shall reassess the Buy-Out Price on an annual or more frequent basis.

(b) Death. Upon the death of any individual Shareholder, the personal representative or administrator of his or her estate shall sell and the Corporation shall purchase all of the deceased Shareholder's shares at a price equal to the greater of any insurance proceeds payable to the Corporation by reason of the death of such Shareholder or the Buy-Out Price.

(c) Disability. In the event an individual Shareholder who is employed by the Corporation in an executive capacity as an officer or director shall become disabled, as defined below, the disabled Shareholder shall sell and the Corporation shall purchase all of the disabled Shareholder's shares at a price equal to the Buy-Out Price. For purposes of this Agreement, a Shareholder is disabled if he or she has been declared legally incompetent by a final court decree, receives disability insurance benefits from any disability income insurance policy, or due to medically determinable disease, injury, or other mental or physical impairment is unable to perform substantially all of his or her regular duties to the Corporation and such disability is reasonably expected to last six (6) months or longer.

(d) Termination of Employment. In the event that a Shareholder voluntarily terminates employment with the Corporation or the Corporation terminates the employment of a Shareholder for cause, as defined below, the terminated Shareholder shall sell, and the Corporation shall purchase, all of the terminated Shareholder's shares at a price equal to one-half (½) of the Buy-Out Price. For purposes of this Agreement, the term "cause" shall mean conviction of a felony, breach of fiduciary duty, proven dishonesty in the course of employment or failure to perform the duties of employment, theft, fraud, or substance abuse. A determination of "cause" may be made only upon the unanimous vote of the remaining Shareholders. The Shareholder sought to be terminated for cause shall have the right to contest the termination in a court of competent jurisdiction during the pendency of which the provisions of this Paragraph 5(d) shall be suspended.

(e) Transfers by Operation of Law. In the event any Shareholder files a voluntary petition under any bankruptcy or insolvency laws or is subjected involuntarily to such a petition or is subjected to any other legal process, including but not limited to, an assignment or transfer pursuant to a divorce decree, the Shareholder shall sell and the Corporation shall purchase all of the Shareholder's shares at a purchase price equal to the Buy-Out Price.

(f) Procedural Requirements. Whenever the Corporation is required to purchase the shares of a Shareholder pursuant to one or more of the events causing a Buy-Out as described in this Paragraph 5, the following procedures shall apply:

(i) The closing upon such purchase shall take place at the offices of the Corporation or at such other place as mutually agreed upon, within sixty (60) days of the event triggering the buy-out.

(ii) The purchase price of any such shares shall be paid as follows:

1. At closing, there shall be a cash payment equal to at least fifty percent (50%) of the Buy-Out Price. The balance of the purchase price shall be made by promissory note by the Corporation in a principal amount equal to the unpaid portion of the Buy-Out Price and carrying interest at the prime interest rate and which note shall be paid in equal quarterly installments, until paid in full. The Corporation shall have the right to prepay, without penalty, all or any part of the amount due under the terms of the promissory note.

2. At closing, the selling Shareholder shall take all steps necessary to legally transfer possession and ownership of the certificate(s) representing all of the shares sold. Delivery of the certificate(s) shall constitute a representation and warranty that good and valid title to the stock is being delivered and that the shares are free and clear or all claims or liens of any kind. Title to and possession of the shares shall pass to the Corporation at the closing, regardless of any balance of the purchase price for such shares which may be payable after the closing.

6. Specific Performance.

Each Shareholder acknowledges that the restrictions contained in this Agreement are reasonable and necessary in order to protect the interests of the Corporation, and that any violation thereof would result in irreparable and substantial harm to the Corporation. The Shareholders understand and acknowledge that the monetary loss or damage which will be suffered by any party by reason of failure to perform the obligations imposed by this Agreement is impossible to determine. Accordingly, it is agreed that in the event of any dispute concerning the sale or other transfer of shares of the Corporation, an injunction may issue restraining any such sale or other transfer pending the determination of such controversy. Such remedy shall not be exclusive and shall be in addition to any other remedies which the parties may have.

7. Binding Nature of Agreement.

This Agreement shall be binding upon the parties hereto and their transferees, assignees, heirs, executors, administrators, and other representatives and it is understood and acknowledged that such transferees, assignees, heirs, executors, administrators, and other representatives shall execute any documents necessary to carry out the intent of this Agreement.

8. <u>Miscellaneous</u>.

(a) This Agreement supersedes all prior agreements and understandings, whether written or oral, relating to the subject matter hereof.

(b) This Agreement may be modified or amended at any time upon written agreement of all the parties hereto.

(c) This Agreement shall be governed by the law of the State of ___________.

(d) Any notice required by this Agreement shall be deemed given when sent certified mail, return receipt requested, first class, postage prepaid to the party to whom such notice is required to be given, at such person's last known address.

IN WITNESS WHEREOF, the parties have executed this Agreement on the date provided herein.

____
Celia G. Spiritos

____
James Hays

____
Mary Jo Stanton

APPENDIX

Letter of Intent

October 19, 2000

Quality Systems, Inc.
Attention: Mr. Francis P. Taylor
340-A Fairfax Road
Boston, MA 01887

Dear Mr. Taylor:

This letter confirms our mutual intention to pursue the proposed business arrangement (the "Transaction") outlined below:

1. *Transaction.* Management Technology Consultants, Inc. ("MTC") wishes to acquire all of the assets of Quality Systems, Inc. ("QSI"), a Massachusetts corporation (the "Transaction"). MTC will assume no liabilities of QSI of any kind or nature but will assume QSI's obligations under scheduled agreements with third parties, subject to review during due diligence. It is our understanding that QSI will liquidate as soon as practicable following the closing of the Transaction.

2. *Purchase Price.* The purchase price (the "Purchase Price") will be Thirty Million Dollars ($30,000,000) payable in cash at the time of the Closing, as herein defined. Five Hundred Thousand Dollars ($500,000) will be held in escrow for ninety (90) days after the Closing to allow for any adjustments to the Purchase Price resulting from shortfalls in assets, inventory, or other issues not uncovered in due diligence (through the exercise of reasonable and good faith efforts by the parties).

3. *Employment.* MTC believes that Mr. Taylor's continued involvement in QSI's operations is critical to the long-term success of the Transaction. Therefore, MTC will offer him employment with MTC with a base annual salary of $150,000, payable in accordance with MTC's normal payroll procedures. He will be eligible for all benefits provided to MTC employees. Historically, MTC has paid bonuses to employees who meet or ex-

ceed company goals and expectations. The parties will use their best efforts to reach mutually satisfactory terms relating to specific and quantifiable performance goals to be achieved by Mr. Taylor and providing that as each goal is met or exceeded, he will be paid a bonus for each such goal for a total aggregate potential bonus payment of $150,000.

4. *Non-Competition Agreements.* QSI shareholders who are employees of QSI will execute customary non-competition agreements in favor of MTC providing that during and upon termination of employment with MTC for any reason former QSI employees will be precluded from performing any work or engaging in any activities that would compete directly or indirectly with MTC's business and operations for five years within a 200-mile radius of any then-existing MTC office location. We will work together to draft appropriate non-competition agreements.

5. *Stock Options.* Mr. Taylor will be granted options to purchase 100,000 shares of MTC stock pursuant to the 1997 MTC Stock Option Plan, exercisable in accordance with the normal vesting schedule applicable to MTC employees.

6. *QSI Employees.* We will discuss issues related to the offer of employment by MTC to various QSI employees and the terms and conditions of such employment. Any individuals who are offered employment with MTC will be granted options to purchase 5,500 shares of MTC stock pursuant to the 1997 MTC Stock Option Plan, exercisable in accordance with the normal vesting schedule applicable to MTC employees. Options are granted at the end of each calendar quarter for newly hired employees. The next meeting of the MTC Stock Option Committee is set for March 31, 2001.

7. *Closing.* The parties desire that closing (the "Closing") of the Transaction occur as soon as practicable, preferably on or before December 31, 2000. Prior to Closing, QSI will conduct its business in the ordinary course.

8. *Due Diligence.* Representatives of MTC will have the opportunity to perform a due diligence investigation of the assets, business, contracts, equipment, inventory, and operations of QSI. A Due Diligence Information Request List is attached hereto. The scope of the investigation will include, but not be limited to, a review of QSI's facilities, material contracts, employee benefit plans, corporate documents, financial statements, and tax returns for prior years. In order to enable MTC to perform and complete its investigation, QSI shall provide representatives of MTC with access to its books, clients, vendors, records, personnel, and premises during normal business hours.

9. *Confidentiality of Discussions.* The parties will keep strictly confidential the existence and content of this letter and the fact that these discussions are taking place, except as required by applicable law and except as agreed to in writing by both parties. MTC and QSI will jointly draft and release a press release announcing the Transaction after this letter of intent has been signed by both parties.

10. *Transaction Fees.* The parties shall bear their own respective costs in connection with the Transaction, including the negotiation and consummation of a definitive agreement.

11. *Definitive Agreement.* During the period prior to Closing, the parties will work in good faith to prepare and execute a definitive agreement for the Transaction contemplated hereby. This letter is intended to serve only as a framework to identify issues and matters that would have to be addressed in such a definitive agreement, which shall contain customary representations, warranties, convenants, and conditions for a transaction of the type contemplated hereby.

12. *Exclusive Dealings.* In consideration of the time, energy, and money that MTC will expend toward consummation of the Transaction, QSI agrees not to solicit other bids for the sale of its stock or assets, accept any bids therefor, whether solicited or unsolicited, or negotiate with any other person or entity with respect to the sale thereof, either in whole or in part, or a similar transaction, through December 31, 2000. Prior to such date, QSI will not dispose of any of its material assets, incur any material indebtedness, issue additional debt or equity securities, declare or pay any dividend or make any other distribution with respect to its capital stock or repurchase any capital stock, agree to any material contract or amend any existing material contract, or agree to any material expenditure out of the ordinary course of business, without the express written consent of MTC. Notwithstanding the foregoing, in the event that either of the parties notifies the other in writing that it wishes to terminate negotiations relating to the Transaction, QSI's obligations hereunder shall terminate ten (10) business days thereafter.

13. *Conditions Precedent.* In order to consummate the Transaction contemplated hereby, and as an express condition precedent to the parties' obligations hereunder, MTC and QSI must each secure approval from their respective boards of directors and lenders for the Transaction. Moreover, QSI must secure the approval of its shareholders to the Transaction. Each party will use its best efforts to secure said approval and will at all times keep the other apprised of the process of obtaining such approval. Moreover, the parties understand and acknowledge that certain government approvals must be secured prior to Closing and the parties will work together and cooperate in making any filings with the government related thereto.

    Except as provided in Paragraphs 9, 10, and 12 hereof, which are intended to be and are legally binding agreements between the parties hereto upon QSI's acceptance below, the parties do not intend for this letter to create any enforceable obligations or rights, and no legal and enforceable obligations or rights shall arise unless and until the parties negotiate, execute, and deliver a definitive written agreement setting forth the specific terms and conditions of the Transaction contemplated hereby.

If this letter is an accurate reflection of our mutual understanding of the proposed Transaction, please indicate your concurrence by countersigning and dating the enclosed copy of this letter in the place provided and returning a fully signed copy to me as soon as possible.

We look forward to working with you on the Transaction and in the years to come.

Very truly yours,

Management Technology Consultants, Inc.
By: Timothy Lyden, President

ACCEPTED AND APPROVED:

Quality Systems, Inc.

________________________ ________________________

Francis P. Taylor, President Date

Glossary

Accredited investor: A bank, a savings and loan, or an investor with a certain net worth, income in excess of $200,000, or otherwise sufficiently sophisticated that they do not require the registration protections afforded by the Securities Act of 1933.

Accrual method of accounting: Accounting method of listing expenses and income in business records when they are incurred or billed rather than when they are actually paid or received.

Accumulated earnings tax: Tax penalty imposed on corporations that retain earnings beyond reasonable business needs.

Actual authority: The grant of authority, either express or implied, by a principal to an agent.

Affiliates: Subsidiaries formed by a common parent corporation.

Agency: Relationship between parties whereby one agrees to act on behalf of another.

Agent: One who acts for or represents another, called a principal.

Agent for service: See Registered agent.

Aggressor: Corporation (or individual) attacking or wishing to acquire control over another corporation, typically called the target.

Alienation: The transfer of some property.

Alien corporation: Corporation formed in a country other than the United States.

Alter ego: When corporate shareholders fail to respect the fact that the corporation is an entity separate and apart from them, they are said to view the corporation as their "alter ego," namely, a mere extension of themselves. Shareholders who treat the corporation as their alter ego may have personal liability imposed on them for the corporation's debts.

Amended articles of incorporation: A document filed with the secretary of state of a corporation's state of incorporation to effect a change in the corporation's articles of incorporation.

Annual meeting: Yearly meeting of shareholders of a corporation to elect directors and conduct other business.

Antitrust: Area of law regulating business competition to ensure fair business conduct and a competitive economy.

Apparent authority: Conduct of a principal causing a third party to believe an agent had authority to act for the principal.

Appraisal rights: Authority given to dissenting shareholders to have their shares appraised, or valued, and bought out.

Arbitrageurs: Individuals or companies trading in a target's stock after announcement of a tender offer or trading in different stocks and bonds in different markets at the same time. Sometimes called risk arbitrageurs or simply "arbs."

Articles of dissolution: Document filed with the secretary of state to effect a dissolution or termination of a corporation as a legal entity. Sometimes called a certificate of dissolution.

Articles of incorporation: Document that creates a corporation.

Articles of merger: Document filed with the secretary of state to effect a merger or other combination of two or more corporations.

Articles of organization: Document filed with the appropriate state official creating a limited liability company.

Asked price: Price at which a corporation will sell its shares.

Asset purchase: Acquisition by one corporation of another's properties.

Assignment: Transfer of all of one's interest in certain property.

Assumed name: See Fictitious business name.

At-will employment: Employment that may be terminated upon the will of an employer or employee, at any time.

Authorized share: Share identified in the articles of incorporation as being capable of and subject to issuance by the corporation.

Back-end transaction: See Mop up.

Bear hug: Approach by an aggressor to a target after the aggressor has acquired a toehold in the target.

Bear market: A declining market.

Bid price: Price at which a share of stock can be purchased.

Black knight: Aggressor attempting to acquire a target.

Blank check: Provision in articles of incorporation authorizing directors to create series of stock.

Blank stock: See Series stock.

Blitz: Lightning and no-notice strike against a target's stock so forceful that the target is sufficiently overwhelmed and cannot adopt any defenses to prevent a takeover.

Block trade: Trade involving at least 10,000 shares of stock.

Blue chip stock: Stock of the elite and nationally known corporations.

Blue sky law: State law regulating the issuance, purchase, and sale of securities.

Board of directors: See Director.

Boilerplate: Standard provisions typically found in contracts or other legal documents.

Bond: Debt security secured by some corporate asset that can be seized by a creditor upon default by the corporation.

Bounty payment: Payment made by the SEC to those who provide information relating to violations of the Securities Exchange Act of 1934.
Broker: Securities firm that acts on behalf of a customer, rather than trading on its own account, as does a dealer.
Bulk transfer: Sale or transfer of the major portion of a company's business outside the scope of its ordinary course of business.
Bull market: A rising market.
Business judgment rule: Court-made rule immunizing directors from liability for their decisions so long as the decision was reasonable and made in good faith.
Business trust: Unincorporated business association governed by the law of trusts in which equitable title to property is held by a trustee for the benefit of others; rarely seen in modern times.
Buy-sell agreement: Agreement entered into by shareholders restricting the transfer or sale of their stock.
Bylaws: Rules governing the management of a corporation.

C corporation: Corporation for profit which is subject to double taxation; one other than an "S" corporation.
Call: Right of a corporation to reacquire stock it has issued to a shareholder (generally, a preferred shareholder).
Cancellation: Elimination of shares reacquired by a corporation.
Capital: Generally, money.
Capital surplus: Amount of consideration in excess of par value of shares that a corporation receives for its shares.
Cash dividend: Distribution of cash by a corporation to its shareholders.
Cash method of accounting: Accounting method of listing expenses and income in business records only when they are paid or received.
Certificate of good standing: Document issued by a secretary of state showing that a corporation is in compliance with that state's laws.
Charter: Name used by some states to refer to a corporation's articles of incorporation.
Chewable poison pill: An anti-takeover defense; a type of poison pill that is of short duration and is triggered only when a bidder buys significant numbers of shares.
Circuit breaker: See Collars.
Class action: Action brought by one or a few shareholders on behalf of numerous other shareholders who are similarly situated.
Class voting: Voting rights given to a class of stock.
Close (closely held) corporation: Corporation whose shares are held by a few people, usually friends or relatives active in managing the business. Some flexibility is permitted with regard to observing corporate formalities.
Collars: Automatic halts to trading at the New York Stock Exchange that occur when the market declines certain percentages (also called curbs or circuit breakers).
Commingling: Combining shareholders' personal funds improperly with those of the corporation; liability can be imposed on shareholders who fail to respect the corporate entity by commingling funds.
Common law trust: A business trust governed by judicial decision rather than state statutes.

Common stock: Stock in a corporation that has no special features, as does preferred stock; usually has the right to vote and to share in liquidation dividends.

Comprehensive Omnibus Budget Reconciliation Act (COBRA): Federal law requiring insurance continuation after employee leaves employment.

Confession of judgment: Provision contained in a promissory note entitling a creditor to obtain an immediate judgment against a debtor in default; not valid in all states.

Consolidation: Combination of two or more corporations into a new corporate entity (example: A + B = C).

Constituent corporations: Corporations that are parties to a merger, consolidation, or other combination.

Contingent voting: Voting which is dependent upon the occurrence of some event such as default by a corporation in the payment of dividends.

Conversion right: 1. Right of preferred shareholders to convert preferred stock into some other security of the corporation, usually common stock.
2. Right of creditors to convert debt security (bond) into equity security (shares).

Copyright: Right given in original works of authorship including literary, artistic, dramatic, and other works.

Corporation: Legal entity existing by authority of state law, owned by its shareholders, and managed by its elected directors and appointed officers.

Corporation by estoppel: Defectively formed corporation which cannot be attacked due to a party's dealing with the corporation as if it were a valid corporation; party is estopped, or precluded, from treating the entity as anything other than a corporation.

Covenant not to compete: Provision in an agreement or an independent agreement prohibiting employees from working in certain industries or in certain geographic areas after termination of employment; to be valid, the clause must be reasonable in scope and duration and can typically be imposed only on employees with special skill and talents.

Cross-purchase insurance: Insurance policies taken out by each shareholder on the life of each other shareholder to provide funds to purchase shares from a deceased shareholder's estate.

Crown jewel defense: Sale by a target of its valuable assets, usually to make itself unattractive to an aggressor.

Cumulative dividend: Distribution which "adds up" over time and must be paid to a preferred shareholder, when the corporation has funds to do so, before any distribution can be made to other shareholders.

Cumulative voting: In an election of directors, a type of voting whereby each share carries as many votes as there are directors' vacancies to be filled; assists minority shareholders in electing representatives to the board of directors.

Curb: See Collars.

Day trading: Trading stock electronically numerous times each day, usually from another's business location.

Dead-hand poison pill: An anti-takeover defense; a type of poison pill that can only be deactivated by the directors who established it (also called a continuing director plan).

Dealer: Securities firm that buys securities for resale to its customers; the firm trades "on its own account."

Debenture: Debt security that is unsecured, such as a simple promissory note.

Debt financing: Borrowing money to raise capital.

Debt security: Instrument evidencing a corporation's debt to another.

De facto: Literally, "in fact"; a corporation with a defect in its incorporation process such that it cannot have de jure status; cannot be attacked by a third party, although the state can invalidate it.

De facto merger: Transaction which has the effect of a merger and must comply with all statutory formalities pertaining to mergers.

Defined benefit plan: Qualified retirement plan that sets a pre-established benefit that will be paid to employees leaving the company.

Defined contribution plan: Qualified retirement plan specifying the amount the employer will place into the plan account each year on behalf of an employee.

De jure: Literally, "of right"; a corporation formed in substantial compliance with the laws of the state of incorporation, the validity of which cannot be attacked by any party or the state.

Derivative action: Action brought by a limited partner or shareholder not to enforce his or her own cause of action but to enforce an obligation due to the business entity; the action "derives" from the claimant's ownership interest in the business entity.

Designated order turnaround (DOT): Computerized trading system used by the New York Stock Exchange.

Direct action: Action brought by a limited partner or shareholder of a corporation for a direct injury sustained by the claimant; for example, being refused the right to examine corporate books and records.

Director: One who directs or manages a corporation; when more than one director exists, they function as a board.

Disproportionate voting: Voting rights which differ in one class from those granted to another class.

Dissenter's rights: See Appraisal rights.

Dissenting shareholder: Shareholder opposing some corporation action, such as amendment to the articles of incorporation, merger, or consolidation.

Dissolution: Termination of a business organization as a legal entity, such as a partnership or corporation; may be voluntary or involuntary.

Distribution: Direct or indirect transfer by a corporation of money or other property (other than its own shares) to or for the benefit of its shareholders, whether a distribution of corporate profits or a distribution at the time of liquidation. The older view used this term to refer to distributions to shareholders *other than* distributions of corporation's own profits.

Dividend: Corporation's distribution of its profits to its shareholders by way of cash, property, or shares. The modern approach is to refer to any distribution as a dividend, whether a distribution of corporate profits or a distribution at the time of liquidation.

Domestic corporation: A corporation created or incorporated in the state in which it is conducting business.

Double taxation: Taxation of corporate income at two levels: once when the corporation earns money and then again when shareholders receive distributions from the corporation.

Dow Jones average: Average of the stock prices of 65 major stocks.

Downstream merger: Merger of a parent and a subsidiary in which the subsidiary survives (example: P + S = S).

Draw: Advance payment to an employee against anticipated compensation.

Dummy directors: Nominal directors in the articles of incorporation, often an attorney and staff members named for the convenience of signing documents; dummies will resign at the organizational meeting and be replaced with the corporation's true directors.

Earned surplus: Total corporate profits earned during some particular accounting period.

Election judge: Neutral party who oversees corporate elections to determine whether a quorum is present, that proxies have been counted, and that a measure has received sufficient votes for approval.

Electronic communication network (ECN): A private electronic trading system allowing quick and inexpensive trading 24 hours per day.

Employee: One who performs services for another for some form of compensation and is subject to the other's control and direction.

Employee Retirement Income Security Act (ERISA): Federal statute regulating retirement plans for employees.

Employee stock ownership plan (ESOP): Retirement plan in which the employer contributes funds (that may be borrowed from a bank or other lender) to a trust. The money is then used to purchase stock in the corporation for employees.

Employment contract: Agreement between employer and employee specifying the terms and conditions of employment.

Equity financing: Issuance of shares to raise capital.

Equity security: Security demonstrating a person's ownership interest in a corporation.

Estoppel: Prohibition imposed on a party to preclude a challenge to some fact or event because such a challenge would be inequitable based on party's conduct.

Ethics: Study of standards of right and wrong.

Ex-dividend: The status of a shareholder or share with no right to receive a declared dividend.

Exempt security: Security that is exempt from compliance with the Securities Act of 1933.

Exempt transaction: Transaction exempt from compliance with the registration requirements of the Securities Act of 1933, such as a small issue.

Express authority: Acts specifically directed or authorized by a principal.

Extinguished corporation: Corporation which does not survive a merger or other combination. Sometimes called a merged corporation.

Family limited partnership: A type of partnership composed of family members and designed to achieve estate and tax planning benefits (also called a "family limited liability company").

Fictitious business name: Name adopted for use by a person, partnership, corporation, or other business which is other than its true or legal name. Sometimes called an assumed name.

Fiduciary relationship: Relationship in which a party owes a duty of good faith to another or to others.

Financing statement: Document recorded with the secretary of state or county recorder to provide notice of a security interest claimed in personal property; also called UCC-1 form.

Fiscal year: Twelve-month reporting period adopted by a business for accounting purposes; it need not be the calendar year.

Floor: Location in the New York Stock Exchange where share transactions occur.

Foothold: See Toehold.

Foreign corporation: Corporation conducting business in a state other than the one in which it is incorporated. Occasionally, corporations formed outside the United States are called foreign corporations, though they are more properly termed alien corporations.

Foreign partnership: Partnership conducting business in a state other than the one in which it is organized.

401(k) plan: Retirement plan funded by the pre-tax contributions of employers and nontaxable contributions of employees.

Fractional share: A portion of a share; typically entitled to proportionate voting and distribution rights.

Franchise: License granted by one party to another enabling the latter to use the licensor's proprietary system and trademark in offering goods or services.

Freeze-out: Impermissible tactic by directors to compel a corporate dissolution in order to dispose of minority shareholders; sometimes called a squeeze-out.

Fringe benefit: Noncash form of compensation for employees.

Front running: An unscrupulous trading practice in which floor brokers trade for themselves before trading on behalf of their clients.

Futures contract: Agreement between two parties to exchange a specified quantity of some asset at a specified price on a specified date.

General agency: Act of a partner in carrying out the usual business of the firm that will bind the partnership unless the person with whom the partner is dealing knows the partner has no authority to perform that act.

General partner: Individual or entity managing or controlling (general) partnership or a limited partnership.

General proxy: A proxy authorizing the proxy holder to vote a shareholder's shares in the proxy holder's discretion.

Going private: See Leveraged buy-out.

Going public: Offering securities to members of the public at large. See Initial public offering.

Golden parachute: Lucrative settlement given to key corporate managers who leave or are let go by a corporation.

Good till canceled order: An order to purchase stock that remains open until it is specifically canceled.

Governance guidelines: Formal written policies relating to management of corporations and often sought by shareholders.

Greenmail: Form of legal corporate blackmail in which an aggressor threatens to take over a target and then sells the toehold back to the target at an inflated price in return for an agreement not to take over the target.

Hart-Scott-Rodino Antitrust Improvements Act: A federal statute requiring pre-merger notification to the government so it can determine if the proposed transaction would have an anticompetitive effect.
Holder of record: Owner of stock as of a particular date. See Record date.
Horizontal restraint: Agreement between business rivals that restrains trade.
Hostile takeover: Acquisition of a corporation against the will of its directors and shareholders.

Illegal dividend: Dividend paid out of an unauthorized account or made while a corporation is insolvent.
Implied authority: Authority to perform acts customarily performed by agents, even if not expressly so directed by a principal.
Incorporator: Person who prepares and signs the articles of incorporation to form a corporation.
Indemnify: Compensating or reimbursing one who has incurred a debt or obligation on another's behalf.
Independent contractor: One who is not subject to the control and direction of another but exercises independent judgment and discretion while performing duties and activities for that party.
Individual retirement account (IRA): Retirement plan funded by an individual not covered under some other retirement plan.
Information returns: Documents filed with the Internal Revenue Service reporting income earned by or distributed to partners or shareholders.
Initial public offering: First offering of securities to the public; usually, the offering by a corporation of its securities to the public as a means of raising capital; often referred to as "going public."
Insider trading: Transaction by corporate insiders, such as directors and officers, to achieve some benefit in the purchase or sale of securities based upon inside information, namely information that is not available to the public at large, prohibited by SEC Rule 10b-5.
Insolvency: Inability to pay one's debts as they become due in the usual course of business or excess of liabilities over assets.
Intellectual property: Property rights in intangibles, such as trade secrets, inventions, copyrights, trademarks, and related intangibles, capable of being owned but which are neither real property nor tangible personal property.
Involuntary dissolution: Dissolution forced upon an entity, such as a partnership or corporation, through a judicial proceeding initiated by either the state or owners of the entity, or perhaps by creditors. Sometimes called judicial dissolution.
Issuance: Process of selling corporate securities.

Joint and several liability: When each member of an association is liable to pay all of a debt or obligation; when a creditor may sue all individuals in an association or pick among them to satisfy a debt.

Joint stock company: Unincorporated association combining features of partnerships and corporations; ownership interests are represented by transferable shares of stock; rarely seen in United States.

Joint venture: Type of partnership formed to carry out a particular enterprise rather than an ongoing business.

Jonestown defense: A target that effectively commits "suicide" by destroying itself rather than be taken over by an aggressor.

Judicial dissolution: See Involuntary dissolution.

Judicial liquidation: Liquidation of a corporation that has been involuntarily dissolved by a court; often performed by a court-appointed receiver or trustee.

Junk bond: Bond below investment grade.

Keogh plan: Retirement plan adopted by a sole proprietor or self-employed individual.

Key person policy: Insurance policy taken out on the life of a senior manager. In the event of the manager's death, the policy proceeds go to the business entity in order to provide sufficient funds to purchase the decedent's ownership interest in the entity.

Killer bees: Attorneys, advisors, and others retained by a target to fight off a takeover.

Legend: Generally, a notation on a stock certificate stating that it is subject to some restriction, typically as to transfer of stock represented by the certificate; a notation on a corporate document such as a prospectus.

Leveraged buy-out: Offer by a target's management to purchase all of the publicly held shares of a target corporation. Sometimes called "going private."

Limited liability: Liability which is confined to that amount contributed by an investor to an enterprise; when personal assets of an investor cannot be used to satisfy business debts or obligations.

Limited liability company: New form of business enterprise, not yet recognized in all states, offering the pass-through tax status of a partnership and the limited liability of a corporation.

Limited liability limited partnership: A limited partnership that files with the secretary of state so its general partner has no liability for partnership obligations.

Limit order: Order given to a broker limiting the broker's authority regarding the price of stock, when to purchase or sell stock, and so forth.

Limited partner: Individual or entity having membership in a limited partnership, but does not manage or control the enterprise, and whose liability is limited to the amount contributed to the limited partnership.

Limited partnership: Partnership formed under statutory requirements which has as members one or more general partners and one or more limited partners.

Limited partnership agreement: Agreement among partners in a limited partnership, usually written, regarding the affairs of the limited partnership, the duties of the general partner, rights of limited partners, and the conduct of the business.

Limited partnership certificate: Document filed with a state agency to create a limited partnership.

Limited proxy: A proxy directing a proxy holder to vote as specified by the shareholder giving the proxy.

Line of credit: A type of pre-authorized loan that the borrower draws against as needed.

Liquidation: Process of completing the affairs of a business; for corporations, the process of collecting corporate assets, discharging debts, and distributing any remains to the shareholders; may be judicial or nonjudicial; precedes dissolution. Sometimes called winding up.

Liquidation distribution: Distribution made to business owners after creditors have been paid upon dissolution of a business entity.

Liquidator: See Receiver.

Load: Additional charge imposed on an investor in a mutual fund, usually imposed when the individual invests in the fund.

Margin: Practice of using a loan or credit for some of the purchase price of stock.

Margin call: Demand by a broker for additional collateral to secure the purchase price of securities bought on margin or credit.

Marshaling of assets: Requirement that partnership creditors must first exhaust partnership assets before attacking a partner's personal assets to satisfy a debt or obligation.

Member:
1. Owner or investor in a limited liability company.
2. Individual or firm holding a seat on the New York Stock Exchange or American Stock Exchange.

Merger: Combinations of two or more corporations into one corporate entity (example: A + B = A).

Midnight raid: Raid by aggressor after the afternoon closing of a stock exchange and concluded before resumption of trading in the morning.

Mining partnership: Partnership formed for the purpose of mining or oil or gas exploration; recognized by statute in some states and by judicial decision in others.

Minutes: Written summary of the proceedings at directors' or shareholders' meetings.

Money maker: Dealers who trade on the NASDAQ market.

Money market fund: Mutual fund that invests in short-term and nearly risk-free investments.

Monopoly: Exclusive privilege or advantage to offer a product or service generally resulting in an illegal restraint of trade.

Mop up: Attempt by a successful aggressor to acquire 100 percent ownership of a target's stock.

Mortgage bond or note: Debt security in which a corporation pledges real estate as security for its promise to repay money borrowed from a creditor.

Mutual fund: Open-end investment management company that continually trades in other issuers' securities for an unlimited number of persons; an entity engaged primarily in the business of investing or trading in the securities of others.

Name registration: Reservation of a corporate name in states in which the corporation intends to do business in the future.

Name reservation: Reservation of proposed corporate name prior to filing of articles of incorporation; generally effective for some specified period.

Name saver: Subsidiary incorporated in a state expressly to ensure name is available for corporate parent in that state.

National Association of Securities Dealers (NASD): Association of dealers involved in the over-the-counter market.

National Association of Securities Dealers Automated Quotation (NASDAQ): Computerized trading system of the National Association of Securities Dealers; has no physical location as does the New York Stock Exchange.

New York Stock Exchange: Largest secondary market for trading of securities; located in New York City.

No-hand poison pill: An anti-takeover device; a poison pill that cannot be removed by any director if control of the board changes hands.

Nonaccredited investor: Investor who is not sophisticated or "accredited"; see Accredited investor.

Noncompetition agreements: See Covenant not to compete.

Nonjudicial liquidation: Liquidation of an entity that has been voluntarily dissolved; in a corporation, such liquidation is performed by corporate directors and officers.

No par value stock: Stock having no stated minimum value; the price can be determined by a corporation's board of directors.

Nonprofit corporation: Corporation formed for some charitable, religious, educational, or scientific purpose or for the mutual benefit of its members, rather than for the purpose of making a profit.

Nonqualified retirement plan: Retirement plan not subject to the extensive regulation governing a qualified plan; does not provide the same tax advantages as a qualified plan.

Nuclear war: Hostile takeover involving numerous large publicly traded companies.

Odd lot: Purchase or sale of less than 100 shares of stock.

Officer: One appointed by corporation's board of directors to carry out management functions as delegated by the board.

Online trading: The practice of trading electronically from one's home computer a few times each day or month.

Operating agreement: Written agreement governing the operation of a limited liability company.

Option: Right to purchase stock or commodities at a specified price during a specified time period.

Organizational meeting: First meeting of a corporation held after incorporation to finalize the incorporation process by electing directors, appointing officers, adopting bylaws, and so forth.

Outstanding shares: Shares issued by a corporation and held by a shareholder.

Oversubscription: Shares tendered to an aggressor in excess of the amount requested in the aggressor's tender offer.

Over-the-counter market: Computerized securities trading network with no physical location.

Pac man defense: Tender offer by a target to acquire an aggressor's stock.

Parent corporation: Corporation that creates another corporation (called a subsidiary) and holds all or a majority of its shares.

Participating preferred stock: Stock which enjoys the right to participate in corporate distributions in addition to those "built into" the preferred stock.

Partnership: An association of two or more persons to carry on a business as co-owners for profit; often called a general partnership to distinguish it from a limited partnership.

Par value: Minimum consideration for which a share of stock can be issued; set forth in a corporation's articles of incorporation.

Patent: A grant by the federal government allowing one to exclude others from making, using, or selling one's new and nonobvious invention or discovery.

Penny stock: A stock selling for less than $5 per share; also called Over-the-Counter Bulletin Board Stock.

Person: According to most statutes, a "person" is a natural individual or a business organization, such as a partnership or corporation.

Personal liability: Liability for debts and obligations in excess of that originally invested, namely, liability extending to one's personal assets.

Piercing the veil: Holding individual shareholders liable for a corporation's debt to prevent fraud or injustice.

Pink sheets: A listing for the sale of stock of companies that do not meet the listing requirements of other exchanges.

Plan of merger: Blueprint for a merger containing all of the terms and conditions of a merger.

Plurality: The number of votes received by a successful candidate who does not receive a majority of votes cast in an election.

Poison pill: Privileges and rights of a target's shareholders triggered by a tender offer that are designed to thwart a takeover.

Pooling agreement: Agreement between or among shareholders specifying the manner in which they will vote.

Porcupine provision: See Shark repellent.

Post: A desk at the New York Stock Exchange where securities are traded.

Preemptive right: Right given to shareholders in articles of incorporation allowing shareholders to purchase newly issued stock in an amount proportionate to their current share ownership.

Preemptive strike: Highly attractive offer made by an aggressor with the intent of obtaining immediate control of a target.

Preferred stock: Corporate stock that has some right, privilege, or preference over another type of stock.

Preincorporation agreement: Agreement entered into between promoters of corporation and some third party prior to creation of the corporation; promoter is bound by the agreement.

Preincorporation share subscription: Offer by a party to purchase stock in a corporation made before the corporation is formed.

Primary market: Investment firms, underwriters, and so forth involved in the process of selling an issuer's initial offering of securities.

Principal: One who appoints another, called an agent, to act for or represent him or her.

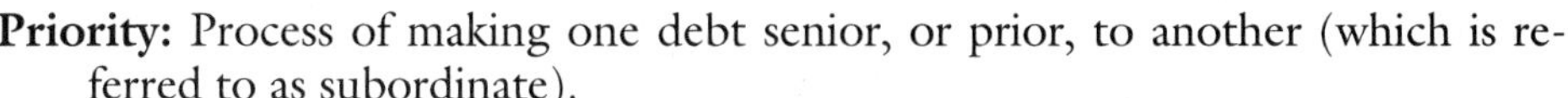

Priority: Process of making one debt senior, or prior, to another (which is referred to as subordinate).

Privately held corporation: Corporation whose shares are not sold to the public but are held by a small group of investors, often family and friends.

Private placement offering: Nonpublic offering of a corporation's stock, generally exempt from the registration requirements of the Securities Act of 1933. Sometimes called a private placement memorandum.

Process: Complaint filed in court by a plaintiff and the summons issued thereafter by the court to the party named as defendant requiring an appearance or response.

Professional corporation: Corporation formed by a person or persons practicing a certain profession, such as law, medicine, or accounting, who retain liability for their own misconduct and those acting under their control.

Profit-sharing plan: Retirement plan funded by employer's profits.

Promissory note: Document evidencing one's debt to another.

Promoter: One who plans and organizes a corporation.

Property dividend: Distribution which is not cash or shares in the issuing corporation but is generally some physical or tangible item.

Prospectus: Document that must be provided to any purchaser of securities registered under the Securities Act of 1933; it includes information relating to the corporation, its management, and the securities being issued.

Proxy: Written authorization by a shareholder directing another to vote his or her shares.

Proxy fight: Solicitation of a target's shareholders by management of the aggressor and management of the target to vote for each party's management slate.

Public corporation: Corporation whose shares can be purchased and sold by members of the general public.

Public offering: Issuance of securities to the general public which generally must first be registered according to the Securities Act of 1933.

Put: Right of a shareholder (usually, a preferred shareholder) to compel a corporation to reacquire stock issued to the shareholder.

Qualification: Process by which a corporation formed in one state is authorized to transact business in another.

Qualified retirement plan: Retirement plan that meets certain Internal Revenue Code requirements and is eligible for special tax treatment.

Qualified small business stock: Stock in certain small businesses (C corporations with less than $50 million) that qualifies for tax advantages by excluding from taxable income one-half of any gain on the sale of the stock.

Quorum: Minimum number of shareholders or directors required to be present at a meeting in order to conduct business; usually a majority.

Ratification: Acceptance or approval of a certain act; may be express or implied from conduct.

Real estate investment trust (REIT): A vehicle usually organized as a trust for investing in real estate by numerous investors who pool their capital to acquire commercial real estate.

Receiver: Individual or firm appointed by a court to oversee a judicial or involuntary dissolution. Sometimes called a liquidator.

Recitals: Preliminary clauses in agreements, often identifying the parties to agreement and the intent or purpose of the agreement.

Record date: Date selected in advance of a meeting used to determine who will be entitled to notice of a meeting and who will be entitled to vote at a meeting.

Redemption right:
1. Right given to corporation to repurchase the stock of preferred shareholders (call) or the right given to a preferred shareholder to compel the corporation to repurchase preferred stock (put).
2. Right of a corporation to pay off, or redeem, debt owed to a creditor before the stated maturity date.

Red herring prospectus: Form of prospectus distributed by an issuer corporation between the filing of a registration statement and its effective date (named for the legend printed in red ink on the prospectus).

Registered agent: Individual or company designated by a business to receive notices, litigation pleadings, documents, and service of process on the business's behalf.

Registered limited liability partnership: Newly recognized form of partnership in which a partner has no personal liability for the misconduct of another partner; formed by filing an application with the appropriate state official.

Registered office: Principal location of a business organization identified in various state forms or filings so that third parties may contact the business.

Registrar: Bank or other institution that maintains a corporation's list of shareholders.

Registration:
1. Process of reserving a corporate name in another state.
2. Process of complying with the Securities Act of 1933 for issuance of securities to the public.

Registration statement: Form or document filed with the Securities and Exchange Commission, pursuant to the Securities Act of 1933, when securities are first offered to the public.

Regular meeting: Routinely scheduled meeting of corporate directors.

Regulations A and D: See Small issues.

Reinstatement: Process of reviving a corporation after it has been dissolved for a technical violation of state law, such as failure to file annual report.

Rent strike: Refusal by a tenant to pay rent, usually due to some defect in the leased premises.

Reorganization: Tax term for mergers, consolidations, and share exchanges.

Representative action: Action brought by numerous shareholders against the corporation or directors; a class action by shareholders.

Reservation: See Name reservation.

Respondeat superior: Latin phrase meaning "let the master answer"; legal theory by which liability is imposed on an employer-principal for an employee-agent's acts committed in the course and scope of the employment or agency.

Restated articles of incorporation: Document filed with the secretary of state to combine previously amended articles into a more comprehensible document.

Restrictive covenant: Clause in an agreement that prohibits or restricts certain activities, such as those prohibiting the disclosure of trade secrets or restricting former employees from working for competitors or in related industries; to be valid, restrictive covenants must be reasonable in scope and duration.

Retained earnings: Undistributed net profits accumulated by a corporation.

Reverse stock split: Reduction by a corporation in the number of its outstanding shares; often done to eliminate smaller shareholders.

Reverse triangular merger: Merger among a parent, its subsidiary, and a target corporation in which the subsidiary merges into the surviving target.

Right: A short-term option, as distinguished from a warrant, a long-term option.

Roth IRA: Retirement plan in which contributions are not deductible and withdrawals are not subject to taxation.

Round lot: Order involving 100 shares of stock.

Saturday night special: Raid by an aggressor made over a weekend so the target cannot marshal its management team.

Scorched earth: Extreme and dramatic efforts by a target to ward off a hostile takeover.

S corporation: Corporation in which all income is passed through to shareholders who pay taxes at appropriate individual rates. Certain eligibility requirements must be met to elect S status.

Scrip: Certificate evidencing a fractional share; scrip does not typically possess voting, dividend, or liquidation rights.

Seat: Membership on the New York Stock Exchange or American Stock Exchange.

Secondary market: Stock exchange where established corporations trade their securities, such as the New York Stock Exchange.

Section 12 company: Company required to register its securities pursuant to Section 12 of the Securities Exchange Act of 1934 (namely, a company traded on a national securities exchange or one having assets of $10 million or more and 500 or more shareholders).

Section 1224 stock: Stock which when sold at a loss provides certain tax advantages; the loss is treated as an ordinary rather than a capital loss. Certain requirements must be met to issue Section 1244 stock.

Secured debt or transaction: Debt secured by some corporate asset that can be seized upon the corporation's default in repayment of its loan obligation.

Securities Act of 1933: Federal law imposing requirements on a company's original issuance of securities to the public.

Securities and Exchange Commission (SEC): Independent federal agency charged with the regulation of securities.

Securities Exchange Act of 1934: Federal law imposing requirements on the trading of stock, primarily the purchase and sale of securities after their original issuance.

Securities Litigation Reform Act: 1995 federal law intended to reduce frivolous shareholder suits for securities fraud.

Security: Share or ownership interest in a corporation (equity security) or obligation of the corporation to an investor (debt security).

Security agreement: Agreement between a debtor and a lender in which debtor pledges personal property (rather than real estate) as collateral to secure repayment of the debtor's loan to the creditor.

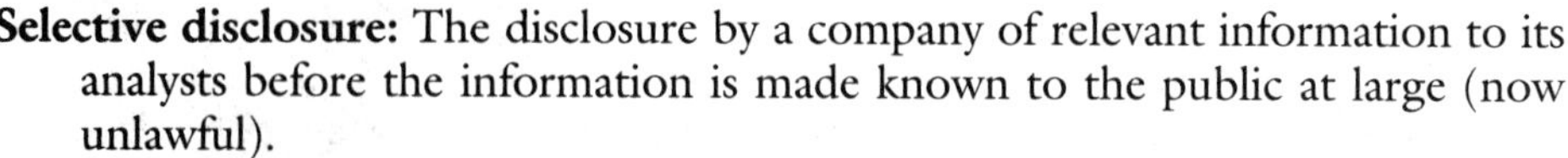

Selective disclosure: The disclosure by a company of relevant information to its analysts before the information is made known to the public at large (now unlawful).

Self-tender: Target's purchase of its own shares in order to prevent a hostile takeover.

SEP-IRA: A retirement plan allowing self-employed individuals to contribute to their retirement.

Series stock: Stock issued within a class including rights and preferences different from those of other series and issues without the necessity of amending the articles of incorporation; sometimes referred to as blank stock.

Service mark: A word, symbol, or device used to identify and distinguish one's services.

Service of process: Delivery of a summons and complaint (i.e., process) upon a defendant or its agent.

Share: Units in which the proprietary interests of a corporation are divided.

Share dividend: Distribution to shareholders of the corporation's own shares.

Share exchange: Process by which the shareholders of a target exchange their shares for those of another corporation.

Shareholder: One who owns an interest in a corporation; synonymous with stockholder.

Share subscription: Agreement whereby a party offers to purchase stock in a corporation.

Shark repellent: Attempts by a target to ward off an aggressor even before a tender offer is made. Sometimes called a porcupine provision.

Short-form merger: Merger between a parent and its subsidiary in which the parent initially owns at least 90 percent of the subsidiary's stock.

Short-swing profits: Profits made by a Section 12 company's officers, directors, or principal shareholders within a six-month period which must be disgorged to the corporation, even without a showing of insider trading or bad faith.

SIMPLE IRA: A retirement plan to which both employer (which has less than 100 employees) and employee contribute.

Sinking fund: Fund of money set aside by a corporation to enable it to redeem or reacquire shares from preferred shareholders or to pay off money borrowed by the corporation from a creditor.

Slow-hand poison pill: An anti-takeover device; a poison pill that bars newly elected directors from deactivating it for some period of time.

Small business corporation: Domestic corporation, with no more than 75 shareholders, all of whom are individuals residing in the United States, which may elect to be treated as an S corporation and thereby avoid double taxation.

Small issue: Offering of stock which does not exceed $5 million and is exempt from the registration requirements of the Securities Act of 1933.

Small order: Order to purchase less than 2,099 shares.

Small-scale merger: Merger not dramatically affecting the survivor corporation's shareholders that is therefore not subject to approval by the survivor's shareholders.

Sole proprietorship: Business managed and owned by one person who has sole authority for all decision-making and faces unlimited personal liability for business debts and obligations.

Solvency: Ability to pay debts as they come due.

Specialist: Individual who handles the stock of one company traded on the New York Stock Exchange.

Special meeting: Any meeting held between the annual meetings of shareholders or regular meetings of directors.

Split-dollar insurance: Insurance policy on the life of an employee, the premiums for which are paid by both the employer and employee.

Squeeze out: See Freeze-out.

Stagger system: Process of varying election dates for board members so that they are not all elected at same time; a stagger system defeats cumulative voting.

Standstill agreement: Agreement by an aggressor not to purchase more shares of the target for some specified period of time; the target may pay greenmail to the aggressor for this agreement.

Stated capital: Amount equivalent to the par value of issued stock or consideration received for stock issued without par value.

Statutory trust: A business trust governed by state statute.

Stock: See Share.

Stock bonus plan: Retirement plan for employees in which the employer's contribution is stock rather than cash.

Stock certificate: Document evidencing an ownership interest in a corporation.

Stock exchange: Marketplace where securities are traded.

Stockholder: See Shareholder.

Stock option plan: Plan used by corporation to compensate employees who have the right to buy the corporation's stock at certain times at fixed prices.

Stock purchase: Acquisition of stock in a corporation.

Stock split: Division by a corporation of its outstanding shares, often done to encourage trading.

Stock watch: Early warning system used by a corporation to detect fluctuations in the market price of its shares that may warn off action by aggressors.

Stop order: Order given to a broker to sell stock when it declines to a certain price or to buy stock when it has increased to a certain price.

Straight voting: The right carried by each outstanding share of record to one vote.

Street sweep: Process by which an aggressor or third party attempts to purchase stock from a risk arbitrageur or speculator in the event an aggressor's takeover bid is unsuccessful.

Strike team: Aggressor's legal counsel, advisors, public relations team, and so forth.

Sublease: Transfer by a tenant of less than all of the interest in leased premises to another party.

Subordination: Process of making one debt junior, or subordinate, to another (which is said to have priority over it).

Subsidiary: Corporation formed by another corporation, called the parent; all or the majority of the subsidiary's stock is owned by the parent.

Suicide pact: Agreement by a target's management team to resign en masse in the event any one of them is fired or demoted after a hostile takeover.

Suitability rule: SEC rule requiring brokers who recommend the purchase or sale of stock to determine the suitability of the investment for the investor.

Surplus: Excess of a corporation's net assets over the corporation's stated capital.

Survivor: Corporation that continues in existence after a merger.

Syndicate: A group of investors, usually banks, that participate in selling an issue of stock.

Takeover: See Hostile takeover.

Target: Corporation being attacked or subject to takeover by another corporation or some third party.

Tender offer: Public offer by an aggressor to shareholders of a target corporation seeking to acquire their shares.

The street: Nickname for Wall Street in New York City.

Thin incorporation: Condition of a corporation's debt being disproportionately higher than its equity.

Tick: The smallest amount by which stock prices normally change.

Ticker: Teletype machine that prints and records stock transactions.

Tin parachute: Moderate settlement given to lower-level corporate employees who leave a company.

Tippee: One who receives a tip or information from a corporate insider about the corporation.

Tipper: Corporate insider who gives tips or information to others about the corporation's finances or operations.

Toehold: Stock of a target purchased by an aggressor wishing to take over the target, usually less than 5 percent. Sometimes called a foothold.

Tombstone ad: Limited advertising offering securities during the twenty-day period between filing of a registration statement with the SEC and its effective date.

Top-heavy plan: Retirement plan that discriminates in favor of more highly compensated employees.

Trademark: A word, symbol, or device used to identify and distinguish one's goods.

Trade secret: Valuable information that gives its owner a competitive advantage, such as a recipe or customer list.

Transacting business: Activities engaged in by a corporation doing business in a state other than its state of incorporation that will require it to formally qualify with that host state to conduct business.

Transfer agent: Bank or other institution that physically issues or cancels stock certificates for large corporations.

Treasury stock: Stock reacquired by a corporation; it is considered issued but not outstanding.

Triangular merger: Merger among a parent, its subsidiary, and a target corporation in which the subsidiary merges with the target, leaving the subsidiary as the survivor.

Triple taxation: Taxation of income when received by a subsidiary, then when received by the parent as a distribution, and finally when received by the parent's shareholders as a distribution.

Trust indenture: Agreement specifying trustee's rights and responsibilities when a corporation issues numerous bonds at one time.

***Ultra vires* act:** Act beyond the purposes and powers of a corporation. The doctrine of ultra vires is limited by modern statutes that allow a corporation to perform any lawful act and that prohibit the corporation or a third party from disaffirming a contract.

Uncertificated share: Share issued without a formal share certificate.

Underwriter: Securities firm used by a corporation issuing stock for the first time. The underwriter buys stock itself for resale to the public or enters into arrangements with dealers for the dealers to sell the stock to their customers.

Underwriting: Process of issuing securities from the corporation to the ultimate shareholder.

Unfair competition: Acts that constitute deceptive and unfair commercial practices.

Uniform Commercial Code (UCC): Statute drafted by National Conference of Commissioners and adopted by every state but Louisiana governing the sale of goods, leases, bulk transfers, secured transactions, and so forth; state variations exist.

Unlimited liability: Liability not limited to a party's investment in an enterprise but rather may be satisfied from the investor's other assets, savings, and property.

Unsecured debt: Debt for which no property is pledged as collateral to secure repayment of the loan; in the event of default, a creditor must sue the debtor to recover money loaned to the debtor.

Upstream merger: Merger of a parent and its subsidiary in which the parent survives (example: P + S = P).

Vertical restraint: Agreement between a buyer and seller restraining trade.

Vesting: Nonforfeitable right of an employee to receive the benefits of a retirement plan.

Vicarious liability: Liability imposed on another for an act that is not his or her fault; typically it is liability imposed on an employer for an employee's torts.

Voluntary dissolution: Dissolution of an entity initiated by the entity itself; with regard to a corporation, a dissolution initiated by corporate directors or shareholders.

Voting agreement: Agreement among shareholders specifying the manner in which they will vote. Sometimes called a pooling agreement.

Voting trust: Agreement among shareholders by which they transfer their voting rights to a trustee to vote on their behalf.

Waiver of notice: Giving up the right to receive notice of some action or event, usually a meeting of directors or shareholders.

War chest: Funds collected or borrowed by an aggressor to acquire a target.

Warrant: Long-term option enabling its holder to purchase shares at a specified price during a specified time period.

Watered stock: Stock issued for less than its par value or for property or services worth less than its par value. Sometimes called discount stock or bonus stock.

White knight: Corporation that saves a target from a hostile takeover.

Williams Act: Federal statute relating to tender offers.

Winding up: See Liquidation.

Withdrawal: Request by an entity wishing to cease being qualified in a state in which it has transacted business.

Work made for hire: Work prepared by an employee in the course of employment and thus owned by the employer.

Written consent: Action taken by board of directors or shareholders without necessity of meeting in person; most states require written consent to be unanimous.

Index